THE
SPECTATOR

THOMAS TICKELL
From the painting by Sir Godfrey Kneller in The Queen's College, Oxford

THE
SPECTATOR

EDITED
WITH AN INTRODUCTION
AND NOTES BY
DONALD F. BOND

VOLUME V

OXFORD
AT THE CLARENDON PRESS
1965

Oxford University Press, Amen House, London E.C.4

GLASGOW NEW YORK TORONTO MELBOURNE WELLINGTON
BOMBAY CALCUTTA MADRAS KARACHI LAHORE DACCA
CAPE TOWN SALISBURY NAIROBI IBADAN
KUALA LUMPUR HONG KONG

© *Oxford University Press 1965*

PRINTED IN GREAT BRITAIN
AT THE UNIVERSITY PRESS, OXFORD
BY VIVIAN RIDLER
PRINTER TO THE UNIVERSITY

CONTENTS

VOLUME I

Joseph Addison. From the Kit-cat painting by Sir
Godfrey Kneller in the National Portrait Gallery,
London. By permission of the Trustees   *Frontispiece*

INTRODUCTION

Beginnings of the *Spectator*   xiii
The Character of the New Journal   xviii
Publishing, Distribution, and Circulation   xx
Contents; *Dramatis Personae*   xxix
Letters from Correspondents   xxxvi
Authorship   xliii
Content and Style: The Relative Contributions of
    Steele and Addison   lix
Success of the *Spectator*: Publication in Volume Form   lxix
The Second Series   lxxiii
Contemporary Readers   lxxxiii
Reputation in the Eighteenth Century—and after   xcvi

THE TEXT   cvi

ABBREVIATED TITLES   cxi

ERRATA   cxiii

NUMBERS 1–125   I

VOLUME II

Sir Richard Steele. From the painting by Jonathan
Richardson in the National Portrait Gallery, London.
By permission of the Trustees   *Frontispiece*

NUMBERS 126–282   I

CONTENTS

VOLUME III

Eustace Budgell. From the engraving by Knight after the portrait by D. Firmin. British Museum, Add. MS. 37232. By permission of the Trustees   *Frontispiece*

NUMBERS 283–426   I

VOLUME IV

John Hughes. From the engraving by G. Van der Gucht after the portrait by Sir Godfrey Kneller (Hughes's *Poems on Several Occasions*, 1735)   *Frontispiece*

NUMBERS 427–584   I

VOLUME V

Thomas Tickell. From the painting by Sir Godfrey Kneller in The Queen's College, Oxford. By permission of the Provost and Fellows   *Frontispiece*

NUMBERS 585–635   I

DEDICATIONS   174

APPENDIXES

    I. Emendation of Accidentals   189
    II. Collation of Textual Variants   196
    III. Advertisements of Books   205
    IV. Sources of Mottoes   225
    V. Documents   233

INDEX   241

> *Ipsi lætitia voces ad sidera jactant*
> *Intonsi montes: ipsæ jam carmina rupes,*
> *Ipsa sonant arbusta . . .*
>
> Virg.

The Sequel of the Story of Shalum *and* Hilpa.

THE Letter inserted in my last had so good an Effect upon *Hilpa*, that she answered it in less than a Twelvemonth after the following Manner:

Hilpa, *Mistress of the Vallies, to* Shalum, *Master of Mount* Tirzah.

In the 789*th Year of the Creation.*

'WHAT have I to do with thee, O *Shalum*? Thou praisest *Hilpa*'s Beauty, but art thou not secretly enamour'd with the Verdure of her Meadows? Art thou not more affected with the Prospect of her green Vallies, than thou wouldst be with the Sight of her Person? The Lowings of my Herds, and the Bleatings of my Flocks, make a pleasant Eccho in thy Mountains, and sound sweetly in thy Ears. What tho' I am delighted with the Wavings of thy Forests, and those Breezes of Perfumes which flow from the Top of *Tirzah*: are these like the Riches of the Valley?

'I know thee, O *Shalum*; thou art more wise and happy than any of the Sons of Men. Thy Dwellings are among the Cedars; thou searchest out the Diversity of Soils, thou understandest the Influences of the Stars, and markest the Change of Seasons. Can a Woman appear lovely in the Eyes of such a one? Disquiet me not, O *Shalum*; let me alone, that I may enjoy those goodly Possessions which are fallen to my Lot. Win me not by thy enticing Words. May thy Trees increase and multiply; mayest thou add Wood to Wood, and Shade to Shade; but tempt not *Hilpa* to destroy thy Solitude, and make thy Retirement populous.'

The *Chinese* say, that a little time afterwards she accepted of a Treat in one of the neighbouring Hills to which *Shalum* had invited

---

[1] *Motto. Virgil, Eclogues,* 5. 62–64:
> The Mountain tops unshorn, the Rocks rejoice;
> The lowly Shrubs partake of Humane Voice. DRYDEN.

her. This Treat lasted for two Years, and is said to have cost *Shalum* five hundred Antelopes, two thousand Ostriches, and a thousand Tun of Milk; but what most of all recommended it, was that Variety of delicious Fruits and Potherbs, in which no Person then living could any way equal *Shalum*.

He treated her in the Bower which he had planted amidst the Wood of Nightingales. This Wood was made up of such Fruit Trees and Plants as are most agreeable to the several Kinds of Singing-Birds; so that it had drawn into it all the Musick of the Country, and was filled from one End of the Year to the other with the most agreeable Consort in Season.

He shewed her every Day some beautiful and surprizing Scene in this new Region of Woodlands; and as by this Means he had all the Opportunities he could wish for of opening his Mind to her, he succeeded so well, that upon her Departure she made him a kind of Promise, and gave him her Word to return him a positive Answer in less than fifty Years.

She had not been long among her own People in the Vallies, when she received new Overtures, and at the same Time a most splendid Visit from *Mishpach*, who was a mighty Man of old, and had built a great City, which he called after his own Name. Every House was made for at least a thousand Years, nay there were some that were leased out for three Lives; so that the Quantity of Stone and Timber consumed in this Building is scarce to be imagined by those who live in the present Age of the World. This great Man entertained her with the Voice of musical Instruments which had been lately invented, and danced before her to the Sound of the Timbrel. He also presented her with several domestick Utensils wrought in Brass and Iron, which had been newly found out for the Conveniency[1] of Life. In the mean time *Shalum* grew very uneasy with himself, and was sorely displeased at *Hilpa* for the Reception which she had given to *Mishpach*, insomuch that he never wrote to her or spoke of her during a whole Revolution of *Saturn*; but finding that this Intercourse went no further than a Visit, he again renewed his Addresses to her, who during his long Silence is said very often to have cast a wishing Eye upon Mount *Tirzah*.

Her Mind continued wavering about twenty Years longer between *Shalum* and *Mishpach*; for tho' her Inclinations favoured the

[1] See *OED*, Convenience, 6 (saving of trouble). The last quotation given in this sense is dated 1796.

former, her Interest pleaded very powerfully for the other. While her Heart was in this unsettled Condition, the following Accident happened which determined her Choice. A high Tower of Wood that stood in the City of *Mishpach* having caught Fire by a Flash of Lightning, in a few Days reduced the whole Town to Ashes. *Mishpach* resolved to rebuild the Place whatever it should cost him; and having already destroyed all the Timber of the Country, he was forced to have Recourse to *Shalum*, whose Forests were now two hundred Years old. He purchased these Woods with so many Herds of Cattle and Flocks of Sheep, and with such a vast Extent of Fields and Pastures, that *Shalum* was now grown more wealthy than *Mishpach*; and therefore appeared so charming in the Eyes of *Zilpah*'s Daughter, that she no longer refused him in Marriage. On the Day in which he brought her up into the Mountains he raised a most prodigious Pile of Cedar, and of every sweet-smelling Wood, which reached above 300 Cubits in Height: He also cast into the Pile Bundles of Myrrh and Sheaves of Spikenard, enriching it with every spicy Shrub, and making it fat with the Gums of his Plantations. This was the Burnt-Offering which *Shalum* offered in the Day of his Espousals: The Smoke of it ascended up to Heaven, and filled the whole Country with Incense and Perfume.

No. 586   *Friday, August 27, 1714*[1]
[BYROM]

. . . Quæ in vita usurpant homines, cogitant, curant, vident, Quæque agunt vigilantes, agitantque, ea cuique in somno accidunt.

Cic. de Div.

B Y the last Post I received the following Letter, which is built upon a Thought that is new, and very well carried on; for

---

[1] *Motto.* Cicero, *De Divinatione*, 1. 22. 45 (altered): Whatever men transact in their lives, whatever employs their thoughts, cares, eyes, or waking actions, these are the subjects of their dreams.

This number, the first of a series of four papers on dreams (the others are Nos. 587, 593, and 597), is assigned by Nichols and later editors to John Byrom, author of the 'Pastoral' in No. 603. Byrom's 'two humorous letters upon dreams' are referred to in the *Biographia Britannica*, vi, part ii, Supplement (1766), pp. 26–28, and identified in Kippis's revised edition (iii. 121) as Nos. 586 and 593. Both of these purport to

which Reasons I shall give it to the Publick without Alteration, Addition, or Amendment.

SIR,

'IT was a good Piece of Advice which *Pythagoras* gave to his Scholars, That every Night before they slept they should examine what they had been a doing that Day, and so discover what Actions were worthy of Pursuit to Morrow, and what little Vices were to be prevented from slipping unawares into a Habit.[1] If I might second the Philosopher's Advice, it should be mine, That in a Morning before my Scholar rose, he should consider what he had been about that Night, and with the same Strictness as if the Condition he has believ'd himself to be in was real. Such a Scrutiny into the Actions of his Fancy must be of considerable Advantage, for this Reason, Because the Circumstances which a Man imagines himself in during Sleep, are generally such as entirely favour his Inclinations good or bad, and give him imaginary Opportunities of pursuing them to the utmost; so that his Temper will lie fairly open to his View, while he considers how it is mov'd when free from those Constraints which the Accidents of real Life put it under. Dreams are certainly the Result of our waking Thoughts, and our daily Hopes and Fears are what give the Mind such nimble Relishes of Pleasure, and such severe Touches of Pain, in its midnight Rambles. A Man that murders his Enemy, or deserts his Friend, in a Dream, had need to guard his Temper against Revenge and Ingratitude, and take heed that he be not tempted to do a vile thing in the Pursuit of false, or the Neglect of true Honour. For my Part, I seldom receive a Benefit, but in a Night or two's Time I make most noble Returns for it; which tho' my Benefactor is not a whit the better for, yet it pleases me to think, that it was from a Principle of Gratitude in me, that my Mind was susceptible of such generous Transport while I thought my self repaying the Kindness of my Friend: And I have often been ready to beg Pardon, instead

be from 'John Shadow' of Oxford, who disclaims authorship of No. 587 (see No. 593 *ad fin.*). The Tickell MS. assigns Nos. 586 and 597 to Byrom, No. 593 to Budgell, and says nothing of No. 587. No. 593 no doubt consists of extracts from John Shadow's letter, revised by Budgell. The authorship of No. 587 remains unknown; No. 597 consists of editorial comments on the dream experiences of several correspondents and cannot be assigned to Byrom. Nos. 586 and 593—and No. 603—are the only papers certainly by him.

[1] See the Commentaries of Hierocles upon the Golden Verses of Pythagoras, printed in André Dacier's *Life of Pythagoras*, published by Tonson in 1707, pp. 304–10. This practice of the Pythagoreans is referred to by Cicero, *De Senectute* ,11. 38.

of returning an Injury, after considering, that when the Offender was in my Power I had carried my Resentments much too far.

'I think it has been observ'd in the Course of your Papers, how much one's Happiness or Misery may depend upon the Imagination:[1] Of which Truth those strange Workings of Fancy in Sleep are no inconsiderable Instances; so that not only the Advantage a Man has of making Discoveries of himself, but a Regard to his own Ease or Disquiet, may induce him to accept of my Advice. Such as are willing to comply with it, I shall put into a way of doing it with Pleasure, by observing only one Maxim which I shall give them, *viz. To go to Bed with a Mind entirely free from Passion, and a Body clear of the least Intemperance.*

'They indeed who can sink into Sleep with their Thoughts less calm or innocent than they should be, do but plunge themselves into Scenes of Guilt and Misery; or they who are willing to purchase any Midnight Disquietudes for the Satisfaction of a full Meal, or a Skin full of Wine; these I have nothing to say to, as not knowing how to invite 'em to Reflections full of Shame and Horror: But those that will observe this Rule, I promise 'em they shall awake into Health and Chearfulness, and be capable of recounting with Delight those glorious Moments wherein the Mind has been indulging it self in such Luxury of Thought, such noble Hurry or Imagination. Suppose a Man's going supperless to Bed should introduce him to the Table of some great Prince or other, where he shall be entertained with the noblest Marks of Honour and Plenty, and do so much Business after, that he shall rise with as good a Stomach to his Breakfast as if he had fasted all Night long; or suppose he should see his dearest Friends remain all Night in great Distresses, which he could instantly have disengaged them from, could he have been content to have gone to Bed without the t'other Bottle: Believe me, these Effects of Fancy are no contemptible Consequences of commanding or indulging one's Appetite.

'I forbear recommending my Advice upon many other Accounts, till I hear how you and your Readers relish what I have already said; among whom, if there be any that may pretend it is useless to them, because they never dream at all, there may be others, perhaps, who do little else all Day long. Were every one as sensible as I am what happens to him in his Sleep, it would be no Dispute whether we past so considerable a Portion of our Time in the Condition of

[1] See Nos. 136, 167, &c. (vol. ii).

Stocks and Stones, or whether the Soul were not perpetually at Work upon the Principle of Thought. However, 'tis an honest Endeavour of mine to persuade my Countrymen to reap some Advantage from so many unregarded Hours, and as such you will encourage it.

'I shall conclude with giving you a Sketch or two of my Way of proceeding.

'If I have any Business of Consequence to do to Morrow, I am scarce dropt asleep to Night but I am in the midst of it, and when awake I consider the whole Procession[1] of the Affair, and get the Advantage of the next Day's Experience before the Sun has risen upon it.

'There is scarce a great Post but what I have some Time or other been in; but my Behaviour while I was Master of a College pleases me so well, that whenever there is a Province of that Nature vacant, I intend to step in as soon as I can.

'I have done many Things that would not pass Examination, when I have had the Art of Flying, or being Invisible; for which Reason I am glad I am not possessed of those extraordinary Qualities.

'Lastly, Mr. SPECTATOR, I have been a great Correspondent of yours, and have read many of my Letters in your Paper which I never wrote to you. If you have a Mind I should really be so, I have got a Parcel of Visions and other Miscellanies in my Noctuary,[2] which I shall send you to enrich your Paper with on proper Occasions.

Oxford, Au-   *I am,* &c.
gust 20.   John Shadow.'

---

[1] I.e. 'onward movement, advance' (cf. *OED*).
[2] This is the first example in *OED* of this word, coined upon the analogy of 'diary'.

. . . intus, et in Cute novi.

Pers.

THO' the Author of the following Vision is unknown to me, I am apt to think it may be the Work of that ingenious Gentleman, who promised me, in the last Paper, some Extracts out of his Noctuary.

SIR,

I Was the other Day reading the Life of *Mahomet.* Among many other Extravagancies, I find it recorded of that Impostor, that in the fourth Year of his Age the Angel *Gabriel* caught him up, while he was among his Play-fellows, and, carrying him aside, cut open his Breast, plucked out his Heart, and wrung out of it that black Drop of Blood, in which, say the *Turkish* Divines, is contained the *Fomes Peccati,* so that he was free from Sin ever after.[2] I immediately said to my self, tho' this Story be a Fiction, a very good Moral may be drawn from it, would every Man but apply it to himself, and endeavour to squeeze out of his Heart whatever Sins or ill Qualities he finds in it.

While my Mind was wholly taken up with this Contemplation, I insensibly fell into a most pleasing Slumber, when methought two Porters entered my Chamber, carrying a large Chest between them. After having set it down in the middle of the Room they departed. I immediately endeavoured to open what was sent me, when a Shape, like that in which we paint our Angels, appeared before me, and forbad me. Enclosed, said he, are the Hearts of several of your Friends and Acquaintance; but before you can be qualified to see and animadvert on the Failings of others, you must be pure your self; whereupon he drew out his Incision Knife, cut me open, took out my Heart, and began to squeeze it. I was in a great Confusion,

---

[1] *Motto.* Persius, *Satires,* 3. 30:

I know thee to thy Bottom; from within
Thy shallow Centre, to thy outmost Skin. DRYDEN.

The authorship of this number is unknown; it may be a genuine contribution inspired by No. 586. Although assigned to Byrom by Nichols, Morley, and Aitken, it is specifically disclaimed by 'John Shadow' in No. 593.

[2] The anecdote is told in *The Turkish Spy,* book iii, letter xx (ed. 1702, v. 200), and by Bayle, art. Mahomet, Remark I. In neither of these accounts, however, is *Fomes peccati* used. (The phrase occurs in Prudentius, *Apophthegmata,* 942, and elsewhere.)

7

to see how many things, which I had always cherished as Virtues, issued out of my Heart on this Occasion. In short, after it had been throughly squeezed, it looked like an empty Bladder, when the Phantome, breathing a fresh Particle of Divine Air into it, restored it safe to its former Repository; and having sewed me up, we began to examine the Chest.

The Hearts were all enclosed in transparent Phials, and preserved in a Liquor which looked like Spirits of Wine. The first which I cast my Eye upon, I was afraid would have broke the Glass which contained it. It shot up and down, with incredible Swiftness, thro' the Liquor in which it swam, and very frequently bounced against the side of the Phial. The *Fomes*, or Spot in the middle of it, was not large, but of a red fiery Colour, and seemed to be the Cause of these violent Agitations. That, says my Instructor, is the Heart of *Tom Dread-nought*, who behaved himself well in the late Wars, but has for these Ten Years last past been aiming at some Post of Honour to no Purpose. He is lately retired into the Country, where, quite choaked up with Spleen and Choler, he rails at better Men than himself, and will be for ever uneasie, because it is impossible he should think his Merit sufficiently rewarded. The next Heart that I examined was remarkable for its Smallness; it lay still at the bottom of the Phial, and I could hardly perceive that it beat at all. The *Fomes* was quite black, and had almost diffused it self over the whole Heart. This, says my Interpreter, is the Heart of *Dick Gloomy*, who never thirsted after any thing but Mony. Notwithstanding all his Endeavours, he is still poor. This has flung him into a most deplorable State of Melancholy and Despair. He is a Composition of Envy and Idleness, hates Mankind, but gives them their Revenge by being more uneasie to himself than to any one else.

The Phial I looked upon next contained a large fair Heart, which beat very strongly. The *Fomes* or Spot in it was exceeding small; but I could not help observing, that which way soever I turned the Phial it always appeared uppermost, and in the strongest Point of Light. The Heart you are examining, says my Companion, belongs to *Will. Worthy*. He has, indeed, a most noble Soul, and is possessed of a thousand good Qualities. The Speck which you discover is *Vanity*.

Here, says the Angel, is the Heart of *Freelove*, your intimate Friend. *Freelove* and I, said I, are at present very cold to one another, and I do not care for looking on the Heart of a Man, which I fear

is overcast with Rancour. My Teacher commanded me to look upon it; I did so, and, to my unspeakable Surprise, found that a small swelling Spot, which I at first took to be *Ill-will* towards me, was only *Passion*, and that upon my nearer Inspection it wholly disappeared; upon which the Phantome told me *Freelove* was one of the best natured Men alive.

This, says my Teacher, is a Female Heart of your Acquaintance. I found the *Fomes* in it of the largest Size, and of a hundred different Colours, which were still varying every Moment. Upon my asking to whom it belonged, I was informed that it was the Heart of *Coquetilla*.

I set it down, and drew out another, in which I took the *Fomes* at first sight to be very Small, but was amazed to find, that as I looked steadfastly upon it, it grew still larger. It was the Heart of *Melissa*,[1] a noted Prude who lives the next Door to me.

I show you this, says the Phantome, because it is indeed a Rarity, and you have the Happiness to know the Person to whom it belongs. He then put into my Hands a large Chrystal Glass, that enclosed an Heart, in which, though I examined it with the utmost Nicety, I could not perceive any Blemish. I made no Scruple to affirm that it must be the Heart of *Seraphina*, and was glad, but not surprised, to find that it was so. She is, indeed, continued my Guide, the Ornament, as well as the Envy, of her Sex; at these last Words, he pointed to the Hearts of several of her Female Acquaintance which lay in different Phials, and had very large Spots in them, all of a deep *Blue*. You are not to wonder, says he, that you see no Spot in an Heart, whose Innocence has been proof against all the Corruptions of a depraved Age. If it has any Blemish, it is too small to be discovered by Human Eyes.

I layed it down, and took up the Hearts of other Females, in all of which the *Fomes* ran in several Veins, which were twisted together, and made a very perplexed Figure. I asked the meaning of it, and was told it represented *Deceit*.

I should have been glad to have examined the Hearts of several of my Acquaintance, whom I knew to be particularly addicted to Drinking, Gaming, Intreaguing, &c. but my Interpreter told me I must let that alone till another Opportunity, and flung down the Cover of the Chest with so much Violence, as immediately awoke me.

---

[1] Both 'Coquetilla' and 'Melissa' appear in No. 377 (vol. iii).

No. 588   *Wednesday, September 1, 1714*[1]
[GROVE]

Dicitis, Omnis in Imbecillitate est et Gratia, et Caritas.
Cicero. De Nat. Deor. L.

MAN may be considered in two Views, as a Reasonable, and as a Sociable Being; capable of becoming himself either happy or miserable, and of contributing to the Happiness or Misery of his Fellow-Creatures. Suitably to this double Capacity, the Contriver of Human Nature hath wisely furnished it with two Principles of Action, Self-love and Benevolence; designed one of them to render Man wakeful to his own personal Interest, the other to dispose him for giving his utmost Assistance to all engag'd in the same Pursuit.[2] This is such an Account of our Frame, so agreeable to Reason, so much for the Honour of our Maker, and the Credit of our Species, that it may appear somewhat unaccountable what should induce Men to represent Humane Nature as they do under Characters of Disadvantage, or, having drawn it with a little and sordid Aspect, what Pleasure they can possibly take in such a Picture. Do they reflect that 'tis their Own, and, if we will believe themselves, is not more odious than the Original? One of the first that talked in this lofty Strain of our Nature was *Epicurus*.[3] Beneficence, would his Followers say, is all founded in Weakness; and, whatever he pretended, the Kindness that passeth between Men and Men is by every Man directed to himself. This, it must be confessed, is of a Piece with the rest of that hopeful Philosophy, which having patch'd Man up out of the four Elements, attributes his Being to Chance, and derives all his Actions from an unintelligible Declination of Atoms. And for these glorious Discoveries, the Poet is beyond Measure transported in the Praises of his Hero, as if he must needs be something more than Man, only for an Endeavour to prove that Man is in nothing superior to Beasts. In this School was Mr. *Hobs* instructed to speak after the same Manner, if he did

---

[1] *Motto.* Cicero, *De natura deorum*, 1. 44. 124: You say all Goodness and Charity are founded in Weakness.

This number is the first of four papers (Nos. 588, 601, 626, and 635) contributed to the *Spectator* by Henry Grove (1684–1738), the dissenting divine. They are reprinted in his *Miscellanies* (1739), in his *Sermons and Tracts* (1740), and in his *Discourses, Tracts and Poems* (1747). See Introduction.

[2] For Pope's statement of this theme see the *Essay on Man*, ii. 53 ff.

[3] Cicero, *De natura deorum*, 1. 43. 121 f.

not rather draw his Knowledge from an Observation of his own Temper; for he somewhere unluckily lays down this as a Rule, 'That from the Similitudes of Thoughts and Passions of one Man to the Thoughts and Passions of another, whosoever looks into himself and considers what he doth when he thinks, hopes, fears, &c. and upon what Grounds; he shall hereby read and know what are the Thoughts and Passions of all other Men upon the like Occasions.'[1] Now we will allow Mr. *Hobs* to know best how he was inclined: But in earnest, I should be heartily out of Conceit with my self, if I thought my self of this unamiable Temper, as he affirms, and should have as little Kindness for my self as for any Body in the World. Hitherto I always imagined that kind and benevolent Propensions[2] were the original Growth of the Heart of Man, and, however checked and overtop'd by counter Inclinations that have since sprung up within us, have still some Force in the worst of Tempers, and a considerable Influence on the best. And, methinks, it's a fair Step towards the Proof of this, that the most beneficent of all Beings is he who hath an absolute Fulness of Perfection in Himself, who gave Existence to the Universe, and so cannot be supposed to want that which He communicated, without diminishing from the Plenitude of his own Power and Happiness. The Philosophers before mentioned have indeed done all that in them lay to invalidate this Argument; for, placing the Gods in a State of the most elevated Blessedness, they describe them as Selfish as we poor miserable Mortals can be, and shut them out from all Concern for Mankind, upon the Score of their having no Need of us. But if He that sitteth in the Heavens wants not us, we stand in continual Need of Him; and, surely, next to the Survey of the immense Treasures of his own Mind, the most exalted Pleasure He receives is from beholding Millions of Creatures, lately drawn out of the Gulph of Non-existence, rejoycing in the various Degrees of Being and Happiness imparted to them.[3] And as this is the true, the glorious Character of the Deity, so in forming a reasonable Creature He would not, if possible, suffer his Image to pass out of his Hands unadorned with a Resemblance of Himself in this most lovely Part of his Nature. For what Complacency could a Mind, whose Love is as unbounded as his Knowledge, have in

[1] Hobbes, *Leviathan*, Introduction (Everyman ed., p. 2).
[2] I.e. propensities. Grove also uses this form of the word in No. 601.
[3] Cf. No. 519 (vol. iv).

a Work so unlike Himself? a Creature that should be capable of knowing and conversing with a vast Circle of Objects, and love none but Himself? What Proportion would there be between the Head and the Heart of such a Creature, its Affections, and its Understanding? Or could a Society of such Creatures, with no other Bottom but Self-Love on which to maintain a Commerce, ever flourish? Reason, 'tis certain, would oblige every Man to pursue the general Happiness, as the Means to procure and establish his own; and yet if, besides this Consideration, there were not a natural Instinct, prompting Men to desire the Welfare and Satisfaction of others, Self-Love, in Defiance of the Admonitions of Reason, would quickly run all Things into a State of War and Confusion. As nearly interested as the Soul is in the Fate of the Body, our provident Creator saw it necessary, by the constant Returns of Hunger and Thirst, those importunate Appetites, to put it in Mind of its Charge; knowing, that if we should eat and drink no oftner than cold abstracted Speculation should put us upon these Exercises, and then leave it to Reason to prescribe the Quantity, we should soon refine ourselves out of this bodily Life. And, indeed, 'tis obvious to Remark, that we follow nothing heartily, unless carried to it by Inclinations which anticipate our Reason, and, like a Biass, draw the Mind strongly towards it. In order, therefore, to establish a perpetual Intercourse of Benefits amongst Mankind, their Maker would not fail to give them this generous Prepossession of Benevolence, if, as I have said, it were possible. And from whence can we go about to argue its Impossibility? Is it inconsistent with Self-love? Are their Motions contrary? No more than the diurnal Rotation of the Earth is opposed to its Annual; or its Motion round its own Center, which may be improved as an Illustration of Self-Love, to that which whirls it about the common Center of the World, answering to universal Benevolence. Is the Force of Self-Love abated, or its Interest prejudiced by Benevolence? So far from it, that Benevolence, though a distinct Principle, is extreamly serviceable to Self-Love, and then doth most Service when 'tis least designed.

But to descend from Reason to matter of Fact; the pity which arises on sight of Persons in Distress, and the Satisfaction of Mind which is the Consequence of having removed them into a happier State, are instead of a thousand Arguments to prove such a thing as a disinterested Benevolence. Did Pity proceed from a Reflection

we make upon our Liableness to the same ill Accidents we see befall others, it were nothing to the present Purpose; but this is Assigning an artificial Cause of a natural Passion, and can by no means be admitted as a tolerable Account of it, because Children, and Persons most Thoughtless about their own Condition, and incapable of entering into the Prospects of Futurity, feel the most violent Touches of Compassion. And then as to that charming Delight which immediately follows the giving Joy to another, or relieving his Sorrow, and is, when the Objects are numerous, and the kindness of Importance really inexpressible, what can this be owing to but a Consciousness of a Man's having done something Praise-worthy, and expressive of a great Soul?[1] Whereas, if in all this he only Sacrificed to Vanity and Self-Love, as there would be nothing brave in Actions that make the most shining Appearance, so Nature would not have rewarded them with this divine Pleasure; nor could the Commendations, which a Person receives for Benefits done upon selfish Views, be at all more Satisfactory, than when he is applauded for what he doth without Design; because in both Cases the Ends of Self-Love are equally answered. The Conscience of approving ones self a Benefactor to Mankind is the noblest Recompence for being so; doubtless it is, and the most interested cannot propose any thing so much to their own Advantage, not-withstanding which, the Inclination is nevertheless unselfish. The Pleasure which attends the Gratification of our Hunger and Thirst, is not the Cause of these Appetites; they are previous to any such Prospect; and so likewise is the desire of doing Good; with this Difference, that being seated in the Intellectual Part, this last, though Antecedent to Reason, may yet be improved and regulated by it, and, I will add, is no otherwise a Virtue than as it is so. Thus have I contended for the Dignity of that Nature I have the Honour to partake of, and, after all the Evidence produced, think I have a Right to conclude, against the Motto of this Paper, that there is such a thing as Generosity in the World. Though if I were under a Mistake in this I should say, as *Cicero* in Relation to the Immortality of the Soul, I willingly err, and should believe it very much for the Interest of Mankind to lie under the same Delusion.[2] For the contrary Notion naturally tends to dispirit the Mind, and sinks

---

[1] Cf. Ronald S. Crane, 'Suggestions toward a genealogy of the "Man of Feeling"', *ELH*, i (1934), 205–30.

[2] Cicero, *De Senectute*, 23. 85. This sentence is used by Addison as the motto for *Freeholder* 51.

it into a Meanness fatal to the Godlike Zeal of doing good. As on the other Hand, it teaches People to be Ungrateful, by possessing them with a Perswasion concerning their Benefactors, that they have no Regard to them in the Benefits they bestow. Now he that banishes Gratitude from among Men, by so doing stops up the Stream of Beneficence. For though in conferring Kindnesses, a truly generous Man doth not aim at a Return, yet he looks to the Qualities of the Person obliged, and as nothing renders a Person more unworthy of a Benefit, than his being without all Resentment of it, he will not be extreamly forward to Oblige such a Man.

No. 589
[BUDGELL]

Friday, September 3, 1714[1]

Persequitur scelus ille suum: labefactaque tandem
Ictibus innumeris adductaque funibus arbor
Corruit. . . .

Ovid.

SIR,

'I AM so great an Admirer of Trees, that the Spot of Ground I have chosen to build a small Seat upon, in the Country, is almost in the midst of a large Wood. I was obliged, much against my Will, to cut down several Trees, that I might have any such thing as a Walk in my Gardens; but then I have taken Care to leave the Space, between every Walk, as much a Wood as I found it. The Moment you turn either to the right or left, you are in a Forest, where Nature presents you with a much more beautiful Scene than could have been raised by Art.

'Instead of *Tulips* or *Carnatians* I can shew you *Oakes* in my Gardens of four hundred Years standing, and a Knot of *Elms* that might shelter a Troop of Horse from the Rain.

'It is not without the utmost Indignation, that I observe several

---

[1] *Motto.* Ovid, *Metamorphoses*, 8. 774–6:
> Not thus restrain'd, he with repeated Blows
> And straining Cords the mighty Tree o'erthrows.

Assigned to Budgell in the Tickell MS.; it may represent an original contribution reworked by Budgell.

prodigal young Heirs in the Neighbourhood, felling down the most glorious Monuments of their Ancestors Industry, and ruining, in a Day, the Product of Ages.

'I am mightily pleased with your Discourse upon Planting,[1] which put me upon looking into my Books to give you some Account of the Veneration the Ancients had for Trees. There is an old Tradition, that *Abraham* planted a *Cyprus*, a *Pine*, and a *Cedar*, and that these three incorporated into one Tree, which was cut down for the building of the Temple of *Solomon*.[2]

'*Isidorus*, who lived in the Reign of *Constantius*, assures us, that he saw, even in his Time, that famous *Oak* in the Plains of *Mambré*, under which *Abraham* is reported to have dwelt, and adds, that the People looked upon it with a great Veneration, and preserved it as a Sacred Tree.[3]

'The Heathens still went farther, and regarded it as the highest Piece of Sacrilege to injure certain Trees which they took to be protected by some Deity. The Story of *Erisicthon*, the Grove at *Dodona*, and that at *Delphi*, are all Instances of this kind.[4]

'If we consider the Machine in *Virgil*, so much blamed by several Criticks, in this Light, we shall hardly think it too violent.[5]

'*Æneas*, when he built his Fleet, in order to sail for *Italy*, was obliged to cut down the Grove on Mount *Ida*, which however he durst not do till he had obtained Leave from *Cybele*, to whom it was dedicated. The Goddess could not but think her self obliged to protect these Ships, which were made of Consecrated Timber, after a very extraordinary Manner, and therefore desired *Jupiter*, that they might not be obnoxious to the Power of Waves or Winds. *Jupiter* would not grant this, but promised her, that as many as

[1] No. 583 (vol. iv).

[2] The material here is to be found in Bayle, art. Abraham, Remark T.

[3] In Remark T of the article 'Abraham' Bayle writes: 'This puts me in mind of the Oak of *Mamre*, under which it is pretended that *Abraham* went sometimes to cool himself. It is said, That that Oak was still to be seen in the Reign of *Constantius* . . .' In the margin a reference is given to 'Isidor. l. 17, c. 7 *Bonifacium Hist. ludicr.* p. 285'.

[4] Erysichthon, the Thessalian, cut down a great oak sacred to Ceres and was punished by a visit from Famine and afflicted with unappeasable hunger (Ovid, *Metamorphoses*, 8. 738–878). Bayle mentions the incident (art. Hamadryades, Remark D). Dodona was a city in Epirus and seat of an ancient oracle of Jupiter, whose responses were given in the rustling of oaks (Ovid, 7. 629; 13. 716). At the shrine of Apollo at Delphi the laurel tree and the quiver borne by Apollo quaked together as the response was given (ibid. 15. 634).

[5] *Aeneid*, 9. 77–122. Cf. Nos. 315 and 351 (vol. iii) for Addison's references to this episode. In No. 351 it is called 'the most violent Machine in the whole *Æneid*', one which 'has given Offence to several Criticks'.

came safe to *Italy* should be transformed into Goddesses of the Sea;
which the Poet tells us was accordingly executed.

> *And now at length the number'd Hours were come,*
> *Prefix'd by Fate's irrevocable Doom,*
> *When the great Mother of the Gods was free*
> *To save her Ships, and finish* Jove's *Decree.*
> *First, from the Quarter of the Morn, there sprung*
> *A Light that sign'd the Heav'ns, and shot along:*
> *Then from a Cloud, fring'd round with Golden Fires*
> *Were Timbrels heard, and* Berecynthian *Quires:*
> *And last a Voice, with more than Mortal Sounds,*
> *Both Hosts in Arms oppos'd, with equal Horror wounds.*
> O Trojan *Race, your needless Aid forbear;*
> *And know my Ships are my peculiar Care.*
> *With greater ease the bold* Rutulian *may,*
> *With hissing Brands, attempt to burn the Sea,*
> *Than singe my sacred Pines. But you my Charge,*
> *Loos'd from your crooked Anchors launch at large,*
> *Exalted each a Nymph: Forsake the Sand,*
> *And swim the Seas, at* Cybele's *Command.*
> *No sooner had the Goddess ceas'd to speak,*
> *When lo, th' obedient Ships, their Haulsers break;*
> *And, strange to tell, like Dolphins in the Main,*
> *They plunge their Prow's, and dive, and spring again:*
> *As many beauteous Maids the Billows sweep,*
> *As rode before tall Vessels on the Deep.*

Dryden's Virg.[1]

'The common Opinion concerning the Nymphs, whom the
Ancients called *Hamadryads*, is more to the Honour of Trees than
any thing yet mentioned. It was thought the Fate of these Nymphs
had so near a Dependance on some Trees, more especially Oaks,
that they lived and died together. For this Reason, they were
extreamly grateful to such Persons who preserved those Trees with
which their Being subsisted. *Apollonius* tells us a very remarkable
Story to this Purpose, with which I shall conclude my Letter.[2]

'A certain Man, called *Rhæcus*, observing an old Oak ready to
fall, and being moved with a sort of Compassion towards the Tree,

---

[1] Dryden's *Aeneis*, ix. 125–48.

[2] Apollonius Rhodius, *Argonautica*, book 2. The story here derives from Bayle,
art. Hamadryades, Remark B. The final sentence is an addition by Budgell.

ordered his Servants to pour in fresh Earth at the Roots, and set it upright. The *Hamadryad*, or Nymph, who must necessarily have perished with the Tree, appeared to him the next Day, and after having returned him her Thanks, told him, she was ready to grant what ever he should ask. As she was extreamly Beautiful, *Rhæcus* desired he might be entertained as her Lover. The *Hamadryad*, not much displeased with the Request, promised to give him a Meeting, but commanded him for some Days to abstain from the Embraces of all other Women, adding, that she would send a Bee to him, to let him know when he was to be Happy. *Rhæcus* was, it seems, too much addicted to Gaming, and happened to be in a run of ill Luck when the faithful Bee came buzzing about him; so that instead of minding his kind Invitation, he had like to have killed him for his Pains. The *Hamadryad* was so provoked at her own Disappointment, and the ill Usage of her Messenger, that she deprived *Rhæcus* of the Use of his Limbs. However, says the Story, he was not so much a Criple, but he made a shift to cut down the Tree, and consequently to fell his Mistress.'

No. 590   *Monday, September 6, 1714*[1]
[ADDISON]

. . . Assiduo labuntur tempora motu
Non secus ac flumen. Neque enim consistere flumen,
Nec levis hora potest: sed ut unda impellitur unda,
Urgeturque prior venienti, urgetque priorem,
Tempora sic fugiunt pariter, pariterque sequuntur;
Et nova sunt semper. Nam quod fuit ante, relictum est;
Fitque quod haud fuerat: momentaque cuncta novantur.
Ov. Met.

The following Discourse comes from the same Hand
with the Essays upon Infinitude.[2]

WE consider infinite Space as an Expansion without a Circumference: We consider Eternity, or infinite Duration, as a

[*For notes 1 and 2 see following page.*

Line that has neither a Beginning nor an End. In our Speculations of infinite Space, we consider that particular Place in which we exist, as a kind of Center to the whole Expansion. In our Speculations of Eternity, we consider the Time which is present to us as the Middle, which divides the whole Line into two equal Parts. For this Reason, many witty Authors compare the present Time to an Isthmus or narrow Neck of Land, that rises in the midst of an Ocean, immeasurably diffused on either Side of it.[1]

Philosophy, and indeed common Sense, naturally throws Eternity under two Divisions; which we may call in *English*, that Eternity which is past, and that Eternity which is to come. The learned Terms of, *Æternitas a Parte ante*, and *Æternitas a Parte post*, may be more amusing to the Reader, but can have no other Idea affixed to them than what is convey'd to us by those Words, an Eternity that is past, and an Eternity that is to come.[2] Each of these Eternities is bounded at the one Extream; or, in other Words, the former has an End, and the latter a Beginning.

Let us first of all consider that Eternity which is past, reserving that which is to come for the Subject of another Paper. The Nature of this Eternity is utterly inconceivable by the Mind of Man: Our Reason demonstrates to us that it *has been*, but at the same Time can frame no Idea of it, but what is big with Absurdity and

---

[1] Cf. Cowley's Pindaric ode, 'Life and Fame', lines 10–13:

> Vain weak-built *Isthmus*, which dost proudly rise
> Up betwixt *two Eternities*;
> Yet canst nor *Wave* nor *Wind* sustain,
> But *broken* and *orewhelm'd*, the endless *Oceans* meet again.

Cowley's note reads: '*Isthmus* is a neck of Land that divides a *Peninsula* from the *Continent*, and is betwixt two Seas. . . . In which manner this narrow passage of *Life* divides the *Past Time* from the *Future*, and is at last swallowed up into *Eternity*' (*Poems*, ed. Waller, pp. 202–3).
[2] In his note on 'The Muse' Cowley writes: 'There are two sorts of *Eternity*; from the *Present backwards* to *Eternity*, and from the *Present forwards*, called by the Schoolmen *Æternitas à parte ante*, and *Æternitas à parte post* (ibid., p. 187).

---

[1] *Motto*. Ovid, *Metamorphoses*, 15. 179–85 (altered):

> Time hastes it self perpetually away.
> No more the fleeting Hours than Tides can stay:
> But as one Billow the preceding drives,
> And as succeeding that a third arrives:
> So fly the rolling Years, and so pursue,
> Each others, ever changing, ever new.
> What once was manifest, no more we see,
> Nor what is present shall hereafter be.
> Each Moment is renew'd . . .

[2] Nos. 565, 571, 580 (vol. iv).

Contradiction. We can have no other Conception of any Duration which is past, than that all of it was once present; and whatever was once present, is at some certain Distance from us; and whatever is at any certain Distance from us, be the Distance never so remote, cannot be Eternity. The very Notion of any Duration's being past, implies that it was once present; for the Idea of being once present, is actually included in the Idea of its being past. This therefore is a Depth not to be sounded by human Understanding. We are sure that there has been an Eternity, and yet contradict our selves when we measure this Eternity by any Notion which we can frame of it.

If we go to the Bottom of this Matter, we shall find, that the Difficulties we meet with in our Conceptions of Eternity proceed from this single Reason, That we can have no other Idea of any kind of Duration, than that by which we our selves, and all other created Beings, do exist; which is, a successive Duration, made up of past, present, and to come. There is nothing which exists after this Manner, all the Parts of whose Existence were not once actually present, and consequently may be reached by a certain Number of Years applied to it. We may ascend as high as we please, and employ our being to all that Eternity which is to come, in adding Millions of Years to Millions of Years, and we can never come up to any Fountain-head of Duration, to any Beginning in Eternity: But at the same time we are sure, that whatever was once present does lie within the Reach of Numbers, tho' perhaps we can never be able to put enough of 'em together for that Purpose. We may as well say, that any thing may be actually present in any Part of infinite Space, which does not lie at a certain Distance from us, as that any Part of infinite Duration was once actually present, and does not also lie at some determined Distance from us. The Distance in both Cases may be immeasurable and indefinite as to our Faculties, but our Reason tells us that it cannot be so in it self. Here therefore is that Difficulty which human Understanding is not capable of surmounting. We are sure that something must have existed from Eternity, and are at the same Time unable to conceive that any thing which exists, according to our Notion of Existence, can have existed from Eternity.

It is hard for a Reader, who has not rolled this Thought in his own Mind, to follow in such an abstracted[1] Speculation; but I have

---

[1] Here, as in No. 47, used in the obsolete sense of 'abstruse, difficult' (*OED*, with dates 1615–1823).

been the longer on it, because I think it is a demonstrative Argument of the Being and Eternity of a God: And tho' there are many other Demonstrations which lead us to this great Truth, I do not think we ought to lay aside any Proofs in this Matter which the Light of Reason has suggested to us, especially when it is such a one as has been urged by Men famous for their Penetration and Force of Understanding, and which appears altogether conclusive to those who will be at the Pains to examine it.

Having thus considered that Eternity which is past, according to the best Idea we can frame of it, I shall now draw up those several Articles on this Subject which are dictated to us by the Light of Reason, and which may be looked upon as the Creed of a Philosopher in this great Point.

First, It is certain that no Being could have made it self; for if so, it must have acted before it was, which is a Contradiction.

Secondly, That therefore some Being must have existed from all Eternity.

Thirdly, That whatever exists after the manner of created Beings, or according to any Notions which we have of Existence, could not have existed from Eternity.

Fourthly, That this eternal Being must therefore be the Great Author of Nature, *the Antient of Days,*[1] who, being at an infinite Distance in his Perfections from all finite and created Beings, exists in a quite different manner from them, and in a manner of which they can have no Idea.

I know that several of the School-men, who would not be thought ignorant of any thing, have pretended to explain the Manner of God's Existence, by telling us, That he comprehends infinite Duration in every Moment; That Eternity is with him a *punctum stans,* a fixed Point;[2] or, which is as good Sense, an *Infinite Instant;* that nothing with Reference to his Existence is either past or to come; To which the ingenious Mr. *Cowley* alludes in his Description of Heaven,

[1] Dan. vii. 9, 13, 22.
[2] The illustrations come from Cowley's notes to *Davideis,* i. 361–2:

Eternity is defined by *Boet.* Lib. 5. *de Consolat. Interminabilis vitæ tota simul & perfecta possessio.* The whole and perfect possession, ever all at once, of a Being without beginning or ending. Which *Definition* is followed by *Tho. Aquin.* and all the *Schoolmen*; who therefore call *Eternity Nunc stans,* a standing *Now,* to distinguish it from that *Now,* which is a difference of *time,* and is alwaies in *Fluxu (Poems,* ed. Waller, p. 273).

Nothing is there to come, and nothing past,
But an Eternal NOW *does always last.*[1]

For my own Part, I look upon these Propositions as Words that have no Ideas annexed to them; and think Men had better own their Ignorance, than advance Doctrines, by which they mean nothing, and which indeed are self-contradictory. We cannot be too modest in our Disquisitions, when we meditate on him, who is environned with so much Glory and Perfection,[a] who is the Source of Being, the Fountain of all that Existence which we and his whole Creation derive from him. Let us therefore with the utmost Humility acknowledge, that as some Being must necessarily have existed from Eternity, so this Being does exist after an incomprehensible manner, since it is impossible for a Being to have existed from Eternity after our Manner or Notions of Existence. Revelation confirms these natural Dictates of Reason in the Accounts which it gives us of the Divine Existence, where it tells us, that he is the same Yesterday, to Day, and for Ever; that he is the *Alpha* and *Omega*, the Beginning and the Ending; that a thousand Years are with him as one Day, and one Day as a thousand Years;[2] by which, and the like Expressions, we are taught, that his Existence, with Relation to Time or Duration, is infinitely different from the Existence of any of his Creatures, and consequently that it is impossible for us to frame any adequate Conceptions of it.

In the first Revelation which he makes of his own Being, he intitles himself, *I am that I am;*[b] and when *Moses* desires to know what Name he shall give him in his Embassy to *Pharaoh*, he bids him say that, *I am* hath sent you.[3] Our great Creator, by this Revelation of himself, does in a manner exclude every thing else from a real Existence, and distinguishes himself from his Creatures, as the only Being which truly and really exists. The ancient Platonick Notion, which was drawn from Speculations of Eternity, wonderfully agrees with this Revelation which God has made of himself. There is nothing, say they, which in Reality exists, whose Existence, as we call it, is pieced up of past, present, and to come. Such a flitting and successive Existence is rather a Shadow of Existence, and something which is like it, than Existence it self.

---

[a] Perfection,] Perfection *Fol.*   [b] *I am that I am;*] *I am, that am; Fol.*

[1] Cowley, *Davides*, i. 361–2.
[3] Exod. iii. 14.   [2] Ps. xc. 4.

He only properly exists whose Existence is intirely present; that is, in other Words, who exists in the most perfect manner, and in such a manner as we have no Idea of.

I shall conclude this Speculation with one useful Inference. How can we sufficiently prostrate our selves and fall down before our Maker, when we consider that ineffable Goodness and Wisdom which contrived this Existence for finite Natures? What must be the Overflowings of that good Will, which prompted our Creator to adapt Existence to Beings, in whom it is not necessary? Especially when we consider, that he himself was before, in the compleat Possession of Existence and of Happiness, and in the full Enjoyment of Eternity. What Man can think of himself as called out and separated from nothing, of his being made a conscious, a reasonable, and a happy Creature, in short, of being taken in as a Sharer of Existence and a kind of Partner in Eternity, without being swallowed up in Wonder, in Praise, in Adoration! It is indeed a Thought too big for the Mind of Man, and rather to be entertained in the Secrecy of Devotion and in the Silence of the Soul, than to be expressed by Words. The Supreme Being has not given us Powers or Faculties sufficient to extol and magnifie such unutterable Goodness.

ᵃIt is however some Comfort to us, that we shall be always doing what we shall be never able to do, and that a Work which cannot be finished, will however be the Work of an Eternity.

No. 591   *Wednesday, September 8, 1714*[1]
[BUDGELL]

. . . Tenerorum lusor amorum.

Ov.

I HAVE just received a Letter from a Gentleman, who tells me he has observed with no small Concern, that my Papers have

ᵃ *No new paragraph in Fol.*

[1] *Motto.* Ovid, *Tristia*, 3. 3. 73: Love is my sportive theme.
This number is assigned to Budgell in the Tickell MS. It is probably a working over of contributed material.

of late been very barren in relation to Love; a Subject which, when agreeably handled, can scarce fail of being well received by both Sexes.

If my Invention therefore should be almost exhausted on this Head, he offers to serve under me in the Quality of a *Love Casuist*; for which Place he conceives himself to be throughly qualified, having made this Passion his principal Study, and observed it in all its different Shapes and Appearances, from the Fifteenth to the Forty fifth Year of his Age.

He assures me with an Air of Confidence, which I hope proceeds from his real Abilities, that he does not doubt of giving Judgment to the Satisfaction of the Parties concerned, on the most nice and intricate Cases which can happen in an Amour; as,

How great the Contraction of the Fingers must be, before it amounts to a Squeeze by the Hand.

What can be properly termed an absolute Denial from a Maid, and what from a Widow.

What Advances a Lover may presume to make, after having received a Patt upon his Shoulder from his Mistress's Fan.

Whether a Lady, at the first Interview, may allow an humble Servant to kiss her Hand.

How far it may be permitted to caress the Maid, in order to succeed with the Mistress.

What Constructions a Man may put upon a Smile, and in what Cases a Frown goes for nothing.

On what Occasions a sheepish Look may do Service, &c.

As a farther Proof of his Skill, he has also sent me several Maxims in Love, which he assures me are the Result of a long and profound Reflection, some of which I think my self obliged to communicate to the Publick, not remembring to have seen them before in any Author.

'There are more Calamities in the World arising from Love than from Hatred.

'Love is the Daughter of *Idleness*, but the Mother of *Disquietude*.

'Men of grave Natures (says Sir *Francis Bacon*) are the most constant; for the same Reason Men should be more constant than Women.[1]

---

[1] Sir Francis Bacon, *Of Marriage and Single Life*: 'Grave Natures, led by Custome, and therfore constant, are commonly loving *Husbands* . . .' (*Essays*, ed. Wright, 1899, p. 27).

'The Gay Part of Mankind is most amorous, the Serious most loving.

'A Coquet often loses her Reputation whilst she preserves her Virtue.

'A Prude often preserves her Reputation when she has lost her Virtue.

'Love refines a Man's Behaviour, but makes a Woman's ridiculous.

'Love is generally accompanied with Good-will in the Young, Interest in the Middle-Aged, and a Passion too gross to name in the Old.

'The Endeavours to revive a decaying Passion generally extinguish the Remains of it.

'A Woman who from being a Slattern becomes over-neat, or from being over-neat becomes a Slattern, is most certainly in love.'

I shall make use of this Gentleman's Skill as I see Occasion;[1] and since I am got upon the Subject of Love, shall conclude this Paper with a Copy of Verses which were lately sent me by an unknown Hand, as I look upon them to be above the ordinary Run of Sonnateers.[2]

The Author tells me they were written in one of his despairing

---

[1] See Nos. 602, 605, 607, 614, 623, and 625.

[2] The tradition that these lines were written by Gilbert Budgell, the younger brother of Eustace, seems to have originated in Theophilus Cibber's *Lives of the Poets* (1753). Apropos of Eustace Budgell the compilers write (v. 14–15):

> As to his brothers, the second, Gilbert, was thought a man of deeper learning and better judgment when he was young than our author, but was certainly inferior to him in his appearance in life; and, 'tis thought, greatly inferior to him in every respect. He was the author of a pretty copy of verses in the VIIIth Vol. of the Spectators, Numb. 591, which begins thus,
>
> > Conceal, fond man, conceal the mighty smart,
> > Nor tell Corinna she has fix'd thy heart.

Gilbert Budgell was born about 1689 and matriculated at Christ Church 17 Nov. 1707, at the age of eighteen, received his B.A. in 1711, his M.A. in 1714, and some time later took orders (John Foster, *Alumni Oxonienses*, Early Series, 1500–1714 (Oxford, 1891), i. 206). The account in the *Lives of the Poets* (v. 15) reports the rumour that the verses are based upon experience:

> It is said that it was a repulse from a lady of great fortune, with whom he was desperately in love whilst at Oxford, and to whom he had addressed these lines, that made him disregard himself ever after, neglect his studies, and fall into a habit of drinking. Whatever was the occasion of his last vice it ruined him.

J. D., writing in the *Gentleman's Magazine*, April 1780 (p. 175), states categorically that 'the verses in No. 591 were by Mr. Gilbert Budgell, Eustace's elder brother'. In a note on this number Nichols (1789) writes: 'This Paper, No. 591, might be written by Mr. G. Budgell or his brother Eustace, for it is said that this whole volume was *published* by him and his kinsman Addison, without the concurrence of Steele.' Nathan Drake (*Essays*, iii. 371) also describes Gilbert Budgell as the author of these 'elegant verses', which describe, 'with no common skill and beauty, his ardent, but almost hopeless, attachment for the fair Corinna'.

Fits; and I find entertains some Hope that his Mistress may pity such a Passion as he has described, before she knows that she is herself *Corinna.*

> *CONCEAL, fond Man, conceal the mighty Smart,*
> *Nor tell* Corinna *she has fir'd thy Heart.*
> *In vain would'st thou complain, in vain pretend*
> *To ask a Pity which she must not lend.*
> *She's too much thy Superior to comply,*
> *And too too fair to let thy Passion die.*
> *Languish in Secret, and with dumb Surprize*
> *Drink the resistless Glances of her Eyes.*
> *At awful Distance entertain thy Grief,*
> *Be still in Pain, but never ask Relief.*
> *Ne'er tempt her Scorn of thy consuming State,*
> *Be any way undone, but fly her Hate.*
> *Thou must submit to see thy Charmer bless*
> *Some happier Youth, that shall admire her less;*
> *Who in that lovely Form, that heav'nly Mind,*
> *Shall miss ten thousand Beauties thou could'st find;*
> *Who with low Fancy shall approach her Charms,*
> *While half enjoy'd she sinks into his Arms.*
> *She knows not, must not know, thy nobler Fire,*
> *Whom she, and whom the Muses do inspire:*
> *Her Image only shall thy Breast employ,*
> *And fill thy captiv'd Soul with Shades of Joy.*
> *Direct thy Dreams by Night, thy Thoughts by Day;*
> *And never, never, from thy Bosom stray.*

No. 592   *Friday, September* 10, 1714[1]
[ADDISON]

. . . *Studium sine divite Vena.*

Hor.

I LOOK upon the Play-house as a World within it self. They have lately furnished the Middle Region of it with a new Sett of Meteors, in order to give the Sublime to many modern Tragedies. I was there last Winter at the first Rehearsal of the new Thunder,

[1] *Motto.* Horace, *Ars poetica*, 409: Study without the rich vein of genius.

which is much more deep and sonorous than any hitherto made use of.[1] They have a *Salmoneus* behind the Scenes, who plays it off with great Success.[2] Their Lightnings are made to flash more briskly than heretofore; their Clouds are also better furbelow'd, and more voluminous; not to mention a violent Storm locked up in a great Chest that is designed for the *Tempest*.[3] They are also provided with above a Dozen Showers of Snow, which, as I am informed, are the Plays of many unsuccessful Poets artificially cut and shreaded for that Use. Mr. *Rimer*'s *Edgar* is to fall in Snow at the next acting of King *Lear*, in order to heighten, or rather to alleviate, the Distress of that unfortunate Prince; and to serve by way of Decoration to a Piece which that great Critick has written against.[4]

I do not indeed wonder that the Actors should be such professed Enemies to those among our Nation who are commonly known by the Name of Criticks, since it is a Rule among these Gentlemen to fall upon a Play, not because it is ill written, but because it takes. Several of them lay it down as a Maxim, That whatever Dramatick Performance has a long Run, must of Necessity be good for nothing; as tho' the first Precept in Poetry were *not to please*. Whether this Rule holds good or not, I shall leave to the Determination of those who are better Judges than my self: If it does, I am sure it tends very much to the Honour of those Gentlemen who have established it; few of their Pieces having been disgraced by a Run of three Days, and most of them being so exquisitely written, that the Town would never give them more than one Night's Hearing.[5]

I have a great Esteem for a true Critick, such as *Aristotle* and *Longinus* among the *Greeks*, *Horace* and *Quintilian* among the *Romans*, *Boileau* and *Dacier* among the *French*. But it is our Misfortune, that some who set up for professed Criticks among us are so stupid, that they do not know how to put ten Words together with Elegance or common Propriety, and withall so illiterate, that they have no Taste of the learned Languages, and therefore criticise upon old Authors only at second-hand. They judge of them by what others have written, and not by any Notions they have of the Authors

---

[1] Cf. Addison's allusion to 'the play-house thunderer' in No. 235 and note.

[2] Virgil, *Aeneid*, 6. 787. Cf. No. 36 (vol. i).

[3] *The Tempest* had been last performed on 4 June at Drury Lane, with Powell in the role of Prospero.

[4] Thomas Rymer's *Edgar, or the English Monarch* (1678). Rymer's censure of Shakespeare is alluded to in 'the next acting of King *Lear*'.

[5] The author's benefit was on the third day.

themselves. The Words Unity, Action, Sentiment, and Diction, pronounced with an Air of Authority, give them a Figure among unlearned Readers, who are apt to believe they are very deep, because they are unintelligible. The ancient Criticks are full of the Praises of their Contemporaries; they discover Beauties which escaped the Observation of the Vulgar, and very often find out Reasons for palliating and excusing such little Slips and Over sights as were committed in the Writings of eminent Authors. On the contrary, most of the Smatterers in Criticism who appear among us, make it their Business to vilify and depreciate every new Production that gains Applause, to descry imaginary Blemishes, and to prove by far-fetch'd Arguments, that what pass for Beauties in any celebrated Piece are Faults and Errors. In short, the Writings of these Criticks compared with those of the Ancients, are like the Works of the Sophists compared with those of the old Philosophers.

Envy and Cavil are the natural Fruits of Laziness and Ignorance; which was probably the Reason, that in the Heathen Mythology *Momus* is said to be the Son of *Nox* and *Somnus*, of Darkness and Sleep.[1] Idle Men, who have not been at the Pains to accomplish or distinguish themselves, are very apt to detract from others; as ignorant Men are very subject to decry those Beauties in a celebrated Work which they have not Eyes to discover. Many of our Sons of *Momus*, who dignify themselves by the Name of Criticks, are the genuine Descendants of these two illustrious Ancestors. They are often led into those numerous Absurdities, in which they daily instruct the People, by not considering that, 1st, There is sometimes a greater Judgment shewn in deviating from the Rules of Art, than in adhering to them; and, 2dly, That there is more Beauty in the Works of a great Genius who is ignorant of all the Rules of Art, than in the Works of a little Genius, who not only knows, but scrupulously observes them.

1st, We may often take Notice of Men who are perfectly acquainted with all the Rules of good Writing, and notwithstanding choose to depart from them on extraordinary Occasions. I could give Instances out of all the Tragick Writers of Antiquity who have shewn their Judgment in this Particular, and purposely receded from an establish'd Rule of the Drama, when it has made way for

[1] 'Momus, was the Son of *Somnus* and *Nox*, he was the God of Liberty, being a Deity that spoke his Mind freely, and controul'd every thing, even the Actions of the Gods themselves, as may be seen in a Dialogue of *Lucian* concerning *Jupiter Tragicus*' (Danet).

a much higher Beauty than the Observation of such a Rule would have been. Those who have surveyed the noblest Pieces of Architecture and Statuary both ancient and modern, know very well that there are frequent Deviations from Art in the Works of the greatest Masters, which have produced a much nobler Effect than a more accurate and exact way of Proceeding could have done. This often arises from what the *Italians* call the *Gusto Grande* in these Arts, which is what we call the Sublime in Writing.[1]

In the next Place, our Criticks do not seem sensible that there is more Beauty in the Works of a great Genius who is ignorant of the Rules of Art, than in those of a little Genius who knows and observes them. It is of these Men of Genius that *Terence* speaks, in opposition to the little artificial Cavillers of his Time;

> *Quorum æmulari exoptat negligentiam*
> *Potiùs, quàm istorum obscuram diligentiam.*[2]

A Critick may have the same Consolation in the ill Success of his Play, as Dr. *South* tells us a Physician has at the Death of a Patient, That he was killed *secundum artem*.[3] Our inimitable *Shakespear* is a Stumbling-block to the whole Tribe of these rigid Criticks. Who would not rather read one of his Plays, where there is not a single Rule of the Stage observed, than any Production of a modern Critick, where there is not one of them violated? *Shakespear* was indeed born with all the Seeds of Poetry, and may be compared to the Stone in *Pyrrhus*'s Ring, which, as *Pliny* tells us, had the Figure of *Apollo* and the Nine Muses in the Veins of it, produced by the spontaneous Hand of Nature, without any Help from Art.[4]

---

[1] In the section on Rome in the *Remarks on Italy* (1705) Addison had commented on the seeming disproportion of the ancient pillars found there. Some, he says, explain this as rather

> an Effect of Art, and of what the *Italians* call the *Gusto grande*, than of any Negligence in the Architect; for they say the Ancients always consider'd the Situation of a Building, whether it were high or low, in an open Square or in a narrow Street, and more or less deviated from their Rules of Art, to comply with the several Distances and Elevations from which their Works were to be regarded (pp. 355–6).

[2] *Andria*, Prologue, 20–21. Terence's critics in censuring him are censuring Naevius, Plautus, and Ennius, 'on whose authority our dramatist may rely, and whose freedom he is far more earnest to imitate than the murky accuracy of his critics' (trans. Sergeaunt, Loeb Lib.).

[3] The phrase occurs in Robert South's 'Sermon preached at Westminster-Abbey, February 22, 1684–5', on chance in the affairs of men (*Twelve Sermons*, 6th ed., 1727, i. 316).

[4] Pliny, *Natural History*, 37. 3: 'Post hunc anulum regis alterius in fama est gemma, Pyrrhi illius, qui adversus Romanos bellum gessit. Namque habuisse dicitur achaten in qua novem Musae et Apollo citharam tenens spectarentur, non arte, sed naturae sponte ita discurrentibus maculis ut Musis quoque singulis sua redderentur insignia.'

[BYROM]

> *Quale per incertam Lunam sub luce maligna*
> *Est iter in Sylvis:* . . .
>
> Virg.

MY dreaming Correspondent, Mr. *Shadow*,[2] has sent me a second Letter, with several curious Observations on Dreams in general, and the Method to render Sleep improving: An Extract of his Letter will not, I presume, be disagreeable to my Readers.

'SINCE we have so little Time to spare, that none of it may be lost, I see no Reason why we should neglect to examine those imaginary Scenes we are presented with in Sleep, only because they have less Reality in them than our waking Meditations. A Traveller would bring his Judgment in Question who should despise the Directions of his Map for want of real Roads in it, because here stands a *Dott* instead of a Town, or a *Cypher* instead of a City, and it must be a long Day's Journey to travel thro' two or three Inches. Fancy in Dreams gives us much such another Landskip of Life as that does of Countries, and tho' its Appearances may seem strangely jumbled together, we may often observe such Traces and Footsteps of noble Thoughts, as, if carefully pursued, might lead us into a proper Path of Action. There is so much Rapture and Extasie in our fancied Bliss, and something so dismal and shocking in our fancied Misery, that tho' the Inactivity of the Body has given Occasion for calling Sleep the Image of *Death*,[3] the Briskness of the Fancy affords us a strong Intimation of something within us that can never die.

'I have wondered, that *Alexander* the Great, who came into the World sufficiently dreamt of by his Parents, and had himself a tolerable knack at dreaming, should often say, that *Sleep was one*

---

[1] *Motto.* Virgil, *Aeneid*, 6. 270–1:
> Thus wander Travellers in Woods by Night,
> By the Moon's doubtful, and malignant Light. DRYDEN.

The main part of this number consists of a second letter by Mr. Shadow, i.e. John Byrom (cf. No. 586). The opening and closing paragraphs are probably by Budgell, since this number is assigned to Budgell in the Tickell MS.

[2] See No. 586.

[3] A frequent comparison; e.g. Ovid, *Amores*, 2. 9. 41.

thing which made him sensible he was Mortal.[1] I who have not such Fields of Action in the Day-time to divert my Attention from this Matter, plainly perceive, that in those Operations of the Mind, while the Body is at rest, there is a certain Vastness of Conception very suitable to the Capacity, and demonstrative of the Force, of that Divine Part in our Composition which will last for ever. Neither do I much doubt but that had we a true Account of the Wonders the Hero last mentioned performed in his Sleep, his conquering this little Globe would hardly be worth mentioning. I may affirm, without Vanity, that when I compare several Actions in *Quintus Curtius* with some others in my own Noctuary, I appear the greater Hero of the two.'[2]

I shall close this Subject with observing, that while we are awake, we are at Liberty to fix our Thoughts on what we please, but in Sleep we have not the Command of them. The Ideas which strike the Fancy, arise in us without our Choice, either from the Occurrences of the Day past, the Temper we lye down in, or it may be the Direction of some superior Being.

It is certain the Imagination may be so differently affected in Sleep, that our Actions of the Day might be either rewarded or punished with a little Age of Happiness or Misery. St. *Austin* was of Opinion, that if in *Paradise* there was the same Vicissitude of sleeping and waking as in the present World, the Dreams of its Inhabitants would be very happy.[3]

And so far at present our Dreams are in our Power, that they are generally conformable to our waking Thoughts, so that it is not impossible to convey our selves to a Consort of Musick, the Conversation of distant Friends, or any other Entertainment which has been before lodged in the Mind.

My Readers, by applying these Hints, will find the Necessity of making a *good Day* of it, if they heartily wish themselves a *good Night.*

I have often considered *Marcia*'s Prayer,[4] and *Lucius*'s Account of *Cato* in this Light.[5]

[1] Plutarch, *Life of Alexander*, 22. 3. The saying is also in Bayle, 'Macedonia', Remark E.

[2] Quintus Curtius wrote an account of Alexander's exploits (*The Life and Death of Alexander the Great*) in ten books, of which two are lost. An incident from it is cited in No. 31 (i. 129).

[3] This has not been located.

[4] Addison's *Cato*, V. iii. 9–13.

[5] Ibid. V. iv. 27–34.

Marc. *O ye immortal Powers, that guard the Just,*
Watch round his Couch, and soften his Repose,
Banish his Sorrows, and becalm his Soul
With easie Dreams; remember all his Virtues!
And show Mankind that Goodness is your Care.

  Luc. *Sweet are the Slumbers of the virtuous Man!*
O Marcia, I have seen thy Godlike Father:
Some Pow'r invisible supports his Soul,
And bears it up in all its wonted Greatness.
A kind refreshing Sleep is fall'n upon him:
I saw him stretcht at Ease, his Fancy lost
In pleasing Dreams; as I drew near his Couch,
He smil'd, and cry'd, Cæsar *thou can'st not hurt me.*

Mr. *Shadow* acquaints me in a Postscript, that he has no manner of Title to the Vision which succeeded his first Letter;[1] but adds, that as the Gentleman who wrote it Dreams very sensibly, he shall be glad to meet him some Night or other, under the great Elm Tree by which *Virgil* has given us a fine Metaphorical Image of Sleep, in order to turn over a few of the Leaves together, and oblige the Publick with an Account of the Dreams that lie under them.[2]

No. 594   *Wednesday, September 15, 1714*[3]
[ADDISON]

Absentem qui rodit amicum,
Qui non defendit, alio culpante; solutos
Qui captat risus hominum, famamque dicacis,
Fingere qui non visa potest, commissa tacere
Qui nequit, hic niger est: hunc tu Romane caveto.
                              Hor.

WERE all the Vexations of Life put together, we should find that a great Part of them proceed from those Calumnies and Reproaches which we spread abroad concerning one another.

[1] The vision succeeding his first letter is contained in No. 587.
[2] *Aeneid,* 6. 282–4.   [*For note 3 see following page.*]

There is scarce a Man living who is not, in some Degree, guilty of this Offence; tho', at the same time, however we treat one another, it must be confessed, that we all consent in speaking ill of the Persons who are notorious for this Practice. It generally takes its Rise either from an Ill-will to Mankind, a private Inclination to make our selves esteemed, an Ostentation of Wit, a Vanity of being thought in the Secrets of the World, or from a Desire of gratifying any of these Dispositions of Mind in those Persons with whom we converse.

The Publisher of Scandal is more or less odious to Mankind, and criminal in himself, as he is influenced by any one or more of the foregoing Motives. But whatever may be the Occasion of spreading these false Reports, he ought to consider, that the Effect of them is equally prejudicial and pernicious to the Person at whom they are aimed: The Injury is the same, tho' the Principle from whence it proceeds may be different.

As every one looks upon himself with too much Indulgence, when he passes a Judgment on his own Thoughts or Actions, and as very few would be thought guilty of this abominable Proceeding, which is so universally practised, and, at the same time, so universally blamed, I shall lay down three Rules by which I would have a Man examine and search into his own Heart, before he stands acquitted to himself of that evil Disposition of Mind which I am here mentioning.

First of all, let him consider whether he does not take Delight in hearing the Faults of others.

Secondly, Whether he is not too apt to believe such little blackning Accounts, and more inclined to be credulous on the uncharitable than on the good-natured Side.

---

³ *Motto.* Horace, *Satires*, I. 4. 81–85:

> He that himself shall blame his absent Friends,
> Or hears them scandaliz'd, and not defends,
> Sports with their Fame, and speaks what e're He can,
> And only to be thought a Witty Man,
> Tells Tales, and brings his Friend in dis-esteem,
> That Man's a *Knave*, be sure beware of him. CREECH.

Although this number, like No. 570, was not reprinted (by an oversight?) in Tickell's edition of Addison's works, it is assigned to Addison in the Tickell MS. and both in content and in style bears the mark of Addison's hand. One of Addison's favourite phrases, 'to wear out of his mind', occurs on p. 33, line 12, and the revisions—including *that* to *which* in two cases—also suggest Addison. Moreover, if we take *secret* to be one of Addison's favourite adjectives, this is to be found twice in the essay (p.33, line 20; p. 34, line 6).

Thirdly, Whether he is not ready to spread and propagate such Reports as tend to the Disreputation[1] of another.

These are the several Steps by which this Vice proceeds, and grows up into Slander and Defamation.

In the first Place, A Man who takes delight in hearing the Faults of others, shows sufficiently that he has a true Relish of Scandal, and consequently the Seeds of this Vice within him. If his Mind is gratified with hearing the Reproaches which[a] are cast on others, he will find the same Pleasure in relating them, and be the more apt to do it as he will naturally imagine every one he converses with is delighted in the same manner with himself. A Man should endeavour therefore to wear out of his Mind this criminal Curiosity, which[b] is perpetually heightened and inflamed by listening to such Stories as tend to the Disreputation of others.

In the Second place, a Man should consult his own Heart, whether he be not apt to *believe* such little blackning Accounts; and more inclined to be credulous on the uncharitable, than on the good-natured Side.

Such a Credulity is very vicious in it self, and generally arises from a Man's Consciousness of his own secret Corruptions. It is a pretty Saying of *Thales*, Falshood is just as far distant from Truth, as the Ears are from the Eyes.[2] By which he would intimate, that a Wise Man should not easily give Credit to the Reports of Actions which he has not seen. I shall, under this Head, mention two or three remarkable Rules to be observed by the Members of the celebrated Abbey *de la Trape*, as they are Published in a little *French* Book.[3]

The Fathers are there ordered, never to give an Ear to any Accounts of Base or Criminal Actions; to turn off all such Discourse if possible; but in Case they hear any thing of this Nature so well attested that they cannot disbelieve it, they are then to suppose that the criminal Action may have proceeded from a good Intention in him who is guilty of it. This is perhaps carrying Charity to an

---

ᵃ which] that *Fol.*   ᵇ which] that *Fol.*

---

[1] Now *obs.* or *arch.* (*OED*).

[2] See Stobaeus, *Anthologium*, 3, cap. 12, no. 14:

Thales. Thales the Milesian on being asked how far falsehood is distant from truth said: as far as the eyes are from the ears.

[3] André Félibien, *Description de l'Abbaye de la Trape* (Paris, 1689), p. 216. For Félibien see *Journal des Savans*, 28 Nov. 1695, pp. 459–65.

Extravagance, but it is certainly much more Laudable, than to suppose, as the Ill-natured part of the World does, that Indifferent, and even good Actions, proceed from bad Principles and wrong Intentions.

In the Third place, A Man should examine his Heart, whether he does not find in it a secret Inclination to Propagate such Reports as tend to the Disreputation of another.

When the Disease of the Mind, which I have hitherto been speaking of, arises to this Degree of Malignity, it discovers its self in its worst Symptoms, and is in danger of becoming incurable. I need not therefore insist upon the Guilt of this last Particular, which every one cannot but disapprove, who is not void of Humanity, or even common Discretion. I shall only add, that whatever Pleasure any Man may take in spreading[a] Whispers of this Nature, he will find an infinitely greater Satisfaction in conquering the Temptation he is under, by letting the Secret die within his own Breast.

No. 595   *Friday, September* 17, 1714[1]

[TICKELL]

. . . Non ut placidis coeant immitia, non ut
Serpentes avibus geminentur, tigribus agni.

             Hor.

IF ordinary Authors would condescend to write as they think, they would at least be allowed the Praise of being intelligible.

[a] spreading] divulging *Fol.*

---

[1] *Motto.* Horace, *Ars poetica*, 12–13:

     Not joyn quite *Opposites*, the Wild and Tame;
     The Snake and Dove, the Lion and the Lamb. CREECH.

This number, the first of a series of twenty-four contributed by Tickell to Vol. viii (Hodgart, p. 373), aroused the indignation of one Nathaniel Castleton, possibly the 'celebrated author' ridiculed in the third paragraph. The *Post-Boy* of Thursday, 30 Dec. 1714, reports that 'Mr. Castleton at the Penny-Post-Office' hopes by Saturday 'to publish several Vindications against the SPECTATOR of the 17th of September, 1714', together with 'the Essay towards a Coalition of Parties in Great-Britain'. Castleton, who seems to have thought Swift was the author of this number of the *Spectator*, published his reply on 18 Jan. 1714/15 (*Post-Boy*, advertisement) under the imprint of John Morphew, in the form of three distinct pamphlets but paged consecutively:

     1. Spectator of the 17th of September 1714. Serpentes avibus geminentur, tigribus

But they really take Pains to be ridiculous; and, by the studied Ornaments of Stile, perfectly disguise the little Sence they aim at. There is a Grievance of this Sort in the Commonwealth of Letters, which I have for some time resolved to redress, and accordingly I have set this Day apart for Justice. What I mean is *the Mixture of inconsistent Metaphors*, which is a Fault but too often found in learned Writers, but in all the unlearned without Exception.

In order to set this matter in a clear Light to every Reader, I shall, in the first place, observe that a Metaphor is a Similie in one Word, which serves to convey the Thoughts of the Mind under Resemblances and Images which affect the Senses. There is not any thing in the World, which may not be compared to several things, if considered in several distinct Lights; or, in other Words, the same thing may be expressed by different Metaphors. But the mischief is, that an unskilful Author shall run these Metaphors so absurdly into one another, that there shall be no Similie, no agreeable Picture, no apt Resemblance, but Confusion, Obscurity and Noise. Thus I have known a Hero compared to a Thunderbolt, a Lion and the Sea; all, and each of them proper Metaphors for Impetuosity, Courage or Force. But by bad Management it hath so happened, that the Thunder-bolt hath overflowed its Banks; the Lion hath been darted through the Skies, and the Billows have rolled out of the *Libyan* Desart.

The Absurdity in this Instance is obvious. And yet every time that clashing Metaphors are put together, this Fault is committed more or less. It hath already been said, that Metaphors are Images of things which affect the Senses. An Image therefore, taken from what acts upon the Sight, cannot, without Violence, be applied to the Hearing; and so of the rest. It is no less an Impropriety to make any Being in Nature or Art to do things in its Metaphorical State, which it could not do in its Original. I shall illustrate what I have said, by an Instance which I have read more than once in Controversial Writers. *The heavy Lashes*, saith a celebrated Author, *that*

agni. Several Preparatory Instances of Mr. Castleton's Way of Writing produced against the intricate Representations of him in the aforesaid Spectator.— nisi lacessitus injuria.

2. An Essay towards a Coalition of Parties in Great Britain.

3. An Explanatory Supplement, addressed to the many Friends, however distinguished, of our excellent Constitution.

See Nichols, *Literary Anecdotes*, i. 111–14. In the *Key to the Lock*, published four months later, Pope included an acrostic poem supposed to be written 'by N. Castleton, A Well-willer to the Coalition of Parties' (*Minor Poems*, ed. Norman Ault and John Butt, p. 133).

have drop'd from your Pen, &c. I suppose this Gentleman having frequently heard of *Gall dropping from a Pen*, and *being lash'd in a Satyr*,
he was resolved to have them both at any Rate, and so uttered
this compleat Piece of Nonsense. It will most effectually discover
the Absurdity of these monstrous Unions, if we will suppose
these Metaphors or Images actually painted. Imagine then a
Hand holding a Pen, and several Lashes of Whip-cord falling from
it, and you have the true Representation of this sort of Eloquence.
I believe, by this very Rule, a Reader may be able to judge of the
Union of all Metaphors whatsoever, and determine which are Homo-
geneous and which Heterogeneous; or, to speak more plainly, which
are Consistent, and which Inconsistent.

There is yet one Evil more which I must take notice of, and that
is the running of Metaphors into tedious Allegories; which, though
an Error on the better hand, causes Confusion as much as the other.
This becomes abominable, when the lustre of one Word leads a
Writer out of his Road, and makes him wander from his Subject for
a Page together. I remember a young Fellow, of this Turn, who
having said by Chance that his Mistress had a *World* of Charms,
thereupon took occasion to consider her as one possessed of Frigid
and Torrid Zones, and pursued her from the one Pole to the other.[1]

I shall conclude this Paper with a Letter written in that enormous[2] Stile, which I hope my Reader hath by this time set his Heart
against. The Epistle hath heretofore received great Applause; but
after what hath been said, let any Man commend it if he dare.

SIR,
'AFTER the many heavy *Lashes* that have fallen from your *Pen*,
you may justly expect in return, all the *Load* that my *Ink* can
lay upon your Shoulders. You have *Quartered* all the foul *Language*
upon me, that could be *raked* out of the *Air* of *Billingsgate*, without
knowing who I am, or whether I deserve to be *Cupped* and *Scarified*
at this rate. I tell you once for all, turn your *Eyes* where you please,
you shall never *Smell* me out. Do you think that the *Panicks*, which
you *sow* about the Parish, will ever *build* a Monument to your Glory.
No, Sir, you may *Fight* these Battels as long as you will, but when
you come to *Ballance* the Account, you will find that you have been
Fishing in troubled Waters, and that an *Ignus fatuus* hath bewildered

---

[1] Possibly a reminiscence of Cowley's poem, 'The Request' (cf. No. 62, vol. i).
[2] Here used in the obsolete sense of 'monstrous'. The last example in *OED* in
this sense is dated 1818.

you, and that indeed you have *built* upon a sandy Foundation, and brought your *Hogs* to a fair Market.

> I am, SIR,
> Yours, &c.'

No. 596   *Monday, September 20, 1714*[1]
[BUDGELL]

> *Molle meum levibus Cor est violabile Telis.*
> Ovid.

THE Case of my Correspondent who sends me the following Letter has somewhat in it so very whimsical, that I know not how to entertain my Readers better than by laying it before them.

SIR,

'I AM fully convinced that there is not upon Earth a more impertinent Creature than an importunate Lover: We are daily complaining of the Severity of our Fate, to People who are wholly unconcerned in it; and hourly improving a Passion, which we would perswade the World is the Torment of our Lives. Notwithstanding this Reflection, Sir, I cannot forbear acquainting you with my own Case. You must know then, Sir, that even from my Childhood, the most prevailing Inclination I could perceive in my self, was a strong Desire to be in Favour with the Fair Sex. I am at present in the one and twentieth Year of my Age, and should have made Choice of a She Bed-fellow many Years since, had not my Father, who has a pretty good Estate of his own getting, and passes in the World for a prudent Man, been pleased to lay it down as a Maxim,[a] That nothing spoils a young Fellow's Fortune so much as marrying early; and that no Man ought to think of Wedlock

---

[a] as a Maxim,] as Maxim *Fol.*

---

[1] *Motto.* Ovid, *Heroides*, 15. 79:
  My tender Heart with ease receives a Wound.

The last of Budgell's contributions, according to the Tickell MS. (Hodgart, p. 379). Budgell at about this date was appointed Clerk of the Council and Secretary of the Lords Justices in Ireland and left for Dublin early in October (Smithers, p. 301). The letter signed Jeremy Lovemore, which makes up almost the whole of this number, may be of course a genuine contribution reworked by Budgell.

till six and twenty. Knowing his Sentiments upon this Head, I thought it in vain to apply my self to Women of Condition, who expect Settlements; so that all my Amours have hitherto been with Ladies who had no Fortunes: But I know not how to give you so good an Idea of me, as by laying before you the History of my Life.

'I can very well remember, that at my School-Mistresses, whenever we broke up, I was always for joining my self with the Miss who *Lay in*,[1] and was constantly one of the first to make a Party in the Play of *Husband and Wife*. This Passion for being well with the Females still increased as I advanced in Years. At the Dancing-School I contracted so many Quarrels by struggling with my Fellow-Scholars for the Partner I liked best, that upon a Ball Night, before our Mothers made their Appearance, I was usually up to the Nose in Blood. My Father, like a discreet Man, soon removed me from this Stage of Softness to a School of Discipline, where I learnt *Latin* and *Greek*. I underwent several Severities in this Place, till it was thought convenient to send me to the University; though, to confess the Truth, I should not have arrived so early at that Seat of Learning, but from the Discovery of an Intrigue between me and my Master's House-keeper; upon whom I had employed my Rhetorick so effectually, that, though she was a very elderly Lady, I had almost brought her to consent to marry me. Upon my Arrival at *Oxford*, I found Logick so dry, that, instead of giving Attention to the Dead, I soon fell to addressing the Living. My first Amour was with a pretty Girl whom I shall call *Parthenope*: Her Mother sold Ale by the Town Wall. Being often caught there by the Proctor, I was forced at last, that my Mistress's Reputation might receive no Blemish, to confess my Addresses were honourable. Upon this I was immediately sent Home; but *Parthenope* soon after marrying a Shooe-maker, I was again suffered to return. My next Affair was with my Taylor's Daughter, who deserted me for the Sake of a young Barber. Upon my complaining to one of my particular Friends on this Misfortune, the cruel Wagg made a meer Jest of my Calamity, and asked me with a Smile, *Where the Needle should turn but to the* Pole?[2] After this I was deeply in Love with a Millener, and at last with my Bed-maker; upon which I was sent away, or, in the University Phrase, *Rusticated*[3] for ever.

[1] Used here in slang sense? The *OED* gives no special meaning which seems appropriate. I have found no references to a play or game called 'Husband and Wife'.
[2] 'The common sign of a barber's shop' (Nichols).
[3] The context implies that this is a recent term. This is the earliest example in

'Upon my coming home, I settled to my Studies so heartily, and contracted so great a Reservedness by being kept from the Company I most affected, that my Father thought he might venture me at the *Temple*.

'Within a Week after my Arrival I began to shine again, and became enamoured with a mighty pretty Creature, who had every thing but Money to recommend her. Having frequent Opportunities of uttering all the soft things which an Heart formed for Love could inspire me with, I soon gained her Consent to treat of Marriage; but, unfortunately for us all, in the Absence of my Charmer I usually talked the same Language to her elder Sister, who is also very pretty. Now I assure you, Mr. SPECTATOR, this did not proceed from any real Affection I had conceived for her; but being a perfect Stranger to the Conversation of Men, and strongly addicted to associate with the Women, I knew no other Language but that of Love. I should however be very much obliged to you, if you could free me from the Perplexity I am at present in. I have sent Word to my old Gentleman in the Country, that I am desperately in Love with the younger Sister; and her Father, who knew no better, poor Man! acquainted him by the same Post, that I had for some time made my Addresses to the Elder. Upon this, old Testy, sends me up Word, that he has heard so much of my Exploits, that he intends immediately to order me to the *South Sea*. Sir, I have occasionally talked so much of dying, that I begin to think there is not much in it; and if the old Squire persists in his Design, I do hereby give him Notice that I am providing my self with proper Instruments for the Destruction of despairing Lovers. Let him therefore look to it, and consider that by this Obstinacy he may himself lose the Son of his Strength, the World an hopeful Lawyer, my Mistress a passionate Lover, and you, Mr. SPECTATOR,

Middle-Temple,	*Your constant Admirer*,
Sept. 18.	Jeremy Lovemore.'

OED in this sense, 'to dismiss or "send down" from a university for a specified time as a punishment'.

No. 597   *Wednesday, September 22, 1714*[1]

. . . *Mens sine Pondere ludit.*

Petr.

SINCE I received my Friend *Shadow*'s Letter,[2] several of my Correspondents have been pleased to send me an Account how they have been employed in Sleep, and what notable Adventures they have been engaged in during that Moonshine in the Brain. I shall lay before my Readers an Abridgment of some few of their Extravagancies, in hopes that they will in Time accustom themselves to dream a little more to the Purpose.

One who stiles himself *Gladio*, complains heavily that his Fair One charges him with Inconstancy, and does not use him with half the Kindness which the Sincerity of his Passion may demand; the said *Gladio* having by Valour and Stratagem put to death Tyrants, Inchanters, Monsters, Knights, &c. without Number, and expos'd himself to all manner of Dangers for her Sake and Safety. He desires in his Postscript to know, Whether, from a constant Success in them, he may not promise himself to succeed in her Esteem at last.

Another who is very prolix in his Narrative writes me Word, That having sent a Venture beyond Sea, he took Occasion one Night to fancy himself gone along with it, and grown on a sudden the richest Man in all the *Indies*. Having been there about a Year or two, a Gust of Wind that forced open his Casement blew him over to his native Country again; where awaking at Six a Clock, and the Change of the Air not agreeing with him, he turned to his Left Side in order to a second Voyage; but e'er he could get on Shipboard, was unfortunately apprehended for stealing a Horse, tryed and condemned for the Fact, and in a fair way of being executed, if some Body stepping hastily into his Chamber had not brought him a Reprieve. This Fellow too wants Mr. *Shadow*'s Advice, who, I dare say, would bid him be content to rise after his first Nap, and learn to be satisfied as soon as Nature is.

The next is a publick spirited Gentleman, who tells me, That on the Second of *September* at Night the whole City was on Fire,

---

[1] *Motto.* Petronius, *Satyricon*, 104: The mind plays free and unoppressed.
This was used as a part of the motto of No. 487. Although this number has often been attributed to Byrom, it is evidently based on contributions from several correspondents. Possibly Budgell is the redactor.
[2] No. 586.

and would certainly have been reduced to Ashes again by this Time, if he had not flown over it with the *New River*[1] on his Back, and happily extinguished the Flames before they had prevailed too far. He would be informed whether he has not a Right to petition the Lord Mayor and Aldermen for a Reward.

A Letter dated *September* the Ninth acquaints me, That the Writer being resolved to try his Fortune, had fasted all that Day; and that he might be sure of dreaming upon something at Night, procured an handsome Slice of Bride-Cake, which he placed very conveniently under his Pillow. In the Morning his Memory happened to fail him, and he could recollect nothing but an odd Fancy that he had eaten his Cake; which being found upon Search reduced to a few Crums, he is resolved to remember more of his Dreams another Time, believing from this that there may possibly be somewhat of Truth in them.

I have received numerous Complaints from several delicious Dreamers, desiring me to invent some Method of silencing those noisy Slaves, whose Occupations lead them to take their early Rounds about the City in a Morning, doing a deal of Mischief, and working strange Confusion in the Affairs of its Inhabitants. Several Monarchs have done me the Honour to acquaint me, how often they have been shook from their respective Thrones by the rattling of a Coach or the rumbling of a Wheel-barrow. And many private Gentlemen, I find, have been baulk'd[a] of vast Estates by Fellows not worth Three-pence. A fair Lady was just upon the Point of being married to a young, handsome, rich, ingenious Nobleman, when an impertinent Tinker passing by, forbid the Banns; and an hopeful Youth, who had been newly advanced to great Honour and Preferment, was forced by a neighbouring Cobler to resign all for an old Song. It has been represented to me, that those inconsiderable Rascals do nothing but go about dissolving of Marriages and spoiling of Fortunes, impoverishing rich and ruining great People, interrupting Beauties in the midst of their Conquests, and Generals in the Course of their Victories. A boisterous Peripatetick hardly goes through a Street without waking half a Dozen Kings and Princes to open their Shops or clean Shooes, frequently transforming Scepters into Paring-Shovels, and Proclamations into Bills. I have

---

[a] baulk'd] baul'd *Fol., 8vo, 12mo*

---

[1] See No. 5.

by me a Letter from a young Statesman, who in five or six Hours came to be Emperor of *Europe*, after which he made War upon the Great Turk, routed him Horse and Foot, and was crowned Lord of the Universe in *Constantinople*; the Conclusion of all his Successes is, that on the 12th Instant, about Seven in the Morning, his Imperial Majesty was deposed by a Chimney-Sweeper.

On the other hand, I have Epistolary Testimonies of Gratitude from many miserable People, who owe to this clamorous Tribe frequent Deliverances from great Misfortunes. A Small-coal-man, by waking of one of these distress'd Gentlemen, saved him from ten Years Imprisonment.[1] An honest Watchman bidding aloud Good-morrow to another, freed him from the Malice of many potent Enemies, and brought all their Designs against him to nothing. A certain Valetudinarian confesses he has often been cured of a sore Throat by the Hoarseness of a Carman, and relieved from a Fit of the Gout by the Sound of *old Shooes*. A noisy Puppy that plagued a sober Gentleman all Night long with his Impertinence, was silenced by a Cinder-Wench with a Word speaking.

Instead therefore of suppressing this Order of Mortals, I would propose it to my Readers to make the best Advantage of their Morning Salutations. A famous *Macedonian* Prince, for fear of for-getting himself in the midst of his good Fortune, had a Youth to wait on him every Morning, and bid him remember that he was a Man.[2] A Citizen who is waked by one of these Criers, may regard him as a kind of Remembrancer, come to admonish him that it is time to return to the Circumstances he has overlook'd all the Night-time, to leave off fancying himself what he is not, and pre-pare to act suitably to the Condition he is really placed in.

People may dream on as long as they please, but I shall take no Notice of any imaginary Adventures that do not happen while the Sun is on this Side the Horizon. For which Reason I stifle *Fritilla's* Dream at Church last *Sunday*, who, while the rest of the Audience were enjoying the Benefit of an excellent Discourse, was losing her

---

[1] Though there is no allusion to music here, editors beginning with Nichols have taken this as a reference to Tom Britton, the 'musical small-coal-man'. Britton, who died very shortly after the publication of this number—his funeral was held on 1 Oct. (*DNB*)—

was universally known to all Lovers of Musick, of what Quality soever; and . . . for 46 Years kept a Consort once a Week at his own House, and at his own Expence, purely for the Entertainment of his Friends and his own Satisfaction (*British Mercury*, 6 October 1714).

[2] Philip of Macedonia. See Bayle, art. 'Daurat', Remark O.

Money and Jewels to a Gentleman at Play, till after a strange Run of ill Luck, she was reduced to pawn three lovely pretty Children for her last Stake. When she had thrown them away her Companion went off, discovering himself by his usual Tokens, a cloven Foot and a strong Smell of Brimstone; which last proved only a Bottle of Spirits, which a good old Lady applied to her Nose, to put her in a Condition of hearing the Preacher's third Head concerning Time.

If a Man has no Mind to pass abruptly from his imagin'd to his real Circumstances, he may employ himself a while in that new kind of Observation which my Oneirocritical Correspondent has directed him to make of himself. Pursuing the Imagination through all its Extravagancies, whether in Sleeping or Waking, is no improper Method of correcting and bringing it to act in Subordinancy to Reason, so as to be delighted only with such Objects as will affect it with Pleasure, when it is never so cool and sedate.

No. 598   *Friday, September 24, 1714*[1]
[ADDISON]

Jamne igitur laudas, quod de sapientibus alter
Ridebat, quoties a limine moverat unum
Protuleratque pedem: flebat contrarius alter?
                  Juv.

MANKIND may be divided into the Merry and the Serious, who, both of them, make a very good Figure in the Species, so long as they keep their respective Humours from degenerating into the neighbouring Extreme; there being a natural Tendency in the one to a melancholy Moroseness, and in the other to a fantastick Levity.

The merry Part of the World are very amiable, whilst they diffuse a Chearfulness through Conversation at proper Seasons and on proper Occasions; but, on the contrary, a great Grievance to

[1] *Motto.* Juvenal, *Satires* 10. 28–30 (altered):
      Will you not now the Pair of Sages praise,
      Who the same end pursu'd by different ways?
      One pity'd, one contemn'd the woful Times,
      One laugh'd at Follies, one lamented Crimes. DRYDEN.

Society, when they infect every Discourse with insipid Mirth, and turn into Ridicule such Subjects as are not suited to it. For tho' Laughter is looked upon by the Philosophers as the Property of Reason, the Excess of it has been always considered as the Mark of Folly.[1]

On the other Side, Seriousness has its Beauty whilst it is attended with Chearfulness and Humanity, and does not come in unseasonably to pall the good Humour of those with whom we converse.

These two Sets of Men, notwithstanding they each of them shine in their respective Characters, are apt to bear a natural Aversion and Antipathy to one another.

What is more usual, than to hear Men of serious Tempers and austere Morals, enlarging upon the Vanities and Follies of the young and gay Part of the Species; whilst they look with a kind of Horror upon such Pomps and Diversions as are innocent in themselves, and only culpable when they draw the Mind too much?

I could not but smile upon reading a Passage in the Account which Mr. *Baxter* gives of his own Life, wherein he represents it as a great Blessing, that in his Youth he very narrowly escaped getting a Place at Court.[2]

It must indeed be confessed that Levity of Temper takes a Man off his Guard, and opens a Pass to his Soul for any Temptation that assaults it. It favours all the Approaches of Vice, and weakens all the Resistance of Virtue. For which Reason a renowned Statesman in Queen *Elizabeth*'s Days, after having retired from Court and publick Business, in order to give himself up to the Duties of Religion; when any of his old Friends used to visit him, had still this Word of Advice in his Mouth, *Be serious*.[3]

An eminent *Italian* Author of this Cast of Mind, speaking of the great Advantage of a serious and composed Temper, wishes very gravely, that for the Benefit of Mankind he had *Trophonius*'s Cave in his Possession; which, says he, would contribute more to the Reformation of Manners than all the Work-houses and Bridewells in *Europe*.[4]

---

[1] Cf. Nos. 249 (vol. ii) and 494 (vol. iv).

[2] *Reliquiae Baxterianae* (1696), lib. i, part i (p. 11). The *Abridgment* by Edmund Calamy (1702) is more likely the direct source, since it has a marginal note (p. 4) on the passage: 'A Great Snare escaped.'

[3] This would be appropriate to one of the Cecil family, whose motto was *Sero sed serio*, but the saying has not been traced.

[4] For Trophonius see No. 505 (vol. iv). John Hughes, in a note in his translation of Fontenelle's *Dialogues of the Dead* (1708), pp. 47–48, explains that Trophonius was

We have a very particular Description of this Cave in *Pausanias*, who tells us, that it was made in the Form of a huge Oven, and had many particular Circumstances, which disposed the Person who was in it to be more pensive and thoughtful than ordinary; insomuch that no Man was ever observed to laugh all his Life after, who had once made his Entry into this Cave.[1] It was usual in those Times, when any one carried a more than ordinary Gloominess in his Features, to tell him that he looked like one just come out of *Trophonius*'s Cave.

On the other Hand, Writers of a more merry Complexion have been no less severe on the opposite Party; and have had one Advantage above them, that they have attacked them with more Turns of Wit and Humour.

After all, if a Man's Temper were at his own Disposal, I think he would not choose to be of either of these Parties; since the most perfect Character is that which is formed out of both of them. A Man would neither chuse to be a Hermit nor a Buffoon: Humane Nature is not so miserable, as that we should be always melancholy; nor so happy, as that we should be always merry. In a Word, a Man should not live as if there was no God in the World; nor, at the same Time, as if there were no Men in it.

No. 599   *Monday, September 27, 1714*[2]

. . . Ubique
Luctus ubique pavor . . .
Virg.

IT has been my Custom, as I grow old, to allow my self in some little Indulgences which I never took in my Youth. Among

the son of Apollo and had a Temple erected in honour of him near Labadia in Boeotia, where he became famous for giving oracles by dreams.

But what is particularly to be remark'd here, is, that 'twas said those who went into this Cave lost, for a time, the Power of Laughing; an Opinion occasion'd by the Mysteriousness of the Solemnity, in which nothing was omitted that cou'd fill a weak Mind with all the Ideas of Fear and Superstition.

[1] Pausanias, *Description of Hellas*, 9. 37. 5–7. Cf. also Cicero, *Tusculan Disputations*, 1. 47. 114.

[2] *Motto*. Virgil, *Aeneid*, 2. 368–9:
    All parts resound with Tumults, Plaints, and Fears. DRYDEN.

Although this essay was not reprinted in Addison's *Works* (1721) and is not

others is that of an Afternoon's Napp, which I fell into in the fifty fifth Year of my Age, and have continued for the three Years last past. By this means I enjoy a double Morning, and rise twice a Day fresh to my Speculations. It happens very luckily for me, that some of my Dreams have proved instructive to my Countrymen, so that I may be said to sleep, as well as to wake, for the Good of the Publick. I was Yesterday meditating on the Account with which I have already entertained my Readers concerning the Cave of *Trophonius*.[1] I was no sooner fallen into my usual Slumber, but I dreamt that this Cave was put into my Possession, and that I gave publick Notice of its Virtue, inviting every one to it, who had a mind to be a serious Man for the remaining part of his Life. Great Multitudes immediately resorted to me. The first who made the Experiment was a *Merry-Andrew*,[2] who was put into my Hands by a neighbouring Justice of Peace, in order to reclaim him from that profligate kind of Life. Poor Pickle-herring[3] had not taken above one Turn in it, when he came out of the Cave, like a Hermit from his Cell, with a penitential Look and a most rueful Countenance. I then put in a young laughing Fop, and, watching for his Return, asked him, with a Smile, how he liked the Place? he replied, Prithee Friend be not impertinent, and stalked by me as grave as a Judge. A Citizen then desired me to give free Ingress and Egress to his Wife, who was dressed in the gayest coloured Ribbons I had ever seen. She went in with a flirt of her Fan and a smirking Countenance, but came out with the Severity of a Vestal, and, throwing from her several Female Gugaws, told me, with a Sigh, that she resolved to go into deep Mourning, and to wear Black all the rest of her Life. As I had many Coquetts recommended to me by their Parents, their Husbands and their Lovers, I let them in all at once, desiring them to divert themselves together as well as they could. Upon their emerging again into Day-light, you would have fancied my Cave to have been a Nunnery, and that you had seen a solemn Procession of Religious marching out, one behind another in the most profound Silence and the most exemplary Decency. As I was very much delighted with so edifying a Sight, there came towards me a great Company of Males and Females laughing, singing and dancing, in such a manner that I could hear them a great while

mentioned in the Tickell MS., it may be by Addison. It is a sequel to his essay constituting the preceding number.   [1] No. 598.
[2] No. 35.   [3] No. 47.

before I saw them. Upon my asking their Leader, what brought them thither? they told me all at once, that they were *French* Protestants lately arrived in *Great Britain*,[1] and that finding themselves of too gay a Humour for my Country, they applied themselves to me in order to compose them for *British* Conversation. I told them, that to oblige them I would soon spoil their Mirth; upon which I admitted a whole Shole of them, who, after having taken a Survey of the Place, came out in very good order, and with Looks entirely *English*. I afterwards put in a *Dutch* Man, who had a great Fancy to see the *Kelder*,[2] as he called it, but I could not observe that it had made any manner of Alteration in him.

A Comedian who had gained great Reputation in Parts of Humour, told me, that he had a mighty Mind to act *Alexander* the Great, and fancied that he should succeed very well in it, if he could strike two or three laughing Features out of his Face:[3] He tried the Experiment, but contracted so very solid a Look by it, that I am afraid he will be fit for no Part hereafter, but a *Timon* of *Athens*,[4] or a Mute in the *Funeral*.[5]

I then clapt up an empty fantastick Citizen, in order to qualify him for an Alderman. He was succeeded by a young Rake of the *Middle Temple*, who was brought to me by his Grandmother; but to her great Sorrow and Surprize, he came out a *Quaker*. Seeing myself surrounded with a Body of Free-Thinkers, and Scoffers at Religion, who were making themselves merry at the sober Looks and thoughtful Brows of those who had been in the Cave; I thrust 'em all in, one after another, and lock'd the Door upon 'em. Upon my opening it, they all look'd as if they had been frighted out of their Wits, and were marching away with Ropes in their Hands, to a Wood that was within Sight of the Place. I found they were not able to bear themselves in their first serious Thoughts; but knowing these would quickly bring them to a better Frame of Mind, I gave them into the Custody of their Friends, till that happy Change was wrought in them.

The last that was brought to me, was a young Woman, who at

---

[1] Nos. 180 (vol. ii), 328 (vol. iii).

[2] The Dutch word for cellar.

[3] *Alexander the Great*, i.e. Lee's *Rival Queens* (No. 36).

[4] This had been performed at Drury Lane on 17 May 1714, with Powell in the title-role, and again at Drury Lane on 16 June, for the benefit of Mrs. Powell and King (a box-keeper).

[5] Steele's comedy (cf. No. 51) had been given on 8 Apr., 11 May, and 9 Dec. 1713 at Drury Lane, but no performances are recorded for the year 1714.

the first Sight of my short Face fell into an immoderate Fit of Laughter, and was forced to hold her Sides all the while her Mother was speaking to me. Upon this I interrupted the old Lady, and taking her Daughter by the Hand, Madam, said I, be pleased to retire into my Closet, while your Mother tells me your Case. I then put her into the Mouth of the Cave, when the Mother, after having begged Pardon for the Girl's Rudeness, told me, that she often treated her Father and the gravest of her Relations in the same Manner; that she would sit giggling and laughing with her Companions from one end of a Tragedy to the other; nay, that she would sometimes burst out in the middle of a Sermon, and set the whole Congregation a staring at her. The Mother was going on, when the young Lady came out of the Cave to us with a composed Countenance, and a low Curtesy. She was a Girl of such exuberant Mirth, that her Visit to *Trophonius* only reduced her to a more than ordinary Decency of Behaviour, and made a very pretty Prude of her. After having performed innumerable Cures, I looked about me with great Satisfaction, and saw all my Patients walking by themselves in a very pensive and musing Posture, so that the whole Place seemed covered with Philosophers. I was at length resolved to go into the Cave myself, and see what it was that had produced such wonderful Effects upon the Company; but as I was stooping at the Entrance, the Door being something low, I gave such a Nod in my Chair, that I awaked. After having recovered my self from my first Startle,[1] I was very well pleased at the Accident which had befallen me, as not knowing but a little Stay in the Place might have spoil'd my *Spectators*.

No. 600   *Wednesday, September 29, 1714*[2]
[ADDISON]

> . . . *Solemque suum, sua sidera norunt.*
> Virg.

I HAVE always taken a particular Pleasure in examining the Opinions which Men of different Religions, different Ages, and

---

[1] A start or shock of surprise or alarm (*OED*). This is the first recorded quotation for this sense in *OED*.   [*For note 2 see opposite page.*

different Countries, have entertained concerning the Immortality of the Soul, and the State of Happiness which they promise themselves in another World. For whatever Prejudices and Errors human Nature lies under, we find that either Reason, or Tradition from our first Parents, has discovered to all People something in these great Points which bears Analogy to Truth, and to the Doctrines opened to us by Divine Revelation. I was lately discoursing on this Subject with a learned Person who has been very much conversant among the Inhabitants of the more Western Parts of *Africk*.[1] Upon his conversing with several in that Country, he tells me that their Notion of Heaven or of a future State of Happiness is this, That every thing we there wish for will immediately present it self to us. We find, say they, our Souls are of such a Nature that they require Variety, and are not capable of being always delighted with the same Objects. The Supreme Being therefore, in Compliance with this Taste of Happiness which he has planted in the Soul of Man, will raise up from time to time, say they, every Gratification which it is in the Humour to be pleased with. If we wish to be in Groves or Bowers, among running Streams or Falls of Water, we shall immediately find our selves in the midst of such a Scene as we desire. If we would be entertained with Musick, and the Melody of Sounds, the Consort rises upon our Wish, and the whole Region about us is filled with Harmony. In short, every Desire will be followed by Fruition, and whatever a Man's Inclination directs him to, will be present with him. Nor is it material whether the Supreme Power creates in Conformity to our Wishes, or whether he only produces such a Change in our Imagination, as makes us believe ourselves conversant among those Scenes which delight us. Our Happiness will be the same, whether it proceed from external Objects, or from the Impressions of the Deity upon our own private Fancies. This is the Account which

---

[1] Identified by Nichols and later editors as Addison's father, Lancelot Addison, author of *West Barbary; or a short narrative of the revolutions of the kingdoms of Fez and Morocco* (Oxford, 1671). Hence Nichols infers an early date of composition for this paper, probably before 1703 (the year of Lancelot Addison's death).

---

[2] *Motto*. Virgil, *Aeneid*, 6. 641:
    Stars of their own, and their own Suns they know. DRYDEN.

This number is Addison's final contribution to the *Spectator*. Since 3 Aug. he had served as Secretary to the Regents, and after this duty ended, on 22 Sept., he was made Secretary to the Lord Lieutenant of Ireland, the Earl of Sunderland (Smithers, p. 297).

I have received from my learned Friend. Notwithstanding this System of Belief be in general very chimerical and visionary, there is something sublime in its manner of considering the Influence of a Divine Being on a Human Soul. It has also, like most other Opinions of the Heathen World upon these important Points, it has, I say, its Foundation in Truth, as it supposes the Souls of good Men after this Life to be in a State of perfect Happiness, that in this State there will be no barren Hopes, nor fruitless Wishes, and that we shall enjoy every thing we can desire. But the particular Circumstance which I am most pleased with in this Scheme, and which arises from a just Reflexion upon Human Nature, is that Variety of Pleasures which it supposes the Souls of good Men will be possessed of in another World. This I think highly probable, from the Dictates both of Reason and Revelation. The Soul consists of many Faculties, as the Understanding, and the Will, with all the Senses both outward and inward;[1] or to speak more Philosophically, the Soul can exert herself in many different ways of Action: She can understand, will, imagine, see, and hear, love, and discourse, and apply herself to many other the like Exercises of different Kinds and Natures; but what is more to be considered, the Soul is capable of receiving a most exquisite Pleasure and Satisfaction from the Exercise of any of these its Powers, when they are gratified with their proper Objects; she can be entirely happy by the Satisfaction of the Memory, the Sight the Hearing, or any other Mode of Perception. Every Faculty is as a distinct Taste in the Mind, and hath Objects accommodated to its proper Relish. Doctor *Tillotson* somewhere says, that he will not presume to determine in what consists the Happiness of the Blest, because God Almighty is capable of making the Soul happy by Ten Thousand different ways.[2] Besides those several Avenues to Pleasure which the Soul is endowed with in this Life; it is not impossible, according to the Opinions of many eminent Divines, but there may be new Faculties in the Souls of good Men made perfect, as well as new Senses in their glorified

[1] The five senses, and the 'faculties' of the mind or soul.
[2] In Sermon 8, 'On the Happiness of a Heavenly Conversation', Tillotson describes the happiness of the blest, who 'shall sing everlasting songs of praise to God':
This, this shall be the employment of the blessed spirits above, and these are the chief ingredients of our happiness which the Scripture mentions. And if there were no other, as there may be ten thousand more for any thing I can tell, yet generous and virtuous minds will easily understand how great a pleasure there is in the improvement of our knowledge, and the exercise of love; and in a grateful and perpetual acknowledgment of the greatest benefits that creatures are capable of receiving (*Works*, 9th ed., 1728, i. 74).

Bodies.[1] This we are sure of, that there will be new Objects offered to all those Faculties which are essential to us.

We are likewise to take Notice that every particular Faculty is capable of being employed on a very great Variety of Objects. The Understanding, for Example, may be happy in the Contemplation of Moral, Natural, Mathematical, and other kinds of Truth. The Memory likewise may turn it self to an infinite Multitude of Objects, especially when the Soul shall have passed through the Space of many Millions of Years, and shall reflect with Pleasure on the Days of Eternity. Every other Faculty may be considered in the same Extent.

We cannot question but that the Happiness of a Soul will be adequate to its Nature, and that it is not endowed with any Faculties which are to lie useless and unemploy'd. The Happiness is to be the Happiness of the whole Man, and we may easily conceive to our selves the Happiness of the Soul, whilst any one of its Faculties is in the Fruition of its chief Good. The Happiness may be of a more exalted Nature in Proportion as the Faculty employ'd is so, but as the whole Soul acts in the Exertion of any of its particular Powers, the whole Soul is happy in the Pleasure which arises from any of its particular Acts. For notwithstanding, as has been before hinted, and as it has been taken Notice of by one of the greatest modern Philosophers, we divide the Soul into several Powers and Faculties, there is no such Division in the Soul it self, since it is the whole Soul that remembers, understands, wills, or imagines.[2] Our manner of considering the Memory, Understanding, Will, Imagination, and the like Faculties, is for the better enabling us to express our selves in such abstracted Subjects of Speculation, not that there is any such Division in the Soul it self.

Seeing then that the Soul has many different Faculties, or in other Words, many different ways of acting; that it can be intensely pleased, or made happy by all these different Faculties, or ways of acting; that it may be endowed with several latent Faculties, which it is not at present in a Condition to exert; that we cannot believe the Soul is endowed with any Faculty which is of no Use to it; that whenever any one of these Faculties is transcendently pleased, the Soul is in a State of Happiness; and in the last Place, considering

---

[1] One of the chief arguments in John Scott's *The Christian Life*, which Addison praises in No. 447.
[2] Locke, *Essay*, II. xxi. 6-20.

that the Happiness of another World is to be the Happiness of the whole Man; Who can question but that there is an infinite Variety in those Pleasures we are speaking of; and that this Fulness of Joy will be made up of all those Pleasures which the Nature of the Soul is capable of receiving?

We shall be the more confirmed in this Doctrine, if we observe the Nature of Variety, with regard to the Mind of Man. The Soul does not care to be always in the same bent. The Faculties relieve one another by Turns, and receive an Additional Pleasure from the Novelty of those Objects, about which they are conversant.

Revelation likewise very much confirms this Notion, under the different Views which it gives us of our future Happiness. In the Description of the Throne of God, it represents to us all those Objects which are able to gratify the Senses and Imagination. In very many places it intimates to us all the Happiness which the Understanding can possibly receive in that State, where all Things shall be revealed to us, and we shall know, even as we are known;[1] the Raptures of Devotion, of Divine Love, the Pleasure of conversing with our Blessed Saviour, with an innumerable Host of Angels, and with the Spirits of just Men made Perfect,[2] are likewise revealed to us in several Parts of the Holy Writings. There are also mentioned those Hierarchies, or Governments, in which the Blest shall be ranged one above another, and in which we may be sure a great Part of our Happiness will likewise consist; for it will not be there as in this World, where every one is aiming at Power and Superiority; but on the contrary, every one will find that Station the most proper for him in which he is placed, and will probably think that he could not have been so happy in any other Station. These, and many other Particulars, are marked in Divine Revelation, as the several Ingredients of our Happiness in Heaven, which all imply such a Variety of Joys, and such a Gratification of the Soul in all its different Faculties, as I have been here mentioning.

Some of the Rabbins tell us, that the Cherubims are a Set of Angels who know most, and the Seraphims a Set of Angels who love most.[3] Whether this Distinction be not altogether Imaginary,

---

[1] 1 Cor. xiii. 12.   [2] Heb. xii. 23.

[3] Cf. Bacon, *Advancement of Learning*, i. 28: 'The first place . . . is given to the Angels of love, which are tearmed Seraphim, the second to the Angels of light, which are tearmed Cherubim' (quoted in *OED*). The patristic explanations point to the Greek meaning of 'cherubim' as 'much knowledge' (Hastings, *Dictionary of the Bible*, 1898, i. 379), while the presumed derivation of 'seraphim' from a Hebrew root meaning 'to burn' led to the view that the seraphim are specially distinguished by fervour

I shall not here examine; but it is highly probable that among the Spirits of good Men, there may be some who will be more pleased with the Employment of one Faculty than of another, and this perhaps according to those innocent and virtuous Habits or Inclinations which have here taken the deepest Root.

I might here apply this Consideration to the Spirits of wicked Men, with Relation to the Pain which they shall suffer in every one of their Faculties, and the respective Miseries which shall be appropriated to each Faculty in Particular. But leaving this to the Reflection of my Readers, I shall conclude, with observing how we ought to be thankful to our great Creator, and rejoice in the Being which he has bestowed upon us, for having made the Soul susceptible of Pleasure by so many different Ways. We see by what a Variety of Passages, Joy and Gladness may enter into the Thoughts of Man. How wonderfully a humane Spirit is framed, to imbibe its proper Satisfactions, and taste the Goodness of its Creator. We may therefore look into our selves with Rapture and Amazement, and cannot sufficiently express our Gratitude to him, who has encompassed us with such a Profusion of Blessings, and opened in us so many Capacities of enjoying them.

There cannot be a stronger Argument that God has designed us for a State of future Happiness, and for that Heaven which he has revealed to us, than that he has thus naturally qualified the Soul for it, and made it a Being capable of receiving so much Bliss. He would never have made such Faculties in vain, and have endowed us with Powers that were not to be exerted on such Objects as are suited to them. It is very manifest by the inward Frame and Constitution of our Minds, that he has adapted them to an infinite Variety of Pleasures and Gratifications, which are not to be met with in this Life. We should therefore at all times take Care that we do not disappoint this his gracious Purpose and Intention towards us, and make those Faculties which he formed as so many Qualifications for Happiness and Rewards, to be the Instruments of Pain and Punishment.

of love (*OED*, s.v. Seraphim). The traditional nine orders are seraphim, cherubim, thrones, dominions, virtues, powers, principalities, archangels, and angels.

No. 601
[GROVE]

Friday, October 1, 1714[1]

ʽΟ ἄνθρωπος εὐεργετικὸς πεφυκώς.

Antonin. Lib. 9.

THE following Essay comes from an Hand which has entertained my Readers once before.

NOTWITHSTANDING a narrow contracted Temper be that which obtains most in the World, we must not therefore conclude this to be the genuine Characteristick of Mankind; because there are some who delight in nothing so much as in doing Good, and receive more of their Happiness at second hand, or by rebound from others, than by direct and immediate Sensation. Now tho' these Heroic Souls are but few, and to Appearance so far advanced above the groveling Multitude as if they were of another Order of Beings, yet in Reality their Nature is the same, moved by the same Springs, and endowed with all the same essential Qualities, only cleared, refined, and cultivated. Water is the same fluid Body in Winter and in Summer; when it stands stiffened in Ice, as when it flows along in gentle Streams gladdening a thousand Fields in its Progress. 'Tis a Property of the Heart of Man to be diffusive: Its kind Wishes spread abroad over the Face of the Creation; and if there be those, as we may observe too many of them, who are all wrap'd up in their own dear selves, without any visible Concern for their Species, let us suppose that their Good-nature is frozen, and by the prevailing Force of some contrary Quality restrained in its Operations. I shall therefore endeavour to assign some of the principal Checks upon this generous Propension[2] of the Human Soul, which will enable us to judge whether, and by what Method, this most useful Principle may be unfettered, and restored to its native Freedom of Exercise.

The first and leading Cause is an unhappy Complexion of Body. The Heathens, ignorant of the true Source of Moral Evil, generally charged it on the Obliquity of Matter, which, being eternal and independant, was incapable of Change in any of its Properties, even

---

[1] *Motto.* Marcus Aurelius, *Meditations*, 9. 42. 4: Man is naturally inclined to do good.

The second of Grove's four contributions; cf. No. 588.

[2] I.e. propensity. In No. 588 Grove also speaks of 'kind and benevolent Propensions'.

by the Almighty Mind, who, when He came to fashion it into a World of Beings, must take it as He found it. This Notion, as most others of theirs, is a Composition of Truth and Error. That Matter is eternal, that from the first Union of a Soul to it, it perverted its Inclinations, and that the ill Influence it hath upon the Mind is not to be corrected by God himself, are all very great Errors, occasioned by a Truth as evident, that the Capacities and Dispositions of the Soul depend, to a great degree, on the bodily Temper. As there are some Fools, others are Knaves, by Constitution; and particularly, it may be said of Many, that they are born with an illiberal Cast of Mind; the Matter that composes them is tenacious as Birdlime, and a kind of Cramp draws their Hands and their Hearts together, that they never care to open them unless to grasp at more. 'Tis a melancholy Lot this; but attended with one Advantage above theirs to whom it would be as painful to forbear good Offices, as it is to these Men to perform them; that whereas Persons naturally Beneficent often mistake Instinct for Virtue, by reason of the Difficulty of distinguishing when one rules them and when the other, Men of the opposite Character may be more certain of the Motive that predominates in every Action. If they cannot confer a Benefit with that Ease and Frankness which are necessary to give it a Grace in the Eye of the World, in requital, the real Merit of what they do is enhanc'd by the Opposition they surmount in doing it. The Strength of their Virtue is seen in rising against the Weight of Nature, and every time they have the Resolution to discharge their Duty, they make a Sacrifice of Inclination to Conscience, which is always too grateful to let its Followers go without suitable Marks of its Approbation. Perhaps the entire Cure of this ill Quality is no more possible than of some Distempers that descend by Inheritance. However, a great deal may be done by a Course of Beneficence obstinately persisted in; this, if any thing, being a likely way of establishing a moral Habit, which shall be somewhat of a Counterpoise to the Force of Mechanism. Only it must be remembered, that we do not intermit, upon any Pretence whatsoever, the Custom of doing Good, in regard if there be the least Cessation, Nature will watch the Opportunity to return, and in a short time to recover the Ground it was so long in quitting: For there is this difference between mental Habits, and such as have their Foundation in the Body; that these last are in their Nature more forcible and violent, and, to gain upon us, need only

not to be oppos'd; whereas the former must be continually reinforc'd with fresh Supplies, or they will languish and die away. And this suggests the Reason why good Habits, in general, require longer time for their Settlement than bad, and yet are sooner displac'd; the Reason is, that vicious Habits (as Drunkenness for Instance) produce a Change in the Body, which the others not doing, must be maintain'd the same way they are acquir'd, by the mere Dint of Industry, Resolution, and Vigilance.

Another Thing which suspends the Operations of Benevolence, is the Love of the World; proceeding from a false Notion Men have taken up, that an Abundance of the World is an essential Ingredient into the Happiness of Life. Worldly Things are of such a Quality as to lessen upon dividing, so that the more Partners there are, the less must fall to every Man's private Share. The Consequence of this is, that they look upon one another with an Evil Eye, each imagining all the rest to be imbark'd in an Interest, that cannot take Place but to his Prejudice. Hence are those eager Competitions for Wealth or Power; hence one Man's Success becomes another's Disappointment; and, like Pretenders to the same Mistress, they can seldom have common Charity for their Rivals. Not that they are naturally disposed to quarrel and fall out, but 'tis natural for a Man to prefer himself to all others, and to secure his own Interest first. If that which Men esteem their Happiness were, like the Light, the same sufficient and unconfined Good, whether Ten Thousand enjoy the Benefit of it, or but one, we should see Mens good Will, and kind Endeavours, would be as universal.

> *Homo qui Erranti comiter monstrat Viam,*
> *Quasi Lumen de suo Lumine accendat, facit,*
> *Nihilominus ipsi luceat, cum illi accenderit.*[1]

But, unluckily, Mankind agree in making Choice of Objects, which inevitably engage them in perpetual Differences. Learn therefore, like a wise Man, the true Estimate of Things. Desire not more of the World than is necessary to accommodate you in passing through it; look upon every thing beyond, not as useless only, but burthensome. Place not your Quiet in Things which you cannot have with-

[1] Ennius, quoted in Cicero, *De Officiis*, 1. 16. 51. The lines are translated by L'Estrange (*Tully's Offices*, 4th ed., 1688):

> To put a Wandring Traveller in's Way,
> Is but to light One Candle with Another:
> I've ne'er the less, for what I Give ——.

out putting others beside them, and thereby making them your Enemies; and which, when attained, will give you more Trouble to keep, than Satisfaction in the Enjoyment. Virtue is a Good of a nobler Kind; it grows by Communication, and so little resembles earthly Riches, that the more Hands it is lodg'd in, the greater is every Man's particular Stock. So, by propagating and mingling their Fires, not only all the Lights of a Branch together cast a more extensive Brightness, but each single Light burns with a stronger Flame. And lastly, take this along with you, that if Wealth be an Instrument of Pleasure, the greatest Pleasure it can put into your Power, is that of doing Good. 'Tis worth considering, that the Organs of Sense act within a narrow Compass, and the Appetites will soon say they have enough: Which of the two therefore is the happier Man? He, who confining all his Regard to the Gratification of his own Appetites, is capable but of short Fits of Pleasure? Or the Man, who, reckoning himself a Sharer in the Satisfactions of others, especially those which come to them by his Means, enlarges the Sphere of his Happiness?

The last Enemy to Benevolence I shall mention, is Uneasiness of any Kind. A guilty, or a discontented Mind, a Mind ruffled by ill Fortune, disconcerted by its own Passions, sowered by Neglect, or fretting at Disappointments, hath not Leisure to attend to the Necessity or Reasonableness of a Kindness desir'd, nor a Taste, for those Pleasures which wait on Beneficence, which demand a calm and unpolluted Heart to relish them. The most miserable of all Beings is the most envious; as, on the other Hand, the most communicative is the happiest. And if you are in search of the Seat of perfect Love and Friendship, you will not find it till you come to the Region of the Blessed, where Happiness, like a refreshing Stream, flows from Heart to Heart in an endless Circulation, and is preserv'd sweet and untainted by the Motion. 'Tis old Advice, if you have a Favour to request of any one, to observe the softest times of Address, when the Soul, in a Flush of good Humour, takes a Pleasure to shew itself pleas'd.[1] Persons conscious of their own Integrity, satisfied with themselves, and their Condition, and full of Confidence in a Supreme Being, and the Hope of Immortality, survey all about them with a Flow of Good-will. As Trees which like their Soil, they shoot out in Expressions of Kindness, and bend beneath their own precious Load, to the Hand of the Gatherer.

[1] Cf. No. 177 (vol. ii).

Now if the Mind be not thus easy, 'tis an infallible Sign that it is not in its natural State: Place the Mind in its right Posture, it will immediately discover its innate Propension to Beneficence.

No. 602   *Monday, October 4, 1714*[1]

. . . Facit hoc illos Hyacinthos.

Juv.

THE following Letter comes from a Gentleman, who, I find, is very diligent in making his Observations, which I think too material not to be communicated to the Publick.

SIR,

'IN order to execute the Office of Love-Casuist to *Great Britain*, with which I take my self to be invested by your Paper of *September* 8,[2] I shall make some further Observations upon the two Sexes in general, beginning with that which always ought to have the upper Hand. After having observed with much Curiosity the Accomplishments which are apt to captivate female Hearts, I find that there is no Person so irresistable as one who is a Man of Importance, provided it be in Matters of no Consequence. One who makes himself talked of, tho' it be for the particular Cock of his Hat, or for prating aloud in the Boxes at a Play, is in a fair way of being a Favourite. I have known a young Fellow make his Fortune by knocking down a Constable; and may venture to say, tho' it may seem a Paradox, that many a Fair One has died by a Duel in which both the Combatants have survived.

'About three Winters ago I took Notice of a young Lady at the Theatre, who conceived a Passion for a notorious Rake that headed a Party of Cat-calls;[3] and am credibly informed, that the Emperor of the Mohocks married a rich Widow within three Weeks after having rendered himself formidable in the Cities of *London* and *Westminster*.[4] Scowring and breaking of Windows[a] have done

---

[a] breaking of Windows] breaking Windows *Fol.*

[1] *Motto*. Juvenal, *Satires*, 6. 110: This transforms those men into Hyacinths.

Although this number is unassigned in the Tickell MS. it is a sequel to the 'Love Casuist' paper No. 591 and may therefore well be by Budgell.

[2] No. 591.   [3] Cf. No. 361 (vol. iii).

[4] His 'manifesto' is given in No. 347 (vol. iii).

frequent Execution upon the Sex;[1] but there is no Sett of these Male Charmers who make their way more successfully, than those who have gained themselves a Name for Intrigue, and have ruined the greatest Number of Reputations. There is a strange Curiosity in the female World to be acquainted with the dear Man who has been loved by others, and to know what it is that makes him so agreeable. His Reputation does more than half his Business. Every one that is ambitious of being a Woman of Fashion, looks out for Opportunities of being in his Company; so that, to use the old Proverb, When his Name is up he may lie a Bed.[2]

'I was very sensible of the great Advantage of being a Man of Importance upon these Occasions on the Day of the King's Entry, when I was seated in a Balcony behind a Cluster of very pretty Country Ladies, who had one of these showy Gentlemen in the Midst of them.[3] The first Trick I caught him at, was bowing to several Persons of Quality whom he did not know; nay, he had the Impudence to hem at a Blue Garter who had a finer Equipage than ordinary, and seemed a little concerned at the impertinent Huzzas of the Mob, that hindered his Friend from taking Notice of him. There was indeed one who pull'd off his Hat to him, and upon the Ladies asking who it was, he told them, it was a Foreign Minister that he had been very merry with the Night before; whereas in Truth, it was the City Common-Hunt.[4]

'He was never at a Loss when he was asked any Person's Name, tho' he seldom knew any one under a Peer. He found Dukes and Earls among the Aldermen, very good-natured Fellows among the Privy Counsellors, with two or three agreeable old Rakes among the Bishops and Judges.

'In short, I collected from his whole Discourse, that he was

---

[1] Cf. No. 276 (vol. ii).

[2] Apperson quotes examples of this proverb from 1611. See also Tilley N28.

[3] George I's royal entry into London occurred on Monday, 20 Sept. Setting out from Greenwich at noon, he arrived in London in the afternoon, and was met at St. Margaret's Hill in Southwark by the Lord Mayor. The following advertisement appears in No. 595, published on the preceding Friday:

The Golden Lion in Cheapside, by Mercers Chappel, is commodiously fitted with Benches, and is to be Let either entire, Balcony and Dining Room seperate, or otherwise in single Places to Gentlemen and Ladies who are minded to see the Royal Entrance of His Majesty. Inquire at the Anchor in Friday-street near Cheapside. N.B. Here Ladies won't be discommoded with the ill Conveniency of being confin'd to their Places, as they must in publick Stands; nor may they fear the Night's Approach ere the Cavalcade be past.

[4] 'The chief huntsman belonging to the lord mayor and aldermen of London' (Chambers' *Cyclopedia*, 1751; quoted in *OED*).

acquainted with every Body, and knew no Body. At the same Time, I am mistaken if he did not that Day make more Advances in the Affections of his Mistress, who sat near him, than he could have done in half a Year's Courtship.

'*Ovid* has finely touched this Method of making Love, which I shall here give my Reader in Mr. *Dryden*'s Translation.[1]

Page the Eleventh.

Thus Love in Theatres did first improve,
And Theatres are still the Scene of Love:
Nor shun the Chariots, and the Courser's Race;
The Circus is no inconvenient Place.
No Need is there of talking on the Hand,
Nor Nods, nor Signs, which Lovers understand;
But boldly next the Fair your Seat provide,
Close as you can to hers, and Side by Side:
Pleas'd or unpleas'd, no Matter; crowding sit;
For so the Laws of publick Shows permit.
Then find Occasion to begin Discourse,
Enquire whose Chariot this, and whose that Horse;
To whatsoever Side she is inclin'd,
Suit all your Inclinations to her Mind;
Like what she likes, from thence your Court begin,
And whom she favours, wish that he may win.

Again, Page the Sixteenth.

O when will come the Day, by Heaven design'd,
When thou, the best and fairest of Mankind,
Drawn by white Horses, shalt in Triumph ride,
With conquer'd Slaves attending on thy Side;
Slaves, that no longer can be safe in Flight;
O glorious Object! O surprising Sight!
O Day of Publick Joy, too good to end in Night!
On such a Day, if thou, and next to thee
Some Beauty sits, the Spectacle to see;
If she enquire the Names of conquer'd Kings,
Of Mountains, Rivers, and their hidden Springs;
Answer to all thou knowest; and, if Need be,
Of Things unknown seem to speak knowingly:

[1] Dryden's translation of the First Book of the 'Art of Love', lines 156–71, 242–60.

This is Euphrates, *crown'd with Reeds; and there*
Flows the swift Tigris, *with his Sea-green Hair.*
Invent new Names of Things unknown before;
Call this Armenia; *that, the* Caspian *Shore:*
Call this a Mede, *and that a* Parthian *Youth;*
Talk probably; no Matter for the Truth.

No. 603   *Wednesday, October 6, 1714*[1]
[BYROM]

Ducite ab Urbe Domum, mea Carmina, ducite Daphnim.
Virg.

THE following Copy of Verses comes from one of my Correspondents, and has something in it so Original, that I do not
much doubt but it will divert my Readers.

I.

MY Time, O ye Muses, was happily spent,[a]
When Phebe *went with me wherever I went;*

---

[a] *The poem is printed in italics in 8vo and 12mo, in roman in Fol.*

---

[2] *Motto.* Virgil, *Eclogues,* 8. 68:

       Restore, my Charms,
My lingring *Daphnis* to my longing Arms. DRYDEN.

The poem which makes up this number is ascribed to John Byrom in the Tickell
MS. Phebe is believed to have been Richard Bentley's youngest and favourite daughter Joanna, called 'Jug Bentley', at that time a child of eleven. She afterwards became
the wife of Denison Cumberland (grandson of the Bishop of Peterborough) and
mother of the dramatist, Richard Cumberland. See Richard Cumberland's *Memoirs*
(ed. 1807, i. 24) and James Henry Monk, *Life of Richard Bentley* (1833), ii. 113–14.
The first printed attribution to Byrom seems to be in the *Biographia Britannica,* vi,
part ii, Supplement (1766), pp. 26–28. Nichols, the first editor of the *Spectator,* writes:

     The author, Mr. John Byrom, was, when he wrote this poem, a student at
     Cambridge, and a candidate for a fellowship. This writer affirms, on good authority,
     that it answered its purpose effectually, which was not so much to win the
     daughter's affections, as to secure her father's interest on the occasion above-
     mentioned. As the poet was not in reality smitten with the charms of *Phoebe,* he is,
     perhaps, more pardonable for the introduction of some ludicrous instances of
     puerility of sentiment and expression which are introduced into his piece; at least
     this information, which may be depended upon, serves to account for them.

When Byrom's *Tunbridgiale, a Poem,* was published in 1726, it was described on the
title-page simply as 'By the Author of *My Time O ye Muses,* &c. SPECTATOR,
Vol. VIII'.
     The poem is reprinted in the *Gentleman's Magazine,* Feb. 1745 (xv. 102–3), with
a Latin translation by G. Walmsley.

Ten thousand sweet Pleasures I felt in my Breast,
Sure never fond Shepherd like Colin *was blest!*
But now she is gone, and has left me behind,
What a marvellous Change on a sudden I find?
When Things were as fine as could possibly be,
I thought 'twas the Spring; but alas! it was she.

II.

With such a Companion, to tend a few Sheep,
To rise up and play, or to lie down and sleep,
I was so good humour'd, so chearful, and gay,
My Heart was as light as a Feather all Day.
But now I so cross and so peevish am grown,
So strangely uneasy as never was known.
My Fair one is gone, and my Joys are all drown'd,
And my Heart—I am sure it weighs more than a Pound.

III.

The Fountain that wont to run sweetly along,
And dance to soft Murmurs the Pebbles among,
Thou know'st, little Cupid, *if* Phebe *was there,*
'Twas Pleasure to look at, 'twas Musick to hear:
But now she is absent, I walk by its Side,
And still as it murmurs do nothing but chide,
Must you be so chearful, while I go in Pain?
Peace there with your Bubbling, and hear me complain.

IV.

When my Lambkins around me would oftentimes play,
And when Phebe *and I were as joyful as they,*
How pleasant their Sporting, how happy the Time,
When Spring, Love and Beauty, were all in their Prime?
But now in their Frolicks when by me they pass,
I fling at their Fleeces an handful of Grass;
Be still then, I cry, for it makes me quite mad
To see you so merry, while I am so sad.

V.

My Dog I was ever well pleased to see
Come wagging his Tail to my Fair one and me;

And Phebe *was pleas'd too, and to my Dog said,*
Come hither, poor Fellow; and patted his Head.
But now, when he's fawning, I with a sour Look
Cry, Sirrah; and give him a Blow with my Crook:
And I'll give him another; for why shoud not Tray
Be as dull as his Master, when Phebe*'s away?*

VI.

When walking with Phebe, *what Sights have I seen?*
How fair was the Flower, how fresh was the Green?
What a lovely Appearance the Trees and the Shade,
The Cornfields and Hedges, and ev'ry thing made?
But now she has left me, tho' all are still there,
They none of 'em now so delightful appear:
'Twas nought but the Magick I find of her Eyes,
Made so many beautiful Prospects arise.

VII.

Sweet Musick went with us both all the Wood thro',
The Lark, Linnet, Throstle, and Nightingale too;
Winds over us whisper'd, Flocks by us did bleat,
And chirp went the Grasshopper under our Feet.
But now she is absent, tho' still they sing on,
The Woods are but lonely, the Melody's gone;
Her Voice in the Consort, as now I have found,
Gave ev'ry thing else its agreeable Sound.

VIII.

Rose, what is become of thy delicate Hue?
And where is the Violets beautiful Blue?
Does ought of its Sweetness the Blossom beguile,
That Meadow, those Daisies, why do they not smile?
Ah! Rivals, I see what it was that you drest,
And made your selves fine for; a Place in her Breast:
To put on your Colours to pleasure her Eye,
To be pluckt by her Hand, on her Bosom to die.

IX.

How slowly Time creeps till my Phebe *return?*
While amidst the soft Zephyrs, cool Breezes, I burn;

Methinks if I knew whereabouts he would tread,
I could breathe on his Wings, and 'twould melt down the Lead.
Fly swifter, ye Minutes, bring hither my Dear,
And rest so much longer for't when she is here.
Ah Colin! *old Time is full of Delay,*
Nor will budge one Foot faster for all thou canst say.

X.

Will no pitying Power that hears me complain,
Or cure my Disquiet, or soften my Pain.
To be cur'd thou must, Colin, *thy Passion remove;*
But what Swain is so silly to live without Love!
No, Deity, bid the dear Nymph to return,
For ne'er was poor Shepherd so sadly forlorn.
Ah! What shall I do? I shall die with Despair;
Take Heed, all ye Swains, how you love one so fair.

No. 604
[TICKELL]

Friday, October 8, 1714[1]

Tu ne quæsieris (scire nefas) quem mihi, quem tibi,
Finem Dii dederint, Leuconoe; nec Babylonios
Tentaris numeros. . . .

Hor.

THE Desire of knowing future Events, is one of the strongest Inclinations in the Mind of Man. Indeed an Ability of fore-seeing probable Accidents is what, in the Language of Men, is called Wisdom and Prudence: But, not satisfied with the Light that Reason holds out, Mankind hath endeavoured to penetrate more compendiously into Futurity. Magick, Oracles, Omens, lucky Hours, and the various Arts of Superstition, owe their Rise to this powerful Cause. As this Principle is founded in Self-Love, every Man is sure to be sollicitous in the first Place about his own Fortune, the Course of his Life, and the Time and Manner of his Death.

[1] *Motto.* Horace, *Odes,* I. II. 1-3:
　　　Seek not to know what fated End,
　　　The Gods for you or me intend,
　　　Nor lend to magick Arts an Ear.

If we consider that we are free Agents, we shall discover the Absurdity of such Enquiries. One of our Actions, which we might have performed or neglected, is the Cause of another that succeeds it, and so the whole Chain of Life is linked together. Pain, Poverty, or Infamy, are the natural Product of vicious and imprudent Acts; as the contrary Blessings are of good ones; so that we cannot suppose our Lot to be determined without Impiety. A great Enhancement of Pleasure arises from its being unexpected; and Pain is doubled by being foreseen. Upon all these, and several other Accounts, we ought to rest satisfied in this Portion bestowed on us; to adore the Hand that hath fitted every Thing to our Nature, and hath not more displayed his Goodness in our Knowledge than in our Ignorance.

It is not unworthy Observation, that superstitious Enquiries into future Events prevail more or less, in proportion to the Improvement of liberal Arts and useful Knowledge in the several Parts of the World. Accordingly we find, that magical Incantations remain in *Lapland*;[1] in the more remote Parts of *Scotland* they have their second Sight, and several of our own Countrymen see abundance of Fairies.[2] In *Asia* this Credulity is strong; and the greatest Part of refined Learning there consists in the Knowledge of Amulets, Talismans, occult Numbers, and the like.[3]

When I was at *Grand Cairo*,[4] I fell into the Acquaintance of a goodnatured Musselman, who promised me many good Offices, which he designed to do me when he became the Prime Minister, which was a Fortune bestowed on his Imagination by a Doctor very deep in the curious Sciences. At his repeated Sollicitations I went to learn my Destiny of this wonderful Sage. For a small Sum I had his Promise; but was required to wait in a dark Apartment till he had run thro' the preparatory Ceremonies. Having a strong Propensity, even then, to Dreaming, I took a Nap upon the Sofa where I was placed, and had the following Vision, the Particulars whereof I picked up the other Day among my Papers.

I found my self in an unbounded Plain, where methought the

---

[1] See John Scheffer, *The History of Lapland* (Oxford, 1674), chap. xi ('Of the magicall Ceremonies of the Laplanders'), pp. 45–60. Magic, Scheffer writes, is 'one of the greatest of their impieties that yet continues among them' (p. 45).
[2] 'Second sight' is also alluded to in Nos. 505 and 524.
[3] This would not hold, however, for China. Le Comte (*Memoirs*, 1697) praises the Chinese for their learning and the purity of their religion, though the *bonzes* do take advantage of the people.
[4] See No. 1.

whole World, in several Habits, and with different Tongues, was assembled. The Multitude glided swiftly along, and I found in my self a strong Inclination to mingle in the Train. My Eyes quickly singled out some of the most splendid Figures. Several in rich Caftans[1] and glittering Turbans bustled through the Throng, and trampled over the Bodies of those they threw down; till to my great Surprize I found that the great Pace they went only hastened them to a Scaffold or a Bowstring. Many beautiful Damsels on the other Side moved forward with great Gaiety; some danced till they fell all along; and others painted their Faces till they lost their Noses. A Tribe of Creatures with busy Looks falling into a Fit of Laughter at the Misfortunes of the unhappy Ladies, I turned my Eyes upon them. They were each of them filling his Pockets with Gold and Jewels, and when there was no Room left for more, these Wretches looking round with Fear and Horror, pined away before my Face with Famine and Discontent.

This Prospect of humane Misery struck me dumb for some Miles. Then it was that, to disburthen my Mind, I took Pen and Ink, and did every Thing that hath since happened under my Office of SPECTATOR. While I was employing my self for the Good of Mankind, I was surprized to meet with very unsuitable Returns from my Fellow-Creatures. Never was poor Author so beset with Pamphleteers, who sometimes marched directly against me, but oftener shot at me from strong Bulwarks, or rose up suddenly in Ambush. They were of all Characters and Capacities, some with Ensigns of Dignity, and others in Liveries; but what most surprized me, was to see two or three in Black Gowns among my Enemies.[2] It was no small Trouble to me sometimes to have a Man come up to me with an angry Face, and reproach me for having lampooned him, when I had never seen or heard of him in my Life. With the Ladies it was otherwise: Many became my Enemies for not being particularly pointed out; as there were others who resented the Satyr which they imagined I had directed against them. My great Comfort was in the Company of half a Dozen Friends, who, I found since, were the Club which I have so often mentioned in my Papers. I laughed often at Sir *Roger* in my Sleep, and was the more diverted with

---

[1] A caftan is a garment worn in Turkey and other eastern countries, 'consisting of a kind of long under-tunic or vest tied at the waist with the girdle' (*OED*).

[2] 'The hirelings and *black gowns* employed by the administration in the last years of the Queen's reign, Dr. Swift, Prior, Atterbury, Dr. Freind, Dr. King, Mr. Oldisworth, Mrs. D. Manley, and the writers of The Examiner, &c.' (Nichols).

Will. Honeycomb's Gallantries, (when we afterwards became acquainted) because I had foreseen his Marriage with a Farmer's Daughter.[1] The Regret which arose in my Mind upon the Death of my Companions, my Anxieties for the Publick, and the many Calamities still fleeting before my Eyes, made me repent my Curiosity; when the Magician entered the Room, and awakened me, by telling me (when it was too late) that he was just going to begin.

N. B. I have only delivered the Prophecy of that Part of my Life which is past, it being inconvenient to divulge the second Part till a more proper Opportunity.

No. 605   *Monday, October 11, 1714*[2]
[TICKELL]

> *Exuerint sylvestrem animum, cultuque frequenti*
> *In quascunque voles artes, haud tarda sequentur.*
> Virg.

HAVING perused the following Letter, and finding it to run upon the Subject of Love, I refer'd it to the Learned *Casuist*, whom I have retained in my Service for Speculations of that Kind.[3] He returned it to me the next Morning with his Report annexed to it, with both of which I shall here present my Reader.

Mr. SPECTATOR,

'FINDING that you have Entertained an useful Person in your Service in quality of *Love-Casuist*, I apply my self to you, under a very great Difficulty, that hath for some Months Perplexed me. I have a Couple of humble Servants, one of which I have no

---

[1] See No. 530 (vol. iv).
[2] *Motto.* Virgil, *Georgics*, 2. 51–52:
   Their Wildness lose, and quitting Nature's part,
   Obey the Rules and Discipline of Art. DRYDEN.

This number is assigned to Tickell in the Tickell MS. Earlier editors, following Nichols, have given it, with some hesitation, to Budgell. Since it is connected with the speculations of the 'Love Casuist' of Nos. 591 and 602, there would be some grounds for connecting it with Budgell—if one may assume that he had left notes behind him before leaving for Ireland. Tickell, however, was by this time in charge of the paper and it seems safer on the whole to assign the essay to him (cf. Hodgart, p. 379).
[3] The 'Love Casuist' of Nos. 591 and 602.

Aversion to; the other I think of very kindly. The First hath the Reputation of a Man of good Sense, and is one of those People that your Sex are apt to Value. My Spark is reckoned a Coxcomb among the Men, but is a Favourite of the Ladies. If I marry the Man of Worth, as they call him, I shall oblige my Parents and improve my Fortune; but with my dear Beau I promise my self Happiness, altho' not a Jointure. Now I would ask you, whether I should consent to lead my Life with a Man that I have only no Objection to, or with him against whom all Objections to me appear frivolous. I am determined to follow the *Casuists* Advice, and I dare say he will not put me upon so serious a thing as Matrimony contrary to my Inclination.

I am, &c.

Fanny Fickle.

P. S. 'I forgot to tell you, that the pretty Gentleman is the most complaisant Creature in the World, and is always of my Mind; but the other forsooth, fancies he hath as much Wit as my self, slights my Lap-dog, and hath the Insolence to contradict me when he thinks I am not in the Right. About half an Hour ago, he maintained to my Face, that a Patch always implies a Pimple.'

As I look upon it to be my Duty rather to side with the Parents than the Daughter, I shall propose some Considerations to my gentle Querist, which may encline her to comply with those, under whose Direction she is: And, at the same time, convince her, that it is not impossible but she may, in time, have a true Affection for him who is, at present, indifferent to her: Or, to use the old Family Maxim, that *If she marries first, Love will come after.*

The only Objection, that she seems to insinuate against the Gentleman proposed to her, is his want of Complaisance, which, I perceive, she is very willing to return. Now, I can discover from this very Circumstance, that she and her Lover, whatever they may think of it, are very good Friends in their Hearts. It is difficult to determine, whether Love delights more in giving Pleasure or Pain. Let Miss *Fickle* ask her own Heart, if she doth not take a secret Pride in making this Man of good Sense look very silly. Hath she ever been better pleased, than when her Behaviour hath made her Lover ready to hang himself? Or doth she ever rejoice more, than when she thinks she hath driven him to the very Brink of a purling Stream? Let her consider, at the same time, that it is not

impossible but her Lover may have discovered her Tricks, and hath a mind to give her as good as she brings.[1] I remember a handsome young Baggage that treated a hopeful *Greek* of my Acquaintance, just come from *Oxford*, as if he had been a *Barbarian*. The first Week, after she had fixed him, she took a Pinch of Snuff out of his Rival's Box, and apparently touched the Enemy's little Finger. She became a profest Enemy to the Arts and Sciences, and scarce ever wrote a Letter to him without willfully mis-spelling his Name. The young Scholar, to be even with her, railed at *Coquettes* as soon as he had got the Word; and did not want Parts to turn into Ridicule her Men of Wit and Pleasure of the Town. After having irritated one another, for the space of five Months, she made an Assignation with him fourscore Miles from *London*. But as he was very well acquainted with her Pranks, he took a Journey the quite contrary Way. Accordingly they met, quarrel'd, and in a few Days were Married. Their former Hostilities are now the Subject of their Mirth, being content at present with that part of Love only which bestows Pleasure.

Women, who have been married some time, not having it in their Heads to draw after them a numerous Train of Followers, find their Satisfaction in the Possession of one Man's Heart. I know very well, that Ladies in their Bloom desire to be excused in this Particular. But when Time hath worn out their natural Vanity and taught them Discretion, their Fondness settles on its proper Object. And it is probably for this Reason, that among Husbands, you will find more that are fond of Women beyond their Prime, than of those who are actually in the Insolence of Beauty. My Reader will apply the same Observation to the other Sex.

I need not insist upon the Necessity of their pursuing one common Interest, and their united Care for their Children; but shall only observe, by the Way, that married Persons are both more warm in their Love, and more hearty in their Hatred, than any others whatsoever. Mutual Favours and Obligations, which may be supposed to be greater here than in any other State, naturally beget an intense Affection in generous Minds. As, on the contrary, Persons who have bestowed such Favours, have a particular Bitterness in their Resentments, when they think themselves ill treated by those of whom they have deserved so much.

[1] The two quotations in *OED* to illustrate this phrase are from Cibber's *She Would and She Would Not* (1703) and *Guardian* 145 (1713, by Steele).

Besides, Miss *Fickle* may consider, that as there are often many Faults concealed before Marriage, so there are sometimes many Virtues unobserved.

To this we may add the great Efficacy of Custom, and constant Conversation, to produce a mutual Friendship and Benevolence in two Persons. It is a nice Reflection, which I have heard a Friend of mine make, that you may be sure a Woman loves a Man, when she uses his Expressions, tells his Stories, or imitates his Manner. This gives a secret Delight; for Imitation is a kind of artless Flattery,[1] and mightily favours the powerful Principle of Self-love. It is certain, that married Persons, who are possest with a mutual Esteem, not only catch the Air and way of Talk from one another, but fall into the same Traces of thinking and liking. Nay, some have carried the Remark so far as to assert, that the Features of Man and Wife grow, in time, to resemble one another. Let my fair Correspondent therefore consider, that the Gentleman recommended will have a good deal of her own Face in two or three Years; which she must not expect from the Beau, who is too full of his dear self to copy after another. And I dare appeal to her own Judgment, if that Person will not be the handsomest, that is the most like her self.

We have a remarkable Instance to our present Purpose in the History of King *Edgar*, which I shall here relate, and leave it with my fair Correspondent to be applied to her self.[2]

This great Monarch, who is so famous in *British* Story, fell in Love, as he made his Progress through his Kingdom, with a certain Duke's Daughter who lived near *Winchester*, and was the most celebrated Beauty of the Age. His Importunities and the Violence of his Passion were so great, that the Mother of the young Lady promised him to bring her Daughter to his Bed the next Night, tho' in her Heart she abhor'd so infamous an Office. It was no sooner dark than she conveyed into his Room a young Maid of no disagreeable Figure, who was one of her Attendants, and did not want Address to improve the Opportunity for the Advancement of her Fortune. She made so good Use of her Time, that when she offered to rise a little before Day, the King could by no means think of parting with her. So that finding her self under a Necessity of discovering

[1] An anticipation of the apophthegm, 'Imitation is the sincerest of flattery', in Charles Caleb Colton's *Lacon: or Many Things in Few Words* (1820–2), No. 217.

[2] For the history of this tenth-century monarch see *DNB*. The story told here follows closely the account given in Sir Richard Baker's *Chronicle* (ed. 1684, page 11).

who she was, she did it in so handsome a Manner, that his Majesty was exceeding gracious to her, and took her ever after under his Protection; insomuch that our Chronicles tell us he carried her along with him, made her his first Minister of State, and continued true to her alone till his Marriage with the beautiful *Elfrida*.

No. 606   *Wednesday, October 13, 1714*[1]

[TICKELL]

> *. . . longum cantu solata laborem*
> *Arguto Conjunx percurrit pectine Telas.*
>   Virg.

Mr. SPECTATOR,

'I HAVE a couple of Nieces under my Direction, who so often run gadding abroad, that I don't know where to have them. Their Dress, their Tea, and their Visits, take up all their Time, and they go to Bed as tired with doing nothing, as I am after quilting a whole Under-Petticoat. The only time they are not idle, is while they read your SPECTATORS; which being dedicated to the Interests of Virtue, I desire you to recommend the long neglected Art of Needle-work. Those Hours which in this Age are thrown away in Dress, Play, Visits, and the like, were employed, in my time, in writing out Receipts, or working Beds, Chairs and Hangings for the Family. For my Part, I have ply'd my Needle these fifty Years, and by my good Will would never have it out of my Hand. It grieves my Heart to see a couple of proud idle Flirts sipping their Tea, for a whole Afternoon, in a Room hung round with the Industry of their great Grandmother. Pray, Sir, take the laudable Mystery of Embroidery into your serious Consideration, and as you have a great deal of the Virtue of the last Age in you, continue your Endeavours to reform the present.

I am, &c.

In Obedience to the Commands of my venerable Correspondent, I have duly weighed this important Subject, and promise my self,

[1] *Motto.* Virgil, *Georgics*, 1. 293–4:
    She sings to drive the tedious Hours away,
    And shoots the flying Shuttle through the Loom. DRYDEN.

from the Arguments here laid down, that all the fine Ladies of *England* will be ready, as soon as their Mourning[1] is over, to appear covered with the Work of their own Hands.

What a delightful Entertainment must it be to the Fair Sex, whom their native Modesty, and the Tenderness of Men towards them, exempts from publick Business, to pass their Hours in imitating Fruits and Flowers, and transplanting all the Beauties of Nature into their own Dress, or raising a new Creation in their Closets and Apartments. How pleasing is the Amusement of walking among the Shades and Groves planted by themselves, in surveying Heroes slain by their Needle, or little *Cupids* which they have brought into the World without Pain!

This is, methinks, the most proper way wherein a Lady can shew a fine Genius, and I cannot forbear wishing, that several Writers of that Sex had chosen to apply themselves rather to Tapestry than Rhime. Your Pastoral Poetesses may vent their Fancy in Rural Landskips, and place despairing Shepherds under silken Willows, or drown them in a Stream of Mohair.[2] The Heroick Writers may work up Battels as successfully,[a] and inflame them with Gold or stain them with Crimson. Even those who have only a Turn to a Song or an Epigram, may put many valuable Stitches into a Purse, and crowd a thousand Graces into a Pair of Garters.

If I may, without breach of good Manners, imagine that any pretty Creature is void of Genius, and would perform her Part herein but very awkardly, I must nevertheless insist upon her working, if it be only to keep her out of Harm's way.

Another Argument for busying good Women in Works of Fancy,[3] is, because it takes them off from Scandal, the usual Attendant of Tea-Tables, and all other unactive Scenes of Life. While they are forming their Birds and Beasts, their Neighbours will be allowed to be the Fathers of their own Children: And *Whig* and *Tory* will be but seldom mentioned, where the great Dispute is, whether Blue or Red is the more proper Colour. How much greater Glory would *Sophronia* do the General, if she would chuse rather to Work the Battel of *Blenheim* in Tapestry, than signalize her self with so much Vehemence against those who are *Frenchmen* in their Hearts![b]

---

[a] successfully,] successively, *Fol.*   [b] Hearts!] Hearts. *Fol.*

[1] Owing to the death of Queen Anne on 1 Aug.
[2] An allusion to Lady Winchilsea?
[3] I.e. needlework (cf. *OED*).

A Third Reason that I shall mention, is the Profit that is brought to the Family where these pretty Arts are encouraged. It is manifest that this way of Life not only keeps fair Ladies from running out into Expences, but is at the same time an actual Improvement. How memorable would that Matron be, who should have it inscribed upon her Monument, 'that she Wrought out the whole Bible[a] in Tapestry, and died in a good old Age, after having covered three hundred Yards of Wall in the Mansion-House.'[1]

The Premises being considered, I humbly submit the following Proposals to all Mothers in *Great Britain.*

I. That no young Virgin whatsoever be allowed to receive the Addresses of her first Lover, but in a Suit of her own Embroidering.

II. That before every fresh Servant, she be obliged to appear with a new Stomacher at the least.

III. That no one be actually Married, till she hath the Child-bed Pillows,[2] *&c.* ready Stitched, as likewise the Mantle for the Boy, quite finished.

These Laws, if I mistake not, would Effectually restore the decayed Art of Needle-work, and make the Virgins of *Great Britain* exceedingly Nimble-Finger'd in their Business.

There is a memorable Custom of the *Grecian* Ladies, in this Particular, preserved in *Homer*, which I hope will have a very good Effect with my Country-women. A Widow, in Ancient Times, could not, without Indecency, receive a second Husband, till she had Woven a Shrowd for her deceased Lord, or the next of Kin to him. Accordingly, the Chaste *Penelope* having, as she thought, lost *Ulysses* at Sea, she employed her time in preparing a Winding-sheet for *Laërtes* the Father of her Husband. The Story of her Web being very Famous, and yet not sufficiently known in its several Circumstances, I shall give it to my Reader, as *Homer* makes one of her Wooers relate it.

> *Sweet Hope she gave to every Youth apart,*
> *With well taught Looks, and a deceitful Heart:*
> *A Web she wove of many a slender Twine,*
> *Of curious Texture, and perplext Design;*

---

[a] Bible] Bible Scripture *Fol. Corrected in Errata (No. 607)*

---

[1] See No. 264 (vol. ii) for this obsolete word.

[2] *OED* gives various uses of 'child-bed' as attributive adjective, though not this one.

My Youths, she cry'd, my Lord but newly dead,
Forbear a while to court my widow'd Bed,
Till I have wov'n, as solemn Vows require,
This Web, a Shrowd for poor Ulysses' *Sire.*
His Limbs, when Fate the Hero's Soul demands,
Shall claim this Labour of his Daughter's Hands:
Least all the Dames of Greece *my Name despise,*
While the great King without a Cov'ring lies.
    Thus she. Nor did my Friends mistrust the Guile.
All Day she sped the long laborious Toil:
But when the burning Lamps supply'd the Sun,
Each Night unravell'd what the Day begun.
Three live-long Summers did the Fraud prevail,
The Fourth, her Maidens told th' amazing Tale.
These Eyes beheld, as close I took my Stand,
The backward Labours of her faithless Hand:
Till watch'd at length, and press'd on every Side,
Her Task she ended, and commenc'd a Bride.[1]

No. 607   *Friday, October* 15, 1714[2]

[TICKELL]

Dicite Iö Pæan, et Iö bis dicite Pæan:
Decidit in casses præda petita meos.
                    Ovid.

Mr. SPECTATOR,

'HAVING in your Paper of *Monday* last published my Report
on the Case of Mrs. *Fanny Fickle*, wherein I have taken
Notice, that Love comes after Marriage; I hope your Readers are
satisfied of this Truth, that as Love generally produces Matrimony,
so it often happens that Matrimony produces Love.

'It perhaps requires more Virtues to make a good Husband or

[1] *Odyssey*, 2. 91–110. The lines here are not from any known translation, and may
be assumed to be Tickell's. His version of the *Iliad* was published on 8 June 1715
(Richard Eustace Tickell, *Thomas Tickell* [1931], p. 41).
[2] *Motto.* Ovid, *Ars amatoria*, 2. 1–2:
        With Io Paeans charm the joyful Air,
        The wisht for Prey is fallen in my Snare.

Wife, than what go to the finishing any the most shining Character whatsoever.

'Discretion seems absolutely necessary; and accordingly we find that the best Husbands have been most famous for their Wisdom. *Homer*, who hath drawn a perfect Pattern of a prudent Man, to make it the more compleat, hath celebrated him for the just Returns of Fidelity and Truth to his *Penelope*; insomuch that he refused the Caresses of a Goddess for her Sake, and, to use the Expression of the best of Pagan Authors, *vetulam suam prætulit Immortalitati*, his old Woman was dearer to him than Immortality.[1]

'Virtue is the next necessary Qualification for this domestick Character, as it naturally produces Constancy and mutual Esteem. Thus *Brutus* and *Porcia* were more remarkable for Virtue and Affection than any others of the Age in which they lived.

'Good-nature is a third necessary Ingredient in the Marriage State, without which it would inevitably sower upon a thousand Occasions. When Greatness of Mind is joined with this amiable Quality, it attracts the Admiration and Esteem of all who behold it. Thus *Cæsar*, not more remarkable for his Fortune and Valour than for his Humanity, stole into the Hearts of the *Roman* People, when, breaking through the Custom, he pronounced an Oration at the Funeral of his first and best beloved Wife.[2]

'Good-nature is insufficient, unless it be steady and uniform, and accompanied with an Evenness of Temper, which is, above all things, to be preserved in this Friendship contracted for Life. A Man must be easie within himself, before he can be so to his other Self: *Socrates*, and *Marcus Aurelius*, are Instances of Men who, by the Strength of Philosophy, having entirely composed their Minds and subdued their Passions, are celebrated for good Husbands, notwithstanding the first was yoked with *Xantippe*, and the other

[1] The Latin phrase seems to originate in Bacon's essay, 'Of Marriage and Single Life' (*Essays*, ed. Wright, 1892, p. 27). The 'best of pagan authors' is apparently Cicero, who (*De legibus*, 2. 1. 3) wrote, 'Siquidem etiam ille sapientissimus vir, Ithacam ut videret, immortalitatem scribitur repudiasse' (and indeed, as you remember, that exceedingly wise man is said to have refused immortality that he might see Ithaca once more—Loeb Library trans.). Cf. also Cicero, *De Oratore*, 1. 44. In Plutarch's 'Bruta Ratione Uti' (*Moralia*, 985F) Circe says to Odysseus, 'Quasi vero non peius iam ante tibi consulueris, qui immortali et senectutis immuni vita, quam apud me licebat degere, dimissa, ad mulierem mortalem, adde etiam vetulam, per infinita quae te manent mala contendis?' (Xylander's version, Frankfurt, 1603, p. 74. Why, haven't you treated yourself in a still stranger fashion, abandoning an immortal and ageless life with me to hasten back, through unnumbered troubles, to a mortal woman, one who I say is, moreover, already an old woman?)

[2] Plutarch, *Life of Caesar*, 5. 2.

with *Faustina*. If the wedded Pair would but habituate themselves for the first Year to bear with one another's Faults, the Difficulty would be pretty well conquered. This mutual Sweetness of Temper and Complacency, was finely recommended in the Nuptial Ceremonies among the Heathens, who, when they sacrificed to *Juno* at that Solemnity, always tore out the Gall from the Entrails of the Victim, and cast it behind the Altar.[1]

'I shall conclude this Letter with a Passage out of Dr. *Plott*'s *Natural History of Staffordshire*, not only as it will serve to fill up your present Paper; but if I find my self in the Humour, may give Rise to another; I having by me an old Register, belonging to the Place here undermentioned.'[2]

Sir *Philip de Somervile*, held the Manors of *Whichenovre*, *Scirescot*, *Ridware*, *Netherton*, and *Cowlee*, all in *Com. Stafford*, of the Earls of *Lancaster*, by this memorable Service. The said Sir *Philip* shall find, maintain, and sustain, one *Bacon-Flitch*, hanging in his Hall at *Whichenovre*, ready arrayed all times of the Year, but in *Lent*, to be given to every Man or Woman married, after the Day and the Year of their Marriage be past, in Form following.

Whensoever that any one such before named will come to enquire for the Bacon, in their own Person, they shall come to the Bayliff, or to the Porter of the Lordship of *Whichenovre*, and shall say to them in the Manner as ensueth.

'Bayliff, or Porter, I doo you to know, that I am come for my self, to demand one *Bacon-Flyke*, hanging in the Hall of the Lord of *Whichenovre*, after the Form thereunto belonging.'

After which Relation, the Bayliff or Porter shall assign a Day to him, upon Promise by his Faith to return, and with him to bring Twain of his Neighbours. And in the mean Time, the said Bayliff shall take with him Twain of the Freeholders of the Lordship of *Whichenovre*, and they three shall go to the Mannor of *Rudlow*, belonging to *Robert Knightleye*, and there shall summon the aforesaid *Knightleye*, or his Bayliff, commanding him to be ready at *Whichenovre* the Day appointed, at Prime of Day, with his Carriage,[3]

---

[1] Plutarch, 'Conjugalia Praecepta' (*Moralia*, 141F). This sentence survives among Addison's 'Papers of Hints' for the eighth volume of the *Spectator* in the Tickell MSS. (see Hodgart, p. 383).

[2] Robert Plot, *Natural History of Stafford-shire* (Oxford, 1686), pp. 440–3. The extract reproduced here is from chap. x ('Of Antiquities'). *The Spectator* modernizes the text generally and omits a word or two here and there, but makes no substantial changes. Sir Philip de Somervile is described as '10 of *Edw*. 3.'

[3] In the old sense of 'a vehicle or means of conveyance of any kind' (*OED*, 'Carriage' 23).

that is to say, a Horse and a Saddle, a Sack and a Pryke,[1] for to convey the said Bacon and Corn a Journey out of the County of *Stafford*, at his Costages. And then the said Bayliff shall, with the said Freeholders, summon all the Tenants of the said Manor, to be ready at the Day appointed, at *Whichenovre*, for to do and perform the Services which they owe to the Bacon. And at the Day assigned, all such as owe Services to the Bacon, shall be ready at the Gate of the Manor of *Whichenovre*, from the Sun-rising to Noon, attending and awaiting for the coming of him who fetcheth the Bacon. And when he is come, there shall be delivered to him and his Fellows, Chapelets; and to all those which shall be there, to do their Services due to the Bacon. And they shall lead the said Demandant with Trumps and Tabours, and other manner of Minstrels, to the Hall-Door, where he shall find the Lord of *Whichenovre*, or his Steward, ready to deliver the Bacon in this manner.

He shall enquire of him, which demandeth the Bacon, if he have brought twain of his Neighbours with him: Which must answer, *They be here ready*. And then the Steward shall cause these two Neighbours to swear, if the said Demandant be a wedded Man, or have been a Man wedded; and if since his Marriage one Year and a Day be past; and if he be a Free-man, or a Villain. And if his said Neighbours make Oath, that he hath for him all these three Points rehearsed; then shall the Bacon be taken down, and brought to the Hall Door, and shall there be laid upon one half Quarter of Wheat, and upon one other of Rye. And he that demandeth the Bacon shall kneel upon his Knee, and shall hold his Right Hand upon a Book, which Book shall be laid upon the Bacon and the Corn, and shall make Oath in this manner.

'Here ye, Sir *Philip* de *Somervile*, Lord of *Whichenovre*, mayntener and gyver of this Baconne: That I *A*. sithe I Wedded *B*. my Wife, and sythe I hadd hyr in my kepying, and at my Wylle, by a Year and a Day after our Marriage, I wold not have chaunged for none other; farer ne fowler; richer, ne pourer; ne for none other descended of greater Lynage; slepyng ne waking, at noo tyme. And yf the seyd *B*. were sole and I sole I would take her to be my Wyfe before all the Wymen of the Worlde, of what condiciones soever they be: good or evylle, as help me God ond his Seyntes, and this flesh and all Fleshes.'

And his Neighbours shall make Oath, that they trust verily he

[1] A goad for oxen.

hath said truly. And if it be found by his Neighbours before-named that he be a Freeman, there shall be delivered to him half a Quarter of Wheat and a Cheese; and if he be a Villain, he shall have half a Quarter of Rye without Cheese. And then shall *Knightleye* the Lord of *Rudlow* be called for, to carry all these things tofore rehearsed; and the said Corn shall be laid on one Horse and the Bacon above it: and he to whom the Bacon appertaineth shall ascend upon his Horse, and shall take the Cheese before him, if he have a Horse. And if he have none, the Lord of *Whichenovre* shall cause him to have one Horse and Saddle, to such time as he be passed his Lordship: and so shall they depart the Manor of *Whichenovre* with the Corn and the Bacon, tofore him that hath won it, with Trumpets, Tabouretts, and other manner of Minstrelsie. And all the Free Tenants of *Whichenovre* shall Conduct him to be passed the Lordship of *Whichenovre*. And then shall they all return; except him, to whom appertaineth to make the Carriage and Journey without the County of *Stafford*, at the Costs of his Lord of *Whichenovre*.

No. 608   *Monday, October* 18, 1714[2]
[TICKELL]

. . . *Perjuria ridet Amantum.*
Ovid.

Mr. SPECTATOR,

'ACCORDING to my Promise, I herewith transmit to you a List of several Persons, who from time to time demanded the *Flitch of Bacon*, of Sir *Philip de Somervile* and his Descendents; as it is preserved in an ancient Manuscript, under the Title of, *The Register of Whichenovre-Hall, and of the Bacon Flitch there maintained.*

'In the Beginning of this Record is recited the Law or Institution in Form, as it is already printed in your last Paper: To which are added Two By-Laws, as a Comment upon the General Law, the Substance whereof is, That the Wife shall take the same Oath as the Husband, *mutatis mutandis*; and that the Judges shall, as they

---

[1] *Motto.* Ovid, *Ars amatoria*, 1. 633: . . . Laughs at the perjuries of lovers.

In the Folio sheets the motto appears as *Ridet Perjuria Amantum*. This number is assigned to Tickell in the Tickell MS.; it may possibly represent a working over of materials left by Addison.

think meet, interrogate or cross-examine the Witnesses. After this proceeds the Register in Manner following.

'Aubry de Falstaff, *Son of Sir* John Falstaff, *Kt. with Dame* Maude *his Wife, were the first that demanded the Bacon, he having bribed twain of his Father's Companions to swear falsely in his Behoof, whereby he gained the Flitch: But he and his said Wife falling immediately into a Dispute how the said Bacon should be dressed, it was by Order of the Judges taken from him, and hung up again in the Hall.*

'Alison, *the Wife of* Stephen Freckle, *brought her said Husband along with her, and set forth the good Conditions and Behaviour of her Consort, adding withall, that she doubted not but he was ready to attest the like of her, his Wife; whereupon he,* the said Stephen, *shaking his Head, she turned short upon him, and gave him a Box on the Ear.*

'Philip de Waverland, *having laid his Hand upon the Book, when the Clause,* Were I sole and she sole, *was rehearsed, found a secret Compunction rising in his Mind, and stole it off again.*

'Richard de Loveless, *who was a Courtier, and a very well bred Man, being observed to hesitate at the Words,* after our Marriage, *was thereupon required to explain himself. He replied, by talking very largely of his exact Complaisance while he was a Lover; and alledg'd, that he had not in the least disobliged his Wife for a Year and a Day* before *Marriage, which he hoped was the same Thing.*

'Rejected.

'Joceline Jolly, *Esq; making it appear by unquestionable Testimony, That he and his Wife had preserved full and entire Affection for the Space of the first Month, commonly called the* Honey-Moon;[1] *he had, in Consideration thereof, one Rasher bestowed upon him.*

'After this, says the Record, many Years passed over before any Demandant appeared at *Whichenovre-Hall*; insomuch that one would have thought that the whole Country were turned *Jews*, so little was their Affection to the Flitch of Bacon.

'The next Couple enrolled had like to have carried it, if one of the Witnesses had not deposed, That dining on a *Sunday* with the Demandant, whose Wife had sate below the Squire's Lady at Church, she the said Wife dropped some Expressions, as if she thought her

---

[1] This is the reading of the Folio and 8vo texts; the 12mo reads Honey-Money. G. Gregory Smith adopts the reading of the 12mo and adds: 'So in the early texts; changed, unnecessarily, by later editors, to Honeymoon.' The *OED* does not record *Honey-Money*, although it gives the obsolete *Honey-month*, the last example of which is from *Tatler* 192 (by Steele).

Husband deserved to be knighted; to which he returned a passionate *Pish!* The Judges taking the Premises into Consideration, declared the aforesaid Behaviour to imply an unwarrantable Ambition in the Wife, and Anger in the Husband.

'It is recorded as a sufficient Disqualification of a certain Wife, that speaking of her Husband she said, *God forgive him!*

'It is likewise remarkable, that a Couple were rejected upon the Deposition of one of their Neighbours, that the Lady had once told her Husband, that *it was her Duty to obey*; to which he replied, *Oh! my Dear, you are never in the Wrong.*

'The violent Passion of one Lady for her Lap-dog; the turning away of the old House-Maid by another; a Tavern-Bill torn by the Wife, and a Taylor's by the Husband; a Quarrel about the Kissing-Crust;[1] spoiling of Dinners, and coming in late of Nights; are so many several Articles which occasioned the Reprobation of some Scores of Demandants, whose Names are recorded in the aforesaid Register.

'Without enumerating other particular Persons, I shall content my self with observing, that the Sentence pronounced against one *Gervase Poacher* is, that *he might have had Bacon to his Eggs, if he had not heretofore scolded his Wife when they were over-boiled.* And the Deposition against *Dorothy Do-little* runs in these Words; *That she had so far usurped the Dominion of the Coal-fire, (the Stirring whereof her Husband claimed to himself) that by her good Will she never would suffer the Poker out of her Hand.*

'I find but Two Couples, in this First Century, that were successful: The First, was a Sea-Captain and his Wife, who, since the Day of their Marriage, had not seen one another till the Day of the Claim. The Second, was an honest Pair in the Neighbourhood: The Husband was a Man of plain good Sense, and a peaceable Temper; the Woman was dumb.'

---

[1] 'The soft part of the crust of a loaf where it has touched another in baking; "also the under-crust in a pudding or pie" (Farmer *Slang*)' (*OED*). Cf. William King, *Art of Cookery* (1708), lines 194–5:

These brought him kissing-crusts, and those
Brought him small-beer before he rose.

No. 609   *Wednesday, October 20, 1714*[1]

... *Farrago libelli.*

Juv.

Mr. SPECTATOR,

'I HAVE for some Time desired to appear in your Paper, and have
therefore chosen a Day to steal into the SPECTATOR, when I
take it for granted you will not have many spare Minutes for
Speculations of your own.[2] As I was the other Day walking with
an honest Country-Gentleman, he very often was expressing his
Astonishment to see the Town so mightily crowded with Doctors
of Divinity: Upon which I told him, He was very much mistaken
if he took all those Gentlemen he saw in Scarfs to be Persons of that
Dignity;[3] for, that a young Divine, after his first Degree in the
University, usually comes hither only to show himself; and on that
Occasion is apt to think he is but half equipp'd with a Gown and
Cassock for his publick Appearance, if he hath not the additional
Ornament of a Scarf of the first Magnitude to intitle him to the
Appellation of Doctor from his Landlady and the Boy at *Child*'s.
Now since I know that this Piece of Garniture is looked upon as a
Mark of Vanity or Affectation, as it is made use of among some of
the little spruce Adventurers of the Town, I should be glad if you
would give it a Place among those Extravagancies you have justly
exposed in several of your Papers; being very well assured that the
main Body of the Clergy, both in the Country and the Universities, who are almost to a Man untainted with it, would be very
well pleased to see this venerable Foppery well exposed. When my
Patron did me the Honour to take me into his Family, (for I must
own my self of this Order) he was pleased to say he took me as a
Friend and Companion; and whether he looked upon the Scarf,
like the Lace and Shoulder-knot of a Footman, as a Badge of Servitude and Dependance, I do not know, but he was so kind as to
leave my wearing of it to my own Discretion; and not having any
just Title to it from my Degrees, I am content to be without the

---

[1] *Motto.* Juvenal, *Satires,* 1. 86: The hodge-podge of the book.

No author is given for this number in the Tickell MS. The three letters of which
it is composed are probably genuine contributions, and combined by Tickell to form
a number.

[2] It was on this day that George I was crowned in Westminster Abbey.

[3] The scarf was the mark of a nobleman's chaplain. See No. 21 (vol. i).

Ornament. The Privileges of our Nobility to keep a certain Number of Chaplains are undisputed, though perhaps not one in ten of those reverend Gentlemen have any Relation to the noble Families their Scarfs belong to; the Right generally of creating all Chaplains, except the Domestick, where there is one, being nothing more than the Perquisite of a Steward's Place, who, if he happens to out-live any considerable Number of his noble Masters, shall probably, at one and the same Time, have fifty Chaplains, all in their proper Accoutrements, of his own Creation; though perhaps there hath been neither Grace nor Prayer said in the Family since the Introduction of the first Coronet.

I am, &c.'

Mr. SPECTATOR,

'I WISH you would write a Philosophical Paper about Natural Antipathies, with a Word or two concerning the Strength of Imagination.[1] I can give you a List, upon the first Notice, of a Rational *China* Cup, of an Egg that walks upon two Legs, and a Quart-Pot that sings like a Nightingale. There is in my Neighbourhood a very pretty prattling Shoulder of Veal, that squawls out at the Sight of a Knife. Then as for Natural Antipathies, I know a General Officer, who was never conquered but by a smother'd Rabbit; and a Wife, that domineers over her Husband by the Help of a Breast of Mutton. A Story that relates to my self on this Subject may be thought not unentertaining, especially when I assure you that it is literally true. I had long made Love to a Lady, in the Possession of whom I am now the happiest of Mankind, whose Hand I should have gained with much Difficulty without the Assistance of a Cat. You must know then, that my most dangerous Rival had so strong an Aversion to this Species, that he infallibly swooned away at the Sight of that harmless Creature. My Friend Mrs. *Lucy*, her Maid, having a greater Respect for me and my Purse than she had for my Rival, always took Care to pin the Tail of a Cat under the Gown of her Mistress, whenever she knew of his coming; which had such an Effect, that every Time he entered the Room, he looked more like one of the Figures in Mrs. *Salmon's* Wax-work,[2] than a desirable Lover. In short, he grew

---

[1] See No. 538 (vol. iv).
[2] See No. 28 (vol. i). 'At the same place, near Temple-Bar, there is still an *Exhibition* of *Wax-work*, by a person of the same name at this day, Feb. 20, 1789' (Nichols).

sick of her Company; which the young Lady taking Notice of, (who no more knew why than he did) she sent me a Challenge to meet her in *Lincoln's-Inn* Chappel,[1] which I joyfully accepted, and have (amongst other Pleasures) the Satisfaction of being praised by her for my Stratagem. I am, *&c.*

From the   Tom. Nimble.'
Hoop.[2]

Mr. SPECTATOR,

'THE Virgins of *Great Britain* are very much obliged to you for putting them upon such tedious Drudgeries in Needlework, as were fit only for the *Hilpa*'s and the *Nilpa*'s that lived before the Flood.[3] Here's a Stir indeed with your Histories in Embroidery, your Groves with Shades of Silk and Streams of Mohair![4] I would have you to know, that I hope to kill a hundred Lovers before the best Houswife in *England* can stitch out a Battel, and do not fear but to provide Boys and Girls much faster than your Disciples can embroider them. I love Birds and Beasts as well as you, but am content to fancy them when they are really made. What do you think of Gilt Leather for Furniture? There's your pretty Hanging for a Chamber; and what is more, our own Country is the only Place in *Europe* where Work of that Kind is tolerably done. Without minding your musty Lessons, I am this Minute going to *Paul's* Church-Yard, to bespeak a Skreen and a Set of Hangings; and am resolved to encourage the Manufacture of my Country.

Yours,
CLEORA.'[5]

---

[1] Completed, according to Hatton (p. 316), in 1626, and noted for its stained-glass windows, described by Hatton, pp. 317–21.

[2] I have found no other reference to this. A coffee-house?

[3] No. 584 (vol. iv).   [4] No. 606.

[5] At the end of an unpublished *Spectator* MS. among the Tickell papers is a reference to this letter: 'N. B. Cleora, whose smart letter I publish'd the 20th instant, needs no answer to it, if she reads this poem thrô.' The poem is Eusden's *Letter to Mr. Addison on the King's Accession*, referred to at the end of No. 618.

No. 610 **Friday, October 22, 1714**[1]
[TICKELL]

> *Sic, cum transierint mei*
> *Nullo cum strepitu dies,*
> *Plebeius moriar senex.*
> *Illi mors gravis incubat,*
> *Qui, notus nimis omnibus,*
> *Ignotus moritur sibi.*
>
> Seneca.

I HAVE often wondered that the *Jews* should contrive such a worthless Greatness for the Deliverer whom they expected, as to dress him up in external Pomp and Pageantry, and represent him to their Imagination, as making Havock amongst his Creatures, and acted[2] with the poor Ambition of a *Cæsar* or an *Alexander*. How much more illustrious doth he appear in his real Character, when considered as the Author of universal Benevolence among Men, as refining our Passions, exalting our Nature, giving us vast Ideas of Immortality, and teaching us a Contempt of that little showy Grandeur wherein the *Jews* made the Glory of their *Messiah* to consist?

Nothing (says *Longinus*) *can be Great, the Contempt of which is Great*.[3] The Possession of Wealth and Riches cannot give a Man a Title to Greatness, because it is looked upon as a Greatness of Mind, to

---

[1] *Motto.* Seneca, *Thyestes*, 398–403:

> Here let my Life, with as much Silence slide,
> As time that measures it, does glide,
> Nor let the Breath of Infamy or Fame,
> From Town to Town eccho about my Name;
> Nor let my homely Death embroider'd be,
> With Scutcheon, or with Elogy.
> An old Plebeian, let me die,
> Alas! all then are such as well as I.

Most of the material for the present number exists among Addison's notes in the Tickell papers (printed by Hodgart, pp. 384–5). Parts have been rearranged and the opening paragraph (as well as the quotation from Cowley) added by Tickell.

[2] I.e. actuated. Cf. No. 287 (vol. iii).

[3] *On the Sublime*, 7. Cf. Boileau's version, chap. v:

In Common Life, we cannot say any thing is Great, when the Contempt of that very thing has it self Greatness in it. 'Tis thus with Riches, Dignities, Honours, Empires, and all those other Good things in Appearance, which have only a Pompous Outside, and will never be thought truly Good by a Wise man, because 'tis on the Contrary, no small Advantage to be able to despise them.

contemn these Gifts of Fortune, and to be above the Desire of them. I have therefore been inclined to think, that there are greater Men who lie concealed among the Species, than those who come out, and draw upon themselves the Eyes and Admiration of Mankind. *Virgil* would never have been heard of, had not his Domestick Misfortunes driven him out of his Obscurity, and brought him to *Rome*.[1]

If we suppose that there are Spirits or Angels who look into the Ways of Men, as it is highly probable there are, both from Reason and Revelation; how different are the Notions which they entertain of us, from those which we are apt to form of one another? Were they to give us in their Catalogue of such Worthies as are now living, how different would it be from that which any of our own Species would draw up?

We are dazled with the Splendour of Titles, the Ostentation of Learning, the Noise of Victories: They, on the contrary, see the Philosopher in the Cottage, who possesses his Soul in Patience and Thankfulness, under the Pressures of what little Minds call Poverty and Distress. They do not look for Great Men at the Head or Armies, or among the Pomps of a Court, but often find them out in Shades and Solitudes, in the private Walks and By-paths of Life. The Evening's Walk of a wise Man is more illustrious in their Sight, than the March of a General at the Head of a hundred thousand Men. A Contemplation on God's Works; a voluntary Act of Justice to our own Detriment; a generous Concern for the Good of Mankind; Tears that are shed in Silence for the Misery of others; a private Desire or Resentment broken and subdued; in short, an unfeigned Exercise of Humility, or any other Virtue; are such Actions as are glorious in their Sight, and denominate Men great and reputable. The most famous among us are often looked upon with Pity, with Contempt, or with Indignation; while those who are most obscure among their own Species, are regarded with Love, with Approbation, and Esteem.

The Moral of the present Speculation amounts to this, That we should not be led away by the Censures and Applauses of Men, but consider the Figure that every Person will make at that Time when Wisdom shall be justified of her Children,[2] and nothing pass for Great or Illustrious, which is not an Ornament and Perfection to humane Nature.

---

[1] After the battle of Philippi in 42 B.C. Virgil was deprived of his farm.
[2] Matt. xi. 19.

The Story of *Gyges* the rich *Lydian* Monarch is a memorable Instance to our present Purpose. The Oracle being asked by *Gyges*, Who was the happiest Man, replied *Aglaüs*. *Gyges*, who expected to have heard himself named on this Occasion, was much surprized, and very curious to know who this *Aglaüs* should be. After much Enquiry he was found to be an obscure Countryman, who employed all his Time in cultivating a Garden, and a few Acres of Land about his House.

Cowley's agreeable Relation of this Story shall close this Day's Speculation.[1]

> Thus Aglaüs (*a Man unknown to Men,*
> *But the Gods knew, and therefore lov'd him then*)
> *Thus liv'd obscurely then without a Name,*
> Aglaüs, *now consign'd t'eternal Fame.*
> For Gyges, *the rich King, wicked and great,*
> *Presum'd at wise* Apollo's *Delphick Seat,*
> *Presum'd to ask, Oh thou, the whole World's Eye,*
> *See'st thou a Man that happier is than I?*
> *The God, who scorn'd to flatter Man, reply'd,*
> Aglaüs *happier is. But Gyges cry'd,*
> *In a proud Rage, Who can that* Aglaüs *be?*
> *We've heard as yet of no such King as he.*
> *And true it was, through the whole Earth around,*
> *No King of such a Name was to be found.*
> *Is some old* Hero *of that Name alive,*
> *Who his high Race does from the Gods derive?*
> *Is it some mighty Gen'ral, that has done*
> *Wonders in Fight, and God-like Honours won?*
> *Is it some Man of endless Wealth? said he:*
> *None, none of these; who can this* Aglaüs *be?*
> *After long Search, and vain Enquiries past,*
> *In an obscure* Arcadian *Vale at last,*
> (*Th' Arcadian* Life *has always shady been*)
> *Near* Sopho's *Town (which he but once had seen)*
> *This* Aglaüs, *who Monarch's Envy drew,*
> *Whose Happiness the Gods stood Witness too,*
> *This mighty* Aglaüs *was lab'ring found*
> *With his own Hands, in his own little Ground.*

[1] 'The Country Life (Lib. iv. Plantarum)', in *Essays*, ed. Waller (Cambridge, 1906), pp. 419–20. Tickell omits the first 22 lines.

> *So, gracious God, (if it may lawful be,*
> *Among those foolish Gods to mention thee)*
> *So let me act, on such a private Stage,*
> *The last dull Scenes of my declining Age;*
> *After long Toils and Voyages in vain,*
> *This quiet Port let my toss'd Vessel gain;*
> *Of heav'nly Rest, this Earnest to me lend,*
> *Let my Life sleep, and learn to love her End.*

No. 611   *Monday, October 25, 1714*[1]

Perfide! sed duris genuit te cautibus horrens
Caucasus, Hircanæque admôrunt ubera tigres.
Virg.

I AM willing to postpone every thing, to do any the least Service for the Deserving and Unfortunate. Accordingly I have caused the following Letter to be inserted in my Paper the Moment that it came to my Hands, without altering one Tittle in an Account which the Lady relates so handsomely her self.

Mr. SPECTATOR,

'I Flatter my self, you will not only pity, but, if possible, redress a Misfortune my self and several others of my Sex lie under. I hope you will not be offended, nor think I mean by this to justify my own imprudent Conduct, or expect You should. No! I am sensible how severely, in some of your former Papers, you have reproved Persons guilty of the like Mismanagements. I was scarce Sixteen, and, I may say without Vanity, Handsome, when courted by a false perjured Man; who, upon Promise of Marriage, rendered me the most unhappy of Women. After he had deluded[2] me from

---

[1] *Motto.* Virgil, *Aeneid,* 4. 366–7:

> False as thou art, and more than false, forsworn;
> Not sprung from Noble Blood, nor Goddess-born,
> But hewn from hardned Entrails of a Rock;
> And rough *Hyrcanian* Tygers gave thee suck. DRYDEN.

There is no mention of this number among the Tickell MSS. It may be a genuine letter, with ensuing comments by Tickell.

[2] Apparently used here in the obsolete sense of 'to disappoint or deprive of by fraud or deceit' (*OED*, 1b).

my Parents, who were People of very good Fashion, in less than three Months he left me. My Parents would not see, nor[a] hear from me; and had it not been for a Servant, who had lived in our Family, I must certainly have perished for want of Bread. However, it pleased Providence, in a very short time, to alter my miserable Condition. A Gentleman saw me, liked me, and married me. My Parents were reconciled; and I might be as happy in the change of my Condition, as I was before miserable, but for some things, that you shall know, which are insupportable to me; and I am sure you have so much Honour and Compassion as to let those Persons know, in some of your Papers, how much they are in the wrong. I have been married near five Years, and do not know that in all that time I ever went abroad without my Husband's Leave and Approbation. I am obliged, through the Importunities of several of my Relations, to go abroad oftner than suits my Temper. Then it is, I labour under insupportable Agonies. That Man, or rather Monster, haunts every Place I go to. Base Villain! By reason I will not admit his nauseous wicked Visits and Appointments, he strives all the ways he can to ruin me. He left me destitute of Friend or Money, nor ever thought me worth inquiring after, till he unfortunately happened to see me in a Front Box sparkling with Jewels. Then his Passion returned. Then the Hypocrite pretended to be a Penitent. Then he practised all those Arts that helped before to undo me. I am not to be deceived a second time by him. I hate and abhor his odious Passion; and, as he plainly perceives it, either out of Spight or Diversion, he makes it his Business to expose me. I never fail seeing him in all publick Company, where he is always most industriously spightful. He hath, in short, told all his Acquaintance of our unhappy Affair; they tell theirs; so that it is no Secret among his Companions, which are numerous. They, to whom he tells it, think they have a Title to be very familiar. If they bow to me, and I out of good Manners return it, then I am pester'd with Freedoms that are no ways agreeable to my self or Company. If I turn my Eyes from them, or seem displeased, they sower upon it, and whisper the next Person; he his next; till I have at last the Eyes of the whole Company upon me. Nay, they report abominable Falshoods, under that mistaken Notion, *She that will grant Favours to one Man, will to a hundred.* I beg you will let those, who are guilty, know, how ungenerous this way of proceeding is. I am sure he will

---

[a] see, nor] see me, nor *Fol.*

know himself the Person aimed at, and perhaps put a stop to the Insolence of others. Cursed is the Fate of unhappy Women! that Men may boast and glory in those things that we must think of with Shame and Horror! You have the Art of making such odious Customs appear detestable. For my Sake, and I am sure, for the Sake of several others, who dare not own it, but, like me, lie under the same Misfortunes, make it as infamous for a Man to boast of Favours, or expose our Sex, as it is to take the Lie or a Box on the Ear, and not resent it.

Your constant Reader,
and Admirer,
LESBIA.'

P. S. 'I am the more Impatient, under this Misfortune, having received fresh Provocation, last *Wednesday*, in the Abbey.'[1]

I entirely agree with the amiable and unfortunate *LESBIA*, that an Insult upon a Woman in her Circumstances, is as infamous in a Man, as a tame Behaviour when the Lie or a Buffet is given; which Truth, I shall beg leave of her to illustrate by the following Observation.

It is[a] a Mark of Cowardise passively to forbear resenting an Affront, the Resenting of which would lead a Man into Danger: it is no less a Sign of Cowardise to affront a Creature, that hath not Power to avenge it self. Whatever Name therefore this ungenerous Man may bestow on the helpless Lady he hath injured, I shall not scruple to give him in return for it, the Appellation of *Coward*.

A Man, that can so far descend from his Dignity, as to strike a Lady, can never recover his Reputation with either Sex, because no Provocation is thought strong enough to justifie such Treatment from the Powerful towards the Weak. In the Circumstances, in which poor *LESBIA* is situated, she can appeal to no Man whatsoever to avenge an Insult, more grievous than a Blow. If she could open her Mouth, the base Man knows, that a Husband, a Brother, a generous Friend would die to see her righted.

A generous Mind, however enraged against an Enemy, feels its Resentments sink and vanish away, when the Object of its Wrath

---

[a] It is] If it is *Fol.*

---

[1] I.e. at the Coronation of George I.

falls into its Power. An estranged Friend, filled with Jealousie and Discontent towards a Bosom Acquaintance, is apt to overflow with Tenderness and Remorse, when a Creature, that was once dear to him, undergoes any Misfortune. What Name then shall we give to his Ingratitude, (who forgetting the Favours he sollicited with Eagerness, and received with Rapture) can insult the Miseries that he himself caused, and make sport with the Pain to which he owes his greatest Pleasure? There is but one Being in the Creation, whose Province it is to practise upon the Imbecilities of frail Creatures, and triumph in the Woes which his own Artifices brought about; and we well know, those who follow his Example, will receive his Reward.

Leaving my fair Correspondent to the Direction of her own Wisdom and Modesty; and her Enemy, and his mean Accomplices, to the Compunction of their own Hearts; I shall conclude this Paper with a memorable Instance of Revenge, taken by a *Spanish* Lady upon a guilty Lover, which may serve to show what violent Effects are wrought by the most tender Passion, when sower'd into Hatred; and may deter the Young and Unwary from unlawful Love. The Story, however Romantick it may appear, I have heard affirmed for a Truth.

Not many Years ago an *English* Gentleman, who in a Rencounter by Night in the Streets of *Madrid* had the Misfortune to kill his Man, fled into a Church-Porch for Sanctuary. Leaning against the Door, he was surprized to find it open, and a glimmering Light in the Church. He had the Courage to advance towards the Light; but was terribly startled at the sight of a Woman in White who ascended from a Grave, with a bloody Knife in her Hand. The Phantome marched up to him, and asked him, what he did there. He told her the Truth without reserve, believing that he had met a Ghost: Upon which, she spoke to him in the following Manner. 'Stranger, thou art in my Power: I am a Murderer, as thou art. Know then, that I am a Nun of a noble Family. A base perjured Man undid me, and boasted of it. I soon had him dispatched; but not content with the Murder, I have bribed the *Sexton* to let me enter his Grave, and have now plucked out his false Heart from his Body; and thus I use a Traitor's Heart.' At these Words she tore it in pieces, and trampled it under her Feet.[1]

[1] The story of the English gentleman in Madrid may be a true one. It has not been traced.

Murranum hic atavos et avorum antiqua sonantem
Nomina, per regesque actum genus omne Latinos,
Præcipitem scopulo, atque ingentis turbine saxi
Excutit, effunditque solo.

Virg.

IT is highly laudable to pay Respect to Men who are descended from worthy Ancestors, not only out of Gratitude to those who have done Good to Mankind, but as it is an Encouragement to others to follow their Example. But this is an Honour to be received, not demanded, by the Descendents of great Men; and they who are apt to remind us of their Ancestors, only put us upon making Comparisons to their own Disadvantage. There is some Pretence for boasting of Wit, Beauty, Strength, or Wealth, because the Communication of them may give Pleasure or Profit to others; but we can have no Merit, nor ought we to claim any Respect, because our Fathers acted well, whether we would or no.

The following Letter ridicules the Folly I have mentioned in a new, and, I think, not disagreeable Light.

Mr. SPECTATOR,

'WERE the Genealogy of every Family preserved, there would probably be no Man valued or despised on Account of his Birth. There is scarce a Beggar in the Streets, who would not find himself lineally descended from some great Man; nor any one of the highest Title, who would not discover several base and indigent Persons among his Ancestors. It would be a pleasant Entertainment to see one Pedigree of Men appear together, under the same Characters they bore when they acted their respective Parts among the Living. Suppose therefore a Gentleman, full of his illustrious Family, should, in the same manner as *Virgil* makes *Æneas* look over his Descendants, see the whole Line of his Progenitors pass in Review before his Eyes.[2] With how many varying Passions,

---

[1] *Motto.* Virgil, *Aeneid*, 12. 529–32:

> *Murranus*, boasting of his Blood, that springs
> From a long Royal Race of *Latian* Kings,
> Is by the *Trojan* from his Chariot thrown,
> Crush'd with the weight of an unweildy Stone. DRYDEN.

[2] *Aeneid*, 6. 756–885.

would he behold Shepherds and Soldiers, States-men and Artificers, Princes and Beggars, walk in the Procession of five thousand Years! How[a] would his Heart sink or flutter at the several Sports of Fortune in a Scene so diversified with Rags and Purple, Handicraft Tools and Sceptres, Ensigns of Dignity and Emblems of Disgrace; and how would his Fears and Apprehensions, his Transports and Mortifications, succeed one another, as the Line of his Genealogy appear'd bright or obscure?

'In most of the Pedigrees hung up in old Mansion Houses, you are sure to find the first in the Catalogue a great Statesman, or a Soldier with an honourable Commission. The honest Artificer that begot him, and all his frugal Ancestors before him, are torn off from the Top of the Register; and you are not left to imagine, that the noble Founder of the Family ever had a Father. Were we to trace many boasted Lines farther backwards, we should lose them in a Mob of Tradesmen, or a Crowd of Rusticks, without hope of seeing them emerge again: not unlike the old *Appian* way, which, after having run many Miles in Length, loses it self in a Bog.

'I lately made a Visit to an old Country Gentleman, who is very far gone in this sort of *Family-Madness*. I found him in his Study perusing an old Register of his Family, which he had just then discovered, as it was branched out in the Form of a Tree, upon a Skin of Parchment. Having the honour to have some of his Blood in my Veins, he permitted me to cast my Eye over the Boughs of this venerable Plant; and asked my Advice in the Reforming of some of the superfluous Branches.

'We passed slightly over three or four of our immediate Fore-fathers, whom we knew by Tradition, but were soon stopped by an Alderman of *London*, who, I perceived, made my Kinsman's Heart go pit-a-pat. His Confusion increased when he found the Alderman's Father to be a Grasier; but he recovered his Fright upon seeing *Justice of the Quorum* at the end of his Titles. Things went on pretty well, as we threw our Eyes occasionally over the Tree, when unfortunately he perceived a Merchant-Tailor perched on a Bough, who was said greatly to have increased the Estate; he was just a going to cut him off, if he had not seen *Gent.* after the Name of his Son; who was recorded to have mortgaged one of the Manors his honest Father had purchased. A Weaver, who was burnt for his Religion in the Reign of Queen *Mary*, was pruned away without

[a] How] Now *Fol.*

Mercy; as was likewise a Yeoman, who died of a Fall from his own Cart. But great was our Triumph in one of the Blood who was beheaded for High-Treason; which nevertheless was not a little allayed by another of our Ancestors who was hanged for stealing Sheep. The Expectations of my good Cousin were wonderfully raised by a Match into the Family of a Knight, but unfortunately for us this Branch proved barren: On the other hand *Margery* the Milk-maid being twined round a Bough, it flourished out into so many Shoots, and bent with so much Fruit, that the old Gentleman was quite out of Countenance.[1] To comfort me, under this Disgrace, he singled out a Branch ten times more fruitful than the other, which, he told me, he valued more than any in the Tree, and bad me be of good Comfort. This enormous Bough was a Graft out of a *Welch* Heiress, with so many *Ap's* upon it that it might have made a little Grove by it self. From the Trunk of the Pedigree, which was chiefly composed of Labourers and Shepherds, arose a huge Sprout of Farmers; this was branched out into Yeomen, and ended in a Sheriff of the County, who was Knighted for his good Service to the Crown, in bringing up an Address. Several of the Names, that seemed to disparage the Family, being looked upon as Mistakes, were lopped off as rotten or withered; as, on the contrary, no small Number appearing without any Titles, my Cousin, to supply the Defects of the Manuscript, added *Esq*; at the End of each of them.[2]

'This Tree so pruned, dressed, and cultivated, was, within a few Days, transplanted into a large Sheet of Vellum and placed in the great Hall, where it attracts the Veneration of his Tenants, every *Sunday* Morning, while they wait till his Worship is ready to go to Church; wondering that a Man, who had so many Fathers before him, should not be made a Knight,[a] or at least a Justice of the Peace.'

---

[a] Knight,] Lord *Fol.*

---

[1] Cf. Will Maple's genealogical tree in No. 203 (vol. ii).
[2] In No. 150 (by Budgell, vol. ii) 'my Banker . . . writes me *Mr.* or *Esq.* accordingly as he sees me dress'd.'

No. 613   *Friday, October* 29, 1714[1]

. . . Studiis florentem ignobilis otî.

Virg.

IT is reckoned a Piece of Ill-breeding for one Man to engross the whole Talk to himself. For this Reason, since I keep three Visiting-Days in the Week, I am content now and then to let my Friends put in a Word. There are several Advantages hereby accruing both to my Readers and my self. As first, Young and modest Writers have an Opportunity of getting into Print: Again, The Town enjoys the Pleasure of Variety; and Posterity will see the Humour of the present Age, by the help of these little Lights into private and domestick Life. The Benefits I receive from thence, are such as these: I gain more Time for future Speculations; pick up Hints which I improve for the publick Good; give Advice; redress Grievances; and, by leaving commodious Spaces between the several Letters that I print, furnish out a *Spectator* with little Labour and great Ostentation.

Mr. SPECTATOR,

'I WAS mightily pleased with your Speculation of *Friday*.[2] Your Sentiments are Noble, and the whole worked up in such a manner, as cannot but strike upon every Reader. But give me leave to make this Remark: That while you write so Pathetically on Contentment, and a retired Life, you sooth the Passion of Melancholy, and depress the Mind from Actions truly Glorious. Titles and Honours are the Reward of Virtue: We therefore ought to be affected with them. And tho' light Minds are too much puffed up with exteriour Pomp, yet I cannot see why it is not as truly Philosophical, to admire the glowing Ruby, or the sparkling Green of an Emerald, as the fainter and less permanent Beauties of a Rose or a Myrtle.[3] If there are Men of extraordinary Capacities who lye concealed from the World, I should impute it to them as a Blot in their Character, did not I believe it owing to the Meanness of their Fortune rather than of their Spirit. *Cowley*, who tells the Story of

---

[1] *Motto.* Virgil, *Georgics*, 4. 564: Affecting studies of inglorious peace.

There is no ascription for this paper among the Tickell MSS. The three letters are probably genuine contributions, with an introductory paragraph by Tickell.

[2] No. 610.

[3] Cf. Pope's First Moral Essay (to Cobham), lines 147-8.

Aglaus with so much Pleasure, was no Stranger to Courts, nor insensible of Praise.

> *What shall I do to be for ever known,*
> *And make the Age to come my own?*[1]

was the Result of a laudable Ambition. It was not till after frequent Disappointments, that he termed himself the Melancholy *Cowley*,[2] and he praised Solitude, when he despaired of shining in a Court.[3] The Soul of Man is an active Principle. He therefore, who withdraws himself from the Scene before he has played his Part, ought to be hissed off the Stage, and cannot be deemed Virtuous, because he refuses to answer his End. I must own I am fired with an honest Ambition to imitate every illustrious Example. The Battels of *Blenheim* and *Ramillies* have more than once made me wish my self a Soldier. And when I have seen those Actions so Nobly celebrated by our Poets, I have secretly aspired to be one of that distinguished Class. But in vain I wish, in vain I pant with the Desire of Action. I am chained down in Obscurity, and the only Pleasure I can take, is in seeing so many brighter Genius's join their friendly Lights, to add to the Splendor of the Throne. Farewel then dear *Spec*, and believe me to be with great Emulation, and no Envy,

> *Your professed Admirer,*
> Will. Hopeless.'

SIR,   *Middle-Temple, Octob.* 26. 1714.

'THO' you have formerly made *Eloquence* the Subject of one or more of your Papers,[4] I do not remember that you ever considered it as possessed by a Set of People, who are so far from making *Quintilian*'s Rules their Practice, that, I dare say for them, they never heard of such an Author, and yet are no less Masters of it than *Tully* or *Demosthenes* amongst the Ancients, or whom you please amongst the Moderns. The Persons I am speaking of are our common Beggars about this Town;[5] and that what I say is true, I appeal to any Man who has a Heart one Degree softer than a Stone. As for my part, who don't pretend to more Humanity than my Neighbours, I have oftentimes gone from my Chambers with Mony in my Pocket, and returned to them not only Pennyless, but

---

[1] Cowley, 'The Motto', lines 1–2 (*Poems*, ed. Waller, p. 15).
[2] 'The Complaint', stanzas 1 and 6 (ibid., pp. 436, 438).
[3] Essay 2, 'Of Solitude' (*Essays*, ed. Waller, pp. 392–7).
[4] Cf. Nos. 407 (vol. iii) and 541 (vol. iv).
[5] See especially Nos. 232 (vol. ii) and 430 (vol. iv).

destitute of a Farthing, without bestowing of it any other way than on these seeming Objects of Pity. In short, I have seen more Eloquence in a *Look* from one of these despicable Creatures, than in the *Eye* of the fairest *She* I ever saw, yet no one a greater Admirer of that Sex than my self. What I have to desire of you is, to lay down some Directions in order to guard against these powerful Orators, or else I know nothing to the contrary but I must my self be forced to leave the Profession of the Law, and endeavour to get the Qualifications necessary to that more profitable one of Begging. But in which soever of these two Capacities I shine, I shall always desire to be your constant Reader, and ever will be

Your most humble Servant,

J. B.'

SIR,

'UPON Reading a *Spectator* last Week, where Mrs. *Fanny Fickle* submitted the Choice of a Lover for Life to your decisive Determination,[1] and imagining I might claim the Favour of your Advice in an Affair of the like, but much more difficult Nature, I called for Pen and Ink, in order to draw the Characters of Seven Humble Servants, whom I have equally incourag'd for some time: But alas! while I was Reflecting on the agreeable Subject, and contriving an Advantageous Description of the dear Person I was most inclined to Favour, I happened to look into my Glass. The sight of the Small-Pox, out of which I am just recovered, Tormented me at once with the Loss of my captivating Arts and my Captives:[a] The Confusion I was in, on this unhappy, unseasonable Discovery, is inexpressible. Believe me, Sir, I was so taken up with the Thoughts of your fair Correspondent's Case, and so intent on my own Design, that I fancied my self as Triumphant in my Conquests as ever.

'Now, Sir, finding I was incapacitated to Amuse my self on that pleasing Subject, I resolved to apply my self to you, or your Casuistical Agent,[2] for Advice in my present Circumstances. I am sensible the Tincture of my Skin, and the Regularity of my Features, which the Malice of my late Illness has altered, are irrecoverable; yet don't despair, but that Loss by your Assistance may in some Measure be reparable, if you'll please to propose a way for the Recovery of one only of my Fugitives.

---

[a] and my Captives:] and Captives: *Fol.*

---

[1] No. 605.　　　　　　　　　　[2] No. 591.

'One of them is in a more particular Manner beholden to me than the rest; he for some private Reasons being desirous to be a Lover Incognito, always Addressed me with *Billet-Doux*, which I was so careful of in my Sickness, that I secured the Key of my Love-Magazine under my Head, and hearing a Noise of opening a Lock in my Chamber, indanger'd my Life by getting out of Bed to prevent, if it had been attempted, the Discovery of that Amour.

'I have formerly made use of all those Artifices, which our Sex daily practises over yours, to draw, as it were undesignedly, the Eyes of a whole Congregation to my Pew; I have taken a Pride in the Number of Admirers at my Afternoon Levée; but am now quite another Creature. I think, could I regain the attractive Influence, I once had, if I had a Legion of Suitors, I should never be Ambitious of Entertaining more than one. I have almost contracted an Antipathy to the trifling Discourses of Impertinent Lovers, though I must needs own, I have thought it very odd of late, to hear Gentlemen, instead of their usual Complacencies, fall into Disputes before me of Politicks, or else weary me with the tedious Repetition of how thankful I ought to be, and satisfied with my Recovery out of so dangerous a Distemper: This, though I am very sensible of the Blessing, yet I cannot but dislike, because such Advice from them rather seems to Insult than Comfort me, and reminds me too much of what I was, which Melancholy Consideration I cannot yet perfectly surmount, but hope your Sentiments on this Head will make it supportable.

'To shew you what a Value I have for your Dictates, these are to certifie the Persons concerned, that unless one of them returns to his Colours, (if I may so call them now) before the Winter is over, I'll voluntarily confine my self to a Retirement, where I'll punish them all with my Needle. I'll be revenged on them by deciphering[1] them on a Carpet, humbly begging Admittance, my self scornfully refusing it: If you disapprove of this, as savouring too much of Malice, be pleased to acquaint me with a Draught you like better, and it shall be faithfully performed

By the Unfortunate,
Monimia.'[2]

[1] Here used in the obsolete sense 'to delineate, portray'. The last quotation in *OED* in this sense is dated 1753.

[2] The name of the heroine in Otway's *Orphan*. For the name of Monimia's lover see No. 619 (below, p. 117).

No. 614   *Monday, November 1, 1714*[1]
[TICKELL]

> *Si mihi non animo fixum, immotumque sederet,*
> *Ne cui me vinclo vellem sociare jugali,*
> *Postquam primus amor deceptam morte fefellit;*
> *Si non pertæsum thalami, tædæque fuisset:*
> *Huic uni forsan potui succumbere culpæ.*
>
> Virg.

The following Account hath been transmitted to
me by the Love-Casuist.[2]

Mr. SPECTATOR,

'HAVING, in some former Papers,[3] taken Care of the two States of Virginity and Marriage, and being willing that all People should be served in their Turn; I this Day drew out my Drawer of Widows, where I met with several Cases, to each whereof I have returned satisfactory Answers by the Post. The Cases are as follow:

'*Q.* Whether *Amoret* be bound by a Promise of Marriage to *Philander,* made during her Husband's Life?[4]

'*Q.* Whether *Sempronia,*[5] having faithfully given a Promise to two several Persons during the last Sickness of her Husband, is not thereby left at Liberty to chuse which of them she pleases, or to reject them both for the Sake of a new Lover?

'*Cleora* asks me, Whether she be obliged to continue single, according to a Vow made to her Husband at the Time of his presenting her with a Diamond Neck-lace; she being informed by a very pretty young Fellow of a good Conscience, that such Vows are in their Nature sinful?[6]

'Another enquires, Whether she hath not the Right of Widowhood, to dispose of her self to a Gentleman of great Merit, who

---

[1] *Motto.* Virgil, *Aeneid,* 4. 15-19:
> —Were I not resolv'd against the Yoke
> Of hapless Marriage; never to be curs'd
> With second Love, so fatal was my first;
> To this one Error I might yield again. DRYDEN.

[2] No. 591.   [3] Nos. 602, 605, 607, 608.

[4] These names happen to be used in a love correspondence in No. 401 (vol. iii), but they are, of course, conventional.

[5] For earlier uses of this name see Nos. 45 (vol. i) and 437 (vol. iv).

[6] Cleora was 'a widow of Ephesus' in No. 233 (vol. ii). The name also occurs in Nos. 377, 392 (vol. iii), and 609.

presses very hard; her Husband being irrecoverably gone in a Consumption?

'An unreasonable Creature hath the Confidence to ask, Whether it be proper for her to marry a Man who is younger than her eldest Son?

'A scrupulous well-spoken Matron, who gives me a great many good Words, only doubts, Whether she is not obliged in Conscience to shut up her two marriageable Daughters, till such time as she hath comfortably disposed of her self?

'*Sophronia*, who seems by her Phrase and Spelling to be a Person of Condition, sets forth, That whereas she hath a great Estate, and is but a Woman, she desires to be informed, whether she would not do prudently to marry *Camillus*, a very idle tall young Fellow, who hath no Fortune of his own, and consequently hath nothing else to do but to manage hers?'[1]

Before I speak of Widows, I cannot but observe one thing, which I do not know how to account for; A Widow is always more sought after, than an old Maid of the same Age. It is common enough among ordinary People, for a stale Virgin to set up a Shop in a Place where she is not known; where the large Thumb-Ring,[2] supposed to be given her by her Husband, quickly recommends her to some wealthy Neighbour, who takes a Liking to the jolly Widow, that would have over-looked the venerable Spinster.

The Truth of it is, if we look into this Set of Women, we find, according to the[a] different Characters or Circumstances wherein they are left, that Widows may be divided into those who raise Love, and those who raise Compassion.

But not to ramble from this Subject, there are two Things in which consists chiefly the Glory of a Widow; the Love of her deceased Husband, and the Care of her Children: To which may be added a third, arising out of the former. Such a prudent Conduct as may do Honour to both.

A Widow, possessed of all these three Qualities, makes not only a virtuous, but a sublime Character.

There is something so great and so generous in this State of Life, when it is accompanied with all its Virtues, that it is the Subject

<hr />

[a] the] their *Fol.*

[1] For Sophronia, cf. Nos. 33 (vol. i), 606; Camillus, No. 263 (vol. ii).
[2] Defined in *OED* simply as 'a ring formerly worn on the thumb. Often engraved with a seal, or inscribed with a posy'.

of one of the finest among our modern Tragedies in the Person of
Andromache;[1] and hath met with an universal and deserved Applause,
when introduced upon our *English* Stage by Mr. *Philips*.

The most memorable Widow in History is Queen *Artemisia*, who
not only erected the famous *Mausoleum*, but drank up the Ashes of
her dead Lord; thereby enclosing them in a nobler Monument than
that which she had built, though deservedly esteemed one of the
Wonders of Architecture.[2]

This last Lady seems to have had a better Title to a second
Husband than any I have read of, since not one Dust of her First
was remaining. Our modern Heroines might think a Husband a
very bitter Draught, and would have good Reason to complain, if
they might not accept of a second Partner, till they had taken such
a troublesome Method of losing the Memory of the first.

I shall add to these illustrious Examples out of ancient Story,
a remarkable Instance of the Delicacy of our Ancestors in Relation
to the State of Widowhood, as I find it recorded in *Cowell's* Interpreter.[3] *At* East *and* West Enborne, *in the County of* Berks, *if a
customary Tenant die, the Widow shall have what the Law calls her* Free
Bench[4] *in all his Copy-hold Lands,* dum sola & casta fuerit; *that is,
while she lives single and chaste; but if she commit Incontinency, she
forfeits her Estate: Yet, if she will come into the Court riding backward upon
a Black Ram, with his Tail in her Hand, and say the Words following, the
Steward is bound by the Custom to re-admit her to her* Free Bench.

> *Here I am,*
> *Riding upon a Black Ram,*
> *Like a Whore as I am;*

[1] See Nos. 290, 335, 338, 341 (vol. iii).

[2] See Cicero, *Tusculan Disputations*, 3. 31. 75. According to Bayle, the monument
to her husband Mausolus at Halicarnassus was one of the seven wonders of the world.
'It is said that she diluted her Husband's Bones and Ashes in Water, and swallowed
them, that she might serve him for a living Tomb.'

[3] The 1701 edition is called *The Interpreter of Words and Terms, used either in the
common or statute laws of this realm, and in tenures and jocular customs.* There was also an
edition in 1708, entitled *A Law Dictionary, or, The Interpreter. . . .* In these the
passage quoted is to be found under the article 'Free Bench', with the jocular poem
and the reference to Torre in Devonshire. John Cowell's *Interpreter* was first published at Cambridge in 1607 and went through several editions in the seventeenth
century. 'Free Bench' or 'Frank Bank' is explained in the early editions, but it is
not until 1684 that the jocular poem begins to be quoted. (It is also to be found in
Thomas Blount's *Law-Dictionary* of 1670 and in his *Fragmenta antiquitatis* of 1679.)

[4] Cowell's *Law Dictionary* (1708) gives the following definition:

Free-bench, Frank-bank, *Francus bancus*, that is, *sedes libera*, signifies that Estate
in Copy-hold Lands, that the Wife being espoused a Virgin hath, after the decease
of her Husband, for her Dower.

And, for my Crincum Crancum,[1]
Have lost my Bincum Bancum,
And, for my Tail's Game,
Have done this worldly Shame;
Therefore, I pray you Mr. Steward, let me have my Land again.

The like Custom there is in the Manor of *Torre* in *Devonshire*, and other Parts of the *West*.

It is not impossible but I may in a little Time present you with a Register of *Berkshire* Ladies and other Western Dames, who rode publickly upon this Occasion; and I hope the Town will be entertained with a Cavalcade of Widows.

No. 615   *Wednesday, November 3, 1714*[2]

[TICKELL]

> . . . *Qui Deorum*
> *Muneribus sapienter uti,*
> *Duramque callet pauperiem pati,*
> *Pejusque letho flagitium timet:*
> *Non ille pro caris amicis*
> *Aut patriâ timidus perire.*

IT must be owned that Fear is a very powerful Passion, since it is esteemed one of the greatest of Virtues to subdue it. It being

---

[1] 'A word applied playfully to any thing full of twists and turns, or intricately or fancifully elaborated' (*OED*). The earliest example in *OED* is the jocular verse quoted here, from Blount's *Law Dictionary* (1670). In Tutchin's *Observator* of 26 May 1703 a cloak given by the French king to the Elector of Bavaria is described as 'Furbeloed, as the Womens Petticoats and Scarfs are at *London*, with *Crincumcrancums* upon 'em'. In Poor Robin's *Almanack* for 1713 (no pagination) we read, 'If . . . thou lye with a Wh— and she pepper thee with the Crinkums . . . .'

[2] *Motto.* Horace, *Odes,* 4. 9. 47–52:

> Who well can use the Gifts of Heav'n,
> That have the generous Skill to bear,
> The hated weight of Poverty;
> Who more than Death doth Baseness fear,
> Who nobly to defend
> Their Country or their Friend,
> Embrace their Fate and gladly dye.

implanted in us for our Preservation, it is no Wonder that it sticks close to us, as long as we have any thing we are willing to preserve. But as Life, and all its Enjoyments, would be scarce worth the keeping, if we were under a perpetual Dread of losing them; it is the Business of Religion and Philosophy to free us from all unnecessary Anxieties, and direct our Fear to its proper Object.

If we consider the Painfulness of this Passion, and the violent Effects it produces, we shall see how dangerous it is, to give way to it, upon slight Occasions. Some have frightened themselves into Madness, others have given up their Lives to these Apprehensions. The Story of a Man who grew grey in the Space of one Night's Anxiety is very famous;

O! Nox, quam longa es, quæ facis una Senem.[1]

These Apprehensions, if they proceed from a Consciousness of Guilt, are the sad Warnings of Reason; and may excite our Pity, but admit of no Remedy. When the Hand of the Almighty is visibly lifted against the Impious, the Heart of mortal Man cannot withstand him. We have this Passion sublimely represented in the Punishment of the *Egyptians*, tormented with the Plague of Darkness, in the *Apocryphal* Book of *Wisdom*, ascribed to *Solomon*:[2]

'For when unrighteous Men thought to oppress the holy Nation; they being shut up in their Houses, the Prisoners of Darkness, and fettered with the Bonds of a long Night, lay there exiled from the eternal Providence. For while they supposed to lie hid in their secret Sins, they were scattered under a dark Veil of Forgetfulness, being horribly astonished and troubled with strange Apparitions— For Wickedness, condemned by her own Witness, is very timorous, and being oppressed with Conscience, always forecasteth grievous things. For Fear is nothing else but a betraying of the Succours which Reason offereth—For the whole World shined with clear Light, and none were hindered in their Labour: Over them only was spread a heavy Night, an Image of that Darkness which should afterwards receive them; but yet were they unto themselves more grievous than the Darkness.'

To Fear, so justly grounded, no Remedy can be proposed; but a Man (who hath no great Guilt hanging upon his Mind, who

[1] Martial, *Epigrams*, 4. 7. 4: A tedious night indeed, that makes a young man old! The question of hair turning grey overnight is discussed in the *British Apollo* of 28 Apr. 1710. See also above, iv. 423.
[2] *Wisdom of Solomon*, 17. 2–3, 11–12, 20–21.

walks in the plain Path of Justice and Integrity, and yet either by natural Complection, or confirmed Prejudices, or Neglect of serious Reflection, suffers himself to be moved by this abject and unmanly Passion) would do well to consider, That there is nothing which deserves his Fear, but that beneficent Being who is his Friend, his Protector, his Father. Were this one Thought strongly fixed in the Mind, what Calamity would be dreadful? What Load can Infamy lay upon us, when we are sure of the Approbation of him, who will repay the Disgrace of a Moment with the Glory of Eternity? What Sharpness is there in Pain and Diseases, when they only hasten us on to the Pleasures that will never fade? What Sting is in Death, when we are assured that it is only the Beginning of Life? A Man who lives so, as not to fear to die, is inconsistent with himself, if he delivers himself up to any incidental Anxiety.

The Intrepidity of a just good Man, is so nobly set forth by *Horace*, that it cannot be too often repeated.

> *The* Man *resolv'd and steady to his Trust,*
> *Inflexible to Ill, and obstinately just,*
> *May the rude Rabbles Insolence despise,*
> *Their senseless Clamours, and tumultuous Cries;*
> *The Tyrant's Fierceness he beguiles,*
> *And the stern Brow, and the harsh Voice defies,*
> *And with superior Greatness smiles.*
>
> *Not the rough Whirlwind, that deforms*
> Adria's *black Gulf, and vexes it with Storms,*
> *The stubborn Virtue of his Soul can move;*
> *Not the Red Arm of Angry* Jove,
> *That flings the Thunder from the Sky,*
> *And gives it Rage to roar, and Strength to fly.*
>
> *Should the whole Frame of Nature round him break,*
> *In Ruin and Confusion hurl'd,*
> *He, unconcern'd, would hear the mighty Crack,*
> *And stand secure amidst a falling World.*[1]

[1] Horace, *Odes*, 3. 3. The translation is apparently Addison's. It was first published, without his name, in the sixth part of Tonson's *Poetical Miscellanies* (1709), pp. 262–70; and later in the reissue of the *Miscellanies* in 1716. It appears, anonymously, in *The Odes and Satires of Horace . . . by the most eminent hands* (Printed for A. Bell and others), 1715. The first nine lines are quoted in Addison's *Dialogues on Medals*, part ii, and assigned to 'Mr. *Creech*' (Guthkelch, ii. 307); but it does not seem to be in any of the editions of Creech. Since Tickell reprints it in the *Works* of 1721 (i. 144) it may be considered to be by Addison.

The Vanity of Fear may be yet farther illustrated, if we reflect,

First, What we fear may not come to pass. No human Scheme can be so accurately projected, but some little Circumstance intervening may spoil it. He, who directs the Heart of Man at his Pleasure, and understands the Thoughts long before,[1] may by ten thousand Accidents, or an immediate Change in the Inclinations of Men, disconcert the most subtle Project, and turn it to the Benefit of his own Servants.

In the next Place we should consider, though the Evil we imagine should come to pass, it may be much more supportable than it appeared to be. As there is no prosperous State of Life without its Calamities, so there is no Adversity without its Benefits. Ask the Great and Powerful, if they do not feel the Pangs of Envy and Ambition. Enquire of the Poor and Needy, if they have not tasted the Sweets of Quiet and Contentment. Even under the Pains of Body; the Infidelity of Friends; or the Misconstructions put upon our laudable Actions, our Minds (when for some Time accustomed to these Pressures) are sensible of secret Flowings of Comfort, the present Reward of a pious Resignation. The Evils of this Life appear like Rocks and Precipices, rugged and barren at a Distance; but at our nearer Approach, we find little fruitful Spots, and refreshing Springs, mixed with the Harshness and Deformities of Nature.

In the last Place, we may comfort our selves with this Consideration; that, as the Thing feared may not reach us, so we may not reach what we fear: Our Lives may not extend to that dreadful Point which we have in View. He who knows all our Failings, and will not suffer us to be tempted beyond our Strength,[2] is often pleased in his tender Severity, to separate the Soul from its Body and Miseries together.

If we look forward to him for Help, we shall never be in Danger of falling down those Precipices which our Imagination is apt to create. Like those who walk upon a Line, if we keep our Eye fixed upon one Point, we may step forward securely; whereas an imprudent or cowardly Glance on either Side will infallibly destroy us.

[1] Cf. Ps. cxxxix. 2.   [2] 1 Cor. x. 13.

Qui bellus homo est, Cotta, pusillus homo est.
Martial.

*C*ICERO hath observed, that a Jest is never uttered with a better Grace, than when it is accompanied with a serious Countenance.[2] When a pleasant Thought plays in the Features, before it discovers it self in Words, it raises too great an Expectation, and loses the Advantage of giving Surprize. Wit and Humour are no less poorly recommended by a Levity of Phrase, and that kind of Language which may be distinguished by the Name of *Cant*.[3] Ridicule is never more strong, than when it is concealed in Gravity. True Humour lies in the Thought, and arises from the Representation of Images in odd Circumstances, and uncommon Lights. A pleasant Thought strikes us by the Force of its natural Beauty; and the Mirth of it is generally rather palled, than heightened by that ridiculous Phraseology, which is so much in fashion among the Pretenders to Humour and Pleasantry. This[a] Tribe of Men are like our Mountebanks; they make a Man a Wit, by putting him in a fantastick Habit.

Our little Burlesque Authors, who are the Delight of ordinary Readers, generally abound in these pert Phrases, which have in them more Vivacity than Wit.

I lately saw an Instance of this kind of Writing, which gave me so lively an Idea of it, that I could not forbear begging a Copy of the Letter from the Gentleman who shewed it to me. It is written by a Country Wit, upon the Occasion of the Rejoycings on the Day of the King's Coronation.[4]

Past two a Clock and
Dear Jack,   *a frosty Morning.*[b],[5]
'*I* HAVE just left the Right Worshipful[6] and his Myrmidons, about a Sneaker[7] of Five Gallons. The whole Magistracy was

---
[a] This] But this *Fol.*   [b] *Past . . . Morning.*] *Two in the Morning is | the Word,* old *Boy. Fol.*

[1] *Motto.* Martial, *Epigrams,* 1. 9. 2: A fop, Cotta, is but a puny fellow.
[2] *De Oratore,* 2. 71. 289.   [3] See No. 147 (vol. ii).
[4] I.e. 20 Oct. 'The Day concluded with Bonefires, Illuminations, Ringing of Bells, and other Demonstrations of a general Joy and Satisfaction' (*Political State,* Oct. 1714, viii. 360).   [5] The watchman's cry.
[*For notes 6 & 7 see next page.*

pretty well disguised[1] before I gave 'em the Slip. Our Friend the Alderman was half Seas over[2] before the Bonfire was out. We had with us the Attorney, and two or three other bright Fellows. The Doctor plays least in Sight.

'At Nine a Clock in the Evening we set Fire to the Whore of *Babylon*.[3] The Devil acted his Part to a Miracle. He has made his Fortune by it. We equip'd the young Dog with a Tester[4] apiece. Honest old *Brown* of *England* was very drunk, and show'd his Loyalty to the Tune of a hundred Rockets. The Mob drank the King's Health, on their Marrow-bones, in Mother *Day's* Double.[5] They whip'd[6] us half a dozen Hogsheads. Poor *Tom. Tyler* had like to have been demolished with the End of a Sky-Rocket, that fell upon the Bridge of his Nose as he was drinking the King's Health, and spoiled his Tip. The Mob were very loyal till about Midnight, when they grew a little mutinous for more Liquor. They had like to have dumfounded the Justice; but his Clerk came in to his Assistance, and took them all down in Black and White.

'When I had been huzza'd out of my Seven Senses, I made a Visit to the Women, who were guzzling very comfortably. Mrs. Mayoress clip'd the King's *English*. Clack was the Word.

'I forgot to tell thee, that every one of the Posse had his Hat cock'd with a Distich: The Senators sent us down a Cargo of Ribbon and Metre for the Occasion.

'Sir *Richard*, to show his Zeal for the Protestant Religion, is at the Expence of a Tar-Barrel and a Ball.[7] I peep'd into the Knight's great Hall, and saw a very pretty Bevy of Spinsters. My dear Relict was amongst them, and ambled in a Country-Dance as notably as the best of 'em.

'May all His Majesty's liege Subjects love him as well as his good People of this his ancient Borough. Adieu.'

---

[1] Archaic slang for 'intoxicated'.

[2] *OED* gives only one quotation earlier for this humorous slang for 'half-drunk'.

[3] In the Protestant demonstrations at this time 'the Pope, the Devil, and the Pretender' were the usual targets. In the rejoicings described in this letter the Church of Rome and the Devil have prominent parts.

[4] The colloquial term for six-pence.   [5] Not identified.

[6] A slang term, 'to drink quickly, toss off' (*OED*).

[7] Some editors have seen this as a reference to Steele's violent Protestant ebullitions. But he was not knighted until April 1715, so that 'Sir Richard' would not particularly suggest Steele.

---

[6] A title applied to mayors, and the sheriffs, aldermen, and recorder of London (*OED*).

[7] A small bowl. A term in common use from about 1710 to 1740 (*OED*).

No. 617   *Monday, November 8, 1714*[1]

[TICKELL]

> *Torva Mimalloneis implerunt cornua bombis,*
> *Et raptum vitulo caput ablatura superbo*
> *Bassaris, & lyncem Mænas flexura corymbis*
> *Evion ingeminat; reparabilis adsonat Echo.*
> Persius.

THERE are two Extreams in the Stile of Humour, one of which consists in the Use of that little pert Phraseology which I took Notice of in my last Paper; the other in the Affectation of strained and pompous Expressions, fetched from the learned Languages. The first savours too much of the Town; the other of the College.

As nothing illustrates better than Example, I shall here present my Reader with a Letter of Pedantick Humour, which was written by a young Gentleman of the University to his Friend; on the same Occasion, and from the same Place as the lively Epistle published in my last *Spectator*.

Dear Chum,[2]

'IT is now the third Watch of the Night, the greatest Part of which I have spent round a capacious Bowl of *China* filled with the choicest Products of both the *Indies*. I was placed at a quadrangular Table diametrically opposite to the Mace-bearer. The Visage of that venerable Herald was, according to Custom, most gloriously illuminated on this joyful Occasion. The Mayor and Aldermen, those Pillars of our Constitution, began to totter; and if any one at the Board could have so far articulated, as to have

---

[1] *Motto.* Persius, *Satires,* I. 99–102:

> Their crooked Horns the *Mimallonian* Crew
> With Blasts inspir'd; and *Bassaris,* who slew
> The scornful Calf, with Sword advanc'd on high,
> Made from his Neck his haughty Head to fly.
> And *Mænas,* when with Ivy-bridles bound,
> She led the *spotted Lynx,* then *Evion* rung around;
> *Evion* from Woods and Floods repairing Eccho's sound. DRYDEN.

(In Persius these are lines of bombast held up to ridicule.)

This number, like No. 616, to which it is a sequel, is assigned to Tickell in the Tickell MS. The translation of the passage from Strada, however, is apparently by Addison; it forms a part of Strada's 'Sessions of the Poets', the translation of which, in Addison's hand, is in the Tickell MSS.

[2] 'A cant word for a chamber-companion and bed-fellow at college' (Nichols). The earliest example in *OED* in this sense is dated 1684.

demanded intelligibly a Reinforcement of Liquor, the whole Assembly had been by this time extended under the Table.

'The Celebration of this Night's Solemnity was opened by the obstreperous Joy of Drummers, who, with their Parchment Thunder, gave a Signal for the Appearance of the Mob under their several Classes and Denominations. They were quickly joined by the melodious Clank of Marrow-bone and Clever,[1] whilst a Chorus of Bells, filled up the Consort. A Pyramid of Stack-Faggots cheared the Hearts of the Populace with the Promise of a Blaze: The Guns had no sooner uttered the Prologue, but the Heavens were brightened with artificial Meteors, and Stars of our own making; and all the *High-street* lighted up, from one End to another, with a Galaxy of Candles. We collected a Largess for the Multitude, who tippled Eleemosynary till they grew exceeding Vociferous. There was a Paste-board Pontiff with a little swarthy Dæmon at his Elbow, who, by his diabolical Whispers and Insinuations, tempted his Holiness into the Fire, and then left him to shift for himself. The Mobile[2] were very sarcastick with their Clubs, and gave the old Gentleman several Thumps upon his triple Head-piece. *Tom Tyler*'s Phiz is something damaged by the Fall of a Rocket, which hath almost spoiled the Gnomon[3] of his Countenance. The Mirth of the Commons grew so very outrageous, that it found Work for our Friend of the *Quorum*, who, by the help of his *Amanuensis*, took down all their Names and their Crimes, with a Design to produce his Manuscript at the next Quarter-Sessions, &c. &c. &c.'

I shall subjoin to the foregoing Piece of a Letter, the following Copy of Verses translated from an *Italian* Poet, who was the *Cleveland* of his Age, and had Multitudes of Admirers.[4] The Subject is an Accident that happened under the Reign of Pope *Leo*, when a Firework, that had been prepared upon the Castle of St. *Angelo*, begun to play before its Time, being kindled by a Flash of Lightning. The Author hath written his Poem in the same kind of Style, as that I have already exemplified in Prose. Every Line in it is a Riddle, and the Reader must be forced to consider it twice or

---

[1] Frequently referred to at this time as instruments of 'rough music'.

[2] The new and shorter form 'mob' is used above in the first sentence of this paragraph.

[3] Used jocularly for the nose, and now obsolete (*OED*).

[4] Eugenius, in Dryden's *Essay of Dramatic Poesy*, describes Cleveland's style as giving 'common thoughts in abstruse words'. 'We cannot read a verse of Cleveland's without making a face at it, as if every word were a pill to swallow: he gives us many times a hard nut to break our teeth, without a kernel for our pains' (Ker, i. 52).

thrice, before he will know that the *Cynick's* Tenement is a *Tub*, and *Bacchus* his Cast-coat a *Hogshead*, &c.[1]

> *'Twas Night, and Heav'n, a Cyclops, all the Day,*
> *An Argus now did countless Eyes display;*
> *In ev'ry Window Rome her Joy declares,*
> *All bright, and studded with terrestrial Stars.*
> *A blazing Chain of Lights her Roofs entwines,*
> *And round her Neck the mingled Lustre shines.*
> *The Cynick's rowling Tenement conspires*
> *With Bacchus his Cast-coat to feed the Fires.*

> *The Pile, still big with undiscover'd Shows,*
> *The Tuscan Pile did last it's Freight disclose,*
> *Where the proud Tops of Rome's new Ætna rise,*
> *Whence Gyants sally and invade the Skies.*

[1] The verses are from Strada's *Prolusiones Academicae Academia secunda* (Leyden, 1627), p. 320. In *Guardian* 103 (9 July 1713) Addison refers to 'an account of a firework, described, if I am not mistaken, by Strada', and in *Guardian* 115 (23 July) he returns to Strada, whose 'prolusion on the style of the most famous among the ancient Latin poets who are extant, and have written in epic verse, is one of the most entertaining, as well as the most just, pieces of criticism that I have ever read'. Strada's prolusion, 'The Session of the Poets', which Addison translated, consists of several imitations of Latin poets—Lucan, Lucretius, Claudian, Ovid, Statius, and Virgil—recited by various members of the assembly. At the end Camillus, the 'poet laureate', is invited to recite; he announces that his verses describe a scene 'which happen'd yesterday when the Hadrian Pile being about to congratulate our Prince with its fire-works was on a sudden struck with a Thunder-bolt from Heav'n and so unexpectedly begun to Play...'. Addison's translation of the verses follows below. It will be noted that Tickell has made but a few changes in printing them in the *Spectator*.

> 'Twas Night and Heav'n, a Cyclops all the Day, }
> An Argos now did all his Eyes display, }
> When glaring Rome's bright windows spoke her joy. }
> A blazing chain of Lights her roofs entwin'd,
> And round her Neck yᵉ mingled flashes shin'd:
> The Cynick's Moveable from High-ways came,
> And Bacchus his Cast-coat increas't yᵉ flame.
> The Pile, still big with undiscover'd shows,
> The Tuscan Pile did last it's Freight expose;
> Here the proud tops of Roman Ætna rise, }
> Whence Giants sally and invade the skies, }
> And Magick here her utmost vertue trie's; }
> Serpents when touch't the changing Quills became
> Serpents they His't, & Serpents belch't out Flame,
> Then on a suddain you might see again
> Nothing of Serpents but the Quills remain.
> Whilst now the Multitude expect the time,
> And theyr tir'd Eyes the lofty mountain climb,

[*For continuation of note see following pages.*

Whilst now the Multitude expect the Time,
And their tir'd Eyes the lofty Mountain climb,
A thousand Iron Mouths their Voices try,
And thunder out a dreadful Harmony;
In treble Notes the small Artill'ry plays,
The deep-mouth'd Cannon bellows in the Bass.
The lab'ring Pile now heaves; and having giv'n
Proof of it's Travail sighs in Flames to Heav'n.

The Clouds invelop'd Heav'n from Human Sight,
Quench'd every Star, and put out every Light;
Now Real Thunder grumbles in the Skies,
And in disdainful Murmurs Rome *defies;*
Nor doth its answer'd Challenge Rome *decline;*
But whilst both Parties in full Consort join,
While Heav'n and Earth in Rival Peals resound,
The doubtful Cracks the Hearer's Sense confound;
Whether the Claps of Thunder-bolts they hear,
Or else the Burst of Canon wounds their Ear;
Whether Clouds rage'd by struggling Metals rent,
Or struggling Clouds in Roman *Metals pent.*
But O, my Muse, the whole Adventure tell,
As ev'ry Accident in order fell.

A thousand Iron mouths theyr voices try
And Thunder out a Dreadfull Harmony;
The smoaking wide-mouth'd Cañon Bellows out
And each small Gun mingle's it's sharper note,
The labring Pile now Heave's, & having giv'n
Proofs of its Travail, sigh's in Flames to Heav'n.
  The Clouds had Clouded Heav'n from human sight
Enlightne'd now by no Appearing Light,
Now Real Thunder grumble's in yᵉ Skies
And in disdainfull murmurs Rome defie's,
Nor dos it's answer'd Challenge Rome decline;
But whilst both parties in full consort join,
Whilst Heav'n & Earth in rival peals resound,
The doubtfull Cracks the Hearer's sence confound,
Whether the Claps of thunder-bolts they hear,
Or else the burst of Cannon strike's theyr ear;
Whether Clouds Rag'd by struling metals rent,⎫
Or struling Clouds in Roman mettals pent: ⎬
In short I'le tell you how the Matter went.   ⎭
  On the high Tow'r where Trees spread out theyr boughs
A Paper Garland on theyr fore-head grows,
These know no Spring, but when theyr Bodys sprout
In Fire, and shoot theyr Gilded blossoms out,
When blazing Woods appear about theyr Head,
And into Branching Flames they bodys spread.
Whilst real Thunder split's the Firmament

[a]*Tall Groves of Trees the* Hadrian *Tow'r surround,*
Fictitious Trees with Paper Garlands crown'd,
These know no Spring, but when their Bodies sprout
In Fire, and shoot their gilded Blossoms out;
When blazing Leaves appear above their Head,
And into branching Flames their Bodies spread.
Whilst Real Thunder splits the Firmament,
And Heav'n's whole Roof in one vast Cleft is rent,
The Three-fork'd Tongue amidst the Rupture lolls,
Then drops and on the Airy Turret falls.
The Trees now kindle, and the Garland burns,
And thousand Thunderbolts for one returns.
Brigades of burning Archers upward fly,   ⎫
Bright Spears and shining Spear-men mount on high, ⎬
Flash in the Clouds and glitter in the Sky.   ⎭
A Seven fold Shield of Spheres doth Heav'n defend,
And back again the blunted Weapons send;
Unwillingly they fall, and dropping down,
Pour out their Souls, their sulph'rous Souls, and groan.

With Joy, great Sir, we view'd this pompous Show, ⎫
While Heav'n, that sate Spectator still till now, ⎬
It self turn'd Actor, proud to Pleasure you.   ⎭
And so 'tis fit, when Leo's *Fires appear,*
That Heav'n it self should turn an Engineer;
That Heav'n it self should all its Wonders show,
And Orbs above consent with Orbs below.

---

[a] *No paragraph in Fol.*

And all it's Pavement into Clefts is rent
The three-forkt Tongue amidst y[e] rupture loll's
This drop's and on the Airy Turret fall's,
The Trees now Kindle, and the Garland burn's,
And thousand Thunder-bolts for One return's:
Partys of burning Archers upwards fly,   ⎫
Bright Spears & shining Spear-men mount on high, ⎬
Blaze in the Clouds, and Glitter in the Sky.   ⎭
Heav'n with a Seav'n-fold shield it self defend's,
And back again the blunted weapons send's.
Unwillingly they fall, and dropping down
Pour out theyr Souls, theyr Sulphrous Souls, & Groan.
   With joy, Great S[r], we view'd this pompous Show, ⎫
Whilst Heav'n, that sate Spectatour still till now, ⎬
It self turn'd Actour, proud to pleasure You.   ⎭
And so tis fit, when Leo's Fires appear,
That Heav'n it self shou'd turn an Engineer,
That Heav'n it self shou'd all it's Triumphs show
And Orbs above Consent with Orbs below.

No. 618   *Wednesday, November 10, 1714*[1]

[PHILIPS; TICKELL]

> *. . . Neque enim concludere versum*
> *Dixeris esse satis: neque siquis scribat, uti nos,*
> *Sermoni propiora, putes hunc esse Poetam.*
>
>   Hor.

Mr. SPECTATOR,

'YOU having in your two last *Spectators* given the Town a couple of remarkable Letters, in very different Styles; I take this Opportunity to offer to you some Remarks upon the *Epistolary* way of writing in Verse. This is a *Species* of Poetry by it self; and has not so much as been hinted at in any of the Arts of Poetry, that have ever fallen into my Hands: Neither has it in any Age, or any Nation, been so much cultivated, as the other several Kinds of Poesie. A Man of *Genius* may, if he pleases, write Letters in Verse upon all manner of Subjects, that are capable of being embellished with Wit and Language, and may render them new and agreeable by giving the proper Turn to them. But in speaking, at present, of *Epistolary Poetry*, I would be understood to mean only such Writings in this Kind, as have been in Use amongst the Ancients, and have been copied from them by some Moderns. These may be reduced into two *Classes*: In the one I shall range Love-Letters, Letters of Friendship, and Letters upon mournful Occasions: In the other I shall place such Epistles in Verse, as may properly be called Familiar, Critical, and Moral; to which may be added Letters of Mirth and Humour. *Ovid* for the first, and *Horace* for the latter, are the best Originals we have left.

'He that is ambitious of succeeding in the *Ovidian* way, should first examine his Heart well, and feel whether his Passions (especially those of the gentler Kind) play easie, since it is not his Wit, but the Delicacy and Tenderness of his Sentiments, that will affect his

---

[1] *Motto.* Horace, *Satires*, i. 4. 40–42:
> 'Tis not enough to fetter Words in Rhime,
> And make a tedious and a jingling Chime;
> 'Tis not enough in numerous Feet t'enclose,
> Familiar plain Discourse and almost Prose,
> To make a Poet ——.

This number is assigned in the Tickell MS. to Ambrose Philips, 'Author of the Pastorals'. The two concluding paragraphs are probably by Tickell.

Readers.[1] His Versification likewise should be soft, and all his Numbers flowing and querulous.

'The Qualifications requisite for writing Epistles, after the Model given us by *Horace*, are of a quite different Nature. He that would excel in this kind must have a good Fund of strong Masculine Sense: To this there must be joined a thorough Knowledge of Mankind, together with an Insight into the Business, and the prevailing Humours of the Age. Our Author must have his Mind well seasoned with the finest Precepts of Morality, and be filled with nice Reflections upon the bright and the dark sides of human Life: He must be a Master of refined Raillery, and understand the Delicacies, as well as the Absurdities of Conversation. He must have a lively Turn of Wit, with an easie and concise manner of Expression; Every thing he says, must be in a free and disengaged manner. He must be guilty of nothing that betrays the Air of a Recluse, but appear a Man of the World throughout. His Illustrations, his Comparisons, and the greatest part of his Images must be drawn from common Life. Strokes of Satyr and Criticism, as well as Panegyrick, judiciously thrown in (and as it were by the by) give a wonderful Life and Ornament to Compositions of this kind. But let our Poet, while he writes Epistles, though never so familiar, still remember that he writes in Verse, and must for that reason have a more than ordinary care not to fall into Prose, and a vulgar Diction, excepting where the Nature and Humour of the Thing does necessarily require it. In this Point *Horace* hath been thought by some Criticks to be sometimes careless, as well as too negligent of his Versification; of which he seems to have been sensible himself.[2]

'All I have to add is, that both these Manners of Writing may be made as entertaining, in their way, as any other Species of Poetry, if undertaken by Persons duly qualified; and the latter sort may be managed so as to become in a peculiar manner Instructive.

I am, &c.'

I shall add an Observation or two to the Remarks of my ingenious Correspondent, and, in the First place, take Notice, that Subjects of the most sublime Nature, are often treated in the Epistolary way

---

[1] Cf. Addison's notes on Ovid (Guthkelch, i. 145): '*Ovid* is very justly celebrated for the passionate speeches of his Poem. They have generally abundance of Nature in them, but I leave it to better judgments to consider whether they are not often too witty and too tedious.'

[2] Dryden, in the *Discourse concerning Satire* (1693), defends Horace on this point against the criticism of Casaubon (*Essays*, ed. Ker, ii. 77 ff.).

with Advantage, as in the famous Epistle of *Horace* to *Augustus*.[1] The Poet surprizes us with his Pomp, and seems rather betrayed into his Subject,[a] than to have aimed at it by Design: He appears like the Visit of a King *Incognito*, with a mixture of Familiarity, and Grandeur. In Works of this kind, when the Dignity of the Subject hurries the Poet into Descriptions and Sentiments, seemingly unpremeditated, by a sort of Inspiration: It is usual for him to Recollect himself, and fall back gracefully into the natural Stile of a Letter.

I might here mention an Epistolary Poem, just Published by Mr. *Eusden* on the King's Accession to the Throne:[2] Wherein, amongst many other noble and beautiful Strokes of Poetry, his Reader may see this Rule very happily observed.

[a] into his Subject,] into it his Subject, *Fol.*

---

[1] *Epistles*, 2. I.

[2] Eusden's poem is advertised in No. 606 (13 Oct.):

This Day is Publish'd, A Letter to Mr. Addison, on the King's Accession to the Throne. By Mr. Eusden. Printed for Jacob Tonson at Shakespear's Head over-against Catherine-street in the Strand.

It is also advertised as 'this day' published in the *Gazette* (12 Oct.), the *Daily Courant* (15 Oct.), and the *Post-Boy* (16 Oct.). Among the Tickell MSS. there is a draft for an unpublished *Spectator* contrasting satire and panegyric, the latter half of which is devoted to praise of Eusden's poem.

That ingenious author has there shown us with success, how hard a thing it is to paint a hero; what a dext'rous nicety is requir'd justly [discreetly *deleted*] to praise the eminent virtues of great Men, & yet to avoid the nauseous dawbings of flattery. But it may be answer'd, that the happy choice of his subject secur'd him from falling into this vice, since there never could be so much commendation given to the Persons he mentions, but the world would still allow them to deserve infinitely more. I must own, I was not a little pleas'd to find in every line, that the author himself seems pleas'd with the theme he had chosen: he shows his joys are not Poetical, but real: Panegyrick indeed looks lovely, when it flows from a heart full of sincerity, & a Poet never charms us so sensibly, as when adorn'd with the truth of an historian.

> *. . . dura*
> *Exerce imperia, et ramos compesce fluentes.*
>   Virg.

I HAVE often thought, that if the several Letters, which are
Written to me under the Character of SPECTATOR, and which
I have not made use of, were published in a Volume, they would
not be an unentertaining Collection.² The Variety of the Subjects,
Stiles, Sentiments, and Informations, which are transmitted to me,
would lead a very curious, or very idle Reader, insensibly along,
through a great many Pages. I know some Authors, who would
pick up a *Secret History* out of such Materials, and make a Bookseller
an Alderman by the Copy.³ I shall therefore carefullyª preserve the
Original Papers in a Room set apart for that Purpose, to the end
that they may be of Service to Posterity; but shall at present content my self, with owning the Receipt of several Letters, lately
come to my Hands, the Authors whereof are impatient for an
Answer.

Charissa, whose Letter is dated from *Cornhill,* desires to be eased
in some Scruples relating to the Skill of Astrologers;⁴ *referred to the
Dumb Man⁵ for an Answer.*

J.C. who proposes a Love-Case,⁶ as he calls it, to the Love-

ª shall therefore carefully] shall carefully *Fol.*

---

¹ *Motto.* Virgil, *Georgics,* 2. 369–70:
>   Let crooked Steel invade
> The lawless Troops, which Discipline disclaim,
> And their superfluous Growth with Rigour tame. DRYDEN.

² In 1725 Richard Lillie, with Steele's permission, published 'near three hundred
letters, wrote by as many different writers', which had been sent in to the *Tatler*
and the *Spectator.* Others remain in the Tickell collection and among the archives at
Blenheim Palace, and a great many doubtless have been destroyed. This number of
the *Spectator,* in which Tickell briefly comments on or answers some of these correspondents, shows indeed 'the variety of the subjects, stiles, sentiments, and informations' in the flood of letters sent in.
³ 'An allusion to John Barber, who had been a bookseller, was at this time an
alderman, and afterwards Lord Mayor of London' (Nichols).
⁴ Charissa's letter, preserved among the Tickell MSS., is dated 'from Cornhill
Oct. 19. 1714' and asks Mr. Spectator's opinion of astrology, chiromancy, and physiognomy. A female acquaintance, after studying the 'lines & crosses' in Charissa's hand,
has volunteered advice as to her rival suitors, Faber and Aprilis.
⁵ Duncan Campbell. See No. 31 (vol. i).
⁶ This letter too, dated 'London No. 1: 1714', is contained in the Tickell MSS.,

Casuist,[1] is hereby desired to speak of it to the Minister of the Parish; it being a Case of Conscience.

The poor young Lady, whose Letter is dated *October* 26, who complains of a harsh Guardian, and an unkind Brother, can only have my good Wishes, unless she pleases to be more particular.

The Petition of a certain Gentleman, whose Name I have forgot, famous for renewing the Curls of decayed Perriwigs, is refered to *the Censor of small Wares.*[2]

The Remonstrance of *T.C.* against the Profanation of the Sabbath by Barbers, Shoe-cleaners, *&c.* had better be offered to *the Society of Reformers.*[3]

A learned and laborious Treatise upon the Art of Fencing, *returned to the Author.*

To the Gentleman of *Oxford,* who desires me to insert a Copy of *Latin* Verses, which were denied a Place in the University Book. Answer. *Nonumque prematur in annum.*[4]

To my learned Correspondent who writes against Master's Gowns, and Poke Sleeves,[5] with a Word in Defence of large Scarves. Answer. *I resolve not to raise Animosities amongst the Clergy.*

To the Lady, who writes with Rage against one of her own Sex, upon the Account of Party-Warmth. Answer. *Is not the Lady she writes against reckoned Handsome?*

I desire[a] *Tom Truelove,* (who sends me a Sonnet upon his Mistress, with a Desire to print it immediately,) to consider,[b] that it is long since I was in Love.

I shall answer a very profound Letter from my old Friend the Upholsterer, who is still inquisitive whether the King of *Sweden* be living or dead, by whispering him in the Ear, *That I believe he is alive.*[6]

---

[a] desire] would have *Fol.*   [b] to consider] consider *Fol.*

---

though half has been torn off. The 'love-case' concerns Lysidor and Euphelia, in love with each other and both without fortune. Each now has the opportunity to marry for money. 'What shall They do? Their Fate seems to be at its Crisis. Should They refuse these Offers either of 'em is Undone: On ye other Hand, all their Happiness is plac'd in each Other. They can be grateful and by a prudent Conduct make the Others happy, but can never love & therefore must be miserable Themselves.'

[1] No. 591.

[2] Addison had suggested this functionary in No. 16.   [3] Cf. No. 8.

[4] Horace's advice, 'Keep it by you till the ninth year', in *Ars poetica* 388.

[5] Cf. John Kersey's revision of Edward Philips's *New World of Words* (1706), quoted in *OED*: 'Pokes were also a sort of long-sleev'd Gowns, which Fashion grew so affected and extravagant, that the wearing of them was forbidden.'

[6] For the Upholsterer see No. 50. The fate of the King of Sweden (Charles XII) is discussed in No. 43.

Let Mr. *Dapperwit* consider, what is that long Story of the Cuckoldom to me?[1]

At the earnest Desire of *Monimia*'s Lover, who declares himself very penitent, he is recorded in my Paper by the Name of *The faithful* Castalio.[2]

The Petition of *Charles Cocksure*, which the Petitioner stiles *very reasonable—Rejected*.

The Memorial of *Philander*, which he desires may be dispatched out of hand, *Postponed*.

I desire *S. R.* not to repeat the Expression *under the Sun* so often in his next Letter.

The Letter of *P. S.* who desires either to have it printed entire, or committed to the Flames. *Not to be printed entire*.

No. 620   *Monday, November 15, 1714*[3]

[TICKELL]

Hic Vir, hic est, tibi quem promitti sæpius audis.
            Virg.

HAVING lately presented my Reader with a Copy of Verses, full of the False Sublime,[4] I shall here communicate to him an excellent Specimen of the True. Tho' it hath not been yet published, the judicious Reader will readily discern it to be the

---

[1] For Dapperwit see No. 482 (vol. iv).

[2] See No. 613. The letter from her lover, signed 'The Faithfull Castalio', is preserved among the Tickell papers. In somewhat involved and high-flown language it attempts to explain why Castalio had endeavoured to shake off 'an Amour, that was very fatal to the quiet of my Mind, and likely to be very fruitless in the Event'. It concludes, however, by asking Mr. Spectator's assistance 'in effecting a Reconciliation, which will compleatly answer your Character and my greatest Hopes of Happiness'.

[3] *Motto*. Virgil, *Aeneid*, 6. 791:
            The Man behold
       Promis'd oft and long foretold.

This number is taken up with the first printing of Tickell's own poem, 'The Royal Progress'. 'Addison may have given his little senator laws about *Spectator* policy; and let us hope that it was he and not Tickell who wrote the editorial blurb for Tickell's poem' (Hodgart, p. 379).

[4] See No. 617.

Work of a Master:[1] And if he hath read that noble Poem on *The Prospect of Peace*, he will not be at a Loss to guess at the Author.[2]

The ROYAL PROGRESS.[a][3]

WHEN BRUNSWICK[4] *first appear'd, each honest Heart,*[b]
Intent on Verse, disdain'd the Rules of Art;
For Him the Songsters, in unmeasur'd Odes,
Debas'd Alcides, and dethron'd the Gods,[5]
In Golden Chains the Kings of India led,
Or rent the Turban from the Sultan's Head.
One, in old Fables, and the Pagan Strain,
With Nymphs and Tritons, wafts him o'er the Main;
Another draws fierce Lucifer in Arms,
And fills th' Infernal Region with Alarms;
A Third awakes some Druid to foretel
Each future Triumph from his dreary Cell:
Exploded Fancies! that in vain deceive,
While the Mind nauseates what she can't believe.
My Muse th' expected Hero[c] *shall pursue*
From Clime to Clime, and keep him still in View:

[a] *Title added in 8vo and 12mo*   [b] *Poem printed in italic in 8vo, 12mo; in roman in Fol.*
[c] *My . . . Hero]* My artless Muse the Hero Fol.

---

[1] This is the first printing of the poem. It was reprinted in Motte's *Miscellaneous Collection of Poems* in 1721 (R. Eustace Tickell, p. 190). Addison may have sent a copy (in manuscript) to Jean de Robethon on 4 Sept. (*Letters*, ed. Graham, pp. 294–5).
[2] *The Prospect of Peace* had been published late in 1712 (dated 1713); it is praised by Addison in No. 523 (vol. iv).
[3] George I set out from Germany on the last day of August (O.S.), travelling through Holland, and embarked for England on 16 Sept. on the *Peregrine*, reaching Greenwich on the 18th. The royal entry was made on Monday, 20 Sept.,

with such Pomp and Magnificence, as can hardly be paralell'd in any other Nation. The Coaches of the Nobility and others, either not coming soon enough, or the Officers of Arms being puzzled how to rank them in their due Order, it was Twelve a-clock before his MAJESTY, accompanied by his ROYAL HIGHNESS the Prince, and the Duke of *Northumberland*, Captain of the Life-Guard in Waiting, set out from *Greenwich*, his Majesty's Coach being preceded by above Two Hundred of those of the Nobility and Gentry all with Six Horses . . . (*Political State*, Sept. 1714, p. 253).

At St. Margaret's Hill in Southwark the King was met by the Lord Mayor (Sir Samuel Stanier), Aldermen, Recorder, Sheriffs, and Officers of the City of London, and thence proceeded to St. James's.
[4] George was elector of Brunswick-Lüneberg, popularly known as Hanover, its capital.
[5] The ridicule of poets who employ classical mythology to praise contemporary heroes recalls Addison's strictures in No. 523 against the use of Apollo, Mars, or Bellona ('downright Puerility, and unpardonable in a Poet that is past Sixteen'). Tickell's aim, 'to paint him, nor presume to praise', is in the vein of Addison's *Campaign*.

His shining March describe in faithful Lays,
Content to paint him, nor presume to praise;
Their Charms, if Charms they have, the Truth supplies,
And from the Theme unlabour'd Beauties rise.

By longing Nations for the Throne design'd,
And call'd to guard the Rights of Human-kind;
With secret Grief his God-like Soul repines,[1]
And Britain's Crown with joyless Lustre shines,
While Prayers and Tears his destin'd Progress stay,
And Crowds of Mourners choak their Sovereign's Way.
Not so he march'd, when hostile Squadrons[a] *stood*
In Scenes of Death, and fir'd his generous Blood;
When his hot Courser paw'd th' Hungarian Plain,
And adverse Legions stood the Shock in vain.[2]

His Frontiers past, the Belgian Bounds he views,
And cross the level Fields his March pursues.
Here pleas'd the Land of Freedom to survey,
He greatly scorns the Thirst of boundless Sway.
O'er the thin Soil, with silent Joy he spies
Transplanted Woods, and borrow'd Verdure rise;
Where every Meadow won with Toil and Blood,
From haughty Tyrants, and the raging Flood,
With Fruits and Flowers the careful Hind supplies,
And cloathes the Marshes in a rich Disguise.
Such Wealth for frugal Hands doth Heaven decree,
And such thy Gifts, Celestial Liberty!

Through stately Towns, and many a fertile Plain,
The Pomp advances to the neighb'ring Main.
Whole Nations crowd around with joyful Cries,
And view the Hero with insatiate Eyes.

---

[a] *Squadrons*] Legions *Fol.*

---

[1] 'The News of being raised to so Powerful a Throne, and of having such vast Dominions added to his own, could not but be pleasing to His Majesty; . . . but yet he received it with that Serenity of Countenance and Composure of Mind, which are peculiar to Heroes' (*Political State*, Sept. 1714, p. 207).

[2] George, as elector of Hanover, had fought in Hungary in the service of the Emperor. He took an honourable part in Sobieski's rescue of Vienna (1683), in 1685 distinguishing himself at the capture of Neuhäusel in Hungary, and in the battle of Neerwinden (29 July 1693), only, escaping with his life through the devotion of General von Hammerstein (*DNB*).

In Haga's *Towers* he waits, till *Eastern Gales*
Propitious rise to swell the British *Sails.*[1]
Hither the Fame of England's *Monarch brings*
The Vows and Friendships of the neighb'ring Kings;
Mature in Wisdom, His extensive Mind
Takes in the blended Int'rests of Mankind,
The World's great Patriot. Calm thy anxious Breast,
Secure in Him, O Europe *take thy Rest;*
Henceforth thy Kingdoms shall remain confin'd
By Rocks or Streams, the Mounds which Heav'n design'd;
The Alps *their new-made Monarch shall restrain,*
Nor shall thy Hills, Pirene, *rise in vain.*[2]

But see! to Britain's *Isle the Squadrons stand,*
And leave the sinking Towers, and lessening Land.
The Royal Bark bounds o'er the floating Plain,
Breaks thro' the Billows, and divides the Main.
O'er the vast Deep, Great Monarch, dart thine Eyes,
A watry Prospect bounded by the Skies:
Ten thousand Vessels from Ten thousand Shores
Bring Gums and Gold, and either India's *Stores:*
Behold the Tributes hastening to thy Throne,
And see the wide Horizon all thy own.

Still is it thine; tho' now the chearful Crew
Hail Albion's *Cliffs, just whitening to the View.*
Before the Wind with swelling Sails they ride,
Till Thames *receives them in his opening Tide.*
The Monarch hears the thundering Peals around,
From trembling Woods and ecchoing Hills rebound;
Nor misses yet, amid the deafening Train,
The Roarings of the hoarse-resounding Main.

As in the Flood he sails, from either Side
He views his Kingdom in its rural Pride;

---

[1] The King had arrived at The Hague on 5 Sept. (O.S.), where he conferred with a deputation from England and received visits from representatives of France, Spain, and Portugal.

[2] One of the conditions of the Peace Treaty of Utrecht was that Philip V of Spain abjure his reversionary claim to the throne of France, so that the Pyrenees in effect would again divide the two kingdoms.

A various Scene the wide-spread Landskip yields,
O'er rich Enclosures and luxuriant Fields:
A lowing Herd each fertile Pasture fills,
And distant Flocks stray o'er a thousand Hills.
Fair Greenwich *hid in Woods, with new Delight,*
(Shade above Shade) now rises to the Sight.
His Woods ordain'd to visit every Shore,
And guard the Island which they grac'd before.

The Sun now rowling down the Western Way,
A Blaze of Fires renews the fading Day;
Unnumber'd Barks the Regal Barge infold,
Brightening the Twilight with its beamy Gold;
Less thick the finny Shoals, a countless Fry,
Before the Whale or kingly Dolphin fly.
In one vast Shout he seeks the crowded Strand,
And in a Peal of Thunder gains the Land.

Welcome, great Stranger, to our longing Eyes,
Oh! King desir'd, adopted Albion *cries.*
For Thee the East breath'd out a prosp'rous Breeze,
Bright were the Suns, and gently swell'd the Seas.
Thy Presence did each doubtful Heart compose,
And Factions wonder'd that they once were Foes;
That joyful Day they lost each hostile Name,
The same their Aspect, and their Voice the same.

So two fair Twins, whose Features were design'd
At one soft Moment in the Mother's Mind,
Show each the other, with reflected Grace,
And the same Beauties bloom in either Face;
The puzzled Strangers which is which enquire,
Delusion grateful to the smiling Sire.

From that fair ★*Hill, where hoary Sages boast*
To name the Stars, and count the heavenly Host,

> ★*Mr.* Flamstead*'s-House.*[a] [1]

[a] ★*Mr.* Flamstead*'s-House.*] ★*Flamstead's-House.* Fol.

[1] John Flamsteed (1646–1719), who had been appointed Astronomer Royal with the opening of the Observatory in Greenwich Park in 1675, moved in 1676 into the house on the hill which had come to be known as Flamsteed House. At this time he was nearly seventy years of age and involved in controversy over what he regarded as unwarranted publication of his astronomical observations.

By the next Dawn doth great Augusta *rise,*
Proud Town! the noblest Scene beneath the Skies.
O'er Thames *her thousand Spires their Lustre shed,*
And a vast Navy hides his ample Bed,
A floating Forest. From the distant Strand
A Line of golden Carrs strikes o'er the Land:
Britannia's *Peers in Pomp and rich Array,*
Before their King, triumphant, lead the Way.
Far as the Eye can reach, the gawdy Train,
A bright Procession, shines along the Plain.

    So haply through the Heav'n's wide pathless Ways
A Comet draws a long-extended Blaze;
From East to West burns through[a] *th' ethereal Frame,*
And Half Heav'n's Convex glitters with the Flame.

    Now to the Regal Towers securely brought,
He plans Britannia's *Glories in his Thought;*
Resumes the delegated Pow'r he gave,
Rewards the Faithful, and restores the Brave.
Whom shall the Muse from out the shining Throng
Select, to heighten and adorn her Song?
Thee, Halifax. *To thy capacious Mind,*
O Man approv'd, is Britain's *Wealth consign'd.*
Her Coin (while Nassau *fought) debas'd and rude,*
By Thee in Beauty and in Truth renew'd,
An arduous Work! Again thy Charge we see,
And thy own Care once more returns to Thee.
O! form'd in every Scene to awe and please,
Mix Wit with Pomp, and Dignity with Ease:
Tho' call'd to shine aloft, thou wilt not scorn
To smile on Arts thy self did once adorn:
For this thy Name succeeding Times shall praise,
And envy less thy Garter, than thy Bays.[1]

    The Muse, if fir'd with thy enlivening Beams,
Perhaps shall aim at more exalted Themes,

---

[a] *burns through*] he burns Fol.

---

[1] Lord Halifax had been named by George as one of the Council of Regents. The lines refer to his services in connexion with the coinage in 1695. Volume II of the *Spectator* had been dedicated to him.

Record our Monarch in a nobler Strain,
And sing the opening Wonders of his Reign;
Bright CAROLINA'*s heavenly Beauties trace,*
Her valiant CONSORT, *and his blooming Race.*
A Train of Kings their fruitful Love supplies,
A glorious Scene to Albion'*s ravish'd Eyes;*
Who sees by BRUNSWICK'*s Hand her Sceptre sway'd,*
And through his Line from Age to Age convey'd.[1]

No. 621   *Wednesday, November 17, 1714*[2]
[TICKELL]

> *. . . postquam se lumine puro*
> *Implevit, stellasque vagas miratur & Astra*
> *Fixa Polis, vidit quanta sub nocte jaceret*
> *Nostra dies, risitque sui ludibria . . .*
>   Lucan.

THE following Letter having in it some Observations out of the common Road, I shall make it the Entertainment of this Day.

[1] Wilhelmina Carola, Princess of Anspach, is described in the *Political State of Great Britain* (Sept. 1714, p. 214) as 'affable and engaging beyond all Expression', with a 'laudable Thirst after knowledge'. Her consort, the future George II, was at this time in his 31st year; their 'blooming race' in 1714 consisted of Frederick (born 1707), Anne, the Princess Royal (born 1709), Amelia (born 1711), and Caroline (born 1713). The Princess arrived at Margate 11 Oct. (o.s.), where she was met by her husband and proceeded to St. James's Palace, accompanied by the two young princesses, Anne and Amelia (*Political State*, Oct. 1714, p. 343).

[2] *Motto.* Lucan, *Pharsalia*, 9. 11–14 (altered):

>   With wonder fill'd,
> The Stars and moving Planets he beheld,
> Then looking down on the Sun's feeble Ray,
> Survey'd our dusty, faint, imperfect Day,
> And under what a Cloud of Night we lay.

The parallels to Pope's *Essay on Man* are so striking in this essay that it is tempting to consider this number as a contribution by him. 'My letter to Mr. Addison on a Future State', Pope told Spence, 'was designed as an imitation of the style of the Spectators; and there are several cant phrases of the Spectator in it' (*Anecdotes*, ed. S. W. Singer, 2nd ed., 1858, p. 126). 'As "Scale of beings," and some others which he mentioned', Spence adds. Elwin and Courthope (vi. 404) cite Pope's letter to Addison of 14 Dec. 1713, but recognize that it does not meet the requirements.

Against this possibility is the fact that the notes for this number exist among the Tickell papers, in a manuscript headed 'Extract of Five Irish Mails from Oct. 26 to Oct. 31' received 6 Nov. 1714. 'This is a short draft in Tickell's hand, with the last

Mr. SPECTATOR,

'THE common Topicks against the Pride of Man, which are laboured by florid and declamatory Writers, are taken from the Baseness of his Original, the Imperfections of his Nature, or the short Duration of those Goods in which he makes his Boast.[1] Though it be true that we can have nothing in us that ought to raise our Vanity, yet a Consciousness of our own Merit may be sometimes laudable. The Folly therefore lies here; We are apt to pride our selves in worthless, or perhaps shameful things; and, on the other Hand, count that disgraceful which is our truest Glory.

'Hence it is, that the Lovers of Praise take wrong Measures to attain it. Would a vain Man consult his own Heart, he would find, that if others knew his Weaknesses as well as he himself doth, he could not have the Impudence to expect the publick Esteem. Pride therefore flows from want of Reflection, and Ignorance of our selves. Knowledge and Humility come upon us together.

'The proper way to make an Estimate of our selves, is to consider seriously what it is we value or despise in others. A Man who boasts of the Goods of Fortune, a gay Dress, or a new Title, is generally the Mark of Ridicule. We ought therefore not to admire in our selves, what we are so ready to laugh at in other Men.[a]

'Much less can we with Reason pride our selves in those things, which at some time of our Life we shall certainly despise. And yet, if we will give our selves the Trouble of looking backward and forward on the several Changes, which we have already undergone and hereafter must try, we shall find that the greater Degrees of our Knowledge and Wisdom, serve only to show us our own Imperfections.

'As we rise from Childhood to Youth, we look with Contempt on

[a] in other Men.] in others. *Fol.*

six words of the text, "sink in our own Esteem hereafter," in Addison's hand. It was written up into *Spectator* 621 of 17 Nov. 1714, which ends with the same six words' (Hodgart, p. 375).

It is impossible therefore to say with any certainty who the original author was. In any case the material seems to have been gone over and arranged for publication by both Addison and Tickell.

[1] In *Guardian* 153 (which has many similarities with this number of the *Spectator*) Addison had insisted that human nature has no claim to pride, since man is a sinful, an ignorant, and a miserable being.

There is not, indeed, any single view of human nature, under its present condition, which is not sufficient to extinguish in us all the secret seeds of pride; and, on the contrary, to sink the soul into the lowest state of humility, and what the schoolmen call self-annihilation.

the Toys and Trifles which our Hearts have hitherto been[a] set upon[1]. When we advance to Manhood, we are held wise in proportion to our Shame and Regret for the Rashness and Extravagance of Youth. Old Age fills us with mortifying Reflections upon a Life misspent in the Pursuit of anxious Wealth or uncertain Honour. Agreeable to this Gradation of Thought in this Life, it may be reasonably supposed, that in a future State, the Wisdom, the Experience, and the Maxims of old Age, will be looked upon by a separate Spirit in much the same Light, as an ancient Man now sees the little Follies and Toyings of Infants. The Pomps, the Honours, the Policies, and Arts of mortal Men, will be thought as trifling as Hobby-horses, Mock-battles, or any other Sports that now employ all the Cunning, and Strength, and Ambition of rational Beings from four Years old to nine or ten.

'If the Notion of a gradual Rise in Beings, from the meanest to the Most High, be not a vain Imagination, it is not improbable that an Angel looks down upon a Man, as a Man doth upon a Creature which approaches the nearest to the rational Nature.[2] By the same Rule (if I may indulge my Fancy in this Particular) a superior Brute looks with a kind of Pride on one of an inferior Species. If they could reflect, we might imagine from the Gestures of some of them, that they think themselves the Sovereigns of the World, and that all Things were made for them.[3] Such a Thought would not be more absurd in Brute Creatures, than one which Men are apt to entertain, namely, That[b] all the Stars in the Firmament were created only to please their Eyes, and amuse their Imaginations. Mr. *Dryden* in his Fable of the *Cock and the Fox*, makes a Speech for his Hero the Cock, which is a pretty Instance for this Purpose.[4]

[a] have hitherto been] have been *Fol.*   [b] entertain, namely, That] entertain, That *Fol.*

---

[1] Cf. Pope's *Essay on Man*, ii. 275–82; and No. 626 (by Henry Grove).
[2] Cf. *Guardian* 153:

If there be anything which makes human nature appear ridiculous to beings of superior faculties, it must be pride. They know so well the vanity of those imaginary perfections that swell the heart of man, and of those little supernumerary advantages, whether in birth, fortune, or title, which one man enjoys above another, that it must certainly very much astonish, if it does not very much divert them, when they see a mortal puffed up, and valuing himself above his neighbours, on any of these accounts, at the same time that he is obnoxious to all the common calamities of the species.

[3] Cf. *Essay on Man*, i. 131–40.
[4] Dryden, 'The Cock and the Fox, or, the Tale of the Nun's Priest, from Chaucer's lines 455–60 (line 457: 'and blue violet spring').

Then turning, said to Partlet, *See, my Dear,*
How lavish Nature hath adorn'd the Year;
How the pale Primrose and the Violet spring,
And Birds essay their Throats, disus'd to sing;
All these are ours, and I with Pleasure see
Man strutting on two Legs, and aping me.

'What I would observe from the Whole is this, That we ought to value our selves upon those Things only which superior Beings think valuable, since that is the only way for us not[a] to sink in our own Esteem hereafter.'[b]

No. 622
[TICKELL]

Friday, November 19, 1714[1]

. . . Fallentis Semita Vitæ.

Hor.

Mr. SPECTATOR,

'IN a former Speculation you have observed, that true Greatness doth not consist in that Pomp and Noise wherein the Generality of Mankind are apt to place it.[2] You have there taken Notice, that

[a] for us not] not for us *Fol.*
[b] *The following two paragraphs in Fol. were omitted in 8vo and 12mo:*

'I shall add to the foregoing Hints a noble Paragraph out of Dr. *Burnet's Theory of the Earth*, which shall conclude this long Letter.*

'*Those sure must be little narrow Souls, that can make themselves a Portion and a Sufficiency out of what they enjoy here; that think of no more, that desire no more. For what is this Life but a Circulation of little mean Actions? We lie down and rise again, dress and undress, feed and wax hungry, work or play, and are weary; and then we lie down again, and the Circle returns: We spend the Day in Trifles, and when the Night comes, we throw our selves into the Bed of Folly amongst Dreams and broken Thoughts, and wild Imaginations. Our Reason lies asleep by us, and we are for the Time as arrant Brutes as those that sleep in the Stalls or in the Field. Are not the Capacities of Man higher than these? and ought not his Ambition and Expectations to be Greater? Let us be Adventurers for another World, 'tis at least a fair and noble Chance; and there is nothing in this worth our Thoughts or our Passions. If we should be disappointed, we are still no worse than the rest of our Fellow-Mortals; and if we succeed in our Expectations, we are eternally happy.*

I am, &c.'

* This passage—except for the first sentence—had been quoted in No. 143, hence presumably the reason for its deletion in 8vo and 12mo.

---

[1] *Motto.* Horace, *Epistles*, 1. 18. 103:
            Or close retirement, and a life by stealth. CREECH.
(The motto of No. 264, vol. ii.)   [2] No. 610.

Virtue in Obscurity often appears more illustrious in the Eye of superior Beings, than all that passes for Grandeur and Magnificence among Men.

'When we look back upon the History of those who have born the Parts of Kings, Statesmen, or Commanders, they appear to us stripped of those out-side Ornaments that dazzled their Contemporaries; and we regard their Persons as great or little, in proportion to the Eminence of their Virtues or Vices. The wise Sayings, generous Sentiments, or disinterested Conduct of a Philosopher under mean Circumstances of Life, set him higher in our Esteem than the mighty Potentates of the Earth, when we view them both through the long Prospect of many Ages. Were the Memoirs of an obscure Man, who lived up to the Dignity of his Nature, and according to the Rules of Virtue, to be laid before us, we should find nothing in such a Character which might not set him on a Level with Men of the highest Stations. The following Extract out of the private Papers of an honest Country-Gentleman, will set this Matter in a clear Light. Your Reader will perhaps conceive a greater Idea of him from these Actions done in Secret, and without a Witness, than of those which have drawn upon them the Admiration of Multitudes.

MEMOIRS.[a]

' "In my 22d Year I found a violent Affection for my Cousin *Charles*'s Wife growing upon me, wherein I was in danger of succeeding, if I had not upon that Account begun my Travels into foreign Countries.

' "A little after my Return into *England*, at a private Meeting with my Uncle *Francis*, I refused the Offer of his Estate, and prevailed upon him not to disinherit his Son *Ned*.

' "*Mem.* Never to tell this to *Ned*, lest he should think hardly of his deceased Father; though he continues to speak ill of me for this very Reason.

' "Prevented a scandalous Law-Suit betwixt my Nephew *Harry* and his Mother, by allowing her under-hand, out of my own Pocket, so much Money yearly as the Dispute was about.

' "Procured a Benefice for a young Divine, who is Sister's Son to the good Man who was my Tutor, and hath been dead twenty Years.

[a] *Title added in 8vo, 12mo*

' "Gave Ten Pounds to poor Mrs. ——, my Friend *H*——'s Widow.

' "*Mem.* To retrench one Dish at my Table, till I have fetched it up again.

' "*Mem.* To repair my House and finish my Gardens, in order to employ poor People after Harvest-time.

' "Ordered *John* to let out Goodman *D*——'s Sheep that were pounded, by Night; but not to let his Fellow-Servants know it.

' "Prevailed upon *M. T.* Esq; not to take the Law of the Farmer's Son for shooting a Partridge, and to give him his Gun again.

' "Paid the Apothecary for curing an old Woman that confessed herself a Witch.

' "Gave away my favourite Dog for biting a Beggar.

' "Made the Minister of the Parish and a *Whig* Justice of one Mind, by putting them upon explaining their Notions to one another.

' "*Mem.* To turn off *Peter* for shooting a Doe while she was eating Acorns out of his Hand.

' "When my Neighbour *John*, who hath often injured me, comes to make his Request to Morrow:

' "*Mem.* I have forgiven him.

' "Laid up my Chariot and sold my Horses, to relieve the Poor in a Scarcity of Corn.

' "In the same Year remitted to my Tenants a Fifth Part of their Rents.

' "As I was airing to Day, I fell into a Thought that warmed my Heart, and shall, I hope, be the better for it as long as I live.

' "*Mem.* To charge my Son in private to erect no Monument for me; but not to put this in my last Will." '

Sed mihi vel tellus optem prius ima dehiscat,
Vel pater omnipotens adigat me fulmine ad umbras,
Pallentes umbras Erebi noctemque profundam,
Ante, pudor, quam te violem aut tua jura resolvam.
Ille meos, primus qui me sibi junxit, amores
Abstulit: ille habeat secum, servetque sepulcro.

                                                    Virg.

I AM obliged to my Friend, the *Love-Casuist*,[2] for the following curious Piece of Antiquity, which I shall communicate to the Publick in his own Words.

Mr. SPECTATOR,

'YOU may remember, that I lately transmitted to you an Account of an ancient Custom, in the Manors of *East* and *West Enborne*, in the County of *Berks* and elsewhere.[3] *If a customary Tenant die, the Widow shall have what the Law calls her* Free Bench *in all his Copy-hold Lands,* dum sola & casta fuerit; *that is,* while she lives single and chaste; *but if she commit Incontinency, she forfeits her Estate: Yet, if she will come into the Court riding a black Ram, with his Tail in her Hand, and say the Words following, the Steward is bound by the Custom, to re-admit her to her Free Bench.*

> Here I am,
> Riding upon a Black Ram,
> Like a Whore as I am;
> And, for my Crincum Crancum,
> Have lost my Bincum Bancum;

---

[1] *Motto.* Virgil, *Aeneid*, 4. 24–29 (altered):
> But first let yawning Earth a Passage rend;
> And let me, through the dark Abyss descend;
> First let avenging Jove, with Flames from high, ⎫
> Drive down this Body, to the nether Sky,   ⎬
> Condemn with Ghosts in endless Night to lye,   ⎭
> Before I break the plighted Faith I gave,   ⎫
> No; he who had my Vows, shall ever have;   ⎬
> For whom I lov'd on Earth, I worship in the Grave. DRYDEN. ⎭

[2] Nos. 591, 602, 605, 614.   [3] No. 614.

And, for my Tail's Game,
Have done this worldly Shame;
Therefore I pray you Mr. Steward, let me have
    my Land again.

'After having informed you that my Lord *Coke* observes, that this is the most frail and slippery Tenure of any in *England*,[1] I shall tell you, since[a] the writing of that Letter, I have, according to my Promise, been at great Pains in searching out the Records of the *Black Ram;* and have at last met with the Proceedings of the Court-Baron,[2] held in that behalf, for the Space of a whole Day. The Record saith that a strict Inquisition having been made into the Right of the Tenants, to their several Estates, by a crafty old Steward, he found that many of the Lands of the Manor, were, by default of the several Widows, forfeited to the Lord, and accordingly would have entered on the Premises: Upon which the good Women demanded the *Benefit of the Ram.* The Steward, after having perused their several Pleas, adjourned the Court to *Barnaby bright,* that they might have Day enough before them.[3]

'The Court being set, and filled with a great Concourse of People, who came from all Parts to see the Solemnity, the first who entered was the Widow *Frontly,* who had made her Appearance in the last Year's Cavalcade. The Register observes, that finding it an easie Pad-Ram,[4] and foreseeing she might have further Occasion for it, she purchased it of the Steward.

'Mrs. *Sarah Dainty,* Relict of Master *John Dainty,* (who was the greatest Prude of the Parish) came next in the Procession. She at first made some Difficulty of taking the Tail in her Hand; and was observed, in pronouncing the Form of Penance, to soften the two most emphatical Words into *Clincum Clancum:* But the Steward took Care to make her speak plain *English,* before he would *let her have her Land again.*

---

[a] since] that since *Fol.*

---

[1] Needless to say, Coke is not among the various authorities cited on the subject of free-bench.

[2] Defined in Cowell's *Law Dictionary* (1708):

Court Baron, *Curia Baronis,* Is a Court that every Lord of a mannor (which in ancient Times were call'd *Barons*) hath within his own Precincts . . . .

[3] St. Barnabas' Day (11 June) was the longest day in the calendar under the Old Style.

[4] A ram for riding.

'The third Widow that was *brought to this worldly Shame*, being mounted upon a vicious Ram, had the Misfortune to be thrown by him; upon which she hoped to be excused from going thro' the rest of the Ceremony: But the Steward being well versed in the Law, observed very wisely upon this Occasion, that the breaking of the Rope does not hinder the Execution of the Criminal.

'The Fourth Lady upon Record was the Widow *Ogle*, a famous Coquette, who had kept half a Score young Fellows off and on for the space of two Years; but having been more kind to her Carter *John*, she was introduced with the Huzza's of all her Lovers about her.

'Mrs. *Sable*, appearing in her Weeds, which were very new and fresh, and of the same Colour with her whimsical *Palfrey*, made a very decent Figure in the Solemnity.

'Another, who had been Summon'd to make her Appearance, was excused by the Steward, as well knowing in his Heart, that the good Squire himself had qualified her for the Ram.

'Mrs. *Quick*, having nothing to object against the Indictment, pleaded her Belly. But it was remembred that she made the same Excuse the Year before. Upon which the Steward observed, that she might so contrive it, as never to do the Service of the Manor.

'The Widow *Fidget*, being cited into Court, insisted that she had done no more since the Death of her Husband, than what she used to do in his Life-time; and withal desired Mr. Steward to consider his own Wife's Case, if he should chance to die before her.

'The next in Order was a Dowager of a very corpulent Make, who would have been excused as not finding any Ram that was able to carry her; upon which the Steward commuted her Punishment, and ordered her to make her Entry upon a black Ox.

'The Widow *Maskwell*, a Woman who had long lived with a most unblemished Character, having turned off her old Chamber-maid in a Pet, was by that Revengeful Creature brought in upon the black Ram, Nine times the same Day.

'Several Widows of the Neighbourhood, being brought upon their Tryal, they showed that they did not hold of the Manor, and were discharged accordingly.

'A pretty young Creature, who closed the Procession, came ambling in, with so bewitching an Air, that the Steward was observed to cast a Sheep's Eye upon her, and married her within a Month after the Death of his Wife.

N.B. 'Mrs. *Touchwood* appeared, according to Summons, but had

nothing laid to her Charge; having lived irreproachably since the Decease of her Husband, who left her a Widow in the Sixty-ninth Year of her Age.

I am, SIR, &c.'

No. 624   *Wednesday, November 24, 1714*[1]

[TICKELL]

*Audire, atque togam jubeo componere, quisquis
Ambitione mala, aut argenti pallet amore,
Quisquis luxuria . . .*

Hor.

MANKIND is divided into two Parts, the Busie and the Idle. The Busie World may be divided into the Virtuous and the Vicious: The Vicious again into the Covetous, the Ambitious and the Sensual. The Idle Part of Mankind are in a State inferior to any one of these. All the other are engaged in the Pursuit of Happiness, though often misplaced, and are therefore more likely to be attentive to such Means, as shall be proposed to them for that End. The Idle, who are neither wise for this World, nor the next, are emphatically called by Dr. *Tillotson, Fools at large.*[2] They propose to themselves no End, but run adrift with every Wind. Advice therefore would be but thrown away upon them, since they would scarce take the Pains to read it. I shall not fatigue any of this worthless Tribe with a long Harangue; but will leave them with this short Saying of *Plato*, that *Labour is preferable to Idleness, as Brightness to Rust.*[3]

[1] *Motto.* Horace, *Satires*, 2. 3. 77–79:

> Sit still and hear, those whom proud thoughts do swell,
> Those that look pale by loving Coin too well;
> Whom Luxury corrupts.   CREECH.

The first two lines formed the motto of *Tatler* 123.
The notes for this essay, with corrections in Addison's hand, are preserved among the Tickell MSS. (Hodgart, pp. 385–6). Like many other numbers (from No. 601 on) published in Oct.–Dec. 1714 they seem to represent materials jotted down by Addison and revised by Tickell.

[2] An allusion to a passage in Tillotson's Sermon i, 'The Wisdom of Being Religious' (*Works*, ed. 1728, i. 27):

> There is a day coming when all these witty fools shall be unhappily undeceived, and not being able to enjoy their delusion any longer shall call themselves fools for ever.

[3] This seems to be a misreading of Plato, *Republic*, 609A. Hughes, in No. 316, calls indolence 'this Rust of the Mind'.

The Pursuits of the active Part of Mankind, are either in the Paths of Religion and Virtue; or, on the other Hand in the Roads to Wealth, Honours or Pleasure. I shall therefore compare the Pursuits of Avarice, Ambition and Sensual Delight, with their opposite Virtues; and shall consider which of these Principles engages Men in a Course of the greatest Labour, Suffering and Assiduity. Most Men, in their cool Reasonings, are willing to allow that a Course of Virtue will in the End be rewarded the most amply; but represent the Way to it as rugged and narrow. If therefore it can be made appear, that Men struggle through as many Troubles to be miserable, as they do to be happy; my Readers may perhaps be persuaded to be Good, when they find they shall lose nothing by it.

First for Avarice. The Miser is more Industrious than the Saint; The Pains of getting, the Fears of losing, and the Inability of enjoying his Wealth, have been the mark of Satyr in all Ages. Were his Repentance upon his Neglect of a good Bargain, his Sorrow for being over-reached, his Hope of improving a Sum, and his Fear of falling into Want, directed to their proper Objects; they would make so many different *Christian* Graces and Virtues. He may apply to himself a great Part of St. *Paul*'s Catalogue of Sufferings, *In journeying often; in Perils of Waters, in Perils of Robbers, in Perils among false Brethren. In Weariness and Painfulness, in Watchings often, in Hunger and Thirst, in Fastings often.*—[1] At how much less Expence might he *lay up to himself Treasures in Heaven*;[2] or if I may, in this place, be allowed to add the saying of a great Philosopher, he may *provide such Possessions, as fear neither Arms, nor Men, nor* Jove *himself*.[3]

In the second Place, if we look upon the Toils of Ambition, in the same Light, as we have considered those of Avarice, we shall readily own that far less trouble is requisite to gain lasting Glory, than the Power and Reputation of a few Years; or in other Words we may with more Ease deserve Honour, than obtain it. The Ambitious Man should remember Cardinal *Wolsey*'s Complaint. 'Had I served God, with the same Application, wherewith I served my King, he would not have forsaken me in my old Age.'[4] The Cardinal here softens his Ambition by the specious Pretence of *serving his King*: Whereas his Words, in the proper Construction,

---

[1] 2 Cor. xi. 26–27.   [2] Matt. vi. 20.
[3] Cf. Ovid, *Metamorphoses*, 15. 871–2.
[4] Cf. Shakespeare, *Henry VIII*, III. ii. 455–7.

imply that if instead of being acted[1] by Ambition, he had been acted by Religion, he should have now felt the Comforts of it, when the whole World turned its back upon him.

Thirdly, Let us compare the Pains of the Sensual, with those of the Virtuous, and see which are heavier in the Balance. It may seem strange, at the first View, that the Men of Pleasure should be advised to change their Course, because they lead a painful Life. Yet when we see them so active and vigilant in quest of Delight; under so many Disquiets, and the Sport of such various Passions, let them answer, as[a] they can, if the Pains, they undergo, do not outweigh their Enjoyments. The Infidelities on the one Part between the two Sexes,[b] and the Caprices on the other, the Debasement of Reason, the Pangs of Expectation, the Disappointments in Possession, the Stings of Remorse, the Vanities, and Vexations attending even the most refined Delights that make up this Business of Life, render it so silly and uncomfortable: That no Man is thought wise till he hath got over it, or happy, but in Proportion as he hath cleared himself from it.

The Sum of all is this, Man is made an active Being. Whether he walks in the Paths of Virtue or Vice, he is sure to meet with many Difficulties to prove[2] his Patience, and excite his Industry. The same, if not greater Labour, is required in the Service of Vice and Folly, as of Virtue and Wisdom: And he hath this easie Choice left him, whether with the Strength he is Master of, he will purchase Happiness or Repentance.

No. 625　　　　　　　　*Friday, November 26, 1714*[3]
[TICKELL]

> . . . *amores*
> *A tenero meditatur Ungui.*
>
> Hor.

THE *Love-Casuist* hath referred to me the following Letter of Queries, with his Answers to each Question, for my Appro-

---

a as] if *Fol.*　　　b between the two Sexes,] *added in 8vo, 12mo*

---

[1] I.e. actuated.
[2] Here, as frequently, in the archaic sense of 'test'.
[3] *Motto.* Horace, *Odes*, 3. 6. 23–24 (altered): 'Plans amours from childhood'.

bation.[1] I have accordingly considered the several Matters therein contained, and hereby confirm and ratifie his Answers, and require the gentle Querist to conform her self thereunto.

SIR,

'I WAS Thirteen the Ninth of *November* last, and must now begin to think of settling my self in the World, and so I would humbly beg your Advice, what I must do with Mr. *Fondle,* who makes his Addresses to me. He is a very pretty Man, and hath the blackest Eyes and whitest Teeth you ever saw. Though he is but a younger Brother, he dresses like a Man of Quality, and no Body comes into a Room like him. I know he hath refused great Offers, and if he cannot Marry me, he will never have any Body else. But my Father hath forbid him the House, because he sent me a Copy of Verses; for he is one of the greatest Wits in Town. My elder Sister, who, with her good Will, would call me *Miss* as long as I live, must be married before me, they say.[2] She tells them, that Mr. *Fondle* makes a Fool of me, and will spoil the Child, as she calls me, like a confident Thing as she is. In short, I am resolved to marry Mr. *Fondle,* if it be but to spite her. But because I would do nothing that is imprudent, I beg of you to give me your Answers to some Questions I will write down, and desire you to get them printed in the SPECTATOR, and I do not doubt but you will give such Advice as, I am sure, I shall follow.

'When Mr. *Fondle* looks upon me for half an Hour together, and calls me *Angel,* is he not in Love?'

Answer, *No.*

'May not I be certain he will be a kind Husband, that has promised me half my Portion in Pin-mony,[3] and to keep me a Coach and Six in the Bargain?'

No.

---

[1] For the Love-Casuist see No. 591.

[2] ' "Miss," in Queen Anne's day, if not used of girls under ten, was a term of reproach, all young unmarried women being described as "Mistress" or "Madam" ' (Austin Dobson, *Steele: Selections,* 1885, p. 461). Lillie (i. 223–4) prints 'A TABLE of Titles and Distinctions for the information of the women of Great-Britain':

'Let all country-gentlewomen, without regard to more or less fortune, be contented to be called and wrote to only by the stile of Mistress.

'Let Madam govern independently in the city, except that the wifes and daughters of all tradesmen indifferently, wheresoever abiding, be admitted on the first demand to list under the said denomination.

'Let no woman accept of the title of Lady, unless her name be added, to prove her right to it.

[*Notes 2 and 3 continued on following page.*

'Whether I, who have been acquainted with him this whole Year almost, am not a better Judge of his Merit, than my Father and Mother, who never heard him talk, but at Table?'

No.

'Whether I am not old enough to chuse for my self?'

No.

'Whether it would not have been rude in me to refuse a Lock of his Hair?'

No.

'Should not I be a very barbarous Creature, if I did not pity a Man that is always sighing for my Sake?'

No.

'Whether you would not advise me to run away with the poor Man?'

No.

'Whether you do not think, that if I won't have him, he won't drown himself?'

No.

'What shall I say to him the next time he asks me if I will marry him?'

No.

The following Letter requires neither Introduction, nor Answer.

Mr. SPECTATOR,

'I WONDER that, in the present Situation of Affairs, you can take Pleasure in writing any thing but News; for, in a Word, who minds any thing else? The Pleasure of increasing in Knowledge, and learning something new every Hour of Life, is the noblest Entertainment of a Rational Creature. I have a very good Ear for a Secret, and am naturally of a communicative Temper; by which Means I am capable of doing you great Services in this way. In order to make my self useful, I am early in the Antichamber, where I thrust my Head into the thick of the Press, and catch the News, at the

'From whence the calling women ladies, without adding the name, will become a banter and scandal.

'Let no woman after the known age of twenty-one presume to admit of her being called miss, unless she can fairly prove she is not out of her sampler.

'Let every common maid-servant be plain Jane, Doll, or Sue, and let the better-born, or higher placed in servitude, be distinguish'd by Mrs. Patience, Mrs. Prue, or Mrs. Abigal.

'Titles flowing from real honour support themselves.'

[3] Cf. No. 295 (vol. iii).

opening of the Door, while it is warm. Sometimes I stand by the Beef-Eaters,[1] and take the Buz as it passes by me. At other times I lay my Ear close to the Wall, and suck in many a valuable Whisper, as it runs in a streight Line from Corner to Corner. When I am weary with standing, I repair to one of the neighbouring Coffee-houses, where I sit sometimes for a whole Day, and have the News, as it comes from Court, fresh and fresh.[2] In short Sir, I spare no pains to know how the World goes. A Piece of News loses its Flavour when it hath been an Hour in the Air. I love, if I may so speak, to have it fresh from the Tree; and to convey it to my Friends before it is faded. Accordingly my Expences in Coach-hire make no small Article; which you may believe, when I assure you, that I post away from Coffee-house to Coffee-house, and forestall the *Evening-Post*[3] by two Hours. There is a certain Gentleman, who hath given me the slip twice or thrice, and hath been before-hand with me at *Child*'s. But I have played him a Trick. I have purchased a Pair of the best Coach-horses I could buy for Money, and now let him out-strip me if he can. Once more, Mr. SPECTATOR, let me advise you to deal in News. You may depend upon my Assistance. But I must break off abruptly, for I have twenty Letters to write.

Yours, in haste,

Tho. Quid-nunc.'[4]

[1] Yeomen of the Guard; also Warders of the Tower.

[2] For this reduplication cf. *OED*. The phrase is also used in No. 452 (iv. 92).

[3] There was a newspaper with this title published in 1706 (*CBEL*, ii. 710), but the allusion here is more likely to the evening mail. 'For the Conveniency of those who live far from the *Post-Office*, there are particular *Post-houses* appointed to take in the Letters till 9 of the Clock at Night, to be sent from thence in due time to the General Post-Office' (Miege, 1707, p. 249).

[4] 'One who is constantly asking, "What now? What's the news?"; hence, an inquisitive person; a gossip, a newsmonger' (*OED*). The earliest example in *OED* is from *Tatler* 10: 'The Insignificancy of my Manners to the rest of the World makes the Laughers call me a *Quid nunc*, a Phrase I shall never enquire what they mean by.'

No. 626   *Monday, November 29, 1714*[1]
[GROVE]

. . . Dulcique animos novitate tenebo.

Ov. Met. *l.* I.

I HAVE seen a little Work of a learned Man, consisting of extemporary Speculations, which owed their Birth to the most trifling Occurrences of Life. His usual Method was, to write down any sudden Start of Thought which arose in his Mind upon the Sight of an odd Gesticulation in a Man, any whimsical Mimickry of Reason in a Beast, or whatever appeared remarkable in any Object of the visible Creation. He was able to moralize upon a Snuff-box, would flourish eloquently upon a Tucker or a Pair of Ruffles, and draw practical Inferences from a full-bottomed Perriwig.[2] This I thought fit to mention, by way of Excuse, for my ingenious Correspondent, who hath introduced the following Letter by an Image which, I will beg Leave to tell him, is too ridiculous in so serious and noble a Speculation.

Mr. SPECTATOR,

'WHEN I have seen young Puss playing her wanton Gambols, and with a thousand antick Shapes express her own Gaiety at the same time that she moved mine, while the old Grannum hath sat by with a most exemplary Gravity, unmoved at all that past; it hath made me reflect what should be the Occasion of Humours so opposite in two Creatures, between whom there was no visible Difference but that of Age; and I have been able to resolve it into nothing else but *the Force of Novelty*.[a]

[b]'In every Species of Creatures, those that have been least Time in the World, appear best pleased with their Condition; for, besides that to a new Comer the World hath a Freshness on it that strikes the Sense after a most agreeable Manner, *Being* it self, unattended with any great Variety of Enjoyments, excites a Sensation of Pleasure. But as Age advances, every thing seems to wither, the Senses are disgusted with their old Entertainments, and Existence

---

[a] *Italics added in 8vo and 12mo*   [b] *No paragraph in Fol.*

---

[1] *Motto.* Ovid, *Metamorphoses*, 4. 284: With sweet novelty your taste I'll please.
EUSDEN.

[2] Morley found an allusion here to the *Meditations* of Robert Boyle.

turns flat and insipid. We may see this exemplified in Mankind: The Child, let him be free from Pain, and gratified in his Change of Toys, is diverted with the smallest Trifle.[1] Nothing disturbs the Mirth of the Boy but a little Punishment or Confinement. The Youth must have more violent Pleasures to employ his Time; the Man loves the Hurry of an active Life, devoted to the Pursuits of Wealth or Ambition; and lastly, old Age, having lost its Capacity for these Avocations, becomes its own insupportable Burthen. This Variety may in part be accounted for by the Vivacity and Decay of the Faculties; but I believe is chiefly owing to this, That the longer we have been in Possession of Being, the less sensible is the Gust we have of it, and the more it requires of adventitious Amusements to relieve us from the Satiety and Weariness it brings along with it.

[a]'And as Novelty is of a very powerful, so of a most extensive Influence. Moralists have long since observed it to be the Source of Admiration, which lessens in proportion to our Familiarity with Objects, and upon a thorough Acquaintance is utterly extinguished.[2] But I think it hath not been so commonly remarked, that all the other Passions depend considerably on the same Circumstance. What is it but Novelty that awakens Desire, enhances Delight, kindles Anger, provokes Envy, inspires Horror? To this Cause we must ascribe it, that Love languishes with Fruition, and Friendship it self is recommended by Intervals of Absence: Hence Monsters, by use, are beheld without loathing, and the most enchanting Beauty without Rapture.[3] That Emotion of the Spirits in which Passion consists, is usually the Effect of Surprize, and as long as it continues, heightens the agreeable or disagreeable Qualities of its Object; but as this Emotion ceases (and it ceases with the Novelty) things appear in another Light, and affect[b] us even less than might be expected from their proper Energy, for having moved us too much before.

'It may not be a useless Enquiry, how far the Love of Novelty is the unavoidable Growth of Nature, and in what Respects it is peculiarly adapted to the present State. To me it seems impossible, that a reasonable Creature should rest absolutely satisfied in any

---

[a] *No paragraph in Fol.* [b] affect] *12mo*; affects *Fol., 8vo*

[1] Cf. Pope, *Essay on Man*, ii. 275–82.
[2] See Clarence D. Thorpe, 'Addison and some of his predecessors on "novelty" ', *PMLA*, lii (1937), 1114–29.
[3] Cf. *Essay on Man*, ii. 217–20.

Acquisitions whatever, without endeavouring farther; for after its highest Improvements, the Mind hath an Idea of an Infinity of things still behind worth knowing, to the Knowledge of which therefore it cannot be indifferent; as by climbing up a Hill in the midst of a wide Plain, a Man hath his Prospect enlarged, and, together with that, the Bounds of his Desires. Upon this Account, I cannot think he detracts from the State of the Blessed, who conceives them to be perpetually employed in fresh Searches into Nature, and to Eternity advancing into the fathomless Depths of the Divine Perfections. In this Thought there is nothing but what doth Honour to these glorified Spirits; provided still it be remembered, that their Desire of More proceeds not from their disrelishing what they possess; and the Pleasure of a new Enjoyment is not with them measured by its Novelty, (which is a thing meerly foreign and accidental) but by its real intrinsick Value. After an Acquaintance of many thousand Years with the Works of God, the Beauty and Magnificence of the Creation fills them with the same pleasing Wonder and profound Awe, which *Adam* felt himself seized with as he first opened his Eyes upon this glorious Scene. Truth captivates with unborrow'd Charms, and whatever hath once given Satisfaction will always do it: In all which they have manifestly the Advantage of us, who are so much governed by sickly and changeable Appetites, that we can with the greatest Coldness behold the stupendous Displays of Omnipotence, and be in Transports at the puny Essays of humane Skill; throw aside Speculations of the sublimest Nature and vastest Importance into some obscure Corner of the Mind, to make Room for new Notions of no Consequence at all; are even tired of Health, because not enlivened with alternate Pain, and prefer the first Reading of an indifferent Author, to the second or third Perusal of one whose Merit and Reputation are established.

'Our being thus formed serves many useful Purposes in the present State. It contributes not a little to the Advancement of Learning; for, as *Cicero* takes Notice, That which makes Men willing to undergo the Fatigues of Philosophical Disquisitions, is not so much the Greatness of Objects as their Novelty.[1] It is not enough that there is Field and Game for the Chace, and that the Understanding is prompted with a restless Thirst of Knowledge, effectually to rouse the Soul, sunk into a State of Sloth and Indolence;

[1] This has not been located.

it is also necessary that there be an uncommon Pleasure annex'd to the first Appearance of Truth in the Mind. This Pleasure being requisite for the Time it lasts, but transient, it hereby comes to pass that the Mind grows into an Indifference to its former Notions, and passes on after new Discoveries, in hope of repeating the Delight. It is with Knowledge as with Wealth, the Pleasure of which lies more in making endless Additions, than in taking a Review of our old Store. There are some Inconveniences that follow this Temper, if not guarded against, particularly this, that through a too great Eagerness of something new, we are many times impatient of staying long enough upon a Question that requires some time to resolve it, or, which is worse, perswade ourselves that we are Masters of the Subject before we are so, only to be at the Liberty of going upon a fresh Scent; in Mr. *Lock*'s Words, *We see a little, presume a great deal, and so jump to the Conclusion.*[1]

ᵃ'A farther Advantage of our Inclination for Novelty, as at present circumstantiated, is, that it annihilates all the boasted Distinctions among Mankind. Look not up with Envy to those above thee. Sounding Titles, stately Buildings, fine Gardens, gilded Chariots, rich Equipages, what are they? They dazzle every one but the Possessor: To him that is accustomed to them they are cheap and regardlessᵇ Things: They supply him not with brighter Images, or more sublime Satisfactions than the plain Man may have, whose small Estate will just enable him to support the Charge of a simple unencumber'd Life. He enters heedless into his Rooms of State, as you or I do under our poor Sheds. The noble Paintings and costly Furniture are lost on him; he sees them not: As how can it be otherwise, when, by Custom, a Fabrick infinitely more grand and finished, that of the Universe, stands unobserved by the Inhabitants, and the everlasting Lamps of Heaven are lighted up in vain, for any Notice that Mortals take of them? Thanks to indulgent Nature, which not only placed her Children originally upon a Level, but still, by the Strength of this Principle, in a great measure preserves it, in spite of all the Care of Man, to introduce artificial Distinctions.

ᵃ *No paragraph in Fol.*   ᵇ cheap and regardless] *12mo*; cheap regardless *Fol., 8vo*

---

[1] This quotation is cited in *OED* solely on the authority of the *Spectator*. I have not traced it in Locke.

'To add no more, Is not this Fondness for Novelty, which makes us out of Conceit with all we already have, a convincing Proof of a future State? Either Man was made in vain, or this is not the only World he was made for: For there cannot be a greater Instance of Vanity, than that to which Man is liable, to be deluded from the Cradle to the Grave[1] with fleeting Shadows of Happiness. His Pleasures, and those not considerable neither, die in the Possession, and fresh Enjoyments do not rise fast enough to fill up half his Life with Satisfaction. When I see Persons sick of themselves any longer than they are called away by something that is of Force to chain down the present Thought; when I see them hurry from Country to Town, and then from the Town back again into the Country, continually shifting Postures, and placing Life in all the different Lights they can think of; *Surely*, say I to my self, *Life is vain, and the Man beyond Expression stupid or prejudic'd, who from the Vanity of Life cannot gather, He is designed for Immortality.*'[2]

No. 627   *Wednesday, December 1, 1714*[3]

[TICKELL]

Tantum inter densas umbrosa cacumina fagos
Assidue veniebat; ibi hæc incondita solus
Montibus et Sylvis studio jactabat inani.
         Virg.

THE following Account, which came to my Hands some time ago, may be no disagreeable Entertainment to such of my Readers, as have tender Hearts and nothing to do.

---

[1] The earliest example of this phrase in *OED* is from *Tatler* 52, paragraph 4.

[2] Johnson thought this essay 'one of the finest pieces in the English language' (Boswell, iii. 33). Among the Tickell papers is a letter dated 4 Dec. 1714 addressed to Mr. Spectator commenting on this number and demonstrating that none of the professions can satisfy this desire for novelty.

[3] *Motto.* Virgil, *Eclogues*, 2. 3–5:
     And underneath the Beechen Shade, alone,
     Thus to the Woods and Mountains made his moan. DRYDEN.

In No. 365 (vol. iii) Zelinda was the name of the lady courted unsuccessfully by the Yorkshire gentleman.

Robert Lloyd's poem, 'An Imitation from the Spectator', is based upon this letter (Robert Anderson, *Select British Poets and Translations* (1794), iv. 695). It begins: 'A month hath roll'd its lazy hours away.'

'*Mr.* SPECTATOR,

'A Friend of mine died of a Feaver last Week, which he caught by walking too late in a dewy Evening amongst his Reapers. I must inform you that his greatest Pleasure was in Husbandry and Gardening. He had some Humours which seemed inconsistent with that good Sense he was otherwise Master of. His Uneasiness in the Company of Women was very remarkable in a Man of such perfect Good-breeding; and his avoiding one particular Walk in his Garden, where he had used to pass the greatest Part of his Time, raised abundance of idle Conjectures in the Village where he lived. Upon looking over his Papers we found out the Reason, which he never intimated to his nearest Friends. He was, it seems, a passionate Lover in his Youth, of which a large Parcel of Letters he left behind him are a Witness. I send you a Copy of the last he ever wrote upon that Subject, by which you will find that he concealed the true Name of his Mistress under that of *Zelinda*.'

[a]*A Long Month's Absence would be insupportable to me, if the Business I am employed in were not for the Service of my* Zelinda, *and of such a Nature as to place her every Moment in my Mind. I have furnished the House exactly according to your Fancy, or, if you please, my own; for I have long since learned to like nothing but what you do. The Apartment designed for your Use is so exact a Copy of that which you live in, that I often think my self in your House when I step into it, but sigh when I find it without its proper Inhabitant. You will have the most delicious Prospect from your Closet-Window that* England *affords; I am sure I should think it so, if the Landskip that shows such Variety, did not at the same Time suggest to me the Greatness of the Space that lies between us.*

The Gardens are laid out very beautifully; I have dressed up every Hedge in Wood-bines, sprinkled Bowers and Arbours in every Corner, and made a little Paradise round me; yet I am still like the first Man in his Solitude, but half blest without a Partner in my Happiness. I have directed one Walk to be made for two Persons, where I promise ten thousand Satisfactions to my self in your Conversation. I already take my Evening's Turn in it, and have worn a Path upon the Edge of this little Alley, while I soothed my self with the Thought of your walking by my Side. I have held many imaginary Discourses with you in this Retirement; and when I have been weary, have sate down with you in the midst of a Row of Jessamine. The many Expressions

---

[a] *The letter is in italics in 8vo and 12mo; in Fol. it is in roman type with double inverted commas.*

of Joy and Rapture I use in these silent Conversations, have made me for some Time the Talk of the Parish; but a neighbouring young Fellow, who makes Love to the Farmer's Daughter, hath found me out, and made my Case known to the whole Neighbourhood.

In planting of the Fruit-Trees I have not forgot the Peach you are so fond of. I have made a Walk of Elms along the River Side, and intend to sow all the Place about it with Cowslips, which I hope you will like as well as that I have heard you talk of by your Father's House in the Country.

Oh! Zelinda, What a Scheme of Delight have I drawn up in my Imagination! What Day-dreams do I indulge my self in! When will the Six Weeks be at an End, that lie between me and my promised Happiness?

How could you break off so abruptly in your last, and tell me you must go and dress for the Play? If you loved as I do, you would find no more Company in a Crowd, than I have in my Solitude.

I am, &c.ᵃ

'On the back of this Letter is written, in the Hand of the Deceased, the following Piece of History.'

Mem. Having waited a whole Week for an Answer to this Letter, I hurried to Town, where I found the perfidious Creature married to my Rival. I will bear it as becomes a Man, and endeavour to find out Happiness for my self in that Retirement, which I had prepared in vain for a false ungrateful Woman.

I am, &c.ᵇ

No. 628
[TICKELL]
Friday, December 3, 1714[1]

Labitur et labetur in omne volubilis ævum.

Hor.

Mr. SPECTATOR,

'THERE are none of your Speculations which please me more than those upon Infinitude and Eternity.[2] You have already

---

ᵃ I am, &c. *om. Fol.*   ᵇ I am, &c. *om. Fol.*

---

[1] *Motto.* Horace, *Epistles*, 1. 2. 43: Still that rouls on and will for ever roul.
[2] Nos. 565, 571, 580 (vol. iv), and 590.

considered that Part of Eternity which is past, and I wish you would give us your Thoughts upon that which is to come.

'Your Readers will perhaps receive greater Pleasure from this View of Eternity than the former, since we have every one of us a Concern in that which is to come, whereas a Speculation on that which is past is rather curious than useful.

'Besides, we can easily conceive it possible for successive Duration never to have an End; tho' as you have justly observed, that Eternity which never had a Beginning is altogether incomprehensible:[1] That is, we can conceive an Eternal Duration which *may be*, though we cannot an Eternal Duration which *hath been;* or, if I may use the Philosophical Terms, we may apprehend a *Potential* though not an *Actual* Eternity.

'This Notion of a future Eternity, which is natural to the Mind of Man, is an unanswerable Argument that he is a Being designed for it; especially if we consider that he is capable of being Virtuous or Vicious here; that he hath Faculties improvable to all Eternity, and by a proper or wrong Employment of them may be happy or miserable throughout that infinite Duration. Our Idea indeed of this Eternity is not of an adequate or fixed Nature, but is perpetually growing and enlarging it self toward the Object, which is too big for human Comprehension. As we are now in the Beginnings of Existence, so shall we always appear to our selves as if we were for ever entring upon it. After a Million or two of Centuries, some considerable Things, already past, may slip out of our Memory; which, if it be not strengthened in a wonderful Manner, may possibly forget that ever there was a Sun or Planets. And yet, notwithstanding the long Race that we shall then have run, we shall still imagine our selves just starting from the Goal, and find no Proportion between that Space which we know had a Beginning, and what we are sure will never have an End.

'But I shall leave this Subject to your Management, and question not but you will throw it into such Lights as shall at once improve and entertain your Reader.

'I have enclos'd sent you a Translation of the Speech of *Cato* on this Occasion, which hath accidentally fallen into my Hands, and which for Conciseness, Purity, and Elegance of Phrase cannot be sufficiently admired.[2]

[1] No. 590 (v. 18–19).
[2] Addison's play; this is the entire first scene of Act V. The Latin translation has

Act. V. Sc. I.

CATO *solus*, &c.

SIC, sic se habere rem necesse prorsus est,
Ratione vincis, do lubens manus, Plato.
Quid enim dedisset, Quæ dedit frustra nihil,
Æternitatis insitam cupidinem
Natura? Quorsum hæc dulcis Expectatio;
Vitæque non explenda melioris sitis?
Quid vult sibi aliud iste redeundi in nihil
Horror, sub imis quemque agens precordiis?
Cur territa in se refugit anima, cur tremit
Attonita, quoties, morte ne pereat, timet?
Particula nempe est cuique nascenti indita
Divinior; quæ corpus incolens agit;
Hominique succinit, tua est Æternitas.
Æternitas! O lubricum nimis aspici,
Mixtumque dulci Gaudium formidine.

Quæ demigrabitur alia hinc in corpora?
Quæ Terra mox incognita? Quis orbis novus
Manet incollendus? Quanta erit mutatio?
Hæc intuenti spatia mihi quaquà patent
Immensa: Sed caliginosa nox premit;
Nec luce clarâ vult videri singula.
Figendus hìc pes; certa sunt hæc hactenus:

been attributed to Bishop Atterbury (*Biographia Britannica*, 2nd ed., 1778, ed. Kippis, i. 50) and one Jenison (*Gent. Mag.*, June 1782, lii. 289), but it is almost certainly by Henry Bland.

This beautiful translation, which fame and Dr. Kippis have attributed to Bishop Atterbury (and which on that authority and on oral tradition in the University of Oxford, I had printed as his in the 'Select Collection of Poems,' vol. V, p. 6), I afterwards found reason (vol. VIII, p. 302) to ascribe to Dr. Henry Bland, head master of Eton school, Provost of the college there, and Dean of Durham (to whom it is also without hesitation ascribed by the last and best Biographer of Addison); and have since had the honour of being assured by Mr. Walpole 'that it was the work of Bland; and that he has more than once heard his father Sir Robert Walpole say, that it was he himself who gave that translation to Mr. Addison, who was extremely surprised at the fidelity and beauty of it' (Nichols).

This note of Nichols had also appeared in *Gent. Mag.*, July 1782, lii. 335–6. Dr. Henry Bland was admitted from Eton to King's College in 1695, was rector of Harpley (Norfolk) from 1715 until his death in 1746, and was appointed headmaster of Eton in 1719. At about the time of the publication of this translation he may have been headmaster of Doncaster School. He was installed Dean of Durham in 1727 and died on 24 May 1746. See Nichols, *Literary Anecdotes*, iii. 661–2. His name is among the subscribers to Lillie's *Letters* in 1725.

Si quod gubernet Numen Humanum genus,
(At, quod gubernet, esse clamant omnia)
Virtute non gaudere certé non potest:
Nec esse non Beata, quâ gaudet, potest.
Sed quâ Beata sede? Quove in tempore?
Hæc quanta quanta terra, tota est Cæsaris.
Quid dubius hæret animus usque adeo? Brevi
Hic nodum hic omnem expediet. Arma en induor
                              [Ensi manum admovens,

In utramque partem facta; quæque vim inferant,
Et quæ propulsent! Dextera intentat necem;
Vitam sinistra: Vulnus hæc dabit manus;
Altera medelam vulneris: Hic ad exitum
Deducet, ictu simplici; hæc vetant mori.
Secura ridet anima mucronis minas,
Ensesque strictos, interire nescia.
Extinguet ætas sidera diuturnior:
Ætate languens ipse Sol, obscurius
Emittet Orbi consenescenti jubar:
Natura et ipsa sentiet quondam vices
Ætatis, annis ipsa deficiet gravis:
At tibi juventus, at tibi immortalitas,
Tibi parta Divûm est vita. Periment mutuis
Elementa sese, et interibunt ictibus:
Tu permanebis sola semper integra,
Tu cuncta rerum quassa, cuncta naufraga,
Jam portu in ipso tuta, contemplabere.
Compage ruptâ, corruent in se invicem,
Orbesque fractis ingerentur orbibus;
Illæsa tu sedebis extra Fragmina.

Act V. Scene I.

CATO alone, &c.

IT must be so—*Plato*, thou reason'st well—
Else whence this pleasing Hope, this fond Desire,
This Longing after Immortality?
Or whence this secret Dread, and inward Horror,
Of falling into Nought? Why shrinks the Soul
Back on herself, and startles at Destruction?

'Tis the Divinity that stirs within us;
'Tis Heav'n itself, that points out an Hereafter,
And intimates Eternity to Man.
Eternity! thou pleasing, dreadful, Thought!

Through what Variety of untry'd Being,
Through what new Scenes and Changes must we pass![a]
The wide, th' unbounded Prospect, lies before me;
But Shadows, Clouds, and Darkness rest upon it.
Here will I hold. If there's a Pow'r above us,
(And that there is all Nature cries aloud
Through all her Works) He must delight in Virtue;
And that which he delights in, must be happy.
But when! or where!—This World was made for *Cæsar*.
I'm weary of Conjectures—This must end 'em.
[*Laying his Hand on his Sword.*

Thus am I doubly arm'd: my Death and Life,
My Bane and Antidote are both before me:
This in a Moment brings me to an End;
But this informs me I shall never die.
The Soul, secur'd in her Existence, smiles
At the drawn Dagger, and defies its Point.
The Stars shall fade away, the Sun himself
Grow dim with Age, and Nature sink in Years;
But thou shalt flourish in immortal Youth,
Unhurt amidst the War of Elements,
The Wrecks of Matter, and the Crush of Worlds.

No. 629   *Monday, December 6, 1714*[1]
[TICKELL]

. . . Experiar quid concedatur in illos,
Quorum Flaminia tegitur cinis atque Latinâ.
Juv.

NEXT to the People who want a Place, there are none to be
pitied more than those who are solicited for one. A plain

[a] *In Fol. these two lines were placed with the preceding paragraph and a new paragraph begun at the following line.*   [For note 1 see opposite page.

Answer, with a Denial in it, is looked upon as Pride, and a civil Answer as a Promise.

Nothing is more ridiculous than the Pretensions of People upon these Occasions. Every thing a Man hath suffered, whilst his Enemies were in play, was certainly brought about by the Malice of the opposite Party. A bad Cause would not have been lost, if such an one had not been upon the Bench; nor a profligate Youth disinherited, if he had not got drunk every Night by toasting an outed Ministry. I remember a Tory, who having been fined in a Court of Justice for a Prank that deserved the Pillory, desired upon the Merit of it to be made a Justice of Peace when his Friends came into Power; and shall never forget a Whig Criminal, who, upon being indicted for a Rape, told his Friends, *You see what a Man suffers for sticking to his Principles.*

The Truth of it is, the Sufferings of a Man in a Party are of a very doubtful Nature. When they are such as have promoted a good Cause, and fallen upon a Man undeservedly, they have a Right to be heard and recompensed beyond any other Pretensions. But when they rise out of Rashness or Indiscretion, and the Pursuit of such Measures, as have rather ruined, than promoted the Interest they aim at, (which hath always been the Case of many great Sufferers) they only serve to recommend them to the Children of Violence or Folly.

I have by me a Bundle of Memorials presented by several Cavaliers upon the Restauration of K. *Charles* II. which may serve, as so many[a] Instances, to our present Purpose.

Among several Persons and Pretensions recorded by my Author, he mentions one of a very great Estate, who, for having roasted an Ox whole, and distributed a Hogshead upon K. *Charles*'s Birth Day, desired to be provided for, as his Majesty in his great Wisdom shall think fit.

Another put in to be Prince *Henry*'s Governour, for having dared to drink his Health in the worst of Times.[1]

A Third petitioned for a Colonel's Commission, for having

---

[a] as so many] as to many *Fol.*

---

[1] Prince Henry, Duke of Gloucester, the third son of Charles I, was born in 1640 and died in Sept. 1660.

---

[1] *Motto.* Juvenal, *Satires,* 1. 170–1: I shall try to see that what I may write is against those whose ashes are covered by the Flaminian and Latin ways.

cursed *Oliver Cromwell*, the Day before his Death, on a publick Bowling-Green.

But the most whimsical Petition I have met with is that of *B. B.* Esq; who desired the Honour of Knighthood, for having Cuckolded Sir *T. W.* a notorious *Roundhead*.

There is likewise the Petition of one, who, having let his Beard grow from the Martyrdom of K. *Charles* the First, till the Restauration of K. *Charles* the Second, desired, in Consideration thereof, to be made a Privy-Counsellor.

I must not omit a Memorial setting forth, that the Memorialist had, with great dispatch, carried a Letter from a certain Lord to a certain Lord, wherein, as it afterwards appeared, Measures were concerted for the Restauration, and without which he verily believes that happy Revolution had never been effected; who thereupon humbly prays to be made Post-Master-General.

A certain Gentleman, who seems to write with a great deal of Spirit, and uses the Words *Gallantry* and *Gentleman like* very often in his Petition, begs, that (in Consideration of his having worn his Hat for ten Years past in the Loyal Cavalier Cock, to his great Danger and Detriment) he may be made a Captain of the Guards.

I shall close my Account of this Collection of Memorials, with the Copy of one Petition at Length, which I recommend to my Reader as a very valuable Piece.

The Petition of *E.H.* Esq; humbly Sheweth,

'THAT your Petitioners Father's Brother's Uncle, Colonel *W.H.* lost the Third Finger of his Left Hand at *Edge-hill* Fight.[1]

'That your Petitioner, notwithstanding the smallness of his Fortune, (he being a younger Brother) always kept Hospitality, and drank Confusion to the Roundheads in half a Score Bumpers every *Sunday* in the Year, as several honest Gentlemen (whose Names are under-written) are ready to testifie.

'That your Petitioner is remarkable in his Country for having dared to treat Sir *P.P.* a cursed Sequestrator,[2] and three Members of the Assembly of Divines,[3] with Brawn and Minced Pies[4] upon *New-Year*'s Day.

[1] For the battle of Edgehill (1642) cf. No. 299 (iii. 70).
[2] Here the reference would be to the depriving the clergy of benefices under the Commonwealth.
[3] The Westminster Assembly, appointed by the Long Parliament in 1643, to aid in settling the government and liturgy of the Church of England.

[*For note 4 see opposite page.*

'That your said humble Petitioner hath been five times imprisoned in five several County-Goals, for having been a Ringleader in five different Riots; into which his Zeal for the Royal Cause hurried him, when Men of greater Estates had not the Courage to rise.

'That he, the said *E.H.* hath had six Duels and four and twenty Boxing-Matches in Defence of His Majesty's Title; and that he received such a Blow upon the Head at a Bonfire in *Stratford* upon *Avon*, as he hath been never the better for from that Day to this.

'That your Petitioner hath been so far from improving his Fortune, in the late damnable times, that he verily believes, and hath good Reason to imagine, that if he had been Master of an Estate, he had infallibly been plundered and sequestred.

'Your Petitioner, in Consideration of his said Merits and Sufferings, humbly requests that he may have the Place of Receiver of the Taxes, Collector of the Customs, Clerk of the Peace, Deputy Lieutenant, or whatsoever else he shall be thought qualified for.

And your Petitioner shall ever pray, *&c.*'

---

[4] The symbols of anti-puritan feasting after the overthrow of the Commonwealth. Cf. Butler's *Hudibras*, I. i. 223–6:

> Rather than fail, they will defie
> That which they love most tenderly,
> Quarrel with *minc'd Pies*, and disparage
> Their best and dearest friend, *Plumb-porridge*.

This humorous account of the petitions to Charles II from persons who had suffered in the Royalist cause during the Civil Wars is obviously pointed toward the contemporary situation after the accession of George I, when the Whig leaders, out of place since 1710, were being besieged with requests for favours from those who had been neglected during the past four years. Among the Tickell MSS. is a 'Letter to J. A——n Esq', protesting against the 'banter' of this number of the *Spectator*:

> How Barbarous—How cruel—& how unworthy of M^r Ad——n is it, to insult over men who are unfortunate enough allready in being neglected by those, who promis'd Them every thing at a time when they had nothing to give? What can any one think of a paper, coming from so considerable a man at Court, but that it is a declaration dictated by some great men, in order to free them from their *place Dunns* all at once?

No. 630   *Wednesday, December 8, 1714*[1]

Favete linguis . . . .

Hor.

HAVING no spare Time to write any thing of my own, or to correct what is sent me by others, I have thought fit to publish the following Letters.

SIR,   *Oxford, Novemb.* 22.

'IF you would be so kind to me, as to suspend that Satisfaction, which the Learned World must receive in reading one of your Speculations, by publishing this Endeavour, you will very much oblige and improve one, who has the Boldness to hope, that he may be admitted into the Number of your Correspondents.

'I have often wondered to hear Men of good Sense and good Nature profess a Dislike to Musick, when, at the same time, they do not scruple to own, that it has the most agreeable and improving Influences over their Minds: It seems to me an unhappy Contradiction, that those Persons should have an Indifference for an Art, which raises in them such a Variety of sublime Pleasures.

'However, though some few, by their own or the unreasonable Prejudices of others, may be led into a Distaste for those Musical Societies which are erected merely for Entertainment, yet sure I may venture to say, that no one can have the least Reason for Disaffection to that solemn kind of Melody which consists of the Praises of our Creator.

'You have, I presume, already prevented me in an Argument upon this Occasion, (which some Divines have successfully advanced upon a much greater) that Musical Sacrifice and Adoration has claimed a Place in the Laws and Customs of the most different Nations: As the *Grecians* and *Romans* of the Prophane, the *Jews* and *Christians* of the Sacred World did as unanimously agree in this, as they disagreed in all other Parts of their Œconomy.

'I know there are not wanting some who are of Opinion, that the pompous kind of Musick which is in Use in foreign Churches is the most excellent, as it most affects our Senses. But I am swayed by

---

[1] *Motto.* Horace, *Odes,* 3. 1. 2: Be silent.
This was used as the motto of *Tatler* 264.
No authorship is assigned for this number in the Tickell MS. The two letters are probably genuine contributions, with an introductory sentence by Tickell.

my Judgment to the Modesty which is observed in the musical Part of our Devotions. Methinks there is something very laudable in the Custom of a *Voluntary* before the First Lesson; by this we are supposed to be prepared for the Admission of those Divine Truths, which we are shortly to receive. We are then to cast all worldly Regards from off our Hearts, all Tumults within are then becalmed, and there should be nothing near the Soul but Peace and Tranquility. So that in this short Office of Praise, the Man is raised above himself, and is almost lost already amidst the Joys of Futurity.

'I have heard some nice Observers frequently commend the Polity of our Church in this Particular, that it leads us on by such easie and regular Methods, that we are perfectly deceived into Piety. When the Spirits begin to languish (as they too often do) with a constant Series of Petitions, she takes care to allow them a pious Respite, and relieves them with the Raptures of an Anthem. Nor can we doubt that the sublimest Poetry, softened in the most moving Strains of Musick, can ever fail of humbling or exalting the Soul to any Pitch of Devotion. Who can hear the Terrors of the Lord of Hosts described in the most expressive Melody without being awed into a Veneration? or who can hear the kind and endearing Attributes of a merciful Father, and not be softened into Love towards him?

'As the rising and sinking of the Passions, the casting soft or noble Hints into the Soul, is the natural Privilege of Musick in general, so more particularly of that kind which is employed at the Altar. Those Impressions which it leaves upon the Spirits are more deep and lasting, as the Grounds from which it receives its Authority are founded more upon Reason. It diffuses a Calmness all around us, it makes us drop all those vain or immodest Thoughts which would be an hindrance to us in the Performance of that great Duty of Thanksgiving, which, as we are informed by our Almighty Benefactor, is the most acceptable Return which can be made for those infinite Stores of Blessings which he daily condescends to pour down upon his Creatures.[1] When we make Use of this pathetical Method of addressing our selves to him, we can scarce contain from Raptures! The Heart is warmed with a Sublimity of Goodness! We are all Piety and all Love!

[1] This may be, as Nichols suggests, a reference to the Proclamation, issued shortly before the publication of this paper, announcing a thanksgiving to be observed on 20 January 1715 for King George's accession. The proclamation is dated from St. James's on 6 Dec. (*Political State*, viii. 523).

'How do the Blessed Spirits rejoice and wonder to behold un-thinking Man prostrating his Soul to his dread Sovereign in such a Warmth of Piety as they themselves might not be ashamed of!

'I shall close these Reflections with a Passage taken out of the Third Book of *Milton*'s *Paradise Lost*, where those harmonious Beings are thus nobly described.'

> *Then Crown'd again their Gold'n Harps they took,*
> *Harps ever tun'd, that glittering by their side*
> *Like Quivers hung, and with Preamble sweet*
> *Of Charming Symphony they introduce*
> *The Sacred Song, and waken Raptures high;*
> *No one exempt, no Voice but well could join*
> *Melodious part, such Concord is in Heav'n.*[1]

Mr. SPECTATOR,

'THE Town cannot be unacquainted, that in divers Parts of it there are vociferous Setts of Men who are called *Rattling Clubs*; but what shocks me most is, they have now the Front to invade the Church and institute these Societies there, as a Clan of them have in late times done, to such a degree of Insolence, as has given the Partition where they reside in a Church near one of the City Gates, the Denomination of the *Rattling Pew*. These gay Fellows, from humble Lay Professions, set up for Criticks without any Tincture of Letters or Reading, and have the Vanity to think they can lay hold of something from the Parson, which may be formed into Ridicule.

'It is needless to observe, that the Gentlemen who every *Sunday* have the hard Province of Instructing these Wretches in a way they are in no present Disposition to take, have a fixt Character for Learning and Eloquence, not to be tainted by the weak Efforts of this Contemptible Part of their Audiences. Whether the Pulpit is taken by these Gentlemen, or any Strangers their Friends, the way of the Club is this: If any Sentiments are delivered too Sublime for their Conceptions,[a] if any uncommon Topick is entered on, or one in use new modified with the finest Judgment and Dexterity, or any controverted Point be never so elegantly handled, in short,

---

[a] their Conceptions,] their shallow Conceptions, *Fol.*

---

[1] *Paradise Lost*, iii. 365-71 (369-70: Their sacred Song, and waken raptures high; / No voice exempt . . .).

whatever surpasses the narrow Limits of their Theology, or is not suited to their Taste, they are all immediately upon their Watch, fixing their Eyes upon each other, with as much Warmth as our Gladiators of *Hockley in the Hole*,[1] and waiting like them for a Hit; if one touches, all take Fire, and their Noddles instantly meet in the Centre of the Pew; then, as by beat of Drum, with exact Discipline, they rear up into a full length of Stature, and with odd Looks and Gesticulations confer together in so loud and clamorous a manner, continued to the close of the Discourse, and during the After-Psalm,[2] as is not to be Silenced but by the Bells. Nor does this suffice them, without aiming to propagate their Noise through all the Church, by Signals given to the adjoyning Seats, where others designed for this Fraternity are sometimes placed upon Tryal to receive them.

'The Folly as well as Rudeness of this Practice is in nothing more conspicuous than this, that all that follows in the Sermon is lost; for whenever our Sparks take Alarm, they blaze out and grow so Tumultuous, that no After-Explanation can avail, it being impossible for themselves or any near them to give an[a] Account thereof. If any thing really Novel is advanced, how averse soever it may be to their way of thinking, to say nothing of Duty, Men of less Levity than these would be led by a natural Curiosity to hear the whole.

'Laughter, where things Sacred are transacted, is far less pardonable than Whining[3] at a Conventicle; the last has at least a Semblance of Grace, and where the Affectation is unseen may possibly imprint wholsome Lessons on the Sincere; but the first has no Excuse, breaking through all the Rules of Order and Decency, and manifesting a Remissness of Mind in those important Matters, which require the strictest Composure and Steadiness of Thought: a Proof of the greatest Folly in the World.

'I shall not here enter upon the Veneration due to the Sanctity of the Place, the Reverence owing the Minister, or the Respect that so great an Assembly as a whole Parish may justly claim. I shall only tell them, that, as the *Spanish* Cobler, to reclaim a profligate Son, bid him *have some regard to the Dignity of his Family*;[4] so[b] they,

---

[a] an] any *Fol.*   [b] so] for *Fol.*

[1] Cf. No. 436 (vol. iv).   [2] Here apparently the hymn following the sermon.
[3] A stock charge against the Dissenters.
[4] See L'Estrange, *Fables*, ii. 133.

as Gentlemen (for we Citizens assume to be such one Day in a Week, are bound for the future to Repent of, and Abstain from the gross Abuses here mentioned, whereof they have been Guilty in Contempt of Heaven and Earth, and contrary to the Laws in this Case made and provided.

I am, SIR,
Your very Humble Servant,
R. M.'

No. 631

[TICKELL]

Friday, December 10, 1714[1]

Simplex Munditiis . . .
Hor.

I HAD occasion to go a few Miles out of Town some Days since in a Stage-Coach, where I had for my Fellow-Travellers a dirty Beau, and a pretty young Quaker Woman. Having no Inclination to Talk much at that time, I placed my self backward, with a design to survey them, and pick a Speculation out of my two Companions. Their different Figures were sufficient of themselves to draw my Attention. The Gentleman was dressed in a Suit, the Ground whereof had been black, as I perceived from some few Spaces that had escaped the Powder which was incorporated with the greatest part of his Coat: His Periwig, which cost no small Sum,[2] was after so slovenly a manner cast over his Shoulders, that it seemed not to have been combed since the Year 1712; his Linnen, which was not much concealed, was daubed with plain *Spanish*[3] from the Chin to the lowest Button, and the Diamond upon his Finger (which naturally dreaded the Water) put me in mind how it sparkled amidst the Rubbish of the Mine where it was first discovered. On the other hand, the pretty Quaker appeared in all the Elegance of Cleanliness. Not a Speck was to be found upon her. A clear, clean, oval Face, just edged about with little thin Plaits of the purest

---

[1] *Motto.* Horace, *Odes*, I. 5. 5: Neat without the help of Art. CREECH.
  A note in Addison's hand, 'Cleanliness 〈 〉 at home', survives among the Tickell MSS. (Hodgart, p. 382). The present number is either an essay by Addison or a reworking by Tickell of notes left him by Addison.
[2] Cf. *Tatler* 54, where a wig is reported as costing forty guineas.
[3] I.e. snuff. Cf. No. 275 (ii. 571).

Cambrick, received great Advantages from the Shade of her black Hood; as did the Whiteness of her Arms from that sober coloured Stuff in which she had Cloathed her self. The Plainness of her Dress was very well suited to the Simplicity of her Phrases; all which, put together, though they could not give me a great Opinion of her Religion, they did of her Innocence.

This Adventure occasioned my throwing together a few Hints upon *Cleanliness*, which I shall consider as one of the *Half-Virtues*, as *Aristotle* calls them,[1] and shall recommend it under the three following Heads. As it is a Mark of Politeness: As it produces Love: and as it bears Analogy to Purity of Mind.

First, It is a Mark of Politeness. It is universally agreed upon, that no one unadorned with this Virtue can go into Company without giving a manifest Offence. The easier or higher any one's Fortune is, this Duty rises proportionably. The different Nations of the World are as much distinguished by their Cleanliness, as by their Arts and Sciences. The more any Country is civilized, the more they consult this part of Politeness. We need but compare our Ideas of a Female *Hottentot* and an *English* Beauty, to be satisfied of the Truth of what hath been advanced.

In the next Place Cleanliness may be said to be the Foster-Mother of Love. Beauty indeed most commonly produces that Passion in the Mind, but Cleanliness preserves it. An indifferent Face and Person, kept in perpetual Neatness, hath won many a Heart from a pretty Slattern. Age it self is not unamiable, while it is preserved clean and unsullied: Like a Piece of Metal constantly kept smooth and bright, we look on it with more Pleasure than on a new Vessel that is canker'd with Rust.

I might observe farther, that as Cleanliness renders us agreeable to others, so it makes us easy to our selves; that it is an excellent Preservative of Health; and that several Vices, destructive both to Mind and Body, are inconsistent with the Habit of it. But these Reflections I shall leave to the Leisure of my Readers, and shall observe in the Third Place, That it bears a great Analogy with Purity of Mind, and naturally inspires refined Sentiments and Passions.

We find from Experience, that through the Prevalence of Custom,

[1] Aristotle, *Ethica Nicomachea*, 4. 9. 8 (1128ᵇ33). Plutarch, 'On Moral Virtue', speaking of temperance, says that the philosophers 'do not account self-control even a virtue in the absolute sense, but less than a virtue' (*Moralia*, 445C).

the most vicious Actions lose their Horror, by being made familiar to us. On the contrary, those who live in the Neighbourhood of good Examples, fly from the first Appearances of what is shocking. It fares with us much after the same Manner as to our Ideas. Our Senses, which are the Inlets to all the Images conveyed to the Mind, can only transmit the Impression of such things as usually surround them. So that pure and unsullied Thoughts are naturally suggested to the Mind, by those Objects that perpetually encompass us, when they are beautiful and elegant in their kind.

In the East, where the Warmth of the Climate makes Cleanliness more immediately necessary than in colder Countries, it is made one Part of their Religion: The *Jewish* Law, (and the *Mahometan*, which in some Things copies after it) is filled with Bathings, Purifications, and other Rites of the like Nature.[1] Though there is the above-named convenient Reason to be assigned for these Ceremonies, the chief Intention undoubtedly was to typifie inward Purity and Cleanness of Heart by those outward Washings. We read several Injunctions of this Kind in the Book of *Deuteronomy*, which confirm this Truth; and which are but ill accounted for by saying, as some do, that they were only instituted for convenience in the Desart, which otherwise could not have been habitable for so many Years.[2]

I shall conclude this Essay, with a Story which I have somewhere read in an Account of *Mahometan* Superstitions.[3]

A *Dervise* of great Sanctity one Morning had the Misfortune as he took up a Chrystal Cup, which was consecrated to the Prophet, to let it fall upon the Ground, and dash it in Pieces. His Son coming in, some time after, he stretched out his Hands to bless him, as his manner was every Morning; but the Youth going out, stumbled over the Threshhold and broke his Arm. As the old Man wondered at these Events, a Caravan passed by in its way from *Mecca*. The *Dervise* approached it to beg a Blessing; but as he stroaked one of the holy Camels, he received a Kick from the Beast, that sorely bruised him. His Sorrow and Amazement increased upon him, till he recollected that through Hurry and Inadvertency he had that Morning come abroad, without washing his Hands.

[1] See Chardin's *Voyages* (Amsterdam, 1711), vii. 105 ff.
[2] I have not located this among the commentators.
[3] Byron Porter Smith (*Islam in English Literature*, 1939) mentions this as an example of the moralistic tale in the Oriental style but says nothing of its source.

. . . Explebo numerum, reddarque tenebris.
Virg.

THE Love of Symmetry and Order, which is natural to the Mind of Man, betrays him sometimes into very whimsical Fancies. *This noble Principle,* says a *French* Author, *loves to amuse it self on the most trifling Occasions. You may see a profound Philosopher,* says he, *walk for an Hour together in his Chamber, and industriously treading, at every Step, upon every other Board in the Flooring.*[2] Every Reader will recollect several Instances of this Nature without my Assistance. I think it was *Gregorio Leti* who had published as many Books as he was Years old;[3] which was a Rule he had laid down and punctually observed to the Year of his Death. It was, perhaps, a Thought of the like Nature which determined *Homer* himself to divide each of his Poems into as many Books as there are Letters in the *Greek* Alphabet.[4] *Herodotus* has in the same manner adapted his Books to the Number of the *Muses,* for which Reason many a Learned Man hath wished there had been more than Nine of that Sisterhood.[5]

Several *Epic* Poets have religiously followed *Virgil* as to the Number of his Books; and even *Milton* is thought by many to have changed the Number of his Books from Ten to Twelve for no other Reason;[6] as *Cowley* tells us, it was His Design, had he finished his *Davideis,* to have also imitated the *Æneid* in this Particular.[7] I believe every one will agree with me, that a Perfection of this Nature hath

---

[1] *Motto.* Virgil, *Aeneid,* 6. 545: I will compleat the number and be gone.

Tickell is named as the author of this number in the Tickell MS., which also assigns 'The Poem on a Lady's Grotto' in this number to 'Mr. Ward of the University of Dublin' (see below).

[2] This has not been identified.

[3] See Bayle, art. 'John Kirchman', Remark B, where examples of this type are given, though not Leti.

[4] See Bayle, art. 'Aristarchus, of Alexandria', Remark B: 'Note, that it's the Opinion of several, that *Aristarchus* was he who divided each of *Homer's* great Poems into as many Books as there are Letters in the Alphabet, and gave to each Book the Name of a Letter.'

[5] The earliest extant letter of Addison's (12 Feb. 1694/5) refers to a projected translation of Herodotus (Graham, p. 1).

[6] There seems to be no evidence that Milton himself made the change from **ten** to twelve books in order to follow Virgil's example. The change (in the second edition) may have been made by the publisher.

[7] Preface to *Works* of 1656 (Spingarn, ii. 86).

no Foundation in Reason; and, with due Respect to these great Names, may be looked upon as something whimsical.

I mention these great Examples in Defence of my Bookseller, who occasioned this Eighth Volume of *Spectators*, because, as he said, he thought Seven a very Odd Number. On the other Side, several grave Reasons were urged on this important Subject; as in particular, that Seven was the precise Number of the Wise Men, and that the most beautiful Constellation in the Heavens was composed of Seven Stars. This he allowed to be true; but still insisted, that Seven was an Odd Number; suggesting at the same time, that if he were provided with a sufficient Stock of leading Papers, he should find Friends ready enough to carry on the Work. Having by this means got his Vessel launched and set afloat, he hath committed the Steerage of it from time to time to such as he thought capable of conducting it.

The Close of this Volume, which the Town may now expect in a little time, may possibly ascribe each Sheet to its proper Author.

It were no hard Task to continue this Paper a considerable Time longer, by the Help of large Contributions sent from unknown Hands.

I cannot give the Town a better Opinion of the SPECTATOR's Correspondents, than by publishing the following Letter, with a very fine Copy of Verses upon a Subject perfectly new.

Mr. SPECTATOR, *Dublin*, Nov. 30. 1714.

'YOU lately recommended to your Female Readers, the good old Custom of their Grandmothers, who used to lay out a great Part of their Time in Needle-Work:[1] I entirely agree with you in your Sentiments, and think it would not be of less Advantage to themselves, and their Posterity, than to the Reputation of many of their good Neighbours, if past many of those Hours in this innocent Entertainment, which are lost at the Tea-Table. I would, however, humbly offer to your Consideration, the Case of the Poetical Ladies; who, though they may be willing to take any Advice given them by the SPECTATOR, yet can't so easily quit their Pen and Ink, as you may imagine. Pray allow them, at least now and then, to indulge themselves in other Amusements of Fancy, when they are tired with stooping to their Tapestry. There is a very particular kind of Work, which of late several Ladies here

[1] No. 606 (above, p. 72).

in our Kingdom are very fond of, which seems very well adapted to a Poetical Genius: It is the making of *Grotto*'s. I know a Lady who has a very beautiful one, composed by her self, nor is there one Shell in it not stuck up by her own Hands. I here send you a Poem to the fair Architect, which I would not offer to herself, till I knew whether this Method of a Lady's passing her Time, were approv'd of by the *British* SPECTATOR, which, with the Poem, I submit to your Censure, who am,

Your Constant Reader

And Humble Servant,

A. B.'

To Mrs. —— on her *Grotto*.[1]

A Grotto *so compleat, with such Design,*
What Hands, Calypso, *cou'd have form'd but Thine?*
Each chequer'd Pebble, and each shining Shell
So well proportion'd, and dispos'd so well,
Surprizing Lustre from thy Thought receive,
Assuming Beauties more than Nature gave.
To Her their various Shapes, and glossy Hue,
Their curious Symmetry they owe to you.
Not fam'd Amphion's *Lute, whose powerful Call*
Made willing Stones dance to the Theban *Wall,*
In more harmonious Ranks cou'd make them fall.[2]
Not Ev'ning Cloud a brighter Arch can shew,
Nor richer Colours paint the heav'nly Bow.

Where can unpolish'd Nature boast a Piece,
In all her Mossie Cells, exact as This?
At the gay parti-colour'd Scene we start,
For Chance too regular, too rude for Art.

Charm'd with the sight, my ravish'd Breast is fir'd
With Hints like those which ancient Bards inspir'd;

---

[1] The poem is by the Rev. James Ward, later Dean of Cloyne. He received the degree of M.A. this year (1714) at Trinity College, Dublin. The poem, 'To Mrs. —— on her Grotto', is reprinted with several poems of Ward, in *Miscellaneous Poems, Original and Translated, by Several Hands: Published by Mr.* [*Matthew*] *Concanen* (1724), pp. 347-9. The only change made is the substitution of 'Clouds' for 'Cloud' in line 12. For Ward's paraphrase of the seventh chapter of Proverbs (also in this collection) see No. 410 (iii. 533-5).

[2] Amphion, son of Jupiter and Antiope, 'was very excellent at Musick, and learn'd of *Mercury* to play upon stringed Instruments, in which he grew so great a Proficient, as the Poets say, That he built the Walls of *Thebes* by the sound of his Harp, and that the Stones put themselves in order to make that Building' (Danet).

All the feign'd Tales by Superstition told,
All the bright Train of fabled Nymphs of Old,
Th' enthusiastick Muse believes are true,
Thinks the Spot sacred, and its Genius You.
Lost in wild Rapture, wou'd she fain disclose,
How by degrees the pleasing Wonder rose:
Industrious in a faithful Verse to trace
The various Beauties of the lovely Place:
And while she keeps the glowing Work in view,
Thro' ev'ry Maze thy artful Hand pursue.

   Oh were I equal to the bold Design,
Or cou'd I boast such happy Art as Thine!
That cou'd rude Shells in such sweet Order place,
Give common Objects such uncommon Grace,
Like them my well-chose Words in ev'ry Line,
As sweetly temper'd, shou'd as sweetly shine.
So just a Fancy shou'd my Numbers warm,
Like the gay Piece shou'd the Description charm.
Then with superior Strength my Voice I'd raise, ⎫
The echoing Grotto shou'd approve my Lays, ⎬
Pleas'd to reflect the well-sung Founder's Praise. ⎭

No. 633
[PEARCE]

Wednesday, December 15, 1714[1]

Omnia profecto, cum se a cœlestibus rebus referet ad humanas excelsius magnificentiusque et dicet et sentiet.

Cicer.

THE following Discourse is printed, as it came to my Hands, without Variation.

[1] *Motto.* Cicero, *Orator*, 34. 119: When a Man descends from celestial to treat of human Affairs, he will both think and speak in a more exalted and magnificent manner.

  This number is by Zachary Pearce (1690–1774), consecrated Bishop of Bangor in 1748 and Bishop of Rochester in 1755. His authorship is revealed in a letter by him dated 5 June 1764 and addressed to either Dr. Birch or Bishop Percy (Add. MS. 4316, ff. 179, 180). In 1714 Pearce was still an undergraduate at Cambridge.

Cambridge, Dec. 12.

'IT was a very common Enquiry among the Ancients why the Number of excellent Orators, under all the Encouragements the most flourishing States could give them, fell so far short of the Number of those who excelled in all other Sciences.[1] A Friend of mine used merrily to apply to this Case an Observation of *Herodotus*, who says, That the most useful Animals are the most fruitful in their Generation; whereas the Species of those Beasts that are fierce and mischievous to Mankind are but scarcely continued.[2] The Historian instances in a Hare, which always either breeds or brings forth; and a Lioness, which brings forth but once, and then loses all Power of Conception. But, leaving my Friend to his Mirth, I am of Opinion, that in these latter Ages we have greater Cause of Complaint than the Ancients had. And since that solemn Festival is approaching, which calls for all the Power of Oratory, and which affords as noble a Subject for the Pulpit as any Revelation has taught us, the Design of this Paper shall be to show, that our Moderns have greater Advantages towards true and solid Eloquence, than any which the celebrated Speakers of Antiquity enjoy'd.

[a]"The first great and substantial Difference is, that their common Places, in which almost the whole Force of Amplification consists, were drawn from the Profit or Honesty of the Action, as they regarded only this present State of Duration. But Christianity, as it exalts Morality to a greater Perfection, as it brings the Consideration of another Life into the Question, as it proposes Rewards and Punishments of a higher Nature and a longer Continuance, is more adapted to affect the Minds of the Audience, naturally inclin'd to pursue what it imagines its greatest Interest and Concern. If *Pericles*, as Historians report, could shake the firmest Resolutions of his Hearers, and set the Passions of all *Greece* in a Ferment, when the present Welfare of his Country, or the Fear of hostile Invasions was the Subject, what may be expected from that Orator, who warns his Audience against those Evils which have no Remedy, when once undergone, either from Prudence or Time. As much greater as the Evils in a future State are than these at present, so much are the Motives to Persuasion under Christianity greater than

---

[a] *No paragraph in Fol.*

[1] Cicero, *De Oratore*, 1. 2. 6 – 1. 4. 16.
[2] *History*, 3. 108.

those which meer moral Considerations could supply us with. But what I now mention relates only to the Power of moving the Affections. There is another Part of Eloquence, which is indeed its Master-piece; I mean the Marvellous or Sublime. In this the Christian Orator has the Advantage beyond Contradiction. Our Ideas are so infinitely enlarged by Revelation, the Eye of Reason has so wide a Prospect into Eternity, the Notions of a Deity are so worthy and refin'd, and the Accounts we have of a State of Happiness or Misery so clear and evident, that the Contemplation of such Objects will give our Discourse a noble Vigour, an invincible Force, beyond the Power of any human Consideration. *Tully* requires in his Perfect Orator some Skill in the Nature of Heavenly Bodies, because, says he, his Mind will become more extensive and unconfin'd; and when he descends to treat of human Affairs, he will both think and write in a more exalted and magnificent manner.[1] For the same Reason that excellent Master would have recommended the Study of those great and glorious Mysteries which Revelation has discovered to us; to which the noblest Parts of this System of the World are as much inferior, as the Creature is less excellent than its Creator. The wisest and most knowing among the Heathens had very poor and imperfect Notions of a future State. They had indeed some uncertain Hopes, either received by Tradition, or gathered by Reason, that the Existence of virtuous Men would not be determined by the Separation of Soul and Body: But they either disbelieved a future State of Punishment and Misery, or, upon the same Account that *Apelles* painted *Antigonus* with one Side only towards the Spectator, that the Loss of his Eye might not cast a Blemish upon the whole Piece;[2] so these represented the Condition of Man in its fairest View, and endeavoured to conceal what they thought was a Deformity to human Nature. I have often observed, that whenever the above-mention'd Orator in his Philosophical Discourses is led by his Argument to the Mention of Immortality, he seems like one awak'd out of Sleep, rous'd and alarm'd with the Dignity of the Subject, he stretches his Imagination to conceive something un-

---

[1] Cicero, *Orator*, 34. 119 (cf. the motto of this number).

[2] Pliny, *Natural History*, 35. 36. 90. Cf. Robert South, Sermon ii (on John xv. 15, preached at Christ Church, Oxon., 1664):

> *Love* is never so *blind*, as when it is to spy faults. It is like the Painter, who being to draw the Picture of a Friend having a Blemish in one Eye, would picture only the other side of his Face. It is a Noble, and a great thing to cover the Blemishes, and to excuse the Failings of a Friend ... (*Twelve Sermons*, 3rd ed., 1704, pp. 60–61).

common, and with the Greatness of his Thoughts, casts, as it were, a Glory round the Sentence: Uncertain and unsettled as he was, he seems fired with the Contemplation of it: And nothing but such a glorious Prospect could have forced so great a Lover of Truth, as he was, to declare his Resolution never to part with his Persuasion of Immortality, though it should be proved to be an erroneous one. But had he lived to see all that Christianity has brought to Light, how would he have lavished out all the Force of Eloquence in those noblest Contemplations which Humane Nature is capable of, the Resurrection and the Judgment that follows it? How had his Breast glow'd with Pleasure, when the whole Compass of Futurity lay open and exposed to his View? How would his Imagination have hurried him on in the Pursuit of the Mysteries of the Incarnation? How would he have enter'd, with the Force of Lightning,[a] into the Affections of his Hearers, and fixed their Attention, in spite of all the Opposition of corrupt Nature, upon those glorious Themes, which his Eloquence had painted in such lively and lasting Colours?

[b]"This Advantage Christians have; and it was with no small Pleasure I lately met with a Fragment of *Longinus*, which is preserved, as a Testimony of that Critick's Judgment, at the Beginning of a Manuscript of the New Testament in the *Vatican* Library.[1] After that Author has number'd up the most celebrated Orators among the *Grecians*, he says, *Add to these* Paul *of* Tarsus, *the Patron of an Opinion not yet fully proved.* As a Heathen, he condemns the Christian Religion; and, as an impartial Critick, he judges in Favour of the Promoter and Preacher of it. To me it seems, that the latter Part of his Judgment adds great Weight to his Opinion of St. *Paul's* Abilities, since, under all the Prejudice of Opinions directly opposite, he is constrained to acknowledge the Merit of that Apostle. And, no doubt, such as *Longinus* describes St. *Paul*, such he appeared to the Inhabitants of those Countries which he visited and blessed with those Doctrines he was divinely commissioned to preach. Sacred Story gives us, in one Circumstance, a convincing Proof of his Eloquence, when the Men of *Lystra* called him *Mercury, because he was the chief Speaker*, and would have paid Divine Worship to him, as to the God who invented and presided

---

[a] Lightning,] Thunder, *Fol.*   [b] *No paragraph in Fol.*

[1] See the first Fragment in Pearce's Longinus, 2nd ed., 1732, p. 260.

over Eloquence.[1] This one Account of our Apostle sets his Character, considered as an Orator only, above all the celebrated Relations of the Skill and Influence of *Demosthenes* and his Contemporaries. Their Power in Speaking was admired, but still it was thought human: Their Eloquence warmed and ravished the Hearers, but still it was thought the Voice of Man, not the Voice of God. What Advantage then had St. *Paul* above those of *Greece* or *Rome?* I confess I can ascribe this Excellence to nothing but the Power of the Doctrines he delivered, which may have still the same Influence on the Hearers; which have still the Power, when preached by a skilful Orator, to make us break out in the same Expressions as the Disciples, who met our Saviour in their Way to *Emmaus*, made use of; *Did not our Hearts burn within us, when he talked to us by the Way, and while he opened to us the Scriptures?*[2] I may be thought bold in my Judgment by some; but I must affirm, That no one Orator has left us so visible Marks and Footsteps of his Eloquence as our Apostle. It may perhaps be wondered at, that in his Reasonings upon Idolatry at *Athens*, where Eloquence was born and flourished, he confines himself to strict Argument only;[3] but my Reader may remember what many Authors of the best Credit have assured us, That all Attempts upon the Affections and Strokes of Oratory were expresly forbidden, by the Laws of that Country, in Courts of Judicature.[4] His Want of Eloquence therefore here, was the Effect of his exact Conformity to the Laws: But his Discourse on the Resurrection to the *Corinthians*,[5] his Harangue before *Agrippa* upon his own Conversion and the Necessity of that of others,[6] are truly Great, and may serve as full Examples to those excellent Rules for the Sublime, which the best of Criticks has left us. The Sum of all this Discourse is, That our Clergy have no farther to look for an Example of the Perfection they may arrive at, than to St. *Paul*'s Harangues; that when he, under the Want of several Advantages of Nature (as he himself tells us)[7] was heard, admired, and made a Standard to succeeding Ages by the best Judge of a different Persuasion in Religion: I say,

---

[1] Acts xiv. 12.　　　　　[2] Luke xxiv. 32.　　　　　[3] Acts xvii. 16–34.

[4] This refers, somewhat inaccurately, to the rule which forbade pleaders before the Areopagus to talk beside the point. See Aristotle, *Rhetoric*, 1. 1. 1354ᵃ23; *Pollux*, 8. 117; Antiphon, *In Defence of the Choreutes*, 9; and Sextus Empiricus, *Adversus Mathematicos*, 2. 77: 'The Athenians in ancient times did not allow persons tried before the council of the Areopagus to present another to plea in their behalf, but each, whether his ability in speaking was great or small, without any distortions or tricks presented his own plea in his own behalf.' My colleague, Professor Benedict Einarson, has very kindly supplied me with these references.　　　　　[5] 1 Cor. xv.

[6] Acts xxvi. 2–23.　　　　　　　　　　　　　　　　　　　[7] 2 Cor. xii. 5–7.

our Clergy may learn, That, however instructive their Sermons are, they are capable of receiving a great Addition; which St. *Paul* has given them a noble Example of, and the Christian Religion has furnished them with certain Means of attaining to.'

No. 634
[TICKELL]

Friday, December 17, 1714[1]

'Ο ἐλαχίστων δεόμενος ἔγγιστα θεῶν.

Socrates apud Xen.

IT was the common Boast of the Heathen Philosophers, that by the Efficacy of their several Doctrines, they made Humane Nature resemble the Divine. How much mistaken soever they might be in the several Means they proposed for this End, it must be owned that the Design was great and glorious. The finest Works of Invention and Imagination are of very little Weight, when put in the Balance with what refines and exalts the rational Mind. *Longinus* excuses *Homer* very handsomely, when he says the Poet made his Gods like Men, that he might make his Men appear like the Gods:[2] But it must be allowed that several of the ancient Philosophers acted, as *Cicero* wishes *Homer* had done; they endeavoured rather to make Men like Gods, than Gods like Men.[3]

According to this general Maxim in Philosophy, some of them have endeavoured to place Men in such a State of Pleasure, or Indolence at least, as they vainly imagined the Happiness of the Supreme Being to consist in. On the other Hand, the most virtuous Sect of Philosophers have created a chimerical Wise Man, whom they made exempt from Passion and Pain, and thought it enough to pronounce him All-sufficient.[4]

---

[1] *Motto.* Xenophon, *Memorabilia*, 1. 6. 10 (altered). He who has the fewest wants most resembles the gods.

[2] *On the Sublime*, 9. 7:

For my part, when I read in *Homer* of the Wounds, the Factions, the Sufferings, the Tears, the Imprisonments of the Gods, and all those Accidents which incessantly befal 'em; it seems to me, that he does his utmost to make Gods of the Men, who were at the Siege of *Troy*; and on the contrary, of the Gods themselves to make Men ...' (Boileau's trans., chap. vii, pp. 26–27).

[3] Cicero, *Tusculan Disputations*, 1. 26. 65.

[4] For the wise man of the Stoics see No. 243 (ii. 444).

This last Character, when divested of the Glare of Humane Philosophy that surrounds it, signifies no more, than that a Good and Wise Man should so arm himself with Patience, as not to yield tamely to the Violence of Passion and Pain; that he should learn so to suppress and contract his Desires as to have few Wants; and that he should cherish so many Virtues in his Soul, as to have a perpetual Source of Pleasure in Himself.

The Christian Religion requires, that, after having framed the best Idea we are able of the Divine Nature, it should be our next Care to conform our selves to it, as far as our Imperfections will permit. I might mention several Passages in the Sacred Writings on this Head, to which I might add many Maxims and wise Sayings of Moral Authors among the *Greeks* and *Romans*.

I shall only instance a remarkable Passage, to this Purpose, out of *Julian's Cæsars*.[1] That Emperor having represented all the *Roman* Emperors, with *Alexander* the Great, as passing in Review before the Gods, and striving for the Superiority, lets them all drop, excepting *Alexander, Julius Cæsar, Augustus Cæsar, Trajan, Marcus Aurelius,* and *Constantine*. Each of these great Heroes of Antiquity lays in his Claim for the upper Place; and, in Order to it, sets forth his Actions after the most advantageous Manner. But the Gods, instead of being dazled with the Lustre of their Actions, enquire, by *Mercury*, into the proper Motive and Governing Principle that influenced them throughout the whole Series of their Lives and Exploits. *Alexander* tells them, That his Aim was to conquer; *Julius Cæsar*, That his was to gain the highest Post in his Country; *Augustus*, To govern well; *Trajan*, That His was the same as that of *Alexander*, namely, To conquer. The Question, at length, was put to *Marcus Aurelius*, who replied, with great Modesty, That *it had always been his Care to imitate the Gods*. This Conduct seems to have gained him the most Votes and best Place in the whole Assembly. *Marcus Aurelius* being afterwards asked to explain himself, declares, That, by imitating the Gods, he endeavoured to imitate them in the Use of his Understanding, and of all other Faculties; and, in particular, That it was always his Study to have as few Wants as possible in himself, and to do all the Good he could to others.

Among the many Methods by which Revealed Religion has advanced Morality, this is one, That it has given us a more just and perfect Idea of that Being whom every reasonable Creature

[1] The Emperor Julian's satire, 'The Caesars', 333C.

ought to imitate. The Young Man, in a Heathen Comedy, might justify his Lewdness by the Example of *Jupiter*; as, indeed, there was scarce any Crime that might not be countenanced by those Notions of the Deity which prevailed among the common People in the Heathen World.[1] Revealed Religion sets forth a proper Object for Imitation, in that Being who is the Pattern, as well as the Source, of all Spiritual Perfection.

While we remain in this Life, we are subject to innumerable Temptations, which, if listen'd to, will make us deviate from Reason and Goodness, the only Things wherein we can imitate the Supreme Being. In the next Life we meet with nothing to excite our Inclinations that doth not deserve them. I shall therefore dismiss my Reader with this Maxim, *viz. Our Happiness in this World proceeds from the Suppression of our Desires, but in the next World from the Gratification of them.*[2]

No. 635   *Monday, December 20, 1714*[3]
[GROVE]

Sentio Te sedem Hominum ac Domum contemplari: quæ si tibi parva (ut est) ita videtur, hæc cœlestia semper Spectato; illa humana contemnito.

Cicero. Somn. Scip.

THE following Essay comes from the ingenious Author of the Letter upon *Novelty*, printed in a late *Spectator*:[4] The Notions

[1] See Bayle, 'Jupiter', Remark D, where a passage from the *Ion* of Euripides is quoted on this point.

[2] Cf. the closing sentence of No. 574 (iv. 565, by Addison).

[3] *Motto.* Cicero, *De republica*, 6. 19. 20: I know you contemplate both Heaven and Earth, which if they seem small to you, as they really are, yet still contemplate the celestial, and despise the terrestrial.

The original manuscript of this number (without Tickell's introductory sentence) survives among the Tickell papers, in the form of a letter postmarked 17 Dec. and directed to Jacob Tonson. The last sheet, containing the final eight sentences of the essay, is missing. Although the manuscript contains a terminal mark to show where the printer has reached the end of the first page in the folio printing and was thus clearly used as printer's copy, the text as set up in the folio sheet shows considerable revisions. Apparently the changes were made in proof. For the text of the original see Appendix V.

This was one of the essays included among the 'Several Discourses' published at the end of Addison's *Evidences of the Christian Religion* (Tonson, 1730).

[4] No. 626.

are drawn from the *Platonick* way of Thinking, but as they contribute to raise the Mind, and may inspire noble Sentiments of our own future Grandeur and Happiness, I think it well deserves to be presented to the Publick.

IF the Universe be the Creature of an intelligent Mind, this Mind could have no immediate Regard to himself in producing it. He needed not to make Trial of his Omnipotence, to be informed what Effects were within its Reach: The World as existing in his eternal Idea was then as beautiful as now it is drawn forth into Being; and in the immense Abyss of his Essence are contained far brighter Scenes than will be ever set forth to View; it being impossible that the great Author of Nature should bound his own Power by giving Existence to a System of Creatures so perfect that he cannot improve upon it by any other Exertions of his Almighty Will.[1] Between Finite and Infinite there is an unmeasured Interval, not to be filled up in endless Ages; for which Reason, the most excellent of all God's Works must be equally short of what his Power is able to produce as the most imperfect, and may be exceeded with the same Ease.

[a]This Thought, hath made some imagine, (what, it must be confest, is not impossible) that the unfathomed Space is ever teeming with new Births, the younger still inheriting a greater Perfection than the elder. But as this doth not fall within my present View, I shall content my self with taking Notice, that the Consideration now mentioned proves undeniably, that the Ideal Worlds in the Divine Understanding yield a Prospect incomparably more ample, various and delightful than any created World can do: And that therefore as it is not to be supposed that God should make a World merely of inanimate Matter, however diversified; or inhabited only by Creatures of no higher an Order than Brutes; so the End for which he designed his reasonable Offspring is the Contemplation of his Works, the Enjoyment of himself, and in both to be happy; having, to this Purpose, endowed them with correspondent Faculties and Desires. He can have no greater Pleasure from a bare Review of his Works, than from the Survey of his own Ideas; but we may be assured that he is well pleased in the Satisfaction derived to Beings capable of it, and, for whose

---

[a] No paragraph in Fol.

---

[1] For this and other illustrations of the 'principle of plenitude' in this essay see A. O. Lovejoy, *The Great Chain of Being*.

Entertainment, he hath^a erected this immense Theatre. Is not this more than an Intimation of our Immortality? Man, who when considered as on his Probation for a happy Existence hereafter is the most remarkable Instance of Divine Wisdom, if we cut him off from all Relation to Eternity, is the most wonderful and unaccountable Composition in the whole Creation. He hath Capacities to lodge a much greater Variety of Knowledge than he will be ever Master of, and an unsatisfied Curiosity to tread the secret Paths of Nature and Providence: But, with this, his Organs, in their present Structure, are rather fitted to serve the Necessities of a vile Body, than to minister to his Understanding; and from the little Spot to which he is chained, he can frame but wandering Guesses concerning the innumerable Worlds of Light that encompass him, which, tho' in themselves of a prodigious Bigness, do but just glimmer in the remote Spaces of the Heavens; and, when with a great deal of Time and Pains he hath laboured a little way up the steep Ascent of Truth, and beholds with Pity the groveling Multitude beneath, in a Moment his Foot slides, and he tumbles down headlong into the Grave.

^bThinking on this, I am obliged to believe, in Justice to the Creator of the World, that there is another State when Man shall be better situated for Contemplation, or rather have it in his Power to remove from Object to Object, and from World to World; and be accommodated with Senses, and other Helps, for making the quickest and most amazing Discoveries. How doth such a Genius as Sir *Isaac Newton*, from amidst the Darkness that involves human Understanding, break forth, and appear like one of another Species![1] The vast Machine we inhabit lies open to him, he seems not unacquainted with the general Laws that govern it, and while with the Transport of a Philosopher he beholds and admires the glorious Work, he is capable of paying at once a more devout and more rational Homage to his Maker. But alas! how narrow is the Prospect even of such a Mind? and how obscure to the Compass that is taken in by the Ken of an Angel; or of a Soul but newly escaped from its Imprisonment in the Body! For my part, I freely indulge my Soul in the Confidence of its future Grandeur; it pleases me to think that I who know so small a portion of the Works of the Creator, and

^a he hath] hath *Fol.*　　^b *No paragraph in Fol.*

[1] Cf. Pope's *Essay on Man*, ii. 35-38.

with slow and painful Steps creep up and down on the Surface of this Globe, shall ere long shoot away with the Swiftness of Imagination, trace out the hidden Springs of Nature's Operations, be able to keep pace with the heavenly Bodies in the Rapidity of their Carreer, be a Spectator of the long Chain of Events in the natural and moral Worlds, visit the several Apartments of the Creation, know how they are furnished and how inhabited, comprehend the Order and measure the Magnitudes, and Distances of those Orbs, which to us seem disposed without any regular Design, and set all in the same Circle, observe the Dependance of the Parts of each System, and (if our Minds are big enough to grasp the Theory,) of the several Systems upon one another, from whence results the Harmony of the Universe. In Eternity a great deal may be done of this kind. I find it of use to cherish this generous Ambition; for besides the secret Refreshment it diffuses through my Soul, it engages me in an endeavour to improve my Faculties, as well as to exercise them conformably to the Rank I now hold among reasonable Beings, and the hope I have of being once advanced to a more exalted Station.

The other, and that the Ultimate end of Man is the Enjoyment of God, beyond which he cannot form a Wish. Dim at best are the Conceptions we have of the Supreme Being, who, as it were, keeps his Creatures in Suspence, neither discovering, nor hiding himself; by which means, the Libertine hath a Handle to dispute his Existence, while the most are content to speak him fair, but in their Hearts prefer every trifling Satisfaction to the Favour of their Maker, and ridicule the good Man for the Singularity of his Choice. Will there not a time come, when the Free-Thinker shall see his impious Schemes overturned, and be made a Convert to the Truths he hates; when deluded Mortals shall be convinced of the Folly of their Pursuits, and the few Wise who followed the Guidance of Heaven, and, scorning the Blandishments of Sense and the sordid Bribery of the World, aspired to a celestial Abode, shall stand possessed of their utmost wish in the Vision of the Creator? Here the Mind heaves a Thought now and then towards him, and hath some transient Glances of his Presence; when, in the Instant it thinks it self to have the fastest hold, the Object eludes its Expectations, and it falls back tir'd and baffled to the Ground. Doubtless there is some more perfect way of conversing with heavenly Beings. Are not Spirits capable of mutual Intelligence unless immersed in

Bodies, or by their Intervention? must superior Natures depend on inferior for the main Privilege of sociable Beings, that of conversing with, and knowing each other? What would they have done, had Matter never been created? I suppose, not have lived in eternal Solitude. As incorporeal Substances are of a nobler Order, so, be sure, their manner of Intercourse is answerably more expedite and intimate. This method of Communication, we call Intellectual Vision, as somewhat Analogous to the Sense of Seeing which is the Medium of our Acquaintance with this visible World. And in some such way can God make himself the Object of immediate Intuition[a] to the Blessed; and as he can, 'tis not improbable that he will, always condescending, in the Circumstances of doing it, to the Weakness and Proportion of finite Minds. His Works but faintly reflect the Image of his Perfections, 'tis a Second-hand Knowledge: To have a just Idea of him, it may be necessary that we see him as he is. But what is that? 'Tis something that never entered into the Heart of Man to conceive; yet, what we can easily conceive will be a Fountain of Unspeakable, of everlasting, Rapture. All created Glories will fade and die away in his Presence. Perhaps it will be my Happiness to compare the World with the fair Exemplar of it in the divine Mind; perhaps, to view the original Plan of those wise Designs that have been executing in a long Succession of Ages. Thus employed in finding out his Works, and contemplating their Author! how shall I fall prostrate and adoring, my Body swallowed up in the Immensity of Matter, my Mind in the Infinitude of his Perfections!

[a] Intuition] Institution *Fol.*

DEDICATIONS

The following dedications were prefixed to the first collected editions of the *Spectator*, in 8vo and 12mo. (The text is that of the 8vo edition.)

To the Right Honourable
John Lord *Sommers*,[1]
Baron of *Evesham*.

My LORD,

I SHOULD not act the Part of an impartial Spectator, if I Dedicated the following Papers to one who is not of the most consummate and most acknowledged Merit.

None but a Person of a finished Character can be the proper Patron of a Work, which endeavours to Cultivate and Polish Human Life, by promoting Virtue and Knowledge, and by recommending whatsoever may be either Useful or Ornamental to Society.

I know that the Homage I now pay You, is offering a kind of Violence to one who is as solicitous to shun Applause, as he is assiduous to deserve it. But, my Lord, this is perhaps the only Particular in which your Prudence will be always disappointed.

While Justice, Candor, Equanimity, a Zeal for the Good of your Country, and the most persuasive Eloquence in bringing over others to it, are valuable Distinctions, You are not to expect that the Publick will so far comply with your Inclinations, as to forbear celebrating such extraordinary Qualities. It is in vain that You have endeavoured to conceal your Share of Merit, in the many National Services which You have effected. Do what You will, the present Age will be talking of your Virtues, tho' Posterity alone will do them Justice.

Other Men pass through Oppositions and contending Interests in the Ways of Ambition, but Your Great Abilities have been invited to Power, and importuned to accept of Advancement. Nor

[1] John, Lord Somers (1652–1716), the great Lord Chancellor under King William, seems to have been—in spite of Queen Anne's personal dislike—generally admired and esteemed by Whig and Tory alike. He had taken a prominent part in the Revolution, and had served successively as Solicitor-General, Attorney-General, Lord Keeper, and finally (1697–1700) Lord Chancellor. Addison dedicated his *Poem to His Majesty* (1695) and his *Remarks on . . . Italy* (1705) to him, and in *Freeholder* 39 (published on the day of Somers's funeral, 4 May 1716) paid warm tribute to his abilities, his generosity to others, and his modesty. 'His Character was uniform and consistent with it self, and his whole Conduct of a Piece. His Principles were founded in Reason, and supported by Virtue; and therefore did not lie at the Mercy of Ambition, Avarice, or Resentment.'

174

is it strange that this should happen to your Lordship, who could bring into the Service of Your Sovereign the Arts and Policies of Ancient *Greece* and *Rome*; as well as the most exact Knowledge of our own Constitution in particular, and of the Interests of *Europe* in general; to which I must also add, a certain Dignity in Your self, that (to say the least of it) has been always equal to those great Honours which have been conferred upon You.

It is very well known how much the Church owed to You in the most dangerous Day it ever saw,[1] that of the Arraignment of its Prelates; and how far the Civil Power, in the Late and present Reign, has been indebted to your Counsels and Wisdom.

But to enumerate the great Advantages which the Publick has received from your Administration, would be a more proper Work for an History, than for an Address of this Nature.

Your Lordship appears as great in your Private Life, as in the most Important Offices which You have born. I would therefore rather chuse to speak of the Pleasure You afford all who are admitted into your Conversation, of Your Elegant Taste in all the Polite Parts of Learning, of Your great Humanity and Complacency[2] of Manners, and of the surprising Influence which is peculiar to You in making every one who Converses with your Lordship prefer You to himself, without thinking the less meanly of his own Talents. But if I should take notice of all that might be observed in your Lordship, I should have nothing new to say upon any other Character of Distinction.

I am,

My Lord,

Your Lordship's

most Obedient,

most Devoted,

Humble Servant,

The Spectator.

---

[1] 29 June 1688, the day on which the Seven Bishops came up for trial (Archbishop Sancroft and Bishops Lloyd, Turner, Lake, Ken, White, and Trelawney). These were the prelates who had signed the petition against James II's order for reading in all churches his 'Declaration for Liberty of Conscience' (May 1688) and had consequently been imprisoned in the Tower. It was largely owing to the eloquence of Somers, their counsel, that the bishops were acquitted.

[2] This word, so frequently occurring in the *Spectator*, does not have the modern meaning of self-satisfaction but the old sense of 'disposition to please' (last recorded example in *OED* is 1749).

To the Right Honourable
Charles Lord *Hallifax*.[1]

My LORD,

SIMILITUDE of Manners and Studies is usually mentioned as one of the strongest Motives to Affection and Esteem; but the passionate Veneration I have for Your Lordship, I think, flows from an Admiration of Qualities in You, of which in the whole Course of these Papers I have acknowledged my self incapable. While I busie my self as a Stranger upon Earth, and can pretend to no other than being a Looker on, You are conspicuous in the Busy and Polite World, both in the World of Men and that of Letters: While I am silent and unobserved in publick Meetings, You are admired by all that approach You as the Life and Genius of the Conversation. What an happy Conjunction of different Talents meets in him whose whole Discourse is at once animated by the Strength and Force of Reason, and adorned with all the Graces and Embellishments of Wit? When Learning irradiates common Life, it is then in its highest Use and Perfection; and it is to such as Your Lordship that the Sciences owe the Esteem which they have with the active Part of Mankind. Knowledge of Books in recluse Men, is like that sort of Lanthorn which hides him who carries it, and serves only to pass through secret and gloomy Paths of his own;[2] but in the Possession of a Man of Business, it is as a Torch in the Hand of one who is willing and able to shew those, who are bewildered, the Way which leads to their Prosperity and Welfare. A generous Concern for Your Country, and a Passion for every thing which is truly Great and Noble, are what actuate all Your Life and Actions;

[1] Charles Montagu (1661–1715), at this time Baron Halifax, was a grandson of the 1st Earl of Manchester. A poet and statesman, he had been Chancellor of the Exchequer and First Lord of the Treasury under William III, and was largely responsible for the founding of the Bank of England in 1694. He had taken a leading part in the negotiations for the Union with Scotland, and in 1706 he had been sent to Hanover with the Acts of Parliament for the naturalization of the Electress Sophia and her family. 'He was one of those Lords who voted Dr. *Sacheverel* guilty in 1710, and spoke in Defence of the *Whig Ministry* in 1711, when falsly accus'd of mismanaging the War in *Spain*' (*Political State*, May 1715, p. 438). He was later made Earl of Halifax, and died on 19 May 1715. Steele dedicated Volume IV of the *Tatler* to Halifax, praising him for his patronage of the arts, his services as an 'able and unbiassed patriot', and his talents for poetry.

[2] A familiar illustration. Cf. Robert Boyle, *Occasional Reflections upon several subjects* (1665), p. 202: 'For there is such a kind of Difference betwixt Vertue shaded by a private, and shining forth in a publick life, as there is betwixt a Candle carri'd aloft in the open air, and inclosed in a Lanthorn; in the former place it gives more light, but in the latter 'tis in less danger to be blown out.' Budgell also uses it in No. 379.

and I hope You will forgive me that I have an Ambition this Book
may be placed in the Library of so good a Judge of what is valuable,
in that Library where the Choice is such that it will not be a Dis-
paragement to be the meanest Author in it. Forgive me, my Lord,
for taking this Occasion of telling all the World how ardently I
Love and Honour You; and that I am with the utmost Gratitude
for all Your Favours,

My Lord,

Your Lordship's

most Obliged,

most Obedient,

and most Humble Servant,

The Spectator.

To the Right Honourable

HENRY BOYLE Esq;[1]

SIR,

AS the profest Design of this Work is to Entertain its Readers in
general, without giving Offence to any particular Person, it
would be difficult to find out so proper a Patron for it as Your self,
there being none whose Merit is more universally acknowledged
by all Parties, and who has made himself more Friends, and fewer
Enemies.[2] Your great Abilities, and unquestioned Integrity, in
those High Employments which You have passed through, would
not have been able to have raised You this general Approbation,
had they not been accompanied with that Moderation in an high
Fortune, and that Affability of Manners, which are so conspicuous
through all parts of Your Life. Your Aversion to any Ostentatious
Arts of Setting to show those Great Services which You have done

---

[1] Henry Boyle, the youngest son of Charles, Lord Clifford, and a grandson of the
1st Earl of Burlington, had been Chancellor of the Exchequer from 1701 to 1708.
From Feb. 1708 until Sept. 1710 he was one of the principal Secretaries of State. He
had been dismissed from office along with Lord Somers and was at this time one of
the Whigs 'out of place'. It was Boyle who requested Addison to write *The Campaign*
to celebrate the victory at Blenheim in 1704.

[2] Boyle was a moderate in politics. Although a friend of Harley and an associate
of the Tories, he had by 1708, when he became Secretary of State for the Northern
Department, become known as a Whig. At the accession of George I he was created
Baron Carleton, and from 1721 until his death in 1725 he was President of the
Council.

the Publick, has not likewise a little contributed to that Universal Acknowledgment which is paid You by Your Country.

The Consideration of this Part of Your Character is that which hinders me from enlarging on those Extraordinary Talents, which have given You so great a Figure in the *British* Senate, as well as on that Elegance and Politeness, which appear in your more retired Conversation. I should be unpardonable, if, after what I have said, I should longer detain You with an Address of this Nature; I cannot, however, conclude it without owning those great Obligations which You have laid upon,

SIR,

Your most Obedient,

Humble Servant,

The Spectator.

TO THE

DUKE

OF

MARLBOROUGH.[1]

My Lord,

AS it is natural to have a Fondness for what has cost us much Time and Attention to produce, I hope Your Grace will forgive an Endeavour to preserve this Work from Oblivion, by affixing it to Your memorable Name.

I shall not here presume to mention the illustrious Passages of Your Life, which are celebrated by the whole Age, and have been the Subject of the most sublime Pens; but if I could convey You to

---

[1] At the time this dedication was written the Duke of Marlborough was in virtual disgrace, having been removed from office in December 1711 as the result of Tory propaganda in the *Examiner* and various political pamphlets, the most important of which was Swift's *Conduct of the Allies*. Steele immediately brought out *The Englishman's Thanks to the Duke of Marlborough*, a two-penny pamphlet dated the day after Marlborough's dismissal and published by Mrs. Baldwin. Shortly after this dedication was published in Volume IV of the *Spectator* (on 11 Nov. 1712) Marlborough went into voluntary exile in the Low Countries, where he remained until the accession of George I in 1714. For the history of Steele's relations with the Duke see Miss Blanchard's edition of Steele's *Correspondence*, pp. 466–7.

Posterity in Your private Character, and describe the Stature, the Behaviour and Aspect of the Duke of *Marlborough*, I question not but it would fill the Reader with more agreeable Images, and give him a more delightful Entertainment than what can be found in the following, or any other Book.

One cannot indeed without Offence, to Yourself, observe, that You excel the rest of Mankind in the least, as well as the greatest Endowments. Nor were it a Circumstance to be mentioned, if the Graces and Attractions of Your Person were not the only Preheminence You have above others, which is left, almost, unobserved by greater Writers.

Yet how pleasing would it be to those who shall read the surprising Revolutions in Your Story, to be made acquainted with Your ordinary Life and Deportment? How pleasing would it be to hear that the same Man who had carried Fire and Sword into the Countries of all that had opposed the Cause of Liberty, and struck a Terrour into the Armies of *France*, had in the midst of His high Station a Behaviour as gentle as is usual in the first Steps towards Greatness? And if it were possible to express that easy Grandeur, which did at once persuade and command; it would appear as clearly to those to come, as it does to His Contemporaries, that all the great Events which were brought to pass under the Conduct of so well-govern'd a Spirit, were the Blessings of Heaven upon Wisdom and Valour; and all which seem adverse fell out by divine Permission, which we are not to search into.

You have pass'd that Year of Life wherein the most able and fortunate Captain, before Your Time, declared he had lived enough both to Nature and to Glory;[1] and Your Grace may make that Reflection with much more Justice. He spoke it after he had arrived at Empire, by an Usurpation upon those whom he had enslaved; but the Prince of *Mindelheim* may rejoyce in a Soveraignty which was the Gift of Him whose Dominions He had preserved.[2]

Glory established upon the uninterrupted Success of honourable Designs and Actions is not subject to Diminution; nor can any Attempts prevail against it, but in the Proportion which the narrow Circuit of Rumour bears to the unlimited Extent of Fame.

We may congratulate Your Grace not only upon Your high Atcheivements, but likewise upon the happy Expiration of Your

---

[1] Julius Caesar. See Cicero, *Pro M. Marcello Oratio*, 8. 25. Addison quotes this in No. 256. [2] Cf. No. 139 (vol. ii).

Command, by which Your Glory is put out of the Power of Fortune: And when Your Person shall be so too, that the Author and Disposer of all Things may place You in that higher Mansion of Bliss and Immortality which is prepared for good Princes, Lawgivers, and Heroes, when HE in HIS due Time removes them from the Envy of Mankind, is the hearty Prayer of,

My LORD,

Your Grace's,

Most Obedient,

Most Devoted

Humble Servant,

The Spectator.

To the Right Honourable
THOMAS Earl of WHARTON.[1]

My LORD,

THE Author of the *Spectator* having prefixed before each of his Volumes the Name of some great Person to whom he has particular Obligations, lays his Claim to Your Lordship's Patronage upon the same Account. I must confess, my Lord, had not I already receiv'd great Instances of Your Favour, I should have been afraid of submitting a Work of this Nature to Your Perusal. You are so throughly acquainted with the Characters of Men, and all the Parts of Humane Life, that it is impossible for the least Misrepresentation of them to escape Your Notice. It is Your Lordship's particular

---

[1] Thomas, Earl of Wharton (1648–1715), as the outstanding leader of the Whigs, is fittingly praised here as 'master of the whole compass of business'; his leadership of the Whig opposition during the last four years of Queen Anne's reign was recognized by both parties. Upon his death, on 12 Apr. 1715, Abel Boyer wrote of him:

> As he was the most active, most stren[u]ous, and most indefatigable *Asserter* of *Liberty*; and the warmest and most inveterate Enemy to *Popery*, *Arbitrary Power*, and *French* Counsels; so was he ever obnoxious to the *Popish*, *Jacobite*, and *Frenchify'd* Faction, who, as far as they dared, aspersed and inveigh'd against him whilst living, and who still calumniate his Memory (*Political State*, Apr. 1715, p. 308).

Addison had served as his secretary when Wharton was Lord Lieutenant of Ireland from 1708 to 1710, and Wharton had proved a serviceable friend to both Addison and Steele. In *Tatler* 4 Steele had praised Wharton's great abilities and described him as a minister 'as industrious and restless for the Preservation of the Liberties of the People, as the greatest Enemy can be to subvert 'em'.

Distinction, that You are Master of the whole Compass of Business, and have signalized Your Self in all the different Scenes of it. We admire some for the Dignity, others for the Popularity of their Behaviour; some for their Clearness of Judgment, others for their Happiness of Expression; some for the laying of Schemes, and others for the putting of them in Execution: It is Your Lordship only who enjoys these several Talents united, and that too in as great Perfection as others possess them singly. Your Enemies acknowledge this great Extent in Your Lordship's Character, at the same Time that they use their utmost Industry and Invention to derogate from it. But it is for Your Honour that those who are now Your Enemies were always so. You have acted in so much Consistency with Your Self, and promoted the Interests of Your Country in so uniform a Manner, that even those who would misrepresent Your generous Designs for the Publick Good, cannot but approve the Steadiness and Intrepidity with which You pursue them. It is a most sensible Pleasure to me that I have this Opportunity of professing my self one of Your great Admirers, and, in a very particular Manner,

My LORD,

Your Lordship's most Obliged,
and most Obedient, Humble Servant,
The Spectator.

To the Right Honourable

CHARLES

Earl of *Sunderland*.[1]

My LORD,

VERY many Favours and Civilities (received from You in a private Capacity) which I have no other Way to acknowledge, will, I hope, excuse this Presumption; but the Justice I, as a *Spectator*,

[1] Charles, Earl of Sunderland (1674–1722), became 3rd Earl on the death of his father in September 1702. He was an important member of the Whig Junto, having married in the previous year Anne Churchill, 'the little Whig', second daughter to the Duke of Marlborough. His library at Althorp in Northamptonshire was already famous. In December 1706 he replaced Sir Charles Hedges as Secretary of State for the Southern Department; in this post he retained Addison, already in office, as his secretary. Steele's position of gazetteer also came under Sunderland's supervision. He was dismissed from office on 14 June 1710, on the eve of the Tories' accession to power.

owe your Character, places me above the want of an Excuse. Candor and Openness of Heart, which shine in all your Words and Actions, exacts the highest Esteem from all who have the Honour to know You, and a winning Condescension to all subordinate to You, made Business a Pleasure to those who executed it under You, at the same time that it heightened Her Majesty's Favour to all who had the Happiness of having it convey'd through your Hands: A Secretary of State, in the Interests of Mankind, joined with that of his Fellow-Subjects, accomplish'd with a great Facility and Elegance in all the Modern as well as Ancient Languages, was a happy and proper Member of a Ministry, by whose Services your Sovereign and Country are in so high and flourishing a Condition, as makes all other Princes and Potentates powerful or inconsiderable in *Europe*, as they are Friends or Enemies to *Great-Britain.* The Importance of those great Events which happened during that Administration, in which Your Lordship bore so important a Charge, will be acknowledg'd as long as Time shall endure; I shall not therefore attempt to rehearse those Illustrious Passages, but give this Application a more private and particular Turn, in desiring your Lordship would continue your Favour and Patronage to me, as You are a Gentleman of the most polite Literature, and perfectly accomplished in the Knowledge of Books and Men, which makes it necessary to beseech your Indulgence to the following Leaves, and the Author of them: Who is, with the greatest Truth and Respect,

My LORD,
Your Lordship's
Oblig'd, Obedient, and
Humble Servant,
The Spectator.

TO

Mr. *METHUEN.*[1]

SIR,

IT is with very great Pleasure I take an Opportunity of publishing the Gratitude I owe You, for the Place You allow me in your

[1] Paul Methuen, son of John Methuen (the Ambassador to Portugal who negotiated the famous Methuen Treaty of 1703), was a prominent member of the Whig party

Friendship and Familiarity. I will not acknowledge to You that I have often had You in my Thoughts, when I have endeavoured to Draw, in some Parts of these Discourses, the Character of a Good-natured, Honest and Accomplished Gentleman. But such Representations give my Reader an Idea of a Person blameless only, or only laudable for such Perfections as extend no farther than to his own private Advantage and Reputation.

But when I speak of You, I Celebrate One who has had the Happiness of possessing also those Qualities which make a Man useful to Society, and of having had Opportunities of Exerting them in the most conspicuous Manner.

The Great Part You had, as *British* Embassador, in Procuring and Cultivating the Advantageous Commerce between the Courts of *England* and *Portugal*, has purchased You the lasting Esteem of all who understand the Interest of either Nation.[1]

Those Personal Excellencies which are over-rated by the ordinary World, and too much neglected by Wise Men, You have applied with the justest Skill and Judgment. The most graceful Address in Horsemanship, in the Use of the Sword, and in Dancing, has been employed by You as lower Arts, and as they have occasionally served to cover, or introduce the Talents of a skilful Minister.

But your Abilities have not appeared only in one Nation. When it was your Province to Act as Her Majesty's Minister at the Court of *Savoy*,[2] at that time encamped, You accompanied that Gallant Prince[3] thro' all the Vicissitudes of His Fortune, and shared, by His Side, the Dangers of that Glorious Day in which He recovered His Capital. As far as it regards Personal Qualities, You attained, in that one Hour, the highest Military Reputation. The Behaviour of our Minister in the Action, and the Good Offices done the Vanquished in the Name of the Queen of *England*, gave both the Conqueror and the Captive the most lively Examples of the Courage and Generosity of the Nation He represented.

and was born in the same year, 1672, as Addison and Steele. He was Minister at Turin in 1705, Ambassador to Portugal 1706–8, and a Lord of the Admiralty 1709–10 and 1714–17. He was appointed Secretary of State in June 1716, a post from which he resigned in April 1717, to be succeeded by Addison. He died at the age of 85, in 1757. Like Addison and Steele he was a member of the Hanover Club.

[1] The treaties with Portugal in 1703, when Paul Methuen was assisting his father, the envoy at Lisbon.

[2] Methuen served as envoy at Savoy, and upon the death of his father was made Envoy Extraordinary to the King of Portugal (*London Gazette*, 12 Sept. 1706).

[3] Victor Amadeus, Duke of Savoy. The reference here is to the battle in September 1706, in which the Duke regained Turin, with the assistance of the Allies under Prince Eugene.

Your Friends and Companions in your Absence frequently talk these Things of You, and You cannot hide from us, (by the most discreet Silence in any Thing which regards your self) that the frank Entertainment we have at your Table, your easie Condescension in little Incidents of Mirth and Diversion, and general Complacency of Manners, are far from being the greatest Obligations we have to You. I do assure You there is not one of your Friends has a Greater Sense of your Merit in general, and of the Favours You every Day do us, than,

SIR,

Your most Obedient, and
most Humble Servant,

Richard Steele.

TO

William Honeycomb, Esq;

THE Seven former Volumes of the *Spectator* having been Dedicated to some of the most celebrated Persons of the Age, I take leave to Inscribe this Eighth and Last to You as to a Gentleman, who hath ever been ambitious of appearing in the best Company.[1]

You are now wholly retired from the busie part of Mankind, and at leisure to reflect upon your past Atchievments; for which reason, I look upon You as a Person very well qualified for a Dedication.

I may possibly disappoint my Readers, and your self too, if I do not endeavour on this occasion to make the World acquainted with your Virtues. And here, Sir, I shall not compliment You upon your Birth, Person, or Fortune; nor any other the like Perfections, which You possess whether You will or no: but shall only touch upon those, which are of your own acquiring, and in which every one must allow You have a real Merit.

Your janty Air and easie Motion, the Volubility of your Dis-

[1] Since Eustace Budgell collaborated with Addison in the revival of the *Spectator* in 1714, the Dedication to Vol. viii has been attributed to him (by Nichols, followed by Morley and Aitken). Gregory Smith assumed it to be by Addison, and the style certainly suggests Addison (cf. 'the secret Ambition of his Heart' and 'the whole Business of their Lives' in paragraph 5).

course, the Suddenness of your Laugh, the Management of your Snuff-Box, with the Whiteness of your Hands and Teeth (which have justly gained You the Envy of the most polite part of the Male World, and the Love of the greatest Beauties in the Female) are entirely to be ascribed to your own personal Genius and Application.

You are formed for these Accomplishments by a happy Turn of Nature, and have finished your self in them by the utmost Improvements of Art. A Man that is defective in either of these Qualifications (whatever may be the secret Ambition of his Heart) must never hope to make the Figure You have done, among the fashionable part of his Species. It is therefore no wonder, we see such multitudes of aspiring young Men fall short of you in all these Beauties of your Character, notwithstanding the Study and Practice of them is the whole Business of their Lives. But I need not tell You that the free and disengaged Behaviour of a fine Gentleman makes as many awkward Beaux, as the Easiness of your Favourite *Waller* hath made insipid Poets.

At present You are content to aim all your Charms at your own Spouse, without further Thought of Mischief to any others of the Sex. I know You had formerly a very great Contempt for that Pedantick Race of Mortals who call themselves Philosophers; and yet, to your Honour be it spoken, there is not a Sage of them all could have better acted up to their Precepts in one of the most important points of Life: I mean in that Generous Disregard of Popular Opinion, which you showed some years ago, when you chose for your Wife an obscure young Woman, who doth not indeed pretend to an ancient Family, but has certainly as many Forefathers as any Lady in the Land, if she could but reckon up their Names.

I must own I conceived very extraordinary hopes of you from the Moment that you confessed your Age, and from eight and forty (where you had stuck so many years) very ingenuously step'd into your Grand Climacterick. Your Deportment has since been very venerable and becoming. If I am rightly informed, You make a regular Appearance every Quarter-Sessions among your Brothers of the *Quorum*; and if things go on as they do, stand fair for being a Colonel of the Militia. I am told that your Time passes away as agreeably in the Amusements of a Country Life, as it ever did in

the Gallantries of the Town: and that you now take as much pleasure in the Planting of young Trees, as you did formerly in the Cutting down of your old ones. In short, we hear from all Hands that You are thoroughly reconciled to your dirty Acres,[1] and have not too much Wit to look into your own Estate.

After having spoken thus much of my Patron, I must take the Privilege of an Author in saying something of my self. I shall therefore beg leave to add, that I have purposely omitted setting those Marks to the End of every Paper, which appeared in my former Volumes, that You may have an opportunity of showing Mrs. *Honeycomb* the Shrewdness of your Conjectures, by ascribing every Speculation to its proper Author: though You know how often many profound Criticks in Stile and Sentiments have very judiciously erred in this Particular, before they were let into the Secret. I am,

SIR,

Your most Faithful
Humble Servant,
The SPECTATOR.

THE

Bookseller *to the* Reader.[2]

*I*N *the Six hundred and thirty second Spectator, the Reader will find an Account of the Rise of this Eighth and Last Volume.*

I have not been able to prevail upon the several Gentlemen who were concerned in this Work to let me acquaint the World with their Names.

Perhaps it will be unnecessary to inform the Reader, that no other Papers,[3] which have appeared under the Title of Spectator, *since the closing of this Eighth Volume, were written by any of those Gentlemen who had a Hand in this or the former Volumes.*

[1] For earlier examples of this expression see *N & Q,* 7th ser., iv (1887), 466; v (1888), 53.

[2] The draft of 'The Bookseller to the Reader' in Tickell's hand exists among the papers in the possession of Major-General Sir Eustace F. Tickell and has been printed in an important article, 'The Eighth Volume of the *Spectator*', by M. J. C. Hodgart, in the *Review of English Studies*, N.S. v (1954), 367–87. This draft is our most valuable piece of evidence for the authorship of Nos. 556–635, which make up the eighth volume. See Introduction, vol. i, p. lxxvi.

[3] The allusion here is probably to the continuation (61 numbers) by William Bond, which ran from 3 Jan. to 3 Aug. 1715 (published on Mondays and Fridays). It later appeared as 'Volume ix' of the *Spectator*.

APPENDIXES

I. Emendation of Accidentals

II. Collation of Textual Variants

III. Advertisements of Books

IV. Sources of Mottoes

V. Documents

APPENDICES

I. EMENDATION OF ACCIDENTALS

As explained in the Introduction (pp. cvii–cviii) the Folio sheets have been used as copy-text for the present edition. All substantive departures from this text are given as footnote variants. As to spelling, punctuation, capitalization, and the like (the 'accidentals' of the text) an attempt has been made to retain those which are common to the early eighteenth century, though now obsolete; errors on the other hand which seem due to the compositor or printing-house rather than to Addison or Steele have been corrected. Such corrections, however, placed at the foot of each page as 'variant readings', would make an edition of the *Spectator* seem an embodiment of the pedantry which Addison so successfully parodies in No. 470. They are instead listed here as Appendix I, where they can be consulted by those interested.

Certain typographical changes are not recorded: the long *s* has been altered to the modern form; inverted commas for quoted material are employed according to present-day usage; accents in Greek words have been silently corrected; *æ* and *œ* in Latin words have been made to conform to modern usage; proper names have been uniformly italicized; faulty punctuation or absence of a full stop at the end of a sentence is silently emended; dates at the head of each number are given in the form 'March 1, 1711' rather than 'March 1. 1711' as in the original sheets; arabic numerals have been uniformly employed in place of the roman numerals which were used for Nos. 1–555. The wrong numbering of several essays in the original sheets (Nos. 155–61, 163–4, 388, 390, 578, 584–6, 590–2, 596–8, 602–4, 607–35) has been silently corrected.

References are to page and line. The reading following the bracket is that of the Folio copy-text.

VOLUME I

9. 16: Marriage-Articles,] Marriages-Articles,
17. 7: *Vires*] *Vires,*
27. 4: *Whittington*] *Wittington*
28. 7: Source] Sourse
30. 35: accommodate] accomodate
61. 10: *Powell*] *Powel*
65. 25: Hay-market] Hay-maaket
75. 5: prominent] promient
80. 24: Graces,] Graces
82. 19: *Di bene fecerunt,*] *Dii benefecerunt*
83. 33: knowledge] kowledge
84. 1: Piece] Peice
89. 10: Laity,] Laiety,
91. 3–4: impaling] impailing
92. 6: *sic,*] *sic*
97. *m.*: *Volscens,*] *Volscens*
     Auctorem,] *Auctorem*
99. 17: Sophy] Sophi

100. 26: *quidam,*] *quidam*
     27: *agis,*] *agis*
101. 10: teized] tiezed
105. 9: *Sydenham's*] *Sidenam's*
105. 12: Phthisical] Pthisical
108. 28: *turres. O beate Sesti,*] *turres, o beate Sexti,*
     29: incohare] inchoare
122. 8: Signior] Seignior
130. 1: *Powell,*] *Powel,*
     3: *Powell*] *Powel*
131. 18: *Turkey*] *Turky*
135. 18: Polls] Poles
142. 15: HONEYCOMB] HONEY-COMBE
143. 20: Hairs,] Heirs,
147. 29: FALSEHOOD.] FALSES-HOOD.
153. 14: Shapes,] Shapes
     26: Faggots] Fagots
154. 14: *Isaac*] *Isaack*

189

166. 20: *Projicit Ampullas*] *Prolicit ampu-*
    lias (corr. in Errata, No. 40)
167. 17: *Otway*] *Ottway*
168. 10: *tractent*] *tractant*
180. 16: Batallions,] Battallions,
182. 10: bottom] botton
189. 32: Parricides] Paracides
190. 24: *Metamorphosis,*] *Metamorposis,*
192. 26–27: HONEYCOMB] HONY-
    COMB
196. 5: Rhapsody] Rapsody
197. 20: *Honeycomb's*] *Honeycombe's*
211. 18: *dicit.*] *dixit.*
221. 4: *neutro, si*] *neutro si,*
230. 32: Dial] Dial.
232. 29: *queo. Surge.*] *queo surge.*
233. 22: *an hunc*] *an hunce* (corr. in Errata,
    No. 58)
234. 11: *Borachio,*] *Boracchio,*
235. 1: *Catiline*] *Cataline*
    27: concerted] conserted
241. 15: Wig;] Whig;
242. 28: Toast] Tost
    29: *Penthesilea*] *Penthesilia*
243. 26: HONEYCOMB] *Honycombe*
244. 8: HONEYCOMB,] Honycombe,
246. 7, 28: Shepherd's] Shephard's
251. 14: *Camden*] *Cambden*
259. *m.*: *equidem hoc studeo,*] *equidem stu-*
    deo,
261. 2: Account] Acount
262. 5: settled,] setled,
269. 19: Rind] Rhind
270. 12: *teneatis,*] *teneatis*
    13: *Credite, Pisones,*] *Credite Pisones*
272. 18: Labyrinths] Labarynths
273. 11: reality] reallity
277. 4: universal] univarsal
278. *m.*: *Demetri, teque, Tigelli,*] *Demetri*
    teque Tigelli
281. *m.*: *Artibus*] *Artubus*
286. 29: HONEYCOMB] HONY-
    COMBE
294. 4: *Swede,*] *Sweed,*
299. 6: Advantages] Advantage
300. 11: hundred] hundreed
303. 20: *miris?*] *miris*
305. 9: *Care,*] *Care*
321. 13: Day?] Day.
328. 12: Looks,] Looks
    25: skilful] skiful
329. 14: of the Power,] of / of the Power,
329. 21: HONEYCOMB] HONEY-
    COMBE
331. 18: HONEYCOMB,] HONEY-
    COMBE,
337. 13: taught] taughs
339. 4: HONEYCOMB] HONEY-
    COMBE
343. 7: Stature,] Stature

351. 24: Honour,] Honour
359. 22: inadvertency,] Inadvertency
392. 11: *Adultery*] *Adultry*
393. 3: accommodate] accomodate
396. 13: considered] considereded
    14: but if] buif
398. *m.*: Mart.] M.
402. 9: *loquuntur,*] *loquuntur*
413. 6: Grass-hoppers] Gras-/hoppers
423. 25: *Isaac*] *Isaack*
426. 6: *dari*] *dari,*
436. 1: HONEYCOMB,] HONY-
    COMB,
449. 18: *Abnormis*] *Ab normis* (corr. in
    Errata, No. 110)
451. 13: Deer-stealers] Dear-stealers
458. 3: *haeres*] *heres,*
    4: *Haeredem*] *Heredem*
467. 6: *Rufus,*] *Rufus*
    Rufo,] *Rufo*
472. 37: Wood-Cocks.] Wood-Cooks.
473. 15–16: *Sydenham*] *Sidenham*
474. 6: Treatise]Treatice
478. 25–26: afterwards] aftewards
486. 15: *Melibœ,*] *Melibæ,*
492. 35: mysterious] misterious
493. 25: *Bayle*] *Bale* (corr. in Errata,
    No. 127)
496. 33: Original,] Original
497. 26: frag.] Frag.
501. 20: Writing] Wrting
508. 10: Oculists] Occulists
511. 32: League,] League.

VOLUME II

10. 16: Gentleman] Gentlemen (corr. in
    Errata, No. 130)
13. 22: *Friezeland*] *Freeze-land*
15. 11: Steenkirk] Stinkirk
21. 6: HONEYCOMB,] HONY-
    COMBE,
    25: HONEYCOMB.] HONY-
    COMBE.
28. 17: thou] thon
29. 22: Beau] Beaux
30. 31: fain] feign
31. 5: Wiseacre.] Wiseaker.
34.35: *rep.*] *reb.*
36. 6: *Spaniards*] *Spaniard*
48. 27: *Alexovitz*] *Alexiwitz*
63. 31: up,] up
65. 22: sitting] sit
69. 19: let her] her let
77. 10: obliterated] oblitterated (corr. in
    Errata, No. 148)
85. 23: *Apud*] Apud.
94. 7: Inability] Inablity
96. 17: Οἴη περ] Ὀιήδη
    30: SENTRY,] SENTREY,

98. 29: Who's] whose
100. 1: Wishes which] which Wishes
   (corr. in Errata, No. 154)
103. 10: he shall be] be shall be
108. 23: Sufferer] Suffererer
128. 12: Bienseance] Bien se'ance
132. 26: always] alwas
135. 21: worldly] wordly
147. 2: unparallel'd] unparelled
149. m.: dabiturque] labiturque
   n. 1: bovem,] bovem
164. 28: Ita] ita
194. 13: Philosophy,] Philosopy,
203. 5: my self,] my self.
207. 28: very] ve-/very
208. 16: Reges,] Reges
219. 27: Jotham's] Jothram's
225. 27: Sleeping,] Sleepinig,
244. 9: Le Comte,] le Conte,
263. 9: καὶ] δὲ
282. 19: when] when,
284. 19: be] be be
286. 25: ἥμισυ παντὸς] ἥμισι παντὰ (corr.
   in Errata, No. 201)
297. 24: Rise from our] Rise our (corr.
   in Errata, No. 205)
315. 3: should] should should
317. 21: οὐδὲν] οὐδὲ
321. 31: cannot] cannnt
323. 18: equally] equallly
328. 15: sum, dic] dic, sum
330. 1: ille] illo
   4: Extimescendum.] Entimescendum.
   5: Gentleman] Genlteman
   24: can] cen
332. 9: Limborch,] Limborck,
337. 16: unaccountable] anacconntable
345. m.: repetitus] repetitur
349. 21: supported] supporeed
355. 9: on one Side,] one one Side,
362. m.: ungui,] ungi,
365. m.: quale in] qualem
370. 25: remarkable:] remarkabe:
382. m.: ὑπακούεις;] ὑπαχούεις;
388. 15: and, Time] And Time
391. 9: aures,] aures.
401. 15: largiundo] largiendo
406. m.: sit] sint
410. 26: thing] think
413. 4: thing] think
417. 4: observe] observe,
420. 16: carenti] carentem
428. 19: December 4,] December 3.
434. 13: December 3d,] December, 3d,
435. 10: videtur] vidatur
439. 6: accersit] arcessit
443. 8–9: Mathematicks.] Mathethicks.
448. 26: Circumstance] Cricumstance
454. 9: μήτηρ·] μήτηρ
461. 11: atræ:] atræ,

471. 20: Ἥρη—] ἥρη—
472. 4: Scintillae] Scinctillae
473. 14: of it,] of / of it,
474. 5: Ramage] Marage (corr. in Errata,
   No. 252)
479. 12: Marriage Ceremony.] Marriage-
   Ceremony?
485. 24: λόφον.] λόφον·
487. 20: the least] the / the least
   23: Imitation;] Imita-/on;
488. 6: transform] tranform
   15: Acquaintance] Acquaintances
491. 30: Sallust's] Salust's
492. 30: Meanness] Meaness
499. 26: proceeded] procedeed
505. 7: Insolence] Inso-/solence
529. 23: One,] Ones,
534. m.: oderit.] oderat.
   2: Desires] Desire,
   25: under one] under in one
535. 22: Women,] Woman,
549. 6: Scanderbeg.] Scanderbag.
550. 18: Neighbours,] Neigbours,
552. 17: Beds] Bed (corr. in Errata,
   No. 271)
553. 32: Instant] instance (corr. in Errata, No. 271)
556. 37: self] self.
558. 12: injuria,] injuria
560. 15: Marriage-Settlement.] Mar-
   riage-Sentlement.
563. 1: Cloanthum:] Cloanthum
568. 14: deserves,] desevers,
576. 26: be sure] besure
583. 20: makes] make
586. 13: meanness] meaness
586. 14: risen] rise

VOLUME III

1. 25: Catiline's] Catlaine's See textual
   note.
4. 5, 18: Rabelais,] Rablais,
10. 33: Idiomatick] Idomatick
11. 8: A while] Awhile
12. 21: Horace] Horae
13. 24: Beëlzebub,] Bëelzebub
15. 6: precedes] preceds
21. 12–13: Government] Goverment
24. 17: of] of / of
25. 29–30: India-Company,] India-Compaay,
27. m.: incohare] inchoare
34. 16: SPECTATOR,] SPECTAROR,
35. m.: Offendar] Offendor
   17: perfected] prefected
40. 29: Virtue-] in Virtue- / in
42. 22: Richelieu] Richlieu
45. 15: Inscription,] Inscripion,
50. 19: reputant] reputat
54. 5: large] lage

56. 29: 1680.] 1780.
61. 5: represented] represent
62. 2: them] them.
62. 24: Words,] Worlds,
70. 17: Countenance] Coutenance
72. 23: of the] of the / the
73. 14: there are any] there any
75. *m.: Possent*] *Possint*
78. 15: *corpore*] *copore*
92. *m.: cœco*] *caro*
94. 8: exercising] excising
95. 16: Receptacle] Recepticle
99. 32: doughty] doubty
101. 9: which] whick
102. 24: same] same.
    26: answered,] answered.
106. 15: insensibly] insensiby
126. 8: Dear Sir,] Dear, Sir,
128. 9: *sibi esse persuaserit ?*] *sibi persuaserit ?*
129. 18: Nature] Nuture
130. 18: impertinent] impertineet
135. 4: Civil] Cilvil
    7: in the] in the the
136. *m.: desine*] *de sine*
    2: I am] I A am
137. 32: Mistakes] Mistake
141. 3: Strength] Strentgh
145. 9: it] t
146. 2: *Circe,*] *Circe*
    16: Natural,] Natural
    18: Penetration.] Penetraction. (corr.
      in Errata, No. 327)
169. 15: *Non*] *Nec*
180. 18: believed] belived
184. 16: *Ancora.*] *Ancoza.* (corr. in Er-
      rata, No. 325)
    21: MONDAY.] MONDAY
    25: within a] within, a
190. 10: *discedat*] *discedet*
193. 17–21: *Indentation regularized.*
194. 30: Spirit,] Sprit,
196. 13: gnaw] knaw
    15: Partridge] Patridge
200. 29: *wide,*] *wid,*
201. 14: they] thy
204. 28: *a labore me*] *me a labore*
212. 8: *quo*] *qua*
214. 13: other] others
219. 19: t'other] to'ther
221. 19: *Ælian,*] *Elian*
227. 15: *Adamantine*] *Adamatine*
237. 25: what is] is what
241. 27: them?] them;
243. *m.: Clament*] *Clamant*
    coner,] *conor,*
244. 34: more,] more.
246. 10: *monstret*] *monstrat*
260. 9: Leviathan] Leviathian
262. 9: a Man,] a / a Man,
267. 23: in] in / in

270. 4: received] recived
    21: further] furthet
271. 14: deserves?] deserve?
    16: than] then
272. 2: Daughter,] Daugher,
    8: truly] trully
284. 26: The Poet] the Poet
294. 21: little] litle
296. 30: *Triplett*] *Tripplett*
299. 30: descanted] discanted
303. 14: *Calais.*] *Calice.*
    18: Cruelty.] Cruelity
306. 27: *Æneid,*] *Eneid*
310. 31: those flaggings] that flaggings
      (corr. in Errata, No. 369)
313. 19: fashionable,] faishonable,
314. 29: perplexity,] *perlexite,*
    30: streight] *stright*
315. 11: drop] *droop*
    34: speaks] *speeks*
320. 7: Occasions:] Occasion:
    11: insipid] insiped
322. 6: speaks] speak
    9: Edifices,] Edifies,
326. 3: and] and / and
327. 17: Doctrine] Doctorine
336. 10: *live,*] *live*
347. 26: Delicacy,] Delicay,
    33: Confusion] Confussion
348. 22: here] hear
349. 12: *omne*] *omnis*
352. 20: seen] seen
353. 8: *Laudibus*] *Lundibus*
354. 10: to give] to / to give
    13: *Cully Mully*] *Mully Mully*
355. 37: knew] know
357. 8: Manner,] Manner.
366. 13: indiscreet] indiscret
368. 31: Policies,] Polices,
    38: Policies] Polices
370. 21: self,] self.
371. 2: Amorous] Amorus
    4: exquisite] enquisite
374. 3: Strawberries] Strawberies
375. 18: the Work] the / the Work
376. 6: agreeably] agreeable
    14: Natives] Natvies
377. 29: too] *to*
    32: here.] *hear.*
381. 2: Billets doux,] Billet-doux,
    13: *France,*] *Fance,*
382. 8: from a] from the a
    25: *mala;*] *mala*
383. 23: lose] loose
    26: stripped] striped
384. 4: off] of
385. 9–10: Misfortune.] Misfottune.
388. 2: Rapture] Raptute
393. 28: shadowy] shadowey
394. 24: knows] know

399. 25: unacceptable] unaccepta-
401. 10: Institution] Institutions
   16: Entertainment] Entertianment
402. 8: to send] to / to send
   19: Judgment] Jugdment
406. 28: Antediluvians:] Antidiluvians:
408. 25: then.] than.
416. *m*.: *quisque vitet*,] *quisque, vitet*
   Cautum] *Cantum*
418. 5: R.F, T.W, S.I, M.P,] R, F.T,
   W.S, I.M, P.
419. 11: *Mossie*] Mossic
420. 2: *hallow'd*] hollow'd
421. 23: *surprize*] suprize
424. 32: *Rosicrucius's*] *Rosicrucias's*
425. 2: *Rosicrucian*] Rosicrosian
   25: *Rosicrucius*,] *Rosicrucias*,
426. 23: distinguish] distingush
   28: another,] onother,
428. 16: then] than
   33: with] within
435. 22: Spirit,] Spirt,
438. 4: Years?] Years;
   31: Peremptory] Peremtory
446. 11: *Æneas*] *Eneas*
456. 12: Head,] *Head.*
462. 22: Ammunition] Amunition
464. 32: *Queen*, says] *Queen* says,
466. 24: *Ebulliat patruus*] *Ebullit patrui*
485. 5: Proceedings,] Proceed-/ceedings,
   15: Mr.] Mr,
   18: surprizing] suprizing
489. 13: *paret*] *pares*
490. 9: forsooth,] forsootb,
491. 5: asked] aked
492. 29: Villain] Villian
493. 26: really] rea-/ly
495. 39: sift] sifft
502. 17: *Philander.*] *Phylander.*
   18: Philander.] *Phylander.*
   23: Repentance] Repentanee
   32: *Philander*,] *Phylander*,
   35: *Philander*] *Phylander*
506. 9: prescribe] prescrbie
508. 17: Kingdom] Kingdon
509. 6: late] *late*
510. 9: Ridicule] Redicule
513. 11: Repugnancy] Repungnancy
518. 7: *Tam*] *Tum*
522. 23: Wigg] Whigg
   28: you] You
523. 22: of humane] of / of humane
528. 26: distinguishing] distingushing
534. 26: *o'er*] *oe'r*
553. 23: Treatises] Treaties
556. 20: *Cymatium*] *Cynatium*
559. 12: Irregularity.] Iregularity.
562. *m*.: *Illum non*] *Non illum*
568. 18: *extinctos*] *extinctus*
571. 2: *innati*] *inanti*

575. 14: Stars] Sars
   19: Labyrinth] Labarynth
576. 25: Chasm,] Charm, (corr. in Errata, No. 421)
596. 22: of] of of
   28: conspicuous] conspicuons
   36: *February*,] *Febrnary*,
598. 2: into] int
600. 5: *Table*] *Taste* (corr. in Errata,
   No. 427)
   9: *the Womb*,] *the the Womb*,

VOLUME IV

7–11: *Inverted commas supplied in No. 429.*
8. 14: lies] i es
   16: Sheweth,] Sheweth.
   22: during] druing
9. 7: Jolly,] Jolly
10. 12–13: impertinent] impertient
   21: Days'] Day's
16. 35: distinguish'd] dishinguish'd
20. 16: Olivia.] Olivio.
   19: ' "IT] 'IT
32. 19: *Amarillis*] *Armarillis*
37. 16: unhappy] unhapy
38. 13: Countenance.] Conntenance.
40. 33: call a peevish] call a peevsh
41. 26: turning] turniug
   28: Chapman,] Chapman
   32: he,] he
   35: Chapman,] Chapman
53. 28: Coquets,] Cocquets,
54. 3: more),] more)
56. 8: Countryman,] Conntryman,
58. *n*. 2: *hiatu?*] *hiatu*
67. 4: afraid] affraid
   17: *Nosses*] *Nosces*
69. 17: anew,] a new,
72. 21: degrees,] degrees
80. 6: decrepid] decripid
85. 19: and] and / and
86. 26: effectually] effectualy
90. 32: Story] Stoty
91. 4: Mail:] Male:
98. 9: *dem*] *duim*
106. 29: know,] know.
108. 33: transferred] tranferred
   37: divide] devide
109. 13–14: destroy'd.] desttoy'd.
118. 26: Pre-eminence] Preminence
119. 15: Religion;] Religon;
134. *m*.: *aurigae*] *aurigis*
135. 10: *put*] *puts*
   17: *now*] *more*
147. 3: her,] her.
150. *m*.: *nec*] *ne*
153. 30: it] it it
159. *m*.: *paupertas*,] *paupertas*
191. 27–28: Hornbeam,] Hornbean,

192–6. *Inverted commas supplied.*
196. 14: exert themselves] exert themseves
198. 22: squawling] squalwing
200. 6: *that*] *ehat*
201. *m.*: *honores*] *honores,*
    se ipso totus, teres] *seipso totus teres,*
205. *m.*: *Compositum*] *Compositus*
214. 13: *Cleobis,*] *Clitobus,*
220. 4: will observe] willo bserve
223. 7: *moechos*] *moechis*
    20: greater] grearer
230. 7: *parvo.*] *parvi.*
233. 8: *Judgment*] *Judgmant*
234. 23: other] other other
237. 11–12. Institution] Institutution
242. 9: *Rhynsault*] *Rhinsault*
243. 26: th' Avenger] th Avenger
249. 35: Word] World
250. 5: Yours,] Yours
255. 9: World,] Word,
259. 33–34: Circumstances] Circum-/cumstance
266. 24: too;] to;
267. 33: Place,] Plaec,
269. 1: HONEYCOMB] HONYCOMB
272. 11: HONEYCOMB.] HONY-COMB.
273. 5: drawn] dawn
    34: As] As / as
    36: Man] Men
274. 14: rode] rod
276. 12: Splendour] Splen-/our
277. 17: upon] up-/pon
280. *m.*: *lubet.*] *lubent.*
282. 15: Mind.] Minds.
285. 32: Countenance.] Countenace.
292. 27: prophesies] Prophecies
302. 12: Superiority] Superio-/ty
305. 7: Understanding,] Understading,
320. 7: *Deo . . .*] *Dei . . .*
329. 14: *Cowley*] *Cowly*
    19: *Xenophon*] *Zenophon*
333. 12: a] a / a
334. *m.*: *credat*] *credit*
    colit . . .] *colat. . .*
338. 14: Stay] Sray
347. 6–7: Perceptive] Preceptive
349. 34: Brethren,] Brethreu,
357. *date: Wednesday,*] *Wedndesay,*
    m.: omnis] *omneis*
359. 33: Heirs] Heris
360. 12: own] owe
366. 25: *Worldly*] *Wordly*
369. 4: bewitching Water,] betwitching Water,
378. 28: rose] rise
386. 12: Learned,] Leaned,
391. 2: not] nor
395. 17: Prophaneness] Prophaness

401. 22: Pert?] Tert?
403. 18–19: Lords *Hallifax, Anglisey* and *Shaftsbury,*] Lord *Hallifax, Anglisey Shaftsbury,*
    22: *Anglisey*] *Anglsey*
405. 28: Mrs.] Mr.
407. 27: *Mr.*] *Mr,*
412. 20: Footmen] Footman
415. 2: HONEYCOMB,] HONY-COMBE,
427. 5: as ever] as / as ever
428. 2: THERE] IHERE
429. 1: *Fairy-Land,*] *Fairy-Eand,*
430. 9: *meet*] *weet*
    9: *somme;*] *soomme;*
431. 17: *Myrrhe*] *Myrhbe*
433. 4: *despairing!*] *dsepairing!*
439. 11: wholly] wholy
445. *m.*: *Quin res, Ætas,*] *Quia res, Ætas novi,*] *novi*
    nescias,] *nescias*
445. 2: SENTRY,] SENTREY,
    20: SENTRY.] SENTREY.
451. 35: Ladies,] Ladies.
455. 1: Thieves.] Theives.
    8: Acknowledgment] Acknowledgent
456. 6: Addition] Adition
461–2. *Inverted commas supplied in first paragraph of No. 548.*
469. 17: HONEYCOMB.] HONEY-COMBE.
    18: HONEYCOMB] HONEY-COMBE
470. 4: SENTRY's] SENTREY's
478. 18: *amabitur*] *amabiter*
486. 18: than] that
493. 20: Gentlemen,] Genntlemen,
494. 5: ANDREW] ANDRRW
502. 4: *Monday, June 21, 1714.*] *From* FRIDAY, *June 18.* to MONDAY, *June 21. 1714.*
520. 19: *sçavoir*] *scavoir*
523. 6: thus,   .] thus
530. 7: annihilated,] anihilated,
531. 23: is Omniscient.] his Omniscient.
533. 11: pretty] pre-/ty
540. 6: *Answer that*] *Answer, that*
541. 20: against] aginst
    24: *laborant,*] *laborent,*
543. 29: *Syrus.*] *Cyrus.* (corr. in Errata, No. 570)
544. 27: *adeò*] *adeó*
547. *m.*: *quaerimus*] *qaerimus*
547–50. *Inverted commas supplied.*
551. *m.*: *Promittunt*] *Promittant*
555. 5: Assiduous] Assidious
    7: Assistance] Assistacce
559. 31: Mr.] Mr
563. 33: he] He

565. 15: Despair] Dispair
571. 1: generally] generallly
    13: Piece] Peice
    22: *Fontenelle's*] *Fontinell's*
573. 20: addressing] ad-/addressing
575. 16: *Identity.*] *Indentity.*
    10–11: *Identity*] *Indentity*
577. 25: communicate] commu-/cate
578. 34: *Zemroude*] *Zamroude*
579. 8: *serenade*] *senerade*
581. 20: compromised] comprimised
591. 14: entitled] entitled,
595. 4: Neighbour] Neigbour

VOLUME V

4. 3: SIR,] IR,
6. 1: perpetually] pre-/petually
10. 5: of] of / of
14. 10: to] to / to
    11: *September* 3, 1714.] *September.* 3
    1714.
19. 32: Understanding] Undestanding
    37: who has] who, has
21. 25: intitles] intiles
22. 6: ineffable] inneffable
    8: prompted] prompred
25. 28: *Friday,*] FRYDAY,
28. 4: Deviations] Diviations
33. 29: Discourse] Discouse
34. 10: Symptoms,] Simptoms,
34. 20: *geminentur,*] *geminenter,*
36. 4: effectually] effectuaily
43. 11: Oneirocritical] Oncicrocritical
    17: *Friday,*] FRYDAY,
44. 10: notwithstanding] nothwith-
    standing
53. 1: examine;] examin ;
54. *m.*: εὐεργετικὸς] ἐυργετὸς
58. 13: *September* 8,] *September* 8.
60. 12: *No*] *Nor*
64. 16: *Friday,*] FRYDAY,
67. 15: *voles*] *voces*
70. 19: to her] to / to her

71. 9: *Conjunx*] *Conjux*
76. 27: thereunto] threunto
79. 6: *his said*] *hiss aid*
80. 15: of] of / of
84. *date*: *Friday,*] FRYDAY,
89. 35: Resentments] Resentmens
90. 22: Rencounter] Recounter
    24: a Church-Porch] a-/ Church-
    Porch
92. 2: thousand] thou-/thousand
94. 29: Meanness] Meaness
98. *m.*: *tædæque*] *tedæque*
100. 18: *At*] *As*
105. *date*: *Friday,*] FRYDAY,
107. *m.*: *superbo*] *superba*
    ingeminat;] *ingeminat*
    5: College.] Collge,
108. 13: Multitude,] Mnltitnde,
    16: Insinuations,] Insi-/uations,
120. 21: *Behold*] ehold
122. 22: *Man*] Mau
124. 12: Heart] Heĕrt
125. 23: Thought] Thoughr
127–8. *Inverted commas supplied.*
135. 8: blackest] blakest
    17–18: confident] coufident
137. 20: Letters] Leters
138. 5: Gesticulation] Gesti-/fication
139. 27: disagreeable] disagree-/ble
140. 6: Desires.] Desirres.
    7: detracts] detacts
    36: not] not not
141. 21: They] The
    36: Distinctions.] Dictinctions.
152. 4: *Novemb.* 22.] *Novemb* 22.
157. 10: Love:] Love;
159. 8: *Gregorio*] *Gregerio*
160. 30: *Dublin,*] *Dublin*
165. 21: Judgment,] Jndgment,
    32: Countries] Conntries
169. *m.*: *contemplari: quae*] *contemplariquae*
170. 29–30: diversified;] de-/versified;
172. 35: Thought] Thonght

II. COLLATION OF TEXTUAL VARIANTS

THE following list of variant readings in the first 8vo and 12mo editions and (for the Milton papers) the 1719 *Notes upon Paradise Lost* is confined to substantives; it does not ordinarily include differences in spelling or punctuation, unless these affect the meaning. The 8vo and 12mo editions frequently modernized or regularized the text, changing, e.g. *o'er* to *over*, *won't* to *will not*. Such changes are not listed here. Many of the rejected variants will be recognized as the source of readings which have persisted down to the present time in reprints of the *Spectator*.

Each item consists first of the reading in the present edition (by page and line), viz. the Folio reading. The reading following the square bracket is, unless otherwise indicated, that of *both* 8vo and 12mo editions and also (for the Milton papers) the *Notes upon Paradise Lost*. When one of the editions has the same reading as the Folio text, this is indicated by a wavy line.

VOLUME I

11. 24: this Way] his way
48. 10: rose,] ∼ *8vo*; arose, *12mo*
51. 6: hold him] hold him awake
53. 22: which] ∼ *8vo*; that *12mo*
90. 6: their] ∼ *8vo*; the *12mo*
107. 12: *Your most Humble*] *Your Humble* 8vo; *Your humble* 12mo
118. 7: make] makes
    13: Countrymen] Country-man
124. 16: Members] Member
144. 14: candid and ingenuous] candid ingenuous
185. 5: nor] ∼ *12mo*; not *8vo*
188. 3: us as a People] ∼ *8vo*; us a People *12mo*
200. 18: divert] ∼ *8vo*; diverting *12mo*
216. 30: know but one] ∼ *12mo*; know not but one *8vo*
222. 25: could both make] could make
242. 23: not I] I not
302. 15: *No paragraph in 8vo and 12mo.*
314. 6: prettily] ∼ *8vo*; pettily *12mo*
317. 14: *To*] ∼ *12mo*; *Tho* 8vo
319. 8: *deadly*] ∼ 12mo; *deeply* 8vo
323. 1–2: Theatrical Air and Tone] ∼ *12mo*; Theatrical Tone *8vo*
332. 7: I had lived,] ∼ *8vo*; I lived, *12mo*
336. 29: your poor Petitioners] ∼ *8vo*; your Petitioners *12mo*
344. 15: in few Days] ∼ *12mo*; in a few Days *8vo*
345. 8: those] ∼ *12mo*; these *8vo*
348. 25: deprive] deprives
351. 16: *New paragraph in 8vo and 12mo.*
385. 19–20: called a Lady] called to a Lady

388. 6: reading this] ∼ *8vo*; reading of this *12mo*
401. 34: with some useful] with useful
424. 3: that it will cool] ∼ *12mo*; that will cool *8vo*
425. 7: at a House] at the House
434. 26: a Part] ∼ *8vo*; Part *12mo*
448. 9: begun] began
450. 15: against] ∼ *12mo*; again *8vo*
464. 13: ride] rid
465. 18: all together,] ∼ *12mo*; altogether, *8vo*
467. 11: lumen] numen,
468. 37: But] Yet
469. 3: into] ∼ *8vo*; in *12mo*
472. 7: Motion] Motions
488. 23: make] ∼ 8vo; makes *12mo*
502. 11: begun] began
503. 5: had not he] ∼ *8vo*; had he not *12mo*

VOLUME II

10. 8: *New paragraph in 8vo and 12mo.*
21. 20: Service to the Knight.] ∼ *8vo*; Service to Knight. *12mo*
23. 19: to be Brideman,] to be the Brideman,
    38: sayeth] said
33. 4: makes] make
35. 20: *Who, which* or *that*,] *whom which* or *they*, 8vo; *whom which* or *they* 12mo. *The Folio reading has been retained here, in spite of the Errata notice in No. 137: 'for that read they', which was apparently intended not for 'that' but for 'it'*

in the same line of the Folio copy ('whether it may have Admission') *and duly corrected in 8vo and 12mo.*

49. 3: Honour, an] Honour, and
53. 1: peculiar] ~ 8vo; perticular *12mo*
53. 2–3: therefore endeavour to imitate] ~ *8vo*; therefore imitate *12mo*

    6: be the Consequence] ~ *8vo*; be Consequence *12mo*
61. 19: Paper,] ~ *8vo*; Papers, *12mo*
63. 30: Admirer] ~ *8vo*; Admirers *12mo*
64. 16: or Misfortune,] of Misfortune, *all edd. The reading adopted here is that of the original letter* (Correspondence, *ed. Blanchard, p. 273*).
66. 31–32: as is his ordinary] ~ *8vo*; as his ordinary *12mo*
69. 8: Subject] Subjects
70. 17: as] ~ *12mo*; is *8vo*
73. 17: need] needs
75. 22–23: For it is of necessity, that one of these two things must be the Consequence.] For it must of necessity be, that one of these two things must be the Consequence. *Fol. The Errata notice in No. 148 corrects 'must' in the first clause to 'is', but this correction was not made in the 8vo and 12mo editions.*
82. 29: not at all] not all
    30: Observations] Observation
86. 17: it is] ~ *8vo*; is it *12mo*
87. 7: take it for granted,] ~ *8vo*; take for granted, *12mo*
92. 10: its] his
    35: Servant] Servants
101. 9: which it is not] ~ *8vo*; which is not *12mo*
104. 5: Occasions] Occasion
108. 2: this] it
111. 35: with her herself.] ~ *8vo*; with herself. *12mo*
117. 6: Lads] ~ *8vo*; Leads *12mo*
122. 13–14: a little Musical] ~ *8vo*; a Musical *12mo*
147. 11: Resolution] Resolutions
148. 32: lie] ~ *8vo*; lies *12mo*
161. 32: *No paragraph in 8vo and 12mo.*
162. 32: come] came
    35: Whisperers,] Whisperers *8vo*; Whispers *12mo*
165. 6: upon one another.] ~ *12mo*; upon another. *8vo*
183. 24: County] ~ *12mo*; Country *8vo*
189. 19: *Signature letter om. in 12mo.*

190. 16: begun] ~ *8vo*; began *12mo*
194. 25: is very frequent] ~ *8vo*; is frequent *12mo*
195. 21–22: This . . . never fails.] ~ *8vo*; om. *12mo*
196. 30: ten thousand thousand] ~ *8vo*; ten thousand *12mo*
200. 26: *not I*] ~ 8vo; *I not* 12mo
202. 16: as if he were] ~ *8vo*; as if he was *12mo*
205. 3: should] ~ *8vo*; would *12mo*
212. 1: though a known] though known
216. 30: Enormities which you] ~ *8vo*; Enormities you *12mo*
218. 23: accused of] ~ *8vo*; accused for *12mo*
219. 12: Harkee, SPEC.] ~ *8vo*; Harkee, Mr. SPEC. *12mo*
    18: *Signature letter om. in 8vo and 12mo.*
223. 3: *upon them both,*] ~ 8vo; *upon both,* 12mo
228. 13: a very keen] ~ *8vo*; a keen *12mo*
232. 12: Foundation.] ~ *8vo*; Foundations. *12mo*
238. 8–9: undistinguishing] ~ *8vo*; undistinguished *12mo*
241. 6: who has said] ~ *8vo*; who said *12mo*
243. 15: Apprehensions] ~ *8vo*; Apprehension *12mo*
248. 8: nauseous to us.] nauseous in us.
253. 10: the future great] the great
259. 23: *glad I see you,*] glad to see you,
266. 15: that great] ~ *8vo*; the great *12mo*
270. 33: *Signature letter om. in 12mo.*
273. 1: begun] ~ *8vo*; began *12mo*
277. 8: *with*] ~ 12mo; *which* 8vo
281. 3: what convenient Corner] ~ *12mo*; what Corner *8vo*
    8: made to it self] ~ *12mo*; made it self *8vo*
    10: of a Debauchée] ~ *8vo*; of the Debauchée *12mo*
284. 27: will] ~ *8vo*; would *12mo*
286. 13–15: wou'd not exceed one Fourth Part of its present Value, or pay more than one Fourth Part of the present Tax.] ~ *8vo*; wou'd not exceed one fourth Part of the present Tax. *12mo*
295. 19: these] ~ *8vo*; those *12mo*
297. 2: Stratagems] ~ *8vo*; Stratagem *12mo*
299. 3: by] ~ *8vo*; through *12mo*
    23: gay] ~ *8vo*; my *12mo*
300. 19: who] ~ *8vo*; that *12mo*

302. 5: in the Day] ~ *8vo*; in Day *12mo*
15: thy] ~ *8vo*; your *12mo*
311. 7: content] ~ *12mo*; contented *8vo*
313. 37: Blessing] ~ *12mo*; Blessings *8vo*
314. 13: *Signature letter om. in 8vo.*
315. 37: insensible] ~ *8vo*; sensible *12mo*
316. 38: *obliged*] ~ 8vo; *Obedient* 12mo
319. 17: *in a separate*] ~ 12mo; *in separate* 8vo
38: *her Looks and her Words*] ~ 8vo; *her Looks and Words* 12mo
320. 2: *a Beast of Burden.*] ~ 12mo; *a Beast of a Burden.* 8vo
16–17: *to her Owner,*] *to the Owner,*
321. 26: bound his] ~ *12mo*; bound to his *8vo*
329. 4: to that Pass,] ~ *8vo*; to pass, *12mo*
331. 15: to a Virtue,] ~ *8vo*; to Virtue, *12mo*
333. 4: makes] ~ *12mo*; make *8vo*
27: that] ~ *8vo*; the *12mo*
334. 33: by want of] ~ *8vo*; for want of *12mo*
337. 8: his Patron] ~ *8vo*; the Patron *12mo*
341. 5: or a *Praxiteles*] ~ 12mo; or *Praxiteles* 8vo
343. 24: Complaisance] ~ *12mo*; Compliance *8vo*
351. 8: wherein] ~ *12mo*; where *8vo*
356. 6: *locus, hora,*] ~ 8vo; *locus, & hora* 12mo
10: those long laborious] ~ *8vo*; those laborious *12mo*
25: into] ~ *12mo*; in *8vo*
363. 5: put beyond] ~ *8vo*; put it beyond *12mo*
364. 9: greatest of Wickedness] ~ *8vo*; greatest Wickedness *12mo*
370. 13: cut out another] cu out another *8vo*; cut another *12mo*
374. 34–35: as it inspires . . . Desires.] ~ *12mo*; as it inspires rational Ambition, corrects Love, and elegant Desire. *8vo*
35: *Signature letter om. in 8vo and 12mo.*
376. 22: his particular Station] ~ *8vo*; his Station *12mo*
378. 5: *Travel:*] ~ 8vo; *Travels:* 12mo
381. 1–2: which, I think, is held] ~ *12mo*; which is held *8vo*
382. 28: one of his] ~ *8vo*; one of the *12mo*
383. 12: with his Life,] with Life,
393. 11: by Sickness,] ~ *8vo*; by his Sickness, *12mo*
395. 3: of this Kind] ~ *8vo*; of that Kind *12mo*

405. 1: *Sorrow, cast*] ~ 12mo; *Sorrow, and cast* 8vo
411. 1: Practices] ~ *12mo*; Practice *8vo*
12: which she herself] which she her self *8vo*; which herself *12mo*
413. 15: *Misdated* November 20 *in 8vo.*
424. 19: Inclinations.] ~ *12mo*; Inclination. *8vo*
427. 21: was Man] ~ *8vo*; was a Man *12mo*
428. 11: beauteous] ~ *8vo*; beautiful *12mo*
429. 17: in *Aristotle.*] ~ 8vo; of *Aristotle.* 12mo
431. 23: his Antagonist] ~ *8vo*; the Antagonist *12mo*
432. 7: full and satisfactory] ~ *8vo*; full satisfactory *12mo*
433. 21: *Your most humble*] ~ 8vo; *Your humble* 12mo
437. 30: begun] ~ *8vo*; began *12mo*
439. 24: shall avenge] ~ *12mo*; shall to avenge *8vo*
448. 29: late] lately
450. 6: Streets] ~ *12mo*; Street *8vo*
18: expresses it,] ~ *12mo*; expresses, *8vo*
452. 34: most Parts] ~ *12mo*; most Part *8vo*
35: into] ~ *12mo*; in *8vo*
457. 15: ought they] ~ *12mo*; they ought *8vo*
460. 6–7: Power, or the] ~ *8vo*; Power, the *12mo*
18: voluble and] ~ *8vo*; voluble or *12mo*
463. 1–2: in their Circumstances] ~ *8vo*; in Circumstances *12mo*
468. 18: is in it self both amiable] ~ *12mo*; is both in it self amiable *8vo*
469. 31: Treatises] ~ *12mo*; Treaties *8vo*
470. 28: Coat.] ~ *12mo*; Cat. *8vo*
471. 9: Title] ~ *8vo*; Titles *12mo*
10: peculiar] ~ *8vo*; particular *12mo*
12: the Cat,] ~ *8vo*; a Cat, *12mo*
472. 1: make] ~ *12mo*; makes *8vo*
5: Turns of Eye-sight,] ~ *12mo*; Turns of the Eye-sight, *8vo*
473. 18–19: within the cognisance] within the Cognizance *12mo*; within Cognizance *8vo*
474. 15: as a Crack and a Projector;] ~ *12mo*; as a Projector; *8vo*
475. 20: of a much] ~ *12mo*; of much *8vo*
24: exceedingly] exceeding
495. 23: Parts] Part
506. 16: Paper,] Papers
515. 32: Equipage,] Equipages,

516. 25: *Signature letter om. in 8vo and 12mo.*
517. 14: Demand for] ~ *8vo*; Demand of *12mo*
   21: propagating Vice] ~ *8vo*; propagating of Vice *12mo*
519. 25: Reasons] ~ *8vo*; Reason *12mo*
520. 26: *Signature letter om. in 8vo and 12mo.*
524. 38: F.T.] ~ *8vo*; E.T. *12mo*
529. 24: gotten thee] ~ *12mo*; gotten the *8vo*
535. 24: and as she] and she
540. 19: his] ~ *8vo, 19*; this *12mo*
541. 7: Besides] ~ *8vo, 12mo*; Beside *19*
   9: breaking the Unity] ~ *8vo, 19*; breaking Unity *12mo*
   21: Progress] ~ *19*; Process, *8vo, 12mo*
545. 2: Nose] ~ *12mo*; Noise *8vo*
548. 4: Youth] Youths
   10: came at] came to
   13: should] shall
550. 3: he had made] he made
   4: County] Country
   11: my own part,] my own Part, *8vo*; my Part, *12mo*
551. 17: a full sight] a full Sight *8vo*; full Sight *12mo*
552. 7: *Discit*] Dicit
   8: *Quod*] ~ 8vo; *Quos* 12mo
   21: the Salutation.] ~ *8vo*; her Salutation. *12mo*
553. 17: has it] ~ *8vo*; it has *12mo*
555. 31: and my Reader.] and Reader.
559. 12: depresses it] ~ *12mo*; depresses him *8vo*
   33: in her Mirth,] ~ *12mo*; in Mirth, *8vo*
560. 16: Pound] ~ *12mo*; Pounds *8vo*
   19: who is] ~ *12mo*; who was *8vo*
561. 10–15: *Advertisement om. in 8vo.*
562. 5: his Poem,] ~ *8vo, 19*; this Poem, *12mo*
573. 9: had passed] ~ *12mo*; has passed *8vo*
574. 18: the same Degree] ~ *8vo*; the Degree *12mo*
579. 13: sets] ~ *12mo*; sits *8vo*
580. 13: exhibit] ~ *12mo*; admit *8vo*
581. 19–20: are all now] ~ *12mo*; are now *8vo*
582. 12: 'twas with her] ~ *12mo*; 'twas her *8vo*
583. 22: proceeds] ~ *8vo*; proceed *12mo*
585. 26: in an Epic Poem] ~ *12mo, 19*; in all Epic Poem *8vo*
588. 12: frequent] ~ *12mo*; frequently *8vo, 19*
   13: Every thing] Every Thing *8vo, 19*; All *12mo*

596. 34: which] ~ *12mo*; that *8vo*
598. 20: of her own,] ~ *12mo*; of our own, *8vo*
   30: of her own] ~ *12mo*; of their own *8vo*
599. 1: had this Time] ~ *12mo*; had by this Time *8vo*
   28: call] ~ *12mo*; calls *8vo*

VOLUME III

1. 24: fittest] ~ *8vo*; fitted *12mo*
3. 28: farther] ~ *12mo*; further *8vo*
7. 35–36: have drank] ~ *12mo*; have drunk *8vo*
8. 13: Yesterday] ~ *12mo*; Yesterday's *8vo*
   31: of a *Gloria Patri*;] ~ 8vo; of *Gloria Patri*; 12mo
12. 6: *in one anothers*] ~ 8vo, 12mo; *in anothers* 19
16. 4: so far from] ~ *8vo*; so from *12mo*
17. 11: Danger of] ~ *12mo*; Danger and *8vo*
26. 28: very great] ~ *12mo*; great *8vo*
28. 4: sometimes be] ~ *12mo*; be sometimes *8vo*
32. 5: throw] ~ *8vo*; threw *12mo*
   9: Examination,] ~ *12mo*; Imagination, *8vo*
   35: find they] ~ *12mo*; find that they *8vo*
33. 5: Sentiment,] ~ *12mo*; Sentiments, *8vo*
39. 6: was] ~ *8vo*; is *12mo*
42. 1: what] ~ *8vo*; when *12mo*
   7: *Signed Z in Fol. and 12mo; unsigned in 8vo.*
47. 1–2: is most apt] ~ *8vo*; is apt *12mo*
48. 25: at her Bosom.] in her Bosom.
49. 7: will] ~ *12mo*; would *8vo*
51. 25: Precedents] ~ *8vo*; Precedent *12mo*
53. 3: Trifles] Trifle
   5: Reasoners] ~ *8vo*; Readers *12mo*
   6: they make] ~ *8vo*; to make *12mo*
   18: your] ~ *8vo*; the *12mo*
54. 1: a great Tract] ~ *8vo*; a Tract *12mo*
   6: improperly] ~ *12mo*; properly *8vo*
   21: County] Country
55. 3: your prefixing] ~ *12mo*; you prefixing *8vo*
   6: effected] ~ *12mo*; affected *8vo*
60. 26: and the *Æneid*] ~ 8vo, 12mo; and *Æneid* 19
61. 17: of unnecessary] of his unnecessary
   23: Complaint of] ~ *8vo, 12mo*; Complaint for *19*
65. 24: profanely] ~ *12mo*; profusely *8vo*

66. 16: among] ~ *12mo*; amongst *8vo*
17: some] ~ *8vo*; *om. 12mo*
67. 1: County,] ~ *12mo*; Country, *8vo*
72. 32: Field for] ~ *8vo*; Field of *12mo*
74. 22: read long since] ~ *8vo*; long since read *12mo*
95. 7: *you*] ~ 12mo; *ye* 8vo
96. 28: interfere] ~ *8vo*; to interfere *12mo*
102. 8: Misfortunes] ~ *12mo*; Misfortune *8vo*
115. 8: in the Assembly,] ~ *8vo, 12mo*; in that Assembly, *19*
116. 13: every way] ~ *12mo*; every where *8vo, 19*
117. 32: the next] ~ *8vo, 12mo*; he next *19*
118. 16: Entertainment] ~ *8vo, 19*; Entertainments *12mo*
119. 28: my Son] ~ *12mo*; thy Son *8vo, 19*
121. 21: *Dobake.*] *Doughbake.* 8vo; *Dowbake.* 12mo
122. 20: in like manner] ~ *12mo*; in a like Manner *8vo*
31: much a better] ~ *12mo*; a much better *8vo*
125. 22: been seen walking] ~ *8vo*; been walking *12mo*
29: after above an Hours search] ~ *12mo*; after an Hour's Search *8vo*
126. 12: *Most Humble*] ~ 12mo; *most obedient humble* 8vo
130. 19: own thou] ~ *12mo*; own that thou *8vo*
134. 24: of Service] a Service
135. 12: go the Western Circuit:] ~ *12mo*; go to the Western Circuit: *8vo*
137. 11: wrightly] writely *8vo*; rightly *12mo*
140. 17: ADVERTISEMENTS.] ADVERTISEMENT.
143. 28: *multitude*] ~ 12mo; *multitudes* 8vo, 19
145. 18: other] ~ *8vo, 12mo*; rather *19*
146. 5: Poet,] ~ *8vo, 12mo*; Poets, *19*
147. 29: *that Globe*] ~ 8vo, 12mo; *the Globe* 19
149. 30: lay] lye
151. 1: my] ~ *12mo*; mine *8vo*
25: *most devoted humble*] ~ 12mo; *most humble* 8vo
156. 11: in such as] ~ *12mo*; as such as *8vo*
166. 3: Tradesman] ~ *12mo*; Tradesmen *8vo*
170. 6: treat of] ~ *8vo, 12mo*; treat on *19*
171. 22: Man] ~ *8vo, 12mo*; Men *19*
179. 23: Time or Place.] ~ *12mo*; Time and Place. *8vo*

184. 10: from Table.] ~ *12mo*; from the Table. *8vo*
189. 17: but is] ~ *12mo*; but it is *8vo*
22: you shall think] you think
191. 26: Observations,] ~ *12mo*; Observation, *8vo*
192. 39: *amiably*] ~ 12mo; *amiable* 8vo
193. 1: *turn'd,*] ~ 12mo; *return'd* 8vo
202. 34: at Table] ~ *8vo, 12mo*; at a Table *19*
203. 3: his] ~ *8vo, 12mo*; this *19*
19: as proceeding] ~ *12mo, 19*; or proceeding *8vo*
26–27: Imagination,] ~ *12mo*; Indignation, *8vo, 19*
217. 9: Riot] ~ *12mo*; Riots *8vo*
219. 4: play'd at trouant,] play'd Truant, *8vo*
223. 1: Extirpation] ~ *12mo*; Expiration *8vo*
224. 8: round him] round about him
17: sufficient,] sufficiently,
225. 6: toward] ~ *8vo*; towards *12mo*
25: these Fellows] those Fellows
226. 12–13: the good Company] the Company
15: Ten of Clock.] Ten a Clock.
227. 26: *pursuit*] ~ 19; *pursues* 8vo; *pursuis* 12mo
228. 22: *Heav'n*] *Heaven's* 8vo; *Heav'n's* 12mo; *Heav'ns* 19
230. 21: savour] ~ *12mo*; favour *8vo, 19*
232. 4: *griding*] ~ 12mo, 19; *girding* 8vo
234. 20: Subject,] ~ *12mo, 19*; Subjects, *8vo*
238. 16: Hammers] ~ *12mo*; Hammer *8vo*
239. 7: as of the young] as to the young
15: *veras*] ~ 12mo; *voras* 8vo
253. 18: most] ~ *12mo*; the most *8vo*
254. 21: *Cœperit,*] ~ 19; *Cœperi,* 8vo, 12mo
255. 18: and have been] ~ *8vo, 12mo*; and been *19*
256. 4: such of these] ~ *12mo, 19*; such as these *8vo*
259. 19: Descriptions] Description
33: *that distance*] ~ 8vo, 12mo; *the distance* 19
261. 2: Resounded,] Resounding,
17: of Imagination.] of the Imagination.
267. 1: *No paragraph in 8vo.*
269. 20: *December 6th*] *December* the 6th
270. 12: natural to such to fancy] natural to fancy
28: any Excuse,] an Excuse
37: for Woman,] ~ *12mo*; for a Woman, *8vo*
275. 3: In my next] ~ *12mo*; In next *8vo*
29: to a Mite,] to a Mite *12mo*; to Mite *8vo*

277. 2: in your] into your
279. 1: Mistress] Mrs.
   24: offers it the Men] ~ *12mo*; offers it to the Men *8vo*
280. *m.: his*] ~ 12mo; *hic* 8vo, 19
286. 2: avoid] ~ *12mo, 19*; void *8vo*
289. 25: who] ~ *12mo*; whom *8vo*
290. 17: from one to whom] ~ *12mo*; from whom *8vo*
296. 26: of Clock:] of the Clock:
301. 11: I meet] ~ *12mo*; I met *8vo*
304. 35: *Signature letter om. in 8vo.*
312. 8: *No paragraph in 8vo and 19.*
   20-21: have more resembled] ~ *8vo, 12mo*; have resembled *19*
313. 7: Knaves] ~ *12mo*; Knave *8vo*
315. 38: *in great*] in his great
320. 22: County,] Country,
334. 9: *No paragraph in 8vo and 19.*
340. 25: in Company] in the Company
342. 11: or make an] or an
   17: *Signature letter om. in 8vo.*
343. 13: County,] Country
   14: says Sir ROGER,] says ROGER,
   14: think she'll] think that she'll
344. 11: things to her, and,] ~ *12mo*; things, and, *8vo*
   31: bore] born
345. 22: *To a fell*] ~ 12mo; *To fell* 8vo
346. 24-25: such Person] such Persons
347. 29: and depth] and the Depth
   34: of the Hat] ~ *12mo*; of a Hat *8vo*
   35-36: has a particular] has parti-/ler *8vo*; has particular *12mo*
348. 1: might with artificial] ~ *12mo*; might / artificial *8vo*
350. 15: Request,] ~ *12mo*; Requests, *8vo*
351. 19: originally] ~ *12mo*; original *8vo*
   27: that] the
352. 3: Works] Words
   35-36. *Footnote om. in 8vo and 12mo.*
355. 11: should] shall
   23: out-run] out-ran
359. 36: *bands*] ~ 12mo, 19; *hands* 8vo
363. 21: *these*] *those*
365. 9: *orcs,*] ~ 12mo, 19; *ores,* 8vo
370. 16: Ominous in] Ominous to
376. 9: lie] live
384. 32: of Clock] of the Clock
387. 16: *and native*] *his native*
389. 22: *meteorous,*] ~ 12mo, 19; *meteors,* 8vo
391. 19: make] makes
392. 33-34: as well . . . Discourses,] ~ *8vo, 12mo*; om. *19*
397. 11: in the Assembly] in an Assembly
398. 31: begun] began
399. 17: begun] began
401. 34: successive,] successively,

408. 7: Interests.] ~ *12mo*; Interest. *8vo*
413. 7: *Signature letter om. in all edd.*
   22: Scream.] ~ *12mo*; Stream. *8vo*
414. 12: her Leader:] the Leader:
433. 20: had] ~ *12mo*; have *8vo*
425. 10-11: the Statue] a Statue
   18: in a thousand] into a thousand
431. 20: It is,] Is it
   22: is it] ~ *8vo*; it is *12mo*
436. *m.:* Juv.] Hor.
438. 10: time of Year.] Time of Year. *12mo*; Time of the Year. *8vo*
441. 5: *my Lord*] *the Lord*
443. 25: *Instrument*] *Instruments*
   39: it to the usual] it the usual
444. 10: and in the first] and the first
452. 15: as to the Soil] ~ *12mo*; as the Soil *8vo*
456. 27: *Eyes*] ~ 12mo; *Eye* 8vo
457. 14-17: *In Fol. and 12mo these lines form part of Stanza IV; in 8vo Stanza V begins at line 14.*
   15: *fainting,*] *fainting* 12mo; *faining* 8vo
463. 1: active] affective
464. 15: for] ~ *12mo*; or *8vo*
472. 16: let] kept
   16: Manner, cover'd] manner, then covered
476. 11: with such a secret] ~ *12mo*; with a secret *8vo*
476. 18: *Signature letter om. in 12mo.*
485. 30: *Signature letter om. in all edd.*
490. 14: Look,] Looks,
   27: in] into
491. 32: Lodgings] Lodging
496. 27: Sidley] ~ *12mo*; Sidney *8vo*
498. 34: Shepherdess] ~ *12mo*; Shepherdesses *8vo*
510. 5: is it] it is
   8: into] in
   10: Affectation] ~ *12mo*; Affection *8vo*
511. 21-22: Vegetables; by . . . Plant,] Vegetables, by the Assistance of Art and an hot Bed: We may possibly extort an unwilling Plant,
514. 18: *Hebraisms,*] ~ *12mo*; *Hebraism,* 8vo
528. 29: with *Sallust*] ~ *12mo*; which *Sallust* 8vo
537. 19: into two] in two
543. 13: *No paragraph in 8vo.*
550. 1: arises] rises
552. 13: laid out by] ~ *12mo*; laid by *8vo*
557. 6: *Angles*] ~ 12mo; *Angels* 8vo
558. 2: arises] rises
559. 19: that] than
   20: sent] ~ *12mo*; send *8vo*

561. 4–5: as free a View] ~ *12mo*; as a free View *8vo*

574. 18: who ever went] ~ *12mo*; who went *8vo*

    21: his Reader] ~ *12mo*; this Reader *8vo*

577. 16: *ignota*] ~ 12mo; *ignotis* 8vo

580. 4: with] ~ *12mo*; which *8vo*

582. 1: *This*] *The*

586. 18: to the Fair,] ~ *12mo*; the Fair, *8vo*

587. 31: the Scheme;] ~ *12mo*; a Scheme; *8vo*

594. 37: moved on to] moved to

598. 2: int] in

599. 37: depend] depending

VOLUME IV

2. 13: *more easily*] ~ 12mo; *more easie* 8vo

3. 12: are ready] and ready

5. 3: exalt,] ~ *12mo*; exult, *8vo*

15. 24: Toll] ~ *12mo*; Toil *12mo*

    29: stuck] ~ *12mo*; struck *8vo*

17. 29–30: owing to the] ~ *12mo*; owing the *8vo*

19. 22: seem] seems

28. 18: saving] ~ *12mo*; saying *8vo*

39. 7: these] ~ *12mo*; those *8vo*

50. 36: which is a kind] ~ *12mo*; which a kind *8vo*

54. 14: Essays] ~ *12mo*; Essay *8vo*

60. 10: had stay'd] staid

62. 6: both] ~ *12mo*; born *8vo*

    17: honestly to promise] ~ *12mo*; honestly promise *8vo*

69. 5: Gentle-man] Gentleman *12mo*; Gentlemen *8vo*

73. 18: upon] ~ *12mo*; up *8vo*

75. 7–8: the gathering] ~ *12mo*; and gathering *8vo*

    20: Promisers] ~ *12mo*; Promises *8vo*

87. 1: But it is] ~ *12mo*; But is *8vo*

90. 16: There are about] ~ *12mo*; There about *8vo*

100. 28: of] ~ *12mo*; on *8vo*

103. 21: *Ego*] *Ergo*

104. 5: moral] modern

105. 30: to be yoked] ~ *12mo*; to yoked *8vo*

106. 9: none of her own] ~ *12mo*; none her own *8vo*

108. 33: of all his Labours] ~ *12mo*; of his Labours *8vo*

109. 32: Mortality,] ~ *12mo*; Morality *8vo*

110. 17: make] ~ *12mo*; makes *8vo*

120. 25: rising] ~ *12mo*; arising *8vo*

122. 18: clear'd up as] cleared as

124. 35: Airs] Arts

141. 12: *Misnumbered 463 in 8vo.*

143. 1: and always] and all always

156. 36: Narrations] ~ *12mo*; Narration *8vo*

166. 22: Besides] Beside

171. 11: transport] ~ *8vo*; transports *12mo*

177. 31: pretended these] pretended that these

178. 20: that] ~ *12mo*; the *8vo*

181. 22: had not he] had he not

187. 7: Skuttle] ~ *12mo*; Cuttle *8vo*

188. 4: Advantages] ~ *12mo*; Advantage *8vo*

193. 24: livelily] ~ *12mo*; lively *8vo*

194. 33: Misfortune,] Misfortune *12mo*; Misfortunes *8vo*

194. 35: be also] also be

196. 23: preferr'd] presented

198. 29: arise] rise

198. 37: Men] ~ *12mo*; Man *8vo*

199. 5–6: come home to Dinner] ~ *12mo*; come to Dinner *8vo*

    8: Year] ~ *12mo*; Years *8vo*

    20: Occasions] Occasion

200. 24: either in] in either

201. 18: Reason] ~ *12mo*; Reasons *8vo*

    26: to take] or take

204. 18: as his] as in his

205. 1: sometimes] ~ *12mo*; something *8vo*

212. 3: Forefather's] Father's

    22: Successes,] Success,

216. 12: your] ~ *12mo*; the *8vo*

217. 1: Strains] Strain

    34: in him] for him

220. 12: as] and

    14: Matters] ~ *12mo*; Matter *8vo*

    19: Men] Friends

221. 1: this our Island] this Island

    24: at other] ~ *12mo*; at the other *8vo*

    24: back his] ~ *12mo*; back of his *8vo*

222. 2: so well fixed] so fixed

223. 19: reign] reigns

224. 39: makes] ~ *12mo*; make *8vo*

226. 22: Intimations] ~ *12mo*; Intimation *8vo*

    27: busie] ~ *8vo*; busied *12mo*

228. 8: than at any other.] ~ *8vo*; than any other. *12mo*

    21: or a Beggar,] ~ *12mo*; or Beggar, *8vo*

    26: active watchful] ~ *8vo*; active and watchful *12mo*

233. 25: rises] ~ *12mo*; arises *8vo*

235. 23: *smooth'd*] ~ 12mo; *smoak'd* 8vo

238. 17: to poetical] ~ *12mo*; to the poetical *8vo*

239. 1: written the] ~ *12mo*; written in
    the *8vo*
    32–33: take its Place] ~ *12mo*; take
    Place *8vo*
240. 13: *doth*] ~ 12mo; *does* 8vo
    29: Mind of Man] ~ *12mo*; Mind of
    a Man *8vo*
242. 13: *save*] ~ 12mo; *serve* 8vo
246. 27: is great] is a great
247. 2: call] ~ *12mo*; calls *8vo*
256. 7: Their] ~ *8vo*; The *12mo*
262. 8: give] ~ *8vo*; gave *12mo*
    10: popularly] ~ *12mo*; peculiarly
    8vo
    17: who] ~ *8vo*; as *12mo*
266. 9: our] ~ *8vo*; the *12mo*
267. 8: these] ~ *8vo*; those *12mo*
270. 28: the City Gates] ~ *8vo*; the
    Gates *12mo*
272. 2: methought,] ~ *12mo*; me-
    thoughts, *8vo*
273. 37: my own Rank] ~ *12mo*; my
    Rank *8vo*
274. 20: mounted] ~ *12mo*; mounting
    8vo
279. 2: Tracts] Tracks
    17: easie] easier
281. 7: meets] ~ *8vo*; meets with *12mo*
286. 6: in Cathedrals] in Cathedrals, *8vo*;
    in the Cathedrals *12mo*
    11: Gold-Pen,] ~ *12mo*; Golden-
    Pen, *8vo*
287. 25: in Country-Halls] ~ *12mo*; in
    the Country-Halls *8vo*
288. 8: had ever] ~ *8vo*; ever *12mo*
    9: great] ~ *8vo*; good *12mo*
    10: arrived at] ~ *12mo*; arrived that
    8vo
293. 28: this] these
294. 21: in the Week] ~ *8vo*; in a Week
    12mo
295. 24: farther] ~ *8vo*; further *12mo*
297. 16: farther,] ~ *8vo*; further, *12mo*
298. 10: pare] ~ *12mo*; pair *8vo*
300. 6: is become] ~ *12mo*; becomes *8vo*
301. 19: has] ~ *12mo*; have *8vo*
    21–22: such a Protestation] ~ *12mo*;
    such Protestation *8vo*
305. 24: Woman] ~ *12mo*; Woman, *8vo*
311. 15–16: our own Interest] ~ *8vo*; our
    Interest *12mo*
312. 4: follow:] ~ *12mo*; follows: *12mo*
    24: *Perswasions*] ~ 12mo; *Perswasion*
    8vo
314. 18: met with] ~ *8vo*; met *12mo*
    25: culled out all the] ~ *8vo*; culled
    out the *12mo*
316. 39: *Signature letter om. in 12mo.*
321. 31: *view*;] *Views*; 8vo; *View*; 12mo
323. 17: Sorrows] ~ 12mo; *Sorrow* 8vo

29: could have] ~ *8vo*; could not
    have *12mo*
324. 17: will] ~ *8vo*; would *12mo*
325. 26: beside] ~ *12mo*; besides *8vo*
327. 15: a Pass] ~ *8vo*; to pass *12mo*
329. 8: sung] ~ *8vo*; sang *12mo*
    18: farther] ~ *12mo*; further *8vo*
330. 19–20: slipping off some of] ~ *8vo*;
    slipping of *12mo*
331. 30: in them:] in them. *8vo*; to them:
    12mo
332. 37: 'Tis to That that our Arms] ~
    8vo; 'Tis to That our Arms
    12mo
333. 31: *obedient*] ~ 12mo; *humble* 8vo
337. 30: Mankind now upon Earth,] ~
    8vo; Mankind upon Earth,
    12mo
340. 12: Hopes] ~ *12mo*; Hope *8vo*
343. 28: I ever] ~ *12mo*; ever I *8vo*
345. 17: *Signature letter om. in all edd.*
349. 21: *downwards*:] ~ 12mo; *downward*:
    8vo
351. 18: Sorrow,] Sorrows,
353. 5: pretty] ~ *12mo*; petty *8vo*
    13: F.J.] ~ *12mo*; F.I. *8vo*
354. 34: attend to them.] ~ *12mo*; attend
    them. *8vo*
355. 27: of Clock,] of the Clock,
356. 16: Fictions;] ~ *12mo*; Factions; *8vo*
368. 5–6: really was] was really
    24: such Terror,] such a Terror,
369. 20: nor] not
    21: *Signature letter om. in all edd.*
373. 21: *Signature letter om. in all edd.*
375. 23: how instructive or diverting so-
    ever] how instructive soever
377. 23: *No. 527 misdated* November 24
    in 8vo and 12mo.
378. 18: of a Relation,] ~ *12mo*; of Rela-
    tion, *8vo*
379. 26: had kiss'd] ~ *12mo*; kiss'd *8vo*
381. 20: *Signature letter om. in all edd.*
383. 14: Country,] ~ *8vo*; County, *12mo*
390. 9: thought] ~ *12mo*; though *8vo*
393. 34: fall] ~ *12mo*; fail *8vo*
402. 30: filthy] ~ *12mo*; silly *8vo*
403. 1: effectual,] effectually,
405. 17: toward Years] towards Years
406. 26: paid us] ~ *12mo*; paid to us *8vo*
418. 1: *No paragraph in 8vo and 12mo.*
419. 30–31: of narrower] of a narrower
420. 15: *Signature letter om. in all edd.*
421. 8: pace] ~ *12mo*; pass *8vo*
422. 9–10: and a Faintness] ~ *12mo*; and
    Faintness *8vo*
    13: gave] ~ *12mo*; give *8vo*
424. 27: *Signature letter om. in all edd.*
427. 31: *Signature letter om. in all edd.*
437. 26: *Signature letter om. in all edd.*

446. 33: that he] ~ *12mo*; and he *8vo*
451. 3: nel] ~ *12mo*; del *8vo*
 24: above a 100] ~ *12mo*; above 100 *8vo*
461. 10: *ille*] ~ 12mo; *illo* 8vo
462. 11: to all such] ~ *12mo*; of all such *8vo*
464. 12: as Tragedy.] ~ *12mo*; as a Tragedy. *8vo*
465. 27: *Signature letter om. in all edd.*
469. 19: Interests] ~ *12mo*; Interest *8vo*
471. 12: opening the Mouth] ~ *12mo*; opening of the Mouth *8vo*
475. 21: keep to them] ~ *12mo*; keep them *8vo*
478. 8: has a Value] ~ *12mo*; has Value *8vo*
 15: *Signature letter om. in all edd.*
486. 33: E.T.] ~ *8vo*; E.F. *12mo*
488. 13: through] ~ *12mo*; though *8vo*
489. 11: Perfections] ~ *12mo*; Perfection *8vo*
491. 16: *Signature letter om. in all edd.*
530. 21: that it is] ~ *8vo*; that is *12mo*
536. 4: I lay] lay
538. 29: this] ~ *8vo*; the *12mo*
540. 2–3: write it at length] ~ *8vo*; write at length *12mo*
557. 29: upon] ~ *8vo*; on *12mo*
558. 12: County,] Country,
 16: begun] ~ *8vo*; began *12mo*
559. 34: engaging] ~ *8vo*; engaged *12mo*
 38: dead] dear
575. 21: or Sameness.] of Sameness.
 25: overflowed] over-flow *8vo*; overflow *12mo*
588. 13: sent] ~ *12mo*; set *8vo*
596. 20: in his] ~ *8vo*; of his *12mo*

VOLUME V

2. 7: This Wood] ~ *8vo*; The Wood *12mo*
7. 23: forbad me.] forbad be.
11. 31: drawn] ~ *8vo*; drown *12mo*

13. 11: but a Consciousness] ~ *8vo*; but Consciousness *12mo*
17. 1: at the Roots,] ~ *8vo*; at the Roots of, *12mo*
19. 20: to all that] to that
20. 22: at an infinite] ~ *8vo*; at infinite *12mo*
21. 26: Embassy] ~ *8vo*; Embassady *12mo*
23. 15: to a Squeeze] ~ *8vo*; to Squeeze *12mo*
 26: Occasions] ~ *8vo*; Occasion *12mo*
27. 24: these] ~ *8vo*; those *12mo*
30. 7: but that had] but had
34. 11: of this] in this
36. 21: to the other.] ~ *12mo*; to other. *8vo*
39. 25: not much] ~ *8vo*; not so much *12mo*
46. 2: three Years last] ~ *8vo*; three last Years *12mo*
48. 33: Religions,] ~ *8vo*; Religion *12mo*
49. 6: bears] ~ *8vo*; bear *12mo*
64. 16: *Misnumbered* 603 *in 8vo.*
77. 20: been a Man wedded;] ~ *8vo*; been a wedded Man; *12mo*
79. 26: Honey-Moon;] ~ *8vo*; Honey-Money; *12mo*
86. 36: Witness too,] Witness to [*In Cowley the reading is* Witness too,]
87. 16: Tittle] ~ *8vo*; Title *12mo*
88. 30: tells] tell
93. 24: within a few] ~ *8vo*; within few *12mo*
105. *date: Misdated* September 5 *in 8vo.*
108. 17: left] ~ *12mo*; let *8vo*
112. 20: for the first,] ~ *8vo*; for first, *12mo*
116. 15: Book.] ~ *8vo*; Books. *12mo*
125. 16: that] ~ *12mo*; than *8vo*
130. 25: Master] ~ *8vo*; Mr. *12mo*
143. 37: Jessamine.] *Jessamines.*
153. 11: Polity] Policy
158. 10: makes] ~ *12mo*; make *8vo*
165. 17: had] hath

III. ADVERTISEMENTS OF BOOKS

O F the more than 800 books advertised in the *Spectator*, the following titles represent, with a few exceptions, all listed as 'this day published'. Following each item is the number of the *Spectator* in which the advertisement appears. Most titles are abbreviated.

An ACCOUNT shewing the Numbers of the Tickets entituled to benefits in the Lottery for 1500000 l. Anno 1711. Printed for Andrew Bell. 313.

ANTIOCHUS, an Opera. Printed for J. Tonson. 245.

ARGUMENTS relating to a Restraint upon the press, fully and fairly handled, in a letter to a Bencher from a young gentleman of the Temple. Printed for R. and J. Bonwicke. 289.

ASGILL, JOHN. Mr. Asgill's Apology for an omission in his late publication. Sold by A. Baldwin. 517. [Refers to next item.]

—— Mr. Asgill's Defence, upon his expulsion from the House of Commons of Great Britain in 1707. Sold by A. Baldwin. 488.

ASHE, ST. GEORGE. A Sermon preached to the Protestants of Ireland . . . October 23,1712, . . . an anniversary thanksgiving for the deliverance of the Protestants of that kingdom from the bloody massacre begun by the Irish Papists on the 23d of October, 1641. Printed for Sam. Buckley. 527.

ASTON, ANTHONY. Pastora, or The coy shepherdess, an English opera. Sold by E. Curll. 515.

The BALLANCE of Power, or a Comparison of the Strength of the Emperor and the French King. Sold by A. Baldwin. 226.

The BARRIER-TREATY Vindicated. Printed for A. Baldwin. 533.

BEAUMONT, FRANCIS, and JOHN FLETCHER. A very neat and correct edition of the Works. In seven vols. 8vo. Printed for J. Tonson. 85.

BEHN, APHRA. Mrs. Behn's Works in 3 Vols. in 8vo. Printed for R. Wellington. 548.

BELLUM Grammaticale: or, the Grammatical Battel Royal. Sold by J. Morphew. 344.

BEVERIDGE, WILLIAM. An Exposition on the Thirty-nine Articles of the Church of England. Printed for R. Smith. 154.

—— Private Thoughts upon a Christian Life. Part II. Printed for and sold by Richard Smith; and sold by William Taylor. 311.

—— Thesaurus Theologicus, or a compleat system of divinity. Vols. III and IV. Printed for Rich. Smith. 65.

—— —— The second edition. Compleat in 4 volumes. Printed for Richard Smith. 189.

—— The Wisdom of being Holy. Good Friday to be kept by all Christians. The Nature and Necessity of Restitution. Printed for Rich. Smith. 43.

BINGHAM, JOSEPH. A Scholastical History of the Practice of the Church in reference to the Administration of Baptism by Laymen. Printed [by W. Downing] for Rob. Knaplock. 547.

BISSE, THOMAS. A Sermon Preach'd before the University of Oxford on Whitsunday 1712. Oxford, Printed at the Theater for Henry Clements. 421.

BLACKMORE, SIR RICHARD. Creation. A Philosophical Poem. Demonstrating the Existence and Providence of God. In Seven Books. Printed for Sam. Buckley, and Jacob Tonson. 313.

—— —— The second edition. 385 (to morrow).

—— The Nature of Man. A Poem. In three books. Printed for Sam. Buckley, and sold by S. Crouch [and others]. 32.

BOILEAU. The Whole Works of Monsieur Boileau. In two volumes 8vo. Made English from the last Paris Edition by several Hands. To which is prefixed his Life; written to Joseph Addison, Esq; by Mr. Des Maiseaux; and some account of this translation by N. Rowe. Printed for E. Sanger, and E. Curll. 272.

BRADBURY, THOMAS. Theocracy. The Government of the Judges, applied to the Revolution in 1688. In a Sermon preached in Fetter-Lane, Nov. 5, 1711. Printed for N. Cliff and D. Jackson. 411.

BRETT, THOMAS. A Review of the Lutheran Principles. Printed for Henry Clements. 609 (just published).

BRIGHTLAND, JOHN. A Grammar of the English Tongue. The second edition. Printed for John Brightland; and sold by the Booksellers of London, &c. 293.

The BRITISH Academy; being a new erected Society for the Advancement of Wit and Learning: with some few observations upon it. Sold by A. Baldwin. 392.

BROOKE and Hillier. A Satyr. Sold by J. Baker. 324.

BROWN, THOMAS. The Fourth Volume of the Works of Mr. Tho. Brown, which compleats the whole sett. Printed for S. Briscoe, and sold by J. Morphew, and J. Woodward. 195 (just published).

BROWNE, JOSEPH. Oratio in Serenissimi Regis Georgii adventum apud villam Virrictem, tradita a Josepho Browne. Or, an Oration upon the happy Arrival of the King, delivered to him at Greenwich. Printed for D. Brown, W. Mears, and J. Brown, and sold by J. Roberts. 598.

BROWNE, SIR THOMAS. Posthumous Works. Printed for E. Cur[ll]. 550.

BUCHANAN, GEORGE. Georgii Buchanani Scoti ad Viros sui seculi clarissimos eorumque ad eundem Epistolae ex MSS accurate descriptae nunc primum in lucem editae. Londini, Impensis D. Brown & Gulielmi Taylor. 237.

BUCKINGHAM, GEORGE VILLIERS, Duke of. A Conference on the Doctrine of Transubstantiation, between His Grace the Duke of Buckingham and an Irish Jesuit. The third edition. Printed for Ferd. Burleigh, and A. Dod. 566.

[BURNET, THOMAS.] The History of Ingratitude, or a second part of Ancient Precedents for Modern Facts. Sold by J. Baker. 393.

[——] Our Ancestors as Wise as We: Or, Ancient Precedents for Modern Facts. Printed for A. Baldwin. 289.

[——] The True Character of an Honest Man. Sold by J. Baker. 399.

BURRAGE, RICHARD. Religio Libertini; or, the Faith of a converted Atheist. Printed for Sam. Briscoe, and sold by John Graves, and J. Morphew. 476 (just published).

[BUTLER, SAMUEL.] Hudibras. To this edition is added Annotations to the Third Part, with a compleat Index to the whole, never before printed. Printed for G. Sawbridge. 112 (just published).

BYSSHE, EDW. The Art of English Poetry. The fifth edition. Printed by S. Buckley; and sold by J. Churchill [and others]. 2 vols. 560.

CAESAR. C. Julii Caesaris quae extant. Accuratissime cum libris editis & MSS optimis collata, recognita & correcta. Accesserunt annotationes Samuelis Clarke. Printed for Jacob Tonson. 346.

CENTLIVRE, SUSANNA. The last new Comedy, call'd the Perplex'd Lovers. Printed for Owen Lloyd [and others]. 306.

CHAPMAN, RICHARD. Britannia Rediviva, or Britain's Recovery, an heroick Poem inscribed to the King. Printed for Bernard Lintott. 604.

CHAUCER, GEOFFREY. The Carpenter of Oxford, or, The Miller's Tale, from Chaucer. Sold by E. Curll. 515.

CIBBER, COLLEY. The Careless Husband, a Comedy. The third edition, revis'd by the Author. Printed for Jacob Tonson. 523.

—— She Wou'd and She Wou'd Not, or, The Kind Impostor. Printed for W. Mears. 579 (just published).

CICERO. A Translation of Part of Tully's 12th Philippic. Sold by A. Baldwin. 231.

—— M. Tully Cicero's Five Books of Tusculan Disputations. Done into English by a Gentleman of Christ Church College, Oxford. Printed for J. Brown. 619 (just published).

CLARKE, SAMUEL. The Scripture Doctrine of the Trinity. Printed for James Knapton. 381.

COCKER, EDWARD. Cocker's Decimal Arithmetick, the fourth edition, corrected. Printed for Richard Wellington. 516.

COKE, SIR EDWARD. An Abridgment of the First Part of my Ld. Coke's Institutes; with some additions. Sold by John Walthoe. 123.

A COLLECTION of all the Addresses, &c. of the Lords and Commons to the Queen, since her Happy Accession to the Throne. Sold by J. Baker. 441.

A COLLECTION of all Her Majesty's Speeches, Messages, &c. from Her Happy Accession to the Throne, to the 12th of June 1712. Sold by J. Baker. 418.

A COLLECTION of Original Poems, by the late E. of Godolphin, Mr. Prior, Mr. Manwaring, &c. Printed for E. Curll, and J. Pemberton. 590.

A COLLECTION of Papers against the Scots Toleration and Patronages that have been Printed or Presented to Her Majesty and the two Houses of Parliament. Printed for A. Bell, and sold by J. Baker. 370.

A COMPANION for the Ladies Closets: Being the Life and Death of the most excellent the Lady ——: By a Minister of the Church of England. [The dedication signed A. B., i.e. Aphra Behn.] Sold by J. Downing. 294.

CONGREVE, WILLIAM. Incognita. Printed for Richard Wellington. 516.

COOKE, EDWARD. A Voyage to the South Sea, and round the World. Printed for B. Lintott [and others]. 337.

—— —— Vol. 2d and last. 404 (to morrow).

The COURT and City Vagaries, being some late (and real) Intreagues of several gentlemen and ladies. Written by one of the fair Sex. Sold by J. Baker. 255.

—— The 2nd part. 426.

The COURT of Atalantis for the last four years. Sold by J. Roberts [and others]. 579.

CRISPE, H. A Congratulatory Poem to the Honourable Matthew Prior, Esq; on his Promotion to the Commission of Her Majesty's Customs. Sold by J. Morphew, and E. Curll. 312.

CROXALL, [SAMUEL]. An Ode: Humbly Inscrib'd to the King. Occasion'd by his Majesty's most auspicious Succession and Arrival: Written in the Stanza or Measure of Spencer. Printed for Bernard Lintott. 604.

[CURLL, EDMUND.] The Life of Dr. Walter Curll, Bishop of Winchester, Lord Almoner to King Charles I. Sold by E. Curll. 515.

[DEFOE, DANIEL.] Armageddon: or, the Necessity of carrying on the War, if such a Peace cannot be obtained as may render Europe safe, and Trade secure. Sold by J. Baker. 209.

[——] Eleven Opinions about Mr. H——y, with Observations clearing some matters. Sold by J. Baker. 65.

[——] An Enquiry into the Danger and Consequences of a War with the Dutch. Sold by J. Baker. 430.

[——] An Essay at a plain Exposition of that difficult Phrase a good Peace. Sold by J. Baker. 218.

[——] An Essay on the South-Sea Trade. Sold by J. Baker. 169.

[——] The History of the Jacobite Club, with the Grounds of their Hopes from the P——t M——y, as also a Caveat against the Pretender. Sold by J. Baker. 537.

[——] The Justice and Necessity of a War with Holland, in case the Dutch do not come in to Her Majesty's Measures, stated and examined. Sold by the Booksellers of London and Westminster. 441.

[——] A Justification of the Dutch from several late scandalous Reflections. Sold by J. Baker. 446.

[——] Reasons why this Nation ought to put a speedy end to this expensive War. Sold by J. Baker. 189.

[——] The Secret History of the October Club. Sold by John Baker. 45.

[——] A Speech for D——sse Younger of Arnistown, if he should be impeach'd of H—h T——n for what he said and did about the Pretender's Medal lately sent to the Faculty of Advocates at Edinburgh. Printed for J. Baker. 157.

[——] The True State of the Case between the Government and the Creditors of the Navy, &c. as it relates to the South-Sea Trade. Sold by J. Baker. 178.

DENNIS, JOHN. An Essay on the Genius and Writings of Shakespear; with some Letters of Criticism to the Spectator. Printed for Bernard Lintott. 221.

—— Reflections Critical and Satyrical, upon a late Rhapsody call'd, An Essay on Criticism. Printed for B. Lintott, and sold by A. Baldwin [and others]. 104 (just published).

DES PERRIERS, BONAVENTURE. Cymbalum Mundi, or Satyrical Dialogues upon several Subjects. Printed for A. Baldwin. 289.

[DIAPER, WILLIAM.] Nereides; or, Sea Eclogues. Printed for E. Sanger. 332 (just published).

DIBBEN, THOMAS. A Sermon Preached at St. John's Church in Utrecht, on Sunday, March 9–20, 1711. Being the Day after the Anniversary of her Majesty's happy Accession to the Throne. Printed for Bernard Lintott. 345.

DITTON, HUMPHRY. A Discourse concerning the Resurrection of Jesus Christ. Printed by J. Darby, and sold by A. Bell and B. Lintott. 318 (just published).

DOUGHARTY, JOHN. The General Gauger: or, the Principles and Practice of Gauging Beer, Wine, and Malt. The second edition. Printed for James Knapton. 433.

D[UMMER], J[EREMIAH]. A Letter to a Friend in the Country on the late Expedition to Canada. Sold by A. Baldwin. 215 (just published).

ECHARD, LAWRENCE. A General Ecclesiastical History. In two volumes 8vo. The third edition. Printed for J. Tonson. 512.

The EFFIGIES of the Right Reverend Dr. William Fleetwood, Lord Bishop of St. Asaph. Curiously done in Mezzotinto, from the original. Painted by Mr. Richardson. Sold by the Printsellers in London and Westminster. 515.

The EFFIGIES of the famous Ben. Johnson . . . Done from the original Picture . . . painted by Gerard Homhorst. Engraved on a copper plate, and sold by George Virtue and Mr. Smith. 118.

[ELSTOB, WILLIAM.] An Essay on the Great Affinity and Mutual Agreement of the two Professions of Divinity and Law, and on the joint Interests of Church and State. Printed for Bernard Lintott, an d sold by Richard Wilkin. 323.

EPICURUS. Epicurus's Morals, translated from the Greek by John Digby, Esq; with comments and reflections taken out of several authors. Also Isocrates his Advice to Demonicus. Done out of Greek by the same Hand. To which is added an Essay on Epicurus's Morals. Written by M. St. Evremont, and made English by Mr. Johnson. Printed for Sam. Briscoe, and sold by J. Morphew, and Ja. Woodward. 307.

An ESSAY upon True Knowledge, and a Sound Judgment in Religion. By a Presbyter of the Church of England. Printed for, and sold by R. Smith. 341.

ESTRADES, GODEFROY D'. Letters and Negotiations of the Count D'Estrades . . . from the year 1663 to the year 1669. Translated by several hands. 3 vols. Printed for D. Brown [and others]. 95.

EUSDEN, LAURENCE. A Letter to Mr. Addison, on the King's Accession to the Throne. Printed for Jacob Tonson. 606.

An EXACT Account of the Form and Ceremony of His Majesty's Coronation. The second edition. Sold by J. Baker. 612.

The EXAMINERS for the Year 1711. To which is prefix'd a Letter to the Examiner. Sold by J. Morphew, and A. Dod. 336 (just published).

The EXAMINER, Number I. Printed for J. Roberts. 615.

[FAIRMAN, Arthur S.?] A Full Confutation of Witchcraft. More particularly of the Depositions against Jane Wenham. Sold by J. Baker. 368.

The FAITHFUL General; a Tragedy. Printed for R. Wellington. 528.

FARQUHAR, GEORGE. Mr. Farquhar's Letters, Poems and Comedies. The second edition. Printed for Bernard Lintott. 251.

—— The fifth edition of the Recruiting Officer, and the fifth edition of the Beaux Stratagem. Printed for Bernard Lintott. 587.

The FARTHINGALE Reviv'd, or More Work for a Cooper. A Panegyrick on the late, but most admirable Invention of the Hoop-Petticoat. Written at the Bath. Sold by J. Baker. 118.

FENTON, ELIJAH. An Epistle from Mr. Fenton to Mr. Southerne. Printed for Benj. Tooke and Bern. Lintott. 83.

[FLEETWOOD, WILLIAM.] The Judgment of the Church of England in the case of Lay Baptism and of Dissenters Baptism. Sold by A. Baldwin. 342 (yesterday).

[——] —— The second edition. Sold by A. Baldwin. 358.

[——] A Sermon on the Fast Day, January 16, 1711-12, against such as delight in War. By a Divine of the Church of England. Printed for Sam. Buckley. Published by A. Baldwin. 279.

[——] —— The second edition. Published by A. Baldwin. 291.

—— Four Sermons. The second edition. Printed for Charles Harper. 388.

—— —— Sold by A. Baldwin. 422.

—— The Bishop of St. Asaph's Charge to the Clergy of that Diocese in 1710. Printed by Sam. Buckley, and sold by D. Midwinter. 422.

The FRENCH King Vindicated. Sold by J. Baker. 517.

[FULLER, FRANCIS.] Medicina Gymnastica; or, A Treatise concerning the Power of Exercise with respect to the Animal Oeconomy, and the great Necessity of it (especially Riding) in the cure of several Distempers. The fourth edition. Printed for R. Knaplock. 86 (this week).

GARDINER, JAMES. A Practical Exposition of the Beatitudes. Printed for Bernard Lintott. 451.

[GARTH, SAMUEL.] The Dispensary: A Poem. The seventh edition. Printed for Jacob Tonson. 556 (just published).

[GAY, JOHN.] The Mohocks: A Tragi-Comical Farce. Printed for Bernard Lintott. 349.

—— The Shepherd's Week, in Six Pastorals. The second edition. Printed for J. Tonson, and sold by W. Taylor. 579.

The GENERAL Cashier'd. Humbly inscribed to his Highness Prince Eugene of Savoy, designed for the Stage. Sold by J. Baker. 285.

GREENWOOD, JAMES. An Essay towards a Practical English Grammar. Sold by S. Keeble [and others]. 106 (just published).

GRIFFIN, BENJAMIN. A new Tragedy call'd, Injur'd Virtue, or, The Virgin Martyr. To be acted this evening at the Play House in Richmond. Printed for Jonas Brown, and J. Richardson. 590 (newly published).

GROVE, HENRY. 1. The Regulation of Diversions. 2. The Duty of Peaceableness explained and enforced. Both printed for John Clark. 368.

HAMLET. An Opera. As it is to be performed next Wednesday at the Queen's Theatre in the Hay-Market. Printed for Jacob Tonson. 311.

—— All the Songs set to Musick in the last new Opera, call'd Hamlet. Printed for J. Walsh, and J. Hare. 358.

[HARE, FRANCIS.] The Allies and the late Ministry defended against France, and the Friends of France, in Answer to a late pamphlet, intitled, The Conduct of the Allies. Printed for A. Baldwin. 242.

[——] —— Part the second, containing a Vindication of the Barrier Treaty, and of our Alliances with Portugal. Printed for A. Baldwin. 255 (just published).

[——] —— Part III. In which are considered all the Objections made against the Emperour, Portugal, and the rest of the Allies. Printed for A. Baldwin. 296.

[——] —— The 4th and last Part of The Allies and the late Ministry defended . . . Containing a Vindication of the late Ministry. Printed for E. Sanger, and sold by A. Baldwin. 318.

[——] Bouchain: in a Dialogue between the late Medley and Examiner. Printed for A. Baldwin. 172.

—— The Charge of God to Joshua. In a Sermon Preached before his Grace the Duke of Marlborough at Avenes le Sec, September 9, 1711. Being the Day of Thanksgiving for passing the Lines, and taking Bouchain. Printed for J. Baker. 179.

—— —— The second edition. 252.

—— The Conduct of the Duke of Marlborough, during the Present War, with Original Papers. Sold by J. Baker. 281 (just published).

—— A Full Answer to the Conduct of the Allies. To which is added some Observations on the Remarks on the Barrier Treaty. Sold by J. Baker. 331.

—— The Treaty betwixt Her Majesty and the States-General . . . consider'd. Sold by A. Baldwin. 300.

HERCULES. A new Opera called Hercules. Printed for Jacob Tonson. 368.

The HERTFORDSHIRE Witchcraft detected, being an Examination of a Book, intituled, A Full and Impartial Account of the Discovery of Sorcery and Witchcraft practis'd by Jane Wenham. Printed for John Pemberton. 430.

The HISTORIAN, Number Eleven, is this Day to be Sold by A. Baldwin at the Oxford Arms in Warwick-Lane, price one Penny, and will for the future continue to be Published every Tuesday, Thursday and Saturday. 311.

The HISTORY of King James's Ecclesiastical Commission. Printed for T· Harrison, and S. Popping. 89.

The HISTORY of Prince Mirabel's Infancy, Rise, and Disgrace; with the sudden Promotion of Novicius. Printed for J. Baker. 310.

—— The 2d part. Printed for J. Baker, and sold by B. Ber[r]ington. 349.

—— The third and last part. Sold by J. Baker. 380.

The HISTORY of the Peace from the Arrival of M. Mesnager, Sept. 8, 1711. to the Return of the Earl of Strafford from Utrecht, May 15, 1712 . . . Done out of French. Sold by J. Baker. 394.

The HISTORY of the Peace with France and War with Holland in the Year 1672. & seq. . . . To which is added a Preface relating to the present times. Printed for A. Baldwin. 229.

The HISTORY of the Proceedings of the Mandarins and Proatians of the Britomartian Empire at their last General Diet, with the Characters of the chief Members. Sold by J. Baker. 446.

The HISTORY of the Reign of Queen Anne. Year the Ninth. Printed for Tho. Ward. 124.

HOADLY, BENJAMIN. The Reasonableness of Conformity to the Church of England. The third edition. Printed for James Knapton. 339.

HOMER. Madam Dacier's Homer, with her Notes . . . Done in[to] English Mr. Ozell. Printed for Bernard Lintott. 251.

—— The Iliad of Homer, with Notes by Madam Dacier. Vol. the 2d. The 4th, 5th, 6th and 8th Books translated by Mr. Ozel, the 7th Book by Timothy, and the 9th Book by Mr. Brome of St. John's College in Cambridge. Printed for Bernard Lintott. 353.

—— The third Volume of Homer, by Madam Dacier. Translated by Mr. Broome. Printed for Bernard Lintott. 403.

—— The Iliad of Homer, with Madam Dacier's Notes, Mr. Johnson's Grammatical Notes, and a large Poetical Index to the whole. 5 vols. 12mo. Printed for B. Lintott. 451.

HOPKINS, EZEKIEL. The Doctrine of the Two Covenants. Printed for Richard Smith. 203.

—— Death disarm'd of its sting . . . A Discourse of Redemption . . . With an Appendix. 2 vols. Printed for Richard Smith. 329.

HORACE. A new Edition of Horace, by the Reverend Dr. Bentley, in 2 vol. Quarto. Published at Mr. Mortlock's and Mr. Bateman's. 281.

—— The Odes of Horace in Latin and English; with a Translation of Dr. Bentley's Notes. To which are added, Notes upon Notes, done in the Bentleian Stile and Manner. Part the 1st. Printed for Bernard Lintott. 423. (Other parts: 433, 445, 461, 499, 541.)

—— The 5th Ode of the 4th Book of Horace imitated, and inscribed to the King. Printed for W. Hinchcliffe. 589 (yesterday).

[HORNBY, CHARLES.] The Caveat against the Whigs: a second part. With a Preface to both parts. Sold by J. Morphew. 251.

HOUGH, JOHN. A Sermon preach'd at St. Bride's before the Lord Mayor and Court of Aldermen, on Monday in Easter-Week, 1712. Printed for Egbert Sanger. 390.

[HUGHES, JOHN.] A Poem intituled, An Ode to the Creator of the World, occasion'd by the Fragments of Orpheus. Printed for Jacob Tonson. 546.

An IMPARTIAL Enquiry into the Management of the War in Spain. Sold by J. Morphew. 218.

An IMPARTIAL View of the two late Parliaments, their proceedings and the late Ministry, fully justified. Together with the Affairs of Convocation. [Dedication signed P. H.] Printed for J. Baker. 167.

The INFANTS Lawyer: or, the Law (Ancient and Modern) relating to Infants. The second edition. Printed for St. John Baker. 425.

The INFORMATION against the Duke of Marlborough, and his Answer. Sold by A. Baldwin. 533.

The INTEREST of Europe, with respect to Peace and War. Sold by S. Popping. 194.

JACOB, GILES. The Accomplish'd Conveyancer. Printed for Bernard Lintott. 562.

—— —— The second part. 618.

JOHNSON, CHARLES. The Wife's Relief: or, The Husband's Cure. Printed for Jacob Tonson. 233.

[KENNETT, WHITE.] A Memorial to Protestants on the Fifth of November. Printed for John Churchill. 525.

KING, WILLIAM. The Works of Dr. King, in 2 volumes 8vo. Printed for Bernard Lintott. 409.

[——] Useful Miscellanies. Printed for Bernard Lintott. 435.

LA BRUYÈRE. The Works of Mr. Bruyere, in 2 vols. compared with the last Paris Edition, and an Original Chapter after the manner of Bruyere. By N. Rowe, Esq. Printed for E. Curll, and J. Pemberton. 590.

LANSDOWNE, GEORGE GRANVILLE, LORD. Poems upon Several Occasions. Printed for Jacob Tonson. 495.

LE CLERC. Monsieur Le Clerc's Extract and Judgment of the Characteristicks of Men, Manners, Opinions, Times, Translated from the French of the 19th, 21st, and 23d Tomes of the Bibliotheque Choisie. Printed for E. Sanger, and sold by A. Baldwin. 296.

—— A Funeral Oration upon the Death of Mons. Limborch, late Professor

of Divinity among the Remonstrants at Amsterdam, who died April 30, 1712. Translated from the Latin. Sold by A. Baldwin. 518 (to morrow).

LEE, NATHANIEL. The Works of Mr. Nathaniel Lee, collected in two volumes. Printed for Richard Wellington. 516.

A LETTER shewing how to reconcile the Churches of England and Rome, by introducing the Pretender. Sold by J. Roberts. 594.

A LETTER to a High-Church Man, in answer to a Pamphlet, intitled, Reasons why this Nation shou'd put a speedy end to this expensive War. Sold by A. Baldwin. 217.

A LETTER to a Member of the October-Club: shewing, that to yield Spain to the Duke of Anjou by a Peace, will be the Ruin of Great Britain. Printed for A. Baldwin. 125 (newly published).
—— The second edition corrected. 240.

LE VASSOR, MICHEL. An Account of the Present State and Government of the Empire of Germany. Printed for Jacob Tonson. 68.

The LIFE, Death, and Character of the Lady Jane Gray. Printed for E. Curll, and J. Pemberton. 590.

The LIFE of Edward Seymour Duke of Somerset, Lord General and Protector of the Realm, with parallel Instances to the case of John D. of M—— Late great Favourite of England. Sold by J. Baker, and B. Berrington. 523.

The LIFE of Mr. John Locke, written by an intimate Friend. Sold by E. Curll. 515.

The LIVES of Mortimer, Earl of March, and of Robert, Earl of Oxford, &c. Prime Ministers in the Reigns of Edward the Second and Richard the Second. Printed for A. Baldwin. 145.

LLOYD, ROBERT LUMLEY. A Sermon preach'd at St. Paul's Covent-Garden on the 30th of January, 1711–12, being the Anniversary-Fast for the Martyrdom of King Charles I. Printed for A. Baldwin. 292.
—— A Sermon preached at St. Paul's Covent-Garden the 5th of November, 1712, being the Anniversary for the happy Discovery of the Gun-powder-Treason, and for the late glorious Revolution in 1688. Sold by A. Baldwin. 534.

LOCKE, JOHN. A neat Edition of Some Thoughts concerning Education. The 7th edition, in 12mo. Printed for and sold by J. Kent. 424 (just published).

[LOCKHART, GEORGE.] Memoirs concerning the Affairs of Scotland. Sold by J. Baker, and by the Booksellers of London and Westminster. 586 (yesterday).

LOCKYER, CHARLES. An Account of the Trade in India. Printed for the Author, and sold by S. Crouch. 80 (just published).

LONG, ROGER. The Musick Speech, spoken at the publick Commencement in Cambridge, July the 6th, 1714. Printed for John Morphew, and Cor. Crownfield in Cambridge. 570.

LONGINUS. The Works of Dionysius Longinus. Translated from the Greek, by Mr. Welsted. Printed for S. Briscoe; and sold by J. Morphew [and others]. 346 (in a few days); 372 (now published).

The LORD MOHUN's Vindication. Printed for A. Dodd. 553.

The LOVERS Secretary, or, The Adventures of Lindamira, a Lady of Quality. Printed for Richard Wellington. 516.

MAITTAIRE, MICHAEL. The English Grammar. Printed for Henry Clements. 210 (to morrow).

MANDEVILLE, BERNARD. A Treatise of the Hypochondriack and Hysterick Passions. Printed and sold by D. Leach [and others]. 52 (just published).

[MANLEY, MARY DE LA RIVIERE.] The Adventures of Rivella. The second edition (to which is added a compleat key). Printed for J. Roberts. 592.

[——] Court Intreagues, in a Collection of Original Letters from the Island of the New Atalantis. Printed for J. Morphew, and J. Woodward. 187 (lately published).

[——] A True Narrative of what pass'd at the Examination of the Marquiss de Guiscard. Printed for John Morphew. 40.

The MARCH of the Chevalier de St. George: or an Account of the Mock Procession of burying the Pope and the Pretender, intended to be performed on the 17th of November 1711. On a Broad Sheet, curiously engraven on Copper. Sold by J. Baker. 271.

[MAYNWARING, ARTHUR.] The History of Hannibal and Hanno in the 2d War between Carthage and Rome. Faithfully collected from the best Authors. Printed for A. Baldwin. 274.

MEMOIRS and Observations of the Occurrences of Europe since the Treaties of Nimeguen and Ryswick, with relation to the present Treaty of Utrecht. Sold by J. Morphew. 436.

MILTON, JOHN. Paradise Lost. The ninth edition. Printed for Jacob Tonson. 29 (just published).

MISCELLANEOUS Poems and Translations. By several Hands. [Edited by Alexander Pope.] Printed for Bernard Lintott. 383.

A MODEST Survey of that celebrated Tragedy, the Distress'd Mother, so often and so highly applauded by the Ingenious Spectator. Printed and Sold by William Redmayne, and John Morphew. 384 (yesterday).

[MOLL, HERMANN.] Geographia classica, the Geography of the Ancients. Sold by Christopher Browne. 255.

—— A View of the Coast, Countries, and Islands within the Limits of the South-Sea Company. Printed for John Morphew. 130.

MONSIEUR LE CLERC's Life. Sold by E. Curll. 515.

The MONTHLY Catalogue of Books, Sermons, and Pamphlets, published in August. Printed for Bernard Lintott. 589.

—— published in September. 604.

—— published in October. 616.

A MORNING's Discourse of a Bottomless Tub. Printed for J. Morphew. 428.

[MORRICE, BEZALEEL.] An Essay on the Poets. Printed for Daniel Browne, and sold by A. Baldwin. 448 (lately published).

[MORRICE, BEZALEEL.] Miscellanies or Amusements in Verse and Prose. Printed for D. Browne, and A. Baldwin. 418.

The MOTTOES to the 5 volumes of Tatlers, and to the four volumes of the Spectators. Printed for Bernard Lintott. 541.

MOTTEUX, PETER. A Poem upon Tea. Sold by J. Morphew. 475 (just published).

MUSARUM Anglicanarum Analecta; sive Poemata quaedam Melioris Notae, seu hactenus inedita seu sparsim edita. Editio Tertia Priori Emendatior. 2 vols. Printed for Henry Clements. 565 (yesterday).

[N., N.] A Full and Impartial Account of the Tryal of the Reverend Mr. Francis Higgins, Prebendary of Christ-Church, Dublin. Printed for Jonah Bowyer. 404.

NEPOS. Cornelius Nepos; or, The Lives of Illustrious Men: Translated from the Latin by Mr. Broome of St. John's College in Cambridge. Printed for Bernard Lintott. 485.

NEW Miscellany Poems, with Five Love Letters from a Nun to a Cavalier, done in Verse. Printed for W. Mears. The third edition. 563.

The OFFERS of France explain'd. Printed for A. Baldwin. 306.

The OLD and New Ministry compar'd. Printed for A. Baldwin. 256.

[OLDISWORTH, WILLIAM.] An Essay on the Nature, Extent, and Authority of Private Judgment in matters of Religion. Printed for Bernard Lintott, and sold by John Friend. 88.

[OLDMIXON, JOHN.] A Letter to the Seven Lords appointed to examine Gregg. Sold by J. Baker. 118.

[OLIVIER, ABBÉ.] Memoirs of the Life and Adventures of Signior Rozelli. The second edition, corrected, enlarged. Printed for J. Morphew and J. Woodward. 516.

ORATIO DOMINICA plus centum linguis, versionibus, aut characteribus reddita & expressa. The Lord's Prayer in above a hundred languages, versions, and characters. Printed for Benj. Motte [and others]. A new edition, with additions. 514.

OTWAY, THOMAS. A very neat Pocket Edition, in two vols. 12mo, of the Works of Mr. Thomas Otway, consisting of his Plays, Poems, and Love Letters. Printed for J. Tonson, and sold by W. Taylor. 385.

OVID. Decerpta ex Ovidii Fastis, per Thomam Johnson usui Scholae Brentfordiensis & quarumvis aliarum. Printed for Bernard Lintott. 215.

—— Ovid's Art of Love. In three books. Translated by Mr. Dryden, Mr. Congreve, &c. Together with the Remedy of Love. To which are added, The Court of Love. A Tale from Chaucer. And the History of Love. Printed for J. Tonson, and sold by W. Taylor. 329 (lately published).

—— Ovid's Metamorphos[e]s. The second edition, with English Notes, by the Author of the Peculiars. Sold by Mr. Guy. 174 (just publish'd).

OZANAM, JACQUES. Mr. Oz[a]nam's Compleat Treatise of Fortification, in

6 parts. Done into English by Mr. Desaguliers of Hart-Hall in Oxon. Sold by M. Hawkins, and J. Morphew. 37.

PALMYRA: Being Poems on Several Subjects. Sold by J. Morphew. 224.

The PARLIAMENT of Birds. Printed for John Morphew. 535.

The PASSION of Sappho, and Feast of Alexander. Set to Musick by Mr. Thomas Clayton. As it is performed at his House in York-Buildings. Printed for Jacob Tonson. 61.

PEACE at Home and Peace Abroad. The second edition. To which is added a Preface, in Answer to a Preface of a Right Reverend Prelate to his Four Sermons. Printed for Thomas Harbin. 397.

PENITENTIAL Meditations of a Soul touched with Remorse for having a long time recited the Lord's Prayer without due Attention and Reflection. Written in French, and translated by W. S. Corrected by Joseph Trapp. The second edition. Printed for Bernard Lintott, and sold by John Harding [and others]. 289.

[PERCY, ELIZABETH, Countess of Northumberland.] Meditations and Prayers to be used before, at, and after the receiving the Holy Sacrament of the Lord's Supper. The fifth edition, with many additions. Printed for F. F. and sold by Tho. Harbin. 353.

PETRONIUS ARBITER. The Works of Petronius Arbiter, in three parts, by several Hands, adorn'd with cuts; with a Key written by Monsieur St. Evremont. Printed for J. Morphew, and J. Woodward. 187 (lately published).

PHILIPS, AMBROSE. The Distrest Mother. A Tragedy. Printed for S. Buckley, and J. Tonson. 338.

—— —— The second edition. 371.

—— An Epistle to the Right Honourable Charles Lord Halifax, one of the Lords Justices appointed by his Majesty. Printed for Jacob Tonson. 589.

—— —— The second edition. 598.

—— The Thousand and One Days Persian Tales. Translated from the French. Printed for Jacob Tonson. 564.

—— The 2d Vol. of Mr. Philips's Translation of the Thousand and one Days Persian Tales. Printed for Jacob Tonson. N.B. The 3d Vol. which compleats the whole, is in the Press, and will be published in a very short time. 585.

PIERS, [SARAH], LADY. George for Britain, a Poem. Printed for Bernard Lintott. 604.

[PITTIS, WILLIAM.] The History of the Present Parliament and Convocation. Printed for J. Baker. 114.

[——] The History of the Proceedings of the Second Session of this Present Parliament. Printed for John Baker, and sold by B. Berrington. 494.

A PLAN of the Town, Fortifications, and Harbour of Dunkirk, with an Historical Description thereof. Sold by J. Baker, and B. Berrington. 435.

A PLAN of the Town of Bouchain; with the situation of the Confederate Army commanded by his Grace the Duke of Marlborough, as also that of

the French Army commanded by the Marshal Villars. Sold by John King, and A. Baldwin. 194.

PLUNDER and Bribery further discover'd. Sold by J. Baker. 287.

A POEM to the Right Honourable Mr. Harley, wounded by Guiscard. Printed for Jacob Tonson. 35.

POINTER, JOHN. A Chronological History of England. 2 vols. 12mo. Printed for Bernard Lintott. 589.

[POPE, ALEXANDER.] An Essay on Criticism. Printed for W. Lewis, and sold by W. Taylor [and others]. 65.

[———] The second edition. Printed for W. Lewis, and sold by J. Morphew. 547.

—— Advertisement to the Subscribers for Mr. Pope's Homer. Whereas it was proposed that the First Volume of this Translation should be published by the beginning of May next. This is to give Notice, that the Undertaker intends it shall be delivered Two Months sooner than the Time promised. Whoever therefore is willing to subscribe for the said Book, is desired to cause the first Subscription (which is two Guineas) to be paid to Mr. B. Lintott at the Cross Keys between the Temple Gates in Fleet-street, and to recieve from him Receipts for the same before the End of January next; at which Time the Subscription will be shut up. All Persons may be assured that no Books will be printed in the same large Volume, with the same Ornaments of Graving, or upon Royal Paper, except just the Number that shall be then subscribed for. 631.

PRINCE Eugene not the Man you took him for; or, a Merry Tale of a Modern Hero. Sold by J. Baker, and B. Ber[r]ington. 471.

The PRINCE's Cabala: or, Mysteries of State. Written by King James I. and some Noblemen in his Reign, and in Queen Elizabeth's. With Socrates's Discourse to a Grecian Prince, on Kingly Government, translated from the Greek. Printed for R. Smith [and others], and sold by R. Burleigh. 608 (to morrow).

PRIOR, MATTHEW. Poems on Several Occasions. Printed for Jacob Tonson. 105.

PROPOSALS for a Lottery of Three Millions (Redeemable by Parliament) containing likewise a Parallel View of all the present Lotteries. Printed by Andrew Bell. 277.

A PROSPECT of the Confederate and French Armies, as they lay the 30th of May 1712. When Prince Eugene was for Fighting. Printed for A. Baldwin. 416.

The PROTESTANT Union, or the main Principles of Religion owned by the Dissenters; agreeable to the Articles, and Homilies of the Church of England, &c. Printed for E. Parker. 395.

[QUILLET, CLAUDIUS.] Callipedia, or the Art of getting Pretty Children. Translated by several Hands, with curious Cuts. Printed for Bernard Lintott. 251.

[———] Callipaedia. A Poem in four Books. With some other Pieces of the same

Author. Written in Latin by Claudius Quillet, made English by N. Rowe, Esq. To which is prefix'd Mr. Bayle's Account of the Author's Life and Writings. Printed for E. Sanger, and E. Curll. 412.

The RATES of Hackney-Coaches and Chairs. Printed by Sam. Buckley for Edward Castle, and sold by A. Baldwin. 183.

The REASONS which induc'd Her Majesty to create Samuel Massan [i.e. Masham], Esq. a Peer of Great Britain: Also the Reasons which induc'd his late Majesty William III to create Charles Mountague, Esq. a Peer of England. Sold by J. Morphew, and E. Curll. 312.

The REASONS which induced Her Majesty to constitute the Right Reverend Father in God John [Robinson] Lord Bishop of Bristol Keeper of the Privy Seal. Printed for E. Curll, and sold by J. Morphew. 178.

RELIGIO CLERICI: or, The Devotions of a Private Country Divine of the Church of England. Printed for N. Cliff and D. Jackson. 189.

RELIGION and Morals: Dedicated to her Grace the Dutchess of Bedford. Sold by J. Morphew. 96.

REMARKS on a false, scandalous, and seditious Libel, entituled the Conduct of the Allies and the late Ministry, &c. Printed for A. Baldwin. 240.

A REPRESENTATION of the Present State of Religion. Printed for Jonah Bowyer. 93.

—— Corrected from the Errors of a former Edition. To which is added the Representation as drawn up by the Upper-House. Printed for John Morphew. 107.

The RE-REPRESENTATION, being an Enquiry into the Plunderers of the Nation. Sold by J. Baker. 118.

The RETIREMENT. A Poem. Printed for Tim. Goodwin. 390.

[RICHARDS, THOMAS.] The (Latin) Description of Hogland: With its Dedication: Imitated in English Verse. Sold by the Booksellers of London and Westminster. 15.

[RIDPATH, GEORGE.] The Present Ministry Justify'd. Printed for J. Morphew. 561.

ROCHESTER. The Works of the Earls of Rochester, Roscommon, and Dorset. 2 vols. Printed for E. Curll, and J. Pemberton. 590.

ROGERS, WOODES. A Cruising Voyage round the World. Printed for A. Bell and Bernard Lintott, and sold by Mr. Horn [and others]. 415.

ROPER, ABEL. Abel Roper's Annals, containing the secret and open advances towards a Peace. Sold by J. Baker, and B. Berrington. 463 (lately published).

ROSE, W[ILLIAM]. The History of Joseph, a Poem in Six Books. Printed for James Knapton. 507.

The ROVER, being English Words made to the most celebrated Air. Sung by Madam Isabella Girardau, in the Opera of Rinaldo. Engraven on a Copper-Plate. Sold by J. Simpson, and J. Baker. 41.

ROWE, NICHOLAS. The Tragedy of Jane Shore, written in imitation of Shakespear's Style. Printed for Bernard Lintott. 587.

The SENSE of the Nation concerning the Duke of Marlborough. Printed for S. Popping. 288.

[SHAFTESBURY, ANTHONY ASHLEY COOPER, EARL OF.] Characteristicks of Men, Manners, Opinions, Times. In 3 volumes. Sold by D. Browne [and others]. 96.

SHAKESPEARE, WILLIAM. The Works of Mr. William Shakespear, in 2 Vols. Compleat. Printed for E. Curll, and J. Pemberton. 590.

SHERLOCK, THOMAS. A Sermon preached before the Rt. Honourable the Lord Mayor, Aldermen, and Citizens of London, at the Cathedral Church of St. Paul's, November 5, 1712. Printed for J. Pemberton. 542.

SHERLOCK, WILLIAM. A neat Elziver Edition of Dean Sherlock's Preservative against Popery in two Parts. Printed for D. Brown [and others]. 589.

The SHINING Sisters, a Poem, written at Tunbridge. Printed for Bernard Lintott. 463.

A SHORT but full Account of the Rise, Nature and Management of the Small Pox, and other putrid Feavers; with their proper Remedies. Sold by J. Morphew. 82.

A SHORT Way to know the World, or the Rudiments of Geography. The second edition. Printed for T. Osborn. 422.

SNELL, CHARLES. Snell's Art of Writing in Theory and Practice, a very useful Copy-Book. Printed for Henry Overton. 344.

[SOMERS, JOHN, BARON.] Anguis in Herba; or, the Fatal Consequences of a Treaty with France. Sold by A. Baldwin. 209.

SOPHIA CHARLOTTE, Queen of Prussia. A Letter against Popery. Printed for A. Baldwin. 307.

SOPHOCLES. Oedipus Tyrannus, a Tragedy, from the Greek of Sophocles, translated into Blank Verse with Notes. Printed for Bernard Lintott. 587 (next week).

A SPECIMEN of Papal and French Persecution . . . exhibited in the cruel sufferings, and most exemplary behaviour of that eminent Confessor and Martyr, Mr. Lewis de Marolles . . . Newly done out of French. Sold by Mr. Brown [and others]. 255.

The SPECTATOR. A Very Neat Pocket Edition of the Spectator, in 2 vol. 12mo. Printed for S. Buckley, and J. Tonson. 278.

—— A Very Neat Pocket Edition of the 3d and 4th Volumes of the Spectator in 12mo. To which is added a compleat Index to the whole 4 Volumes. Printed for S. Buckley, and J. Tonson. 537 (just published).

The SPECTATOR Inspected, or a Letter to the Spectator from an Officer of the Army in Flanders, touching the Use of French Terms, in Relations from the Army: Occasioned by the Spectator of the 8th of September 1711. Written by the Author of the Spy upon the Spectator. [London: Printed in the Year 1711.] 223 (just published).

STANYAN, ABRAHAM. An Account of Switzerland, written in the Year 1714. Printed for J. Tonson. 570 (yesterday).

A STATE of the Bewdley Case. Sold by S. Popping. 228.

STEELE, RICHARD. The Christian Hero. The sixth edition. Printed for J. Tonson. 517 (just published).

[——] The Englishman's Thanks to the Duke of Marlborough. Sold by A. Baldwin. 266, 269.

[——] The French Faith, represented in the Present State of Dunkirk. Printed and sold by Ferd. Burleigh. 562.

—— A very neat Pocket Edition of Mr. Steele's two Comedies, viz. The Funeral, and The Tender Husband. Printed for J. Tonson and sold by Owen Lloyd. 181.

[——] A very neat Pocket Edition of the Lying Lover, a Comedy. Printed for Bernard Lintott. 187.

—— Mr. Steele's 3 Comedies, viz. Funeral, Lying-Lover, and Tender-Husband. Printed for Bernard Lintott. 215.

—— A Book, (formerly so often mentioned in the Spectator) intituled, The Ladies Library. Written by a Lady. Published by Mr. Steele. Consisting of general Rules for Conduct in all the Circumstances of the Life of Women. Printed for Jacob Tonson. 604 (to morrow).

[——] In a neat Pocket Volume, (the same with the Spectator, Guardian and Englishman) The Lover; to which is added the Reader, by the same Author. N.B. There are a small Number printed in 8vo upon Royal and Demy Paper to compleat Setts of the Author's Works. Printed for Jacob Tonson. 634 (to morrow).

—— Mr. Steele's Apology for himself and his Writings; occasioned by his Expulsion from the House of Commons. London: Printed, and sold by R. Burleigh. 610.

[——] The Prologue at the Opening of the Theatre Royal in Drury Lane the Day after His Majesty's Publick Entry, spoken by Mr. Wilks. Printed for Jacob Tonson. 598.

—— The Romish Ecclesiastical History of late Years. Printed for J. Tonson. 565 (just published).

STEVENS, WILLIAM. A Sermon Preached to the Protestants of Ireland now residing in London, at their Anniversary Meeting, October 23, 1711, in Commemoration of their Deliverance from the barbarous Massacre committed by the Irish Papists in the Year 1641, in the Parish Church of St. Paul's Covent-Garden. Sold by A. Baldwin. 209.

—— —— The second edition. 235.

STURMY, D[ANIEL]. A Theological Theory of a Plurality of Worlds. [Publisher's name not given.] 114.

[SWIFT, JONATHAN.] The Conduct of the Allies and the late Ministry, in beginning and carrying on the present War. Printed for John Morphew. 234 (yesterday).

[——] —— The third edition. 238.

[——] Miscellanies in Prose and Verse. Printed for John Morphew. 10 (just published).

[——] A New Journey to Paris. Sold by John Morphew. 194 (just published).

[SWIFT, JONATHAN.] Some Remarks upon a Pamphlet, Entitl'd, A Letter to the Seven Lords of the Committee, appointed to examine Gregg. Printed by J. Morphew. 148 (just published).

[——] Some Remarks on the Barrier-Treaty. Printed for John Morphew. 304 (next week).

[——] A True Relation of the Several Facts and Circumstances of the intended Riot and Tumult on Queen Elizabeth's Birth-day. Printed for J. Morphew. 242 (just published).

[—— and Mrs. Manley.] A Learned Comment upon Dr. Hare's excellent Sermon preach'd before the D. of Marlborough on the surrender of Bouchain. Sold by J. Morphew. 194 (just published).

SYDENHAM, THOMAS. The whole Works of that excellent Physician, Dr. Thomas Sydenham. The fifth edition, by J. Pechey. Printed for R. Wellington. 405.

SYNGE, RICHARD. The Good Man's Refuge in Distress, and the Right Way to secure and perpetuate the Blessings of our present Establishment. Delivered in two Sermons at the Savoy, the former August 8, 1714, on Occasion of the Death of Queen Anne, the latter October 3 following, on the happy Arrival of King George. Printed for J. Tonson. 613.

TALBOT, WILLIAM. The Bishop of Oxford's Charge to the Clergy of his Diocese, at his Visitation in the Year 1712. Printed for Jonah Bowyer. 534.

TASSONI. La Secchia: The Bucket. A Mock-Heroic. Done from the Italian by Mr. Ozell. Sold by Mr. Lintott and Mr. Sanger. 455 (lately published).

A TASTE of Philosophical Fanaticism, in some Speculations upon the four first chapters of Mr. Green's Principles of natural Philosophy. By a Gentleman of the University of Gratz in Germany. Translated from the Original. Printed for J. Morphew. 532.

THEOBALD, LEWIS. The Mausoleum, a Poem, sacred to the Memory of her late Majesty, Queen Anne. Printed for Jonas Brown. 585 (yesterday).

—— —— The second edition. 601.

THEOPHRASTUS. A New Translation of the Characters of Theophrastus. Translated from the Greek by Eustace Budgell, Esq. The second edition. Printed for Jacob Tonson. 571.

THREE Articles of the Grand Alliance; with the late Preliminaries of Peace, in the Year 1709. Sold by S. Popping. 194.

TICKELL, THOMAS. A Poem to his Excellency the Lord Privy-Seal, on the Prospect of Peace. Printed for J. Tonson. 521.

—— —— The second edition. 528.

—— —— The third edition. 532.

—— —— The fourth edition. 552.

TILLY, WILLIAM. Dr. Tilly's Sermon on the Parable of the Pharisee, preached before the Lord Mayor, November 11, 1711. Printed for Bernard Lintott. 263.

[TINDAL, MATTHEW.] The Nation Vindicated from the Aspersions cast on it in a late Pamphlet, intituled, A Representation of the present State of Religion. Part I. Printed for A. Baldwin. 171 (just published).

[——] —— The Second Part. 341.

TOLAND, JOHN. An Account of the Courts of Prussia and Hanover: Sent to a Minister of State in Holland. . . . To which are added, The Ordinances and Statutes of the Royal Academy erected by the King of Prussia at Berlin. And the Declaration of the Elector Palatine in favour of his Protestant Subjects. All three publish'd by Mr. Toland. Sold by J. Roberts [and others]. 578.

TORY Partiality detected: or a True State of the Pole and Scrutiny of Broad-street-Ward, on the Election of an Alderman in the room of Sir Joseph Wolf deceas'd. Printed for J. Baker. 251.

[TRAPP, JOSEPH.] Abra-Mule; or, Love and Empire, a Tragedy. Printed for W. Mears [and others]. 579 (just published).

—— Praelectiones Poeticae: in schola naturalis philosophiae Oxon. habitae. Oxonii e Theatro Sheldoniano. Impensis Bernardi Lintott. 6 (just published).

A TRUE and Particular Account of a Storm of Thunder and Lightning which fell at Richmond in Surrey on Whit-Sunday last in the Afternoon, being May the 20th 1711. Printed for John Morphew. 86.

The TUNBRIDGE Miscellany, consisting of Poems, Letters, &c. Panegyrical and Satyrical, Written at the Wells this Summer: With a particular Account of the swinging Ladies. Sold by E. Curll. 515.

VAN OOSTEN, HENRY. The Dutch-Gardener; or, the Compleat Florist. Translated into English. The second edition, with great amendments. Printed for D. Midwinter. 32 (now published).

VERSES written to the Duke of Marlborough upon his leaving England. Now first printed, and recommended to Sir Anthony Crabtree, who is best able to supply what is wanting in them. Printed for R. Burleigh. 625.

VERTOT D'AUBŒUF, ABBÉ. The History of the Revolutions in Portugal. Translated from the French Original. Printed by Sam. Buckley: Sold by S. Crouch [and others]. 332.

—— The History of the Revolutions in Sweden. Written originally in French, and translated into English by J. Mitchel, M.D. The third edition. Printed for Tim. Childe. 12 (just published).

VERTUE, GEORGE. A Print of the Right Honourable John Lord Sommers Baron of Evesham. Engraved from a Painting lately done by Sir Godfrey Kneller. Printed for Jacob Tonson. 281.

A VINDICATION of the Reverend Mr. William Richardson, from the Aspersions cast upon him by Ellenor Kirk, a common Prostitute, and in two Libels intituled, The Goat in Sheeps Cloathing, and The Preaching Weather-cock. Sold by J. Baker. 488.

A VINDICATION of the Earl of Nottingham from the vile Imputations and malicious Slanders which have been cast upon him in some late Pamphlets. Printed for J. Roberts. 561.

A VINDICATION of the present Negotiations of Peace from the Imputation of Trifling. Sold by J. Baker. 399.

[WARD, EDWARD.] The History of the Grand Rebellion. Printed for J. Morphew. 3 vols. 547 (on Monday next).

[——] The Poetical Entertainer; or, Tales, Satyrs, Dialogues and Intrigues, &c. Serious and Comical, all digested into such Verse as is most agreeable to the several Subjects. To be Publish'd as often as Occasion shall offer. Numb. I. Sold by J. Morphew. 438 (just published).

[——] —— Part First and Second. 468 (just published).

[——] —— Numb. III. Sold by T. Woodward, and J. Morphew. 515 (just published).

WATS, WILL. The Clergyman's Law; or, The Compleat Incumbent. The second edition. Printed for D. Brown [and others]. 230.

[WEAVER, JOHN.] An Essay towards a History of Dancing. Printed for Jacob Tonson. 476.

[WELLS, EDWARD.] An Essay towards an Impartial Account of the Holy Trinity, and the Deity of our Saviour, as contained in the Old Testament. Printed for Henry Clements. 423.

—— An Historical Geography of the Old Testament, in three volumes. Vol. II. Printed for James Knapton. 129.

—— The Young Gentleman's Astronomy, Chronology, and Dialling. Printed for James Knapton. 433.

WHISTON, WILLIAM, and Humphrey Ditton. A New Method for Discovery of the Longitude both by Sea and Land. Printed for John Phillips. 566 (this week will be published).

WILKINS, W. A Poem on the Arrival of the King. Sold by J. Morphew. 596.

WRIGHT, SAMUEL. To be every where spoken against, at first the Case of the Christians themselves, and now of the Protestant Dissenters. Considered in Two Sermons Preach'd at Black Fryars, March the 9th and 16th, 1711–12. The second edition. Printed for J. Clark, and E. Matthews. 366.

WYCHERLEY, WILLIAM. The Works of Mr. Wycherley, collected into one volume. Printed for Richard Wellington. 516.

XENOPHON. Hiero; or the Condition of a Tyrant, translated from the Greek of Xenophon, with Observations. Printed for Bernard Lintott. 541.

—— The Memorable Things of Socrates. Translated into English. To which are prefixed the Life of Socrates: From the French of Monsieur Charpentier. And the Life of Xenophon, collected from several Authors. With some Account of his Writings. By E. Bysshe. Printed for G. Sawbridge, and sold by J. Woodward. 248 (yesterday).

YOUNG, EDWARD. The 2d Edition of Mr. Young's Poem, intituled, The Force of Religion; or, Vanquish'd Love. Printed for E. Curll, and J. Pemberton. 590.

—— A Poem on the Late Queen's Death, and His Majesty's Accession to the Throne. Inscribed to Joseph Addison, Esq., Secretary to their Excellencies the Lords Justices. Printed for Jacob Tonson. 595.

IV. SOURCES OF MOTTOES

OVER half the mottoes in the *Spectator* are drawn from Horace and Virgil; roughly a third are from Horace alone. For most eighteenth-century readers (at least among the male sex) the quotations from the classics must have struck a responsive chord, since many were familiar tags known from school days—the *Mens sibi conscia recti* or *Nugaeque canorae* which adorn many an eighteenth-century sermon or political address. How much the *Spectator* contributed to making them increasingly a part of the middle-class reader's stock of 'familiar quotations' it is impossible to say.

Since almost none of the essays in the *Spectator* bear titles, the motto obviously serves in many instances in lieu of such a title. Often it is so closely connected with the body of the essay as to serve as a starting-point, or (as before Addison's Saturday 'lay sermons') as a kind of text. At times it provides an ironic commentary on the subject-matter of the paper and thus serves to orient the reader. In any case it is clearly thought of as an integral part of the paper.

How was the motto chosen? Addison affords us a glimpse at the opening of No. 221.

> When I have finished any of my Speculations, it is my Method to con-sider which of the Ancient Authors have touched upon the Subject that I treat of. By this means I meet with some celebrated Thought upon it, or a Thought of my own expressed in better Words, or some Similitude for the Illustration of my Subject. This is what gives Birth to the Motto of a Speculation. . . . (ii. 358.)

This seems definite enough, and there can be no doubt that this was the frequent practice of Addison. On occasion, however, it seems clear that an essay might be written with the motto itself as a starting-point. In No. 139, by Steele, we read, 'But let us consider what is truly Glorious, according to the Author I have to Day quoted in the Front of my Paper' (i. 50). Similarly in No. 153, which has a motto from *De senectute*, Steele writes: 'It is (as my Author has it) as absurd in an old Man to wish for the Strength of a Youth, as it would be in a young Man to wish for the Strength of a Bull or a Horse' (i. 100). The motto of No. 150 is from Juvenal's third satire, and Budgell in his first paragraph after quoting from this satire remarks: ''Tis on this Occasion that he afterwards adds the Reflection which I have chosen for my Motto' (i. 90). As for contributed essays, while we may assume that the motto would generally be supplied by Steele or Addison, it is quite possible that a contribution might be sent in with a motto already prefixed. There are examples of this practice in the collection of unused letters published by Lillie, as well as in No. 404, for which the original manuscript is extant (see iii. 513, n. 3, and Appendix V).

The following analytical index shows in tabular form the relative frequence of the authors drawn upon for mottoes. The references, in parentheses, are

to numbers of the *Spectator*; those marked with an asterisk indicate mottoes in the original Folio numbers which were changed later in the 8vo and 12mo editions.

HORACE

Satires, Book 1
1. 1–19 (558)
   20–22 (559)
2. 37–38 (274, 486)
3. 6–7 (221)
   18–19 (338)
   29–30 (268, 332)
   41 (234)
   42 (276)
   44–48 (373*)
   68–69 (548)
   117–19 (564)
4. 17–18 (19)
   40–42 (618)
   43–44 (160)
   81–85 (594)
5. 44 (100, 462)
   64 (32)
6. 23–24 (224)
   63 (99)
   66–67 (297)
7. 19–21 (481)
9. 3–4 (24)
10. 9 (135)
    23–24 (29)
    90–91 (65)

Satires, Book 2
1. 1–2 (538)
2. 3 (109)
3. 9 (457)
   13 (348)
   77–79 (624)
   156 (488)
   271 (398)
6. 33 (220*)
   58 (4)
7. 2–3 (96)
   85–86 (480)
   91–92 (212)
   101 (244)

Epistles, Book 1
1. 11 (16)
   20–26 (27)
   36–37 (255)
   53–54 (450)
   90 (319)
2. 14 (180)
   27 (317)
   43 (628)
   62–63 (438)
   64–65 (337)
4. 5 (459)
5. 28 (21)
6. 10 (288)

27 (329)
65–66 (30)
7. 98 (174*)
8. 17 (76)
11. 27 (80)
    28 (54, 284*)
    28–29 (364)
    30 (196, 424)
14. 36 (550*, 553)
16. 24 (458)
    52 (79)
17. 3–5 (250)
    23 (75)
    35 (280)
    43–44 (360)
    62 (430)
18. 5 (300)
    6 (474)
    15–20 (197)
    24 (114)
    25 (202)
    29 (145)
    68 (218)
    69 (228)
    76–77 (493)
    86 (214*)
    97–99 (465)
    102 (387)
    103 (264, 622)
19. 6 (362)
    12–14 (473)
    42 (296)

Epistles, Book 2
1. 5–10 (101)
   13–14 (552)
   63 (70)
   76–77 (253)
   80–85 (336)
   112 (136)
   115–16 (572)
   117 (442)
   127 (51)
   128 (168)
   148–50 (451)
   166 (290*)
   168–9 (242)
   187–8 (18, 141)
   197 (208*)
   202–7 (42)
   208–13 (40)
   250–1 (278)
   262–3 (270)
2. 45 (111)
   55 (260)
   61–63 (92)
   102–3 (39)

128–40 (167)
133 (178)
140 (419)
149–51 (547)
183–4 (222)
187–9 (157)
208–9 (7)
212 (148)
213 (440)
216 (318★)

Ars Poetica
1–8 (63)
5 (5)
12–13 (595)
25 (205, 460)
39–40 (307)
41 (476)
48, 50–51 (165)
71–72 (478)
81–82 (235)
92 (529)
97 (290)
99 (321)
100 (420)
108–11 (541)
110 (322)
119 (538★)
126–7 (162, 338★)
138 (444★, 553★, 550)
139 (444)
142 (403)
143–4 (1)
153 (44)
156 (273)
180–1 (369)
181–2 (402)
188 (22)
191–2 (315, 483)
227–30 (285)
240–2 (103)
300 (275)
304–5 (532)
308 (446)
309 (62)
316 (279, 357★)
317–18 (335)
319–22 (85)
322 (570)
338 (245)
341–4 (179)
344 (512)
351–3 (291)
359 (53)
360 (184)
361 (58, 226★)
363–4 (303)
398 (236, 479)
400–1 (551)
409 (592)
410–11 (414)

417 (428)
434–6 (569)
451 (155)

Odes, Book 1
3. 38 (186)
4. 13–17 (26)
   15 (289)
5. 5 (631)
   12–13 (187)
11. 1–3 (604)
    6–8 (93)
    7 (535)
12. 15–18 (531)
13. 4 (194)
    18 (142)
17. 14–16 (106)
19. 7–8 (204)
22. 17–18, 23–24 (366)
23. 11–12 (314)
24. 1–2 (133, 520)
    19–20 (501)
30. 5–8 (33)
33. 10–12 (530)

Odes, Book 2
2. 19–21 (429)
3. 1–4 (381)
5. 15–16 (308)
8. 5–7 (156)
   18 (190)
10. 5–8 (464)
    19–20 (28)
13. 13–14 (377)
14. 21–22 (490)
20. 1–2 (453)

Odes, Book 3
1. 2 (630)
3. 7–8 (441)
4. 5–8 (477)
6. 21–24 (66)
   23–24 (625)
11. 35 (234★)
16. 1–5 (326)
    21–22 (206)
24. 32 (443)
26. 1. (423)

Odes, Book 4
2. 27–30 (455)
3. 1–4, 10–12 (417)
4. 33–36 (123)
   50–52 (198)
   57–60 (495)
7. 9–12 (425)
9. 10–12 (229)
   45–49 (574)
   45–50 (375)
   47–52 (615)
12. 28 (358)
13. 26–28 (301)

Epodes 17. 24 (328)

227

VIRGIL
Eclogues:
 1. 19–20 (119)
    27 (316)
 2. 3–5 (627)
    17 (87)
    63–64 (359)
 3. 16 (88)
    60 (121)
    89 (418)
    93 (400)
    103 (252★)
 4. 48 (378)
 5. 62–64 (585)
 6. 33–36 (339)
 7. 17 (284)
    69 (174)
 8. 63 (318, 404)
    68 (603)
    108 (117)
 9. 34 (461)
    36 (432)
 10. 42–43 (584)
    60–61 (233)
    63 (131)

Georgics
 1. 54–61 (69)
    60–61 (404★)
    201–3 (10)
    293–4 (606)
    412 (393)
    415–16 (120)
    513–14 (498)
 2. 51–52 (605)
    155 (415)
    174–5 (388)
    369–70 (619)
    461–2 (193)
    527–34 (161)
 3. 8–9 (554)
    43–44 (116)
    99–100 (90)
    244 (91)
    272 (365)
    291–3 (514)
 4. 6 (353)
    112–15 (583)
    208–9 (72)
    221–2 (565)
    226 (575)
    494, 497–8 (164)
    564 (613)

Aeneid
 1. 11 (185)
    73 (310)
    74–75 (52)
    202–3 (341)
    316–17 (104)
    328 (73)
    341–2 (272)

    405 (466)
    411–13 (8)
    464 (83)
    604 (213)
    661 (557)
    720–2 (561)
 2. 6, 8 (357)
    6–8 (84)
    145 (181)
    368–9 (363, 599)
    471–5 (556)
    521–2 (305)
    570 (252)
    604–6 (159)
    755 (110)
 3. 56–57 (426)
    318 (491)
    583–4 (36)
    660–1 (472)
 4. 2 (304)
    4 (113)
    10–11 (340)
    15–19 (614)
    24–29 (623)
    64 (281)
    73 (118)
    88 (74)
    99–100 (545)
    132 (579)
    285 (140)
    366–7 (611)
    373 (298)
    376–9 (523)
    466–8 (241)
    701 (271)
 5. 343–4 (302)
 6. 50–51 (513)
    86 (239)
    143 (540)
    172 (333)
    264–7 (309)
    266 (31)
    270–1 (593)
    436 (97)
    493 (567)
    545 (632)
    625–6 (251)
    641 (600)
    728–9 (519)
    791 (620)
    823 (200)
    832–3 (125)
    852–3 (43)
    878 (517)
 7. 44 (327)
    514–15 (361)
    748–9 (130)
    805–6 (37)
 8. 580 (282)
 9. 294; 10. 824 (189)

420–1 (23)
617 (536)
10. 108 (126)
824 *see* 9. 294
11. 659–63 (434)
12. 46 (25)
59 (351)
228 (220)
529–32 (612)

OVID

Heroides
4. 10 (71, 199)
15. 79 (596)

Ars Amatoria
1. 99 (208)
159 (15)
175 (511)
241–2 (269)
633 (608)
2. 1–2 (607)
24 (165*)
233 (566)
539 (380)
3. 7 (265)

Remedia Amoris
10 (395)
135–6 (272*)
625 (175)

Metamorphoses
1. 9 (46)
76–78 (345)
175–6 (580)
355 (68)
521–2 (134)
654–5 (41)
746 (560)
758–9 (372)
2. 13–14 (543)
36–38 (203)
72–73 (576)
127 (526)
430 (542)
447 (86)
3. 432–6 (325)
4. 280 (323)
284 (626)
287 (413)
294–5 (421)
378–9 (435)
428 (277)
591 (14)
5. 216–17 (173)
6. 182–4 (500)
428–9, 431 (320)
7. 826 (171)
8. 774–6 (589)
9. 163 (528)
12. 57–58 (439)
13. 127 (407)

141 (219)
228–9 (397)
14. 652–3 (48)
15. 165–8 (343)
167–8 (578)
179–85 (590)
871–2 (166)

Tristia
1. 3. 66 (385)
2. 563 (355)
566 (262)
3. 3. 73 (591)

Epistulae ex Ponto
2. 9. 47–48 (215)

JUVENAL, *Satires*

1. 18 (367)
75 (383)
86 (609)
170–1 (629)
2. 35 (573)
46 (507)
63 (11)
82 (448)
83 (154)
3. 1–2 (549)
33 (82)
36–37 (436)
100 (45)
124–5 (214)
152–3 (150)
182–3 (64)
6. 110 (602)
138–9 (311)
167–71 (299)
168–9 (354)
178–9 (306)
181 (182)
252–3 (57)
259 (320*)
327–8 (217)
362–5 (295)
501 (98)
614–15 (577)
7. 51–52 (582)
167–8 (2)
237–8 (313)
8. 73–74 (534)
76–77 (518)
10. 1–4 (207)
28–29 (371)
28–30 (598)
191 (17)
349–50 (356)
356 (115)
365 (225)
11. 11 (344)
13. 54–55 (6)
14. 47 (330)
109 (373)

Juvenal, *Satires* (*cont.*)
321 (50)
15. 34, 36–38 (516)
140–2 (177)
159–60 (34)
163–4 (9)
164 (324*)

Cicero

Orations:
Pro Quinctio 15. 50 (456)
Pro Archia 7. 16 (406)
Post Reditum ad Quirites 1. 2 (431)
Pro M. Caelio 3. 8 (427)
6. 13 (386)
Pro Q. Ligario 1. 2 (382)
12. 38 (230)
Rhetorical Works:
De Oratore 1. 26. 120 (390)
1. 61. 258 (334)
2. 4. 17 (132)
Orator 34. 119 (633)
Philosophical Works:
De republica 6. 19. 20 (635)
De finibus 2. 35. 117 (151)
Tusculan Disputations 1. 15. 33 (210)
1. 48. 115 (368)
2. 6. 16 (312)
4. 25. 55 (494)
4. 32. 68 (149)
De natura deorum 1. 44. 124 (588)
2. 66. 167 (146)
De senectute 1. 1 (163)
23. 85 (153)
De divinatione 1. 22. 45 (586)
1. 58. 132 (505)
De officiis 1. 5. 15 (243)
1. 15. 49 (248)
1. 19. 62 (350)
1. 19. 63 (172)
1. 27. 94 (259)
1. 28. 99 (342)
1. 34. 124 (408)
2. 5. 16 (138)
2. 12. 43 (139)
2. 16. 57 (394)
2. 18. 63 (346)
3. 5. 21 (469)
3. 8. 35 (352)
3. 12. 51 (546)
Correspondence:
Epistulae ad Familiares 7. 1. 6 (422)
11. 28. 3 (137)
12. 16. 1 (263)
15. 6. 1 (188)
See also *Rhetorica ad Herennium*

Terence

Andria 60–61 (105)

62–66 (169)
96–98 (192)
694–7 (522)
910–13 (437)
Heauton Timorumenos 90 (454)
131–3 (496)
260–1 (515)
579 (509)
643 (502)
Eunuchus 50–55 (216)
57–58 (475)
59–61 (170, 401)
76–78 (510)
192 (562)
296 (503)
426 (504)
566 (144)
930–3 (266)
934–40 (410)
Adelphoe 855–8 (544)

Martial, *Epigrams*

1. 9. 2 (616)
16. 1–2 (581)
16. 2 (240)
38. 2 (568)
86. 8–10 (77)
117. 18 (445)
2. 41. 1 (47)
86. 9–10 (470)
3. 68. 1 (449)
4. 13. 7–10 (506)
82. 8 (412)
6. 29. 8 (38)
70. 15 (143)
8. 78. 4 (231)
10. 4. 10 (49)
23. 7–8 (94)
12. 92. 4 (13)
13. 2. 8 (158)
14. 183 (433)

Persius, *Satires*

Prologue 10 (283)
1. 1 (127)
27 (379)
40–41 (499)
99–102 (617)
2. 3–13 (391)
28 (331)
61 (324)
3. 30 (587)
85 (60)
4. 23 (399)
50–51 (238)
51 (555)
5. 19–20 (61)
64–71 (89)
71–72 (129)

92 (12)
129–30 (55)
6. 11 (376)

ARATUS OF SOLI, *Phainomena* 5 (537)

CAECILIUS STATIUS, quoted in Cicero, *Tusculan Disputations* (149)

CALLIMACHUS, *Fragments* 359 (124)

CATULLUS, *Carmina* 39. 16 (35)

CLAUDIAN, *Poems* 27 (Panegyricus De Sexto Consulatu Honorii Augusti, Praefatio), 1–6, 11–12 (463)

CURTIUS RUFUS, QUINTUS, *History of Alexander the Great*, 7. 8. 15 (485)

ENNIUS, quoted in Cicero, *De senectute* (163); quoted in Cicero, *De divinatione* (505)

EURIPIDES, *Ino, Fragment* 7 (471); *Cresphontes*, quoted in Cicero, *Tusculan Disputations* (368); *Stheneboia, Fragment* 671 (525)

EVENUS PARIUS, quoted in Winterton (447)

GELLIUS, AULUS, *Noctes Atticae*, 4. 9 (201)

HESIOD, *Theogony*, 27–28 (183)
39–40 (247)
Works and Days, 40–41 (195)
317 (458)
761–2 (256)

HOMER, *Iliad*, 1. 225 (20)
472–4 (405)
2. 6 (191)
6. 146 (152)
16. 33–35 (246)
21. 195 (489)

LUCAN, *Pharsalia*, 1. 8 (347)
98 (128)
135 (563)
459 (56)
459–62 (349)
2. 657 (374)
9. 11–14 (621)
579 (571)

LUCRETIUS, *De rerum natura*
1. 926–8 (411)
934 (409)
3. 11 (482)
4. 750 (416)
962–5 (3)
1162 (176)

MARCUS AURELIUS ANTONINUS, *Meditations*, 9. 42. 4 (601)

MENANDER, *Eunuchus, Fragment* (497)
Monostichoi 88 (249)
102 (261)
462 (293)
Naucleros 349 (287)

NEPOS, CORNELIUS, *De viris illustribus*, 1. 8. 3 (508)

PETRONIUS ARBITER, *Satyricon*:
7 (328★)
80 (521)
104 [= *Poems*, 31. 3–4] (487, 597)
118 (392)
130 (382)

PHAEDRUS, *Fables*
1. Prologue 7 (211)
2. 5. 3 (108)
[Epilogue 1–3 (107)
3. 1. 5–6 (223)
14. 12–13 (102)

PHOCYLIDES, *Poema admonitorium* 62 (254)

PLATO, quoted in Cicero, *De officiis* (172)

PLAUTUS, *Stichus* 109–10 (527)
550–1 (533)

PLINY THE ELDER, *Natural History*, 12. 5 (452)

PLINY THE YOUNGER, *Epistles*
3. 21 (468)
6. 23 (484)

PROPERTIUS, *Elegies*, 2. 34. 65 (267)

PUBLILIUS SYRUS, *Sententiae* 116 (122)

PYTHAGORAS, *Carmina Aurea* 1–2 (112); 'Pythag. apud Ovid', [*Met.* 15. 165–8] (343)

Rhetorica ad Herennium, formerly (and in the *Spectator*) attributed to Cicero:
1. 2. 3 (147)
4. 17. 24 (294)
4. 28. 39 (see note to No. 226)

SALLUST, *Bellum Catilinae*, 25. 2 (67)
54. 3 (232)

SENECA, *De brevitate vitae*, 13. 1 (59)
Epistles, 99. 17 (524)
Natural Questions, 7. 31. 2 (492)
Hippolytus 607 (95)
Oedipus 295 (237)
Thyestes 398–403 (610)

SIMONIDES (SEMONIDES), *Iambics* 3 (209)

SOCRATES, quoted in Xenophon, *Memorabilia* (634)

STATIUS, *Thebaid*, 2. 128–9 (81)

STOBAEUS, *Anthology*, i. 3. 9 (257)

TACITUS, *Annals*, 14. 21 (286)

TERTULLIAN, *De poenitentia*, 12. 9 (282*)

THEOCRITUS, *Idylls*, 3. 24–27 (227)

TIBULLUS, *Elegies*, 4. 1. 24–27 (467)
2. 7–8 (292)

'TREBONIUS APUD TULL' = CICERO, *Epistulae ad Familiares*, 12. 16. 1 (263)

XENOPHON, *Memorabilia*, 1. 6. 10 (634)

Other Sources

BACON, FRANCIS, *Advancement of Learning*, I. iii. 3 (78)

Post Boy (384)

SMALRIDGE, GEORGE, 'Auctio Davisiana' (389)

'Divide & impera' (258)

'Mutum est pictura poema' (226)

'Totus mundus agit histrionem' (370)

'Heteroclyta sunto . . . Quae Genus', in Lily's *Latin Grammar* (539); 'Pliny apud Lill.' (452)

'Barbara, Celarent, Darii, Ferio, Baralipton' (396)

V. DOCUMENTS

No. 402

The Letter from Dorinda

(Blenheim Palace Archives)

Mr Spectator—

your Generosity to your Correspondents in printing thare Letters, has made me ventuer to write to you in hopes of ye like Sucksess, I doubt not but you have sufficient matter for many papers to come but would be glad to see mine Incerted very Shortly, having noe other way of exposeing my unfaithfull Lover, and Returning my very thankfull Acknowlidgments to my kind & friendly Adviser. the matter of fact is as follows, about five years since I was courted by a young Gentleman of a good Estate, I then being about Fiveteen years of Age my person not Disagreable or Birth Inferior to his though my fortune was, the Superiority of that being on his side he Judg'd my Affections might be gained, as after two years triall they really ware, so much that I thought my self ye happyest woman in the world in having his Love, which he no sooner perceive'd but according to the fallshood so naturall in ye Sex, his Lessens, & my Sparks Honourable Courtship ended. the bright scein now closes & he begins to think noe Longer of Mariage but Courts me for a Mistriss, I bore this for three years in hopes of bringing him to his first proposall, but all in vain for he has now nothing of Honour nor Gratitude left, but Still persisted in his baseness & offer'd all a Woman that way Inclin'd Could wish for. my Stedfast Refusealls so Inrage'd him that he had the Assurance to tell me he never Repented of any thing in his Life but that he had let Slip so many oppertunity's and had not forc'd me to yeild, at these words I Left ye Roome & vow'd I would never see him more. In all ye perplexity in ye World I went to a Lady of my Intemite Acquaintance & told her ye whole affair, her Husband comeing In, & seeing me in a great Concern desiered to know ye Reason I haveing been before Inform'd of his Honour & tenderness to our Sex I made noe Scruple but frankly told him all. he was pleased to tell me that every word I Spoke plainly Show'd ye Love I had for him, & fearing what time might doe, he did with ye greatest earnestness, Honesty, Faithfullness, & Ingenuety, Disswade me from entertaining any kind thoughts towards such a wrech, & Read me so fine a Lecture on vertue that I hardly think any man besides himself can come up to, which at that time struck me dumb & So Confounded me that I could give him noe Answer but that I would returne him thanks in ye Spectator. it was as we say Reckoning without ones host, but believeing you to be Such a Favouror of gratitude that you will not faile me, I am throughly perswaded a man of your parts will easeyly See ye good Such a Letter may doe in ye world, in ye first place I hope it will make all young Ladies take care how they Discover their Passion before hand, and may it deter all Gentlemen from Serveing those, whose Affections they have gain'd in ye Like manner not only from a fear of being expos'd but from that

233

of transgresing against ye Laws of Vertue and Modesty, if not may all that are soo atack'd as I have been Resist with as great Resolution (but you'l say I am now praising my Self) and may they have the helps of my very good Adviser

> In hopes of being Obliged by you in
> Printing this my Letter
>
> I am Your Most Humble
> Servant & Admirer

May ye 12: 1712   Unfortunate Dorinda

[On verso:]

Dorinda discovers a Tenderness for her Lover, He thereupon attacks her virtue. She consults a friend &c

used

The Original for No. 404

(Blenheim Palace Archives)

Quid est aliud, Gigantum modo bellare cum diis, nisi naturæ repugnare?   Tull: de Senectute.

It has been held as a very ancient and a very certain maxim among the philosophers That Nature dos nothing in vain; That wise being who created the Universe has appointed evry thing to a certain use and purpose, and determind it to a settled course and sphere of action from which if it the least deviates it becomes unfitt to answer those ends for which it was designd: In like manner is it in the dispositions of society, evry man when he's sent into the world is designd for a particular station and has qualifications givn him suitable to it; Nature who wrote the play best knows how to dispose the parts, but if like refractory actors we refuse to submitt to her disposition we can expect but little harmony in the performance; and it is I think pretty plain that most of the impertinence and ridicule we meet with in the world is generally owing to the absurd affectation of excelling in characters men are not fitt for, and for which nature never designd them.

Evry man has one or more qualities which may make him usefull both to himself and others, Nature never fails of pointing 'em out, and while the infant continues under her guardianship she brings him on in his way, and then offers her self for a guide in what remains of the journy, if he proceeds he can then scarce miscarry; for Nature reckons her self oblidgd to make good her own engagements, and as she never promises what she is not able to perform so she never fails of performing what she promises. But the misfortune is men despise what they may be masters of and affect what they are not fitt for; they reckon themselves already possessd of what their Genius inclines 'em to, and so bend all their ambition to excell in what is out of their reach; Thus they destroy the use of their natural talents in the same manner as covetous men do their quiet and repose, they can enjoy no satisfaction in

what they have, because of the absurd inclination they are possessd with to what they have not.

Cleanthes had good sense a great memory and a constitution capable of the closest application, in a word, there was no profession in which Cleanthes might not have made a very good figure; but this wont satisfie him, he takes up an unaccountable fondness for the character of a fine gentleman, all his thought and application is bent upon this; instead of attending a dissection frequenting the courts of Justice or studying the fathers, Cleanthes reads plays, dances, dresses, and spends his time in drawing rooms, instead of being a good physician lawyer or divine, Cleanthes is a downright Coxcomb, and will remain to all that knew him a contemptible example of talents mis-applied. It is to this affectation the world owes its whole race of Coxcombs, Nature in her whole Drama never drew such a part, she has sometimes made a fool, but a coxcomb is allways of a mans own making by applying his talents otherwise than nature designd, who ever bears an high resentment for being putt out of her course and never fails of taking her revenge on those that do so. Opposing her tendency in the application of a mans parts has the same success as declining from her course in the production of Vegetables, by the assistance of art and an hott bed we may possibly extort an unwilling plant or an untimely sallad, but how weak how tastless and insipid? Just as insipid as the poetry of Valerio: Valerio had an universal character, he was genteel, had learning, thought justly spoke correctly, twas believd there was nothing in which Valerio did not excell, and twas true there was but one, Valerio had no Genius for poetry, yet hes resolvd to be a poet, he writes verses, and takes great pains to convince the town that Valerio is not that extraoirdnary person he was taken for. Behold how industrious a man is to his own disadvantage, and how artfull an enemy his vanity proves in exposing him most where he is least guarded.

If men wod be content to graft upon nature and assist her operations what mighty effects might we expect, Our age shod then boast of productions equall to those of Virgill and Tully: To build upon nature is laying the foundation upon a rock, evry thing disposes it self into order as it were of course, and the whole work is half done as soon as undertaken; Ciceros Genius in-clind him to Oratory Virgills to follow the train of the Muses, they piously obeyd the admonition, and were rewarded; they had the Vis ignea in their soul and all they had to do, was to blow it into a flame, in vain might they have labourd, in vain attempted to raise a superstructure if Nature had not first laid the foundation, and given em that particular Genius, from which only those mighty effects cou'd arise, and which as Mr Dryden says—Must be born and never can be taught. and certainly wherever Nature designs a production she allways disposes seeds proper for it which are as absolutely necessary to the formation of any Moral or intellectuall excellence as they are to the being and growth of plants; and I know not by what fate and folly it is that men are taught not to reckon him equally absurd that will affect a character in spite of Nature with that gardner that shod undertake to raise a junquil or tulip without the help of their respective seeds.

As there is no good or bad quality that dos not in some measure affect both sexes, so it is not to be imagind but the fair sex must have sufferd by an

affectation of this nature att least as much as the other; the ill effect of it is in none [. . .]spicuous as in the two opposite characters of Cælia and Iras; Cælia has all the charms of person together with an abundant Sweetness of nature, but is excessive silly and has a very ill voice; Iras is ugly and ungenteel but has a great deal of witt and good sense; If Cælia wod be silent her beholders wod adore her, if Iras wo'd talk her hearers wod admire her, but Cælias tongue runs incessantly while Iras gives her self silent airs and is coquetish; so that tis difficult to persuade one self that Cælia has beauty and Iras witt, each neglects her own excellence and is ambitious of the others character; Iras wod be thought to have as much beauty as Cælia, and Cælia as much witt as Iras.

The great misfortune of this affectation is, that men not only loose a good quality but also contract a bad one, they not only are unfitt for what they were designd, but they assign themselves to what they are not fitt for, and instead of making a very good figure one way make a very ridiculous one another. In a word, coud the world be reformd to the obedience of that famd dictate Follow Nature, which the Oracle of Delphos pronouncd to Cicero when he consulted what course of studies he shod follow, we shod see allmost evry man as eminent in his own sphere as Tully was in his; and shod in a very short time find impertinence and affectation banishd from among the women, and coxcombs and false characters from among the men.

[On verso:]

To the Spectator.
follow nature

No. 520

The Letter from F. J.

(Blenheim Palace Archives)

Mr Spectator—

The just value and esteeme you have alwayes showne for a matrimoniall State, incourages my Address to you for directions to me and others who may be in that sorte of single State I am now in—

About 3 months since dyed the dearest partner of my Life, my Wife; A loss of the greatest weight I e're yet mett with—and to recover which, if I know my own heart I could most willingly bee stripp't of all (which is not a little) I enjoy in the World: All! but the dearest Offspring of our Loves, the first borne of our Joys, and now the only surviveing of a numerous Traine; a Youth in whome I am as much blest and honour'd as ever parent was, and by whose conduct and counsell my loss which otherwise would bee insupportable is rendred more easy: ffor if my Eyes stand in Teares as frequently they doe at sight of the picture of my Love, the sight of him who has soe great a share of her Vertues sensibly dryes them, and administers secret joy to my declyneing spiritts—

236

'Tis true the memory of this departed Creature will most certainly bee ever most deare and valueable to me—But inasmuch as yor truely valued advice will live and flourish in yor happy papers to many generations, and may make others equally happy with myself, I intreat you in their names alsoe, that you will give us some few and speedy directions how to make the memory of such a wife not only deare but delightfull And you will thereby not only obleige me and the World I hope, but add to the just veneration you have always had from S^r

Yo^r disconsolate and
most humble Servt
F: J:

Norwich
7°: 8^{bris} 1712.

No. 528

The Letter from Bellmour in reply to Rachel Welladay

(Blenheim Palace Archives)

Middle Temple Nov^{br} 6

Mr Spectatour—

You have convinced me of the gracefullness and M^{rs}: Rachell Welladay of the necessity of Marriage, and I am so truly become a Convert that I hate to live alone any longer: The reason why I have not been hitherto a friend to it has been occasioned by the false artifices and sly Endeavours made use of to trick[1] me into it; You have professed yourself an Advocate for the fair sex, and a friend in dehorting them from those little follies and mistakes in the pursuit whereof they are too Eager and Ungovernable. And though you have avowedly acted in behalf of the other Sex, yet I have some reason to hope you won't intirely neglect your own. I beg you to insert this among your Speculations (tis realy matter of fact) for a Certain Lady's instruction who ha's wilfully mistaken conversation for Courtship, and by a designed and industrious way of discovery ha's wrought it into a common and almost received opinion, So that if it spreads too far I am in danger of loosing the the liberty of Choice and the benefit of my Conversion. I take therefore this way to Let her know that I never intended any addresses to her, or ever made ~~any~~ such to any Woman living, and therefore insist on the freedom and liberty of the Subject, and

---

[1] ~~trepan~~ trick

hope that when this appears to have the sanction of your Authority (which I beg it may) she will be induced in Justice to me to retract from her present Errour for I assure you that tho' I am a man yet never was a Lover   Pray Melinda take notice o'nt

I am S^r
Your very humble Servt
Bellmour

my humble Service to Mrs Welladay

[On verso:]

To the Authour of the Spectatour
to be left at Mr Charles
Lillies at the Corner of
Beaufort buildings
Strand

No. 539

The Letter from Eustace

(Blenheim Palace Archives)

Dear Mr Spectator—
If your ffriendship to Virtuous Love be any thing but Pretence, You will immediatly Answer the Design of this letter, wch comes from One most exceedingly tho' Unfashionably in Love with a Young Lady upon the Pure Consideration of her Own Merit, I mean the Beauty of her Person & the Endowments of her Mind. These are so Excellent that they Entitle Her to the Character of Most Agreable. Tho' Her ffamily and ffortune are in divers Respects Valuable, Yet did You know Us, You wou'd absolve my Love from any Tincture of either Avarice or Ambition. No, Cupid did not take Aim from either of those Eminencies. The Innocent Beauty and Pleasantries of her blooming Youth gain'd an Easy Entrance into my affections, and by a Continued Conversation of some Years her growing Virtues have taken so deep Root, that she is Now sole Mistresse of my Heart Yet so it is, that to obtain her I must be Assisted either by You or an Act of Parliament. ffor the Only Objection to my being accepted as a Lover is her being too Young for a Wife. Now there are so many Particulars, besides the Common Accidents of Love and Life, to hinder the Prospect of our being Joyned three Years hence that 'tis next to Impossible to Expect it. If therefore You have any Compassion for a sincere Lover, or Regard for a ffriend, be pleased soon to Notifie it Under Your Hand, that Parents may permit a Handsome discreet Daughter of 18^{teen} to Marry, without Offence either to Prudence or Humanity. If You oblige me in this and I succeed, I promise You a Place at my Wedding and a Treatment sutable to Your Great Age and Dignity, if Not, I shall endeavour

238

to get it Enacted Next Sessions that She is One and Twenty, and then You
shall never see the Charming Eugenia nor receive any thanks from

Her ffaithfull humble Servant

Eustace

Toms. Novemb^r 13

[On verso:] To

The Honble the Spectator

of

Great Britain

This.

No. 545

*Copia di lettera del Re della Cina al Papa, interpretata del padre Secretario
della Compagnia di Gesù*

Girolamo Gigli, *Il Gazzettino* (Lanciano, 1913), pp. 3-5.

A VOI benedetto sopra i benedetti, padre ed imperator grande de' pontefici
e pastori cristiani, dispensatore dell'olio de' Re d'Europa, Clemente XI.

Il favorito amico di Dio, Gionata VII, potentissimo sopra i potentissimi
della terra, altissimo sopra gli altissimi sotto il sole e la luna, che siede nella
sieda di smeraldo della Cina, sopra cento scaloni d'oro, ad interpetrare la
lingua di Dio a tutti i discendenti fedeli d'Abramo, e che dà la vita e la morte
a centoquindici regni, ed a centosettanta isole, scrive con la penna bianca dello
struzzo vergine e manda salute ed accrescimento di vecchiezza.

Essendo arrivato il tempo, in cui il fiore della nostra gioventù reale deve
maturare i frutti della nostra vecchiaia, e confortare con quelli il desiderio
de' nostri popoli devoti, e propagar il seme di quella pianta che deve proteg-
gerli, aviamo stabilito d'accompagnarci con un'eccelsa amorosa vergine,
allattata alle mammelle della leonessa forte, e dell'agnella mansueta. Perciò,
essendoci stato figurato il vostro popolo europeo romano per padre di donne
invitte e caste, allunghiamo la nostra potente mano a stringere una di loro;
e questa sarà una vostra nipote, o nipote di qualche altro gran sacerdote
latino, che sia guardato dall'occhio diritto di Dio. Sarà seminata in lei
l'autorità di Sara, la fecondità di Rachele, la fedeltà d'Ester, la sapienza di
Saba. La vogliamo con l'occhio della colomba, che guarda il cielo e la terra,
e con la bocca della conchiglia, che si pasce della rugiada della mattina. La sua
età non passi i 200 corsi della luna; e la sua statura sia alta quanto la spiga del
grano verde; e la grossezza sia quanto un manipolo del grano secco. Noi la
manderemo a vestire per i nostri manderini ambasciatori, i quali la condur-
ranno a noi; e noi l'incontraremo alla riva del fiume grande, facendola salire
nel nostro cocchio. Ella potrà appresso di noi adorare il suo Dio, assieme con
ventiquattro ancelle a sua elezione; e potrà cantare con loro come la tortora
la primavera. Sodisfacendo voi, padre ed amico nostro, a questa nostra brama,
sarete cagione d'unire in perpetua amistà cotesti vostri regni d'Europa al

nostro dominante impero; e si abbracceranno le nostre leggi come l'ellera abbraccia la pianta; e noi medesimi spargeremo del nostro seme reale in coteste provincie, riscaldando i letti de' vostri principi col fuoco amoroso delle nostre Amazzoni, d'alcune delle quali i nostri mandarini ambasciatori vi porteranno le somiglianze dipinte. Vi confortiamo a tener in pace le due buone religiose famiglie de' missionari neri figliuoli d'Ignazio, e de' bianchi e neri figliuoli di Domenico; il cui consiglio degli uni e degli altri ci serve di scorta, come appunto fa lume l'olio che si getta nel mare.

Abbracciandovi intanto dal nostro trono, vi dichiaramo nostro congiunto e confederato, ed ordiniamo che sia segnato questo foglio col nostro sigillo imperiale.

Dalla nostra città capo del mondo, il quinto giorno della terza lunazione, l'anno nono del nostro impero.

INDEX

Entries for noblemen will be found under their titles rather than family names. Proverbs and foreign words are italicized. Names of the fictional characters of the *Spectator* and of correspondents with obviously invented names are printed in capital and small capital letters. Italic numerals indicate footnote references. Attention is called to certain group headings, notably 'Coffee-houses', 'London', and 'Poems'. Throughout the index *PL* = *Paradise Lost*; *m*=*motto*.

Aaron's serpent, i. *45.*

Abba, the wisdom of, iv. 452.

Abbey, ruins of an, at Sir ROGER's, i. 453.

Abbey de la Trappe, Rules of, v. 33–34.

Abdiel, the loyal angel, a pattern to mankind, iii. 204.

Abdon, judge of Israel, his many children, iv. 274.

Abel: murder of, occasioned by a religious controversy, ii. 228; Adam's vision of Cain and, iii. 362.

Abigails, male, in fashion among the ladies, i. 192.

Abilities: religion gives a man room to exert his, ii. 374; men of greatest a. most fired with ambition, ii. 490–1; few men furnished with outstanding, ii. 491.

Abney, Sir Thomas, a director of the Bank, a subscriber, i. xc.

Abracadabra, as a signature for *Spectator* (?), ii. 360.

Abradatas: Panthea, wife of, iv. 526.

Abraham: interceded for Sodom, iii. 131; figure of in old tapestry, iii. 221; described in *PL*, iii. 387; tradition of his planting trees, v. 15; dwelt under an oak in Plains of Mambré, v. 15. *See also* Isidorus.

Abraham, men with surname of, i. *40.*

Abroad, to be, iii. 69.

Absence: called by poets death in love, ii. 436, 452; contrivances of lovers in, ii. 436–9, 452–3; a wife's behaviour in a. of husband, iii. 269–72; jealousy caused by lover's a. described by Spenser, iv. 430.

Absence (inattention), i. *330.*

Absences among the best preservatives of love, iv. 296.

Absent (absent-minded) man, character of, i. 329–33; causes and cure of absent-mindedness, i. 330–1; character of, described by La Bruyère, i. 332–3; an assembly of 'absent men', i. 126;

absent from what they were doing, iii. 7; the 'absent actor', iv. 436.

Absolute monarchy dangerous to a nation, iii. 20–21.

Absolution, in Book of Common Prayer, ii. 79, 420.

Abstinence: days of, advisable for health, ii. 266; as a virtue, ii. 445, 599; advised in May, iii. 374; of the Jews, iv. 257.

Abstracted (abstruse): too a. in my speculations, i. 203; speculation, v. 19; subjects of speculation, v. 51.

Absurdity (-ies): laughter caused by reflection on, ii. 466; impieties of Satan in *PL* I big with, iii. 86; of a rich fool represented on stage, iii. 394.

Abuse: in nursing of children, ii. 454–8; Locke on a. of words, iii. 403–4; terms of a. in modern pamphlets, iv. 536–8.

Academics, a crowd of at Astrop, ii. 104.

Académie française. *See* French Academy.

Académie galante, L', i. *382.*

Academy: for training women in exercise of the fan, i. 426–9; needed to settle controversies in language, ii. 35; a well-conducted school almost a little, ii. 396; project for a political a. in France, iii. 96. *See also* French Academy.

Academy of Compliments, in LEONORA's library, i. 155.

Academy of Painting, in London, iv. 495.

Acarnania, a promontory in, ii. 366, 382.

ACASTO, has the art of being agreeable, iii. 449.

Accent: differs from country to country, i. 120; in reading aloud, ii. 79–80; a preacher with something particular in his, ii. 120.

Accidents: unforeseen in human life, iii. 44; iv. 219–20; variety of, in an implex fable, iii. 58; surprising a. in *PL*, iii. 88.

Accomplishments: must serve virtue and honour, ii. 179; prizes for useless, ii. 185; to be taught to youth, ii. 395–6; pride in, iii. 75; of a wife, iii. 205.

Account of Charity Schools, An, iii. 48.
Account of the Works of the Learned, iv. 14; *Account of the Works of the Unlearned* proposed, iv. 14.

Accounts (Accompts): books of, ii. 37; keeping, ii. 187; iii. 104; 'has not kept true a.', ii. 187; balancing one's, ii. 188; 'upon the balance of', ii. 232; a tradesman's books of, iii. 26; value of a. and shorthand, iii. 319.

Accursius, Franciscus, ii. 454.

ACETUS, cruel in his raillery, iii. 584.

Achates (friend of Aeneas): does nothing to deserve the title, ii. 562; does not give advice or strike a blow throughout the *Aeneid,* iii. 446.

Achilles: *Nulli gravis est percussus A.,* i. 197; a prince of Greece, i. 300; as personification of anger, ii. 221; Joshua Barnes the A. of the modern Grecians, ii. 453; anger of, the theme of the *Iliad,* its consequences, ii. 541; son of a goddess, ii. 562; of special interest to Greek readers, ii. 585; battle with Hector, iii. 173; iv. 134; Alexander called A. by Lysimachus, iii. 247; tradition of, in time of Homer, iii. 305; friend of Patroclus, iii. 446; persuaded by Phoenix to lay aside resentments, iii. 466–7; his character only 'poetically good', iv. 464; mentioned, iii. 60.

Achilles, Thomas Inkle's ship, i. 49, 196.

Acids, a constitution abounding in, iv. 460.

Acknowledgement of faults, iii. 433–5.

Acorns: grow naturally in England, i. 295; a doe eating a. out of a servant's hand, v. 128.

Acosta, Uriel, his answer to Limborch on religious ceremonies, ii. 332.

Acquaintance: breaking off, ii. 316; enlarging, as aid to success, iii. 349.

Acrostic(s): satires and panegyrics in, i. 245; examples of false wit, i. 255; simple and compound, i. 255–6; handed about town, i. 262; Tory and Whig, i. 262; based on resemblances of letters, i. 265; iii. 560; a group of, in allegory of true and false wit, i. 272; laborious fools who write, iv. 146.

Act: our business to act rather than to know, ii. 421.

Act of Deformity, for use of Ugly Club, i. 76.

Acts of Parliament: i. 337; against Occasional Conformity, Sir ROGER's praise of, ii. 550–1; against illicit lotteries, iii. 548; against wagers, iv. 354; collection of bequeathed by Sir ROGER,

iv. 341; for establishing public funds, i. 15; for importing French wines, i. 181; for rewarding discovery of longitude, iv. 589; Act of Settlement, i. 15, 16; iii. 444; Act of settlement of the poor, ii. 404; Act of Toleration, i. 15; does not allow nonconformity in singing, ii. 306; Act of Uniformity, i. 15; passages in it marked by Sir ROGER, iv. 341.

Act-tune, to an incorrigible play, iii. 353.

Acting: on stage, ii. 56–57; iv. 453–4; children to be taught, ii. 396; Estcourt's skill in, iv. 157; suggestions on (from Cicero), iv. 432–7, 440.

Action: love of praise a principle of, i. 312; felicity of soul consists in, i. 475; tracing out principles of, ii. 370; common principle of, in all men, ii. 490; some cannot discern between a noble and a mean, ii. 491; on the stage, ii. 504–5; three qualifications of, in an epic, ii. 539; additional graces in, iii. 38–41; religion as an uniform tenor of, iii. 80; beginning of in *PL* and *Aeneid,* iii. 203; the Templar's essay on pronunciation and, iv. 432–7, 440; 'a kind of universal tongue', iv. 437; two principles of, in man, v. 10.

Actions: a fine gentleman is honest in his, i. 278; of Earl Douglas suitable to an epic hero, i. 301; life 'a circulation of little mean', ii. 67; time and place to be considered in all our, ii. 120; our best a. must be seen with grains of allowance, ii. 166; influence of intentions on, ii. 331–4; religion animates to laudable, ii. 374; men differ in their secret thoughts and public a., ii. 388; pleasure in generous, ii. 393–6; great a. possible in every station, ii. 462–5; lose their lustre when self-displayed, ii. 492; difficulty of judging, ii. 499–502; iv. 525–8; love gives a certain grace to, ii. 559; in *PL* appropriate to characters, ii. 564–5; iii. 113–18; giving fair names to foul, iii. 15–17; additional graces in, iii. 38–41; inconsiderable a. of life, iii. 156; can be understood by studying the passions, iii. 523–6; weighed by the Almighty, iv. 134; Epicurus and Hobbes on the source of all, v. 10–11.

Activity, natural to the soul, iii. 226.

Actor(s): letters from, i. 93–96; a company of strolling a. at Epping, i. 207–8; 'corporeal and intellectual', ii. 56; applause due a good a. when he leaves the scene, ii. 103; an a. overcome by shyness, ii. 397; expression used by

Roman a. at their exit, iii. 152; subdued by the cat-call, iii. 352; who put in words of their own, iv. 282, 427; rank among, iv. 388.

Ad eundum, admitted, i. 336.

Adam: his first impressions of Eve, i. 140–1; 'Adam, Sheth, Enosh', ii. 361; could not laugh before the Fall, ii. 466; character of in *PL*, ii. 563, 565; described by Milton, iii. 10; lived 930 years, iii. 28; mentioned, iii. 167; speeches of in *PL* IV, iii. 171; his part in *PL* IV, iii. 174–7; in *PL* V, iii. 197–203; in *PL* VII, iii. 256; conversation with Raphael, iii. 280–7; the Fall, iii. 308–12; behaviour after the Fall, iii. 333–6; his speech to Eve quoted, iii. 345; in last two books of *PL*, iii. 359–66, 385–91; 'the sun's first setting view'd', iv. 233; hearkened to voice of his wife, iv. 312; would have kept holy the Sabbath, iv. 586; labour enjoined on, and on his descendants, iv. 592; his delight on first seeing beauty of creation, v. 140; 'like the first man in his solitude', v. 143.

Adam and Eve: roving the walks of Paradise like the first happy pair, ii. 487; not only our progenitors but our representatives, ii. 565; a different species before the Fall, ii. 587; Milton's reflection on their going naked, iii. 61; beauty of description of, in *PL*, iii. 566; a garden their habitation before the Fall, iv. 192.

Adapting oneself to humour of others, iii. 448–9.

Adda (river), aqueduct from, to Milan, iv. 489.

Addison, Joseph: early career, i. xvi; launching of *Spectator*, i. xvii–xviii; papers in *Spectator*, i. xliii–xlv, lvii–lxix; in 2nd series, i. lxxiii–lxxxii; later reputation of, i. xcvii–cv; character of in Mr. SPECTATOR, i. 1; member of Kit-Cat Club, i. 42; advice to Pope, i. 242; not a 'preromantic', i. 322; 'Atticus' in No. 150(?), ii. 91; drew a prize in lottery, ii. 249; assistance to Budgell, ii. 274; visit to St. Peter's, ii. 290; his wife, ii. 328; assisted Philips in translating Sappho(?), ii. 367; diffidence in public speaking, ii. 398; reminiscence of stay in Dublin(?), ii. 460; of tour on Continent, ii. 466; and Pope, ii. 483, 485; assisted Budgell in Epilogue to *Distressed Mother*(?), iii. 31, 251; Desmaizeaux's life of Boileau addressed to, iii. 91; friendship with Whiston, iii. 485; praise of Nicolini, iii. 514; vexation over No. 410, iii. 531; iv. 339; 'Callisthenes' in No. 422(?), iii. 583–4; his method of raillery admired by Stella, iii. 583; and the Scriblerians, iv. 161–2; his decision to kill Sir ROGER, iv. 339; his productions brought to light by Steele, iv. 396; the 'British Virgil', iv. 399; friendship with Steele, iv. 399; and Hughes's 'Ode to the Creator', iv. 420; author of papers marked C,L,I,O, iv. 492; assisted Steele in *The Tender Mother*, iv. 493; his view of the French, iv. 499.—WORKS: *Account of Greatest English Poets*, i. 265; ii. 221; *Campaign*, i. xvi; iii. 530; iv. 399; v. 118; *Cato*, i. lxxiii; i. 452; iv. 280; Epilogue to, iii. 253; Latin translation of scene in, v. 145–8; Powell as Portius in, i. 130; quoted, iv. 38; v. 30–31; 'Defence of Newtonian Philosophy', iv. 346; *Dialogues on Ancient Medals*, i. 250, 256, 263; iii. 43; iv. 63; v. 103; *Discourse on Ancient and Modern Learning*, ii. 565; iii. 230, 446; *Drummer*, i. 53, 172, 182, 375, 453; ii. 20, 412; *Essay on Virgil's Georgics*, iii. 258, 560; iv. 595; *Evidences of Christian Religion*, v. 169; *Freeholder*, i. xciii, 72, 346; ii. 230; iii. 19, 43, 287; v. 13, 174; *Guardian*, i. 139, 160, 423; ii. 219, 387, 438; iii. 25, 48, 90, 202, 255, 418; iv. 589; v. 109, 124, 125; *Letters*, i. 123, 505; ii. 205, 249; iv. 499; v. 118, 159; 'Machinae Gesticulantes', iii. 572; 'Milton's Style Imitated', ii. 376; *Musarum Anglicanarum Analecta*, iii. 459; *Notes on Ovid*, i. 263; iii. 63, 87, 176; v. 113; *Notes upon Paradise Lost*, ii. 538; 'Poem to His Majesty', v. 174; *Present State of the War*, iii. 407; Prologue to *Phaedra and Hippolitus*, i. 81; *Remarks on Italy*, i. 480; iii. 369, 556, 557; v. 28, 174; *Rosamond*, i. 79; ii. 596; iii. 296–7; *Whig-Examiner*, i. xiv–xv, xvii; iv. 520.
— BOOKS IN LIBRARY OF, i. 164, 368, 390, 478; ii. 176, 220, 367; iii. 461, 576; iv. 567.

Addison, Lancelot, referred to in No. 600(?), v. 49.

Address, by Sir ROGER, presented at County Sessions, iv. 339.

Address: in imposing upon mankind, ii. 180; lack of, in applying knowledge, ii. 362; in dissembling poverty, iii. 593; persuasive a. of shopkeepers, iii. 94.

Address to the Unmarry'd Women, ii. 106.

Addresses: women's easy admittance of, iii. 64; women imposed on by false, iii. 73; to Louis XIV after battle of Ramillies, iii. 102.

Adept, in hermetic mysteries, iii. 598.

Adin, Thomas (weaver), iv. *458*.

Admiration: kinds of, ii. 239; passion of, portrayed by Raphael, ii. 380; one of our most pleasing passions, ii. 420; a short-lived passion, ii. 495–6; the most pleasing passion, iii. 145; a pleasing motion of the mind, iii. 545; lessens with familiarity, v. 139. *See also* Praise, love of.

Admiration (wonder): in her face, ii. 235; desire for annihilation deserves our, ii. 323; matter of, ii. 363.

Admirers: every man desirous of a set of, ii. 351; vanity of women in tormenting, ii. 553; desert PARTHENISSA after her small-pox, iii. 101.

Admonitions, example more persuasive than, iii. 82.

Adonis: loves of Venus and, i. 66; and Venus in modern prints, ii. 60; paintings of Venus and, iv. 298.

Adrian, Emperor. *See* Hadrian.

Adulteration of wine, iii. 353–5.

Adultery: now a 'modest word', iii. 16; account of an 'innocent' a., iv. 579; punishment of, iv. 580.

Adversity: we may in some measure defend ourselves from, ii. 88; the 'storms and tempests' of, ii. 374; not in itself an evil, ii. 421–3; the post of honour in human life, ii. 422; addresses to Louis XIV in, iii. 102; right way of regarding, iii. 128–30; benefits of, v. 104.

Advertisements: cost of, i. lxix–lxx; usual to publish a. of cures, ii. 30; many dealers turn authors and write quaint, iii. 25; in newspapers read with curiosity, iv. 92; of cures for blindness, iv. 173; sometimes dictated in anger, iv. 356; for elixirs and pills, hung up in coffee-houses, iv. 553; number of in *Spectator*, i. lxx–lxxi; read with interest, iii. 26; generally read by women, ii. 316; preferable to letters from readers, iii. 124; some of them named, iv. 129–30.

Advertisements in *Spectator* text: The *Cruelty of Atreus* (opera), i. 65; an Italian chirurgeon, i. 96; changes in St James's Coffee-house, i. 104; a school for birds of the loquacious kind, i. 151–2; benefit performance of *The Indian Emperor*, i. 172–3; a young woman who paints and mixes ribbons, i. 176–7; a sale of pictures, i. 288; a meeting of critics, i. *372*; instruction in exercise of the snuff-box, ii. 46–47; a horse called Caesar, ii. 117; a horse-race, ii. 182; Nicholas Hart, the sleeper, ii.

225; Mr. Sly, haberdasher, ii. 237–8; Nath. Cliff, for a lottery ticket, ii. 250; a painter from Italy, ii. 382; from the parish vestry, ii. 561; asking information about a young equestrian, iv. 222–3; testifying to cures from reading *Spectator*, iv. 457–62.

Advice: can be given to all, i. 143; giving of, causes uneasiness, ii. 293; ridicule a better expedient against love than sober, ii. 385; an old beau's a. to his son, ii. 593; manner of giving, iii. 41; pride prevents us from taking, iii. 82; to women in month of May, iii. 372–5; difficulty in giving, iii. 447–8; iv. 317.

Aeacus (judge of the dead), ii. 76.

Aegis of Minerva, in Homer, iii.258,337.

Aegisthus, said to have been nursed by a goat, ii. 455.

Aegrescitque medendo, i. 105 m., 197.

Aelianus, Claudius, ii. *266*; iv. *581*; on the beard of Zoilus, iii. 221.

Aeneas: and Hudibras, i. 170; and Dido, Virgil's and Ovid's treatment of, i. 268–9; founder of Rome, i. 300; his lamentation over Lausus, i. 303; wounded, i. 319; phantom of, ii. 304; first appearance in *Aeneid*, ii. 540; settlement in Italy and its consequences, ii. 541; a perfect character, ii. 562; of interest to Roman readers, ii. 565; and Dido, ii. 587; mentioned, iii. 61; his fleet turned into a shoal of water-nymphs, iii. 145; tore up myrtle that dropped blood, iii. 145; battle with Turnus, iii. 174; iv. 134; his sword broke that of Turnus, iii. 231; as a subject for schoolboys' essays, iii. 248; and the Sibyl, iii. 282; superior to Turnus in piety, iii. 304; Virgil's knowledge of, iii. 305; history of by Dionysius Halicarnasseus, iii. 305; his vision of his future descendants, iii. 361–2; v. 91; and Achates, iii. 446; his voyage traced on a map by a mathematician, iii. 529; his recognition of Venus, iv. 145; glowed 'with more than mortal charms', iv. 399; cured by Iapis, iv. 555–6; cut down grove on Mt. Ida, v. 15–16.

Aeolus: gave bags of wind to Odysseus, i. 17; Virgil's ruler of winds, ii. 415.

Aeschines, his tribute to Demosthenes, iii. 522.

Aeschylus: guilty of the false sublime, iii. 11; allegorical figures of Strength and Necessity improper agents in *Prometheus Bound*, iii. 338.

Aesculapius, Socrates desired to offer a cock to, ii. 234.

Aesop, i. *48, 58, 143, 262*; iii. 243; a celebrated 'ill face', i. 77; an early writer of fables, ii. 220.

Aesop at the Bear-Garden, iv. *32*.

Aesop Naturaliz'd, i. *143, 220*; fable of Earth, ii. 455. *See also* L'Estrange.

Aeternitas a parte ante and *a parte post*, v. 18.

Aethiopia, the English factory in, iii. 276.

Affability: good breeding is a. reduced into an art, ii. 165; of Germanicus, ii. 425–6; of Augustus, ii. 592; and benevolence of Sir ROGER, iii. 590; of Henry Boyle, v. 177.

Affectation: an enemy to beauty, i. 139, 159, 206; ii. 69; turns wit into absurdity, i. 159; ill effects of, i. 159–63; found in the wise man as well as the coxcomb, i. 161; of mispronouncing words, i. 193; of appearing greater than we are, i. 276; ill effect of on taste, i. 297; of delicacy, i. 420; account of a wife over-run with, ii. 11; in reading aloud, ii. 79; of Caesar, ii. 260; of loving solitude, ii. 525; of singularity, ii. 525–6; of closeness and covetousness in IRUS, ii. 527–8; of most men during the day, ii. 553; of negligence, iii. 6; of greatness hurts perspicuity of style, iii. 11–12; false delicacy is a., not politeness, iii. 15–17; deceitful a. of love, iii. 23–24; genteelest demeanour may degenerate into, iii. 40; of strangeness in a friend, iii. 74; of singularity in Saint-Evremond, iii. 299–300; of courage, iii. 303–4; of smartness, wit, and courage, iii. 322; lessened by foreign travel, iii. 368; of excelling in characters men are not fit for, iii. 510; allegorical figure of, iv. 123; 'our greatest charms are owing to', iv. 332; of wit absent from the *Fairie Queene*, iv. 429; an example of pedantic, v. 107.

Affection: rooted out of soldiers, ii. 99; the parent who extinguishes, ii. 214; not to be ashamed of, towards a wife, ii. 418; of a husband, ii. 435; the eye and, ii. 471–2, 478–9; constancy of, to be supported, ii. 521–3; true delicacy consists of purity of, iii. 15; women who rail at, iv. 331.

Affection (affectation), people are got into a way of, ii. 113.

Afflavit Deus & dissipantur, iii. 45.

Afflicted, the: our duty to comfort, i. 395; pleasure of helping, ii. 526–7.

Affliction(s): and sorrow not always expressed by tears, i. 403; supporting oneself under, ii. 139–43; generally

lead men to books of morality, ii. 141; made heavier by cruelty of others, ii. 164–5; nothing more unhappy than a man who had never known, ii. 422; some virtues seen only in, ii. 500; sympathy for a. of others, iii. 80; folly of judging a. of others, iv. 211–14.

Africa: woody parts of, i. 76; deserts of, i. 116; Pyrrhus' design to conquer all, ii. 212; part of setting of *Aeneid*, iii. 332; exotic plants from, iv. 104; Jews settled in, iv. 256; opinions of heaven among inhabitants of, v. 49.

African Company, Y. Z. has 21 shares in, iv. 469.

Africanus Major, Scipio: in Cicero's *De Senectute*, iv. 419.

AFTERDAY, EVE, letter from (kept by a jealous tyrant), ii. 247.

AFTERDAY, JACK, letter from (on growing old), ii. 510–12.

After-expectations, iii. 66.

After-game, iv. 38.

After life. *See* Eternity.

'After love and unseasonable youth', i. 387.

After-psalm, in the church service, v. 155.

Agamemnon: that great prince, against Troy, ii. 76; rapacious and imperial, his soul transformed into that of an eagle, ii. 326; his son Orestes, iii. 579.

Aganippe (fountain), protects against all harms but envy, iv. 328.

Age: ii. 100–3, 510–12; respect to, i. 30–31; equality of, an essential in friendship, i. 291; of patriarchs, iii. 28; and love, iii. 75–78; tyranny of, iii. 243–5. *See also* Old Age.

Age (period of time): the present a loose age, ii. 554; Homer's faults due to his, ii. 586.

Ages of man's life: vices and imperfections associated with, ii. 271; toys and trifles in each, v. 124–5; each requires new amusements, v. 138–9.

Ages of the world: authors who describe, ii. 317–18; great souls produced in the first, ii. 467; impossible for us to be original who live in the later, ii. 483–4.

Agesilaus, i. *334*.

AGLAURA, full of nameless graces, iii. 40–41.

Aglauros, in Ovid, iii. *40*.

Aglaüs, story of (the happiest man), v. 86–87, 95.

Agreeable man: defined, ii. 591; must also be easy within himself, ii. 445;

to succeed with others, one must be agreeable or considerable, ii. 336–7, 599; art of being agreeable with others, iii. 448–51; makes his friends enjoy themselves rather than him, iii. 583–4.

Agreeable sensations, why pleasing, iii. 453.

Agreeables, The, the beauties, or, iv. 314.

Agréemens upon a sign, i. 118.

Agreement between friends the greatest pleasure of life, iii. 590.

Agriculture: manufactures, trade and a. employ nineteen men out of twenty, i. 472.

Agrippa, St. Paul's harangue before, v. 166.

AGRIPPA, CORNELIUS, letter from (on fortune-telling), iv. 512–13.

Agrippa von Nettesheim, Henry Cornelius, iv. *513*.

Agues, shaking the human fabric, ii. 159.

Agur's prayer, iv. 139.

Air: a good air and mien, ii. 159; good nature gives a certain air to the countenance, ii. 165; a gallant and polite, ii. 427; a soft, ii. 433; a bride's languishing, ii. 479; a forbidding air preventing a salutation, ii. 508; a pert, ii. 534; a gallant and *dégagé*, ii. 579; a cheerful air, of advantage to a poor dependant, ii. 593; of melancholy, ii. 598; an indisposed, iii. 6; a serious and instructive, iii. 37; and beauty in human actions, iii. 39; shopkeepers' beseeching, iii. 94; Mr. PRIM's soft, iii. 415; the finest pitty-pat, iv. 286; WILL HONEYCOMB's janty, v. 184.

Airs: and graces, i. 415; and motions, ii. 46; of a Jezebel, ii. 190; fine and reserved, ii. 434; a wife's demure and serious, ii. 488; of virtue, ii. 555; young fellows' blustering, iii. 321; MATILDA MOHAIR's nice, iv. 261; such violent, iv. 286; of merit, iv. 332.

Airiness of temper in women, ii. 193.

Air-pump: stifling of cats in an, i. 91; invention of, by Royal Society, ii. 519.

Airy: the dull and, i. 42; in his behaviour, i. 146; manner, i. 434; women who affect being brisk and, ii. 8; gentlemen, iii. 162.

AIRYE, Lady, a session of scandal in her drawing-room, iii. 296–7.

Ajax: suffered from iniquity of his judges, ii. 76; all wrath and fierceness, his soul transformed into that of a lion, ii. 326; mentioned, ii. 485; iv. 473.

Akenside, Mark, iii. *536*.

Alabaster, William: preached on 'Adam, Sheth, Enosh', ii. 361.

A-la-mode: now common in English, ii. 152; *à la mode de Paris*, ii. 579; 'a la mode disease', advertisement for cure of, iv. *61*.

ALBACINDA, a tyrannical beauty, ii. 69–70, 110.

Albert, St., Bishop of Ratisbon (Albertus Magnus), saw a 'substantial form' in a blue vapour, i. 237.

ALBINA, has six votaries in the Amorous Club, v. 127.

Albion, v. 120, 123.

Albius, son of, example in Horace, iii. 248.

Alcaeus, wrote an ode on Sappho, ii. 409.

Alchemist: ruined by misemployed hopes, iv. 410; and the philosopher's stone, iv. 562.

Alchemy, iii. 479; jargon of, iii. 600.

Alcibiades: his dialogue with Socrates on prayer, ii. 310–13; Plato's *Alcibiades* quoted, iii. 53–54.

Alcoran, i. 360; story of Mahomet's journey in, i. 400; commands the Grand Signior to practise a handicraft trade, iii. 319.

Alderman, i. 293; v. 92; gravity of, v. 47; on the stage usually a cuckold, iv. 68; wealth of, i. 91; v. 115.

Aldermen: 'that foolish beaten road of satirizing', i. 142; satires against mayors and, iv. 18.

Aldhelm, St., ii. *450*.

Aldrich, Henry, i. *363*.

Aldus Manutius, the Elder: fine printing by, iii. 381; 'Aldus reads . . .', iv. 163.

Ale: glass of, i. 119; butts of, i. 310; a run of, i. 310; hogshead of, ii. 132; full-pots of, ii. 164; Burton-Ale, iii. 438; a tub of, set abroach, iv. 93.

Ale-house, ii. 164, 402; incident in an, i. 374–5; a box at an, iv. 80.

Alerte young fellow, an, iii. 507.

Alexander the Great: events of his life worked into a projected opera, i. 128–32, 150–1; wore his head a little over left shoulder, i. 135; charms of his conversation, i. 167; buried large suits of armour, ii. 7; aided by others, ii. 44; would contend 'if he had kings to run against him', ii. 114; his cruelty arose from his education, iii. 247; Prince Eugene compared to, iii. 264; his letter to Aristotle, iii. 423; statues of, iii. *555*; and Callisthenes, iii. *583*; Persian soldier rebuked for reviling, iv. 2; had a mind above unmerited reproaches, iv. 44; a saying of, iv. 166 & n.; sleep made him aware he was mortal, v. 29–30; poor ambition of an, v. 84; his chief aim to conquer, v. 168.

Alexander the Great. See Lee, *The Rival Queens.*

Alexander VII, Pope, iv. *449.*

Alexandrine, Pope's illustration of the, ii. *484.*

Alexandrinus Valentinus. *See* Valentinus.

Algiers, ii. 278; iii. 273; pirates of, ii. 277–8.

Alimony, pin-money a kind of, iii. 53.

'All face', ii. 387.

All-fours, footmen playing, at the theatre, ii. 163.

Allcraft's (Allcroft's) toy-shop, in Cornhill, iv. *5, 130, 460, 554.*

Allcroft, —— (apothecary?), i. *139.*

Allegorical figures: in poetry, iii. 573; in epic poetry, ii. 563–4; iii. 337–9, 393, 573; in mock-heroic poems, ii. 564; in *PL*, ii. 563; iii. 61, 120–1, 145–6.

Allegories in *Spectator*: Decay of Public Credit, i. 14–17; True and False Humour, i. 147; Luxury and Avarice, i. 234–5; True and False Wit, i. 270–4; Vision of the Painters, i. 354–6; Vision of MIRZAH, ii. 121–6; Pleasure and Pain, ii. 222–3; A Sultan's Exercise, ii. 263; Dissection of a Beau's Head, ii. 570–3; Dissection of a Coquette's Heart, ii. 594–7; Love and Old Age, iii. 76–78; Prayers the Daughters of Jupiter (in Homer), iii. 468–9; Folly of Men's Desires, iii. 468–70; Transformation of FIDELIO into a Looking-Glass, iii. 470–3; The Seasons, iii. 594–7; Plants and Human Life, iv. 104–5; The Paradise of Fools, iv. 121–4; The Golden Scales, iv. 135–8; Chremylus: Wealth and Poverty, iv. 139–41; The Modern Women of Hensburg, iv. 270–2; The Grotto of Grief, iv. 276–9; A Sale of London Women, iv. 316; A Vision of Mt. Parnassus, iv. 324–30; Heavenly and Worldly Wisdom, iv. 365–9; Exchanging of Human Miseries, iv. 506–11; An Examination of Hearts, v. 7–9; Trophonius' Cave, v. 46–48; Men's Reactions to the *Spectator*, v. 65–67. *See also* Dream-Visions.

Allegory (-ies): 'after Plato's manner', i. 146; Virgil cast Platonic philosophy into, i. 382; and fable, ii. 219–21; Jesus taught by parable and, iii. 327; not suitable in epic, iii. 336–9; and fables proper for instruction, iii. 467; value of in prose works, iii. 577–8; among finest compositions of ancients, iv. 275; popularity of, iv. 364–5; in *PL (see* Sin and Death).

Allen, Thomas, ii. *28.*

Allestree, Richard: *The Ladies' Calling*, i. 155, *159*; *The Government of the Tongue*, i. 391; *The Whole Duty of Man*, iv. 541.

Alliance, proposed between Chinese and Roman churches, iv. 448–53; Treaty of the Grand, iii. 51.

Allusion: a species of wit, i. 264–5; 'strength of', i. 291; consequence of a forced, ii. 53; witty a. of an eminent author, ii. 401.

Allusions: of the ancients lacking in correctness, ii. 127; *bienséance* in, ii. 128, 318; (metaphors), ii. 302, 318–19, 338, 353; in *Essay on Criticism*, ii. 483; in *PL* I, iii. *90*; writer's art shown in choice of, iii. 578.

Alma Mater, a son of, iv. 344.

Almahide (opera), i. *23, 56, 79*; the young singer in, ii. 397–8.

Almanac: short minutes from, ii. 262; Latin verses prefixed to, ii. 357; astrological prescriptions in, iii. 374. *See also* Edward Pond, Poor Robin, Richard Saunders.

Almanza, battle of, i. 32.

Almanzor, in *Conquest of Granada*, ii. 159; iii. 352.

Almonds, sold in London streets, iii. 354.

Alms: man who lives upon, ii. 351; giving of, ii. 401–5; 'the wages of idleness', ii. 403.

Almshouse, 'of idle people', ii. 405; Sir ANDREW's plan for one, iv. 468.

Alnaschar (glass-man), fable of, iv. 410–12.

Alone: *never less a. than when a.* (prov.), i. 19; get into the crowd in order to be, ii. 20–21; those who lack courage to go, iv. 196.

Alpheius of Mytilene, his epitaph on Homer quoted, iv. 473.

Alpheus, in a French opera, i. 123.

Alps: traveller upon, a symbol of life, ii. 322; Eugene's march over, iii. 263; the hoary Alpine hills, iv. 235; the clown who led Eugene over, iv. 327; 'their new-made monarch shall restrain', v. 120.

ALTAMIRA, letter from (on *The Amorous Widow*), iii. 370–1.

Altar, poems in shape of, i. 246–7, 265, 271; iii. 560.

Altro volto (encore), iii. 138.

AMANDA, history of, iii. 409–13.

Amaranths, iii. 569.

AMARYLLIS (AMARILLIS), a well-bred woman, ii. 69; subject of a challenge, iv. 32.

Amazonian enchantress, in *Rinaldo*, i. 25.

Amazons (women in hunting garb), i. 434; iv. 28, 37–38; a bold A. with a fan, ii. 31; Commonwealth of, and Republic of Males, iv. 21–26; 'with the amorous fire of our', iv. 452.

Amazons (political partisans), i. 347.

Amazons: and Scythians, iv. 22; River of, iv. 22.

Ambassador of Bantam, letter from, iv. 503–5.

Ambassadors: factors are like, i. 293; excellence or perfection, the title given to, ii. 352; French generals transformed into, iii. 97.

Ambition: natural to soul of man, i. 458–9; ii. 370–1; iv. 544; occasions factions, i. 511–12; pulls one way, interest another, ii. 136; of Louis XIV, ii. 209–12, 282–3; most men subject to, ii. 351, 370; of use when rightly directed, ii. 370–1; role of, in human life, ii. 370–4; of Philip, ii. 396; exhibited by a beau at the theatre, ii. 434–5; difficulty of attaining, ii. 490–2; easily lost and rarely satisfied, ii. 493–8; rewards of, ii. 499–502; freedom from, ii. 553; thrift disappoints ends of, iii. 5; extinguished by considerations of eternity, iii. 29; little a. of distinguishing ourselves, iii. 277; takes all faculties into its service, iv. 242; allegorical figure of, iv. 326; incapable men rail at, iv. 331; worthy and unworthy kinds of, iv. 544–6; letter in praise of, v. 94–95; pains of, v. 133–4. See also Fame, Praise.

Amelot de la Houssaye, Abraham Nicolas, iii. 477.

Amen: uttered with gravity, iii. 8; from the parish-clerk, iii. 402.

America: story from (INKLE and YARICO), i. 50; greed of Europeans in, i. 51, 240; drugs from, i. 295; Dampier on travellers to, i. 494; stories of jealousy from, ii. 172; want of inhabitants in, ii. 297; behaviour of Negroes in plantations, ii. 339; messages delivered by painting in, iii. 559; exotic plants from, iv. 104; Jews settled in inner parts of, iv. 256.

American (West-Indian), i. 50.

Americans (Indians): their opinion of souls, i. 236–7; vision of one, i. 237–40; burial customs of, i. 236–7.

Amiable: Cato's character awful rather than, ii. 166; nature of virtue, ii. 443; virtue appears a. in EMILIA, iii. 81.

AMILCAR, his letter to CORINNA, iii. 102–3.

Amity, between man and woman, iii. 499.

Amleto (opera), i. 23.

Ammonio, Andrea (Andrew Ammonius), an author quoted by Bayle, ii. 431.

AMORET: and PHILANDER, letters between, iii. 500–2; bound by promise of marriage to PHILANDER (?), v. 98.

Amory, Thomas (nephew of Henry Grove), i. lxxx.

Amphion's lute, 'made willing stones dance', v. 161.

AMPLE, Lady, fears to eat too much, i. 134.

Amsterdam, ii. 17; Sign of the Gaper at, i. 200; news from Gazette of, iii. 96.

Amulets: against evil eyes, ii. 360; and other superstitions in Asia, v. 65.

Amusements: of women, i. 46; in London, i. 127–8, 149–50; in a box of pictures, ii. 29; of fallen angels in PL, ii. 421; described by TIMOTHY DOODLE, ii. 450–2; allegorical depiction of gleams of, iv. 279.

Anabaptist, who designs to come over to Church of England, ii. 510.

Anacharsis, claimed the prize for drinking, iv. 541–2.

Anacreon, in Vision of Parnassus, iv. 329; Antipater's epitaph on, quoted, iv. 473.

'Anagram of a Man', epithet given to a distorted man, i. 254.

Anagrams: examples of false wit, i. 254; Tory and Whig, i. 262; consist in resemblances of letters, i. 265; iii. 560; a regiment of, i. 271; laborious fools who write, i. 146.

Anarchy, allegorical figure of, i. 16.

Anatomy, human: rules of, in a good picture, ii. 447; of a female eye, requested, ii. 481; observations in, by a virtuoso, ii. 570; the work of a wise Providence, iv. 441–4; described in Blackmore's Creation, iv. 444; Leonardo da Vinci skilled in, iv. 489.

Anaxarchus of Abdera, 'Thou dost but beat the case of', iv. 492.

Ancestry, undue pride in, v. 91–93.

Ancients: The TEMPLAR familiar with, i. 9; that 'beautiful simplicity in writings of', i. 268; natural geniuses found among, ii. 127–8; human nature as described by, ii. 318; quotations from in Spectator, why used, ii. 358–9; most of their writers swallowed up in ocean of time, ii. 365; had fewer poems dealing with ghosts and spirits, iii. 572; hymns to deities by, iv. 94–95; scholars studying costume of, iv. 195; opinions of, on modesty, iv. 216–17; lenient toward excesses in each

stage of life, iv. 259; fine allegories among, iv. 275; their studies of anatomy, iv. 441; their solutions of the problem of evil, iv. 565; their veneration of trees, v. 15.

Ancients and Moderns: contrasted in genius, i. 261; moderns have advantage of Scripture and revelation, ii. 75; ancients lack nicety and exactness of moderns, i. 128, 318; more raillery among moderns, more good sense among ancients, ii. 467; ancients superior to moderns, iii. 11; iv. 105, 137; v. 26–27; moderns have more advantages for eloquence, v. 164.

Ancora (encore), iii. 184, 266.

'And so Sir', a redundant phrase in conversation, iii. 398.

ANDIRON, Mrs., a panegyric on her left shoulder, i. 77.

Andrewes, Lancelot, his sermons full of puns, i. 260.

Andromache: Hector's advice to, i. 241; a rural, i. 241–2; in Juvenal, i. 414; letter from, ii. 60–61; in epitaph on Homer, iv. 473. *See also* Philips, *The Distressed Mother.*

Angel, an: in the sun, iii. 147; phantom of, v. 7; looks down upon man with a kind of pride, v. 125; ken of, superior to man's, v. 171.

Angel, a bawd living at the sign of the, i. 117.

Angelic Snuff, iii. *278.*

Angels: extravagant imagination in descriptions of, iii. 201; hosts of in Paradise, iv. 583; existence of probable, from reason and revelation, v. 85; in *PL*: their amusements, ii. 421; battle of, ii. 540; iii. 227–34, 566; well diversified, ii. 565; rallying of, by evil spirits, ii. 589; Milton's reflection on their eating, iii. 61; their nine-days' astonishment, iii. 84; Satan's call to, iii. 85; return to heaven after Fall of Adam, iii. 330; metamorphoses of, iii. 566; beauty of description of, iii. 566.

Angels, Guardian, ii. 77; iii. 83; worthy patrons like Plato's, ii. 337.

Anger: Achilles a symbol of, ii. 221; to be avoided in disputation, ii. 274–5; more easily transferred to children than love, ii. 523; of Achilles described in *Iliad*, ii. 541; allegorical depiction of, iii. 596; conquest of, the worthiest discipline, iv. 39; scene of, in a bookshop, iv. 41; causes inaccuracy in reports, iv. 356; example of, in *King Lear*, iv. 433–4; in a husband, iv. 524–5.

Angle-rods, furnished by WILL WIMBLE, i. 447.

Anglesey, Arthur Annesley, Earl of: anecdote of, iv. 403.

Angling, i. 499.

Anguish, allegorical figure of, iv. 278.

Animal spirits: motions of, and the face, i. 367; necessary for proper exertion of intellectual faculties, i. 471; of women, more light and volatile, ii. 8; irradiation of the mind from, ii. 197; a new motion to, ii. 383; in the tongue, ii. 460; effect of sadness and cheerfulness upon, iii. 451; effect of colours upon, iii. 452; circulation of, necessary to health, iii. 525; set in agreeable motions by pleasures of the fancy, iii. 539; and trains of ideas, iii. 563.

Animals: men who resemble a. in physiognomy, i. 366–7; their ideas of time and duration, i. 399; arrive at a point of perfection, i. 457–8; ii. 322; observations upon, i. 489–97; instinct in, i. 490–7; ii. 136–7; lust and hunger in, i. 489–90; care of young, i. 490–2; ii. 244, 457; arms of defence in, i. 495; millions still unknown to us, i. 497; not capable of sinning, ii. 137; keep to one dish, ii. 265; have glimmerings of reason, but not devotion, ii. 288; pre-existence of women in, described by Simonides, ii. 319; more excellent than men (Boileau), ii. 321; transmigration of men into, ii. 324–6; iii. 272–3, 525; cunning in, ii. 377; qualities of eyes named from, ii. 471; males more highly coloured, ii. 531; form a huge army: not a species lost, iii. 28; monstrous a. produced in hell, iii. 119; contemplation of world of, iii. 346; made for use and delight of man, iii. 452; notions of beauty in, iii. 542–3; contemplation of minute, iii. 574–7; digestion in, iv. 165; not conscious of past or future, iv. 291; reading fortunes in entrails of, iv. 292; range of, in the universe, iv. 345–9, 442–4; most useful a. are most fruitful in their generation, v. 163.

Animism, Americans' belief in, i. 236–7.

Anjou, Duke of, claimant to Spanish throne, iii. 508.

ANNA BELLA, letter from (on relationship between men and women), i. 225–6.

ANNABELLA, letter from (on education of girls), i. 404–5.

Anne, St., i. 509.

Anne, Queen: assigns interpreters to Indian Kings, i. 213; her reign described

by a future historian, i. 424; victories
of her armies, ii. 209; alluded to(?), ii.
227; 'the greatest and most pious
Sovereign in the world', ii. 380; prohibits persons behind the scenes in
theatre, ii. 435; touching for the evil,
ii. *456*; her birthday, iii. 48; the birthday ball, iii. *418*; accession of, iii. *440*;
Bishop Fleetwood's tribute to, iii. 444;
mourning for, v. 72.

Annesley, Arthur. *See* Anglesey.

Annihilation: horror of, an argument for
immortality, i. 457; hope of, 'pitifully
mean', ii. 323.

Annuity, i. 441; iii. 155.

Anodine Fotus, of quack doctors, iv. 553.

Anodyne, for gout, iv. 169

Anonymous writings, reasons for, iv. 87.

Anselm, St., *Meditations*, ii. *121*.

Antanaclasis, a form of punning, i. 261.

Antechamber, catching the news in the,
v. 136-7.

Antediluvian novel, An, iv. 595-8; v.
1-3.

Antelopes, v. 2.

ANTENOR, a rival of PHILANDER, iii.
502.

Anthem: in cathedrals, where one person
sings alone the, iv. 286; effect of, in
church service, v. 153.

'Anthony, Trusty', of the Bumper Tavern
(Anthony Aston?), ii. *529*, *534*.

Antigonus, Apelles' painting of, v. 164.

Antiluminaries, iv. 592.

Antimony, Boyle on, i. 398.

Antiochus (opera), i. *23*; iii. *513*.

Antiochus and Stratonice, ii. 393.

Antipater of Sidon, his epitaphs on
Orpheus and Anacreon quoted, iv.
472-3.

Antipater of Tarsus (Stoic philosopher),
iv. *454*.

Antipathies, iv. 421-2; v. 82-83; to puns,
iv. 48; to cats, iii. 352; iv. 48, 422;
v. 82; of serious and merry persons to
each other, v. 44.

Antiphanes, on death (quoted), iii.
28-29.

Antiphon (orator), v. *166*.

Antiquaries: one a friend of Mr. SPECTA
TOR, i. 326, 357; opinion of, concerning origin of the May-Pole, iii. 372.

Antiquities of St. Peter's, Westminster, i. *109*.

Antiquity: pieces of, at Rome, ii. 390;
old words used by Milton to give an
air of, iii. 13; visiting places associated
with authors of, iii. 369; writings of,
as a test of taste, iii. 528.

Antisthenes, the Cynic, ii. *240*; his
remark to a beautiful youth, ii. 71.

Antitheses: points, turns, and a. as a
kind of wit, ii. 270; witty authors' love
of quaint, ii. 53; absence of forced
a. in the *Faerie Queene*, iv. 429.

ANTONIO, kept in subjection by his
father, iv. 260.

Antony, Mark, i. *144*; ii. *200*; 'Anthony
and Cleopatra for that', ii. 40; summoned Herod to Egypt, ii. 176;
Atticus a friend to, iii. 447; his witty
mirth, ii. 450; his description of Cleopatra (Dryden), iii. 497.

Antrum, or cavity, in a beau's head, ii.
571.

ANVIL, JACK (ENVILLE), story of his
marriage, ii. 68-71, 111.

Anvil: 'upon the a.', iii. 506; iv. 364;
a wooden a. proposed for the trunk-
maker, ii. 415.

Ap, in Welsh names, v. 93.

Apartments (rooms), i. 454; ii. 24, 27,
215, 235, &c.; of women of the town,
ii. 248; of Rosamond's bower, ii. 596.

Apelles: works of, lost, ii. 154; painted
Antigonus with one side only towards the spectator, v. 164.

Apes: women who resemble, ii. 320;
account of a set of them, ii. 448-9;
referred to, iii. 320.

APICIUS, pleased with the account of a
delicious meal, i. 217.

Apollo: bestowing a vizard, i. 136; temple
to, at Leucate, ii. 366, 385, 406-8; a
composition of Hercules and, ii. 416;
and Bacchus in Lilly's grammar, ii. 529;
his punishment of the critic who only
found faults, iii. 38; and the Hours, in
Homer, iii. 337; oracle of, consulted
by Chremylus, iv. 139-40, by Gyges,
v. 86; in the Vision of Parnassus, iv.
327-9; invocations to Phoebus in
modern poems, iv. 362-3; Pantheus
a priest of, iv. 464; picture of, surrounded by Muses, iv. 474; and the
Muses in Pyrrhus' ring, v. 28.

Apollodorus of Gela: the comic poet,
contemporary with Menander, ii. 296;
quoted, ii. 296-7.

Apollonius Rhodius, story of Rhaecus
and the Hamadryad from, v. 16-17.

Apoplexy, iv. 290, 561.

Apostles, The, paintings of, by Raphael,
ii. 379.

Apothecaries: needed to countermine
the cook and vintner, ii. 264; funeral-
men have their vintners and, iii. 166;
the apothecary's shop, iii. 189, 210;
disdain of physicians when a. give
advice, iv. 454; Mr. Moore, iv. 457.

Appearance(s): vanity of keeping an a.

of wealth, i. 468; we are judged by our first, ii. 307; value of, iii. 347–8; a. of virtue necessary to women, iii. 464–5.

Appetite(s): lust and hunger the most violent, i. 489; cravings of, in the man of pleasure, ii. 94; abandoned resignation in the young to, ii. 101; command of, in Lucceius, ii. 309; sooner moved than the passions, ii. 315; command of, ii. 364; increase of, in the wicked, without means of satisfaction, ii. 421, 510–11; the eye as the seat of, ii. 471; for coal and chalk, in young girls, iv. 15–17; necessary to man, v. 12; governed by our sickly and changeable, v. 140.

Appian way, iii. 369; loses itself in a bog, v. 92.

Applause: desired even by the man of sense, i. 161; of others and self-approbation, ii. 135–6, 181, 238–40, 370–3; CINNA's desire of, ii. 307; effect of, ii. 424–6; greatness of soul above the a. of the multitude, ii. 492–3; 'best and most significant of applauses' at the last Judgement, ii. 502; true greatness not measured by men's, v. 85. *See also* Praise.

Apple(s): no greater than crabs in English climate, i. 295; the Golden A. formerly the prize of beauty, ii. 182–3; buying in London streets, ii. 477; vendors of, at the Royal Exchange, iv. 307.

Application: to studies caused Pascal's ill health, i. 478–9; of talents in the interests of virtue, ii. 178–81.

Applications, medical: blistering, cupping, bleeding, and inward a., ii. 264.

Appointments, neglect in keeping, iv. 74.

Apprentice(s): dispute of a blacksmith's a. with a hackney-coachman, ii. 291; grave and solid a. of the law, iii. 348; useful reading for an, iv. 4–6; Captain SENTRY's assistance to, iv. 446.

Approbation: of others not to be neglected, i. 433; a great satisfaction to an honest mind, i. 497; only of what is honourable, ii. 179; intention should be considered as the measure of, ii. 180; pleasure from a. of others, ii. 349; of the Supreme Being our only concern, ii. 500; sincerity forces a. even of opponents, ii. 592.

Apricots: imported into England and naturalized, i. 295; apricock boats on the Thames, iv. 99; preserving, iv. 210.

April: 'the month of fools', i. 223; allegorical description of, iii. 595.

April fool jests, i. 197, 202–3; iv. 20.

Apron(s): working-aprons, ii. 345; iii. 206; a short working apron, ii. 580.

Apron-strings, hanging at their (prov.), iv. 297.

Apuleius: 'Speak that I may see thee', i. *366*; on the Indian Gymnosophists' training of their disciples, iii. 249.

Aqueduct from River Adda to Milan, designed by Leonardo da Vinci, iv. 489.

Arabella, Congreve's lines on, quoted, iv. 56.

Arabian (a horse), Mr. Courant's, ii. 117.

Arabian Nights' Entertainment: story of physician exercising with mallet and ball, ii. 263; story of Alnaschar, the Persian glass-man, iv. 410–12.

ARABLE, BETTY, and her mother: stage-coach companions of Mr. SPECTATOR, ii. 22.

Aranda, Countess of. *See* Padilla, Luisa de.

Araspas (a young Persian), anecdote of, iv. 526–7.

Arbuthnot, John: *John Bull still in his Senses*, i. 59; *Proposals for . . . a Treatise . . . of Political Lying*, iii. 100; iv. 299.

Arcana: or secrets of prudence, iii. 423; of the fair sex, iv. 113.

Arch, effect of, in architecture, iii. 557.

Archilaus, King (father of Glaphyra), i. 455.

Archimedes, ii. 130.

Architecture: laws of, how deduced, i. 123; Goths in, i. 268; enjoyment of, as a useful diversion, i. 397; less permanent than literature, ii. 154; rules of, in a good picture, ii. 447; we fall short of the ancients in, ii. 467; greatness important in, ii. 542; terms of, used by Milton, iii. 64; and primary pleasures of the imagination, iii. 553–8; Leonardo da Vinci a master in, iv. 489; frequent deviations from the rules in, v. 28.

ARETHUSA, 'may hear further', iv. 588.

Aretino, Pietro, European kings and Sophy of Persia subject to his pen, i. 99.

Argantes, in *Rinaldo*, i. 64.

Argentré, Bertrand d', on head-dresses, i. 415.

Argument(s): those who raise a. over obvious points, ii. 45–46; a young lawyer who argued on both sides of a question, ii. 272–3; rules for managing, ii. 273–5; information and truth the true end of, ii. 275; kinds of, ii. 428–32; used by wives, iv. 313–14.

Argumentation, THOMAS SUDDEN too much given to, iv. 8.

Argumentum Baculinum, or Club-Law, ii. 429.

Argus, hundred-eyed: pimp for Juno, ii. 470; implies only that the eye is in every part, ii. 479; (in Strada), v. 109.

Ariadne and Bacchus, in modern prints, ii. 60.

ARIDAEUS, his leap into the Ionian sea, ii. 407.

ARIETTA, 'Inkle and Yarico' told at her salon, i. 47.

Ariosto, Ludovico, iii. 60; iv. 429.

Aristaenetus: *Letters of Love and Gallantry*, i. lii & n.; his description of a fine woman, i. 263; 'Philopinax to Chromation' quoted, ii. 427–8.

Aristippus (of Cyrene): in Horace, i. 322 m.; his 'free and easy' air, iv. 153; his reflection on loss of a farm, iv. 563.

ARISTIPPUS: his kind invitation received, iv. 588.

Aristophanes: ridiculed Socrates, i. 98; *Frogs*, i. *178*; his allegory of wealth and poverty (*Plutus*), iv. 139–41.

Aristotle: The TEMPLAR familiar with his works, i. 9; Dyer 'our A. in politics', i. 183; not every schoolboy fitted to study, ii. 115; a learned genius, ii. 129; his soul transformed into an ass or beau (Congreve), ii. 326; many of Horace's precepts to be found in, ii. 484; his rules had been more perfect could he have studied the *Aeneid*, ii. 566; 'the best critic, and one of the best logicians', iii. 35; Homer has charmed more readers than, iii, *538*; wrote with regularity and method, iv. 185–6; Alexander's letter to, iv. 423; a true critic, v. 26; mentioned, i. *73*, 229; ii. *322*. — DOCTRINES: man a sociable animal, i. 39; iambic verse proper for tragedy, i. 164; expression to be laboured in unactive parts of the fable, i. 165–6; on unhappy endings in tragedy, i. 169; iv. 465; on dresses and decorations of the stage, i. 177; on puns or paragrams, i. 259; on physiognomy, i. *365*; ii. 68; ideas a transcript of the world, ii. 153; a statue lies hid in a block of marble, ii. 338; on fable of the epic, ii. *539*; on unity in the epic, ii. 539–43; treats fable, characters, sentiments, and manners, ii. 562, 585; admired the part of Ulysses in *Odyssey*, ii. 564; on raising pity and terror, ii. 565–6; iii. 567; iv. 465; on language of epic, iii. 10–14; on simple and implex fable, iii. 58; on repetition of sounds as a rhetorical device, iii. 63; on Pericles' oration, iii. *105*; 'credible and astonishing' in the epic, iii. 144; on using names of actual men in tragedy, iii. 146; ornaments of diction to be lavished on weak parts of the fable, iii. 170; on 'magnitude and order', iii. *540*; man's instant recognition of works of God, iv. 144; all art an imitation of nature, iv. 146; rated the epic below tragedy, iv. 388; a poet more delighted with his productions than any other writer, iv. 593; the 'half-virtues', v. 157; on pleading before the Areopagus, v. *166*.

Aristotelian method of argument, compared with Socratic, ii. 429; Aristotelian substantial forms, i. 237.

ARISTUS and ASPATIA, a happily married couple, ii. 11.

Arithmetic: study of by women recommended, i. 391, 404; 'a man conversant in', ii. 355.

Arm: bold tongue and feeble arm of Drances, ii. 399; sound judgment and strong arm of the trunk-maker, ii. 416; called by Cicero the orator's weapon, iv. 436.

Armada, medal on defeat of the, iii. 45.

Armenian, study of, iv. 104.

Armenians, at the Royal Exchange, i. 294.

Armida, an Amazonian enchantress in *Rinaldo*, i. 25, 64.

Armies: represented on stage, i. 179; their pillaging, ii. 99; junction of French and Bavarian at Blenheim, ii. 152; Her Majesty's a. conquered Louis XIV, ii. 209.

Armstrong, W., 'the famous fine writer of music' (i.e. copyist), ii. 329, 342.

Army: Captain SENTRY advises *Spectator* not to touch upon, i. 143; desertion in, ii. 23; executive part of, ii. 97; a standing army, ii. 133; at end of campaign has commonly lost a fifth of its men, ii. 210; Catiline's exhortation to his, ii. 1; the whole animal world like a huge, iii. 28; Satan's review of his infernal in *PL*, iii. 89; 'before the disbanding of the', iii. 126.

Arne, Thomas (upholsterer), i. 212; v. 116.

Arrack, 'and other Indian goods', iii. 25.

Arrianus Maturius. *See* Maturius.

Arrogance: insolent a. in youth, ii. 100; of Mr. SPECTATOR objected to, ii. 118; of infidels, ii. 233; lies told out of, ii. 410; of a scholar, ii. 554; shocking

and offensive to men and God, iii. 45–46.

Arsinoe, 'the first opera that gave us a taste of Italian music', i. 79; brought from Italy by Clayton: Dieupart and Haym helped promote it, ii. 506; iii. *296–7*.

Art: to conform to taste, i. 123; universality the test of, i. 297–8; a ballad without the helps and ornaments of, i. 362; additional advantages of, i. 364; little tricks of, ii. 128; corrections and restraints of, ii. 129; of value only in service of virtue, ii. 179; of painting, ii. 446–8; a character drawn with much art and humour, ii. 553; printing, the noblest and most beneficial, iii. 381; works of, deficient in vastness, iii. 548–9; poet should be well versed in productions of, iii. 564; all art an imitation of nature, iv. 146.

Art: of being a politician, iii. 95–100; of being agreeable, iii. 449–50; of bestowing favours, iii. 39–41; of cavilling, ii. 432; of growing old, ii. 511; of growing rich, iii. 2; of managing mankind, iv. 60; of pleasing, ii. 590–3; iii. 92–93; of praising justly, ii. 425; of writing unintelligibly, iii. 424.

Artemisia, Queen, the most memorable widow in history, v. 100.

Artery, a surgeon's error in opening an, iii. 383–4.

Arthegal, Spenser represented justice in, iv. 429.

Arthur, Prince, in Spenser, iv. 429.

Artifice(s): disappoints him that practises it, i. 432; a husband misled by tricks and, ii. 169; and refinements obscure human nature, ii. 318; and modes of false wit, ii. 355; of the flatterer, ii. 424.

Artificially (artfully), ii. 150, 263, 453; iii. 471; &c.

Artillery, i. 438; in *PL*, ii. 589; iii. 229.

Artisans, British, ii. 181.

Arts, terms of: French military, ii. 152–3; in Milton, iii. 63–64; in accounts of trade, iv. 6.

Arts: which all men are masters of, i. 365; Peter the Great's cultivation of mechanic, ii. 49; last a shorter time than books, ii. 154; in which the ancients excelled, ii. 467; ambition the motive for invention and improvement of, ii. 490; Milton's display of knowledge of, iii. 62; our schools should teach the practical, iii. 318.

As in praesenti, ii. 360.

Ascalaphus, in Lully's opera, i. 123.

Ascanius, in the *Aeneid*, ii. 563; iii. 306.

Ascham, Mrs., of Connington, iii. *78*.

Asclepius, god of medicine, iv. *551*.

Ashe, Edward, a subscriber, i. lxxxix.

Ashe, St. George, Bishop of Clogher: on lying, iv. *301*; his sermon to the Protestants of Ireland, iv. 334–5.

Ashes, pale as (prov.), i. 53, 175, 371; ii. 521.

Ashley, Lord. *See* Shaftesbury.

Ashurst, Sir William, director of the Bank, a subscriber, i. *xc*.

Asia, i. 129; Lacedemonian dancing famous in, i. 284; setting of part of the *Aeneid*, iii. 332; exotic plants from, iv. 104; the lesser A. planted by Cyrus, iv. 593; superstitions abound in, v. 65.

Asparagus: 'ducklins and sparrow-grass', iii. 397.

Aspasia: instructed Socrates in eloquence, ii. 458.

ASPATIA and ARISTUS, a happy couple, ii. 11.

Aspect: woman's, ii. 68–71; we are often judged by our, ii. 307; the preventing a. which discourages salutations, ii. 508; of Marlborough, v. 179.

Ass(es): in lion's skin (fable), i. 58; better suffer from paw of lion than hoof of, i. 262; in a field of corn, in Homer, ii. 127–8; a plate to be run for by, ii. 182; *between two bundles of hay* (prov.), ii. 248, 270, 286; women who resemble, ii. 320; the famous ass-race, iii. 320; Aristotle's soul 'may now be damn'd to animate an ass', ii. 326; Balaam's, iv. 514.

Assault and battery, an action of, iv. 208.

Assemblies, i. 19, 22, 44, 68, 124, &c.; of the fair sex, i. 208; about town, i. 282; public, i. 87; ii. 107, 163, 397, &c.; religious, ii. 510.

Assembly: Clarinda's, i. 314; of duchesses, i. 487; of the clergy of Sion College, ii. 79; of ladies, ii. 440, 556; of virtuosos, ii. 570; of divines (the Westminster Assembly), v. 150, &c.

Assizes: The PERVERSE WIDOW at, i. 464; Sir ROGER at, i. 499; at Exeter, ii. 135.

Association proposed, of honest men above party, i. 512; ii. 1–2.

Assurance: distinguished from modesty, iii. 404–6; liveliness and a., qualities of the French, iv. 29.

Assurance upon Lives, Monthly Society of, i. *118*; freight and a. of a cargo to Turkey, ii. 188.

ASTERIA: letter from (on husband's absence), ii. 435-6; referred to, iii. 269.

Asterisk, use of in pamphlets, iv. 538-9.

Astragal, term in architecture, iii. 556.

Astrologers: their prescriptions for May, iii. 374; frequent in London, iv. 292; CHARISSA's scruples regarding, v. 115.

Astrology: a student of, ii. 357; Ramsay's Vindication of, iv. 591.

Astronomy: in education, ii. 396; Milton's ostentatious references to, iii. 62; terms of, used by Milton, iii. 64; pleasure in reading books on, iii. 575; wonders of, iv. 170, 529-30.

Astrop, visited by SIMON HONEYCOMB, ii. 104.

Astyanax, in The Distressed Mother, iii. 241; iv. 434.

ATALANTA, her leap into the Ionian sea, ii. 407.

Ate, the goddess: signifies injury, or divine justice, iii. 467.

Atheism: allegorical figure of, i. 16; hypocrisy in one age succeeded by a. in another, i. 488; zealots in, ridiculous and perverse, ii. 229-30; the five great points of, ii. 230; the unreasonableness of, ii. 231-4; iii. 459-63; a prejudice towards a. is not impartiality, ii. 413; defined, iii. 431; destructive of cheerfulness, iii. 431.

Atheist(s): the shoe-maker in The Man of Mode an, i. 280; VOCIFER a coxcomb and, i. 324; and tithe-stealers, i. 462; as full of zeal as the Christian, ii. 229; and the free-thinker, ii. 412; made up of pride, spleen and cavil, iii. 431; TOM PUZZLE an a. 'as much as his parts allow', iv. 187; does God less dishonour than the man who believes Him cruel, iv. 254; the Spectator's conversion of, iv. 398.

Atheistical author, story of an, ii. 155-6.

ATHENAIS, letter from, inquiring about lover's leap, ii. 384.

Athenian Mercury, i. xxxvii.

Athenians: 'understand what is good, but Lacedemonians practise it', i. 31; regulations of their stage, i. 172; iv. 66; Pericles' oration on, i. 349; war with Lacedemonians, i. 349; ii. 312; Phocion and 'this injury of the', ii. 26; the oracle's reply to, ii. 312; Raphael's painting of St. Paul preaching to, ii. 379-80; iii. 521; and Philip, ii. 396, 431-2; man who brought false news of victory to, ii. 410; Pericles' funeral oration on, iii. 105; Diagoras and the mariners, iv. 213.

Athens: incident in theatre at, i. 30-31; the plague in, ii. 266; St. Paul preaching at, ii. 379-80; iii. 521; v. 166; Philip confuted the statesmen of, ii. 431-2; Cicero's son educated at, iii. 106; anecdote of Pisistratus, the tyrant of, iv. 379; nobleman of, his compliment to Plato, iv. 448; in epigram on Menander, iv. 475.

Athos, Mount, proposal to cut it into a statue of Alexander, iii. 555.

Atkyns, Sir Robert, iv. 527.

Atmosphere: dispute concerning pressure of, ii. 442; weather-glass shows variations of, ii. 595.

Atom, imagination unable to grasp idea of, iii. 576-7.

Atomical philosophers, their regard for religion, ii. 234.

Atoms, Epicurus derived man's actions from an unintelligible declination of, v. 10.

Atreus: an opera call'd The Cruelty of, i. 65; in Horace, i. 190.

Atterbury, Francis: v. 66, 146; referred to (?), iv. 71.

Atticus, Titus Pomponius: dressed moderately, ii. 91; maintained friendships with both parties, iii. 446-7; avoided extremes of two parties, iv. 152.

Attorneys: a club of, iii. 402-3; disdain of lawyers when a. give advice, iv. 454.

Attractives (attractions), iii. 80.

Auction: in Covent-Garden, i. 288; in Somerset House Yard, i. 329; in Shandois Street, ii. 381; of Persian women, iv. 314-15.

Auction-pulpit, at Lloyd's, i. 196.

Audience(s): wretched taste of, i. 59; ii. 314-15; more affected by a tragedy ending unhappily, i. 169; iii. 59; well disposed to a modest speaker, ii. 397-8; in Venice contrasted with those in England, iv. 55-56; composed of two sorts of people, iv. 282.

Audience of leave, a curtsy as an, iii. 60.

Augurs, Cicero busied himself in the College of, iv. 292.

August, allegorical depiction of, iii. 595-6.

Augustan age, ii. 482; Horace the greatest wit and critic in the, ii. 220.

Augustine, St.: splendida peccata, ii. 331; on dreams in Paradise, v. 30.

Augustus (C. Julius Caesar Octavianus), i. 144; had intrigues with wives of senators out of stratagem, ii. 247; the age of, ii. 220, 482; candor and affability of, ii. 592; degeneracy of Romans

under, iii. 22; asked if he had acted his part well, iii. 152; Atticus a friend to, iii. 447; Louis XIV more like A. or Nero(?), iii. 509; great geniuses arose in time of, iii. 529; his speech of censure to bachelors, iv. 382–3; Horace's tact in delivering his book to, iv. 485; style of Horace's famous epistle to, v. 113–14; his chief aim, to govern well, v. 168. *See also* Solon.

Aumont, Duc d', i. *62*.

Aunt: Pliny's tribute to an, iv. 372; one of those who read plays with spectacles on, iv. 401.

AURELIA, delights in the privacy of country life, i. 68.

Aurelius, Marcus. *See* Marcus Aurelius Antoninus.

Aurora: robed in saffron, ii. 533; an attendant of Summer, iii. 595.

Austen, Jane, on the *Spectator*, i. c–ci.

Austria, House of, i. 277; iv. 207.

Author(s): vanity of, i. 18; draw themselves in their chief characters, i. 218–19; ignorant of ultimate fate of their books, i. 361; ignorance and envy of (one a. a mole to another), i. 508; over-witty, ii. 52–53; fame their greatest reward, ii. 154–5; who propagate vice, ii. 155, 517; story of an atheistical, ii. 155–6; a discreet a. will avoid immorality, ii. 206; the *Spectator* has refrained from ridiculing, ii. 519–20; dealers turn a. and write quaint advertisements, iii. 25; reflections of, to be admitted sparingly in epic, iii. 60–61; who writes on, though in his dotage, iii. 75; precedency among, iv. 386; fame of, increases after death, iv. 472; fond of their own productions, iv. 587.

Autumn: best in France, iii. 474; allegorical depiction of, iii. 596.

Avarice: fear of want degenerates into, i. 232; allegory of luxury and, i. 235–6; allegorical representation of, in Vision of Painters, i. 355; allegorical depiction of, ii. 124; conflict between love and, ii. 270; ill effects of, ii. 372–3; moves in the eyes, ii. 471; extinguished by consideration of eternity, iii. 29; represented in *Volpone*, iii. 394; balanced against poverty, iv. 136; of old men, excused by the ancients, iv. 259; makes it difficult for some to retire from the world, iv. 466; pains involved in, v. 133.

Aversion: passion of, mentioned, ii. 455; to business and attention, iii. 6. *See also* Antipathies.

Aviary of nightingales, Sir ROGER's, iii. 438.

'Awakened' behaviour of women in France, i. 193.

Awe, inspired by public assemblies, ii. 397–8.

Awful, Cato's character a. rather than amiable, ii. 166.

Axe, poems in shape of an, i. 246, 265, 271.

Ayloffe, Captain, i. *264*.

Aysenby, Mr., iii. 211.

Azazel, description of in *PL*, iii. 89.

B., A.: his advice on ladies' reading, i. 392; letter from (a clergyman's wife), ii. 348; letter from (on choice in marriage), ii. 545–6; his paraphrase of *Proverbs*, iii. 533–5; letter from (on fashions), iv. 192–6; testimonial from, praising No. 193, iv. 459; letter from (on grottoes), v. 160–1.

B., B.: whimsical petition of, v. 150.

B., C.: letter from (on knotting), iv. 412–13.

B., F.: letter from (on immodest conversation), iv. 57–58.

B., J.: letter from (on eloquence of beggars), v. 95–96.

B., N.: letter from (on qualifications of a poet), iii. 138; letter from (on idleness), iii. 168–9.

B., R.: 'fishmonger in the Strand', i. 52; letter from (to the CLERGYMAN), i. 114–15; letters from (on beauty in women), i. 138–41, 224–5.

B., T.: letter from (on masquerades), i. 35–37; letter from (on the Amorous Club), i. 125–7; letter from (on equanimity), ii. 268–9; letter from (on lovers' talismans), ii. 452–3; letter from (on the eyes), ii. 469–72; letter from (on railing), ii. 513; letter from (on a wife's whims during pregnancy), iii. 195–7; letter from (on coquetry of a milkmaid), iii. 427–8; letter from (on control of the passions), iii. 523–6; letter from (on fathers and sons), iv. 258–60.

B., W.: letter from (on illegitimacy), ii. 298; letter from (on the pipe of Licinius), ii. 388–9.

Baal, votaries of, i. 313.

Babbler, endangers credit of the tradesman, ii. 350.

Babel, Tower of, ii. 553; iii. 386, 555; builder of Babels, ii. 159.

Babes in the Wood (ballad), i. 362–4.

Baboon, ii. 184.

Baby (-ies), i.e. dolls, i. 342; a new wax,

ii. 190; a jointed b. from France, ii. 578; dressed out in fashion, iv. 194; girls tutoring their, iv. 274.

Babylon, Babylonia: 'the crooked morals of this our', ii. 577; walls and Hanging Gardens of, iii. 554; its temple to Jupiter Belus, with observatory, iii. 554; in ruins, iii. 579; King of, weighed in the balance, iv. 134; publicizing of cures in, iv. 552–3; burning the 'whore of', v. 106.

Bacchanal, painting of, ii. 379.

Bacchus: and Ariadne in modern prints, ii. 60; and Apollo in Lily's grammar, ii. 529; an attendant of Autumn, iii. 596; in modern poems, iv. 363; cast-coat of, in Strada, v. 109.

Bachelor(s): an ill-bred, ii. 73–74; children of, ii. 295; unhappy old age of a, ii. 510–12; account of an impotent old, ii. 575–6; Inquisition on maids and, iii. 165–8; Augustus' address of censure to, iv. 382–3; evils of bachelordom, iv. 382–5; marriage comes as a judgement to, iv. 389.

Back-gammon, i. 5; 333, 441; ii. 528; iii. 478; iv. 258. *See also* Tables.

Back-sword, fighting with, iv. 31, 133, 212.

Bacon, Francis: a well-written book 'like Moses's serpent', i. 45; on the envious eye, i. 83; on the 'fruits of friendship', i. 289; a learned genius, ii. 129; on a cunning solicitor, ii. 197; complied with public forms of worship, iii. 460; prescribes poems and prospects for health, iii. 539; on taste, iii. 70–71; on disadvantages of eldest and youngest children in a family, iv. 274; amazing breadth of knowledge in, iv. 487–8; on constancy in men of grave natures, v. 23; *Advancement of Learning*, i. 45, 334; v. 52; Apophthegms of, ii 37, 430, 575; *Essays*, i. 83, 289, 339; ii. 197; iii. 45, 539; iv. 71, 274; v. 23, 75; *Sylva Sylvarum*, iv. 70.

Bacon, Roger, the speaking head erected by, in Oxford, iv. 514.

Bacon: a flitch of, i. 462; dined on a knuckle of veal and, iii. 154; a flitch of, awarded to a happily married couple at Whichenovre, v. 76–80.

Baggage (young women): an idle, ii. 17; this abandoned, ii. 304; idle baggages, iv. 84; a pert young, iv. 513; a handsome young, v. 69.

Baghdad: high hills of, ii. 122; long hollow valley of, ii. 126.

Bagnio: a 'walking b.' contrived by the Mohocks, iii. 224; orthography of the

word, iii. 225; in Newgate Street and in Chancery Lane, iii. 225; six in London, iii. 225.

Bailey, Nathan, *Dictionary*, iv. 85.

Bailiff's house, confined for debt in a, iii. 217.

Baius, example of, in Horace, iii. 248.

Baker, J., *The Medley* printed by, iii. 380.

Baker, Sir Richard: *Chronicle*, in LEONORA's library, i. 156; Sir ROGER's observations from, ii. 551; iii. 212, 215–16; cited, i. 135; ii. 135, 596; iii. 215; iv. 212; v. 70; mentioned, iii. 209.

Baker, Thomas, *The Fine Lady's Airs*, i. 373–4.

Balaam's ass, iv. 514.

Balances: examples of in Homer, Virgil, and the Bible, iv. 134; in Milton, iv. 134–5; vision of, iv. 135–8.

Baldwin, Anne: distributor of the *Spectator*, i. xxi–xxiv, 74; iv. 459; association with Buckley, i. xxi–xxiii, 6; *The Historian* sold by, iii. 111; *The Medley* printed and sold by, iii. 380.

Balk, a town in Tartary, iii. 30.

Ball(s): a great help to discourse, i. 67; dancing at a b. at M. Rigadoon's, i. 285–6; the 'pleasure of plays, balls, and opera', ii. 299; a British lady dressed for a, ii. 531; 'slain by a lady's glance at a', iii. 417; the red wax of b. tickets, iv. 15; Charles II fond of balls and plays, iv. 132; a b. night at a dancing-school, v. 38.

Balls, boys playing with, in the streets, iv. 307.

Ballads: universal appeal of, i. 297–8; *Chevy Chase*, i. 298–303, 315–22; *The Two Children in the Wood*, i. 361–4; Lord Dorset's 'numerous collection' of, i. 363–4; admired by Dryden and Molière, i. 364; *The Wanton Wife of Bath*, ii. 461; beggars and ballad singers in London, iv. 101; Elizabeth's minister of state on, iv. 281; a genius for the modern ballad indicated by an unequal pace, iv. 345.

Balon (French dancer), i. 194 & n.

Balzac, Jean-Louis Guez de: his letter to the Chancellor of France quoted, iii. 324.

BAMBOO, BENJAMIN, his efforts to tame a shrew, iv. 209.

Bands: remarkable for great wisdom and his broad, ii. 207; 'who washes and can clear-starch his', ii. 528.

Bandbox(es), i. 361; ii. 217; iii. 125.

Bandy legs, iv. 510.

Banker: bows lowest when I wear my full-bottom'd wig, ii. 92; in Lombard Street, iii. 275.

Bankrupt(s): phrase used for, in Holland, ii. 187; ruined by misemployed hopes, iv. 409–10.

Bankruptcy: follows the pursuit of pleasure, ii. 95; 'that most dreadful of all humane conditions', iv. 6; unhappiness caused by, iv. 107–11.

Banks, John, *The Unhappy Favorite, or Earl of Essex*: acted at Epping, i. 207.

Bank-stock, rise and fall of, iii. 348.

Banquo, in *Macbeth*, i. 194.

Bantam, Ambassador of: letter of, describing his visit to London, iv. 504–5.

Bantry Bay, the action at, iii. 437.

Bar, pitching the, i. 214, 239; ii. 133; iv. 24; (metaphorically), iv. 422.

Bar (of the coffee-house), i. 371; iii. 509; the bar-keeper there, iv. 407.

Barachel the Buzite, iii. 244.

Barbadian merchant, i. 51.

Barbadoes: Ligon's account of, i. 49; the products of, i. 295; residence of PHILLIS and BRUNETTA, i. 343; send citron-water to whisperers about men in power in London, iii. 479.

Barbadoes waters. *See* Citron.

Barbarisms (in language): pedants' concern with, i. 250; in street cries, ii. 475.

Barbarity: the ignorance of true honour, ii. 49; connexion between despotic government and, iii. 21; practised by the Mohocks, iii. 187.

Barber, John (alderman), referred to(?), v. 115.

Barber(s's): periwig powdered at the, i. 10; barber's pole, i. 197; v. 38; broad pair of shoulders thrown away upon, iii. 109; snaps his fingers, iii. 109; with an improvised barometer, iv. 60; a young, v. 38; profanation of Sabbath by, v. 116.

Barbier, Mrs. (singer): in *Almahide*, ii. 397–8; in *Calypso and Telemachus*, ii. 398.

Barcelona, i. 277; 'a pinch of right and fine' (snuff), iv. 345.

BAREFACE, a woman's man, ii. 112.

Baretti, Giuseppe, on the *Spectator*, i. lxxx.

Bargain(s): as they say in a b., 'Let the buyer look to it', ii. 180; drinking at driving of, iv. 85; a marriage not to be considered a common, iv. 360.

Barge: 'If I was a Lord or a Bishop, and kept a', iii. 436; Antony's description of Cleopatra in her, iii. 497.

Barker, Henry, on wit, i. 265.

Barnaby bright (St. Barnabas' Day), court adjourned to, v. 130.

Barn-Elms, Surrey, i. 42.

Barnes, Joshua (professor of Greek): an enemy of the 'Trojans', ii. 453.

Barnet, Clench of, i. 102, 129; ii. 206.

Barnet Wells, ii. 206.

Barometer: 'the glass fell', ii. 262; invention of, ii. 519; a weather-glass, ii. 595; a barber's improvised, iv. 60.

Baronet: Sir ROGER DE COVERLEY a, i. 7; WILL WIMBLE younger brother to a, i. 447; Sir ANTHONY LOVE, a young, ii. 600.

Barrel(s): a lover peeping out of, in English comedy, i. 191; tubs and b. thrown out to a whale, ii. 519.

Barrett, John: song by, iii. 438.

Barrister, iii. 348, 418.

Barrow, Isaac, his sermons preached by Sir ROGER's chaplain, i. 442; ii. 549.

Barrow, Dr. Samuel, ii. 537.

Barry, Elizabeth (actress), i. 81.

Bartholomew Fair, i. 102, 119; ii. 56, 206.

Bashfulness: of behaviour in the English, ii. 82; iv. 102, 116; without merit is awkward, ii. 398; 'bashful grace' in women readers, ii. 567; regarding religion, iv. 116; effect of clothes on, iv. 193; an unmanly, iv. 217.

Basilisks, women as b. that destroy with their eyes, iii. 416.

Basilius Valentinus. *See* Valentine family.

Basin: of water as a looking-glass, iii. 191; in a China shop, iii. 245; or artificial lake, at Babylon, iii. 554.

Basket-hilt sword, i. 450; Fraternity of Basket-hilts, iv. 81.

Basnage de Beauval, Jacques: *History of the Jews*, iv. 256–8.

Bassas, Turkish, at the masquerade, i. 96.

Bass-viol, i. 450; ii. 184; iv. 546.

Basset (game at cards), iii. 182.

Bastards, ii. 295–8.

Bastardy, and cuckoldom looked upon as reproaches, ii. 297.

Bastile, incident of a prisoner in, i. 475.

BASTO, RACHEL, letter from (on female gamesters), ii. 54.

Batallia (order of battle), iv. 6.

Bateman, James (Director of the Bank), a subscriber, i. xc.

Bath, i. 61; ii. 104; 'now to Bath, now to Tunbridge', i. 231; ii. 104; a whistling-match at, ii. 206–7; an under-citizen of, ii. 207; 'The Wanton Wife of', ii. 461; long-chinned persons assembled

at, iii. 396–7; insinuations against Powell at, iii. 401.

Bath-faggots, i. 17.

Bathing: women who pass their time in, ii. 320; and purification, in the Jewish and Mahometan laws, v. 158.

Baths, cold, for distempers, iii. 383.

BATHYLLUS, and HIPPARCHUS' wife, ii. 408.

Battle: of Almanza, i. 32; of Blenheim, i. 110; ii. 151–2; v. 72, 95; of Edgehill, iii. 70; of Ramillies, iii. 102; v. 95; of the angels, in *PL*, ii. 540; iii. 227–34, 566; of the Lapithae and Centaurs, iii. 596.

Battle(s): more killed in flight than in, i. 107; and bloodshed foretold by the hoop-petticoat, ii. 6; 'to cover thy beloved face in the day of', ii. 302; gallantry and generosity in a day of, ii. 591; not always to the strong, iii. 44; poorly described by historians, iv. 6.

BATTUS, his leap into the Ionian sea, ii. 406.

Bavaria, Guelphus, Duke of, iv. 269; Max Emanuel, Duke of, at Blenheim, ii. 152.

Bavarian Red Liquor, i. *222*; advertisement for, iv. *130, 460*.

Bavius, enemy of Virgil, ii. 482.

Bawd(s): should not live at the sign of the Angel, i. 117; in a brothel, ii. 246; account of, ii. 304, 535–7, 567–70; 'those hags of hell', ii. 535; letter from a b. to a noble lord, ii. 569–70.

Bawdry: pert style of the pit b., i. 63; in poetry owing to dearth of invention, i. 216; allusions to in drama, ii. 315.

Bawdy-house(s): account of a girl in a, ii. 245–7; greatest politicians of the age visiting, ii. 247; men who visit b. to 'see the world', ii. 248; 'education' in, ii. 536; protected by the Mohocks, iii. 188.

Bawlers, and loud speakers, ii. 83.

Baxter, Richard: a page of, under a Christmas pie, i. 361; *Last Words of*, iv. 63; congratulated himself on not getting a place at court, v. 44.

Bayes, Mr., in *The Rehearsal*, i. 345; iii. 571.

Bayhuysen, Bernard van (Bauhusius), inscription to the Virgin Mary, i. *254*.

Bayle, Pierre: 'one of the most learned Men of the present age', i. 382; the *Dictionary* suggested for ladies' reading, i. 390; 'a modern philosopher, quoted by Monsieur Bayle', i. 493; 'an author quoted by Monsieur Bayle',

ii. 431; 'a man of great freedom o thought, as well as of exquisite learning and judgment', iv. 89; Monsieur Bayle's opinion of the hymn by Des Barreaux, iv. 323; i. *98, 99, 221, 257, 263, 327, 330, 346, 347, 382, 415, 455, 491, 494*; ii. *166, 215, 228, 248, 249, 250, 260, 276, 297, 318, 334, 361, 365, 366, 369, 373, 382, 393, 399, 407, 409, 410, 430, 431, 450, 454, 530*; iii. *28, 42, 44, 45, 152, 249, 258, 324, 371, 407, 424, 446–7*; iv. *2, 89, 116, 146, 213, 226, 229, 241, 256, 264, 319, 323, 392, 565*; v. *7, 15, 16, 30, 42, 100, 159, 169*.

Bayly, Richard, surgeon in Arundel Street, iv. *61*.

Bayly, Thomas, *Witty Apophthegms*, ii. *37, 430, 575*; iii. *300*.

Bayne, Alexander, i. *392*; ii. *364–5*; iii. *409*.

Beadle: should take care of beggars, iv. 12; disciplining boys in the streets, iv. 307.

Beagles, in fox-hunting, i. 476.

Bear, living at the sign of a, i. 118.

Bear-garden: spectators proper at, i. 86; masters of ceremonies in, i. 269; bodily actors should be dismissed to, ii. 56; reason and good manners absent from, ii. 59; a trial of skill at, iv. 30–35.

Beard(s): letting b. grow, i. 76; old woman with a, i. 197; fashions in, iii. 220–3; Licander's prayer to increase his wisdom and, iii. 468; one who let his b. grow from martyrdom of Charles I, v. 150.

Beardwell, Lucy, printer of the *Post Boy*, i. *244*.

Beasniffe, Francis, author of letter in No. 443 (?), iv. 56.

Beating up: a lewd woman's quarters, i. 436; for recruits, ii. 514.

Beattie, James, iii. *536*.

Beau(x): loaden with excrescences, i. 71; eternally playing with a snuff-box, i. 185; proposed for membership in the Ugly Club, i. 205; among servants, i. 374; iii. 69; DICK CRASTIN 'the only surviving b. of the last age', i. 385–6; TOM TULIP 'almost the only one that keeps up that order of men in this', i. 386; my fair readers deeper scholars than the, i. 393, 404; a country, ii. 13–14; mentioned, ii. 29; of ancient Rome, ii. 89; who have raised up children before marriage, ii. 295; Aristotle's soul may be 'doing painful penance in some b.', ii. 326; behaviour of a b. at the theatre, ii. 434–5;

an old beau's advice to his son, ii. 593; story of ESCALUS, an amorous old b., iii. 157–60; transmigration into a, iii. 276; rivalry between factions of b. and belles, iv. 17–18; old b. as leaders of fashion, iv. 196; knotting proposed as employment for, iv. 413; a dirty b. in a stage-coach, v. 156.

Beau monde, grown more childish, not more innocent, i. 60.

Beau's head: dissection of a, ii. 570–3; referred to, ii. 594, 596; iii. 161.

Beaufort, Henry, Cardinal, his death described by Shakespeare, ii. 323–4.

Beaumont and Fletcher, iv. *427*; Dryden on, ii. 58; a new edition of, advertised, ii. *58*; *Philaster*, ii. 434; *The Scornful Lady*, ii. 552–5; iv. *62*.

Beauties, of nature, ii. 447; hidden b. of a soul, ii. 500.

Beauties (of literature): in Sappho, ii. 367; criticism should discover b. rather than faults, ii. 519–20; in the epic, ii. 539, 565; iii. 60; little b. and niceties, iii. 5; greater b. atone for small blemishes, iii. 10; the critic should discover the concealed b. of a writer, iii. 36–37, 527–8; kinds of, in *PL*, iii. 392; rational and manly, iii. 530; ancient critics discovered, v. 27.

Beauties (women): history of the rival, i. 342–4; generally untractable, i. 369; often discourage salutations, ii. 508; the whole circle of, at the theatre, ii. 511; often ill-natured, iii. 103–4.

Beautiful, The: as a source of aesthetic pleasure, iii. 542–4; depiction of, in Virgil, iii. 565.

Beauty: WILL HONEYCOMB on, i. 20–21; women's undue concern for, i. 137–41; must be heightened by virtue, i. 139–41, 224–5, 315, 338–41; ii. 533; spoiled by pride and affectation, i. 139, 159–60; too brief for 'demurring', i. 378; pleases the eye, i. 433; definitions of, ii. 68; dangers of, ii. 68–71; silent flattery of, ii. 480; is transitory, ii. 511; in distress, iii. 80; disfigured by small-pox, iii. 101; v. 96; and good-nature, iii. 104; unlovely without innocence, iii. 482; pre-eminent in British ladies, iv. 30; the force of, iv. 311–14; the 'eloquence' of, iv. 332; that sage who demanded what b. was, iv. 589.

Beauty, A (woman): a little spite natural to, ii. 111; grows wrinkled while we are yet gazing, ii. 511; disadvantages of marrying a celebrated, ii. 515; CANIDIA a haughty b. of the last age, iii. 75; an imperious b. humbled and neglected, iii. 76; education of a, iv. 405–6; letter describing a, iv. 589; may lose her charm through familiarity, v. 139.

Beauty of holiness: Raphael's depiction of, ii. 379; the justest title to, iii. 40.

Beauvoir, W., iv. *416*.

Beaver hat, i. 361; ii. 132; iii. 522; edged with silver, i. 433.

BEAVER, the haberdasher, an authority on news, i. 209.

Beaux Esprits: of the Middle Ages, i. 254; tribe of free-thinking, ii. 412.

Beck, Justus, Director of the Bank: a subscriber, i. *xc*.

Bed: receiving visits in, i. 192–3; of Procrustes, i. 247.

Bed-maker, JEREMY LOVEMORE in love with his, v. 38.

Bedford, Francis Russell, 2nd Earl of, iii. 214.

Bedfordshire, letter from, ii. 164.

Bees: kept by the PERVERSE WIDOW, i. 486; women who resemble, ii. 320, 326–7, 348; simile of, in *PL*, iii. 91; hung upon tongue of Menander, iv. 474.

Beef: cold b. upon the table at Christmas, ii. 550; overcorned, iii. 155; a slice of hung b., iii. 438.

Beef-Eaters, 'sometimes I stand by the', v. 137.

Beef-steak Club, i. 42.

Beelzebub: form of word used by Milton, iii. 13; his character in *PL*, iii. 116–17.

Beer: mild, i. 374; small, i. 106, 310; ii. 225, 550; iii. 111, 155; iv. 542.

Beggar(s): in Lincoln's Inn Fields, i. 28; at bridges and church porches, i. 208; upon the road, ii. 17; Sir ANDREW on charity to, ii. 402–3; Sir ROGER's conversation with a beggar man in London, ii. 549; who exposes his sores, ii. 593; scorn of the wealthy for, iii. 47–48; tripping up a b. on crutches, iii. 322; impostors among, iv. 11–12; and ballad-singers in London, iv. 101; at the Royal Exchange, iv. 307; eloquence of, v. 95–96; 'gave away a dog for biting a', v. 128.

Behaviour: rusticity of, i. 226; openness of, a mark of good breeding, i. 487; abandoned b. successful with women, ii. 105; of patron to client, ii. 337; indelicate b. of a young woman, ii. 346–7; inconsistency of, ii. 362–4; decorum in, iii. 38–41; to be suited to one's age, iii. 75–76; strict b. laughed

at in our age, iii. 271; singularity in, iv. 569–74.

Behn, Aphra: *Emperor of the Moon*, i. 93–94; *The Rover*, i. 218; translated Fontenelle, iv. *346*.

Bel and the Dragon, i. 118, 313.

Bel Esprit, contrasted with natural genius, ii. 127.

Belch, muddy (stale beer), use of, a cause of punning, iii. 484.

Belial: his scoffing speech to Satan, ii. 590; iii. 115–16; his character in *PL*, iii. 87, 115; his sentiments in the infernal assembly, iii. 115–16.

Believe what we wish, We are easy to (prov.), iv. 143.

BELINDA: and CLEANTHES, ii. 558–60; character of, iii. 356–7; a dimple in her left cheek, iii. 418. Cf. BELLINDA.

Belisarius (Byzantine general), *Date obolum Belisario*, iv. 129.

Bell, Adam Schall von, iv. *449*.

Bell(s): use of as a sign, i. 116–18; ringing of, in English tragedies, i. 186; ringing to dinner, i. 448; ii. 530; signalling information to a quack doctor, ii. 257–8; calling to prayers twice a day, ii. 526; a chorus of, v. 108.

Bellair, in *The Man of Mode*, i. 279, 280.

BELLAMOUR, transformed into a sober husband, ii. 488.

Bellamy, Edward, translated Huarte, iii. *106*.

Bell-Savage: origin of the sign, i. 118; mentioned, i. 281.

Belles-lettres, appearance of a man interested in, iv. 345.

BELLFRY, RALPH (sexton), letters from, i. 61–62; iii. 400–1.

BELLINDA: letter from (to the Sothades), ii. 299–300; an affected beauty, iii. 104; poem to, iv. 176. Cf. BELINDA.

Bellman, cry of, iv. 103.

Bellona: Homer's description of, iii. 337; in modern poems, iv. 363.

Bellows-mender, cries of, in London streets, ii. 477.

Belly and the limbs, fable of, ii. 185, 220.

Belshazzar, iv. 134.

Belvedere Torso, in the Vatican, ii. 390.

BELVIDERA, letter from (on female panders), ii. 303–5; in *Venice Preserved*, iv. 108; in a song, iv. 163.

Bembus (Bembo), Pietro, iv. *438*.

Bencher of the Temple: story told by, ii. 464; account of an old, ii. 575–6.

Benchers, of Inns of Court, i. 90.

Benches, in the theatre, ii. 414.

Bender (Tighina): Charles XII fled to, i. *182*; advices from, iv. 93.

Benefice: offer of, by 'an endowed female', iii. 66–67; 'procured a b. for a young divine', v. 127.

Benefit: of five hundred pounds in the lottery, ii. 441; 'of the ram', v. 130; b.-days of plays and operas, iii. 26; a b.-play, i. 103; the great b.-ticket, ii. 348.

Benevolence: enjoined upon R. O., i. 113–14; *Spectator* to be written in spirit of, i. 145; of EUCRATE, i. 357–8; practice of social virtues recommended, i. 395; 'the secret and incomparable pleasure of doing good', i. 404; to dependants, i. 443–5; universal b. of Sir ROGER, i. 498; ii. 549–51; iii. 216, 437–8, 590; and good nature, ii. 164–7; charity the test of, ii. 197–201; 'the noblest power, that of doing good', ii. 394; the result of the most amiable virtues, ii. 445; to be practised in all stations of life, ii. 462–5; inward pleasure resulting from, ii. 500; as a motive for pleasing others, ii. 591; to be done with a good grace, iii. 38–41; 'the godlike pleasure of', iii. 39; expressed in charity, iii. 47–50; MANLIUS an example of, iv. 151–4; opportunities for, in men of great place, iv. 159–61; and good-will the aim of the *Spectator*, iv. 501; and self-love, the two principles of action, v. 10; pleasures of, v. 12–14; principal checks upon, v. 54–58; Jesus the author of, v. 84.

BENEVOLUS, the best and best-beloved of husbands, iii. 371–2.

Bennet, Madam (procuress), *The Plain Dealer* dedicated to, ii. 537.

Bentley, Joanna, the 'Phebe' of No. 603, v. *61*.

Bentley, Richard: 'the phrase of a great modern critic', ii. 151 & n.; satire on his edition of Horace, iv. *162*; *Dissertation on … Phalaris*, iv. *520*; his daughter Joanna, v. *61*.

BENTSTAFF, SAMPSON, has sent a puzzling letter, iv. 588.

Berenger, Richard, *History and Art of Horsemanship*, ii. *31*.

Berington, B. (news-shop), i. lxxxiv.

Berkeley, George, iii. *538*.

Berkshire, custom of the ram in, v. 100, 129.

Bermudas, The, iv. 225.

Bernard, Charles, sale of his library, iii. *459*.

Bernard, Jacques, on animals, i. *494*.

Berwick (Sussex), i. 35; -upon-Tweed, a letter received from, iv. 484.

Betis (governor of Gaza), iii. 247.

Betterton, Thomas: his *Amorous Widow*, i. *72*; iii. 370–1; his *King Henry IV*, i. *75*; in *Phaedra and Hippolitus*, i. *81*; in *Macbeth*, i. *194*.

BETTY: sweetheart of WILLIAM, Sir ROGER's master of the game, i. 484; BELINDA's maid, ii. 560; proposed as a wife, iv. 401.

Beveridge, William, 'the pious and learned' Bishop of St. Asaph, ii. 45.

Bey, Alexander. *See* Scanderbeg.

Bèze, Théodore de, version of Psalm 134, ii. *305*.

Bias(es): fixed in minds by nature, ii. 8; in relations between parents and children, ii. 521; towards knowledge in every mind, iii. 107; a wrong b. hung on the mind, iii. 495.

'Biberius Mero', Nero called, ii. 455–6.

Bible: O.T. and Apocrypha written in a perriwig, i. 248; Psalms written in a picture of Charles I, i. 247–8; worked in tapestry, ii. 60; v. 73; elevated style of O.T.: far-fetched comparisons in, ii. 127; old and new versions of Psalm 100, ii. *305*; Beza's version of Psalm 134, ii. *305*; a sermon preached on 1 Chron. 1. 1, ii. 361; a sermon preached on Ecclesiastes 2. 2. ii. 466; the old version of Psalm 14, iii. *131*; paraphrase of Isaiah in Pope's *Messiah*, iii. 419–22; paraphrase of Song of Solomon 2, iii. 455–9; Hebrew style and language of O.T., iii. 514–15; paraphrase of Proverbs 7, iii. 533–5; paraphrase of Psalm 23, iv. 50–51; hymns and divine odes of O.T., iv. 95; paraphrase of Psalm 114, iv. 127–8; paraphrase of Psalm 19, iv. 144–5; an error in printing the Seventh Commandment, iv. 580; ceremonies of purification in Deuteronomy, v. 158; Vatican MS. of N.T., v. 165.—QUOTATIONS FROM: Gen., i. 497; ii. 333, 353; iii. 28, 30, 131, 350, 389, 555; iv. 171; Exod., i. 45; iii. 386; iv. 322; v. 21; Num., i. 413; iv. 254, 514; Deut., i. 497; Judg., ii. 219; iv. 274; 1 Sam., iv. 134, 593; 2 Sam., ii. 148, 220; 1 King, iv. 583, 584; Job, ii. 200–1; iii. 244–5, 258, 260; iv. 134, 349, 532, 549, 584; Psalms, i. 401, 453, 458, 497; ii. 333, 351, 353, 374; iii. 30, 200, 493, 496; iv. 144, 168, 234, 250, 322, 529; v. 104; Prov., i. 507; ii. 199; iv. 72, 139, 219, 501; Eccl., ii. 426; iii. 44, 349; iv. 43, 138, 488; Song Sol., iv. 127; iii. 198; Isa., iii. 258, 419; iv. 134, 213, 583; Ezek., iii. 201, 233, 358, 386, Dan., iii. 174; iv. 134; v. 20; Hab., iii. 338–9;

Zech., iii. 256; Wisd., i. 109; ii. 354, 378; v. 102; Ecclus., i. 290–1; ii. 170, 375; iii. 261, 557; iv. 215, 394; v. 102; Bel & Dr., i. 313; 2 Macc., iii. 231; Matt., ii. 199, 405, 502; iii. 328, 329; iv. 117–18, 273; v. 85, 133; Mark, iv. 73; Luke, i. 491, 510; ii. 314; iii. 514; v. 166; John, ii. 313; iii. 256; iv. 550; Acts, ii. 73; v. 165–6; Rom., ii. 331; 1 Cor., ii. 333, 422; iv. 125, 322, 585; v. 52, 104, 166; 2 Cor., iv. 321, 583, 585; v. 133, 166; Eph., iii. 256; 1 Thess., ii. 127; Heb., ii. 137; iii. 256; iv. 550, 584; v. 21, 52; 2 Pet., ii. 127; iv. 585; v. 21; 1 John, ii. 577; Rev., ii. 77, 250; iii. 147, 331, 358; iv. 583; v. 21.

Bible and Three Crowns (bookseller's shop), ii. 250.

BIBLIS, every woman's rival, ii. 237.

Bicknell, Mary (actress): her dancing, iii. 395; MARIAMNE in No. 466(?), iv. 148.

Bienséance, ii. 128, 318.

Bigotry: allegorical figure of, i. 16; of atheists and infidels, ii. 230; of freethinkers, ii. 412; criminal in its nature, iii. 495.

Bill 'for the better preserving of the female game', iii. 194.

Bill(s) of mortality: made up by parish-clerks, ii. 67; iii. 402; of those who have taken the Lovers' Leap, ii. 406–9; an argument for Providence, iii. 27–28; of those who have 'died from love', iii. 417–18; politicians within the, iii. 507.

Bills of fortune-tellers, ii. 250.

Billet(s)-doux, i. 120, 375; ii. 571; iii. 381, 478; iv. 513, 598; v. 97.

Billets: little brown b. of quack doctors, iv. 58.

Billiard-tables, i. 231.

Billingsgate, our satire only ribaldry and, iv. 88.

Bincum Bancum, v. 101, 129.

Bin-Ortoc, father of Fadlallah, iv. 576.

Biographia Britannica, i. xxvi; iv. *252*; v. *3*, *61*, *146*.

Biography: interest in b. of an author, i. 1; boys may learn notions of courage, &c., from, iii. 247.

Bion (of Borysthenes), a saying of, iv. 564.

Birch, Thomas, iii. *208*, *366*; iv. *551*; v. *162*.

Bird, William (servant at St. James's Coffee-house), i. 104.

Birds: use of, in opera, i. 24–27; of England practise singing under b. of

warmer climates, i. 121; a school for b. 'of the loquacious kind', i. 151-2; on fans, i. 427; males alone have voices and beautiful head-dresses, ii. 9; duties of males and females in care of young, ii. 9; catching b. by imitating their voices, ii. 111; and invention of musical instruments, iii. 352; courtship of, often determined by colour, iii. 542-3; music of, pleasing to imagination, iii. 544; encouraged to nest in a garden, iv. 189-92; reading fortunes in flights of, iv. 292; understanding language of, iv. 319; an imitator of singing, iv. 546; bird-catchers, iv. 578; a consort of singing, v. 2.

Birth: advantages of, to be supported by collateral eminence, ii. 292; b., title or riches constitute quality of fortune, ii. 352; not to be ashamed of, ii. 401; high b. involves obligations of doing good, ii. 462; gifts of, so-called and actual, iv. 390-1.

Birthday: furnishes conversation, i. 67; 'dressed for a ball or a', ii. 531; the last b. massacre (the Queen's birthday ball), iii. 418.

Birth-night (evening of a royal birthday), appearing *à la mode de Paris* on the next, ii. 579.

Birth-right, selling the b. of Britons 'for a shilling', ii. 285.

Births, nice proportion between deaths and, iii. 27-28.

BISCUIT, EDWARD (Sir ROGER's butler), letter from, iv. 339-41.

Bishops: addicted to puns in reign of James I, i. 260; the 'burthensome finery' of, iii. 348; trial of the seven, v. *175*.

Bitch, example of parental love in a, i. 491.

'Bite the hand that feeds him', i. 148.

'Biting' and 'Biters': defined, i. 203, 223; iv. 289; a common bite of WILL HONEYCOMB's, ii. 111; anecdote of, iv. 290.

Biton and Cleobis, story of, iv. 214.

Black: hood used by CORNELIA, ii. 532; recommended for dark complexion, ii. 533; clothes of parish clerks, iii. 401-2; wig, iv. 222; gowns among Mr. SPECTATOR's enemies, v. 66.

Black (man, men), i. 1; ii. 518; iii. 240; a b. swarthy French man, ii. 183; the Trunk-maker a large, ii. 414; a b. gentlewoman, iii. 569; letter from a, iv. 220-2; 'tall or short, black or fair', iv. 356; a tall, broad-shouldered, impudent, b. fellow, iv. 515.

Black Prince, the: military exploits of, ii. 151; Sir ROGER gave us the whole history of, iii. 215.

Black River, at Coverley Hall estate, i. 446.

Black (proverbial phrases): *in black and white*, iii. 17; *to say b. is her eye*, i. 341; *to call b. white, or white b.*, ii. 1.

Black-a-moor(s), i. 273; ii. 29; iii. 69.

Blackbirds, in a garden, iv. 189.

Blacking for shoes, the author of, iv. 129.

Blackmore, Sir Richard: i. *141, 262*; ii. *46, 356, 379*; Preface to *Prince Arthur* quoted, i. 29-30; *The Creation* 'one of the most useful and noble productions in our English verse', iii. 261; *The Nature of Man*, iii. *461*; Book 6 of *The Creation* describes human anatomy 'with great perspicuity and elegance', iv. 444.

Blacksmith: man who put his son to a, ii. 335; Care described as a b. in Spenser, iv. 430.

Blacksmith's apprentice, his dispute with a hackney-coachman, ii. 291.

Blackstone, Sir William, i. *480*; ii. *214*; iv. *290-1*.

Blackwell, Lambert (a director of S. Sea Co.), a subscriber, i. *xci*.

Bladder, stone in the, iv. 510.

Bladders, filled with wind and froth, in a beau's head, ii. 571.

Blade, Gentlemen of the: a letter received from, iv. 533.

Bladen, Martin, translation of Caesar, i. *90*.

Bladud, History of King (puppet show), i. *61, 130*.

Blair, Hugh: on Addison's style, i. xcix; *Lectures*, iii. *550*.

Bland, Henry, Latin translation of passage in *Cato*, v. *146*.

Blandishment(s): little arts of b. given by nature to the French, ii. 9; of the man of pleasure, ii. 94.

BLANK, T., letter from (on family of BLANKS), iv. 522-4; referred to, iv. 575.

Blank spaces in party pamphlets, iv. 536-41.

Blank verse: best for English tragedy, i. 164; alternating with rhyme a solecism, i. 164-5; needs assistance to keep it from flatness of prose, iii. 14.

Blanks: of Society, i. 18, 46; the ancient family of, iv. 522-4, 575.

BLAST, Lady, a whisperer of scandal, iv. 113.

Bleeding: advertised for threepence, iv. 59; seldom of use but to the idle

and intemperate, iv. 264; to prevent fever, iv. 559.

Blemishes: to be found in most shining characters, ii. 466; publishing b. in characters of others, ii. 494; and imperfections revealed after marriage, ii. 516.

Blenheim, battle of, i. 110; ii. 151–2; in tapestry, v. 72; and Ramillies, v. 95.

Blenheim Palace, iii. 339; collection of letters from, i. xl; rebus on, i. 251; gardens at, iv. 191.

Blessings: apparent b. may have dreadful consequences, ii. 311; balanced against calamities, iv. 136; hard to distinguish from calamities, iv. 214.

BLIGHT, the Widow, and JOHN MILLDEW, iv. 93.

Blind: Raphael's painting of the man born b., ii. 379; can trace lines in an image, iii. 559; an establishment for treatment of, desirable, iv. 168–9; the b. at the Royal Exchange, iv. 307.

Blind Man's Buff: account of a game, ii. 452; the play of, iv. 100.

Blindness: Milton's complaint of his, iii. 61; iv. 172; counterfeited by beggars, iv. 11–12; cures of, iv. 168–73.

BLINKO, ROGER, 'slain by a whitewash', iii. 418.

Blistering: seldom of use but to the idle and intemperate, iv. 264.

BLITHE, Lady, iii. 182–4.

Blois, PHARAMOND's court at, i. 412.

Blondes and brunettes, which more attractive (?), iii. 17–18, 483–5.

Blood: of women more refined (?), ii. 8; a 'milkiness of b.', ii. 197; effect on, of a cold bath, ii. 383; 'as the b., so is the milk', ii. 456; of the gods not real b., ii. 570; iii. 232; letting b. to prevent fevers, iii. 383; iv. 559; good-nature a sweetener of, iv. 460.— Circulation of, promoted by exercise, ii. 264; discovery of, iv. 441; checked by ligatures of English dress, iv. 571.— Blood-vessels, ii. 572.

Blood, runs in the (prov.), iv. 105–6.

Bloodshed on the stage, i. 187–9.

Blots: standers-by discover, i. 5; persons shrewd at hitting, ii. 467.

Blount, Thomas: Les Termes de la Ley, iii. 189; Law Dictionary, v. 100, 101; Fragmenta antiquitatis, v. 100.

Blount, Sir Thomas Pope, i. 162; ii. 127.

Blue hoods, ii. 532, 557; sky-coloured garments, ii. 533.

BLUEGARTER, ALICE, letter from (on MATILDA MOHAIR), iv. 261.

BLUEMANTLE, Lady, a malicious gossip, iv. 2.

Blundel, ——, notes on Spectator, i. 97; iii. 289.

Blunderbuss: a horse, ii. 117; a politician called a bl–nd–rb–ss, iv. 538; blunderbusses, iii. 194.

Blunt, Charles, a Director of S. Sea Co., a subscriber, i. xc.

Blunt, John, a Director of S. Sea Co., a subscriber, i. xc; iv. 538.

Blunt, Ned, in The Rover, i. 218.

Blush, a, now out of fashion, i. 193; 'slain by a', iii. 418.

Blushing, injures the complexion, i. 282; a beau deprived of the faculty of, ii. 572; 'that ambiguous suffusion', iii. 464.

Blusterers, carrying away the praise of speaking, iv. 218.

Boar: the wild b. in Camilla, letter from, i. 93; referred to, i. 438; blue b. as a sign, i. 116, 197.

Board, man who trod on every other b. in the flooring, v. 159.

Board wages for servants, evil effects of, i. 373–4, 406.

Boarding, ladies and gentlemen b. in the same house, iii. 57.

Boarding school for young gentlewomen, near Stepney, iii. 140, 226, 254.

Boaster: character of the, iv. 36–40; referred to, iv. 75; 'empty boasts and ostentations', ii. 492.

Boat news, an example of, iv. 93.

Boats, making paper b. with his sisters, iv. 210.

Bob (refrain), iii. 413.

Bob wigs, ii. 14; iii. 321.

Boccalini, Traiano: his story of a critic, iii. 38; his fable of traveller and grasshoppers, iii. 325; Dispatches from Parnassus, iv. 329.

Bodenham, John, Wit's Commonwealth, ii. 378; iii. 94.

Bodice, a neat, ii. 576.

Bodkin, stabbing with a, iii. 472; iv. 305.

Body, the human: a system of tubes and glands, i. 471; exercise necessary to, i. 471–4; fable of sedition of members of, ii. 185, 220; fortuitous organization of, one of the great points of atheism, ii. 230; juices of, and disease, ii. 424; a virtuous mind in a fair, ii. 445; an active b. without a quick conception, ii. 504; reading the future from 'signatures' on, iv. 292; the work of an all-wise Providence, iv. 441–4.

Body cloaths, asses kept in, ii. 182.
Boece (or Boethius), Hector: a source of *Macbeth*, ii. 58.
Boethius, Anicius Manlius Severinus, v. 20.
Boeotia, plains of, iv. 325.
Boevey, Catherine. *See* Bovey.
Bohea. *See* Tea.
BOHUN, Lady MARY, an anagram on, i. 255.
Boileau, Nicolas Despréaux: on Virgil and the *clincant* of Tasso, i. 26; satirized stage and court, i. 142; death of, i. *142*; iii. *508*; Dennis's translation of a couplet on, quoted, i. 201; rejected mixed wit, i. 265; on true wit, i. 268; ii. 483; his anecdote of Molière, i. 297; on style of Longinus, i. *430*, *484*; on a simile of Homer, ii. *128*; 'the most correct poet among the moderns', ii. 220; fables of, ii. 220; erred in writing sweeping, condemnatory satires, ii. 320–1; his translation, or rather imitation, of Sappho's ode *Ad Lesbiam* quoted, ii. *391*; translation of *Le Lutrin*, ii. *467*; allegorical figures in *Le Lutrin*, ii. *564*; his answer to Perrault on Homer's similes, iii. 91; on comparisons in epic poems, iii. 91; English translation of *Works*, iii. *91*; on beard of Zoilus, iii. *221*; says 'all men are fools' (*Sat.* iv. 39–40 quoted), iv. 463; a 'true critic', v. 26; mentioned, i. 372; iii. 529; iv. *362*.
Boiled dumpling, affair of the, iv. 588.
Bold: b. tongue and feeble arm of Drances, ii. 399; b. but just metaphors in *PL*, iii. 12.
Bold, Charles the. *See* Burgundy.
Boldness: of Lucifer in *PL*, iii. 114; of carriage, and wantonness, iii. 496.
Boleyn, Anne, her letter to Henry VIII quoted, iii. 487–9.
Bolingbroke, Henry St. John, Viscount: and Swift, i. xvii; referred to (?), ii. 247; iv. 398.
Bologna, Giovanni (sculptor), i. *59*.
Bolonia lap-dog, iv. 271.
Bolus, or electuary, i. 353.
Bombast, in English tragedy, i. 166, 171.
BOMBYCA, the musician, ii. 406.
Bona Dea, Clodius intruding on rites of, ii. 346.
Bond, John, notes on Horace, iii. 18.
Bond, Mrs., news-shop: *Spectator* sold by, i. xxiv; locations of, i. *xxv*.
Bond, William, continuation of *Spectator*, i. lxxvi.
Bone-lace, i. 271, 416.
Bonfire: of head-dresses, i. 414; to cele-

brate the Coronation, v. 106; in Stratford-upon-Avon, v. 151.
Bonnet, small b. (of men) in Henry VII's time, i. 450.
Bononcini, Antonio, composer of *Camilla*, i. *79*; ii. *397*.
Bononcini, Giovanni, composer of *Almahide*, i. *79*; ii. *397*.
Bonosus (a Gaul), 'not a man but a bottle', iv. 542–3.
Booby: 'like a great surprized', i. 404; 'the b. his heir', ii. 254.
Book: effect of a well-written, i. 45; *a great b. a great evil* (prov.), i. 506; Clarke's edition of Caesar 'the finest b. that I have ever seen', iii. 382.
Bookish husband, XANTIPPE married to a, iv. 209.
Book-learning, a youth's comprehensive knowledge of all, iii. 367.
Book-pedant, the most supportable of all pedants, i. 438.
Books: counterfeit b. of wood, i. 153; useful contrasted with diverting, i. 158; of devotion for women, i. 340–1; ignoble fate of some, i. 361; of chivalry, i. 417; iii. 129; now judged by party standards, i. 510–11; the legacies a great genius leaves to mankind, ii. 154; ambition the motive for writing, ii. 490; frequently given at funerals, iv. 232; Gregorio Leti published as many b. as he was years old, v. 159; knowledge of, like a dark lantern, v. 176. See also Lady's Library; Women, Reading for.
Bookseller(s): their recommendations of books for women, i. 389–91; books upon the rails of ANTHONY TITLE-PAGE's shop, iii. 94; erudite sign-posts of, iii. 348; incident in a French b.'s shop, iv. 41–42; Mr. SPECTATOR's encounter with a young woman in a b.'s shop, iv. 412.
BOON, Lady MARY, an anagram on, i. 255.
Boot, a cook living at the sign of the, i. 117.
Booth, Barton: as Othello, i. *170*; iii. *236*; in *The Lancashire Witches*, ii. 57; Welford in *The Scornful Lady*, ii. 554; Pyrrhus in *The Distressed Mother*, iii. *31*, 236; other roles of, iii. *236*.
Boots, little, i. 451.
Borysthenes, the (Dnieper), interest in people who live upon, iv. 91.
Boscawen, Hugh, a subscriber, i. *lxxxviii*.
Bosom: of mistress compared to snow, i. 264, 273; the finest neck and, ii. 535; 'to be taught the risings of the', ii. *581*.

Bossuet, Jacques-Bénigne, Sermon *sur la mort*, iii. *28*.

Boswell, James, on the *Spectator*, i. xcvii.

Bothmar, Johann Caspar von (Elector of Hanover's Envoy), iii. *439*, 440, 441.

Bottle: to crack a, ii. 411; after the second, iii. *398*; a mistress brings sorrow, a b. madness, iii. 407; 'drunk a full b. to her share', iii. 532.

Bottle-companion, i. 377; *The Bottle-Companion*, iii. *438*.

Bottle-conversation, iv. 299.

Bottoms, Winding up your (prov.), iv. *462*.

Bouchain, besieged by the French, iv. 407.

Bouhours, Dominique: 'the most penetrating of all the French critics', i. 268; on the basis of true wit, i. 268; referred to, iv. *362*.

Boul, Mr. (in Chandos Street), ii. 381.

Boulter, Mrs., news-shop: *Spectator* sold by, i. xxiv; appeared before Queen's Bench, i. xxv.

Bounce(s), at the door, iii. 414, 436.

Bounty (-ies): given to MOLL WHITE, i. 482; for taking excess of corn off our hands, ii. 285; to foreigners of no name or merit, ii. 381.

Bourbon, House of, discussed in St. James's Coffee-house, iii. 507.

Bourgeois, Louis, ii. *305*.

Boutell, Mrs. (actress), in Dryden's *Tyrannic Love*, iii. *266*.

Bouts-rimés: examples of false wit, i. 256–8; example of, from *Mercure Galant*, i. 257; Ménage on, i. 258; ridiculed by Sarasin, i. 258.

Bovey, Catherine, the original of the PERVERSE WIDOW?, iv. *463*.

Bow (weapon): Persian boys instructed in use of, i. 418; English statute regarding the long, ii. 133.

Bow (inclination of body or head): party-spirit displayed in return of the, ii. 2; in salutation, ii. 433–4; persons unwilling to confer a, ii. 508; making a b. out of a coach in full speed, ii. 508–9; politicians taught the, iii. 90.

Bow-window, iii. 417.

Bowden, Mr., his 'Issue-Pease and Plaisters' advertised, iv. *61*.

Bowen, William (actor): as a witch in *Macbeth*, i. *194*; as the shoemaker in *The Man of Mode*, i. *278*.

Bower(s): woods twisted into, i. 158; Rosamond's, ii. 596; contrivers of, like romance writers, iv. 190; of Bliss in Spenser, iv. 429.

Bowles, Brig. Phineas, a subscriber, i. lxxxix.

Bowling-Green, i. 231, 446; party-spirit at a, ii. 3–4; public, v. 150.

Bowman, John (actor), Phoenix in *The Distressed Mother*, iii. *239*.

Bowyer, William, iii. *409*.

Box(es): for alms for prisoners, i. 350; of pictures in which a face can be changed into a variety of representations, ii. 29; at an inn, ii. 536; a show of midgets carried in a, ii. 557; at an ale-house, iv. 80; at Christmas, iv. 307.

Box(es) at the theatre: i. 194; ii. 59; immodest conversation in, ii. 440; in the hinder part of the, ii. 531; handing a lady out of a, ii. 532; like beds of tulips, ii. 552; the Queen's, iii. 418; men prating aloud in, v. 58. — FRONT BOXES: at the opera, iii. 184; in Drury Lane, iii. 417; seats in, retained by servants for their masters, iv. 523; mentioned, v. 88. — SIDE BOXES: i. 346, 375; on the stage, ii. 434; 'taken his stand in a', iii. 127. — MIDDLE BOXES, i. 347.

Box on the ear, ii. 407; iii. 155; iv. 224.

Boxing, i. 474; part of the Roman Pentathlon, ii. 133; men who have boxed before Charles II, iv. 133; boxing-matches, v. 151.

Boy: of the coffee-house, i. 196, 371; ii. 92, 552; a smock-faced, i. 197; story of b. stolen by gypsies, ii. 17–18; Spartan b. and the fox, ii. 116; praising the wit of her little b. before he is able to speak, ii. 459; a little chub-faced, iii. 70; who forms parties at school, iii. 133.

Boyer, Abel, ii. *86*, 427.

Boyle, Henry (afterwards Lord Carleton), Vol. iii dedicated to, v. 177.

Boyle, John (afterwards 5th Earl of Orrery), ii. *183*.

Boyle, Robert: on wit and judgement, i. *263*; on study of a mineral, i. 398; on the mole, i. 496; quoted, ii. *128*; v. *176*; and thermometric experiments, ii. *426*, *519*; complied with public forms of worship, iii. 460; Burnet's sermon at his funeral, iv. 394–5; always paused at name of God, iv. 395; a devout scientist, iv. 488; referred to(?), v. 138.

Boys: fable of b. and the frogs, i. 100; we adorn their minds and neglect their bodies, i. 282; their lack of social graces ('a man's life half spent before he is taken notice of'), i. 282; education of Persian, i. 418; in charity school at St. Bride's, iii. 49; treatment of, in school, iii. 134. *See also* Education.

Bracelet(s): a lover's gift, ii. 407; and lockets, iv. 84; set with jewels, iv. 340.

Brachman. *See* Brahmin.

Bracknock, Mrs. (apothecary), i. *139*; iii. *418*; iv. *130*.

Bracton, Henry de, on correction of wives, iv. 199, 209.

Bradbury, Thomas, referred to (?), iv. *251-2*.

Bradshaw, Lucretia: as Monimia in *The Orphan*, i. *169*; in *The Lancashire Witches*, ii. *57*.

Brady, Nicholas: praised as schoolmaster, ii. 162 & n.; Tate and Brady's new version of Psalms, ii. *305*.

Brag-table, members of the, iii. 112.

Brahmin(s): a college of, iii. 274; a secret imparted by a, iv. 577.

Brandenburg, Albert Frederick of, iv. *571*.

Brandy: gives a flush to the face, i. 243; barrels of, i. 310; mirth compared to, ii. 268.

Brass: youth who admired his figure in, ii. 71; twanking of a b. kettle, ii. 475; and pewter, iii. 189, 210.

Brave man: spectacle of, superior to his sufferings, i. 163-4; ii. 422; often appears timorous before public, ii. 398.

Bravery: true b. marked by greatness of mind, iii. 304; of Isadas in Sparta, iv. 528.

Bravoes: dogged by b. in Rome, ii. 38.

Brawl, the French, i. 284.

Brawn, and minced-pies on New Year's Day, v. 150.

Brazil (snuff), iii. *278, 279*.

Breach, of promise between two courtiers, ii. 180; of Leagues, ii. 186.

Bread, and butter, iii. 182; iv. 231.

Break (fail in business): how referred to in Holland, ii. 187; tradesmen b. who have met with no misfortune, ii. 252; in danger of breaking, ii. 327.

Break measures, ii. 519.

Break one's mind (to propose), ii. 357, 513.

Break the ice (prov.), ii. 560; iv. 224.

Breakfast, *Spectator* served with the coffee at, iv. 230.

Breast: a small patch worn on her, ii. 580; the open b. and the art military, iv. 345.

Bredes: YARICO dressed in shells, bugles, and, i. 50.

Breeches, i. 215; ii. 276; *wearing the b.* (prov.), i. 435; iv. 210; trunk b., ii. 7; and doublet of one piece of cloth, iv. 571.

Breeding: fine *v.* good, i. 282; a man of,

ii. 574; pedants in, iii. 15; a kind of dancing-school b., iv. 371.

Breeding, Good: importance of knowing rules of, i. 285-7; effect on our conversations, i. 467; in town and country, i. 486-9; an outward show of, ii. 3; and ceremony turning upon matters of ill-health, ii. 67; in AMARYLLIS, ii. 69; which is exclusive of morality, ii. 112; request for a *Spectator* wholly writ upon, ii. 120; an imitation and mimicry of good nature, ii. 165; 'a kind of artificial humanity', ii. 165; French, admired by 'Salamanders', ii. 276; human nature now lost under, ii. 318; salutation as a piece of, ii. 358; politeness which recommends impudence as, ii. 400; towards a wife, ii. 418; in the country, ii. 433; has made the tongue falsify the heart, ii. 479; accomplishments which go with, iii. 205; the *Spectator* has made learning a part of, iv. 128; the court the standard of, iv. 534.

Bribing: as a method of persuasion, ii. 431; as a method of making one's court, iv. 478-9; street-venders, ii. 476.

Brick-dust: cries of retailers of, ii. 475; Rabelais's wrapping b. in papers as poison, iii. 4.

Bride: to give the, ii. 23; gives her hand and says 'I do', ii. 479.

Bride-cake, sleeping on a slice of, v. 41.

BRIDEGROOM, ROBIN, letter from, iii. 370.

Brideman, at a wedding, ii. 23.

Bridewells, and work-houses, in Europe, v. 44.

Bridge(s): beggars at the end of, i. 208; of human life, ii. 123; greatest conquerors break down b. behind them, iii. 53; an half-way, iv. 316.

Bridges, Brook (a Director of the Bank), a subscriber, i. *xc*.

Bridges, John, offers a reward, iii. *302*.

Bright: 'what they call b. to entertain her', i. 159.

BRILLIANT, Mrs., her necklace, iii. 183.

Brisk: and airy, ii. 8; and lively, ii. 425.

Bristow, Robert (a Director of the Bank), a subscriber, i. *xc*.

Britannick Beautifier: advertisement for, iv. *130, 459-60*; testimonial to, iv. 459.

British Apollo, iv. *173*; v. *102*; distribution of, i. *xxiv*; materials in, i. xxxvii; advertisements in, i. lxix; quoted, i. *33, 199*; ii. *91, 225, 234, 572*; iv. *15, 61*.

British: army in Caesar's time, i. 90; artisans, ii. 181; blood spoiled with

foreign mixtures, ii. 285; 'The B. Common' (the sea), i. 10; B. Hippocrates, cosmetic of, i. 221–2; B. Journal, ii. 238; ladies contrasted with Picts, i. 174; ladies who write Pindarics, iii. 376; manufacture, i. 296; B. Merchant, i. lii; B. Mercury, ii. 423; iii. 383, 395, 439; v. 42; French truth and B. policy make a conspicuous figure in Nothing, iii. 100; B. Schools of Politics (coffee-houses), iii. 100; B. Senate, v. 178; B. Spectator, iii. 558.

Britomartis, in Spenser, represents chastity, iv. 429.

Britons, ancient, saw their defeat celebrated on the Roman stage, ii. 150.

BRITTLE, BARNABY, letter from (on his wife), ii. 327.

Britton, Thomas, the small-coal-man in No. 597(?), v. 42.

Broad expressions, offensive, iii. 497.

BROADBRIM, HEZEKIAH, letter from (on his daughter TABITHA and his wife SUSANNA), ii. 577.

Brocas, Sir Bernard, tomb of, iii. 214.

Brocades: and ribbons from France, i. 192, 225; petticoats of, i. 295, 344; and silks in Motteux's shop, iii. 26; iv. 479; and embroidery, iv. 271; b. versus grogram, iv. 390.

Brockbank, Thomas, Diary, i. 56.

Broken credit, allegorical figure of, iv. 124; broken officer, suitor of the Widow WILDFIRE, iv. 517; broken views, acting by, ii. 136.

Broker, letter from a, iii. 401–2.

Brome, Dr. ——, the BROMIUS of No. 302(?), iii. 79.

Brome, Richard, The Northern Lass, Bullfinch in, ii. 240; iv. 157.

BROMIUS (clergyman), and EMILIA, iii. 81.

Brook and Hellier, ii. 529; iii. 155; a letter in praise of, iii. 353–5.

Brooke, Thomas (wine merchant). See Brook and Hellier.

Broth: and soup, iii. 111; a mess of, at the chop-house, iv. 102.

Brothel: account of a girl in a, ii. 245–7; men who visit, to see the world, ii. 247; indigent wickedness expelled the harbours of the, ii. 537; iii. 16.

Brother: of the Quill, iv. 478; complaint regarding an unkind, v. 116.

Brothers: 'all the b. were valiant', i. 417; of the Whip, iv. 267.

Brow: politicians taught to draw the b. up in wrinkles, iii. 98; a contracted b. a sign of learning, iv. 344.

Brown, Thomas ('Tom'), i. 264, 450; ii. 456; iii. 214, 215, 216, 397; on Bully Dawson, i. 8; Letters, i. 59, 102, 202; Amusements, i. 116; Dialogues, i. 254; translation of Lucian, iii. 468; 'of facetious memory', iv. 537; on the Dutch, iv. 564.

BROWN, ——: 'Old Brown of England', v. 106.

Brown complexion: Ovid recommends a white hood for, ii. 533; a fair or a b. woman more beautiful(?), iii. 17–18.

Brown study, in a (prov.), iii. 18.

Browne, Sir Thomas: Religio Medici quoted, ii. 199, 227–8; Pseudodoxia epidemica, iii. 195.

Browne, William, epitaph on Sir Philip Sidney's sister quoted, iii. 185.

Bruin, in Hudibras, i. 252–3.

BRUNETTA and PHILLIS, rivalry of, i. 342–4.

Brunettes: superior to blondes(?), iii. 17–18; a punning letter on, iii. 483–5.

Bruno, Giordano, plan of his Spaccio de la Bestia trionfante, iii. 459–60.

Brushes, ii. 237; iv. 195.

Brussels, advices from, iv. 90.

Brutum fulmen, ii. 416.

Brutus, D. Junius (husband of Sempronia), iv. 36.

Brutus, L. Junius, iv. 304.

Brutus, M. Junius: represented by Shakespeare without trappings and equipage, i. 180; his apostrophe to virtue, iii. 43–44; mentioned, iii. 369; received aid from Atticus, iii. 447; a saying of, iv. 115; tried to free Rome from tyranny, iv. 304; on Cicero's vanity, iv. 519; and Portia remarkable for virtue and affection, v. 75.

Bubble, 'she has bubbled him out of his youth', i. 377.

Bubbles: pursuit of, ii. 124; cheats and b. in every generation, iv. 58.

Bubo, accompanying a clap, iv. 59.

Bucephalus (Alexander's horse), i. 130, 197.

Buck, Timothy (prize-fighter), iv. 30–35.

Buckingham, George Villiers, 1st Duke: assassinated by Felton, iv. 220.

Buckingham, George Villiers, 2nd Duke, i. 264; ii. 138; iv. 403; on the project of a Dutch mechanic, iii. 357; his jests on long-chinned persons(?), iii. 396; Advice to a Painter, iii. 397; manufacture of glass, iv. 308. — The Rehearsal: dance of sun, moon and earth in, i. 16; Drawcansir in, i. 72; Thunder in, i. 150; army in, i. 179; 'Egad and all that', i. 345; epilogue to,

iii. 267; 'spirits must not be confined to speak sense', iii. 571; Estcourt as Bayes in, iv. 155.

Buckle: letting a wig lie in, ii. 14; tongue to a shoe-buckle, iii. 154, 155.

Buckley, Samuel, i. xx–xxi, 6; iii. 124; letters to be left with, i. 35; 'my publisher', i. 44; printer of Daily Courant, i. 52; 'my bookseller', i. 245; ii. 241; letter addressed to, ii. 241; moved to Amen-Corner, iv. 502.

Buckram, a prude armed in whale-bone and, ii. 346.

Bud, nip him in the (prov.), iv. 374.

Buda, Siege of, iii. 70.

Budgell, Eustace: contributions to Spectator, i. li–lii; to 2nd series, i. lxxiv, lxxvii–lxxviii; a subscriber, i. lxxxviii; member of the Temple, i. 9; Letter to Cleomenes, i. 30; iv. 528; assisted by Addison, ii. 274; Letters of Love and Gallantry dedicated to, ii. 427; The Bee, iii. 265, 531; iv. 339; No. 425 attributed to, iii. 597; on death of Sir ROGER, iv. 339; letter in No. 539 attributed to, iv. 425; author of papers signed X, iv. 493; No. 591 attributed to, v. 24; departure for Dublin, v. 37. — Epilogue to 'The Distressed Mother': iii. 31, 239; iv. 493; attacked, iii. 250–4; defended by PHILOMEIDES, iii. 265–9.

Budgell, Gilbert, verses in No. 591 attributed to, v. 24–25.

Buff, made b. of his skin, i. 185.

Buffoon(s): b. readers, i. 320; Thersites a mimic and, ii. 326; who ridicule writings of others, ii. 467; figure made by, iii. 152; Leo X fond of, iv. 263–4.

Buffoonery, passing for wit, iv. 58.

Bugles: YARICO dressed in shells, b. and bredes, i. 50.

Bulfinch, in The Northern Lass, ii. 240; iv. 157.

Bull, Richard, and family, subscribers, i. xcii.

Bull, eye of, applied to Hera, ii. 471.

Bull-baiting, i. 129.

Bull-beggars, invented to frighten wives and daughters, iii. 292.

Bull-dogs, tame only when not offended, iv. 40.

Bull-fights, in Spain, i. 417.

Bull-rush, shaking of a, i. 54.

Bullock, Christopher (actor), as Statira, i. 128.

Bullock, Gabriel, letter to Margaret Clark, iii. 189, 209.

Bullock, Hildebrand (actor), i. 151.

Bullock, William (actor): as Sir Martin Mar-All, i. 24; as Roxana, i. 128; petitions to be Hephestion, i. 151 [may refer to Bullock, jun.]; Boniface in The Beaux' Stratagem, i. 151; iv. 388; a witch in Macbeth, i. 151, 194; Sir Bookish Outside in Injured Love, i. 151; 'in a short coat', i. 191; in The Lancashire Witches, ii. 57; descended from Gabriel Bullock, iii. 209; as Sir Thomas Testy in Doggett's Country Wake, iv. 283; his height and gracefulness, iv. 388; Sir Harry Gubbin in The Tender Husband, iv. 388; inserting words of his own, iv. 427.

Bullock, William, jun. (actor): Hephestion in The Rival Queens, i. 151; Young Bell-Air in The Man of Mode, i. 278; in The Lancashire Witches, ii. 57.

Bully (-ies): country, i. 306; rakes and, i. 345; a dwarf who is a, ii. 557; and scowrers among the Mohocks, iii. 188.

BUMPER, FILL, cousin of TOM NIMBLE, iv. 587.

Bumper, drinking a, ii. 530; iv. 177, 180; v. 150.

Bumpkin, a country, and his sister, ii. 537.

Bunyan, John, i. xcv, 59; not a master of the sublime, iv. 365.

Burden, a fellow with a b. on his head, iii. 322.

Burdock, Samuel, servant at St. James's Coffee-house, i. 104.

Burges, Thomas (druggist), advertises snuff, iii. 278.

Burgundy, Charles, Duke of, his punishment of Rhynsault, iv. 241–4.

Burgundy and champagne, iii. 207.

Buridan's ass, ii. 248, 270, 286.

Burleigh, Ferdinand (bookseller), i. 52.

Burlesque: a form of wit, i. 265; moderns exceed ancients in, ii. 467; and comedy distinguished, ii. 467; two kinds of, ii. 467–8; use of heroic verse or doggerel in, ii. 468; examples of, in Homer, ii. 589; in Claudian, iii. 230; writers of, ranked below writers of epic, iv. 388; pictures 'which Italians call Caracaturas', iv. 417; account of a b. musician, iv. 545–6; little b. authors abound in pert phrases, v. 105.

Burlington, Richard Boyle, 3rd Earl of, a subscriber, i. lxxxviii.

Burnaby, Eustace, iii. 379.

Burnaby, William: The Ladies Visiting-Day, i. 104; The Modish Husband, iii. 191; The Reform'd Wife, iii. 214.

Burnet, Gilbert, i. xxvi; on the English language, i. 162; an inscription quoted

in his *Travels*, i. 198; his *History* quoted, ii. *48*; iii. *263, 264*; his *History of the Reformation*, iv. 142; his funeral sermon on Robert Boyle, iv. 394–5.

Burnet, Dr. Thomas, 'that admirable writer', ii. 75; his *Theory of the Earth* quoted, i. 160; ii. *67–68, 76–77*; v. 126.

Burnet, Thomas (son of Gilbert): *Second Tale of a Tub*, i. *56–57, 64, 130*; iv. *107*; letters, i. *41*; iii. *186–7, 253*.

Burning-glasses: in Cowley's poems, i. 266; in poems of mixed wit, i. 273.

Burton, Robert, *Anatomy of Melancholy*, i. *263*; ii. *20, 450, 451*; iv. *86, 166, 239, 506*; iv. *521*.

Burton, Jonathan (linen-draper), iii. *162*.

Burton Ale, iii. 438.

Bury, visited by SIMON HONEYCOMB, ii. 104.

Burying tickets, black wax from, iv. 15.

Busby, Richard: his tomb in Westminster Abbey, iii. 214; severity of, iii. 134.

Bush, flaming: Moses and, ii. 600; a great genius compared to, iii. 526.

Busie, in *The Man of Mode*, i. 279.

BUSIE, MARTHA, letter from, iii. 226.

Business: letter from a man of, i. 113–14; dull fellows, good men of, i. 184; language used in, ii. 109; dull rogues of, ii. 219; the pleasure of some men, ii. 296; a dull man's application to, ii. 364; Sir ANDREW alternates between b. and pleasure, ii. 401; a man out of all, ii. 474; desirable to be no man's competitor in, ii. 553; in b. fools sometimes pretend to be knaves, ii. 567; method in, as a means of gaining riches, iii. 2; methods of selling, iii. 94–95; man of b. best formed by public education, iii. 133; following b. and pleasure, iii. 395; men of b. use mean and familiar allusions, iii. 578; men of learning who take to, iv. 161.

Business (general occupation): the 'Lowngers' enemies to, i. 230; the great should regard b. rather than ostentation, ii. 257; men of b. and bustle in the world, ii. 268; aversion to all manner of, iii. 6; Wharton 'master of the whole compass of', v. 181.

Buskin, the dignity of the, iv. 388.

Bussy d'Amboise, anecdote of, iv. 153.

Busy, the: contrasted with the learned, ii. 362; mankind made up of the b. and the idle, v. 132.

Butcher(s), i. 230; raillery with the barbarity of, iii. 585.

BUTLER, ROBERT, petition of, ii. 294.

Butler, Samuel, *Hudibras*: Hudibras a celebrated ill face, i. 77; 'the incomparable H.' admired more for its double rhymes, i. 258; has a passage ridiculing *Chevy Chase*, i. 320; imitating doggerel expressions in, ii. 35; new edition of, advertised, ii. *35*; on wagerers, ii. 71; effectual to cure the extravagances of love, ii. 385; speaks of wagers used as arguments, ii. 430; compares the tongue to a race-horse, ii. 460; would have been more agreeable if set out in heroic verse, ii. 468; quoted, i. 230, 252–3, 258; ii. 273; iii. *127, 222*; iv. 514; mentioned, i. *254, 262, 451, 509*; ii. *2, 467*; iii. *292*; iv. *414*; v. *151*.

Butler, i. 408; Miss JENNY had run away with, iii. 344; 'in love with her father's', iv. 261; — Sir ROGER'S. *See* BISCUIT and COVERLEY.

Butter-making, hindered by witches, i. 481.

Butterflies, collectors of, i. 91.

Button, Daniel, iv. 499.

Button, the frosted, on men's coats, iii. 163.

Buttons: small, i. 451; silver hasps instead of, ii. 193; on men's dress, ii. 526.

Button-makers, petition of, ii. 193.

Butts in conversation, i. 204, 223; ii. 191.

Buy cheap and sell dear (prov.), ii. 403.

Buyer look to it, Let the (prov.), ii. 180.

Buz (busy rumour): of politics, iii. 507; 'take the buz', v. 137.

By-coffee-house, in a narrow lane, iii. 509.

Byfield, Dr., his Sal Oleosum Volatile advertised, iv. 61.

Byrom, John, contributions to *Spectator*, i. lxxx–lxxxi; v. *3–4, 61*.

Bysshe, Edward, *Art of English Poetry*, i. *258*; ii. *436*.

C., speculation on *Spectators* signed, ii. 360; letter from, iv. 220–2.

C., A.: letter from. *See* CARBUNCLE, ALEXANDER.

C., J.: proposes a love-case, v. 115.

C., R.: letter from (on tradesmen), iv. 56–57; epitaph on, iv. 343–4.

C., S.: letter from (on 'starers'), i. 86.

C., T.: remonstrance of (against profanation of the Sabbath), v. 116.

C., W.: letter from (on a generous benefactor), iv. 455–6.

Cabal, a certain female (the Widow-Club), iv. 515.

Cabalistic(al): letters (C, L, and X), ii. 361; words uttered by the dervish, iv. 577.

Cabbages and coleworts, in a garden, iv. 189.

Cacoethes scribendi, or 'itch of writing', iv. 590.

Cacus (son of Vulcan), Sappho compared to, ii. 366.

Caecilius, Longinus' criticism of, i. 245.

CÆLIA: a name used by correspondents, i. 71; of CÆLIA, a beauty who affects the character of a wit, iii. 512.

Caernarvonshire, Wales, ii. 384.

Caesar, Gaius Julius: his generous treatment of Catullus, i. 98; behaviour of, and that of Mr. SPECTATOR, i. 197; and rebus of elephant, i. 250; and Pompey, i. 423; and Cato, i. 423; ii. 166; reported to have lain with Cato's sister, ii. 72; 'If you sing, you sing very ill', ii. 81; mentioned, ii. 114, 396; dictated to three writers at once, ii. 260; might have made an excellent wrestler, ii. 371; covered baldness with laurels, ii. 401; satisfied with his share of life and fame, ii. 497; iv. 150; v. 179; his polite reply, 'a careless fellow', ii. 575; depicted by Shakespeare, ii. 586–7; Cato's suicide when C. destroyed Roman liberty, iii. 33; his regard for decorum in death, iii. 41; prologue to a play on, quoted, iii. 74; Sulla saw many Mariuses in, iii. 99; Prince Eugene compared to, iii. 264; the first to give a tolerable account of England, iii. 382; new edition of his *Commentaries*, iii. 381–2; 'thought nothing done while anything left for him to do', iii. 407; notes for his conduct, iii. 407–8; his reflections on Calpurnia's dream, iii. 408; Atticus a friend to, iii. 447; warned against Ides of March, iii. 480; his genius inclined him to war, iii. 512; had a mind above unmerited reproaches, iv. 44; Cicero's praise of, iv. 150; a 'saying' of, iv. 166; assassination of, iv. 519; his funeral oration on his first wife, v. 75; the poor ambition of a, v. 84; his aim, to gain the highest post in his country, v. 168; Marlborough compared to, v. 179.

Caftan (oriental garment), v. 66.

Cain: murdered Abel because of a religious controversy, ii. 228; Adam's view of C. and Abel, iii. 362; COHU thought to signify, iv. 596.

Cairo, Grand, Mr. SPECTATOR's voyage to, i. 2, 38, 76, 197, 294, 425; ii. 121; v. 65.

Calais, governor of, iii. 303.

Calamity (-ies): one common c. brings men together, i. 124; attendant on poverty, ii. 89; of mankind greater than private griefs, ii. 142; the common c. aggravated by men's cruelty to one another, ii. 164–5; relieving c. of others, ii. 463–4; fickleness of fortune blamed for our, ii. 597; which a weak man suffers from wrong measures, iii. 68; of youth and old age compared, iv. 14; of men laid in a balance, iv. 134–6; impossible always to distinguish blessings from, iv. 214; vision of exchanging human, iv. 506–11; more arise from love than from hatred, v. 23. *See also* Misfortunes.

Calamy, Dr. Benjamin, his sermons preached by Sir ROGER's chaplain, i. 442.

Calamy, Edmund, i. *442*; v. *44*.

Calends of December, Cicero quashed conspiracy of Catiline in, iv. 519.

Calentures, frequent in May, iii. 373.

Caliban, Shakespeare's genius in inventing, ii. 586–7.

Calicoes, iii. 42.

Calidore, in Spenser, iv. 428.

Caligula: wished the city of Rome had but one neck, i. 72; ii. 456; iv. 29; imbibed cruelty from his nurse, ii. 456.

CALLICLEA, full of nameless faults, iii. 40–41.

Callimachus, a great book a great evil, i. *505*.

CALLISTHENES, agreeable in his raillery, iii. 584.

CALLOW, EDWARD, slain by the ogle of a widow, iii. 417.

Calpurnia, wife of Caesar, iii. 408.

Calumny (-ies): and party-spirit, i. 510–11; of a good man concerns all society, ii. 349; and defamation, iv. 86–90; Spenser quoted on avoidance of, iv. 431; evils caused by, v. 31–34.

Calverley, Edmund (stationer), advertises snuff, iii. *278*.

Calvinists, their devotions prompted by fear, ii. 332.

Calvus, Gaius Licinius, style of, criticized by Seneca, iii. 62.

CALYPSO, poem to, on her grotto, v. 161–2.

Calypso and Telemachus (opera), i. *23*; ii. *398*; praised, iii. 514.

Cambray, Archbishop of. *See* Fénelon.

Cambric: and muslins, i. 241; in commodes, ii. 531; in Motteux's shop, iv. 479; thin plaits of, v. 156–7.

Cambridge: Staincoat Hole, iii. 484–5; Hobson's choice originated in, iv. 309.

Cambridge University: the 'Lowngers' at, i. 229–32; formerly infested with puns, i. 261; fens and marshes drained, i. 261; Club of Ugly Faces originally

at, i. 335; Clare Hall, formerly ugliest, now the neatest, i. 335; King's College, i. 335; sermon preached before, ii. 361; Trojan–Grecian hostilities at, ii. 453–4; 'to speak in the language of', ii. 470; letter from Trinity College, iii. 17–18; letter from St. John's College, iii. 483–5; where they grow dumb in study of eloquence, iv. 218; epitaph in King's College Chapel, iv. 343; letter from (on physiognomy), iv. 344–5; Mr. Eusden, of Trinity College, iv. 494; letter from (on Christianity), v. 163–7.

Cambridge Jests, iv. 522.

Camden, William: 'our learned Camden in his *Remains*', i. 250; i. 126, 250–1, 254; ii. 200, 387, 456; iii. 185; iv. 566.

Camels, ii. 126; v. 158.

Camera obscura, at Greenwich, iii. 550.

CAMILLA: party rage in, i. 242; painted in mannish garb, i. 435; letter from (Mrs. Tofts), iv. 55–56.

Camilla, in the *Aeneid*: an example of female passion for dress and show, i. 69; her death described, i. 302; a beautiful improvement on Homer, ii. 563.

Camilla (opera): the famous song in, i. 79–80; killing of the wild boar in, i. 93; Camilla's charms, i. 93; King Latinus in, i. 95–96, 228; song in, ii. 82; Mrs. Tofts in, iv. 55.

CAMILLUS: happy relation with his son, ii. 522; an idle tall young fellow, v. 99.

Camisards, a 'sister' among the, ii. 129.

Camlet: a coat and waistcoat of blue, i. 434; blue c., iii. 163; dark c. of parish clerks, iii. 401.

Campbell, David (contractor to the army), a subscriber, i. *xci*.

Campbell, Duncan: 'the dumb conjuror', i. 129 & n.; 'the handsome sloven', ii. 90; Clarinda visits, iii. 184; account of a visit to, iv. 181–2; whereabouts inquired after, iv. 182; alluded to, iv. 293, 365; delivers his oracles in writing, iv. 512; account of, iii. 184; 'the Dumb Man', v. 115.

Camperfelt, Colonel, to be welcomed at Coverley Hall, iv. 447.

Camphor, Virtues of, recommended to ladies, i. 391.

Campley, in *The Funeral*, i. 216.

Canaan: Milton's account of idols in, i. 313; spies sent by Moses into, iv. 254.

Candi, Giovanni (librettist), i. 56.

Candle, lighting a pipe at the same c. an overture of friendship, iv. 539.

Candle-snuffer, in role of the lion, i. 57.

Candle-sticks, a fringe for, i. 361.

Candour: wit tempered with, i. 363; candid behaviour, ii. 239; iii. 102; c., sense and ingenuity, ii. 431; fame should be built on c. and ingenuity, ii. 482; critical remarks to be communicated with, ii. 520; of critics of Homer, ii. 586; and affability of Augustus, ii. 592; c. rather than cavilling in the ancient critics, iii. 10; *Spectator* famous for c. of its criticisms, iii. 266; natural to an ingenious mind, iii. 433; critical remarks to be received with, iii. 531.

Cane(s): and snuff-boxes, the usual helps to discourse, i. 124; a beau with his, ii. 434; double-headed, ii. 471; Old JACK TAWDERY should buy, ii. 512; a little oaken, ii. 527; a new head to, iii. 155; cane-shops, iii. 166; FRANK JOLLY weaning himself from his, iv. 9; mentioned, iv. 511, 524.

CANIDIA, a superannuated coquette, iii. 75–76.

Canine particles, women who were made of, ii. 319.

Caning servants, i. 375.

CANNIBALL, letter from (a case of jealousy), iii. 504.

Cant, Rev. Andrew, a Presbyterian minister, ii. 80.

Cant: of an impatient lover, ii. 52; etymology of the word, ii. 80; of words in critics, iii. 36; of lawyers, iii. 402; iv. 477–8; of particular trades, iii. 578; of hackney-coachmen, iv. 101; WILL HONEYCOMB'S little cant-phrases, iv. 390; of a Rosicrucian, iv. 562; of humorous language, illustrated, v. 105–7.

Cantrell, Mrs., iii. 189.

Cap, servant's hair under a, iii. 296.

Cap and bells of the jester, i. 200.

Capacity (-ies): hard to judge our own, ii. 114; of a child easy to discover, ii. 114; gold adapts itself to the meanest, ii. 431; methods of gaining riches attainable by persons of the meanest, iii. 2; why men of greatest c. fail to become rich, iii. 3; no man ever provoked his c. as far as possible, iv. 487.

Capers: out-of-the-way c. of JOHN TROTT, iii. 57; on the stage, iii. 237; Mr. TROTT raises six or seven c. with ease, iii. 415; cut capers *coupée*, iv. 332.

Capitol (in Rome), iv. 433; saved by geese, iv. 17.

Capping verses, iv. 287.

Caprice: and industry the companions of

dullness, i. 271; in making choices, ii. 249.

Captain: burnt in his ship, i. 309; a stage-coach companion, ii. 22–25, 73; his conquest over a female neighbour, iii. 55; immodest offer from a, iii. 65; indecent conversation of a, iv. 402; a C. of Dragoons a rival of Mr. SPECTATOR, ii. 514; C. of the Guards, i. 375; v. 150.

Caravaggio, Polidoro Caldara da (?) (painter), iv. 44.

Caravansary, a palace mistaken for a, iii. 30–31.

Carbanado: victims of Mohocks 'cut and carbanado'd', iii. 187.

CARBUNCLE, ALEXANDER: letter from (on the Ugly Club), i. 76–78; letter from (welcoming Mr. SPECTATOR as a probationer), i. 133–6; 'faces of Dr. CARBUNCLE's die', i. 221.

Carbuncle, iv. 510.

Cardan, Girolamo, on the mole, quoted by Henry More, i. 495–6.

Carders (card-players), at York, iii. 112.

Cardinal(s): an intrigue with a c.'s mistress, ii. 38; pope and c., iv. 19; anecdote of a c. and his spy, iv. 43–44; opening of a c.'s mouth, iv. 92, 471.

Card-matches: 'cry fish and', i. 152; cries of venders of, ii. 476.

Cardmatch-makers, the whole tribe of, ii. 476.

Card-playing: waste of time in, i. 396–7; ladies 'the veriest wasps in nature' at ombre, ii. 54; until morning, iii. 465.

Cardonnel, Adam, a subscriber, i. lxxxviii.

Cards: 'a great consumption of', i. 310; 'has another hold her cards while she prays', i. 341; time spent in shuffling and dividing a pack of, i. 396–7; to take up a pack of, i. 428; Sir ROGER sends a pack of, to every poor family at Christmas, ii. 550; throwing down c. in a rage, iv. 10; and dice, iv. 102; a huge bale of, iv. 271; anecdote of Locke and, iv. 403–4.

Care(s): in allegory of luxury and avarice, i. 235; and cheerfulness balanced in husband and wife, ii. 9; allegorical depiction of, ii. 124; iv. 278; of the world extinguish devotion, ii. 287; a wife divides her husband's, ii. 546; and solitude, ii. 599; and discontent banished by cheerfulness, iii. 451; C. and his house described by Spenser, iv. 430–1.

CARELESS, AURELIA, letter from (on use of the window), iii. 55–56.

CARELESS, CHARLES, slain by a lady's glance, iii. 418.

Carew, Richard, iii. 106.

Carey, Henry, i. liii; Sally in Our Alley, ii. 247.

Carey, Walter, contributions to Spectator, i. liii–liv; iii. 151; iv. 494.

Caricatures, burlesque pictures which the Italians call, iv. 417.

Carlile, James, The Fortune Hunters, i. 93.

Carman (-men): rivalry of c. and coachmen in streets, ii. 187; cobblers and, iv. 315; waked by, v. 42.

Carnations, cultivation of, iv. 105; v. 14.

Carneades, on beauty, ii. 68.

Carnival: at Venice, i. 96; spring the great c. of nature, iii. 374.

Caroline of Anspach (Princess of Wales), v. 123.

Carpet: on the pulpit, ii. 510; Eastern traveller spreads his, iii. 30; lovers deciphered in a, v. 97.

Carracci, Annibale, in Vision of Painters, i. 356.

Carrel, Sir Charles, slain at Chevy Chase, i. 320.

Carriage: of a well-bred man, i. 323; a man's, i. 326; an agreeable c. pleases the eye, i. 433; an unconstrained c. the mark of good breeding, i. 487; a melancholy, dejected, ii. 175; wanton, ii. 179; her unaccountable, ii. 235; of a seaman, ii. 271; of IRUS, ii. 528.

Carrier(s): and stage-coachmen, iv. 179; a book sent by the, iv. 341.

Carte blanche: a French term imported, ii. 151–3; 'a charte blanche, as our news papers call it', iii. 69; 'insist upon carte blanche', iv. 536.

Cartel, a French term imported, ii. 151–2.

Carter, the Widow OGLE more than kind to her, v. 131.

Carteret, John, Baron (afterwards Earl Granville), iii. 533.

Cartesians: their doctrine that the soul always thinks, ii. 460; the pineal gland as the seat of the soul, ii. 571; their explanation of a train of ideas, iii. 562–3; sermons that should only have been preached before, iii. 578.

Carthage: Pyrrhus' designs on, ii. 212; birth of, described in Aeneid, ii. 541.

Carthaginian faith, a proverbial phrase explained by Sir ANDREW, ii. 186–7.

Cartoons of Raphael, at Hampton Court, ii. 379–80, 446.

CARUS, his cheerful manner of doing a kindness, iii. 39.

Carving, pretended ignorance of, iv. 175.

Cary, John, *Essay on Trade*, i. 294.

Caryll, John, ii. 255.

Casaubon, Isaac, v. 113.

Cascades: in a garden, iii. 569; contrivers of, like romance writers, iv. 190.

Case: horses in case, iv. 331; what they call *a case in point*, ii. 214.

Case-knife, whistling with a, iv. 545.

CASH, Mr., ii. 350.

Cash-book, ever poring on his, ii. 188.

CASSANDRA (a gypsy fortune-teller), ii. 16.

Cassani, Giuseppe, in *Rinaldo*, i. 25.

Cassini, Giovanni Domenico (astronomer), iv. 481.

Cassini, Jacques, iv. 481.

Cassius, Gaius, anecdote of, as a child, ii. 114.

Cast: a measuring, iv. 422.; of the head, ii. 235; of the eyes, ii. 235, 470, 471; iii. 397; of horror and melancholy, ii. 421; a mirthful c. in Sir ROGER, i. 8; the mind with a c. towards devotion, ii. 142; or turn to the mind, ii. 271; of mind in a discreet man, ii. 377; of temper, ii. 417; and turn of disposition, ii. 425; of mind towards ridicule, ii. 466; a serious c. of mind, v. 44; an illiberal c. of mind, v. 55.

Cast (p.p.): TOM TOUCHY 'has c. and been c. so often', i. 498; having c. great quantities of ribbon, ii. 531; c. clothes given to servants, i. 444; cast-off clothes given to others, iii. 378; 'our parts will be *new cast*', ii. 353.

CASTALIO, THE FAITHFUL: MONIMIA's lover, v. 117.

Castile, kingdom of, impoverished by wars, ii. 277.

Castilian and his unfaithful wife, ii. 277-9.

Castle-builders: account of, ii. 157-60; letter from one, ii. 158-60; referred to, iv. 75; schemes of, to promote the public good, ii. 285.

Castle-soap, the present duties on, iv. 230.

Castle-Yard Bagnio, iii. 225.

Castleton, Nathaniel (Controller of the Penny Post-Office), v. 34-35.

Castriota, George. *See* Scanderbeg.

Casual or eternal formation of the world, one of the great points of atheism, ii. 230.

Caswall, George (a Director of S. Sea Co.), a subscriber, i. *xc*.

Cat (or Catling), Christopher, i. 42.

Cat(s): stifling of, in an air-pump, i. 91; C. and Fiddle as a sign, i. 116; an old woman's in the straw, i. 230; 'grey as a cat', i. 378; a witch's, i. 482; 'a cat and a whoremaster will find a way through a door', ii. 296-7; women who resemble, ii. 320, 327; its contribution to music, iii. 351; roasting of a, iii. 351; antipathy to, iii. 352; iv. 48, 422; v. 82; 'young puss playing her wanton gambols', v. 138.

Cat's eye, denotes a greedy, rapacious aspect, ii. 471.

Catalogues, of ships, &c., in the epic, iii. 87.

Catamountain (leopard), i. 136.

Cataracts, a doctor who pretends to cure, iv. 61.

Cat-call: account of, iii. 349-53; as a cure for the itch of writing, iv. 590; a party of cat-calls headed by a rake, v. 58.

Catch: widows 'upon the c.', iv. 515.

Catches (songs), i. 311; ii. 372.

Catechetical method of arguing, introduced by Socrates, ii. 428.

Catechism, questions and responses of the, ii. 536.

Catechizing-day, i. 461.

Caterwauling, iii. 349.

Cathedral(s): Gothic c. less affecting than the Pantheon, iii. 556; in c., where one person sings alone the anthem, iv. 286.

Catherine, St., in Dryden's *Tyrannic Love*, ii. 266.

Catiline: his fall would have been glorious if in service of his country, i. 168; coveted wealth of others while squandering his own, i. 235; his conspiracy discovered by a courtesan, ii. 247; his exhortation to his army, iii. 1; lived with the sad severely . . ., iii. 448; his actions based on ambition, iii. 524; scene in Jonson's play, iv. 312-13; his conspiracy quashed in Calends of December, iv. 519.

Cato, Marcus Porcius (the Censor): in Cicero's Dialogue of Old Age, iii. 60; iv. 418; taught his son himself, iii. 132.

Cato, Marcus Porcius (of Utica): and Caesar both virtuous, i. 423; his sister and Caesar, ii. 72; his character contrasted with Caesar's, ii. 166; a reminder of decency, ii. 400; preserving his integrity amidst ruins of his country, ii. 422; considered only the virtuous handsome, ii. 444; the less he coveted glory the more he acquired it, ii. 490; suicide of, iii. 33, 300; mentioned, iii. 369; Martial's epigram

on, iv. 67; his reputation for sincerity, iv. 502; quotation from Addison's play, v. 30–31, 146–8.

Cattle (live stock): sufficiency of, in Great Britain, ii. 285; customers for, ii. 402; Hobson's stable of, iv. 310.

Catullus, Gaius Valerius: Caesar's kind treatment of, i. 98; compliments made to Lesbia, i. 125; no mixed wit in, i. 266; his translation of Sappho's *Ad Lesbiam* quoted, ii. 390–1; diminutive epithets in, iv. 397.

Caudle: a young man who can make a, i. 241; a porringer of, ii. 65.

Caul, of a wig insanitary, iv. 571.

Caution: women have less c. than men, i. 243; charity to be managed with prudence and, ii. 198; and prudence should temper heats of devotion, ii. 289; and prudence often hinder a man from success, iii. 44; in securing a retreat, iii. 53.

Cavaliers: feuds with Round-heads, i. 509; memorials of, to Charles II, v. 149–51.

Cave(s): and grottoes, iv. 325; of Trophonius, v. 44–45, 46–48.

Caveat to the Fair Sex, iii. 372, 481.

Cavil(s): and scruples raised by infidels, ii. 233; atheists marked by pride, spleen and, iii. 431; envy and c. the fruits of laziness and ignorance, v. 27.

Cavilling: the whole art of, ii. 432; ancient critics marked by candour rather than, iii. 10.

Cecil, William (Lord Burleigh), statue of, iii. 214.

CECILIA, the beauteous, iii. 489.

Cedar(s): women's head-dresses like a forest of, i. 415; on the top of Tirzah, iv. 598; an altar of, v. 3; planted by Abraham, v. 15.

Celia, in *As You Like It*, ii. 132.

CELIA: letter from (objecting to licentious language), ii. 575; shewed FIDELIO her teeth, iii. 471; requests advice from LEONILLA, iv. 183; reply to letter from, iv. 588.

Celibacy: condemned by the Jews, iv. 257; 'the great evil of our nation', iv. 382.

CELIMENE, letter from (on education of a young girl), i. 281–2.

CELINDA, letter from (on an inconsiderate husband), ii. 201–3.

Censor of Marriages: proposed, iii. 110–11; memorandum to, iii. 123; report from, on a case, iii. 166.

Censor of Small Wares: considered, i. 70, 115; a petition referred to, v. 116.

Censorious, the, i. 347; character of, ii. 459.

Censoriousness: a virtuous mind to be kept from souring into, ii. 445; jarrings and dissonances arising from, ii. 461.

Censure(s): the tax a man pays for being eminent, i. 422; of the world and self-reproach, i. 497; women who bestow c. on others, ii. 449; and approbation as helps to discourse, ii. 459; we should not be affected by c. or applauses of men, ii. 492; v. 85; exposing c. in characters of others, ii. 494. See *also* Reproach.

Centaurs, Battle of Lapithae and, iii. 596.

Centlivre, Susannah, i. *62*; iii. *499–500*.

Centurion (in the Bible), language of the, iv. 273.

Cephalic Tincture: of quack doctors, iv. 460, 553; the *Spectator*'s, iv. 460.

Cephalus and Procris, story of, iv. 380–1.

Cerberean, a word coined by Milton, iii. 13.

Cerecloths (plasters in surgery), iii. 206.

Ceremonial: more prominent in country than in city, i. 486–8; in religion, ii. 332–3.

Ceremony(-ies): foreign to true affliction, i. 403–4; of the snuff-box taught, ii. 46–47; among women turns upon matters of ill health, ii. 67; ridiculous c. in Roman Catholic Church, ii. 289–90; human nature now lost under form and, ii. 318; Acosta's defence of religious, ii. 332; of the green gown, iii. 372.

Ceres, an attendant on Summer, iii. 595.

Cervantes Saavedra, Miguel de: Addison compared to, i. xxxv–xxxvi. — *Adventures of Don Quixote*: Don Q. the patron of the Amorous Club, i. 125; Don Q. and the puppet-show, i. 207; recommended for comfort in grief, ii. 141–2; a cure for the extravagances of love, ii. 385; an example of burlesque, ii. 467–8; translated by Motteux, iii. 26; behaviour of the Knight of the Sorrowful Countenance, iii. 268; effect of, upon romances, iv. 69; Don Q.'s raptures in contemplation of Dulcinea, iv. 238; 'a knight errant without a mistress is like a tree without leaves', iv. 371.

Chabrias (Athenian commander), iii. 299.

Chaffinches, in the opera, i. 64.

Chain of being: and progress of finite beings to perfection, i. 459; 'from the highest angel to the lowest worm', ii.

101; beings above and below us, ii. 136–7; the whole circle of being, ii. 542; also in the civil economy, iii. 510; iv. 7; man the middle link between angels and brutes, iii. 524–5; range of, iv. 345–9; diversity of creation, iv. 441–4; created beings rise one above another in the scale of existence, iv. 531; the notion of a gradual rise in beings, v. 125; between finite and infinite 'an unmeasured interval', v. 170.

Chain of events, many of the links lost to human sight, ii. 422.

Chair(s): the third c. in an opera, i. 93; a mathematical, i. 106; as actors upon the stage, i. 149, 425; cry of mender of, ii. 476; a great, ii. 512; a wife who changes c. every two years, iii. 111; easy, iii. 206.

Chairmen, noises of coaches and, ii. 189–90.

Chalk: a pregnant wife eating, iii. 196; a young girl licking, iv. 15; 'chalk-lickers', iv. 17.

Challenge: sending and accepting a, i. 412; to a trial of skill, iv. 31.

Chamade, a French word imported, ii. 151–2.

Chamber-fellow, disputes with a, iii. 17–18.

Chamberlain of an inn, ii. 22, 536.

Chamberlayne, Edward, *Magnae Britanniae Notitia*, i. xciii; iii. 521; iv. 370, 387.

Chamberline, Dr. Paul, his Chrystal Cosmetick, i. *139*, *222*; iii. *418*; iv. *130*.

Chambermaid: *The Nineteen Plagues of a*, ii. 89; a wife confined to conversation of husband and, ii. 486; letter from a discontented, iii. 378–9; 'he kissed my c. before my face', iv. 556–7; turned off in a pet, v. 131.

Chamber-practice, among lawyers, i. 90.

CHAMBERS, ABIGAIL, petition of, ii. 294.

Chamfort (pseud. for Sébastien-Roch Nicolas): *La Jeune Indienne*, i. 49.

Chamont, in *The Orphan*, quoted, ii. 277; iii. 482.

Champagne: 'I have drank champaign at Versailles', ii. 159; burgundy and, iii. 207; three glasses of, iv. 542.

Chance: the goddess who presides over anagrams, i. 254; histories composed by politicians leave nothing to, ii. 171; proportion between births and deaths, males and females, not due to, iii. 27–28; human wisdom often overruled by, iii. 44; cannot account for wonders of creation, iv. 442–4; Epicurus attributed man's being to, v. 10.

Chance-medley (manslaughter), i. 138; ii. 479; iii. 355.

Chancel (in church), Sir ROGER's seat in the, i. 461.

Chancellor of France, Balzac's letter to, iii. 324.

Chancery, Court of, erected to adjust legal hardships on individuals, iv. 528.

Chancery-bill, ii. 82.

Chancres, accompanying a clap, iv. 59.

Changing one's condition (getting married), iv. 357, 370.

Changing sides, in religion or party, ii. 135.

Chaos: 'like the world in its', i. 196; Satan's voyage through, iii. 120; imaginary persons in, iii. 145; a bridge over, iii. 337.

Chapel, iii. 184.

Chaplain(s): in *The Scornful Lady*, ii. 553–4; improper language in prayer of, iii. 130–1; in noblemen's families, v. 82. See also COVERLEY.

Chaplets of flowers (roses), i. 421; ii. 65.

Chapman, —— (Director of S. Sea Co.), iv. *538*.

Chapmen, chaps (purchasers), i. 92; iv. 41, 84, 85, 315.

Character(s): in *Spectator* fit a thousand people, i. 145; exposing weaknesses in c. of others, ii. 494–6; imaginary names of, in *Spectator*, ii. 518; influence of a good, ii. 522–3; most men affect c. during the day, ii. 553; in *PL*, ii. 561–6; most of Milton's lie out of nature, ii. 586–7; qualities of, iii. 33; novelty and variety of in English comedy, iii. 396.

'Characters' in the *Spectator*: the envious man, i. 82–85; the valetudinarian, i. 105–8; the 'Pict', i. 174–6; ii. 303; the 'Idol', i. 312–15; ii. 303; the 'Demurrer', i. 377–80; ii. 303; the absent man, from La Bruyère, i. 332–3; the woman's man, ii. 110–13; the castle-builder, ii. 158–60; the jealous husband, ii. 168–72; the henpecked husband, ii. 194–6; the charitable man, ii. 198–9; the jilt, ii. 234–7; the courtier, ii. 256–62; the mercurial friend, ii. 262–3; 'Salamanders', ii. 275–7; ii. 303; of women, after Simonides, ii. 318–20; the inconsistent and extravagant, ii. 362–4; the inquisitive, ii. 386–8; the free-thinker, ii. 411–13; the tyrannical husband, ii. 417–19; the talkative, ii. 458–62; the ambitious man, ii. 490–502; the frugal, retired man, ii. 527–8, 593; the agreeable man,

INDEX

ii. 591; iii. 449; the affectedly unconcerned and the affectedly busy, iii. 6–7;
the male jilt, or fribbler, iii. 23–25; the
virtuous woman, iii. 79–83; the *dévote*,
iii. 320–1; the match-maker, iv. 36–37;
the angry man, iv. 39–42; the unduly
curious, iv. 45; the model daughter,
iv. 78–80; the pleasant fellow, iv.
130–1; the benevolent man, iv. 151–4;
the cott-quean, iv. 209–10; the punster, iv. 288; the biter, iv. 289–90; the
club-tyrant, iv. 302–4.

CHARAXUS or CHARIXUS (brother of
Sappho), ii. *407*.

Chardin, Sir John, *Travels into Persia*, i. *48*,
410; ii. *121*; iii. 30–31, *46*; v. *158*.

Chariot, i. 43 & n.; Sir ANDREW's, ii.
402; to bespeak a fine, iii. 165; and a
stately pair of horses, iii. 195; a gilt c.
and new liveries, iii. 502; 'on foot or in
a', iv. 554; a gilt c. and six, iv. 558;
'laid up my c. and sold my horses',
v. 128. — The Messiah's c., iii. 232,
256–7. — Bacchus in a c. drawn by
tigers, iii. 596.

CHARISSA, her scruples regarding astrologers, v. 115.

Charity: statue of, i. 187; Sir ROGER
on, ii. 186, 550–1; monuments repre-
senting, ii. 187; good-nature finds
expression in, ii. 197–201; Sir ANDREW
on, ii. 401–5; one of the superior
virtues, ii. 445; 'the salute of', ii. 450;
an example of, in the Temple, ii. 464–5;
practised in secret by IRUS, ii. 527–8;
the duty of all mankind, iii. 47–50;
appeals for, in London, iii. 11–13;
balanced against zeal, iv. 137; a proposal for, iv. 168–9; Jesus the highest
pattern of, iv. 334; Sir ROGER's
legacies, iv. 340–1; Captain SENTRY's,
iv. 445–8; Sir ANDREW's, iv. 467–8;
examples of, by a country gentleman,
v. 127–8.

Charity schools: value of, iii. 48–50; a
laudable feature of the present age,
iii. 108; Martin Powell's benefit for,
iii. 400; of girls, iii. 428–9; contributions for, iv. 12–13.

CHARLES, a young gentleman in the
army, addicted to French phrases, ii.
153.

CHARLES's wife, Cousin, v. 127.

Charles I: picture of, at Oxford, i. 247–8;
and country wakes, ii. 135; martyrdom of, v. 150; mentioned, iv. 580.

Charles II: character of, iv. 131–2; 'not
a king a quarter of an hour together',
iv. 133; incident of, and Sir Robert
Viner, iv. 131–3; restoration of, v. 150;

reign of, i. 23, 41, 142, 184, 191, 310,
335, 377; ii. 14, 91, 118; iii. 76, 240,
313; Ambassador of Bantam to court
of, iv. 503; memorials presented by
Cavaliers to, v. 149–51.

Charles II, King of Spain: death of, i. 276;
iii. *508*; will of, ii. *211*.

Charles XII, King of Sweden: 'conjunction with infidels', i. 182; retired to
Bender, ii. *36*; query about, v. 116.

Charles, Archduke ('Charles III' of
Spain): afterwards Emperor Charles
VI, ii. *549*; claimant to Spanish throne,
iii. 508.

Charles of Burgundy, and Rhynsault,
iv. 241–4.

Charles the Great (Charlemagne), and
Eginhart, ii. 215–16.

Charlett, Dr. Arthur, i. *183*.

Charmer: i. 388; ii. 112; 'my lovely c.',
ii. 62, 63; the c. of his soul, ii. 235;
success of male charmers, v. 59.

Charms: a Jezebel's pernicious, ii. 190;
virtue makes the beautiful sex all over
c., ii. 445; the insolence of beauty
without its, iii. 76; beauties encumbered with their, iii. 104; 'our greatest
c. are owing to affectation', iv. 332.

Charms against evil eyes, ii. 360.

Chart (canvas, picture) of Raphael, ii.
380.

Chase, the: cost and returns of, ii. 188–
9; most healthy parts of the world,
where they subsist by, ii. 264.

Chastity: the great point of honour in
women, i. 416; women's contempt for
c. in men, ii. 103–4; a Salamander a
kind of heroine in, ii. 275–6; walking
on burning plowshares as a test of, ii.
276; iii. 481; attitudes toward breach
of, ii. 534; habitual c. of thought, ii.
591; dangers to, iii. 16, 480–2; valetu-
dinarians in, iii. 481; c. of renown, iv.
203; representation of, by Spenser, iv.
429; story of dogs capable of detecting, iv. 581–2.

Chaucer, Geoffrey, anecdote from
pseudo-C. *Remedie of Love*, i. 314. *See
also* Dryden.

Cheapening (bargaining, trading): goods
at the New Exchange, i. 408; fans at
the Change, iii. 182; tea in China
shops, iii. 245; a beaver, iii. 522; a bad
face for a lost reputation, iv. 510.

Cheats: women who engage in, ii. 320;
and bubbles, iv. 58; practised in
selling, iv. 454–5.

Cheek: lady who turned her c. when
offered a kiss, ii. 561; a dimple in
BELINDA's left, iii. 418.

Cheerfulness: of temper maintained by communication with God, i. 396; our duty in conversation with others, i. 419–22; ii. 64–68; and care balanced in wife and husband, ii. 9; equanimity is above c. and below mirth, ii. 268; and good-nature the two chief ornaments of virtue, ii. 445; and good humour of Sir ROGER, ii. 551; in obliging others, iii. 39; compared with mirth, iii. 429–32; natural advantages from, iii. 451–4; inspired by scenes of nature, iii. 475–6; desirable in religious persons, iv. 254.

Cheese: Cheshire, ii. 208, 530; a great, ii. 537; effect of effluvia of, iv. 421; antipathy to, iv. 421.

Cheese-cakes, ii. 191; a gentleman making, ii. 443.

Chemical: medicine advertised for venereal maladies, iv. 59; method practised by essay-writers, i. 506; art and diligence in a c. operation, i. 492.

Chemistry, 'having formerly dabbled in', iii. 479.

Cherries: imported into England and naturalized, i. 295; in May, iii. 196; sold single like c. upon the stick, iv. 231–2; begin now to crowd the market, iv. 486.

Cherry-brandy, orange-flower and, iii. 206–7.

Cherry-coloured: hood, ii. 556; gown and petticoat, ii. 580.

Cherubim: perfection of, will ultimately be surpassed by man, i. 459; a set of angels who know most, v. 52.

Cheshire cheese, ii. 530; yawning for, ii. 208.

Chess, a game of, iii. 578.

Chetwood, W. R., General History of the Stage, ii. 529; iii. 350.

Chevy Chase, critique on, i. 298–303, 315–22.

CHEZLUY, JEAN, letter from, to PHARAMOND, iv. 201–3.

Chicken, 'Madam, you are now past a', ii. 344.

Chickens: a couple of, eaten, iii. 532; Cicero observed, for omens, iv. 292.

Chiffinch, Thomas (carpenter), iv. 458.

Child and father: relation between, like that of a creature and Creator, ii. 214.

Child-bed pillows, embroidering of, v. 73.

Childermas-day, unlucky for beginning projects, i. 32, 196.

Children: in English tragedy, i. 187; education of, the duty of women, i. 312; weep and laugh readily, i. 403; and parents, ii. 241–4, 252–6, 336, 521–5; iii. 597; iv. 198–200; devotion to be implanted in, ii. 287; nursing of, ii. 454–8; benefited by charity-schools, iii. 48–50; influence of manners of servants upon, iii. 49; playing with, iii. 70; iv. 199; a wife's neglect of her, iii. 207–8; education of, iii. 217–20; frightened with 'Raw-head and Bloody-bones', iii. 202; care of, iv. 14–17; the blessings of having many, iv. 273–5; eldest and youngest often spoiled, iv. 274; show compassion for others, v. 13. See also Boys, Girls, Parents.

Children in the Wood, The Two: critique of, i. 362–4; the tune of, ii. 207.

Chili, ladies of, dress their heads over a basin of water, iii. 191.

Chilo (Cato's servant), iii. 132.

Chimera, a: in painting, i. 354; 'C. and confusion', ii. 102.

Chimerical: grandeur, ii. 252; correspondence between two friends, ii. 437–8.

Chimney-pieces, glazed with looking-glass, iii. 69.

Chimney-sweepers: cry of, in London streets, ii. 475; their raillery with a fruit-wench, iv. 99; waked by, v. 42.

CHIN, Sergeant, former president of the Ugly Club, i. 222.

Chin(s): youth who learned to beat the Grenadiers' March on his, iii. 3; persons with long c. invited together as a jest, iii. 396–7.

China: inhabitants of, laugh at European formal plantations, iii. 552; Wall of, still to be seen, iii. 555; Jews settled in remotest parts of, iv. 256; letter from Emperor of, to the Pope, iv. 448–53; a story from (HILPA and SHALUM), iv. 595–6.

China (porcelain): jars of, in LEONORA's library, i. 153; china ware, i. 153; iii. 25; pyramids of, i. 295; breaking a c. cup, ii. 458; piles of, ii. 480; broken by a woman's squirrel, ii. 480–1; heaps of, in every corner, iii. 69; a blue c. cup, iii. 183; to furnish an India shop, iii. 196; a prized possession, iv. 271; broken by a choleric husband, iv. 524–5; bowl of, v. 107.

China-houses, iii. 166.

China plant, the infusion of a, i. 295.

China shops: Motteux's, iii. 25–26; iv. 479; behaviour of women in, iii. 245–6.

China women: one of the top China women about town, iii. 245.

Chinese, the: Sir ANDREW calls them our potters, i. 296; their punishment of children's disobedience, ii. 244.

Chinese, study of, iv. 104.

Chinese: buildings, round pillars and vaulted roofs in, iii. 557; idols, whipped for refusing to answer prayers, i. 313; women, the Tartar general's sale of, iv. 315–16; writing, in a perpendicular line, i. 255.

Chippenham, Wilts., R. M. of, ii. 113.

Chirurgeon, advertisement of an Italian, i. 96. See also Surgeon.

Chit-Chat Club, iv. 513.

Chivalry, books of, chastity and courage their theme, i. 417.

CHLOE: T. D.'s fondness for, i. 114; a jilt, ii. 237; her indifferent familiarity, ii. 308; CHLOE's foot, iii. 471; a silly dancer, iv. 149; enters a room with a familiar run, iv. 245; CHLOE's toilet, iv. 398. See also CLOE.

CHLORIS: won by the same compliments made a thousand years ago to Lesbia, i. 125; and PHILOTAS, iii. 25.

Chocolate: 'drank two dishes of c. in bed', iii. 182, 183; coffee and, iii. 207; an inflamer of passion, iii. 374, 480; a dish of, iv. 459.

Chocolate-house, iv. 198.

Choice: irresolution in making a, ii. 136; difficulties in making a, ii. 248–9; necessity made to look like, iii. 596.

Choler: 'over-run with cholers against me', ii. 384; a heart choked up with spleen and, v. 8.

Choleric: dwarf, ii. 557; father, ii. 242; fellow, i. 118; husband, iv. 518, 524–5; lover, i. 377; temper, i. 58.

Chop-house, dining at the, iii. 111; iv. 102.

Chremylus, story of (from Aristophanes), iv. 139–41.

Christenings: a gossip who launches out into descriptions of, ii. 459; drinking at, iv. 85; presents at, iv. 232.

Christian(s): connotation of the word, iii. 326; the ordinary duties of a, iii. 327; rancour among, iv. 334; music in worship of, v. 152–3.

Christian's Overthrow Prevented, The. See Moss, Robert.

Christianity: advantages of belief in, ii. 232–3; the great art and secret of, ii. 331; greatest mysteries of, set forth in PL, iii. 142; not contrary to civil liberties, iii. 442; history of the Jews a strong argument for, iv. 257; the only source of contentment, iv. 565; superiority of, to paganism, v. 163–7;

compared to paganism in imitation of Deity, v. 167–9.

Christmas: pie, i. 361; gambols at Twelfth-Night, ii. 208; games, ii. 513, 547; at Sir ROGER's, ii. 550–1; church decorations at, ii. 600; iii. 8–9; mutton-pie at, iii. 380.

Chromatic ears, music not designed to please only, i. 123.

Chromation, letter from Philopinax to, ii. 427–8.

Chronograms: examples of false wit, i. 256; based on resemblances of letters, i. 265; in allegory of true and false wit, i. 272.

Chronology, a short scheme of, proposed, ii. 395–6.

Chrystal Cosmetick, advertisement of, iii. 418; iv. 130.

Chub-faced boy, iii. 70.

Chuck-farthing (child's game), iv. 147, 307.

'Chum', v. 107.

Church, the: (as a profession) over-crowding in, i. 88–89, 449.

Church of England: freedom from enthusiasm and superstition in, ii. 288–90; Tory cry of 'The Church in danger', ii. 446; ceremony in, disturbing to dissenters, ii. 509–10; late act of parliament for securing, ii. 550–1; its superiority, iii. 18; purity of worship in, iv. 496: music in services of, v. 152–3; 'the most dangerous day it ever saw', v. 175.

Church(es), Parish: interior of, beautified by Sir ROGER, i. 460; eve-feast of dedication of, ii. 131; decoration of, at Christmas, ii. 600; iii. 8–9; the fifty new c. in the city, iii. 437.

Church, behaviour in: 'Starers' in, i. 86, 227; 'Peepers' in, i. 227–8; bowing and curtsying in, i. 213; iii. 8; sleeping in, i. 213, 461; v. 42–43; 'Idols' in, i. 313; Sir ROGER at, i. 461; crowded with hoop-petticoats, ii. 7; display of dress in a country c., ii. 14; giggling and ogling in, i. 120; v. 48; manner of singing in, ii. 305; audible repetition of prayers, ii. 419–20; immodest conversation in, ii. 440; salutations in, ii. 509–10, 552; iv. 124–5; new-fashioned hoods in, ii. 561; flirtation in, hindered by decorations, ii. 600; iii. 8–9; a lady's bow to EUPHUES in, iii. 56; behaviour of beauties in, iii. 104; taking of snuff in, iii. 279, 427; neglecting to join in service, iii. 427; diverting eyes of the congregation, iv. 284–7; knotting not to be done in, iv. 413;

artifices to attract attention in, v. 97; levity and irreverence in, v. 154–6.

Churchmen (Tory sympathizers), ii. 195.

Church music, v. 152–4; 'a merry jigg from the organ-loft', iii. 253–4, 268; neglect of, iii. 514–16.

Church porches, beggars at, i. 208.

Church service. *See* Prayer, Common.

Churchwarden: to hold up his wand, ii. 120; illegitimate children fathered upon, ii. 295; election for, at Putney, iv. 93.

Church work is slow (prov.), iii. 437.

Churchyard, general meeting-place on Sunday, i. 460.

Churchill, A. and J., *Collection of Voyages*, iii. 461.

Cibber, Colley: *The Careless Husband*, ii. 15; acted at Epping, i. 207; Lord Foppington in, i. 207; Cibber's acting Lord Foppington in, iii. 394; *Love Makes a Man, or The Fop's Fortune*, Penkethman's acting in, iii. 394–5; *Ximena*, rehearsal of, iv. 453–4; one of the managers of the Haymarket, i. 25; *Apology*, i. 194; iii. 351; as Aesop, i. 77; in *The Pilgrim*, i. 94; burlesque of *The Rival Queens*, i. 128; as Alexander, i. 128; on rants in tragedy, i. 171; Sir Fopling Flutter, i. 278; on Estcourt, ii. 529; iv. 157; on Wilks, ii. 545; Sir Roger in *The Scornful Lady*, ii. 554; on Mrs. Oldfield, iii. 252; on Mrs. Tofts, iv. 55; on Doggett, iv. 283.

Cibber, Theophilus, *Lives of the Poets*, i. li, lxxv; ii. 538; v. 24.

Cicero, Marcus Tullius: The TEMPLAR familiar with his works, i. 9; 'never less alone than when alone', i. 19; iii. 151; rebus used by, i. 250; used puns, i. 259–60; wrote before rules of art were codified, i. 261; on friendship, i. 289; *morum comitas* necessary in friendship, i. 291; on ambition, i. 312; on Socrates and the physiognomist, i. 368; on Socrates conquering tendency to vice, i. 368; 'virtue and decency allied', i. 433; on instinct in a lamb, i. 494; gives an admirable sketch of natural history, i. 497; his reply to the man 'forty years old', ii. 37; on an author who proved the obvious, ii. 44; on the perfection of glory, ii. 50; truth and good sense in his philosophy, ii. 75; Socrates' address to his judges quoted, ii. 75–76; on old age, ii. 100, 102; 'so great with Tully of late', ii. 106, 118; a learned genius, ii. 129; wrote allegorical fables, ii. 221;

on lessening one's paternal estate, ii. 364; 'live with your enemy as if he might become your friend . . .', ii. 375; on an orator's diffidence, ii. 398; thought virtue amiable, ii. 444; on Caesar, ii. 497; iv. 150; v. 179; on mixed government, iii. 19; easy to ridicule a *verbum ardens*, iii. 37; no time of life in which a duty may not be practised, iii. 39; recommended Pompey on three accounts, iii. 43; quoted by Tillotson, iii. 45; on old age, iii. 60; and Calvus, iii. 62; education of his son Marcus, iii. 106; on Possidonius' defiance of pain, iii. 130; laboured to acquire eloquence, iii. 150; on Catiline, iii. 448; on Antony's witty mirth, iii. 450; complied with public forms of worship, iii. 460; his genius inclined him to oratory, iii. 512; on following nature, iii. 513; impaired health by vehemence of action, iii. 522; brilliance of language, iii. 528; a benefit to be made as diffusive as possible, iii. 548; on people who delight in wrangling, iii. 590; on prevalence of scandal, iv. 2; on parental affection, iv. 14; on gladiatorial combats, iv. 35; could visit the refined Roman playhouses, iv. 67; on libels and lampoons, iv. 88; on approving a crime, iv. 89; his papers written with regularity and method, iv. 186; affection to wife and children, iv. 238; weakness for divination, iv. 293; on death, iv. 418–20; a friend of Roscius and a good judge of dramatic performances, iv. 432; his rules for oratory, iv. 432–4, 436–7, 440, 487; delight in food consists in desire, not satiety, iv. 448; a nobleman's compliment to Plato, iv. 448; his love of glory, iv. 490; his works run very much in the first person, iv. 519; on immortality of the soul, v. 13; 'the best of pagan authors', v. 75; a master of eloquence, v. 95; on jesting with a serious countenance, v. 105; on novelty, v. 140; an orator should know heavenly bodies, v. 164; wishes Homer had tried to make men like gods, v. 167; mentioned, i. 26; ii. 90, 115, 154, 396; iii. 318, 369; iv. 71, 306, 514; *Academica*, ii. 431; *De Amicitia*, iv. 68; *De Divinatione*, i. 255; *De Natura Deorum*, i. 489, 490, 492–5; iii. 223, 452; iv. 144, 213, 392, 442; v. 10; *De Officiis*, i. 475, 490; ii. 491; iii. 126; iv. 144; *De Oratore*, iii. 535; v. 75, 163; *De Senectute*, i. 30; v. 4; *Paradoxa Stoicorum*, ii. 444; a passage from, set to

music, ii. *329–30*; *Pro L. Murena*, ii. *444*; *Pro C. Plancio*, ii. *449*; *Tusculan Disputations*, i. *44, 294, 368*; ii. *49, 455*; v. *45, 100*; Cicero paraphrased, iii. 288–9; quotation from, iii. 290–1; v. 56.

Cider: Pomona with a glass of, iii. 596; barrels of, iv. 542.

CINAEDUS, not allowed to make the lovers' leap, ii. 408.

Cincinnatus, left the camp to follow the plow, iv. 535.

Cinder-wench, v. 42.

Cinesias (Athenian poet), iv. *95*.

CINNA, on self-esteem, ii. 307–8.

Circe, story of, often regarded as allegory, iii. 146.

Circumforaneous wits, i. 201.

Circumstantial in speech, persons who are over-, ii. 45.

'Cit', the penurious, iv. 398.

Cithaeron, Mount, iii. 358.

Cities: dwellers in, fancy a country abode, iii. 270; contrasted with the country, iv. 143–4.

Citizen: journal of a sober, iii. 153–5; an empty fantastic, v. 47.

'Citizen of the World', i. 294.

Citron, citron-water: a drachm of, i. 340; used by Barbadoes as a bribe, iii. 479.

City feasts, drinking at, iv. 85.

City Rake, The (puppet show), i. *61*.

CIVIL, SUSAN, letter from (on voluntary counsellors), ii. 293.

Civil list, and the military, ii. 187, 258.

Civil war: results from party spirit, i. 510; ii. 4.

Civil Wars: i. 309, 452; iii. 222; two friends on opposite sides in, iii. 134–5; sectaries in the Great Rebellion, iv. 117; the general officer in, who adjudicated decisions, iv. 262.

Civil Wars of Rome: prodigies preceding, iii. 61; Atticus' conduct in, iii. 447.

Civility (-ies): excessive way of speaking, i. 429; courtiers' cold and repeated, ii. 257; towards one's wife, ii. 418–19; kissing by way of, ii. 434; outward c. and salutations, ii. 508; returning 'the c. of the hat', iii. 347.

CLACK, Lady BETTY, a member of the Chit-Chat Club, iv. 513.

'Clack was the word', v. 106.

Clap, the, in the theatre, ii. 414–15.

Claps, medicine for, advertised, iv. 59.

Clarendon, Edward Hyde, 1st Earl of: 'the famous Captain mentioned in', i. 309; *History* quoted, ii. 42; iv. 45, 219. Claret: a dose of, i. 101; French, i. 182; ii. 578; iv. 46; taste for, gradually acquired, iv. 70–71.

CLARINDA: an 'Idol', i. 314–15; journal of, iii. 181–5; slays with a glance, iii. 418.

Clark, —— (posture-master), i. *128*; ii. *504*.

Clark, J., in Ave-Mary Lane, i. *40*.

Clark, Margaret, letter from a countryman to, iii. 189–90, 208–12.

Clark, Sir Samuel (Director of S. Sea Co.), iv. *538*; a subscriber, i. *xc*.

Clark, Samuel (of Edinburgh), iii. 5.

Clarke, Samuel: his edition of Caesar, iii. 381.

Classics: *see* Greek, Latin.

Claudia, power of chastity in, iv. 380.

Claudian (Claudius Claudianus): swelling sentiments in, ii. 588; guilty of the false sublime, iii. 11; wildness of imagination in his description of the Giants' War, iii. 230; mentioned, v. *109*.

Claudius Nero. *See* Tiberius.

Clavell, Mr., of the Middle-Temple, iii. *459*.

Clavigny de Saint Honorine, Jacques, *Usage des livres suspects*, iv. 89.

Clavis apocalyptica. See Mede, Joseph.

Clavius, Christopher, his talent for geometry, iii. 107.

Clay, Stephen, death of, ii. 27–28.

'*Clay, moisten their*', i. 311.

Clayton, Thomas: i. lvi; music for *Arsinoe* and *Rosamond*, i. *79*; music for *The Passion of Sappho*, ii. *365, 506*; entertainments of music at his house, ii. 505–7; entertainments of music at York-Buildings, ii. 584–5.

Cleanliness, benefits of, v. 157–8.

CLEANTHE, story of, i. 66.

CLEANTHES: letter from (on his affair with BELINDA), ii. 558–60; affects character of a fine gentleman, iii. 511.

Clearness and perspicuity: in epic language, iii. 10; necessary to the critic, iii. 35.

Cleland, William, an original of WILL HONEYCOMB (?), i. *12*.

Clement XI. *See* Pope.

Clench of Barnet: his nightly meeting, i. 102; introduced into a projected opera, i. 129.

Cleobus, story of Biton and, iv. 214.

CLEOMIRA, a graceful dancer, i. 283.

CLEONE, letter of CLYTANDER to, iii. 151.

Cleopatra: 'a mind as wild as', ii. 70; Antony's description of, iii. 497.

Cleopatra (Martial's wife), epigram on, iv. 238–9.

CLEORA: a widow of Ephesus, ii. 407; PHILANDER 'mortally wounded' by, iii. 417; brandished her diamond, iii. 471; letter from (on needlework), v. 83; query from, regarding a second marriage, v. 98.

Clergy, The: its 'generals, field-officers, and subalterns', i. 88–89; reverence, the title given to the inferior, ii. 352; raillery on, ii. 488; pedants among, ii. 553; many unqualified, iii. 108; concern for honour of, in Spectator, iii. 130; inappropriate language in prayers of, iii. 130-1; attacks on Spectator by men in black gowns, v. 66; Spectator not to raise animosities among, v. 116. See also Divines.

CLERGYMAN, THE (in Spectator Club): character of, i. 13; letters received by, i. 113; commends Spectator for attacking vice and folly, i. 143; on dissimulation and compliment, i. 429–32; submits an essay on atheism, ii. 231; suspected of writing essays signed 'C', ii. 360; contributes 'a thought in sickness', iv. 320; is dying, iv. 440; candidates for his place in the Club, iv. 470; the world not worthy of, iv. 485.

Clergyman: unnatural portrayal of, in The Scornful Lady, ii. 553–5; immodest offer of a benefice to, iii. 66–67.

Clergyman, a country, letter from (on singing psalms), ii. 305–6.

Clergyman's wife, letter from (on women like bees), ii. 348.

Clergymen's scarves, i. 89; iii. 131; iv. 427; v. 81–82, 116.

Clerk: an attorney's, ii. 82; to a conveyancer, ii. 560; to a lawyer, iv. 204.

Clerk(s), parish: raises the psalm, i. 122–3; of Sir ROGER's parish church, i. 462; make up bills of mortality, ii. 67; iii. 402; has decorated church with greens, ii. 600; letter from one, iii. 8–9; calls out two staves 'proper to the discourse', iii. 254; a club of, iii. 401–2.

Clerk of the Peace, v. 151.

Cleveland, John: favoured brunettes, iii. 18; Strada 'the C. of his age', v. 108.

Clients and patrons, form a third of the nation, ii. 335.

Cliff, John (stationer), i. 310.

Cliff, Nathaniel (bookseller), advertises for a lottery ticket, ii. 250–1.

Climacteric: 'am turned of my great c.', iii. 50; 'has passed her grand c.', iii. 481; 'in his', iv. 259; WILL HONEYCOMB 'in his grand c.', v. 185.

Climate, effect of: on literary productions, ii. 128; on jealousy, ii. 172; on love poetry, iii. 376; on industry, iii. 554. See also English climate.

Clincant of Tasso, i. 26.

Clinches, clenches (puns): Bishops and Privy Counsellors addicted to, i. 260; 'a little pretender to clenching', iii. 483. See also Puns.

Clinch of Barnet. See Clench.

Clio, the muse, Spectators signed with letters in name, iv. 492.

CLITOPHON, letter from (is being rejected by LYDIA), iii. 122–3.

Cloak: and upper coat, ii. 43; philosopher who carried something hidden under his, ii. 360; a blue, ii. 442.

Cloak-bag, ii. 22.

Cloanthus, a colourless character in the Aeneid, ii. 562.

Clock: sounding of, in Venice Preserved, i. 186; that stands still, points right once in twelve hours, ii. 12; a great, ii. 52; story of an idiot and striking of a, iv. 69–70.

Clod, a character in The Lancashire Witches, ii. 58.

CLODIUS: pleased when you describe a wanton beauty, i. 217; an ageing dancer, iii. 75.

Clodius Pulcher, P., i. 217; intruding on rites of the Bona Dea, ii. 346.

Clodpate, Justice, in Epsom Wells, i. 207.

Cloe: in The Humorous Lieutenant, ii. 535–6; WILL HONEYCOMB's letter to (on old age and love), iii. 76–78. See also CHLOE.

Close hunks, a, worth money, ii. 528.

Closet: a pretty furnished, i. 340; Spectator read by PARTHENIA in her, ii. 55; 'called me into her c.', ii. 237; approbation of a good man in the cool reflections of his, ii. 239; retiring into, ii. 438; a poetical virtuoso's, ii. 469.

Clothes: giving cast c. to servants, i. 444; iii. 378–9; second-hand c. for sale in Long-lane, ii. 527; black c. of parish clerks, iii. 401; importance of, in human life, iv. 192–7; effect of new c. upon the wearer, iv. 221. See also Dress.

Clotilda (opera), i. 23.

Cloud for a Juno, i. 38.

Clouds: stains of light in, pleasing, iii. 544; the Almighty knowing the balancing of, iv. 134; and storms in the playhouse, v. 26.

Clown(s): conversation of lewd, i. 488; drunken, ii. 254; an enthusiast in religion like an obstinate, ii. 289;

drinking with, iii. 476; and lubbards imitated by Mr. Prince, iv. 146; who led Prince Eugene over the Alps, iv. 327; 'in youth a coxcomb, and in age a', iv. 398.

Club, to pay one's, i. *43*; iv. 303.

Club-law, ii. 429.

Club(s): account of these nocturnal assemblies, i. 39–42; ii. 345; regulations of an old Roman, i. 43; impertinent assemblies in taverns, i. 101–2; always contain butts, i. 203; 'merry-meetings', i. 203; 'mirthful meetings', i. 208; conversation in, i. 289; frequented by servants, i. 374; *Spectator* read in a, ii. 306; conversation in, falling upon vanity, ii. 427; tyrants in, iv. 302–4; a young rake initiated into half a dozen, iv. 569.

Club, the Spectator. *See* Spectator Club.

Club, the Ugly (at Oxford): account of, i. 76–78; Mr. SPECTATOR elected probationer of, i. 133, 197; Mr. SPECTATOR's letter of acceptance to, i. 205; an old beau and a Pict proposed for, i. 205; HECATISSA wishes to join, i. 205–6; letter from HUGH GOBLIN, president, i. 221–3; was originally at Cambridge, i. 335–6; why its secrets were exposed, i. 369; ROSALINDA's application to join, i. 370; mentioned, iv. 486.

Clubs: of fat men, i. 39; of scarecrows and skeletons, i. 39–40; of the Kings, i. 40; of the Georges, i. 40–41; street-clubs, i. 41; the Hum-Drum, i. 41; the Mum, i. 41; of Duellists, i. 41; iii. 188; Kit-Cat, i. 42, 310; iv. *517*; Beef-Steak, i. 42; October, i. 42, 310; Two-Penny, rules of, i. 43; Punning, i. 76; Witty, i. 76; Handsome, i. 76; Amorous, i. 124–7, 197; the Fringe-Glove, i. 125; Hebdomadal Meeting at Oxford, i. 181–3; 'Lowngers' at Cambridge, i. 229–32, 336; Everlasting, i. 308–11; of She-Romps, ii. 345–6; a 'lazy club' near the Temple, iii. 168–9; of female rakes in China-shops, iii. 245–6; of parish-clerks, iii. 401–2; of lawyers, iii. 402–3; of the metaphorically defunct, iv. 178; of hunters, iv. 178–9; of the Henpecked, iv. 208–9; formed to reread the *Spectator*, iv. 486; the Chit-Chat, iv. 513; the Widow-Club, iv. 515–18; Rattling, v. 154.

CLYTANDER: letter from (on wealth as a factor in marriage), iii. 92–93; 'C. to CLEONE', iii. 151.

Coach(es): hired, ii. 107; noises of c. and chairmen, ii. 189–90; 'can loll in her c.', ii. 237; rattling in London streets, ii. 477; v. 41; footmen hanging behind, iii. 69; &c.

Coach and horses, as a means of wasting time, i. 231.

Coach and six, i. 67, 384; iv. 554; &c.

Coach-box, ii. 23.

Coach-hire, a shilling for, ii. 199.

Coach-horses, a pair of, ii. 459.

Coach-makers, iii. 166.

Coachman (-men): Sir ROGER's, i. 439, 445; ii. 3; *The Plagues of a*, ii. 89; rivalry of carmen and c. in city streets, ii. 187; dispute between a hackney-c. and a prentice-boy, ii. 291; sign-language of, iv. 100; amateur, iv. 265–8, 373–7, 402; practices of, iv. 330; a widow who has buried a husband and two c., iv. 516.

Coal(s): a pan of burning, ii. 547; a young girl eating, iv. 16; c.-carts, iii. 210; c.-fire, a wife who usurped dominion of, v. 80; c.-pit on Sir ROGER's estate, iii. 54; 'c.-scranchers', iv. 17.

Coat(s), embroidered, i. 67; ii. 595; turned up with blue, i. 197; of blue camlet trimmed with silver, i. 434; jetting c. of Henry VII's time, i. 450; red c. and laced hat, i. 488; red c. to go a wooing in, ii. 14; with long pockets and slit sleeves, ii. 14–15; upper, ii. 43; skirt of, ii. 74; bunch of fold on each side of, ii. 74; silver hasps instead of buttons on, ii. 193; strutting in a laced, ii. 217; effect of, on a coquette's heart, ii. 595; with close sleeves, iii. 163; story of the long and short c. in Xenophon, iii. 249; TOM TAWDRY's laced, iv. 298; &c.

Coat of arms: husband adds those of his mistress, i. 117; with tools of forefathers, i. 117; mentioned, ii. 132.

Cob, Mother: 'Mother Cob's Mild', iii. 154.

Cobbler(s): ii. 238; iv. 271; winner of a grinning-match, ii. 184; smoking a c. in a frolic, iii. 341; c. and carmen, iv. 315; waked by a, v. 41; saying of a Spanish, v. 155.

Cobweb, working a rich embroidery upon a, iii. 369.

Cock: rebus of c. and lion on Blenheim House, i. 251; symbol of the French, i. 251; 'Sir ANDREW is grown the c. of the club', ii. 21; a c. to Aesculapius, ii. 234; c.-and-bull story, ii. 21; c.-loft, iii. 69, 71; c.-matches, ii. 3; iv. 18, 132; c.-pheasant, i. 448; c.-sparrow, iii. 275.

Cock, to: the chin, i. 136; the hat, i.

161; ii. 91; iii. 508; iv. 29; v. 106; the nose, ii. 572.

Cock(s) (of the hat): a beaver hat in a smart, i. 434; the Monmouth, ii. 14; reveal whimsicality of male sex, iii. 161; twirl the c. of a squire's hat behind him, iii. 322; show party allegiance, iv. 17–18; the military, iv. 377, 400; John Sly's report on, iv. 400; admired by women, v. 58; the loyal Cavalier, v. 150.

Cocker, Edward, *English Dictionary*, i. 155.

Cocking: young fellow, ii. 100; youths, iii. 303; a young officer c. upon the company, iii. 584.

Cockle: Locke on the senses of, i. 495; cockleshell merchants, i. 91.

COCKSURE, CHARLES, petition of, rejected, v. 117.

Codfish, a dish of, i. 77.

Cœur de Lion, a terror to the Saracens, i. 135.

Coffee: i. 52, 183, 371; sitting about a pot of, ii. 4; sugar in, ii. 82; a dish of, ii. 551; and snuff, iii. 97; laced, iii. 155; iv. 230; and chocolate, iii. 207; taste for, gradually acquired, iv. 70–71; *Spectator* served with the c. at breakfast, iv. 230; c.-room at Squire's, ii. 552.

Coffee-house(s): i. 44, 331; ii. 389; popularity of, i. *3*; a projector in a, i. 127–32; and their conversation, i. 208–11; and chocolate-houses, i. *232*; lawyers idling in, i. 209; EUBULUS presides in, i. 210–11; 'shift c. from hour to hour', i. 232; incident in a, i. 331; 'Idols' in, i. 371–2; ii. 107; iv. 407; places to do business or talk politics in, i. 371; behaviour in, i. 371; ii. 107–8; iii. 245; 'a dirty crowd of busy faces' in, ii. 63; disputation in, ii. 71–73; singing and whistling in, ii. 73; immodest conversation in, ii. 107–8; entertained with an account of a grinning match, ii. 183; 'pass his evening in a', ii. 199; theorists, ii. 251; IRUS and a justice of the peace meet at, ii. 528; 'our British Schools of Politics', iii. 100; reading the news at, iii. 154–5; v. 137; each has its particular statesmen, iii. 507; a 'by-coffee-house', iii. 509; 'laid down my penny at the bar', iii. 509; no variety of, in the country, iii. 590; PETER HUSH a whisperer in, iv. 112–13; witlings come to c. which have left off the *Spectator*, iv. 129; disputants in, iv. 187; leaders of fashions in, iv. 196; Rechteren–Mesnager

controversy discussed in, iv. 206–8; critics in, iv. 268; inaccurate reports in, iv. 355; letter from a bar-keeper in a, iv. 407–8; Mr. SPECTATOR in the, iv. 499–500; catching the news from court at, v. 137; advertisements of quacks in, iv. 553.

Coffee-houses:
Amsterdam, behind the Royal Exchange, ii. *57*.
Baker's, in Cornhill, ii. *74*.
Batson's, in Cornhill, i. *120*; iii. *510*.
The Bear, in Holborn (?), ii. 45.
Black-Boy, in Ave-Maria Lane, iii. *459*.
Blacknell's, in Hatton Garden, i. lxxxv.
Blue-Coat. *See* Joe's.
Button's, in Covent-Garden, iii. *485*; iv. 499.
Child's, in St. Paul's Church-yard, v. 137; Mr. SPECTATOR smokes a pipe at, i. 3; discourses at, iv. 355; letters from, iv. 470; a Tory resort, iv. 499; the boy at, v. 81.
Cock and Bottle, in Little Britain (?), ii. 225.
Cocoa-Tree, in Pall-Mall: Mr. SPECTATOR very well known at, i. 4.
Cross-Keys, in Holborn (?), ii. 45.
Edlin's, in St. Ann's Lane near Aldersgate, i. *509*.
Elford's, in George Yard, Lombard Street, iii. *278*.
Garraway's, in Exchange Alley: i. *4*, *120*; ii. *108*; iii. *510*; iv. *102*; a toyshop near, ii. 46; receives news of health of French king, iii. 509; PETER HUSH at, iv. 113.
George's, without Temple Bar, ii. *238*.
Giles's, in St. James's Street: discusses report of death of Louis XIV, iii. 507.
Golden-Lion, in Drury-Lane (?), iv. 182.
Grecian, in Devereux Court, i. xviii, *3*, 404; iv. *265*; Mr. SPECTATOR very well known at, i. 4; 'adjacent to the Law', i. 209.
Grecian's Head, in the Strand, i. *129* ii. *441*.
The Hoop (?), letter from, v. 83.
Italian, in the Strand, ii. *474*.
Jacob's, behind the Royal Exchange, iv. 5.
Joe's, 'the Blue-Coat Coffee-house in Sweething's Alley', letter from, iv. 478.
John's, near the Royal Exchange, iv. 5.
Jonathan's, in Exchange Alley: Stock-Jobbers at, i. 4; the stocks at, iv.

Coffee-Houses (*cont.*)
355–6; a Jew at, iv. 500; mentioned, ii. *108*; iv. *102*.
Lloyd's, in Lombard Street: iii. *353*; 'where the Auctions are usually kept', i. 196.
Man's, Jenny (Tilt-Yard), in White-hall: i. 450; discusses report of death of Louis XIV, iii. 507–8; letters received from, iv. 470.
Margaret's, in Cheapside, i. *153*.
Mitchel's, in Crutched Friars, i. *156*.
Nando's, in Fleet Street, iii. *206*.
Old Man's, at Charing Cross, i. *xxv*.
Pall-Mall, in Pall Mall, iii. *125*.
Rainbow, in Fleet Street: i. *258*; ii. *57*; iii. *206*; silver garters seen at, i. 70.
Robin's, in Exchange Alley: i. *120*; iii. *510*; bills for the value of large estates given at, iv. 102.
St. James's, in St. James's Street: i. xix, 3, *120*; iii. *279*; 'committee of politics in the inner room at', i. 4; advertisement of changes among servants at, i. 104; politicians at, iii. 100; 'the fountain-head of poli-tics', iii. 507; TOM TAWDRY pares his nails at, iv. 298.
St. Paul's, iv. *61*.
Sam's, in Ludgate Street, i. *120*; iii. *278*; iv. *5*.
Searle's, in Searle Street, Lincoln's Inn Fields: 'adjacent to the Law', i. 209.
Smyrna, in Pall Mall: i. *120*; iii. 100; PETER HUSH at, iv, 113.
Squire's, in Fullwood's (Fuller's) Rents, Holborn: 'adjacent to the Law', i. 209; Sir ROGER at, ii. 551, 557; the high table at, ii. 551.
Three Chairs, in Covent Garden (?), an auction of paintings at, i. 288.
Tilt-Yard. *See* Man's, Jenny.
Tom's, in Devereux Court, i. 404.
White's (chocolate-house), in St. James's Street: i. xviii, 3; iii. 163; TOM THE TYRANT at, i. 211; lovers and men of intrigue at, i. 375; TOM TAWDRY pares his nails at, iv. 298.
The Widow's, in Devereux Court: i. *372*; letters from, iv. 265, 374.
Will's, in Covent Garden: i. xviii, *185*; ii. 37; iv. 113; the round of politi-cians at, i. 3; the TEMPLAR takes a turn there before the play, i. 10; gentlemen that make a figure at, i. 393, 404; letters from, ii. 561; iii. 111–12; iv. 406; Robin the porter at, iii. 490; deaths of French poets discussed at, iii. 508; discourses at, iv. 102, 355.
Will's, in C rnhill, i. *120*.
Young Man's, at Charing Cross, i. *156*.
'A c. at Westminster', iv. 553.
'A little c. beyond Aldgate', ii. 348.
'A c. in Cheapside', iii. 509.
'A c. in Fish Street', iii. 508.
'A c. in St. Paul's church-yard', iv. 470.
'A c. near the Temple', letter from, ii. 73; further report from, ii. 81; incident at, ii. 92; disputation in, ii. 273; a 'lazy club' at, iii. 168; discussion of Spanish succession at, iii. 508.
'A c. not far from the [Royal] Ex-change', iii. 428; iv. 539.
'A c. not far from the Hay-Market Theatre', i. 127.
Coffee-man, his last week's bill of mor-tality, iii. 27.
COHU, race of, iv. 596.
Coiff, Brother of the (a serjeant-at-law), i. 377.
Coiffure: now in fashion, i. 414; the French, ii. 579. *See also* Hair.
Coin, Pay in his own (prov.), i. 230.
Coinage, reform of, by Charles Montagu, v. 122.
Coke, Sir Edward: The TEMPLAR's knowledge of, i. 9; iv. 485; 'Cook and Littleton', iii. 126; and other vener-able authors, iii. 168; on the Law of Free-Bench, v. 130.
Colbert, Jean-Baptiste. *See* Torcy.
Colchester, Lord Lucas of, i. 417.
Cold, a: the woman's man never at a loss what is good for, ii. 111; fear of catch-ing, ii. 385, 386; iv. 210.
Cold: and heat, why made agreeable to man, iii. 453; baths for distempers, ii. 383; fits of a mistress, ii. 512; wash-ing the head with c. water, ii. 387.
Coldness: of a mistress, ii. 512–13; of a friend, iii. 74; that usually comes on after marriage, iii. 490.
COLE, KATE (mother of WILLIAM, RICHARD, and REBECCA), in WILL MAPLE's genealogy, ii. 296.
Cole, Mrs., letter received by, iii. *189*.
Coleburt, Dr., his elixir advertised, iv. *61*.
Coleshill-Heath, Warwickshire, grin-ning contest at, ii. 182.
Coleworts, rows of, in a garden, iv. 189.
Colic, iv. 509; cordials and strong waters for, iv. 517.

COLIN's lament for PHEBE's absence (poem), v. 61–64.

Collar (for a girl), used in learning to dance, i. 283.

Collector of Customs, petition to be made, v. 151.

Collet, Joseph: a contributor (?), i. xli; and the *Spectator*, i. lxxxvi, xcv.

COLLIDAN, reply to letter from, iv. 588.

Collier, Jeremy: *Dissuasive from the Play-House*, recommended to women for reading, i. 391; Essay 'Of Musick' quoted, iii. 352.

Collier, William, and Drury Lane Theatre, ii. *504*.

Colly-Molly-Puff (Cully Mully Puff), the pastry-man, ii. 477; 'of agreeable and noisy memory', iii. 354.

Colmar, ——, fans 'must be mounted by no body but C.', iii. 206.

Colour(s): entertain the eye but do not affect the heart, i. 140; hanging out false, i. 347; no such thing as c. in nature, ii. 46; hung in Westminster Hall after Blenheim, ii. 50; in painting set off by shades, ii. 399; only the infractions of the rays of the sun, ii. 442; use of just and natural c. in painting, ii. 447; in head-dresses, ii. 530–3, 552; to purchase a c., iii. 4; why made agreeable to man, iii. 453; gaiety and variety of, pleasing to the imagination, iii. 544; have no existence in matter, iii. 547. *See also* Hoods.

Colour-shop, ii. 447.

Colson, Tom, described in No. 346 (?), iii. *289*.

Comb(s): ivory, i. 193; tortoise-shell, iii. 183; and brushes, iv. 195.

COMB-BRUSH, CONSTANTIA: letter from (a chambermaid), iii. 378–9.

Comedians, always ranked below tragedians, iv. 388.

Comedies, English: devices for comic effect in, i. 191; gentlemen in, disguised as painter or dancing master, iii. 319; excel in novelty and variety of characters, iii. 396.

Comedy: allegorical figure of, i. 274; should move mirth rather than sorrow and indignation, i. 280; distinguished from burlesque, ii. 467; true spirit of c. in *The Humourous Lieutenant*, ii. 536; less safe than tragedy for women, iii. 374.

Comeliness, and decorum, iii. 40–41.

Comet: the great c. of 1680, i. 423; draws a long-extended blaze, v. 122.

COMFITT, JEREMY (a grocer), letter from, iv. 407.

COMFITT, MARY, letter from (on a suitor), iii. 195.

Comfort: pleasures expressed by the word, ii. 269; allegorical figure of, iv. 279.

Commandant, a French word imported, ii. 152.

Commander(s), military: distinguished from the gross of soldiery, ii. 97; tribute to a, ii. 99; must not let their orders be disputed, ii. 344.

Commandments, the: in the church service, ii. 420; insult upon all the ten c. in plays, ii. 554.

Commendation: how to be bestowed, ii. 238–41; only despised when we cease to deserve it, iv. 150.

Commendatory verses, practice of publishing, iv. 484.

Commerce (intercourse, dealings): of witches, i. 482; of lovers, ii. 109; of friendship, ii. 180; between great men and courtiers, ii. 257; between husband and wife, ii. 260–1; all parts of human life a, ii. 292; unlawful c. of the sexes, ii. 534; the c. of life, ii. 559; of sin, ii. 568.

Commerce (exchange of goods). *See* Trade.

Commercy, in Lorraine, iii. 440.

Commode(s) (head-dress): Conecte's crusade against, i. 414; a c. at Staines not half a foot high, ii. 13; in the northern countries, ii. 15; *Spectator's* censure of, iii. 161; and a night-raile, iv. 29; mentioned, ii. 531. *See also* Head-dress.

Commodus (son of Faustina), often portrayed as a Hercules, ii. 10–11.

COMMON, MOLL, slays with her tears, iii. 418.

Common, living upon the, ii. 295.

Common expressions, shunned by epic poets, iii. 11.

Common-Hunt, the City, v. 59.

Common life, heroic virtue in, ii. 433.

Common sense: lack of, in audiences, i. 59; fashion often leads against, i. 275; best literature appeals to reader of, i. 297; of a nation destroyed by party-spirit, i. 510; ii. 4; seldom in high fortune, ii. 259; wanting in free-thinkers, ii. 412; of mankind, the material of criticism, ii. 484; two meanings of, ii. 508; music now without any passion or, ii. 584.

Common thoughts, i. 506.

Commoner (member of House of Commons), i. 13.

Commonplace: book, ii. 114; talker, i. 48; commonplaces in oratory, v. 163.

Commonwealth: allegorical figure of genius of, i. 16; of letters, i. 245, 438; iv. 387; v. 35; constitution of Roman, iii. 20; of Amazons, iv. 21–26.

Commonwealth's men, Sir ANDREW likely to convert his friends to, ii. 21.

Communication between absent lovers, ii. 437–9.

Communion-table, railed in, i. 460.

Companion: a troublesome c. to himself not an agreeable one to others, ii. 54; a good c. not easily found, ii. 260; marks of a pleasant, iii. 340–1, 448–51.

Company: putting c. on others, ii. 54; necessary to women, ii. 119–20; 'to see c.', ii. 246; iii. 69; 'the purest goodest c. in the world', iii. 72; behaviour of married couples before, iii. 72; iv. 13–14; art of being agreeable in, iii. 448–51; choice of, iii. 589; fear of appearing singular in, iv. 116; effects of pleasantry in, iv. 130–1.

Comparaisons à longue queue, iii. 90.

Comparisons: must not be too obvious, i. 264; Milton's c. censured by ignorant readers, iii. 90; Perrault and Boileau on Homer's, iii. 90–91; art of making c. and allusions, iii. 578. *See also* Similes.

Compass: living within, i. 468; ii. 252; real pleasures of life lie within a narrow, iv. 563.

Compasses, golden, in Homer and *PL*, iii. 258.

Compassion: mutual offices of c. needed, ii. 165; good natured man shows, ii. 167; and love of parents for children, ii. 213; of God, ii. 214; for others, ii. 394; iv. 511; to be exercised towards the vicious, ii. 534; tenderest sensations of love and, iii. 80; refines and civilizes human nature, iii. 486; sources and rewards of, v. 12–14. *See also* Pity.

Competitions: races and grinning-matches at country wakes, ii. 131–5, 182–5; whistling and yawning matches, ii. 206–8; motives in, ii. 371.

Complacency, i. 358, ii. 11; iii. 92, 143; in manner of the PERVERSE WIDOW, i. 465; in proclaiming errors of the great, ii. 494; in doing good, ii. 500; inspired by beauties of nature, iii. 475, 542; derived from a garden, iv. 192; habitual c. of BENEVOLUS, iv. 372; sweetness of temper and c. necessary in married couples, v. 76; of manners, v. 175, 184.

Complaint: Milton's c. of his blindness, iii. 61, 147–8; examples of sorrow and c. from Shakespeare and from Philips, iv. 434.

Complaints of ill health, intolerable in society, i. 420–1; ii. 64–67; iv. 9–10.

Complaisance: 'with my usual c.', i. 206; words of, i. 429; a mutual, i. 486; of a companion, ii. 61; 'in c. to', ii. 90; good breeding is c. reduced into an art, ii. 165; of clients towards patrons, ii. 337; an eye of proper, ii. 470; of Catiline, iii. 448; practised in courts, iii. 478; of ERASTUS, iv. 297; lack of, in a gentleman, and in a lover, iv. 304–5; v. 18; exact c. when he was a lover, v. 79.

Compleat Jockey, The, i. 390.

Compleat Ogler, manuscript of the, i. 199.

Complexion (disposition), ii. 417; iv. 312; too warm a, ii. 158; men of a serious, ii. 314; vigour of, determines ambition, ii. 370; religion sometimes expressed in a melancholy, iii. 80; checks and restraints caused by one's, iii. 405.

Complexion (colour and texture of skin): cosmetic aids for, i. 139, 221–2; party zeal bad for, i. 242; injured by blushing, i. 282; beautiful c. of English women, ii. 532; colours to suit different c., ii. 533; an assumed, ii. 574; worn by ladies in Paris, ii. 580.

Compliment, and dissimulation, i. 429–32; iv. 503.

Compliments: in use at tea-tables, i. 152; mechanical acts of devotion are c. made to virtue, i. 341; return of c. and salutations, ii. 508–9; insincere c. an offence, iv. 7–8; well-turned c. of Estcourt, iv. 155.

Compos mentis, ii. 153.

Composition: feats of, in authors, ii. 355–7.

Compositions (medicines), ii. 263.

Composure (composition), of music, ii. 505.

Comptroller-general of London Cries: proposed, ii. 474–5, 503–5; referred to, iv. 11.

Comus (god of revels), an attendant on Winter, iii. 596.

Concanen, Matthew, *Miscellaneous Poems*, i. lxxxii; iii. 533; v. 161.

Concave: the hoop-petticoat blown up into an enormous, ii. 5; and convex in architecture, iii. 557.

Conceit(s): in modern Italian writers, i. 26; in the sign of Cat and Fiddle, i. 116; monstrous, i. 145–6; the rebus a kind of, i. 250–1; echo poem a kind of,

i. 252; and puns i. 262–3; preferred to solid sense, i. 269; ingenious, i. 378; in modern lyrics, ii. 366; of free-thinkers, ii. 412; in a letter from PETER DE QUIR, iii. 483; taste in England for forced, iii. 530; dressed up in smooth quaint language, iv. 82. *See also* False Wit.

Conception: a man may have an active body but not a quick, ii. 504; limitations of human, iv. 530–1.

Condé, Louis II de Bourbon, Prince of: his face like an eagle's, i. 367; and the Chevalier de Flourilles, ii. *98*.

Condescension(s): as a part of fashionable life, i. 486; humanity and c. of superiors, ii. 354; dignity and c. of Raphael in *PL*, ii. 564–5.

Condition, people of, i. 324; iii. 47; &c.

'Conditions, ill', defined, i. 308.

Conduct: inconsistency of, ii. 136–9; the learned often lack skill in c. of life, ii. 362–4; value of discretion in c. of life, ii. 375–8.

Conecte, Thomas, his crusade against head-dresses, i. 414–15.

Confections (confects): and fruits in a modern meal, ii. 265; and cordials, iii. 206.

Confidant(s): the PERVERSE WIDOW's, i. 465–6, 484; the most impertinent of all people, i. 484.

'Confirmation, This wants', a common sentence in newspapers, ii. 388.

Confucius, i. 289; ii. 155.

congé d'élire, iv. 183.

Congreve, William: and the Haymarket, i. 4; a member of the Temple, i. 9; a member of the Kit-Cat Club, i. 42; referred to (?), iv. 66. — WORKS: *The Double Dealer*, Lady Touchwood in, i. 77; *Doris* quoted, a masterpiece of good-humoured satire, iii. 585–6; *Love for Love*, i. 262; Sir Sampson in, ii. 242; 'one of the finest comedies', ii. 242; Epilogue to, quoted, ii. 326; benefit performance of, for Estcourt, iii. 342; *The Mourning Bride*, a noble tragedy which ends happily, i. 170; *The Old Bachelour*, Doggett as Fondlewife in, iv. 68; wit and humour in, iv. 389; *On Mrs. Arabella Hunt Singing*, quoted, iv. 56; *The Way of the World*, ii. 300, 527.

Conjugal: caresses and endearments, ii. 177; morality, ii. 203; women who refuse c. endearments, ii. 320; averse to c. friendship, ii. 417; 'c. liberty of conscience', iii. 65; c. love refines life, iv. 369–73.

Conjuror: a Christian c. in *Armida*, i. 25,

196; Mr. SPECTATOR suspected of being a, ii. 19; mentioned, ii. 29; a house in Moorfields tenanted by a, iv. 293. *See also* Campbell, Duncan.

Connivances (winkings), iii. 397.

CONQUEST, DEBORAH: member of the Widow-Club, iv. 516.

CONQUEST, Sir SAMPSON, Justice of the Quorum, iv. 516.

Conquest(s): of the man of pleasure unsatisfactory, ii. 94; the vanity of military, ii. 208–12, 282–7; an eye wandering after new, ii. 300; making c. in church, ii. 600; HONORIA's thoughts bent upon, iii. 81; difficult for a beauty or a hero to resign, iii. 102.

Conrade III, and the Siege of Hensburg, iv. 269.

Conscience: value of a good, i. 54; approval of, the highest step to which human nature can arrive, ii. 181; testimony of a good, ii. 238; 'conjugal liberty of', iii. 65; terrors of an evil c. depicted in *PL*, iii. 120.

Conscience (consciousness): follows every thought, i. 160; of a good fame, ii. 101; of worthy enterprizes, ii. 180; of doing good, ii. 526.

'Conscious beauty adorned with conscious virtue', ii. 21.

Consciousness: sometimes leads to affectation, i. 161; of worthy actions itself an ample reward, ii. 370; Locke on importance of, in personal identity, iv. 575–6.

Consent of mankind, as to existence of God, ii. 230, 233–4, 288, 322; iii. 461.

Consistency: disdained by free-thinkers, ii. 412; of characters in *PL*, ii. 565; iii. 114.

Consolation: in grief, ii. 139–43; a letter of, ii. 256; on loss of beauty, iii. 102–4; letter of, by Phalaris, iii. 298–9.

Consort (wife), WILL HONEYCOMB's opinion of the word, iv. 239.

Consort (concert): of birds, i. 158; of music, i. 228; of hounds, i. 476; director of a, ii. 415.

Conspiracy, pronunciation of the word, ii. 33.

Constable(s): knocking down a, i. 436; v. 58; with his attendants, ii. 218; 'an invader of c.' in his youth, ii. 576.

Constancy: the old topic of c. in love, i. 48; a qualification of a good friend, i. 291; and love make a good spouse, ii. 515; of affection to be supported, ii. 523; praise of Louis XIV's heroic, iii. 102; greater in men of grave natures, v. 23.

CONSTANTIA and THEODOSIUS, ii.143–8.
Constantine (emperor), v. 168.
Constantini, Angelo, *Vie de Scaramouche*, iii. 3.
Constantinople, v. 42.
CONSTANTIUS, reply to letter from, iv. 588.
Constantius (emperor), v. 15.
Constellations: grow thin at rising of sun, i. 274; in the celestial globe, iv. 481.
Constitution(s): affected by cloud or sunshine, ii. 137; good nature one of the blessings of a happy, ii. 166, 197; which flag without use of brandy, ii. 268; humours affect the body differently according to, ii. 371; a crazy c. in an old man, ii. 512; a good c. marked by soundness and vigour of the parts, iii. 15; an easy, iii. 80; naturally abounding with acids, iv. 460.
Consuls: authority of, i. 185; powers of the Roman, iii. 20
Consumption(s): momentary, i. 15; children brought into, ii. 456; mentioned, i. 105; iv. 559; v. 99.
Contemplation: of another life, a rational pleasure, ii. 101; of Divine Wisdom, in a future state, ii. 420; reading and c., the two great sources of knowledge, iii. 21; allegorical figure of, iv. 326.
Contempt: attendant on poverty, ii. 89–90; for Negroes inexcusable, ii. 339; depresses a noble spirit, ii. 426; of religion and decency in plays, ii. 554–5; cocking the nose as a sign of, ii. 572; of pleasure a preparatory for contempt of pain, iii. 130; ways of expressing, iii. 322; haughty, iv. 246.
Content, contentedness, contentment: the utmost we can hope for in this world, ii. 139; Epictetus's motive to, ii. 353; secret rest and c. of mind, ii. 500; balanced against riches, iv. 136; how acquired, iv. 561–5; is natural wealth, iv. 563–4.
Continency, Hobbes on, iv. 245.
Contradiction: troubled with an humour of, ii. 72; in the great points of atheism, ii. 230; spirit of, in some men, ii. 525–6.
Contrast, and opposition of incidents, delightful in poetry, iii. 363.
Contrition: for behaviour towards parents, ii. 521–5; of a reformed prodigal in *Henry IV*, iii. 394.
Controversies: and disputes about nothing, i. 474; in religion, ii. 229; methods of managing, ii. 428–32; Jesuits' practice in, iii. 98.

Controversy: books of c. unsettling to faith, iv. 141–2; between Rechteren and Mesnager, iv. 206–8.
Conundrums (puns), in reign of James I, i. 260.
Conventicle(s): meetings and, ii. 7; a neighbouring, iii. 509; whining at a, v. 155.
Conventicler, a female, i. 197, 198–9.
Conventual: Father FRANCIS, a venerable, ii. 146; sermon of a, ii. 466.
Conversation: secret of, to listen attentively, i. 208; best c., with a friend, i. 289, 397; of a gentleman should be clean, i. 324; ill health not a proper subject for, i. 420; should present nothing but in its excellence, i. 422; lack of sincerity in, i. 429–32; coarser in town than in the country, i. 488; of military men, ii. 23–24, 96; iv. 402; of the English falls into pauses and intervals, ii. 32; undue exactness about trifles in, ii. 44–46; our duty to be cheerful in, ii. 64–68; coffee-house c., ii. 71–72, 81–82; immodest c., ii. 107–8, 439–40; iv. 58, 402–3; lawyers too argumentative in, ii. 272–5; with a friend is only *thinking aloud*, ii. 375; of the inquisitive, ii. 386–9; by the eyes, ii. 478–80; in the country, ii. 486; art of pleasing in, ii. 590–3; with equals necessary in education, iii. 133; examples of redundant phrases in, iii. 398; with men of polite genius, a method of improving taste, iii. 529; unkind raillery in, iii. 582–6; should not be monopolized by one, iv. 4; country c., iv. 177–8; of MANILIUS, iv. 153–4; method in, iv. 186–7; substitutes for wit in, iv. 287–90; of women, iv. 499; sincerity in, iv. 502–5; egotists in, iv. 521–2; singularity in, iv. 570. *See also* Language.
Conversation (intercourse, manners): between men and women, i. 225–6; an unbecoming levity in, i. 326; has become simplified in town, i. 486–7.
Conversation-piece, a green, iv. 178–9.
Converts, and renegadoes, in religion and politics, ii. 135.
Convex and concave in architecture, iii. 557.
Conveyancer(s), in marriage-settlements, ii. 87; iii. 110; clerk to a, ii. 560.
Conveyances, lawyers employed in drawing up of, i. 90.
Convicts, fined, iv. 384.
Convocation, refused to alter wording of Lord's Prayer, i. 337.
Convulsions: of an infant, ii. 524; dis-

tortions and c. practised by beggars, iv. 12.

Conyers, Gerard (a Director of the Bank), a subscriber, i. *xc*.

COOK, HARRY, petition of, ii. 294.

Cook and Littleton. *See* Coke.

Cook: should not live at sign of the Boot, i. 117; apothecary employed in countermining the c. and the vintner, ii. 264.

Cook-maid: DIAGORAS in love with his, ii. 408; 'in love, and grown careless', iii. 154; squabbles with the, iv. 210.

Cooksey, Richard, iii. *366*.

Cooper, Mr., print-seller, ii. *381*; toy-shop, iv. *5*.

Cooper, cries of the, in London streets, ii. 476.

Cope, Sir John (a Director of the Bank), a subscriber, i. *xc*.

Copenhagen, a letter from, iii. 473–4.

Copernican hypothesis, described in *PL*, iii. 281.

Copiers of men, like copiers of authors, iv. 19.

Copiousness: of expression in the censorious, ii. 459; Milton copies Homer in c. of his phrases, iii. 15.

Coptic, Mr. SPECTATOR not versed in, i. 294; study of, iv. 104.

COQUETILLA: on reading for ladies, i. 392; kills by a tap of the fan, iii. 417; examination of her heart, v. 9.

Coquetry: and childishness of behaviour, i. 194; a dash of, i. 382; jarrings and dissonances arising from, ii. 461.

Coquette: 'the most airy', i. 67; a country, i. 306; life not long enough for all her tricks, i. 378; 'a c. lady', i. 437; woman often degenerates into a, ii. 9; an old c. married to a morose rustic, ii. 11; to be regarded with contempt or indifference, ii. 179; compared with a jilt, ii. 234–5; behaviour of in the theatre, ii. 315; character of, ii. 459; a dwarf who is a, ii. 557; dissection of a c.'s heart, ii. 594–7; iii. 161; behaviour of a c. in low life, iii. 427; behaviour of a c. at church, iv. 284–7, 330; often loses her reputation whilst she preserves her virtue, v. 24; the Widow OGLE a famous, v. 131.

Coquettes: a sisterhood of, i. 37; introduced custom of receiving visits in bed, i. 193; a few fantastical, i. 347; *petits-maîtres* and, i. 354; a satire upon, i. 426; and jilts, ii. 234–5; who break up affairs of other lovers, ii. 559–60; male c. or 'friblers', iii. 23–25, 73;

superannuated, iii. 75; restrained by fear of gossip, iii. 465; and prudes, iv. 316; behaviour of, iv. 331–3; in Cave of Trophonius, v. 46.

Coral, a child's rattle and, i. 2.

Corbaccio (in *Volpone*), Johnson as, iii. 394.

Cordials, cordial waters: receipts for distilling, ii. 487; confects and, iii. 206; and anodyne for gout, iv. 169; and strong waters for colic, iv. 517.

Corelli, Arcangelo, ii. *506*.

CORINNA: charming though inconstant, ii. 119; an unsuccessful jilt, ii. 235; torments her husband with indifference, ii. 261; her fond approach, ii. 308; her billet to her lover, iii. 102; her letter to a young lady, iii. 166; in 'My love was fickle . . .', iv. 163; verses addressed to, v. 25.

Corinth, a drinking match at, iv. 541–2.

Corinthian order of pillars, iv. 122.

Cormorant(s): symbols of cares and passions, ii. 124; Satan's transformation into a, in *PL*, iii. 172.

Corn: ruined by hunters, ii. 189; sufficiency of, in Great Britain, iii. 285; the critic who separated chaff from, iii. 38; fields of c. make a pleasant prospect, iii. 552; man who learned to throw a grain of c. through the eye of a needle, iv. 146.

Cornaro, J. (Venetian ambassador), ii. 267.

Cornaro, Luigi, his book on attaining a long and healthful life, ii. 266–7.

Corn-cutter: cry of, in London streets, ii. 477; who might have made an excellent physician, iii. 109.

Corneille, Pierre: the thought bears up the expressions in his tragedies, i. 165; an improbability in his *Horace*, i. 188–9; death of, iii. 508; mentioned, iii. 529; Cibber's *Ximena* based on the *Cid*, iv. 453.

CORNELIA: puts on a black hood when her husband goes into the country, iii. 532.

Cornelia, wife of Caesar, iii. *99*.

CORNELII, family of, the father and sons on good terms, ii. 254–5.

Cornelison, William Henry (a Director of the Bank), a subscriber, i. *xc*.

Cornice: a term of art used by Milton, iii. 64; features of, in architecture, iii. 556–7; (cornish) in a repository for fashions, iv. 194.

Cornishman, letter from a, ii. 13.

Cornwall, fashions in, ii. 14–15.

Coronation: chairs in Westminster

Abbey, iii. 215; letters describing rejoicings at c. of George I, v. 105–8.

'Corporeal wits' on the stage, ii. 504.

Corps: a French word imported, ii. 151–2; 'innumerable c., if I may use that term', iii. 28; *c. de réserve*, ii. 151–2.

Correctness: moderns excel ancients in, i. 261; ii. 127–8; Boileau the most correct poet among the moderns, ii. 220; works of a great genius superior to authors of mere, iii. 37–38.

Correggio [Antonio Allegri], in Vision of Painters, i. 356.

Correspondence, between absent lovers, ii. 437–8.

Correspondence (intercourse): of WILL WIMBLE with gentlemen about him, i. 447; 'good c.', ii. 235, 255; unreserved c. between father and son, ii. 255; with France interrupted by war, ii. 577.

Corruption(s): true delicacy opposed to, iii. 15; among men of great place, iv. 160–1.

Cosmetic(s): use of, i. 139, 173–7, 221–2; a whitewash, iii. 418; advertisement for, iv. 129, 130. *See also* Chrystal Cosmetick.

Coste, P., *Life of Condé*, ii. 98.

Costume. *See* Dress.

Cotterell, Sir Charles, translated La Calprenède, i. 154.

COTTILUS: a man of equal spirit, ii. 65–66; an elderly fortune-hunter, iii. 127.

Cottius, followed Cato in suicide, iii. 33.

Cotton Library: letter from Anne Boleyn in, iii. 487; a manuscript in, iv. 163.

Cott-quean, description of a, iv. 210.

Counsellors: nuisance of voluntary, ii. 293; safety in a multitude of, iv. 501.

Countenance: keeping in, ii. 400; putting in, ii. 515; out of, iii. 70. *See also* Face.

Counter-tenor, i. 476.

Counterparts: men and women made as c. to one another, ii. 9; immoral writers the c. of a Confucius or a Socrates, ii. 155.

Countess of Kent's Receipts. See Kent.

Country, love of one's: the noblest of principles, but capable of mischief, i. 512; an honest prejudice, iii. 18.

Country, country life: i. 67–68; ii. 486–9; iv. 143–4, 390–1; problem of educating a c. girl, i. 281–2; *Pleasures of a C. Life* recommended, i. 391; useful diversions and 'reliefs' of, i. 397; pleasures of, i. 439, 470–1, 483; Sunday in, i. 459–62; most healthful because of physical exercise, i. 471–4; good breeding (salutations) in, i. 486–9;

ii. 433–4; fashions of dress in, out of date, i. 486–9; ii. 12–15; party-spirit reigns more in, ii. 2–4; account of festivals in, ii. 130–5; Sir ANDREW divides himself between town and, ii. 401–2; visits paid in, ii. 448–9; married life in, ii. 486–9; letter from three c. maidens, iii. 226; city dwellers fancy a retreat in, iii. 270; dancing round Maypole in, iii. 372; how to be a leading man in, iii. 478; poets always in love with, iii. 549; poets must be conversant with, iii. 563; good humour necessary to enjoyment of, iii. 590; excessive drinking in, iv. 177–8; scheme of a, iv. 180–1; WILL HONEYCOMB on simplicity of manners in, iv. 390–1; motions of the eye practised by c. beauties, iv. 425.

Country dances, i. 285–6; ii. 82, 512; iii. 112–13; v. 106; the 'Sir Roger de Coverley', i. 7; Mr. Fert's instructions for, i. 157; intricacies of, i. 272; a country jig, ii. 207; delight in, iv. 331–2.

Country gentleman (gentlemen): seldom hunts on his own grounds, ii. 18–19; excessive eating and drinking of, ii. 96, 225; iv. 448; ridiculed in London, iii. 322; letter from (on catcalls), iii. 349; conversation of, iv. 177–81; letter from, to PHARAMOND, iv. 201; often apply themselves wholly to hunting, iv. 593; their duty to plant, iv. 593–5; the 'Memoirs of an Honest', v. 127–8.

Country Gentleman's Courant, i. lxx.

Country Justice. See Dalton.

Countryman: fable of Jupiter and, i. 108; letter from a (to his mistress), iii. 189, 209.

Country-putt, ii. 524.

Country seat: of Sir ROGER, i. 439–40; of Sir ANDREW, ii. 401; a traveller viewing a fine, iv. 421.

Country wake, account of a, ii. 130–2. *See also* Doggett.

Country wife, an excellent, i. 451.

Country wits, iii. 57.

Coup d'éclat, iii. 187.

Coup d'essai, iii. 163.

Coupée, capers (a dance step), iv. 332.

Courage: the great point of honour in men, i. 416; of military men, ii. 96–99; exerted as fierceness in savage nations, ii. 339; kinds of c. in Homer's characters, ii. 562; and magnanimity inseparable, iii. 303; of Turnus and Aeneas contrasted, iii. 304; of young men of Sparta, iii. 321; example of, from Dry-

den, iv. 435; and patience among soldiers, iv. 534.

Courant. See *Daily Courant.*

Courant, Mr., owner of horse 'Arabian', ii. 117.

COURIER, STEPHEN, letter from, to a friend, iii. 7.

Coursing: dressing for hunting or, ii. 111; the time of c. is come on, ii. 164.

Court: follies of, not too sacred for ridicule, i. 142; a c. physician, ii. 253; effect of, on manners, ii. 522–3; Gracián's maxims for advancing at, iii. 42; method of making one's way at, iii. 477–8; its method of gathering intelligence, iv. 43; a c. lady and her crazy young husband, ii. 134; and city contrasted with country, iv. 143–4; motives for appearing at, iv. 201–2; the standard of good breeding, iv. 534.

Court: proceedings of the c. baron, v. 130; of judicature, ii. 458; 'within the verge of the c.', i. 425, 437.

Courtesan: OMNAMANTE, a prodigal, ii. 70; discovered Catiline's conspiracy, ii. 247; RHODOPE, the, ii. 407.

Courtesy: of Lacedaemonians, i. 30–31; represented by Calidore in Spenser, iv. 428.

Courtier(s): tawdry, ii. 11; making professions of esteem, ii. 180; at a great man's levée, ii. 256–60; a superstitious man like an insipid, ii. 289; new fashions in salutations introduced by, ii. 433–4; Horace knew how to be a skilful, ii. 592.

COURTLY, FRANCIS: letter from (protesting against too specific discussion of vice), ii. 574–5; referred to, iii. 15, 65.

COURTLY, NED, slain by a lady's curtsy, iii. 418.

Courtship: women who spin out the time of, i. 376–80; in this age contrasted with the former, i. 386; problems of, ii. 52; iii. 503–5, 586–9; v. 35–37, 405–8, 425–6; as practised by men of gallantry, ii. 105–6; a long c. makes a happy marriage, ii. 514–15; distinguishing between c. and conversation, iii. 426; of birds determined by colour, iii. 542–3; STREPHON's covert way of, iii. 587–8.

Cousins, a visit between two, iv. 378–9.

Coventry, a prize-fighter from, iv. 31.

Coventry, Anne, Countess of, the original of EMILIA (?), iii. 78.

COVERLEY, Sir ARTHUR DE (father of Sir ROGER), iv. 340.

COVERLEY, Sir HUMPHREY DE: character of, i. 452; wise management of his affairs, i. 470.

COVERLEY, Lady (mother of Sir ROGER), lived to a great age, i. 454.

COVERLEY, Sir ROGER DE: a baronet, i. 7; ii. 187; (elsewhere referred to as knight: i. 425, 439, 440, 448; ii. 551, 557; iii. 343; 'Knight of the Shire', iii. 437); character of, i. 7–9; thinks only men of fine parts deserve hanging, i. 28; objects to *Spectator*'s criticism of country squires, i. 143; encloses a letter to LEONORA, i. 152–3; management of LEONORA's estate left to, i. 158; orders a posset drink for persons out of order, i. 420; at home, i. 439–40; his servants, i. 439–40, 443–5; his chaplain and his sermons, i. 441–2; and WILL WIMBLE, i. 446–9; his blunt way of speaking, i. 449; his portrait-gallery and ancestors, i. 449–52, 470; and haunted places, i. 453–6; at church, i. 459–62; that inconsistency in his speech, i. 466; conversation at dinner (LAERTES and IRUS), i. 467–70; an indefatigable hunter, i. 472–3, 475–6; a hunt with, i. 475–9; and witchcraft (MOLL WHITE), i. 479–82; on confidants, i. 483–6; comical familiarity of speech or odd phrase in, i. 486; and good breeding: ceremonial at his table, i. 487–8; and the animal economy, i. 489–97; universal benevolence of, i. 498; iii. 437–8, 590; thinks 'much might be said on both sides', i. 499, 500; at the assizes, i. 499–500; and education of young persons (EUDOXUS and LEONTINE), i. 501–5; on party-spirit (anecdote of Sir ROGER as a boy), i. 509–12; a stronger Tory in country than in town, ii. 3; inclined to the landed interest, ii. 3, 186; reads Dyer's news-letter, ii. 4–5; a married couple who live near, ii. 11; and the gipsies, ii. 15–18; mentioned, ii. 57, 131, 328; suspected of writing *Spectators* signed 'R', ii. 360; disturbed by cries of London, ii. 474; letter to Dick Estcourt (on wines and food), ii. 529–30; always keeps open house at Christmas, ii. 550–1; visits London to see Prince Eugene, ii. 548–52; has been seen at Squire's Coffee-house, ii. 557; oddness and singularity of, iii. 54; iv. 445; visits Westminster Abbey, iii. 212–16; at the theatre, iii. 239–42, 251; at Spring-Garden, iii. 436–9; his custom of saluting everybody, iii. 437; as

a Justice of Peace is busier in month of May, iii. 480; his meeting with a woman of the town, iii. 531-3 (this incident misunderstood by many readers, iv. 445); a lady equestrian seen at Sir ROGER's, iv. 28; warmth of heart of, iv. 445; 'I laughed often at', v. 66. — THE PERVERSE WIDOW: i. 8, 462-7; the cause of Sir ROGER's fox-hunting, i. 473; the grove sacred to, i. 483; Sir ROGER's reflections on, i. 483-6; TOM TOUCHY once went to law with, i. 498; cruelty and perverseness of, ii. 328; proposed 'pin-money' gifts to, iii. 54; Sir DAVID DUNDRUM has been making a visit to, iii. 343; Sir ROGER's thoughts of, iii. 438; Sir ROGER's bequests to, iv. 340. — SIR ROGER's BUTLER: i. 439-40, 445, 453; and gipsies, ii. 16; always shaves Sir ROGER, iii. 212; accompanies him to the play, iii. 240; letter from, on Sir ROGER's death, iv. 339-41. — SIR ROGER's CHAPLAIN: i. 440-2, 476, 482; ii. 549; iv. 339; exorcises haunted rooms, i. 454-5; good relations with Sir ROGER, i. 462. — SIR ROGER's COACHMAN, ii. 548. — SIR ROGER's STEWARD, iii. 343. — DEATH OF SIR ROGER: letter from Sir ROGER's butler on, iv. 339-41; comment on, iv. 342, 440; disposition of his servants, iv. 446; 'the wisest thing he ever did', iv. 485.

Coverley, Sir Roger de (country dance), i. 7.

Coverley church, i. 459-62; iv. 340.

Covetous: c. man will call himself poor, ii. 373; wishful eye of the c. spirit, ii. 471; the ambitious and the c. are madmen, iv. 571.

Covetousness: in Sir JEOFFREY FOIBLE, ii. 246; pretended c. in IRUS, ii. 527-8; the folly of, iv. 563.

Cow, eye of, applied to Hera, ii. 471.

Coward: who is afraid to be thought virtuous, ii. 400; every man called a man of honour who is not a, iii. 466; one who affronts a lady he has injured, v. 89.

Cowell, John: The Interpreter (law dictionary), ii. 40; quoted, v. 100-1, 130.

Cowlee, manor of, v. 76.

Cowley, Abraham: mixed wit abounds in, 'more than in any author that ever wrote', i. 265; had as much true wit 'as any author that ever writ', i. 267; a reader of plain common sense would neither relish nor comprehend a poem of, i. 297; magnanimity of ('I always read Mr. C. with the greatest pleasure'), i. 469; his admirers imitate only his turns and antitheses, ii. 53; tried to rival Pindar, then imitated Horace and Anacreon, iv. 329; defined wit by negatives, i. 146; on dancing, i. 287; compared a beautiful woman to a porcupine, iii. 416; condemned Persius for obscurity, iii. 424; on two kinds of eternity, v. 18. — WORKS: 'The Chronicle', iii. 127; 'The Complaint', v. 95; Davideis, i. 116, 348; iii. 147, 364, 425; iv. 464; v. 20, 21, 159: 'Epitaphium vivi authoris' quoted, iv. 475-6; Essays, i. 19, 469-70, 502; ii. 49, 214, 260, 263, 286, 525, 591; iii. 424, 448, 518; iv. 170, 475-6, 519; v. 86-87, 95; The Mistress, i. 175, 266-7; iii. 127; v. 36; 'The Motto' quoted, v. 95; Pindaric Odes quoted, ii. 353; iv. 139, 152; v. 18; Preface to Poems quoted, iii. 21; 'The Resurrection' quoted, ii. 154; works were published by Sprat, i. 470.

Cowper, William (Earl Cowper), i. 162; iv. 151.

Cowpland, William (soap-maker), advertisement of, iv. 230.

Cowslips, v. 144.

Cox, Mrs. (actress): in The Lancashire Witches, ii. 57; Cleone in The Distressed Mother, iii. 239.

Coxcomb(s): i. 38, 161, 206, 347, 393; ii. 112; iii. 23; English less obsequious than Irish, i. 88; at the theatre, i. 203; iv. 282; Dorimant (in The Man of Mode) a, i. 280, 323; noise and nonsense of, i. 323; VOCIFER an empty, i. 324; succeeds through loving by sight, i. 339; among servants, i. 374; 'within a month of a', i. 393; language of, i. 488; preferred by women to a man of sense, ii. 9, 103-6, 303; a whining, ii. 60; 'this blundering', ii. 98; to be regarded with contempt or indifference, ii. 179; who visit brothels to see the world, ii. 248; produced by flattery, ii. 425; indecent conversation of a, ii. 439-40; ridiculous in old age, ii. 489; in the coquette's heart, ii. 595; complaint against a, iii. 56-57; iv. 304-5; CLEANTHES a downright, iii. 511; who over-ride men of modesty, iv. 218; a tribe of fashionable young fluttering, iv. 391; 'in youth a c. and in age a clown', iv. 398; jests of a young, iv. 521; a public nuisance in the army, iv. 534.

'Crab', of King's College, Cambridge, i. 335.

Crab (apple), i. 295; ii. 184.

CRABTREE, BARBARA, letter from (on a debauched husband), ii. 480.

Crack (crazy fellow), ii. 474.

'Crack a bottle', ii. 411.

Crackers, and squibs, i. 361.

Cradle to the grave, From the (prov.), v. 142.

Craftsman, The, ii. 451.

Craggs, James, the Elder, a subscriber, i. lxxxix, xci.

Craggs, James, the Younger, i. xci.

Crakanthorp, Richard (divine), iii. 485.

Crambo, game of, i. 272; iv. 287.

Crape: hatband, i. 276; on the fontange, i. 414.

CRASTIN, DICK, an old beau, suitor to HONORIA, i. 385-8.

Cratippus, Cicero's son educated by, iii. 106.

Cravat(s), i. 351; ii. 217; iv. 195; a well-tied, i. 161; a paper, i. 207; of lace, i. 434; ii. 236; lace for, ii. 217; knotted, iii. 163; burning c. in a frolic, iii. 341; a beau's, iii. 381; 'adjust his c. at the glass', iv. 198.

Crawley, Sir Ambrose: the original of JOHN ENVILLE, iii. 68.

CRAZY, Sir CHRISTOPHER, Bart., hurt by a whalebone petticoat, iii. 417.

CRAZY, MARY, iv. 458.

CRAZY, WILLIAM, testimonial from, praising Nos. 170-1, iv. 458-9.

Crazy: young husband of a court lady, ii. 134; constitution of an old man, ii. 512; a frame grown c. with toil, iii. 598.

Creation (the world): a perpetual feast to the mind of a good man, iii. 475; man's delight in the beauty of, v. 140.

Creation of the world: an episode in *PL*, ii. 540; as reported in *PL*, iii. 117-18, 566; described in *PL*, iii. 255-61; Moses' account of, praised by Longinus, iii. 255-6; Blackmore's poem on, iii. 261.

Credit: discourses concerning decay of public, i. 14; allegorical figure of, i. 15; of the trader endangered by loose talk, ii. 350-1; is ready cash to a trader, ii. 591; allegorical figure of broken, iv. 124; importance of, iv. 309.

Creech, Thomas, translation of Horace, i. 136; v. 103.

Creek of salt waters, ii. 383.

Cremer, Acton, translation of Scheffer's *Lapponia*, iii. 376.

Cremona, surprised by Prince Eugene, iii. 263.

Cricket (insect), superstition concerning, i. 33, 196.

Cries, in streets of London, i. 152; ii. 474-8; iv. 11; v. 41-42; Comptroller of, proposed, ii. 475, 503; iv. 11, 438; criers distinguished by particular tones, iii. 413.

Crime, not the individual, to be attacked, i. 72.

Criminal: at the bar obtains mercy by admitting his faults, iii. 434-5; pleasure in reading of a c. overtaken, iv. 240; who tricked a surgeon, iv. 290.

Crimp (card game), iii. 183; iv. 113.

Crincum crancum, v. 101, 129.

Cripples, from the wars, ii. 335.

Critic(s): advertisement of a meeting of, i. 372; Horace the greatest c. in the Augustan age, ii. 220; many c. incapable of writing well themselves, ii. 467; Horace, Petronius, Quintilian, Longinus, the best of the Latin, ii. 484; little pedantic c., ii. 554-5; ancient c. acted by candour rather than cavilling, iii. 10; requirements of a good, iii. 35-38; v. 26-28; verses addressed to little, iii. 74; in coffee-houses, iv. 268; acquaintance with the best, a means of cultivating taste, iv. 530; Aristotle, Longinus, Horace, Quintilian, Boileau, Dacier the true c., v. 26; faults of modern dramatic, v. 26-28.

Critic (critique), i. 298.

Criticism: *Spectators* on, well received, i. 245; early authors destitute of rules and arts of, i. 261; vitiated by party-spirit, i. 510-11; Pope's *Essay on C.* praised, ii. 482-6; impossible to make original observations in, ii. 483-4; to discover beauties rather than faults, ii. 519; iii. 36-38, 170; upon *PL* announced, ii. 520; 'I do not naturally affect critical learning', iii. 208-9; Sir ROGER's 'natural c.' of *The Distressed Mother*, iii. 241-2; the whole art of, expressed in cat-calls, iii. 352-3; absurdities of textual c. illustrated, iv. 161-5.

Crocodile: finds a place to deposit its eggs, i. 490; its eggs broken by the ichneumon, ii. 2; worshipped by Egyptians, ii. 2; the 'river-dragon' in *PL*, iii. 386.

Crocus, in Homer, iii. 311.

Croesus, son of, formerly tongue-tied, iv. 498, 514.

Cromwell, Oliver, iii. 135; iv. 252; v. 150.

Crooke, John, an opponent of Brooke and Hellier, iii. 353.

CROSS, Miss, too thin to be accounted a beauty in Holland, i. 135.

Cross-purposes (game), ii. 451; iv. 287.

CROSS-STITCH, BETTY, letter from (on a French doll), ii. 580.

CROSSTITCH, SUSANNAH, SAMUEL FELT 'wounded' by, iii. 418.

CROTCHET, KIT, ii. 504.

CROTCHETT, RALPH: asks to be Comptroller of London cries, ii. 474–8; letter from (proposing a theatre of ease), ii. 503–5.

Crow and her egg (Greek proverb), ii. 243.

Crowley, Sir Ambrose. *See* Crawley.

Crown (coin): wenches for a c. apiece, ii. 93; cut in two as token for absent lovers, ii. 452; given to a prostitute, ii. 535; Cloe in *The Humorous Lieutenant* purchased with 350 crowns, ii. 536; to Robin for his afternoon's work, iii. 493.

Crows: cawing of, a kind of natural prayer, i. 453; a parcel of, iii. 196.

Croxall, Samuel (poet), iii. 455.

Crozier, introduced by a Gothic bishop, ii. 290.

CRUEL, PENANCE, letter from (on indecent conversation), iv. 402–4.

Cruelty: man's c. to man, ii. 164–5; of Herod to Mariamne, ii. 178; of Caligula imbibed from his nurse, ii. 455–6; supported by fashion, ii. 458; in absolute monarchs, iii. 20–21; of Alexander, iii. 247; of a French captain, iii. 308; delight in c. of combats, iv. 34–35.

Cry but little wool, Much (prov.), ii. 476.

Crystal Cosmetic. *See* Chrystal Cosmetick.

Cuckold(s), i. 43; ii. 219; v. 150.

Cuckoldom: fostered by masquerades, i. 37; the *Spectator* not to be a publisher of, i. 72, 142; and bastardy looked upon as reproaches, ii. 297; the basis of most modern plays, iv. 68; those who think c. inseparable from marriage, iv. 273; Mr. DAPPERWIT's story of, v. 117.

Cucumbers, pickling of, ii. 477.

Cudgel(s): and bamboos, i. 197; query, whether c. may be used by a female orator, ii. 480; taking up c. for Gloucestershire, iv. 283.

Cudgel-player(s): a quarrelsome, i. 306; a ring of, breaking heads, ii. 131; desire of glory in a ring of, ii. 371.

Cuffe, Mr., of Nine-Elms, consigns melons to Covent Garden, iv. 99.

Cully, cullyism, i. 38, 408; iv. 225.

Culpeper, Nicolas, *Directory for Midwives*, i. 155.

Culture, allegory of modern, iv. 104–5.

Cumberland family, v. 61.

Cumberland, a fashion makes its progress slower into, ii. 15.

Cunning: a c. temper as a source of jealousy, ii. 171; wisdom exerts itself as c. in savage nations, ii. 339; selfish c. an effect of ambition, ii. 371; contrasted with discretion, ii. 375–8; and suspicion inseparable in little minds, ii. 419; c. people incapable of agreeable conversation, ii. 592; highly regarded in present age, iii. 313–14.

Cunning man (men): Mr. SPECTATOR suspected of being a, ii. 20; frequent in England, iv. 292.

Cupid(s): gilded c. on a coach, i. 66; Amorous Club votaries of, i. 126; Venus and C. on a fan, i. 227, 427; ii. 113; paintings of, i. 246; ii. 379; iii. 373; 'little winged boys', ii. 124; offering of a silver C., ii. 407; frequent in lovers' letters, ii. 438; a heart held by a, ii. 453; of Hudibras, iii. 127; as name of lap-dog, iii. 183; iv. 271; attends the fair sex, iii. 472; as attendant of May, iii. 595; as self-conceit, iv. 122–3; Venuses, Graces, and, iv. 196; in embroidery, v. 72.

Cupping (medicine), ii. 264; v. 36.

Curate(s): who might have been aldermen of London, i. 91; of the parish, ii. 153; and the atheistical author, ii. 155–6.

Curatii and Horatii, Corneille's play on, i. 188.

Cureau de la Chambre, Marin, i. 258; ii. 465; on poetic composition, i. 257.

Cures: usual to publish advertisements of, ii. 30; iv. 457; custom of an Eastern nation to advertise, iv. 552–3.

Curiosities, Repository of, ii. 7.

Curiosity: Mr. SPECTATOR's prevailing passion, ii. 111; of the inquisitive, ii. 386–8; iv. 42–45; a strong and lasting appetite, ii. 420; to behold a man of heroic worth, iii. 262; sketch of a man who teased himself with an absurd, iv. 45; occasioned by jealousy, as described by Spenser, iv. 430.

Curius and Fulvia, in Jonson's *Catiline*, iv. 312.

Curling-irons for moustaches, iii. 222.

Currants, sold in London streets, iii. 354.

Curtains, window, ii. 190.

Curtius Rufus, Quintus, iii. 247, 554; on tenacity of dogs, i. 129; account of Alexander's exploits, v. 30.

Curtsy (-ies), i. 342; ii. 270, 433; iii. 8, 66, 428; unwilling to confer a bow or a, ii. 508; doing honour by a, ii. 552; taught the c. and recovery, ii. 581;

slain by a, iii. 418; HARRIOT must not c. to folks she does not know, iv. 588.

Cushion-dance, i. 286.

Custom(s): of other countries seem ridiculous, i. 215; power of, i. 275; force of, in duelling, i. 359; nature gives place to, ii. 458; effects of, iv. 69–73, 105; v. 139–40; *is second nature* (prov.), iv. 69; deference due to, in little intercourses of life, iv. 569–70; establishes both vicious and good actions, v. 157–8.

Customs duty: to the Queen, ii. 188; and excises, ii. 283.

Cutberd, Dr., in *The Silent Woman*, i. 173.

Cuthbert, Mr., benefit for, i. 120.

Cutlers, i. 246.

Cutters (bullies), the world filled with, ii. 364.

Cuttle-fish, disputants like the, iv. 187.

Cybele: Ovid's account of C.'s image, iv. 380; grove on Mt. Ida sacred to, v. 15.

Cymbals, in a morris dance, iii. 595.

Cymon and Iphigenia: Dryden's fable of, quoted, i. 304–5.

CYMON, WILL, letter from (in love with BELINDA), iii. 355–7.

Cyneas (minister of Pyrrhus), ii. 212.

Cynic: sullen and morose, ii. 9; saying of a, ii. 46, 71.

Cynical humour, of the Lowngers, i. 229.

CYNISCA, her leap into the Ionian sea, ii. 406–7.

CYNTHIO and FLAVIA, exchange of letters between, iii. 489–93.

Cypress(es): a crown of, in Roman Pentathlum, ii. 133; a wordy orator compared to a, iv. 75; yews and, iv. 325; planted by Abraham, v. 15.

Cyrus: aided by others, ii. 44; his good nature, ii. 166; death and burial of, ii. 166; offered sacrifices before his death, ii. 234; punished for 'the long and the short coat', iii. 249; on immortality, iv. 418–19; and Araspas, iv. 526; planted all the Lesser Asia, iv. 593.

Czar of Muscovy: a subject of, at the Royal Exchange, i. 293. *See also* Peter the Great.

D., B: letter from (on books of devotion for women), i. 340–1; letter from (on grief), i. 402–4; letter from (asking advice about marriage), iv. 184–5.

D., C.: letter from (on Sir ROGER's visit to London), ii. 557.

D——, Goodman, v. 128.

D., J.: in *Gent. Mag.*, ii. 141; iii. 14, 102, 135, 483; v. 24.

D——, Lady, iii. 502.

D., M.: letter from (on preferment), iv. 204.

D., R.: letter from (on over-witty authors), ii. 52–53.

D., T.: letter from, to the CLERGYMAN (on CHLOE), i. 114; letter from (on stage properties), i. 149–50; letter from (a love-letter), ii. 300; letter from (on immortality), ii. 321–4; letter from (on salutations), ii. 358; letter from (on the poor), iv. 12–13; letter from (on the *Spectator*), iv. 514.

Dacier, André: translation of Aristotle, i. 164, 166; on allegory in Homer, ii. 220; *Life of Pythagoras*, ii. 233, 361, 444; iii. 238, 274; iv. 71, 471; v. 4; work of, ii. 367; on narration and duration of action in the epic, ii. 543; on Ulysses, ii. 564; on the wonderful and probable in the epic, iii. 144, 145; defended Homer against Scaliger, iii. 201; on Aeschylus' use of allegorical figures, iii. 338; on tragedy, iii. 568; on manners in the epic, iv. 464; a true critic, v. 26.

Dacier, Mme (Anne Lefèvre): work of, ii. 365, 367; on Sappho's Ode to Venus, ii. 367, 369, 391; assisted Huet in the Delphin classics, iii. 219.

Daciers, the two: try to vindicate everything censured in Homer, iii. 201; mentioned, iii. 529.

DACINTHUS, a 'pleasant fellow', iv. 130–1.

Dactyls, a line of, in Homer, ii. 485.

Daffy, Thomas: his Elixir advertised, iv. 61.

Dagger: ruffian with lantern and, ii. 350; or cup of poison in tragedy, ii. 397.

Dahl, Michael (artist), iv. 495.

Daily Courant: printed by Samuel Buckley, i. xx, 6; Mr. SPECTATOR's landlord inserts an advertisement in, i. 52; an advertisement in regarding Nicholas Hart, ii. 284–5; news article from Paris quoted from, iii. 96; mentioned, iii. 153, 380.

Daintry, Captain John (amateur musician), iv. 545.

DAINTY, JOHN, v. 130.

DAINTY, MARY, memorial of, iv. 7–8.

DAINTY, SARAH, riding the black ram, v. 130.

'Dainty weather', iii. 321.

Dairy-maid(s): making butter, i. 481; consulting gipsies, ii. 16; one of Sir ROGER's, ii. 21.

Daisies: picking of, ii. 21; and doves in

romance writers, iii. 18; in Byrom's poem, v. 63.

Dalrymple, Sir David. *See* Hailes.

Dalton, Michael, *The Country Justice*, recommended, i. 389.

Damascus, ii. 127.

DAMON: 'wounded' by a diamond necklace, iii. 417; and STREPHON, their plot against GLORIANA, iii. 587–9.

Damp: on my spirits, ii. 159; caused by fear, ii. 521; and faintness, iv. 422.

Dampier, Sir William, *Voyages*, cited, i. 494; iii. 461.

Dance: of sun, moon, and earth in *The Rehearsal*, i. 16; 'what a dance she has led me!', i. 377; leading up a d. in a full court, ii. 470; simile of the fairy d. in *PL*, iii. 91.

Dancer: FLAVIA a fine, i. 339; JOHN TROT a 'minuit', iii. 112; MARIANNE a graceful, iv. 148–9; CHLOE a silly, iv. 149; a good d. must have a good understanding, iv. 149.

Dances: Pyrrhic, i. 284; the Lacedaemonian Hormus, i. 284; the French brawl; i. 284; 'Hunt the Squirrel', i. 285, 'Mol Pately', i. 286; kissing, i. 286–7; of witches in *The Lancashire Witches*, ii. 57; a country jig, ii. 207; pricked, ii. 571; Highland d. in a puppetshow, iii. 401. *See also* Country *and* French dances.

Dancing: distortions in, i. 150; walking a kind of recitative, i. 281–2; Lucian on, i. 284; emblematical figures in, i. 285; immodest, i. 286–7; benefits from knowledge of, i. 287; iii. 235–9, 415; iv. 145–9; at Maypoles, i. 306; 'a public ball', i. 344; in the midst of the room, ii. 196; as an accomplishment for youth, ii. 395; in order not to misbehave in church, ii. 510; a pretty untaught step in, ii. 576; dancing a jig, iii. 104; in education of girls, iii. 140, 239; singing and, iii. 205; value to the stage, iii. 395; letter on, iii. 414–15; a morris, iii. 595; pretenders in, iv. 145–6; affectation of neglect for, iv. 174; 'dances like an angel', iv. 184; a d. walk, iv. 245; verses on, sent in, iv. 587; ambling in a country dance, v. 106; Methuen's skill in, v. 183. See also JOHN TROTT.

Dancing-masters, i. 123; education of girls by, i. 282–3, 284–7; M. RIGADOON, i. 285; TETTYX the dancingmaster, ii. 408; Mohocks as, iii. 187, 223.

Dancing-school: 'a kind of d. breeding', iv. 371; quarrels at a, v. 38.

Dane, a, at the Royal Exchange, i. 294.

Danet, Pierre, *Dictionary of Greek and Roman Antiquities*, ii. 10; iii. 342; &c.

Danube, interest in people who live upon the, iv. 91.

Danvelt, Paul, his wife Sapphira seduced by Rhynsault, iv. 241–4.

Danzig, the sickness at, iii. 213.

DAPHNE and LAETITIA, i. 137–8, 224.

DAPHNIS: in love with MELISSA, ii. 406; the Myndian, ii. 407; the loves of Leucothoe and, iv. 329.

DAPPERWIT, ABRAHAM, query from, and reply, iv. 406–7.

DAPPERWIT, TOM: looks on marriage as a purgatory, iv. 209; comments on women of Hensburg, iv. 270; his volume of Herodotus, iv. 314; suggested to replace WILL HONEYCOMB in the Club, iv. 391.

DAPPERWIT, Mr., reply to, v. 117.

Darcey, James (of Sedbury, Yorkshire), breeder of the horse 'Caesar', ii. 117.

Darius, iv. 2; tent of, in a projected opera, i. 129.

Dark expressions, ii. 151.

Darkness: the mind's associations with, i. 454; Plague of, and the Egyptians, v. 102.

Darling: WILL WIMBLE the d. of the country, i. 447; of his mother, ii. 31; 'fond of this', ii. 195.

Darts, against a coquette's heart, ii. 594.

Dashes in pamphlets, to pique the reader, iv. 536–41.

Date Obolum Belisario, iv. 129.

Daughter: account of a dutiful, ii. 254; Pliny's gift to Quintilian's, iii. 40; character of FIDELIA, a model, iv. 78–81. *See also* Girls.

Dauphin: Rabelais' 'poison' for the, iii. 4; edition of classic authors prepared for the, iii. 219; acecdote of a, iii. 433–4; ill health of the, iii. 439.

Davenant, Sir William, *Gondibert*, iii. 499.

David: Nathan's reproof of, ii. 220; set his psalms to music, iii. 515; his reliance on God, iv. 50; his contemplation of the heavens, iv. 529.

Davies, John, i. 105, 156; iii. 597.

Davis, Richard (Oxford bookseller), iii. 459.

Dawks, Ichabod: his News-Letter, i. 202; 'an epistolary historian', iv. 111.

Dawson, 'Bully', i. 8.

Dawson, Joshua, i. lxxv.

Day, Mother: 'drank the King's health in Mother Day's Double', v. 106.

Day and night, vicissitude of, pleasing to the imagination, iii. 453.

Day is long, As happy as the (prov.), iv. 16.

Day of Judgement, ii. 331, 352, 502; iv. 213; solemnity of such a prospect, iv. 320–1.

Day-dreams, of a castle-builder, ii. 158–60.

'Day-goblins', disarrange wares in a China shop, iii. 245.

Day-watchman, with a goose, iii. 413.

Dead, the: may still have a sense of what passes below, ii. 301–2; we are not to grieve for, iii. 29–30.

Dead languages, advantage of, over living, iii. 11.

'Dead men': 'for so we call all those fragments and tatters', ii. 346.

Dean, Mr., benefit for, i. 228.

Death: apprehension of, begets superstitions, i. 34; neither fearing nor wishing for, the perfection of happiness, i. 108; reflections on, i. 108–11, 325; ii. 25; iv. 320–4; Sherlock upon, i. 155; ii. 29; iv. 321–2; of foreign sovereigns, effect on trade, i. 277; of great men, ii. 25–26; of Stephen Clay, ii. 27–28; calm attitude of URANIUS toward, ii. 66; Socrates on, ii. 75–76; military men do not fear, ii. 97–99; youth has more chances to be near it than age, ii. 102–3; trap-doors in the bridge of life, ii. 123–4; consolations against grief over, ii. 139–48; iii. 298–302; Milton's personification of in *PL*, ii. 183, 563; iii. 60, 119–20, 145, 336–9, 573; a wife's reflection on, iii. 301–2; of Cardinal Beaufort, ii. 323–4; shows emptiness of titles, ii. 352; an essay upon, iii. 27–31; accounts of behaviour at, iii. 28–29; concern for decency in, iii. 41; of the young like destruction of the Spring, iii. 105; of Augustus, iii. 152; fixes a man's reputation, iii. 299; contemplation of d. of Christ, iii. 329; Adam's view of, in *PL*, iii. 362–3; of Mme de Villacerfe, iii. 383–5; does not deserve name of evil, iii. 431–2; trust in God at hour of, iv. 50–51; of Dick Estcourt, iv. 154–8; comfort of hope at hour of, iv. 167; account of d. of a wife, iv. 350–3; verses written at d. of Hadrian, iv. 396–7; Cato and Cyrus on, iv. 418–20; account of d. of Leonardo da Vinci, iv. 489.

Death-watches, the superstitious hear, i. 34.

Deaths and births, nice proportion between, iii. 27–28.

Debates: methods of managing, ii. 428–32; among ladies of the British fishery, ii. 458.

Debauchees: common refuse of all the rakes and, ii. 246; pleasures of, short-lived, ii. 281; among husbands, ii. 480; a town full of ranters and, iv. 224.

Debauchery: the occupation of the man of wit and pleasure, ii. 93–96; effect of the *Spectator* upon, iv. 128.

Debt: misfortune of running into, i. 350–3, 468; ii. 362–3; our gentry generally in, i. 352; imprisonment for, ii. 180; confined to a bailiff's house for, iii. 217.

Debtor, sneaking away like a fearful, ii. 470.

Debts: of honour to be first discharged, ii. 335; contracted by extravagances, ii. 546; play-debts of a wife, iii. 51.

Deceit: OMNAMANTE made for, ii. 70; no d. in language of the eyes, ii. 479; dangers of d. and dissimulation, iii. 314–16; an element of the female heart, v. 9.

December: allegorical figure of, iii. 596; Cicero quashed conspiracy of Catiline in Calends of, iv. 519.

Decency: decorum, or a regard to, i. 432; and virtue nearly related, i. 433; 'publicly decent, privately dissolute', ii. 112; of similitudes, ii. 127–8; and common sense wanting in free-thinkers, ii. 412; contempt of, in plays, ii. 554; in all our actions, iii. 38–41, 463–6.

DECENT, SUSANNA, letter from (on behaviour of married couples), iii. 71–72.

Deception: of women by male jilts, iii. 23–25; of OCTAVIA, iii. 178–80.

Decker, Matthew (a Director of East India Co.), a subscriber, i. xc.

Declaimers in coffee-houses, iv. 355.

Decorum. *See* Decency.

Dedication: absurd panegyrics in, ii. 240; 'the inimitable d. of *The Plain Dealer*', ii. 537.

Deer: hunting, i. 472; character in Homer with heart of a, ii. 399; d.-stealers, i. 451; iii. 194.

Defamation: and scandal, ii. 493–8; iv. 1–3, 86–90; defamatory whispers by domestics, iii. 49; the sexes equally inclined to, iii. 296; the true way to avoid, iii. 464–5; defamatory papers and pamphlets, iv. 86.

Defence, the noble science of, iv. 31.

Deference(s): in fashionable life, i. 486; paid to the old, ii. 102, 522; to superiors, ii. 354; due a great assembly, ii. 398.

Defile: a French word imported, ii. 151–2, 429.

Definitions: a schoolman a great friend to, ii. 272; necessary in moral discourses, iii. 403–4.

Defoe, Daniel: *Defence of the Allies*. iv. 32–33; *Essay upon Public Credit*, i. 14; *History of Duncan Campbell*, i. 129; ii. 90; iii. 184; *History of Peter Alexowitz*, ii. 47; *Journey through England*, ii. 46; *Mercator, or Commerce Retrieved*, i. lii; ii. 208; *Review*, i. xiv, xxxvii, xxxviii, 42, 47, 277, 419, 505–6; ii. 51, 186, 214, 431; iii. 186, 251, 261, 380; *Secret History of the October Club*, i. 42; warehouse of, ii. 74.

Deformity (-ies): and ugliness, i. 74–78; not criticized by a gentleman, i. 279, 324; 'many an amiable piece of', i. 367; of husband as a cause of jealousy, ii. 170–1; of body banished by virtue, ii. 444; as source of aesthetic pleasure, iii. 540–2; dream-vision of discarding, iv. 508.

Dégagé, an air altogether gallant and, ii. 579.

DEIDAMIA, her pensive attention at a tragedy, iv. 333.

Deism, atheists now retired into, ii. 232.

Dejectedness, a sheepish, ii. 470.

Dejection: caused by love, ii. 478; allegorical figure of, iv. 278.

Delany, Mrs. Mary, i. 56.

Delia: in Philips' pastorals, iii. 499; in Pope, iv. 381.

Delicacy: an affected, i. 420; men of, ii. 248; lack of, in Simonides, ii. 318–19; lack of, in a young woman, ii. 346–7; lack of, in Homer, ii. 586; of sentiments, ii. 591; true and false, iii. 15–17; a word which gives effect of immense reading, iii. 347; in conferring benefits, iv. 455–6.

Delight: and surprise essential to wit, i. 264; the Persian Emperor 'the Nutmeg of', ii. 128; and surprise in detecting appearances of Satan in *PL*, ii. 564; enhanced by novelty, v. 139.

Delius, Horace's advice to, iii. 129, 429 m.

Della Porta, Giovanni Battista, *De humana physiognomonia*, i. 366.

Delme, Peter (a Director of the Bank), a subscriber, i. xc.

Delphi: oracle at, i. 129, 150; that famed dictate of, iii. 513; pronounced Socrates the wisest of all men living, iii. 523; grove at, v. 15; consulted by Gyges, v. 86.

Delphin editions, iii. 219.

Deluge, the: described by Ovid and Milton, iii. 363–5; Mr. W—n's comments upon, iii. 485.

Demetrius, a noble saying of, ii. 422.

Demi-culverin, iii. 463.

Democritus: Sir Thomas More 'a second D.', iii. 300; on understanding language of birds, iv. 319.

Demolishing a prude, in the Club of She-romps, ii. 346.

Demon(s): conversation with a, iii. 274; writings about d. and departed spirits, iii. 570; of good thoughts, iv. 153.

Demosthenes: The TEMPLAR familiar with his orations, i. 9; overcame defects of nature, iii. 150; vehemence of action in, iii. 522; St. Paul a greater orator than, v. 166; mentioned with Cicero, ii. 396; iii. 318; v. 95.

Demurrage, the folly of, i. 378.

'Demurrers', i. 376–80; ii. 303.

Denain: debates about Douai or, iv. 187; French victory at, iv. 206.

Denham, Sir John: *Cooper's Hill* quoted, i. 351; 'beautiful lines' on Fletcher's Works quoted, ii. 482.

Denial: a feeble d. is a modest assent, iii. 159; 'an absolute d. from a maid, and from a widow', v. 23.

Denmark, a letter from, iii. 473.

Dennis, John: translation of Boileau quoted, i. 201; 'Upon our great victory at sea' quoted, iv. 38; on Italian opera, i. 22–23; on poetic justice, i. 168–70; iv. 461–5; alluded to (?), i. 204; iii. 37; iv. 361–2; defence of *The Man of Mode*, i. 280–1; *Original Letters*, i. 322; on Milton, ii. 129, 537–8, 563, 587; new way of making thunder, iii. 414; v. 25–26; *Reflections on Pope's Essay on Criticism*, ii. 486; on action of the epic, ii. 539; the Devil the hero of *PL*, iii. 59; *Essay on Shakespear*, iii. 74–75; on Milton's infernal characters, iii. 118; on 'admiration' in the epic, iii. 145; on episodes in the epic, iii. 280; on Virgil's allegorical figures, iii. 337–8; on the later books of *PL*, iii. 365; on English melancholy, iii. 454; on 'wearisome uniformity', iii. 541.

Dentry, John. *See* Daintry.

Denying to visitors, i. 103; a servant's duty, i. 409; ii. 329.

Dependant(s): on great men, ii. 334–8; account of a poor, iii. 593.

Deputy Lieutenant, Petition to be made, v. 151.

Deputy of the Ward, iv. 284.

De Quincey, Thomas, on Addison's style, i. ci.
Derham, William, *Astro-Theology*, i. *493*.
Dering, Sir Cholmondeley, duel with Thornhill, i. *359*.
Dernier Ressort, i. 183.
Dervise [dervish]: who mistook a palace for a caravansary, iii. 30–31; and Fadlallah, iv. 576–9; anecdote of a d. who failed to wash his hands, v. 158.
Desaulnais. *See* Disney.
Des Barreaux, Jacques Vallée, Seigneur, his hymn quoted, iv. 323–4.
Descartes, René: *Les Passions de l'âme*, iii. *560–1*; *Six Metaphysical Meditations*, iii. *576*; his theory of the universe, iv. *170*. *See also* Cartesians.
Description: in *PL*, iii. 169–74, 256–60; in Homer more charming than a chapter in Aristotle, iii. 538; a secondary pleasure of the imagination, iii. 558–61.
Desdemona (in *Othello*), ii. 105; iv. 219.
Deserts: a source of aesthetic pleasure, iii. 453, 540; savage prospects of vast, iii. 564.
Desertion (in the army), ii. 23.
Deshabille, i. 209; iii. 82.
Designing, proposed as an accomplishment for youth, ii. 395.
Desire(s): a play written on d. of multiplying our species, i. 216–17; moderation of, i. 467–70; ii. 65–67, 252, 433; iv. 258–9, 562–5; God has given us no d. which has not its object, ii. 323; passion of, ii. 455; ambition an object of d. incapable of fruition, ii. 497; if we do not leave our d., they will leave us, ii. 511; the first heats of, ii. 515; looking at beauty not as the object of, ii. 553; happiness in this world arises from the subduing of, and in the next world from the gratification of, iv. 565; v. 169; awakened by novelty, v. 139.
Desmaizeaux, Pierre, Life of Boileau, iii. 91.
Despair: allegorical depiction of, ii. 124; Shakespeare's portrayal of, ii. 323–4; representation of, in *The Distressed Mother*, iii. 33; of Satan in *PL*, iii. 84.
Despondings, religion sometimes expressed in, iii. 80.
Despotic rule, dangerous to a nation, iii. 19–22.
Destinies: convert Fidelio into a looking-glass, iii. 472; in modern poems, iv. 363.
Detraction: party-spirit breaks out in, i. 510; a man who turned d. into flattery, ii. 411; envy and d. among poets, ii. 481.
Detur tetriori, motto for a grinning-match, ii. 183.
Deus est anima brutorum, i. 493–4.
DEUTERERASTUS, letter from (a problem in marriage), iv. 400–2.
Devil: *is at home* (prov.), i. 230; MOLL WHITE advised to shun the, i. 482; worship of, in *The Lancashire Witches*, ii. 58; of lust, ii. 567; rebuked by Zephon, iii. 41; the hero of *PL* (Dryden), iii. 59; and Eve, iv. 99; works through women, iv. 312; usual tokens of, v. 43; practises upon frail creatures, v. 90; and the Pope in the Coronation festivities, v. 106, 108. *See also* Satan.
Devils of the play-house, Petition of, i. 151.
Devoirs, pay their, iii. 23.
Devonshire, William Cavendish, 1st Duke of: referred to(?), i. 418.
Devonshire: letter written from, ii. 411; mentioned, iii. 455; custom of riding the black ram in, v. 101.
Dévote, character of a, iii. 320–1.
Devotion: books of, for women's reading, i. 340, 392; a source of consolation in sorrow, ii. 142–3; to be implanted early in a child, ii. 287; distinguishes man from animals, ii. 286–7; errors caused by mistaken, ii. 288–90; notions of the heathens on, ii. 310–14; music as an aid to, iii. 514–16; responsible for the noblest buildings in the world, iii. 555; undue modesty regarding, iv. 116; and hypocrisy, iv. 117; balanced against superstition, iv. 136; is heightened and inflamed in dreams, iv. 228.
Devotionists, behaviour of, iv. 125.
De Wit, Jan, always did one thing at once, iii. 2.
Dextro tempore, what Horace calls, iv. 485.
Diabetes, i. 371.
Diagoras the Atheist, his reply to the Athenian mariners, iv. 213.
DIAGORAS, a usurer, in love with his cook-maid, ii. 408.
Dial, cut in a window, iii. 318.
Dial-plate and a loadstone, use of a, ii. 437–8.
Dialect (language, speech), i. 430; iv. 503.
Dialects: pedants' concern with, i. 250; Homer's use of, iii. 12.
Diamond: necklace, i. 295; iii. 417; iv. 558, 561; v. 98; writing with a d. upon glass, ii. 356; ring, v. 156.

Diana: a heathen hymn to, iv. 95; dogs presented by, to Vulcan, iv. 581.

Diapason, interval called, iii. 238.

Dice: playing at, i. 407; cards and, iv. 102; Xenophanes on playing at, iv. 116; improbability of repetition in throwing of, iv. 443–4.

Dicky. *See* Norris, Henry.

DICTAMNUS and MORIA, a squabbling couple, iv. 238.

Diction: ornaments of, to be lavished on weak parts of epic, iii. 170; beauty of, in *PL*, iii. 333; beauty of, in *The Faerie Queene*, iv. 429; of verse different from that of prose, v. 113.

Dictionary: for explanation of hard words, i. 155; at Westminster School, i. 406; Hector's life 'at the end of the', iii. 240.

Dido: Virgil's and Ovid's treatment of, i. 268–9; in Dryden's Virgil, ii. 384; her character in the *Aeneid* 'cannot be sufficiently admired', ii. 563; and Aeneas, ii. 587; her yielding to temptation, iii. 311.

Diet: nature delights in most plain and simple, ii. 265; a plain and simple d. advised in month of May, iii. 374.

Dieupart, Charles, i. lvi; and *Arsinoe*, i. 79; letters from, ii. 505–7, 584–5.

Differences: in men, ii. 274, 525; between private and public behaviour of men, ii. 388; in men often result in friendships, iii. 447; causes of d. in men, iv. 490.

Diffidence (want of confidence; mistrust), i. 353; ii. 201.

Diffidence (distrust of oneself): and presumption, on account of our persons, equally faults, i. 370; of St. Thomas, ii. 380; and modesty generally accompany merit, ii. 381; in public speaking, ii. 397; a man diffident of himself, ii. 410; of CAMILLUS' son, ii. 522.

Digby, Sir Kenelm, i. 225; iii. 425.

Dignity: of human nature, ii. 118, 233, 321–2; iv. 416–20; and novelty of Homer's characters, ii. 562; and condescension of Raphael in *PL*, ii. 564–5; and weight conferred by wealth, iii. 1; true delicacy consists in d. of sentiment, iii. 15.

Digression(s): not allowable in the epic, iii. 60–61; the longest d. in the *Aeneid*, iii. 61; frequent in Lucan, iii. 61; too many in *PL*, iii. 61–62.

Dilatations, bodily, i. 472.

Diligence: makes more lasting acquisitions than valour, i. 10; as a means of gaining riches, iii. 2; allegorical figure of, iv. 327.

Dill and cucumbers, pickling of, ii. 477.

Dillon, Mr. (optician), sells perspective glasses, ii. 475.

Diminutive epithets, in Latin, iv. 397.

DIMMACHUS, the Miletian, ii. 407.

DIMPLE, ELIZABETH, a toast of the Amorous Club, i. 126.

Dimple: spelt with a single or a double 'p' (?), ii. 53; in BELINDA's left cheek, iii. 418.

Dinner: hour of, i. 211; iii. 153, 155, 182–4, 465; bell ringing for, i. 448; ii. 530; never asked a favour of a great man before, ii. 197; spoiling of d. a source of marital quarrels, v. 80.

Diodorus Siculus: on the ichneumon, ii. 2; on Nero and Caligula sucking in cruelty from their nurses, ii. 455–6; on buildings in Babylon and Egypt, iii. 554–5.

Diogenes the Cynic: and his tub, i. 229; v. 109; 'a citizen of the world', i. 294; prevented a youth from going to a feast, ii. 264; 'to plant men', ii. 297; looking for an honest man, ii. 264.

Diogenes Laertius, *Lives of Eminent Philosophers*: a new edition to be published, i. 230; cited, i. 229, 294; ii. 68, 71, 240, 264, 266, 338, 359; iii. 238, 322; iv. 200, 471, 492, 502, 564, 565, 591.

Diomedes: mist removed from his eyes by Minerva, ii. 312; wounding the gods, iii. 232; followed by Victory, iii. 337.

Dionysius, tyrant of Sicily: his dungeon called 'Dionysius's Ear', iv. 44; asked Simonides to tell him what God was, iv. 392.

Dionysius of Halicarnassus: preserved Sappho's Ode to Venus, ii. 369; on a passage in Homer, ii. 485; retold the story of Aeneas, iii. 305.

DIONYSIUS, tyrant of a club, iv. 302–4.

Dipped (mortgaged), i. 468; iii. 226.

'Dirty acres', v. 186.

Dis, Proserpine captured by, iii. 373.

Discipline: Spartans famous for, iii. 109; of the strap for a wife, iv. 271.

DISCIPULUS, JAMES, letter from (on parental discouragement of learning), iii. 219–20.

Discord: *Iliad* begins with d. of princes, ii. 540; Homer's description of, iii. 173; encompassed Minerva's buckler, iii. 337; mother of funerals and mourning, iii. 337; daughter of Sin, in *PL*, iii. 338; spirit of, in England in 1712, iii. 444–5.

Discourse, helps to, i. 124; ii. 459.

Discretion: in women now out of fashion, i. 193–4; women have less than men, i. 243; a qualification of a good friend, i. 291; contrasted with cunning, ii. 375–8; value of, ii. 446–7, 462; and good nature to be exercised after marriage, ii. 516; a love marked by judgement and, ii. 545; years of, iii. 73, 128; necessary in a husband, v. 75.

Discretion, At: a French phrase imported, ii. 151–2; armies living, ii. 209; to surrender, ii. 429; iv. 408.

Diseases: the legacy of men of pleasure, ii. 95; most proceed from too much tenderness, ii. 386–7; love of flattery one of the d. of the mind, ii. 424; contracted by children, ii. 456–7; a quack doctor who offers to cure all, iv. 58–62.

Diseurs de bonne avanture, ii. 250.

Disguise: used by generals, ii. 6; Germanicus in d. listened to his soldiers, ii. 425–6.

Disguised (intoxicated), v. 106.

Dishforth, ——, iii. 211.

Dishumour (ill humour), iii. 591; iv. 197, 249.

Disinheriting an elder son, ii. 463.

Disney, Col. Henry (or Desaulnais), a subscriber, i. lxxxix.

Dispensations of Providence: mysterious, ii. 422–3; a kind of proportion in, ii. 491.

Disposition (arrangement): of the epic, ii. 540; of business, iii. 2; arrangement and d. of bodies, pleasing to the imagination, iii. 544.

Disposition (turn of mind): of the child to be consulted in education, i. 91, 448–9; ii. 114–17; a sweet, i. 421; of mind called good nature, ii. 165; warm and amorous d. of Mariamne, ii. 176; an ingenious, ii. 370; a rude and untractable, ii. 425; a grutching uncommunicative, iii. 39; living with all kinds, iii. 449; a virtuous d. necessary to married happiness, iv. 357.

Disposition (inclination) to be pleased, one of the blessings of life, i. 419–22.

Disputants: frivolous, ii. 44–46, 71; in a coffee-house, ii. 273; iv. 186–7; immethodical, iv. 187.

Disputation: among lawyers, ii. 272–3; rules for managing, ii. 273–5; methods of, ii. 428–32; noise and violence in, iv. 48; for argument's sake, iv. 500.

Dispute(s): between a prentice-boy and a hackney coachman, ii. 291; concerning rank and precedence, iv. 205–8,

386–8; public d. in the University, iv. 500.

Disquiet, the greatest cause of our, ii. 136.

Disquietude, love the mother of, v. 23.

Dissection: of dogs, i. 91; of a woman's tongue, proposed, ii. 460, 481; of a female eye, requested, ii. 481; of a beau's head, ii. 570–3; of a coquette's heart, ii. 594–7.

Dissembling in women, i. 49; ii. 459.

Dissenter(s): 'Gospel-gossips' frequent among, i. 198; canting tones of, ii. 80; a zealous d. an enemy of Popery, ii. 249; have strong tinctures of enthusiasm, ii. 289; opinion of a d. on salutations in Church of England, ii. 509–10; a rigid d. eating plum-porridge, ii. 551; hypocrisy of, iv. 117; their jargon of enthusiasm, iv. 117.

Dissimulation, i. 429–32; iii. 313–16, 393.

Dissolute: 'publicly decent, privately d.', ii. 112.

Dissolution (dissoluteness), iv. 384.

Dissuasive from the Play-House. See Collier.

Distemper(s): physicians usually convert one d. into another, i. 105; fashionable, i. 437; pains and, i. 479; attitude toward, ii. 64–67; caught more easily by youth, ii. 102; exercise and temperance the cure for, ii. 263–7; cold baths for, ii. 383; love of flattery a d. of the mind, ii. 424; of a nurse affecting the child, ii. 456.

Distich, hats cocked with a, v. 106.

Distinction: desire of, universal, ii. 370–4; few men furnished with abilities for, ii. 491; methods of attaining wealth and, iii. 477.

Distinctions, worldly: sources of, ii. 351–2; among mankind merely titular, iii. 16; when useful to men, iv. 203; annihilated by love of novelty, v. 141.

Diston, Josiah (a Director of the Bank), a subscriber, i. xc.

Distortions: and grimaces in a dance, ii. 207; practised by beggars, iv. 12; and mimicries to be avoided in dancing, iv. 146.

Distrait, what the French call a *reveur* and a, i. 329.

Distress(es): an authority due to, i. 359; and woes of life, common to all, ii. 139–43; Raphael's depiction of generous, ii. 379; 'elegant d.' (modesty in public speaking), ii. 397; relieving d. of others, ii. 462–5; beauty in d. moving, iii. 80; virtue in, iii. 412.

Ditties, of street vendors, ii. 476.

Ditton, Humphrey, ii. *470*; iv. *589*.

Diurnal: 'little d. essays', i. 424; 'your diurnals', ii. 118; 'in my diurnal', iv. 78.

Diversions: fashionable *v.* reasonable, i. 158; useful and innocent d. recommended, i. 396–7; public shows and, ii. 413, 502–3; 'innocent', ii. 450–2; in the *Aeneid*, ii. 589; of fallen angels in *PL*, iii. 118; of life a source of pleasure, iii. 453. *See also* Amusements.

Diversity: of colours and of complexions, ii. 532–3; of animals show the goodness of the Creator, iv. 347–8.

Diverticula in Lucan, iii. 61.

Divide & impera (prov.), ii. 502 m.

Divination: in dreams, iv. 229, 292–3; folly of, iv. 291–4.

Divine(s): dictates with authority in private company, ii. 272; sermon of a rabbinical, ii. 361; who plays a part, iii. 393; young d. about town, in the cock military, iv. 400; assembly of, v. 150. *See also* Clergy.

Divisions, Running: in music, ii. 305; upon a head-dress, ii. 459; upon the same ground, iv. 443.

Divorce, grounds for, i. 173.

Do that by proxy which you can do yourself, Never (prov.), iii. 2.

DOBAKE, BIDDY, letter from (on a love-problem), iii. 121.

DOBSON, SISLY, 'who made the miller make away with himself', iv. 406.

Dockwra, William, and the penny post, ii. *84.*

Doctor: degree of, in the three learned professions, iv. 387; 'the invisible d.' (Steele), iv. 460.

Doctors. *See* Physicians.

Dodd, Ann, the *Spectator* sold by, i. xxiv.

Dodona, grove at, reverenced by the ancients, v. 15.

Dodwell, Henry, the Elder, iv. *155.*

Doe: Fadlallah's soul translated into that of a, iv. 577; shooting a, v. 128.

Dog: and gridiron as a sign, i. 116; a house-dog, i. 196; Sir ROGER DE COVERLEY's house-dog, i. 439; iv. 341; frenzy produced by biting of a mad, ii. 384; character in Homer with eyes of a, ii. 399; a Bolonia lap-dog, iv. 271; given away for biting a beggar, v. 128.

Dog, Love me, love my ('the old Sicilian proverb'), iv. 581.

Dog, an impudent young, i. 286.

Dog-days, i. 428; ii. 262.

Dog-star, levels his rays in August, iii. 595.

Dog's sleep (prov.), ii. 226.

Dogs: howling of, unlucky, i. 34; cutting up alive, i. 91; tenacity of, described by Quintus Curtius, i. 129; a pack of, for fox-hunting, i. 232, 352, 447; musical sound of, i. 476; women who resemble, ii. 319; 'keeping mistresses, horses, and hounds', ii. 546; honest creatures, iv. 179–80; 'first with the d. and king amidst the squires', iv. 398; varieties of, in the animal world, iv. 442–3; capable of detecting chastity, iv. 581.

Doggerel: rhymes an example of false wit, i. 258, 265; expressions of *Hudibras* imitated by poets, ii. 35; moderns excel ancients in, ii. 467; when suitable for burlesque, ii. 468; rhymes, iii. 560. *See also* Double rhymes.

Doggett, Thomas: one of the managers of the Haymarket Theatre, i. *25;* iv. *283;* writer of the letter in No. 36(?), i. *149;* a witch in *Macbeth*, i. 151; admired by the Trunk-maker, ii. 415; *Hob, or The Country Wake*, ii. *415;* iv. *283;* Ben in *Love for Love*, ii. 415; Hob in *The Country Wake*, ii. 415; iv. 282–3; one of the managers of Drury Lane Theatre, ii. 504; possible roles for, iii. 394; as cuckold, iv. 68; Fondle-Wife in *The Old Batchelor*, iv. *68;* *The Country Wake*, iv. 282–3.

Doily, iii. 163. *See also* Doyly.

Dolabella, in *All for Love*, iii. 497.

'Doleful Being' (Grief), allegorical figure of, iv. 277–8.

DOLITTLE, DOROTHY, applied for the flitch of bacon, v. 80.

Doll. See Baby.

Dolphins, i. 271.

Dome, effect of, in architecture, iii. 557.

Domestic: gratifications of d. life, ii. 269; d. sciences (preserving, &c.), iii. 205; d. virtues concern all the world, iii. 32.

Domestics. *See* Servants.

'Domesticks' of Socrates, iv. 223.

DOMINIC (Dr. Bernard Gardiner), i. 183.

Dominicans, in China, iv. *452.*

Dominion: Duncan's abstinent use of (*Macbeth*), ii. 308; gratifying to the mind of man, iv. 273.

Dominicus, white and black sons of (Dominicans), iv. 452.

Domitian, the Emperor: his desires turned upon catching flies, ii. 373.

Don Cholerick Snap Shorto de Testy, Penkethman as, iii. 394–5.

Doncaster (Yorkshire), epitaph at, ii. *200.*

Donne, John: quoted, i. 176; *Letters*, iii. *430.*

DOODLE, TIMOTHY, letter from (on innocent diversions), ii. 450–2.

Dorchester, Evelyn Pierrepont, Marquis of: a subscriber, i. *lxxxviii*.

Dorigny, Nicholas, engraved cartoons of Raphael, ii. 380–1.

Dorimant, in *The Man of Mode*, i. 278–80, 322–4.

DORINDA: letter from (on men's wigs and hats), iii. 161–2; letter from (complaining of a fiancé's behaviour), iii. 504–5.

Doris, character of Congreve's, iii. 585.

Dormer, Brig. James: a subscriber, i. *lxxxix*.

Dormouse, a lady's, in her pocket, iii. 320.

DOROTHY, Mrs., proposed as a wife, iv. 401.

Dorset, Charles Sackville, 6th Earl of: Epilogue by, i. 59; his collection of ballads, i. 363–4.

Douai: debates about D. or Denain, iv. 187.

Double-headed canes and spoons, ii. 471.

Double meanings: in plays, i. 217: in conversation, iv. 288.

Double plots, in English tragedy, i. 170–1.

Double rhymes: an example of false wit, i. 258, 272; in *Hudibras*, i. 258.

Doubles: of a hare, i. 477; 'false steps or', ii. 171.

Doublet(s), i. 58; 'learned men in plush d.' (quack-doctors), ii. 28–29; and breeches of one piece of cloth, iv. 571.

Doubt(s): and scruples raised by infidels, ii. 233; gold dissipates every d. and scruple, ii. 431; the freethinker has enough knowledge to raise d. but not to clear them, iv. 187; caused by jealousy, iv. 458.

Douglas, Capt. Archibald, i. 309.

Douglas, James Douglas, 2nd Earl of, in *Chevy Chase*, i. 300, 317–20.

Douglas, James. *See* Hamilton.

Dove(s): a man made up wholly of the d. without a grain of the serpent, ii. 450; in romance writers, iii. 18; a mean between being wasps and d. in public, iii. 72; her eye like that of a, iv. 452.

Downes, John, *Roscius Anglicanus*, ii. 57.

Doxy, 'a warm fire and his', i. 28.

Doyly, Thomas (linendraper), raised a fortune, iii. 4.

Drachmas: Persian, iv. 410; Greek, iv. 528.

Dragon(s): in the opera, i. 64; and giants in romances, iii. 129; river-dragon in *PL* (crocodile), iii. 386; in Spenser, iv. 429.

Dragoons: a captain of, ii. 514; indecent conversation of, iv. 402.

Draining fens and marshes, ii. 285.

Drake, Nathan: quoted, i. lxv, cii–ciii; v. 24.

Drama. *See* Comedy, Playhouse, Plays, Tragedy, Stage.

Drams: sips, d., and whets, iv. 542.

Drances (in the *Aeneid*), bold tongue and feeble arm of, ii. 399.

Drapery: lace and d. in men's dress, iii. 376.

Draught: an evening's, i. 309; a morning's, i. 310.

Drawcansir (in *The Rehearsal*), charged whole armies, i. 72.

Drawing, proposed as an accomplishment of youth, ii. 395.

Drayman (-men), i. 95; iii. 109.

DREAD-NOUGHT, TOM: examination of his heart, v. 8.

Dream(s): of Mr. SPECTATOR's mother, i. 2; portend misfortune, i. 31–32; and visions a species of wit giving delight and surprise, i. 265; Glaphyra's, i. 455–6; affect our spirits, ii. 137; Homer said to have had golden, ii. 226; of Nicholas Hart, ii. 227; determining choice of a lottery ticket, ii. 251; of Eve in *PL*, ii. 199; fanciful visions in, iii. 579; usually mix mirth with gravity, iv. 137; as evidence of immortality, iv. 226–30; divination in, iv. 229, 292–3; an inundation of, sent in to *Spectator*, iv. 364–5; Epictetus' advice to dreamers, iv. 365; reports from JOHN SHADOW on, v. 3–6, 29–31; the result of our waking thoughts, v. 4; benefits from, v. 29; accounts of, from correspondents (GLADIO's, FRITILLA's), v. 40–43.

Dream-visions: public credit, i. 14–17; true and false wit, i. 270–4; painters living and dead, i. 354–6; MIRZAH (the bridge of life), ii. 121–6; dissection of a beau's head, ii. 570–3; dissection of a coquette's heart, ii. 594–7; love and old age, iii. 76–78; FIDELIO's transformation into a looking-glass, iii. 470–3; the seasons, iii. 594–7; the paradise of fools, iv. 121–4; the golden scales, iv. 135–8; the modern women of Hensburg, iv. 270–2; the grotto of grief, iv. 276–9; a sale of unmarried women, iv. 316; Mount Parnassus, iv. 324–30; heavenly and worldly wisdom, iv. 365–9; exchanging misfortunes, iv. 506–11; examination of hearts, v. 7–9; the cave

INDEX

of Trophonius, v. 46–48; men's reactions to the *Spectator*, v. 65–67.
Drench (drink): ill effects of a, iv. 178.
Dress: the *Spectator* to avoid descending to particularities of, i. 70; ii. 7; and equipage proper subjects for raillery, i. 142; English d. 'barbarous', i. 214–15; English d. checks circulation of blood, iv. 571; of other countries seems ridiculous, i. 215; variety of, as a means of wasting time, i. 231; mourning, i. 275–7; of Sir ROGER's ancestors, i. 449–52; in the country old-fashioned and behind the times, i. 488–9; ii. 13–15, 192–3; Roman d. in portrait painting, ii. 12; modes and apparels but trifles, ii. 25; desire of distinction through, ii. 372; gaudy draperies not a mark of the well-dressed, ii. 447; vanity of mankind laid out in, iv. 193; a 'Repository for Fashions' proposed, iv. 194–6; as an indication of character, iv. 344–5. — NEGLIGENCE OF: less offensive than coarse language, i. 324; a real disadvantage, ii. 90–92; the bane of conjugal love, iii. 82; iv. 295–6.
Dress, men's: extravagance in, admired by women, i. 66–67; 'the dressing part of our sex' extravagant, i. 161; of law students, i. 209; 'barbarous', i. 214; effeminate effect of, i. 435; 'Gothic architecture' of, ii. 74; in Charles II's reign, ii. 91; of a 'woman's man', ii. 111; affectation of singularity in, ii. 526; modest d. of IRUS, ii. 527; of the fortune-hunter, iii. 126–7; importance of, iii. 346–9; 'two plain suits a year', iii. 347; laced and embroidered, iii. 347; lace and drapery in, iii. 376; plain d. of MANLIUS, iii. 152–3; of Bussy d'Amboise, iii. 153; Osborne's advice to his son on, iv. 194. *See also* Coats, Hats, &c.
Dress, women's: the product of a hundred climates, i. 295; rivalry in, i. 343–4; mannish riding-dress, i. 434–5; iv. 28–29, 37–38; *Spectators* on particular extravagances in, ii. 303; iv. 27; articles of, ii. 345–6; iii. 206; woman an animal that delights in finery, ii. 530–1; manners and not d. the ornaments of a woman, ii. 533, 556; thin and tawdry d. of a prostitute, ii. 535; ornaments of, in a box at the play, ii. 552; of a French doll described, ii. 578–9; and trifles uppermost in women's thoughts, iii. 53; adopt fashions of men, iii. 223; 'the naked shoulder'd', iv. 38. *See also* Head-dresses, Hoop-petticoats, &c.

Dressing-room, description of a lady's, i. 340–1.
Drigelling: 'COLLIDAN must explain what he means by his', iv. 588.
Dring, Mrs., picture-shop in Fleet Street, iv. *130, 459*.
Drinking: and gaming, i. 58; ii. 546; v. 9; healths, ii. 126, 226, 487; iv. 505; the Queen's health, i. 206; the King's health, iv. 570; for complexion, i. 221; 'uncertain whether to stand or sit while my lord drank to him', i. 287; of the Everlasting Club, i. 310–11; 'grow immortal by', i. 311; and rowdiness, i. 350, 407; to remove humours, ii. 54; of country gentlemen, ii. 96, 225; iv. 177–80; Greeks made slaves drink to excess as examples to youth, ii. 242; makes men appear monstrous and irrational, ii. 242; Sir William Temple's rule for, ii. 266 (an 'emendation' of this, ii. 306); of beggars, ii. 402; habit of, acquired from the nurse, ii. 455; effect of habit upon, iv. 70; at christenings, City feasts, and driving of bargains, iv. 85; false modesty to refuse, iv. 115; feats of, iv. 541–4; on the King's coronation, v. 105–6.
Drole, Rabelais an eminent, iii. 4.
Droll (farce), speeches of Bulfinch in the, ii. 240.
Drolls (fools, jesters): names and actions of in different countries, i. 201; always placed at lower end of table, iv. 388; Dutch excel in painting, iv. 496.
Dromedary, in a projected opera, i. 130, 197.
Drone(s): without stings, ii. 226; letter from MELISSA, married to a, ii. 326–7.
Dropsy: 'my body hydropical', i. 107; resulting from intemperance, ii. 265; a quack doctor who offers to cure, iv. 59.
Drowning man catches at every twig (prov.), iv. 551.
Drugger, Abel (in *The Alchemist*), i. 118.
Druid(s), i. 126; v. 118.
Drum(s) (musical instrument), i. 132; ii. 22; a type of the empty talkative person, ii. 23; 'to purchase a', iii. 4; a set of d. serenading a bridal couple, iii. 370.
Drums (the sound), and enchantments in Lapland, iii. 376.
Drum (drummer), a French term imported, ii. 151–3.
Drummer(s), ii. 22; iv. 33.
Drum-sticks, i. 197.
Drummond, John (an East India Co. Director), a subscriber, i. *xc*.

304

Drummond, William: Jonson's conversations with, i. *298*.

Drunk, drunken: with the scorn that a sober person sees a man d., ii. 66; in good company, ii. 105; d. clowns, ii. 254; getting d. twice a day, ii. 372, 412; 'He that's d. is as great as a King' (the old song), iv. *132*; come home roaring d. at five in the morning, iv. 557; we generally conclude that man d. who takes pains to be thought sober, iv. 574.

DRY, WILL, a man of a clear methodical head, iv. 187-8.

Dryden, John: at Will's, i. *9*; Italian epitaph quoted by, i. 107; on rhyme and blank verse, i. *164*; on *Venice Preserved*, i. 167; most of his tragedies end happily, i. 170; his tragic heroes, i. 172; has little mixed wit, i. 265; his definition of wit, i. 267-8; 'Egad and all that', i. 345; liked ballads, i. 364; copied after Sappho, ii. 390; on the action of the epic, ii. *539*; on duration of action in *Iliad* and *Aeneid*, ii. *543*; on Shakespeare's Caliban, ii. *586*; on Lucan and Statius, ii. *588*; on Milton's 'antiquated' words, iii. *13*; his 'prose-criticks', iii. 15; on criticism, iii. *37*; on Longinus, iii. *38*; on the unhappy ending of *PL*, iii. *58*; thought the Devil the hero of *PL*, iii. 59; on terms of art in the epic, iii. *63*; on 'flats' in *PL*, iii. *141*; on 'the fairy way of writing', iii. 570; on 'golden verses', iv. *287*; rated epic above tragedy, iv. 388.

—WORKS: *Absalom and Achitophel*, quoted, i. 330; ii. 138-9, 363-4; 'one of the most popular poems in English', iv. 318; *All for Love*, a successful tragedy which ends unhappily, i. 170; recommended to ladies, i. 392; mentioned, ii. 40; quoted, iii. 36, 497; *Arviragus Reviv'd* (Prologue), ii. *163*; *Aurengzebe*, quoted, i. 345; recommended to ladies, i. 392; read by Clarinda, iii. 183; Epilogue to, praised, iii. 267; *Cleomenes*, quoted, ii. 197; Epilogue to, praised, iii. 267; *Conquest of Granada*, ii. 397; Almanzor in, ii. 159; iii. 352; *Discourse concerning Satire*, i. *261*; ii. *538*, *543*; iii. *424*; v. *113*; *Don Sebastian*, quoted, i. 140; iv. 435; Epilogue to, praised, iii. 267; source, iii. *301*; *Duke of Guise*, Epilogue to, praised, iii. 267; *Essay of Dramatic Poesy*, i. *170*; v. *108*; *Fables*, quoted, i. 304-5; iii. 373; v. 125-6; *The Indian Emperor, or The Conquest of Mexico*, benefit performance of, i. 172-3; mentioned, i. 345; *Juvenal*, frontispiece to, i. *136*; in LEONORA's library, i. 154; quoted, ii. 90; *Love Triumphant*, Epilogue to, praised, iii. 267; *Mac Flecknoe*, quoted, i. 247; *The Medal*, ii. 20; *Oedipus* (see Lee); *Ovid*, mentioned, ii. 113; quoted, ii. 325-6; tells of Polypheme, iii. 191; passage from *Art of Love* quoted, v. 60-61; *Parallel of Poetry and Painting*, i. *221*; ii. *543*; *Persius*, quoted, i. 233-4; *Sir Martin Mar-All*, trick practised by Sir Martin, i. 24; quoted, ii. *90*; *The Spanish Fryar, or the Double Discovery*, iv. *87*; its double plot admired, ii. 541; Estcourt in, iv. 155; *The State of Innocence and Fall of Man*, i. *166*; passage in, compared with *PL*, iii. 285-6; 'Sylvia the Fair', quoted, i. 387; *The Tempest*, quoted, ii. 58; *Tyrannic Love*, incident of Nell Gwyn and the Epilogue in, quoted, ii. 266; *Virgil* (*Eclogues*), quoted, ii. 384; (*Georgics*), quoted, ii. 150; (*Aeneid*), Dedication to, quoted, i. 107, 268-9, *506*; iv. *464*; the Phantom in the Tenth Book, ii. 304; Iris in, ii. 532; sometimes misrepresents Virgil, ii. 588; quoted, ii. 382; iii. 64; iv. 555-6; v. 16.

DUALL, BETTY, and her two lovers, iv. 226.

Du Bartas, Guillaume de Salluste, Seigneur, false wit in translation of, i. 247.

Dublin, letter written from, with poem, v. 160.

Du Bos, Jean-Baptiste, ii. *127*.

Duckett, George: letters to, i. *41*; iii. *186-7*, 253; *Second Tale of a Tub*, i. *56-57*, *64*, *130*; iv. *107*.

Ducks, ducklings: and sparrow-grass, iii. 397; at a club dinner, iv. 303.

Dudley, Sir Matthew, a subscriber, i. lxxxix.

Duel: Sir ROGER had fought, i. 8; DICK CRASTIN challenges TOM TULIP to, i. 387-8; the English peer who refused a d. in Paris, i. 418; an officer killed in a, iv. 559.

Duelling: i. 41, 126; ii. 237; v. 151; complaint of SPINAMONT, i. 358-60; PHARAMOND's edict against, i. 410-12; false honour in, i. 418-19; Louis XIV's edict against, i. 418-19; every man has his defence in his own arm, ii. 349; the *Spectator's* declaiming against, ii. 439; admired by women, v. 58.

Duellists, Club of, i. 41; iii. 188.

Duff, William, iii. *536*.

Dufoy (in Etherege's *Comical Revenge*), i. *191*.

Du Fresny, Charles Rivière, editor of the *Mercure Galant*, i. xxxvii, *257*.

Dugdale, Sir William, i. *90*.

DULCEORELLA, her art of staring at young men, iv. 246.

DULCIAMARA, her scornful approbation at a comedy, iv. 333.

DULCIANARA, most insolent of all creatures, i. 341.

Dulcinea (in *Don Quixote*), iv. 238.

DULCISSA: a beauty by art, ii. 69; her familiarity of manner, iv. 245.

Dull: 'the d. and the airy', i. 42; the *Spectator* to cease when it grows, i. 47; 'will sometimes be dull', i. 85; d. fellows, i. 180, 184; d. poets resort to bawdry, i. 217; d. parasites and their patrons, i. 217; an author ought to be d. sometimes, i. 505; men of d. tempers often become wealthy, iii. 2; 'd. with design', iii. 251.

Dullness: the spleen an excuse for, i. 226; a Gothic temple consecrated to the god of, i. 271.

Dulot,——, inventor of *bouts-rimés*, i. *258*.

Dumb: conversation with the, i. 20; d. bell, exercise with, i. 473–4; d. man, the Trunk-maker thought to be a, ii. 414; TITUS TROPHONIUS not d., iv. 294. For Dumb Conjurer, Dumb Man, *see* Campbell.

Dummer, Thomas (Deputy Master of the Great Wardrobe), a subscriber, i. xcii.

Dumpling, affair of the boiled, iv. 588.

Dumps, in the, ii. 195.

Duncan (in *Macbeth*): moderation of, ii. 308; murder of, ii. 315; iv. 434.

Duncombe, Rev. John, i. *1*; ii. *364*; iii. *409*; iv. *420*.

Duncombe, William, i. xlix–l, *141*, *225*, *281*, *388*, *435*; ii. *59*, *357*, *393*, *397*, *480*; iii. *102*, *126*, *151*, *409*, *514*; iv. *428*.

DUNDRUM, Sir DAVID, a rival of Sir ROGER for the hand of the widow, iii. 343.

Dungeons: wretches shut up in, ii. 142; as instruments of religious zeal, ii. 229; as methods of persuasion, ii. 431.

Dunghill, description of, may be pleasing to the imagination, iii. 567.

Dunkirk, demolishing of, debated in a coffee-house, ii. 273.

Dunlop, Alexander, a contributor (?), i. lvii; iv. *364–5*.

Dunners, iv. 101.

Duns Scotus, Johannes: a celebrated 'ill face', i. 77; followers of, in Oxford, ii. 429.

Dunton, John, i. xx–xxi, *364*; iii.*153*; and the *Athenian Mercury*, i. xxxvii.

Du Perron, Jacques Davy, ii. 297.

Dupuy (Van de Putte), Henri, hymn to the Virgin Mary, i. *254*.

D'Urfey, Thomas, i. *364*; *Banditti*, iii. *350*; *Don Quixote*, i. *125*; iv. *132*, *238*; *The French Prophets*, ii. *129*; *The Marriage-Hater Matched*, iv. *391*; *Tales*, in LEONORA's library, i. 156.

Durley, Henry (a Director of S. Sea Co.), a subscriber, i. *xc*.

Du Rondel, Jacques, ii. 297.

Dutch (=German): Motteux speaks D. and French, iii. 26.

Dutch, the: their good taste in monuments, i. 111; famous for industry, i. 200; sign of the Gaper a jest at Amsterdam, i. 200; destroy surplus spices, ii. 286; insolent to the French, iv. 207; excel in painting drolls, iv. 496; gravity of, v. 47.

Dutch: atlases (silk-satin), iii. 26; boors brought over in herds, i. 269; great globes, iv. 482; holly, iv. 104; mail, i. 46; ii. 476; iii. 27; mechanic's project to make verses, ii. 357; painter (Minheer Grotesque), i. 176; ii. 183; painting, i. 135, 355.

Dutchman (men): at the Royal Exchange, i. 294; represents industry in vision of painters, i. 355; anecdote of one who broke his leg, ii. 564; not altered by cave of Trophonius, v. 47.

Dutton, Sir Richard, referred to (?), iv. 248.

Duty(-ies): a court can make d. and fashion walk together, i. 359; animals are out of the possibilities of, ii. 137; of man, ii. 181, 233, 353, 443; iv. 569; want of, in children, how punished by Chinese, ii. 243–4; opinion of Persians on, ii. 244; of religion, ii. 331–4; decency accompanying every, iii. 39; ordinary d. of a Christian, iii. 326–7; each station of life has its, iv. 592.

Duty (tax) on Castle-soap, iv. 230.

Dwarf(s): in books of chivalry, i. 417; a show of, ii. 557–8; marriage of the, iii. 167; and squires carry impresses of giants or knights, iv. 18.

D'ye hear me and *D'y'see*, redundant phrases in conversation, iii. 398.

Dyer, John: 'our authentic intelligence, our Aristotle in politics', i. 182–3; his news-letter read aloud by Sir ROGER, ii. 4–5; an epistolary historian, iv. 111.

'Dying for love', iii. 416–18.

Dying man: one whom sooner or later we shall certainly resemble, iii. 29; sustained by religious hope, iv. 167.

E Tow O Koam, 'King of the Rivers', i. 212.

Eagle: Condé's face compared to that of an, i. 367; Agamemnon's soul transformed into that of an, ii. 326; the eye of an, ii. 470; pursuing its prey in Paradise, iii. 359.

Ear(s): a box on the, ii. 407; treatises on, ii. 470; dungeon in Sicily called 'Dionysius' Ear', iv. 44; pertness of one ear as a mark of reprobation, iv. 344.

EARLY, ALICE (a house-maid), letter from, iii. 226.

Earnings (yearnings): of distress, i. 402; of heart in a father, ii. 521.

Earth: must be laboured before it gives its increase, i. 472; the mother of all things, ii. 166, 457; women who were made out of, ii. 319; Aesop's fable of, ii. 455; action in PL executed upon, ii. 541; sweated out bitumen, iii. 554; decay of moisture in, iv. 542; diurnal and annual rotation of, compared to self-love and benevolence, v. 12.

Ease: a gentleman-like, i. 325; of mind necessary to our well-being, ii. 65; lacking to the man of pleasure, ii. 94; a translation with the e. of an original, ii. 367; desire of e. and disencumbrance, ii. 526; and plenty the great cherishers of knowledge, iii. 22.

Ease, Theatre of, proposed, ii. 503.

EASIE, BENJAMIN: petition from, ii. 31; answer to, ii. 46; referred to, ii. 269.

Easiness: and credulity fatal to JACK TRUEPENNY, i. 353; of temper and good-breeding, ii. 165; of Waller has made many insipid poets, v. 185.

East Enborne, Berks., custom at, v. 100, 129.

East India Company, Directors of, subscribers to Spectator, i. xc.

East Indies, reports of witchcraft in, i. 480.

East wind: effects of, ii. 436; brings melancholy, iii. 454; and unsociable temper, iv. 48; Lady BLAST's whisper blights like an easterly wind, iv. 113.

Eastcourt, Dick. See Estcourt.

Eastern: allegory, ii. 263; king's device, iii. 550; parts of the world, natural geniuses in, ii. 127; salutations, iv. 418, 485; style of writing, ii. 128; iv. 134, 576; way of thinking, iii. 231.

Eastern nations: tyranny of princes in,

iii. 22; monuments of, iii. 324; importance of cleanliness among, v. 158.

EASY, CHARLES: letter from (on a beau's behaviour in the theatre), ii. 434–5; testimonial from to Spectators on hypochondria, iv. 459.

EASY, JAMES, letter from (on nose-pulling at the theatre), ii. 544–5.

Easy: a man should try to make himself e. now and happy hereafter, ii. 139; e. to oneself and agreeable to others, ii. 197, 445; v. 75; an e. fortune, ii. 253; let your precept be, Be easy, ii. 268; an e. temper, ii. 281, 328; iii. 446; an e. companion for life, ii. 515; an e. philosophy, ii. 553; and pleasant manner, iii. 56; an e. constitution, iii. 80; conversation, iii. 81; iv. 82; an e. mien defined, iv. 332.

Easy writer: or a sonneteer, i. 451; Anacreon an e. gay author, iv. 473.

Eating: Milton's digression on the angels', iii. 61; 'e. fashionably', iii. 111; e. contests, iii. 277–8; a humorist who disregarded hours for, iv. 570.

Eating and drinking: are points wherein most men agree, i. 42; temperance in, ii. 264–7; an eminent physician's rules for, ii. 265.

Echard, Laurence, Roman History, quoted, iv. 382.

Echo poems: examples of false wit, i. 252, 271; iii. 560; example from Hudibras quoted, i. 252–3; consist of resemblances of syllables, i. 265.

Eclipse of sun, simile of, in PL, iii. 91.

Economy: a good economist, i. 276; compared to good breeding, i. 467; of the merchant and the gentleman, ii. 188; EUGENIUS prudent in, ii. 198; Mr. SPECTATOR talks well of, but is suspected of profuseness, ii. 349; Tigellius a mighty pretender to (in Horace), ii. 363; of Providence, ii. 422; of whoredom, described by Fletcher, ii. 535; 'ripe for', iii. 136.

Ecstasies and raptures the result of enthusiasm, ii. 289.

-ed, dropping of vowel in words ending in, ii. 33–34.

Eden, Garden of, iv. 192. See also Milton.

Edgar, King, anecdote of, v. 70–71.

Edgar (in King Lear). See Rymer.

Edgcumbe, Richard, a subscriber, i. lxxxix.

Edgehill, Battle of, iii. 70; v. 150.

Editors, textual: overpraised by pedants, i. 438; of Sappho, ii. 393; among the unlearned, iv. 14; pedantry in, iv. 161–5.

Education: for trade rather than learned professions recommended, i. 91–92; to be adapted to the genius of the child, i. 91–92; iii. 105–9; mistakes in, i. 281–3; a liberal, i. 285; ii. 100, 340, 372, 412, 432; of their children the duty of women, i. 312; among ancient Persians, i. 418; iii. 248–9; of a young heir to an estate, i. 501; reading aloud neglected in, ii. 78; flogging in, ii. 115–17, 160–2; improper e. produces pedants, ii. 162; may improve but not produce good nature, ii. 166; suggested for illegitimate children, ii. 297; like polish and sculpture to a block of marble, ii. 338–9; proposal for a new method of, ii. 395–6; in charity schools, iii. 48–50, 108; at a public school *v.* e. at home, iii. 132–5; methods of inculcating virtue in, iii. 246–50; iv. 274–5; by Indian Gymnosophists, iii. 249; in practical arts, iii. 316–19; through travel, iii. 367–70; advantages of, and moral culture, iv. 104–5; should not encourage undue modesty in speaking, iv. 218.

Education of a Daughter. See Fénelon.

Education of women: hypocrisy the foundation of, i. 49; fine breeding *v.* good breeding, i. 281–3; importance of, iii. 139–40; accomplishments of, iii. 205; benefits of dancing in, iii. 414–15; of a wealthy young woman, iv. 405–6.

Edward the Confessor: his tomb in Westminster Abbey, iii. 215; the first who touched for the evil, iii. 215.

Edward I, called 'long-shanks', i. 135.

Edward III: his victories over the French, ii. 151; his sword in Westminster Abbey, iii. 215; Sir Richard Baker's opinion of, iii. 215.

EDWARD, your uncle, iv. 359.

Eels, antipathy to, iv. 421.

Effeminacy: account of an effeminate young gentleman, i. 241; a man who affects the softness and e. of a woman, i. 435; tenderness toward a wife not softness or e., ii. 418; account of an effeminate husband, iv. 209–10.

Effingham, Thomas Howard, 6th Baron, iii. *102.*

Effluviums of cheese, effect of, iv. 421.

'Egad and all that' (in Mr. Bayes), i. 345.

Egerton, William, *Memoirs of Mrs. Oldfield,* iii. *251, 351.*

Egg(s): poems in shape of, i. 246, 265, 271; care of, varies with different animals, i. 490; a hen's care of, i. 492; of the crocodile broken by the ichneumon, ii. 2; the shepherd who juggled, ii.130; Leda's, ii. 539; a hypochondriac fancying himself an, iv. 415.

Eginhart and Imma, ii. 215–16.

Ego & Rex meus, of Cardinal Wolsey, iv. 520.

Egotism: to be avoided in conversation, ii. 521–2; a word coined by the 'Gentlemen of Port-Royal', iv. 519–20; Montaigne the most eminent egotist, iv. 520; referred to, iv. 572.

Egypt: controversies over antiquities of, i. 2; merchant of, at Royal Exchange, i. 294; story of Sultan of, i. 400–1; would be overrun by crocodiles but for the ichneumon, ii. 2; plagues of, described in *PL,* iii. 386; pyramids and labyrinth of, iii. 555; journey of Israel from, iv. 126–8.

Egyptian, study of, iv. 104.

Egyptian mummy, i. 383; useful in physic, iii. 149.

Egyptian temple, the monkey enshrined in an, ii. 7.

Egyptian woman in Lincoln's Inn Fields, gingerbread sold by, iii. 94.

Egyptians: serpent of, swallowed up by that of Moses, i. 45; worship the crocodile, ii. 2; their simile of a dark lantern, iii. 424; troubled with plague of darkness, v. 102.

EITHERDOWN, BRIDGET, letter from (to a friend), iii. 7–8.

Ela, milk generally sold in a note above, ii. 475.

Elbow-chair, i. 197, 309, 335, &c.; politicians to be taught the importance of the, iii. 99.

Elcock, Mrs., iii. 211.

Elder brother: born a mere, ii. 38; restoration of an estate to an, ii. 463.

Elder-bushes, i. 453.

Elders and betters, saluted first, ii. 433.

Eldest child, often spoiled by prospect of an estate, iv. 274.

Eleemosynary (almonry), 'the multitude tippled e.', v. 108.

ELEONORA: letter from PARTHENIA referring to, ii. 54–55. Cf. LEONORA.

Elections for Parliament, i. 89; ii. 3; riots and tumults at, iii. 218; behaviour of candidates at, iii. 476–7.

Elector of Hanover's Memorial, iii. *439.*

Electuary (-ies): a bolus or, i. 353; of quack doctors, iv. 553.

Elegance: of Catullus' translation of Sappho, ii. 391; of lovers' sentiments, ii. 437; and perspicuity of Pope's *Essay on Criticism,* ii. 483; and delicacy of language in ancient critics, iii. 36.

Elegant: expression and solid sense, i. 269; satisfactions flow from reason and virtue, ii. 87; and knowing part of mankind, ii. 349; distress (modesty in public speaking), ii. 397; entertainments, ii. 413; figure in Holy Writ, ii. 422; 'simple truth elegantly recommended', ii. 447; many e. phrases become debased by common use, iii. 11.

Elephant: antipathy of rhinoceros and, i. 213; rebus of, used by Caesar, i. 250; in Bartholomew Fair, iv. 106-7.

Elevation of style: in the Old Testament, i. 127; in the epic, iii. 11-15.

'Elevator muscle', which turns the eye towards Heaven, ii. 572-3.

Elfrida, wife of King Edgar, v. 71.

Eligible: the latter part of life more, ii. 101; commemoration of great actions, which kind more, ii. 239; shade and privacy a more e. portion, ii. 462.

Elihu, his thoughts on old age and youth quoted, iii. 244-5.

Elisions in *PL*, iii. 15.

Elixirs of quack doctors, iv. 553.

Elizabeth I: poetry in time of, i. 316; a rabbinical divine in reign of, ii. 36; glorious name of, ii. 216; a saying ascribed to, ii. 359; 'in old Queen Bess's days', ii. 465; letter of Anne Boleyn, mother of, ii. 487; struck a medal on defeat of Spanish Armada, iii. 45; tomb of a maid of honour to, iii. 214; fashions in time of, iv. 195; ballads brought before a minister of state in reign of, iv. 281; compliment to, in *Faerie Queene*, iv. 429; saying of a statesman in days of, v. 44.

Elizabeth Farnese, Queen of Spain (wife of Philip V), i. 277.

ELIZABETH: letter from JAMES to, i. 305-8.

Elm(s): at Sir ROGER's, i. 453; a knot of, v. 14; metaphorical image of sleep in Virgil, v. 31; a walk of, v. 144.

Elmsly, Peter (bookseller), iv. *41*.

Elogiums, funeral orations and, iii. 152.

Eloquence: of lawyers unjustly employed, ii. 180; modesty in public speaking a kind of mute, ii. 397; of women, ii. 458-62; of the eye, iv. 479; of tears and fainting fits, ii. 480-1; rules for, iii. 520-3; iv. 432-7; of beauty, iv. 332; of beggars, v. 95; moderns have greater advantages towards than ancients, v. 164-7.

Elrington, Thomas, in *The Lancashire Witches*, ii. 57.

Elysium, of Virgil, iii. 564.

Elzeviers: a set of, in LEONORA's library, i. 156; fine printing by, iii. 381.

Embassy (-ies): of Indian Queens, ii. 532; secretaries to, iii. 96.

'Embellishers', a variety of liars, iv. 355.

Embellishments: fashionable in conversation, ii. 467; mixed e. of Tasso, ii. 588.

Emblematical: figures in dancing, i. 285; persons (allegorical figures), iii. 573.

Embroidered: coat, effect of on women, i. 67; ii. 595; e. and laced suits, iii. 347.

Embroidery, i. 46, 271; in a beau's head, ii. 571; and needle-work, iii. 205; working a rich e. upon a cobweb, iii. 369; ribbons, brocades, and, iv. 271; the 'laudable mystery' of, recommended, v. 71-74; histories worked in, v. 83.

Embryon atoms, a word coined by Milton, iii. 13-14.

Emendations and different readings, iii. 208; iv. 161-5.

Emerald: spirit living within an, iv. 562; sparkling green of, v. 94.

Emerson, William (prize-fighter), iv. *31*.

EMILIA: a model wife, iii. 78-83; a ward in danger from her guardian, iii. 504.

Eminence, Men of. *See* Great Men.

Emma, Queen, her ordeal by fire, ii. 276; iii. *481*.

Emmaus, disciples on the way to, v. 166.

Emmet, transmigration into an, iii. 275.

Emotion: vehemence and e. in Sappho, ii. 392; players overcome by, iii. 32, 34.

Emperor: death of (Joseph I), i. 276; argument with Roman (Hadrian), ii. 430; of the Mohocks, iii. 187, 224, 293-5; of Mexico, iii. 559; doctor who had lost an eye in service of, iv. 61-62; of China, letter from, iv. 448-53.

Emperors, Roman, ambitions of the different, v. 168.

Empires: the four first e. of the world, ii. 227.

Empiric, ignorance and inhumanity of an, iv. 158.

Empty spaces of life, methods of filling up, i. 395-9.

Emulation: in country sports, ii. 131-5, 370-4; in learning, iii. 22; opposed to envy, iv. 19; ambition posing as, iv. 326.

Enborne, Berks., custom of riding the black ram at, v. 100, 129.

Enchantments: in the reign of false wit, i. 271; in Lapland, iii. 376.

INDEX

Enclosures, the merchant throws down no man's, ii. 188.

Encore: or *Altro Volto*, at the opera, iii. 138; 'Mr. FROTH cried out *Ancora*', iii. 184.

End: necessity of adhering steadfastly to one great, ii. 136; being useful to mankind the chief e. of being, ii. 432; of life compared to that of a play, iii. 299.

'Endorsing' with the whip, iv. 267.

Enemy (-ies): Plutarch says a man should not hate even his, i. 510; a secret e. more dangerous than a declared one, ii. 83; 'live with an e. as if he might become a friend . . .', ii. 375; we should esteem virtue though in an, ii. 445–6; forgiveness of, iii. 323; benefits which we may receive from, iii. 323–4, 494; a generous e. sometimes commends, iv. 45.

Energy of expression, more necessary to blank verse than to rhyme, iii. 14.

Engineers, military, and the art of scaling, iii. 126.

England: a barren country, except for advantages of commerce, i. 295; free from extremities of weather, i. 296; a trading nation, i. 449; its climate induces melancholy, ii. 205; produces men of integrity rather than statesmen, iii. 100; fine printing in, iii. 381–2; famous for whims and humorists, iii. 396; taste for epigrams and conceits in, iii. 530; not a village in, without a ghost, iii. 572; practice of hiring party writers 'a kind of national crime', iv. 87. *See also* Great Britain.

English, the: gallant to women, i. *21*; a polite nation, but lacking in good sense and religion, i. 30; delight in bloodshed, i. 188; observations of the Four Indian Kings on, i. 211–15; cunning in handicraft, i. 214; very idle, i. 214; a lion the emblem of, i. 251; character of, in *Chevy Chase*, i. 300, 320; plainness and sincerity of, i. 430; taciturnity of, ii. 32, 82; boasted liberty of, ii. 115; not delicate eaters, ii. 264–5; reflections on idolatry of no use to, ii. 290; love of fighting, ii. *291*; genius of, iii. 382; French opinion of, iii. *396*; 'one Englishman could beat three Frenchmen', iii. 437; naturally fanciful, iii. 572; the proudest nation under heaven, iv. 18; their fondness for news, iv. 90; natural bashfulness or sullenness of, iv. 102; fear of hypocrisy in religion, iv. 116–17; good nature peculiar to, iv. *370*; 'let out

their wives to all encounters', iv. 379; excel in portrait painting, iv. 497; afflicted with the itch for writing, iv. 590; excel in embroidery, v. 83.

'English Artist' (a showman), i. *128*.

English beauty, a female Hottentot contrasted with an, v. 157.

English climate, i. 295; makes entertainments of mirth and laughter necessary, ii. 205; rule for temperance in, ii. 265; mildness of, iii. 474.

English constitution, superiority of, iii. 18–22.

English fleet: a security against Popery, iii. 437; formerly the terror of the ocean, iv. 538; destruction of trees for, iv. 594.

English gardens, compared with French and Italian, iii. 551–3.

English language: tone of, differs from Welsh and Scotch, i. 120; characteristics of, ii. 32–36; rapidity of pronunciation in, ii. 33; adulterated with French words and phrases, ii. 149–53; cultivation of, a concern of education, ii. 395–6; carried to greatest height by Milton, iii. 14; unequal to Milton's greatness, iii. 62–63; enriched by infusion of Hebraisms, iii. 514–15; not very capable of good compound words, iv. 38; cant language in, illustrated, v. 105–6; 'clipping the King's English', v. 106; pedantic language in, illustrated, v. 107–11.

English melancholy: caused by climate, ii. 205; a demon that haunts our island, iii. 454; and gloominess so frequent in our nation, iii. 572.

English modesty, i. 435; ii. 35; noticed by foreign writers, iii. 520; 'our distinguishing character', iv. 29; bashfulness or sullenness, iv. 102.

English oak, iv. 104.

English octavo, heavier than a French folio, iv. 137.

'English Pills', of quack doctors, iv. 553.

English women: excel those of all nations in beauty, i. 349; beautiful complexions of, ii. 532–3.

Englishman: impudence in an E. sullen and insolent, i. 87; 'gratifies my vanity as an', i. 292–3; Mr. SPECTATOR happy that he was born an, ii. 32.

Enigmas, a species of wit giving delight and surprise, i. 265.

Enipeus, river on Mount Ida, iii. 230.

Enjoyment(s): incapacity of finding e. in our own minds, ii. 363; a perpetual succession of, in eternity, ii. 420; glory the greatest of mortal, ii. 426;

a happy marriage has all the e. of sense and reason, ii. 516; the luxurious man gains only uneasiness from his, ii. 599.

Ennius, Quintus, v. *28, 56.*

Enosh, ii. 361.

Enquiry after Truth. See Malebranche.

Ens rationis, at the sign of an, i. 116.

Entail: of estate, ii. 598; in marriage settlements, iv. 359–60.

Enter into thy Closet, i. *391.*

Enthusiasm: and superstition, ii. 288–90; that divine e. so natural to devotion, iii. 200; vagaries of, among Quakers, iii. 484; the bellowings and distortions of, iii. 522; jargon of, among sectaries, iv. 117; 'a humorist or enthusiast', iv. 319.

Entrails of beasts, divination from, iv. 292.

ENVILLE, JOHN, Kt.: letter from (on his marriage), iii. 68–71; this letter praised, iv. 438; his wife, Lady MARY; his children, the Hon. ODDLY and HARRIOT, iii. 69.

Envious eye, beliefs regarding, i. 83.

Envious man, character of, i. 82–85.

Envy: allegorical depiction of in Vision of Painters, i. 355; in authors, i. 508; likely to take up our minds, ii. 67; allegorical depiction of, ii. 124; prevalence of, ii. 165; 186–7, 411, 426, 491, 493–5; iv. 19; reigns among bad poets, ii. 481–2; strokes of, in Pope's *Essay on Criticism,* ii. 482–3; of an old man for the follies of the young, ii. 512; and revenge of Satan in *PL,* iii. 84; banished by friendship, iii. 446; allegorical figure of in Ovid, iii. 573; an affectation contrary to, iv. 174; fountain Aganippe protects against all harms but, iv. 328; of authors ceases after their death, iv. 472; the fruit of laziness and ignorance, v. 27; provoked by novelty, v. 139.

Epaminondas (Theban general): noble death of, ii. 26; anecdote of, iii. 299.

Epeus, and building of the Trojan horse, i. 246.

Ephesian widow: story of, i. 48, 49, 51; CLEORA, a widow of Ephesus, ii. 407; cruelty of an, iii. 468.

Ephori, chief magistrates of Sparta, iv. 528.

EPHRAIM, the Quaker: a stage-coach companion, ii. 22, 73, 439.

Epic poetry: puns unsuitable in, i. 251; similitudes in, seldom contain wit, i. 264; allegorical figure of, i. 274; to be founded on a precept of morality, i. 299; should celebrate persons and actions which do honour to their country, i. 300; the fable in, ii. 537–44; iii. 58–60; the actors in, ii. 561–6; imaginary (allegorical) persons in, ii. 563–4; iii. 337–9, 393, 573; thoughts or sentiments in, ii. 585–90; iii. 61–62; language of, iii. 9–15, 62–64; an unhappy ending not so proper for, iii. 59, 388; the author of should seldom speak himself, iii. 60; digressions in, iii. 60–61; use of similes in, iii. 90–91; fable should be filled with the probable and the marvellous, iii. 144; dispute for precedency between writers of, and tragedy, iv. 388; poetical justice not a feature of, iv. 464–5; women writers of, v. 72. *See also* Homer, Milton, Virgil.

Epictetus: 'those little familiar instances and illustrations so much admired in', i. 291; quoted, on women's desire to please, i. 224; on our duty to act our part in the theatre of life, ii. 353; on criticism from others, iii. 323–4; on not sorrowing over troubles of others, iii. 486; on relating dreams, iv. 365; mentioned, ii. 205.

Epicureans: their regard for the religion of their country, ii. 234; emulated the pleasure of the gods, v. 167.

Epicurus: the gods of, indifferent to mankind, ii. 337–8; thought sensual pleasure best attained in gardens, iv. 595; his view of human nature, v. 10.

Epigram: the only province for mixed wit, i. 267; allegorical figure of, i. 274; little fanciful authors and writers of, i. 297; epigrammatical turns, i. 316; epigrammatic wit on glass, ii. 356; epigrammatic turns of Lucan, ii. 588; too much nicety in comparisons savours of the epigrammatist, iii. 91; taste in England for, iii. 530; makers of parterres are like epigrammatists, iv. 190; women writers of, v. 72.

Epigrams: 'The Witches' Prayer', i. 262; Tate's e. on the *Spectator,* iv. 232–3; Greek, iv. 472–6. *See also* Martial.

Epilogues of tragedies: reflections on facetious, iii. 252–4; defence of facetious, iii. 265–9; of *The Distressed Mother,* iii. 266; iv. 493; Dryden's happy turn for, iii. 267.

Épine, Marguerite de l': in *Almahide,* ii. *398;* Bernice in *Hydaspes,* iii. *514.*

Epirus: ARIDAEUS of, ii. 407; Scanderbeg, Prince of, iii. 149.

Episodes: in the epic, ii. 540–1; like so many short fables, iii. 91.

Epistolary verse, remarks on, v. 112–14.
Epitaphs: on a valetudinarian, i. 107; in Westminster Abbey, i. 109–11; by Ben Jonson, i. 141; on Troilus, i. 246; on Duchess of Newcastle, i. 417; on a charitable man ('What I spent I lost'), ii. 200; on Countess Dowager of Pembroke, iii. 185; in Stepney churchyard (on Thomas Sapper and Daniel Saul), iv. 343; on R. C., iv. 343–4; in Pancras churchyard (on a child), iv. 424; on Greek writers, iv. 472–6; of Cowley on himself, iv. 475–6.
Epithets: of Homer and Virgil compared, iii. 564–5; of Homer much admired by antiquity, iv. 431; Spenser's e. of trees, iv. 431.
Epping, a letter from, i. 207–8.
Epsom, ii. 104; Epsom Old Wells, i. 102. See also Shadwell.
Equability ('evenness of behaviour'), a qualification of a good friend, i. 291; of COTTILUS, ii. 65–66.
Equality: of age and fortune necessary to friendship, i. 291; of mind necessary to enjoyment of life, ii. 67; in human nature and civil government, iii. 19.
Equanimity desirable, ii. 43–44, 64–68; above cheerfulness and below mirth, ii. 268; fortitude, e., and moderation the great rule, iii. 406–8.
Equipage: women's love of, i. 66–69, 197; ii. 303, 545–6; vanity of, in court of Louis XIV, ii. 48; of the tea-table, ii. 454; the world is intent on, ii. 515.
Equipage (retinue): 'thought me an e. ready to his hand', i. 407; a captain's, ii. 22; regular visitants the pleasantest parts of a woman's, ii. 112; merit serves in place of e. to a gentleman, ii. 591.
Er, son of Armenius, ii. 326.
Erasistratus, recognized symptoms of love from Sappho's writings, ii. 393.
Erasmus, Desiderius: an echo poem by, i. 252; on Socrates' death, ii. 334; on 'Greeks and Trojans' in the universities, ii. 429–30; his tribute to Sir Thomas More, iii. 300.
ERASTUS and LAETITIA, a happily-married couple, iv. 297–8.
Error: and prejudice the foundation of the world's opinion, ii. 280; the wicked in eternity bewildered in labyrinths of, ii. 421; vagaries of, among Quakers, iii. 484; allegorical figure of, iv. 121.
Error personae, as a cause of separation, i. 173.
Errors: vulgar e. ridiculed by the virtuosos, ii. 442–3; pleasure in pro-claiming e. of a great man, ii. 494; in Milton's syntax to be excused, iii. 10; the critic not to be chiefly concerned with, iii. 36–37; an e. in printing of the Bible, iv. 580.
Erysichthon, story of, v. 15.
ESCALUS and ISABELLA, story of, iii. 157–60.
ESCHINES, his leap into the Ionian sea, ii. 406–7.
Escritoire. See Scrutore.
ESCULAPIUS: letter from (on the Lovers' Leap), ii. 383–4; the famous golden beard of, iii. 223; restores the sight of Plutus, iv. 140.
Esprit, Jacques, Traité de la fausseté des vertus humaines, iv. 416.
Esq.: my banker writes me Mr. or Esq. as he sees me dressed, ii. 92; 'Thomas such a one, Esquire', ii. 226; 'Esq., if you please', iv. 376; added to names, v. 93.
Essays: essayers upon friendship, i. 289; of a man of quality, i. 361; little diurnal e. (the Spectator), i. 424; difficulties of writing, i. 505–8; looseness and freedom of, ii. 465; serious e. v. occasional papers, iv. 27; methodical discourses and e. in the Spectator, iv. 185; a wild kind of composition, iv. 185; Montaigne's celebrated e. written about himself, iv. 520; moral and divine e. in the Spectator, iv. 547.
'Essays' in Spectator: upon virtue, ii. 443; upon laughter and ridicule, ii. 465; upon love and marriage, ii. 514; upon the art of growing rich, iii. 2; upon the civil part of our constitution, iii. 18–19; upon death, iii. 29; towards an history of dancing, iii. 237; a loose e. upon friendship, iii. 45; on the pleasure the mind conceives from nature, iii. 475; on the pleasures of the imagination, iii. 530; the TEMPLAR's e. on pronunciation and action, iv. 432; against quacks, iv. 551; on singularity, iv. 571; on benevolence, v. 54.
Essence, the beau's pineal gland smelt strong of, ii. 571.
Essex, Earl of, his chaplain, ii. 361.
Essex: Duncan Campbell's wonders reported in, iv. 181; indecent conversation in a stage coach out of, to London, iv. 402.
Estate(s): raising, i. 294; ii. 363; encumbering, i. 352; and health ruined by gallantry, ii. 105; lack of, an obstacle to marriage, ii. 140; getting an e. by industry better than losing it by negligence, ii. 189; a husband who

raised an e. by snoring, ii. 226; men of e., why reduced to poverty, ii. 252; squandered away by spendthrifts, ii. 295; Cicero, on lessening a paternal, ii. 364; restoration of, to an elder brother, ii. 463; the chief consideration in an arranged marriage, ii. 515; calculation of, ii. 597–9; methods of arriving at great, iii. 2–5; Themistocles preferred a man without an e. to an e. without a man, iii. 126; education as a means of acquiring, iii. 317–18; care of, by planting, iii. 551–2; settlement of an, iv. 359–60.

Estcourt, Richard: Providore of the Beef-Steak Club, i. 42; and opening of Bumper Tavern, i. 42; ii. 529; letter from, ii. 529; Sir ROGER's letter to, ii. 529–30; his interlude, *Prunella*, iii. 182; his jovial humour, iii. 342; benefit for, iii. 342; his talent in acting, iii. 394; death of, iv. 154–8; Bulfinch in *The Northern Lass*, iv. 157; Pounce in *The Tender Husband*, iv. 157; his other roles, i. 75, 128, 173, 218; ii. 240, 242, 529; iii. 278, 342; iv. 155, 157.

Esteem: courtiers making professions of, ii. 180; marks of, from enemies, ii. 426; to be sought from God, not men, ii. 500; and love the first principles of friendship, iii. 445; the due point of, iv. 124; love seldom continues long after, iv. 298.

Esteem, Passion for. *See* Praise, Love of.

Esther, the fidelity of, iv. 451–2.

Estienne, Robert (Stephanus), a variant reading by, iv. 164.

Estrades, Count d', *Letters and Negotiations of*, recommended, iv. 390.

Eternity: perpetual progress of the soul in, i. 458–9; iii. 432; v. 140, 145, 171–3; Socrates on, ii. 75–76; in the Vision of Mirzah, ii. 123–5; the pleasures of, ii. 231; iii. 27; our knowledge of, ii. 301; v. 17–22, 48–53, 144–5, 585–6; we should value ourselves as heirs of, ii. 321–2; rank and precedence in, ii. 352–3; the discreet man's view of, ii. 377; rewards and punishments in, ii. 420–1; happiness in, prevented by love of fame, ii. 499–502; happiness in, often determined by choice in marriage, ii. 515; to be kept constantly in mind as our goal, iii. 29; speculations of, pleasing to the understanding, iii. 541; pleasures of, must be prepared for in this life, iv. 72; weighed against temporal considerations, iv. 136; the blessed behold God face to face,

iv. 549; duration of, iv. 567–8; e. past and future, or actual and potential, v. 144–8, 170–3; the heathens had but an imperfect idea of, v. 164. *See also* Immortality.

-eth, substitution of *-s* for words ending in, ii. 34, 79.

Ether: fields of, iii. 575; blueness of the, iv. 529.

Etherege, Sir George: Sir ROGER often supped with, i. 8; 'the polite', i. 217; *The Comical Revenge; or Love in a Tub*, a scene in, i. 191, 361; 'Etheridge's way of making love in a tub', ii. 6; Estcourt in, iv. 155; *The Man of Mode, or Sir Fopling Flutter*, i. 8, 193; ii. 218, 477; iii. 57; immodesty in, i. 278–80; character of Dorimant, i. 322–4; *She Would if She Could*, iv. 155, 333; innuendo in its title, i. 216–17.

Etna, Mount: Cowley compares his heart to, i. 266; temple to Vulcan on, iv. 580.

Eton: WILL WIMBLE had been at, i. 447; flogging at (?), ii. 161.

Etymology: of *cant*, ii. 80; examples of popular, iv. 195.

EUBULUS, presides at the coffee-house, i. 210–11.

Euclid, i. 267, 331; Aristotle's criticism of, iii. 14–15.

EUCRATE: friend of PHARAMOND, i. 328, 357–8, 410; iv. 201; on duelling, i. 410–11.

EUCRATIA, a true beauty, ii. 70.

EUDAMIA, STREPHON's riddle to, iii. 25.

EUDOSIA: has all the arts of life and good breeding, i. 339; a commanding beauty, ii. 70, 110.

EUDOXUS and LEONTINE, account of, i. 502–5.

Eugene, Prince: Sir ROGER comes to see, ii. 549; Sir ROGER's praise of, ii. 551; his visit to England, iii. 263–5; the peasant who showed him the way over the Alps and is drawn in the map, iii. 263; iv. 327; appearance and character of, iii. 263–5; iv. 354; friendship with Marlborough, iii. 265; iv. 399; captured Douai, iv. 187; defeated at Denain, iv. 187; surprised Fort Knocke, iv. 355; a favourite of Mars in modern poems, iv. 363.

EUGENIUS, a charitable man, ii. 198–9; comments on the *Spectator*, iv. 230.

EUNICA, her leap into the Ionian sea, ii. 408.

Eunuchs in the opera, i. 65.

Euphrates, artificial lake formed in (at Babylon), iii. 554.

EUPHUES, letter from (on a lady's behaviour in church), iii. 56.

EURILLA, ESCHINES in love with, ii. 406–7.

Euripides, epitaph on, iv. 474; *Ion*, v. 169.

Euryalus, Nisus and: their characters beautiful but common, ii. 563; come to unfortunate ends, iv. 464.

EURYBATES, EUNICA in love with, ii. 408.

Eusden, Laurence: contributions to *Spectator*, i. lv, *334*; named as a contributor, iv. 494; letter on Lowngers by (?), i. 229–31; letter on Ugly Club at Cambridge by (?), i. 335–7; letter on Idols in coffee-houses by (?), i. 372; *Letter to Mr. Adddison on the King's Accession*, v. *83*, 114.

EUSTACE, letter from (on delay in marriage), iv. 426.

EUTERPE, her defence of wives, iv. 209.

EUTRAPELUS, makes a Mohock of a man, iii. 347.

Evance, Sir Stephen (goldsmith), iii. *289*.

Evander, Pallas and, in the *Aeneid*, ii. 563.

Eve: Adam's description of, i. 140–1; modesty of, an example to her daughters, i. 379; character of, in *PL*, ii. 563, 565, 587; described by Milton, iii. 10; speeches of, in *PL*, iii. 171, 174–7; her first action, to run to a looking-glass, iii. 191; her speech to Adam quoted, iii. 192–3; her dream, iii. 197–200; ministering at table, iii. 202; Adam's account of, iii. 284–7; temptation and fall, iii. 307–12; behaviour of, after the Fall, iii. 333–6, 357–60, 388–90; and the Devil, iv. 99; the cause of Adam's downfall, iv. 312. *See also* Adam.

Eve-feast, of dedication of a church, ii. 131.

Evelyn, John, i. *59*, *407*; iii. *21*; iv. *308*; on physiognomy, i. *365*, *366*; translation of Fréart, iii. *556*; sketched a plan for an Academy, iv. *495*.

Evening: pleasing reflections in, ii. 94; enjoyment of a cool, iii. 592.

Evening-Change (the Royal Exchange at evening), iv. 307.

Evening-Post, v. 137.

Evening's draught, i. 309.

Evenness: of behaviour, a qualification of a friend, i. 291; of temper, necessary in marriage, ii. 515–16; v. 75–76; and tranquillity of mind, the effect of virtue, iii. 430.

Evergreens: 'of the sex' (elderly ladies), iii. 481; and other movable plants, iii. 553; in an English garden, iv. 191.

Everlasting Club, i. 308–11.

Evil: no e. without some good attending it, i. 192; in men makes us ashamed of our species, ii. 394; promiscuous distribution of good and, ii. 421–2; natural horror we have to, iii. 16; mixed with good, Locke's explanation of, iii. 454; women should avoid appearance of, iii. 463–6; in this life to be rectified in another, iv. 213.

Evil, problem of: apparent misfortunes may prove blessings, ii. 142; insoluble in this life, ii. 421–3; heathen solutions to, afford no real comfort, iv. 565; obstacles to benevolence, how accounted for, v. 54–58.

Evil (the King's Evil): produced by nurse's milk, ii. 456; Edward the Confessor the first who touched for, iii. 215.

Evil eye, fascination of, ii. 360, 472.

Evil speaking, Tillotson's sermon on, iv. 427.

Evil spirits: intercourse with among witches, i. 480, 482; carry away a piece of the house they are about to leave, ii. 448–9; rallying the angels in *PL*, ii. 589; catalogue of, in *PL*, iii. 87.

Evils: shame the greatest of all, i. 360; of life can be borne with fortitude, ii. 431–2; *out of two e. the least must be chosen* (prov.), ii. 457; appear more painful in prospect, iv. 291–2; v. 104.

Exactness: undue e. about trifles in speech, ii. 44–46; and nicety in literature of colder climates, ii. 128; true delicacy consists in e. of judgment, iii. 15; works of great genius superior to authors of, iii. 37–38; v. 27–28.

Examiner, The, i. xiv, xviii, *4*; ii. *106*, *451*; iii. *37*, *251*, *380*, *441*; iv. *413*, *499*; v. *66*.

Example(s): 'I love to shelter myself under the e. of great men', i. 285; more effective than precept, ii. 78; iii. 67–68; iii. 82; women who are e. or the first of the mode, ii. 315; how to be taught to pupils, iii. 247.

Excellence: the title given to ambassadors, ii. 352; of virtue, as represented by Stoics, ii. 444.

Excelling: vanity in e. not a good motive, ii. 591; every one capable of e. in something, iv. 491.

Exchange, Rate of, between French and English money, iii. 97.

Exchanging calamities, vision of, iv. 505–11.

Execution(s): meditated by a beauty, ii. 69; at Smithfield increased price of

wood, ii. 431; with the eyes, ii. 479; iii. 416–18.

Exercise: of the fan, i. 426–9; benefits of physical, i. 471–4, 478–9; ii. 65, 133–4, 263–4; of the snuff-box taught, ii. 46–47.

Exeter, i. 35; ii. 135; out-of-date fashions at, ii. 192–3; trial of rebels at, iii. 135.

Existimation (estimation), iv. 110.

Exorcizing of haunted rooms, i. 454–5.

Expletives: of oaths, i. 345; in the newspapers, ii. 388; illustration of, in Pope's *Essay on Criticism*, ii. 484; curing men of their favourite, iii. 398.

Export of manufactures, i. 296; ii. 402–3.

Expression: turn of, in Greek poetry, ii. 391; copiousness of, in the censorious, ii. 459; rather than invention, admired in poetry, ii. 483–4; methods of, in poetry, iii. 10–11; energy of e. more necessary to blank verse than to rhyme, iii. 14; *verbum ardens*, or a glowing bold, iii. 37.

Expressions: flat, i. 506; dark, ii. 151; common, iii. 11.

Extravagance: and reason responsible for mixed wit, i. 267; in living beyond one's means, i. 467–70; in art, ii. 447; of expression in love, ii. 478; of a wife, iii. 204–8; the old rail at the e. of the young, iv. 195; in telling stories, iv. 420–4.

Extravagances: of human reason, ii. 250; of the male sex, ii. 325; of the wise man and the fool, ii. 375; of love, ii. 385; and follies depicted in *Spectator*, ii. 450; debts contracted by, ii. 546.

Extravagant: and wild quality of the natural genius, ii. 127; Mr. SPECTATOR reported to be an e. creature, ii. 349; character of the, ii. 362–4; e. men sometimes esteemed, ii. 445.

Eye(s): beliefs regarding envious, i. 83; Cowley compares his mistress's e. to burning-glasses, i. 266; the language of, i. 281; ii. 478–80; iii. 321; iv. 436; affection taken in at the, i. 339; 'I have seen an eye curse for half an hour', i. 365; and expression of grief, i. 403; *The Discipline of the Eye*, i. 426; of the mole, i. 496; a sly surveying, ii. 113; a schoolboy's honest, ii. 116; of the world, ii. 135; of our great Judge, ii. 137; the first shot of the eye toward a patron, ii. 258; are spectacles to others to read our hearts, ii. 307; fascination of the evil eye, ii. 360, 472; discretion like a well-formed, ii. 376; a speaker feels a fascination in the e. of the audience, ii. 397; a man with e. of a dog (Homer), ii. 399; believing

one's e. a sure way to be deceived, ii. 443; pictures that are made only for the, ii. 447; a treatise of, ii. 469–72; 'killing eyes', ii. 472, 478–80; iii. 416–18; dissection of a woman's e. requested, ii. 481; wan and eager e. of a prostitute, ii. 535; muscles in a beau's, ii. 572–3; in a coquette, ii. 459, 596; iii. 75; revolving her e. round about in church, iii. 8; politicians taught how to connive with either, iii. 98; unlucky casts in, iii. 397; a pair of blue, iii. 418; green pleasing to, iii. 452; doctor who had lost an e. in the Emperor's service, iv. 61–62; maladies of, cured by Read and Grant, iv. 168, 173; judging the brains from the, iv. 344; compliments paid to bright, iv. 405; a woman skilled in the downcast, iv. 425; are the epitome of the face, iv. 436; providential design of two e. in animals, iv. 443; Mr. FONDLE's black, v. 135. *See also* Sight.

EYE-BRIGHT, RACHEL, frequents Powell's puppet-show, i. 61.

Eyebrow: can call a man scoundrel, i. 365; contempt shown by the elevated, iii. 322.

Eye-shot: avoiding one another's, ii. 411; many a young man preserved from her, iii. 9.

Eye-sight, various turns of, ii. 472.

Eye-water, iii. 206.

Eyles, Sir Francis (Director of the Bank and of East India Co.), a subscriber, i. xc; and his sons referred to (?), ii. 254–5.

Eyles, Sir John, Bart., i. xc.

Eyles, Sir Joseph, Kt., i. xc.

Ezekiel, vision of, iii. 201, 232–3, 358. *See also* Bible.

F., R., slain by a lady's glance, iii. 418.

F., T., letter from (in praise of *Spectator*), iv. 486.

F., W., letter from, acknowledged, iv. 588.

Fable(s): old women's, i. 53; a species of wit giving delight and surprise, i. 265; and songs from father to son, i. 297; Eastern, i. 401; antiquity of, ii. 219–20; kinds of, ii. 219–21; allegorical, ii. 220–1; reflecting upon the gods, ii. 421; 'it would look like a f. to report', ii. 526; frequent allusion to heathen f. a blemish in *PL*, iii. 62; proper for instruction, iii. 467; iv. 317–18. *See also* Allegory.

Fables (told or referred to): the lion and the man, i. 48–49, 60; the ass in the

lion's skin, i. 58; the frogs and the boys, i. 100; of Jupiter and the countryman, i. 108; the old man and his two wives, i. 143; of tongs and grid-iron, i. 197; of luxury and avarice, i. 235–6; the paw of a lion rather than the hoof of an ass, i. 262; Cymon and Iphigenia (Dryden), i. 304–5; the mole, i. 508; sedition of members of the body, ii. 185, 220; Jotham's f. of the trees, ii. 219; Nathan's f. of the poor man and his lamb, ii. 220; the sultan's exercise, ii. 263; Polyphemus, ii. 376; earth and plants, ii. 455; the pearl swallowed by an oyster, iii. 46; the traveller and grasshoppers, iii. 325; a heathen f. relating to prayers, iii. 467–70; the woman who broke her looking-glass, iv. 86; Pandora's box, iv. 166–7; wealth the father of love, iv. 295; the vizier who understood language of birds, iv. 318–19; Alnaschar, the Persian glass-merchant, iv. 410–12; the cock and the fox (Dryden), v. 125. *See also* Aesop.

Fable (in the epic): three qualifications of, ii. 539; of *PL*, ii. 539; iii. 58–59; the soul of the epic, iii. 91; should be probable and marvellous, iii. 144–6; as historical background of the epic, iii. 305–7; contrivance of, the principal beauty of *PL*, Book IX, iii. 307.

Face: we take our idea of character from the, i. 365–6; resemblance of human features to those of animals, i. 366–7; nature has laid out all her art in beautifying the, i. 415; *a good face a letter of recommendation* (prov.), ii. 68, 359; good nature gives a certain air to, ii. 165; a man wears the picture of his mind in his, ii. 307; the Indian who said 'I am all face', ii. 387; saw my mistress's f. stark-naked, ii. 548; a very fine f. laid waste, ii. 598; reading the future in the features, iv. 292; emotions expressed by the f. in acting, iv. 436–7. *See also* Physiognomy.

Face-painting (portrait-painting), iv. 495.

Faces: not of our own choosing, i. 74–75, 134; contortions of, in a grinning contest, ii. 183–4; guessing at pursuits and interests from men's, ii. 256; silent flattery of women's pretty, ii. 480; patches placed for fat or lean, long or oval, iii. 415.

Factors in the trading world, like ambassadors in the politic world, i. 293.

Faculty (-ies): of talking in the pulpit, ii. 80; put in good humour by mirth and laughter, ii. 205; assembling the f. to make a judgement, ii. 447; laughter weakens the, ii. 466; no f. in the soul adapted to ambition, ii. 497; many f. in the soul, v. 50; gratification of, in this life and in eternity, v. 50–53; man's f. improvable to all eternity, v. 145.

Faculty (the medical profession), satires upon the religion of, iv. 18.

FADDLE, Lady: her dog CUPID, iii. 183; promises me her woman to cut my hair, iii. 183.

FADDLE, Mrs. FIDDLE, a gossip, ii. 459.

FADDLE, TOM, and his wife: their behaviour in public, iii. 72.

Fadlallah and the dervish, story of, iv. 576–9.

Faggots: i. 272; filling a ditch with, ii. 151; fire and f. as methods of persuasion, ii. 431; a pyramid of stackfaggots, v. 108.

Faggots (in muster of a regiment), i. 153.

Fahrenheit, D. G., invention of thermometer, ii. 426, 519.

Fainting, faintness, ii. 342, 441, 480–1; iv. 422.

FAIR, Lady, iv. 360.

'Fair, The' (the fair sex), ii. 113, 236; iii. 23, &c.

Fair sex, the: ii. 5, 9, &c.; a caveat to, iii. 372; affectation in, iii. 512; key to behaviour of, iv. 29; their reflections on marriage, iv. 209; greater tyrants over lovers than husbands, iv. 223.

Fairies: writings about, iii. 570, 573; belief in, in England, v. 65.

Fairs, in Persia, for sale of unmarried women, iv. 314–15.

Fairy dance, simile of, in *PL*, iii. 91.

Fairy favours, iv. 87.

Fairyland, where knights errant have full scope to range, iv. 429.

Fairy way of writing, iii. 570.

Faith: less important than morality, iv. 118–20; balanced against morality, iv. 137; methods of strengthening, iv. 141–5.

Faithful Shepherd. See *Pastor Fido.*

Faithfulness and constancy the chief qualifications of a friend, i. 291.

Falchions, fighting with, iv. 31.

Fall of man: tradition of, represented in story of Pandora's box (?), iv. 166. See *also* Milton.

'Fall of the leaf', iv. 63.

Falls of water, pleasing to the imagination, iii. 542, 544.

False Triumph, or The Destruction of Troy, The (puppet opera), iii. 400.

Falsehood(s): founder of family of false humour, i. 147; goddess of, rules over region of false wit, i. 271; allegorical figure of, i. 273–4; and dissimulation in speech, i. 430–2; party spirit breaks out in, i. 510; an inclination to, in 'Liars', ii. 36–40; justifiable when it makes others happy, ii. 410–11; a beau's head filled with, ii. 571; as far distant from truth as the ears are from the eyes, v. 33.

FALSTAFF, AUBRY and MAUDE DE, apply for the flitch of bacon, v. 79.

Falstaff, Sir John: his ridicule of leanness, i. 75; his description of himself, i. 204; Powell to play this role, iii. 291.

Fame: neglect of, shows you arrogant and abandoned, i. 433; an author's greatest reward, ii. 154; not a primary basis for happiness, ii. 158; less valuable than self-approval, ii. 180–1; a babbler, ii. 241; with respect to the hero, the gentleman, and the tradesman, ii. 348–51; and envy among authors, ii. 481–3; difficulties in attaining, ii. 490–3; brings little happiness, ii. 493–8; an enemy to virtue, ii. 499–502; allegorical figure of in the Aeneid, ii. 564; iii. 173, 573; a follower of merit, iv. 1; Ovid's Palace of, iv. 43; of writers increases after death, iv. 471–2.

Fame, love of, i. 311–12; ii. 370–4; iv. 490–1. See also Glory; Praise.

Familiar phrases, not suitable for epic, iii. 10–11.

Familiar spirit, ii. 83.

Familiar way of writing, iv. 177.

Familiarity (-ies): degrees of, ii. 47; indifferent f. of CHLOE, ii. 308; lessens admiration, ii. 496; v. 139; coquettes who contract f. out of malice, ii. 560; and forwardness, ii. 568; nauseous allusions to private, iii. 72; neglect of apparel creates a f. too low and contemptible, iii. 82–83; disagreeable f. prohibited, iv. 10; of manner in young women, iv. 245; too great f. in dress in married couples, iv. 295–6.

Family (-ies): care of their f. the duty of women, i. 312, 349; a well-balanced f. like a ship duly trimmed, ii. 9; pictures of f. life, ii. 252–6; few without feuds and animosities, iii. 591.

Family-book, mentioned by Montaigne, ii. 464.

Family-madness (pride in ancestors), an old gentleman far gone in, v. 92.

Family-piece: request for a, iii. 591; Pliny's letter to Hispulla an agreeable, iv. 372.

Famine in France, during the last war, ii. 210.

Famous men. See Great men.

Fan(s): a blow of the, i. 13; a broken f. as a love-token, i. 124; mentioned, i. 160, 194, 295, 314–15, &c.; immodest figures on a, i. 227; Titus Oates's picture among the sticks of a, i. 244; poem in shape of a, i. 248; 'that little modish machine', i. 427; cupids, garlands, &c. on, i. 427; reproved with a blow of the, ii. 105; 'let him reckon the sticks of one's', ii. 113; flirtation with, ii. 301; iv. 333; a coquette playing with her, ii. 459; the side-peep through hood or, ii. 472; and other Indian goods, iii. 25; of the PERVERSE WIDOW, iii. 54; cheapened a couple of f. at the Change, iii. 182; mounted by Colmar, iii. 206; 'to twerl, slip, or flirt a', iii. 415; 'killed' by a, iii. 417; 'hold up her f. to a hackney coach', iv. 286; play of the, iv. 333; history of Procris and Cephalus on a, iv. 383; a pat upon the shoulder from, v. 23; a flirt of the, v. 46. — EXERCISES OF THE FAN, i. 426–9; ii. 30, 31, 46, 269–70, 303; iv. 438.

Fanatic, Mr. SPECTATOR suspected of being a, ii. 4.

Fancies, wild irregular, i. 145; of jealous husbands, ii. 171; and imaginations, ii. 498; of authors of inferior genius, iv. 234; hypochondriacal, iv. 415; exploded, v. 118; whimsical, v. 159.

Fanciful authors, i. 297.

Fancy: works of (false wit), i. 249; extravagances of an irregular, i. 268; a liar a person of pregnant, ii. 39; luxuriance of, produces too witty authors, ii. 53; men of sober and moderate, ii. 128; ungoverned f. in liars and castle-builders, ii. 158–60; chimerical happiness from paintings of, ii. 159; of the debauchee soon sated, ii. 281; of the inquisitive, ii. 386; light pieces that ask more of f. than of judgement, ii. 396; extravagant f. of freethinkers, ii. 412; work of, in dreams, ii. 570; iii. 76; iv. 366; v. 4, 29; flights of, iii. 21; life and spirits which raise an author's, iii. 75; vagaries of, iii. 103; strength of, in Milton, iii. 202; something in poetry that elevates and astonishes, iii. 530; and imagination synonymous, iii. 536–7; and judgement both necessary for proper taste, iii. 561; noble extravagance of f. in Shakespeare, iii. 572; allegorical figure of, iv. 328, 507, 509; wit the offspring

of f. and judgement, iv. 328; briskness of, an intimation of immortality, v. 29; works of (embroidery), v. 72; extravagances of, in hypochondriacs, v. 82; 'so just a f. should my numbers warm', v. 162.

FANFLY, Mr., an obsequious woman's man, iv. 332.

FANNY, sister of AMANDA, iii. 411.

Fantasque, in the vision of painters, i. 354.

Fantastic(al): behaviour of women in France, i. 193; objects removed from sight of young women, ii. 60; handsome people are fantastically pleased with themselves, ii. 69; figure, ii. 95; evil of castle-building, ii. 160; passion of Philopinax for a picture, ii. 427; a beau dressed in a very f. manner, ii. 596; hearts bent upon f. advantages, ii. 597.

Farquhar, George: *The Beaux' Stratagem*, iv. *388*; *The Constant Couple, or, The Trip to the Jubilee*, iv. *558*; Wilks in, iii. 394; a blush in the third act of, iii. 418.

Farthing(s), ii. 576; iv. 60; the insolence to owe no tradesman a, ii. 505; 'not care a', iv. 332.

Farthingale: appeared in England a little before the ruin of the Spanish monarchy, ii. 6; popular etymology of the word, iv. 195.

Farthingale Reviv'd, The, i. 5.

Fascines, filling a ditch with, ii. 151.

FASHION, WILL, Letter from (on meeting Mr. SPECTATOR in the Park), i. 102–3.

Fashion: contest between f. and reason, i. 115; in allegory of luxury and avarice, i. 235; the force of, i. 275; as a subject of conversation, ii. 289; a court can make f. and duty walk together, i. 359; the man of, ii. 93; cruelty supported by, ii. 458; allegorical figure of, iv. 123; variableness of, iv. 193.

Fashionable Society, The, proposed, iv. 196.

Fashionable wife, account of a, iii. 68–71, 111.

Fashionable world, the, is grown free and easy, i. 487.

Fashions: affected by sovereigns, i. 135; from France, i. 192–5, 225; ii. 577–81; Sir ROGER on, i. 449–50; out-of-date f. in the country, i. 486–9; ii. 12–15, 192–3; changes and innovations in, ii. 12; a Society for Inspection of, proposed, ii. 193; absurd f. attacked by *Spectator*, iv. 27; use of, iv. 193–6; a repository for, iv. 194.

Fasting and abstinence, in order to give to the poor, ii. 199.

Fat: Club of Fat Men, i. 39; jests upon fat and lean, i. 75; fashions in fat and lean vary with nations, i. 134; fat persons admired in Holland, i. 134.

Fate, Necessity the mother of, iii. 596.

Fates, the, in modern poems, iv. 363–4.

Father: relationship with son, i. 235; ii. 92, 387, 521–4; iii. 219–20, 597–600; iv. 259–60; of his country, i. 359; displeasure of an inexorable, ii. 212–13; account of an unnatural, ii. 241–3; and his children, ii. 252–6; iv. 272–5; of ten children a benefactor to his country, ii. 287; injustice of an extravagant, ii. 364; affection of God like that of a wise, ii. 422; who is 'plagued with deer-stealers and fops', iii. 194; tenderness of a f. in *Macbeth*, iii. 393–4; relationship between f. and daughter, iv. 78–80, 147–8.

Fathers, one of the, his abhorrence of lying, iv. 301.

Fauquier, John Francis (a Director of the Bank), a subscriber, i. *xc*.

Fault-finding: by little conceited wits, i. 364; inferior critics look for faults and errors, iii. 36–37; with food, a mark of ill humour, iv. 48.

Faults: to be overlooked in private, not public, affairs, ii. 166–7; in love and friendship, ii. 260–3; liking a woman for her, ii. 300; imitation of f. of the great, ii. 337; to be scrutinized before, not after, marriage, ii. 516; criticism should discover beauties rather than, ii. 519–20; polite raillery against a man's, ii. 574–5; I had much rather prevent f. than find them, ii. 580; in *PL*, iii. 58–64, 74, 83; acknowledgement of, iii. 433–5; difficulty in pointing out f. in a friend, iii. 447–8; danger in listening to reports of, in others, v. 31–34.

Faults on Both Sides, i. *131*.

Fauns, paintings of, ii. 379; accompanying Bacchus, iii. 596; and satyrs not necessary to the pastoral, iv. 362.

Faustina (wife of Marcus Aurelius), ii. 10; v. 75–76.

FAVILLA, married to a dolt, iv. 35–36.

Favour: 'to ask the', i. 383; the proper time for asking a, ii. 197; v. 57; 'to own the', ii. 304; in the fifth or sixth degree of f. with a minister, ii. 508; 'a clear stage and no', iv. 32; a necessary consequence to a shame-faced man, iv. 216; well bestowed, an honour to him who confers it, iv. 262.

Favourite, a female (i.e. a favourite with women), ii. 9–10, 110–11. *See also* Woman's man.

Favourite-woman (confidante), i. 484.

Favours: at a wedding, iii. 501; a mistress's, in combats, iv. 33.

Favours: receiving of creates less goodwill than conferring, ii. 243; poured on a parasite a form of self-love, ii. 424; bestowed on such as least want them, iii. 1; the art of bestowing and receiving, iii. 38–40; disposal of, by the powerful, iv. 262–3; she that grants f. to one man, will to a hundred, v. 88.

Fawners: among tradesmen, iii. 95; and jobbers, iii. 378.

Fear(s): and ignorance natural to the soul of man, i. 34; dispelled by reason and religion, i. 34–35, 54–55; tender f. desirable in woman, ii. 70; Calvinists actuated by, ii. 332; the gentle gales of hopes and, ii. 373; makes husbands tyrannical, ii. 418; of a lover, ii. 514; freedom from, necessary to the poet and scholar, iii. 21; religion in many expressed in, iii. 80; of wrinkles and old age, iii. 81; depicted by Homer, iii. 337; concerned with the future, iv. 165–8; effects of, iv. 423; example of, from *Macbeth*, iv. 434–5; caused by jealousy, iv. 458; vanity of, and methods of subduing, v. 101–4.

Feather, Light as a (prov.), v. 62.

Feathers: plumes of, on the stage, i. 123, 178; on the hat, i. 434, 464; iii. 223; iv. 222; effect of, on a coquette's heart, ii. 595; young fellows wearing, iii. 162.

February, allegorical figure of, iii. 596.

Feeling, sense of: for ever exercising their, ii. 364; modesty a quick and delicate f. in the soul, ii. 399; more limited than that of sight, iii. 536.

Feet: ambition has taught some to write with their, iv. 544; of a bed, i. 53; of trees, iv. 277.

FEILD, CONSTANTIA, letter from (on female 'apes'), ii. 448–9.

Feilding, Robert ('Beau'), his *Tryal* in LEONORA's library, i. 157.

Félibien, André, *Description de l'Abbaye de la Trape*, v. 33.

Felix, or fortunate, a title of Roman emperors, iii. 43.

Fell, Bishop John: his biography of Dr. Hammond quoted, iv. 564–5.

Fellowes, John (a Director of South Sea Co.), a subscriber, i. xc.

FELT, JOHN (haberdasher), suitor of the Widow WILDFIRE, iv. 517.

FELT, SAMUEL (haberdasher), 'wounded' by sight of a lady, iii. 418.

Felton, Henry, i. xiv.

Felton, John: villainy of, against Buckingham, iv. 220.

Female 'apes' (women who ridicule others), ii. 448–9.

Female orators, ii. 458–62; query, whether a cudgel may be used by, ii. 480.

Female Tatler, The, i. xxi, 126, 409.

Females: nice proportion between males and, iii. 27–28; fortune, like other f., favours the young, iii. 44.

Fencers, raillery with barbarity of butchers rather than skill of, iii. 585.

Fencing: affectation of neglect of, iv. 174; schools, iv. 425; the art of, iv. 500; treatise on, returned to the author, v. 116.

Fénelon, François de Salignac de la Mothe (Bishop of Cambray): i. 159, 195; his *Education of a Daughter* recommended, i. 405; his *Telemachus*, iii. 249–50.

Fens and marshes, schemes for draining, ii. 285.

Ferments: exercise raises proper f. in the humours, ii. 264; of youthful blood, ii. 372; in the blood caused by repinings, iii. 451.

Fern, Thomas (quack doctor); advertisement of, iv. 61.

Ferocity, resulting from brutality in education, ii. 116.

Ferrers, Benjamin (painter); advertisement of, iv. 495.

Fert, Anthony (dancing-master): his *Instructions for Country Dances* in LEONORA's library, i. 157; advertisements of, i. 157.

Fervours, the mind cannot be always in its, i. 396.

Festeau, M., and death of Mme de Villacerfe, iii. 383.

Feuds, between parson and squire, i. 462; between parties, i. 509–12; in the universities, ii. 429–30, 453; few families without, iii. 591.

Fever(s): Sydenham's treatise on, i. 105; of the spirits, i. 222; mentioned, i. 371, 406; ii. 140, 148, 159; dreams in, ii. 101; resulting from intemperance, ii. 265; agonies of a, ii. 302; of a lover, ii. 513; Estcourt's wine excludes surfeits and, ii. 530; letting blood to prevent, iv. 559.

Fibres: of women more delicate, ii. 8; of women's tongues, ii. 460; of a

coquette's heart turned and twisted, ii. 595.

FICKLE, FANNY, letter from (problem of marriage), v. 67–68, 74, 96.

Fickleness of fortune, blamed for our calamities, ii. 597.

Fiction, or poetical ornament, i. 363; addition of poetical, ii. 75; truth dashed with, in Homer and Virgil, ii. 543.

Fictions, a beau's head filled with, ii. 571.

Fiddle(s): heard in the street, iii. 125; a barber with a broken, iv. 60.

Fiddle faddle: abundance of, iii. 70; Mrs. FIDDLE FADDLE (a gossip), ii. 459.

Fiddlers, at dances, i. 286.

FIDDY, Miss (FIDELIA), proposed as a wife, iv. 401; FIDELIA, a model daughter, iv. 78–80.

FIDELIO, transformation of, into a looking-glass, iii. 470–3.

FIDGET, Mrs., her inclination to motion, iii. 149; the Widow F., riding the black ram, v. 131.

Fielding, Henry, i. 9, *176*; ii. *467*.

Fielding's *Tryal*. *See* Feilding, Robert.

Fifteen Comforts of Cuckoldom, The, ii. *89*.

Fifteen Comforts of Matrimony, The, ii. *89*; in LEONORA's library, i. 155.

Fifteen Plagues of a Maiden-Head, The, ii. *89*.

Fifteen Pleasures of a Virgin, The, ii. *89*.

Fifth of November, Sir HARRY tells the story of the, ii. 530.

Figs: imported into England and naturalized, i. 295; sold in streets, iii. 354.

Figure, people of, ii. 104, 226, 304, 575, 591, &c.; we make a f. proportionable to what we may be, not what we are, ii. 251–2; men of the most considerable figures, iii. 5; those of the highest, iii. 32; persons of tolerable f. as times go, iii. 65; consider what f. we make in the world, iii. 152; ingredient for making a considerable f. in the world, iii. 477.

Figures of rhetoric, ii. 458.

Figure(s) of speech: puns reckoned among, i. 260; mood or figure in Aristotle, ii. 429; a cudgel as a, ii. 480; invented by ancient critics, ii. 10.

Final causes, of aesthetic pleasure, iii. 545–7.

Findley, Robert (contractor to the army), a subscriber, i. *xci*.

Finery: woman an animal that delights in, ii. 530; the burthensome f. of judges, nobles, and bishops, iii. 348.

Finger(s): 'reckoned the pretty pieces of ivory over and over', ii. 120; snapping, iii. 109; the extended f. of the prentice, iii. 322.

Fingers-ends, at his (prov.), ii. 113.

Finis coronat opus, iv. *468*.

Finishing Stroke, The. See Leslie, Charles.

Fiorilli. *See* Fiurelli.

Fire(s): and flame as a similitude of love, i. 266–7, 273, 313; ii. *468*; and impetuosity of Pindar, ii. 128; and sword, ii. 228, 350; v. 179; of devotion never entirely quenched, ii. 287; and faggot as methods of persuasion, ii. 431; affirming that f. is not hot, ii. 442; crying of, ii. 476; *light your fire at both ends* ('the old kitchen proverb'), ii. 531; burns dimly in light of sun, ii. 533; warm f. at Christmas, ii. 550; a coquette's heart not singed by, ii. 597; a man who stands afore the, iii. 57; the sea of, in *PL*, iii. 84–85, 118, 121; one of the words to suggest immense reading, iii. 347; the man who dreamed the city of London was on, v. 40–41.

Fire, the Great, i. 309; iv. 83.

Fire-Office, servants of the, ii. 57.

Fireworks: in *Rinaldo*, i. 24–25; squibs and crackers, i. 361; in celebration of the Coronation, v. 106, 108.

First: ages of the world produced great souls, ii. *467*; impressions often erroneous, i. 368–9; sight, dislike conceived at, ii. 23; steps toward evil, to be avoided, iv. 74.

Fish: to cry f. and card-matches, i. 152; cast their eggs as chance directs them, i. 490; *neither f., flesh, nor good red herring* (prov.), ii. 153; fowl, f., and flesh in a modern meal, ii. 264; with wings, iv. 349; variety of species of, iv. 443.

Fishery, British: debates among ladies of the, ii. 458; disturbed by French privateers, iii. 508.

Fishing in troubled waters (prov.), v. 36.

Fishmonger in the Strand, i. 52.

Fishponds, Sir ANDREW's, iv. *467*.

Fit(s): falling in a, ii. 342; fainting away in a, ii. 441; of the gout, ii. 442, 530; children brought into, ii. 456; eloquence of tears and fainting, ii. 480; of melancholy, ii. 498; cold f. of a mistress, ii. 512; of laughter, ii. 547; and sallies of devotion, iii. 80.

Fitzgerald, Thomas, translator of Addison's *Machinae gesticulantes*, iii. *572*.

Fiurelli (Fiorilli), Tiberio (actor), iii. *3*.

Five-bar gate(s), ii. 504–5; iv. 178.

Five-penny ordinary, iv. 102.

Flageolets, a consort of, i. 24.

Flag-officer: at a great man's leveé, ii. 259; her great-grandfather a, iii. 71.

Flames (of love), ii. 215, 478.

Flaming bush, great geniuses compared to the, iii. 526.

Flamsteed, John: iv. 5; astronomical observations of, iv. 481; house of, v. 121.

Flanders: the army in, i. 182; a soldier's fingers buried in, ii. 102; conquest of by Louis XIV, and its population, ii. 209.

Flanders lace, iii. 26; iv. 271.

Flanders mares, i. 23.

Flap: the scollop f. on men's coats, iii. 163.

Flash and *Froth*, pedants describe writings of a polite author as, i. 249.

Flat expressions, i. 506.

Flatterers: of coffee-house potentates, i. 208; of Scipio, ii. 114; in families of humorists, ii. 292; why successful, ii. 424–5; pride lays us open to, iv. 131.

Flattery (-ies): an accompaniment of eminence, i. 423; by servants and domestics, i. 502; ii. 254; 'insnared by', ii. 62; by women's men, ii. 112; a man who turned detraction into, ii. 411; love of, ii. 424–5; 'silent' f. of women's pretty faces, ii. 480; a beau's head filled with, ii. 571; encouraged by those who listen to it, iii. 73; used by Lysimachus to Alexander and Philip, iii. 247; allegorical figure of, iv. 123; the result of pride, iv. 131; of kings, iv. 182; practised by Fulvia (in *Catiline*), iv. 312–13; of a wealthy young woman, iv. 405–6.

FLAVIA: a fine dancer, i. 339; a rival to her mother, i. 384–8; slays with a curtsy, iii. 418; coloured her hair, iii. 471; and CYNTHIO, iii. 489–93.

FLAVILLA: a taker of snuff in church, iii. 279; and TOM TAWDRY, an unhappy married couple, iv. 298.

Flavius Vopiscus, iv. *542*.

Flaws: everyone has, ii. 466; discovering f. in characters of the great, ii. 494–5; politicians taught how to find f. in solemn compacts, iii. 98.

Fleet, of Aeneas built from consecrated timber, v. 15. *See also* English fleet.

Fleetwood, William, Bishop of St. Asaph: i. *159*; a contributor, i. lvi; on the circulation of the *Spectator*, i. xxvi; Sir ROGER's chaplain to read a sermon by, i. 441; the preface to his *Four Sermons*, iii. 440–5; his *Sermon on the Fast-Day*, iv. *63*.

Flesh: broiled on coals, a simile in Homer, ii. 128; and blood, ii. 203, 567; fowl, fish, and f. in a modern meal, ii. 264; Pythagoras dissuaded his hearers from eating, ii. 325.

Fletcher of Saltoun, Andrew, iv. *281*.

Fletcher, John: Denham's poem on, quoted, ii. 482; *The Humorous Lieutenant*: Leucippe's soliloquy quoted, ii. 535–6; a performance of, iii. 349; *The Pilgrim*: the mad scene in, i. 94. *See also* Beaumont and Fletcher.

Flies, desires of Domitian turned upon catching, ii. 373.

Flight and Fear, as depicted by Homer iii. 337.

Flirt(s): Mrs. TAPERTY an eternal, ii. 293; the young f. about town, iv. 559; proud idle f. sipping their tea, v. 71.

Flirts (of the fan), i. 427; iii. 415.

Flitch of bacon: Sir ROGER's gift of, i. 462; awarded to a happily married couple at Whichenovre, v. 76–80.

Flogging of schoolboys, ii. 114–17, 160–2.

Flood, the: the age of man before, i. 378; Milton's account of, contrasted with Ovid's, iii. 363–5; Mr. W—n's comments upon, iii. 485; mentioned, iv. 575; one who lived before, iv. 595.

Flora, a companion of Spring, iii. 594.

Floralia in Roman theatre, Cato's visit to, iv. 67.

FLORELLA, on reading for ladies, i. 392.

Florence (wine), iii. 402.

FLORINDA, letter from (on her marriage), ii. 583–4.

FLORIO: son of EUDOXUS, brought up by LEONTINE, i. 503–5; and STREPHON as suitors, ii. 86–88.

Florus, Lucius Annaeus: his saying about Catiline quoted, i. 168; a *populus virorum*, as Florus elegantly expresses it, iii. 28; cited, iii. *44*.

Flounces and furbelows, ii. 13 ('flounced and furbelowed'), 345.

Flourilles (or Tourille), Chevalier de, anecdote of his death, ii. 98.

Flower, Joseph, ii. *235*.

Flower dyers, i. 197.

Flower-garden(s): description of a, iv. 188–92; makers of, like sonneteers, iv. 190.

Flower-pot(s): letter from one, i. 94, 197 (referred to, iv. 438): as actors, i. 425.

Flowers, cultivation of, iv. 104–5.

Floyer, Sir John, ii. *383*.

Flustered (slightly drunk), i. 101, 371; iv. 115, 249.

Flutter, Sir Fopling (in Etherege), i. 280, 323.

Flutter: of a fan, i. 428; in the female favourite, ii. 9; 'fluttering tribe of young fellows', iii. 126.

Flying: 'f. the country' (a hunting term), i. 477; actors f. in the air, ii. 57; transmigration into a f.-fish, iii. 275; borne away with f. colours, iii. 344; dreaming of, v. 6.

Flying Post, i. lxxxv; iv. *112, 173, 206, 310, 449, 460–1.*

Fob, putting the hand into the, ii. 549; iv. 345.

Focus perennis esto, i. 310.

FOIBLE, Sir JEOFFREY, a visitor to a brothel, ii. 246.

Foiling a fish, i. 448.

Foils, schools for learning to use, iv. 425.

Foley, Thomas, Baron: a subscriber, i. *lxxxviii.*

Folly (-ies): laughter a daughter of, i. 147; made supportable by good nature, ii. 165; one of the foundations of infidelity, ii. 232; superstition has in it something of, ii. 289; innocence with a dash of, ridiculous, ii. 449; of the world depicted in *Spectator*, ii. 450; ridicule laughs men out of vice and, ii. 467; envy of the old for the f. of the young, ii. 512; cracklings of mirth and, iii. 432; men fond of their own, iv. 121; allegorical figure of, iv. 124.

Fomes peccati, removed from Mahomet's heart, v. 7.

FONDLE, Mr., love-queries with regard to, v. 135–6.

Fondness: for oneself, ii. 114; display of, by married couples, iii. 72; iv. 13–14.

Fontana, Prospero (painter), ii. 154.

FONTANGE, CLARINDA's tire-woman, iii. 183.

Fontanges, formerly rose an ell above the head, i. 414.

Fontenelle, Bernard le Bovier, Sieur de: *Dialogues des morts*, ii. *373*; iv. *294*; quoted, iv. 487, 571; trans. by John Hughes, v. 44; *Entretiens sur la pluralité des mondes*, iii. *576*; quoted, iv. 346; *Histoires des oracles*, iv. *294.*

Fonvive, Jean de, writer of the *Post-Man*, i. *4.*

Food(s): variety of, over the world, i. 294–6; the gluttony of a modern meal, ii. 264–5; consumption of, a source of revenue, ii. 283–4; delight in, consists in desire, not satiety, iv. 448.

Fool: reflections of, compared with those of the wise, i. 311; time spent by a, i. 401–2; the woman's man neither a

man of sense nor a, ii. 112; to play the, ii. 196, 583; and the superstitious, ii. 250; an indiscreet talker, ii. 375; a fond, ii. 524; in fine clothes will be heard with attention, iv. 193.

Fools: multiply evils of life by superstition, i. 34; two amusements of f. of eminence, i. 184; dressed in petticoats, i. 200; kept in German courts, i. 200, 223; sometimes pretend to be knaves, ii. 567; allegory of Paradise of, iv. 121–4; mischiefs done by, iv. 219; Leo X's fondness for, iv. 263–5; Boileau says all men are, iv. 463; 'f. at large' (Tillotson), v. 132.

Foot: put things on a right, ii. 218; upon the common f. of humanity, ii. 339; of an account, iii. 288; behaviour of persons walking on, iv. 376–7; *to know the length of the* (prov.), iv. 414; stamping of, in acting, iv. 436.

Foot-ball: match on the green, ii. 132; spirit of rivalry in, iv. 18.

Footboy, THOMAS TRUSTY a f. at fourteen, i. 406.

Footman (-men): i. 193, 333, 453; ii. 44, 343, &c.; powdered, i. 66; letter by an enamoured f. in the country, i. 305–8; who borrowed his master's clothes, i. 373; *The Plagues of a*, ii. 89; who keep places at the theatre, ii. 163; iv. 523; who won the prize at a whistling-match, ii. 207; 'with child by my', ii. 236; letters from, ii. 293, 513; 'order them to breathe their saucy', ii. 316; hires himself for bodily labour, ii. 305–2; of Lady MARY ENVILLE, iii. 69; love makes a f. talk like Oroondates, iii. 416; women of quality marrying their, iv. 113; quarrels between f. at Utrecht, iv. 206; lace and shoulder-knots of, v. 81.

Footnotes, learned and useless, iv. 162.

Fop: Lord Foppington as, i. 207; an affected, i. 287; medium between f. and sloven desirable, ii. 91; a young f. buying a pair of gloves, ii. 108; defined, ii. 591; can find out faults in plays, iii. 74; soon becomes a fortune-hunter, iii. 126; a soft gentle young f. of the town, iii. 167; complaint against an insolent, iv. 304–5; a young laughing f. in Cave of Trophonius, v. 46.

Fops: among servants, i. 374; essenced, ii. 11; elderly, iii. 75; fraternity of, iii. 167; a father plagued with deer-stealers and, iii. 194.

Fopling: 'and with his tailor share the f.'s heart', iv. 398.

Fopperies, French, importation of, i. 192–5, 225.

Foppington, Lord (in *The Careless Husband*), acted at Epping, i. 207; Cibber as, iii. 394.

Forbearance and gentleness to be practised, ii. 308.

Forbidding air, preventing a salutation, ii. 508.

Force: want of, in literature of colder climates, ii. 128; Socrates conquers you by stratagem, Aristotle by, ii. 429.

Force of Love, The. See Lee.

Ford, Charles, i. 4.

Forehead: of a mountain, ii. 385; the most material organ of the orator, ii. 398.

Foreign: words and phrases, importation of, ii. 149–53; Milton's use of f. words, iii. 12–13, 62; ornaments, iii. 40; correspondents of the *Spectator*, iii. 96; style proper for a f. minister, iii. 98.

Foreigners: at the Royal Exchange, i. 293–4; comments of, on the English, ii. 32, 474; fear lest one should carry away the honour of the day, ii. 183; allowing f. into England, ii. 284–5; who are deceived into thinking they have affairs with women of title, ii. 304–5; bounties to, ii. 381; should learn English, ii. 507.

Forester (uncouth country girl), i. 282.

Forewarn'd, forearm'd (prov.), iii. 480.

Forfeit, paying, iii. 215.

Forgery of a deed to bar an inheritance, ii. 350.

Forgiveness of injuries: 'the greatest act of the human mind', i. 411; to be practised, ii. 166, 212–16; 'difference between giving and forgiving', ii. 243; satisfaction in, iii. 323.

Formosa: Mr. Psalmanazar, lately arrived from, i. 65.

Fornication: 'I designed only f.', ii. 219; 'the present state of', ii. 567; and adultery 'modest words', iii. 16.

Fort Knocke, conflicting reports of, in coffee-houses, iv. 355.

Fortifications abound in foreign terms, ii. 150.

Fortitude: and dancing compared, i. 284; improved through adversity, ii. 421–2; of a martyr, ii. 500; f., equanimity, and moderation, the great rule, iii. 406; a good mind will bear up under evils with, iii. 431.

FORTIUS, has the art of pleasing, iii. 585.

FORTUNATUS, a dishonest tradesman, iv. 57.

Fortune (chance): danger of anticipating

our good, ii. 251–2; gratitude toward God for good, ii. 288; iii. 44–46; fickleness of, blamed for our calamities, ii. 597; role of, in human life, iii. 42–46, 128–30; favours the young, iii. 44; gifts of, to be condemned, v. 84–85; Marlborough now out of the power of, v. 180.

Fortune (wealth): equality of, a qualification of friendship, i. 291; importance of, in marriage, ii. 85–88, 279–82, 583–4; iii. 92–93; iv. 357–60; common sense seldom in high, ii. 259; advantages of, must be supported by collateral eminence, ii. 292; one of the elements of 'quality', ii. 352; the ways to raise a man's, iii. 1–5, 317–19, 476–9; laying a proper value upon, iii. 47–48.

Fortune (woman of wealth), i. 484; ii. 22, 598; education of a, iv. 405–6.

Fortune-hunters: Irish, i. 87–88; iii. 125; and fortune-stealers, iii. 124–8, 193–5.

Fortune-teller(s): and wizards, ii. 20; should predict outcome of lotteries, ii. 250; letter from a, iv. 512–13; visit to a f. at Grand Cairo, v. 65.

Fortune-telling: by gypsies, ii. 16–17; a screen for, ii. 357; methods of, iv. 292–3; by sleeping on a slice of bride-cake, v. 41.

Forty: 'after f. there is no dallying with life', i. 502.

Forward: air and fashion in assemblies, i. 215; youth, iii. 367; obtrusion, iii. 497.

Forwardness: women who regard a salutation as, ii. 358; familiarity and, ii. 568.

Fossé, a French word imported, ii. 151–2.

Fotus, Anodine, of quack doctors, iv. 553.

Fountain(s): pleasing to the imagination, iii. 452; in a garden, iv. 189.

Four, a number highly regarded by Pythagoreans, ii. 361.

Fourberia della scena, the knavery or trickish part of the drama, i. 180.

Fowlers, imitate voices of birds, ii. 111.

Fowls, fish, and flesh in a modern meal, ii. 264.

Fox(es): and goose as a sign, i. 116; and seven stars as a sign, i. 116; noses of, patched on stable doors, i. 472–3; ii. 189; Sir ROGER's enmity to, i. 472–3, 475; seldom preys near his own home, ii. 19; Spartan boy and the, ii. 116; women who resemble, ii. 319; fable of the cock and, v. 125. See also *Volpone*.

Fox-gins, planted in garden, iii. 194.

Fox-hunter(s): i. 60, 232, 472–3, 475; iv. 177–9, 535; a female, i. 241–2; Tory, ii. 3; run away from their own thoughts, iii. 149; a wild roaring, iii. 167; tricks of, iii. 240; JOHN WILD-FIRE, iv. 516; JOHN STURDY, iv. 558.

Fraigneau, —— (confectioner), i. 157.

Frailty: 'sure some excuse for', ii. 113; of an author, ii. 155–6.

France: love of display in 'that fantastick nation', i. 66; 'this ludicrous nation', i. 192, drolls in, called 'Jean Pottages', i. 201; vineyards of, i. 295–6; decline of duelling in, i. 418–19; mannish riding-habit imported from, i. 435; iv. 29; coarse language in, i. 488; quarrels of the League in, i. 511; iv. 91; freedom of conversation in, ii. 38; story of two lovers in, ii. 142–8; mentioned, ii. 159; famine in, during the last war, ii. 210; goods imported from, iii. 26; project of a Political Academy in, iii. 95–100; formerly the terror of Europe, now the object of pity or contempt, iii. 96; Balzac's letter to the Chancellor of, iii. 324; tour of F. and Italy, iii. 367; anecdote of Dauphin of, iii. 433–4; news from, iii. 439–40; autumn best in, iii. 474; report of death of King of, iii. 507–9; deplorable state of, during minority of Louis XIV, iii. 508; has infected all Europe with its levity, iv. 29; monthly pamphlets published in, iv. 113–14; Englishmen go to, for fashion and breeding, iv. 195; painting in, iv. 496; prestige of military profession in, iv. 533–4.

Francham, John, of Norwich, i. lvii; iv. 350.

Francis, St., anecdote of, ii. 450.

FRANCIS, FATHER (THEODOSIUS), ii. 146.

FRANCIS, Uncle, v. 127.

Francis I, at death-bed of Leonardo da Vinci, iv. 489.

FRANK: an undutiful son, ii. 524; letters between F. and his mother, ii. 524–5; CLARINDA's servant, iii. 183.

FRANKAIR, CHARLES, overcomes others of more modesty, iv. 218.

Franklin, Benjamin, and the Spectator, i. lxxxv–lxxxvi.

Fraternity: of fops, iii. 167; of basket-hilts, iv. 81; of the henpecked, iv. 208, 223; of heathen gods, iv. 364.

Fréart de Chambray, Roland, Parallel of the Antient Architecture with the Modern, quoted, iii. 556–7.

FRECKLE, STEPHEN and ALICE: apply for the flitch of bacon, v. 79.

Free agents, men are, v. 65.

Free and easy (prov.), i. 487.

Free-Bench, a widow's right of, v. 100, 129.

Freedom(s): of passages in The Lancashire Witches, ii. 58; agreeable f. and indifference, ii. 357; of conversation with a friend the greatest pleasure, ii. 375; licentiousness is not, ii. 413; decent f. and good humour, iii. 82; of married couples in company, iv. 13–14; with men on the part of young women, iv. 244–5.

Freeholds, splitting of, i. 89.

Free livers, rakes pretending to be, ii. 412.

FREELOVE, ——, examination of his heart, v. 8–9.

FREELOVE, JACK: letter from to his mistress (on transformations of PUGG), iii. 273–6; 'murder'd by MELISSA in her hair', iii. 418.

FREEMAN, ANTONY, revolt of, ii. 328–30, 342–4 (referred to, iv. 461).

Freeman of London, sounds made by a, ii. 475.

FREEPORT, Sir ANDREW: character of, i. 10–11; thinks the Spectator should not criticize aldermen and citizens, i. 142; often smiles upon Mr. SPECTATOR at the Exchange, i. 294; on importations into England, i. 295–6; never a defendant in a lawsuit, i. 352; mentioned, i. 144, 451, 486; iii. 343, 532; inclined to the moneyed interest, ii. 3; is grown the cock of the club, ii. 21; will make Commonwealth's men out of his friends, ii. 21; and Sir ROGER on the landed v. commercial interests, ii. 186–9; iii. 212; suspected of writing Spectators signed 'T', ii. 360; his discourse on economic aspects of charity, ii. 401–5; suspected of having a hand in the Pope's procession, ii. 551; his republican doctrines, ii. 551; showed us a citizen's journal, iii. 153; read to the club Sir ROGER's billet to SUKEY, iii. 532; scrupulous in keeping promises, iv. 75–76; receives a letter on death of Sir ROGER, iv. 339; Sir ROGER left a collection of Acts of Parliament to, iv. 341; announces his retirement, iv. 466–8; his successor proposed, iv. 469–70; the language of, iv. 494.

Free-thinker(s): description of a, ii. 411–13; TOM PUZZLE sets up for a, iv. 187–8; changed by Cave of Trophonius, v. 47; impious schemes of, to be overturned, v. 172.

Free will: absence of, illustrated by ass between two bundles of hay, ii. 248–9; Milton's ostentatious excursions on, iii. 62; abstruse doctrine of, in *PL*, iii. 142; determines outcome of our actions, v. 65.

Freher, Marquard, 'an old chronicle published by', ii. 215.

Freind, Dr. John, v. 66.

French, the: Punch's reflections on, i. 65; their love of equipage and show, i. 66; addicted to grimace, i. 78; iv. 207; 'a gay airy people', i. 122; fond of *bouts rimés*, i. 256; decay of wit and learning among, i. 256–7; characterized by vanity, i. 354; a vain and lively people, i. 418–19; gaiety of, i. 435; 'are taught to do anything so it be with an assurance', i. 435; light talkative humour of, has infected their tongue, ii. 36; 'knows all the F. are doing', ii. 40; *bel esprit*, ii. 127; *bienséance* in allusions, ii. 128; already cowed and accustomed to flight, ii. 159; vivacity of, ii. 278; their activities published daily, iii. 476; TERAMINTA a great lover of, ii. 578–9; their polite taste, iii. 267; liveliness, assurance, and vivacity, their distinguishing characters, iv. 29; communicative temper of, iv. 499; laughing, singing, and dancing, v. 46–47.

French Academy, founded by Richelieu, iii. 96.

French agriculture, a great part done by women and children, ii. 210–11.

French army, at Blenheim, ii. 151–3; at Bouchain, iv. 407.

French aspen, always in motion, iv. 104.

French authors, rules extracted out of, iii. 36.

French bookseller's shop, an incident in a, iv. 41–42.

French brawl, the, i. 284.

French claret, i. 182; iv. 46.

French costume, a doll from Paris dressed in, ii. 577–81.

French court: under Louis XIV, ii. 47–48; motions taught at, ii. 581; at Marly or Versailles, iv. 92; Leonardo da Vinci invited to, iv. 489.

French critics: object to bloodshed upon English stage, i. 188; *bienséance*, ii. 318; acquaintance with, not sufficient, iii. 35; what they call 'marvellous', iii. 88; on the probable and the marvellous, iii. 144; on the 'tender', iii. 333.

French dances, i. 284–5; ii. 82; iii. 112.

'French disease', a certain cure for the, iv. 59.

French fashions, importation of, i. 191–5; ii. 577–81.

French flowers, gaudy-coloured but faint and languid, iv. 105.

French folio, lighter than an English octavo, iv. 137.

French fopperies, importation of, i. 192–5, 225; ii. 303.

French gardens, an agreeable mixture of garden and forest, iii. 551.

French generals, transformed into ambassadors, iii. 97.

French good-breeding, admired by 'Salamanders', ii. 276.

French hats, John Sly's report on, iv. 453.

French Huguenots: brought over in herds, but not naturalized, i. 269; subjected to torture, ii. 430. *See also* French Protestants.

French industry, deplorable state of, ii. 211.

French King, the: wenches of, setting fashions, i. 12; head of, before door of a sword-cutler, i. 117; the hoop-petticoat portends the downfall of (?), ii. 6; Rabelais' 'poisons' for, iii. 4; report of his death, iii. 507–9.

French language: birds taught to speak, i. 152; reflects humour of the people, ii. 36; young ladies learn to speak, ii. 395; Motteux speaks 'Dutch' and, iii. 26; in education of girls, iii. 140; a wife who is perfect mistress of, iii. 205; a lawyer's clerk who has learned Italian and, iv. 204; hideous French of lawyers, iv. 478.

French music, now preferred to English, i. 82; perfect in its kind, i. 122.

French novelist, on English melancholy, iii. 454.

French opera, account of, i. 122–3.

French privateer(s): barbarous behaviour of a, iii. 302–3; disturb British fishery, iii. 508.

French prophets. *See* Camisards.

French Protestants: number destroyed or banished by Louis XIV, ii. 211; employed in making quilts, &c., iii. 206; in Cave of Trophonius, v. 47. *See also* French Huguenots.

French renegado, and the Castilian's wife, ii. 278–9.

French romance, an old, i. 118.

French soldier, his raillery upon his superior officer, ii. 98.

French tragedy. *See* Tragedy.

French truth, a conspicuous figure in *Nothing*, iii. 100.

French wines, importing of, i. 181; ii. 578.

French words and phrases, importation of, ii. 149–53.

Frenchman (-men): at the Royal Exchange, i. 294; *agréments* on signboard of, i. 118; represents Vanity in vision of painters, i. 354; eminent person who thanked Heaven he was born a, ii. 32; in a grinning-match, ii. 183; talking in chorus with a parcel of, iv. 499; 'Frenchman, Papist', &c., help to sell a pamphlet, iv. 537.

Frenchwoman (-women): fashions and fopperies of, i. 191–5; ii. 577–8; employ *valets de chambre*, i. 192; custom of receiving visits in bed, i. 192–3; levity of their conversation, i. 193–4; affectation of mispronouncing words, i. 195; talkative, ii. 581; a servant of Lady MARY ENVILLE, iii. 69; offering to dress and undress, in a modern comedy, iv. 296.

Frenzy (-ies): descended from Nonsense, i. 147; produced by love and by biting of a mad dog, ii. 383–4; of love, described by Sappho, ii. 393.

Fresh: news 'fresh and fresh', iv. 92; v. 137; news 'fresh from the tree', v. 137.

Fret, gamesters eternally upon the, ii. 230.

Fretwork of rocks and grottoes, iii. 550.

FRIBBLE, JOSIAH: letter from (on pin-money), iii. 50–51; mentioned, iii. 68, 113.

FRIBBLE, Sir NICHOLAS, married the President of the Widow-Club, iv. 557–8.

Friblers (male coquets), iii. 23–25, 73, 165.

FRIDAY, Lord, married the President of the Widow-Club, iv. 559.

Friend: qualifications of a, i. 291–2; a mercurial, ii. 262–3; iii. 74; talking with a f. is thinking aloud, ii. 375; treat a f. as though he may some time be an enemy, ii. 375.

Friends: best conversation, between two, i. 289, 397; ii. 375; art of making, i. 289–92; choice of, i. 290–2; story of two, i. 502–5; cares and distresses not to be obtruded upon our, ii. 65; bringing f. together through beneficent falsehood, ii. 410–11; a chimerical correspondence between two, ii. 437–8; grief for deceased, iii. 29–30; and enemies both help us to see ourselves, iii. 394; iv. 45; falling out of, iii. 499.

Friends. *See* Quakers.

Friendship, pleasures of, i. 289–92; iii. 445–8, 590; of EUDOXUS and LEON-
TINE, i. 502–5; a happy marriage has all the pleasures of, ii. 516; contracted at public schools, iii. 134; Spenser on, iv. 239–40; recommended by intervals of absence, v. 139.

Friesland hen, a woman in flounces and furbelows looks like a, ii. 13.

Frieze: a term of art used by Milton, iii. 64; part of entablature, iv. 192.

Frieze coat, iv. 340.

Fringes: a pair of fringed gloves, i. 67, 70; iii. 125; Fringe-Glove Club, i. 125; effect of fringed gloves on a coquette's heart, ii. 595; fringe-makers, iv. 193; knotted fringes, iv. 413.

FRITILLA, her dream at church, v. 42–43.

Frog(s): fable of boys and, i. 100; rebus of, on Greek buildings, i. 250–1; eaten in France, iii. 99.

Frolic(s): The f., who are slaves to their wives or mistresses, ii. 196; frolicsome practices, ii. 372; pulling noses by way of, ii. 544–5; mistaken ideas of a, iii. 340–1.

Frontispiece: mottoes prefixed to f. of *Spectators*, iii. 55; as motto, iv. 219.

FRONTLY, Widow, riding the black ram, v. 130.

FROST, CHARITY, letter from (on a man who stands before the fire), iii. 57.

FROST, SUSANNA (an old maid), letter from, ii. 347–8.

FROTH, ABRAHAM (Arthur Charlett), letter from (on the Hebdomadal Meeting), i. 181–3.

FROTH, Mr., in CLARINDA's Journal, iii. 182–5.

Froth, bladders filled with, in a beau's head, ii. 571.

Froward: man cured, ii. 30; a f. mistress, ii. 42–43; wives, ii. 194; bearing with a f. woman, iv. 224.

Frowde, Philip, referred to (?), iv. 396.

Frown: a coquette's forbidding, iii. 75; 'murdered by a', iii. 417; in what cases a f. goes for nothing, v. 23.

Frugality: the support of generosity, i. 444; and parsimony the virtues of the merchant, ii. 186.

Fruit(s): few grow originally in England, i. 295; care in cultivating finer, ii. 116; confections and f. in a modern meal, ii. 265; a young woman who ate greedily of a basket of, ii. 347; fruit-shop and fruit-wenches in Covent Garden, iv. 99; fruit-trees, v. 144. *See also* Gardens.

Frying-pan: twanking of, in London streets, ii. 475; music played upon a, ii. 545–6.

Fuddled, i. 467.

Fuller, Francis, *Medicina gymnastica*, i. 473.

Fuller, Thomas, story of Dr. Alabaster from, ii. 361.

FULVIA: thinks only of pleasure and show, i. 68–69; the courtesan who discovered Catiline's conspiracy, ii. 247; and Curius (in *Catiline*), iv. 312–13.

Funds, public: Acts of Parliament for establishing, i. 15.

Funeral(s): oration by Pericles quoted, i. 349; oration over this globe by Burnet, ii. 77; orations and elogiums, iii. 152; f. men, iii. 166; books frequently given at, iv. 232; f. procession, iv. 277; of Sir ROGER, iv. 340–1; oration on a country gentleman, iv. 595; oration by Caesar on his first wife, v. 75.

FUNNELL, WILL, prodigious drinking of, iv. 542.

Funnels of conversation (the inquisitive), ii. 387.

Furbelow: of precious stones, i. 67; popular etymology of, iv. 195. *See also* Flounces.

Furnese, Henry (a Director of the Bank and East India Co.), a subscriber, i. lxxxix, xc.

Furniture: for his horse, ii. 153; magnificent f. demanded by wives, ii. 546; Lady MARY's reforms of, iii. 69.

Furs: those who smooth and clean f. of Lapland, iii. 376.

Fury (-ies): and monsters represented in art, ii. 180; vice the offspring of the, ii. 222; allegorical figure of, iii. 337; progress of a f. in modern poems, iv. 362.

Fustian: the f.-note taught, iii. 353; a young fellow in a f. jacket, iv. 267.

Future, the: ignorance of, a source of our happiness, i. 34–35; v. 65; superstitious inquiries into iv. 291–4; v. 64–65.

Future prospects, danger of relying upon, ii. 251–2.

Future state: prospect of, doubles our pleasures and supports us under afflictions, ii. 231–2; our proper concern, ii. 321–4, 377; of rewards and punishments the measure of man's merit, iii. 43–44; the poor to be compensated in, iii. 50. *See also* Eternity.

G., Mr.: reply to, who has sent in a letter, iv. 587.

G., D.: letter from (praising Milton papers), iii. 74.

G., R.: letter from (on a gospel-gossip), i. 198–9.

Gabble, the language of the Hottentots a confused, iii. 461.

Gabriel, the Angel: conducted Mahomet on a journey, i. 400; always in character in *PL*, ii. 565; his conference with Satan, iii. 172–3; iv. 135; his part in the battle in Heaven, iii. 232; cut the *fomes peccati* from Mahomet's heart, v. 7.

Gadding: like others of her sex, ii. 452; addicted to motion and, iv. 244.

Gai, the *toujours*, i. 354.

Gaiety: of women, i. 193; music now only an impertinent, ii. 584; and cheerfulness conducive to long life, iii. 451.

Gain, love of, i. 50.

Gait: of a tailor, ii. 271; of one interested in belles-lettres, iv. 345.

Galaxy (Milky Way), iv. 170, 529.

Galbinius, Caesar's behaviour to, iii. 408.

Galen: writers who prescribe 'after the Galenick way', i. 506; converted to belief in God by his dissections, iv. 441, 444; 'these itinerant Galens', iv. 552; a distemper not mentioned by, iv. 590.

Galilei, Galileo, invention of thermometer, ii. 426.

Galimatias, in a beau's head, ii. 572.

Gall, torn out from entrails in nuptial sacrifices to Juno, v. 76.

Galland, Antoine, an Arabian fable translated by, iv. 410–12.

Gallant: a lap-dog or a, i. 243; married her, ii. 408; a modern woman of Hensburg carries off her, iv. 271.

Gallanting: a fan, i. 429; ii. 30; a familiar acquaintance, iii. 532.

Gallantries: of the age, i. 436; the tour of, ii. 112; of crafty men, ii. 567; a poor man who attributes thinness to, ii. 593; in Charles II's reign, iii. 76; of Paradise in *PL*, iii. 175.

Gallantry: women to beware of thoughtless, iv. 8; false notion of g. in love, ii. 60; SIMON HONEYCOMB's progress in, ii. 103–6; education to a certain g. of soul, ii. 395; WILL HONEYCOMB's insights into, ii. 532; haunts of beauty and, ii. 537; in day of battle, ii. 591; false g. proceeds from impotence of mind, iii. 24; justness in point of, iii. 304; use of feigned names in letters of, iii. 489; allegorical figure of, iv. 122. *See also* Wit and Pleasure, Men of.

Galleys: as instruments of religious zeal, ii. 229; gibbets and g. as methods of

persuasion, ii. 431; a punishment in France, iii. 4, 507; iv. 207; a galley-slave in his chains, iv. 509–10.

Galliard, John Ernest, composed music for Hughes's opera, iii. *514*.

Galligaskins, 'each lateral pocket of the', iv. *345*.

Galloons, silver and gold, i. 67.

Gallus, Gaius Cornelius, Virgil praised by, ii. 482.

Galway, Henri de Massue de Ruvigny, Earl of, defeat at Almanza, i. *32*.

Game: preservation of, i. 158; party-spirit tends to destruction of, i. 509; variety of g. sought by *Spectator*, i. 448; ii. 19; iii. 399; preserved in one's own grounds, ii. 18–19; pursuing the g. with the husband abroad, iii. 66.

Game-Act, the: Sir ROGER explained a passage in, i. 9; a yeoman of an hundred pounds a year 'just within the', i. 498.

Games: account of country, ii. 131–5; in Greece and Rome, ii. 133; all-fours, ii. 163; 'little sordid g. of schoolboys', ii. 395; old-fashioned (hot-cockles, questions & commands, mottoes, similes, cross-purposes, blind man's buff), ii. 451; 'not so innocent' (whist, lanterloo, one and thirty), ii. 451; in the *Aeneid* and *Iliad*, ii. 542; 'the parson has lost his cloak', ii. 547; and diversions in the *Aeneid*, ii. 589; in country-halls (cross-purposes, questions & commands, crambo or capping verses, making golden verses), iv. 287.

Gamesters: letter from RACHEL BASTO on female, ii. 54; eternally upon the fret, ii. 230; and spendthrifts, iv. 315; 'from felon g. the raw squire is free', iv. 398.

Gaming: in London, i. 36; and drinking, i. 58; ii. 546; v. 9; has little to recommend it, i. 396–7; among women, ii. 54; in presence of women, ii. 105; effect of habit on, iv. 70; Rhaecus addicted to, v. 17.

GANDER, MICHAEL, letter from (on a watchman and his goose), iii. 413–14.

Ganges, river, iii. 274.

GAPE, ANTHONY, letter from (describing an accident), ii. 547.

GAPELY, RALPH, 'wounded' by a lady's glance, iii. 417.

Gaper, sign of the, at Amsterdam, i. 200, 223.

Garden(s): descriptions of, i. 158; iii. 592–3; iv. 188–92; the learned genius like a formal, ii. 129; English g. compared with French and Italian, iii.

551; hanging g. of Babylon, iii. 554; the *Aeneid* like a well-ordered, iii. 564; made from a gravel-pit at Kensington, iv. 190; benefits from a, iv. 192; many old philosophers spent most of their lives among, iv. 595.

Gardeners, a fleet of, bound for market-ports of London, iv. 99.

Gardening: a useful diversion in country life, i. 397; letter from a humorist in, iv. 188–92; and poetry, iv. 190.

Gardiner, Dr. Bernard (Warden of All Souls, Oxford), i. *183*.

Gardiner, Stephen (Bishop of Winchester), iii. 222.

Gardiner, W., translated Fontenelle, iv. *346*.

Gardner, Robert (contractor to the army), a subscriber, i. *xci*.

Garlands on fans, i. 427.

GARLICK, PILL: letter from (master of neither money nor wife), iv. 106.

Garret, ——, sells snuff, iii. *278*.

Garrick, David, iii. *251*.

Garter, Order of the, iv. 315; v. 59, 122.

Garters: i. 134; ii. 345; silver g. buckled below the knee, i. 70; knitted by WILL WIMBLE, i. 447; something curious in the tying of her, ii. 581; glimpses of ladies', iv. 246; decent ornament of a leather g., iv. 377; embroidering of, v. 72.

Garth, Dr. Samuel: a subscriber, i. lxxxix; member of Kit-Cat Club, i. *42*; referred to (?), iv. 556.—*The Dispensary*: in heroic verse, ii. 468; allegorical figures in, ii. 564; quoted, ii. 46; iv. 187.

Gasconnade: a French term imported, ii. 151–2; 'guilty of a', iv. 266.

Gate(s): a five-bar, ii. 504–5; a six-bar, i. 241; iv. 516; of Hell, in *PL*, iii. 120; of Heaven, in *PL* and Homer, iii. 200, 257.

'GATTY': one of the naked-shouldered, iv. 38; the 'Phantom', iv. 284–7, 330–3.

Gay, John: *Beggar's Opera*, i. *362*; *Epistle to Pulteney*, i. 122; *Fables*, i. *375*; *The Fan*, i. 426; *The Mohocks*, iii. *186*; *The Present State of Wit*, i. xiv, xxix–xxx; *The Shepherd's Week*, i. 298, 451; ii. 16, 513; iii. *372*; iv. *260*; *Trivia*, i. *434*; ii. 461; iii. *187*.

Gazers, a warning to, ii. 547.

Gazette(s), ii. 79; of Amsterdam, iii. 96; Paris, iii. 97, 98; foreign, iv. 471.

Gazette, The London: Steele's writing for, i. xvii; mentioned, i. 276, 438, 502; ii. *60*; iii. *187*; iv. 92, *168, 173, 444*; v. *114*.

Geese, saved the Capitol at Rome, iv. 17.

Gelding(s), i. 473; ii. 182; iii. 276; Sir ROGER's white, i. 477; iv. 340.

Gellius, Aulus: on Sallust, i. 234; on Socrates, ii. 266; an old heathen saying quoted by, ii. 289; on abuses in rearing of children, ii. 454; Alexander's letter to Aristotle, iii. 423.

Gemini, dangers to women when the sun is in, iii. 374.

Genealogy: of true and false humour, i. 147; WILL MAPLE's, ii. 296; kinds of characters found in a, v. 91–93.

General(s): dress others in their own habit to avoid attack, ii. 6; dependent upon assistants, ii. 44; saying of a Greek g. regarding fortune, ii. 45; the wise g. looks to both front and rear, ii. 471; over-cautious g. always secure a retreat, iii. 53; French g. become ambassadors, iii. 97; shameful to be surprised in winter quarters, iii. 482; confidence of, aided by belief in divine powers, iv. 50; of the Tartars who sold Chinese women in sacks, iv. 315; in the Civil Wars who dispensed favours equitably, iv. 262–3.

Generality (the public), i. 323, 350; ii. 99, 115, 205, &c.

Generosity: roused by the Spectator, ii. 29; romantic, ii. 252; and pity in drama, ii. 314; of a benefactor described, ii. 432–3; iv. 455–6; even false g. highly esteemed, ii. 445; among Augustan writers, ii. 482; in day of battle, ii. 591; the proper kind of, iii. 288–91; in Mme de Villacerfe, iii. 383; of human nature proved, v. 13–14.

Generous: a candid and g. spirit, i. 239; actions dependent on g. thoughts of ourselves, ii. 321; pleasure in g. actions, ii. 394; a g. mind the most sensible of praise and dispraise, ii. 426; a g. and constant passion in an agreeable lover, iii. 502, &c.

Genius (demon, spirit): of a Commonwealth, i. 16; of Great Britain, i. 17; the haunt of a, ii. 122; my ill, ii. 191; of the garden, iii. 594; who presides at our births, iv. 327; my good, iv. 559.

Genius (inclination, bent), for raillery, ii. 191.

Genius (natural ability): of the child to be consulted in education, i. 91, 449; ii. 114–17; iii. 105–9; schoolboys bred to learning who have not a g. for it, ii. 162; want of, not to be imputed to any man, ii. 254; spark of, in youth, ii. 396; arts and sciences which depend more on g. than experience, ii. 467;

critics without, ii. 484; for music, ii. 507; importance of following one's own, ii. 525–6; iii. 510–13; room for g. in acquiring wealth, iii. 3.

Genius (creative power, opp. to talent): writers who want, resort to bawdry, i. 217; ii. 206; false wit the product of industry rather than, i. 246, 249; ancients excel moderns in greatness of, i. 261; poets wanting g. hunt after foreign ornaments, i. 268; Shakespeare's g. shown in invention of Caliban, ii. 586–7; sublime g. of Milton, iii. 89; Milton's g. strengthened by learning, iii. 234; marks of, in writing, iii. 304; one of the words to suggest immense reading, iii. 347; in Shakespeare, iii. 572–3.

Genius, geniuses: the natural and the learned, ii. 126–30; books the legacy of a great, ii. 154; often fail in management of life, ii. 362–4; in Augustan age, ii. 482; can't always mind little beauties and niceties, iii. 5; their works preferable to those of exact authors, iii. 38; French Academy founded to divert them from politics, iii. 96; strong affections in, iii. 525; have faults mixed with virtues, like the flaming bush, iii. 526; arise at certain periods and in groups, iii. 529; a great g. springing out of Ireland, iv. 18; Sir Francis Bacon an extensive and improved, iv. 487; Leonardo da Vinci a universal, iv. 488; sometimes lost for want of education, iv. 490; a great g. may ignore rules of art, a little g. observes them, v. 28.

Gens d'Arms, a French word imported, ii. 151–2.

Gent., written after a name, v. 92.

Gentil, F., Le Jardinier solitaire, i. 27.

GENTLE, READER, letter from (recommending The Historian), iii. 111–12.

Gentleman: conversation of the, i. 324; occupations of an English, i. 352; ii. 225; WILL HONEYCOMB on the learning of a, i. 436; Mr. SPECTATOR 'does not write like a', ii. 119; and the merchant contrasted, ii. 185–9; the prentice-boy who said he was a gentleman's son, ii. 291; reputation the portion of the, ii. 349; one of your gay g. of the town, ii. 411; to be civil not beneath the character of, ii. 418; going on like a g. of the town, ii. 524; acknowledged merit gives distinction to, ii. 591; the accomplished g. in modern comedy, iv. 69.

Gentleman, fine: WILL HONEYCOMB

a well-bred, i. 13; as represented in plays, i. 219–20; actions and language of, i. 278; Dorimont as, i. 322–3; character of the, i. 323–5; 'that sort of creature, whom the sillier part of woman call', i. 386; 'Pray, Jack, be a', ii. 593; CLEANTHES tries to be a, iii. 511; now neither a keeper nor an infidel, iv. 128; sets up for hardness of heart, iv. 352–3.

Gentleman's Journal, i. xxxvii, *120*; iv. *38, 386, 413, 414.*

Gentleman-usher, i. 275.

Gentlemen of the robe, ii. 117, 272; iv. 574.

Gentleness: and forbearance to be practised, ii. 308; of behaviour in Marlborough, v. 179.

Gentlewoman, qualities of a, i. 405.

Gentlewomen, boarding-school for young, near Stepney, iii. 140.

Gentry, are constantly in debt, i. 352.

Geography: wagers on questions in, ii. 72; in education, ii. 396; Milton's ostentatious references to, iii. 62; writers on, and the pleasures of the imagination, iii. 574.

Geometry: a good picture is begun on a foundation of, ii. 447; Plato calls God the divine geometrician, iii. 258; value of practical, iii. 318; Savilian Professor of, in Oxford, iv. 481.

George, Prince, of Denmark, i. xvii.

George I: in allegory of public credit, i. 17; entry into London, v. 59, 117–23; coronation of, v. 81, 105–8; Eusden's poem on accession of, v. *114;* Thanksgiving for accession of, v. *153;* mentioned, iv. *169, 173.*

George II, v. 123.

George's Day, St., i. 41.

Georges, Club of the, i. 40–41.

Gerard, William: *Essay on Genius*, iii. *536.*

German, represented by stupidity in Vision of Painters, i. 354.

German Artist, the, i. 130.

German chronicle, story from an old, ii. 215.

German count, deceived by bawds, ii. 304.

German empire, iii. 600.

German holly, iv. 104.

German language: the lion to act a part in High-Dutch, i. 57; reflects the blunt honest character of the people, ii. 36. *See also* Dutch.

German manuscript, a variant reading in a, iv. 164.

German medals, chronograms on, i. 256.

German music, preferred to English, i. 82.

German Princes, 'are all well', i. 277.

German wits: fond of chronograms, i. 256; long laborious nothings of, ii. 356.

Germanicus, listened in disguise to his soldiers, ii. 425–6.

Germany: fools for jesters in courts of, i. 200, 223; 'I have cursed the inns of', ii. 38; Emperors in, who learned handicraft trades, iii. 319; family of Valentines in, iii. 597; monthly pamphlets published in, iv. 113–14.

Geryoneo, in Spenser, represents Philip II, iv. 429.

Gesta Romanorum, ii. *423.*

Gesture(s): affectation in, i. 159–60; should follow thought, i. 283; proper in offering snuff, ii. 46–47; a man more full of, than ordinary, ii. 113; in oratory, ii. 159; iii. 520–3; importance of, in behaviour, iii. 235–6; little used by English orators and preachers, iii. 520–3; in acting, iv. 432–7.

Gew-gaws, i. 67, 416; iv. 26; v. 46.

Ghibellines, strife of Guelphs and, i. 511.

Ghost(s): seen by the superstitious, i. 34, 453; stories of, i. 53; in Drury Lane Theatre, i. 149, 150; in tragedy, i. 186; ii. 397; iv. 283; in *Hamlet*, i. 186; ii. 414; in *Macbeth*, i. 194; haunt cemeteries, i. 381; appearance of, i. 453–6; ii. 254; iii. 292; as evidence of immortality, i. 455–6; stories dealing with, pleasing to the imagination, iii. 570–3.

Giant(s): in romances and books of chivalry, i. 84, 417; iii. 129; impresses of, iv. 18.

Giants' war against the gods: described by Hesiod, Homer, and Claudian, iii. 229–30; a sin against Heaven, iii. 513.

Gibbeting. *See* Hanging in chains.

Gibbets: as instruments of religious zeal, ii. 229; as methods of persuasion, ii. 431.

Gibbon, Edward (a Director of S. Sea Co.), a subscriber, i. *xc.*

Gibbon, Edward, *Decline and Fall*, iv. *129.*

Gibbons, Grinling, i. *251.*

Gibbosity of figure, i. 77.

Gibson, —— (painter), i. *243.*

Gibson, Edmund (later Bishop of London), a subscriber, i. *lxxxviii.*

Gibson, Thomas, *Anatomy*, ii. *571, 572.*

GIDDY, PATIENCE (a maidservant), letter from), ii. 42–43.

Gift(s): of nature, when valuable, ii. 179; Pliny's g. to Quintilian's daughter,

iii. 40; laying proper value upon g. of fortune, iii. 47; to charity schools, iii. 48; of birth, so-called and actual, iv. 390–1; doubled when accompanied with delicacy of address, iv. 456.

Gigglers, ii. 85; in church, ii. 120.

Gigli, Girolamo, author of letter in No. 545, iv. 449–51.

Gimcrack, Sir Nicholas (in Shadwell's *Virtuosi*), i. 91; ii. 245.

Ginger-bread; bought in London streets, ii. 477; hieroglyphics wrought in, iii. 94.

'Gionnata VII', Emperor of China: letter from, to the Pope, iv. 450, 451.

Gipsies: Sir ROGER and, i. 8, 207; ii. 15–17; story of a boy stolen by, ii. 17–18; frequent in England, iv. 292.

Girard, Paul: advertisement for cordials, iii. 206–7.

Girardeau, Isabella (singer), i. 25; in *Almahide*, ii. 398.

Girdle(s): as a love-token, i. 124; exclamation on a, ii. 120–1; given by Venus to Juno, iii. 311; country squires in white, iii. 321.

Girls: education of, i. 281–3, 404–5; ii. 60; iii. 414–15; we take care of their persons and neglect their minds, i. 282–3; early acquire social graces, i. 282; training of, by dancing-masters, i. 283, 285–6; innocent diversions for wives and daughters, ii. 451.

Give her as good as she brings (prov.), v. 69.

Giving and forgiving, a difference between, ii. 243.

Gladiator, the younger Faustina admired a common, ii. 10.

Gladiatorial shows, Cicero on cruelty of, iv. 35.

GLADIO, his exploits in dreams, v. 40.

Glance(s): of ill-nature, ii. 206; false g. of a coquette, ii. 235; leers and sly, ii. 470; the mind summed up and expressed in a, ii. 478; an artful, ii. 574; iii. 16; half-glances, iv. 246.

Glands, the body a system of tubes and, i. 471–2.

Glanvill, John, translated Fontenelle, iv. 346.

Glanvill, Joseph, *Scepsis scientifica*, iii. 536.

Glaphyra's dream, i. 455–6.

Glasgow, letter from (vision of heavenly and worldly wisdom), iv. 369.

Glass, Clear as the (prov.), ii. 385.

Glass, taking the, i. 310; 'the first g. for myself', ii. 266.

Glass, a poet upon, ii. 356; manufacture of, iv. 308. *See also* Looking-glass.

Glass-house fires, i. 310.

Glass-man, fable of Alnaschar, the Persian, iv. 410–12.

Glasses: cries of retailers of broken g. in London, ii. 475; a wife's dislike of g. of last year, iii. 111.

Glasses (microscopes): a virtuoso's discoveries by the help of, ii. 570; applied to a coquette's heart, ii. 594, 596.

Glasses, put down and pulled up in coaches, i. 103–4; ii. 329; iii. 490.

Globes: trees cut in shape of, iii. 552; celestial, iv. 326; proposals for a pair of, iv. 481–3.

GLOOM, GEORGE, testimonial from (the *Spectator* a cure for spleen), iv. 460–1.

Gloom, gloominess: of mind dispersed by pictures, i. 353; of minds of best men needs incitements to mirth, ii. 205; man not created for g. and melancholy, iii. 453–4; in religion, iv. 251–4.

GLOOMY, DICK, examination of his heart, v. 8.

Gloria Patri, in the midst of a, iii. 8.

GLORIANA, ostentation of, ii. 308; courtship of, by DAMON and STREPHON, iii. 586–9; in the *Faerie Queene*, iv. 429.

Glory: true and false ideas of (Peter the Great and Louis XIV), ii. 47–50; Persian Emperor 'the Sun of', ii. 128; true g. resides in self-approbation, ii. 180–1; the greatest of mortal enjoyments, ii. 426; the less Cato coveted g. the more he acquired it, ii. 491; ambition posing as emulation or, iv. 326; pursuit of by Louis XIV and William III, iv. 335–8; of Marlborough not subject to diminution, v. 179.

Glory, love of: the most ardent affection attending human life, ii. 47–50; love towards EUDOSIA a sentiment like, ii. 70; in military men, ii. 97–98; in wrestlers, ii. 132–3; a universal passion, ii. 370–4, 490–502; iv. 17–19; an imperfection of character, ii. 492–3; to be encouraged, iv. 490–1; in Cicero and the younger Pliny, iv. 490–1.

Glossographia Anglicana Nova, i. 155.

Gloucester, Duke of (son of Queen Anne), death of, iii. 440, 443.

Gloucestershire, i. 40; iii. 502; iv. 283.

Glove(s): fringed, i. 67, 70; ii. 595; silver-fringed, iii. 125; a young fop buying a pair of, ii. 108; to let fall, ii. 190; iii. 418; given at a wedding, ii. 280; iii. 501; mourning, iii. 401; a woman's hand playing with the g. off, iii. 417.

GLOWORM, MARTHA, testimonial from (praising No. 231), iv. 459–60.

Gluttons: women who are g. at their table, ii. 319.

Gluttony: of a modern meal, ii. 264–5; dangers of, iii. 277–8.

GLYCERA, her dancing walk, iv. 245.

Glynne, Sir John, iii. *135*.

Gnomon (the nose), v. 108.

Goat: as a sign before a perfumer's door, i. 117; a lamb sucking a, ii. 455; Aegisthus nursed by a, ii. 455; a wild, iii. 274; effect of goat's milk upon a religious man, iii. 525.

Go-betweens, of women of intrigue, iv. 281.

GOBLIN, HUGH (President of the Ugly Club), letter from, i. 221–3.

Goblins: and sprites associated with darkness, i. 454; night-goblins that overturn plates and dishes, iii. 245.

Go-cart, ladies now walk as if they were in a, i. 451.

God: trust in, i. 34–35; iii. 43–46; iv. 49–51, 529–33; v. 103–4; love of, towards man, i. 54–55; ii. 213–14, 232–4; iii. 432; iv. 234–6, 547–50; worship of, our concern, i. 395–6; ii. 232–4, 288, 331–4; iv. 150, 394–5, 547–50; v. 20–22, 170–3; nature of, an argument for immortality, i. 457; 'the soul of brutes', i. 494; justice agreeable to nature of, mercy to that of man, ii. 166; charity to the poor an offering to, ii. 198; gratitude due towards, ii. 288; iv. 94–98, 234–6; wisdom of, inscrutable, ii. 420–3; approbation of, our only concern, ii. 499–502; iii. 326; character of, in *PL*, ii. 564; iii. 141–2; omnipotence of, acknowledged by Satan, iii. 86; faith in, and morality, iii. 118–20; iv. 141–5; Plato's description of, iii. 258; iv. 298; the source of our happiness, iii. 431–2, 545; iv. 94–98, 254; presence of, depicted in Psalm cxiv, iv. 126–7; infinite goodness of, iv. 345–9, 392–5; v. 170–1; our ideas of, iv. 392–5, 530–1; v. 168–9, 171–3; omniscience and omnipresence of, iv. 529–33, 547–50, 582–6; v. 20–22; 'a Being whose centre is everywhere and his circumference nowhere', iv. 531; habitation of, in Heaven, iv. 582–6; v. 52; imitation of, our duty, v. 168–9.

God, evidences for existence of: this 'almost the only truth we are sure of', iii. 431; from apparitions and ghosts, i. 456; from natural history of animals, i. 489–97; iv. 441–4; from propensity of the mind to worship, ii. 288; from the universal concurrence of nations, ii. 288; iii. 460–1; from statistics in bills of mortality, iii. 27; from man's imperfection, iii. 44; from external nature, iii. 475–6; iv. 144–5, 233–4, 529–33; from our ideas of eternity past, v. 17–22; from the frame and constitution of our minds, v. 53.

'God's blessing, With', the formula in quack medicines, iv. 554.

God: our apocryphal heathen, i. 118; of love, i. 246.

Godfrey, Brigadier Francis, a subscriber, i. *lxxxviii*.

Godolphin, Sidney, 1st Earl of: member of Kit-Cat Club, i. *42*; fall of, referred to(?), iv. 23; mentioned, iv. *155*.

Gods, the: Seneca on the innate goodness of, ii. 116; virtue the offspring of, ii. 222; negligent patrons like Epicurus's, ii. 337–8; paintings of, ii. 378–9; men appear like g. in practice of benevolence, ii. 394; Plato on the benevolence of, ii. 421–2; Lucian's burlesque depiction of, ii. 467–8; Argus king-at-arms to, ii. 470; anger of Achilles engaged all the g. in factions, ii. 541; in Homer suitably individualized, ii. 562; blood of, not real, ii. 570–1; motions of, described by Heliodorus, iii. 389; making men like g., the heathen boast, v. 167–8.

Godwin, William, on Addison's style, i. c.

Gold: Europeans' desire of, in America, i. 240; word of a merchant the g. of Ophir, ii. 351; 'a wonderful clearer of the understanding', ii. 431; a modern woman of Hensburg carries off a bag of, iv. 271.

Golden: beard of Aesculapius, iii. 223; dreams of Homer, ii. 226; expedition of G. Fleece described by Valerius Flaccus, i. 300; number, ii. 250; pen, iv. 286; rule, i. 510; scales, iii. 173; iv. 135; making g. verses, iv. 287.

Golding, ——, author of letter in No. 250(?), ii. 472.

Goldsmith, Oliver, ii. *464*.

Goldsmith near Temple Bar, John Warner, iv. 483.

Goldsmith's shop, the heaps upon the counter in a, ii. 471.

Goldsmiths, subscribers to *Spectator*, i. xc.

Goliah (Goliath), words of, quoted, iv. 593.

Gols, Conrade de, a subscriber, i. xc.

Gombauld, Jean Ogier de, his criticism of Ménage's rhymes, i. 257, *258*.

Good: ambition reaches after an empty imaginary, ii. 498; discerning of g. and

evil, ii. 310–12, 421–2; 'for the g. of the public', in quack doctors' advertisements, iv. 59.

Good, doing: 'the secret and incomparable pleasure', i. 404; a worthy object of ambition, ii. 374; virtues which dispose us to, ii. 445; inward pleasure felt in, ii. 500; iii. 423; v. 13–14; carries its own reward, iii. 423; practised by MANILIUS, iv. 152–3; opportunities for, in men of great place, iv. 159. Cf. Benevolence.

Good bodies, 'those whom they call', iii. 72.

Good companion, figure made by the, iii. 152.

GOODFELLOW, ROBIN, letter from (on drinking), ii. 306.

Good Hope, Cape of, iii. 462.

Good housewifery, iii. 53.

Good humour: importance of, i. 419–22; portable quality of, i. 421; and sprightliness of the wife, ii. 9; necessary in conversation with others, ii. 64–68, 204–6; the officious liar and, ii. 409–11; necessary to happiness in marriage, ii. 545–6; of Sir ROGER, ii. 551–2; of EMILIA, iii. 80; virtue consistent with, iii. 82; a stock of, to be carried into country solitude, iii. 590.

Good nature: and humanity the mark of a gentleman, i. 324–5; 'a whorish unresisting', i. 352; and humanity of Sir ROGER, i. 440, 478; necessary in marriage, ii. 87, 515–16; iv. 357–8; v. 75; benefits of, ii. 164–7; in Cyrus and Caesar, ii. 166; as a moral virtue, ii. 197–201; iv. 460; charity the test of, ii. 198–201; an endless source of pleasure, ii. 269; incompatible with avarice, ii. 372; of youth, ii. 396; and cheerfulness the two great ornaments of virtue, ii. 445; the tongue to be tuned by, ii. 462; accompanying benevolence, iii. 38–39; supplies the absence of beauty, iii. 104; and good sense go together, iv. 37; and anger, iv. 39–40; a term peculiar to the English language, iv. 370; has come almost to mean folly, iv. 370; a sweetener of the blood, iv. 460.

Good-natured: my landlord a jolly g. man, i. 52; more honourable to be a g. man than a wit, i. 100; reader, i. 363; WILL WIMBLE a g. officious fellow, i. 447; men pity rather than ridicule infirmities of others, ii. 167; a g. man whom rakes call hen-peckt, ii. 194; wives wheedling g. husbands, iv. 518.

Good-neighbourhood: spoiled by party-spirit, i. 509; 'jollity, and what they call', ii. 20.

Good sense. See Sense.

Good will: praise from an ignorant man is only, ii. 238; and benevolence the aim of the Spectator, iv. 501; love in the young generally accompanied with, v. 24.

Goodwin, John, his capture by a French privateer, iii. 302–3.

Goodwin, Thomas (President of Magdalen College), referred to (?), iv. 251–2.

Goose, following the day-watchman, iii. 413–14.

GOOSEQUILL, FRANCIS, slain by an ogle, iii. 417.

GOOSEQUILL, WILL, Clerk of the Lawyers' Club, iii. 402.

Gordian knot, twisted like a (prov.), ii. 595–6.

Gore, John (Director of the Bank and S. Sea Co.), a subscriber, i. xc.

GORGON, GILES, winner of a grinning match, ii. 184.

Gorman, Timothy (prize-fighter), iv. 34.

Gospel-gossip, account of a, i. 198–9.

GOSSELIN, JOHN, slain by a lady's smile, iii. 418.

Gosselin, William (a Director of E. India Co.), a subscriber, i. xc.

Gossiping, evils of, ii. 459–62, 558–60; iii. 123–4, 296–8, 463–6.

Gossips (female companions), ii. 458.

GOSSLING, GEORGE, letter from (on lotteries), ii. 251.

Gothic architecture: ('extravagances of an irregular fancy'), i. 268; monstrous and barbarous, i. 271; the fontange a Gothic building, i. 414; architecture of men's dress 'mere Gothic', ii. 74; meanness of a Gothic cathedral, iii. 556.

Gothic bishop, introduces a ridiculous dress in R.C. Church, ii. 290.

Gothic king, like the figure of an old, iii. 215.

Gothic manner in writing, i. 297, 321.

Gothic taste of English poets and readers, i. 269; iii. 530.

Gothic temple, consecrated to god of dullness, i. 271.

Goths: from the Northern hive, i. 90; in poetry and architecture, i. 268; the Spectator not to engage with Goths and Vandals, iii. 382.

Gould, Nathaniel (Governor of the Bank and Director of E. India Co.), a subscriber, i. lxxxix, xc.

Gould, Robert, 'The Play-house', i. 331.

Goulston, Theodore, Latin version of Aristotle's *Poetics*, i. *164*.

Goust, Bon, gentlemen of the, iii. 485.

Goût: of French tire-women, ii. 578; barbarous g. of the great vulgar and the small, iv. 170.

Gout, the: i. 105, 206; ii. 442, 530; iv. 554, 564; v. 42; resulting from intemperance, ii. 265; a proposal to sufferers from, iii. 169; 'gout pills' advertised, iv. *61*.

Governesses, maladministration of, iii. 139.

Government: obedience of children to parents the basis of all, ii. 244; superiority of English, iii. 18–22; patriarchal origin of, iv. 273.

Government of the Tongue. See Allestree.

Governor, colonial: anecdote of a, iv. 248–9.

Gown(s): and staff of a servant, i. 409; sale of, advertised, ii. *74*; 'madam in her grogram', ii. 486; silks for a dwarf's, ii. 557; a cherry-coloured, ii. 580; ceremony of the green, iii. 372; a correspondent has written against Masters', v. 116.

Gracchus: employed a servant with an ivory pipe, ii. 388–9; iv. 437; exclamations of, iv. 432–3.

Grace: the title given to Archbishops, ii. 352; in actions which follow nature, ii. 425; love gives a certain g. to actions, ii. 559; bashful g. in my women readers, ii. 567; a benefaction done with a good, iii. 40; doctrine of, in *PL*, iii. 142.

Grace at table, many Englishmen too bashful to say, iv. 116–17.

Graces: of novelty in Pope's *Essay on Criticism*, ii. 483; secret g. of the soul, ii. 500; additional g. in actions, iii. 38–41; unstudied g. of behaviour, iii. 79–80; particular g. thrown into an ogle, iii. 126; quavers and g. in playing of a cat-call, iii. 351; beautifying g. in stories, iv. 421; and attractions of person in Marlborough, v. 179.

Graces, the: Venus dressed by, iii. 337; attendants on Spring, iii. 594; and Cupids, iv. 196; attending Hymen, iv. 326; in Greek epitaphs, iv. 474–5.

Gracián, Baltasar: recommends associating with the fortunate, iii. 42; Luisa de Padilla angry with, iii. 423–4; recommends the 'fine taste', iii. 527; *El Discreto(Art of Prudence)*, publication of, iii. 423–4; quoted, ii. *401*; iii. *477*.

Graecisms in *PL*, iii. 12.

Graecum est non potest legi, ii. 454.

Graham, George, inventor of the orrery, iv. *481*.

Graham, J. (auctioneer), letter from, i. 288.

Grammar: an Academy to settle controversies between idiom and, ii. 35; a little slip in, to be overlooked in great poetry, iii. 10; taking a lad from g. and taw, iii. 368.

Grammarian, every one that speaks is a, i. 365.

'Granajah', King of, i. 212.

Grand Alliance (1701), Treaty of, iii. 51.

Grand Climacteric. *See* Climacteric.

Grand-Jury-man, iii. 210.

Grand Monarque. *See* Louis XIV.

Grand remedy (death), iv. 559.

Grand Signior. *See* Signior.

Grandeur: chimerical, ii. 252; and respect from circle of friends, ii. 351; arising from greatness of sentiments, iii. 33; that little showy g. which the Jews expected of their Messiah, v. 84; easy g. of Marlborough, v. 179.

Granger, James; *Biographical History*, iv. *251*.

Grant, Roger (oculist): referred to (?), iv. 61; testimonies to, iv. 173, 457.

Grantorto, in Spenser, iv. 429.

Grasshoppers: 'we appeared as g. before them', i. 413; anecdote of the traveller and, iii. 325.

Grate, a wife's dislike of an old-fashioned, iii. 111.

Gratitude: towards God, ii. 288; iv. 94–98, 234–6; letters of, on generous benefactors, ii. 432–3; iv. 455–6; cheerfulness a constant g. to God, iii. 430, 475–6.

Grave: or sullen temper, ii. 174; the merry and the, ii. 204; men of g. natures the most constant, v. 23.

Grave-digger in *Hamlet*, petition of, i. 151.

Gravel, the: a treatise upon, i. 105; Widow TRUEBY's water best for, iii. 212–13.

'Gravel-diggers', iv. 17.

Gravel-pits at Kensington, ii. 46; iv. 190.

Graves, Thomas: *Spectator* sold by, i. xxiv.

Gravitation: principle of, in bodies, i. 493; of matter one of the great points of atheism, ii. 230.

Gravity: characteristic of men, ii. 8; of a husband tempers the vivacity of the wife, ii. 9; of a privy-counsellor, ii. 130; of ROXANA's entrance into a room, ii. 308; often mistaken for wisdom, ii. 377; balanced against wisdom, iv. 136; undue appearance of, iv. 263.

Gray, S. (printer), i. 52.

Grazier, found among one's ancestors, v. 92.

Great, the truly, neglect applause of the multitude, ii. 180-1.

Great, by the, i. 96, 152; iv. 294, 342; &c.

Great, living (imposingly), ii. 86, 88.

Great Britain: genius of, i. 17; drolls in, i. 202; population and wealth of, ii. 282-7. See also England.

Great horse, ride the, iv. 24.

Great man: strange stories of a certain, ii. 4; asking a favour of, after dinner, ii. 197; pleasure in discovering infirmities in a, ii. 494-8.

Great men: liable to censure and flattery, i. 422-3; their true characters not drawn until after death, i. 423; their sense of the merit of their dependants, i. 445; subjects of admiration rather than example, ii. 25; deaths of, ii. 25-26; iii. 28-29, 299-302; the two most eminent now in Europe, ii. 47; some have sacrificed themselves to pleasure, ii. 95; recital of actions of, ii. 239; levées of, ii. 256-60; dependants on, ii. 334-8.

Great Mogul: woods belonging to, i. 119; a subject of, at the Royal Exchange, i. 293.

Great point of view, in the, ii. 183.

Great Secret, discourse with a Rosicrucian about the, iv. 561.

Great Vulgar (Cowley), i. 470; iv. 170.

Greatness: Pascal on our endeavours after, i. 478; true and false, ii. 351-4, 370-4; v. 84-87, 94-95, 126-7; of action necessary in the epic, ii. 541-3; in architecture, ii. 542; iii. 553-8; superior g. of Lucifer in PL, iii. 114; as a source of primary pleasures of the imagination, iii. 540-1, 545, 553-8, 564-5, 578, 580-1; iv. 233-4. See also Sublime.

Greatness of mind: the mark of true bravery, iii. 304; induced by poetry, iii. 530; necessary to married happiness, v. 75.

Greatness of soul: in Negroes of American plantations, ii. 339; shown in benevolence, ii. 418; above applauses of multitude, ii. 492; in Milton, iii. 62-63.

Greatness of spirit: shown in admission of error, iii. 433-5.

Greaves, John, Pyramidographia, i. 2-3.

Greece: dancing in, i. 284; iii. 237-8; discords in, in time of Homer, i. 299; women not allowed at Olympic games,

i. 348-9; bodily exercises and games encouraged in, ii. 133; the fable written in most distant ages of, ii. 220-1; suicides among women prevented in, ii. 399-400; liberty in ancient G. contrasted with present slavery, iii. 22; how Sparta became mistress of, iii. 109; great geniuses in, in time of Socrates, iii. 529; blind Teresias in, iv. 512; fidelity of women in, v. 73-74. See also Ancients.

Greek, a young, just come from Oxford, v. 69.

Greek architects, not allowed to inscribe their names on their works, i. 251.

Greek author(s): no mixed wit in, except among epigrammatists, i. 265; many now lost, ii. 365; outweighs a whole library of moderns, iv. 137; superior in wit, iv. 328; epitaphs on, iv. 472-6.

Greek buildings, use of rebus on, i. 251.

Greek critics: knowledge of, necessary to the modern critic, iii. 35; were masters of elegance and delicacy of language, iii. 36; full of praises of their contemporaries, v. 27.

Greek epigrams: the only form of Greek literature containing mixed wit, i. 265; examples of, from Greek Anthology, iv. 472-6.

Greek evergreens, iv. 104.

Greek language: on monuments, i. 110; an opera to be performed in, i. 131; Sir Roger afraid of being insulted with Latin and, by his chaplain, i. 440; in Spectator, ii. 360, 453-4, 556; iii. 54-55; proposal to teach 'that more difficult sister language', ii. 396; in universities in time of Erasmus, ii. 429-30; a shop-keeper's wife enamoured of, ii. 582; forms of, in Virgil and Horace, iii. 12; and Greek virtues, iii. 250; and Latin learnt at a country school, iv. 204; 'spells uncouth Latin, and pretends to', iv. 398; 'deep and sonorous, and conducive to expectoration', iv. 571; and Latin learnt at school, v. 38. See also Translations.

Greek law, an old, forbidding neutrality, i. 72.

Greek manuscript, describing the Lovers' Leap, ii. 385, 406.

Greek mottoes in Spectator: women pleased with, ii. 360; disliked, ii. 453-4; iii. 54-55.

Greek oratory: gestures used in, iii. 521; attempts upon the affections forbidden in, v. 166.

Greek particle, the critic who has only rectified a, i. 438.

Greek plays: prologue and epilogue were real parts of, iii. 266; written with a regard to morality, iv. 66–67.

Greek poems in typographical shapes, i. 246–7.

Greek poetry and poets: knowledge of, necessary to the critic, iii. 35; composed both words and music, iii. 515; diversions filled with songs and hymns to deities, iii. 516; iv. 94–95; did not deal much with fairies and ghosts, iii. 572; on man's happiness, iv. 463.

Greek proverbs, i. 506; ii. 243.

Greek sophisters, ii. 385.

Greek tragedy. *See* Tragedy.

Greek (unintelligible speech): *this is heathen Greek* (prov.), ii. 479.

Greeks: at present the only musicians in the Turkish empire, i. 131; caused slaves to drink to excess, as warning to children, ii. 242; and Trojans in universities, ii. 429–30, 453–4; favoured education in public schools, iii. 132; their siege of Troy, iii. 481; music in worship among, v. 152.

GREEN, SABINA. *See* RENTFREE.

Green: our eyes refreshed with g. field of Britain, i. 296; hoods, ii. 532; helps the eyes, iii. 452; said to be cheerful, iii. 452.

Green gown, ceremony of the, iii. 372.

Green tea. *See* Tea.

GREENBAG, MOSES: letters from (on amateur coachmen), iv. 265–8, 374–6.

Greene, Robert, iv. *514*.

Greenfield, Dr. ('college physician' in the Old Bailey), advertisement of, iv. *61*.

Green-house, ii. 600; iv. 189.

Greens, decoration of church with, ii. 600; iii. 8–9.

Green-sickness: symptoms of, iv. 16; a quack doctor who offers to cure, iv. 59.

Gregory the Great, Pope: established love-feasts in England, ii. 134; on calumny, iv. 89.

Grenadiers' March, youth who learned to beat the, on his chin, iii. 3.

Grey, Elizabeth, *Countess of Kent's Receipts*, recommended, i. 391.

Grey, Zachary, iii. *135*.

Grey: man whose hair grew g. in one night, v. 102.

Greyhounds, a brace of, ii. 164.

Gridiron: fable of tongs and, i. 197; music of the, iv. 546.

Grief: for decease of friends, i. 95; iii. 29–30; mourning costume as expression of, i. 275–6; true g. beyond relief of tears, i. 402–4; demonstrations of, i. 403; ii. 301–2; consolation in, ii. 139–48, 256; of Asteria for husband's absence, ii. 435–6; iii. 269; of Orestes in *The Distressed Mother*, iii. 34; has a natural eloquence superior to art, iii. 486–7; Grotto of, iv. 276–9; upon death of a wife, iv. 350–3.

Griefs and calamities, each finds his own most bearable, iv. 506–11.

Grimace(s): 'no further than a bow and a', i. 294; of a country girl, ii. 132; in a grinning contest, ii. 184; and distortions in a dance, ii. 207; capers and original g. of JOHN TROTT, iii. 57; politicians taught the whole art of political, iii. 98.

Grimaldi, Nicola. *See* Nicolini.

Grimalkin, JOSIAH HENPECK married to a, ii. 327.

Grinders of knives and scissors, cries of, in London streets, ii. 477.

Grinning contest, at Coleshill, Warwickshire, ii. 182–5, 206, 224; iii. 321.

Gripes, a fit of the, iv. 509.

Groat, ii. 226; iv. 305.

Groat, not worth a (prov.), iii. 183, 469.

Grocer, letter from a, with account of his wooing, iv. 407.

Grogram: 'Madam in her g. gown', ii. 486; versus brocade, iv. 390.

Groom(s): carelessness of, i. 373; Sir ROGER's, i. 439; ii. 22.

Groom Porter's, money lost at, iv. 558.

Gross, in (the), iii. 478; iv. 29, 474, 527.

Gross, the (the majority), of mankind, ii. 97; of the soldiery, ii. 99; of the room, ii. 433; &c.

Grossness, true delicacy opposed to corruption and, iii. 15.

'GROTESQUE, Minheer', a Dutch painter in the Barbican, i. 176.

Grotesque: figures in a grinning match, ii. 184; parts of nature, aesthetic pleasure in, iii. 453; works in LEONORA's library, i. 153.

Grotius, Hugo, iii. 51; on Ezekiel, iii. 233.

Grotto(es): LEONORA's, i. 158; fretwork of rocks and, iii. 550; contrivers of, like romance writers, iv. 190; of Grief, iv. 276–9; and caves, iv. 325; poem 'To Mrs. —— on her', v. 161–2.

Grouler, The, i. 95.

Grove, Henry, contributions to *Spectator*, i. lxxix–lxxx; v. *10*.

Grove, Col. Hugh: unhappy enterprise of, in the Civil Wars, iii. 135.

Grove: sacred to the PERVERSE WIDOW, i. 483; at Dodona and at Delphi

venerated by the ancients, v. 15; on Mt. Ida cut down by Aeneas, v. 15.

GRUEL, Doctor, prescribes for Lord FRIDAY, iv. 559.

GRUMBLE, GRACE, letter from, received, iv. 588.

Grutching uncommunicative disposition, a, iii. 39.

Guard-coat, i. 375.

Guardian, The, i. 77, 259; ii. 91, 240, 297, 412, 442, 468; iii. 163; iv. 280, 488, 499; cost of advertisements in, i. *lxx*. *See also* Addison, Steele.

Guardian: angel, ii. 77, 302; angels of Paradise, iii. 330; who has fallen in love with his ward, iii. 504; complaint regarding a harsh, v. 116.

Guelphs and Ghibellines, strife of, i. 511.

Guelphus, Duke of Bavaria, besieged at Hensburg, iv. 269.

Guericus, iii. *28*.

Guido Reni, in Vision of Painters, i. 355.

Guillaume de Cabestan, iv. *571*.

Guilt: and solitude most unfit for each other, ii. 281; of Adam and Eve in *PL*, ii. 563; iii. 333–6; indicated by bashfulness or impudence, iii. 405–6; sense of, deprives us of cheerfulness of heart, iii. 431; spread among many is only multiplied, iv. 300; division of, like that of matter, iv. 300.

Guinea: a leap and trial, for a horse, ii. 117; the prize at a whistling match, ii. 206; for a criminal's body, iv. 290.

Guiscard, Antoine de, ii. *129*.

Gulston, Jane, i. li.

Gulston, Bishop William, i. li.

Gumley, John (glass-merchant), iv. 308–9.

Guns, of several kinds, at Sir ROGER'S, i. 472.

Gust (enjoyment), v. 139.

Gustavus Adolphus (King of Sweden), a chronogram medal of, i. 256.

Gusto, ii. 390; ill g. of an extravagant painter, ii. 448; 'what the Italians call the *gusto grande*', v. 28.

Gutter, falling in a, ii. 191; iii. 155.

Guyon, in Spenser, iv. 428–9.

Gwyn, Eleanor, her performance in *Tyrannic Love*, iii. 266.

GWINIFRID, Mrs., a heart full of love for, ii. 384.

Gyas, a colourless character in the *Aeneid*, ii. 562.

Gyges (Lydian monarch), anecdote of, v. 86–87.

Gymnosophists, Indian, education of their disciples, iii. 249.

H—'s widow, v. 128.

H., E.: petition of, quoted, v. 150–1.

H., Colonel W., v. 150.

Haarlem, prevalence of fat ladies in, i. 134.

Haberdasher, i. 202, 223; BEAVER, i. 209; 'like a haberdasher's shop', ii. 132; John Sly, ii. 237–8; iv. 376; SAMUEL FELT, iii. 418; who was oracle of the coffee-house, iii. 509; any h. in Cheapside, iv. 91; JOHN FELT, iv. 517.

Habit(s): good h. long to acquire, ii. 116; role of, in reading, iii. 235–6; effects of, iv. 69–73; how confirmed, v. 55–56.

Hack(s), iv. 101, 311; hackneys, i. 388.

Hackney-boat, in Holland, ii. 17.

Hackney-coach, i. 376; ii. 217, 345; iii. 213, 490; iv. 286, 478.

Hackney-coachman (men), ii. 291; iv. 47, 99; Sir ROGER demands an elderly, iii. 213; amateur, iv. 265–8, 374–6.

Hackney-horses, Hobson the first to let, iv. 309–10.

Hadrian, Emperor, ii. *430*; iv. 256; dying words of, iv. 396–7; the H. Tower, v. 111.

Haemus mountains, cool shades and retirements of, iv. 325.

Hags: whose bloom was given up to WILL HONEYCOMB'S arms, ii. 94; industrious h. in service of lust, iii. 567.

Hague, The: dispatch from, iii. 439; advices from, iv. 91; Haga's Towers v. 120.

Hailes, Lord (Sir David Dalrymple), iv. *251*.

Hair: curling, i. 12; adjusting of, women's principal employment, i. 46; tied up in a knot, i. 214; well curled and powdered, i. 434; thrown into the nicest curls, ii. 320; a ring containing mistress's, ii. 453; my own h. woven in ringlets, ii. 576; cut and divided very prettily, ii. 580; a woman to cut my, iii. 183; JACK FREELOVE slain by MELISSA in her, iii. 418; the author of powder for colouring, iv. 129; a lock of grey, iv. 510.

Hair, men's: grey and black h. plucked out by wives, i. 143; going in his own h. at home, ii. 14; short h. formerly fashionable, ii. 91; TOM TOWNLEY has red, iii. 183; turning grey from fear, iv. 423; v. 102.

Hair-coloured silk, iii. 595.

Hal, Prince: jests with Falstaff, i. 75; Wilks as, iii. 393–4.

Half: Hesiod's paradox, the h. is more than the whole, ii. 286; h.-crown paid

at the theatre, iii. 252, 268; h.-glances, iv. 246; saving a h.-penny each day, iv. 231; a captain's h.-pike, ii. 22; *half seas over* (prov.), v. 106; cleanliness one of the h.-virtues, v. 157; the h.-virtuous and the h.-wise, ii. 592; a h.-way bridge, iv. 316; a creature of h. wit, iii. 394.

Halifax, Charles Montagu, Baron, i. xxx; a subscriber, i. *lxxxviii*; member of Kit-Cat Club, i. 42; lines by (?), i. 340; friendship for Budgell, iii. 265; complimented by Tickell, v. 122; dedication to, v. 176–7.

Halifax, George Savile, Marquis of: Dryden's dedication of *King Arthur* to, iii. 570; anecdote of Locke in company with, iv. 403; *Advice to a Daughter*, i. 156, 159; ii. 168.

Hall, John, translation of Sapphic fragments, ii. 365.

Halley, Edmond; iv. 5, 365; astronomical observations of, iv. 481.

Halley, Robert, iv. 252.

Halsey, Edmund, M.P., a subscriber, i. lxxxix, *xc*.

Halsey, R. (bookseller), iv. 130, 459.

Hamadryad(s): legends of, v. 16; story of Rhaecus and the, v. 16–17.

Hamilton, Elizabeth, Duchess of, a subscriber, i. *lxxxviii*.

Hamilton, James Douglas, 4th Duke of, duel with Mohun, iii. 438.

HAMMERCLOTH, TOM, an amateur coachman, iv. 376.

Hammond, Dr. Henry, his reflection on his illness, iv. 564–5.

Hampshire, iv. 225.

Hams, and Portugal onions, ii. 530.

Hand: making love by squeezing the, i. 451; the PERVERSE WIDOW 'has the finest', i. 463, 466; silks and laces sold 'at the best h.', iii. 26; a woman's h. playing with the glove off, iii. 417; *living from h. to mouth* (prov.), iv. 83; he has the whitest h. you ever saw, iv. 210; reading the future in lines of a man's, iv. 292; one h. in the fob, and a negligent swing of the other, iv. 345; knotting shows a beau's white h. to advantage, iv. 413; motion of, in acting, iv. 436; 'what constitutes a squeeze of the', v. 23; when to allow a suitor to kiss a lady's, v. 23.

Hands: a horse of fourteen h. high, ii. 182; pomatum for, iv. 129; ambition has taught some to walk upon their, iv. 544; whiteness of WILL HONEYCOMB'S, v. 185.

Handel, George Frederick, 'the Orpheus of our age', i. 26. See also *Pastor Fido*, *Rinaldo*.

Handicraft(s): of an idle man, i. 447; need for learning, i. 185; English skill in, i. 214; a project to improve h. trades, ii. 133–4, 181; letter from a plain h. man, ii. 327; importance of, even to the great genius, iii. 319.

Handkerchief(s), i. 351; use of, in English tragedy, i. 187; throwing of, in *Ibrahim*, i. 218; picture of Titus Oates in plaits of a, i. 244; Othello's uneasiness over a, i. 244; iv. 219; poetical, i. 248; and weeping, i. 403; an unfolded h. formerly fashionable, ii. 91; CLARINDA'S flowered, iii. 183; neck-h., iv. 195.

Handmaid: decency the h. to religion, iii. 40; an h. in a straw-hat, iii. 95.

Handsome: powers and responsibilities of the, ii. 68–69; Cato would not allow any but a virtuous man to be, ii. 444; the H. Club, i. 76.

Handwriting: of the merchant a portable coin, ii. 351; write a good hand, iii. 104; a hand generally used for engrossing bills in Chancery, iii. 207; reading the future from, iv. 292.

'Hang up a client a whole term' (legal jargon), iv. 478.

Hanger, John (a Director of the Bank), a subscriber, i. *xc*.

Hanging: Gardens of Babylon, iii. 554; in chains, iv. 290; for stealing sheep, v. 93.

Hangings: in *The Emperor of the Moon*, i. 93, 94, 149; in a lady's dressing-room, i. 175; for closets, beds, window-curtains, iii. 206; embroidered in needlework, v. 71–73, 83.

Hangman, writings burnt by the common, ii. 219.

Hanmer, Sir Thomas (Speaker of the House), ii. 552; iv. 392.

Hannam, John, a toy-shop in Cheapside, iv. 129.

Hannibal, contrasted with Pyrrhus, ii. 444.

Hannibal's Overthrow. See Lee, *Sophonisba.*

Hanover: succession of house of, iii. 441, 444; minister of (*see* Bothmar).

Happiness: to be found in retirement and obscurity, i. 67; v. 85–86; Martial on the perfection of, i. 108; doubled by friendship, i. 289; in marriage, ii. 87–88, 279–82, 514–16, 545; iv. 197–200; inquiries after, less useful than arts of consolation, ii. 139; not to be found in this world, ii. 139, 268; iii. 128–9; iv. 561–5; fame, glory, wealth, and

honour only secondary ingredients towards, ii. 158, 545–6; the mother of pleasure and the child of virtue, ii. 222; most men pursue outward show rather than real, ii. 257; inquiry after, has something restless in it, ii. 268; doubled by moderation, ii. 306–9; virtue the source of, ii. 443–6; incompatible with fame, ii. 493–8; in after-life prevented by love of fame, ii. 499–502; over-sanguine expectations of, ii. 597–9; in this world proceeds from suppression of our desires, in the next world from gratification of them, iv. 565; v. 169; and unhappiness the result of our own actions, v. 64–65.

Happy: 'for making a man h.: £10', ii. 465; 'this happy man (as the phrase is)', iv. 225; 'those happy few', iv. 327; that man is most h. who is least miserable, iv. 463.

Harbin, R., printer of Lillie's collection of letters, i. xxiii.

Harcourt, Simon, Lord, a subscriber, i. lxxxviii–lxxxix.

Hard: 'to buy hard', ii. 108; h. words and dark expressions, ii. 151; h. features, ii. 183.

Hardness(es): a result of brutality in education, ii. 116; of heart towards one's children, ii. 213.

Hardwicke, Earl of. See Yorke.

HARDY, Colonel, and MARINET, iii. 499.

Hare, Francis, The Charge of God to Joshua, advertised, ii. 51.

Hare(s), iii. 274; hunting, i. 447, 473, 477; ii. 19, 164; witches helping a h. to escape from hounds, i. 481; qualified to kill an h. or a pheasant, i. 498; is constantly breeding, v. 163.

Harford, Mr., at the Acorn in York Street, Covent Garden, i. 433.

Harington (or Harrington), James: 'my wife answers me out of H's Oceana', ii. 195.

Harleian Miscellany, iii. 372.

Harlequin(s): at the masquerade, i. 63; in The Emperor of the Moon, i. 93–94; tickled to death, iii. 268.

Harley, Edward (a Director of S. Sea Co.), a subscriber, i. xc.

Harley, Robert. See Oxford.

Harley, Thomas, iv. 501.

HARMLESS, BOB: letter from (a love problem), iii. 136.

Harp, invented by Sappho, ii. 408.

HARPATH, brother of SHALUM, iv. 596–7.

Harper, Charles (bookseller), iii. 440.

Harper, Robert (conveyancer), a contributor (?), i. lvi; iv. 204.

Harpsichord, iii. 205, 352.

Harpy (-ies): symbols of cares and passions, ii. 124; prophecy of the, in Aeneid, iii. 306; the consequence of vanity, iv. 123–4.

Harrington, James. See Harington.

Harriot: in The Funeral, i. 216; in The Man of Mode, i. 279.

HARRIOT: letter to, and reply, ii. 486–9; reply to letter from, iv. 588.

Harris, ——, in Steele's employ, i. xli.

Harris, Renatus, his proposal for an organ at St. Paul's, iv. 479.

HARRY: King H. laying his leg on the queen's lap in the puppet-show, i. 65; Sir H. 'has stolen all your songs', ii. 530; 'my nephew H.', v. 127.

Hart, Moses, a subscriber, i. xc.

Hart, Nicholas (the sleeper'), ii. 224–7; iv. 438.

Hasps, little silver h. instead of buttons, ii. 193.

Hastiness (ill-temper), toward a servant, ii. 293.

Hasty-pudding, receipt for, i. 451.

Hat(s), men's: cocked with unusual briskness, i. 161; broad and narrow brimmed, in comedy, i. 191; beavers, i. 361; iii. 522; laced, i. 488; iii. 341; iv. 552; party-spirit displayed in, ii. 2–3; now decreased in size, ii. 74; broad-brimmed formerly fashionable, ii. 91; to cock up the, ii. 91; a pinched, ii. 113; a beaver-hat as a prize in wrestling, ii. 132; removing the h. to women, ii. 358; various cocks of, iii. 162; to appear at White's in a cherry-coloured, iii. 163; twirl the cock of a squire's h. behind him, iii. 322; return the civilities of the, iii. 347; the button on, iii. 522; cocks and pinches to show party allegiance, iv. 17–18; the h. and feather, iv. 28; John Sly's reports on, iv. 399–400, 408, 453; French h. of a prodigious magnitude, iv. 453; monstrous broad-brimmed, iv. 484; cocked with a distich, v. 106.

Hat(s), women's: buttoned with a diamond, i. 67; a little beaver h. edged with silver, i. 434; an hand-maid in a straw, iii. 95; women who adopt the h. and feather, iv. 28.

Hat-band(s), iv. 246; crape, i. 276; mourning, iii. 401.

Hat-case, i. 361.

Hatred: Plutarch on, i. 510; the wise man hates no body, ii. 444; of virtue

and vice, ii. 445–6; rancour and h. among Christians, iv. 334.

Hatton, Edward, *A New View of London*, i. *4*, *36*; ii. *57*, *102*, *200*, *579*; iii. *48*, *93*, *94*, *149*, *225*, *294*, *344*, *417*; iv. *101*, *221*, *293*, *306*, *311*, *342*, *343*, *483*, *536*; v. *83*.

Hatton, Sir Thomas: Harriet, wife of, iii. *78*.

Haunch of venison, the best sauce for a, iv. 210.

Haunted places, i. 453–6.

Hautboy, ii. 73.

Hauteur, a French word imported, ii. 152.

Havers, G., translation of Scudéry, i. *156*.

Hawes, Francis (a Director of S. Sea Co.), i. *xc*.

Hawkins, Sir John, *General History of Music*, iv. 55.

Hawkins & Young's *Spelling Book*, i. *155*.

Hawkers, street, ii. 89.

Hawk's eye, denotes a sharp piercing nature, ii. 471.

Haws, grow naturally in England, i. 295.

Hay-harvest, iii. 189, 210.

Haym, Nicolino Francesco, i. lvi; letters from, ii. 505–7, 584–5. See also *Arsinoe*, *Camilla*, and *Pyrrhus and Demetrius* (operas).

Hazel-twigs, i. 447.

Hazlitt, William, ii. *381*.

Head, Richard, i. *78*.

Head(s): beautiful appearance of the, i. 415; breaking, ii. 371; iv. 282–3; washing with cold water, ii. 387; dissection of a beau's, ii. 570–3; the various leanings and bendings of the, ii. 581; Friar Bacon's speaking, iv. 514.

Head(s) (head-dresses), ii. 525, 531; iii. 182; extremely high, ii. 580; will shoot up again, iv. 484.

Head-clothes, ii. 195.

Head-dress(es), i. 342; ii. 247, 459; bushy, i. 71; fashions in, i. 413–16; ii. 5, 12–15, 530–3, 580; Conecte's crusade against, i. 414–15; old-fashioned high, i. 488; with a hooped petticoat, ii. 14; made of a cherry-coloured ribbon, ii. 192–3; lappets of, ii. 345; colours of, ii. 530–1; of birds, ii. 531; of the PERVERSE WIDOW, iii. 54; stocks rise or fall in proportion to, iv. 18. *See also* Commodes, Fontanges.

Head-strings, i. 134.

Health: undue anxiety about, i. 105–8; complaining about, in company, i. 420; ii. 64–68; preservation of, by exercise, i. 471–4, 478–9; ii. 263–4; and estate ruined by gallantry, ii. 105; influence of, on our bodies and minds, ii. 137, a great cherisher of good nature, ii. 165–6; temperance a preservative of, ii. 264–7; of mothers encouraged by nursing of children, ii. 457; no one can enjoy h. who is only not sick, iii. 38; cheerfulness the best promoter of, iii. 451; pleasures of the fancy conducive to, iii. 539; cleanliness a preservative of, v. 157.

Hearne, Thomas, iii. *381*, *459*; quoted, i. *183*, *298*, *359–60*, *363*; iii. *186*, *339*; No. 133 sent to, ii. *28*.

HEART, ANN, iii. *493*.

Heart(s): in love has its foundations sapped, ii. 141; 'An Hue and Cry after a stray', ii. 317; avarice a passion of the, ii. 372–3; breaking one's, ii. 383; figure of a h. as a token for absent lovers, ii. 452–3; good-breeding has made the tongue falsify the, ii. 479; to make the h. better, the purpose of the *Spectator*, ii. 517; 'earnings' of h. in a father, ii. 521; dissection of a coquette's, ii. 594–7; broken, iii. 24; a warm h. superior to great talents, iv. 445; dream-vision of examination of, v. 7–9.

HEARTFREE, MARY, letter from (on the language of the eye), ii. 478–80.

'Hearty neighbours, Those whom they call', iii. 72.

Heat: of summer and hoop-petticoats, ii. 5–6; and cold, why made agreeable to man, iii. 453.

Heathcote, Sir Gilbert: a subscriber, i. lxxxix; as an original of Sir ANDREW FREEPORT, i. *10*.

Heathen philosopher, the vulgar definition of a, ii. 91.

Heathen virtues, so many 'shining sins', ii. 331.

Heathens, the: their notions of religion, ii. 310–14; precepts of, to reinforce a paper on morality, ii. 334; valued a man for his good fortune, iii. 43; recognized omnipresence of God, iv. 583; their high regard for sacred trees, v. 15; had an imperfect knowledge of a future state, v. 164.

Heats: a woman's face breaking out in, i. 243; and extravagances, i. 243; and prepossessions that cleave to parties, ii. 1; of youth temporarily extinguish devotion, ii. 287; of devotion to be tempered with caution and prudence, ii. 289; the first h. of desire, ii. 515; valetudinary friendship, subject to h. and colds, iii. 74.

Heaven(s) (vault overarching the earth):

pleasing to the imagination, iii. 541; the handiwork of God, iv. 143–5; beauty of, at night, iv. 529–30.

Heaven(s) (habitation of God and angels; state of the blessed hereafter): pleasure, happiness, and virtue, residents of, ii. 222; belief in, is to our interest, ii. 231; government in, monarchical, iii. 21; beauty of description of, in *PL*, iii. 566; the natural effect of a religious life, iv. 72; our knowledge of, iv. 582–6; Cowley's description of, v. 20–21; notions of, v. 48–53. *See also* Eternity, Immortality.

Heaven (Providence, God): action in *PL* punished by, ii. 541.

Heavenly bodies: Milton's account of, iii. 64; knowledge of, requisite to the orator, v. 164.

Heavenly wisdom, vision of, iv. 365–9.

Hebdomadal meeting at Oxford, i. 181–3.

Hebdomadal societies at Oxford, i. 76.

Hebraisms: in *PL*, iii. 12; infusion of, in English, iii. 514.

Hebrew language: on monuments, i. 110; beauty of, iii. 514–15.

HECATISSA: asks to be admitted to the Ugly Club, i. 205–6; suggestion that Mr. SPECTATOR marry her, i. 220–3; letter from, i. 339–41; mentioned, i. 370; 'the heroic H.'s rival', iii. 34.

HECTICK, Lady, iii. 183.

Hectick, a lingering, i. 105.

Hector: his advice to Andromache, i. 241; and Priam imitated in Pallas and Evander, ii. 563; wife of, in *The Distressed Mother*, iii. 32–33; battle with Achilles, iii. 173; iv. 134, 473; Sir ROGER had read his life, iii. 240.

Hectoring, the, a subdivision of the angry, iv. 41.

Hecuba, mother of Troilus, i. 246.

HEDGEDITCH, ISAAC, letter from (a poacher), ii. 164.

Hedges, Sir Charles, i. xvi.

Hedges: trespass in breaking of, i. 498; rows of, set off by trees and flowers, iii. 552.

Heedlessness(es): of a wife, ii. 261; attentive, iv. 246.

Heels: red, i. 70; higher h. to his shoes, ii. 388; sent him out of the house with his h. foremost, iv. 518.

Heidegger, John James, i. *132*.

Height of stature, in EUDOSIA, ii. 70.

Heir(s): mourning now worn by h. and widows, i. 275; WILL WIMBLE a favourite of all the young, i. 447; education of h. to estates, i. 501–2; an h. of a great house who seduced a girl,

ii. 245; good and bad, ii. 253–4; extravagant, iv. 315; prodigal young h. who destroy trees, v. 14–15.

Helen of Troy: rape of, ii. 539; in modern poems, iv. 362.

Heliodorus, on the motion of the gods, iii. 389.

Hell: a Platonic, i. 382; 'in an hell', ii. 87; pain, misery, and vice residents of, ii. 222; in *PL*, ii. 541–2; iii. 84–90, 114–20; Milton's description of, less pleasing than that of Paradise, iii. 567; pains of, prepared for in this life, iv. 72–73.

Hell-doom'd, a word coined by Milton, iii. 13.

Hell-hounds: produced by Sin and Death, iii. 119; in a stage-coach, iv. 402.

Hellenisms, used by Virgil and Horace, iii. 12.

Hellier, John (wine-merchant). *See* Brook and Hellier.

Helmet of Minerva, covered a whole army, iii. 258.

Hemistich, speeches that close with a, i. 165.

Hempen manufacture, i. 36.

Hemsly Turk (a horse), ii. 117.

Hen: care of her nest and chickens, i. 492; and a brood of ducks, i. 493; a Friesland, ii. 13.

Hendecasyllabi, Catullus and the authors of, iv. 397.

Henley, Anthony: writer for the *Medley*, iii. *380*; referred to(?), iv. 251.

Henley, John ('Orator'): a contributor(?), i. lvi–lvii; iii. *483*; iv. 345; on punning in Cambridge, i. *261*.

HENPECK, JOSIAH, letter from ('married to a grimalkin'), ii. 327.

Henpecked, the, ii. 193–6, 303; iv. 197–200, 208–9; the revolt of a h. husband, ii. 328–30, 342–4; iv. 461; the fraternity of, iv. 208, 223; h. lovers, iv. 223–6.

Henri IV: equestrian statue of, i. 59; opposed by the League, iv. *91*; assassinated by Ravaillac, iv. 220.

HENRIETTA, letter from to her suitor, ii. 355.

HENROOST, NATHANIEL (a slave to his wife): letter from, ii. 194–6; this letter praised, iv. 460.

Henry, Prince, Duke of Gloucester (son of Charles I), v. 149.

Henry III, iii. 215.

Henry IV: and the Duchy of Lancaster, i. *73*; in *Chevy Chase*, i. 300, 321; his 'tomb in Westminster Abbey', iii. 215.

Henry V: silver head stolen from his monument, iii. 215; glorious name of, iii. 216.

Henry VI, and Cardinal Beaufort, ii. 323.

Henry VII, costume in time of, i. 450.

Henry VIII, letter of Anne Boleyn to, quoted, iii. 487.

Henry the Proud, Duke of Bavaria, iv. 269.

Hensburg, women of, iv. 269.

Hephaestion, Bullock's petition to be, i. 151.

Hera: eye of an ox, bull, or cow applied to, ii. 471.

Heraclitus, his comment on dreams, iv. 229.

Heraldry: a libertine with a smattering of, ii. 296; the Herald's office, ii. 296; spangles of Herald's coat, ii. 470.

Herbert, Edward (first Baron Herbert of Cherbury), De Veritate, ii. 288.

Herbert, George: false wit in poetry of, i. 247; borrowing from, iv. 98.

Herbert, Philip. See Pembroke.

Herbs: salads of twenty different h. in a modern meal, ii. 264–5.

Hercules: task of, clearing city from monsters, i. 116, 150; and Hylas in Hudibras, i. 252; statues of Commodus as, ii. 11; 'Choice of', ii. 221; statue of (Belvedere Torso), ii. 390; the Trunk-maker to combine H. and Apollo, ii. 416; Telephus, son of, ii. 455; mentioned, ii. 562.

Hercules (opera), i. 23; iii. 514.

Herefordshire (wine), iii. 355.

Hermaphrodites (women in mannish dress), iv. 28.

Hermes Trismegistus, the Smaragdine Table of, iii. 600.

Hermetic mysteries, knowledge of, iii. 598.

Hermione (in The Distressed Mother), iii. 241; Mrs. Porter as, iii. 371.

Hermit, anecdote of a youth and a, iv. 566.

Hermit, The (periodical), ii. 60, 106.

Hero and Leander, i. 265; ii. 383.

Hero(es): often lies hid in the plebeian, ii. 338; glory, the fame of, ii. 349; treatment of, in burlesque, ii. 467; Homer's and Virgil's directed by some deity, iii. 43; the Messiah the h. of PL, iii. 59; always drawn struggling with adversities, iii. 129; compared to a thunderbolt, a lion, and the sea, v. 35.

Herod and Mariamne, story of, ii. 176–8.

Herodotus: iii. 554; iv. 506; often applies judgement impertinently, iv. 212;

adapted his books to the number of the Muses, v. 159; on the Persians' instruction of their sons, i. 418; on the Persians' opinions of parricide, ii. 244; story of Amazons and Scythians in, iv. 22; story of Biton and Cleobis, iv. 214; story of Persian fairs for sale of unmarried women, iv. 314–15; Croesus' release from being tongue-tied, iv. 498, 514; on publicizing of cures in Babylonia, iv. 552–3; 'the most useful animals are the most fruitful in their generation', v. 163.

Heroic: actions possible to all, ii. 462–3; Heroic Daughter by Cibber: see Cibber, Ximena; Heroick Love (puppet show), i. 61; minds disregard unmerited reproaches, iv. 44; poetry: see Epic Poetry; an h. scribbler called a great genius, ii. 126; verse, when suitable for burlesque, ii. 468; virtue in common life, ii. 433.

Heroicism, always surrounded with a shade of distress, iii. 129.

Heroine ('as the phrase is'), the, ii. 553.

Herrings, pickled: as drolls in Holland, i. 201; at a whistling match, ii. 207; of the quack doctor, iv. 552; in Cave of Trophonius, v. 46.

Hervey, John, Lord, iv. 392.

Hesiod: compared with Milton, i. 55; iii. 84; praises dancing, i. 284; mentioned, ii. 76; 'the half is more than the whole', ii. 286; sublime description of the Giants' War, iii. 229; represents the Muses surrounding Jupiter, iii. 516; 'labour placed before virtue', iv. 72.

HESPERUS, his leap into the Ionian sea, ii. 408.

Hessebon, form of the word used by Milton, iii. 13.

Heterodox, wrong notions of religion ranked under name of, ii. 472.

Heteroptics (varieties of glances), ii. 472.

Hevelius, Johannes, astronomical observations of, iv. 481.

Hewet, Mrs., i. 56.

Hexameters: hymn in, to the Virgin Mary, i. 254; a table for composing, ii. 357.

Heylyn, Peter: Ecclesia Restaurata, iii. 487; History of the Sabbath, iv. 586.

Heywood, James (linen-draper): a contributor, i. lvi; ii. 545; referred to (?), i. 209; mentioned, iv. 546.

Hickes, William, Oxford Jests, iii. 300; iv. 522.

Hickford's dancing-room, ii. 506.

Hierarchies: in Paradise, iv. 583; appropriate h. in Heaven, v. 52.

Hierocles: quoted, ii. 444; commentaries on Pythagoras, v. 4.

Hieroglyphics: a good courtier's habit and behaviour is hieroglyphical, i. 275–6; wrought in gingerbread, iii. 94: art of political characters and, iii. 98; used by Egyptians, iii. 424.

Higgins, —— (posture-master), i. 128; ii. 504.

Higgs, T. (apothecary), medicine advertised, iv. 61.

High Change, i. 293.

High Mall, walking the park at, iv. 38.

High Priest, prophecy by the, ii. 313.

High Street, Oxford, ii. 429; v. 108.

High Treason, beheading for, v. 93.

Highland dances, in a puppet-show, iii. 401.

Hill, Aaron, i. 25; translated Rinaldo, i. 63–64.

Hill, William, sen., 'historiographer' of Nicholas Hart, ii. 224–5.

HILPA and SHALUM, story of, iv. 596–8; v. 1–3, 83.

Hint, a man slow at a, iii. 65.

Hinton, Moll, i. 331.

HIPPARCHUS: his leap into the Ionian sea, ii. 407–8; his duel with PHILANDER, iv. 183.

Hipped (depressed), iii. 8.

Hippocrates: the British, i. 222; a distemper not mentioned by, iv. 590.

Hips and haws, grow naturally in England, i. 295.

Hiram, inspired with wisdom to build the Temple, iv. 584.

Hirst, James, the 'enamour'd footman' in No. 71 (?), i. 305.

Hispulla, Pliny's letter to, iv. 372–3.

Hissing: sounds in English, ii. 34; at the opera, iv. 56.

Historian, The, a new paper recommended, iii. 111.

Historian(s): natural h. on the barrenness of England, i. 295; account of Queen Anne's reign by a future, i. 424–6; liars might be called, ii. 38–39; proposal to teach the best Roman, ii. 395; describe Rosamond's Bower, ii. 596; the art of the, iii. 574; usually unable to give a clear narration of a battle, iv. 6; their interpretation of disasters, iv. 212–13.

Histories written by politicians, derive every action from some plot or contrivance, ii. 171.

History: we fall short of the ancients in, ii. 467; Milton's ostentatious references to, iii. 62; treatment of, by Homer, Virgil, and Milton, iii. 305–7; the art of writing, iii. 574; more instructive than newspapers, iv. 91.

History of Bretagne. See Argentré, d'.

History of Infant Baptism. See Wall, William.

History of Providence, i. lvii.

History of the Mohocks, iii. 186.

History of the Works of the Learned, iv. 114.

History-Painter, iii. 386.

History-Painting: Leonardo da Vinci a great master of, iv. 488–9; Italians excel in, iv. 496.

History-Picture of a fan, iv. 378.

History-Piece (painting), an instructive lecture, ii. 379.

Hive, a glass, i. 486.

Hoadly, Benjamin, i. 244; iv. 155.

Hoadly, John, i. 352; ii. 238.

Hob, in The Country Wake, iv. 282–3.

Hobbes, Thomas: the Discourse of Human Nature the best of his works, i. 200; his definition of laughter quoted, i. 200–1, 223; ii. 466; Leviathan, i. 431; iii. 536–7; on terms of art in the epic, iii. 63; on the imagination, iii. 576; on continent persons, iv. 245; his philosophy derived from observation of his own temper, v. 10–11.

Hobblers and skippers (dancers), iii. 112.

Hobby-horse(s), i. 272; iv. 274; v. 125.

Hobson's choice, iv. 309–10.

Hodges, James, Essays, ii. 449.

Hog in armour (prov.), i. 116, 197.

Hogs: eight killed for Christmas at Sir ROGER'S, ii. 550; brought your h. to a fair market (prov.), v. 37.

Hogs-puddings, sent by Sir ROGER to every poor family, ii. 550.

Hogarth, William, on time as an improver of paintings, i. 356.

Hole, a whispering, in coffee-houses, iv. 112.

Holiness: the title given to the Pope, ii. 352; the beauty of, represented by Raphael, ii. 379; the beauty of, created by grace and decorum, iii. 40; represented by Spenser in the Red-Cross Knight, iv. 428–9.

Holland: a tumbling monkey from, i. 119; ladies of ample proportions admired in, i. 134; sign of the Gaper in, i. 200; drolls in, called Pickled Herrings, i. 201; a story of gipsies, still fresh in, ii. 17; 'that exact nation', ii. 187; phrase used in, for bankrupts, ii. 187; Prince Eugene's arrival in, ii. 263; importing goods from, iii. 26; fine printing in, iii. 381; actors in,

contribute to charity, iii. 400; monthly pamphlets published in, iv. 113–14; represented as Belge in Spenser, iv. 429; style of painting in, iv. 496. *See also* Dutch.

Holland (linen): drawers, i. 218; 'fine H.', iii. 348; 'finest pieces of', iii. 380; an audacious display of the H. shirt, iv. 345.

HOLLIDAY, SUSAN; BETTY's rival in WILLIAM's affections, i. 485.

Holly: decorating a church, ii. 600; German and Dutch, iv. 104; in a winter garden, iv. 191.

Holy of Holies, as the habitation of God, iv. 583.

'Holy officiousness', in our most indifferent actions, ii. 333.

Holy Spirit, Milton's invocation to, iii. 84.

Holy Week, set apart for serious thoughts, i. 100.

HOME, MARY, letter to LYDIA (on her marriage), ii. 488–9.

HOMEBRED, PHILIP, letter from (on travel), iii. 366–70.

Homer: pleases the reader of common sense, i. 297; founded his poems on a precept of morality, i. 299; mentioned, i. 319; ii. 76, 154, 395; iii. 169, 219; iv. 171, 329; a natural genius, ii. 127–8; some critics consider his poems entirely allegorical, ii. 220–1; iii. 146; said to have had golden dreams, ii. 226; starts in the midst of things, ii. 539–40; superior to all other poets in variety and consistency of his characters, ii. 562; lack of delicacy in his sentiments, ii. 586–9; varies diction and metre to achieve the sublime, iii. 12–15; his similitudes ridiculed by Perrault and defended by Boileau, iii. 90–91; his heroes always directed by some deity, iii. 43; iv. 363; compared with Milton, iii. 59–60; no ostentatious display of learning in, iii. 62; Milton follows H. in plain and simple invocation to *PL*, iii. 84; his use of similes, iii. 91; Zoilus wrote against, iii. 221; sublimity of, iii. 230; parts of Ezekiel similar to, iii. 233; Alexander's passion for, iii. 247; lived near 300 years after Trojan War, iii. 305; speaks as little as possible in his own person, iii. 307; his use of allegorical figures, iii. 337; a description in H. has charmed more readers than a chapter in Aristotle, iii. 538; strikes the imagination with what is *great*, iii. 564–5; his epithets admired by antiquity, iv. 431; epitaphs on, iv. 473,

476–7; seven towns contended for his birthplace, iv. 473; 'that divine poet', iv. 477; Greek tongue deep and sonorous in, iv. 571; wrote on gardening, iv. 595; divided his poems into number of letters of Greek alphabet, v. 159; made his gods like men, that his men might appear like gods, v. 167. — *Iliad*: Thersites a celebrated ill-face, i. 77; quoted, i. 109, 284; iii. 565; Hector bids his wife concern herself about spinning, i. 241; mentioned, i. 246; calls Merion a fine dancer, i. 284; based on discords of Greek princes, i. 299; a striking simile in, ii. 127–8; cited, ii. 312 (*bis*); epithet for a man both timorous and saucy, ii. 399; 'the ox-eyed Juno', ii. 471; starts in the midst of things, ii. 539–40; action of, ii. 539–44; defective unity of, ii. 540; on the blood of the gods, ii. 570–1; burlesque images in, ii. 589; catalogue of ships, iii. 87; two deities on an oak, like vultures, iii. 172; description of Discord, iii. 173; Jupiter's weighing event of battle in scales, iii. 173; iv. 134; speeches begin directly, iii. 177; passage quoted by Longinus, iii. 177; tripods on golden wheels, iii. 201; Milton's imitation of, iii. 203–4; battles still 'rise one above another', iii. 228; ichor flowing from wounds of gods, iii. 232; the wounded Mars, iii. 232; description of the fight of the gods, iii. 233; on opening of gates of Heaven, iii. 257; description of arms and armour of gods, iii. 258; converse of Jupiter and Juno in Book XIV, iii. 311; calculation of time in, iii. 391; Achilles and Patroclus in, iii. 446; Phoenix speaks in allegory, and prayers called daughters of Jupiter, iii. 466–7; represents Muses surrounding Jupiter, iii. 516; iv. 583; reading it, like travelling through a great and wild country, iii. 564; Achilles morally vicious and only poetically good, iv. 464; Machaon in, iv. 551. — *Odyssey*: hero receives bags of wind from Aeolus, i. 17; an *Odyssey* by Tryphiodorus, i. 249–50; a striking simile in, ii. 128; as a moral allegory, ii. 221; iii. 146; description of stone of Sisyphus, ii. 485; Irus, the beggar, in, ii. 527; role of Ulysses in, ii. 564; burlesque images in, ii. 589; fable of, iii. 58; Ulysses' ship turned into a rock, iii. 145; piling of Ossa on Olympus and Pelion on Ossa a sublime passage, iii. 230; calculation of time in, iii. 391; description of a storm at sea

praised by Longinus, iv. 234; description of Penelope's web quoted, v. 73–74; character of Ulysses in, v. 75.

Honest men above party, an association of, proposed, i. 512; ii. 1–2.

HONESTUS, a judicious tradesman, iv. 57.

Honesty: undervalued in the present age, iii. 313–14; in trade, iv. 453–5.

HONEYCOMB, SIMON, letter from (describing his amours), ii. 103–6.

HONEYCOMB, WILL: character of, i. 12–13; his remarks on a 'young thing' at the play, i. 20–21; takes Mr. SPECTATOR to see ARIETTA, i. 48; reports that some ladies are offended by Mr. SPECTATOR's remarks, i. 142; mentioned, i. 144; and the 'Pict', i. 175–6; takes Mr. SPECTATOR to a lady's ruelle, i. 192; coat-pocket of, i. 197; visits Mrs. TRUELOVE with Mr. SPECTATOR and hears of Titus Oates, i. 243–4; on 'kissing dances', i. 286–7; his absent-mindedness, i. 329–30, 331–2; and Mr. SPECTATOR in a coffee-house, i. 331; on women's postscripts, i. 339; his 'studying of mankind' and dislike of pedantry, i. 436–7; his letter rallying Mr. SPECTATOR on a country life, ii. 21; his idea of a man of wit and pleasure, ii. 93; on 'good women' he has enjoyed, ii. 94–95; a common 'bite' with, ii. 111; pleased with cries of London, ii. 474; on women's hoods, ii. 532; on the 'outragiously virtuous', ii. 534; to examine the haunts of vice, ii. 537; always consulted in matters of fashion, ii. 581; his account of three sisters ruined by over-sanguine expectations, ii. 598–9; at a reading of The Distressed Mother, iii. 31; admires gallantries of Charles II's reign, iii. 76; sends the Spectator a letter from a wit to his mistress (allegory of love and old age), iii. 76–78; his proposals to widows, iii. 127; would like to know WILL SPRIGHTLY, iii. 164; his anecdote of a looking-glass in a snuff-box, iii. 190; on the usefulness of looking-glasses, iii. 191; on transmigration of souls, iii. 272–3; on the vices of the young, iii. 313; his unsuccessful courtships, iii. 343–5; behaviour in church of a friend of, iii. 427; says it is easier to steal an elderly woman, iii. 481; with SIR ROGER encounters a woman of the town, iii. 531–3; is now on the verge of threescore, iv. 183; thinks of marrying Lady BETTY SINGLE, iv. 183–4; his translation of an epigram

by Martial, iv. 239; letter from (on modern women of Hensburg), iv. 269–72; letter from (on auction of women at fairs), iv. 314–16; his marriage to a farmer's daughter, iv. 389–91, 440, 485; v. 67, 185; suggests TOM DAPPERWIT for the Club, iv. 391; may have been a 'cast shoeing-horn', iv. 415; did not take sufficient care of ladies' interests in the Club(?), iv. 469; last volume of Spectator dedicated to, v. 184–6.

Honeymoon: the first h. over, iii. 70; a battle in the, iii. 370; a young husband who did not outlive the, iv. 516; the first month of marriage, v. 79.

Honeysuckles and tuberoses in summer, iii. 595.

HONORIA: story of FLAVIA and ('the rival mother'), i. 384–8; contrasted with EMILIA, iii. 81.

Honour: mistaken h. in duelling, i. 359, 412, 419; in men is courage, in women chastity, i. 416; strained to madness in books of chivalry, i. 417; true and false, i. 418–19; iv. 201–3; women's h. protected by hoop-petticoats, ii. 6; contrasted with fame, ii. 48–49; sense of shame and h. in children, ii. 115; glorious sense of, in the Spartan boy, ii. 116; in women only peevishness(?), ii. 118; only a secondary ingredient towards happiness, ii. 158; debts of h. to be first discharged, ii. 335; virtue the source of, ii. 352; the title given to peers, ii. 352; the secret spring in competitions, ii. 371; education should infuse early notions of, ii. 374; adversity the post of h. in this life, ii. 422; and applause invigorate a noble spirit, ii. 426; the name given by men of the world to virtue, ii. 443; men of h. defamed by party attacks, ii. 446; ambition stimulates procuring of, ii. 490; 'to do h.' by curtsying, ii. 552; the 'point of h.' sometimes placed in the beard, iii. 222; undervalued in the present age, iii. 313; allegorical figure of decreasing h., iv. 122; revenge stalking in the robe of, iv. 326; TOM DREAD-NOUGHT vainly seeking a post of, v. 8; we may with more ease deserve h. than obtain it, v. 133.

Honours: and their relation to merit, ii. 352; and titles balanced against vanity, iv. 136.

Hood(s), i. 12, 177; the side-peep through a thin, ii. 472; of different colours worn by Whig and Tory ladies, ii. 531–3, 556–7; iii. 161; iv. 27, 460;

of all colours worn by ladies, ii. 547; a cherry-coloured, ii. 556; new-fashioned, ii. 561; a flame-coloured h. in a coquette's heart, ii. 596; peace or war expected 'as the white or red h. hath prevailed', iv. 18; the black h. of a young Quaker, v. 157.

Hooke, Robert: work on thermometer, ii. *426*, *519*; his 'wheel barometer', ii. *519*.

Hoop, throwing oneself through a, iv. 544.

Hoop-petticoat. *See* Petticoat.

'Hoot and hollow, I do not', ii. 20.

Hope(s): in youth and old age, ii. 102–3; danger in over-sanguine, ii. 251–2, 597–9; *the man who lives by h. will die by hunger* (prov.), ii. 252; the gentle gales of h. and fears, ii. 373; the discreet man's, ii. 377; exclusion of h. from hell, in *PL*, iii. 84; influence of, in human life, iv. 165–8; misapplied on temporal objects, iv. 409–12.

HOPEFULL, LAZARUS, an imaginary letter from, iv. 169.

HOPELESS, WILL letter from (on ambition), v. 94–95.

HOPEWELL, Mrs. MARTHA, a demurrer who married, i. 377–8.

HOPEWELL, SAM, letter from (on his marriage), i. 377–8.

Hopkins, John: version of the Psalms (with Thomas Sternhold): *eke* and *aye* in, ii. 305; replaced by Tate and Brady, ii. *305*.

Horace: satirized stage and court, i. 142; copied most of his criticisms from Aristotle, i. 166; very little mixed wit in, i. 266; precepts and illustrations in, i. 291; the greatest wit and critic in the Augustan age, ii. 220; and Virgil friends and admirers of each other, ii. 482; an excellent judge of human life, ii. 592; John Bond's notes on, iii. 18; mentioned, iii. 219; iv. 306, 468; travelling the Appian road with H. as a guide, iii. 369; a literal translation of reads awkwardly, iii. 515; takes fire when he has Homer in his view, iii. 565; Cowley's imitations of, iv. 329; wrote on gardening, iv. 595; a true critic, v. 26; the best original for familiar, critical, and moral epistolary verse, v. 112; some think he occasionally fell into vulgar diction and was negligent of versification, v. 113. — *Satires*: Tigellius the most humorous character in, an example of inconsistency, ii. 137–8, 363; mentions an author who wrote while standing on

one leg, ii. 355–6; ridicule of wise man of the Stoics, ii. *444*; Canidia in, iii. *75*; tells how his father pointed out living examples of virtue or vice, iii. 248; says that all men are vicious to a certain degree, iv. 462–3; our own misfortunes are more easy to us than those of any other person could be, iv. 506–7; quoted, ii. 137–8, 356; iii. 220; iv. 485, 500, 544. — *Odes*: Bentley's edition of, satirized, i. 117, *500–1*; iv. *162*; Cowley's imitation of, i. *470*; on difficulty of imitating Pindar, ii. 128; jealousy admirably described in, ii. 173; on Prometheus' man of clay, ii. 324–5; Venus the goddess who delights in laughter, ii. 468; Hellenisms in, iii. 12; advice to Dellius, iii. 129; advises us not to hope for anything which lies at a great distance from us, iv. 409; quoted, i. 317, 363; ii. 173, *496*; v. 103. — *Epodes*: Canidia in, iii. *75*; account of an old usurer (Alfius) in, iv. 466. — *Epistles*: considered the *Odyssey* an allegory, ii. *220*, 221; on conversing with the great, ii. 592; Horace's letter of recommendation to Claudius Nero, iv. 250–1; the famous Epistle to Augustus, v. 114; quoted, i. 458; ii. *498*, 520; iii. 549; iv. 485. — *Carmen saeculare*, quoted, iv. 232. — *Ars Poetica*: some incidents to be told, not represented, ii. 166; established rule not to have unnatural murders on stage, i. 189; mentioned, ii. 416; precepts in, ii. 483–4; the business of the stage is to instruct and please, ii. 503; Homer starts in the midst of things, ii. 539; little blemishes to be pardoned when the thought is great, iii. 10; advises plain and simple invocations, iii. 84; the poet should consider the nature and force of his genius, iii. 141; on stirring up pity, iii. *486*; quoted, ii. 166, 179, 189–90, 230; ii. 503; iii. 571; iv. 216; v. 116.

Horatii and Curatii, Corneille's play concerning the, i. 188.

Horizon: a spacious h. an image of liberty, iii. 541.

Hormus, a dance of the Lacedemonians, i. 284.

Horn: music of the sow-gelder's, ii. 475; of plenty, iii. 595–6; a drench tendered in the, iv. 178.

Hornbeam, in a winter garden, iv. 191.

Hornpipe, on a festival day, iii. 113.

Horrid (shaggy, rough), to make your visage less, iv. 5.

Horror: Raphael's depiction of, ii. 379;

and melancholy in fallen angels, ii. 421; a pleasing kind of, induced by writings about spirits, iii. 571; inspired by novelty, v. 139.

Hors d'œuvre, a frenzy, iv. 571.

Horse(s): breaking a, i. 239; building of the Trojan, i. 246; abuse of, by servants, i. 373; Persian boys instructed to manage the, i. 418; witches riding, i. 481; to ride the great, ii. 31; iv. 24; advertisement of a chestnut, ii. 117; whistle to a h. to make his waters pass, ii. 207; killing a great number of, ii. 372; a jockey's conversation about his, ii. 386; keeping mistresses, h. and hounds, ii. 546; a show of midgets, consisting of a man, a woman, and a h., ii. 557; a piebald h. strayed near Islington, iv. 92; clapped into the pound at Knightsbridge, iv. 93.

Horse-coursers, speeches of, in selling horses, ii. 246.

Horse-flesh, profoundly learned in, ii. 117.

Horse-hair, added to the wig, iv. 221.

Horse-matches, -races: at Newmarket, ii. 117; advertised at Coleshill, ii. 182; Charles II at, iv. 132.

Horseman, Oliver, i. xli.

Horsemanship, Methuen's address in, v. 183.

HORTENSIUS and SYLVANA, anecdote of, iii. 269–71.

Hospital: of invalids, ii. 405; Adam's vision of a h. or lazar-house, iii. 362.

Hot-cockles: an innocent diversion, ii. 451; an incident at, ii. 513.

HOTSPUR, letter from (on a *dévote*), iii. 320–1.

Hotspur (in Shakespeare), ii. 586.

HOTSPUR, Mr., and his wife, their behaviour in public, iii. 72.

HOTSPUR, JEOFFRY, petition of, iv. 10–11.

Hottentot: a female H. contrasted with an English beauty, v. 157.

Hottentots: a nation of atheists (?), iii. 461; their language a confused gabble, iii. 461.

Houdar de la Motte, Antoine, ii. *367*.

Hough, John (Bishop of Lichfield), iv. *499*.

Houghton, John: *Collection*, i. *241*.

Hounds. *See* Dogs.

Hour-glass, Saturn with a scythe and an, iii. 596.

House of Commons, i. 13; students of the, i. 209.

'Household stuff', iii. 189, 210.

Housekeepers (householders), libertine, iv. 384.

Housemaid: behaviour of a, ii. 513; turning away of an old, v. 80.

House-warming, a treat at a, iv. 342.

Houses, numbering of, i. *116*.

HOUSEWIFE, MARTHA, her letter to her husband, ii. 204.

Housewifery: COQUETILLA on Books of, i. 392; of Eve in *PL*, iii. 202; good, iii. 53, 206; a martyr to good, iii. 214.

Howard, Edward, *The British Princes*: the 'incomparable' poem, i. 184; quotation from, i. 185.

Howard, Edward. *See* Suffolk, 8th Earl of.

Howard, Henry. *See* Norfolk, 6th Duke of.

Howard, Sir Robert: on rhyme and blank verse, i. *164*. — *The Committee*: 'a good Church of England comedy', iii. 239; Estcourt as Ned Blunt in, iv. *155*.

Howard, Thomas. *See* Effingham, Lord.

Howdee's, ii. 67.

How-d'ye servants, ii. 67.

Huarte, Juan de San, *Examen de Ingenios*, iii. 106–7.

Huddled (disguised), ii. 218.

Hue and cry: 'after a stray heart', ii. 317; after a daughter, iii. 125.

Huet, Pierre Daniel, iii. *219*.

Hughes, —— (singer), i. *80*; iii. 297.

Hughes, John: contributions to *Spectator*, i. xlix–li; essays or portions attributed to, i. *388*; iii. *102*, 151; iv. *154*, *425*, *428*; *Letters* quoted, i. *23*; ii. *364–5*; iii. *514*; iv. *420*; *Siege of Damascus*, i. *339*; 'Barn-Elms', i. *387*; referred to (?), ii. *65*; iv. *396*; translation of Vertot, iii. *301*; *Calypso and Telemachus*, iii. *514*; story by, in *Tatler*, iv. *398*; *Ode to the Creator of the World*, iv. 420, 487; poem on Peace of Ryswick, iv. *479*; translation of Fontenelle, v. *44*.

Huguenots: brought over in herds, but not naturalized, i. 269; subjected to torture, ii. 430.

Hum, a, where the point is touched in a speech, i. 409.

Human Invention, road of (in vision of heavenly and worldly wisdom), iv. 369.

Human life, allegory of plants and, iv. 103–5.

Human nature: the same in all reasonable creatures and in all ages, i. 297, 357; inconsistency the greatest weakness of, ii. 137; immoral writers deprave, ii. 155; consciousness of doing

right the highest step to which it can arrive, ii. 181; a mixture of virtue and vice, ii. 223, 393–4; iv. 416–18, 463–4, 526–8; now lost under form and ceremony, ii. 318; as a whole not a proper subject for satire, ii. 320–1; reflections upon, the best means for self-improvement, ii. 341; *Spectator* represents it in all its changeable colours, ii. 450; masterpieces of, produced in first ages of the world, ii. 467; Milton had a perfect insight into, ii. 588; errors in Milton's syntax due to weakness of, iii. 10; equality in h.n. and civil government the basis of civil liberty, iii. 19; perfection of, the great end of government, iii. 22; excellence of, shown in attitude towards misfortune, iii. 128–9; the most useful object of study, iii. 523–4; tragedy corrects the insolence of, iv. 463; the ancients endeavoured to conceal weakness of, v. 164; heathen philosophers boasted they made it resemble the divine, v. 167. — DIGNITY OF HUMAN NATURE: objection to *Spectator*'s stress on, ii. 118; enforced by Christianity, ii. 232–3; and the idea of immortality, ii. 321; supported by the ancients, iv. 259; views on, iv. 416–20; arguments for, v. 10–14.

Human society, mutual dependence of, iv. 7.

Human virtues, books written to show the falsity of all, iv. 416.

Humanity: the ornament of our nature, i. 164; and good nature the mark of a gentleman, i. 324; a reader of common, i. 363; and good nature of Sir ROGER, i. 440; iii. 437; the *Spectator* inculcates, ii. 29; good breeding a kind of artificial, ii. 165; tender h. represented in portraiture, ii. 179–80; dependence a perpetual call upon, ii. 214; want of, is a man's own fault, ii. 254; an imitable piece of, ii. 350; and condescension of superiors, ii. 354; benevolence and h. the greatest compliment to our own being, ii. 394; giving vent to the h. which rose in him, iii. 32; the heart confesses its h. and flows out into tears, iii. 80; balanced against justice, iv. 137.

Humbledon Hill, Battle of, i. 301.

Hum-drum Club, i. 41.

Hume, Patrick, iii. 63, 174, 176; iv. 254.

Humility: always attended with a certain homage, i. 432; frequent instances of a proud, ii. 373; and majesty of Jesus portrayed by Raphael, ii. 380.

Hummums: in Covent Garden, iii. 225, 294; of the Mohock 'sweaters', iii. 294.

Humour (comicality): true and false, i. 145–8; to be controlled by reason and judgement, i. 146; genealogies of true and false, i. 147; *Spectators* on, well received and made up in sets, i. 245, 507–8; a woman's man has a wonderful deal of wit and, ii. 112; exquisite strokes of, in *Love for Love*, ii. 242; moderns excel ancients in, ii. 467; egotism allowable in works of, iv. 521; most effective when concealed in gravity, v. 105; an example of pedantic, v. 107. *See also* Laughter, Wit.

Humour(s) (mental disposition, temperament): changes and vicissitudes of, i. 292; obliging little h. of WILL WIMBLE, i. 447; labour or exercise ferments the, i. 471; of a sick person often driven out of one limb into another, ii. 5; taciturn h. of the English, ii. 32; folly of drinking to remove, ii. 54; of appearing in the fashionable world, ii. 102; Tigellius the most humorous character in Horace, ii. 137; histories which leave nothing to chance or, ii. 171; squeamish, ii. 246; exercise raises proper ferments in the, ii. 264; variety of, in man, ii. 324–5, 371; varieties of, in false wit, ii. 355; of the inquisitive, ii. 386–9; inquisitive h. of youth, ii. 396; child imbibes gross h. of its nurse, ii. 455; disparity in, the chief cause of unhappy marriages, ii. 515; a woman's h. revealed by colour of her head-dress, ii. 532; of affected negligence, iii. 6; indulgence in particularities of, iv. 10, 570–1; types of, iv. 53; h. so opposite in two creatures, v. 138; inconsistent with good sense, v. 143.

Humorist(s): a set of, i. 12; in every tavern, i. 102; Sir ROGER a, i. 440; Mr. SPECTATOR 'a great h. in all parts of his life', i. 425; flatterers in families of, ii. 292; an untractable, iii. 336; who invent songs and tunes of their own, ii. 477; the witty man sinks into a, ii. 511; account of a, ii. 526–7; England noted for whims and, iii. 396; evils of indulging, iv. 7–11; no h. allowed in the Infirmary for the Ill-natured, iv. 10; letter from a h. in gardening, iv. 188–92; or enthusiast, iv. 319; account of a h. who disregarded stated hours for eating and sleeping, iv. 570–1.

Humoursome: 'an old h. father', i. 9; 'an h. rich man', ii. 292.

Hump on the back, iv. 508, 510.

Humphrey, Duke of Gloucester (in *2 Henry VI*), murder of, ii. 323.

Hundredth Psalm, the ('All People'), manner of singing, ii. 305.

'Hung up by a writ of error' (legal jargon), iv. 478.

Hung-beef, a slice of, iii. 438.

Hungary, the malcontents in, i. 182.

Hungary water, a bottle of, in LEONORA's library, i. 156.

Hunger: in allegory of avarice and luxury, i. 235; and lust the most violent appetites in all creatures,i. 489; allegorical figure of, in Ovid, iii. 573.

Hunks: 'a close h. worth money', ii. 528.

Hunt, Arabella: Congreve's lines to, quoted, iv. 56.

Hunt, Mrs., stock of citron waters advertised, i. *340*.

'Hunt the Squirrel' (a dance), i. 285–6.

'Hunters', among the Mohocks, iii. 295.

Hunting: i. 232, 352, 447, 472–3, 473–9; Pascal's severity upon, i. 478; a country gentleman seldom hunts on his own grounds, ii. 18–19; cost and returns of, ii. 188–9; benefits of, ii. 264; h.-match in *Philaster*, ii. 434; an occupation of country gentlemen, iv. 177–9, 593.

Hurd, Richard (Bishop of Worcester): on Addison's style, i. xcviii; *Letters on Chivalry and Romance*, i. 26; comments on *Spectators*, i. *240*; ii. *151*; iii. *468, 539*; iv. *51*.

Hurley, Patrick, an expert at brag, iii. *113*.

Hurry, affectation of always being in a, iii. 6–7.

Hurt, William (printer of the *Flying Post*), iv. *112*.

Husband(s): books recommended by, for women, i. 391; account of a morose, ii. 11; letters from a constant (Steele's letters to Prue), ii. 60–64; crazy young h. of a court lady, ii. 134; types discussed by Halifax, ii. 168; jealous, ii. 168–72, 261–2; rules for behaviour towards a jealous, ii. 173–6; who gives his wife cause for jealousy, ii. 201–4; the considerate, ii. 203, 418–19; an improvident and lazy, ii. 326–7; the unkind and tyrannical, ii. 417–18; grief over an absent, ii. 435–6; complaint concerning a debauched, ii. 480; of great beauties hate their wives, iii. 104; a grave or elderly h. on the stage usually a cuckold, iv. 68; advice to, iv. 197–200; who is a cott-quean, iv.

209–10; saved by women of Hensburg, iv. 269–70; behaviour to his wife, iv. 313–14; story of a jealous, iv. 378–9; the Widow-Club's rules for management of a, iv. 518; a choleric h. who breaks china-ware, iv. 524–5; the six h. of the President of the Widow-Club, iv. 556–61; qualities necessary to a, v. 75–76. *See also* Henpecked, Marriage, Wife.

Husband (thrifty person): Sir ROGER a good, i. 444.

Husband and wife: often divided between luxury and avarice, i. 235; contrasting characters of, ii. 8–11; not terms of reproach, iv. 273.

'Husband and wife' (a school game), v. 38.

Husbandman: Sir HUMPHREY DE COVERLEY an excellent, i. 452; and country life, iii. 453; 'you may trace him' in improvements he has made, iv. 595.

Husbandry, good: in moral life, ii. 332.

HUSH, PETER: a whisperer in coffee-houses, iv. 112–13.

Hush-note: to be used against long stories, swearing, obscenities, &c., ii. 389.

Hussars, costume of, iv. 571.

Hussy, i. 485; ii. 442–3; iv. 224, 406.

Huygens, Christian, on the light of stars, iv. 530.

Hyacinths, iii. 311–12.

HYAENA, a melancholy and indolent jilt, ii. 237.

Hydaspes (opera), i. 23, 79; iii. 514; Nicolini's combat with the lion in, i. 55–59, 93; iii. 138–9.

Hydropical (dropsical), 'my body is become', i. 107.

Hylas, and Hercules, in *Hudibras*, i. 252.

Hymen: allegorical figure of, iv. 326; takes his revenge in kind, iv. 389.

Hymn(s): in hexameters to the Virgin Mary, i. 254; to Venus, by Sappho, ii. 367–9; hymn-tunes, iii. 8; by pagan poets and Jews, iv. 94–95; praise of h. in the *Spectator*, iv. 126; passions raised by, iv. 515. For 'Hymns' in the *Spectator see* Poems.

Hyperbole usual among the Rabbins, iv. 256.

Hypochondria: 'Hypo', i. 15; hypochondriacal fancies, iv. 415; cure for hypochondriac melancholy in *Spectators*, iv. 459.

Hypocrisy: in education of women, i. 49; in one age succeeded by atheism in another, i. 488; in religion, like good breeding without good nature, ii. 165;

more detestable than professed impiety, ii. 165; does great honour, or rather justice, to religion, ii. 443–4; to be judged only by God, ii. 500–1; iv. 253; and the art of pleasing others, ii. 592; Milton's digression upon, in *PL*, iii. 148; of self-deception, iii. 493–6; of Dissenters, iv. 117; preferable to open impiety, iv. 117; balanced against religion, iv. 136; guilt often leads to, iv. 300–1; at court of Louis XIV, iv. 336.

Hypocrites: promoting their own advantage under colour of public good, ii. 1; incapable of pleasure of agreeable conversation, ii. 592.

I., S. : 'slain by a lady's glance', iii. 418.
Iambics: in Greek most proper for tragedy, i. 164; of Simonides, ii. 318.
Iapis: a physician in Virgil, iv. 551; cured Aeneas, iv. 555–6.
Ichneumon, breaks eggs of crocodile, ii. 2.
Ichor, flowing from wounds of the gods, ii. 570; iii. 232.
Id populus curat scilicet, iv. 521.
Ida, Mount: torn up by one of the giants, iii. 230; a bed of flowers on, iii. 311; grove on, cut down by Aeneas, v. 15.
Ideas: Platonists' improbable talk of world of, i. 237; resemblance of, the source of wit, i. 263–5; iii. 559–60; opposition of, produces a kind of wit, i. 270; flow of, in the mind, i. 330; trains of, give us our notion of time and duration, i. 399; Locke on association of, i. 454; strike forcibly upon the imagination, ii. 25; transcripts of, ii. 153–4; innocent and pleasing, from contemplation of women, ii. 552–3; furnished to the imagination by the sense of sight, iii. 536–7; comparing, iii. 550, 559–60, 566–7; trains of, iii. 563; imagination receives, retains, and ranges, iii. 563; multitude and variety of, in dreams, iv. 228; Locke on complex and simple, iv. 393; the senses the inlets to, v. 158; are enlarged by revelation, v. 164; of God, v. 173.
Identity, theories concerning personal, iv. 575–6.
Idiom: an academy to settle controversies between grammar and, ii. 35; 'our vernacular', ii. 151; one of the words to suggest immense reading, iii. 347.
Idioms: mean phrases or, in Homer and

Virgil, iii. 12–13; Milton's use of foreign, iii. 62.
Idiomatic ways of speaking to be avoided in the epic, iii. 10–13.
Idiot: in *The Pilgrim*, i. 95; and the striking of a clock, iv. 69–70.
Idiots (jesters), i. 200, 223.
Idle, the: handicrafts of, i. 447; charity to, condemned, ii. 405; 'not idle' a modern phrase for studying hard, iii. 348; few know how to be idle and innocent, iii. 538–9; are apt to detract from accomplishments of others, v. 27; called 'fools at large' by Tillotson, v. 132.
Idleness: of Englishmen, i. 214; the 'Lowngers', i. 229–32; of younger sons, i. 447–9; 'meer gaps and chasms' in life, i. 395; a motive to fortune-hunting, iii. 126; a general distemper, iii. 148–51, 168; a 'lazy club', iii. 168–9; love is the daughter of, v. 23; compared by Plato to rust, v. 132. *See also* Indolence, Time.
Idol(s): in the Apocrypha, i. 313; in China whipped and scourged, i. 313; of a beau in a coquette's heart, ii. 596; HONORIA demands veneration as an, iii. 81.
'Idols' (women actuated by vanity): character of, i. 311–15; description of one, i. 340; referred to, i. 369; iv. 407; behaviour of those who serve in coffee-houses, i. 371–2; letter from one, ii. 107–8.
Ignatius, black sons of (i.e. Jesuits), iv. 452.
Ignis fatuus, v. 36.
Ignorance: and fear natural to the soul, i. 34; pedantry and, i. 262; ill effect of, on taste, i. 297; and heaviness in minds of ordinary men, i. 508; and rusticity of country people, ii. 15; of schoolmasters, ii. 115; of husband as cause of jealousy, ii. 170; most men blinded with, ii. 310; means of recovering our souls from, ii. 341; virtues obscured by, ii. 491; the effect of slavery, iii. 21; invincible, iv. 119; envy and cavil the fruits of laziness and, v. 27; of the future, a blessing, v. 65.
Ignorant, the: silly competitions among, ii. 185; minds of, unsettled by infidels, ii. 233; praise from, is only good-will, ii. 238; and the unwary to be warned by the *Spectator*, ii. 302.
IGNOTUS, a gentleman, character of, i. 324–5.
'Ill conditions', i. 306, 308.
Ill men naturally suspicious, iii. 599.

Illegitimate: propagation of i. children, ii. 295–7; letter from an i. son, ii. 298.

Ill-humoured: an Infirmary for the, described, iii. 591–2; histories of persons there, iv. 7–11, 46–48.

Ill nature: prevalence of, causing lampoons and satires, i. 71, 97; among ordinary observers passes for wit, ii. 167; and envy among all classes, ii. 186–7; avoided by a careful author, ii. 206; often passes for religious zeal, ii. 229; less harmful than indiscretion, ii. 293; of mankind, iii. 1; in critics, iii. 36; the *Spectator* a cure for, iv. 458.

Ill-natured: and froward, ii. 30, 194; i. man seems more witty than the good-natured, ii. 167; old saying concerning an i. fellow, ii. 455; take pleasure in crossing our inclinations, ii. 492; discover weaknesses in others' characters, ii. 494.

Ill will: towards those of different opinions, ii. 512; taking up that of our parents a sort of self-love, ii. 523; in FREELOVE's heart, v. 9.

Illness. *See* Sickness.

Illuminations: once a week with wax-candles, iii. 69; in Pandemonium, iii. 90.

Images: indelicate i. in plays, i. 216; in paintings, ii. 378–9; effect of, in epic poetry, iii. 90–91; 'fine i.' one of the phrases to suggest immense reading, iii. 347; compounded by the imagination, iii. 537; inconsistent, v. 35; the senses the inlets of all, v. 158.

Imaginary: invalids, i. 105–8; pleasure and pain i. distinctions, ii. 442; mourning for i. losses, ii. 597; i. persons in Chaos (Milton), iii. 120–1, 145–6; i. (allegorical) persons in epic poems, ii. 563–4; iii. 337–9, 393, 573; i. persons in *PL* Book XI, iii. 362; writings about fairies and other i. beings, iii. 570–3.

Imagination: value of a sound, i. 54; and judgement needed in writing works of humour, i. 145–6; books which only divert, i. 158; 'on the stretch', i. 159; objects of love which both inflame and chastise the, i. 304; a well-corrected lively, i. 421; and fear of goblins, i. 454; kept untroubled by physical exercise, i. 471; crazed, in witches, i. 480; in the formation of 'liars', ii. 36–40, 157; Shakespeare's, in *Macbeth*, ii. 58; a brisk i. in a schoolboy, ii. 115; in natural geniuses, ii. 128; Pindar's noble sallies of, ii. 128; in 'castle-builders', ii. 157–60; of a jealous husband, ii. 175; in sleep and dreams, ii. 227, 570; iv. 226–30; v. 29–30, 40–43; and religious enthusiasm, ii. 288–9; the painter's, ii. 378; in children, ii. 396; sallies of, when excusable, ii. 555; creative, ii. *586*; Caliban drawn from Shakespeare's, ii. 586–7; in Milton, ii. 587; iii. 147, 170–1, 201, 227, 332; incidents in *PL* which raise and terrify the reader's, iii. 85; in a pregnant wife, iii. 196; wildness of, in Claudian, iii. 230; pleased by natural sights and sounds, iii. 452, 475; warmed by Antony's description of Cleopatra, iii. 497; pleasures of the, iii. 535–82; synonymous with fancy, iii. 536–7; pleasures of, defined, iii. 535–9; primary pleasures of, iii. 540–4; iv. 233; secondary pleasures of, iii. 558–61; can enlarge, compound, and vary ideas, iii. 559; ranges ideas together, iii. 563; sometimes makes new worlds of its own, iii. 573; limited in contemplating infinity, iii. 575–7; the very life of poetry, iii. 578–9; has something in it like creation, iii. 579; disorders of, iii. 579; Table of Contents of 'Pleasures of', iii. 580–2; goes beyond sight in exploring the heavens, iv. 170; creative power of, in dreams, iv. 226–30; affected by sight of ocean, iv. 233–4; cannot comprehend Paradise, iv. 584; our happiness or misery dependent on, v. 5; strength of, v. 82; works of, v. 167; swiftness of, v. 172.

Imaginations: crazed by stories of ghosts, i. 53; dazzled by instances of virtue, ii. 462; men of lively i. often puzzle their affairs, iii. 2; wanton i. in Ovid, iii. 364; men of warm i. and towering thoughts, iv. 410.

Imitation: did not teach the bird to build its nest, i. 490; good breeding an i. of good nature, ii. 165; of the faults of the great, ii. 336–7; of qualities of others to be avoided, ii. 424–5; iv. 19, 196; of good characters, iv. 150–1; Estcourt's skill in, iv. 157; a kind of artless flattery, v. 70; of the Divine Nature required of Christians, v. 168–9.

Imitation (in literature and art): often breaks out in puns, i. 259; of Milton, Cowley, and Ovid, ii. 52–53; of other authors, ii. 128–9; iii. 255; of the best authors not to compare with a good original, ii. 129–30; compared with a translation, ii. 392; of nature, produces the best painting, ii. 447; of Homer and Virgil by Milton, ii. 540;

iii. 12–15; judgement required in i. of the ancients, iii. 177; servile i. of authors or painters, iv. 19.

Imma and Eginhart, story of, ii. 215–16.

Immateriality of the soul, an argument for immortality, i. 456–7.

Immodest: expressions learned by birds, i. 152; practices given soft and harmless names, iii. 65.

Immodesty: in plays, i. 215–20; in dancing, i. 285–7; in conversation, ii. 107–8, 439–40; iv. 57–58, 402–3.

Immorality: writers who propagate, ii. 155; to be a wit without i. requires genius and invention, ii. 205–6; immoral thoughts avoided in *Spectator*, ii. 517–18; the immoral man the object of derision in *Spectator*, iv. 65. *See also* Licentiousness.

Immortality: expectation of, in IGNOTUS, i. 324; arguments for, i. 455–9; ii. 321–4; iii. 43–44, 454; iv. 416–20, 489; v. 29, 142, 144–8, 170–1; ideas of, ii. 75–77; Socrates' discourse on, ii. 75–76; the discreet man's hopes are full of, ii. 377; poets give and receive, ii. 425; Cato and Cyrus on, iv. 418–20; Cicero on, iv. 418–20; v. 13, 164–5; capacity of the human mind an argument for, iv. 489, 566–9; v. 48–53; heathen notions of, imperfect, v. 164. *See also* Eternity.

Imperfection of man: an argument for immortality, i. 456–9; iii. 43–44, 454; makes it difficult to comprehend God, iv. 531.

Imperfections: false shame of one's, ii. 401; of others not to be ridiculed, ii. 466–7; revealed after marriage, ii. 516; false pride in one's, iv. 174–5; of nature sometimes pleasing, iv. 541. *See also* Faults.

Imperial Majesty, His. *See* Charles VI.

Impertinence(s): of staring, i. 86, 227; ii. 472–3; in visiting, i. 100–4; shown to women who sell in shops, ii. 108–9; made supportable by good nature, ii. 165; of rakes, ii. 217; only i. regarded at the play, ii. 314; women who regard a salutation as an, ii. 358; in conversation, ii. 386; of being always in a hurry, iii. 6.

Impertinent: mirth, ii. 67; wishes, ii. 100; coxcombs, ii. 248; self-love, iii. 16; no i. fellow allowed in the Infirmary for the Ill-natured, iv. 10.

Impertinents: types of, ii. 81–85; in public assemblies, ii. 162–4; immodest behaviour of, ii. 439–40.

Impiety: professors of, iii. 493; hypocrisy preferable to open, iv. 117–18.

Impostors: and incendiaries, ii. 39; among beggars, iv. 11–12.

Impotence after debauchery, ii. 94; of the old, ii. 100–1; false gallantry proceeds from i. of mind, iii. 24.

Imprecations, a beau's head filled with oaths and, ii. 571.

Impresses of giants and knights, iv. 18.

Impressions, first: always the strongest, iii. 249.

Impropriety: of language, i. 226; of sentiments in Homer, ii. 589; of speech in prayers, iii. 130–1.

Imprudent, Cardinal Richelieu's view of the, iii. 42.

Impudence: in 'Starers', i. 86; differs according to nationality, i. 87; of a recruiting officer, ii. 23–24; contrasted with modesty, iii. 303–4; not to be confounded with assurance, iii. 404–5; in gay fellows about town, iii. 434; in Congreve's Doris, iv. 57–58; now out of fashion, iv. 128.

Impudent: how SIMON HONEYCOMB became an i. fellow, ii. 104; behaviour in a coffee-house, ii. 107–8; no creature more i. than a coward, ii. 398–9; an i. fellow mistaken for a man of true courage, ii. 447.

In aeternitatem pingo, i. 221.

In forma pauperis, i. 337; iv. 408.

In rerum Naturâ, ii. 442.

In usum Delphini, iii. 219.

Inadvertency (-ies): an irreligious i. complained of, ii. 420; a pardonable i. in Milton's syntax, iii. 10; work of a great genius, with many lapses and, iii. 38; and neglects cast a blemish upon a great character, iii. 82; childish i. of coquettes, iv. 246.

Inamoratos: in the Amorous Club, i. 124; all our poets are professed, iv. 371.

Inattention or dishumour, marks of ill nature, iii. 591.

Incarnation, The: contributes to heightening of morality, ii. 232–3; represented in *PL*, iii. 142; mysteries of, v. 165.

Ince, Richard, a contributor, i. lv–lvi; iv. 497.

Incendiary (-ies): and impostors, ii. 39; looked upon as an, ii. 344.

Incidents: *PL* filled with astonishing but credible, ii. 540–1, 543; contrast of, delightful in poetry, iii. 363.

Inclination(s): the best rule of life (?), ii. 118; ambition pulls one way, i. another, ii. 136; and duty, ii. 203,

300, 418–19; extravagancy of, in free-thinkers, ii. 412; of children determined by their nurses, ii. 455; no one has power over his, iii. 24; likeness of, not a requisite to friendship, iii. 447; draw the mind, like a bias, v. 12.

Inclinations (bows), politicians taught, iii. 99.

Incog., i. 176; ii. 465; a curtailment of *incognito*, ii. 34.

Inconsiderateness, inconsideration: towards women, ii. 109; and folly, the foundations of infidelity, ii. 232.

Inconsistency: of men, i. 112–13, 326; with ourselves in use of time, i. 394; the greatest weakness of human nature, ii. 136–9; of behaviour, ii. 234–7, 362–4; between private and public behaviour, ii. 388.

Inconstancy: disadvantages of, ii. 135–9; in heroine of *The Scornful Lady*, ii. 553.

Inconstant: a woman's man the most i. creature living, ii. 112; account of an i. friend, iii. 74.

Inconvenience, better to suffer a mischief than an (legal maxim), iv. 527.

Incurabili, large endowments given for, in Popish countries, ii. 245.

Indamora (in *Aurengzebe*), iii. 183.

Independent minister, gloomy behaviour of an, iv. 251.

Indeserts, men regard fame of others as a reflection on their own, ii. 493.

India: part inhabited by pygmies, i. 130; warehouse, ii. 480; cannibals in, called Mohocks, iii. 187; shop, iii. 196, 245; kings of, v. 118; 'either India's stores', v. 120.

India company, iii. 25.

Indian: maid (YARICO), i. 50; story of MARRATON and YARATILDA, i. 237–40; pith of I. cane, i. 295; canopies, i.295; expedition of Alexander, ii. 7; pine, ii. 82; who said 'I am all face', ii. 387; queens, ii. 532; iii. 162; goods, iii. 25; silks, iii. 26; princes, iii. 162; pagod, iii. 196; gymnosophists, iii. 249; Brachman, iii. 274; tax-gatherer, iii. 275; missionaries, iv. 453; ware, iv. 479.

Indian Kings, four, i. 61; their visit to London, i. 211–15; their story of MARRATON's visit to the world of spirits, i. 237–40.

Indians, uncultivated minds of, iv. 489–90.

Indies, the, iv. 305; v. 40; products of both the, v. 107; a Father Jesuit, Secretary of, iv. 451. *See also* East Indies, West Indies.

Indifference: and heedlessness of a wife,

ii. 261; agreeable freedom and, ii. 357; of a husband will grow into contempt, ii. 418; of a mistress, ii. 512–13; 'a modish state of i. between vice and virtue', iii. 181; to reports spread about one, iv. 44; as a reproof to the teller of extravagant stories, iv. 423. *See also* Ease.

INDIGO: 'Honest I. of the Change', ii. 40.

Indiscretion: more hurtful than ill-nature, i. 100; ii. 293; folly of, ii. 375–8; men led into indiscreet actions by false modesty, iv. 115–16.

Indisposition: of a sultan cured by exercise, ii. 263; abstinence destroys the first seeds of an, ii. 266; to company a mark of ill-nature, iii. 591.

Indolence: of the 'Lowngers', i. 231; an unbecoming quality, i. 420–1; of one of Sir ROGER's ancestors, i. 451; in the woman's man, ii. 110–12; preferable to striving after happiness, ii. 268; of a henpecked husband, ii. 328–9; unmanly, ii. 373; and coldness of a mistress, ii. 512–13; a pleasing and indolent old age, ii. 522; a stream which undermines the foundation of every virtue, iii. 149; a rust (and slumber) of the mind, iii. 149; as a support against evils, iii. 431; of humour conducive to long life, iii. 451; the ideal of the Epicureans, v. 167–8.

Indoles, ii. 114; *bona indoles*, ii. 117.

Indostan, diamond necklace from, i. 295.

Induitur, formosa est . . ., i. 263.

Industry: in allegory of avarice and luxury, i. 235; false wit the product of, i. 246, 249; and caprice the companions of dullness, i. 271; allegorical depiction of, in vision of painters, i. 355; in younger brothers, i. 449; leads to tranquillity, ii. 269; children put into, from charity schools, iii. 48.

'Infallible', a favourite word in medical advertisements, iv. 553.

Infamy: and scorn the consequences of vanity, iv. 124; product of vicious and imprudent acts, v. 65.

Infant baptism. *See* Wall, William.

Infant mortality, ii. 123–4.

Infants, abuses in nursing of, ii. 454–8.

Inferiors, method of pleasing, ii. 592.

Infidel(s): zeal and bigotry of, ii. 229–30; the free-thinker and, ii. 412; a fine gentleman now need not be an, iv. 128.

Infidelity: essay on, ii. 231–4; no fashionable touches of, in *Spectator*, ii. 517; marital i. not a proper subject for comedy, iv. 68; not as bad as immorality, iv. 119.

Infinitude: speculations of, pleasing to the understanding, iii. 541; pleasure in contemplating, iii. 574–6; of the universe, iv. 529–30; v. 17–18; *Spectator* essays on, pleasing, v. 144. *See also* Eternity.

Infirmary for the ill-humoured: described, iii. 591–2; histories of persons in, iv. 7–11, 46–48; approved, iv. 180–1.

Infirmities: of husbands, ii. 170–1; of men not to be concentrated upon, ii. 466–7; pleasure in proclaiming i. of a great man, ii. 494–5.

Informers buzzing about a great man, iv. 43.

Informis Societatis Socius, i. 136.

Ingenious: disposition, ii. 370; and learned man, ii. 556; device of Rabelais, iii. 4.

Ingenuity (ingenuousness): candour, sense, and, ii. 431; fame should be built on candour and, ii. 482; truth and, iii. 314; modesty and, in a young prince, iii. 404.

Ingenuous: behaviour, ii. 108; schoolboy, ii. 115–16; minds shy in public speaking, ii. 397; methods of pleasing which are worthy and, ii. 592; candour natural to an i. mind, iii. 433.

Ingoltson, Charles, a 'doctor' in Barbican, iv. 62.

Ingratitude: that vice which is said to comprehend all others, ii. 449; a vice inseparable to a lustful man, iv. 241.

Injured Love, or The Lady's Satisfaction, ii. 451.

Injustice, ii. 165; of a father, ii. 364; the gods not authors of, ii. 421; in princes, not encouraged by Christianity, iii. 442.

INKLE, THOMAS, and YARICO, i. 49–51, 196.

Inkle, an half-penny worth of, i. 202.

Inn: Sir ROGER would not bait at a Whig, ii. 3; the world an, ii. 353; the traveller who mistook a palace for an, iii. 30–31.

Inn-signs, i. 500; mottoes in the *Spectator* like, ii. 359.

Innocence: a melancholy carriage the usual effect of injured, ii. 175; leads to tranquillity, ii. 269; a woman who has given up, ii. 337; with a dash of folly, ridiculous, ii. 449–50; of St. Francis, ii. 450; *PL* shows man and woman in highest, ii. 563; often betrayed by beauty, iii. 79–80; the true safeguard of reputation, iii. 464–5; importance of, to the female sex, iii. 482.

'Innocent diversions', letter on, ii. 450–2.

Innocent as bread, a panacea as, iv. 458.

Innocent Adultery. See Southerne, *The Fatal Marriage*.

Innuendo: use of, in party-writing, iv. 537.

Inquietude(s): and doubts, ii. 235; only to be avoided in this life, ii. 268; induced by ambition, ii. 308–9.

Inquisition on Maids and Bachelors, iii. 165–6.

Inquisitive, the: and the malicious, ii. 350; character of, ii. 386–8 (testimonial to this paper, iv. 459); exercised with problem of evil, ii. 421.

Inquisitive: humour natural to youth, ii. 396; before marriage we should be i. in the faults of the person beloved, ii. 516; unwise to be i. about what others say of us, iv. 44–45.

Inquisitors, a circle of female, ii. 193.

Insects: impaled on a needle for microscopical observations, i. 91; cast their eggs as chance directs them, i. 490; detractors are like imperceptible, iv. 65.

Insensibility of a mistress, ii. 513.

Insensible, my pretty, ii. 236.

Insignificant persons, dangers from, iv. 219–20.

Insignificants, iv. 223.

Insipid: causes of i. life in marriage, ii. 87; ANTONY FREEMAN's i. way of life, ii. 329; smoothness in poetry, ii. 484; Euclid's i. mirth, iii. 14.

Insolence: of servants, i. 375; protest against, ii. 575; the crime every man is most apt to rail at, iii. 47; of beauty without its charms, iii. 76; of office, iv. 303; of beauty in women, v. 69.

Insolent: DULCIANARA an i. beauty, i. 341; 'all the blooming charms of an i. beauty', i. 367; equipage, iii. 599.

Inspector of Signs, i. 115–16; iii. 354, 413; iv. 438.

Inspector of Wonders, iv. 182.

Instinct: in animals, i. 489–97; ii. 136; iv. 347; of parental love, ii. 214, 243, 522; for devotion in the soul, ii. 288; of immortality, ii. 323; cunning a kind of, ii. 377. *See also* Reason.

Integrity: the chief ornament of the male sex, i. 30; of Cato preserved amidst ruins of his country, ii. 422; England produces men of i. rather than statesmen, iii. 100; better than dissimulation, iii. 314; defence of one's, iii. 479; bears in itself its reward, iv. 338; one of the great social virtues, iv. 502–3.

Intellects, judging the size of, by the nose, iv. 344.

Intelligence: necessary to the orator, ii. 398; every orb has its, iii. 147.

Intemperance: of country gentlemen, ii. 96; to sleep off an, ii. 202; not the same as drunkenness in polite circles, ii. 574.

Intention(s): to be considered as measure of approbation, ii. 180; influence of, upon our actions, ii. 331–4; actions measured by sincerity of, ii. 500–1.

Intents and purposes, To all (prov.), i. 484.

Interest (self-interest): friendship turned into commerces of, ii. 48; often passes for religious zeal, ii. 228–9; prejudices of party and, ii. 273; knowing one's true, ii. 377; a marriage of, ii. 516; love in the middle-aged generally accompanied with, v. 24.

Intrepidity: of Sappho, ii. 408; of Lucifer, iii. 114, 172; which attends heroic virtue, iii. 204; of Muly Moluc, iii. 301; of a just good man, set forth by Horace, v. 103; and steadiness of Wharton, v. 181.

Intrigue(s): not to be published by *Spectator*, i. 72; 'not yet blown upon by common fame', i. 437; Mr. SPECTATOR sometimes examines the course of, ii. 111; a husband bewildered in a crooked, ii. 171; a taste towards, ii. 236; of Augustus with wives of senators, ii. 247; the inquisitive fond of searching out, ii. 388; women are attracted by men with a reputation for, v. 59.

Intriguing: drinking, gaming, and, v. 9.

Intuition, in beings above us, ii. 136.

'Invader of constables', in days of yore, ii. 576.

Invention: dearth of, causes bawdry in poetry, i. 216; ii. 206; feats of, in a modern poet, ii. 355–6; fluency of, in the censorious, ii. 459; expression rather than i., what we admire in poetry, ii. 484; of incidents used sparingly in *PL*, ii. 543; most of Milton's characters formed purely by his own, ii. 586–7; Milton a poet of unbounded, ii. 587; iii. 84, 228; power of, in attaining wealth, iii. 3; of characters outside nature, iii. 570–3; method a great help to a writer's, iv. 186; a painful action of the mind, but easy in dreams, iv. 227.

Inventions of the Royal Society, ii. 519.

Ion, epitaph on Euripides, iv. 474.

Ionian sea, ii. 382, 406; iii. 469.

Ionic dialect, i. 131.

Iphicrates, Athenian commander, iii. 299.

Iphigenia, Cymon and (Dryden), i. 305–6.

Ipswich, letter from, iii. 302.

IRAS, a wit who affects the character of a beauty, iii. 512.

Ireland, ii. 286; a great genius from, iv. 18.

Irena, in Spenser, iv. 429.

Iris, in Dryden's Virgil, ii. 532.

Irish, the: terror spread by, some years since, iii. 292.

Irish: fortune-hunter, i. 8*y*; ii. 598; iii. 125; iv. 518; coxcomb more obsequious than an English, i. 88; letter from an Irish gentleman on ogling, i. 199; an Irish fellow who struts in a laced coat, ii. 217; shambrogue, iv. 104; rebellion, iv. 334–5; widow-hunter, iv. 518.

Irishman: impudence in an, i. 87; the most successful 'Starer', i. 87; on women's tongues, ii. 460.

Iron: JACK ANVIL began with a small parcel of rusty, iii. 68; *strike while the iron is hot* (prov.), iii. 163; superstitions regarding a rusty piece of, iv. 292.

Irony: the 'snarler' deals mightily in the, iv. 41; the finest palliative of praise, iv. 477.

Irresolution: in a man's affairs, ii. 95–96; on the schemes of life the cause of unhappiness, ii. 136; of mind more contemptible than impotence of body, iii. 24.

IRUS: and LAERTES, i. 468–9; the frugal, retired man, ii. 527; in Homer, ii. 589.

Irving, David, on Addison's style, i. cii.

Isaac, figure of, in old tapestry, iii. 221.

Isaac, Mr., new dance by, i. *285*.

ISABELLA, story of ESCALUS and, iii. 157–60.

Isadas, and the defence of Sparta, iv. 528.

Isidore of Seville, iv. *512*; v. *15*.

Isinglass, ii. 29.

Islands of the Blessed, ii. 125–6.

Isocrates, wrote before rules of art were codified, i. 261.

Israel: iv. 213; journey of, from Egypt, iv. 126–8; Abdon, judge of, iv. 274.

Isthmus, life on earth compared to an, v. 18.

Italian actors: introduction of, into English opera, i. 80.

Italian airs: introduced into psalm-singing, ii. 305; scale of, ii. 329–30.

Italian allegories, ii. 221.

Italian author(s): florid style of, i. 26; tells story of a shepherd juggling eggs,

ii. 130; allegories written by, ii. 221; tells story of a cardinal and a spy, iv. 43; who wished he owned Trophonius's cave, v. 44.

Italian chirurgeon, an advertisement from an, i. 96.

Italian comedian: story of Scaramouche, the first famous, iii. 3.

Italian critics, iii. 35.

Italian epitaph, i. 107.

Italian flowers, iv. 105.

Italian gardens, an agreeable mixture of garden and forest, iii. 551.

Italian language: quoted (from preface to *Rinaldo*), i. 25–26; tone of spoken, i. 121; birds taught to speak, i. 152; reflects the addiction to music and ceremony of the people, ii. 36; Latin as old Italian, iii. 55; a wife studying, iii. 205; a lawyer's clerk who has learned, iv. 204; letter in, iv. 450–1.

Italian music, i. 79; preferred to English, i. 81; character of, i. 119–23; in church, ii. 305; ANTONY FREEMAN's wife far gone in, ii. 329; grafted upon English poetry, ii. 506; in its perfection shown by Nicolini, iii. 513–14. *See also* Opera.

Italian paintings, iv. 285; auction sale of, i. 288; postures expressed in, iii. 521.

Italian poets, full of mixed wit, i. 265.

Italian proverbs, ii. 252; iii. 2.

Italian recitativo, i. 119–23; iii. 352.

Italian sonata, ii. 207.

Italian solo, on a case-knife, iv. 545.

Italian trips, i. 58.

Italic, printing in for emphasis, iv. 106, 537.

Italy: drolls in, called Maccaronies, i. 201–2; long torn by Guelphs and Ghibellines, i. 511; people addicted to music and ceremony, ii. 36; Pyrrhus's ambition to conquer, ii. 212; ancient writers of, lost, ii. 365; advertisement of a painter from, ii. 382; Clayton's studies in, ii. 506; Aeneas's settlement in, ii. 540–1; iii. 305–6; v. 15–16; the tour of France and, iii. 367; Addison's *Remarks* on, recommended, iii. 369; spring best in, iii. 474; appreciation of music in, iv. 55–56; excels in history-painting, iv. 496; the *gusto grande* in, v. 28.

Itch of writing, iv. 590.

Ithaca, Ulysses' injunction to the nobles of, iii. 249.

Ithuriel, in *PL*, iii. 172.

Ivory: comb, i. 193; in romance writers, iii. 18.

Ivy: covering a ruined abbey, i. 453; decorating a church, ii. 600; walls covered with, in a winter garden, iv. 191; caves encompassed with, iv. 325; 'as the ivy embraces the tree', iv. 452.

Ixion, i. *38*.

J., F., letter from (on death of his wife), iv. 350–3.

Jack (man's name): i. 333; ii. 53, 101, 593; iii. 508; iv. 401; in French is *Janot*, ii. 35; letter to, v. 105.

Jack (fish), i. 446, 448.

Jack-boots, breeches and, iv. 29.

Jack Puddings, merry drolls in England called, i. 202.

Jackal, transmigration into a, iii. 274.

Jackanapes, iii. 71, 125, 276.

Jacket: the modish, with close sleeves, iii. 163; a fustian, iv. 267.

Jackson, John (apothecary), i. *139*; iii. *418*; iv. *130*.

Jackson, Philip (a Director of the Bank), a subscriber, i. *xc*.

Jackson, Mrs. Samuel, i. *340*.

Jacksprat, i. 337.

Jacob: figure of, in old tapestry, iii. 221; Jacob's Pillow, underneath the Coronation chair, iii. 215.

Jacob, Giles, iii. *74*.

Jacobite, in a grinning-match, ii. 184.

Jacobson, Jacob (a Director of S. Sea Co.), a subscriber, i. *xc*.

Jacobus (coin), iv. 181.

Jade(s), ii. 16, 39.

Jaffier, in *Venice Preserved*, iv. 107.

James I, of Scotland, i. 300.

James I: a tolerable punster, i. 260; few beards in reign of, iii. 222.

James Francis Edward Stuart, the 'Old Pretender', i. 16.

JAMES: a love-letter to ELIZABETH, i. 305–8.

JANE, Mrs., meddling of, ii. 558–60.

Janot, the French form of *Jack*, ii. 35.

Janssen, Sir Theodore, a subscriber, i. xc, xci.

Janty. *See* Jaunty.

January: allegorical figure of, iii. 596; fine days in, iv. 191.

Janus, double-sighted capacity of, ii. 470.

Japan: table, i. 153; inhabitant of, at Royal Exchange, i. 293; workmanship of, i. 295; screens, ii. 480; ware, iii. 25.

Japis. *See* Iapis.

Jargon: of French phrases, ii. 149; of lawyers, iii. 402–3; iv. 477–8; of alchemists, iii. 600; of enthusiasm, among dissenters, iv. 117.

Jarrings and dissonances arising from anger, ii. 461.

Jaundice, a quack doctor who offers to cure the yellow, iv. 59.

Jaunty ('janty'): and lively in her impertinence, i. 322; laugh, iii. 343; from a j. part of the town, iv. 286; gay, j. fluttering pictures, iv. 496; WILL HONEYCOMB's j. air and easy motion, v. 184.

Jays and thrushes in a garden, iv. 190.

Jealousy: defined, ii. 168; in a husband, ii. 168–76 (these papers referred to, ii. 201, 261; iv. 458–9); rages most in warm climates, ii. 172; of Herod towards Mariamne, ii. 176–8; in a wife, ii. 201–4; iv. 380–1; between rival Negroes, ii. 470; Argus a spy in affairs of, ii. 470; in BELINDA, ii. 560; of a keeper, ii. 576; account of a jealous husband, iv. 378–80; described by Spenser, iv. 429–30; wives amusing jealous husbands, iv. 518.

Jean Pottages, merry drolls in France called, i. 201.

Jeffreys, George, *Father Francis and Sister Constance*, ii. *149*.

Jellies, i. 46; iv. 210.

Jenison, ——, v. *146*.

Jennets, Spanish, impregnate by the wind, ii. 5.

JENNY: one of WILL HONEYCOMB's loves, iii. 344; letter to, from 'the Phantom', iv. 331–3.

Jeremiah, Maccabeus dreams of receiving sword from, iii. 231–2.

Jerome, St., his definition of woman, ii. 530.

Jerusalem: King of, in *Rinaldo*, i. 64; Jesus's entry into, iii. 328.

Jessamines, i. 158; iii. 569; v. 143.

Jest(s): licentious j. in *The Lancashire Witches*, ii. 58; played by Rabelais, iii. 4; a series practised by a wit of the last age, iii. 396–9; unkind j. in conversation, iii. 582–3; most effective when accompanied with a serious countenance, v. 105; repeaters of stale, iv. 521–2; the *Oxford* and *Cambridge*, iv. 522.

Jesters, in homes and courts, i. 200.

Jesting: the rich man has a sly way of, i. 10; on others' deformities, i. 74–75.

Jesuit: Mr. SPECTATOR mistaken for, i. 18, 332; ii. 20; Secretary of the Indies, iv. 451.

Jesuits: their practice in evasion, iii. 98; their education of Clavius, iii. 107; experiments of, in China, iv. *449*, *452*.

Jesus Christ: recommended charity, ii. 199–200, 405; example of, ii. 232–3; predicted by Socrates (?), ii. 313; prayer of, ii. 314; painted by Raphael, ii. 379–80; the hero of *PL*, iii. 59; the model for Christian conduct, iii. 326–7, 494; death of, iii. 328–9; never seen to laugh, iii. 430; never subverted the law, iii. 442; the highest pattern of meekness and charity, iv. 334; 'A Testimony concerning', iv. 385; glorified body of, in Paradise, iv. 583; true character of, v. 84; and the disciples on way to Emmaus, v. 166. *See also* Messiah.

Jet (swagger), the agreeable, ii. 581.

Jetteaus: in the opera, i. 24; pleasing to the imagination, iii. 542.

Jetting (jutting) coat, of Henry VII's time, i. 450.

JETT-WELL, ELIZABETH: 'slays' by a glance, iii. 418.

Jeux d'esprit, iii. 99.

Jew, a: in assembly of stock-jobbers at Jonathan's, i. 4; at the masquerade, i. 63, 197; offer of, to Betty Lemon, iii. 428; at Jonathan's, iv. 500.

Jewish rabbins, on the murder of Abel, ii. 228.

Jewish tradition concerning Moses, ii. 423.

Jews: at the Royal Exchange, i. 294; 'hold out to the conversion of the', i. 378; Limborch's objection to their religious ceremonies, and Acosta's defence, ii. 332; hymns and divine odes among, iv. 95; history and sufferings of, iv. 255–8; venerated name of God, iv. 395; salutation of, to their kings, iv. 418; their aversion to bacon, v. 79; the kind of Messiah they expected, v. 84; music in their worship, v. 152; their law prescribed bathings and purification rites, v. 158.

Jewstrump (a horse), ii. 117.

Jewels, ii. 552; iii. 48.

Jezebel at the window, a, ii. 190–1.

JEZEBELL: letter from ('proud and vain'), iii. 41–42.

Jig: Miss LIDDY can dance a, iii. 104; a merry jig from the organ-loft, iii. 254, 268; taught by Mr. TROTT, iii. 415.

Jilt(s): character of the, ii. 234–7; male, iii. 23–25; 'the most incorrigible part of the most incorrigible sex', iii. 500; a 'reformed' jilt, iii. 500–2; in modern comedies, iv. 68; mentioned, iv. 225.

Jingle of words in Milton, iii. 63.

Jobbers and fawners, iii. 378.

Jockey(s): Whig j. and Tory foxhunters, ii. 3; conversation with a, ii. 386.

John, St., painted by Raphael, ii. 380.

JOHN: Sir JOHN, i. 408, 447; 'John such a one, gentleman', ii. 226; 'we've lost old JOHN', ii. 530; (Sir ROGER's coachman in London), iii. 240; a servant, v. 128; a neighbour, v. 128; a carter, v. 131.

John a Styles and John a Nokes (prov.): came in with the Conqueror, iv. 523; the humble petition of, iv. 574–5.

John of Gaunt, Duke of Lancaster, i. 95, 96.

John-apple, a face like a, i. 222.

Johnson, Benjamin (actor): in *The Rehearsal*, i. 150; the Grave-Digger in *Hamlet*, i. 151; in *Epsom Wells*, i. 207; almost lamed in *The Lancashire Witches*, ii. 57; as Old Corbaccio in *Volpone*, iii. 394.

Johnson, Charles: *Love in a Chest*, iii. 24.

Johnson, Samuel: on No. 626, i. lxxx, v. 142; on Addison's share in *Spectator*, i. lxxxii–lxxxiii; on the *Spectator*, i. xcv–xcvi, xcvii–xcviii; on Addison's style, i. xcix–c; *Dictionary*, i. 261; iii. 56, 183, 598; iv. 16, 85, 414; Life of Ambrose Philips, iii. 251; Life of Milton, iii. 336; on No. 364, iii. 366; Life of Addison, iii. 530; iv. 339, 494; on an epitaph in No. 518, iv. 343; on No. 576, iv. 571.

Johnson, Thomas, publisher at The Hague, i. *xxxvii*.

Join-hand, in penmanship, i. 32.

Joint-stool, 'in the very lowest place at the table', i. 370.

Jointure(s): a widow's, ii. 524; Mrs. SNAPP's, iv. 516.

Jollities: of country gentlemen, ii. 95–96; of youth, ii. 512.

Jollity and good-neighbourhood, ii. 20.

JOLLY, FRANK, memorial of, iv. 9.

JOLLY, JOCELINE, applies for the flitch of bacon, v. 79.

Jolly man, 'what the mob call a handsome', iv. 221.

Jones, John, translation of Ovid, iv. 492.

Jones, W., translation of Cornaro, ii. 267.

Jones, William (of Newington), 'cured' by Dr. Grant, iv. 173.

Jonquil, iii. 512.

Jonson, Ben: *Leges Convivales* of, i. 43; epitaph by, i. 141; thought highly of *Chevy Chase*, i. 298; his club, where the fire was to be always kept in, i. 310; epitaph attributed to, iii. 185; mentioned, iv. 427.—*The Alchemist*: Abel Drugger, i. 118; Sir Epicure Mammon, iii. 278; *Bartholomew Fair*: Justice Overdo, i. 207; *Catiline*: scene between Fulvia and Curius in, iv. 312–13; *The*

Silent Woman, i. 130; cited on causes of separation, i. 173; behaviour of La Foole in, ii. 509; *Staple of News*, i. 104; *Volpone*: Wilks as Mosca in, iii. 394; Johnson as Old Corbaccio in, iii. 394; quoted, iv. 379.

Joseph (uncle of Herod), put to death, ii. 177.

Joseph I, Emperor, death of, i. 192, 276.

Josephus, Flavius: story of Glaphyra's dream, i. 455–6; story of Herod and Mariamne, ii. 176.

Jotham, fable of the trees, ii. 219.

Journal: of Nicholas Hart, the 'sleeper', ii. 225; of a sober citizen, iii. 153–5, 181; of one's actions for a week, recommended, iii. 156; of a fashionable lady, iii. 182–5; of three country maidens, iii. 226.

Journal littéraire de la Haye, i. xcvi.

'Journals' received by the *Spectator* ('Rake's Journal', &c.), iii. 181.

Journeyman, a young sprightly, iii. 66.

Joys: a wife who will divide her husband's cares and double his, ii. 546; supernumerary, arising from practice of religion, iv. 72. *See also* Happiness.

Jubal, discovery of music by, iii. 350; iv. 171.

Jubilee, the great year of (1700), i. 309.

Judah, iv. 127, 213.

Judge: costume of, at the masquerade, i. 63; *serious (grave) as a* (prov.), i. 147; v. 46; a fellow who bowed and smiled in the face of a, ii. 509; the guilty man honours the, ii. 592. *See also* Lawyers.

Judges: Socrates' speech to his, ii. 75–76; examination of women at j.'s chambers, iii. 110; the burthensome finery of, iii. 348.

Judgement: value of a clear, i. 54; should control humour, i. 146; Locke's distinction between wit and, i. 263–4; 'shew their j. by finding fault', i. 364; distorted by party-spirit, i. 510–11; an imagination unguided by the check of reason and, ii. 157; Boileau a man of excellent, ii. 321; light pieces that ask more of fancy than of, ii. 396; our j. of events limited, ii. 420–3; pride in singularity of, ii. 494; only God can make a right j. of our actions, ii. 500–1; of epic poets in choice of heroes, ii. 565; Milton's, ii. 587; iii. 13, 88, 228; and taste at court of Augustus, ii. 592; of the poet in combining perspicuity with sublimity, iii. 11; true delicacy consists in exactness of, iii. 15; lack of, in the male coquet, iii.

24; the mark of genius in a writer, iii. 304; and fancy both necessary for proper taste, iii. 561; necessary to wit in conversation, iii. 583; balanced against wit, iv. 137; allegorical figure of, iv. 328; corrects errors of fancy, iv. 328. Judgement Day, see Day of Judgement.

Jugs: use of brown j. a cause of punning, iii. 484.

Juices: of the body, ii. 424; in the tongue, ii. 460.

Julep: given for fever, i. 406; for gout, iv. 169; prescribed for Lord FRIDAY, iv. 559.

Julia, aunt of Caesar, iii. 99.

Julian, Emperor, his satire The Caesars quoted, v. 168.

Julian, Count, iii. 425.

July, allegorical figure of, iii. 595.

JUMPER's lady, Colonel, iii. 415.

Junction, a French word imported, ii. 152.

June: to January, wrangle from, iii. 168; flourishing like a rose in, iii. 482; allegorical figure of, iii. 595.

Junket: a late j. which he was invited to, iii. 66.

Junketings with servants, iv. 147.

Juno: mistaking a cloud for a, i. 38; Argus a pimp for, ii. 470; Lucina, iii. 72; conversation with Jupiter, iii. 311; a priestess to, iv. 214; in modern poems, iv. 362; gall removed in nuptial sacrifices to, v. 76.

Jupiter: and the countryman, fable of, i. 108; life of, saved by dancing, i. 284; his judgement of the good and bad, ii. 222–3; prayer to, ii. 311; oracle of, ii. 312; pleasure of, in observing Cato, ii. 422; Virgil's account of, iii. 142; weighed outcome of battle between Turnus and Aeneas, iii. 173–4; iv. 134; thunders over combatants in battle, iii. 233; conversation with Juno, iii. 311; and naming of stars, iii. 460; prayers to, iii. 467–70; surrounded by Muses, iii. 516; temple to, at Babylon, iii. 554; magnificent portrayal of, in the Iliad, iii. 564; in Plutus, iv. 140–1; in modern poems, iv. 362–4; imaginary proclamation of, iv. 507–11; an example of lewdness, v. 169.

Jus trium liberorum, granted by Roman laws, ii. 295; iv. 25.

ust: no thought can be beautiful which is not, i. 268; iv. 362; and sublime, i. 290; iii. 303; and natural, ii. 53, 447, 585–6.

Justice: administration of, restricted to men, i. 312; the part of, never to do violence, i. 433; party spirit results in a partial administration of, i. 510; most agreeable to nature of God, and mercy to that of man, ii. 166; mercy to one may be cruelty to others in administration of, i. 410; ii. 167; lawyers should use their talents only in contending for, ii. 180; education should infuse early notices of, ii. 374; a superior virtue, ii. 445; balanced against humanity, iv. 137; the mind of man naturally a lover of, iv. 240; the first consideration in awarding favours, iv. 262; represented in Arthegal in Spenser, iv. 429.

Justice, a: plaguing of, in The Lancashire Witches, ii. 58; reconciling a minister of the parish and a Whig j., v. 128.

Justice of the Peace: ii. 20, 57, 183, 218, 528; iv. 339; v. 93, 149; Mr. SPECTATOR's father a, i. 2; Sir ROGER as, i. 499; ii. 15; a Justice of Peace's Lady, ii. 13; a clerk a necessary counsellor to, ii. 15.

Justice of the Quorum. See Quorum.

Justices' wives, place and precedency among, i. 487.

Justness: in point of gallantry, iii. 304; and variety of Spenser's epithets, iv. 431.

Juvenal: the frontispiece of the English Juvenal, i. 136; satirized follies of stage and court, i. 142; Dryden's J. in LEONORA's library, i. 158; satirized women's head-dresses, i. 414; tells how the beaux of Rome ridiculed the dress of a poor man, ii. 89–90; mentions a drowsy husband who raised an estate by snoring, ii. 226; says there is seldom common sense in high fortune, ii. 259; Plato's Alcibiades II gave occasion to J.'s tenth satyr, ii. 310; his sixth satire condemns the female sex in general, ii. 320; says that virtue is real honour, iii. 15–16; mentioned, iii. 219; tenth satire on vanity of men's wishes the finest satire in his whole works, iii. 470; would have satirized women in riding-habits, iv. 28; calls the itch of writing a cacoethes, iv. 590; quoted, i. 197, 414; ii. 89–90, 175.

KATE, BLACK, ii. 131, 134.

KATHERINE, Mrs., proposed as a wife, iv. 401.

Keene, Edward, benefit performance for, iii. 291.

Keeper(s): the thraldom of kind, ii. 196:

a tyrannical old, ii. 246; kind, ii. 568; an impotent old, ii. 575–6; a fine gentleman now need not be a, iv. 128.

Keepers (of a park), left-handed, iii. 194.

Keeping: 'in the days when k. was in fashion', ii. 236.

Kelder (cellar), v. 47.

Kempenfelt, Magnus, as an original of Captain Sentry, i. *11*; iv. *447*.

Ken, Thomas (Bishop of Bath and Wells), v. *175*.

Kennett, Basil: translation of Pascal, iv. *417*, *527*.

Kennett, White (Dean of Peterborough), *Parochial Antiquities*, ii. 134–5, *276*.

Kent, *Countess of Kent's Receipts* recommended, i. 391.

Kent, letter written from, iv. 182.

Kentish men: Roman Catholics imagine a Kentish man is known by his tail, ii. 182; how they evaded the Conqueror, iii. 8–9.

Kept mistress(es): letter from a, ii. 575–6; examples of, iv. 225–6.

Kerry, Lady (Anne), iii. *439*.

Kersey, John: *Dictionary*, iii. *206*; revision of Philips's *New World of Words*, v. *116*.

Ketch, John (Jack), iv. 290.

Kettle, twanking of a brass, ii. 475.

Kettle-drum(s): i. 65; ii. 415.

Kick the beam (prov.), iv. 136.

Kidney, Humphrey, waiter at St. James's Coffee-house, i. 104.

Kilderkin of small beer, i. 310.

'Kill at first sight, as the phrase is', ii. 69.

'Killing' in love: 'upon sight of a fine woman, I have killed with a good air and mein', ii. 159; k. eyes, ii. 472, 479; examples of, iii. 416–18.

KIMBOW, THO. (a tavern-frequenter), letter from, i. 101–2.

Kind, to be, 'as the phrase is', iv. 384.

Kindness: the great are slow in receiving impressions of, ii. 336; ways of doing an office of, iii. 39; necessary to effective raillery, iii. 584.

King, —— (a box-keeper), benefit for, v. 47.

King, John, i. *40*.

King, Dr. William: a Tory party-writer, v. *66*; *Useful Transactions in Philosophy*, i. xiv, *286*; *Art of Cookery*, i. 42, *451*; v. *80*; letter to Dr. Lister, iv. *310*; translation of *Persian Tales*, iv. 576.

King: and his physician, story of, ii. 263–4; Persian king and the dervish, story of, iii. 30–31.

King Arthur (opera), i. *27*.

King-at-arms to the gods (Argus), ii. 470.

King of Clubs (punning name for Mr. SPECTATOR), iv. 470.

King of Rome, represented by the consul, iii. 20.

King without a head (Henry V), iii. 215.

King's English, Clipping the (prov.), v. 106.

Kings: Club of the, i. 40; visit of the four Indian, i. 211–15; majesty the title given to, ii. 352; 'the logic of', ii. 430; chosen by Benchers of the Temple, ii. 464; regal power one of the three branches of government, iii. 19–20; salutation of Jews to their, iv. 418. *See also* Sovereigns.

Kirleus, Susanna (quack doctor), advertisement of, iv. *61*.

Kirleus, Thomas, iv. *61*.

Kiss(es): snatching k. by surprise, ii. 73; St. Francis mistook the k. of a lover for the salute of charity, ii. 450; the lady who turned her cheek when offered a, ii. 561; poem on snatching a, iv. 176.

Kissing: as a mode of salutation, ii. 433–4; iv. 379; Pisistratus on k. in public, iv. 379; k. the hand of a lady, v. 23.

Kissing-crust, a quarrel about the, v. 80.

Kissing-dances, i. 286–7.

Kissing-strings, ii. 580.

Kit (small fiddle), iv. 60.

Kit-Cat Club: said to have taken its original from a mutton-pie, i. 42; mentioned, i. 310; portraits of members of, iv. *517*.

Kitchen, atmosphere of, iii. 485.

Kitchen garden, description of a, iv. 189.

Kitchen music, a master of, iv. 545–6.

Kitchen proverb, ii. 531.

Kite: a paper k. lined with reading-matter, i. 361.

KITTY: an accomplished jilt, ii. 236; one of ABRAHAM THRIFTY's nieces, ii. 442; Miss KITTY, iii. *184*; reply to, who has sent in a letter, iv. 587.

Knapton, James, the *Spectator* sold by, i. xxiv.

Knaves: Spanish proverb about fools and, i. 512; fools in business sometimes pretend to be, ii. 567; *knave*, *villain*, &c., in pamphlets, iv. 537.

Knee-strings, iii. 153.

Kneller, Sir Godfrey: a subscriber, i. lxxxix; portrait of Steele, i. *75*; pictures of ladies at Kneller's, i. 140; and the Academy of Painting, iv. *495*; praise of, iv. 497.

Knife and fork, superstition regarding position of, i. 32–33.

Knife-grinder, cries of, in London streets, ii. 477.

Knives, poems inscribed by cutlers upon, i. 246.

Knight, Frances: in *The Unhappy Favourite*, i. *207*; Lady Cockwood in *She Would if She Could*, i. 217; in *All for Love*, i. *392*; Lady Macbeth, ii. *308*; Cephisa in *The Distressed Mother*, iii. *239*.

Knight, the Red Cross, in Spenser, iv. 428-9.

Knight of the Shire: Sir HUMPHREY DE COVERLEY, i. 452; Sir ROGER, iii. 437.

Knight of the Sorrowful Countenance. *See* Cervantes, *Don Quixote*.

Knight-Errant(s): behaviour of, in books of chivalry, i. *417*; a necromancer generally in train of, ii. 438; have full scope to range in fairy-land, iv. 429.

Knight-Errantry: a noble piece of, ii. 161; combats in ages of, iv. 32.

Knight's Head, as an inn-sign, i. 500.

Knights, impresses of giants and, iv. 18.

Knights of the post (perjurers), ii. 180; iv. 553.

Knightleye, Robert, and the flitch of bacon, v. 76.

Knocke, Fort, conflicting reports of, in coffee-houses, iv. 355.

Knot(s): a true-lover's, ii. 453; Gordian, ii. 595-6; swords with fine, iv. 195.

Knotting, proposed as employment for women's men and beaux, iv. 412-13.

Know what's what, to (prov.), ii. 23.

Knowledge: of oneself, i. 45; a qualification of a good friend, i. 291; pursuit of, recommended, i. 397-8; WILL HONEY-COMB's k. of the town, i. 436; of men and books, i. 502; disseminated by books and periodical publications, i. 505-7; unjustly employed, ii. 180, 370; lack of address in applying, ii. 362-3; human k. limited, ii. 420-3; v. 171; of the world desirable, ii. 449-52; pedantic pride in one's, ii. 554-5; reading and contemplation the two great sources of, iii. 21-22; ease and plenty the great cherishers of, iii. 22; necessary to the critic, iii. 35-36; a poet's k. should seem born with him, iii. 63; worth nothing if communicated(?), iii. 423; Alexander's passion for, iii. 423; kept to oneself like a dark lantern, iii. 424; v. 176; enough k. to raise doubts but not to clear them, iv. 187; of Bacon, Boyle and Newton, iv. 487-8; the mind's constant search for, v. 140-1; our k. of God, v. 170-3.

Knox, John, Anglo-Genevan Psalter, ii. 305.

Knox, Vicesimus, on Addison's style, i. xcviii-xcix.

Koenig, Johann, *A Royal Compleat Grammar*, i. *4*, *8*, *293*.

Koran. See *Alcoran*.

L, speculations on *Spectators* signed, ii. 360.

L., B., letter from (on masquerades), i. 37-38.

L—y, Mr.: his refining upon Shakespeare's points and quibbles, iii. 485; his plays condemned by the pit, iii. 485.

Labour: two kinds of bodily, i. 471; necessary to welfare, i. 472; vicissitudes of l. and rest, ii. 269; wit as well as l. should be made cheap, ii. 357; relation of, to prices of manufactures, ii. 402-4; Sir William Petty's theory of division of, ii. 404; benefits of l., disappointment, and pain, ii. 422; we should expect nothing beyond our own property or, ii. 599; preferable to idleness, as brightness to rust, v. 132.

La Bruyère, Jean de: papers in style of, i. lx; character of Menalcas quoted, i. 332-3; on affectation of mispronouncing of words, i. 195; character of Arrias, ii. *40*; on inconsistency of character, ii. *136*; iv. *526*; comparison of passages with, ii. *307, 375, 386*; on modesty, ii. *399*; on trivial occupations, iii. 153; mentioned, iii. 529; on taking satisfaction in one's imperfections, iv. 174.

Labyrinth(s): of error for the wicked in eternity, ii. 421; and recesses in a coquette's heart, ii. 594; of vice and folly, iii. 81-82; of a parterre, iii. 552-3; remains of one in Egypt still to be seen, iii. 555.

La Calprenède, Gautier de Coste, Sieur de: *Cassandra* and *Cleopatra* in LEONORA's library, i. 154; *Faramond*, i. *327*; female readers recommend *Faramond* and *Cassandra*, i. 392; Oroondates in *Cassandra*, ii. *280*; iii. 416.

Lace(s): adding a supernumerary, i. 67; and ribbons as lures to women, i. 67; in head-dresses, i. 414, 416; cravats, i. 434; ii. 217, 236; on a gentleman's dress, i. 451; and ribbons, iii. 346, 531, 571; iv. 101; and drapery in men's dress, iii. 376; a bundle of Flanders, iv. 271; in Motteux's shop, iv. 479; and shoulder-knot of a footman, v. 81.

Lace (in coffee), iv. 230; bad for the head, iii. 155.

Laced liveries, iii. 69; and embroidered suits, iii. 347.

Lacedaemonians: their courtesy to the old, i. 31; war with Athenians, i. 349;

ii. 312; the bravest people in Greece, i. 284; encouraged dancing, i. 284; sacrificed to the Muses when entering upon a great enterprise, ii. 239; a form of prayer used by, ii. 311–12.

Laceman (-men), i. 276; iii. 509; iv. 193.

La Chambre. *See* Cureau de la Chambre.

Lachesis, iii. 596.

Lacqueys, i. 375; iv. 207.

La Croze, J. de, *Memoirs for the Ingenious*, i. xxxvii.

Lacy, John, iii. 485–6.

Ladder of ropes, iii. 126.

Ladder-dance, i. 128.

Ladder-walkers on the stage, ii. 504.

Ladies' Calling. See Allestree.

Lady (-ies), fine, i. 393; ii. 449; iv. 333.

Lady's library, a: suggestions for, i. 153–7, 197, 340–1, 389–93; promised by Mr. SPECTATOR but not given, ii. 54–55; iv. 382.

Lady's New-Years Gift. See Halifax, Marquis of.

Lady-Day, iv. 470.

LADYLOVE, BARTHOLOMEW: petition of, iii. 94–95.

Laelius, Gaius (friend of Cicero), iv. 68, 418.

LAERTES and IRUS contrasted (LAERTES lives beyond his means), i. 468–9.

Laertes (father of Ulysses), v. 73.

LAETITIA: and DAPHNE, i. 137–8, 224; has been the finest woman in town these three months, iii. 489; her remarks on the *Spectator*, iv. 231; and ERASTUS, a happily-married couple, iv. 297–8.

La Ferte. *See* Fert.

La Fontaine, Jean de: i. 48, 143; iii. 529; vogue of, ii. 220.

La Foole, in *The Silent Woman*, ii. 509.

Laguerre, Louis, iv. 495.

La Hogue, the glorious action at, iii. 437.

Lais: not Lais but the harlot to be exposed, i. 72.

Lake, John (Bishop of Chichester), v. 175.

Lake(s): the burning l. in *PL*, iii. 85; and rivers pleasing to the imagination, iii. 452; artificial l. at Babylon, iii. 554.

Lamb, Sir David, slain at Chevy Chase, i. 320.

Lamb: and Dolphin as a sign, i. 116; as a sign, i. 118; instinctively butts, i. 495; sacrifice of the black l. in *The Lancashire Witches*, ii. 58; Nathan's fable of the poor man and his, ii. 220; sucking a goat changes its nature, ii. 455; in Emperor of China's letter, iv. 451.

Lambarde, William, *Perambulation of Kent*, ii. 182.

Lambert, Sir John (a Director of S. Sea Co.), a subscriber, i. xc, xci.

Lame: Raphael's painting of the l. who are healed, ii. 379; and the halt, at the Royal Exchange, iv. 307.

Lameness: counterfeited by beggars, iv. 11–12; a quack doctor who offers to cure, iv. 59.

Lampooner, to be attacked by every honest man, i. 148.

Lampoons: sent in to *Spectator*, i. 71; ill effects of, i. 97; well figured by an axe, i. 246; men resent being left out of, ii. 372; pretenders to wit who write, ii. 56; the effect of spleen, iv. 86; as a cure for the itch of writing, iv. 590.

Lamps of the ancients, ever-burning, iii. 425.

Lamy, Bernard, praise of a hymn by Des Barreaux, iv. 323.

Lancaster, Duke of. *See* Henry IV.

Lancaster, Earls of, v. 76.

Lancaster, Dr. William, i. 183.

Landed interest: *v.* the moneyed interest, ii. 3; and the commercial classes, ii. 185–9; and sale of wool, corn, and cattle, ii. 402.

Landskip(s), i. 353, 402, 470; the natural genius like a beautiful l. without order or regularity, ii. 129; sunshine in l. of Titian, iii. 39; cut out into rivers, woods, rocks, and meadows, pleasing to the imagination, iii. 541; in veins of marble, iii. 550; made by an experiment in optics, iii. 550–1; in Virgil's *Georgics*, iii. 565.

Land tax. *See* Tax.

Langhorne, John, ii. 149.

Language: impropriety of, i. 226; indelicate and immodest, i. 241–2, 323–4; ii. 107–8, 254, 346–7, 439–40, 574; iv. 57–58, 402–3; a fine gentleman is refined in, i. 278; teaching a girl the visible graces of speech, i. 281; extravagant l. addressed to 'Idols', i. 313; of *Chevy Chase* very sounding, i. 316–21; of *Two Children in the Wood* mean, i. 362; obscurity in, i. 488; 'speculations' on the English, ii. 32–36; reflects genius and temper of a people, ii. 35–36; of the eye, ii. 478–80; iii. 321–2; of *PL*, iii. 9–15, 62–64, 566; of the Hottentots, iii. 461; of dissenters, iv. 117; understanding l. of birds, iv. 319–20; justness and purity of, in Menander, iv. 475.

Language-master, for politicians, iii. 98.

Languages: idioms of other l. used to

elevate poetical style, iii. 12; affectation of contempt for modern, iv. 174; prettinesses of foreign l. picked up by travellers, iv. 179.

Languishing: air of a bride, ii. 479; the soul, without passions, is l. in its executions, ii. 490.

Languishings: sighs and, ii. 177; of a mind infected with love, iii. 416.

Languishment: music now only a l. of notes, ii. 584; that easy posture which expresses the very top and dignity of, iv. 221.

LANQUICELSA, her lowly aspect at a sermon, iv. 333.

Lansdowne, George Granville, Baron: on rants in tragedy, i. *171*; *The Jew of Venice*, iv. *34*.

Lanterloo (a game), ii. 451.

Lantern: ruffian with the l. and dagger, ii. 350; the recluse man like a dark, iii. 424; v. 176.

Lantern-jaws, ii. 184.

Lap-dog(s), i. 243; ii. 459; iii. 273; iv. 24, 578-9; v. 68, 80; a Bolonia, iv. 271.

LAPIRIUS, turned over his estate to his elder brother, ii. 463.

Lapithae and Centaurs, Battle of, iii. 596.

Lapland: witchcraft in, i. 480; iii. 376; love-songs, iii. 376-8, 518-20; Scheffer's history of, iii. 376, 518; surprise that fine odes have been written in, iv. 18; magical incantations remain in, v. 65; Odes referred to, iv. 329.

Laplanders, have a place on Parnassus, iv. 329.

Laponian language, wilder graces suit the genius of the, iii. 377.

Lappets of head-dresses, ii. 345.

La Quintinie, J. de, *Compleat Gard'ner*, i. *27*.

Larceny, petty, and murder not to be punished alike, iii. 16.

Large, men who live at, ii. 105.

Larger than life, a picture, iii. 81.

LARISSA, her leap into the Ionian sea, ii. 407.

Lark(s): to be introduced in the puppet-show, i. 64; and nightingales, i. 158; ii. 474; a wife who cannot bear the noise of, ii. 11; pestle of a, iii. 196; and the linnet, v. 63.

La Rochefoucauld, François VI, Duc de, i. *416*; ii. *444*; iv. *416*; on military manners, iv. 534.

Laroon (or Lauron), Marcellus, the Elder, *Cryes of the City of London*, i. *128*, *152*; ii. *474*, *505*; iii. *372*.

La Rue, Captain de, iv. *355*.

Larvati, or *larva donati* of the ancients, i. 136.

Lash: of a whip, i. 446; educating by the, ii. 117.

'Last words', popularity of, iv. 63.

Lastanosa, John, iii. *424*.

Laterum contentio (Cicero), iii. 522.

LATH, 'Squire, thin legs of, i. 135.

Latimer, Hugh, anecdote of, iv. 142.

Latin: Sir ROGER afraid of being insulted with, by his chaplain, i. 440; a cousin who contradicts because he knows, ii. 53; love of, prevalent in our common people, ii. 359-60; rival preachers who quoted, ii. 359-60; a method of learning, ii. 395; using words only with L. derivations, ii. 442; women prefer L. to Greek, iii. 55; politicians instructed in Treaty-L., iii. 98; and the Roman virtues, iii. 250; less useful to average boys than English, iii. 318; Spanish secretary of state who knew L. better than the king, iii. 477; public are impressed by, iv. 62; Mr. SHAPELY 'can talk L. as fast as English', iv. 184; and Greek learnt at a country school, iv. 204; diminutive epithets in, iv. 397; 'spells uncouth L., and pretends to Greek', iv. 398; lawyers subscribe to false, iv. 478; and Greek learnt at school, v. 38.

Latin authors: who are guilty of the false sublime, iii. 11; outweigh moderns, iv. 137; uncommon passages in, iv. 138; superior in wit, iv. 329. *See also* Ancients.

Latin critics: the best of the, ii. 484; knowledge of, necessary to the modern critic, iii. 35; were masters of elegance and delicacy of language, iii. 36.

Latin evergreens, iv. 104.

Latin epitaph, iv. 343.

Latin grammar, introduced into sermons, ii. 359-60.

Latin mottoes in *Spectator* perplex readers, iii. 393.

Latin poetry and poets: mixed wit in, i. 265-6; knowledge of, necessary to the critic, iii. 35; largely devoted to praise of deities, iv. 94-95.

Latin proverbs, i. 330, 508.

Latin quotations, in discussing *Chevy Chase*, i. 321-2.

Latin school, iii. 219.

Latin translation: of Sappho, ii. 390-1; of Cato's soliloquy, v. 146-7.

Latin verses: false quantity in making, ii. 116; tables for composing, ii. 356-7; sent by a gentleman of Oxford, v. 116.

Latin words terminating in -*osus*, ii. 289.

Latinisms in *PL*, iii. 12.

Latinus, King (in *Camilla*): sung by Turner, i. 79; drafted into army, i. 95–96, 197; letter from, i. 228.

Latitudinarians in wedlock, iii. 65.

Latium: settling of Aeneas in, the action of the *Aeneid*, ii. 540.

La Trappe, Abbey de: rules of, v. 33–34.

'Latter spring', a kind of, in blood of an old woman, i. 379.

Laud, Archbishop William: objected to abolishing country-wakes, ii. 135; fined the Stationers' Company for an error in the Bible, iv. 580.

Laugh: the one l. in the *Aeneid*, ii. 589; not one passage in the *Self-Tormentor* that could raise a, iv. 280; suddenness of WILL HONEYCOMB's, v. 184.

Laughers, a set of, in public assemblies, ii. 163.

Laughing: Mr. SPECTATOR would not willingly laugh, but to instruct, ii. 205; a coquette laughs when she is not merry, ii. 459; metaphor of, applied to fields and trees, ii. 468; Jesus never seen to laugh, iii. 430.

Laughter: loud and excessive, a mark of false humour, i. 147; the daughter of folly, i. 147; devices for, in comedy, i. 191; provocatives of, i. 200–4; Hobbes on the source of, i. 200–1, 223; ii. 466; 'that secret elation and pride of heart', i. 203; does not proceed from profound joy, i. 403; as unmanly as weeping, ii. 67; gravity and mirth both appealed to by *Spectator*, ii. 204–6; account of a grinning match, ii. 206–7; loud l. condemned, ii. 268; in the audience at the theatre, ii. 314–15; distinguishes man from animals, ii. 465; iv. 254; an essay on l. and ridicule, ii. 465–9; unsuitable to the epic, ii. 589–90; effect of, on a coquette's heart, ii. 595; the rabble of mankind ready to laugh, iii. 37; and cheerfulness, iii. 429–32; the property of reason, but not to be carried to excess, v. 44; the Cave of Trophonius a cure for, v. 46–48; less pardonable in church than whining, v. 155.

Laughter-loving, the title given to Venus, ii. 468.

Laurel: in a winter garden, iv. 191; by the throne of Apollo, iv. 329.

Lausus: Aeneas's lamentation over, i. 303; and Mezentius almost parallels to Pallas and Evander, ii. 563; and Pallas come to unfortunate ends, iv. 464.

Lavinia, in Otway's *Caius Marius*, iv. 435.

Law, the: overcrowding in, i. 89–90; of separation and divorce, i. 173; the law-pedant, i. 438; TOM TOUCHY takes the law of everybody, i. 498; *the law is open* (prov.), ii. 73; for poor relief, ii. 404; 'the perplexed style and matter of', iii. 348–9; careful to restrain prosecution, iv. 108–9; a maxim of, iv. 527.

Lawrence, —— (singer), i. 132.

Lawrence's toy-shop, i. 221.

Laws: ineffectual in duelling, i. 359; against exorbitant power should be made in a good reign, i. 415; regarding use of the long bow, ii. 133; persons who watch over our, ii. 149; of parish settlements, ii. 284; against profanity, iii. 398; *of the Medes and Persians* (prov.), iv. 303.

Law-students: idling in coffee-houses, i. 209; as amateur coachmen, iv. 266, 374–5.

Lawyer: a Brother of the Coiff, i. 377; letter from a, ii. 13–15; who can argue on both sides, ii. 272–3; letter from a practitioner in the law, ii. 480–1; importance of appearance to the, iii. 348; who is vehement and loud in a cause he does not believe in, iii. 393; besieging LUCINDA PARLEY, iv. 407–8.

Lawyer's chamber, with rails before it, iii. 348.

Lawyer's clerk, letter from a, iv. 204.

Lawyers: in Westminster Hall, i. 58, 89; embracing one another when out of the court-room, i. 58; overcrowding in the profession, i. 89–90; account of 'peaceable', i. 90; eating once a day and dancing once a year, i. 90; affectation in, i. 162; complained of, by 'who' and 'which', i. 337; judge and justices at the assizes, i. 499; often misuse their talents in defending an ill cause, ii. 180; strife and contention in, ii. 272–3; women would carry eloquence of the bar to greater heights, ii. 458; many unqualified, iii. 109; a club of, iii. 402–3; English l. use little gesture or action, iii. 521; importance of modesty in, iv. 215–17; illiberal cant of, iv. 477–8; litigious temper of, iv. 574–5.

Lazar-house, Adam's vision of a hospital or, iii. 362.

Lazars and diseased persons, iii. 400.

Laziness, complaints of, in husband and wife, ii. 326–7.

Leach, Dryden, printer of the *Post-Man*, i. 4.

League, The (in France), quarrels of, i. 511; iv. 91.

Leanness: jests upon fat and lean, i. 75;

a quack doctor who advertises a cure for, iv. 554.

Leander, Hero's passion for, ii. 383.

Leaping, a feature of the Roman Pentathlum, ii. 133

Learned, the: their controversies about nothing, i. 474; often lack skill in conduct of life, ii. 362–4; *Account of the Works of*, iv. 114.

Learned ladies: account of two female virtuosos, ii. 442–3.

'Learned men in plush doublets' (quack doctors), ii. 28.

Learned professions, the three, i. 88–92; iv. 274, 387.

Learned societies, now marked by party-spirit, i. 511.

Learned wife, a would-be, ii. 582–3.

Learned world, the: divided upon Milton's language, iii. 9; rank and precedence in, iv. 386–8.

Learning: a man may appear learned without talking sentences, i. 21; effect of, on LEONORA, i. 158; decay of, follows declension of empire, i. 256–7; makes the silly man more insufferable, i. 438; the *Spectator* 'so learned there is no enduring you', ii. 53; schoolboys bred to, who have not a genius for it, ii. 162; without discretion is pedantry, ii. 376; pedantic pride in, ii. 554–5; flourishes only under liberty, iii. 22; all parts of, to be mastered by the critic, iii. 36; without additional graces degenerates into pedantry, iii. 40; ostentation of, a fault in *PL*, iii. 62; abundance of, in catalogue of evil spirits in *PL*, iii. 87; services of French Academy to polite, iii. 96; Milton's genius strengthened by, iii. 234; a boy who showed his l. on all occasions, iii. 367; the glory of a nation, iii. 382; dissemination of, iii. 422–5; display of, iii. 578; the *Spectator* has made l. a part of good breeding, iv. 128; balanced against pedantry, iv. 136; compared with natural parts, iv. 136–7; honesty of men of l. in business, iv. 161; is the chief advantage of men over women, iv. 296; practical *v.* classical, iv. 306–10; examples of extensive, iv. 487–91.

Leather: decent ornament of a l.-garter, iv. 377; gilt l. for furniture, v. 83.

Leaves, words compared to, iv. 75, 104.

Lebanon, Tower of, ii. 127.

Le Bas, Charles (contractor to the Army), a subscriber, i. *xci*.

Le Bossu, René: on example of Camilla in *Aeneid*, i. *69*; the epic to be founded on a precept of morality, i. 298–9; iii.

144, 390–1; on Homer's similes, ii. *128*; definition of fable, ii. *539*; and the rules of epic poetry, ii. 539; on the theme of the *Aeneid*, ii. *541*; on duration of action in the epic, ii. *543*; iii. 391; on 'manners' in the epic, ii. *562*; on the happy endings of the epic, ii. 566; iii. 59; on meanness of Homer's sentiments, ii. *586*; warns against pedantry, iii. *62*; on the propositions in the epic, iii. *84*; on 'admiration' in the epic, iii. *145*; on Homer's allegories, iii. *146, 337*; tries to vindicate Homer by parallels in Holy Writ, iii. 201; his method in dating action of the epic, iii. 203; on episodes in the epic, iii. *280*; on courage in Aeneas and Turnus, iii. 304; mentioned, iii. 529.

Le Clerc, Jean, *Life of Locke*, iv. *403*.

Le Comte, Louis, *Memoirs of China*: i. *313*; ii. 244; iii. *555*; iv. *315*; v. 65.

Lector, Theodorus, *Anagnostes*, iv. 497.

Lectures, example more persuasive than severity of, ii. 205; iii. 82.

Leda's egg, Homer did not begin with, ii. 539.

Lee, Nathaniel: should have kept impetuosity of his genius within its proper bounds, i. 166–7; pleases the ladies by his heroes, i. 172; guilty of the false sublime, iii. 11—*Mithridates, King of Pontus*, a favourite with the ladies, i. 392; *Oedipus* (by Dryden and Lee): a tragedy with an unhappy ending, i. 170; two contrasting passages from, quoted, i. 172; a fine satire on woman in (quoted), ii. 10; suicide of Oedipus in, iii. 358; quoted (on the magpie), iv. 512; *The Rival Queens, or the Death of Alexander the Great*: burlesques of, i. *128*; Powell as Alexander in, i. *130*; iii. 291; petition of Bullock to be Hephaestion in, i. 151; Statira's speech quoted, i. 167; a tragedy with an unhappy ending, i. 170; acted at Epping, i. 207; a favourite with the ladies, i. 392; quoted (passion 'in a mad hero, drawn by a mad poet'), iv. 40; a comedian who had a mighty mind to act Alexander, v. 47; *Sophonisba, or Hannibal's Overthrow*, a favourite with the ladies, i. 392; *Theodosius, or The Force of Love*: a tragedy with an unhappy ending, i. 169–70; Epistle dedicatory to, i. *176*; most popular with the ladies, i. 392, 405.

Leek, as green as a (prov.), ii. 385.

Leers: kinds of, ii. 472; a town leer, iii. 112.

Leeuwenhoek, Antony van, iv. *346*.

Leeward Islands, story from the, ii. 339.

Lefèvre, Anne. *See* Dacier, Madame.

Left-handed keepers (of a park), iii. 194.

Leg(s): thin, i. 135; in wrestling, ii. 132; iv. 283; composing poetry while standing upon one, ii. 355; crooked, iv. 261; bandy, iv. 510; 'long trapsticks without calfs', iv. 510–11.

Legend, Sir Sampson (in *Love for Love*), ii. 242.

Leges convivales of Ben Jonson, i. 43.

Le Grand, Antoine: *Man without Passion*, iii. 526; *Entire Body of Philosophy*, iv. 328.

Leicestershire, Swepstone in, iii. 210.

Leigh, John (actor), Clodpate in *Epsom Wells*, i. 207.

Leisure, methods of employing, i. 394–402.

Le Jeune, Jean: *Scala Coeli*, ii. 423.

Lelius. *See* Laelius, Gaius.

Lemnos, thrown to the skies by a giant, iii. 230.

LEMON, BETTY, letter from (encounter with a Jew), iii. 428.

Le Neve, John: *Memoirs*, iv. 251.

Lennox, Charlotte. *See* Ramsay.

Le Nôtre, André, designer of gardens at Versailles, iii. 551; iv. 191.

Lent in Roman Catholic countries, charity practised in, iii. 400.

Lent, Rules to Keep, recommended for ladies' reading, i. 391.

Leo X, Pope: his fondness for buffoons, iv. 263–5; an accident in reign of, v. 108.

LEODACIA: spreads her charms only for her husband, iv. 331.

Leonardo da Vinci, a universal genius, account of his death, iv. 488–9.

LEONILLA: daughter of LEONTINE, i. 503–5; her advice to CELIA, iv. 183.

LEONORA: her library and garden, i. 153–8; requests a list of books, i. 389; referred to (as ELEONORA), ii. 54–55; letter from (on death of her lover), ii. 140–1; advice to, ii. 141–3; the eye of, slyly watchful, while it looks negligent, ii. 479.

LEONTINE and EUDOXUS, i. 502–5.

Leopold I (Emperor of Germany): worked in wood, iii. 319; his son Charles, iii. 508.

Lepidum caput, true form and dimensions of the, iv. 400.

Lepidus, i. 144.

Lesbia: compliments made to, a thousand years ago, i. 125; Sappho's ode to, ii. 390–2; letter from (a ruined reputation), v. 87–89.

Leslie, Charles, *The Finishing Stroke*, recommended for ladies' reading, i. 391.

L'Estrange, Roger: fable of boys and frogs, i. 100; pruned words of superfluous letters, ii. 35; *Fables of Aesop*, i. 48, 58, 77, 262; ii. 186, 455; *Fables and Storyes Moralized*, i. 508; ii. 211, 399; iii. 28, 325; iv. 310, 543, 552; v. 155; *Seneca's Morals*, in LEONORA's library, i. 157; translation of Josephus, ii. 176; *Select Colloquies out of Erasmus*, ii. 334; translation of Quevedo, iii. 222; iv. 15, 492; translation of Cicero, v. 56.

LETACRE, Mr. (a servant), ii. 524.

Lethargies, resulting from intemperance, ii. 265.

Leti, Gregorio, i. 99; had published as many books as he was years old, v. 159.

Letter-droppers. *See* Lipogrammatists.

Letters (of alphabet), resemblance of, as source of false wit, i. 265; iii. 560.

Letters (epistles): the best revelation of character, i. 113; practice in writing, a concern of education, ii. 396; discover a person's true temper, iii. 7; politicians taught how to open, and fold them up again, iii. 97; students should be taught to write English, rather than Latin, iii. 318; a professional l.-writer, iv. 225; of recommendation, iv. 247–51; to wives and mistresses compared, iv. 371; kinds of epistolary verse, v. 112–14.—Letters to *Spectator*: see *Spectator*.

Letters (other than those addressed to *Spectator*): from MARY TUESDAY to an acquaintance, i. 103–4; from R. O., T. D., and R. B., to the CLERGYMAN, i. 113–15; from JAMES, a footman, to ELIZABETH, i. 305–8; to ANDROMACHE (Steele to Prue), ii. 60–64; from THEODOSIUS to CONSTANTIA, ii. 144, 147–8; from a young gentleman in the army to his father, ii. 152–3; from MARTHA HOUSEWIFE to her husband, ii. 204; from a gentleman to a lady who had commended him, ii. 240–1; from an angry father to his son, ii. 241–2; to a young man who has lost a worthy father, ii. 256; from STATIRA to OROONDATES, ii. 280–2; from BELINDA to the Sothades, ii. 299–300; from T. D. to ——, ii. 300; from —— to ——, ii. 301; from PHILLIS to ——, ii. 301; from a wife to Colonel R—s in Spain, ii. 301–2; from Pliny to Maximus, ii. 394–5; from Philopinax to Chromation, ii. 427–8; from P. T. to his brother, ii. 463; from W. S. to a trader, ii. 464; from LYDIA to HAR-

RIOT, ii. 486–8; from MARY HOME to LYDIA, ii. 488–9; to a cold mistress, ii. 513; between FRANK and his mother, ii. 524–5; from a bawd to a noble lord, ii. 569–70; from Pliny to Quintilian, iii. 40; from a wit to CLOE, iii. 76–78; between CORINNA and AMILCAR, iii. 102–3; between LYDIA and CLITO-PHON, iii. 122–3; from CLYTANDER to CLEONE, iii. 151; between ESCALUS and ISABELLA, iii. 159–60; from CORINNA to a lady, iii. 166; from Gabriel Bullock to Margaret Clark, iii. 189, 209–10; from George Nillson to Mary Norton, iii. 210–12; from PUGG to his mistress, iii. 274–6; a consolatory letter from Phalaris, iii. 298–9; from Ipswich to Capt. SENTRY, iii. 302–3; from Balzac to the Chancellor of France, iii. 324; from Paul Regnaud to a gentleman in London, iii. 383–5; from Alexander to Aristotle, iii. 423; from a friend in Denmark, iii. 473–4; between CYNTHIO and FLAVIA, iii. 491–3; between AMORET and PHILANDER, iii. 501–2; from a gentleman to a friend, on solitude, iii. 517–18; Sir ROGER's billet to SUKEY, iii. 533; from DAMON to STREPHON, iii. 588; from NICODEMUNCIO to OLIVIA, iv. 20; between a citizen who had failed and his friend who helped him, iv. 109–11; from M. CHEZLUY to PHARAMOND, iv. 201–3; of recommendation from JACK TOPER, iv. 249–50; from Horace to Claudius Nero, iv. 250–1; between GATTY and JENNY, iv. 331–3; from T. W. and B. T., proposing marriage, iv. 359–60; from Pliny to Hispulla, iv. 372–3; from Emperor of China to the Pope, iv. 450–2; from Ambassador of Bantam to his master, iv. 504–5; between SHALUM and HILPA, iv. 598; v. 1–3; written in mixed metaphors, v. 36–37; two, describing the Coronation rejoicings, v. 105–8; from a countryman to ZELINDA, v. 143–4.

Lettres historiques, iv. 449.

Leucas, Leucate: scene of Lovers' Leap, ii. 366, 382, 385, 406, 409.

Leucippe, in *The Humorous Lieutenant,* ii. 535.

Leucothoe and Daphnis, the loves of, iv. 329.

Levée: account of a great man's, ii. 256–60; iv. 459; of the sun, ii. 470; manners of politicians at, iii. 99; attention paid to insignificant fellows at a great man's, iv. 220; a cure for l.-haunting, iv. 459; admirers at my afternoon, v. 97.

Level: persons above the common, ii. 426; Providence sets men upon a, ii. 491; the envious try to reduce the successful to a l. with themselves, ii. 493–4.

Levelling: satires of no use to the world, ii. 320; pleasure in l. superior persons, iv. 320.

Leviathan: simile of the sleeping, in *PL,* iii. 91; one of the noblest productions in nature, iii. 260.

Levity: sprightliness of women should not degenerate into, i. 193; in choice of husbands, ii. 9–10, 303; of temper, ii. 135; of behaviour, degrading, ii. 164; of women at the play, ii. 314–15; of thought in young women of quality, ii. 486; of childhood, indulged by the ancients, iv. 259; and seriousness, v. 43–45. *See also* The French.

Lewd: beating up a l. woman's quarters, i. 436; fellow will debauch your sister or lie with your wife, ii. 93; men suspect all women of misbehaviour, ii. 171; devices perpetuated by painters and sculptors, ii. 179; anecdote of a l. young fellow and a hermit, iv. 566.

Lewdness: in London, i. 36; in youth and old age, ii. 100–3; effect of *Spectator* on, iv. 128; justified by example of Jupiter, v. 169.

Lewis, David, *Miscellaneous Poems,* iv. 522.

Lewis, William, *Spectator* sold by, i. xxiv.

Leyden, ii. 17.

Liar(s): history of an inveterate, ii. 36–40; ii. 157; a 'castle-builder' a liar in soliloquy, ii. 158; the officious l. to be excused, ii. 410–11; who fails to keep a promise, iv. 74–76; kinds of, iv. 355–6; *liar, rogue,* &c., in pamphlets, iv. 537.

Libel(s): on the eminent never fail of success, ii. 494–5; Balzac's attitude towards, iii. 324; defamatory, iv. 86–90; dispersers of, condemned by Roman law, iv. 89–90; mock example of a political, iv. 537–8 (comment on, iv. 539–40). *See also* Lampoons, Satire.

Libeller, to be attacked by every honest man, i. 148.

Liberal arts: give a turn or cast to behaviour, ii. 271–2; flourish under liberty, iii. 21–22.

Liberality: to be performed with cheerfulness, iii. 39; should be based on frugality, iii. 288–9; of MANILIUS, iv. 151–2.

Libertine: women, ii. 236, 303–4; who drew up a genealogical tree of his illegitimate children, ii. 295–6; is ashamed to read a serious discourse, ii. 400; disputes existence of God, v. 172.

Libertinism of young men in England, iv. 384.

Liberty: allegorical figure of, i. 17; pronunciation of the word, ii. 33; civil l. defined, iii. 19; the fruits of, iii. 21–22; 'conjugal l. of conscience', iii. 65; danger of loss of, iii. 442.

Libidinous man, ii. 101; full of stratagems, ii. 297.

Library, a person more famous for his l. than his learning, iv. 439. *See also* Lady's Library.

Libyan desert, v. 35.

Licander, prayer of, to Jupiter, iii. 468.

Licence, impertinent l. in speech of married women, iii. 72.

Licentious: passages in *The Lancashire Witches*, ii. 58–59; behaviour, ii. 439–40; language has something brutal in it, iii. 498.

Licentiousness: among servants, i. 373; is not freedom, ii. 413; prevalence of, iii. 64–67.

Licinius, the pipe of, ii. 388–9; iv. 437.

LIDDY, a cheerful good-humoured creature, iii. 104.

Lie(s): 'giving the lie' the greatest insult from man to man, i. 418; kinds of, ii. 409–11; the officious, when excusable, ii. 410; one of the Fathers on telling a, iv. 301; telling a lie at Charing Cross and following it through the town, iv. 355–6.

Life, Human: preservation of, a secondary concern; the direction of, our principal concern, i. 108; conduct of, i. 112–13; duration of, uncertain, i. 113, 325; too short for 'demurring', i. 378; we complain of shortness of, yet wish every period of it at an end, i. 394; ii. 322; emptiness of most men's, i. 395; may be lengthened by pursuit of knowledge, i. 401–2; largely made up of sickness, ill humour or idleness, i. 419–20; enjoyment of, ii. 64–68, 100–3; an education for Heaven, ii. 76; allegory of (Vision of Mirzah), ii. 122–6; the great articles of, ii. 135; a pilgrimage, ii. 353; iii. 30; the art of enjoying ordinary, ii. 364; a state of probation, ii. 420–3; our business in, to act rather than to know, ii. 421; man only a passenger in, iii. 29; scene of sorrow, iii. 129; cannot be judged before its conclusion, iii. 299; end of, compared to winding up of a well-written play, iii. 299; like a game at tables, iii. 518; shortness and uncertainty of, iv. 409, 566; vanity of, an argument for immortality, v. 142.

Ligatures in English dress, check circulation of blood, iv. 571.

Liger, L., *Le Jardinier fleuriste*, i. 27.

Light: and shadows in a picture, ii. 447–8; descriptions of, in *PL*, iii. 89–90; overflow of, among Quakers, iii. 484; stains of, in clouds, pleasing to the imagination, iii. 544; and colours have no existence in matter, iii. 547; the shadow of God, iv. 298.

Light (linkman), iv. 103.

LIGHTFOOT, JACK, letter from (on the Mohocks), iii. 223–5.

Lightning: raptures of passion like, ii. 281; mirth like a flash of, iii. 429; *a l. before death* (prov.), iv. 340; and storms in the play-house, v. 26.

Ligon, Richard, *History of Barbados*, i. 49; iii. 479.

Lilies, violets, and amaranths may bloom together, in poetry, iii. 569.

Lillie, Charles: connexion with *Spectator*, i. xxii–xxiv; his collection of *Letters*, i. xxii–xxiii, 6, 74; iii. 94; v. 115; *The British Perfumer*, i. xxii, 74, 156, 314; iii. 279; letter from (offering to take in letters and advertisements), i. 73–74; advertises 'Exercise of the Snuff-Box', ii. 46; replies to be left with, ii. 53; iii. 454; receives subscriptions for Dorigny's engravings, ii. 381; agent for musical entertainments in York Buildings, ii. 507; comments on mosaic discovered at Stunsfield, iii. 339–40; mentioned, i. 197; iii. 124, 441.

Lily, William: Latin grammar: preacher who used sentences from, ii. 359–60; mentioned, ii. 395; 'how sweetly Bacchus and Apollo run in a verse', ii. 529; 'he sold you your first Lilly's Grammar', iii. 93; mentioned, iv. 90.

Lilybeum, promontory of, iv. 582.

Limbeck (alembic), i. 266.

Limbo of Vanity in *PL*, improbability of, iii. 60, 144.

Limborch, Philippe de: his objection to Jewish religious ceremonies, ii. 332; Acosta's answer to, ii. 332.

Limning, iii. 206.

Lincoln: county of, ii. 117; city, iv. 588.

LINDAMIRA, complexion of, i. 176.

Linen, i. 241, 351; ii. 16; iii. 189, 210; delicate l. of advantage to a poor

dependant, ii. 593; in Motteux's shop, iii. 26; iv. 479; clean, iii. 54; dirty, the bane of conjugal love, iii. 82; metamorphoses of, into paper, iii. 380–1; John Moreton, well known in the l. trade, iv. 455; daubed with snuff, v. 156.

Linen-draper, an arrant, iii. 162.

Lines, mathematical: that draw nearer to each other without touching, i. 459.

Link-boy, conversation with a, iv. 103.

Linnet and the lark, v. 63.

Lintot, Bernard, shop of, i. 70.

Linus, quoted, iv. 166.

Lion: fable of l. and man, i. 48–49, 60; and Nicolini, i. 55–60; will not hurt a virgin, i. 57; actors as, i. 57–58; letter from, i. 60 (referred to, iv. 438); red l. as a sign, i. 116, 197; a tailor living at the sign of, i. 117; rebus of cock and l. on Blenheim House, i. 251; rather suffer from paw of, than hoof of ass, i. 262; particles of, in man's make-up, ii. 325; soul of Ajax transformed into that of a, ii. 326; one of the noblest productions in nature, iii. 260; a jackal in service of a, iii. 274; pursuing his prey in Paradise, iii. 359; shop-sign with a lion's heart in each hand, iv. 4.

'Lion, Tipping the', iii. 187, 294.

Lioness: suckled by a wild, iv. 451; brings forth but once, v. 163.

Lions: in the Tower, i. 56, 127; in china ware, i. 153; Amazonian ladies play with, iv. 24; varieties of, iv. 442–3.

Lion-tippers, iii. 223.

Lipogrammatists, or letter-droppers, i. 249–50, 272.

Lipograms, a type of false wit, i. 265.

Lipsius, Justus, i. 43.

Liquorice powder, bought at apothecary's shop, iii. 189, 209–10.

Lister, Dr. Martin, iv. 310.

Liszynski, Casimir, execution of, for atheism, iii. 462.

Literature: transmits ideas of a genius to posterity, ii. 154; less readily understood than painting, ii. 378.

Litterati: correspondence with, i. 228; to be consulted on project for discovery of longitude, iv. 589.

Little: excellencies, thorough contempt of, i. 324; mind, behaviour of, i. 350; man, easy and pleasant manner of, iii. 56; many a l. makes a mickle (prov.), iv. 309.

Littleton, Sir Thomas: a case in, iii. 249; 'Cook and', i. 9; iii. 126.

Liturgy, the: a pattern for clergymen's devotions, iii. 130.

Liveliness and assurance, the qualities of the French, iv. 29.

Lively: the brisk and, ii. 425; lights in pictures represent bright and l. thoughts, ii. 447–8.

Livery (-ies): servants', ii. 43, 592; iii. 69; impertinent behaviour turns a fine coat into a, ii. 164; of an equipage, ii. 251; mentioned, iii. 109; Mr. FROTH passed by in his new, iii. 182.

Living: in the world and out of it at the same time, i. 115; folly of l. beyond one's means, i. 467–70; dangers of l. above our circumstances, ii. 251–2.

Livre, French: value of, iii. 97.

Livy (Titus Livius): History of Rome, i. 348; iv. 17; fable of members of the body, ii. 185; his excellence lies in his manner of telling a story, iii. 528; excels in vividness, iii. 574.

Lizard: rebus of, on Greek building, i. 250–1.

Lloyd, Rev. John, i. lvii.

Lloyd, O., Spectator sold by, i. xxiv.

Lloyd, Robert, paraphrase of No. 627, v. 142.

Lloyd, William (Bishop of Worcester), v. 175.

Loadstone: Albertus Magnus's dissertation upon, i. 237; correspondence by means of a, ii. 437–8; dispute concerning magnetical virtue of, ii. 442.

Locke, John: 'a lady that reads L. and understands the mathematics', ii. 443; complied with public forms of worship, iii. 460; anecdote of (on time wasted in playing cards), iv. 403–4; mentioned, iii. 485; iv. 252. — Essay concerning Human Understanding: a copy in LEONORA's library, i. 155; distinction between wit and judgement quoted, i. 263–4; comment on our ideas of time quoted, i. 399; on association of ideas quoted, i. 454; observation that the oyster, &c., has as many sensations as are good for it, quoted, i. 495; of great value to the critic, iii. 36; on the abuse of words, quoted, iii. 403–4; his explanation of mixture of evil with good in nature, quoted, iii. 454; distinction between primary and secondary qualities, iii. 537; 'that great modern discovery' that light and colours are ideas in the mind and not qualities in matter, iii. 547; on the chain of beings, quoted, iv. 348–9; his explanation of how we form our ideas of God, quoted, iv. 392–3; on stupidity of choosing a course of vice, quoted, iv. 568–9; remarks on personal identity

puoted, iv. 575-6; the whole soul remembers, understands, wills, or imagines, v. 51. — *Some Thoughts concerning
Education*: on harsh treatment of children in schools, ii. *115*; on Greek in
schools, ii. *396*; on education at public
school and at home, quoted, iii. *132*;
unwise to hazard innocence and virtue
of children for a little Greek and Latin,
iii. *250*. — quotation from (unidenti-
fied), v. 141.
Lockets and bracelets, iv. 84.
Lodgings, at ten shillings a week, ii. 526.
Lodgements, the military man always
talking of making, i. 438.
LOFTY, Mrs., a prude, iii. 297.
Logarithms, a kind of poetical, ii. 356.
Logic: kinds of, in disputation, ii. 428-9;
of kings (*Ratio ultima regum*), ii. 430;
a clear and logical head necessary for
the critic, iii. 35; marks of a person
perfect in, iv. 344-5.
Logic-Lane, in Oxford, ii. 429.
Logician(s): everyone that reasons is a,
i. 365; their distinction of material and
formal, iii. 379.
Lokman (Luqmān), Arabian physician,
iii. *597*.
LOLLER, Lady LYDIA: memorial of, iv. 8.
Lolling-table, at the Lazy Club, iii. 168.
London, George: to be appointed gardener of the play-house, i. 27; Wise and
L., our heroic poets, iv. 190.
London (and Westminster): Mr. SPECTA-
TOR's familiarity with, i. 3; vice in
streets of, i. 36; trained-bands in, i.
183; smoke of, i. 195; ii. 21; comments
on, by the Four Indian Kings, i. 211-
15; an emporium for the whole earth,
i. 293; the great field of game for the
Spectator, ii. 19; 'the populous and
wealthy city of', ii. 194; population of,
ii. 283; taxes paid by, ii. 283; seduction in, ii. 295; 'my law-suits have
brought me to', ii. 385; 'female apes'
frequent in, ii. 448; the cries of, ii. 474-
8; a freeman of, ii. 475; 'the crooked
morals of this our Babylon', ii. 577;
a square at the other end of the town,
iii. 71; within the city-walls, iii. 111;
iv. 5; suburbs beyond the Tower, iii.
413; the fifty new churches, iii. 437;
the fashionable end of the town, and
the City, iii. 493, 506; the different
worlds of, iii. 506; iv. 99; variety of
amusements in 'this dear town', iii.
590; Sheriff of the City of, iv. 4;
scandalous appearance of the poor in,
iv. 11; the Court-end of, iv. 84; a
twenty-four hours' ramble in, iv. 98-

103; Lord-Mayor's Day in, iv. 132;
account of, by the Ambassador of
Bantam, iv. 504-5.
'London City's Triumph; or, my Lord
Mayor's Show' (song), iv. *283*.
London Dispensary, iv. 590.
London Prentice, i. 59.
London and environs, places in:
Aldgate, ii. 348.
Bank: Directors of, subscribers to
Spectator, i. xc; directors, secre-
taries, and clerks of, i. 14; a billet-
doux understood at the, iii. 478;
'selling out of the', iii. 509. See also
Grocers' Hall.
Barbican: a Dutch painter in, i. 176;
a quack doctor, next door to the
Harp in, iv. 62.
Barn Elms, as a place for duels, i. 387.
Bartholomew Fair, i. *63*, *201-2*, 218;
an elephant in, iv. 106-7.
Bear-Garden. See Hockley-in-the-Hole.
Beaufort Buildings in the Strand, i. *73*,
74, &c. See Lillie.
Bedlam, in Moorfields, i. *56*, 146; ii.
583; iv. *293*, 571.
Billingsgate, ii. 458; iv. 88; v. 36.
Birchin Lane, letter addressed from,
iii. 370.
Bishopsgate Street, an inn in, iv. 310.
Bloomsbury Square, 'next the Fields
in a good air', i. 151.
Bow Street, Covent Garden: Will's
Coffee-house in, i. *3*; Sir ROGER's
lodgings in, iii. 533.
Bread Street, iv. *306*.
Bridewell, Hospital of, i. 36.
Bridges Street, near Russell Court, i.
10.
Broad Street, letter addressed from,
iv. *306*.
Brompton: news from, iv. 93; Bromp-
ton Park, i. *27*.
Chancery Lane, the bagnio in, iii. 225.
Chandos Street: auction of Mr. Boul
'in Shandois-street', ii. 381.
'Change, i. 285, 331, 365, 371, 460;
ii. 110; iii. 125, 182, 450; 'Honest
INDIGO of', ii. 40; 'greater estates
got about C., than at Whitehall or
St. James's', iii. 4-5.
Change Alley, ii. 108; iv. 4.
Charing Cross, i. 118, 119; noise in
Haymarket theatre heard in, i. 179;
from C.C. to the Royal Exchange, i.
365; between C.C. and Covent
Garden, iii. 508; following a lie from,
through the town, iv. 355.
Cheapside, i. *40*, 381, 404; BRUNETTA
and PHILLIS born in, i. 342; Nath.

INDEX

London and environs (*cont.*)
Cliff, at the Bible and Three Crowns in, ii. 250; letter addressed from, ii. 327; inhabitants of, different from those of St. James's, the Temple, and Smithfield, iii. 506; a coffee-house in, iii. 509; any haberdasher in, iv. 91; an honest tradesman in, iv. 208.

Chelsea: Addison's retreat at, i. xvii; the five fields towards, ii. 43; Hospital, ii. 102; to C. by water, ii. 191; 'to go as far as Chelsey', iv. 267.

City, The: Sir ANDREW a merchant of eminence in, i. 10; approves of the *Spectator*, i. 142; always the province of satire, i. 142; a dancing-master in, i. 285; supplying want of eloquence with cash, ii. 109; a genteel trade in, ii. 432; 'a city romance', ii. 463; a tavern in, iii. 402; thick set with churches, iii. 437; a woman kept by a merchant in, iv. 225; JEREMY COMFITT a wealthy grocer in, iv. 407.

Clare Market, Timothy Buck of, iv. 31.
Cornhill: shop of John Moreton in, iv. 455; letter addressed from, v. 115.
Counter, the (a prison), i. 36.
Courts of Justice, i. 375.
Covent Garden: Will's Coffee-house in, i. 3, &c.; a fine lady who lives near, i. 36, 38; Powell's puppet-show in, i. 61; iii. 400; SALMONEUS of, i. 150-1; auction of pictures in, i. 288; letter addressed from, ii. 446; mentioned, ii. 503; Richard Estcourt's house in, ii. 529; meeting with a prostitute near, ii. 534; the Piazza in, ii. 534; iii. 490; iv. 546; from Charing Cross to, iii. 508; purveyors for market in, iv. 99; a player in, iv. 281; the Queen's Arms in, iv. 546.
Cripplegate, letter addressed from, iv. 169.
Custom-House, the, i. 371; ii. 578.
Dark-House, the, iv. 99.
Deptford, lodging of the Czar there, ii. 37.
Devereux Court in the Strand, i. 4; iv. 265; John Sly in, ii. 237; iv. 376.
Doctors' Commons, iv. 369.
Downs, The, i. 49.
Drury Lane: letters addressed from, i. 94, 150; Mohocks to be confined to, iii. 295; a quack doctor's place in, iv. 59; the Half-Moon Tavern in, iv. 182. — Drury Lane Theatre: i. lxxxiii, 4, 10, 149-50; iii. 351, 417;

the motto at top of the stage in, iii. 393.
Essex-Street, iv. 249.
Exchange: 'I have been taken for a merchant upon the', i. 4; young merchants about the, ii. 46; letters both from the Royal and the New, ii. 108; taverns about the, iii. 401; a coffee-house near the, iii. 428; 'centre of the world of trade', iv. 102; her husband gone to the, iv. 378; mentioned, iii. 590; iv. 377, 408. — EXETER EXCHANGE, i. 4. — NEW EXCHANGE: cheapening goods at, i. 408; they are eloquent for want of cash at the, ii. 109; 'that great hive of females', ii. 326; the petition of, iii. 95; mentioned, ii. 108; 'the Change' (probably the New Exchange), iii. 125, 182. — ROYAL EXCHANGE: description of, i. 292-6; shops of agreeable females in, iv. 102; neglect of, iv. 307-8; mentioned, i. 365; ii. 108; iv. 57, 539. *See also* 'Change.
Fish Street, iii. 508.
Fleet Street, i. 70, *128, 129*; Mohocks in, iii. 224, 240; lucubrations of law-students in, iv. 375.
Fox-Hall (Vauxhall). *See* Spring Garden.
Fulham, news from, iv. 93.
Fuller's Rents, a coffee-house in, i. 372.
Garlick Hill, St. James's church, ii. 78.
Gates, one of the North, i. 86.
Gerard Street, iv. 311.
Gravel Pits, at Kensington, ii. 46; iv. 190.
Gray's (Grey's) Inn, i. 61; iv. 497.
Gray's-Inn-Lane, fresh air in, iv. 375.
Gray's-Inn-Walks, Sir ROGER takes a turn in, ii. 549.
Greenwich, iii. 550; v. 121.
Grocers' Hall, 'where the Bank is kept', i. 14.
Grub Street: orators of, ii. 89; one of the most eminent pens in, ii. 227.
Guildhall Yard, incident in, iv. 132.
Haberdashers' Hall, a consort of music to be held at, i. 228.
Hackney, letter addressed from, ii. 269; Hackney Church, ii. 31.
Hammersmith: news from, iv. 93; practices of a quack at, iv. 552.
Hampstead, ii. 344; H.-Heath, iv. 266.
Hampton Court: cartoons of Raphael at, ii. 379; mentioned, iii. 521.
Hay Market, the Queen's Theatre in the: Mr. SPECTATOR well known in, i. 4; the owner of, i. 25; Nicolini's

371

London and environs (*cont.*)
combat with the lion in, i. 55–59;
letter from the lion there, i. 60;
scenes and machinery in the opera,
i. 65; noise of battle in, i. 179; formerly used for plays, i. *179*; party-
patches in, i. 346; mentioned, i. 127;
iii. *513*.

Hockley-in-the-Hole, ii. 56, 59; 'all
the diversions of', i. 129; a match at
the Bear Garden, iv. 30–35; cheat-
ing at, iv. 80–81; 'our gladiators of',
v. 155.

Holborn, the 'Bear' in, ii. 45.

Hyde Park: servants congregate at
entrance to, i. 375; as a place for
duels, i. 387; a strange-windowed
house near, ii. 576; the mannish
equestrienne in, iv. 29. *See also* The
Ring.

India Company, iii. 25.

Inns of Court, i. 90, 504; the TEMPLAR
thinks they should not be ridiculed,
i. 143; members of, at the coffee-
house, i. 209; idle young fellows of,
ii. 71–72; nurseries of statesmen
and law-givers, ii. 273; a Bencher
of one of the, ii. 575; 'trifled away a
whole year' there, iii. 217; young
gentlemen from, as amateur hackney-coachmen, iv. 266; lawyers in,
iv. 574.

Islington: Mr. SPECTATOR seen going
towards, i. 52; took a walk to, iii.
154; in his walk to, iii. 418; a horse
strayed out of a field near, iv. 92.

James Street, Covent Garden, ii. 534;
iv. 100.

Kensington: nursery at Brompton
Park near, i. 27; gravel pits at, ii.
46; work of London and Wise at,
iv. 190.

King Street, Covent Garden, i. *129*;
'the Seven Stars in', ii. 578–9; we
drove for, iv. 100.

Knights-bridge, a horse clapped into
the pound at, iv. 93.

Lancaster, Duchy of, i. 73.

Leadenhall Street, iii. 25.

Liberties, within the, ii. 475.

Lincoln's Inn, ii. 225; the chapel at,
v. 83.

Lincoln's-Inn-Fields: the beggar in,
i. 28; a stationer in the centre of,
iii. 93; Theatre, i. *24*.

Little Britain: Samuel Buckley's shop
in, i. xx, 6, 59; the Cock and Bottle
in, ii. 225.

Lombard Street, an eminent banker in,
iii. 275.

London Bridge, i. 371; 'a greater piece
of work than any of the Seven
Wonders of the World', iii. 437; a
church not far from, iv. 284.

Long Acre, ii. 473; iv. 100.

Long Lane: second-hand dresses
hanging in, ii. 527; tradesmen in,
iii. 95.

Lords, House of, i. 374.

Lothbury Street, iii. 93.

Ludgate Prison, i. 350.

Lyon's Inn, an attorney in, iii. 344.

Mall, The: walk the Park at high
Mall, iv. 38; solacing himself in,
iv. 259; talking with Frenchmen in,
iv. 499.

Mile-End-Green, near Stepney: a
boarding school formerly at, iii. 140,
226, 254; a letter addressed from,
iii. 195.

Monmouth Street, tradesmen in, iii.
95.

Montague House, a place for duels behind, i. 387.

Moorfields: a fortune-teller in, ii. 257;
the habitation of prophetic philomaths, iv. 293; TITUS TROPHONIUS
writes from, iv. 293–4.

Mouse Alley near Wapping, a doctor
in, iv. 61.

Mulberry Garden, i. 407.

New River, i. 24; v. 41.

Newgate Prison, the officer of, iv. 290.

Newgate Street, the bagnio in, iii. 225.

New Inn, i. 10.

Newington, Jones of, iv. 173.

Newport Street, iv. 100.

Nine Elms, 'put in at, and taken in
melons', iv. 99.

Norfolk Buildings, Sir ROGER's lodging in London, iii. 216.

Norfolk Street: the New Inn near, i.
10; Sir ROGER and the Mohocks in,
iii. 240.

Ormond Street, a club in, i. 41.

Paddington, news from, iv. 93.

Pall Mall: the Cocoa-Tree chocolate
house in, i. *4*; at a person of quality's
in, ii. 579.

Pankridge. *See* St. Pancras.

Paper Buildings. *See* Temple.

Park, the: Duke of Monmouth at
head of his troop in, i. 12; walking
in, i. 101, 102; ii. 53; iii. 34; iv. 38;
meeting in, iii. 166.

Parsons Green, a tub of ale set abroach
at, iv. 93.

Pass, the: at St. Martin's Lane, iv. 100;
at St. Clement's Church, iv. 267,
374, 408.

London and environs (*cont.*)

Paul's Churchyard: Child's Coffee-house in, i. *3*; discussions of the Spanish succession in, iii. 508; a stop of coaches in, iv. 330; a coffee-house in (probably Child's), iv. 470; screens and sets of hangings sold in, v. 83.

Piazza, The. *See* Covent Garden.

Piccadilly: letter addressed from, ii. 327; THYRSIS 'shot from a casement in', iii. 417.

Putney, news from, iv. 93.

Red Lion Square: letter addressed from, iv. 536.

Ring, the (in Hyde Park), i. 68, 199, 312, 375; ii. 487; iii. 417.

Rosamond's Pond, iii. 125.

Round Court, the, in parish of St. Martin's in the Fields, iii. 94.

Round-house: put into the, ii. 218; letter addressed from, ii. 218–19.

Russell Court, i. 10; a quack doctor in, iv. 59.

St. Anne's Lane, Sir ROGER as a school boy inquiring for, i. 509.

St. Bartholomew's Hospital, where Nicholas Hart 'slept', ii. 225.

St. Bride's Church, i. *36*; charity school at, iii. 49, 428; iv. 12.

St. Clement's Church, the 'streight' at, iv. 267.

St. Dunstan's in the West, the clock at, iii. 294.

St. James's: the parish of, i. 195; iv. 330, 460; people of, different from those of Cheapside, iii. 506; mentioned, ii. 46; iii. 5; iv. 100.

St. James's Church, 'shot through the sticks of a fan at', iii. 417.

St. James's, Garlick-Hill, Church, the service read well at, ii. 78.

St. James's Park, sauntering in, ii. 487.

St. John Street, IRUS lives in, ii. 527.

St. Martin's, letter addressed from, ii. 419–20.

St. Martin's Lane, i. *61*; iv. 100.

St. Martin's in the Fields: New Version of Psalms first used at, ii. *305*; Round Court in parish of, iii. 94.

St. Olave's, Hart Street, epitaph in, ii. *200*.

St. Pancras in the Fields: weddings in, iv. 93; epitaph in churchyard, iv. 424.

St. Paul's Cathedral described by the Four Indian Kings, i. 212–13; 'company coming out of the Cathedral', iv. 330; proposal for an organ in, iv. 479–81.

St. Paul's, Covent Garden: letters from the under-sexton, i. 61–62; iii. 400–1.

Savoy in the Strand, the, letter addressed from, i. 95, 228.

Sion College, Annual Assembly of clergy of, ii. 79.

Smithfield: executions there, ii. 431; a S.-Bargain in marriage, iii. 92; inhabitants of Cheapside distinct from those of, iii. 506.

Soho Square, Sir ROGER's town house in, i. 7–8.

Somerset Garden, i. 330.

Spittlefields, ii. 440; iv. 343.

Spring Garden (Vauxhall), i. *36*; Sir ROGER at, iii. 436–9.

Stationers' Hall, i. *120*; iv. 483.

Stebon-Heath, 'commonly called Stepney', iv. 342.

Stepney: boarding school near, iii. 140, 254; epitaphs in St. Dunstan's churchyard, iv. 342–4.

Stocks Market, i. *56*; iv. 99.

Strand, the: 'R. B., fishmonger in', i. 52; the Savoy in, i. 95; Beaufort Buildings in, ii. 46; Devereux Court in, ii. 237; mentioned, ii. 326; iv. 267, 408.

Strand Bridge, iv. 99.

Temple, The, i. *61*, 88, 371, 377; the walks in, i. 407; proficients in wind-music at, ii. 73; a coffee-house near, ii. 73, 81, 92, 273; iii. 168, 508; a nest of Jezebels near, ii. 191; a tradition of choosing kings in, ii. 464; MULES PALFREY lodges at, iii. 110; idleness in, iii. 168–9; Mohocks to be confined to purlieus of, iii. 295; TOM POTTLE in his third year at, iii. 353–5; inhabitants of Cheapside distinct from those of, iii. 506; letter addressed from Paper-Buildings, iv. 220; JACK TOPER of, iv. 249; young gentlemen of, as amateur hackney coachmen, iv. 266, 374; a gay gentleman of, iv. 379.

Temple Bar, i. *73*; iii. 437; iv. 408, 483, 546.

Temple Cloister: walking in, ii. 465 scene of Sir ROGER's meeting with SUKEY, iii. 531.

Temple Gate, iv. 267.

Temple Stairs, iii. 109, 436.

Temple, Inner: The TEMPLAR a member of, i. 9; THOMAS SUDDEN, of, iv. 8; WILL TRAP and JACK STINT chamber-fellows in, iv. 76.

Temple, Middle: letters from, i. 37–38; ii. 13; iv. 330, 514; v. 39, 95;

London and environs (*cont.*)
JOHN PLEADWELL of, iii. 418; a young rake of the, v. 47.

Thames, the, i. 330; ii. 73; language of watermen on, ii. 439; 'the noblest river in Europe', iii. 437; T.-ribaldry, iii. 438; loaded with the product of each shore, iv. 99; overflowing of, iv. 575; George I's arrival on, v. 122.

Tilt-Yard: 'now a common street before Whitehall', i. 450; the coffee-house there, i. 450.

Tower, the: animals in, i. 56, 127; costume of Yeomen of the Guard, i. 450, the T.-guns, ii. 150; suburbs lying beyond, iii. 413; Anne Boleyn's letter written in, iii. 487–9; the Beef-Eaters, v. 137.

Tower Hill, letter addressed from, ii. 29–30.

Tyburn: speeches after every sessions at, ii. 95; Paul Lorrain, iii. 254, 268.

Vauxhall. *See* Spring Garden.

Vinegar Yard, letter addressed from, i. 228.

Wapping: letter addressed from, ii. 327–8; a doctor in Mouse Alley near, iv. 61.

Warwick Lane, Anne Baldwin's shop in, i. xx–xxi, 6, 40.

Warwick Street, iv. 101.

Water-works. *See* Winstanley.

Westminster, i. 73, 209, 384, &c.

Westminster Abbey: a rendezvous in, i. lxxxiii; reflections in, i. 108–11; monument to Duke and Duchess of Newcastle in, i. 417; Sir ROGER's visit to, iii. 212–16, 220; mentioned, i. 197; v. 89.

Westminster Hall: lawyers in, i. 58, 89, 209; iv. 215, 408; transactions of, i. 438; the colours in the Westminster schoolboy, ii. 49–50; a Counsellor in, iii. 522; 'the late shake of the roof', iv. 8; being driven to, iv. 266; term-time at, iv. 377; illiberal cant of lawyers in, iv. 477; causes depending in, iv. 574.

Westminster School: HARRY RACK-RENT attends, i. 406; the colours in Westminster Hall and the Westminster schoolboy, ii. 49–50; the curtain which used to separate the upper school from the lower, iii. 134; friendship between two schoolboys at, iii. 134–5.

Whitehall, i. 450; ii. 190; iii. 5.

Workhouse, the, ii. 242.

York Buildings, entertainments of music in, ii. 506, 585; iii. 291.

Long: bow, statute regarding, ii. 133; chins, persons with, invited together as a jest, iii. 397; *home, to his* (prov.), iii. 418, 600; life, gaiety and cheerfulness conducive to, iii. 451; robe, gentlemen of the, ii. 272; story, a hush-note to be used against, ii. 389.

Longevity: of philosophers the result of temperance, ii. 266; Cornaro's book on, ii. 267; of HILPA and SHALUM, iv. 596–8; v. 1–3.

Longing: natural causes of, in women, iii. 195–7.

Longinus: the TEMPLAR familiar with his work, i. 9; his censure of Caecilius, i. 245; and Quintilian the only ancient authors who separated puns from true wit, i. 262; wrote of the sublime in a style suitable to it, i. 430; ii. 484; a true critic, v. 26; 'the best of critics', v. 166; on Sappho, ii. 369 & n., 391, 393; on Homer, ii. 587–8; iii. 173, 177, 230, 255; iv. 234; v. 167; says that the great genius who sometimes errs is preferable to the inferior author who follows the rules, iii. 5, 38; observes there may be a loftiness in sentiments where there is no passion, iii. 254–5; recommends considering how Homer would have spoken on such an occasion, iii. 255; his praise of Moses' account of the Creation, iii. 255–6; on modesty of Spartan youths, iii. 321; one of the few critics to see in poetry something that elevates and astonishes the fancy, iii. 530; says that nothing can be great, the contempt of which is great, v. 84; a fragment of, preserved in a MS. in the Vatican, v. 165.

Longitude, the: 'the late noble inventor of', iv. 5; project for discovery of, iv. 589.

'Long-shanks' (Edward I), i. 135.

Long-tailed comparisons, Perrault on Homer's, iii. 90–91.

Look(s): gay, ii. 94; beauty in, ii. 300; a kind l. imparts a year's discourse in a moment, ii. 478; blustering airs and big, iii. 321; contempt shown by the scornful, iii. 322; a lumpish downcast l. as a sign of learning, iv. 344.

Lookers-on see more . . . . *See* Standers-by.

Looking-glass(es): shivered into pieces because they tell the truth, i. 134; effect on a jealous husband, ii. 171; 'grinning in their glasses', ii. 182; women looking in, ii. 202, 236, 327; a

person placed between two opposite, ii. 470; chimney-pieces glazed with, iii. 69; the fop who admires his person in a, iii. 126; WILL HONEYCOMB'S dissertation on, iii. 191; transformation of FIDELIO into a, iii. 470–3; fable of the woman who broke a, iv. 86; 'pelvis' used by ancient comic writers for, iv. 164; broken by a choleric husband, iv. 525.

Loops and buttons in men's dress, ii. 526.

Loose: hopes, i. 283; desires, ii. 172; looser part of mankind, ii. 205; and ungoverned mind, ii. 238; tribe of men (profligates), ii. 295; conduct, ii. 432; thoughts avoided in *Spectator*, ii. 517; 'a l. age', ii. 554; singing a l. air, ii. 576; looser part of the female sex, iii. 64.

Loquacity: English aversion to, ii. 32–36; in women, ii. 458–62.

Loquet, —— (master of languages), i. 157.

'Lord of the Ring', among wrestlers, ii. 133.

Lord-Mayor's Day, Charles II dined with citizens on, iv. 132.

Lord's Prayer, the: proposed alteration in wording, i. 337; quoted, ii. 214.

Lorrain, Paul (ordinary of Newgate Prison), iii. 254, 268.

Lorraine, Commercy in, iii. 440.

Lot and his family, in *PL*, iii. 389.

Lot (prize in a lottery), 'the great lot', ii. 250, 251.

Lotus, crocus, and hyacinth, iii. 311.

Lottery, the Public: i. 370; choice of numbers in, ii. 248–52, 348; the Spittle-fields weaver who sold his wife's ticket, ii. 440–1; 'the great benefit ticket', ii. 348.

Louis XIII, iv. 452.

Louis XIV: mistresses of, i. *12*; 'my Brother Lewis of France', i. 96; reduction of duelling under, i. 419; the hoop-petticoat portends the downfall of(?), ii. 6; contrasted with Peter the Great, ii. 47–49; debauchery of his youth succeeded by superstition of his old age, ii. 48; 'an hardened sinner', ii. 208; poor economy of his military victories, ii. 209–11, 283; his seizure of Spain, ii. 211; motto on his arms (*ratio ultima regum*), ii. 430; to establish an Academy for Politics, iii. 96; at Versailles or Marly, iii. 98; addresses to, after Ramillies, iii. 102; his strut, iii. 241; encouraged fine printing, iii. 381; reactions to rumours of his death, iii. 507–9; his attitude to the Mesna-

ger–Rechteren controversy, iv. 207; contrasted with William III, iv. 335–8; mentioned, iv. 499.

Louis d'or, iii. 98.

'Lousy cur', a tradesman called a, i. 242.

Louvre, The, ii. 159; iii. 96; books printed at, iii. 381.

LOVE, SIR ANTHONY, his pew covered with greens, ii. 600; iii. 8–9.

Love: the greatest concern, i. 22, 124; the cement of society, i. 22; the old topic of constancy in, i. 48; love-tokens, i. 124, 306; ii. 452–3; iii. 210; compared to fire and flame by witty poets, i. 266–7, 273, 313; is refined by the force and dignity of the object, i. 304; burns with greatest fury in a virtuous and noble heart, i. 504; a long-lasting (letters to Prue), ii. 60–64; allegorical depiction of, ii. 124; disables the heart from bearing up against distresses, ii. 141; a strong ingredient in jealousy, ii. 168–9; Roman Catholics actuated by, and Calvinists by fear, ii. 332; described in all its symptoms by Sappho, ii. 366, 393; frenzy produced by, and by biting of a mad dog, ii. 383–4; moves the eyes, ii. 471; extravagant effects of, ii. 478; iii. 375–6, 416; as a factor in marriage, ii. 514–16, 545–6; iv. 369–73; the predominant passion, ii. 559; that noble passion, iii. 23; allegory of l. and old age, iii. 76–78; good effects of, in a lover, iii. 92–93, 356–7; a periodical love-fit spreads through the whole sex in May, iii. 373; the mother of poetry, iii. 416; 'dying for', iii. 416–18; and esteem the first principles of friendship, iii. 445; the most witty, and most delightful, passion, iii. 484, 486; a discourse on, which only a chemist could understand, iii. 578; giving advice to those in, iv. 182–5; success of Socrates' discourse on, iv. 272–3; wealth the father of, iv. 295; seldom continues long after esteem, iv. 298; allegorical figure of virtuous, iv. 326; the daughter of idleness but mother of disquietude, v. 23; 'nice and intricate cases in', v. 23–24; Ovid's advice on, v. 60–61; comes after marriage, v. 68, 74; languishes with fruition, v. 139; cleanliness the foster-mother of, v. 157.

Love, parental: in animals, i. 490; descends from parent to child, i. 491; upholds the world of life, ii. 213–14; stronger than filial gratitude, ii. 243; vicissitudes of, ii. 521–5.

Love of country: the noblest of principles, but capable of mischief, i. 512; pleasure from, ii. 511; an honest prejudice, iii. 18.

Love Casuist, the: letter from a gentleman offering to serve as, v. 22–24; observations by, v. 58–61; reports from, v. 67–71, 74–78, 98–101, 129–32, 134–6; appealed to for advice, v. 96, 115–16.

Love-feasts: established in England by Pope Gregory the Great, ii. 134.

Love-letters, volumes of, read by girls, ii. 11; a beau's head filled with, ii. 571; advice to PARTHENISSA on, iii. 102; frequent in spring, iii. 373.

Love poetry: wit and turn, out of place in, iii. 375–6; in hot and cold climates, iii. 376.

Love: proverbial sayings connected with: *I love you so that I could eat ye*, i. 201–2; *He will love me long, if he love me little*, ii. 52.

Love's Triumph (opera), i. 23; ii. 506.

LOVEBANE, Mrs. JUDITH, iii. 56.

LOVEBANE, SUSANNAH, letter from (on a coxcomb), iii. 56–57.

LOVEDAY, Lady, to be married to a young fellow, iii. 183.

Loveday, Robert, translation of La Calprenède, i. 154.

Loveit, Mrs. (in *The Man of Mode*), i. 279, 323.

LOVEIT, SARAH, petition of, refused, iv. 588.

Lovel, Mr. (apothecary?), iv. 61.

Lovelace, Mr., benefit for, i. 120.

LOVELENGTH, AMANDA, letter from (on the *Spectator*), iv. 589.

LOVELESS, BIDDY, letter from (which suitor to marry?), ii. 269–70.

LOVELESS, RICHARD DE, applies for the flitch of bacon, v. 79.

LOVELESS, TOM, testimonial to letter by, iv. 461.

LOVELY, RELICTA, letter from (on pert suitors), iv. 425–6.

LOVEMORE, JEREMY, letter from (history of his amours), v. 37–39.

Lover: should be educated to esteem virtue, i. 225; in *The Way of the World*, ii. 300; St. Francis mistook the kiss of a, for the salute of charity, ii. 450; the true l. often makes a poor figure, ii. 514; how may one know a ?, iii. 426; 'the submission of a son with the impatience of a', iv. 401; the Widow-Club concerned with how to treat a, iv. 518.

Lover, The: a letter concerning a late number of, iv. 588.

Lovers: communicating in dumb show, i. 365; language of, ii. 52, 438–9; iv. 507; gifts of, ii. 407; correspondence between absent, ii. 435–9; that whimsical tribe of mortals, iii. 469; griefs of, begin to flow in spring, iii. 473; best described in plays, iv. 312–14; whimsical burthens of, iv. 507; always allowed the comfort of soliloquy, iv. 574; complaints from, iv. 587–8.

Lovers' Leap, at Leucate, ii. 366, 382–5, 406–9.

LOVESICK, DICK, letter from (a love-problem), iii. 121–2.

LOVEWORTH, CHASTITY, letter from (offers of love received), iii. 64–67.

LOVEWORTH, SUSANNA. *See* DECENT, SUSANNA.

Low condition, men of, iii. 5; iv. 205.

Low Countries, i. 135; iv. 536.

Low life: an unhappy story in, ii. 440; behaviour of a coquette in, iii. 427.

Low thoughts to be avoided in epic poetry, ii. 588–9.

Lowndes, William (Secretary to the Treasury): a subscriber, i. xcii; Mr. SPECTATOR 'the Lowndes of the learned world', iv. 111; mentioned, iv. 537.

'Lowngers, the', at Cambridge, i. 229–31, 336.

Loyola, Ignatius, 'the old gentleman in Oldham', i. 77.

Lozenges, elixirs, and pills of quack doctors, iv. 553.

Lubbards and clowns, iv. 146.

Lubin (in *Georges Dandin*), iii. 267.

Lucan: his epigrammatic turns, ii. 588; and Ovid have many common and vulgar expressions, iii. 10–11; often drops his story for digressions, or *diverticula*, iii. 61; imitation of by Strada, v. 109.

Lucas, Lord, of Colchester, i. 417.

Lucas, Margaret. *See* Newcastle, Duchess of.

Lucas, Richard: *The Duty of Servants*, i. 372–3.

Lucas, Theophilus: *Memoirs of Gamesters*, ii. 276, 451; iii. 112–13, 478.

LUCCEIUS, moderate behaviour of, ii. 309.

Lucceius, L., Cicero's request to, iv. 490.

Lucetta (in *The Rover*), i. 218.

Lucian: dialogue in praise of dancing, i. 284; reading of, recommended, ii. 142; burlesque treatment of the gods, ii. 467–8; on riches, iii. 1; on philosophers' rivalling one another in beards,

iii. 221; a fable in the manner of, iii. 467–8.

Lucilius, Seneca's letter to, iii. 150.

LUCINA: an outspoken lady, iii. 72; her immodest conversation, iv. 13.

Lucius (in *Cato*), his account of Cato's sleep, v. 30–31.

'Lucky hit', iv. 466.

'Lucky hours' and inquiries into the future, v. 64.

Lucretia (Lucrece), ii. 70; concern for decorum when she stabbed herself, iii. 41; and Portia, iv. 28.

Lucretius Carus, Titus: no mixed wit in, i. 265; did not doubt the reality of apparitions, i. 455; an exercise in the style of, ii. *438*; his account of men and gods, v. 10; imitation of by Strada, v. *109*.

Lucubrations of law-students in Fleet Street, iv. 375.

Lucus a non lucendo, i. 249.

Lucy, Mrs., iii. 212; v. 82.

Luke, St.: the Blessed Virgin descended, to sit to, iv. 497.

Lully, Jean-Baptiste: adapted Italian music to French taste, i. 122; his opera, *Proserpine*, i. 123.

Lumber of human race, the, ii. 87.

'Lump, in the', i. 506; iv. 231, 357.

Lumpish, iv. 47, 344.

Lunar years, measuring time by, iv. 25.

Lurch, in the (prov.), i. 488.

Luscious (voluptuous): expressions in plays, i. 216; nothing l. in Antony's description of Cleopatra, iii. 497; a l. account, iv. 239.

LUSITANIA: the eye of, an instrument of premeditated murder, ii. 479.

Lust: and hunger the most violent appetites, i. 489; dedication of *The Plain Dealer* a masterpiece of raillery on, ii. 537; prostitution and, ii. 534–7, 567–70; in absolute monarchs, iii. 20–21; takes in all the faculties to its service, iv. 242; allegorical figure of, iv. 326; love in the old generally accompanied with, v. 24.

Lusty: young fellow, ii. 131; protest against the words 'lusty fellow', ii. 575.

Lute: playing on the, iii. 205; iv. 78, 373; Sappho added two strings to the, iv. 546.

Lute-string (for clergymen's scarves), price of, i. 89.

Luttrell, Narcissus, ii. *164*; iv. *308*, *503–4*.

Luxembourg, François-Henri de Montmorency-Bouteville, Duc de: de-feated William III at Steenkirk, iii. *240*.

Luxuriant (excessively prosperous), iii. 217.

Luxury: and avarice, i. 232–6; money profused in, ii. 511; wealth not to be used only for pomp and, iii. 47; of the present age, iii. 223; advantageous to labour, iv. 193; is artificial poverty, iv. 564.

LYCUS, CYNISCA in love with, ii. 406.

Lydia: Horace's ode to, quoted, ii. 173–4; letters between LYDIA and HARRIOT, ii. 486–9; letters between L. and CLITOPHON, iii. 122–3.

Lydia: king of, his golden touch, i. 16; king of, his offer to Pittacus, iv. 563; Gyges, monarch of, v. 86–87.

Lying: to make others happy, ii. 409–11; the heinousness of, iv. 298–9; party-lying, iv. 299–301.

Lying-in: in a quack doctor's advertisement, iv. 59; 'the miss who *lay in* at school', v. 38.

LYSANDER: 'slain at a puppet show', iii. 417; an admirable husband, iv. 358.

Lysimachus, his flattery of Alexander, iii. 247.

Lysippus, his statues of Alexander, iii. 555.

Lystra, men of, called St. Paul Mercury, v. 165.

M., J.: letter from (on Greek mottoes), iii. 54–55; iv. *317*.

M., R.: Mr. SPECTATOR's thanks to, ii. 113; letter from (on rude behaviour in church), v. 154–6.

Macaulay, Thomas Babington, on Addison, i. ciii–civ.

Maccabeus dreams of receiving sword from Jeremiah, iii. 231–2.

Maccaronies, merry drolls in Italy, i. 201–2.

Macedon: court of Alexander the Great, i. 135; troops of, on stage, i. 150; Philip of, ii. 431; v. 42.

Machaon, a physician in Homer, iv. 551.

Machiavelli, Niccolò: a politician borrowing a Tacitus or a, iii. 98; 'these young Machiavels', iii. 99; advises a state to be perpetually jealous of its neighbours, iii. 525; Machiavilian scheme, iv. 335–6; a society of she-Machiavils, iv. 518.

Machine, machinery: the witches a proper m. in *Macbeth*, ii. 58; of gods in the epic, ii. 543; in the epic, iii. 144–6; the most violent m. in the *Aeneid*, so much blamed by critics, iii.

145, 306; v. 15–16; in *PL*, iii. 171–4; of the ancients in mock-heroic poetry, iv. 362; v. *118*.

Mackerel fisheries, disturbed by French privateers, iii. 508.

Macky, John, *Journey through England*, i. *346, 350*; iv. *265*.

Macrobius, on the origin of music, iii. *236, 238*.

Maddox, Mrs., in Wine-Office-Court, advertises a cosmetic, iv. *129*.

Mademoiselle, the wooden (a French doll), ii. 578–81.

Madmen, the ambitious and the covetous are, iv. 571.

Madness: scenes of, on the stage, i. 95; enthusiasm has in it something of, ii. 289; in love compared to m. produced by biting of a mad dog, ii. 383–4; in Lee's plays, iv. 40.

Madrid: Count d'Olivarez disgraced at court of, iii. 43; story of an Englishman in, v. 90.

Maevius, enemy of Virgil, ii. 482.

Magic: world of, the region of false wit, i. 273; oblique vision the mark of magical fascination, ii. 472; a ridiculous piece of, from Democritus, iv. 319; arose from desire to know the future, v. 64; magical incantations remain in Lapland, v. 65.

Magicians: in *Rinaldo*, i. 25; burned their books after St. Paul's preaching, i. 414; writings about fairies, witches, and, iii. 570.

Magistrates: keep peace in a tumult, ii. 120; worship, or venerable behaviour, the title given to, ii. 352; should take care of beggars, iv. 12.

Magna Charta, i. 15.

Magnanimity: of Cowley, i. 469; and courage of military men, ii. 96; acts of, the result of ambition, ii. 371; inseparable from courage, iii. 303; modesty always joined to, iii. 321; of Mme de Villacerfe, iii. 385.

Magnificence: in every part of *PL*, ii. 542; a great poet is full of most magnificent ideas, iii. 5; a rude kind of m. in works of nature, iii. 540.

Magpie(s): a school for, i. 151; a great fortune-teller among the ancients, iv. 512.

Mahmoud and his vizier, story of, v. 319.

Mahomet: journey of, and vision of the seven Heavens, i. 400; his coffin suspended between two magnets, ii. 248–9; the *fomes peccati* removed from his heart, v. 7.

Mahometan: custom of treating women as if they had no souls, i. 224; custom of preserving papers, i. 360–1; custom of washing before prayers, i. 401; Spring Garden a kind of M. Paradise, iii. 438; law, filled with bathings and purifications, v. 158; anecdote from an account of M. superstitions, v. 158.

Mahometans: are clothed in British manufacture, i. 296; purchase freedom of birds confined in cages, iii. 273; propriety of their demeanour in worship, iv. 125.

Maid: a young man rallied upon being a, ii. 103–4; in *The Scornful Lady*, ii. 554; in a milliner's shop, ii. 580; *caress the m. in order to succeed with the mistress* (prov.), v. 23.

Maid's Vindication, The, ii. *89*.

Maids and bachelors, the Inquisition on, iii. 165–6.

Maids, ladies', behaviour of, iv. 406.

Main chance (prov.), ii. 270.

Maintenon, Françoise d'Aubigné, Marquise de: her first husband (Scarron), i. 75; petticoat politicians, brought up at the feet of, iii. 97.

Majesty: the title given to kings, ii. 352; humility and m. of Jesus portrayed by Raphael, ii. 380; effect of, on mind of the beholder, iii. 555; of Messiah in *PL*, iii. 566; majestatic presence of God, iv. 583.

Make (= train): 'a setting-dog that he has *made*', i. 447.

Make-bates: and liars, ii. 39; support the economy of a humoursome rich man, ii. 292.

Mal à propos, i. *331*.

Malcontent(s): in Hungary, i. 182; in a grinning-contest, ii. 183–4.

Male charmers, success of, v. 59.

Male jilts, iii. 23–25 (comment, iii. 73, 165).

Male widowhood, subject of, iv. 350.

Malebranche, Nicolas: his *Search after Truth* in LEONORA's library, i. 155; on relative duration of time, i. 399; on pedantry, i. *437*.

Males and females, nice balance between, iii. 27–28; iv. 21.

Males, the Republic of, and Commonwealth of Amazons, iv. 22–26.

Malice, ii. 165; and zeal, ii. 229; of infidels, ii. 233; a person crazed with pride or, ii. 288; of evil eyes, ii. 360; a curiosity without m. or self-interest, ii. 388; lies told out of, should be exposed, ii. 410; imbibing m. with

nurse's milk, ii. 455; and insinuation of servants, ii. 523; volunteers in, ii. 559.

Mallet, E., i. *xx*.

Malt: a double quantity of, in small beer at Christmas, ii. 550.

Maltby, Edward (Bishop of Durham), i. cii.

MALVOLIO, his uneasiness a form of praise, ii. 426.

Mambré, Abraham's oak in plains of, v. 15.

Mammon, in *PL*, iii. 89, 116.

MAMMON, EPICURE, letter from (on eating contests), iii. 277–8.

Man, Jenny. *See* Coffee-houses.

Man: a sociable animal, i. 39; iv. 17; of the town, i. 278, 323, 437; iv. 225; of the world, i. 278; ii. 280; essential and comparative perfection of, i. 311; imperfection of, an argument for immortality, i. 456–9; v. 170–2; *one m. a wolf to another* (Latin prov.), i. 508; of merit should be our friend, regardless of party, i. 512; but a shadow, ii. 122; given away to misery and mortality, ii. 124; not made in vain, who has prospect of Paradise, ii. 125; the most changeable being in the universe, ii. 137; iv. 417, 526; subject to pains and sorrows, ii. 164; justice most agreeable to nature of God, and mercy to that of, ii. 166; letter from a m. of pleasure about town, ii. 218–19; of mode, ii. 218; iii. 163 (*see also* Etherege); too virtuous to be miserable and too vicious to be happy, ii. 222; of merit should desire to be tried only by his peers, ii. 239; distinguished from animals by devotion, ii. 287–8; satires against, ii. 320–1; iv. 18; of clay made by Prometheus, ii. 325; reason the distinguishing characteristic of, ii. 417; the merriest species of the creation, ii. 465; iv. 254; old age of a m. of pleasure, ii. 510–12; language of a m. of breeding, ii. 574; of figure, ii. 575; a short-sighted creature, iii. 44; easy and pleasant manner of a little, iii. 55–56; ignorant of futurity and unable to bear prosperity with moderation, iii. 61; *rather a man without an estate, than an estate without a man* (prov.), iii. 126; the world made for use and pleasure of, iii. 452; v. 125, 170–1; a middle link between angels and brutes, iii. 524; iv. 348; v. 125; subject to calamities and misfortunes, iv. 49; *is known by the company he keeps* (prov.), iv. 110; *must have his mare*

again (prov.), iv. 205; distinguished by faculty of laughter, iv. 254; reflects on what is passed and fears what is to come, iv. 291–2; 'sunk to slav'ry, tho' to glory born', iv. 399; designed for two lives, a temporal and an eternal, iv. 566; in his primeval state cultivated gardening, iv. 595; two principles of action in, v. 10; should be neither hermit nor buffoon, v. 45; imperfections of, v. 124–6; an active being, v. 134; designed for eternity, v. 145; capacities and imperfection of, v. 170–2; ultimate end of, the enjoyment of God, v. 172–3. *See also* Mankind, Men.

Man, Woman's. *See* Woman's Man.

Man's cruel treatment of his fellowmen, ii. 164–5.

Management: men of genius often fail in m. of affairs, ii. 362–3; the Widow-Club's rules for m. of a husband, iv. 518.

Mancini, Francesco (composer), i. 56.

Mandarin(s): in china ware, i. 153; sister to a great, iv. 316; ambassadors of, iv. 452.

Mandelslo, John Albert de, *Voyages and Travels*, iii. 273.

Mandeville, Bernard, i. 15.

Mandeville, Sir John, iv. 428.

Manes of war, iv. 533.

Manhood: wisdom and valour essential to character of, ii. 70; schemes of thought in, lost in old age, ii. 137; growth toward, desirable to all, ii. 522; ambition of, excused by ancients, iv. 259.

Manifesto of Emperor of Mohocks, iii. 293–5.

MANILIUS, character of, iv. 151–4.

Manilius, Marcus, *Astronomica*, ii. 175.

Mankind: divided between the pleasure-loving and the serious, i. 208–10; greatest part of m. die before resolving how to live, ii. 136; divided between the mercurial and the saturnine, ii. 204–6; divided into different sexes by Providence, ii. 210; instructive to view m. in ancient and modern times, ii. 317–18; our thoughts, words, and actions to be aimed at the good of, ii. 332; fame, as it regards the different orders of, ii. 349; mixture of good and evil in, ii. 393–4; business of m. in this life to act rather than to know, ii. 421; being useful to m. the chief end of being, ii. 432; fate of all m. the subject of *PL*, ii. 541–2; the good of m. the great end of government, iii. 22; regular increase and diminution of,

iii. 27; Milton gives a glimpse of m. 'even before they are in being', iii. 118; different employments of, iii. 393; art of managing m. 'to make them stare a little', iv. 60; divided between the merry and the serious, v. 43–45; divided between the busy and the idle, v. 132–4.

Manley, Mary de la Rivière, ii. *518*; v. *66*; the *New Atalantis* in LEONORA's library, i. 156.

Manlius Capitolinus, Marcus, iv. *17*.

Manly (in *The Plain Dealer*), behaviour of, ii. 425.

Manly: modesty in my men readers, ii. 567; rational and m. beauties, iii. 530; a m. panegyric, iv. 362.

Manners: neglect of, i. 29; in country and in town, i. 486–9 ; of ancient and modern times, ii. 317–18; art of painting should improve m., ii. 378; changes in, within ten or fifteen years, ii. 511–12; and not dress, the ornaments of a woman, ii. 533, 556; similitude of, required for happiness in marriage, ii. 545; miseries that flow from degeneracy of, ii. 554; in *PL*, ii. 561–6; schoolboys to be instructed in, iii. 250; travelling assists in unlearning peculiarities in our, iii. 368; simplicity of, the source of wealth, iv. 306–7.

Mansion-house(s): of a tailor's widow, ii. 527; embroidering tapestry for one's, v. 73; old, v. 92.

Manslaughter, chance-medley or, iii. 355.

Mantua(s): black silk, i. 344; without leads in the sleeves, ii. 579; and petticoats, iii. 206; a black tabby m. and petticoat, iii. 532.

Mantua-maker(s), ii. 580; iii. 125, 183.

Manufacture: agriculture, trade and m. employ nineteen men out of twenty, i. 472; relation of costs of labour to, ii. 402–4; of paper, iii. 379.

Manumission of servants, i. 444.

Manuzio (Manutius), Aldus. *See* Aldus.

Map(s), of spots in the sun, iii. 83; showing Prince Eugene crossing the Alps, iii. 263; iv. 327; following Aeneas's voyage by the, iii. 529; symbols on, v. 29.

MAPLE, WILL, genealogy of his illegitimate children, ii. 296.

MAPLE, MARY, wife of WILL MAPLE, ii. 296.

Mar-all, Sir Martin (in Dryden), the trick he practised upon his mistress, i. 24.

Maraud, a French term imported, ii. 152.

Marble: in the quarry compared to the soul without education, ii. 338; in romance writers, iii. 18; two 'intellectual beings' engaged in polishing, iii. 153; accidental landscapes found in veins of, iii. 550.

March: Caesar warned of the Ides of, iii. 480; allegorical depiction of, iii. 595; Brutus did not perpetually talk of the Ides of, iv. 519.

March, the Grenadiers', iii. 3.

Marcia, her prayer in *Cato*, v. 30–31.

Marcus, son of Cicero, could not be improved by the best education, iii. 106.

Marcus Aurelius Antoninus: rebus of owl, on statue of, i. 251; 'one of the greatest, wisest, and best of the Roman emperors', ii. 10; married to the younger Faustina, ii. 10; a good husband, v. 75–76; desired to imitate the gods, v. 168.

Mare(s), i. 197; ii. 182; women who resemble, ii. 320, 327; Pelias nursed by a, ii. 455.

MARGERY, the milkmaid, found in a genealogy, v. 93.

Mariamne: and Herod, ii. 176–8.

MARIAMNE, a graceful dancer, iv. 148–9.

MARINET, the agreeable, her friendship for Lord WELFORD, iii. 499.

Marius: his future greatness discerned by Scipio, ii. 114; Sulla saw many Mariuses in Caesar, iii. 99; his father, iii. 447; Atticus's friendship toward, iii. 447.

Marks: Sir ROGER deposits 30 m. with his chaplain to be distributed among his poor parishioners, ii. 549.

Mark Antony. *See* Antony.

Markham, —— (apothecary), iv. *554*.

Marlborough, John Churchill, Duke of: and battle of Blenheim, i. xvi; v. 72; connexions of, among subscribers, i. *lxxxviii*; member of Kit-Cat Club, i. *42*; the nation's ungrateful treatment of, ii. *2*, *50*; Prince of Mindelheim, ii. 50; passing the *Ne plus ultra* lines, ii. 50; tribute to(?), ii. 99, 308; levée of, ii. *258*; interview with Prince Eugene in London, ii. 263; Tory attacks on, ii. *494*; Estcourt a favourite with, ii. *529*; dismissed from all his offices, ii. 549; iii. 265; compared to Hector, iii. *31*; Clarke's edition of Caesar dedicated to, iii. *381*; his victories in Europe, iii. 444; fall of, referred to(?), iv. 23; captured Douai, iv. *187*; friendship with Prince Eugene, iv. 399; and Bouchain, iv. *407*; allusions to, in pamphlets, iv.

536–7; volume of *Spectator* dedicated to, v. 178–80.

Marly, French court at, iii. 98; iv. 92.

MARRATON's visit to the world of spirits, i. 237–40.

Marriage: between a man of sixty-five and a lass of fifteen, i. 222; ridicule of, in *The Man of Mode*, i. 279–80; girls' training for, i. 282–3; destructive of 'Idols', i. 315; marriage-articles, i. 347; iii. 69, 111; iv. 360; first offer of, to be rejected, i. 379; mutual obligations and duties in, ii. 8–9; of children without parents' consent, ii. 59, 212–13; rules for happiness in, ii. 87–88, 417–20, 514–16, 545–6; iii. 53; iv. 197–200, 237–40, 272–5, 295–8, 357–60, 369–73; v. 67–71, 74–76; of convenience, ii. 145; for money, ii. 279–82, 419, 479, 515; arranged without consulting children, ii. 355; railing and laughing at, ii. 417, 486–90; gossip about, ii. 459; the m. ceremony 'an offering of the sacrifice', ii. 479; no satires upon, in the *Spectator*, ii. 517; Milton's panegyric on, in *PL*, iii. 61; the Inquisition on Maids and Bachelors, iii. 164–6; story of a private and secret, iii. 178–80; coldness that usually comes on after, iii. 490; unsuitable m. forced on children, iv. 37; the completest image of heaven and hell, iv. 200; rather like purgatory to TOM DAPPERWIT, iv. 209; presents given at, iv. 232; frequent among the Jews, iv. 257; effect of *Spectator*'s discourses on, iv. 273, 369–70; raillers upon, eventually marry, iv. 389; letter on delay in, iv. 426. *See also* Matrimony.

Marriage, choice in: not to be determined by the eyes only, i. 339; made on wrong basis, ii. 8–11, 545–6; the wealthy STREPHON or the poor FLORIO (?), ii. 85–88; the wealthy WILL or the handsome TOM (?), ii. 269–70; a woman of fortune or one simply in love (?), ii. 279–82; between pleasing others and pleasing oneself, ii. 489; role of friends in, ii. 515; good qualities of the person beloved the only foundation, ii. 545; advice sought by FLORINDA, ii. 583–4; advice sought by CHASTITY LOVEWORTH, iii. 64–67; wealth as a determining factor, iii. 92–93; iv. 315; mistakes made in, iv. 35–37; conditions for, iv. 357–60; forcing children to marry contrary to their inclinations, iv. 400–2; use of 'shoeing-horns', iv. 414–15. *See also* Love-Casuist.

Marriage-finger, i. 248.

Marriage-Hater matched, the tune of, iv. 391.

Marriage-licences, taken out in Doctors' Commons, iv. 369.

Marriage-settlements: ii. 560; do not regard the young lady's person, ii. 87; and pin-money, iii. 52; terms of, iv. 359–60.

Marriage-treaty: articles of, broken off by small-pox, iii. 102.

Marriages, Censor of: MULES PALFREY proposes himself for this office, iii. 110–11; ordered to consider CLITOPHON's letter, iii. 123; reports on a case, iii. 166.

Married couples: indolence in (HARRY TERSETT and his wife), i. 421; behaviour in company and alone, ii. 87; 'wasps' or 'doves' in public, iii. 72; immodest behaviour in company, iv. 13; come to resemble each other, v. 70; qualifications of, v. 75–76; sources of quarrels between, v. 79–80.

Married life: a wife who tortures her husband with indifference, ii. 261–2; in the country, ii. 486–9; of Sir JOHN ENVILLE, iii. 68–71; care in dress important to, iii. 82; iv. 295–6. *See also* Husbands, Wives.

Marrow-bone(s): for dinner, iii. 155; 'on their', v. 106; music of m. and cleaver, v. 108.

Marry first, and love will come afterwards (prov.), v. 66.

Mars: Homer's story of M. and Venus, an example of burlesque, ii. 589; Venus always kind to, iii. 65; in the *Iliad* and Milton's Moloch, iii. 232–3; and Venus attending Spring, iii. 594; in modern poems, iv. 363.

Marsh(es): schemes for draining, ii. 285; overgrown with willows, beautiful and beneficial, iii. 552.

MARTHA, an uneasy, splenetic woman, iii. 104.

Martial (Marcus Valerius Martialis): i. 108, *144*, *217*; ii. 572; scarce anything but mixed wit in, i. 266; Segrais's contrast between M. and Virgil quoted (from Dryden), i. 269; language of Homer, Virgil, or Milton 'will please a reader of plain common sense, who would neither relish nor comprehend an epigram of', i. 297; mentioned, ii. 79; [a phrase wrongly attributed to M.], i. 89; *Epigrams* quoted: on drinking toasts, i. 126; on an old woman, i. 221; on a changeable friend, i. 291–2; on physiognomy, i. 366; on Rufus and

Naevia, i. 467; on Cato visiting the theatre, iv. 67; on his wife, iv. 239; on hair turning grey in a night, v. 102.

Martin, Martin: *Description of the Western Islands*, i. 212; *A Late Voyage to St. Kilda*, ii. 214.

Martyn, Henry: contributions to *Spectator*, i. lii–liii; a subscriber, i. lxxxix; referred to (?), ii. 65, 208; *The British Merchant*, ii. 208; author of material in No. 200, ii. 283.

Marvell, Andrew, i. 459; reminiscence of 'To his Coy Mistress', i. 378.

Marvellous: a term of the French critics, iii. 88; the probable and the m. in the epic and in Milton, iii. 88, 144–6, 200–1.

Mary, the Virgin: a hymn in hexameters to, i. 254; descended from Heaven to sit to St. Luke, iv. 497.

MARY: letter from (on gossip and scandal), iii. 296–8.

Mary, Lady (rope-dancer), i. 218.

Mary I, Queen: persecutions under, ii. 431; beards flourished in reign of, iii. 222; conference between Protestants and Papists in reign of, iv. 142; a weaver burnt for his religion in reign of, v. 92.

Mary II, Queen, iii. 440; Bishop of St. Asaph's tribute to, iii. 443.

Mask (= a woman masked), Sir Roger's reply to, in Spring Garden, iii. 438.

Mask(s): and vizards worn by wits, i. 136; worn by women, i. 375; iv. 100; the actor's m. not liked by the best judges in Rome, iv. 436.

MASKWELL, the Widow, riding the black ram, v. 131.

Masquerade: evils of the midnight masque, i. 36–38; incongruity of costumes at, i. 62–63; masquing habits, i. 96; within the verge of the court, i. 425.

Mass production: Sir William Petty's example of watch-making, ii. 404.

Massacre(s): mainly caused by a furious pretended zeal, ii. 228–9; allegorical figure of, iii. 337; of the Jews by Romans and Turks, iv. 256; instigated by Church of Rome, iv. 334.

Massue de Ruvigny, Henri de. *See* Galway, Earl of.

Master: of the Hounds, i. 481; Sir ROGER's M. of the Game, i. 484; one must be m. of himself to be a proper m. of another, ii. 43; qualities necessary in m. of a family, ii. 291–3; *confuted by one who is m. of fifty legions*

(prov.), ii. 430; m. of the ceremonies, to instruct politicians, iii. 99.

Masters' gowns, a correspondent has written against, v. 116.

Masters, Harcourt (a Director of S. Sea Co.), iv. 538; a subscriber, i. xc, xci.

Mastiffs, i. 451; ii. 164.

Match-maker: SEMPRONIA, a professional, iv. 35–37.

MATCHWELL, Madam, her opinion of 'shoeing-horns', iv. 414.

Materiality of a thinking substance, one of the great points of atheism, ii. 230.

Mathematical: chair, i. 106; lines that draw nearer to each other without touching, i. 459; infidels' objections to anything incapable of m. demonstration, ii. 233; trees cut into m. figures, iii. 552; m. demonstrations called by Plato the cathartics of the soul, iv. 299; schemes of m. theorems, iv. 326.

Mathematician, a: who was uncertain whether to stand or sit while my lord drank to him, i. 287; Archimedes, ii. 130; project of, for composing poetry, ii. 356–7; who traced Aeneas's voyage by the map, iii. 529.

Mathematicians: often absent-minded, i. 330; require demonstration even in common discourse, ii. 272; Clavius one of the greatest, iii. 107; proceed upon propositions once demonstrated, iv. 142.

Mathematics: a lady that reads Locke and understands the, ii. 443; marks of a person perfect in, iv. 344–5; in construction of globes, iv. 482; Leonardo da Vinci skilled in, iv. 489.

Mather, Charles (toyman): miniatures set by, iii. 206; his fine tablets, iv. 286; 'the famous', iv. 546.

Mather, Cotton, a contributor (?), i. xl–xli, lxxxv.

MATHEWS, JOHN, reprimanded by Sir ROGER at church, i. 461.

Matrimony: *The Fifteen Comforts of*, in LEONORA's Library, i. 155; *The Plagues of*, ii. 89; the suburbs of, ii. 196. *See also* Marriage.

Matter: motions and gravitation of, one of the great points of atheism, ii. 230; how made fluent, iii. 479; division of, iv. 300; all parts of, are filled with animals, iv. 346; variety of systems of, iv. 443; fortuitous concourse of, cannot produce the body of an animal, iv. 444; eternity of, an error, v. 55.

'Matter for that, No', ii. 442.

Matter of Fact Man, defined, iv. 353.

Matthias, Olaus, iii. 376.

Maturius, Arrianus, Pliny's letter recommending, ii. 394–5.

Maundrell, Henry, *Journey from Aleppo to Jerusalem*, iii. 88.

Mausoleum, erected by Artemisia, v. 100.

Maxim(s): of Sir ANDREW, i. 10; of Plato, on apparent evils, ii. 421–2; for gaining wealth, iii. 2; of conduct important in character-building, iii. 33; of Gracián, iii. 42; less effective than examples, iii. 67–68; a stage m., iv. 388; of the Love-Casuist, v. 23–24.

Maximus, Pliny's letter to, ii. 394–5.

Maximus Planudes, on Aesop, i. 77.

Maxwell, John, iii. *461*.

May: queens of, i. 343; dangers in month of, iii. 371–5, 480–2; iv. 221; allegorical depiction of, iii. 595; PRETTYMAN's behaviour in, iv. 221.

May-day customs, iii. 372–3.

May-dew for complexion, i. 139.

May-Fair, i. *119*; ii. *56*.

May-fly: WILL WIMBLE makes a m. to a miracle, i. 447.

Maynard, Samuel, iv. *458*.

Mayne, Zachary, iii. *537*.

Maynern, Sir Theodore, his 'Imperial Snuff', iii. *278*.

Maynwaring, Arthur: Vol. I of *Tatler* dedicated to, i. xvii; a subscriber, i. lxxxix; Mrs. Oldfield mistress of, iii. *252*; writer for the *Medley*, iii. *380*.

Maynwaringe, Dr. (quack), advertisement of, iv. *61*.

Mayo, J., printer of *British Apollo*, i. *xxiv*.

Mayoress, Mrs., 'clip'd the King's English', v. 106.

Mayors and aldermen, satires against, iv. 18.

Maypole: dancing at, i. 306; antiquarians' opinion concerning, iii. 372.

Mazarin, Jules, Cardinal, his generous treatment of Quillet, i. 98.

Mead, John, a subscriber, i. *xc*.

Mead, a bottle of, iii. 438.

Meadows, ii. 158; metaphor of laughing applied to, ii. 468.

MEAGER, MAT., forced to feed upon green tea, iii. 480–1.

Mean: persons dressed as heroes, in one kind of burlesque, ii. 467; and narrow minds least actuated by ambition, ii. 491; and vulgar to be avoided in the epic, ii. 589; phrases in ancient authors no longer shocking, iii. 11.

Meanders, rivers in, pleasing to the imagination, iii. 570.

Meanest capacities: gold accommodates itself to the, ii. 431; methods of gaining riches attainable by persons of, iii. 2–3.

Meanness: desire of fame as a m. and imperfection, ii. 492; obvious phrases contract a kind of, iii. 10.

MEANWELL, MARY, letter from (on proper notification when one is in town), ii. 316 (testimonial to this letter, iv. 461).

MEANWELL, T., letter from (on freedoms taken by married couples), iv. 13–14.

MEANWELL, WILLIAM, slain by the ogle of a widow, iii. 417.

Measom, George, *Light from the East*, ii. *122*.

Measurable step, a, ii. 113.

Measures, to break, ii. 519.

Meat: in the Jewish religion, ii. 332; a dish of, ii. 459; a chop of, iv. 102: antipathy to shape of a joint of, iv. 421.

Mecca: Mahomet's burying-place at, ii. 248; a caravan from, v. 158.

Mechanic: the poorest m. gets him his set of admirers, ii. 351; project of a Dutch, iii. 357; the most ordinary plebeian or m. in love, iii. 416; Mr. SPECTATOR a famous m., iv. 404; John Rowley the best m. of my acquaintance, iv. 481.

Mechanic: behaviour of a m. being, i. 470; Peter the Great's cultivation of m. arts, ii. 49; courage of soldiers, ii. 97; education for m. way of life advisable for some boys, ii. 117; usefulness of m. arts, iv. 4, 57.

Mechanics, Leonardo da Vinci skilled in, iv. 489.

Medal(s): chronograms on German, i. 256; and statues of Commodus, ii. 11; 'a little view of', in education, ii. 396; of Roman emperors, ii. 43; on defeat of Spanish Armada, iii. 45.

Mede, Joseph, *Clavis Apocalyptica*, recommended, i. 390.

Medea, i. 190; ii. 243.

Medes and Persians, laws of, iv. 303.

Medicina gymnastica. See Fuller, Francis.

Medicine(s): medicaments enclosed in a wooden ball, ii. 263; a substitute for exercise or temperance, ii. 264; medicinal preparations, iii. 206; expensiveness of, in London, iii. 354; for venereal maladies advertised, iv. 59; which are 'infallible, and never fail of success', iv. 553. *See also* Physicians, Quacks.

Medicine (figurative uses): a faithful

friend the m. of life, i. 290; testimonial to m. of the *Spectator*, ii .29–30; iv. 457–61.

Medicine, profession of: overcrowding in, i. 90–91; 'divinity, law, and physic', i. 449.

Medina, Moses de, a subscriber, i. xci–xcii.

Medina, Sir Solomon de: a subscriber, i. xci–xcii; referred to (?), iii. *428*.

Meditation: upon the Divine Perfections wonderfully transporting, ii. 288; as a means of strengthening faith, iv. 143–4.

MEDLAR, Mrs., member of Widow-Club, iv. 516, 558.

Medley (in *The Man of Mode*), i. 280, 323.

Medley, The, i. xiv, xviii, xxi, *83*, *442*; ii. *51*, *186*; iii. *279–80*, 380, *439*, *440*.

MEGGOT, TOM: friend of ANTONY FREEMAN, ii. 329–30; letter from, ii. 342–4 (praise of this letter, iv. 461).

Mein, Charles (wine-examiner in the Customs), a subscriber, i. lxxxix, xcii.

MELAINIA, letter from (on male jilts), iii. 23–24 (comment, iii. 73, 165).

'Melancholies, in my', ii. 385.

Melancholy: and dejected carriage, ii. 175; needs to be dispersed by little incitements to mirth, ii. 205; women of a m. nature, ii. 320; in Orpheus, ii. 326; Greek women seized with an unaccountable, ii. 399; in fallen angels, ii. 421; a reserved and m. temper at times agreeable, ii. 425; to be kept out of a virtuous mind, ii. 445; shadows in painting represent the serious and, ii. 447; a fit of, ii. 498; an air of, ii. 598; in religion, iii. 80; mirth often succeeded by, iii. 429; a kind of demon that haunts our island, iii. 454; and spleen in religious persons, iv. 251–4; cure for, in *Spectators*, iv. 459; and despair of DICK GLOOMY, v. 8.

MELESINDA, reveals her humours by colours of her hood, ii. 532.

MELISSA: letter from (is married to a drone), ii. 326–7; leap into the Ionian sea, ii. 406; slays by her hair, iii. 418; asks advice of her friends on marriage, iv. 183; examination of her heart, v. 9.

Mellitus (first Bishop of London), Pope Gregory's letter to, ii. 134.

Melmouth, William, on Addison's style, i. xcviii.

Melons: imported into England and naturalized, i. 295; consigned to Covent Garden, iv. 99.

Melpomene, iii. 562 m.; iv. 327.

Memnon (general of Darius's army), iv. 2.

Memoirs: authors of, a tribe of egotists, iv. 520; 'of an honest country-gentleman', v. 127–8.

Memoirs for the Ingenious, i. xxxvii.

Memorials: of persons in the Infirmary for the ill-natured, iv. 7–10; from RACHAEL WELLADAY, iv. 382–5; of PHILANDER, postponed, v. 117; presented to Charles II, v. 149–51.

Memory: a thought in poetry is more portable to the, ii. 358–9; of good and worthy actions a feast to the soul, ii. 512; affectation of having a bad, iii. 6; iv. 174; impaired by old age, iii. 75; heightens the delightfulness of trains of ideas, iii. 562–3; function of, iv. 165; the guilty man willing only to discard his, iv. 508; in eternity, v. 51.

Men (humanity): differ from themselves, ii. 135–9, 325, 363–4, 388; iv. 526–7; setting a right value upon, ii. 178–81; differ from each other, ii. 274–5, 393–4, 525–6; iv. 52; set upon a level by Providence, ii. 491; must know sorrow and pain, iii. 128; most are forgotten as though they had never been, iii. 152–3; all are vicious (Horace) and fools (Boileau), iv. 462–3; making m. like gods, the heathen boast, v. 167. *See also* Man, Mankind.

Men (males): integrity the chief ornament of, i. 30; effeminate, i. 241; courage the great point of honour in, i. 416; more grave and serious than women, ii. 8; of light and volatile humour preferred by women, ii. 9, 85; of rakish and gallant character preferred by women, ii. 103–6, 110–13; women's attitude towards chastity in, ii. 103–4; refined by contacts with women, ii. 119; iv. 21; of honour should endeavour only to please the worthy, ii. 238–9; falsehood among, not reproachful, ii. 245; false by nature, ii. 277; their conversation superior to tattle of women, ii. 296–7; particles of the lion in, ii. 325; satires against women and against men, iv. 18; should not give way to charms and flattery of women, iv. 313.

Men of letters, illiberal sauciness of, ii. 116.

Ménage, Giles: a learned man talking seriously on *bouts rimés*, i. 257; *Menagiana*, on making of rhymes, i. 257; on dangers in month of May, iii. 371; quoted or cited, i. *117*, *248*, *249*, *257–8*, *263*, *265*, *366*; iii. *364*, *477*; iv. *591*.

MENALCAS, an absent-minded man (from La Bruyère), i. 332–3; the Sicilian, ii. 406.

Menander: Apollodorus a contemporary with, ii. 296; wrote with justness and purity of language, ii. 475; quoted on women's ornaments, ii. 533, 556, 583; quoted on the happiness of man, iv. 463; epitaph on, iv. 474–5.

Mender of chairs, the sad and solemn cry of, ii. 476.

Menippus, of Gadara: listens to prayers offered to Jupiter, iii. 468.

Mental reservations, Jesuits well read in controversies of, iii. 98.

MERAB, an affected beauty, ii. 69.

Mercers, i. 46, 276.

Mercerus (= Josias Mercier), his rendering of Aristinetus' description of a fine woman, i. 263.

Merchant(s): useful members of a commonwealth, i. 296; 'honest INDIGO', ii. 40; young m. about the Exchange, ii. 46; who are impertinent when buying of women in shops, ii. 108–10; frugality and parsimony the virtues of, ii. 186–7; value of, contrasted with noblemen, ii. 186–9; monuments of charity and public spirit erected by, ii. 187; suffer by want of punctuality in dealings of persons above them, ii. 334–5; credit of, ii. 350–1; should not encourage beggars, ii. 402; letter from a generous m. to a trader, ii. 463–4; worth and importance of, to his country, iv. 4–7; Jews now wandering m. by profession, iv. 257; has never enough till he has got a little more, iv. 467; a m.-tailor found among one's ancestors, v. 92.

Mercure Galant: a prototype of Spectator, i. xxxvii–xxxviii; bouts rimés in, i. 257.

Mercurial, the: and the dull, i. 184; and the saturnine, ii. 204; a mercurial friend, ii. 262–3.

Mercurialis, Hieronymus, De arte gymnastica, i. 474.

Mercury (the god): in Aristophanes' Plutus, iv. 140; in modern poems, iv. 363; St. Paul called, by men of Lystra, v. 165; in Julian's Caesars, v. 168.

Mercury (the metal): contracted or delated in thermometer, ii. 426, 595; in a beau's head, ii. 573; in a coquette's heart, ii. 595.

Mercy: to particulars is cruelty in the general (prov.), i. 410; ii. 166–7; justice most agreeable to nature of God, and m. to that of man, ii. 166; the man lacking m., an enemy to the world, iv. 109.

Merion, called a fine dancer by Homer, i. 284.

Merit: regard for, rather than party, ii. 1–2; of the merchant above that of all other subjects, ii. 351; modesty and diffidence generally accompany, ii. 381, 397–8; recompence of, in the poet's praise, ii. 425; only God can esteem us according to our, ii. 500–1; iii. 43; acknowledged m. gives immediate distinction to a gentleman, ii. 591; measured by future state of rewards and punishments, iii. 43; neglected, misapplied, or misunderstood, in Estcourt, iii. 394; consciousness of our own m. sometimes laudable, v. 124.

Mermaids, i. 271; iv. 349.

Merry: they who resolve to be m., seldom are so, ii. 65; the m. grin, ii. 183; the m. and the grave, ii. 204; v. 43–45; 'tis merry in the hall, when beards wag all (prov.), iii. 397; 'Merry Monarch' (Charles II), iv. 133.

Merry-Andrew: a monkey as a, i. 119; as jocular as a, i. 147; mentioned, i. 223; ii. 29; antic postures of a, ii. 206; a Pickled Herring, ii. 207; v. 46; necessary to a quack doctor, iv. 552; in the Cave of Trophonius, v. 46.

'Merry Beggars, The' (song), ii. 405.

Merry Club. See Ugly Club.

Merry fellow(s): among the ancients, i. 421; 'quite spoiled me for a', ii. 75.

Merry-meeting or club, i. 203.

Merry men, 'a cheerful word for companions', i. 302.

Merrythought (wishbone), plucking of a, i. 33.

Mesnager and Rechteren, dispute between, iv. 205–8.

Messala (a lawyer in Horace), iv. 216.

Messalina, ii. 70.

Messiah: the hero of PL, iii. 59; role in PL, iii. 232–4, 257–60, 358, 387–8, 566; Pope's poem, iii. 419–22; Jews marry early, hoping the M. may descend from them, iv. 257; Jews' conception of, v. 84.

Metals, treatises on, pleasure in reading, iii. 575.

Metaphors: hard m., i. 166; a species of wit, i. 264; of fire and burning applied to love, i. 266; of laughing applied to meadows and trees, ii. 468; Milton's use of, iii. 12; in Scripture, iii. 30; value of, in prose, iii. 578; mixture of

INDEX

nconsistent, v. 35–37; defined, v. 35.
See also Similitudes.

Metaphysics, marks of a person perfect in, iv. 344–5.

Meteors, treatises on: pleasure in reading, iii. 575; a new set of, in the playhouse, v. 25.

Method: in business as a means of gaining riches, iii. 2; advantages of, in writing and conversation, iv. 185–8.

Methuen, Sir Paul: and treaty of 1703, i. *181*; ii. *578*; volume of *Spectator* dedicated to, v. 182–4.

Methuselah, lived 969 years, iii. 28.

Mexico, Emperor of, Spaniards sent messages to, in paint, iii. 559.

Mezentius and Lausus (in the *Aeneid*), ii. 563.

Mezzotinto, i. 135.

Michael (in *PL*): always in character, ii. 565; sword of, from armoury of God, iii. 231–2; in Book XI, iii. 359–60.

Michelangelo: ii. 154; 'learned his whole art from' the Belvedere Torso, ii. 390; envied Leonardo da Vinci, iv. 489.

Microscope: for observing insects, i. 91; applied to a coquette's heart, ii. 596. *See also* Glasses.

Midas, touch of, i. 16.

Middle Ages: false wit flourished in 'times of monkish ignorance', i. 253–4; superstition of, iii. 572.

Middle-aged, the, love generally accompanied with interest in, v. 24.

Middle condition, most advantageous: for gaining knowledge, iii. 21–22; for improving virtue, iv. 139.

Middlesex, iv. 516.

Midgets, a show of, ii. 557–8.

Midnight: disturbing people with m. serenades, i. 436; m. quarrels, ii. 512. *See also* Masquerades.

Midwife: cannot deliver a woman unless she is first with child, iii. 107; advertisement for a, iv. 551.

Midwives, A Directory for (by Culpeper), in LEONORA's library, i. 155.

Miege, Guy, *Present State of Great Britain*, i. *3, 21, 43, 293*; ii. *84, 172, 205, 402*; iii. *27*; iv. *181, 212, 271*; v. *137*.

Mien: noble and majestic m. of Germanicus, ii. 426; of IRUS, ii. 528; genteel and childish m. of a prostitute, ii. 535; a good m. heightened by force of reason, iii. 235; an easy m. easily affected, iv. 332.

Might overcomes right (prov.), ii. 242.

Milan, aqueduct from the river Adda to, iv. 489.

Mild beer, i. 374.

Mildness, serenity or m. of temper, the title given to princes, ii. 352.

Milfris, Elizabeth, iv. *168*.

Military: stupidity of m. writers, i. 184; the m. pedant, i. 438; eloquence, ii. 151; use of French m. terms, ii. 152–3; the civil and m. list regard each other with ill nature, ii. 187; engineers use art of scaling, iii. 126; La Rochefoucauld on m. manners, iv. 534.

Military men: conversation of, ii. 23, 96; iv. 402; their contempt of death, ii. 97; leaders contrasted with gross of soldiery, ii. 99; private men in horse and foot regard each other with ill will, ii. 187; exposing themselves undressed at their levée, ii. 258; praise of, iv. 533–5. *See also* Soldiers.

Military profession: the way to advance in, i. 11; manners and morals in, iv. 403; honoured in France and ancient Rome, iv. 534.

Militia, the, ii. 14.

Milk: influence of, on animals and children, iii. 455–6; cry of the seller of, in London, ii. 475; in romance writers, iii. 18; effect of drinking goat's, iii. 525; antipathy caused by m. of nurse, iv. 421.

Milk score, a husband acquainted with the, iv. 210.

Milking a ram, laborious disputation like, ii. 46.

Milkiness of blood (Dryden), ii. 197.

Milkmaid: under a pyramid of silver tankards, iii. 372; coquetry of a, iii. 427–8; found in a genealogy, v. 93.

Milksop, a woman was never designed to be a, ii. 328.

Milky Way, iv. 170, 529.

Mill(s): project of a, to make verses, ii. 357; paper m. in England, iii. 379–80.

MILLDEW, JOHN, and the Widow BLIGHT, iv. 93.

Miller, James, 'master of the noble science of defence', iv. 31.

Miller, SISLY DOBSON, who made the m. make away with himself, iv. 406.

Milliner(s), i. 276; ii. 108, 192, 577; letter from a pretty m. in the City, ii. 110; a m.'s shop, ii. 569; in Oxford, iv. 38.

Mills, John: Medley in *The Man of Mode*, i. *278*; in *The Lancashire Witches*, ii. 59; as Macbeth, ii. 308; Pylades in *The Distressed Mother*, iii. 239.

Mills, Mrs., in *The Lancashire Witches*, ii. 57.

Milo Papinianus, T. Annius: 'the cause of Milo', ii. 396.

386

INDEX

Milton, John: had a genius much above mixed wit, i. 265; Homer, Virgil, or M. will please the plain reader, i. 297; imitators of, follow him only in uncouth or antique words, ii. 52; one of the 'learned geniuses', ii. 129; 'the first place among our English poets is due to', ii. 520; 'I have drawn more quotations out of him than from any other', ii. 520; his genius turned to the sublime, iii. 141; full of hints and translations from Greek and Latin poetry, iii. 173; 'Mr. FROTH's opinion of', iii. 183; a master of both the sublime and the pathetic, iii. 255; 'that sublime imagination so peculiar to', iii. 332; 'the greatest poet which our nation or perhaps any other has produced', iii. 530; 'a perfect master in all these arts of working on the imagination [i.e. the Great, the Beautiful, and the Strange]', iii. 566; placed with Homer and Virgil, iv. 135, 171, 329. — L'Allegro, quoted, ii. 468-9. — Il Penseroso, quoted, iii. 593. — Comus [figure of Comus, iii. 596].— Samson Agonistes, quoted, iv. 172. — Paradise Lost: the eighteen papers on, announced, ii. 520; the fable of, ii. 537-44; the characters of, ii. 561-6; the sentiments of, ii. 585-90; the language of, iii. 9-15; approach to [on criticism], iii. 35-38; the defects or faults of, iii. 58-64; Book I, iii. 83-91; Book II, iii. 113-21; Book III, iii. 141-8; Book IV, iii. 169-77; Book V, iii. 197-204; Book VI, iii. 227-34; Book VII, iii. 254-61; Book VIII, iii. 280-7; Book IX, iii. 305-12; Book X, iii. 329-39; Book XI, iii. 357-66; Book XII, iii. 385-92; praise of PL papers, iii. 74; iv. 428; 'this noble poem', ii. 540; 'the Devil never ashamed but once', iii. 41; the Messiah the hero of, iii. 59; compared to the sun, iii. 83; its subject the noblest that could have entered into the thoughts of man, iii. 141; regarded as the noblest work of genius in our language, iii. 169; Milton's subject the most sublime that could enter into the thoughts of a poet, iii. 234; WILL HONEYCOMB reads aloud a passage from, iii. 345; Tonson's edition of, advertised, iii. 345; those rational and manly beauties in that divine work, iii. 530; falls short of the Aeneid or Iliad only in its language: 'so divine a poem in English is like a stately palace built of brick' (compared to one in marble),

iii. 566; most readers more charmed with the description of Paradise than that of Hell, iii. 567; its diction could not consist of common ordinary words, iv. 429; Milton probably changed the number of books from ten to twelve to agree with Virgil's number, v. 159; reminiscences of, ii. 486-7; v. 140, 143; allegorical figures in, ii. 563; iii. 61, 120-1, 145-6, 573; Book I quoted, iv. 304; Book II quoted, ii. 183, 421; iii. 484; iv. 573; Book III quoted, iv. 172; v. 154; Book IV quoted, i. 55; iii. 41, 192-3, 373, 474; iv. 135, 529; Book V quoted, ii. 481; Book VIII quoted, i. 140-1, 379-80; iv. 14; Book X quoted, iii. 345; other allusions to, i. 313; v. 140, 143.

Mimic: Thersites a m. and a buffoon, ii. 326; cunning only the m. of discretion, ii. 376-7.

Mimic(s): among women, their behaviour at the theatre, ii. 315; women who m. faces, dresses, and behaviour of their neighbours, ii. 449; among men as well as women, ii. 459-60.

Mimicry: a form of false wit, i. 265; iii. 560; good breeding a m. of good nature, ii. 165; Estcourt's talent in, iii. 342; iv. 156-7; pleasure derived from, iii. 560.

Minced pies: upon the table at Christmas, ii. 550; and brawn, on New Year's Day, v. 150.

Mind(s): must not be allowed to lie fallow, i. 44; immediately aware of its thoughts, i. 160; thoughts of, continue in sleep, i. 270; clothing of our m. more important than of our bodies, i. 324; of an absent-minded person, i. 330; cultivation of, will outweigh defects of body, i. 367; must be allowed relaxations, i. 396-7; effect of physical exercise upon, i. 471-2; the secret springs of, ii. 29; affections of the, ii. 79, 221; effect of disappointment in love upon, ii. 141-2; ideas in, are a transcript of the world, ii. 153; of best men often gloomy and in need of diversion, ii. 204-5; devotion opens the m. to great conceptions, ii. 287; a man wears the picture of his m. in his countenance, ii. 307; of men very differently disposed, ii. 314, 525; its appetite for knowledge and duration, ii. 321-4; iv. 487-91; v. 140-1; embellishing the mind more praiseworthy than adorning the outside, ii. 370-1; constantly active, ii. 373-4; iv. 165; discretion v. cunning in

387

INDEX

the, ii. 376–7, 419; of men are chequered with truth and falsehood, ii. 421; love of flattery one of the diseases of, ii. 424; laughter slackens and unbraces the, ii. 466; whole strength of, sometimes seated in the eye, ii. 478–9; desire of fame breeds several vicious habits in, ii. 499; improvement of, the purpose of the *Spectator*, ii. 517; women urged to cultivate their, ii. 533; a m. too lazy to raise one to anger, iii. 6; false gallantry proceeds from impotence of, iii. 24; similes amuse and relax the reader's, iii. 91; greatness of, induced by poetry, iii. 530; hates restraint, iii. 540–1; most pleased in actions which prove its perfections and abilities, iv. 318.

Mindelheim, Prince of [Marlborough], v. 179.

Mineral(s): Boyle's comments on a certain, i. 398; pleasure in reading treatises on, iii. 575.

Minerva: an axe consecrated to, i. 246; removed mist from Diomedes' eyes, ii. 312; hurled a rock at Mars in battle, iii. 233; her armour, iii. 258; her aegis, iii. 258, 337; in modern poems, iv. 363.

Miniature, paintings in, set by Charles Mather, iii. 206.

Minister (clergyman): the fellow who smiled in the m.'s face in church, ii. 509; gloomy behaviour of an Independent, iv. 251–3; reconciling the m. of the parish and a Whig justice, v. 128.

Minister(s) (officer of state): dependent upon assistants, ii. 44; Eginhart, first m. to Charles the Great, ii. 215; in the fifth or sixth degree of favour with a, ii. 508; twilight visits by m. of state, iv. 112.

Ministry, defamatory scribblers employed by a, iv. 87.

Ministry, the late (Whig): attacked and defended in a coffee-house, ii. 273; diligence and abilities of, iii. 444; accomplishments of, v. 182.

Minos (judge of the dead), ii. 76.

Minshul, Mr., owner of the horse, 'Jews-trump', ii. 117.

Minuet: at the masquerade, i. 37, 63; led his mistress half a, i. 387; the gentleman who practised m.-steps in a coffee-house, ii. 82; CLODIUS still loves to hobble in a, iii. 75; JOHN TROTT has set up as a m.-dancer, iii. 112.

Minutes (memoranda): for the *Spectator*, i. 196–7; from John Sly, iv. 408.

MINUTIUS, tactful in his raillery, iii. 584–5.

Minx, MATILDA MOHAIR a malicious, iv. 261.

MIRABELL, TOM, i. 13.

'Miracle, To a', i. 447; ii. 452.

Miracles: reconciling m. with credibility in the epic, iii. 144–5; performed by Jesus, ii. 327.

MIRANDA: letter from (on a temperamental friend), iii. 74; sweetheart of DEUTERERASTUS, iv. 401.

Mirth: the parent of wit, i. 146; in allegory of luxury and avarice, i. 235; impertinent m. likely to take up our minds, ii. 67; authors who stir up, recommended by Saint-Evremond, ii. 141–2; a fit of, ii. 204; little incitements to, ii. 205; of *Spectator* will be instructive and innocent, ii. 205; equanimity is above cheerfulness, and below m., ii. 268; to a prudent man should always be accidental, ii. 268; induced in drama, ii. 314–15; causes of, ii. 465–6; band of, described by Milton, ii. 468; painful to be exposed to m. of public, ii. 518; the sole piece of m. in the *Aeneid*, ii. 589; pretenders to, ii. 591; Euclid's insipid, iii. 14; unseasonable in a critic, iii. 37; contrasted with cheerfulness, iii. 429–32; witty m. of Antony, iii. 450; rustic m. unfit for polite conversation, iv. 9; sober and polite m. in Terence, iv. 280. *See also* Laughter.

MIRTILLA: soft regularity in her motion, ii. 308; letter from (what constitutes a real lover?), iii. 426.

MIRZA, Vision of, ii. 121–6.

Misanthrope(s): character of Molière's, i. 364; the Mohocks, these m., iii. 187.

Miscarriages: which happen in conversations over wine, ii. 54; of men set in a strong light by satire, ii. 318.

Miscarriages (of women): caused by sight of a master of grinning, ii. 184; future m. prevented by nursing of children, ii. 457; a quack doctor who offers cures for, iv. 59, 61.

Miscellany: the late m. published by Mr. Pope, iv. 361.

Miscellany poem(s): ii. 113; iv. 225.

Mischief: better suffering a m. than an inconvenience (legal maxim), iv. 527.

Miscreated, a word coined by Milton, iii. 14, 484.

Miser: i. 19; a husband who is a, iii. 53; the pains of the, v. 133.

Miseries: marriage enlarges the scene of our happiness and, ii. 516; vision of the mountain of human, iv. 507–11.

Misery: vale of, in Vision of MIRZA, ii. 123; the child of vice and parent of pain, ii. 222–3; something sacred in, iv. 108–9. *See also* Grief, Pascal.

Misfortune(s): *never come single* (prov.), i. 32; Seneca on spectacle of a virtuous man struggling with, i. 163–4; ii. 422; iii. 409; happen to both good and evil men, i. 169; ii. 421; iv. 213, 463–5; kinds to which the life of man is exposed, i. 358; *happen in all families* (prov.), i. 451; consolation under, ii. 139–42; bring a man to himself, ii. 287; a virtuous unbeliever under pressure of, iii. 43–44; our own should be regarded as little, those of others as great, iii. 128; folly of judging m. of others, iv. 211–14; allegorical figure of, iv. 276; each finds his own most bearable, iv. 506–11; are always less than they might be, iv. 564. *See also* Calamities.

MISPACH, a suitor of HILPA, v. 2–3.

Mispronouncing words, affectation of, i. 195.

'Miss': 'My elder sister would call me *Miss* as long as I live', v. 135.

Missionaries in China, iv. 452.

Misson de Valberg, Henri, *Mémoires et observations faites par un voyageur en Angleterre*, i. *3*, *68*; ii. *3*, *32*, *84*, *131*, *132*, *265*, *291*, *402*, *430–1*, *439*, *456*, *511*; iii. *292*, *370*, *372*.

Mist's Weekly Journal, i. 322.

Mistress(es) (woman illicitly occupying place of wife): of SIMON HONEYCOMB, ii. 104; KITTY, m. of CHARLES YELLOW, ii. 236; choice between m. and wife, ii. 280–2; keeping m., horses and hounds, ii. 546; letter from a kept m., ii. 575–6; no better than a strumpet, iii. 16; and pin-money, iii. 52; brings sorrow, iii. 407; a fiancé who proposes making DORINDA his m., iii. 504–5; passion of love to a m. contrasted with that to a wife, iv. 371–2.

Mistress (sweetheart): ii. 192; indelicate behaviour of a, ii. 347; coldness of a, ii. 512–13; incident at a m.'s toilet, ii. 548; his m. a lovely fair, mine a lovely brown, iii. 17; letter from CLYTANDER on his, iii. 92–93.

Mithridates, King of Pontus. See Lee.

Mitre, introduced by a Gothic bishop, ii. 290.

Mnestheus, a colourless character in the *Aeneid*, ii. 562.

Mob (rabble): a curtailment of *mobile*, ii. 34; in the street, ii. 291; humour of the, iv. 101; what the m. call a jolly man, iv. 221; the huzzas of the, v. 59; drank the King's health, v. 106, 108.

Mob (attire): 'all that huddled oeconomy of dress', iii. 82; 'went in our mobs to the dumb man', iii. 184.

Mobile, the: curtailed into *mob*, ii. 34; used their clubs, v. 108.

Mob-readers, i. 269.

Mock-battles of children, v. 125.

Mockery and scorn, the best weapons against atheists, iii. 463.

Mock-heroic poems: and burlesque, ii. 467–8; allegorical figures admitted in, ii. 564; heathen mythology excusable in, iv. 362.

Mode: corruption of m. and gallantry, i. 30; professed followers of the, iii. 65; *See also* Fashion.

Mode (one who sets or displays the fashion), iv. 194.

Modes: a Society for Inspection of M. and Fashions, proposed, ii. 193.

MODELY, Lady BETTY, her scuttle, iii. 183.

Moderation: allegorical figure of, i. 17; men of, i. 209–10; of desires, i. 470; necessary to enjoyment of life, ii. 64–68; the source of happiness, ii. 306–9; recommended by Horace, iii. 129; fortitude, equanimity, and m. the great rule, iii. 406; FRANK JOLLY endeavouring to learn to act with, iv. 9; between seriousness and levity the ideal, v. 45; of Henry Boyle, v. 177.

Moderator, The, i. 15.

Moderator, the part of, esteemed by all men, ii. 275.

Moderns. *See* Ancients and Moderns.

Modest Survey of . . . The Distrest Mother, i. lxxxiv; iii. *34*.

Modesty: false m. a hindrance to advancement, i. 11; the chief ornament of the female sex, i. 30; ii. 568; iii. 482; beauty ungraceful and wit detestable without, i. 88; in women now out of fashion, i. 193–4; the part of, never to commit offence, i. 433; in conversation now out of fashion in town, i. 488; ignorance of, in court of Louis XIV, ii. 48; in men, displeasing to ladies, ii. 103–4; and coolness great assets in disputation, ii. 274; blessings brought by, ii. 306–9; virtuous and vicious m., ii. 397–401 (this paper praised, iv. 459–60); and diffidence generally accompany merit, ii. 381, 397–8; manly m. in my men readers, ii. 567; in Prince

Eugene, iii. 262–5; contrasted with impudence, iii. 303–4; of Spartan young men, iii. 321; is always joined to magnanimity, iii. 321; distinguished from assurance, iii. 403–6; defined, iii. 404, 464; of a young prince before Roman Senate, iii. 404; usually attending faultless poverty, iii. 409–10; opposed to wantonness, iii. 496–8; the national virtue of the English, iii. 520; iv. 29; true and false, iv. 115–18; the *Spectator* has made m. fashionable, iv. 128; in the legal profession, iv. 215–18; opinions of the ancients concerning, iv. 216.

MODISH, JACK, letter from (on fashions in Exeter), ii. 192–3.

MODISH, Mrs., ii. 488.

Modish: machine (the fan), i. 427; world, i. 487; part of the world, ii. 372.

Mogul, the Great, i. 119, 293.

MOHAIR, MATILDA, letter from (on behaviour of young women), iv. 244–7 (comments on this letter, iv. 260–1).

Mohair, in embroidery, v. 72, 83.

Mohocks: 'Journal of a Mohock', received, iii. 181; Mr. FROTH's account of, iii. 183; accounts of, iii. 186–8, 223–6; Sir ROGER followed by, iii. 240, 253, 268; existence of, doubted by some, iii. 292; mentioned, iii. 347. — Emperor of, iii. 187, 224; his manifesto, iii. 293–5; married a rich widow, v. 58.

Moisture, decay of, in the earth, iv. 542.

Mol. Pately (a dance), i. 286.

Mole, the: Henry More, on the senses of, i. 495–6; Boyle, on the sight of, i. 496; fable of, i. 508.

Molesworth, Robert Molesworth, 1st Viscount: letter from Copenhagen by (?), iii. 473.

Molière (Jean-Baptiste Poquelin): used to read his comedies to his housekeeper, i. 297; fondness for old ballads, i. 364; mentioned, iv. 529. — *L'Avare*, iv. 43; *L'Etourdi*, i. 24; *Georges Dandin*: i. 417; Lubin in, iii. 267; Betterton's *Amorous Widow* based on, iii. 370; *Le Misanthrope*, Alceste in, i. 364.

MOLLY: friend of JAMES and ELIZABETH, i. 306, 307; one of ABRAHAM THRIFTY's nieces, ii. 442; T. B.'s daughter, iii. 196.

Moloch: worshipped in fires and flames, i. 313; offerings to, iii. 17; his character in *PL*, iii. 87, 114; flying from battle, wounded, iii. 115, 232.

Moluc, Muly (Emperor of Morocco), death of, iii. 301.

Momus: statue of a, lately dug up at Rome, iii. 351; on scandalous stories of the gods, iii. 460; modern sons of, among critics, v. 27.

Monarchy: allegorical figure of, i. 17; absolute m. dangerous, iii. 21; a monarchical form of government in Heaven (?), iii. 21.

Money: suitors with, are saucy and cold, ii. 52; as a method of persuasion, ii. 431; essays on, invited, iv. 54; essay on means of acquiring, iv. 81–86; letter on, iv. 106, 306–10; 'every married man's m.', iv. 208; 'every ordinary man's m.', iv. 232; DICK GLOOMY, who thirsts after, v. 8.

Moneyed interest, Sir ANDREW inclined to the, ii. 3.

Monimia (in *The Orphan*): her lament, ii. 436; MONIMIA, letter from (on loss of beauty by small-pox), v. 96–97; her lover, v. 117.

Monkey(s): proposed for an entertainment, i. 119; dancing, i. 127, 129; characteristics of, i. 148; in china ware, i. 153; on the shoulder of Caprice, i. 271; enshrined in an Egyptian temple, ii. 7; the image of a, ii. 184; soul of Thersites transformed into that of, ii. 326; Lady HECTICK's m. leaping out at window, iii. 183; and lapdogs of ladies, iii. 273; account of a m.'s former incarnations, iii. 273–6; a modern woman of Hensburg carries off her favourite, iv. 271; avoid speaking to evade work (?), iv. 513.

Monks: in medieval times produced much false wit, i. 253–5; god of dullness dressed in monk's habit, i. 271; passed judgements on kings who opposed them, iv. 212.

Monmouth, Duke of: amours of, i. 12; the M. cock still fashionable in the country, ii. 14; 'danced at court with', iii. 70.

Monoetes, a ludicrous incident of, in the *Aeneid*, ii. 589.

Monosyllables: English language abounds in, ii. 32; Pope's illustration of use of, in poetry, ii. 484.

Monsoons, depicted in a terrestrial globe, iv. 482.

Monster(s): in region of mixed wit, i. 273; represented in art, ii. 180; of the poet's own forming, ii. 554; of lust and cruelty among absolute monarchs, iii. 20–21; 'those deceitful m. [male jilts]', iii. 119; produced in hell, iii. 119; in romances, iii. 129; may be pleasing because of strange-

ness, iii. 541; incapable of propagating its likeness, iii. 546; depicted in Ovid, iii. 565–6; created by a disordered imagination, iii. 579; by use, are beheld without loathing, v. 139.

Montagu, Charles. *See* Halifax.

Montagu, Edward. *See* Sandwich.

Montagu, Edward Wortley: Volume II of *Tatler* dedicated to, i. xvii; a subscriber, i. lxxxix; letter written by his footman (?), i. 305; letter from Addison to, i. 505; courtship of Lady Mary, iii. 52; referred to (?), iv. 556.

Montagu, John Montagu, 2nd Duke of, a subscriber, i. lxxxviii.

Montagu, Lady Mary Wortley: a contributor, i. lxxxi; iv. 556; *Letters*, i. 56; ii. 8; iii. 536; courtship of, iii. 52; introduced inoculation, iii. 101.

Montaigne, Michel de: mentions a family-book, recording occurrences in one particular house, ii. 464; and Seneca are patterns for writing essays, iv. 186; perhaps the most eminent egotist that ever appeared in the world, iv. 520; *Essays*, i. 294, 459; ii. 211, 387, 399, 464; iii. 299; iv. 146; mentioned, ii. 142.

Montgomery, ——, No. 524 attributed to, i. lvii; iv. 364.

Montgomery, Sir Hugh, slain at Chevy Chase, i. 319, 320.

Month, 'Within a m. of', i. 393; ii. 335–6.

Monthly accounts, printed in one of our, ii. 17.

Monthly pamphlets, published in France, Germany, and Holland, iv. 113–14.

Monthly Register, printed for Sam. Buckley, i. xx, xxi, 6.

Months, allegory of the, iii. 594–7.

Monument(s): in Westminster Abbey, i. 108–11; to Sir Cloudesley Shovell, i. 110–11; to Duke and Duchess of Newcastle, i. 417; erected by merchants, ii. 187; of Eastern nations, iii. 324–5; in memory of the friendship of Steele and Addison, iv. 493.

Moon: 'The m. takes up the wondrous tale', iv. 144; beauty of, in clouded majesty, iv. 529.

Moonshine: sleep, that m. in the brain, v. 40.

'Moor, the apothecary'. *See* More, John.

Moore, John (Bishop of Ely), a subscriber, i. lxxxviii.

Moors, victory of, over Portuguese, iii. 301–2.

Moose, Richard (quack of Ipswich), advertisement of, iv. 61.

Moral: of *Chevy Chase* contained in four last lines, i. 299; of *The Lancashire Witches*, ii. 59; very title of a m. treatise shocking to the careless, ii. 205; derived from paintings, ii. 378–9; of *PL*, iii. 390–1; necessity of definition in m. discourses, iii. 403; of a fable is unobtrusive, iv. 317–18.

Moralists faulty in always teaching happiness, ii. 268.

Morality: moral instruction in literature, i. 298–9; immortality of the soul the basis of, i. 456; *Spectators* on, made up in sets, i. 507–8; the three great branches of, ii. 233; duties of, ii. 331–4, 443–6; undermined by politicians, ii. 400; impossible to make original observations in, ii. 483–4; discourses of, in *Spectator*, well received, ii. 517; precepts of, less effective than examples, iii. 67–68; capable of demonstration as well as mathematics, iii. 404; and faith compared, iv. 118–20, 137; strengthens faith, iv. 143.

Morality, books of: writers of, prescribe after the Galenic way, i. 506; men generally draw consolation from, ii. 141; the best means of self-improvement, ii. 341.

Moralize: how to m. pleasure, iii. 475–6; a man who could m. upon trifles, v. 138.

Morals: effects of party-spirit upon, i. 510; the crooked m. of London, ii. 577.

Morass, a French word imported, ii. 152.

Morat (in *Aurung-zebe*), i. 345 and n.

More, Henry: on taking a prejudice against a man for his looks (a *prosopolepsia*), i. 368–9; on the structure of the mole, i. 495–6; *Antidote against Atheism*, i. 480; iv. 349; *Divine Dialogues*, ii. 423.

More, John (apothecary): testimonials to his cures, iv. 457; his advertisement of medicine for 'weakness', iv. 553.

More, Sir Thomas: gaiety of humour in death, iii. 300; story from, iv. 566.

Morecraft, Thomas, original of WILL WIMBLE (?), i. 446.

Mores hominum multorum, i. 230.

Moreton, John (linen merchant): referred to (?), ii. 464; his linen shop fitting up anew, iv. 455.

MORIA and DICTAMNUS, a squabbling couple, iv. 238.

Morning's draught, i. 295, 310.

Morning's dream, i. 354.

Morocco: courtiers of, know emperor's disposition by the colour of his dress, ii. 532; 'the lord who cut off the King

of M.'s head', iii. 214; death of Muly Moluc, Emperor of, iii. 301.

Morose and covetous, the, iv. 181.

Moroseness: affected m. of the unkind husband, ii. 418.

Morphew, John: and the *Tatler*, i. xxii, 74; publisher of *Post Boy* and *Supplement*, ii. *549*.

Morris dance, iii. *595*.

Morris-dancer, in the masquerade, i. 96.

Mortality of the soul, one of the great points of atheism, ii. 230.

Mortality, Bills of: ii. 406; made by parish clerks, ii. 67; iii. 402; an argument for Providence, iii. 27–28; made up of those who 'died for love', iii. 417.

Mortgaging of estates, i. 352, 468; ii. 40; mortgages the legacy of men of pleasure, ii. 95.

Mortier, D., translation of *Spectator*, iv. 23.

MORTMAIN, Mr., attorney, iv. 174.

Moreton-Hampstead, Devonshire, iii. 455.

Morum comitas, a requirement for friendship, i. 291.

Mosaic, discovered at Stunsfield, iii. 339.

Mosca (in *Volpone*), Wilks as, iii. 394.

Moscow, a young merchant bred at, ii. 37.

Moses: his serpent swallowed up those of the Egyptians, i. 45; Jewish story concerning, ii. 423; hearing the word out of a bush, like Moses, ii. 600; the Muse who inspired, iii. 84; his description of the Creation praised by Longinus, iii. 255–6; crossing the Red Sea, iii. 386–7; spies sent by, into the Promised Land, iv. 254; God's revelation to, v. 21; mentioned, iv. *256*.

Moss, Robert: *The Christian's Overthrow prevented*, recommended, i. 391.

Mother: obedience to a, ridiculed in *The Man of Mode*, i. 279; rivalry of a m. and daughter, i. 384–8; *every m.'s son of us* (prov.), ii. 21; prosperity like the too great indulgence of a fond, ii. 422; letters between a m. and son, ii. 524–5; portrayal of, in *The Distressed M.*, iii. 32; carrying a boy to travel in his m.'s lap, iii. 368.

Mother (hysteria), i. 147.

Mother Cob's Mild, iii. 154.

Mother Day's Double, v. 106.

Mother-in-law: Antiochus in love with his, ii. 393.

Mothers: who whip children till they cry and then whip them for crying, ii. 336; should nurse their children, ii. 454–8.

Motion(s): 'the dumb eloquence of', i. 281; giddy, ii. 62; that m. which we call strutting, ii. 113; little heedless unguarded, ii. 235; soft regularity of, in MIRTILLA, ii. 308; ambition stirs up uneasy m. in the mind, ii. 498; of the gods, described by Heliodorus, iii. 389; objects in m. pleasing to the imagination, iii. 542; beauty of, in dancing, iv. 146; WILL HONEYCOMB's easy, v. 184.

Motions (puppet shows), i. 63.

Motte, Benjamin: *Miscellaneous Collection of Poems*, v. *118*.

Motteux, Peter Anthony: a contributor, i. lvi; letter from, on his wares, iii. 25–26; has dedicated a poem on tea to Mr. SPECTATOR, iv. 478–9; description of his warehouse, iv. *479*; and the *Gentleman's Journal*, i. xxxvii, *120*; iv. *386, 413, 414*; wrote libretto of *Arsinoe*, i. 79; translation of *Don Quixote*, i. *125*; on punning, i. *259*; *Love's Triumph*, ii. *506*; translation of Rabelais, iii. 4.

Mottoes: a species of wit, i. 265; an innocent diversion, ii. 451.

Mountain(s): huge heaps of, pleasing to the imagination, iii. 540; shaded with oaks, beneficial, iii. 552; weighed in scales by the Almighty, iv. 134; of the Muses described, iv. 325–7; vision of the m. of human miseries, iv. 507–11.

Mountebank(s): a m.'s stage, i. 269; practices of quacks, iv. 552; fantastic habit of, v. 105.

Mountfort, William (actor), in *The Fortune-Hunters*, i. *94*.

Mourning: costume, i. 275–7, 402; for deaths of rulers, i. 276–7; effect on mercers, &c., i. 276–7; inward m. the mark of true grief, i. 402–4; in sack-cloth instead of fine Holland, iii. 348; gloves and hat-bands, iii. 401; an agreeable second-m., iii. 532; fashionable mourners, iv. 279; a sort of second m., iv. 281; suits at Sir ROGER's funeral, iv. 340–1; for Queen Anne, v. 72.

Mousel, Kingdom of: ruled over by Fadlallah, iv. 576.

Mouth: opening the m. of a Cardinal, and of Mr. SPECTATOR, iv. 471.

Mouths, 'to make m. at', iv. 207, 208.

Moving picture: i. 128; ii. 441, 471; iii. 550–1; advertisement for, i. *128–9*; ii. *441–2*; iii. *550–1*.

Moving sentries proposed, iv. 408.

Mr. or *Esq.*, ii. 92.

Mucro, or point, of a coquette's heart, ii. 595.

Muff(s): the little m. now in fashion, i. 70; last year's little, ii. 13; mentioned, i. 295.

Mulgrave. *See* Sheffield.

Mullineaux, Sir Vivian, iv. 567.

Multa Renascentur, the: in words, iv. 429.

'Multiplication Table', Steele's proposal for a, iii. 547-8.

Multitude, the: approval of, as test of a work of art, i. 297; applause and favour of, less important than self-approbation, ii. 181, 238, 492-3; men love to dazzle, ii. 515.

Mum Club, i. 41.

Mummers, i. 78.

MUMMIUS, his grudging way o consenting to a benefaction, iii. 39.

Mummy, Egyptian, useful in physic, iii. 149.

Mumpers (beggars), at the Royal Exchange, iv. 307.

Mundus agit histrionem, Totus, iii. 393.

Murder: the first m. occasioned by a religious controversy, ii. 228; and petty larceny not to be punished alike, iii. 66; allegorical depiction of, iii. 596; celibacy a form of, iv. 383.

Murphy, Arthur, i. lvi, lvii.

Murrain, 'a m. to her', i. 464.

Murrel, Sir Charles, slain at Chevy Chase, i. 320.

Musaeus (author of *Hero and Leander*), strokes of mixed wit in the little poem ascribed to, i. 265.

Musaeus (legendary poet), ii. 76; iv. 329.

Muscles: of the female tongue, ii. 460; ogling and elevating m. in the eye, ii. 572-3.

Muscovites, at Battle of Pultowa, ii. 37.

Muscovy, i. 45, 293.

Musculi amatorii, or the ogling muscles, ii. 572.

Muse: Sappho called the Tenth, ii. 366; who inspired Moses, iii. 84.

Muses, the: Blackmore wrote to rescue, i. 29-30; Lacedaemonians sacrificed to, ii. 239; teasers of, iii. 26; surrounding Jupiter, iii. 516; as companions of those in solitude, iii. 518; mountain of, described, iv. 325-7; surrounding Apollo, iv. 329, 474; v. 28; invocation of, in modern poems, iv. 363; surrounding the supreme deities, iv. 583; Herodotus adapted his books to the number of, v. 159.

Mushroom, ii. 265.

Music: of kettle-drums, i. 65; ii. 415; Italian and English, i. 79-81; effects of, i. 81-82; banished by Plato, i. 82; differences between Italian, English, and French, i. 119-23; its laws to be deduced from general sense and taste of mankind, i. 123; concerts in Haberdashers-Hall, i. 228; as a useful diversion, i. 397; sounds of words compared to notes in, ii. 33; proficients in windm., ii. 73; of a shepherd's pipe, ii. 122; played to departed souls on arrival in Paradise, ii. 122; in church, ii. 305-6; iii. 253-4, 268, 514-16; iv. 285-6; v. 152-4; Armstrong, the famous fine writer of, ii. 329; proposed as an accomplishment for youth, ii. 395; softens and disarms the mind, ii. 424; of the tongue, ii. 461; of cries of London, ii. 474-8; poetry and m. in public diversions, ii. 503-5; concerts in Clayton's house in York Buildings, ii. 505-7, 584-5; iii. 291; arose from sounds of a smith's hammer, iii. 238; iv. 171; and the cat-call, iii. 349-53; iv. 590; Collier's essay on, quoted, iii. 352; on a bridal night, iii. 370; Italian m. in its perfection shown us by Nicolini, iii. 513-14; as an aid to devotion, iii. 514-16; of birds, pleasing to the imagination, iii. 544; descriptive effects in, iii. 559; invented by Jubal, iv. 171; sight, and development of, iv. 171; kitchen-m., iv. 545-6; v. 108; ravishes and transports the soul, iv. 585; as cure for bite of tarantula, iv. 590; of marrow-bone and cleaver, v. 108.

Musical instrument(s): a shepherd with a, ii. 122; invented by Sappho, ii. 408; in a beau's head, ii. 571; origin of, iii. 350-2.

Musical societies, merely for entertainment, v. 152.

MUSIDORUS, slain by 'an arrow that flew out of a dimple', iii. 418.

Muslin(s): cambric and, i. 241; and other Indian goods in Motteux's shop, iii. 25; iv. 479; 'her linen was striped m.', iii. 532.

Mussulman, i. 360; at Grand Cairo, v. 65.

Mustachio, the: curling-irons for, iii. 222; treatise on, in manuscript, iii. 223.

Mustard, ii. 530.

Muster-master, a new sort of, ii. 30.

Mutton: Kit-Cat Club took its original from m.-pie, i. 42; leg of, iii. 154; m.-pie at Christmas, iii. 380.

Myndian, DAPHNIS the, ii. 407.

Myrrh: in every hedge, iii. 569; bundles of, v. 3.

Myrtle(s): a garland of, ii. 408; the bleeding m. in *Aeneid*, iii. 145; oaks or, iii. 569; oranges and, iii. 593; mentioned, v. 94.

Mystery (occupation), ii. 582; iii. 380.

Mythology, heathen: in poetry condemned, iv. 361–4; 'the pagan strain', v. 118.

Mytilene, Alpheus of: his epitaph on Homer, iv. 473.

Naevia (in Martial), i. 126, 467.

Naevius, Gnaeus (early playwright), v. 28.

Nail(s): superstition concerning a rusty, i. 33; *hits the right n. upon the head* (prov.), ii. 416; Jews are like pegs and n. in a building, iv. 255.

Nails: TOM TAWDRY paring his, iv. 298.

Naked: our Saviour's injunction to clothe the, ii. 200, 405; reply made by a n. Indian to a European, ii. 387; bodies of female suicides threatened to be exposed n. in Greece, ii. 400; Milton's reflection on Adam and Eve's going, iii. 61; 'to see fellows running races n.', iii. 320–1; rakes jesting themselves stark n. in a frolic, iii. 341; the n.-shouldered, iv. 38.

Name: sincerity the foundation of a good, ii. 239; virtue and service the foundation of a high, ii. 349; a good n. fitly compared to a precious ointment, ii. 426; pleasure in attacking an established, ii. 494–5; difficulties in preserving a great, ii. 496–8; a good n. to be valued as life itself, iv. 88; veneration due to n. of God, iv. 395; *when his n. is up, he may lie abed* (prov.), v. 59.

Names: familiar forms of, in English, are short, in other languages, long, ii. 35; corresponding under n. of love, ii. 559; iii. 489; calling n. does no good, ii. 568; giving fair n. to foul actions, iii. 16; which begin and end with same letters, iv. 293.

Namur, siege of, ii. 183; iii. 399.

Nantes, Revocation of Edict of, ii. 211.

Nap, afternoon, iii. 153, 154.

Napier, Sir Theophilus, iii. *102*.

Naples, ii. 277; iii. 369.

NARCISSA: lovers of, iii. 471–2; her cabinet of love-letters, iv. 371.

Narcissus: love of self, ii. 427; fable of, adapted by Milton, iii. *176*; the flower, iii. 594.

Narrations, inaccurate, iv. 353–6.

Narrative: mixture of vision and n. in *PL* regrettable, iii. 386.

Nash, Richard ('Beau'), referred to (?), ii. 464.

Nathan: his fable of the poor man and his lamb, ii. 220.

Natural: 'that n. way of writing, that beautiful simplicity', i. 268; and wonderful, i. 304; and poetical, i. 315–16; just and n. opposed to point or turn, ii. 52–53; just and n. colouring in painting, ii. 447; sentiments in the epic must be n. and sublime, ii. 587; n. but not obvious, 'the true character of all fine writing', iii. 284.

Natural genius. *See* Genius.

Natural historians: on the barrenness of England, i. 295; on male and female birds, ii. 9.

Natural history: a body of, proposed, i. 496; an admirable sketch of, in Cicero, i. 497.

Natural History of Coffee, iii. *372*.

Natural knowledge, disquisitions of, by the Royal Society, ii. 519.

Natural objects, pleasing to the imagination, iii. 451–2, 538.

Natural parts, compared with learning, iv. 137.

Natural philosophers, and the pleasures of the imagination, iii. 574–5.

Naturalists, i. 261.

Naturalization of Foreign Protestants, Bill for, ii. *285*.

Naturals, 'a monstrous birth in', ii. 362.

Nature (as object of imitation in art): shadows and realities not to be mixed together, i. 23; a kind of n. to be observed in humorous writings, i. 146; wit must have its foundation in, i. 268; strokes of, in Ecclesiasticus, i. 290; copyings after, in *Chevy Chase*, i. 316; *Two Children in the Wood* a plain simple copy of, i. 362; to be admired in her simplicity, i. 364; flights of, ii. 128; touches of, in a letter, ii. 212; Sappho followed n. in all her thoughts, ii. 366; Sappho's *Ode to Lesbia* an exact copy of, ii. 393; in painting, ii. 447; *The Distressed Mother* is everywhere n., iii. 32–33; the poet mends and perfects, iii. 569–70.

Nature (as dominating power in men or animals): to follow n. brings one an equal spirit, ii. 66; all that n. has prescribed must be good, ii. 97; should direct in all things not contradictory to justice, law or reason, ii. 100; temperance gives n. her full play, ii. 264; gives grace to every action wherein

she is complied with, ii. 425; gives place to custom, ii. 458; following n. insufficient in relationship of parents and children, ii. 522; most men follow n. only while they are in their night-gowns, ii. 553; alone can qualify a man for learning, iii. 106; he who follows n. can never be improper or unseasonable, iii. 450; 'follow n.' the command of the oracle, iii. 513.

Nature (as creative power in the physical world): disseminates her blessings in different regions, i. 294–5; *does nothing in vain* (prov.), ii. 322; iii. 510; makes the earth gay and delightful to carry on her great work, iii. 452–3.

Nature (contrasted with art): superior to art in portraying grief, iii. 486–7; works of n. and art as they affect the imagination, iii. 548–53; rough careless strokes of n. superior to nice touches of art, iii. 549; beautiful wildness of n. without the nicer elegancies of art, iv. 190–1; a scene of n. more beautiful than that of art, v. 14; the spontaneous hand of n., without any help from art, v. 28.

Nature (the material world): dissolution of, described by Burnet, ii. 76–77; books will perish only in the general wreck of, ii. 154; everything great in n. has a place in *PL*, ii. 542; the whole circle of, ii. 563; the Holy Spirit operating in the first production of, iii. 84; love of, implanted early in our natures, iii. 473–4; God revealed in, iii. 475–6; everything in, created for a certain use, iii. 510; pleases the imagination, iii. 535–53; the poet must gain a due relish of works of, iii. 563; inspires devotion, iv. 144–5; all parts of n. invigorated by presence of God, iv. 548.

Ne quid detrimenti res capiat publica, i. 181.

Near (stingy), iii. 219, 505.

Nebuchadrezzar, iii. 554.

Necessities: of the poor supplied by the superfluities of the wealthy, i. 277; of one country supplied by superfluities of another, i. 294; neglect of, an extravagant vice, i. 469; regard for n. of poor, ii. 405; iii. 48–49; provision of necessaries man's first concern, iii. 21.

Necessity: allegorical figure of in Aeschylus, iii. 338; the mother of fate, iii. 596.

Neck(s): 'put his hand in our', ii. 73; the pole of the, ii. 508; the finest n. and bosom, ii. 535; 'to play with my',

ii. 576; exposure of women's n. in public, iv. 38.

Neck-handkerchiefs, iv. 195.

Necklace: diamond, i. 295; iii. 417; iv. 558, 561; of an immoderate length, ii. 580; Mrs. BRILLIANT's n. false stones, iii. 183; a great pearl n. bequeathed by Sir ROGER, iv. 340.

Necromancer, generally in train of a knight-errant, ii. 438.

NED, v. 127.

Need makes the old wife trot (prov.), iv. 309.

Needful, 'to write the n.', iv. 306.

Needle(s): sympathetic n. and loadstone, ii. 437–8; n.-money, iii. 53; the man who could throw a grain of corn through the eye of a, iv. 146; always turns to the pole, v. 38.

Needlework: in education of girls, iii. 140; embroidering and, iii. 205; the neglected art of, recommended, v. 71–74; letter on, v. 83; mentioned, v. 97, 160.

Neglect: of dress prejudicial, ii. 90–92; iii. 82; and contempt depress a noble spirit, ii. 426; never in. small matters and expenses ('Italian proverb'), iii. 2; in keeping promises and appointments, iv. 74–75.

Negligence(s): of what others think of you, i. 433; an agreeable n. is now modish, i. 487; in a woman's man, ii. 113; a little n. can spoil us, ii. 116; complaint of a husband's sloth and, ii. 326–7; childish n., ii. 521; affectation of, iii. 6; a certain n. 'that is so becoming', iii. 104. *See also* Ease.

Negroes, story of rival, ii. 339–40.

Neighbourhood, good, i. 509.

Neighbourhoods, those little communities called, i. 210.

Neighbours: a gentleman's hospitality among his, ii. 186; our duty towards our, ii. 232–3.

Nelson, Robert: a disclaimer by, iv. 385.

NEMESIS, passes judgement on afflictions of others, iv. 211–12.

Nemine contradicente, i. 310; iii. 66; iv. 46, 458.

Nepos, Cornelius: *De viris illustribus*, ii. 26; quoted, iii. 446–7.

NEPOS, CORNELIUS, letter from (on his nephews), iii. 506.

Neptune: Pelias, son of, ii. 455; raises a tempest in time of battle, iii. 233; in modern poems, iv. 364.

Nero: called Biberius Mero because of his drinking, ii. 455–6; resemblance to Louis XIV(?), iii. 509.

Nerves: perfume intended to refresh the, ii. 426; little n. in the heart, ii. 596.

Nesbit, Rev. Mr., iii. 153.

Nestor, a novel character in the Iliad, ii. 562.

Nests of birds, structure of, derived from instinct, i. 490.

Netherton, manor of, v. 76.

NETTLETOP, REBECCA, letter from (history of a prostitute), ii. 245–7 (testimonial to this letter, iv. 461).

Network, a curious piece of, ii. 571.

Neuter(s): i. 235, 273; Greek law forbade any man to stand as a, i. 72; some opinions in which a man should stand n., i. 479; Spectator stands a n. between both sexes, iii. 160.

Neutrality Army, i. 182.

New England, iv. 343.

New Forest, judgement of William the Conqueror's race in, iv. 212.

New style in dating, iii. 480.

New Year's Day, brawn and minced-pies on, v. 150.

Newberry, Mr., rebus of, i. 251.

Newcastle, William Cavendish, Duke of: translated Molière, i. 24; monument to Duke and Duchess in Westminster Abbey, i. 417.

Newcastle, Margaret Lucas, Duchess of, her epitaph, i. 417.

Newcastle, 'the steenkirk arrived but two months ago at', ii. 15.

Newmarket, i. 231, 335; ii. 117.

News, contemporary: inquirers after, i. 46; as a subject of conversation, i. 289; ii. 386–8; the state-pedant wrapped up in, i. 438; crying of, in streets, ii. 476; not a single word of, in Spectator, ii. 517; 'in the hottest seasons of', iii. 27; delight in, iv. 90–94; private history and scandal the chief qualifications in, iv. 112; letter from THO. QUID-NUNC, on his fondness for, v. 136–7.

News-gatherers, in the employ of courts, iv. 43.

News-letter of whispers, proposed, iv. 111–14.

Newsmonger(s): among men as well as women, ii. 459–60; Mr. W——, 'that learned', iii. 485; our modern n. in coffee-houses, iv. 91.

Newspaper(s): read in coffee-houses, i. 3–4, 198, 276–7; should instruct men in wisdom and virtue, i. 507; French terms in, ii. 151; iii. 69; common phrases in, ii. 388; necessary to politicians, iii. 97; distributed by men, women, and children, iii. 380;

the stamp act fatal to many, iv. 62–63; project for a n. of occurrences within the verge of the penny-post, iv. 92–94; project of a n. of whispers, iv. 111–14.

News-writers, and zealots of parties, i. 507.

Newton, Henry, ii. 466.

Newton, Sir Isaac: a subscriber, i. lxxxix; his works in LEONORA's library, i. 154; his calculations on the heat of the comet of 1680, i. 423; 'the miracle of the present age, can look through a whole planetary system', iv. 442; the glory of our nation, worthy to be named with Bacon and Boyle, iv. 488; calls infinite space the sensorium of the Godhead, iv. 532; like one of another species, yet his view is narrow compared to an angel's, v. 171; Opticks, i. 493; iv. 442; Principia, i. 493; referred to(?), i. 330; iii. 529; iv. 488; mentioned, iv. 5.

Newton, John, The English Academy, iii. 483.

Newton, Thomas, edition of PL, ii. 538; iii. 121, 201.

Nexus utriusque mundi, iv. 349.

Nice: Sir ROGER 'so n. in this particular', i. 476; Mr. SPECTATOR 'so n. there is no enduring you', ii. 53; some women 'too n. to be quite alive', ii. 66; the n. Puritans objected to country wakes, ii. 135; in such n. circumstances, ii. 249; so n. an affair as between man and wife, ii. 343; n. proportion, iii. 27. — Nicely, ii. 494, 596.

Nicety (-ies): and correctness of the moderns, ii. 127; and exactness in literature of colder climates, ii. 128; the great poet does not always mind little, iii. 5; too much n. in epic similes condemned by Boileau, iii. 91.

NICHARAGUA, Prince, i. 238.

Niches, grottoes, and caves, iv. 325.

Nicholas, Robert (judge), iii. 135.

Nichols, John, Literary Anecdotes, i. 6; v. 35, 146.

Nick: in Italian is Nicolini, ii. 35.

Nicknames: short in English, long in other languages, ii. 35; disgraceful appellations, commonly called, ii. 449.

Nicocrean, tyrant of Cyprus, iv. 492.

NICODEMUNCIO, letter from, to OLIVIA, iv. 20.

Nicolas, Sébastien-Roch. See Chamfort.

Nicolini, the Italian form of Nick, ii. 35.

Nicolini (Nicola Grimaldi): sailing on a sea of paste-board in Rinaldo, i. 23; combat with the lion in Hydaspes, i. 55–59, 60; iii. 138–9; acting ability, i. 59;

Prenesto in *Camilla*, ii. *82*; graces of, ii. 305; applauded by the Trunk-maker, ii. 415; clapped, iii. 184; is about to leave the stage, iii. 513; has shown us Italian music in its perfection, iii. 513–14.

Nieces: ABRAHAM THRIFTY's, ii. 442–3; who run gadding abroad, v. 71.

Nieremberg, Juan Eusebio, S.J., iv. *567*.

Night: made before day, iii. 17; vicissitude of day and n. pleasing to the imagination, iii. 453; the 'sweet vicissitudes' of n. and day, iii. 594; beauty of the sky at, iv. 529; coming in late at n. a source of marital quarrels, v. 80.

Night-cap(s), i. 332; ii. 388, 512; half-a-dozen upon his head, iv. 252.

Night-cap (a wig), ii. 14; iii. 161.

Night goblins, that overturn plates and dishes, iii. 245.

Night-gown(s) (dressing-gown), i. 192, 209, 383; ii. 553; iii. 168; iv. 221, 225.

Nightingale(s): i. 50, 158, 306; ii. 474; iii. 593; v. 2; a countryman's description of (*Vox et praeterea nihil*), i. 263; a wife who cannot bear the noise of, ii. 11; song of, not heard above two months, ii. 477; Sir ROGER's aviary of, iii. 438; Milton's description of singing of, iii. 338, 481; in Spring Garden, iii. 438–9; a man who can imitate the song of, iv. 546; Prince Fadlallah's soul in body of a, iv. 578–9; the throstle and, v. 63.

Nightmare, a witch giving maids the, i. 482.

Night-pieces (paintings), i. 355.

Night-rail, i. 272; iv. 29.

Night-walkers, female, i. 36; iii. 225.

Nigidius, on the Latin termination -*osus*, ii. 289.

NIGRANILLA, a Tory partisan, i. 347.

Nile, the, Egypt derives its plenty from, iii. 386; iv. 152.

Nillson, George, letter from, to Mary Norton, iii. 211.

NIMBLE, TOM: reply to, who has sent in a letter, iv. 587; letter from (how he triumphed over a rival), v. 82–83.

Nimrod: 'has spoken some things of N. with too great freedom', ii. 227; the *Spectator* the N. of writers, iii. 399.

Nineteen Plagues of a Chambermaid, The, ii. 89.

Ninety-nine Plagues of an Empty Purse, The, ii. 89.

Niocles, allowed to drink the death potion before Phocion, ii. 26.

NISBY, Mr., his opinions on current affairs, iii. 153–5.

Nisus and Euryalus: their characters beautiful, but common, ii. 563; came to unfortunate ends, iv. 464.

Nitocris, Queen of Babylon, iii. *554*.

Nitrous particles in snow, ii. 442.

No better than she should be (prov.), ii. 11; iv. 286; no wiser than he should be, ii. 38.

Noah's flood, the Ark and, iv. 575.

Noble: sentiments, ii. 372; spirit, ii. 426; science of defence, iv. 31.

Nobleman: value of the n. contrasted with the merchant, ii. 188; a n. who has improved several estates, iv. 593.

Nobles: of Rome represented by the Senate, iii. 20; the burthensome finery of, iii. 348.

Noctuary, of JOHN SHADOW, v. 6, 30; of a correspondent, v. 7.

No-customers, in India and China shops, iii. 245.

Noddle (head), v. 155.

Noddle-case (wig), loaden with pulvil, iv. 345.

NOEWILL, A., letter from (on Mrs. FREEMAN), ii. 342.

Noisy, the, insults of, ii. 389.

[*Nolo episcopari*], i. 379.

Nonconformity, and the Act of Toleration, ii. 306.

Non-existence, the prospect of, hardly endurable, iii. 431.

Non-juror, i. 43; iii. 509.

Nonsense: not the same as humour, i. 145; mother of frenzy, i. 147; love makes men talk n., ii. 478; n. verses in poetry, ii. 505; in a beau's head, ii. 572.

Nooning (a midday drink), i. 309.

Norfolk, Henry Howard, 6th Duke of, iii. *149*.

Norman line, beards discouraged under the, iii. 222.

Norris, Henry (actor): Spruce in *The Fortune-Hunters*, i. *94*; Cutberd in *The Silent Woman*, i. *173*; 'N. in a long coat', i. 191; a witch in *Macbeth*, i. *194*; in *The Lancashire Witches*, ii. *57*; Dick in *The Country Wake*, iv. 283.

Norris, John, *Reflections upon the Conduct of Humane Life*, i. 259.

Norris, Robert (quack doctor), advertisement of, iv. *61, 554*.

North, the: 'things go ill in', iii. 153; 'more work in', iii. 154.

Northamptonshire, iii. *189*.

North-Briton, a, iii. 399.

Northern Circuit, the, ii. 15.

Northern countries: why less populous, i. 90; physicians in, i. 90; less subject to jealousy, ii. 172.

'Northern Hive, The', Sir William Temple on, i. 90.
Northern Lass, The. See Brome, Richard.
Northumberland. *See* Percy, Earl.
Norton, Mary, iii. 211.
Norway, stories of witches in, i. 480.
Norwich, letter addressed from, iv. 353.
Nose: shape of, in the Ugly Club, i. 77; Solomon compares the n. of his beloved to Tower of Lebanon, ii. 127; of ARIDAEUS a little 'flatted' by his fall, ii. 407; pinching and pulling the, ii. 544–5; 'chanced to run my n. directly against a post', ii. 547; cocking the, ii. 572; muscle which draws the n. upwards, ii. 572; a fellow without a, iv. 59; judging size of the intellects from the, iv. 344.
Nose-pullers and nose-wringers, at the theatre, ii. 545.
Noses: Roman n. revived under William III, i. 135; a treatise of, ii. 469–70; red n. discarded, iv. 507.
Nostrils: the swelling n. of the proud and prosperous, iii. 322.
'Not at home', iii. 183.
Notable people: 'Those whom they call', iii. 72.
Nothing(s): long laborious n. of German wits, ii. 356; women can talk whole hours on, ii. 458; Rochester's admirable poem on, iii. 100.
Nottingham, Daniel Finch, 2nd Earl of: referred to(?), ii. 526.
Nouvelles de la République des Lettres, i. 494.
Novel: 'rather like a n. than a true story', i. 502; each letter contains a little n. or adventure, ii. 427; opening of a French, iii. 454; a new-fashioned, iv. 69; an antediluvian, iv. 595.
Novels: a book of, in LEONORA's library, i. 155; brains disordered with romances and, ii. 487; and romances inflamers of passion, iii. 374.
NOVELL, LYDIA, letter from (a love problem), ii. 52.
Novelty: wit consists not in advancing things that are new, ii. 483; variety and n. of characters in Homer, Virgil, and Milton, ii. 562–3; the grace of, iii. 29; and variety of characters in English comedy, iii. 396; as a source of aesthetic pleasure, iii. 540–4; in works of architecture, iii. 558; in poetry, exemplified in Ovid, iii. 564–6; as a source of pleasure to faculties of the soul, v. 52, 138–9; the force of, v. 138–42.
November: 'in the gloomy month of',

iii. 454; allegorical figure of, iii. 596; fine days in, iv. 191.
Now or never (prov.), iii. 508.
Nox, Momus the son of, v. 27.
Nullum magnum ingenium sine mixtura dementiae, i. 330.
Number of the Beast, ii. 250.
Numbers: the most infallible way of measuring things, ii. 187; the measure of everything valuable, ii. 188; choice of, in the lottery, ii. 249–50; Pythagoras on the mystery of, ii. 361; on coaches, iv. 268; belief in occult n. in Asia, v. 65; interest in, v. 159–60.
Numbers (in poetry): power of, ii. 75; harmonious, ii. 359; beauty of, ii. 485; rules of poetical, ii. 505; variety of, in *PL*, iii. 15; loose and unequal n. in Pindarics, iii. 376; exquisite n. in the *Faerie Queene*, iv. 429.
Numerousness of verse, iii. 330.
Numici. *See* Minucius.
Nunquam minus solus, quam cum solus, i. 19; iii. 151.
Nun(s): in the masquerade, i. 96; Three N. and a Hare, as a sign, i. 117; picture of a, ii. 29; CONSTANTIA in a sisterhood of, ii. 145.
Nurse: dry-nurse, iii. 207; antipathy caused by milk of, iv. 421.
Nursery of statesmen proposed in France, iii. 96.
Nursing of children, ii. 454–8; legendary n. by animals, ii. 455.
Nut-crackers, a pair of, ii. 184.
Nutmeg of Delight, the Persian Emperor calls himself the, ii. 128.
Nutt, John, printer of *Tatler*, i. lxvi.
Nutt, Richard, employed with his father in printing *Tatler*, i. lxvi; iii. 162.
Nymphs: paintings of, iii. 379; in sky-coloured garments, ii. 533; ships transformed into sea-n., iii. 145, 306; v. 15–16; wood- and water-n. not necessary to the pastoral, iv. 362; hamadryads or wood-n., v. 16–17; and Tritons, v. 118; fabled n. of old, v. 162.

O., J., letter from (on improper language in prayers), iii. 130–1.
O., R.: letter from, to the CLERGYMAN, i. 113–14; letter from (on an Infirmary for the ill-humoured), iii. 589–92.
O., W., bookseller, i. 59.
Oak: branches of, endure all seasons of the year, ii. 181; 'beauty flourishes as a mountain oak', iv. 598; Abraham's, in plains of Mambré, v. 15.
Oaks: on Sir ROGER's estate, iii. 54; a

mountain shaded with, beneficial, iii. 552; or myrtles, iii. 569; 'Britain owes her rescued oaks to thee', iv. 398; of four hundred years' standing, iv. 595.

Oaken pipes and cymbals in a morris dance, iii. 595.

Oaken plant(s): of the Trunk-maker, ii. 414; of Sir ROGER's servants, iii. 240.

Oates, Titus: 'when Dr. Titus Oates was in all his glory', i. 243; 'about the time of Oates's plot', ii. 44.

Oaths, a beau's head filled with, ii. 571. *See also* Profanity.

Oaths, refused by a Jacobite, ii. 184.

Oatmeal, a young girl eating, iv. 15; 'oatmeal-chewers', iv. 17.

Obedience: to a mother ridiculed in *The Man of Mode*, i. 279; of children to parents the basis of all government, ii. 244; and tenderness of a wife, ii. 281; our existence to be one continued act of, ii. 333; to the will of God, the moral of *PL*, iii. 391.

Oblige: whether to, or receive an obligation, ii. 87; and having the obligation multiplied in returns, ii. 255.

Oblique vision the mark of bewitchery, ii. 472.

Oblivion, River of, in *PL*, iii. 118–19.

Obloquy: men of honour exposed to, by party attacks, ii. 446; and praise frequently proceed from the same mouth, iv. 45.

Obnoxious (liable) to, ii. 311; iii. 299, 429; &c.

Obscene: songs learned by birds, i. 152; no o. ideas in *Spectator*, ii. 517; witticisms, ii. 591; conversation in a stage-coach, iv. 402.

Obsceneness, obscenity: in speech, i. 488; a hush-note to be used against, ii. 389.

Obscurity: in Milton's writing, iii. 62–64; of Persius, iii. 424; that quiet which Cowley calls the companion of, iii. 518; true greatness often found in, v. 84–87, 126–7.

Obsequiousness: in conferring salutations, ii. 508; as it sits upon a companion in pleasure, iii. 448; slaves to, iv. 196.

'Observation, on the': 'I am a woman turned of thirty, and am on the observation a little', ii. 479.

Observator, The, iii. 439.

Observator Reformed, The, i. lxx.

Observatory: Babylonian, iii. 554; John Sly's, iv. 376, 399, 408, 453.

Obsolete words and phrases, pedants' concern with, i. 250.

Obstinacy: in parents, ii. 213; resolution exerting itself as, in savage nations, ii. 339; conquered by gold, ii. 431; of EMILIA's goodness, iii. 83; of Satan depicted in *PL*, iii. 84; the mark of little minds, iii. 435.

Occasional Conformity, Bill against: ii. 249; Sir ROGER's praise of, ii. 550.

Occult numbers, and other superstitions in Asia, v. 65.

Occupations: effect of, upon personality, ii. 271–2.

Ocean: of Eternity, ii. 125; of Time, ii. 365; Book VI of *PL*, like a troubled, Book VII, like the o. in a calm, iii. 255; a troubled o. pleasing to the imagination, iii. 540; iv. 233–4; poetic descriptions of, iv. 233–6.

Oceana, 'my husband is pleased to call me his', ii. 327.

OCTAVIA, letter from (account of her seduction), iii. 178–80.

October, allegorical figure of, iii. 596.

October (ale): a barrel of, iv. 469; hogsheads of, iv. 542.

October Club, i. 42, 310.

Odd: and uncommon characters most interesting to the *Spectator*, i. 448; ii. 9; an o. kind of fellow, ii. 517; Sir ROGER o. and singular, iii. 54.

ODDLY, Lady MARY, married to Sir JOHN ANVIL, iii. 69.

Ode: Sappho's, to Venus, ii. 367; Sappho's, to Lesbia, ii. 390; Alcaeus', to Sappho, ii. 409; with variant readings, iv. 163; a divine o., made by a gentleman after his travels, iv. 235; a genius for the o. indicated by an unequal pace, iv. 345; Hughes's *Ode to the Creator of the World*, announced, iv. 420; on the subject of a late *Spectator*, received, iv. 588.

Odes: use of similes in, iii. 91; written in Lapland, iii. 376, 518; iv. 18; 'the songsters, in unmeasured', v. 118.

Odysseus. *See* Ulysses.

Oedipus: prayed for dissension between his sons, ii. 310; story of, most proper for tragedy, iii. 58–59; wished to end his life on Mount Cithaeron, iii. 358; Dacier on, iii. 568.

'Off and on', iv. 85.

Office: of kindness, two manners of doing, iii. 39; the insolence of, iv. 303.

Officer: a dying French soldier's raillery upon his superior, ii. 98; who shares dangers of his men, ii. 308; in the French army and the Dauphin, iii.

433–4; in the Civil Wars who was famed for justice and impartiality, iv. 262; a broken, suitor of the Widow WILDFIRE, iv. 517; letter from a half-pay, iv. 535; a young o. in the Guards, married President of Widow-Club, iv. 558.

Offices: mutual, ii. 87, 165; kind, ii. 93; iii. 39; good, ii. 94, 389; iii. 39, 288–91, 522, 523; of life, ii. 349; indirect, ii. 411.

Officious: WILL WIMBLE a good-natured o. fellow, i. 447; the *Spectator* has caused GEORGE TRUSTY to become hospitable and, ii. 30; acts of a daughter, iv. 79.

Officiousness: a 'holy o.' in our most indifferent actions, recommended by St. Paul, ii. 333; of an artful servant in *Volpone*, iii. 394.

Officiousnesses: little pretty o. in the woman's man, ii. 111.

Ogilby, John, his translation of Virgil in LEONORA's library, i. 158.

OGLE, the Widow, riding the black ram, v. 131.

Ogle: types of (the 'church', the 'play-house', the 'new flying'), i. 199; the Idol glances an, i. 314; the fop who throws particular graces into his, iii. 126; 'slain by an o.', iii. 417.

Ogler: *The Compleat Ogler*, i. 199; LEONORA's eye turned against an, ii. 479; a set of oglers brought together in jest, iii. 397.

Ogling: in church, i. 86–87, 227–8; ii. 120 (*see also* Starers); the art of, i. 199; Idols suffer from, i. 371; 'o. all the young fellows', ii. 300; the o. muscles in a beau's eye, ii. 572; mentioned, iv. 26, 246; Mr. FANFLY very soft in his, iv. 332.

Ogle-Master, the, i. 197.

Ogling-Master, letter from an, i. 199.

Oil(s): *throwing oil upon the fire* (prov.), i. 266; imported into England, i. 295; and vinegar, i. 374; and vinegar in a modern meal, ii. 264.

Old: *He that would be long an old man, must begin early to be one* (prov.), ii. 102.

Old, the: rail at extravagance of youth, iv. 195; love in, accompanied with a passion too gross to be named, v. 24.

Old age: lack of respect for, i. 30–31; a great decayer of Idols, i. 315; of the licentious, ii. 95; enjoyment of, ii. 100–3; often leads us back into our infancy, ii. 137; of a husband as a cause of jealousy, ii. 170–1; avarice common in, ii. 372; iv. 259; natural coldness of, ii.

497; JACK AFTERDAY on the art of growing old, ii. 510–12; and relationship between parents and children, ii. 521–5; CAMILLUS enjoys a pleasing and indolent, ii. 522; lust in, ii. 567–8; Cicero's Dialogue on, iii. 60; clings to habits and pleasures of youth, iii. 75; allegory of love and, iii. 76–78; gallantry in, iii. 157–60; tyranny of, iii. 243–5; does not deserve the name of evil, iii. 431; calamities of youth and, compared, iv. 14; those who are loath to grow old, iv. 196–7; ridiculous when imitating youth, iv. 258–60; and cleanliness, v. 157.

Old maid: who is troubled with vapours, i. 34; 'a state of tranquillity which few people envy', ii. 347–8; ATALANTA, ii. 407; letter from an, iii. 56–57; 'the senseless rude phrase', iv. 384; less sought after than a widow, v. 99.

'Old Man's Wish, The', sung by SUKEY to Sir ROGER, iii. 532.

'Old shoes', the cry of, v. 42.

'Old woman', to be pulled out of our hearts, i. 54.

Oldfield, Mrs. Anne: in *The Amorous Widow*, i. 72; iii. 370; Loveit in *The Man of Mode*, i. 278; in *The Scornful Lady*, ii. 552; Andromache in *The Distressed Mother*, iii. 31, 239, 352; her gaiety in speaking the Epilogue to *The Distressed Mother*, iii. 251–2; Egerton's *Memoirs* of, iii. 251, 252; Lady Betty Modish in *The Careless Husband*, iii. 252; Ismena in *Phaedra and Hippolitus*, iii. 252, 267; benefit for, iii. 349; in *The Constant Couple*, iii. 418; praise of her acting in *Ximena*, iv. 454.

Oldham, John: *Satyrs upon the Jesuits*, i. 77; translation of Ovid, i. 386.

Oldisworth, William, v. 66.

Oldmixon, John, iii. 131, 292; writer for the *Medley*, iii. 380; *Reflections on the English Tongue*, iii. 381.

Oldys, William, i. 8; iii. 341.

Olearius, Adam, story of Basilius and Alexandrinus, from, iii. 597.

Olivares, Gaspar de Guzmán, Count of, disgraced at court of Madrid, iii. 43.

Olive beauties, iii. 484, 513.

OLIVIA, letter from (enclosing a letter), iv. 20.

OLPHIS, the fisherman, his leap into the Ionian sea, ii. 383, 407.

OLYMPIA, TETTYX in love with, ii. 408.

Olympiad, ii. 406, 409.

Olympic games: Greek women not allowed at, i. 348–9; Alexander the Great and, ii. 114; nothing in them

like an ass-race or a grinning-match, ii. 182.

Olympus, Ossa thrown upon, iii. 230.

Ombre: 'all the incidents, turns, and revolutions in', i. 437; turns women into wasps, ii. 54; mentioned, iv. 24; ombre table, ii. 54.

OMNAMANTE, OMNIAMANTE, a false beauty, ii. 70, 179.

'Once a King and always a King' (a stage maxim), iv. 388.

One and thirty (game), ii. 451.

Oneirocritic (interpreter of dreams), iv. 293; v. 43.

Onions, Portugal, ii. 530.

Open house, kept by Sir ROGER at Christmas, ii. 550.

Opening the mouth of a Cardinal, and of Mr. SPECTATOR, iv. 471.

Openness of behaviour, a mark of good breeding, i. 487.

Opera: its only design, to gratify the senses, i. 22–23; absurd decorations of, i. 22–27; forced thoughts, cold conceits, and unnatural expressions of, i. 59; one of the two leading diversions of the town, i. 63; absurdity of singing partly in Italian, partly in English, i. 78–82, 132, 425; improbabilities in, i. 92; the third chair and flower-pots in an English, i. 93; Italian recitativo seemed strange at first, i. 119–20; differences between Italian, English, and French, i. 119–23; absurdities of, satirized in a projected, i. 127–32, 149; and the puppet-show, i. 142, 243, 331; Italian recitativo and air, i. 165; subscribing to, i. 209; Spectators on, well received, and bound up in sets, i. 245, 507–8; in region of false wit, i. 271; party patches at the, i. 346–7; keeping time with a cudgel in the gallery, i. 409; a husband who dislikes the fooleries of plays and, ii. 11; set of impertinents at the, ii. 163; mentioned, ii. 199, 487; the pleasure of plays, balls, and, ii. 299; young ladies learn to sing Italian, ii. 395; the Trunk-maker sometimes plies at the, ii. 415; throwing away time at the, ii. 451; subscriptions to a new, ii. 481; Italian introduced by Clayton, Haym, and Dieupart, ii. 506, 584; women in coloured hoods at the, ii. 531–2; 'all the plays, operas, and songs that come out', ii. 576; benefit days of, iii. 26; ladies charmed with sounds abstracted from ideas, iii. 55; 'the opera subscription is full', iii. 123; CLARINDA hears Nicolini at the, iii. 184; less safe than puppet-shows for

women, iii. 374; WILL SIMPLE smitten at, by a lady's glance, iii. 417; more appreciated in Italy, iv. 55; vast sums laid out upon, only to suspend or vitiate our understandings, iv. 480.

Opera-airs: the newest, i. 152; introduced into psalm-singing, ii. 305.

Opera-glasses, ii. 473.

Opera score, ii. 82.

Opera tunes, sung by a young gentleman in a coffee-house, ii. 73, 82.

Operas. See Almahide, Amleto, Antiochus, Arsinoe, Calypso and Telemachus, Camilla, Clotilda, Hercules, Hydaspes, King Arthur, Love's Triumph, Il Pastor Fido, Proserpine, Pyrrhus and Demetrius, Rinaldo, Rosamond, The Tempest, Thomyris.

Ophir, the word of a merchant the gold of, ii. 351.

Opinion, popular: the wise man indifferent to, iv. 44–45; allegorical figure of, iv. 121.

Opinions: we often embrace and reject the very same, ii. 136; differing from others in religious, ii. 228; respect for those of others, ii. 274; changing those of others by arguing, ii. 431; ill will towards men of different, ii. 512.

Opium, a dose of, iv. 561.

Optics: a treatise on, ii. 469–72; an experiment in, described, iii. 550–1.

Oracle: darkness of an, ii. 17; IRUS the oracle of a neighbouring justice of peace, ii. 528; of a coffee-house, iii. 509.

Oracle of Apollo at Delphos: i. 129, 150; 'that famed dictate of', iii. 513; called Socrates the wisest of all men living, iii. 523; consulted by Chremylus, iv. 139–40; consulted by Gyges, v. 86.

Oracle of Jupiter Ammon: reply to the Athenians, ii. 312.

Oracles, arose from a desire to know the future, v. 64.

Orange-flower (water), ii. 571; iii. 206–7.

Orange-girl, adventure of an, iii. 428.

Orange-tree(s), iii. 593; iv. 105.

Orange-wench(es), i. 324; ii. 59.

Orange-woman, i. 279, 280.

Orangery, iv. 189.

Oranges growing wild, iii. 569.

Orator: pronunciation of the word, ii. 33; the forehead the most material organ of the, ii. 398; the best, not the one who speaks loudest, ii. 447; a wordy o. like a tree without fruit, iv. 75; should have skill in the heavenly bodies, v. 164.

Orators: of Grub Street, ii. 89; boys to be taught the best Roman, ii. 395–6;

female, ii. 458–62; in England use little gesture or action, iii. 521; motions used by Greek and Roman, iii. 521; few in numbers among the ancients, v. 163.

Oratory: its laws to be deduced from general sense and taste of mankind, i. 123; apt gesture and proper cadence in, ii. 159; diffidence in, desirable, ii. 397–8; we fall short of the ancients in, ii. 467; women better qualified to succeed in, than men, ii. 480; use of gestures in, iii. 520–3; the TEMPLAR's essay on pronunciation and action in, iv. 432–7; St. Paul's skill in, v. 165–7; strokes of, forbidden in law-courts of Greece, v. 166.

Orb, belief that every orb had its *intelligence*, iii. 147.

ORBICILLA, has lost sense of innocence, not of shame, iii. 464.

Orchard: robbing an o. as training for greater matters, iii. 133; in flower, more beautiful than a finished parterre, iii. 552–3.

Ordeal by fire, ii. 276; iii. 481.

Order: and distinction to be kept up in the world, ii. 354; religion consults the harmony and o. of the community, ii. 374; the support of society, ii. 554; love of symmetry and, natural to mind of man, v. 159.

Ordinary: dining at a common, i. 374; the five-penny, iv. 102.

Ordinary expressions, shunned by epic poets, iii. 11.

Ordonnance of the whole, iv. 479.

Orestes: in *The Distressed Mother*, i. *130*; iii. 34, 236, 242, 291; in *Electra*, compared with Hamlet, i. 189–90; in Racine's *Andromaque*, iii. 267; and Pylades, iii. 498; Dacier on, iii. *568*; in Virgil, iii. 579.

ORESTILLA, a great fortune, i. 484.

Organ: board of an, i. 132; a voluntary played by, iv. 285; proposal for, in St. Paul's, iv. 479–81.

Oriental: manuscripts, ii. 121; warmth of o. style, iii. 514–15; examples of o. style, iv. 448–53, 596–8; v. 1–3; salutations, iv. 485. *See also* Eastern.

Orientals, the (languages), iv. 175.

Original, a good: imitation of best authors is not to compare with, ii. 129–30; better to become, than a miserable copy, ii. 425.

Originality: the best writers have something peculiar to them and entirely their own, ii. 130; wit consists not in advancing things that are new, ii. 483.

'Orlando's' in tales of knight-errantry, iv. 429.

Ormonde, James Butler, Duke of, referred to (?), ii. 258.

Ornament(s): forms of punning as o. in discourse, i. 260; foreign o. in poetry, i. 268; helps and o. of art, i. 362; a little poetical o. in a ballad, i. 363; superfluity of, in dress, ii. 5; foreign or affected, in poetry, ii. 367; religion an o. to human nature, ii. 443–4; cheerfulness and good-nature the two great o. of virtue, ii. 445; silent perfections great o. to human nature, ii. 500; poetical o. in the epic, ii. 543; of jewels, silks, and colours, ii. 552; without foreign, iii. 40; poetic in *PL*, iii. 170–1; studied o. of style, v. 35.

Ornamental: 'something o. in what men utter before women', ii. 119.

Orobio, Isaac, iii. *332*.

OROONDATES: a letter from STATIRA to, ii. 280–2; love makes a footman talk like Oroondates, iii. 416.

Orpheus: Handel the O. of our age, i. 26; and wild beasts, i. 57; mentioned, ii. 76, 143 m.; was musical, melancholy, and a woman-hater, ii. 326; his soul transformed into that of a swan, ii. 326; invention of the cat-call ascribed to, iii. 351; Hughes's *Ode occasioned by the Fragments of*, iv. 420, 487; epitaph on, by Antipater, iv. 472–3.

Orpheus' Journey to Hell (puppet show), i. *61*.

Orra, in a Lapland song, iii. 377–8.

Orrery, Roger Boyle, 1st Earl of, iii. *102*; Charles Boyle, 4th Earl of, iv. *481*.

Orrery, the, iv. *481*.

Orsin, in *Hudibras*, i. *252*.

Os cribriforme, in a beau's head, ii. 572.

Osborn, Mrs., her toy-shop, i. *226*.

Osborne, Francis: on dressing well, ii. 91; training youth in circumspection, iii. 133; advises his son to dress above his fortune rather than under it, iv. 193–4.

Oscitancy (drowsiness) of transcribers, iv. 165.

Ossa upon Olympus, and Pelion upon, iii. 230.

Ostentation: of courage in despising terrors of another world, ii. 232; senseless, ii. 252; the great should regard business rather than, ii. 257; of GLORIANA, ii. 308; lies told out of, should be detected, ii. 410; a vain o. of wit, ii. 494; of learning, a fault in *PL*, iii. 62; of Turnus, iii. 304; allegorical

figure of, iv. 122; Boyle's aversion to, v. 177.

Ostentations, ii. 492.

Ostrich(es): finds a place to deposit its eggs, i. 490; a letter written with quill of a virgin, iv. 451; mentioned, v. 2.

Others: respect for opinion of, in disputation, ii. 274–5; only two ways of gaining by, ii. 599; merit of acknowledging praise of, iv. 395–6.

Otter, Dr. (in *The Silent Woman*), i. 173.

Otter-hunting, i. 472.

Otway, Thomas: little pomp but great force in his language, i. 167. — *Caius Marius*, quoted, iv. 435; *Friendship in Fashion*, in which a man trips up a beggar on crutches, iii. 322; *The Orphan*: a successful tragedy which ends unhappily, i. 169; quoted, i. 481; ii. 277, 436; iii. 482 (letter signed Monimia, v. 97); *Venice Preserved*: founded on a wrong plot, i. 167; a successful tragedy which ends unhappily, i. 169; sounding of the clock in, i. 186; to be acted for Mrs. Rogers's benefit, iii. 395; quoted, iv. 107–8.

Ounce of mother is worth a pound of clergy (prov.), iv. 136.

Out of sight, out of mind (prov.), i. 332.

'Outragiously virtuous', WILL HONEYCOMB on the, ii. 534.

Overdo, Justice (in *Bartholomew Fair*), i. 207.

Overseers of the poor, living as well as the, iii. 402.

Overton, Henry (print and map seller), ii. 379.

Overwise, the: refiners upon incidents, ii. 171; in detecting satire, iv. 540.

Ovid (Publius Ovidius Naso): a great deal of mixed wit in, i. 266; his imitators admire only his turns and far-fetched antitheses, ii. 52–53; the woman's man has the translation of his Epistles by heart, ii. 113; his Epistles full of complaints of absent lovers, ii. 436; little points and puerilities frequent in, ii. 588; and Lucan have many common and vulgar expressions, iii. 10–11; Strada's imitation of, v. 109; the best for love-letters, letters of friendship, and letters upon mournful occasions, v. 112; his versification soft, and his numbers flowing and querulous, v. 113. — *Amores*, v. 29; — *Ars Amatoria*: contains all the forms of worship to an 'Idol', i. 313; praises Virgil, ii. 482; gives advice on colours of hoods, ii. 533; quoted, i. 386; v. 60–61; — *Fasti*: iii. 72; quoted, iii. 41; iv.

380; — *Heroides*: ii. 383; iv. 468; his depiction of Dido compared with Virgil's (from Dryden), i. 268–9; — *Ibis*, iv. 492; — *Metamorphoses*, i. 123, 198, 382; ii. 479; iii. 40, 299, 594, 596; iv. 17, 329, 512; v. 15, 133; introduces Echo as a nymph, i. 252; story of Pygmalion and the statue, i. 427; fable of Narcissus adapted by Milton, iii. 176; tells of Polyphemus, who used the sea as a looking-glass, iii. 191; copies Homer's description of piling Pelion upon Ossa, iii. 230; metamorphosis of Trojan fleet into water-nymphs, iii. 306; change of Satan in *PL* is described after Ovid's manner, iii. 332–3; Milton's description of the Flood superior to Ovid's, iii. 363–4; strikes imagination with the strange: in the *M.* we are walking on enchanted ground, iii. 565–6; personifications of Hunger and Envy, iii. 573; description of Palace of Fame, iv. 42–43; effect on modern poets, iv. 361–2; story of Procris and Cephalus, iv. 380–1; quoted, i. 17; ii. 228, 325–6, 461; iii. 363–4; v. 133.

Owen, John (Dean of Christ Church, Oxford), iv. 252.

Owen, Thankful (President of St. John's, Oxford), iv. 252.

Owl(s): rebus of, on statue of Marcus Aurelius, i. 251; the eye of the, ii. 470; story of the Sultan's Vizier and the two, iv. 318–19.

Ox, oxen: in valley of Baghdad, ii. 126; eye of, applied to Hera, ii. 471; ox-cheek for dinner, iii. 155.

Oxford, Robert Harley, Earl of: and Swift, i. xvii; and Guiscard, ii. 129; referred to (?), ii. 258; and the *Review*, iii. 380; allusions to, in pamphlets, iv. 536–7.

Oxford: Ugly Club in, i. 76, 133–6, 197, 205, 221–3; St. John's men, i. 76; mentioned, i. 88; ii. 583; Amorous Club in, i. 124–7; Hebdomadal meeting in, i. 181–3; port wine at honest George's in, i. 181–2; a young scholar, i. 197; wasters of time at, i. 231; picture of Charles I at, i. 247–8; Logic Lane and High Street in, ii. 429; PATETIA the reigning toast in, ii. 547; false modesty inculcated in, iv. 218; Savilian Professor of Geometry in, iv. 481; *Spectator* well received in, iv. 485; New College and Queen's College, iv. 494; JEREMY LOVEMORE's amours in, v. 38; a hopeful Greek just come from, v. 69; illuminations in High Street,

v. 108; copy of Latin verses sent from, v. 116.— Letters from, i. 181; ii. 547; iv. 17, 485, 514; v. 6, 107, 152.

Oxford Jests, iv. 522.

Oxfordshire, Stunsfield, or Stonesfield, in, iii. 339.

Oyster, Locke on the senses of the, i. 495.

Ozell, John: *The Monthly Amusement*, i. xiv; translation of Boileau, ii. *467*.

P., M., 'Slain by a lady's glance', iii. 418.

P., Sir P., a cursed sequestrator, v. 150.

P., S.: letter from (on assistance to young men), iii. 216–18; letter from (on self-disparagement), iv. 174–5.

Pace, kinds of, for different kinds of genius, iv. 344–5.

Pacer (horse), i. 434.

Pack, George (actor), ii. *57, 535*; iv. *283*.

Packington, Sir John, as an original of Sir ROGER, i. *7, 463*.

Pack-thread, ii. 557; the counsellor who could not speak in public without a certain piece of, in his hand, iii. 522–3.

Pacquet from Will's, A, i. *218*.

Pactolus in stockings, i. 197, 198.

Pad (horse), i. 373, 439, 476; ii. 536.

Pad-ram, v. 130.

Padilla, Luisa de, and Gracián, iii. 423–4.

Padlock proposed to prevent indecent conversation, iv. 404.

Pagan: many will listen to a p. philosopher, rather than to a Christian writer, ii. 334; works of p. poets largely hymns to deities, iv. 94–95; mythology in modern poetry condemned, iv. 361–4.

Page, Susanna, iv. 32.

Pagod, an Indian, iii. 196.

Pain: URANIUS's calm attitude to, ii. 66; Socrates on, ii. 221–2; allegory of pleasure and, ii. 222–3; we should try to allay, not to obtain happiness, ii. 268; benefits of labour and, ii. 422; and pleasure imaginary distinctions, ii. 442; Posidonius's indifference to, iii. 130; and sickness not evils, iii. 431; mixed with pleasure, Locke's explanation of, iii. 454; in the shoulder as a sign of rain, iv. 47; the result of vicious and imprudent acts, v. 65.

Painter(s): dream of living and dead, i. 353–6; great p. never care for drawing people in the fashion, ii. 12; lewd devices by, ii. 179; of landskips, buildings, or single figures, ii. 381; advertisement of a, from Italy, ii. 382; softens the picture with an agreeable likeness, ii. 425; depiction of spring by, iii. 373; keep a green cloth near, to ease the eye, iii. 452; sight and the work of the, iv. 171.

Painting: its laws to be deduced from general sense and taste of mankind, i. 123; an auction of Italian, i. 288; as a useful diversion, i. 397; less permanent than literature, ii. 154; should be used for worthy ends, ii. 179–80, 378–9; of Raphael, ii. 378–81, 446–7; of Michelangelo, ii. 390; shades in painting compared to modesty, and to serious thoughts, ii. 399, 447–8; art of, ii. 446–8; we fall short of the ancients in, ii. 467; a wife who paints prettily, iii. 205; a less natural kind of representation than statuary, iii. 559; used to convey messages in Mexico, iii. 559; disposition of figures in, iv. 186; ERASTUS's good taste in, iv. 297–8; Academy of, lately established in London, iv. 495; kinds of, iv. 495–6; England excels in portrait-p., iv. 496–7.

Paiston, —— (stationer), iv. 5.

Palace: the traveller who mistook a p. for an inn, iii. 30–31; the infernal p. in *PL*, iii. 88; of Fame in Ovid, iv. 43.

Palamedes, suffered from iniquity of his judges, ii. 76.

Palatine Anthology, The: a prayer in, ii. 311.

Paleness, allegorical figure of, iv. 278.

PALFREY, MULES, letter from (proposing a Censor on Marriages), iii. 110–11.

Palfrey: in books of chivalry, i. 417; a pair of dwarfs and their whimsical, ii. 557.

Pallas Athene, in the *Iliad* a symbol of Reason, ii. 221.

Pallas (in the *Aeneid*): and Evander, ii. 563; Turnus dressing himself in spoils of, iii. 61; and Lausus come to unfortunate ends, iv. 464.

Palmer, Samuel, *Moral Essays on Proverbs*, i. *512*.

Palmes, Lieut.-Gen. Francis, a subscriber, i. *lxxxix*.

Palmquist, ——, envoy of Charles XII, i. 182.

PAMPHILIO, a considerate master, ii. 43–44.

Pamphlets: in LEONORA's library, i. 153; which have appeared against the *Spectator*, ii. 432; v. 66; lowly position of writers of, iv. 387; methods of making them sell, iv. 536–7.

Pan and Ceres, attendants on Summer, iii. 595.

Panacea, advertisement of a, iv. 458.

Pandemonium (in *PL*): description of,

iii. 89, 90, 566; Mammon the architect of, iii. 116.

Panders and libertines among women, ii. 303–4.

Pandora's box, story of, and tradition of Fall of Man, iv. 166–7.

Panegyric(s): in acrostic, i. 245; in dedications, ii. 240; on marriage, in *PL*, iii. 61; a manly p., with all the colours of truth, iv. 362.

PANTHEA: heaved her bosom before FIDELIO, iii. 471; Panthea and Araspas, iv. 526.

Pantheon, Penkethman's, i. 130–1, 150.

Pantheon at Rome, more affecting than a Gothic cathedral, iii. 556.

Pantheus (in the *Aeneid*), a pious man, but comes to an unfortunate end, iv. 464.

Pantomimes, on the ancient stage, iii. 237–8, 342.

Paper: a quire of gilt, i. 153; printed p. on walls, i. 361–2; ignoble uses of printed, i. 362; uses of, in printing, iii. 379–82.

Paper-mills, now in England, iii. 379–80.

Paphos, ii. 408; sighs from the Isle of, iii. 469.

Papist(s): fined, iv. 384; *Papist, Plunderer*, &c., help to sell a pamphlet, iv. 537. *See also* Roman Catholics.

Parable(s): a species of wit, i. 265; concerning Moses, ii. 423; Jesus taught by, iii. 327.

Paracelsus, Theophrastus, iv. 591.

Paradin, Guillaume, *Annales de Bourgongne*, i. 414–15.

Paradise: communion of men and spirits in, i. 55; music played to departed souls on arriving in, ii. 122; MIRZAH's vision of the blessed in, ii. 125; 'roving among the walks of, like the first happy pair', ii. 487; Adam's vision of restoration to a happier, iii. 59; description of, in *PL*, iii. 170–1, 566–7; expulsion of Adam and Eve from, iii. 359–66, 387–90; allegory of P. of Fools, iv. 121–4; the particular residence of God, iv. 583; St. Augustine's opinion of dreams in, v. 30.

Paradisiacal, the thoughts of Adam and Eve always, iii. 171.

Paradox of Hesiod, ii. 286.

Paragrams: kinds of puns described by Aristotle, i. 259; Mr. Swan 'the greatest paragrammatist among the moderns', i. 260–1.

Paraphrase: better than literal translation, iii. 515; *on History of Susanna*, recommended, i. 391; of Isaiah by

Pope, iii. 419–22; of Solomon's Song, iii. 455–9; of Proverbs, iii. 533–5; of Psalm 23, iv. 51.

Parasite(s): and their patrons, i. 217; ii. 591–2; favours given to, a form of self-love, ii. 424; in ancient comedy, iv. 68.

Pardon, pardoning: we pass our whole life in offending and asking, ii. 137; of faults to be exercised in private not public affairs, ii. 166–7.

Parents and children: relationship between, ii. 214, 241–4, 252–6, 521–5; iii. 597; iv. 35–37; *Spectator*'s attitude in controversies between, ii. 243.

Paring-shovel, ii. 573; v. 41.

Paris: statue on Pont-Neuf at, i. 59; incident at opera in, i. 418; the most eminent toasts in, ii. 578; *à la mode de*, ii. 579; fashions in, ii. 580; advices from, iii. 96; iv. 90; mentioned, i. 384; iii. 3–4, 508; v. 19.

Paris *Gazette*, i. 331; iii. 97.

Parish(es): taking relief from the, ii. 403; rivalry between neighbouring, iv. 18.

Parish politics, discussed on Sunday, i. 460.

Parish settlements, laws of, ii. 284.

Parker, ——— (of Merton College), iii. 151.

Parker, Richard (vicar of Embleton), iv. 181.

Parker, Sir Thomas (afterwards Earl of Macclesfield): a subscriber, i. *lxxxviii*; letter from Hughes to, iv. 420.

Parkes, John. *See* Sparks.

Parliament: a disagreeable vote in a former, ii. 4; 'could one but lay asleep a few busy heads . . .', ii. 226; mentioned, ii. 474; Henry Boyle's great figure in the British Senate, v. 178.

Parliament-man, franked by a, ii. 13.

Parlour, ii. 480, 522.

PARLY, LUCINDA, letter from (on a besieger), iv. 407–8.

Parnassus: poets sleeping on, ii. 226; a vision of, iv. 324–30.

Parnell, Thomas: a contributor, i. lv; iv. 121, 276, 494; *The Hermit*, ii. 423; essay attributed to, iii. 597.

Paronomasia, a form of pun, i. 261.

Parot, Michael, iv. 457.

Parr, Rev. John, iii. 455.

Parricide, punished by Chinese and ancient Persians, ii. 244.

Parrot(s): a school for, i. 151, 197; the coquette talks to her, ii. 459; and lapdogs of ladies, iii. 273.

Parsimony and frugality, the virtues of the merchant, ii. 186.

Parsley, a crown of, in the Roman Pentathlum, ii. 133.

Parsnips, antipathy to, iv. 421.

'Parson has lost his cloak' (game), ii. 547.

Parsons, a Templar who was very arch
upon, iv. 18.

Parsonage of the parish, i. 441.

Part: our duty to act our p. in perfection,
ii. 353; religion gives a man room to
play his, ii. 374.

Parterre(s): the learned genius like a soil
laid out in walks and, ii. 129; labyrinths of a, iii. 552–3; in a garden, iii.
593; makers of, like epigrammatists,
iv. 190.

Parterre (in a theatre), i. 122. See also
Pit.

PARTHENIA, letter from (on reading for
women), ii. 54–55.

PARTHENISSA, letter from (on loss of her
beauty by small-pox), iii. 100–2.

Parthenius, ii. 391.

PARTHENOPE: letter from (objecting to
Spectators), ii. 53; one of JEREMY
LOVEMORE's sweethearts, v. 38.

Particles, suppression of, in English, ii. 35.

Partridge(s): i. 158; iii. 196; hunting, i.
472, 498; ii. 19; coveys of, i. 475; gift
of a, to Mr. SPECTATOR, ii. 113; for
a club dinner, iv. 303; taking the law
of a farmer's son for shooting a, v. 128.

Parts (abilities), i. 159, 312, 406; ii. 2,
253, 362, 374, 376; iii. 15; natural,
i. 232; ii. 127, 129; great p. and learning, ii. 143; writers who employ their
p. in propagating vice, ii. 155, 517;
a boy with p. of the middle size, iii.
367. — Men of Parts: more liable to
blame when they offend, i. 28; often
fail in management of affairs, ii. 362–4;
iii. 2.

Party (-ies): neutrality of Spectator towards, i. xviii, 5, 72–73, 262; ii. 2, 517;
iv. 65; our duty to mitigate the fierceness of, i. 395; zealots of, and periodical papers, i. 507; iv. 64–65; the mischief they do, i. 509–12; an association
of honest men above p. proposed, i.
512; ii. 1–2; narrow p.-humour, ii. 3;
changing sides in, ii. 135–6; animosities between, ii. 185; Spectator draws
men's minds off from bitterness of, ii.
519; iv. 458; marks and devices to
distinguish, iv. 17–18; behaviour of
p. zealots, iv. 64–65.

Party-lying: the abominable practice of,
iv. 298–301; how protected, iv. 354.

Party-spirit: i. 5, 72–73, 509–12; ii. 1–4;
iii. 414, 495; iv. 18, 87–88; observed
by the Four Indian Kings, i. 213;

among women, i. 242–4, 346–9; ii. 532;
iv. 27; v. 72, 116; heat of, in England,
i. 423–4; reigns more in country than
town, ii. 2–3; prevents judgement of
virtue and vice, ii. 445–6; iii. 289; in
criticism of Spectator, iv. 65; and place-
hunting, v. 149–51; strong in England,
iv. 501.

Party-writers: hiring of, in England, 'a
kind of national crime', iv. 87–88;
among the unlearned, iv. 114; their
methods of writing, iv. 536–41.

Pas, to yield the, iv. 388.

Pascal, Blaise: Addison compared to, i.
xxxv; on our aversion to scrutiny of
self, i. 478–9; man's greatness and his
meanness must both be shown him,
iv. 417; cited, iv. 527, 530, 531.

Pasiphae, ii. 427.

Pasquin, statue of, in Rome, i. 99; iv. 3.

Passion(s): exemption from, is the only
pleasing solitude, i. 19; of mankind,
the province of the Spectator, i. 70; get
the better of reason, in grief, i. 95;
books which rectify, to be preferred,
i. 158; entire conquest of, difficult, i.
304; shown in the face, i. 365; contracted in life, remain after death, i.
380; Platonic notion of, i. 380–2; in
animals, adapted to their needs, i.
494–5; subside in old age, ii. 101, 522;
allegorical depiction of, ii. 124; as
characters in allegory, ii. 220; sexual
p. short-lived, ii. 281; of children to be
seasoned with devotion, ii. 287; most
men blinded with, ii. 310; appetites
sooner moved than the, ii. 315; avarice
the most absurd, ii. 372; love and
desire of glory the most natural, ii.
373; the gales, ii. 373; iii. 524–5; children imbibe passions of their nurses,
ii. 455–6; government of, ii. 433; iv.
39–42; expressed by the eyes, ii. 470–
2; inflamers of, iii. 374; cheerfulness
soothes and composes, iii. 451; put the
soul in action, iii. 524–5; should not be
repressed but controlled, iii. 526;
affected by descriptions and by poetry,
iii. 567; more active in dreams, iv. 228;
expressed in oratory, iv. 432–7; a
mind free from, necessary to sleep,
v. 5; effect of novelty upon, v. 139;
effect of music upon, v. 153.

Passion of Sappho, and Feast of Alexander,
The, ii. 365.

Past, the: the wise man's and the fool's
views of, contrasted, i. 401–2; folly of
reflecting unduly on, iii. 406; our
conceptions of, v. 18–22.

Paste, raising, ii. 443; iii. 104; iv. 210.

Pastor Fido, Il (The Faithful Shepherd) (opera), i. *23*.

PASTORA, a name used by correspondents, i. 71.

Pastorals: of Ambrose Philips, ii. 367; iii. 498–9; iv. 362–3; the thoughts should take a tincture from woods, fields, and rivers, iii. 171; and the lower kinds of poetry, iii. 564; women writers of, v. 72.

Pastry: art of, taught to young women, iii. 140, 226, 254; and preserving, iii. 205.

Pastry-cooks, unused letters might be used by, iii. 94.

Pastry-man, song of, in London streets, ii. 477.

Patch(es): i. 193; a paper of, i. 155; 'little black spots', i. 214–15; to indicate Whig or Tory, i. 346–9, 371, 425; ii. 303; iv. 18, 27; a patched lady, ii. 29; 'you cannot place a p. where it does not hide a beauty', ii. 548; a small p. worn on her breast, ii. 580; worn by a fortune-hunter, iii. 126; in CLARINDA's journal, iii. 184; how to place, taught, iii. 415; sale of p., pins, and wires, iv. 102; 'always implies a pimple', v. 68.

Patch-boxes, iv. 195.

Patchwork, poem in, i. 197.

Pately, Mol., a dance, i. 286.

Paterson, William, as an original of Sir ANDREW FREEPORT, i. *10*.

PATETIA, the reigning toast at Oxford, ii. 547.

Pathetic: simplicity peculiar to Ambrose Philips, ii. 367; not essential to the sublime (Longinus), iii. 254–5.

Patience: as sullenness and despair in savage nations, ii. 339; under suffering, iii. 128–30; in Mme de Villacerfe, iii. 383; promoted by trust in God, iv. 50; allegorical figure of, iv. 276–7, 511; and courage in soldiers, iv. 534.

Patriarchal model of government, iv. 273.

Patriotism the noblest of principles, but capable of mischief, i. 512.

Patroclus, Greece preserved by Achilles' friendship for, iii. 446.

Patron(s): absurd dedications to, ii. 240; and clients include a third of the nation, ii. 335; methods of pleasing a, ii. 592–3, 599; of young men, iii. 217–18; their difficulty in awarding favours, iv. 262–3.

Pattern poems. *See* Poems in typographical shapes.

Paul, St.: his preaching caused magicians to burn their books, i. 414; his argu-

ments for advancing of morality, ii. 233; his precept, regarding all our actions, ii. 333; Raphael's painting of, ii. 379; never subverted the law, iii. 442; quoted, iv. 321; his catalogue of sufferings, v. 133; Longinus on, v. 165; eloquence of, v. 165–7.

PAULINO, an elderly man retaining the foppery of youth, iv. 259.

Paulus, L. Aemilius, and his son (in Cicero, *De Senectute*), iv. 419.

Pausanius, gives a description of Trophonius' cave, v. 45.

Payn, Payne, —— (toyshop), i. *222*; iii. *278*; iv. *130*, *460*, *462*, *554*.

Peace with the French, approaching: will inundate us with French fopperies, i. 191–2, 225; preliminaries debated in a coffee-house, ii. 273; mentioned, iii. 154; reported, iii. 439–40; the right and wrong kind of, iii. 444–5; white or red hood as portent of, iv. 18; will dry up the great fountain of news, iv. 63, 92; discussion of, iv. 207; effect on fashions, iv. 377; Tickell's poem on the prospect of, iv. 361; in modern poems, iv. 363.

Peaches, imported into England and naturalized, i. 295; peach-tree, v. 144.

Peacock, less colourful than a British lady, ii. 531.

Pearce, Dicky, jester to Earl of Suffolk, i. *200*.

Pearce, Zachary, a contributor, i. lxxxi; iv. *551*; v. *162*.

Pearl, fixed on top of Persian diadem, iii. 46.

Peasant(s): made merry by the gentleman, ii. 187; who showed Prince Eugene the way over the Alps, iii. 263; iv. 327.

Pease, green, in April, iii. 196.

Pechy, John, M.D., i. *105*.

Peco. *See* Tea.

Peculiarities: travel helps us unlearn p. in our manners, iii. 368.

Pedantry: attempts at wit by pedants, i. 249; WILL HONEYCOMB on p. in spelling, i. 437; kinds of, i. 437–8; *Spectator* accused of, ii. 120–1; results from improper education, ii. 162; learning without discretion is, ii. 376; of female virtuosos, ii. 442–3; stoicism the p. of virtue, ii. 444; in holy orders, ii. 553; characteristics of, ii. 554; the pedantic Stoic, who thinks all crimes are alike, ii. 568; in breeding, iii. 15; without additional graces, learning would degenerate into, iii. 40; balanced

against learning, iv. 136; illustrated in variant readings, iv. 161–5; example of pedantic humour, v. 107–8.

Pedigree: whispering a, ii. 388; description of a, v. 91–93.

Peep: the side-peep through hood or fan, ii. 472.

'Peepers' in church, i. 227–8.

Peep-show. See Rary show.

Peer(s): at the midnight masque, i. 36; who refused a duel in France, i. 418; Honour, the title given to, ii. 352; 'in pomp and rich array', v. 122.

Peers, Charles (a Director of the Bank), a subscriber, i. xc.

Peevishness: of spirit, i. 468; honour in women, only, ii. 118; natural to the sick, ii. 156; assumed p. of IRUS, ii. 528; as acted by Penkethman, iii. 394; 'the peevishest hussy breathing', iii. 466; a peevish fellow described, iv. 40–41.

PEGGY (T. B.'s daughter), iii. 196.

Pegs and nails in a building, the Jews resemble, iv. 255.

Pekoe. See Tea.

Peleus: and Telephus, i. 166; the name given by Lysimachus to Philip, iii. 247.

Pelias (son of Neptune), said to have been nursed by a mare, ii. 455.

Pelion: upon Ossa, iii. 230; called εἰνοσίφυλλον by Homer, iii. 230.

Pellegrini, Antonio, iv. 495.

Pelvis, used by several ancient comic writers for a looking-glass, iv. 164.

Pemberton, Henry, A View of Sir Isaac Newton's Philosophy, i. 425.

Pembroke, Mary Herbert, wife of 2nd Earl of: epitaph on, iii. 185. See also Sidney, Arcadia.

Penelope: the web of, v. 73–74; constancy of Ulysses to, v. 75.

Penkethman, William: his new theatre in Greenwich, i. 93; account of, and roles, i. 129–30, 151, 278; to personate King Porus in a projected opera, i. 129; his Pantheon of Heathen Gods, i. 130, 150; Bullock's petition to be Hephaestion to, i. 151; in Love Makes a Man, iii. 394, his varied expressions, iii. 394–5; on an elephant's back in Bartholomew Fair, iv. 107; in The Country Wake, iv. 283; 'mending a play of Shakespeare and Jonson', iv. 427. — Pinkethman's Jests, ii. 451; iv. 288.

Penmaenmawr, 'the glory of all Wales', ii. 384–5.

Penmanship ('join-hand'), i. 32.

Penny: 'laying down my p. upon the bar'

at the coffee-house, i. 132; iii. 509; Penny wise and pound foolish (prov.), iii. 53; iv. 309; A penny saved is a penny got (prov.), Sir ANDREW's favourite maxim, iv. 309.

Penny post, i. 118; ii. 84; iii. 433; iv. 92, 111.

Pennyworths (bargains), iv. 83.

Penruddock, John, unhappy enterprise of in the Civil Wars, iii. 135.

Pensioner-matrons, iii. 194.

Pentameters, a table for composing, ii. 357.

Pentathlum, Roman, ii. 133.

PENTHESILEA, 'the fierce and beautiful', i. 242.

Pentheus (in Virgil), iii. 579.

People, the source of wealth, ii. 283–7; of Rome represented by Tribunes, iii. 20.

Pepusch, Dr. J. C., a subscriber, i. lxxxix.

Pepys, Samuel, i. 63; ii. 451; iii. 350, 436; iv. 308.

Percy, Earl (in Chevy Chase), i. 300–1, 316–17.

Percy, Thomas, iii. 409; v. 162.

Perfect man: of the Stoics, ii. 444; v. 167; not to be introduced upon the stage, iv. 463–5.

Perfection(s): essential p. of man little, but comparative p. considerable, i. 311; Cyrus portrayed by Xenophon as a pattern of, ii. 234; excellence, or p., the title given to ambassadors, ii. 352; Stoics comprehended all possible p. in virtue, ii. 444; many silent p. in the soul of a good man, ii. 500; PL shows man and woman in highest, ii. 542, 563; of human nature the great end of government, iii. 22; our ideas of, iv. 393; plenitude of p. in God, v. 11.

Perfumer(s): the sign of a goat before the door of a, i. 117; and toy-men, iii. 166.

Perfumes, perfuming: women who pass their time in dressing, bathing, and, ii. 320; Scaramouche's mingling of, iii. 3; fragrancy of, pleasing to the imagination, iii. 544.

Pericardium of the heart, ii. 594–5.

Pericles: his funeral oration on Athenian youth, i. 349; iii. 105; his advice to women, i. 349; aided by others, ii. 44; could shake the finest resolutions of his hearers, v. 163.

Periodical writers, no species of scribblers more offensive and incurable, iv. 590.

Periodicals, periodical essays, i. xiii; difficulties of writing and publishing,

i. 505–8; the Stamp Act fatal to many, iv. 62–63.

Periods: Milton copies Homer in length of his, iii. 15; 'structure of p.' one of the phrases to suggest immense reading, iii. 347.

Periwig(s): i. 10, 110; ii. 236, 344; iv. 198, 221, 371; v. 156; full-bottomed, i. 71, 123, 248; v. 138; with a high foretop, i. 76; styles in, ii. 13–14; a prentice-boy's, ii. 291; long, ii. 388; effect of an ill-shaped p. on a coquette's heart, ii. 595; women who adopt the riding-coat and, iv. 28; 'turning grey from fear', iv. 423; a humorist who wore a turban instead of a, iv. 571; renewing curls of decayed, v. 116.

Perplexity, example of, from Shakespeare, iv. 435–6.

Perquisites to servants, iii. 378.

Perrault, Charles, his ridicule of Homer, ii. 589; iii. 90.

Perronet, —— (surgeon), his medicine advertised, iv. 61.

Perry, Micaiah, a subscriber, i. lxxxix.

Persecution: for religious beliefs, ii. 228–9; for any party or opinion, to be avoided, iii. 495; evil of p. for conscience' sake, iv. 120; of the Jews by Romans and Turks, iv. 256.

Persepolis, burning of, on the stage, i. 151.

Persia: Sophy of, under contribution to Aretino, i. 99; Emperor of, in Homeric times, i. 299; Emperor of, now 'the Nutmeg of Delight', ii. 128; sacrifices in, ii. 234; caravansaries in, iii. 30; tracts in, set aside for the queen's dress, iii. 54; sale of unmarried women at fairs in, iv. 314–15; desolation of Persian empire, iv. 319; 'luxury of a Persian', iv. 335.

Persian diadem, pearl fixed on top of, iii. 46.

Persian fable, of the drop of water, iii. 46.

Persian glass-man, fable of Alnaschar, iv. 410–12.

Persian Jupiter, sacrifices to, ii. 234.

Persian nobleman, anecdote of Araspas, a young, iv. 526–7.

Persian silk, adorers of the sun in, ii. 470.

Persian soldier, rebuked for reviling Alexander, iv. 2.

Persian Tales, story of Fadlallah from, iv. 576–9.

Persians, Sir ANDREW calls them our silk-weavers, i. 296.

Persians, Ancient: education of their children, i. 418; iii. 248–9; their horror of parricide, ii. 244; laws of Medes and, iv. 303.

Persico and ratafia, iii. 206.

Persius Flaccus, Aulus: his second and fourth satires based on Plato's two Alcibiades dialogues, ii. 310; condemned by Cowley for his obscure way of writing, iii. 424; his second satire, on vanity of men's wishes, the finest in his whole works, iii. 470; quoted, i. 54, 96, 232–4; ii. 238.

Person(s) (human beings): in Homer and Virgil compared, iii. 565; types of, iv. 53–54; theories of personal identity, iv. 575; Locke's definition of, iv. 575–6.

Person (the body): less important than character, i. 74–78, 369–70; we should not be ashamed of our, ii. 401; a good p. not only raises but continues love, ii. 515; comeliness of p. adds weight to speech, iii. 41; a fit lodging for a fair and lovely mind, iii. 80; an agreeable p. necessary to happiness in marriage, iv. 357; graces and attractions of, in Marlborough, v. 179.

Perspective glasses, to avoid the impertinence of staring, ii. 473.

Perspicuity: and elegance of Pope's Essay on Criticism, ii. 483; and sublimity necessary in language of epic, iii. 10; and clearness necessary to the critic, iii. 35; of style in PL, iii. 142; of style balanced against depth of sense, iv. 137.

Perspicuity (transparency) of humours of the eye, iv. 171.

Persuasion: torture as a method of, ii. 431; feminine arts of, ii. 480–1.

PERT, Mr., iv. 401, 589.

Pert: creatures with vivacity and little understanding, i. 421; the p. and talkative, ii. 82; the shop-maid a p. wench, ii. 581; 'from p. to stupid sinks supinely down', iv. 398.

Peru, the brocade petticoat rises out of the mines of, i. 295.

Peruke, a fall of one wing of a, iv. 345.

Pervigilium Veneris, an edition of satirized (?), iv. 161.

Pescetti, Orlando, Proverbi italiani, ii. 252.

Pestilence, allegorical figure of, iii. 338–9.

Pestle: and Mortar, the British Hippocrates of, i. 222; of a lark, iii. 196.

Peter, St.: painted by Raphael, ii. 380; reprimanded by Jesus, iii. 328; never subverted the law, iii. 442.

Peter II, King of Portugal, death of, i. 276.

Peter Alexowitz (Peter the Great) of Russia: defeated Charles XII at Pultowa, i. *182*; ii. *36*; contrasted with Louis XIV, ii. 47–49.

Peter, John: satire on his *Artificial Versifying*, ii. 356.

PETER, a servant, v. 128.

Pétis de la Croix, François, iv. *576*.

Petite pièce, followed a French tragedy, iii. 267.

Petits Esprits, Les, i. 269.

Petits-maîtres, i. 354.

Petitions: from the Playhouse, i. 151; of *who* and *which*, i. 336–7, 344–5; of BENJAMIN EASIE, ii. 31; of JOHN STEWARD *et al.*, ii. 294; manner of granting, iii. 39; of ANTHONY TITLE-PAGE, iii. 93–94; of BARTHOLOMEW LADYLOVE, iii. 94–95; of the New Exchange, iii. 95; against unnecessary letters in *Spectator*, iii. 124; of JOHN A NOKES and JOHN A STOKES, iv. 574–5; of P. S., iv. 588; of SARAH LOVEIT, iv. 588; a p. referred to the Censor of Small Wares, v. 116; of CHARLES COCKSURE, rejected, v. 117; from Cavaliers to Charles II, v. 149–51; to Whig leaders in 1714, v. *151*.

'Petrifyed with the love of this world', iii. 328; iv. 169.

Petronius Arbiter, Gaius (or Titus): his story of the Ephesian Matron, i. 48, 49, 51; recommended, ii. *142*; among the best of the Latin critics, ii. 484; his courage at death praised by Saint-Evremond, iii. 300.

Petticoat(s), hooped petticoats: frailty covered by, i. 12; brocade, i. 67, 295, 344; part of a riding-habit, i. 434; changes in fashion of, i. 450–1; ii. 13–14; enormous size of, ii. 5–8, 74; iv. 24; quilted, ii. 74; 'avoided hampering my spurs in their', ii. 433; female projectors taken up with improvement of, ii. 531; without whalebone, ii. 579; 'hurt by the brush of a whalebone p.', iii. 417; a mantua and p. without ribbons, iii. 532; DULCISSA's manner of letting her hooped p. fall, iv. 245; quilting a whole under-p., v. 71.

Petty, Sir William: on population, ii. 286–7; his theory of division of labour, ii. 404.

Petty Jury, Foreman of the, i. 498.

Petty larceny, punishment for, ii. 161; iii. 16.

Petulance, petulancy: and wit learned at our great schools, ii. 116; of a peevish old fellow, acted by Penkethman, iii. 394; of young gentlemen, iv. 383.

Pew(s): immodest conversation in, ii. 440; news of fashion whispered in, ii. 578; decoration of, with greens, ii. 600.

Pew-door, the scholars stand in rows at PATETIA's, ii. 548.

Pewter: changed every half-year, iii. 111; p.-dish, iii. 154; brass and, iii. 189, 210; reduced to downright, iv. 559.

Phaedra, unhappy in her love, ii. 427. *See also* Smith, Edmund.

Phaedria, his request to his mistress (in Terence), ii. 169; iv. 486.

Phaeton, the fate of, iv. 266.

Phalaris, a consolatory letter of, iii. 298–9.

'Phantom, The': her behaviour at church, iv. 284–7; further account of, with her letter, iv. 330–3.

Phantom(s): of a castle-builder, ii. 159; in Dryden's Virgil, ii. 304; in dream-vision of examination of hearts, v. 8.

Phaon and Sappho, ii. 366, 408–9.

PHARAMOND: whims of, with his companion EUCRATE, i. 326–9; complaint of SPINAMONT to, i. 357–60; his edict against duelling, i. 410–12; a letter from a country gentleman to, iv. 201–3.

Pharaoh, King of Egypt, iii. 386; iv. 127; Moses' embassy to, v. 21.

Pharsalia, battle of, iii. 407.

Pheasants, i. 158, 448, 472, 498.

PHEBE, COLIN's lament for her absence, v. 61–64.

Phidias: works of, lost, ii. 154; mentioned, ii. 341; iii. 555.

PHILAGNOTES, letter from (on his cousin and her jealous husband), iv. 378–80.

PHILANDER: in love with SYLVIA, a demurrer, i. 377; 'mortally wounded' by CLEORA, iii. 417; letters between AMORET and, iii. 500–2; his duel with HIPPARCHUS, iv. 183; whether AMORET be bound by a promise of marriage to, v. 98; memorial of, postponed, v. 117.

PHILANTHROPOS: letter from (on men's flattery of women), iii. 73; letter from (on an elderly tale-bearer), iii. 123–4; letter from (on Mohocks), iii. 186–8; reply to letter from, iv. 588.

PHILANTHROPUS: letter from (on sight and blindness), iv. 170–3.

Philanthropy: Xenophon always celebrating the p. or good nature of his hero, ii. 166; deserves title of a moral virtue, ii. 197.

PHILANTHUS, letter from (on the naked-shouldered), iv. 37–38.

PHILARITHMUS: letter from (on French military conquests), ii. 209–12; his comment on Louis XIV, ii. 283.

PHILAUTIA, an 'Idol', i. 340.

Philip of Macedonia: ambition of, ii. 396; used gold to win over his opponents, ii. 431–2; flattered by Lysimachus under name of Peleus, iii. 247; had a youth to bid him remember that he was a man, v. 42.

Philip II of Spain, iii. *106*, *477*; as Geryoneo in Spenser, iv. 429.

Philip V of Spain. See Anjou, Duke of.

PHILIPATER, letter from (on his daughter), iv. 147–8.

Philippick Islands, give a flavour to our European bowls, i. 295.

Philips, Ambrose: a contributor, i. lxxxi–lxxxii; his translation of Sappho's Hymn to Venus, ii. 366–9; his translation of Sappho's *Ad Lesbiam*, ii. 392; translation of Lapland songs by (?), iii. *376*, *519*; *Pastorals* praised, ii. 367; iv. 362; *Pastorals* quoted, iii. 497–9; his *Winter-Piece* praised, ii. 367; letter from Copenhagen by (?), iii. 473; referred to (?), iv. 396; his translation of the *Persian Tales*, iv. 576; *Collection of Old Ballads*, i. *362*. — The *Distressed Mother*: Powell as Orestes in, i. *130*; iii. 34, 291; praise of, iii. 31–34; Booth as Pyrrhus in, iii. 236; Sir ROGER's visit to a performance of, iii. 239–42; Prologue to, iii. 250–1; Epilogue to, iii. 250–4, 265–9; iv. 493; Mrs. Oldfield in, iii. 252, 266; disturbance at a performance of, iii. *351*; passage from, quoted, iv. 434; 'one of the finest among our modern tragedies', v. 99–100.

Philips, Edward, *New World of Words*, v. *116*.

Philips, John, *Cyder*, ii. *52*.

PHILLIS: a name used by correspondents, i. 71; rivalry of BRUNETTA and, i. 342–4; letter from (incident of a fan), ii. 301; STREPHON and, ii. 464.

PHILO-BRITANNICUS, letter from (on servants), i. 372–3.

PHILOBRUNE, letter from (on brunettes), iii. 17–18 (comment on, iii. 483–4).

Philoctetes, iii. *568*.

PHILOGAMUS, letter from (on pleasures of fatherhood), iv. 272–5.

Philomaths, in Moorfields, iv. 293.

PHILOMEDES, willing to pay sixpence for the *Spectator*, iv. 231.

PHILOMEIDES, letter from (defending Epilogue to *The Distressed Mother*), iii. 265–9.

Philomot (feuillemorte) hoods, ii. 532.

PHILONICUS, letter from (on illiberal cant of lawyers), iv. 477–8.

PHILONOUS, letter from (on free-thinkers), ii. 411–13.

Philopinax, letter to Chromation, ii. 427–8.

Philoponus, iii. *559*.

Philosopher: who discovered a monkey in an Egyptian temple, ii. 7; vulgar definition of a heathen, ii. 91; a man must be a p. to know how to pass time agreeably, ii. 269; often lies hidden in the plebeian, ii. 338; a map of spots in the sun by a modern, iii. 83; tries to subdue his passions and lay aside his prejudices, iv. 525; the philosopher's stone of the alchemist, iv. 562; more to be esteemed than a potentate, v. 127; a whimsical p. treading upon every other board, v. 159.

Philosophers: a new sect of, at Cambridge, i. 229; sayings of, on beauty, ii. 68; attitude of atomical p. towards religion, ii. 233–4; temperance of, brought them long lives, ii. 266; attitude towards riches, iii. 1; spent much of their lives among gardens, iv. 595.

Philosophy: the business of religion and, ii. 374; authors of the new, iii. 574–5; balanced against religion, iv. 137; appeal of novelty in study of, v. 140–1.

PHILO-SPEC, letter from (on the dissolution of the Club), iv. 440–1 (comment on, iv. 485).

Philo Strategos, *Churchill's Annals*, ii. *51*.

PHILOTAS and CHLORIS, iii. 25.

Phiz (face), i. 133; iv. 344; v. 108.

Phlebotomy, moderate use of, advised in May, iii. 374.

Phocion: his dignified conduct in death, ii. 26; his distrust of applause, ii. 240; likened a wordy orator to a tree without fruit, iv. 75.

PHOEBE. See PHEBE.

Phoebidas, Isadas, son of, iv. 528.

Phoenix: in *The Distressed Mother*, iii. 242; name given by Lysimachus to himself, iii. 247; his speech to Achilles, iii. 466–7.

Photius, ii. *409*.

Phthisical distempers, i. 105.

PHYLADELPHUS, reply to query from, iv. 587.

PHYLLIS. See PHILLIS.

PHYSIBULUS: letter from (on epilogues), iii. 251–4; answered, iii. 265–9.

Physic: Estcourt's wine excludes surfeits, fevers, and, ii. 530; Mr. SPECTATOR

sometimes taken for a doctor of, iii. 27. *See also* Medicine.

Physical exercise, i. 471–4.

Physician(s): 'titular', i. 45; work of, and of surgeon, i. 71; some slay in chariots and some on foot, i. 90; a mountebank doctor, i. 96; Dryden on origin of, i. 479; assisting death, ii. 124; a court, ii. 253; the famous doctor in Moorfields, ii. 257–8; who prescribed exercise for the sultan, ii. 263; an eminent p.'s rules for eating, ii. 265; dictates with authority in private company, ii. 272; letter from ESCULAPIUS, on cures for love, ii. 383–4; Erasistratus, ii. 393; allowed to lie to their patients, ii. 410; many unqualified, iii. 109; doctor who will give no advice for less than a guinea, iii. 354; satires upon the religion of the Faculty, iv. 18; to the Fashionable Society, iv. 197; profession of, both honourable and advantageous, iv. 551; anecdote of a p. who went on foot, iv. 554; whose patient was killed *secundum artem*, v. 28. *See also* Quacks.

Physician (student of physics), iii. 72.

Physiognomy, i. 365–9; ii. 307; reading the future in features of the face, iv. 292; letter on, iv. 344–5.

Pick-axes, iv. 263.

Picket. *See* Piquet.

Pickle, pickling: of dills and cucumbers, ii. 477; preserving and, iii. 205; the best p. for a walnut, iv. 210.

Pickle(d) Herring(s): merry drolls in Holland, i. 201; at a whistling-match, ii. 207; of quack doctors, iv. 552; in Cave of Trophonius, v. 46.

Pickpocket(s), i. 335; ii. 17, 219.

Pickthank, ii. 558.

Pict, the 'painted vest' of the naked, i. 185.

'Picts' (women with borrowed complexions), i. 173–7, 197, 205, 221, 228.

Picture(s): may entertain the eye but not affect the heart, i. 140; ii. 446–7; a sale of, announced, i. 288, *329*; fill the mind with gay ideas, i. 353; at Sir ROGER's, i. 445, 449–52; a box of, ii. 29; as a lover's gift, ii. 407; Philopinax, who fell in love with a, ii. 427–8; a fine p. in a good light, ii. 445; how to judge, ii. 446–7; shadows and lights in, ii. 447–8; sold by Motteux, iii. 25; drawn larger than life, iii. 81; some men, like p., fitter for a corner than a full light, iii. 518; Italian p. cannot be relished by untravelled Englishmen,

iii. 521; conversing with a, iii. 538; in motion described, iii. 550–1; a lady's p. on which different dresses could be clapped, iv. 148–9; burlesque p. which the Italians call *caricaturas*, iv. 417: *See also* Paintings.

Pie: a Christmas, i. 361; and piety, i. 361.

Pied Piper: cleared a great town in Germany of mice, i. 27.

Pierault's Bagnio, iii. *225*.

Pierre (in *Venice Preserved*), iv. 107.

Piety: a strong steady masculine p. desirable, ii. 290; rational p. of EMILIA, iii. 80; of Aeneas contrasted with courage of Turnus, iii. 304; a whimsical sort of, in great lovers of money, iii. 600.

Pig: in the puppet-show, i. 64; Flying P. as a sign, i. 116; a shoe-maker living at the sign of the Roasted, i. 117; on a spit, iii. 196.

Pig-nuts, grow naturally in England, i. 295.

Pigs, care of poultry and, a great enemy to the countenance, iv. 333.

Pilchards, fisheries disturbed by French privateers, iii. 509.

Pilgrimage, human life a, ii. 353; iii. 30.

Pillar(s): *Doric Pillars* a term of art used by Milton, iii. 64; effect of round p. in architecture, iii. 557; the radiant p. in the vision of heavenly and worldly wisdom, iv. 367–9.

Pillory: recommended for duellists, i. 419; as a cure for the itch of writing, iv. 590; a prank that deserved the, v. 149.

Pillow(s): the Stone of Scone called Jacob's, iii. 215; embroidering of child-bed, v. 73.

Pills, 'English Pills' of quacks, iv. 553.

Pimp(s), i. 219; Argus a p. for his mistress Juno, ii. 470; skilful, ii. 568.

Pin(s): superstition concerning a crooked, i. 33; accepting a pin from a witch, i. 481; a witch making children spit, i. 482; *a pin a day is a groat a year* (prov.), iii. 52; *care not a pin* (prov.), iii. 53; 'The Pins' as a name for part of every estate, iii. 54; sale of patches, pins, and wires, iv. 102.

Pincushion(s), i. 193; ii. 190, 557; iii. 183, 206; iv. 195.

Pin-money, iii. 50–54, 68, 113, 196; 'Mr. FONDLE promises me half my portion in', v. 135.

Pinch (of the hat): a pinched hat, ii. 113; cocks and pinches to show party allegiance, iv. 17–18.

Pindar: 'the gorgeous eloquence of'

(Sidney), i. 298; a great unlearned genius, ii. 129; ridiculous modern imitators of, ii. 129; a literal translation of, reads awkwardly, iii. 515; Second Olympic Ode quoted, iv. 152; joined with Cowley, iv. 329.

Pindaric: writers, fit to excel in typographical wit, i. 248; readers, 'confined to no set measure', ii. 79; numbers as loose and unequal as those in which the British ladies sport their Pindariques, iii. 376; my compositions in gardening, after the P. manner, iv. 190–1.

Pine, planted by Abraham, v. 15.

Pineal gland, as the seat of the soul, ii. 571.

Pinkerton, John ('Robert Heron'), on Addison's style, i. c.

Pinkethman. See Penkethman.

'Pinking', a practice of the Mohocks, iii. 294.

Pinks of good breeding, ii. 54.

Pinto, Ferdinand Mendez, iv. 428.

Pioneers, in expedition of Alexander, i. 151.

Pipe: poems in shape of shepherd's, i. 246; quail-pipe, i. 448; of Licinius, ii. 388–9; iv. 437.

'Pipe-champers', iv. 17.

Piper, Count, captured at Battle of Pultowa, ii. 37.

Pipes: Sir ROGER loves to clear his p. in good air, ii. 549; and tubes in the brain, ii. 573; oaten, in a morris dance, iii. 595. See also Smoking.

Pipkin, a hypochondriac fancying himself a, iv. 415.

Pippin, a golden, ii. 530.

Pippin-woman, story of the, ii. 461.

Piquet: plays a whole afternoon at, ii. 276; engaged at, iii. 491; ombre or, iv. 24; 'we sate down to', iv. 378.

Pisistratus, on kissing in public, iv. 379.

Pistol-shot, reach out their hands at, iii. 95.

Pit (of the theatre): i. 94, 194, 217; ii. 57, 545; iv. 76; 'style of the pit bawdry', i. 63; men in, regarding ladies in the boxes, i. 219, 385; ii. 511, 532; Sir ROGER sits in the, iii. 241; at Drury Lane, iii. 351; 'as she looked down into the', iii. 418; the gentlemen of the bon goust in the, iii. 485; in the Bear-Garden, iv. 33; the whole pit in a chuckle, iv. 282.

Pitty-pat air, iv. 286.

Pitt, Thomas (Governor of Madras), iii. 289.

Pittacus, an example of content, iv. 563.

Pity: 'the under passion of a noble spirit', ii. 314; weeping should be reserved to adorn generous, ii. 481; the vicious should arouse our, ii. 534; is love softened by sorrow, iii. 486; exercise of, in pugilistic encounters, iv. 34; the softest and most generous of all passions, iv. 52. See also Compassion.

Pity and terror: devices for inducing, on the stage, i. 177–9, 185–91; Aristotle on the kind of character proper for inducing, ii. 565–6; aroused by the more serious kinds of poetry, iii. 567.

Pix, Mrs. Mary, Ibrahim, i. 218.

Place: and precedency more regarded in the country, i. 487; right of, on the road, ii. 24; qualifications of men in great, iv. 159–61.

Place-hunters, petitions of, v. 149–51.

Plagiarism, should be acknowledged by an author, iv. 453.

Plague(s): in Athens, ii. 266; of Egypt, iii. 386; v. 102; of 1665, iv. 83.

Plagues: books with this title, ii. 89.

Plain Dealer, The (periodical), i. lxxxiv; iii. 440–1, 509–10.

Plain dealing, allegorical figure of, iv. 123.

Plain man (men, people), i. 498; ii. 117, 544.

Planets: study of, less important than study of human nature, iii. 523; motions and revolutions of, iv. 170; may be inhabited, iv. 346; Newton's view of the, iv. 442.

Plant, oaken, of the Trunk-maker, ii. 414.

'Plant men, to' (Diogenes' phrase), ii. 297.

Plantations: behaviour of Negroes in American, ii. 339; desirable in English estates, iii. 551–2; in China and in Europe, iii. 552–3; methodical discourses, like regular, iv. 186; afford lasting pleasure, iv. 593–4.

Planting, delights and benefits of, iv. 592–5 (this essay praised, v. 15).

Plants: care in cultivation of better, ii. 116; the most important are the most beautiful, iii. 452–3; pleasure in reading treatises on, iii. 575; allegory of p. and human life, iv. 104–5.

Plate: eating in, i. 67; a present of, ii. 536; changed every twelve-month, iii. 111.

Plate, running for a, of six guineas value, ii. 182.

Plato: banished music from his commonwealth, i. 82; an allegory, after P.'s manner, i. 146; wrote before rules of art were codified, i. 261; taught that

the passions remain in a soul after death, i. 380–2; called beauty a mere gift of nature, ii. 68; one of the learned geniuses, ii. 129; the finest prose writers of antiquity, such as Cicero, P., Xenophon, wrote allegories, ii. 221; 'that divine author', ii. 222; 'like P.'s guardian angels', ii. 337; said it was allowable in physicians to lie to their patients, ii. 410; denied that the gods were authors of injustice, ii. 421–2; Zoilus wrote against, iii. 221; calls God the Divine Geometrician, iii. 258; complied with public forms of worship, ii. 460; wrote on the vanity of men's wishes, iii. 470; 'if the gods were to talk with men, they would speak in P.'s style', iii. 515; said of God 'truth is his body, and light his shadow', iv. 298; called mathematical demonstrations the cathartics or purgatives of the soul, iv. 299; the spirit of, iv. 329; compliment paid him by an Athenian nobleman after supping at his house, iv. 448; said that nothing is so delightful as the hearing or speaking of truth, iv. 502; said labour is preferable to idleness, as brightness to rust, v. 132; 'Plato, thou reasonest well', v. 147. — *Alcibiades II*: analysis of ('Plato's discourse on prayer'), ii. 310–14; *Alcibiades I*: cited, iii. 53–54; — *Apology*: on Socrates' professed ignorance, i. 229–30; whatever befalls a just man conduces to his good, ii. 421–2; 'content is natural wealth', iv. 564; — *Laws*, ii. 242; — *Phaedo*: Socrates' reference to Aristophanes' lampoons, i. 98; subsistence of passions after death, i. 381; death of Socrates, ii. 25, 221–2, 234; on guardian angels, ii. 337; — *Republic*: i. 82; records some beautiful transmigrations in the Vision of Erus, ii. 326; cited, ii. 410; iii. 596; iv. 298, 299; v. 132; the virtuous man a good subject for Plato's Republic, iii. 133; — *Symposium*: Socrates' appearance, i. 368; 'wealth the father of love', iv. 295; — *Theaetetus*: anecdote of Socrates, iii. 107.

Platonic love: TOM TULIP's sly commendation of, i. 387; 'I have but a low opinion of', iii. 499; the waist of a Platonist has lately swollen, iii. 500.

Platonism: extravagant and chimerical talk of Plato's followers, i. 237; Platonic writers on the number ten, ii. 361; Platonists' high regard for truth, iv. 298–9; the ancient Platonic notion of perfect existence, v. 21; an essay on immortality, drawn from the Platonic way of thinking, v. 169–70.

Plautus, *Asinaria*, i. 508.

Play: behaviour at the, ii. 552–3; a first-rate toast at a, iii. 427; go to the p. and sit at cards, iii. 465; an incident in a, iv. 281; rehearsal of a p. by Cibber, iv. 453–4. See also Theatre.

Play (verb): the fool, ii. 583; 'he played a couple of black riding wigs upon me', iii. 161–2; *playing fast and loose* (prov.), iii. 165; 'playing them off, as our phrase is', iv. 264.

Play-bills, iii. 183.

Play-debts, of a wife, iii. 51.

Player(s): are under patronage of *Spectator*, iii. 291; the whole world acts the, iii. 393. See also Actors.

Playford, Henry, iii. 532.

Playhouse, no one rises in it by merit, i. 93; petitions from, i. 151; the upper-gallery audience in, i. 269; the seat of wit, to the man of the world, i. 278; frequently filled with 'Idols', i. 313; a *Dissuasive from the*, recommended, i. 391; adventures in gallantry about the, ii. 104; a set of impertinents at, ii. 162–3; footmen keeping places at, ii. 163; the Trunk-maker in the upper gallery at, ii. 413–16; side-boxes, entering-doors, and curtain, ii. 434; on persons allowed behind the scenes, ii. 435; immodest conversation in, ii. 440; throwing away time at, ii. 451; motions of the eye at, ii. 472; where some go to see, others to be seen, ii. 479; the Latin sentence at the top of the stage, iii. 393; none in the country, iii. 590; knotting may be done in, iv. 413; new scenic effects in, v. 25–26. See also Stage, Theatre.

Plays: improbabilities in modern, i. 92; in LEONORA's library, i. 153; improvement from, i. 173; immodesty in, i. 215–20; effect of, on manners, i. 278; recommended for women, i. 392; a husband who dislikes the fooleries of, ii. 11; poverty of taste in, ii. 314; of 1711/12 season not approved by the Trunk-maker, ii. 415; contempt of religion and decency in, ii. 554; benefit days, iii. 26; every fop can find faults in, iii. 74; immorality of modern, iv. 66–69; new stage effects in modern, v. 25–26; critics now condemn p. which are successful, v. 26; a run of three days, v. 26; critics of modern, v. 26–28.

PLEADWELL, JOHN, 'slain' by KITTY SLY, iii. 418.

Pleasantness: of temper a qualification of a good friend, i. 291; character of a pleasant fellow, iv. 131.

Pleasantry (-ies): flat impertinent, ii. 108; of the inquisitive, ii. 388; the only piece of, in *PL*, ii. 589; unfair p. in criticism, iii. 37; effects of, in company, iv. 130.

Pleased, disposition to be: to be cultivated by every man, i. 420; ii. 65; necessary to happy married life, iv. 197; promoted by religion, iv. 254.

Pleasing others: desire of, a laudable motive in women, i. 139; methods of, ii. 590–3, 599; iii. 38–41, 104, 476–9.

Pleasure(s): love of, degenerates into luxury, i. 232; in allegory of luxury and avarice, i. 235–6; not necessary to enjoyment of life, ii. 65; the highest we are capable of enjoying with composure, ii. 75; sensual p. an unlasting satisfaction, ii. 93–96, 100–3, 296–7, 599; character of men of wit and, ii. 93–96; rational and worthy, ii. 101; men of wit and p. preferred by women, ii. 103; Socrates on p. and pain, ii. 221–2; allegory of p. and pain, ii. 222–3; mean and inordinate, ii. 254; doubled by moderation, ii. 308–9; relation of p. and business, ii. 364; conversation with a friend the greatest, ii. 375; in doing good, ii. 394, 500, 526–7; iii. 39, 423; iv. 151–3; v. 13–14; Sir ANDREW alternates between business and, ii. 401; and pain imaginary distinctions, ii. 442; laughter a great p. of life, ii. 466; ambition produces unsatisfying, ii. 498; and recreation necessary to mind and body, ii. 502; of reading and contemplation, iii. 21; constant pursuit of, insolent and improper, iii. 129; ideas of, among the Romans, iii. 340; to be moralized, iii. 475–6; of the imagination, iii. 535–82; derived from a garden, iv. 192; expression of, from Otway, iv. 435.

Pleasures of a Country Life, recommended, i. 391.

Plebeian: benefits of education to the, ii. 338; the p. or mechanic in love, iii. 416.

Pleiades: the most beautiful constellation, v. 160.

Plenitude, principle of, iv. 347–8, 531; v. 11–12, 21–22, 170–1.

PLENTY, BASIL, an imaginary letter to, iv. 169.

Plenty: in allegory of luxury and avarice, i. 235–6; in countries of the greatest p. there is the poorest living, ii. 286; the fruit of liberty, and cherisher of knowledge, iii. 21; allegorical figure of, iii. 595–6; the horn of, iii. 596.

Pleurisy, iv. 553.

PLEXIPPUS and LARISSA, ii. 407.

Pliny the Elder: *Natural History*: on understanding language of birds, iv. 319; on Pyrrhus's ring, v. 28; Apelles' painting of Antigonus, v. 164.

Pliny the Younger: the greatest lawyer and most elegant writer of his age, iv. 216; one of the finest gentlemen and politest writers of his age, iv. 372; carried a commonplace book with him, iii. 150–1; his speech in praise of Trajan, iv. 150; on modesty in speaking, iv. 216; his passion for fame, iv. 490–1. — *Letters*, ii. 295; quoted, ii. 394–5; iii. 40; iv. 216, 372–3, 490–1.

Ploce, a form of pun, i. 261.

Plot, Robert: *Natural History of Staffordshire*, i. 174; ii. 182; iii. 572; story of the idiot and the clock, iv. 69–70; story of the flitch of bacon, v. 76–80; *Natural History of Oxfordshire*, i. 248; iii. 521.

Plough, the farmer inspecting his, iv. 572.

Ploughman: in a grinning-match, ii. 184; in a whistling-match, ii. 206–7.

Ploughshares, walking on burning, as test of chastity, iii. 481.

Plum (£100,000), iv. 82.

Plum-porridge, a dissenter eating plentifully of, ii. 551.

Plums: growing in Britain, i. 295; 'too many p. and no suet', iii. 153; vendors of, at the Royal Exchange, iv. 307.

Plume of feathers: in French opera, i. 123; in English tragedy, i. 178; effect of, on a coquette's heart, ii. 595.

'Plunderer', a word which helps to sell a pamphlet, iv. 537.

Plush-doublets, learned men in (i.e. quacks), ii. 28.

Plutarch: and Seneca, moral writers, ii. 142; and Herodotus often apply impertinent judgements on disasters, iv. 212; compares Sappho to Cacus, son of Vulcan, ii. 366; mentioned, ii. 190; iv. 306. — LIVES: *Agesilaus*, i. 334; anecdote of Isadas, iv. 528; *Alexander*: i. 135; ii. 7, 114, 596; iii. 423, 555; iv. 166; v. 30; Lysimachus' flattery of Alexander, iii. 247; *Antony*, i. 68, 144; *Marcus Brutus*, ii. 114; a saying of, iv. 115; *Caesar*, ii. 260; iii. 99; v. 75; *Marcus Cato*: Cato taught his son himself, iii. 132; *Cato the Younger*: ii. 72; one witness not enough, though it were Cato himself, iv. 502; *Cicero*, i. 144;

ii. *398*; iii. *150, 513, 515*; iv. *519*; Demosthenes, iii. *150, 452*; Demetrius, ii.
242, 410; how Erasistratus discovered
symptoms of love in Antiochus, ii.
393; *Tiberius Gracchus*: Caius Gracchus
and the pipe of Licinius, ii. *388*;
Lycurgus, ii. *116, 239, 242*; iii. *99, 109*;
Caius Marius, ii. *114*; *Pericles*, i. *221*; ii.
458; *Phocion*, ii. *26, 240*; iv. *75*; *Pompey*,
iv. *301*; *Pyrrhus*, ii. *211*; *Solon*, i. *72*;
iv. *214*; *Sulla*, iii. *43, 45*; *Themistocles*,
iii. *126*. — *Moralia*, i. *30, 221, 263*; ii.
*116, 239, 240, 242, 373, 378, 388, 399,
444*; iii. *99, 299, 555*; iv. *2, 75, 116,
214, 379, 506, 542, 563, 564*; v. *75, 76,
157*; a man should not hate even his
enemies, i. *510*; has written an essay
on benefits to be received from enemies,
iii. *494*; human life like a game at tables:
one must play as well as one can, iii.
518; story of the man singing a hymn to
Diana, iv. *95*; a saying of Brutus, iv.
115; Heraclitus' saying about dreams,
iv. *229*; the atheist does less dishonour
to God than the man who believes
Him to be cruel, iv. *254*. — *On the
Life and Poetry of Homer*: on Homer's
coining new words, iii. *14*. — *Sympo-
siaca*, iii. *258*.

Pluto: in Lully's opera, i. *123*; affrighted
at shock of battle, iii. *233*.

Plutus (god of riches), story of, from
Aristophanes, iv. *139–41*.

Plymouth, i. *344*.

POACHER, GERVASE: applied for the
flitch of bacon, v. *80*.

Poacher, letter from a, ii. *164*.

Pocket-authors, iv. *386*.

Pocket-book, i. *157*; carried by Pliny,
iii. *150*.

Pocket-pistol, i. *428*.

Pockets: coats with long, ii. *14–15*; iii.
163; and loops, ii. *526*.

Poems: inscribed on rings, i. *185, 248*; ii.
183; inscribed on knives, i. *246*; in
typographical shapes, i. *246–8, 265,
271*; iii. *560*; iv. *288*; inscribed on
wedding-rings, i. *378*; 'has read all the
miscellany p.', ii. *113*.

Poems in the *Spectator*:
A grotto so compleat, with such de-
sign (Ward)   v. *162*
Adeste, o quotque sunt, Veneres,
Gratiae, Cupidines   iv. *196*
Anacreon, On (Antipater)   iv. *473*
Animula vagula, blandula (Hadrian)
                      iv. *397*
As when in Sharon's field   iii. *456*
Bellinda, see from yonder flowers
                      iv. *176*

Poems (*cont.*)
Blest as th'immortal gods is he
(Sappho–Philips)   ii. *392*
Come gentle air! th'Eolian shepherd
said (Pope)   iv. *381*
Conceal, fond man, conceal the
mighty smart   v. *25*
Crine ruber, niger ore, brevis pede,
lumine laesus (Martial)   i. *366*
Difficilis, facilis, jucundus, acerbus es
idem (Martial)   i. *292*
Divine Euripides, this tomb we see
(Ion)   iv. *474*
Epitaphium Vivi Authoris (Cowley)
                      iv. *475*
Euripides, On (Ion)   iv. *474*
Grand Dieu, tes jugemens sont remplis
d'équité (Des Barreaux)   iv. *324*
Haste my rein-deer, and let us nimbly
go   iii. *519*
Here I am, / Riding upon a black
ram   v. *100, 129*
Here innocence and beauty lies, whose
breath   iv. *424*
Here lies the body of Daniel Saul
                      iv. *343*
Here Thomas Sapper lyes interr'd,
Ah why!   iv. *343*
Heureux! qui prés de toi (Sappho–
Boileau)   ii. *391*
Hic, O Viator, sub Lare parvulo
(Cowley)   iv. *475*
Homer, On (Alpheus)   iv. *473*
How are thy servants blest, O Lord!
(Addison)   iv. *235*
Ille mi par esse deo videtur (Sappho–
Catullus)   ii. *390*
In all thy humours, whether grave or
mellow (Martial–Addison)   i. *292*
In courts licentious, and a shameless
stage (Tickell)   iv. *397*
Lapland Odes   iii. *377, 519*
Lesbiam, Ad (Sappho–Catullus)
                      ii. *390*
Menander, On   iv. *474*
Messiah (Pope)   iii. *419*
My love was fickle once and changing
                      iv. *163*
My son, th'instruction that my words
impart (Ward)   iii. *533*
My time, O ye Muses, was happily
spent (Byrom)   v. *61*
No longer, Orpheus, shall thy sacred
strains (Antipater)   iv. *472*
Noble, generous, great, and good
                      ii. *317*
Nosses jocosae dulce sacrum Florae
(Martial)   iv. *67*
O Venus, beauty of the skies (Sappho–
Philips)   ii. *367*

Poems (*cont.*)

Orpheus, On (Antipater) iv. 472

Peculiar therefore is her way (Congreve) iii. 585

Proverbs, Paraphrase of (Ward) iii. 533

Scit thalamo servare fidem, sanctasque veretur (Addison) iii. 543

Solomon's Song, Paraphrase of iii. 456

Sophocles, On (Simonides) iv. 474

Spectator, On the (Tate) iv. 232

Spectator, To the Supposed Author of the (Tickell) iv. 397

Still in our ears Andromache complains (Alpheus) iv. 473

Tacta places, audita places, si non videre (Martial) i. 221

The Lord my pasture shall prepare (Addison) iv. 51

The man resolv'd and steady to his trust (Horace–Addison) v. 103

The Royal Progress (Tickell) v. 118

The spacious firmament on high (Addison) iv. 144

The very bees, O sweet Menander, hung iv. 474

This tomb be thine, Anacreon: all around (Antipater) iv. 473

Thou rising sun, whose gladsome ray iii. 377

Thy beard and head are of a diff'rent die (Martial–Addison) i. 366

To Mrs. —— on her Grotto v. 161

'Twas night, and Heav'n, a cyclops, all the day (Strada–Addison) v. 109

Underneath this marble hearse (Browne) iii. 185

Underneath this stone doth lye (Jonson) i. 141

Venus, An Hymn to (Sappho–Philips) ii. 367

When all thy mercies, O my God (Addison) iv. 96

When Brunswick first appear'd, each honest heart (Tickell) v. 118

When first the Tatler to a mute was turn'd (Tate) iv. 232

When Israel, freed from Pharaoh's hand (Watts) iv. 127

When my bright consort, now nor wife nor maid (Martial–Steele) iv. 239

When rising from the bed of death (Addison) iv. 322

Whilst in the dark on thy soft hand I hung (Martial–Steele) i. 221

Who first transcrib'd the famous Trojan war iv. 476

Why dost thou come, great Censor of thy Age (Martial–Addison) iv. 67

Poems (*cont.*)

Winde, gentle ever-green, to form a shade (Simonides) iv. 474

Ye nymphs of Solyma! begin the song (Pope) iii. 419

Poet: Boileau the most correct, among the moderns, ii. 220; usually begins by attacking reputation of others, ii. 482; the great p. does not always mind little niceties, iii. 5; chief qualifications of a, iii. 138, 563–4; more delighted with his productions than any other writer or artist, iv. 593; work of poetical ladies, v. 160.

Poetic justice, i. 168–70; iv. 461–5.

Poetical logarithms, ii. 356–7.

Poetical prose, a kind of, ii. 427.

'Poetically good, if I may use the phrase of our modern critics', iv. 464.

Poetry: its laws to be deduced from general sense and taste of mankind, i. 123; and politics the two amusements for all fools of eminence, i. 184; bawdry in, owing to lack of invention, i. 216; true and false wit in, i. 244–74; our modern smatterers in, i. 248; readers of, distinguished into three classes, i. 269; the property of every man in love, i. 386; feats of poetical activity, ii. 355–7; points, conceits, and turns of wit in modern, ii. 366; we fall short of the ancients in, ii. 467; the decay of, a favourite topic in the beginning poet, ii. 482; and music in public diversions, ii. 502–7; greatness in architecture and, ii. 542; clothes abstracted ideas in images, iii. 258; rules may prevent ill poets but never make good ones, iii. 450–1; something in, that elevates and astonishes the fancy, iii. 530; kinds of, iii. 563–4; divine imagery of, owing to sight, iv. 171; as many kinds of gardening as of, iv. 190; and physiognomy, iv. 344–5; use of pagan mythology in, iv. 361–4; to please is the first precept in, v. 26; kinds of epistolary, v. 112–14; popularity of love p., iv. 371.

Poets: Pindaric p. advised to write typographical poems, i. 248; Gothic taste of modern, i. 269; value themselves for sleeping on Parnassus, ii. 226; give a finer turn to a thought than prose writers, ii. 358–9; give and receive immortality, ii. 425; envy and detraction common in bad, ii. 481; turns of wit in modern, iii. 90; borrow more of their epithets from colours, iii. 544; heathen mythology allowed to women,

iv. 364; women p. ought to apply themselves to tapestry, v. 72.

Point(s) in poetry: as a kind of wit, i. 270; of wit, i. 316; in Cowley and Ovid, ii. 52–53; in modern lyrics, ii. 366; a rare example in Homer, ii. 399; and puerilities of Ovid, ii. 588; some of Milton's sentiments 'too much pointed', iii. 61; refining upon Shakespeare's, iii. 485. See also Turns.

Point of view, in the great, ii. 183.

Poison(s): the dagger or cup of p. in tragedy, ii. 397; pretended p. prepared by Rabelais, iii. 4; vended in London streets, iii. 354–5; men who have taken p. before Charles II, iv. 133.

Poke sleeves, a correspondent has written against, v. 116.

Poland: 'to hear what passes in Muscovy or', i. 45; the King of, i. 438; Casimir Liszynski, an atheist of, iii. 462; the Polish nettle, iv. 104.

Pole, Reginald, Cardinal, bearded figure of, iii. 222.

Pole, the, the tippet comes from beneath, i. 295.

Pole: a man who balances a p. on his chin or forehead, iv. 544.

Polite: most p. ages the least virtuous, i. 30; reading the most p. authors, ii. 127; a gallant and p. air, ii. 427; a man of figure in the p. world, iii. 437; what is gay and, ii. 567; the politer parts of the town, iii. 95; services of the French Academy to p. learning, iii. 96; advantages of a man of a p. imagination, iii. 538.

Politeness: excessive in the country, i. 487; which recommends impudence as good-breeding, ii. 400; false delicacy is affectation, not, iii. 15; cleanliness a mark of, v. 157; and elegance of Henry Boyle, v. 178.

Political: an essay in p. arithmetic, ii. 282–7; project of a p. academy in France, iii. 95–100; the whole practice of p. grimace, iii. 98; Swift and Arbuthnot on p. lying, iii. 100; sample of a p. treatise, iv. 536–8; the p. scratch, iv. 538.

Political State of Great Britain, i. lxxxix, xci, 27, 32, &c.

Politician(s): at Will's, i. 3; iv. 102; at the masquerade, i. 62; looks eagerly ahead to change, i. 395; histories composed by, ii. 171; visiting bawdy-houses, ii. 247; more reserved at their levées than military men, ii. 258; talkative p. among men as well as women, ii. 459–60; looks of p. and courtiers cannot de-

ceive, ii. 479; a seminary of petticoat p. in France, iii. 96–97; the art of being a, iii. 96–99; and coffee-houses, iii. 100, 506–9; iv. 90, 206; give only welcome advice to their sovereigns, iv. 182; 'the grave, solemn stalking pace' of the, iv. 345; their cynical view of human nature, iv. 416.

Politics: Spectator neutral in, i. 5, 72–73, 262; ii. 2, 517; iv. 65; and poetry the amusements for fools of eminence, i. 184; the state-pedant lost in, i. 438; wisdom and virtue more important than, i. 507; husband and wife talking, ii. 195; the Royal Society designed to divert men from, ii. 519; talk of, not encouraged for women, iii. 73; French Academy established to divert men of genius from, iii. 96; of the Widow-Club, iv. 518.

Politics (politicians), Persian, iv. 315.

Pollexfen, John, Discourse of Trade, i. 294.

Poltava. See Pultowa.

Polybius, on government, iii. 19.

POLYCARPUS, an agreeable man, ii. 591.

Polydorus and the myrtle (in the Aeneid), iii. 145.

Polypheme, Polyphemus: a man with great talents but void of discretion is like, ii. 376; paintings of, ii. 379; story of, regarded by many critics as an allegory, iii. 146; used the sea for a looking-glass, iii. 191; in modern poems, iv. 362; mentioned, ii. 562.

Pomatum for the hands, iv. 129.

Pomona, an attendant of Autumn, iii. 596.

Pomp(s): in allegory of luxury and avarice, i. 235; in church services, ii. 509–10; outshining others in, ii. 546; of sound more necessary to blank verse than rhyme, iii. 14; and triumphs balanced against vanity, iv. 136.

Pompey (the Triumvir): and Caesar both considered great by posterity, i. 423; recommended to the Romans by Cicero, iii. 43; his visit to Posidonius, iii. 130; at battle of Pharsalia, iii. 407–8; war with Caesar, iii. 447; 'it is necessary for me to sail, but not necessary for me to live', iv. 301.

Pond, Edward, Pond's Almanac, iii. 374.

Pontignan, the love-adventure of, i. 382–4.

Pont-Neuf at Paris, the equestrian statue on, i. 59.

Pontoons, a French term imported, ii. 151.

Pontus, Mithridates, King of, i. 392.

Poor, the: raising a fine for, i. 36; necessities of, supplied by superfluities of the wealthy, i. 277; relief of, ii. 199–201,

402–5; work only that they may live, ii. 286; a painter who paints them for nothing, ii. 382; relief to, at Christmas, ii. 550; foul play to be feared more from the indigent than the wealthy, iii. 1; *a dreadful thing to be poor and proud* (prov.), iii. 42; regard for the, iii. 47–49; to be compensated in the next world, iii. 50; living as well as Overseers of, iii. 402; scandalous appearance of, in London, iv. 11; virtues and vices of, iv. 139; 'For the benefit of', iv. 459; Sir ANDREW's plans to aid, iv. 467–8. *See also* Charity.

Poor Robin's Almanack, v. 101.

Pope, Alexander: contributions to *Spectator*, i. xlviii–xlix; iii. *419*, *517*; iv. *92*, *114*, *381*, *396*; other contributions attributed to, ii. *374*; iii. *74–75*, *510*, *526–7*, *597*; iv. *154*; v. *123*; Addison's advice to, i. *242*; on the *Spectator*, ii. *255*; 'an author, who is very justly esteemed among the best judges', ii. *482*; 'that ingenious gentleman', iv. *361*; edited *Works of John Sheffield*, iii. *75*; the late Miscellany published by, iv. *361*; referred to (?), iv. *396*; mentioned, iv. *32*, *309*. — *Critical Specimen*, i. *201*, *473*; ii. *414*; iii. *37*; — *Dunciad*: i. *9*, *260*; ii. *207*, *338*, *414*, *483*; iii. *350*; — *Eloisa to Abelard*, ii. *148*; — *Epistle to Dr. Arbuthnot*, ii. *91*, *483*; iii. *478*; — *Essay on Criticism*, i. *20*; ii. *322*; iii. *36*, *236*, *511*; iv. *500*; praise and analysis of, ii. *481–6*; — *Essay on Man*, iii. *452*, *526–7*; v. *10*, *123*, *125*, *139*, *171*; — *Guardian* essays, i. *77*; ii. *240*; — *A Key to the Lock*, v. *35*; — *A Letter to a Noble Lord*, iii. *206*; — *Letters*, ii. *483*, *485*; iii. *419*; iv. *114*, *361*, *396*; — *Messiah*, iii. *419–22*; query regarding authorship and reply, iv. *406–7*; — *Moral Essays*, iv. *466*, *527*; v. *94*; — *Narrative of Dr. Robert Norris*, i. *168*; — *Rape of the Lock*, i. *15*, *36*, *71*, *226*, *295*, *346*; ii. *6*, *276*, *436*; iv. *361*, *362*, *415*; — *The Temple of Fame*, 'an admirable poem which, I hope, will shortly see the light', iv. *396*; — *To Mr. John Moore*, iv. *458*.

Pope, Walter, 'she sung the Old Man's Wish to Sir ROGER', iii. 532.

Pope: Sixtus V, i. 99; Gregory the Great, ii. 134; puts on and off different accoutrements while officiating, ii. 290; Holiness the title given to, ii. 352; 'Procession of his Holiness', ii. 518, 551; who objected to effigy of a saint without a beard, iii. 221; and Cardinals, iv. 19; a very good hand at fomenting a division, iv. 206; Leo X, who delighted in buffoons, iv. 263–4; v. 108; letter from Emperor of China to, iv. 448–53; and the Devil burned in effigy, v. 106, 108.

Popery: country wakes a remnant of, ii. 135; treatment of prostitutes in countries where p. prevails, ii. 245; 'a zealous dissenter, an enemy of', ii. 249; the English fleet a security against, iii. 437; England's deliverance from arbitrary power and, iii. 443.

Popish: Plot, i. *243*, 331; 'a young P. cur', i. *509*; Mr. SPECTATOR suspected of being a P. priest, ii. 20; refinements in using force in persuasion, ii. 431.

Poppies, Widow TRUEBY's water distilled from, iii. 213.

Popular errors: the *Spectator's* campaign against, iv. 293.

Population: of Flanders 100 years ago, ii. 209; the source of wealth, ii. 209–12, 283, 402–3; of Great Britain, about eight million, ii. 284; balance of births and deaths, males and females, iii. 27–28.

Populus virorum (Florus), iii. 28.

Porcia: a model wife, ii. 487; and Lucretia, iv. 28; and Brutus a virtuous couple, v. 75.

Porcupine: a beautiful woman compared to a, iii. 416; a simile about, iv. 38.

Porpoises, have warm blood and entrails of a hog, iv. 349.

Port (wine): 'good solid edifying', i. *181*; hogsheads of red, i. 310; hogsheads of neat, ii. 529; *Herefordshire* poured into *Port O Port*, iii. 355; four tun of, iv. 542.

Porter, Mary: Emilia in *The Man of Mode*, i. *278*; Hermione in *The Distressed Mother*, iii. *239*, 371; Philadelphia in *The Amorous Widow* (to be acted for her benefit), iii. 370–1, 395.

Porter: a lady's, i. 192; a nobleman's, i. 406; speaks his disrespect by stealing out his tongue, iii. 322; 'Robin' at Will's Coffee-house, iii. 490; in *The Fatal Marriage*, iv. 205; at Lady Betty Clack's, iv. 513; to a quack, iv. 553.

Portland, Richard Weston, 1st Earl of, Clarendon's sketch of, iv. 45.

Portmanteau, iv. 504.

Portrait- or face-painting: ii. 425; English superiority in, iv. 496–7.

Portraits: in De Coverley Hall, i. 449–52; done in Roman costume, ii. 12.

Port-Royal, Gentlemen of, coined the term *egotism*, iv. 519–20.

Portugal: death of King of, i. 276; fruits of, i. 295; a Portuguese word, ii. 299; mail, ii. 476; onions, ii. 530; treaty with, ii. *578*; v. *183*; snuff, iii. *278*; Vertot's history of Revolutions in, iii. 301; Don Sebastian of, iii. 301; iv. 263; James Miller, lately come from, iv. 32.

Portuguese wines, importation of, i. *181*; ii. *578*.

Porus, King, to be personated by Pen-kethman, i. 129, 150, 151.

'Pos' (positive), ii. 34, 301.

Posidonius: his indifference to pain, iii. 130.

Posie: of a ring, i. 185, 248; ii. *183*; inscribed on a knife, i. 246; on a wed-ding-ring, i. 378.

Positive: manner of Mr. SPECTATOR objected to, ii. 119–20; dangers of being too p. in disputation, ii. 274; critics who write in a p. dogmatic way, ii. 484.

Posset-drink, i. *241*, 420; ii. 65.

Possets, receipts for salves and, ii. 487.

Post (situation): we should fill honour-ably the p. in which Providence has placed us, ii. 352–3, 374; adversity the p. of honour in human life, ii. 422.

Post Boy: i. *32*; ii. *106*; iv. *112, 206, 385, 458, 459*; v. *34, 114*; circulation of, i. xxv; advertisements quoted from, ii. 182, 250; mentioned, iii. 380; dis-patch from, iii. 439–41.

Posterity: adjusts characters of illus-trious persons, i. 423; an author's duty towards, ii. 155; 'would fain see p. do something for us', iv. 594.

Post-existence, or transmigration, ii. 325.

Post-Man: circulation of, i. xxv; read at Child's, i. 4; quoted, i. *56*; iv. *308, 449, 458, 460*; mentioned, ii. 198, 277; iii. 380; iv. *173*; the famous cosmetic mentioned in, i. 221.

Postmaster-General, petition for being made, v. 150.

Postscript, a woman writes her mind in her, i. 339.

Posture(s): of a Merry-Andrew, ii. 206; a woman in a toying, iii. 55; which expresses languishment, iv. 221; polite p. for listening to a narrative in a coffee-house, iv. 354–5.

Posture-makers on the stage, ii. 504–5.

Posture-man, i. 128.

Posture-master, to instruct politicians, iii. 97–98.

Potatoes, as bread for beggars, ii. 402.

Potcheare, Captain. *See* Pottiere.

Pot-herbs, in a garden, iv. 189; fruits and, v. 2.

Potion, given to a horse, ii. 386.

Pottages, Jean, as drolls in France, i. 201.

Pottiere, Dominick, his cruelty, iii. 302–3.

POTTLE, TOM, letter from (on adultera-tion of wines), iii. 353–5.

Poultices, receipts for applying, ii. 487.

Poultry: Sir ROGER's, i. 489; care of, a great enemy to the countenance, iv. 333.

Pounce (in *The Tender Husband*), Estcourt as, iv. 157.

Pound at Knightsbridge, a horse clapped into the, iv. 93.

Poverty: in allegory of luxury and avarice, i. 235–6; fear of, and shame of, i. 469; shame of, in court of Louis XIV, ii. 48; inconveniences and morti-fications of, ii. 89; men of estates, why reduced to, ii. 251–2; only an apparent evil to a just man, ii. 421–2; obscures virtues of liberality and munificence, ii. 500; skill in dissembling, ii. 593; and want accompany slavery, iii. 22; stands in our imaginations in place of guilt, iii. 48; silence of our p. is a re-commendation, iii. 346; modesty usually attending faultless, iii. 409–10; and old age not evils, iii. 431; scorn and p. the consequences of vanity, iv. 124; balanced against avarice, iv. 136; virtue covered by, iv. 138; and wealth, iv. 138–41; allegorical figure of, iv. 140; as a misfortune, iv. 507; natural product of vicious and impu-dent acts, v. 65.

Povey, Charles: *Visions of Sir Heister Ryley*, i. *10*; *General Remark*, ii. 594.

Powder(s): vendor of p. and washballs, ii. 477; and other medicinal prepara-tions, iii. 206; for colouring the hair, iv. 129; and ball, in modern warfare, iv. 363.

Powder-bags, iv. 195.

Powder-Watt, the vendor of powder and washballs, ii. 477.

Powell, George: in *Sir Martin Mar-All*, i. *24*; to represent Alexander in a pro-jected opera, i. 130; Alexander in *The Rival Queens*, i. *130, 151*; Orestes in *The Distressed Mother*, i. *130*; iii. *239*; Portius in *Cato*, i. *130*; Lear, i. *170*; often raises himself a loud clap by ranting, i. 171; benefit for, i. 172–3; letter from, on his role as Orestes in *The Distressed Mother*, iii. 34; the haughty G. P. to play Falstaff, iii. 291; Prospero in *The Tempest*, v. 26.

Powell, Jeremiah (a Director of the Bank), a subscriber, i. *xc*.

Powell, Martin (puppeteer): his puppet-

show under the Piazzas in Covent-Garden, i. 61–65, 78; iii. 400; iv. 281, 514; 'the ingenious Mr. Powell', i. 130; ii. 581; his benefit performance for charity children, iii. 400; insinuations made against, at Bath, iii. 401.

Powell, Mrs.: in *The Lancashire Witches*, ii. 57; benefit for, v. 47.

Power: laws against exorbitant p. should be made in a good reign, i. 415; application, not possession, makes it honourable, ii. 239; rules for conversing with men of, ii. 592; danger of unlimited p. in a ruler, iii. 20–21; gratifying to the mind of man, iv. 273.

Powers, division of, in Roman and English constitutions, iii. 19–20.

Pox, medicine for treatment of, advertised, iv. 59.

Pragmatical, lacqueys are saucy and, iv. 207.

Praise: of an ignorant man is only good-will, ii. 238; one of the attendants of virtue, ii. 374; the art of praising, ii. 425; iv. 457, 475; from God, not from men, our only concern, ii. 500–1; soliciting p. from the undiscerning, iii. 449; and obloquy frequently proceed from the same mouth, iv. 45; merit of acknowledging p. of others, iv. 396.

Praise, love of: right and wrong effect of, i. 160–2; letter to a man over-run with, i. 163; often has good consequences, i. 312; stronger in women than in men, i. 312; how to be valued, ii. 238–9; a universal passion, ii. 370–4; unmixed with flattery, a desirable pleasure, ii. 425; leads to contests for superiority, iii. 277–8; found in extraordinary persons, iv. 150–1.

Pranks committed in London, iii. 340–1.

PRATE-APACE, Mr., iv. 513.

PRATER, THOMAS, 'practitioner in the law', i. 151.

Prater, danger done by a giddy, ii. 350.

Pratt, Mrs. John, iii. 439.

PRAXINOE, wife of THESPIS, ii. 407.

Praxiteles, ii. 341.

Prayer: affectation in, i. 162; an exercise of virtue, i. 395–6; cawing of rooks and crows a kind of natural, i. 453; praying of the Presbyterians, ii. 80; Plato's dialogue on, ii. 310–13; absent lovers who offered up a certain p. for each other, ii. 437; examples of, iii. 466–70; advantages of set forms of, iii. 470; Agur's, iv. 139.

Prayer, Book of Common: the General Confession in, 1. 337; ii. 79; reading of, ii. 78–81; the Absolution in, ii. 79, 420; the Thanksgivings in, ii. 79; 'the best prayers that ever were compos'd', ii. 80; as perfect as any thing of human institution, ii. 80–81; the Commandments, ii. 420.

Prayer, the Lord's, i. 337; ii. 313–14; we pray for forgiveness as we forgive others, ii. 214, 313.

Prayer, the Soldier's, i. 197.

Prayer, the Witches', i. 262.

Prayer-book, in LEONORA's library, i. 156; 'together lie her p. and paint', i. 340; each parishioner given a, i. 460; mentioned, iii. 9.

Prayers: witches saying p. backwards, i. 481; audible repetition of, in church, ii. 419–20; the bell which calls to p. twice a day, ii. 526; titles and epithets in, iii. 130–1; 'the daughters of Jupiter', iii. 467; improved by use of Biblical phrases, iii. 514–15; a congregation reproved for standing at, iv. 106.

Preacher, 'The great British' (Tillotson), iv. 503.

Preachers: affectation among, i. 162; addicted to punning in time of James I, i. 260; contentions between parson and squire, i. 462; their subject-matter commands respect, ii. 56; rival p. who quoted Latin, ii. 359–60; English p. sparing in gesture, iii. 521.

Preaching: a handsome elocution more important than originality of sermons, i. 442; undue exactness about details in, ii. 45–46; of the Presbyterians, ii. 80; manner in, iv. 427.

Precedence, rank and: in this world and the next, ii. 351–4; late disputes concerning, iv. 386.

Precepts: few original p. in Horace's *Art of Poetry*, ii. 483; exemplified by Pope in the *Essay on Criticism*, ii. 484–5; of morality less effective than examples, iii. 67–68.

Precipices: high rocks and p. pleasing to the imagination, iii. 540; mis-shapen rocks and, iii. 564.

Precise: unfashioned fellow, ii. 105; humour of the Puritans, ii. 135; a p. set of people (parish-clerks), iii. 401.

Predestination: Milton's ostentatious excursions on, iii. 62; abstruse doctrine of, in *PL*, iii. 142.

Pre-eminence: in ourselves, as a motive of laughter, i. 200–1, 223; ii. 466; absurd ideas of, ii. 185; based on quality of fortune, body, or mind, ii.

351–2; pedantic scorn of fortune and, ii. 554; of Marlborough, v. 179.

Pre-existence of women in animals (Simonides), ii. 319, 325.

Preface to Bishop of St. Asaph's Sermons, iii. 440–5.

Prefaces, modern, savour strongly of egotism, iv. 521.

Preferment: that market for, a great man's levée, ii. 257; a letter on, iv. 204; methods of awarding, iv. 262–4.

Pregnancy: the hoop-petticoat a concealment for, ii. 6–7; a dwarf's demands during, ii. 557–8; letter from T. B., describing his wife's whims during, iii. 195–7.

Prejudice(s): against foreign customs and dresses, i. 215; derived from a stranger's appearance, i. 368–9; and passions of a contemporary author, i. 424; and error the foundation of the world's opinion, ii. 280; want of, in LUCCEIUS, ii. 309; most men blinded with, ii. 310; good to clear our minds of p. and prepossession, ii. 318; means of recovering our souls from, ii. 341; towards atheism is not impartiality, ii. 413; virtues obscured by, ii. 491; received from parents, ii. 523; against Milton's language, iii. 14; honest p. in favour of one's country, iii. 18; souls too large to be taken with popular, iii. 48; honest p. in the heart of a true Englishman, iii. 437; the inlets of, to the mind, iii. 495; strength of, iv. 17–18; letter on, received, iv. 588.

Prelates, arraignment of the seven, v. 175.

Prenesto (in Camilla), i. 93; ii. 82.

Prentice: attempted seduction of a p. seamstress, ii. 216–19, 316; disputing with a hackney coachman, ii. 291; saved from seduction by reading a Spectator, ii. 316; 'speaks his disrespect by an extended finger', iii. 322.

Preparation-Sermons, i. 199.

Preparations, weekly, devotional books entitled, i. 341.

Prepossession(s): and heats that cleave to parties, ii. 1; good to clear our minds of prejudice and, ii. 318.

'Prerogative', use of the word, iv. 202–3.

Presbyterians, their praying and preaching, ii. 80.

Present, the: our restlessness in, ii. 322–3; alone is ours, iii. 150; has been compared to an isthmus in eternity, v. 18.

Present State of England, The, iv. 387.

Preserving: art of, taught to young women, iii. 140, 226, 254; and pickling, iii. 205–6.

'Preserving of the Female Game, A Bill for the Better', iii. 194.

President of the Widow-Club: has disposed of six husbands, iv. 516; letter from, iv. 556–61.

Pressed as a common soldier, i. 96.

Prester John's country, iv. 256.

Preston, Christopher, iv. 32.

Preston, Elizabeth, iv. 32.

Presumption: and diffidence, i. 370; our lack of knowledge should check our, ii. 423.

Pretender, the (James Francis Edward Stuart): in allegory of public credit, i. 16; report of death of, iii. 439–41.

Pretenders: to mirth, ii. 591; to negligence, iii. 6.

Preterperfect tense, spelling of, ii. 33.

Prettiness: example of a, in PL, below the genius of Milton, iii. 174.

Pretty: fellows, i. 393; ii. 105, 514; iii. 182; gentleman, i. 437; rake among the men, ii. 105; 'the prettiest sort of woman in the world', iii. 465; has made a p. penny, iv. 62.

PRETTYMAN: his behaviour in the month of May, iv. 221.

'Prevailing gentle art, the', caution against, iii. 496–7.

Prevent (anticipate), iii. 47; iv. 326; &c.

Preventing aspect, which discourages salutations, ii. 508.

Priam, ii. 312, 562; Hector and, copied in Pallas and Evander, ii. 563.

Prick-eared cur, i. 509.

Pricked dances, a beau's head filled with, ii. 571.

Priddon (or Prydden), Sarah, alias Sally Salisbury, ii. 246–7.

Pride: destroys all symmetry and grace in woman, i. 139; and prejudices, i. 491; often passes for religious zeal, ii. 228; the peacock in all his, ii. 531; PATETIA's favourite passion, ii. 547; sourness and p. causing untractable tempers, ii. 568; prevents us from taking advice, iii. 82; as an obstacle to self-knowledge, iii. 326; the mark of the atheist, iii. 431; the most ordinary spring of action among men, iii. 477; the universal passion, iv. 131; natural p. and ambition of the soul, iv. 318; the Spectator a cure for, iv. 458; undue p. in ancestry, v. 91.

Priesthood, no satires upon p. and marriage in the Spectator, ii. 517.

Prig: 'the old Prig is dead' (Louis XIV), iii. 508; Mesnager called an insignificant, iv. 207; 'the old Prig', iv. 500.

PRIM, Madam, an alderman's lady, iii. 415.

PRIM, Mr. (dancing-master), his soft air in dancing, iii. 415.

Prime Minister, a Mussulman who hoped to become, v. 65.

Primroses and violets, iii. 594; iv. 189; v. 126.

Prince, Mr., his dancing on the stage, iv. 146.

Prince, anecdote of, defending his father before Roman Senate, iii. 404.

Printing: a method of instructing in virtue, i. 507; invention of, has given permanence to ideas, ii. 154; the noblest and most beneficial of arts, iii. 381; fine p. in Europe today, iii. 381-2; used for scattering prejudice and ignorance, iv. 591.

Prints, our common (newspapers), i. 507; ii. 153.

Prints, mythological figures in, ii. 60.

Prior, Matthew: a writer for the Examiner, i. xvii; 'Hans Carvel's Wife' quoted, ii. 59; satirized(?), ii. 139; mentioned, iii. 100; his Epilogue to Phaedra and Hippolitus, iii. 267; 'An Epitaph', iv. 462; mentioned, v. 66.

Prisoners for debt, i. 350.

Private: 'privately dissolute, publicly decent', ii. 112; differences between p. and public behaviour, ii. 388; silent perfections which are transacted in, ii. 500; joys and satisfactions of a p. life, iii. 517-18.

Privy Counsellor(s), i. 260, 392, 439; ii. 130; v. 150.

Probability: passages in PL lacking in, ii. 563; iii. 60; in stories dealing with spirits, iii. 571.

Probable: and the marvellous in the epic, iii. 88, 144-6; Jesuits well read in controversies of p. doctrines, iii. 98.

Probatum est, iv. 459.

Procession of his Holiness: 'the late designed affair', ii. 518; Sir ROGER thinks Sir ANDREW had a hand in, ii. 551.

Procrastination: dangers of, i. 112-15; and addiction to pleasure, ii. 95; an enemy to thrift, iii. 2.

Procris and Cephalus, iv. 380-1.

Procrustes, iron bed of, i. 247.

Procuress: taking in a girl at a brothel, ii. 246; in The Humorous Lieutenant, ii. 535-6; conversation between a p. and a country girl at an inn, ii. 536-7;

letter from a p. to a noble lord, ii. 569-70.

Prodicus, author of 'The Choice of Hercules', ii. 221.

Prodigality, arises from shame of poverty, i. 469.

Prodigy (-ies): and enchantments in region of false wit, i. 271; the hoop-petticoat regarded as a, ii. 6; preceding the civil war in Rome, iii. 61.

Prodigies, great natural geniuses the p. of mankind, ii. 126-7.

Profaneness, profanity: 'the expletives of oaths', i. 345; 'talked and swore loud', i. 350; a device to cure men of, iii. 398-9; effect of Spectator on, iv. 128; our prevailing impiety, iv. 394-5. See also Swearing.

Professions: origin of, in love of pleasure or fear of want, i. 232; effect on men's behaviour, ii. 271-2; regulation wanting in, iii. 108-9. — The Three Learned Professions: i. 88, 449; iii. 108; iv. 274; overcrowding in, i. 88-92, 197; precedency in, iv. 387; hats for, iv. 400.

Progne, Metamorphosis of (Horace), i. 190.

Project, a: for regulating shop-signs, i. 115-18; for an opera, i. 127-32; for devices for making poetry, ii. 356-7; for regulating cries of London, ii. 474-8; for a Political Academy in France, iii. 95-100; for a newspaper, iv. 92-94; for a news-letter of whispers, iv. 111-14; for discovery of the longitude, iv. 589. See also Proposals.

Projector(s): letter from a, i. 115-18; female, ii. 531; Dr. T. W., iii. 484; 'apt to turn', iv. 85; ruined by misemployed hopes, iv. 410; schemes from, iv. 587.

Projects, a book of, proposing annual prizes for handicraft trades, ii. 133-4, 181.

Prometheus: his man of clay, ii. 325; nailed to a rock (in Aeschylus), iii. 338.

Promise, breach of, between two courtiers, ii. 180.

Promise, Land of: Abraham travelling towards (in PL), iii. 387; spies sent by Moses into, iv. 254; apostasies of the Jews in, iv. 256-7.

Promisers, impertinent, iv. 75.

Promises: a beau's head filled with, ii. 571; neglect of, iv. 75-76.

PRONE, THOMAS (the wild boar killed by Mrs. Tofts), letter from, i. 93 (referred to, iv. 438).

Pronunciation: affectation of mispronouncing words, i. 195; rapidity of English, ii. 33; talk with a friend on the force of, ii. 398; The TEMPLAR's essay on p. and action, iv. 432–7 (referred to, iv. 440, 487).

Propertius, Sextus, Virgil praised by, ii. 482.

Property: precarious in France, ii. 211; about seven-eighths of the people without, ii. 284; we should expect nothing beyond our own p. or labour, ii. 599.

Prophecy (-ies): of the coming of Jesus, ii. 313; iv. 258; of the Harpy in the *Aeneid*, iii. 306; of the Sybils, iv. 258.

Proposals: for sale of perspective-glasses, ii. 472–3; of marriage, quoted, iv. 359–60; for an organ in St. Paul's, iv. 479–81; for a pair of new globes, iv. 481–3. *See also* Projects.

Propriety: speculation in p. of speech, ii. 469; of sentiments in Virgil, ii. 586.

Prose: a kind of poetical, ii. 427; methodical regularity of, absent in Pope's *Essay on Criticism*, ii. 483; avoiding style of p. in the epic, iii. 11–15; blank verse needs more assistance, to keep it from flatness of, iii. 14.

Proserpine: in Lully's opera, i. 123; captured by Dis, iii. 373.

Proserpine (opera), i. *122*, 123.

Prosopolepsia, More's account of, i. 368–9.

Prospect(s): and points of view, ii. 436; a variation of the, ii. 552; a beautiful p. as delightful as a demonstration, iii. 538; kinds of, which please the imagination, iii. 541, 549–52; savage p. suggested by the *Iliad*, iii. 564.

PROSPER, WILL: a tale-bearer, i. 83; ordered to out-stare 'starers', i. 86.

Prosperity: a great cherisher of good-nature, ii. 165; of the guilty and foolish, ii. 421; like too great indulgence of a fond mother, ii. 422; some virtues seen only in, ii. 500; man unable to bear p. with moderation, iii. 61.

Prostitute(s): OMNAMANTE a witty, ii. 70; treatment of, in Roman Catholic countries, ii. 245; history of several, ii. 245–8; Mr. SPECTATOR's meeting with a, ii. 534–5; poor and public, ii. 534–7; the same easy creature in all months of the year, iii. 374–5; Sir ROGER's encounter with a, iii. 531–3.

Prostitution, ii. 216–19, 244–8, 303–5, 316, 534–7.

Protestant(s): 'Were I less a', ii. 159;

a very good P. who lies with a Roman Catholic, ii. 247; demonstrations, ii. 518, 551; v. 106; conference between P. and Papists, in reign of Queen Mary, iv. 142; French King should be obliged to tolerate, iv. 207.

Protestations, a beau's head filled with, ii. 571.

Protier, Paul (quack), iv. *61*.

'Proud stomach', i. 468.

Proverbs, Book of: Ward's paraphrase of chap. vii, iii. 533–5.

Proverb(s): 'the old kitchen', ii. 531; three Italian, iii. 2; proverbial simplicity, iv. 306; short p. one way of conveying advice, iv. 317; a Sicilian, iv. 581.

Providence: the great design of, ii. 214; discretion like an under-agent of, ii. 375; inscrutable, ii. 420–3; iv. 211–14; a garden gives us a great insight into the wisdom of, iv. 192; conduct of, in formation of a human body, iv. 441–4. *See also* God.

Proving matters which no one would deny, ii. 46, 71–73.

Prude(s): and coquettes, i. 375, 429; ii. 29; iv. 316; v. 24; books written against, i. 392; acts always in contradiction, ii. 315; 'demolishing a', ii. 345–6; at Lady AIRY's session of scandal, iii. 297; letter from a, iii. 370–1; MATILDA MOHAIR an insufferable, iv. 261; MELISSA, a noted, v. 9; often preserves her reputation after losing her virtue, v. 24; mentioned, v. 48; SARAH DAINTY, the greatest p. of the parish, v. 130.

Prudence: charity to be managed with, ii. 198; prudential considerations, ii. 215; the prudent man's mirth, ii. 268; acting in the prudential way, ii. 282; should temper heats of devotion, ii. 289; necessary in managing servants, ii. 292; and human success, iii. 42–45; a prudent friend to be preferred to a zealous one, iii. 446; proposal of marriage by a man of, iv. 359–60. *See also* Caution, Discretion.

Prudentius Clemens, Aurelius, *Apophthegmata*, v. 7.

Prue, Steele's letters to, ii. 60–64.

PRUE, Miss, gone into the country, iii. 183.

Pruriency; of inordinate desire, ii. 94; indulging a, ii. 567.

Prydden, Sarah. *See* Priddon.

Psalm(s): raised by the parish clerk, 1. 122–3; tunes, i. 461; iii. 8; the Singing-Psalms, i. 461; introducing Italian airs

into singing of the Hundredth, ii. 305–6; Addison's paraphrase of Psalm xxiii, iv. 51 (set to music, iv. 236); Watts's paraphrase of Psalm cxiv, iv. 127–8; 'when the p. was given out', iv. 285.

Psalmanazar, George: to play in an opera, i. 65.

'Pshaw': FRANK JOLLY endeavouring to forget the word, iv. 9; pishes and pshaws, iv. 40.

Ptolemaic hypothesis, described in *PL*, iii. 281.

Public, the: readily distinguishes between wit and ill-nature, ii. 167; painful to be exposed to derision of, ii. 518; relishes ridicule of eminent writers, ii. 519.

'Public, For the Good of the': a favourite phrase of quacks, iv. 551.

Public: zeal for p. cause, apt to breed passions, i. 510; assembly, ii. 107; day, ii. 112; place, ii. 112; prints, ii. 153; spirit, ii. 187; incident in a p. room, ii. 386–7; men differ in their secret thoughts and p. actions, ii. 388; modesty in p. speaking, ii. 397–8; some virtues seen only in a p. capacity, ii. 500; support of p. funds, a patriotic duty, iii. 290.

Public good: zeal for, induces uncharitable and barbarous notions, i. 512; projects of virtuosi for, ii. 357.

Public house, ii. 108.

Public peace: disturbing the, ii. 226, 233; and tranquillity, iii. 19.

Public spirit: men of, ii. 463; charity schools instances of, iii. 48.

Public table: keeping a, i. 352; dining at a, i. 466.

'Publicly decent, privately dissolute', ii. 112.

Publilius Syrus, ii. *359, 375, 449*; maxim upon drunkenness, iv. 543.

PUCELLA, (kept by an old bachelor): letter from, ii. 575–6.

Puckle, James, *The Club*, i. *39*.

Pudding: I love thee like (prov.), i. *201*; *the proof of the p. is in the eating* (prov.), iv. 538.

Puddings, 'gave her name to two sorts of', iii. 206.

Puddings, Jack, drolls in Great Britain, i. 202.

Puddle, 'makes the p. boil', i. 184.

Puerility (-ies): of Ovid, ii. 588; of Claudian, iii. 230; in modern pastorals, iv. 363.

Pufendorf, Samuel, iii. 51.

Puffs: powder-bags and, iv. 195.

PUGG: former incarnations of, iii. 273; a lady's monkey, iv. 271.

Pullets and, iii. 402.

Pulpit: at Lloyd's coffee-house, i. 196; p.-cloth, i. 460; the carpet of a, ii. 510; decorated with greens, ii. 600. *See also* Preachers, Preaching.

Pulse: an irregular, i. 105; a regular, ii. 197.

Pulteney, William (afterwards Earl of Bath), iv. *309*.

Pultowa, Battle of, i. *182*; ii. 36.

Pulvil, pulvillio (powder for wig), i. 271; iv. 345.

Pump, the, in *The Fortune Hunters*, i. 93.

Pumps (slippers), i. 388.

Pun(s), punning: Punning Club at Oxford, i. 76; in a heroic poem, like a rebus on a noble building, i. 251; the seeds of, in all men, i. 259; as a species of false wit, i. 259–63; Mr. Swan, the famous punster, i. 261; consists in resemblances of words, i. 265; iii. 560; and true wit combine to form mixed wit, i. 267; those who prefer a quibble to solid sense and elegant expression, i. 269; allegorical figure of, i. 273; 'one word made to look two ways', ii. 53; in *PL*, ii. 590; iii. 61–63; monopoly of, in St. John's Coll., Cambridge, iii. 483; causes of, iii. 484–5; antipathy to, iv. 48; and 'bites', iv. 288–9; absence of, in *The Faerie Queene*, iv. 429; men whose reputation depends on, iv. 544. — Examples of, in the *Spectator*, i. 361; ii. 305; iii. 17–18; iv. 63, 102, 288, 470; v. 38.

Punch: and a pig dance a minuet together, i. 64; his reflections on the French, i. 65; to be reprimanded when extravagant, i. 144; Punch's Theatre, i. *198. See also* Punchinello.

Punch, four hundred bowls of, iv. 542.

Punch-bowl: and angels, as a sign, i. 118; in a China shop, iii. 245.

Punchinello, i. 62, 64, 65; iii. 401; iv. *290*.

Punctuality: of the merchant, ii. 186; merchants suffer by want of, in dealings of persons above them, ii. 334–5.

Punctum stans, a fixed point: Eternity with God a, v. 20.

Punic faith (prov.), ii. *186*.

Punishment(s): in grammar schools, ii. 115, 160–2; proposed for profligates, ii. 297; of children, ii. 336; murder and petty larceny require different, iii. 16; rewards and p. after death, iii. 43; of atheists, iii. 462; designed more for deterring the innocent than chastising

the guilty, iv. 151; Sparta exact in distributing rewards and, iv. 528.

Punting (a term in basset), iii. 182.

Puppet: a jointed doll from France, ii. 378–81.

Puppet-show(s): popularity of, i. 61, 197; 'Whittington and his Cat', i. 63; 'Susanna, or Innocence Betrayed', i. 65; spectators proper at, i. 86; 'an artificial composition of wood and wire', i. 119; to be introduced into a projected opera, i. 130 (this essay praised, ii. 303); some ladies offended at *Spectators* on, i. 142; Don Quixote and the, i. 207; party-patches at, i. 348; women of quality spend whole mornings at, i. 425; children staring and gaping at, iii. 368; safer than opera for women, iii. 374; charity performance by, iii. 400–1; LYSANDER 'slain' at a, iii. 417; mentioned, i. 127, 142, 243, 331, *391*; iv. *514*.

Puppy, WILL WIMBLE exchanges a p. between a couple of friends, i. 447.

'Puppy', impertinence of a noisy, v. 42.

Purcell, Henry: passing from song to speaking in his operas, i. 120; his compositions not admired by Italian artists, i. 121.

Pure, purest (excellent), ii. 219, 530; iii. 72; iv. 182, 314, 406.

Purgatory, ii. 87; a ridiculous notion, ii. 155; vicious writers continuing in, while their books influence posterity, ii. 155; the married state compared to, iv. 209.

Puritans: objected to country-wakes, ii. 135; their precise humour, ii. 135; enthusiasm and hypocrisy of, iv. 117.

Purity: of thought sanctifies a virtuous man, ii. 500; a mind with a habit of innocence and, ii. 559; true delicacy consists in p. of affection, iii. 15; of descriptions of love in *PL*, iii. 286; cleanliness and p. of mind, v. 157.

Purl: a double mug of, i. 374; 'drank a glass of p. to recover appetite', iii. 155.

'Purling stream, the': in LEONORA's garden, i. 158.

Purple: for mourning, i. 275; hood, ii. 532.

Purse: skill of the p. the cardinal virtue of this life, i. 444; *Ninety-nine Plagues of an Empty*, ii. 89.

Purses: separate p. between man and wife unnatural, iii. 53; needlework on, iii. 206; v. 72.

Pursuit: allegorical figure of, encompassing Minerva's buckler, iii. 337.

PUSH, PETER, letter from (is laying siege to an obstinate female), iv. 536.

Puss (a hare), i. 477.

Put: 'the old put', iii. 343; 'queer old put', iii. 438.

Puttenham, George, i. *254*.

PUZZLE, TOM, an immethodical disputant, iv. 187–8.

Pygmalion and the statue (in Ovid), ii. 427.

Pygmy (-ies): that part of India inhabited by, i. 130; a woman but a p. without her head-dress, i. 414; pun in Milton's description of, iii. 61–62.

Pylades: in *The Distressed Mother*, iii. 242; and Orestes, iii. 498.

Pyper, John, translation of d'Urfé, i. *154*.

Pyramid(s): one measured by Mr. SPECTATOR, i. 3, 425; head-dresses in shape of, i. 414; pyramidical form of women's dress, ii. 74; trees in cones, globes, and, iii. 552; of Egypt, still to be seen, iii. 555.

Pyrrhus: his victory over the Romans and conversation with Cyneas, ii. 211–12; 'this ambitious madman', ii. 212; contrasted with Hannibal, ii. 444; stone in ring of, v. 28.

Pyrrhus (Neoptolemus): gained reputation by inventing a dance, i. 284; as portrayed by Booth in *The Distressed Mother*, iii. 236 ('the King of France had not a better strut', iii. 241).

Pyrrhus and Demetrius (opera), i. 23, 24; ii. *329*, *506*.

Pythagoras: his first rule, ii. 233–4; on transmigration, ii. 325; iii. 274; on the mysteries of numbers, ii. 361; his discovery of musical sounds, iii. 238; his precept to his disciples, iv. 71; form used, in breaking silence, iv. 471; his advice to his scholars, v. 4; Dacier's *Life* of, ii. *233*, *361*, *444*; iii. *238*, *274*; iv. *71*, *471*; v. *4*.

Pythian records, ii. 408.

Pythian Apollo, temple of, ii. 406.

Python, Apollo's victory over the serpent, iv. 329.

Q, as signature in *Spectator*, ii. 360, 473.

Q–p–t–s, Lady, iv. 538, 540.

Quacks, medical: 'stragglers from the body of regular troops', i. 90; and pretenders, i. 139; 'learned gentlemen in plush doublets', ii. 28; vend their wares from a stage at Tower Hill, ii. 28–29; account of, iv. 58–62, 551–5.

Quack-Vintners, The, iii. *353–4*.

Quadrant, invention of, by the Royal Society, ii. 519.

Quae Genus, the whole book of, digested into sermons, ii. 360.

Quail, iii. 196.

Quail-pipe, i. 448.

Quaker(s): costume of, at the masquerade, i. 37, 63; trimmed close and almost cut to the quick, i. 71; 'Gospel-Gossips' frequent among, i. 198; EPHRAIM, a stage-coach companion, ii. 22–25, 439; a Quaker's visit to an Anglican service, ii. 510; letter from HEZEKIAH BROADBRIM, ii. 577; their vagaries of error and enthusiasm, iii. 484; a letter in the style of, iv. 514–15; a rake transformed into a, v. 47; a young Quaker woman in a coach, v. 156–7.

Quality: the, i. 119; persons of q., i. 129, 142, 176, &c.

Quarrel(s): a beau succeeds by quarrelling impertinently, ii. 111; a coquette has false q. with men, ii. 459; midnight, ii. 512; of Scaramouche with a Swiss officer, iii. 3; now on foot in London, iii. 435; of the Swiss cantons, iv. 91, 206; between Rechteren and Mesnager, iv. 205–8; sources of marital, v. 79–80; of the League, iv. 91.

Quarter-day, i. 395.

Quarter-Session(s): Sir ROGER fills the chair at, i. 9; suing at a, i. 498; party-spirit at, ii. 3; chairman at a, iii. 355.

Quarter-staff, iii. 194; iv. 31.

Quarto, author of a, sets himself above author of an octavo, iv. 386.

Quartos, in LEONORA's library, i. 153.

'Quash an indictment' (legal jargon), iv. 477.

Quavers and graces in playing a cat-call, iii. 351.

Queen of Persia: pin-money of, iii. 54; 'Queen's Girdle' and 'Queen's Veil' in Persia, iii. 54.

Queen's Bagnio, iii. *225*.

Queen's Birthday (ball), iii. 418.

Queen's Box at the theatre, iii. 418.

Queens, an embassy of Indian, ii. 532.

Queerity (quearity) in his aspect, i. 76.

QUERY, CHRISTOPHER, testimonial praising *Spectator* 228, iv. 459.

Questions, a cure for asking unnecessary, iv. 459.

Questions and Commands, iii. 320; iv. 287; an innocent diversion, ii. 451; 'that laudable and primitive diversion', iv. 270.

Quevedo Villegas, Dom Francisco de, iii. 222; iv. *15*, *492*.

Quibbles. *See* Puns.

QUICK, Mrs., ii. 441.

QUICK, the Widow: member of the Widow-Club, iv. 516; riding the black ram, v. 131.

QUICKLY, Rebecca, i. 421.

QUICKSET, Squire, a stage-coach companion, ii. 22.

Quick-set hedge(s), i. 238; ii. 82.

Quick-silver, in a beau's head, ii. 573.

QUID-NUNC, THOMAS, letter from (a gatherer of news), v. 136–7.

Quiet: the wealthy are most concerned for q. and interest of a commonwealth, iii. 1; which Cowley calls the companion of obscurity, iii. 518.

Quill, Brother of the, iv. 478.

Quillet, Claude, Cardinal Mazarin's generous treatment of, i. 98.

Quilling a ruff, iv. 195.

Quilts, iii. 206.

Quinault, Philippe, i. *24*.

Quincy, John, i. *106*.

Quintilian, Marcus Fabius: and Longinus the only ancient authors who distinguished between puns and true wit, i. 262; 'the incomparably wise', ii. 161; among the best of Latin critics, ii. 484; a true critic, v. 26; eloquence possessed by some who have never heard of his rules, v. 95; Pliny's letter to, iii. 40; quoted, i. *249*; ii. *38*, *81*, *161*; iii. *134*.

Quinze Joies de Mariage, i. *155*.

QUIR, PETER DE, letter from (on punning), iii. 483–5.

Quit-rents, upon Sir ROGER's estate, iv. 341.

Quoit (coit), tossing a, i. 239.

Quorum, Justice of the, i. 208; iv. 68; v. 92, 108; Sir ROGER a, i. 9; iii. 438; at Sir ROGER's funeral the pall held up by six of the Quorum, iv. 341; Sir SAMPSON CONQUEST a, iv. 516; WILL HONEYCOMB among his brothers of the Q., v. 185.

Quotations, Latin and Greek, why introduced in *Spectator*, ii. 360.

R., *Spectators* signed: speculations on, ii. 360; 'to be examined', iii. 124, 220.

R., B., letter from (on opening of Mr. SPECTATOR's mouth), iv. 514.

R., F., 'slain' by a lady's glance, iii. 417.

R., G., letter from (with epigram on Homer), iv. 476–7.

R., H., letter from (on a club of lawyers), iii. 402–3.

R., J., letter from (on country life), iv. 177–81.

R., Q., letter from (on laughter), i. 223.

R., S., desired not to repeat the expression 'under the sun' so often, v. 117.

R—s, Colonel: letter to, ii. 301–2.

Rabbinical: preaching of a r. divine, ii. 361; secret of the Jesuits taught to politicians, iii. 98.

Rabbins: on the murder of Abel, ii. 228; their account of the persecution of the Jews, iv. 256; on cherubim and seraphim, v. 52.

Rabbits, coupling of fat and lean, i. 40.

Rabble, the: of a nation as a criterion of taste, i. 297; flung stones, i. 415; of mankind, their opinion of the ridiculous, iii. 37; of evil spirits in *PL*, iii. 88.

Rabelais, François: anecdote of, iii. 4; translated by Motteux, iii. 26.

Race not always to the swift (prov.), iii. 44.

'Race of mankind, the whole', inappropriate in prayers, iii. 130.

Races, fellows running naked in, iii. 320–1.

Race-horse(s): in a match at Coleshill, ii. 182; the tongue like a, ii. 460.

Racine, Jean: the thought bears up the expressions in his tragedies, i. 165; Orestes (in *Andromaque*), iii. 267; death of, iii. 508; mentioned, iii. 529. *See also* Philips, *The Distressed Mother.*

Racine, Louis, translation of Addison's notes on *PL*, ii. *538.*

Rack: jealousy puts a man on the, ii. 169; a servant stretched upon the, ii. 177; in religious persecutions, ii. 229, 431.

RACKRENT, HARRY, i. 406.

RACKRENT, Sir STEPHEN, patron of TOM TRUSTY, i. 406–7.

Radcliffe, Dr. John, 'a triumphant empiric's ignorance and inhumanity', iv. 158.

Ragamuffin(s), iv. 356; at the Royal Exchange, iv. 307.

Railing: 'our dears sometimes whine, at others rail', ii. 194; Whigs r. at the times, ii. 195; Mrs. FREEMAN's, ii. 342; mutual, ii. 410–11; and laughing at marriage, ii. 417; an indication of love (?), ii. 513; at the rich, iii. 41.

Raillery: with a butt, i. 203–4; ii. 191–2; strokes of, sometimes suppressed by a discreet author, ii. 205–6; more r. among the moderns, more good sense among the ancients, ii. 467; on matrimony, ii. 488; iv. 370–1; Dedication of *The Plain Dealer* a masterpiece of, ii. 537; the rule of polite, ii. 574; against Homer for homeliness of his sentiments, ii. 589; kinds of, iii. 582–6.

RAINBOW, ELIZABETH, testimonial to *Spectator* 265, iv. 460.

Rainbow(s): on fans, i. 427; appeals both by figure and colours, iii. 557; 'the heavenly bow', v. 161.

Rainbow hood, ii. 532.

Raisins, rotten r. sold in London streets, iii. 354.

Rake(s): at the masquerade, i. 62; in one of Shadwell's plays, i. 146; oaths of r. and bullies, i. 345; characteristics of, ii. 93–96, 295–8; 'a very pretty', ii. 105; common refuse of r. and debauchees, ii. 246; pretending to be free-thinkers, ii. 412; association with, ii. 527; women's encouragement of, iii. 64–65; a 'Rake's Journal' received, iii. 181; a club of female r. in China shops, iii. 245–6; of WILL HONEYCOMB's acquaintance, iii. 481; picture of a converted r. (WILL HONEYCOMB), iv. 390; marks of an agreeable, iv. 569; heading a party of cat-calls, v. 58.

Rakeshames, at the Royal Exchange, iv. 307.

Raleigh, Sir Walter, quotation from his *History of the World*, iv. 311–12.

RALPH: advertisement from (regarding new-fashioned hoods), ii. 561; a servant, iii. 153, 155.

Ram, custom of widow riding on a black, v. 100–1, 129–32.

Ram: impertinent disputation like milking a, ii. 46.

Ramage de la ville, WILL HONEYCOMB calls the cries of London the, ii. 474.

Ramillies: battle of, iii. 102; Blenheim and, v. 95; a hat shaped in 'the Ramillie cock', ii. 13.

Ramsay, Charlotte (afterwards Mrs. Lennox), iv. *596.*

Ramsey, William, *Vindication of Astrology*, iv. 591–2.

Ramus, Peter, iii. 485.

Rancour: breaking out as religious zeal, ii. 229; and hatred among Christians, iv. 334.

Randall, David, i. *129.*

Ranging one's thoughts, art of, necessary to the critic, iii. 36.

Rank: and precedency in this world and the next, ii. 351–4; in the Republic of Letters, iv. 386–8; persons of r. often reminded of their obligations, iv. 416.

Rant, Sir William (in *The Scowrers*), i. *218.*

Rant, a philosophical, ii. 444.

Ranters (rakes), a town full of r. and debauchees, iv. 224.

Rants, in English tragedy, popular with the audience, i. 171.

Rape: of Helen, ii. 539; on the wedding-night, iii. 110; the Whig criminal indicted for, v. 149.

Raphael (in *PL*): character of, ii. 564–5; iii. 200–3; his discourse to Adam, iii. 280–2; 'the sociable spirit', iii. 360.

Raphael Sanzio: 'the inimitable Raphael', ii. 446; in dream-vision of painters, i. 355; mentioned, ii. 154; cartoons of, at Hampton Court, ii. 379–81, 446–7; picture of St. Paul preaching at Athens, ii. 379–80; iii. 521; universal admiration for, iv. 152; learnt from Leonardo da Vinci, iv. 489.

Rapidity of composition in a modern author, ii. 355–6.

Rapin, René: on Homer and Virgil, ii. *127, 537*; on one of Homer's similes, ii. *128*; on Tacitus, ii. *291*; on meanness of Homer's sentiments, ii. *586, 589*; on episodes in the epic, iii. *280*; on Livy, iii. *574*.

Rapture(s): of a Christian and a man of honour, ii. 60; 'my heart melted away in secret r.', ii. 122; of innocent passion are like lightning to the day, ii. 281; and ecstasies the result of enthusiasm, ii. 289; poems of Sappho filled with bewitching tenderness and, ii. 366.

Rarities: in a virtuoso's closet, ii. 469; a rary-show, i. 128; advertisement of a show of, ii. 557–8.

'Rascal, knave', &c., in modern pamphlets, iv. 537.

Rashness, a happy r. often succeeds where prudence fails, iii. 44.

Ratafia and persico, iii. 206.

Ratio ultima regum, ii. 430.

Ratsbane, i. 372.

RATTLE, TOM, 'slain' by a lady's glance, iii. 417.

Rattle(s): a child's, i. 2; the God of Dullness with a, i. 271; made for children's ears, ii. 447; of children, ii. 506.

'Rattling Clubs' in church, v. 154; the 'Rattling Pew', v. 154.

Ravens: feeding of, i. 453; symbols of cares and passions, ii. 124.

Ravaillac, François, villainy of, against Henri IV, iv. 220.

Raw-head and Bloody-bones, to frighten children (prov.), iii. 292.

Rawlinson, Thomas, referred to (?), iv. 439.

Ray, John, i. *493*.

Rayner, John, *The Paul's Scholar's Copy Book*, i. *32*.

Razors, the author of strops for, iv. 5, 309.

Read, Sir William: his 'cures' of the blind, iv. 168, 457.

Readers: Gothic taste of, i. 269; three classes of r. of poetry, i. 269; the best writing appeals to r. of all conditions (of common humanity), i. 297, 321, 363; of the *Spectator*, ii. 204, 567, 577; of the epic, ii. 543; iii. 58, 60, 91; why they have a different relish of the same description, iii. 561; their pleasure in applying characters and circumstances, iv. 318.

Reading: benefits of, i. 397–8, 507; ii. 75; the PERVERSE WIDOW 'a reading lady and a desperate scholar', i. 465; of prayers, ii. 78–81; of polite authors the mark of the *bel esprit*, ii. 127; and contemplation the two great sources of knowledge, iii. 21; role of habit in, iii. 235–6; words which give the effect of immense, iii. 347; trash or treasure met with in, iv. 180; 'loitering way' of, iv. 240; reactions to, iv. 280; the man who read poetry aloud, iv. 572–3.

Reading suggested for women. See Women.

Readings, variant, pedantry of, iv. 161–5.

Reapers dancing a morris, iii. 595.

Reason: should govern passion, i. 29; and religion arm us against fear, i. 54; living according to the rules of, i. 113, 114; ii. 87, 136, 197–8, 288, 333; iii. 432, 479, 524; iv. 115; contest between r. and fashion, i. 115; should govern humour, i. 146; rather than imagination in entertainments, i. 210; subdues the seeds of punning, i. 259; and extravagance responsible for mixed wit, i. 267; r., truth and nature the measures of praise and dispraise, i. 278; and good sense determine the carriage of the well-bred man, i. 323–5; 'r. and good sense', i. 469; ii. 94, 101, 119, 143, 522; not found in animals, i. 491–7 (but glimmerings of, ii. 288); and reflection rooted out by pursuit of pleasure, ii. 94; more powerful in old age, without disturbance of passions, ii. 101, 281, 522; Mr. SPECTATOR's high evaluation of, objected to, ii. 118; and judgement, ii. 157, 179; Pallas (in the *Iliad*) as a symbol of, ii. 221; notions that fall in with the common r. of mankind, ii. 230; vanity rather than r. the guide of infidels, ii. 233; so busy it will exert itself in meanest

trifles, ii. 250; to be kept as cool as possible, ii. 289; enthusiasm and superstition the weaknesses of human, ii. 290; and choice inducing moderation in our wishes, ii. 308–9; the light of, in Socrates, ii. 313; passions operate variously, as rectified and swayed by, ii. 339; discretion the perfection of, ii. 376–7; disdained by free-thinkers, ii. 412; the distinguishing characteristic of man, ii. 417; blinded by flattery, ii. 424; common sense sometimes signifies right r. and what all men should consent to, ii. 508; a happy marriage has all the enjoyments of sense and, ii. 516; affection grounded upon principles of, ii. 523; and conviction as opposed to prejudice, iii. 18; religion as founded in, and enlivened with hope, iii. 80; and the passions, iii. 523–6; a humorist who followed the pure dictates of, iv. 570; revelation confirms the natural dictates of, v. 21, 48–53; and goodness, the only things wherein we can imitate God, v. 169.

Reason and instinct: differences between, i. 491–7; ii. 136, 214, 288, 377; iv. 347–8; in relationship of parents and children, ii. 522–3; example of alliance between, iii. 414.

Reasoning, advantages of Socratical way of, ii. 274.

Reasonings: our r. broken and imperfect, ii. 422; avoiding the r. of the prejudiced, ii. 450.

REBECCA 'the distress'd', letter from (on women's behaviour in china-shops), iii. 245–6.

Rebellion(s): in *Philaster*, ii. 434; swarms of sectaries during the Great, iv. 117; Jews always involved in, iv. 257. *See also* Civil Wars.

Rebequi, Troseme, ii. *487*.

Rebuke: the art of bestowing, iii. 41; Zephon's r. to the Devil, iii. 41.

Rebus, an example of false wit, i. 250–1, 272.

Receipts (recipes): the Countess of Kent's, i. 391; for a hasty-pudding and a whitepot, i. 451; for salves and possets, &c., ii. 486–7; an hereditary book of, iii. 206; writing out, v. 71.

Receiver of the Taxes, petition to be made, v. 151.

Recentibus odiis, i. 424.

Rechteren, Count, controversy with Mesnager, iv. 205–8.

Recitativo, i. 56, 96; Italian, i. 119–23; iii. 352.

'Reciters', a variety of liars, iv. 355.

Recommendation, letters of, iv. 247–51; Pliny's letter of r. quoted, ii. 394–5.

Reconciliation of friends, by means of beneficent lying, ii. 410–11.

Reconnoître, a French word imported, ii. 151–2; iii. *194*.

Records, searching in rolls and r. may become pleasant, iv. 71.

Recovery, to be taught the curtsy and, ii. 581.

Recreation, and pleasure necessary to mind and body, ii. 502.

Recruiting officer, a stage-coach companion, ii. 22, 73.

Recruits: beating up for, ii. 514; and losses of a nation, iii. 27–28.

Red-Cross Knight (in Spenser), iv. 428–9.

Red: silk for pale complexion, ii. 533; heels, the mark of the fortune-hunter, iii. 126; breeches, a sign of valour, iii. 322.

Red Sea: ghosts conjured into the, i. 53.

Redemption: represented in *PL*, iii. 142, 388.

Redundant phrases in conversation, examples of, iii. 398.

Refinements: artifices and r. obscure human nature, ii. 318; Popish r. in methods of torture, ii. 431; false r. in the epic, ii. 588.

Reflection: follows every thought, i. 160; on ideas gives us the notion of time or duration, i. 399; the *bel esprit* refined by, ii. 127; persons who find something too solemn in, iii. 6; the longest r. in the *Aeneid*, iii. 61; beauty often made a privilege against thought and, iii. 81.

Reflections: an author's r. to be admitted sparingly in epic, iii. 60–61; on a whole people unjust, iv. 29

Reflections on Courtship and Marriage, ii. *178*.

Reformation, the: retrenched superfluities of the Church, i. 487; monuments erected by merchants since, ii. 187; Latimer's share in, iv. 142.

Reformation: of a young man, ii. 432–3; of an elder brother, ii. 463; of the stage proposed, ii. 503–5; not to be deferred till old age, ii. 511; of BROMIUS by EMILIA, iii. 81–83.

Reformation of Manners, Society for, i. 35; Society of Reformers, v. 116.

Refugees, the poor (French Huguenots), ii. 430.

Refuse: 'giving a vast r. of his superfluities', ii. 527.

Regardless (unregarded), 'cheap and r. things', v. 141.

Regnaud, Paul: letter to a French gentleman in London (on death of Mme de Villacerfe), iii. 383–5.

Reindeer, Lapland song to, iii. 519–20.

Rejoicing-Day, i. 361.

Relatives, omission of, in English, ii. 35.

Religentem esse oportet, religiosum nefas, ii. 289.

Religion: allegorical figure of, i. 17; and reason arm us against fear, i. 54; formerly observed in England, i. 213; a mechanical observance of, i. 341; changing sides in, ii. 135; abates grief, ii. 140–2; mischiefs of zeal in, ii. 227–30; 'is left to us silly women', ii. 280; without devotion is mere philosophy, ii. 287; enthusiasm and superstition in, ii. 288–90; notions of, among heathen, ii. 310–14; duties of, ii. 331–4; its effects on human life, ii. 374; a consolation to absent lovers, ii. 437; the name given by devout men to virtue, ii. 443; hypocrisy's tribute to, ii. 443–4; and politics, ii. 446; contempt of, in plays, ii. 554; without additional graces becomes sour and ill-humoured, iii. 40; expressed in various passions, iii. 80; the most honourable incentive to good actions, iii. 326; satisfaction arising from practice of, iv. 72; English bashfulness concerning, iv. 116–17; faith and morality in, iv. 118–20; balanced against hypocrisy, iv. 117, 136; balanced against philosophy, iv. 137; hope and, iv. 166–8; gloominess in, iv. 251–4; produces good-will and charity towards others, iv. 211; Jews' firm adherence to their, iv. 257; as practised by William III and Louis XIV, iv. 335–8. *See also* Christianity.

Religious ceremonies, Acosta's defence of Jewish, ii. 332.

Remedium efficax & universum, iv. 458.

Remedy: for restoring taste, iv. 462; 'the grand r.' (death), iv. 559.

'Remember thou art but a man', v. 42.

Remonstrance: 'the just r. of *That*', i. 344–5.

Remus and Romulus nursed by a wolf, ii. 455.

Renaissance. *See* Revival of Letters.

Renatus Valentinus, story of, iii. 599–600.

Rencounter, i. 416, 436; v. 90.

Renegado, a French, and the Castilian's wife, ii. 278–9.

Renegadoes and converts, in religion and politics, ii. 135–6.

RENTFREE, RICHARD and SABINA, letters from ('the history of a boy and girl to their wedding day'), iv. 14–17.

RENTFREE, TOBY, letter from (on Nicolini and the lion), iii. 138–9.

Rep., a curtailment of *reputation*, ii. 34.

Repentance, terrors of a death-bed, ii. 142.

Reports, inaccurate, iv. 353–6.

Repository: of curiosities, ii. 7; of dissections, ii. 573; for fashions, iv. 194.

Reproach: a concomitant to greatness, i. 423; the ambitious man hates, ii. 498; the proper attitude toward r. by an enemy, iii. 323–4; shame and r. not evils, iii. 431; of a friend, iii. 447; heroic minds disregard unmerited, iv. 44. *See also* Censure.

Reptiles, diversity of species among, iv. 443.

Republic of Letters: crisis in, iv. 63; persons of eminence in, iv. 162; a young adventurer in, iv. 252; distinctions in, iv. 388.

Republic of males, and the Commonwealth of Amazons, iv. 22–26.

Republican: and anti-monarchical principles, i. 40; doctrines of Sir ANDREW, ii. 551; Sir DAVID DUNDRUM a noted, iii. 343.

Reputation: curtailed to *rep.*, ii. 34; avoiding injury to another's, ii. 205–6; do things laudable rather than purchase r., ii. 239; the portion of every gentleman, ii. 349; the beginning poet usually attacks r. of others, ii. 482; arouses envy of others, ii. 494–5; of others never attacked by *Spectator*, ii. 517–20; some women guard their r. rather than their modesty, iii. 464; to gain a merited r. whilst we are living, the greatest happiness, iv. 150.

Resentment(s): of true love, ii. 514; heroic minds are above, iv. 44–45.

Reserve, reservedness: women have less caution and r. than men, i. 243; a just r. accompanying mirth, ii. 559; religion in some is little better than sullenness and, iii. 80.

Reserved: and melancholy temper at times agreeable, ii. 425; to be r. among strangers, a point of good breeding, iii. 347.

Resignation: in a father, ii. 522; pleasure in r. from the world, ii. 599.

Resolution: exerting itself as obstinacy in savage nations, ii. 339; enterprises of spirit and, ii. 447; needed to develop good qualities, iii. 149.

Resolutions, conversation of a friend animates good, i. 397.

Resolves, the soul without passions, slow in its, ii. 490.

Respect: of dependants, how obtained, ii. 292; from circle of friends, ii. 351.

Responsibility, rightly entrusted to the wealthy, iii. 1.

Rest: points of, in life, i. 395; ii. 322; vicissitudes of labour and, ii. 269; youth neither can nor ought to remain at, ii. 373; secret r. and contentedness of mind, ii. 500; man not to set up his r. here, iii. 29.

Resting-places, in *PL*, iii. 234.

Restoration, the, a reaction against religious practices of Puritans, iv. 117.

Resurrection, the: Cowley's poem on, quoted, ii. 154; Raphael's painting of Jesus after, ii. 380; St. Paul's discourse on, to the Corinthians, v. 166.

Retainers, party, their implicit submission to their leaders, ii. 1.

Retentive power, lacking in women(?), ii. 460.

Retinue and grandeur, the farce of, i. 352.

Retirement: pleasures of, among crowds, i. 18–19; true happiness in, i. 67–68, 470; ii. 525–8, 599; iii. 517–18; v. 84–87; desire for, i. 114–15; iv. 466; raillery against, ii. 486–9; effect of habit upon love of, iv. 70; strengthens religious faith, iv. 143–4; JEAN CHEZLUY on, iv. 201–3; of Sir ANDREW, iv. 466–8; not always commendable, v. 94–95.

Retroprospective cast of Janus, ii. 470.

Revelation: the lights of reason and, ii. 76; proves the received articles of Christianity, ii. 232; ratifies men's ideas of immortality, ii. 322; and our knowledge of God, iv. 394; confirms the natural dictates of reason, v. 21, 48–53; our ideas enlarged by, v. 164.

Revelations, Mede on the, i. 390.

Revenge: allegorical figure of, iv. 326; a Spanish lady's, v. 90.

Reverence, the title given to the inferior clergy, ii. 352.

Reveries: of a 'castle-builder', ii. 158–60; pass through the mind of the wise man and the fool, ii. 375.

Rêveur: 'what the French call a *r*. and a *distrait*', i. 329.

Revival of Letters: punning revived with, i. 262; Revival of Greek Letters, ii. 429.

Rewards and punishments: after death, the measure of man's merit, iii. 43; Spartans exact in distributing, iv. 528.

Rhadamanthus (judge of the dead), ii. 76.

Rhaecus and the Hamadryad, v. 16–17.

Rhea (goddess), invented dancing, i. 284.

Rheni, Guido. *See* Guido.

Rhetoric: writers of, treat punning with respect, i. 260; allegorical figure of, i. 274; Tillotson abhors pomp of, i. 430; of beggars, ii. 402; she-professors for chairs of, ii. 458; springs of, possessed by women, ii. 480.

Rhetorician(s): recommend modesty to the orator, ii. 398; too much nicety in comparisons savours of the, iii. 91.

Rhinoceros: antipathy of elephant and, i. 213; playing the (cocking the nose), ii. 572.

RHODOPE: the courtesan, ii. 407; FIDELIO has tied the garters of, iii. 471.

RHUBARB, JOHN: memorial of, iv. 9–10.

Rhyme: less suitable than blank verse for English tragedy, i. 164; suitable for close of acts, i. 165; in *bouts rimés*, i. 236–7; needs less assistance to keep it from flatness of prose, iii. 14; perpetual returns of, monotonous, iii. 15.

Rhymes, double: as a kind of false wit, i. 258, 272; iii. 560; in *Hudibras*, i. 258; ii. 468.

Rhynsault, Claudius: and Sapphira, iv. 241–4.

Rialton, Francis, Viscount (later 2nd Earl of Godolphin), a subscriber, i. *lxxxviii*.

Ribaldry: learned by birds, i. 152; at the Exchange, ii. 108; with which women are entertained, ii. 119; on the Thames, iii. 437–8; our satire only r. and Billingsgate, iv. 88.

Ribbons, ribbands: sorting of a suit of, i. 46; iii. 183; as lures to women, i. 67; a piece of, as a love-token, i. 124; mixed to suit colour of face, i. 177; and brocades from France, i. 192, 225; a wholesale dealer in silks and, i. 277; in head-dresses, i. 414, 416; ii. 531; a scarlet r. to tie the hair, i. 434; for his wrist-bands, ii. 110; cherry-coloured, ii. 192; 'almost ruins me in', ii. 327; laces and, ii. 346; iv. 101; and embroidery in a beau's head, ii. 571; r. stuck up and down in her hair, ii. 580; a mantua and petticoat without, iii. 532; women who tie up their hair in a bag or, iv. 28; a r. tied round the sword-arm, iv. 33; pretty hands busy in the foldings of, iv. 102; curling locks with bows of r. sloping over them, iv. 194; sacrifice a single ribband to pay for the *Spectator*, iv. 231; r., bro-

cades, and embroidery, iv. 271; gay-coloured r. of a citizen's wife, v. 46.

Rich, Christopher (manager of Drury Lane Theatre): refuses to allow an opera on Whittington to be performed, i. 27; brought in ladder-dancers, i. 128; petition of devils referred to, i. 151; inventory of movables of, i. 177; 'Kit Crotchet', ii. 504.

Rich: 'Be rich', a short method of pleasing, ii. 593; methods of growing, iii. 1–5.

Rich, the: jests of, would make no great figure otherwise, i. 10; need not care for any body, as the vulgar say, ii. 73; flatterers of, ii. 292; railing at, iii. 41; virtues and vices of, iv. 139–41; are only those who have more than they want, iv. 563.

Riches: ordinary people dazzled with, i. 462; where suitors are equal, r. ought to be a reason for preference, ii. 86–88; application, not possession, makes them honourable, ii. 239; the world's regard for, ii. 280, 352; wrongly considered a requirement for happiness in marriage, ii. 545–6; to be considered real goods (?), iii. 1; and plenty the natural fruits of liberty, iii. 21; proper use of, iii. 47–49; iv. 107–11; methods of acquiring, iv. 81–86; balanced against wisdom, iv. 136; balanced against content, iv. 136, 561–5. See also Money, Wealth.

Richard I (Cœur de Lion), terrible to the Saracens, i. 135.

Richard III, set up half the backs of the nation, i. 135.

RICHARD, Sir, at the Coronation festivities, v. 106.

Richardson, Jonathan, iv. 495.

Richardson, Samuel: Pamela, iii. 409; Sir Charles Grandison, i. 419.

Richelieu, Armand Du Plessis, Cardinal de: saying attributed to, ii. 430; on good and ill fortune, iii. 42; his politics made France the terror of Europe, iii. 96; founding of the Academy, iii. 96.

Richmond: letter addressed from, ii. 162; Mr. SPECTATOR at, iv. 98.

Richmond (Yorkshire), ii. 117.

Rickets, in children, ii. 456.

'Ride the great horse', ii. 31; iv. 24.

Riddle: clashing metaphors turn a sentence into a, iii. 12; presented by STREPHON to EUDAMIA, iii. 25.

Ridicule: sources of, i. 200–4; a better expedient against love than sober advice, ii. 385; improper fear of, ii. 400–1; essay on laughter and, ii. 465–

9; two great branches of (comedy and burlesque), ii. 467–8; of the eminent and successful, ii. 494–5, 519; of marriage, ii. 516, 517; of other writers, iii. 36–37; the Spectator has new-pointed all the batteries of, iv. 65; stronger when concealed in gravity, v. 105.

Riding, recommended as a healthful exercise, i. 473–4.

Riding-habits, mannish, i. 432–5 (this paper praised, ii. 303); iii. 223; iv. 28–29, 37–38, 222–3.

RIDINGHOOD, REBECCA: letter from (on immodest conversation), ii. 439–40.

Riding-hood, a black, iv. 340.

Ridout, Mr. (surgeon), iii. 279.

Ridpath, George (writer of the Flying Post), iv. 112.

Ridware, manor of, v. 76.

RIGADOON, Monsieur, a dancing-master in the City, i. 285.

Rigaudon, a dance, i. 285.

Right hand from their left, Do not know their (prov.), iv. 387.

'Right worshipful', v. 105.

Rigid: men often affect character of being r. and severe, ii. 8; rebukes and advice of old r. persons, iii. 41.

Rigidly virtuous, iii. 122, 466.

Rigids (strict or precise persons), 'as the fellows call us', iv. 247.

Rinaldo (opera), i. 23; iii. 514; thunder and lightning, illuminations and fireworks in, i. 24–25; sparrows in, i. 24, 26–27, 64; Armida and Cassani in, i. 25; Preface to, quoted, i. 25–26; account of performance of, i. 63–65.

Ring(s): posie of (in), i. 185, 248, 378; ii. 183; a gold r. as a prize in a grinning match, ii. 182, 184; competitors for, at a whistling match, ii. 206; writing poems on glass with a diamond r., ii. 356; bracelet, or little picture, ii. 407; containing mistress's hair, ii. 453; Sir ROGER's proposed diamond r. for the WIDOW, iii. 54; and mourning left by Sir ROGER, iv. 341; a beau's white hand and diamond r., iv. 413; the stone in Pyrrhus's, v. 28; a thumb-r., v. 99.

Riot: and prodigality arise from shame of poverty, i. 469; and excess not becoming to princes, ii. 212.

Ripheus (in the Aeneid), his death, i. 320; iv. 464.

Rival factions, frequency of, iv. 17–19.

Rival Queens, The. See Lee.

Rival(s): history of BRUNETTA and PHILLIS, i. 342–4; history of the r. mother, i. 384–8; account of the r.

Negro slaves, ii. 339–40; r. preachers who quoted Latin, ii. 359–60.

Rivell'd, 'a sour r. face', i. 366.

River: of Oblivion in *PL*, iii. 118–19; stained with Adonis's blood, iv. 88; allegorical figure of R. of Tears, iv. 276.

River-dragon (in *PL*), the crocodile, iii. 386.

River-god: exploits of a, in modern poems, iv. 362.

Rivers: in red stockings in the French opera, i. 123; in ancient poets, iii. 87; the four r. in hell (in *PL*), iii. 118; pleasing to the imagination, iii. 452, 542.

Road, rules of the, ii. 24.

Road of Superstition, in the vision of heavenly and worldly wisdom, iv. 369.

Roarers, unpleasant conversation of, in the country, iv. 178–9.

Roaring: by country gentlemen till they cannot hear, ii. 96; r. drunk, iv. 557.

Robberies, frequent on the high road and in our own houses, i. 373.

Robe: our learned men of either, ii. 117; gentlemen of the, ii. 272; iv. 574.

Roberts, J., publisher of 'vol. ix' of *Spectator*, i. lxxvi.

Robethon, Jean de, v. *118*.

Robin, the porter at Will's Coffee-house, iii. 490.

Robin-red-breast, in *The Children of the Wood*, i. 363.

Robinson, ——, the 'master ladder-dancer of England', i. *128*.

Robinson, John (Bishop of Bristol and Lord Privy Seal), Tickell's poem dedicated to, iv. *361*.

Rochester, John Wilmot, 2nd Earl of: Sir ROGER had often supped with, i. 8; 'the three critics who settled the characters of my Lord R. and Boileau', i. *372*; *Allusion to the Tenth Satire of the First Book of Horace* quoted, i. 386–7; iii. 496; his 'admirable poem' on 'Nothing', iii. 100.

Rock(s): wildness of r. and deserts as a source of aesthetic pleasure, iii. 453; high r. and precipices pleasing to the imagination, iii. 540; fretwork of r. and grotto, iii. 550; at Babylon cut into figure of Semiramis, iii. 554; mis-shapen r. and precipices, iii. 564.

Roderick, Dr. Charles (master of Eton), referred to (?), ii. 161.

Roderigo, King of Spain, iii. *425*.

Roderigo (in *Othello*): 'these foolish Roderigos', ii. 304.

Roger, Sir (in *The Scornful Lady*), ii. 554.

Rogers, Jane (actress), iii. *351*; Belinda in *The Man of Mode*, i. *278*; benefit for, iii. *395*.

Rogers, Capt. Woodes, *A Cruising Voyage round the World*, iv. 22.

'Rogue, Rascal', &c., in modern pamphlets, iv. 537.

Rolle, Henry (judge), iii. *135*.

Roman actors: expression used by, at exit, iii. 152.

Roman augur, warned Caesar against Ides of March, iii. 480.

Roman Catholic: gentleman on treatment of prostitutes, ii. 245; a very good Protestant who lies with a, ii. 247; Erasmus an unbigoted, ii. 334.

Roman Catholic Church: sermon of a conventual in the, ii. 466; massacres instigated by, iv. 334. *See also* Romish Church.

Roman Catholic churches, reverent behaviour in, iv. 125.

Roman Catholic religion: one huge overgrown body of childish and idle superstitions, ii. 289; ridiculous use of vestments in, ii. 290. *See also* Romish religion.

Roman Catholic superstitions, Saint-Evremond's defence of, ii. 332.

Roman Catholics: their view of Purgatory, ii. 155; imagine Kentishmen have tails, ii. 182; contrasted with Calvinists, ii. 332; the wealthy, during Lent, attend the poor and ill, iii. 400; conference between Protestants and, in reign of Queen Mary, iv. 142.

Roman club, regulations of an old, i. 43.

Roman commonwealth, Constitution of, iii. 19–20.

Roman consuls: authority of, i. *181*; lack of power of, iii. 20.

Roman costume in portraits, ii. 12.

Roman emperors: an argument with one, ii. 430; called themselves 'Felix', iii. 43; slaughter of Jews under, iv. 256; ambitions of different, v. 168.

Roman fable, ii. 185–6, 220.

Roman games and gladiatorial combats, ii. 133; iv. 35.

Roman historians: proposal to teach, to the young, ii. 395.

Roman History. See Echard.

Roman law(s): the *jus trium liberorum*, i. 295; the Twelve Tables, iv. 88; condemned dispersers of libels, iv. 89–90; two witnesses required in, iv. 502.

Roman matron, habit and air of a, ii. 487–8.

Roman money, rebus on, i. 250.

INDEX

Roman mosaic, discovered at Stonesfield, iii. 339.

Roman noses, revived in 1688, i. 135.

Roman orators: proposal to teach, to the young, ii. 395; gestures used by, iii. 521.

Roman poets: proposal to teach, to the young, ii. 395; their hymns to deities, iv. 94. *See also* Latin.

Roman proverb, on the Carthaginians, ii. 186–7.

Roman Senate, anecdote of young prince defending his father before, iii. 404.

Roman Senators, costume of, at the masquerade, i. 62.

Roman theatre: curtain of, depicted defeat of Britons, ii. 150; regulation of, iv. 66–68; Cato's visit to, iv. 67.

Roman triumph, satires and invectives an essential part of a, i. 423.

Roman Triumvirate, sacrificed friends 'to furnish out a decent execution', i. 144.

Roman women: prevented fighting between Romans and Sabines, i. 348; contributed rings and jewels to the state, i. 349; funeral elegies allowed for, i. 349; Sabine and Roman wives, models, ii. 487.

Romance(s): the envious man like the seat of a giant in a, i. 84; an old r. translated out of the French, i. 118; effect of, on LEONORA's taste, i. 158; JAMES a reader of, i. 306; dressed according to some description in a, i. 434; volumes of love-letters and, ii. 11; 'if I do not succeed it shall look like r.', ii. 280; accounts of lovers in, ii. 438; a city r., ii. 463; brains disordered with r. and novels, ii. 487; 'it would look like r. to tell you', ii. 526; phrases used in, iii. 18; conception of heroism in, iii. 129; iv. 32; and novels inflamers of passion, iii. 374; metaphorical deaths in, iii. 416; an enchanted hero in, iii. 546; dwarfs and squires in, iv. 18; *Don Quixote*'s effect upon, iv. 69.

Romans: and Sabines at war, i. 348; Scipio's advice to, ii. 114; defeated by Pyrrhus, ii. 211–12; thought education of children a business of parents, iii. 132; dances of, iii. 237; ideas of pleasure among, iii. 340; paid honours to him who had saved life of a citizen, iii. 354–5; pugilistic contests of, iv. 35; punished lampoons by death, iv. 88; grandeur of, in warfare and politics, iv. 280; music in worship among, v. 152.

Romantic: imagination, i. 20; situation, i. 318; humour in Spain, i. 417; clothes, i. 435; 'whose vein is on the', ii. 39; hero or a whining coxcomb, ii. 60; generosity, ii. 252; spice of r. madness, ii. 462; account of Thammuz in *PL* finely r., iii. 87; ludicrous epilogues 'downright silly and', iii. 253; a most r. wretch, iii. 473; the world enchanted with r. and improbable achievements, iv. 4; &c.

Rome: statue of Pasquin in, i. 99; iv. 3; republic sunk into luxury and avarice, i. 234; an intrigue with a Cardinal's mistress at, ii. 38; destruction of 'the Empress of the World', ii. 77; the beaux of, ii. 89; trunk of a statue in, ii. 390; prodigies preceding Civil War in, iii. 61; statue of a Momus dug up in, iii. 351; the Pantheon, iii. 556; great geniuses in, in time of Augustus, iii. 529; the Capitol saved by geese, iv. 17; few capital punishments in Twelve Tables of, iv. 88; military profession honoured in, iv. 534; fireworks at (in Strada), v. 108–11.

Romish Church, anecdote of a great man in the, iii. 28.

Romish religion: encumbered with ceremony, i. 487; 'a wrong religion and a misguided devotion', ii. 143.

Romp(s): BETTY, a r. at stool-ball, i. 306; a romping girl, ii. 236; a club of she-romps, ii. 345–6; Mrs. Bicknell, iii. 395–6; who developed into a graceful young woman, iv. 147–8; a set of familiar, iv. 246; half a dozen, iv. 316.

Romp, romping, i. 451; a bachelor whose pleasantry consists in, ii. 73.

Rompishness, ii. 236.

Romulus and Remus, nursed by a wolf, ii. 455.

Roofs, vaulted, effect of, in architecture, iii. 557.

Rooke, Sir George, i. *314*.

Rooks and crows, cawing of, a kind of natural prayer, i. 453.

Room, entering a: a boy so lacking in social graces he is afraid of, i. 282; a man should be capable of, with a good grace, i. 287; a good air at, ii. 106; Mr. FONDLE's manner of, v. 135.

Rope: breaking of, does not hinder execution of a criminal, v. 131.

Rope-dancer(s), i. 119; ii. 56, 504.

Roper, Abel (writer of the *Post Boy*), iii. *439, 441*.

ROSALINDA: a Whig partisan, i. 347; her application to the Ugly Club, i. 370.

Rosamond (opera). *See* Addison.

435

Rosamond's bower, ii. 596.

Roscius (actor), a friend of Cicero, iv. 432.

Roscommon, Wentworth Dillon, 4th Earl of: translation of Horace quoted, i. 166, 179, 190; *Essay on Translated Verse*: a masterpiece, ii. 486; points out beauties in Milton, iii. 231.

Rose(s), iii. 482, 569; v. 63, 94.

Rosemary: decorating a church, ii. 600; hedges of, in a churchyard, iv. 277.

Rosicrucian: sepulchre, discovery of, iii. 424–5; discourse with a, on the great secret, iv. 561.

Ross, Alexander, i. 258.

Rossi, Giacomo, preface to *Rinaldo* quoted, i. 25–26.

Rotheram, Elizabeth, iii. *102*.

Rotheram, John (of Much Waltham, Essex), iii. *102*.

Rotonda, the hoop-petticoat a new-fashioned, ii. 7.

Rotunda. *See* Pantheon at Rome.

Round, James, *Spectator* sold by, i. xxiv.

Round pillars, effect of, in architecture, iii. 557.

Roundheads: feuds with Cavaliers, i. 509; drinking confusion to the, v. 150.

Rout, allegorical figure of, encompassing Minerva's buckler, iii. 337.

Rowe, Elizabeth Singer, i. lxxix; *Miscellaneous Works*, iii. *376*.

Rowe, Nicholas: *Tamerlane* and *Ulysses* noble tragedies with happy endings, i. 170; *The Biter*, i. 203; *Account of Shakespeare*, i. *260*; ii. *323*, 586; iii. *572*; translation of Pythagoras, ii. *233*; mentioned, iv. *233*.

Rowe, Rev. Thomas, i. lxxix.

Rowley, John, his proposals for a pair of new globes, iv. 481–3.

ROXANA, gravity of her entrance, ii. 308.

Royal Bagnio, in Newgate Street, iii. 225.

Royal Snuff, true, advertised, iii. *278*.

Royal Society, the: Fellows of, i. 45; should compile a natural history, i. 496; an ingenious artist who works for, ii. 389; designed to divert men from party politics, ii. 519; a Fellow of, on the origin of the cat-call, iii. 350.

Royalty, exchanging salutations during the royal presence, ii. 509.

Rozinante (in *Don Quixote*), iv. 238.

Rub, there's the (prov.), iv. 401.

Rubbers, sold by John Sly, ii. 237.

Rubens, Peter Paul, in vision of painters, i. 356.

Ruby (-ies): English wool exchanged for, i. 296; the glowing, v. 94.

Rude: and untractable disposition, ii. 425; magnificence in works of nature, iii. 540.

Rudeness, artificial r. of French and Italian gardens, iii. 551.

Rudge, John (Deputy-Governor of the Bank, and Director of S. Sea Co.), a subscriber, i. *xc*.

Rudlow, manor of, v. 76.

Ruelle: i. 192; WILL HONEYCOMB formerly an *homme de ruelle*, iv. 391.

Ruff, washing and quilling a, iv. 195.

Ruffian, with the lantern and dagger, ii. 350.

Ruffles, a man who could write eloquently upon a pair of, v. 138.

Rufus and Naevia, Martial's epigram on, i. 467.

Ruins: pictures of, i. 288; of an old Abbey at Sir ROGER'S, i. 453.

Rules: of the Two-penny Club, i. 43; eternal r. of reason and good sense in behaviour, i. 323; married persons are under particular, ii. 202; some things which do not need, ii. 508; Horace's r. for conduct of conversation with men of power, ii. 592; for acquiring taste, iii. 529–30; for self-examination with regard to scandal, v. 32–33; observed in the Abbaye de la Trappe, v. 33.

Rules of art: first race of authors destitute of, i. 261; a natural genius not disciplined and broken by, ii. 127; learned geniuses have formed themselves by, ii. 129; in poetry and music, ii. 505; *PL* to be examined by, ii. 539; laid down by Aristotle need to be qualified by later epics, ii. 566; of French authors, used by English critics, iii. 36; works of great genius superior to authors who conform to, iii. 38; may prevent ill poets but can never make good ones, iii. 450–1; something in poetry more essential than, iii. 530; greater judgement sometimes shown in deviating from, v. 27–28; a great genius may be ignorant of, v. 28.

Rules to Keep Lent, recommended, i. 391.

Rumour: too short-lived to compete with glory, ii. 349; the narrow circuit of, v. 179.

RUNNET, Mrs., a member of the Widow-Club, iv. 517.

Running, a part of the Roman Pentathlum, ii. 133.

Ruptures, advertisement for cure of, iv. 61.

RURICOLA, has an unworthy heir, ii. 254.

RUSSEL, iv. 559.

Russell, Elizabeth, monument to, in Westminster Abbey, iii. 214.

Russell, Francis. *See* Bedford.

Russell, John, Lord, iii. *214.*

Russia, reforms in, by Peter the Great, ii. 48–49.

Russian nettle, iv. 104.

Rust, indolence and idleness compared to, iii. 149; v. 132.

Rustic(s): a morose r. married to an old coquette, ii. 11; boisterous r. who infest our streets in turnip season, ii. 476; love converts a brutal r. into a gentle swain, iii. 416.

Rustic: phrase, i. 471; part of the species, i. 486; fierceness, ii. 2; mirth unfit for polite conversation, iv. 9.

Rusticated, 'the university phrase', v. 38.

Rusticities (in language): pedants' concern with, i. 250; in *The Country Wake*, iv. 282.

Rusticity of behaviour, i. 226; among country people, ii. 15; a shrewd, iii. 112; offensive, iii. 497.

RUSTY, SCABBARD, letter from (on sports at the Bear-Garden), iv. 80–81.

Ryan, Lacy, in *The Lancashire Witches*, ii. 57.

Rycaut, Sir Paul, on Mahometans' freeing birds from cages, iii. 273.

Ryder, Dudley, on the *Spectator*, i. xli, lxxxvi–lxxxvii, xcv, *163.*

Rymer, Thomas: *Edgar*, v. 26; his censure of Shakespeare, v. 26.

Ryswick, Treaty of, iii. 97; iv. *479;* marked end of Louis XIV's triumphs, ii. 209.

S sounds in English, ii. 34.

S., A., papers of, returned, iv. 588.

S., E., letter from (on a young woman who turned her cheek when offered a kiss), ii. 561.

S., G., letter from (in praise of the *Spectator*), iv. 485–6.

S., J., letter from (on behaviour in church), iii. 427.

S., Marchioness of, iii. 371.

S., P.: petition of, granted, iv. 588; letter received from, v. 117.

S., R., letter from (on behaviour in church), ii. 305–6.

S., T.: letter from (a schoolboy), ii. 162; letter from (on behaviour in church), ii. 419–20; 'wounded by ZELINDA's scarlet stocking', iii. 417.

S., W., letter from, to a trader, ii. 464 (referred to (?), iii. 289).

S—e, Dr., ii. 80.

Sa Ga Yean Qua Rash Tow (one of the Indian Kings), his comments on London, i. 212.

Sabbath: Adam would have kept holy the, iv. 586; profanation of, by barbers, shoe-cleaners, &c., v. 116.

Sabine women, prevented war between Romans and Sabines, i. 348; Sabine and Roman wives, models, ii. 487; rape of the, iv. 282.

Sabio muda conscio, Il (Spanish prov.), i. 337.

SABLE, Mrs., riding the black ram, v. 131.

Sacharissa, every poet has his, iv. 371.

Sacheverell, Dr. Henry: visit to a female admirer of, i. 243–4; his *Speech* in LEONORA's library, i. 157; referred to (?), ii. *553–4;* mentioned, v. *176.*

Sack-posset: a young man who can make a, i. 241; mentioned, ii. 442.

Sackcloth, mourning in, iii. 348.

Sackville, Charles. *See* Dorset.

'saddled with costs' (legal jargon), iv. 477.

Sa'di, Muslih al-Din, Shaikh (Persian poet), fable from, iii. 46.

Saffin, Thomas, iv. *343.*

Sailors: sight of disabled s. in London, iv. 11.

Saint: 'this sly saint' (a Quaker), ii. 23; Erasmus could scarce forbear regarding Socrates as a, ii. 334; represented without a beard, iii. 221; was formerly of a sorrowful countenance, iv. 251.

St. Angelo, Castle of, v. 108.

St. Asaph, Bishop of. *See* Fleetwood.

St. Barnabas' Day, v. 130.

St. Christopher's, story of rival Negroes in, ii. 339–40.

Saint-Evremond, Charles de Marguetel de Saint-Denis de: an invention of, i. *93;* on women's vanity, i. 138; on Racine, i. *165;* thought *Don Quixote* could give more relief to a heavy heart than Plutarch or Seneca, ii. 141–2; his defence of Roman Catholic ceremonies and duties, ii. 332; 'Idée de la Femme', iii. *78–79;* praised the constancy and courage of Petronius at death, iii. 299–300; 'affectation of appearing singular in his remarks', iii. 300; 'Letter to Duchess of Mazarin', iv. *153,* referred to, i. 224.

St. George, Chevalier de. *See* Pretender.

St. John, Henry. *See* Bolingbroke.

St. John's College, Cambridge, monopoly of puns in, iii. 483.

Sainte-Marthe, Scévole de, i. 98.

St. Mauro (modern name of the island of Leucas), ii. 382.

St. Peter's, Rome, the Pope officiating in, ii. 290; praise of, iii. 556, 557.

'Sal'. *See* Salisbury, Sally.

Salads: of twenty different herbs, in a modern meal, ii. 264–5; a frog or a, iii. 99. *See also* Sallet.

'Salamanders': women who defy temptations against their chastity, ii. 275–7; 'salamandrine quality' in a coquette's heart, ii. 597.

Salic Law, to be established in every family (?), iv. 209.

Salisbury, Sally ('Sal'), courtesan and procuress, ii. 246.

Salisbury, dress of a woman near, ii. 13.

Salisbury, Bishop of. *See* Burnet, Gilbert.

Sallet (salad): a trusse of s. eaten, iii. 532.

Sallust (Gaius Sallustius Crispus): 'the most elegant and correct of all the Latin historians', i. 234; enters into 'those internal principles of action which arise from the characters and manners of the persons he describes', iii. 528; on Catiline's coveting wealth of others while squandering his own, i. 234–5; that celebrated passage, where Caesar and Cato are placed in such beautiful but opposite lights, ii. 166; remarked of Cato that the less he coveted glory the more he acquired it, ii. 491; other references to *Bell. Catil.*: i. 181, 193; ii. 247, 499; iii. 1, 524; iv. 36.

Salmasius. *See* Saumaise.

Salmon, Mrs.: sign of the ingenious, i. 117; to supply waxworks for a projected opera, i. 129; 'like a figure in Mrs. Salmon's wax-work', v. 82.

Salmon, fishing for, i. 475.

SALMONEUS: letter from ('thunderer to the play-house'), i. 150–1; a new S. in the play-house, v. 26.

Salop (Shrewsbury), letter addressed from, iii. 239.

Salt, spilling s. unlucky, i. 32.

Salutation: 'the business of', ii. 358, 508–10; iv. 379; kissing as a mode of, ii. 433–4; in church, ii. 509; at the play, ii. 552; familiar arts of, in church, iv. 124–5; of the Jews to their kings, iv. 418; to Eastern monarchs, iv. 485.

Salute(s), saluting: at a loss how to s. a lady, i. 287; 'after the first s. were over', i. 448, 504; St. Francis mistook the kiss of a lover for the s. of charity, ii. 450; a civil, ii. 536; Sir ROGER's custom of, iii. 437.

Salver of *Spectators* and a s. of sweetmeats, iv. 232.

Salves, ii. 486–7; iii. 206.

Samian expedition, Athenian youth who perished in the, iii. 105.

Sampson, Sir. *See* Legend, Sir Sampson.

Sampson (the porter, in *The Fatal Marriage*), iv. 205.

Sancho Panza (in *Don Quixote*), iv. 238.

Sancroft, William (Archbishop of Canterbury), v. 175.

Sanctorius: 'that ingenious discourse of', i. 105; his mathematical chair, i. 106.

Sanctum Sanctorum, in Solomon's Temple, iv. 583.

Sand (for blotting ink), i. 333.

Sanderson, Robert (Bishop of Lincoln): his sermons used by Sir ROGER's chaplain, i. 442.

Sands of the sea, More in number than the (prov.), i. 148; ii. 125.

Sandwich, Edward Montagu, 1st Earl of, i. 309.

Sanger, Egbert, *Spectator* sold by, i. xxiv.

Sanguine temper: dangers of a, ii. 252; often achieves success where prudence fails, iii. 44.

Santlow, Hester: Harriet in *The Man of Mode*, i. 278; Flora in *The Country Wake*, iv. 283.

Sap: taking a town by, ii. 429; laying siege by storm or, iv. 535.

Sapper, Thomas, epitaph on, iv. 343.

Sapphic Ode, turn of expression peculiar to, ii. 391.

Sapphira, Claudius Rhynsault and, iv. 241–4.

Sappho: account of, ii. 365–9; her *Hymn to Venus* (in Philips' translation), ii. 367–9; her *Ode to Lesbia* (three translations, by Catullus, Boileau, and Philips), ii. 390–3; an authority on symptoms of love, ii. 393; her brother Charaxus, ii. 407; and Phaon, ii. 408; legend of her suicide, ii. 408–9; Alcaeus in love with, ii. 409; 'adding two strings to the lute', iv. 546.

Saracen's Head, as an inn-sign, i. 500.

Saracens, Richard I a terror to, i. 135.

Sarah, 'the authority of', iv. 451.

Sarrasin, Jean-François, ridiculed *bouts rimés*, i. 258.

Sarsenet, white s. recommended for pale features, ii. 533.

Sash, lawyer in a strawberry, i. 209.

Satan (in *PL*): his role, ii. 564; Milton's description of, iii. 84–87, 114, 566; ashamed but once, iii. 41; not the hero of *PL*, iii. 59; his flight to the earth, iii. 143–8; his speech to the sun, iii. 171; wounded by Michael, iii. 232; temptation of Eve, iii. 307, 310; his actions in Book IX, iii. 307, 310; his return to Hell, iii. 332–3; miserable in the height of his triumphs, iii. 388; his conference with Gabriel in Book IV, iv. 135.

Satiety, quickly follows passion, ii. 281.

Satire: should aim at the vice, not the person, i. 144, 148; iv. 585; allegorical figure of, i. 274; an abusive scurrilous style now passes for, i. 511; instructs us in manners of the times, ii. 318; of Simonides the oldest s. now extant, ii. 318; should expose nothing but what is corrigible, ii. 321; men resent being left out of, ii. 372; on the eminent never fails of success, ii. 495; ill-natured applications of, ii. 518; raillery and, iii. 582–6; Congreve's *Doris* a masterpiece of, iii. 585–6; the *Spectator* accused of secret, iv. 64–65; and defamation, iv. 86–90; panegyrical s. on oneself, iv. 174; the over-wise in detecting, iv. 540–1; strokes of, in epistolary verse, v. 113. *See also* Humour, Ridicule.

Satires: sent in to *Spectator*, i. 71–72; ill effects of lampoons and, i. 97; in acrostic, i. 245; and invectives a part of a Roman triumph, i. 423; general levelling s. of no use to the world, ii. 320–1; iv. 18, 416–17: no s. upon priesthood and marriage in the *Spectator*, ii. 517; against woman, man, the religion of the Faculty, mayors and aldermen, parsons, iv. 18; and lampoons as a remedy for the itch of writing, iv. 590.

Satisfaction(s): which flow from reason and virtue, ii. 87; inward s. in proclaiming errors of the great, ii. 494; secret s. and complacency from beauties of nature, iii. 475–6.

Saturn: father of Jupiter, i. 284; in allegory of love and old age, iii. 76; allegorical depiction of, iii. 596; reign of, iv. 326.

Saturn (the planet), iii. 575; v. 2.

Saturnine and the mercurial, the, ii. 204.

Satyr(s): presenting a vizard, i. 136; on a fan, i. 227; represented in art, ii. 180, 379; accompanying Bacchus, iii. 596; and fauns not necessary to the pastoral, iv. 362.

Sauce(s): the food often grows in one country, the s. in another, i. 295; of an hundred ingredients in a modern meal, ii. 265; for a haunch of venison, iv. 210.

Saucebox, 'encouraged my s. to be witty upon me', ii. 327.

Sauciness, illiberal s. in men of letters, ii. 116.

Saucy: men of late years have been, ii. 6; pride of youth, ii. 100; Homer's description of a man both timorous and, ii. 399.

Saudades, ii. 299.

Saul, Daniel, epitaph on, iv. 343.

Sault, R., translation of Malebranche, i. 155.

Saumaise, Claude de (Salmasius), a variant reading by, iv. 164.

Saunders, Richard, *Apollo Anglicanus*, iii. 374; iv. 591–2.

SAUNTER, BETTY, letter from (on spelling of *dimple*), ii. 53.

SAUNTER, Mrs., a taker of snuff, iii. 279.

Saunter, in the gait of a person interested in belles-lettres, iv. 345.

Savage: philosophy, ii. 8; greatness of soul in Negroes, ii. 339.

Savile, George. *See* Halifax.

Saving, as a means of gaining wealth, iii. 2.

Savoy, Victor Amadeus, Duke of, recovery of his capital, v. 183.

Sawbridge, Jacob (a Director of S. Sea Co.), a subscriber, i. *xc*, *xci*.

Saxon, WILL FUNNELL, the West, iv. 542.

Saxon Heptarchy, beards flourished in the, iii. 222.

Say, Rev. Samuel, ii. *141*.

Scale of being. *See* Chain of being.

Scales, golden, in Milton, Homer, and Virgil, iii. 173–4; iv. 134.

Scaliger, Joseph Justus: on 'Hero and Leander', i. *265*; referred to (?), iv. 163; his objection to Montaigne's egotism, iv. 520.

Scaliger, Julius Caesar: on Musaeus, i. *265*; on Homer, ii. *127*; on Lucan's unnecessary digressions, or 'diverticula', iii. 61; rallying of Homer's *tripodes*, iii. 201; on the English, iii. *521*; a variant reading by, iv. 163.

Scaling, art of, used by military engineers and fortune-hunters, iii. 126.

Scallop: tops of shoes, ii. 15; flap, iii. 163.

'Scamperer, a scowrer and', ii. 576.

Scandal: the *Spectator* not to deal in, i. 71; inflamed by party-spirit, i. 511; a dealer in antique, ii. 72; discovering

s. in some past action of the eminent, ii. 493–4; no private s. in the *Spectator*, ii. 517; a woman without enough curiosity to listen to, iii. 6; prevalence of, iii. 296–8; spreaders of, iv. 1–3; evils of printed, iv. 86–90; a newsletter of whispers proposed, iv. 111–14; seasonings of, in political pamphlets, iv. 536–41; from ladies, iv. 587; ill effects of, v. 31–34; the usual attendant of tea-tables, v. 72.

Scandalum magnatum, iv. 540.

Scanderbeg (George Castriota): Sir ROGER thinks Prince Eugene a greater man than, ii. 549; his bones worn by the Turks, iii. 149.

Scaramouche: in *The Emperor of the Moon*, i. *94*; a Venetian S. in vision of the painters, i. 354; his *tabac de mille fleurs* (samples of snuff), iii. 3.

Scaramouches: in the masquerades, i. 96; in china ware, i. 153.

Scarborough, ii. 104.

Scarecrow, the beggar in Lincoln's-Inn-Fields, i. 28.

Scarecrow, vicious character set up as a, ii. 302.

Scarf, the clergyman's, i. 89; iii. 131; iv. 427; v. 81, 116.

Scarf, woman's: comes from the Torrid Zone, i. 295; a spinster in a coloured, iii. 95.

Scarlatti, Alessandro, i. *23*; ii. *506*.

Scarron, Paul: jested on his deformity, i. 75; a celebrated ill face, i. 77; mentioned, iv. *158*.

Scawen, Thomas (a director of the Bank), a subscriber, i. *xc*.

Scawen, William, the generous merchant of No. 248(?), ii. 464.

Scenes: side s. in the opera, i. 65; no one allowed behind, in the theatre, ii. 435.

Scetanus, example of, in Horace, iii. 248.

Scheffer, John, *Lapponia*, Lapland songs from, iii. 376–8, 518–20.

Schemes: of thought in stages of life, ii. 136–7; laid by human wisdom often perverted by accidents, iii. 44; wrong measures and ill-concerted s. of life, iii. 68.

Schiavonetti, Elisabetta Piloti (opera singer), i. *25*.

School(s): children sent to, to keep them out of harm's way, ii. 39; of equity in Xenophon, iii. 248; fail to teach practical arts, iii. 317–19; for learning to use foils, iv. 425.

'School, Michelangelo's', ii. 390.

Schoolboy(s): an awkward s. and his new sword, ii. 30; flogging of, ii. 114–17, 160–2; letters from, ii. 162; iii. 219–20; little sordid games of, ii. 395; friendship between two at Westminster, iii. 134–5; success of two, iii. 317–18.

Schoolmaster(s): ignorance and brutality of, ii. 114–17, 160–2; account of a kind s. at Richmond, ii. 162; a schoolman learned in Greek, ii. 582; improvement in quality of, iii. 134; account of two rural, iii. 134; inventions in deluding the, iv. 378.

Schoolman (-men): a case put by some ludicrous (Buridan's ass), ii. 248; great friends to definitions and syllogisms, ii. 272; a question started by (concerning eternity), iv. 567–8; ideas of, concerning God, v. 20.

Schoppe, Caspar (Scioppius), a variant reading by, iv. 164.

Schuyler, Col. Peter, i. *211*.

Sciences: each one great enough to occupy a man's whole life, i. 398; we fall short of the ancients in, ii. 467; Milton's display of knowledge of, iii. 62.

Scioppius. *See* Schoppe.

Scipio Africanus Major, Publius, in Cicero's *De Senectute*, iv. 419.

Scipio Africanus Minor, Publius: discerned future greatness of Marius, ii. 114; 'a Scipio or Lelius', iv. 68; in Cicero's *De Senectute*, iv. 418–19.

Scirescot, manor of, v. 76.

Scissors-grinder, cries of, in London streets, ii. 477.

Sclerotes, in the eye, iv. 171.

Scold(s): women who resemble dogs, ii. 319; description of a, iv. 105–6; a toast who was also a, iv. 316.

Scorn: generous s. attending heroic virtue, iii. 204; and mockery the best weapons against atheists, iii. 463; infamy and s. the consequences of vanity, iv. 124.

Scot, Thomas (contractor to the Army), a subscriber, i. *xci*.

Scotch: impudence in a Scotchman untractable and rapacious, i. 87; tone differs from English and Welsh, i. 120; feuds between S. and English the basis of *Chevy Chase*, i. 299; in battle of Chevy Chase, i. 299–300, 317–20; a S. tune, ii. 207; thistle, iv. 104; a saying among the, iv. 136; 'a S. Highlander, and second-sighted', iv. 293.

Scotists and Smiglesians at Oxford, ii. 429.

Scotland: some illiterate part of, ii. 80; Highlands of, ii. 286; Coronation chair

from, iii. 215; a dream-vision sent from, iv. 365; second sight in remote parts of, v. 65.

Scott, John: *The Christian Life* 'one of the finest and most rational schemes of divinity' in any language, iv. 73; its thesis, iv. 73; used in *The Ladies' Library*, i. 159; quoted or cited, i. *457, 459, 490, 492*; ii. *231*; iii. *431, 452*; iv. *120, 348, 566*; v. *51*.

Scourer(s): and breaker of windows, ii. 576; among the Mohocks, iii. 188.

Scouring (turning a suit), i. 276.

Scourings: boundings, friskings, and s. of a dog, iv. 180.

Scouring (roistering): 'scowred all the witty hours of the night', iii. 341; s. and breaking of windows admired by women, v. 58–59.

Scrunching (crunching) coals, iv. 16.

Scratch, master of the political, iv. 538.

Screech-owl, superstition concerning, i. 33, 196.

Screen(s): a fortune-telling, ii. 357; Japan, ii. 480; buying a s. in a China shop, iii. 245; bespeaking a s. in Paul's Church-yard, v. 83.

SCRENE, WILLIAM, letter from (on roles he has played), i. 93–94.

Scribbler(s): an heroic s. called a great genius, ii. 126; of the age a favourite topic in a beginning poet, ii. 482; of lampoons, iii. 56; 's., liar', &c., in modern pamphlets, iv. 537.

Scribendi, Cacoethes, iv. 590.

Scriblerus Club, iv. 161–2.

Scriptores Historiae Augustae, iv. 542.

Scripture: stories in tapestry hangings, ii. 60; and revelation give a modern writer an advantage over an ancient, ii. 75. *See also* Bible.

Scruples, 'perspired five ounces and four s.', i. 106.

Scruples and doubts: raised by infidels, ii. 233; dissipated by gold, ii. 431.

Scrutore (escritoire), ii. 235.

Scudéry, Georges and Madeleine de: *Clelia* and the *Grand Cyrus* in LEONORA's library, i. 154, 156; *Ibrahim*, i. *218*; story of two lovers from 'one of Scudéry's romances', ii. 437–8.

Sculptor(s): lewd devices perpetuated by painters and, ii. 179; art of the s. compared to education, ii. 338–9; sight and the work of the, iv. 171.

Sculpture: of Michelangelo, ii. 390; Leonardo da Vinci a master in, iv. 489.

Scurrility now passes for wit, iv. 88.

Scurvy, the: produced by nurse's milk,

ii. 456; a quack who offers to cure, iv. 59.

Scuttle: Lady BETTY MODELY's, iii. 183; an easy, iv. 412.

Scuttle-fish. *See* Cuttle-fish.

Scythians and Amazons, iv. 22.

Sea: called 'the British common' by Sir ANDREW, i. 10; scheme for banking out the, ii. 285; women who were made out of the, ii. 319, 327; of fire in *PL*, iii. 84–85.

Sea-captain: a woman kept by a, iv. 225; and his wife happily married, v. 80.

Sea-coal, 'immersed in sin and', iv. 390.

Seal (of letter), politicians instructed how to take off the impression of a, iii. 97.

Seals, live on land and at sea, iv. 349.

Seaman, identifiable by his carriage, ii. 271.

Seamen, mermaids or, iv. 349.

Sea-monster, a barber with a dried, iv. 60.

Seamstress, attempted seduction of a prentice, ii. 216–19.

Sea-nymphs, ships transformed into (in the *Aeneid*), iii. 145, 306; v. 15–16.

SEAROOM, Mr., a 'general merchant', ii. 350.

Seasons: change of, pleasing to the imagination, iii. 453, 473–6; allegorical dream-vision of the, iii. 592–7.

Sebastian, Don (King of Portugal): his invasion of Morocco, iii. 301; mentioned, iv. 263; speech of (in Dryden), iv. 435.

Second mourning, an agreeable, iii. 532.

Second sight, among the Scotch, iv. 293, 365; v. 65.

Secret history: some pieces of, dealing with Pharamond, i. 326; offered to *Spectator*, ii. 479–80; could be made from letters sent to *Spectator*, v. 115.

Secret Treaties . . . of the Marshal d'Estrades, i. 390.

Secret(s): betraying of, destroys friendship, i. 291; ii. 375; telling of, ii. 83–4; ii. 388; of numbers, ii. 361; a great rabbinical s. of the Jesuits, iii. 98; Telemachus taught to keep a, iii. 249.

Secretary, Mr., to a wench, iv. 225.

Sectaries: enthusiasm of, ii. 288–9; zeal of, iii. 463; enthusiastic jargon of, iv. 117.

Secundum artem, a patient killed, v. 28.

Sedan chairs, i. 51, 214.

Sedbury (Yorkshire), ii. 117.

Sedley, Sir Charles: Rochester's description of, i. 386; iii. 496; frolics of, iii. *341*; *The Mulberry Garden*, i. *407*; 'Phillis knotting', iv. *413*.

Seduction: account of an attempted, ii. 216–19, 316; account of a, ii. 245–6; v. 87–89; of unfortunate females, ii. 295; a woman who plans s. of others, ii. 303–4.

Segrais, Jean Regnauld de, on the three classes of poetry readers (from Dryden), i. 269.

Séguier, Jean (Chancellor of France), iii. 324.

Selden, John, iii. 209.

SELF, SAMUEL, testimonial praising *Spectator* 177, iv. 460.

Self: man cannot bear a view of himself (Pascal), i. 478; avoidance of self-reproach, a man's first care, i. 497; self-pity, in old age, ii. 100; self-sacrifice in order to relieve the poor, ii. 197–201; our duty towards, ii. 231–2; the best means for self-improvement, ii. 341; self-praise, in the ambitious man, ii. 492–3; *Never do that by proxy which you can do your self* (prov.), iii. 2; a stroke of self-pity in *The Distressed Mother*, iii. 34; hypocrisy of self-deception, iii. 493–6; self-confidence promoted by trust in God, iv. 50; allegorical figure of self-conceit, iv. 123; self-disparagement to be reproved, iv. 174–5; egotism, iv. 519–22; the law of self-defence, iv. 560; Locke's definition of, iv. 575–6.

Self-denial: attended with blessings, ii. 306–9; the great foundation of civil virtue, ii. 462.

Self-esteem: Cinna's, ii. 307–8; in women, ii. 308; proper, ii. 321.

Self-examination: value of, iii. 156; advised by Pythagoras, v. 4; rules for, with regard to scandal, v. 32–34.

Self-interest: one that demurs from, i. 377; brings disappointment, ii. 373–4.

Self-knowledge: importance of, i. 45, 369–70; best means of gaining, ii. 341; rules for arriving at, iii. 494–6.

Self-love: sensitiveness to ridicule, one of the weaknesses of, i. 75; ii. 498; in woman's passion for man, ii. 9–10; and reason direct us to promote our own interest, ii. 231–2; good relations between father and son a transplanted, ii. 255; and flattery, ii. 424; v. 70; taking up ill-will of our parents a sort of, ii. 523; unrecognized by most men, iii. 326; how it may become a virtue, iii. 479; in care of children, often punished, iii. 599; the source of passions (?), iv. 35; shown in men's impatience of being mimicked, iv. 157; allegorical spring of, iv. 366; and bene-

volence, the two principles of action in man, v. 10; the source of benevolent actions (Epicurus and Hobbes), v. 10–11; desire of knowing the future, founded in, v. 64; imitation favours the powerful principle of, v. 70.

Selling: arts of buying and, iii. 94–95; cheats practised in, iv. 453.

SEMANTHE: affects the character of a painted beauty, iii. 512–13.

Seminary of petticoat politicians, in France, iii. 96–97.

Semiramis: rocks cut into figure of, at Babylon, iii. 554; her works of war and peace, iii. 554.

Semonides (of Samos): author of the oldest extant satire, ii. 318; on different types of women, ii. 318–20 (referred to, ii. 324, 448).

SEMPRONIA: a woman addicted to French foppery, i. 193; a matchmaker, iv. 36–37; whether at liberty to choose a new husband, v. 98.

Senate, Roman, represented the nobles, iii. 20.

Senator(s): a grave, ii. 29; Augustus's intrigues with wives of, ii. 247.

Seneca, Lucius Annaeus (the Elder), his objection to style of Calvus, iii. 62.

Seneca, Lucius Annaeus (the Philosopher): 'read S. and quote him against me if you think fit', ii. 121; or Plutarch, ii. 142; or Epictetus, ii. 205; 'be true to love and burn your', ii. 219; death of, iii. 300; or Socrates, iii. 461; and Montaigne patterns for writing essays, iv. 186; mentioned, ii. 268; iv. 306. — *Dialogues*: *De Providentia*: a virtuous man struggling with misfortunes a spectacle the gods might look upon with pleasure, i. 163; ii. 422; iii. 409; *De Ira*, i. 72; iii. 452; *De Consolatione ad Marciam*, ii. 353; *De Otio*, iii. 545; *De Tranquillitate Animi*, i. 330; *De Brevitate Vitae*, we are always complaining our days are few, and acting as though there would be no end of them, i. 394; *De Consolatione ad Polybium*, iv. 565; — *Moral Treatises*: in LEONORA's library, i. 157; *De Beneficiis*, ii. 200, 449; — *Epistles*: on the shortness of time, i. 394; on some men's natural propensity to good, ii. 116; on practice of modesty in secret ('we should fancy that Cato stands before us'), ii. 400; made a practice of writing something every day, iii. 150; on men who shrink into dark corners, iii. 518; 'drunkenness does not produce but discover faults', iv. 543;

'there is a Holy Spirit residing in us', iv. 550; other epistles quoted or cited, ii. 49, 353; iii. 299; — Natural Questions: criticism of Ovid, iii. 364; — Hercules Furens, quoted, i. 89.

Sense: pity, the best and worthiest part of our, ii. 315; discretion found only in men of strong, ii. 377; a happy marriage has all the enjoyments of s. and reason, ii. 516; degrees of, in animals, iv. 348–9; a moral s., iv. 352–3.

Sense, man of, i. 217, 220, 262, &c.; women prefer a coxcomb to a, ii. 9; tries to keep a medium between a fop and a sloven, ii. 91; the woman's man neither a fool nor a, ii. 112; and a coxcomb, ii. 595; in a dress of negligence, iv. 193.

Sense, men of: often absent-minded, i. 330; among servants, i. 406; among soldiers, ii. 96; should give women their company, ii. 119; may become rich, iii. 3; arrogance shocking to, iii. 45.

Sense, good: the father of wit, i. 146; subdues the seeds of punning, i. 259; the ground-work of wit, i. 269; reason and, i. 323, 325, 469–70; overflowing of, thought to produce over-witty authors, ii. 53; and truth in Cicero, ii. 75; more raillery among the moderns, more g. s. among the ancients, ii. 467; and virtue make an agreeable friend, ii. 515; women urged to excel in virtue and, ii. 533; and good nature always go together, iv. 37.

Sense(s): those who lack one s., possess the others with greater force, i. 19–20; in animals adapted to their needs, i. 493–7; fallibility of, ii. 442–3; the outward and the inward, v. 50; 'out of my seven', v. 106; the inlets to all images conveyed to the mind, v. 158.

Sensibility, modesty an exquisite, ii. 399.

Sensitive plant, ii. 8.

Sensitiveness: to ridicule, one of the weaknesses of self-love, i. 75; to praise in a generous mind, ii. 425–6.

Sensoriola, of men and brutes, iv. 532.

Sensorium: infinite space the s. of the Godhead, iv. 532.

Sentence(s): talking s. not the only mark of learning, i. 21; a good s. in a play received with indifference, ii. 315; making s. and observations, ii. 559; in histories more moving than fiction, iii. 487.

Sentiment(s): vulgarity of, in English drama, i. 165; in ballads, i. 315–22, 362–3; avarice kills all the noble s.

that adorn human nature, ii. 372; great s. of Roman writers, ii. 396; music must express some passion or, ii. 505–6; in The Scornful Lady, ii. 554; in the epic, ii. 585–90; swelling s. in Statius and Claudian, ii. 588; delicacy of s. flowing from chastity of thought, ii. 591; sublimity of Milton's style equal to that of his, iii. 14; true delicacy consists in dignity of, iii. 15; greatness of, in The Distressed Mother, iii. 33; defects in s. in PL, iii. 61–62; of Satan in PL appropriate, iii. 86; having worthy s. the test of greatness, iv. 280; in drama, iv. 280–3.

Sentries: moving s. proposed, iv. 408.

SENTRY, Captain (WILLIAM): character of, i. 11–12; nephew and next heir to Sir ROGER, i. 11; iv. 341; commends the Spectator for not attacking the Army, i. 143; on courage in military men, ii. 96–99; on envy among all classes of men, ii. 186–7; a man of good sense but dry conversation, ii. 272; on argumentative conversation of lawyers, ii. 272–3; goes with Sir ROGER to the play, iii. 240; the sword he used at battle of Steenkerke, iii. 240; on magnanimity and courage, iii. 302–4; a letter received from, iv. 339; inherits Sir ROGER's estate, iv. 341, 440; letter from, iv. 445–8; candidates for his place in the Club, iv. 470; mentioned, i. 144; ii. 344.

September, allegorical figure of, iv. 596.

Septimius, Horace's letter recommending, iv. 250.

Sepulchre of Rosicrucius, discovery of, iii. 424–5.

Sequestrator, a cursed, v. 150; an estate sequestered, v. 151.

Seraphim, a set of angels who love most, v. 52.

SERAPHINA, examination of her heart, v. 9.

Serenade: of cat-calls, iii. 352; of a newly-married couple, iii. 370.

Serenity: the title given to princes, ii. 352; of mind, ii. 599; iii. 454; cheerfulness brings a steady and perpetual, iii. 429.

Sergestus: a colourless character in the Aeneid, ii. 562.

Serious: mercurial persons call everything s. stupid, ii. 204; the shadows in pictures represent the s. and melancholy, ii. 447; part of mankind, the most loving, v. 24; mankind divided into the merry and the, v. 43–45.

Seriousness and gravity of a Privy Counsellor, ii. 130.

Serjeant-at-law, in love with a 'demurrer', i. 377; in Westminster Hall, iv. 215, 477-8.

Sermon(s): affected wit in, i. 162; preparation-sermons, i. 199; Sir ROGER's chaplain reads printed, i. 441-2; Latin grammar introduced into, ii. 359-60; of a rabbinical divine, ii. 361; of a Roman Catholic conventual, ii. 466; on 30 January, iii. 21; Dr. Snape's s. on charity schools, iii. 50; Preface to s. of Bishop of St. Asaph, iii. 440-1; learned allusions in, understood only by Cartesians, iii. 578; reflections on a, iv. 365; preached at funeral of Robert Boyle, iv. 394-5; one of Tillotson's delivered with too many changes, iv. 427.

Serpent: of Moses swallowed up that of the Egyptians, i. 45; finds a place to deposit its eggs, i. 490; a man made up of the dove, without the least grain of the, ii. 450; eating of a s. to understand language of birds, iv. 319-20; Apollo's victory over the python, iv. 329.

Servant: experiences of a, i. 405-9; a spruce s., whose hair is under a cap, iii. 296; officiousness of an artful s. in The Fox, iii. 394; JACK TOPER's recommendation of his, iv. 249-50.

'Servant, Humble' (male companion of women), i. 408; ii. 245; iii. 161, 375; v. 67, 96; (professed servants of the fair, ii. 236).

'Servant, Humble' (polite phrase between men), iv. 570.

Servants: corruption of manners in, i. 372-6, 405; imitate manners of their masters, i. 374-6, 409, 443; borrow their masters' clothes, i. 375; Sir ROGER's treatment of his, i. 439-40, 443-5, 500; ii. 41; giving cast clothes to, i. 444; ii. 378-9; children flattered by, i. 502; ii. 254; complaints of, ii. 40-43, 293; treatment of, ii. 43-44, 291-4; how-d'ye, ii. 67; sent to hold seats in the theatre, ii. 163; iv. 523; respect of, how obtained, ii. 291-3; spies upon, ii. 294; misunderstandings created by malice of, ii. 523; of the wealthy look with scorn on the poor, iii. 47; good and useful s. produced by charity schools, iii. 49; influence of manners of, upon children, iii. 49; behaviour of Sir JOHN ENVILLE's, iii. 69; 'politicians' in liveries, iii. 109; speaking impatiently to, iii. 591; iv. 41; swearing at, iv. 46.

Service: virtue and, the foundation of a high name, ii. 349; professors of, to the wealthy, ii. 526.

Servile, a courtier knows how to be s. with an air, ii. 257.

Servilia (Cato's half-sister), ii. 72.

Servitude to a patron, ii. 591-2.

Seth, lived 912 years, iii. 28.

Setting, an impudent and lascivious dance-step, i. 286.

Setting-dog, i. 447; ii. 118.

Settlement(s): the legacy of men of pleasure, ii. 95; important in marriage of widows, iv. 515.

Seven: Champions, i. 59; Punch's Theatre at the Seven Stars, i. 61; Heavens, i. 400; a seventh son, ii. 295; iv. 516; Stars, King Street (a shop), ii. 578-9; Wonders of the World, iii. 437; 'out of my s. senses', v. 106; an odd number, v. 160; Wise Men, v. 160; s. stars form the most beautiful constellation, v. 160.

Sevennight, ii. 78.

Severity: absence of, in men of pleasure, ii. 94; of temper in a worthless man, monstrous, ii. 166; authors of professed, ii. 205; and distance of a father, ii. 254; avoid souring into s. and censoriousness, ii. 445; the severer sects of philosophers, iii. 1; a graceful and becoming, iii. 41; religion in some, expressed in, iii. 80; example more persuasive than the s. of lectures, iii. 82.

Sewell, Sarah, and Co., stall in Covent Garden, iv. 99.

Sewing and embroidery, i. 46.

'Sex, the' (women), ii. 10, 308, 320, 324, &c.

Sex, a kind of s. in the soul itself(?), ii. 8.

Sexes: difference between the, ii. 8-9; unlawful commerce of, the hardest to avoid, ii. 534; equal balance in numbers between, iii. 27-28; mutual benefits of the, iv. 21; balanced against each other, iv. 137; distinction between, the work of Providence, iv. 444.

Sexton: letters from s. of St. Paul's, Covent Garden, i. 61; iii. 400; at Sir ROGER's, ii. 530; 'sometimes taken for a parish s.', iii. 27; letter from s. of St. Bride's, iii. 428-9.

Sextus Empiricus, v. 166.

Seymour, Jane, iii. 487.

Seymour, Richard, The Compleat Gamester, ii. 451; iii. 113, 182, 478.

Seymour, Lieut.-Gen. William, a subscriber, i. lxxxix.

Shades in painting: set off the colours, ii. 399; represent the serious or melancholy, ii. 447.

SHADOW, JOHN: letters from (on sleep and dreams), v. 4–6, 29–31 (referred to, v. 40).

Shadow, fighting with one's, i. 474.

Shadwell, Thomas: his excellent talent of humour, i. 146; ii. 57; breaking of windows by rakes in his plays, i. 146. — *Bury Fair*, i. *346*; ii. *104*; iii. *26*; — *Epsom Wells*: Clodpate in, i. *45*, 207; Frible in, i. *130*; acted at Epping, i. 207; cited, i. *506*; ii. *104*; iii. *292*; — *The Humourists*, i. 202, 375, 407; ii. *8*; — *The Lancashire Witches*: i. *480*; description of a performance of, ii. 57–59; Preface to, ii. *586*; — *The Libertine*, ii. *356*; — *The Miser*, iv. *132*; — *The Scowrers*, i. *218*; ii. *576*; iv. *15*; — *The Squire of Alsatia*, Captain Hackum in, i. *8*; — *The Sullen Lovers*, i. *202*, *298*, *436*; — *A True Widow*: iv. *333*; Young Maggot in, i. *9*, *106*; — *The Virtuoso*, i. *139*; ii. *245*, *532*; — *The Volunteers*, i. *139*; ii. *245*, *356*, *532*; iii. *182*.

Shaftesbury, Anthony Ashley Cooper, 1st Earl of: anecdote of Locke in company with, iv. 403.

Shakespeare, William: noble instances of madness in, i. 94–95; his thoughts often obscured by sounding phrases, hard metaphors, and forced expressions, i. 166; many of his tragedies end happily, i. 170; his tragedies full of puns, i. 260; 'the inimitable': Dryden would not allow even Beaumont and Fletcher capable of imitating him, ii. 58; a remarkable instance of the natural, unlearned genius, ii. 128; audiences have such poor taste that they take little notice of the most exalted parts of his best tragedies, ii. 314; proposal to teach young people to act scenes of, ii. 396; the Trunk-maker's enthusiasm for S.'s tragedies, ii. 415; displayed greater genius in drawing Caliban than Hotspur or Julius Caesar, ii. 586–7; and Lee were guilty of the false sublime, iii. 11; his points and quibbles, iii. 485; 'S. himself could not have made [Anne Boleyn] talk in a strain so suitable', iii. 487; his noble extravagant fancy, in portraying ghosts, fairies, witches, &c., iii. 572–3; Bullock or Penkethman, when they mend a noble play of, iv. 427; 'our inimitable S.' a stumbling-block to rigid critics concerned with the rules, v. 28. — *As You Like It*, quoted, ii. 132; — *Hamlet*: the grave-digger's petition, i. 151; appearance of the ghost a masterpiece in its kind, and appeals to the Trunk-maker, i. 186; ii. 414; compared with *Electra* of Sophocles, i. 189; quoted, i. 186–7; ii. 251, 348; iv. 155–6, 303(?) ('the insolence of office'), 435–6 (Hamlet's celebrated soliloquy); mentioned, i. 331; — *1 Henry IV*: Prince Henry and Falstaff jest on fat and lean, i. 75; Powell as Falstaff, iii. 291; Estcourt as Falstaff, iv. *155*; Hotspur mentioned, ii. 586–7 (also 'Mr. and Mrs. Hotspur', iii. 72); quoted, ii. 450; iii. 349; — *2 Henry IV*: Wilks as the reformed prodigal in, iii. 394; quoted, i. 204; — *2 Henry VI*, quoted, ii. 323–4 (death of Cardinal Beaufort); — *Henry VIII*, quoted, iv. 434, 520; v. 133; — *Julius Caesar*: majesty of character of Brutus, i. 180; character of Caesar mentioned, ii. 586–7; Sheffield's adaptation, iii. 74; quoted, i. 121; — *King John*, quoted, iv. 179, 355; — *King Lear*: an admirable tragedy, except as rewritten to conform to 'poetical justice', i. 170; acted by George Powell, iii. 291; 'the next acting of', v. 26; quoted, iv. 434; — *Macbeth*: a woman's silly actions at a performance of, i. 194; the incantations and witches in, ii. 58; story derived from Hector Boethius, ii. 58; audience's wrong reactions to, ii. 314; Lady Macbeth, ii. 315; iv. 434; Wilks as Macduff in, iii. 393–4; quoted, ii. 308; iv. 434–5; — *A Midsummer Night's Dream*, quoted, i. 476; iv. 217; — *Othello*: a successful tragedy which ends unhappily, i. 170; Othello's uneasiness over a handkerchief, i. 244; iv. 219; 'foolish Roderigos', ii. 304; quoted, ii. 105; mentioned, i. 331; — *The Tempest*: creation of character of Caliban, ii. 586–7; new stage properties for, v. 26; — *Timon of Athens*: acted by George Powell, iii. 291; v. 47; mentioned, v. 47.

Shakings and distortions practised by beggars, iv. 12.

Shales, Charles, a subscriber, i. *xc*.

SHALLOW, JOHN, Esq., letter from (on the cat-call), iii. 349–50.

SHALUM, HILPA and, iv. 596–8; v. 1–3 (mentioned, v. 83).

Shame: the greatest of all evils, i. 360; the false s. of appearing what one really is, i. 468; after debauchery, ii. 94; sense of s. and honour, ii. 115; fear

of, in the Spartan boy, ii. 116; fear of, in women of ancient Greece, ii. 400; raised in the profligate, iii. 41; and reproach do not deserve name of evils, iii. 431; and infamy the consequences of vanity, iv. 124.

Shamefaced: people, who avoid decency of behaviour, ii. 400; favour a necessary consequence to the s. man, iv. 216.

Shamrock, the Irish, iv. 104.

SHAPELY, Mr.: B. D. in love with, iv. 184.

Shark, iii. 275.

Sharp: a s. fellow, i. 407; to look, ii. 22; *sharp's the word* (prov.), iii. 508; and biting, 'as the term is', iii. 583.

Sharper(s), ii. 356; iv. 289.

Sharp-set (hungry), Rabelais's expedient when, iii. 4.

She: 'the happiest She in Kent', iv. 182; 'the fairest She I ever saw', v. 96; She-Romps, ii. 345–6; She-Professors, ii. 458; She-Slanderers, iii. 465; She-Disciples of the *Spectator*, iv. 29; She-Machiavils, iv. 518.

Sheep: in valley of Baghdad, ii. 126; on Sir ROGER's estate, iii. 54; hanging for stealing, v. 93; Goodman D.'s, pounded, v. 128.

Sheepish: dejectedness, ii. 470; look s., when it may do service, v. 23.

Sheepishness: modesty not to be confounded with, iii. 404; passing for modesty, iv. 217.

Sheep's eye (prov.); denotes an amorous roguish look, ii. 471; the Steward was observed to cast a, v. 131.

Sheffield, John (later 3rd Earl of Mulgrave; Duke of Buckingham and Normanby): his *Essay on Poetry* a masterpiece, ii. 486; verses from his Prologue to *Julius Caesar*, iii. 74; his character of Charles II, iv. 133.

Shell-fish: just above dead matter, iv. 347; the mouth of a, iv. 452.

Shells: bugles, bredes, and, i. 50; in china ware, i. 153.

SHENKYN, DAVYTH AP, letter from (his love for Mrs. Gwinifrid), ii. 384–5.

Shepard, Thomas, *Theses Sabbaticae*, iv. 586.

Shephard, the Misses, ii. 55, *141*.

Shepherd, Sir Fleetwood, ii. 55, *141*; lines by, i. *340*.

Shepherd, Samuel (a Director of the Bank), a subscriber, i. xc; mentioned, iv. *538*.

Shepherd(s): who juggled eggs, ii. 130; in Theocritus, ii. 382–3; in Philips'

Pastorals, iv. 362–3; Cephalus, the Eolian, iv. 381; Colin, in Byrom's poem, v. 62.

Shepherd's pipe: poems in shape of, i. 246; music of, in Vision of Mirzah, ii. 122.

Shepherdesses, at the masquerade, i. 63.

Sheriff: 'serving s.', i. 335; Sir ROGER S. of the county, i. 464; of City of London, iv. 4; knighted for bringing up an address, v. 93.

Sherlock, William: *A Practical Discourse on Death*: in LEONORA's library, i. 155; 'one of the strongest persuasives to a religious life' in any language, iii. 29; discussion of Heaven and Hell in, iv. 73; quoted, iv. 321–2.

Sheth, 'Adam, S., Enosh' (a preacher's text), ii. 361.

Shift, a lady's, iii. 381; sleeves, ii. 190.

Shilling: 'a s. the man' in an advertisement, ii. 117; a s. for coach-hire, ii. 199; a crooked s. as a token for absent lovers, ii. 452.

Shine, 'in constant good humour and s., as we call it', i. 325.

Ship(s): of Sir ANDREW, i. 11; carry British manufactures over the world, i. 91–92; duly trimmed, wants neither sail nor ballast, ii. 9; plundering of a s. which struck upon a rock in the West, iii. 47; greatest conquerors always burn their, iii. 53; Homer's catalogue of, iii. 87; transformed into sea-nymphs (in the *Aeneid*), iii. 145, 306; v. 15–16.

Shipman, John (a Director of the Bank), a subscriber, i. xc.

Shipping trade, ii. 404.

Shipton, Mother, NELL TROT the counterpart of, i. 78.

Shirt(s), i. 351; ruffled down to his middle, ii. 14; an audacious display of the Holland, iv. 345.

Shiver, DULCISSA's pretty, iv. 245.

Shock-dog: a lady's, iii. 276; a white, with bells, iii. 320.

Shoe(s): high-heeled, with a glazed waxleather instep, i. 206; with high scollop tops, ii. 15; many a sixpence for wiping his, ii. 92; particular s. used by a Gothic bishop, ii. 290; thick enough for the weather, ii. 386; higher heels to his, ii. 388; the housemaid who struck her lover with her, ii. 513; effect of a clumsy pair of s. on a coquette's heart, ii. 595; double-soled, iii. 154; tongue of shoe-buckle, iii. 154–5; the laced, iv. 100; a low-

heeled, iv. 377; cleaning, v. 41; the street-cry of 'old shoes', v. 42.

Shoe-cleaners, profanation of Sabbath by, v. 116.

'Shoeing-horns', young men used as, iv. 414–15.

Shoemaker, i. 117, 202; the real hero of *The Man of Mode*, i. 280; PARTHENOPE marrying a, v. 38.

Shoe-strings, wearing, with great success, ii. 91.

SHOOESTRING, RACHEL, letter from (describing the Swingers), iv. 260.

Shoot flying, i. 498; iii. 418.

Shop, *Keep your shop, and your shop will keep you* (prov.), Sir William Turner's rule, iv. 308.

Shop-keeper(s): difficulties of, ii. 108–10, 245–6; letter from a, ii. 582–3; methods of, to entice customers, iii. 94–95.

Shop-maid, ii. 581.

Shop-signs. *See* Signs.

Shops: letter from MELISSA (has a shop in the New-Exchange), ii. 326–7; a history of s. in London desirable, iv. 5; wealthy s. in London, iv. 101–2.

SHORT, BOB, letter from, iv. 177.

Short, Thomas, *A Dissertation upon Tea*, iii. *207*.

SHORT, TOM, a football player, ii. 132, 134.

SHORTER, ROBIN, letter from, iv. 222.

'Short-Face', letter to Mr. SPECTATOR as, iii. 223.

Short-hand: value of, iii. 319; mentioned, iii. 397.

Short-sighted: perspective-glasses for the, ii. 473; man a s. creature, iii. 44.

Short-sightedness, cunning a kind of, ii. 376.

Shoulder(s): the princess who carried her lover over the snow on her, ii. 215–16; politicians taught how to shrug up their, and how to elevate the left, iii. 97–98; a pair of round, iv. 510.

Shoulder-belt, as a device in comedy, i. 191.

Shoulder-knot, the footman's, v. 81.

Shovell, Sir Cloudesley: his monument in Westminster Abbey, i. 110; iii. 214.

'Show' of Midgets, a, consisting of a man, a woman, and a horse, ii. 557–8.

Show, outward: pursued by most men, ii. 257; and pomp often derided, ii. 526; outshining others in pomp and, ii. 546.

Shrew, BENJAMIN BAMBOO's efforts to tame a, iv. 209.

Shrewsbury. *See* Salop.

Shrimp, transmigration into a, iii. 276.

Shrug, politicians taught how to, iii. 97–98.

Shuttlecocks, a set of, i. 448.

Shuttleworth, John, *Treatise of Opticks*, ii. *470*.

Sibyl(s): 'those antiquated', i. 34; in Virgil, ii. 129; Aeneas and the S. before the adamantine gates, iii. 282; 'I would have you tell the town the story of the', iv. 129; prophecies of the, iv. 258.

Sicilian: MENALCUS, the, ii. 406; proverb, iv. 581.

Sicily: Pyrrhus' designs on, ii. 212; Sappho's voyage into, ii. 366; 'Dionysius' Ear' in, iv. 44; women of, and the dogs of Vulcan, iv. 581–2.

Sick: humours of the s. driven out of one limb into another, ii. 5; peevishness natural to the, ii. 156; obligation of visiting a s. friend, iii. 406–7; JOHN RHUBARB's habit of complaining that he is, iv. 9–10.

Sickness: excessive concern over, i. 105–8; not a subject for conversation, i. 420; is the portion of our very make, ii. 88; more violent and dangerous in youth, ii. 102; influence of, on our bodies and minds, ii. 137; often results from gluttony and intemperance, ii. 264–7; only an apparent evil to the just man, ii. 421–2; iii. 431; a woman who professes s. upon all occasions, iii. 6; imagination in dreams and, iii. 579; 'a thought in', iv. 320–4; Dr. Hammond's reflections on, iv. 564.

Side-face, PRETTYMAN obliges sometimes only with a, iv. 221.

Side-peep, through a hood or fan, ii. 472.

'Sides, Much might be said on both', i. 499, 500.

Sidney, Sir Philip: his praise of the ballad of *Chevy Chase*, i. 298, 316; erred in commenting on its 'rude style', i. 316; epitaph (by William Browne) on S.'s sister, iii. 185. — *Arcadia*, i. 63; in LEONORA's library, i. 155.

Siege, ii. 150; taking a town by sap, ii. 429; of Buda, iii. 70; of Hensburg, iv. 269; of a barmaid by a lawyer, iv. 407–8; of Bouchain, iv. 407; methods of laying s. to women, iv. 535–6.

Sighs, sighing: in the Amorous Club, i. 126, 197; teaching a girl to sigh when she is not concerned, i. 281; part of the devotion paid to 'Idols', i. 313; of lovers, ii. 177; iii. 469, 595; a coquette sighs when she is not sad, ii. 459; of grief, iv. 277.

Sight: a treatise on, ii. 469–72; iv. 170–3; the most perfect and delightful of the senses, iii. 535; source of pleasures of the imagination, iii. 536; iv. 170; cases of men restored to, iv. 168–9, 173; cannot comprehend Paradise, iv. 584.

Sight, pleasures of: Mr. SPECTATOR's pleasures those of sight, i. 21, 288; ii. 446; improved by study of pictures, ii. 446–8.

Signior, the Grand: Charles XII took refuge with, i. *182*; obliged to learn a handicraft trade, iii. 319.

Signs (in streets and on shops): a project for reformation of, i. 115–18 (this letter praised, iv. 438); Superintendent or Inspector of, i. 116; iii. 354, 413; Sign of the Gaper, at Amsterdam, i. 200; tradesmen's, iii. 348; iv. 4, 101, 422.

Silence: now ill-bred, i. 193; a beautiful eye makes s. eloquent, ii. 479; of our poverty is a recommendation, iii. 346; eating in s. at the chop-house, iv. 102; allegorical figure of, iv. 326; as a reproof to tellers of extravagant stories, iv. 422–3.

Silent: flattery of women's pretty faces, ii. 480; perfections in the soul of a good man, ii. 500; smiles carrying a s. reproof, iii. 80.

Silenus: the drunkard, rather than S., whom I shall try to expose, i. 72; Socrates resembled S. in appearance, i. 368.

Silius Italicus and Horace, Addison's guides through Italy, iii. 369.

Silk(s), i. 91; ii. 346, 557; iii. 42; a wholesale dealer in, i. 277; a s. waistcoat, ii. 14; *soft as s.* (prov.), ii. 327; ornaments of jewels, s., and colours, ii. 552; importation of, iii. 26; turning over s., laces, and ribbands, iv. 101; and brocades in Motteux's shop, iv. 479; and mohair in embroidery, v. 83.

Silkmen, i. 276.

Silk-weavers: Sir ANDREW calls the Persians our, i. 296.

Silkworm: after spinning, lays her eggs and dies, i. 458; a cant-phrase for a woman who turns over goods without buying, iv. 101.

Silver: coat and waistcoat trimmed and embroidered with, i. 434; a beaver hat edged with, i. 434; in romance-writers, iii. 18.

SILVIA and THYRSIS, iii. 480.

SIMAETHA, her leap into the Ionian sea, ii. 407.

Simias of Rhodes, i. *247*; his epitaph on Sophocles, iv. 474.

Simile(s): of the top in the *Aeneid*, ii. 542; quaint s. in vogue among modern poets, iii. 90; in *PL*, iii. 91, 310; ignorance in use of, iv. 106.

Similes (a game), ii. 451.

Similitude(s): a species of wit, i. 264; in epic poetry seldom contain wit, i. 264; of the ancients extravagant rather than correct, ii. 127–8, 318; chosen for illustration in *Spectator*, ii. 358; Jesus taught by, iii. 327.

Similitude of manners: required for happiness in marriage, ii. 545; one of the strongest motives to affection and esteem, v. 176.

Simonides of Ceos, anecdote of, iv. 392. *See also* Simias of Rhodes.

Simonides of Samos. *See* Semonides.

SIMPER, JENNY, letter from (on decorating church with greens), ii. 600 (comment on, iii. 8–9).

Simper, a kind of, ii. 207.

SIMPLE, RALPH, letter from (on roles he has taken), i. 94.

SIMPLE, WILL, smitten by a lady's glance, iii. 417.

Simple: truth elegantly recommended, ii. 447; and implex fable, iii. 58; opening lines of *PL* s. and unadorned, iii. 84.

Simplicity: native s. of aspect, in AMARYLLIS, ii. 69; an art which leads to tranquillity, ii. 269; and coarseness of age of Semonides, ii. 318; in worldly affairs, often ridiculous, ii. 449–50; noble s. of behaviour in first ages of world, ii. 467; Homer's faults due to s. of his age, ii. 589; impositions on s. of young women, iii. 73.

Simplicity (in writing): a mark of good writing, i. 268, 287; iii. 530; of style in *Chevy Chase*, i. 303, 316; in the verse of *Two Children in the Wood*, i. 362; in Tillotson's sermons, i. 430; in Ambrose Philips, ii. 367; pleasure of greatest variety and s. in *PL*, ii. 540–1.

Simson, Robert: No. 524 ascribed to, iv. *364–5*.

Sin: properly the Portress of Hell, iii. 120; Discord the daughter of, in *PL*, iii. 338; 'immersed in s. and sea-coal', iv. 390.

Sin and Death, Allegory of (in *PL*): lacking in probability, ii. 563–4; iii. 61, 119, 145–6, 336–9; mentioned, iii. 331, 573.

Sincerity: lack of, in conversation, i. 429–32; Tillotson on, i. 429–32; iii.

314–16; iv. 503; honest plainness and, ii. 449; the tongue to be tuned by, ii. 462; goodness of actions weighed by s. of intentions, ii. 501; necessary in pleasing others, ii. 592.

Singing: of catches, i. 311; ii. 372; in a coffee-house objected to, ii. 73, 81–82; 'if you sing, you sing very ill', ii. 81; theatrical manner of s. psalms, ii. 305-6; and dancing, iii. 205.

Singing-Master, an itinerant, i. 461.

Singing-Psalms, the, i. 461.

SINGLE, Lady BETTY, one of the greatest fortunes about town, iv. 184.

Single Life, The Plagues of a, ii. 89.

Singular: a mind to appear, ii. 517; Sir ROGER odd and, iii. 54; the fear of appearing, iv. 116, 196, 569; the epithet, iv. 181.

Singularity: in dress, ii. 90–93, 110–11; iv. 570; pride in s. of judgement, ii. 494; affectation of, ii. 525–8; when laudable and when vicious, iv. 569–71.

Sinner, more to be condemned than a heretic, ii. 228.

Sinning, man's addiction to, ii. 136–7.

Sinon (in the *Aeneid*), a beautiful improvement on Homer, ii. 563.

'Sins, shining' (heathen virtues), ii. 331.

Sion, songs of, iii. 515.

'Sippers', the world filled with, ii. 364.

SIPPET, JACK, negligent in keeping appointments, iv. 74.

Sips, drams, and whets, iv. 542.

Sirach, son of, quoted, ii. 375; iii. 261; iv. 394. *See also* Bible.

Sirens, the, story of, regarded by many as an allegory, iii. 146.

Siris, P. (dancing-master), i. *285*.

Sirloin, iv. 340.

Sisters: 'all the s. were virtuous', i. 417; three s. ruined by over-sanguine expectations, ii. 598–9.

Sisyphus, ii. 76, 485.

Six Nations, King of the, i. 212.

Sixpence, a silver, iv. 60.

Sixtus V, Pope, his inhuman treatment of Pasquin, i. 99.

'Skill of the purse', the cardinal virtue of this life, i. 444.

Slans, Mr., advertises citron water, iii. *479*.

Skippers (dancers), hobblers and, iii. 112.

Skylark, a man who imitates the singing of a, iv. 546.

Sky-rocket, falling on TOM TYLER, v. 106, 108.

SLACK, SAMUEL: letter from (on use of time), iii. 148–51 (referred to, iii. 169).

Slander and gossip, i. 97–100; ii. 558–60; iii. 296–8, 463–6; iv. 1–3, 86–90; v. 31–34, 87–90.

Slashes, about a man's clothes, i. 451.

Slated house, iii. 189, 210.

Slattern(s): women who resemble swine, ii. 319; description of a, iv. 100; effects of love upon the, v. 24.

Slavery, above nine parts of the world in ten in a state of, iii. 21.

Slaves: killed to attend obsequies of their kings, i. 276; men who are s. to affection, ii. 194–6; account of Negro s. at St. Christopher's, ii. 339–40; who approve and smile at all a great man says, iii. 478.

Sleep: no perception of time, in. i. 399–401; of Nicholas Hart, ii. 224–7; as a personage in the *Iliad*, iii. 337; the mind's activity in, v. 4–6, 29–31, 40–43; has been called the image of death, v. 29.

Sleeve(s): a coat with slit, ii. 14–15; a mantua without leads in the, ii. 579; *to have something in your* (prov.), iv. 60.

Sleeveless errand (prov.), i. 202.

Slippers, ii. 247, 290, 576.

Sloe (fruit of the blackthorn), i. 295.

Sloper, William (contractor to the Army), a subscriber, i. *xci*.

Sloth: 'has ruined more nations than the sword', i. 10; complaint of a husband's, ii. 326–7.

Sloven: commencing a s. to become a wit, ii. 90; medium between a fop and a s. desirable, ii. 91; a husband who is a s. at home, ii. 202; slovenly dress of a beau, v. 156.

Slow but sure (prov.), ii. 52.

Slut(s), ii. 16, 39, 441; women who resemble swine, ii. 319.

Sly, John (haberdasher and tobacconist), i. lvi; advertisement of, ii. 237–8; death of, ii. *238*; 'a pipe of John Sly's best', ii. 530; appointed by Mr. SPECTATOR to keep an eye on coachmen, iv. 374, 376–7; his reports, iv. 399–400, 408, 453.

SLY, KITTY, slays with a glance, iii. 418.

Slyboots (Dr. William Lancaster), i. 183.

Smalbroke, Richard (later Bishop of St. David's . . .), a subscriber, i. *lxxxviii*.

Small-coal, cries of retailers of, ii. 475.

Small-coal man, a sleeper waked by a, v. 42.

Smallpox: advertisement for cure of, iii. *101*; fatal to Thomas Sapper, iv. 343; mentioned, iv. 590; as a destroyer of beauty: i. 139, iv. 211; in Mrs. VIZARD, i. 77; in PARTHENISSA, iii. 101;

in NARCISSA, iii. 472; in MONIMIA, v. 96.

Smalridge, George (Bishop of Bristol), iii. *459*; referred to (?), ii. 80.

Smaragdine Table of Hermes, iii. 600.

Smarts, and all sorts of wits, iv. 53.

Smatterers: in poetry, i. 248; in tragedy, ii. 126; in anatomy, ii. 595; in criticism, v. 27.

Smelling: 'to a lock of hay', ii. 21; a tincture to restore sense of, advertised, iv. *462*.

Smells and sounds: why made agreeable to man, iii. 453; pleasing to the imagination, iii. 544.

Smiglecius, Martin, ii. *429*.

Smiglesians and Scotists at Oxford, ii. 429.

Smile(s): teaching a girl to s. when she is not pleased, i. 281; carrying a silent reproof, iii. 80; JOHN GOSSELIN slain by a lady's, iii. 418; what constructions may be put upon a, v. 23.

Smirk: a smirking air, i. 354; an allusion to bawdry produces a pleasing, ii. 315.

Smith, Father Bernard (organ-builder), iv. *479–80*.

Smith, Edmund, *Phaedra and Hippolitus*: an admirable tragedy, scarcely given a third day's hearing, i. 81; a noble tragedy with a happy ending, i. 170; Epilogue to, praised, iii. 267.

Smith, John (a Director of the Bank), a subscriber, i. *xc*.

Smith, Joseph, married Mrs. Tofts, iv. 55.

Smithfield bargain (prov.), a marriage of interest, iii. 92.

SMOAKY, THOMAS, letter from (a footman), ii. 293 (this letter praised, iv. 461).

Smock, a prize for running, ii. 134.

Smock-faced, i. 197; iii. 221.

'Smoke' (to smell or suspect): WILL TRIPPIT begins to be smoaked, i. 393.

'Smoke' (to ridicule, banter): fearing lest they should smoak Sir ROGER, iii. 242; smoking a cobler in a frolic, iii. 341.

Smoking, i. 41, 58, 134, 209, 226, &c.; in coffee-houses, i. 3; ii. 551; iv. 539; a monkey who takes a pipe of tobacco, i. 119; Mr. SPECTATOR smokes his pipe, i. 198; my morning's pipe, ii. 29; by country gentlemen till they cannot see, ii. 96; tobacco and taking snuff, ii. 364; a pipe in quiet, ii. 442; a pipe of John Sly's best, ii. 530; three pipes of Virginia, iii. 153; a pipe and a half, iii.

154; a roll of best Virginia, iii. 213; effect of habit on, iv. 70; lighting a pipe at the same candle an overture of friendship, iv. 539.

'Smoky' (shrewd, suspicious): 'a smoaky old fellow', ii. 24; 'the uncle smoaky, rotten, poor', iii. 166.

SMOOTHLY, FRANK, within a month of a coxcomb, i. 393.

Smoothness, Pope's illustration of insipid s. in poetry, ii. 484.

Smug (smooth, sleek), iv. 5.

Smut-note taught, iii. 353.

Smutting, ii. 550.

Smyrna: our factory at, i. 131; advice from, iii. 155.

Snails, drawing in their horns, i. 415.

Snake in the grass (prov.): Virgil's warning of, iii. 374.

Snape, Dr. Andrew, sermon on charity-schools, iii. 50.

SNAPP, Mrs., a member of the Widow-Club, iv. 516.

'Snapp'd a judgment' (legal jargon), iv. 477.

Snarler, the, description of, iv. 41.

Sneaker (bowl), of five gallons, v. 105.

Snow: *white as s.* (prov.), i. 264; ii. 408; persons who try to prove that s. is white, ii. 46; the princess who carried her lover on her shoulders over the, ii. 215–16; to say s. is white a vulgar error, ii. 442; in romance writers, iii. 18; showers of, in the play-house, v. 26.

Snuff: i. 65, 314; ii. 434; iii. 492; the best plain or perfumed, ii. 46; the 'careless', 'scornful', 'politic', and 'surly' pinch of, ii. 47; smokers of tobacco and takers of, ii. 364; kinds and prices of, iii. *278*; 'right Spanish' in the beau's head, ii. 571; Scaramouche's new kind 'of a thousand flowers', iii. 3; women taking, iii. 55, 278; coffee and, iii. 97; disagreeable sights and sounds caused by taking, iii. 279; taking a pinch of, in church, iii. 279, 427; 'Apoplectic' s. advertised, iv. *61*; effect of habit on, iv. 70; 'right and fine Barcelona', iv. 345; she took a pinch of s. out of his rival's box, v. 69; a beau's linen daubed with plain Spanish, v. 156.

Snuff-box(es): and canes, 'the usual helps to discourse', i. 124; of silver, shaped like a book, i. 153; a beau eternally playing with his, i. 185; mentioned, i. 241, 248, 385; iii. 165; with Titus Oates's picture in the lid, i. 244; management of, ii. 31; exercise

and ceremony of, taught, ii. 46–47; rules for offering to a stranger, a friend, or a mistress, ii. 47; with a picture in the lid, ii. 453; iii. 183; with a mirror in the lid, iii. 190–1; behaviour in presenting a s. taught, iii. 415; a man who could moralize upon a, v. 138; WILL HONEYCOMB's management of the, v. 184–5.

Soap, the late tax upon, iv. 230.

Soap-boiler, a, his remarks on the *Spectator*, iv. 230.

'Sober man', has come to mean 'a spiritless fellow', iv. 370.

Sobriety: of heart which is above all pleasures, ii. 67; without devotion, insipid, ii. 287; importance of temperance and, iv. 448.

Social virtues, the, i. 395.

Society: kind of men formed for, i. 210; kept up by good nature, ii. 165; concerned in the calumny of a good man, ii. 349; religion consults the harmony and order of, ii. 374; order is the support of, ii. 554; iii. 510.

Society for the Inspection of Modes and Fashions, proposed, ii. 193.

Society for the Reformation of Manners, letter from a director of the, i. 35.

Society of Reformers, v. 116.

Society, the Fashionable, officers in, iv. 196.

Socinian: a most impudent S. for half an hour, iv. 500.

Socrates: brought philosophy down from Heaven, i. 44; sensitive to satire of Aristophanes, i. 98; confessed that he knew nothing, i. 230; called the wisest of men, i. 284; iii. 523; learnt to dance, i. 284; 'a citizen of the world', i. *294*; pronounced lewd and libidinous by a physiognomist, i. 368; his death, ii. 25–26, 334; iii. 300; on beauty, ii. 68; 'the greatest mere man that ever breath'd', ii. 76; his speech to his judges, ii. 75–76, 334; an immoral man the counterpart of, ii. 155; and Xantippe, ii. 196, 459; iv. 199–200, 209, 223; v. 75–76; his reflections on pleasure and pain, ii. 221–2; asked his friends to sacrifice a cock to Aesculapius, ii. 234; resisted the plague, ii. 266; his method of reasoning, ii. 274, 428–9; iii. 107; on prayer, ii. 310–13; iii. 470; compared to Jesus, ii. 314; 'that divine philosopher', ii. 334; Erasmus's admiration of, ii. 334; instructed by Aspasia, ii. 458; Antiphanes lived before, iii. 29; on tracts in Persia reserved for the queen's

dress, iii. 53–54; his mother, a midwife, could not deliver a woman unless she was first with child, iii. 107; overcame defects and improved gifts of nature, iii. 150; and Seneca, iii. 461; appearance of great geniuses in time of, iii. 529; frequented Athenian plays, iv. 67; some further account of, requested, iv. 209; his 'Domestics', iv. 223; practical success of his discourse on love, iv. 272–3; on Mt. Parnassus, iv. 329; on the misfortunes of mankind, iv. 506.

Sodom, Abraham's interceding for, iii. 131.

Soft: gentleman, i. 451; and indolent manner, ii. 111; names, ii. 113; and tender hypocrisy, ii. 169; insinuations, ii. 424; Mr. PRIM's s. air in dancing, iii. 415.

SOFTLY, Sir SIMON, murdered by a frown, iii. 417.

Softness: a man who affects the s. and effeminacy of a woman, i. 435; gentle s. desirable in woman, ii. 70; tenderness towards a wife is not s. or effeminacy, ii. 418; of behaviour in a shopkeeper, iii. 94; caused by grief, iv. 350.

Sohemus, put to death by Herod, ii. 177–8.

Soldier(s): affrighted at his own shadow, i. 54; the S.'s Prayer, i. 197; of fortune, ii. 23; true character of, ii. 96–99; iv. 447–8; repines at the courtier's power, ii. 187; Moses' vision of the s. killing an old man, ii. 423; Germanicus listened in disguise to his, ii. 425–6; insolence of the man in a red coat, iii. 322; appearance of destitute s. in London, iv. 11; the vainglorious s. in ancient comedy, iv. 68; Capt. SENTRY's provision for retired, iv. 447–8; letters from, iv. 533–6.

Solitude: exemption from passions the only pleasing, i. 19; the source of true happiness, i. 67–68; ii. 88, 525–6; an unnatural being to women, ii. 119; and guilt most unfit for each other, ii. 281; in s. we should fancy that Cato stands before us, ii. 400; contrasted with public life, iii. 517–18; allegorical figure of, iv. 325; Cowley's praise of, v. 86–87, 94–95.

Solomon: compares nose of his beloved to Tower of Lebanon, ii. 127; on charity, ii. 199; cautions against careless talk, iv. 43; modesty in days of, iv. 216; on mischief done by fools, iv. 219; sinned through love of women,

iv. 312; Temple of, iv. 583; v. 15. *For
Solomon's Song and* Wisdom of Solomon *see* Bible.

Solon: iv. *506*; his law forbidding neutrality, i. 72; his reply to a friend who advised him not to grieve, iv. 565.

SOMBRIUS, a gloomy religious man, iv. 253.

Somers, John, Lord, i. xxx; a subscriber, i. *lxxxviii*; member of Kit-Cat Club, i. *42*; encouraged Tonson to publish *PL*, ii. *538*; referred to(?), iv. 39; first volume of *Spectator* dedicated to, v. 174–5.

Somerset, Elizabeth, Duchess of, a subscriber, i. *lxxxviii*.

Somervile, Sir Philip de, and the Flitch of Bacon, v. 76–80.

Somnus, Momus, son of, v. 27.

Son: relationship to parents, ii. 252–6, 521–5; Andromache's care for her, iii. 32; a modern woman of Hensburg with her s. on her back, iv. 271; 'the submission of a s. with the impatience of a lover', iv. 401; actions of an undutiful, iv. 509.

Song(s): obscene s. learned by birds, i. 152; and fables that are come from father to son, i. 297; and tunes of itinerant tradesmen, ii. 477; a loose trivial s. gains the affections, iv. 246; women writers of, v. 72.

Songs: 'The Merry Beggars', ii. 405; 'The Fifth of November', ii. 530; 'The Old Man's Wish', iii. 532; 'London City's Triumph', iv. 283. *See also* Ballads.

Sonnet(s): a bundle of, in a beau's head, ii. 571; TOM TRUELOVE has written a, v. 116.

Sonneteer(s): 'like an easy writer, or a', i. 451; a little s. called a fine genius, ii. 126; makers of flower-gardens are like, iv. 190; verses above the ordinary run of, v. 24.

Soon, Thomas (prize-fighter), 'the bold Welshman', iv. *33*.

Sophia, Electress of Hanover, i. *15*.

SOPHIA, letter from (on seeing Mr. SPECTATOR), iii. 34 (reply, iii. 34).

Sophists, sophisters, ii. 385; v. 27.

Sophocles, ii. 396; sometimes guilty of the false sublime, iii. 11; epitaph on, iv. 474. — *Electra*, compared with Hamlet and Corneille's *Horace*, i. 189–90; — *Oedipus the King*: proceeds upon a story most proper for tragedy, iii. 58–59; incident in, iii. 358.

Sophonisba, or Hannibal's Overthrow. See Lee.

SOPHRONIA: her real loveliness, i. 140; advised to do needlework, v. 72; query from, regarding a second marriage, v. 99.

SOPHROSUNIUS, letter from (on insolence in London streets), iii. 321–2.

Sophy of Persia, a 'tributary' of Aretino, i. 99.

Sorbière, Samuel, *Voyage to England*, i. *247–8*.

Sorcerer, Raphael's painting of the, ii. 379.

Sorites, a pile of faggots as a kind of, ii. 431.

Sorrow: none of human race above the reach of, i. 359; ii. 164–5; consolation in, ii. 139–43; iii. 486; representation of, in *The Distressed Mother*, iii. 32–33; iv. 434; condemned by Stoics, iii. 486; expression of, in poetry and history, iii. 486–7; raised by hymns and anthems, iii. 515; depicted by Shakespeare in *Henry VIII*, iv. 434.

Sot: 'I have a sot of a husband', ii. 480; a 'Sot's Journal', received by the *Spectator*, iii. 181.

'Sothades, To the', letter from BELLINDA, ii. 299–300.

Soul(s): in inanimate objects, i. 236–7; the body as the habitation of the, i. 367; is the same, before and after death, i. 381; immateriality of, an argument for immortality, i. 456–7; perpetual progress of, to perfection, i. 457–9; ii. 322; iv. 72–73, 393, 577; felicity of, consists in action, i. 475; some have imagined a kind of sex in, ii. 8; burning the body to save the, ii. 229; mortality of, one of the great points of atheism, ii. 230; Semonides on the s. of women, ii. 318–20; without education, like marble in the quarry, ii. 338; modesty a quick and delicate *feeling* in, ii. 399; greatness of, seen in benevolence, ii. 418; Cartesian doctrine that the s. always thinks, ii. 460; laughter causes a kind of remissness in, ii. 466; without passions, of a remiss and sedentary nature, ii. 490; many silent perfections in the s. of a good man, ii. 500; pineal gland as the seat of, ii. 571; cheerfulness keeps the soul in a perpetual calm, iii. 451; constant activity of, iv. 226–7; v. 6; Hadrian's address to his, iv. 397; of men all naturally equal(?), iv. 490; a rough diamond which must be polished, iv. 490–1; we seem to have two, iv. 526–7; various faculties of,

v. 50–52; though divided into faculties, the s. acts as one, v. 51; dispositions of, depend on bodily temper, v. 54–56. *See also* Immortality, Transmigration.

Sound(s): and sense in poetry, ii. 484–5; pomp of s. necessary to blank verse, iii. 14; abstracted from ideas, in opera, iii. 55; and smells, why pleasing, iii. 453, 544; of the voice in acting, iv. 432–7.

Soup and broth, iii. 111.

Sourness: men who affect singularity out of, ii. 525–6; and pride causing untractable tempers, ii. 568; and ill humour in religion, iii. 40.

South, Dr. Robert, i. 260; ii. 250, 449; iii. 540; v. 164; his sermons preached by Sir ROGER's chaplain, i. 441; says many preachers might have been better at a plough-tail, iii. 108; on the physician whose patient was killed *secundum artem*, v. 28.

South Britain, i. 139.

South Sea, v. 39.

South Sea Company, Directors of, subscribers to *Spectator*, i. xc–xci.

Southern countries, most subject to jealousy, ii. 172.

Southerne, Thomas: *The Fatal Marriage, or The Innocent Adultery*, a favourite with the ladies, i. 392; the porter's decision in, iv. 205; — *Oroonoko*, a tragedy which ends unhappily, i. 170.

Southwell, Robert, Jonson on, i. 298.

Southwell (hymn tune), iii. 8.

Sovereigns: mourning ceremonial of, i. 275–7; relations with their subjects, ii. 47–50, 283.

Sow-gelder, WILLIAM SQUEAK, the, iv. 93.

Sow-gelder's horn, music of the, ii. 475.

Sowton, John, servant at St. James's Coffee-house, i. 104.

Space: contemplation of unfathomed, iii. 574–7; views of infinite, iv. 529–33; unfathomed s. ever teeming with new births, v. 170–2.

Spain: death of King of, i. 276; the new Queen of, i. 277; courtship in, i. 417; iii. 194; the King of, i. 438; bigotry in, ii. 211; Castile impoverished by wars, ii. 277; letter 'to Colonel R—s in', ii. 301; King of, and the Armada, iii. 45; invasion of, by Moors, iii. 425; best in winter, iii. 474; Philip II of, represented by Spenser, iv. 429. *See also* Almanza, Barcelona.

Spalding (Lincolnshire), the *Spectator* read at, i. lxxxv.

Spaniards: stateliness and gravity of, reflected in their language, ii. 36; cruelty of, ii. 161; particular about beards, ii. 222; in Mexico, iii. 559.

Spaniel, i. 435, 498; ii. 164.

'Spanish' (snuff), ii. 571; iii. 278; v. 156.

Spanish: wool, used in make-up, i. 175–6; proverbs, i. 337, 512; jennets impregnate by wind, ii. 5; farthingale appeared in England a little before ruin of S. monarchy, ii. 6; story related by a S. officer, ii. 277; mail, ii. 476; medal on defeat of S. Armada, iii. 45; 'the S. Doctor' (Huarte), on education, iii. 106–7; discussions of S. monarchy in coffee-houses, iii. 507–8; anecdote of S. Secretary of State, iii. 477; myrtle, iv. 104; Blacking for Shoes, advertised, iv. 129; story of a S. lady's revenge, v. 90; a S. cobbler's advice to his son, v. 155.

Spark: a wealthy, iv. 84; every s. should be a 'shoeing-horn', iv. 414; a young s. of a clergyman, iv. 427; my s. is a favourite of the ladies, v. 68.

Sparkes, John (pugilist), of Coventry, iv. 30.

SPARKISH, WILL, distracted by noise of his children, iv. 198.

Sparrow-grass, at a dinner, iii. 397.

Sparrows: for the opera, i. 24, 26, 64; of Venus, ii. 368.

Sparta: an officer of, ii. 407; famous for civil and military discipline, iii. 109; modesty and courage of young men of, iii. 321; distributed rewards and punishments according to merit, iv. 528; war between Thebes and, iv. 528.

Spartan: virtue among the Lacedaemonians, i. 31; boy who hid fox under his coat, ii. 116; virgin, ii. 408; moderation of William III, iv. 335.

Spartans: looked upon theft as honourable if it succeeded, iii. 99; bringing up of their children, iii. 109.

Speakers, loud, ii. 83.

Speaking in public, modesty in, ii. 397–8.

Spear of Minerva, overturned whole squadrons, iii. 258.

SPEC, CONSTANTIO, letter from (on his 'dear angel'), iv. 589.

Species: not a s. lost from the whole animal world, iii. 28; gradations of, iv. 345–9; diversity of, in the animal world, iv. 441–4.

Spectacle, in English tragedy, i. 177–80.

Spectacles (glasses), ii. 511; iii. 481; a man who wore two pairs at once, iv. 263.

Spectateur moderne, Le, iv. 252.

SPECTATOR, Mr. [The following entries list references to 'Mr. Spectator' primarily as the central figure of the Club, and only incidentally as author of the essays, dream-visions, 'speculations', stories, &c., which constitute the *Spectator*.]

I. EARLIER LIFE

Childhood and youth, i. 1–2; his father, i. 2; ii. 514; travels: to Grand Cairo, i. 2, 38, 76, 197, 294, 425; ii. 121; v. 65; in France, i. 66, 297; ii. 142–3; in Rome, ii. 290, 390; often in storms at sea, iv. 234; met many Jews in travel, iv. 255; formerly concealed shortness of face by a wig and letting beard grow, i. 76; was with the Four Indian Kings, i. 211; formerly practised with dumb-bell and did shadow boxing, i. 473–4; visited a lady who admired Titus Oates, i. 243–4; had been at Oxford, i. 248; recalls Blenheim and Ramillies, ii. 151; iii. 102; his unsuccessful courtship, ii. 514; early reading and first essays in Spectatorship, iii. 93–94; formerly dabbled in chemistry, iii. 479; used to frequent Westminster Hall, iii. 522; recalls death of Richard Baxter, iv. 63; other recollections, iv. 248, 262; received favours from Earl of Sunderland, v. 181.

II. CHARACTER

1. *General traits.* A spectator of mankind, i. xxxi–xxxii, i–6; ii. 388; neutral in politics, i. 5; others' opinions of, i. 18–19; ii. 19–20, 348–9; mistaken for a Jesuit, i. 18, 332; ii. 20; pleasures chiefly those of sight, i. 21, 288; always serious but never melancholy, i. 111; knows nothing of women but from seeing plays, i. 217; a lover of mankind, i. 294; enjoys popular songs and fables, i. 297; method of asking the time, i. 329; overcame absentmindedness, i. 331; a 'humourist', i. 425; suspected of being a fanatic, ii. 4; 'variety of game' pursued by, ii. 19; iii. 399; a sage in morality, ii. 29; a person of some consequence, ii. 51; a man pretty well made for secrets, ii. 83; 'my banker bows lowest when I wear my full-bottomed wig', ii. 92; 'great with Tully', ii. 106; curiosity 'my prevailing passion', ii. 111; a bachelor, ii. 193; would not willingly laugh but to instruct, ii. 205; his rules for managing an argument, ii. 273–5; ever contriving schemes for the public good, ii. 285; 'generally in the theory of mankind', ii. 291; is become the courier of love, ii. 299; a great casuist, ii. 344; skill in paintings inconsiderable, ii. 381; inquisitive after everything curious in nature, ii. 557; 'a professed friend to love', iii. 23; opinions on dancing, iii. 57, 113, 239; a visitant of boarding schools for young women, iii. 140; 'I do not naturally affect critical learning', iii. 208; interested in the theatre, iii. 393–6; 'the lady's philosopher', iii. 426; has a low opinion of Platonic love, iii. 499; 'a kind of guardian to the fair', iii. 586; often mistakes date of an engagement, iv. 75–76; salutes any person whom he likes, iv. 98; 'the Lowndes of the learned world', iv. 111; in the service of honour and virtue, iv. 149; indifferent to external appearances, iv. 157; a philosopher, iv. 224; a gentleman-usher to the arts and sciences, iv. 396; a famous mechanic as well as looker-on, iv. 404; scrupulous in acknowledging passages from other authors, iv. 439, 453–4; may be called the King of Clubs, iv. 470; a stranger upon earth and a looker-on, v. 176.

2. *Appearance.* Face 'not quite so long as it is broad', i. 75; face 'none of the longest', i. 85; a candidate for the Ugly Club, i. 133, 206, 221; a man of a very short face, i. 331, 425; ii. 131, 557; iii. 34; iv. 80, 412, 485, 508, 510, 513; short face a cause of mirth, v. 48.

3. *Taciturnity.* Distinguished at the University 'by a most profound silence', i. 2; a silent man, i. 5, 13, 19, 48, 52, 75; 'I hate long speeches', i. 157; taciturnity, i. 192, 196, 198, 208, 322, 329–31, 350–1, 361, 374, 425, 449, 477, 488, 500; ii. 19–20, 22, 32, 83, 191, 346, 389, 469, 514, 529; iii. 112, 523; iv. 182, 265, 374, 455, 470, 485, 589; v. 176.

4. *Customary habits.* Smokes a pipe, i. 198; is at the coffee-house at 6 in the morning, i. 209; often dances with his landlady's eldest daughter, i. 287; visits the Royal Exchange, i. 292; diversions, i. 353; often dines at a common ordinary, i. 374; exercises with a dumb-bell, i. 473; keeps a commonplace-book, ii. 114; frequents Inns of Court, ii. 273; reads bills of mortality in the coffee-house, iii. 27; loves to ramble about London, iii. 506–7; since his 55th year has taken an afternoon nap, v. 45–46.

5. *Lodgings and associates.* Various lodgings, i. 52, 425; his landlady's

SPECTATOR, Mr. (*cont.*)

(eldest) daughter, i. 197, 202–3, 287; ii. 548; iii. 380; landlady's eldest son, i. 202; landlady's children, i. 474; iii. 436; landlady a victim of April Fool jests, i. 202–3; his neighbour the Haberdasher, i. 202; his 'mistress' HECATISSA, i. 222, 339; iii. 34; his friend the Antiquary, i. 326, 357; his steward and laundress, i. 351; his library, i. 361; has a young kinsman proficient in the law, ii. 273; his good friend a Fellow of the Royal Society, iii. 350.

6. '*Account of, by a future historian*', i. 424–5.

III. ACTIONS (during the course of the *Spectator*)

Visits the Bank, i. 14; to the play with WILL HONEYCOMB, i. 20; meets a fellow with cage of birds for the opera, i. 23–24; visits a superstitious family, i. 31; visits ARIETTA, i. 48; behind the scenes at the opera, i. 57; walks in the Park, i. 102–3; visits Westminster Abbey, i. 108–11; encounters a projector in a coffee-house, i. 127; received into the Ugly Club, i. 133, 205, 221–3, 370; visits LEONORA, i. 152–3; at a lady's *ruelle*, i. 192–3; loses paper of minutes at Lloyd's, i. 195–8; walking with WILL HONEYCOMB in Somerset Garden, i. 329; to the opera and puppet-show, i. 346, 348; accosted by a prisoner in Ludgate, i. 350; visits a picture-gallery, i. 354; observes physiognomies, i. 365; witnesses servants drinking at a victualling-house near the House of Peers, i. 374; in the country at Sir ROGER's, i. 439–512; ii. 1–22 (at church, i. 459–62; the hunt, i. 476–9; Moll White, i. 480–2; at the assizes, i. 499–500; visit to gipsies, ii. 15–17); returns to London by stage-coach, ii. 22–25; witnesses death of Stephen Clay, ii. 27–28; walking towards Chelsea, ii. 43; observes a father and son in a coffee-house, ii. 92; walking in the fields with Captain SENTRY, ii. 96; thanks R. M. for gift of partridges, ii. 113; designs to go out of town, ii. 203; visits a father with a large family of children, ii. 252; sees a prentice-boy disputing with a hackney-coachman, ii. 291; has lately been 'among the mercantile part of the world', ii. 307; overhears comments on himself in a coffee-house, ii. 348–9; recalls the cartoons of Raphael at Hampton Court, ii. 379; visits Sir ANDREW in his country

retreat, ii. 402; encounters a prostitute, ii. 534–5; observes a bawd and a country girl, ii. 536–7; 'to examine the haunts of vice', ii. 537; receives a visit from Sir ROGER, ii. 548–52; visits Squire's Coffee-house with Sir ROGER, ii. 551–2; to the play, ii. 552; in an assembly of virtuosos, ii. 570; visits Mrs. CROSS-STITCH, ii. 580; goes with WILL HONEYCOMB to a reading of *The Distressed Mother*, iii. 31–33; 'was very ill and kept my chamber', iii. 34; not seen at the chop-house of late, iii. 111; visited by a messenger from York, iii. 112; visits Westminster Abbey with Sir ROGER, iii. 212–16; goes with Sir ROGER and Captain SENTRY to a performance of *The Distressed Mother*, iii. 239–42; has seen Prince Eugene, iii. 263; is given an engraving of a Roman pavement by Charles Lillie, iii. 339; has received a gift of wine from a correspondent, iii. 433; visits Spring-Garden with Sir ROGER, iii. 436–9; listens in coffee-houses to discussions of rumoured death of Louis XIV, iii. 507–9; dines with a friend in the country, iii. 597; recalls seeing an equestrian lady at Sir ROGER's, iv. 28; visits the Bear-Garden, iv. 30–35; sees FAVILLA in her chariot, iv. 35; overhears a conversation at a French bookseller's, iv. 41–42; dines with JACK SIPPET, iv. 74; leaves Richmond and takes a twenty-four-hour ramble about London, iv. 98–103; hears in a coffee-house of the Rechteren–Mesnager dispute, iv. 206–8; meets a young woman on horseback, iv. 222–3; sees a young coquette in Gerard Street, iv. 311; meets a correspondent in a bookseller's shop, iv. 412; with a company who are discussing antipathies, iv. 421–2; attends a rehearsal of Cibber's *Ximena*, iv. 453–4; his mouth 'to be opened in form', iv. 471, 483–4; a poem on tea by Motteux dedicated to him, iv. 478; his farewell to his readers, iv. 491–4; the new 'talkative' SPECTATOR, iv. 498–502; overhears comments on himself in a coffee-house, iv. 539–41; visits a master of kitchen-music, iv. 545–6; witnesses the first rehearsal of the 'new thunder' in the playhouse, v. 25–26; dreams of men's reactions to his paper, v. 65–67; travels in a stage-coach with a dirty beau and a pretty young Quaker woman, v. 156–7. *For his sessions with the Club see* Spectator Club.

Spectator, *The*, ADDISON'S SHARE IN, i. lviii–lxix, lxxiv–lxxviii.

ADVERTISEMENTS, i. lxx–lxxii, lxxxiii; read by Motteux, iii. 26; petition for more a. and fewer letters, iii. 124.

AUTHORSHIP, i. xliii–lviii; in Second Series, i. lxxiv–lxxxii; use of signature letters to indicate, ii. 360–1; 'many of the most beautiful papers are contributed', iii. 434; contributors in first series named, iv. 492–4, 497; contributors in second series may be revealed later, iv. 501; v. 160; signature letters purposely omitted in second series, v. 186.

BEGINNINGS, i. xiii–xviii.

CIRCULATION, i. xxv–xxvii, lxix–lxxiii, lxxxiii; three thousand distributed every day, i. 44; the demand increases daily, i. 507; 'my late going into the country has increased the number of my correspondents', ii. 130; the demand has increased every month, ii. 517; effect of stamp tax on, i. xxv–xxvi; iv. 63–65, 128–9, 137, 230–2, 494; nine thousand copies each of the first two volumes sold, iv. 494.

COMPOSITION, METHODS OF: 'minutes' for essays, i. 195–6; such materials as memory suggests, ii. 221; in papers on morality, ii. 334; some papers written 'in the looseness and freedom of an essay', others 'in a particular order and method', ii. 465, 499; iv. 185–6; two kinds: serious essays and discourses, and occasional papers, iv. 27; an incident during c. of a *Spectator*, iv. 41–42; 'loitering way of reading' in preparation for writing, iv. 240; 'related in my Historical Dictionary', iv. 269; authors of quoted passages always acknowledged, iv. 439, 453.

CONTENTS (AND CHARACTERS OF THE SPECTATOR CLUB), i. xxix–xxxvi, lix–lxiv, lxxvii–lxxxiii.

CONTINUATION (SPURIOUS 'VOL. IX'), i. lxxvi.

DISTRIBUTION: agents in London, i. xxi–xxv; received at Epping the morning it comes out, i. 207; delivered in the country, iv. 174.

LETTERS AND OTHER CONTRIBUTIONS: i. xxxvi–xliii; invited, i. 6, 73, 159; 'to be left with Mr. Buckley', i. 59; essays on gain, husbandry, and thrift, invited, iv. 4–7; essays on 'money' invited, iv. 52–54; use of letters, i. 196; iv. 52–53; iv. 438–9; a letter 'which I have castrated in some places', ii. 206; 'scattered up and down your works', ii. 303; 'encouraged by l. from unknown hands', ii. 341; several presented in their 'artless dress', ii. 544; advantages derived from printing them, ii. 555; v. 94; some thought to be written by Mr. SPECTATOR himself, ii. 555–6; iv. 438; request for unused, iii. 93–94; my 'foreign correspondents', iii. 96; petition for fewer, iii. 124; instructions to lovers who write to *Spectator*, iii. 140; some papers bring in a great return of, iv. 208; *Spectators* 'so prettily laced down the sides with little c's', iv. 375; one delivered in my bookseller's shop, iv. 412; five reasons for 'casting my thoughts into a letter', iv. 438–9; many from unknown hands, iv. 493; variety of, received, iv. 587; unused ones would make an entertaining collection, v. 115.—*Salutations* (a selection): 'Dear Spec', ii. 251; 'Dear Dumb', iv. 265; 'Honest Spec', iv. 514; 'Dear Mr. Prate-apace', iv. 513; 'Brother Spec', iv. 589; 'Good Mr. Pert', iv. 589. — *Replies* (a selection): i. 223; ii. 84–85, 86–88; iii. 34, 104, 587–8; short answers to various correspondents, iv. 587–9; v. 115–17. See also Lillie, Charles.

MOTTOES: read first, ii. 29; uses of, ii. 358–60; Greek, ii. 453–4; iii. 54–55; Latin, puzzling to readers, iii. 393; iv. 62.

POLITICAL NEUTRALITY, i. xviii, 5, 72–73, 262; ii. 2, 517; iv. 137, 499, 501, 539–41; not always held to (?), i. 197; iv. 64–65.

PRICE OF ORIGINAL NUMBERS, i. xxiii–xxiv; a penny, ii. 30; iv. 459; raised to twopence, iv. 128–9, 230–2.

PRINTING OF ORIGINAL NUMBERS, i. xx–xxix.

PUBLICATION IN VOLUMES, i. lxxii–lxxiii, lxxv; 'your speculations are now swelling into volumes', iii. 105; third and fourth volumes ready, iv. 232; will give me a respectable position in the Republic of Letters, iv. 386–7; a half-dozen to be published, iv. 386–7; 'the two last volumes in large paper', iv. 458; four published, and three others in the press, iv. 494; an eighth to be published, v. 160.

Spectator, The (cont.)

PURPOSE, i. xviii–xx; programme stated, i. 44–47, 70–73; (to cease when it grows dull), i. 47; not to attack particularities of dress, i. 70; ii. 7; to attack the vice, not the individual, i. 72 (one exception to this, i. 148); to correct impudence, i. 85; to attack vice and folly in all ranks of society, i. 143–4; iii. 181; to banish vice and ignorance 'the great and only end of these my speculations', i. 245; to reform the stage, ii. 56–57, 413; iii. 393–4; to give readers an insight into the ways of men, ii. 450; to view immorality and actions of men not as a pedantic Stoic but as an impartial Spectator, ii. 568; iv. 525; to correct ideas of the married state, iv. 237; to revive the allegorical way of writing, iv. 275; to root out popular errors, iv. 293; 'to restore proper ideas of things', iv. 370; to encourage young authors, iv. 396. — The 'material' and 'formal' benefits of the *Spectator*, iii. 379–81; — general reviews of the *Spectator*'s programme and campaign, ii. 516–20; iii. 530; iv. 27–28; — frequent references to 'Spectatorial' authority, wisdom, dignity, &c., iii. 243, 354; iv. 80, 106, 245, 247, 363, 373, 385, 426, 438–9, 478, &c.

READERS: contemporary, i. lxxxiii–xcvi; two classes (the mercurial and the saturnine), ii. 204; manly modesty and bashful grace in my men and women readers, ii. 567; must have something diverting or uncommon, iv. 580.

READERS, WOMEN: aimed largely at their service, i. xix, xcii–xciii, 21, 46, 242; ii. 119–21, 533; iii. 52; letters from, complaining of neglect, i. 282; 'a part of my tea-equipage', i. 389; on women's dress, ii. 5, 7–9, 74, &c. (*see* Women); read 'when alone in my closet', ii. 55; 'a friend to women', ii. 279; 'since you are so sharp upon other women, let me know what materials your wife is made of, if you have one', ii. 328; 'as you never spare your own sex, do not be afraid of reproving what is ridiculous in ours', ii. 348; urged to renew its correction of the sillier branch of women, iii. 65; accused of favouring men over women, iii. 161; 'drank a dish of Bohea, read the *Spectator*', iii. 182; its campaign to reform jilts, iii. 500; has treated the fair sex with too much severity, iv. 78; women's fondness for the *Spectator*, iv. 272; concerned for their happiness and quiet, iv. 377.

RECEPTION: i. lxxxiii–xcvi; at first, mixed, i. 18, 85; varied reactions by members of the Club, i. 141–5; by my mercurial readers and by my saturnine, ii. 204–5; review of various reactions, iv. 437–41; Mr. SPECTATOR's dream-vision of reactions to second series, v. 65–67. — *Favourable reactions (see also* Circulation): read aloud, i. lxxxv; iii. 57; increasing popularity, i. 44, 507; 'your endeavours to adorn the fair sex are well received', i. 224; critical papers well received, i. 245; iv. 461–2; papers are having a good effect on women and beaux, i. 393; your pen 'a public benefit', especially in directing women's reading, i. 404–5; 'rural speculations' and other groups of papers made up in sets, i. 507–8; moral benefits (testimonial from GEORGE TRUSTY), ii. 29–30; papers on wit praised, ii. 52; 'my late going into the country has increased the number of my correspondents', ii. 130; particular numbers praised (letter from BELVIDERA), ii. 303–5; read in a club, ii. 306; No. 182 put in a frame and glass and 'hung behind my counter', ii. 316; papers on morality praised, ii. 341; demand has increased every month, ii. 517; papers on *PL* praised, iii. 74; *261*; 'your agreeable manner of working up trifles', iii. 105; 'you are so generally read, that what you speak of will be read', iii. 112; 'we fly to you for redress', iii. 188; 'you are the daily endeavourer to promote learning and good sense', iii. 243; famous for the candour of its criticisms, iii. 266; praise from *The Medley*, iii. 279–80; uncommon demand for *PL* papers, iii. 392; 'you are the Lowndes of the learned world', iv. 111; hymns in *Spectator* praised, iv. 126; 'modesty is become fashionable', iv. 128; *Letter from Dick Estcourt to the Spectator*, iv. 155; continued demand in spite of increased price, iv. 230–2; Epigram on the *Spectator*, by Tate, iv. 232–3; discourses on marriage have had a very good effect and been well received, iv. 273, 369; allegorical

Spectator, The (cont.)

papers in great demand, iv. 275; testimonial from the CLERGYMAN (on the Saturday papers), iv. 320; 'those many excellent discourses upon a marriage-life', iv. *391;* 'To the Supposed Author of the *Spectator*', by Tickell, iv. 397–9; testimonials from various persons to particular papers, iv. 457–61; 483–6; a lady has 'the two last volumes in large paper interleafed for her own private use', iv. 458; my name found 'in foreign gazettes', iv. 471; dismay at impending cessation of, iv. 484–6; a society formed at Oxford for re-reading, iv. 485–6; complaint that second series appears only thrice a week, iv. 589; papers on infinitude and eternity praised, v. 144–5. — *Adverse reactions*: female correspondents angry for abridging their pleasures, i. 338; 'you are often so nice there is no enduring you, and so learned there is no understanding you', ii. 53; new evils still arise every day, ii. 81; 'you do not write like a gentleman', ii. 119; papers and pamphlets which have appeared against the *Spectator*, ii. 432; v. 66; protest against discussion of vice, ii. 574–7; Mr. SPECTATOR's attitude towards detractors, iii. 323–5; charged with flattering the powerful on the stage, in order to fill their benefit-days, iv. *395;* charged with 'having prostituted learning to the embraces of the vulgar', iii. 423; criticism for publishing No. 384, iii. *440–1;* accused of political bias, iv. 539–41; 'two or three in black gowns among my enemies', v. 66.

REPUTATION, i. xcvi–cvi; French translation, iv. *23.*

REQUESTS FOR PAPERS ON PARTICULAR TOPICS (a selection): on good-breeding, ii. 120; on consolation in grief, ii. 140–1; on 'castle-building', ii. 160; on the hen-pecked, ii. 194–6; on advice to husbands and wives, ii. 201–3, 417; on lottery subjects, ii. 251; on choice of husband, ii. 270, 583–4; on the business of salutation, ii. 358; on perspective-glasses, ii. 473; on behaviour of parents and children, ii. 521–3; on kissing, ii. 561; on how to deal with male jilts, iii. 23–24; on 'valetudinary friendship', iii. 74; on mercenary marriage arrangements, iii. 122–3; on fortune-hunters, iii. 126; on the right use of time, iii. 151; on the natural causes of longing in women, iii. 195; on beggars, iv. 11–12; on behaviour in church, iv. 124; on modesty, iv. 217; on employment for women's men, iv. 413; on the proper approach to a rich widow, iv. 535.

REVISIONS, i. lxvi–lxix.

SECOND SERIES, i. lxxiii–lxxxiii.

STEELE'S SHARE IN, i. lviii–lxix.

SUBSCRIBERS, i. lxxxviii–xciii.

TEXT, i. cvi–cix.

Spectator Club, the, i. xix, xxxi–xxxiv; 'those gentlemen who are concerned with me in this work', i. 6; meets on Tuesdays and Thursdays, i. 6; members of, i. 7–13; Sir ROGER comments on degeneracy of manners, i. 28–31; reactions of members to the *Spectator*, i. 141–5; WILL HONEYCOMB 'told us, one day, an adventure he once had with a *Pict*', i. 175; 'a little before our Club-time last night', i. 329; were last night engaged in a discourse upon honour, i. 416; the CLERGYMAN made a discourse against complaisance, i. 429; frequently catches WILL H. for his ignorance of books, i. 436–7; discussions between Sir ROGER and Sir ANDREW often divert the rest o the Club, ii. 3, 86; 'Sir ANDREW is grown the cock of the Club', ii. 21; 'Sir ANDREW, as we were sitting in the Club last night, . . .', iii. 153; WILL HONEYCOMB diverted us last night . . . , iii. 190; Sir ROGER, when we last met together at the Club . . . , iii. 239; WILL HONEYCOMB told us yesterday at the Club . . . , iii. 272–3; Captain SENTRY was last night at the Club, and produced a letter from Ipswich, iii. 302; WILL HONEYCOMB's account of his amours 'at the Club last night', iii. 342–5; Sir ROGER's encounter with SUKEY related to the Club by WILL HONEYCOMB, iii. 531–3; news of Sir ROGER's death received, iv. 339–41; news of WILL HONEYCOMB's marriage received, iv. 389–91; rumours of dissolution, iv. 440–1; sentiments cultivated in, iv. 448; Mr. SPECTATOR and Sir ANDREW 'the sole remaining members', iv. 466; suggestions for new members, iv. 469–70; project for a new Club, iv. 470–1; a new Club formed, iv. 498.

Spectator Inspected, The, ii. *151–2.*

Spectators, the fraternity of, i. 45.
Speech: differences in, i. 120; more easily disguised than the countenance, i. 366; undue exactness about trifles in, ii. 44-46; organs needed by the orator, ii. 398; and behaviour of Raphael in *PL*, ii. 564-5; epic should avoid ordinary phrases of, iii. 11-15.
Speeches in *PL*: appropriate to the speakers, iii. 114; in Book III less poetic, iii. 141-2; of Adam and Eve in Book IV always *paradisiacal*, iii. 171.
Speed, John, iii. *209*.
Spelling: pedants' concern with absurd, i. 250; women's, i. 393; WILL HONEY-COMB on pedantry in, i. 437; reform of, ii. 35; query regarding s. of *dimple*, ii. 53; poor s. in JOHN TROTT's letter, iii. 137.
Spelling-book: in LEONORA's library, i. 155; assistance of a, iii. 55.
Spence, Joseph, i. liii, lxv; iv. *162*; v. *123*.
Spendthrifts, ii. 295; iv. 315.
Spenser, Edmund: had a genius above mixed wit, i. 265; allegories in Ariosto and, iii. 60; had an admirable talent in allegory, iii. *573*; *Faerie Queene*: one continued series of allegory, ii. 221; quoted, iii. 464-5; iv. 239-40; a letter on, with quotations, iv. 428-31.
Spenser, Edmund, 'the younger', i. *76*.
Spent I lost, What I (prov.), ii. 200.
Sphinx(es), i. 466; ii. 379; iv. 194.
Spice-Islands, Sir ANDREW calls them our hot-beds, i. 296.
Spice(s): imported into England, i. 295; wines and, in a modern meal, ii. 264-5; surpluses of, destroyed by the Dutch, ii. 286; *Spectators* good for wrapping s. in, iii. 380; a grove of, iii. 569.
Spider, ii. 237; spider-catchers, i. 91.
Spies: heads of families keep about them certain mischievous animals called, ii. 294; sent by Moses into the Promised Land, iv. 254.
Spikenard, sheaves of, v. 3.
Spikes, leaping over the s. on the stage, ii. 434.
SPINAMONT, story of (killed his friend in a duel), i. 358-60.
SPINDLE, JAMES, a youth married to Lady WADDLE, iv. 516.
Spindle pair of legs, WILL HONEY-COMB's, iii. 344.
Spinet, playing the, ii. 196; iv. 78, 80.
Spinster: in a coloured scarf, iii. 95; ELIZABETH JETT-WELL, iii. 418.
Spirit: men who game, to appear men of, ii. 105; want of force and s. in literature of colder climates, ii. 128; a

translation with all the ease and s. of an original, ii. 367; a noble, ii. 426; enterprises of, ii. 447; music now without just, ii. 584; affectation of being thought a person of, iii. 6; politicians taught to distinguish between s. and letter, iii. 98.
'Spirit up' a person, to, iii. 70; iv. 209.
Spirits: a bottle of, in case of any sudden indisposition, ii. 111; applied to the nose, v. 43.
Spirits: and apparitions, i. 53; all regions of nature swarm with, i. 54; MARRATON's visit to the world of, i. 236-40; reasonableness of belief in, i. 455-6; communication with a familiar spirit, ii. 83; in eternity, ii. 420-1; existence of, iii. 571-2; have a faculty by which they apprehend one another, iv. 549; communication with, v. 172-3.
SPITELY, Mrs., iii. 183.
Spleen: i. *15*, 292; iii. 168; as an excuse for dullness, i. 226-7; frequent in men of studious and sedentary tempers, i. 471-2; physical exercise helps to evaporate the, i. 474; produced by party-spirit, i. 510; vented upon servants, ii. 41; or ill-humour to be avoided, ii. 65; laughter a good counterpoise to, ii. 465; actuated by a violent, iii. 6; a particular s. against Mrs. SIMPER, iii. 8; in Madam MARTHA, iii. 104; diverting the, iii. 245; infidels made up of pride, cavil, and, iii. 431; and melancholy in religious persons, iv. 251; manifestations of, iv. 415-16; the *Spectator* as a cure for, iv. 458, 460; a complication of all diseases, iv. 508; choked up with s. and choler, v. 8.
Splendida peccata, ii. *331*.
Splenetic, ii. 30, 476; iv. 559.
Spoiling of children, iv. 274.
Spoke in his wheel, Clapt such a (prov.), iv. 268.
Spondees, effect of, in Homer, ii. 485.
Spoons, double-headed, ii. 471.
Sports: country, i. 472-3, 475-9; ii. 131-5, 371; Pascal on, i. 478; of condemned spirits in *PL*, ii. 421; innocent s. and pastimes, ii. 451; English youth exercising in s. of the field, iii. 94.
Spout, face of a, ii. 184.
Sprat, Thomas, the elegant author who published Cowley's works, i. 469-70.
Sprightliness of women, i. 193; balanced against men, ii. 8-9.
SPRIGHTLY, RUSTICK, letter from (on salutations), ii. 433-4 (praise of this letter, iv. 461).

SPRIGHTLY, WILL, letter from (on men's fashions), iii. 163–4 (referred to, iii. 225).

Spring (the season): dangers to women in, iii. 371–5, 480–2; the most beautiful season, iii. 473–4, 542; best in Italy, iii. 474; allegorical figure of, iii. 594–5.

Spring(s): tones and s. of the vessels of the body, ii. 266; and sluices of the eye, ii. 481; secret s. of detraction, ii. 494; of self-love, iv. 366.

Sprouts, with veal and bacon, iii. 154.

Spruce (in *The Fortune-Hunters*), i. 93–94.

Spruce servants, junketings with, iv. 147.

Spurs: 'avoided hampering my s. in their petticoats', ii. 433.

SPY, ABRAHAM, letter from (on perspective-glasses), ii. 472–3.

Spy: Argus a s. in affairs of jealousy, ii. 470; character of a, iv. 43; and the cardinal, iv. 43–44.

Spy upon the Spectator, A, ii. 151–2.

Squab (sofa, ottoman), iv. 386.

Squatting of a hare, i. 477.

SQUEAK, WILLIAM, the sow-gelder, iv. 93.

Squeamishness: squeamish humours, ii. 246; of stomach not the mark of a good constitution, iii. 15.

SQUEEKUM, Squire: by his voice seems to be cut out for an Italian singer, ii. 305.

Squeezing the hand: the first that made love by, i. 451; the Love Casuist determines what constitutes, v. 23.

Squibs and crackers, i. 361.

Squir away his watch, i. 330.

Squires and dwarfs carry impresses of giants or knights, iv. 18.

Squire(s), country, i. 41; ii. 29, 132; Sir ROGER thinks the *Spectator* should not meddle with, i. 143; contentions between parson and, i. 462; politeness of, i. 487; dress of, ii. 14–15; frightened by cries of London, ii. 474; on pin-money, iii. 53; anecdote of a, iii. 65–66; the illiterate body of the nation, iv. 387; 'first with the dogs, and king amidst the', iv. 398. See also Country gentleman.

Squirrel: 'Hunt the S.' (a dance), i. 285; a lady's, ii. 480; iii. 320.

Stabbing, statute against, iii. 341.

Stack-faggots, a pyramid of, v. 108.

Staffordshire, Plot's *Natural History of*, iv. 69; v. 76.

Stag-hunting, i. 214.

Stag's horns, in the great hall, ii. 189.

Stage, the: to be reprimanded if it becomes a nursery of folly and impertinence, i. 144–5; disposal of 'animated utensils' (properties), i. 149–50; coxcombs, i. 203; in its original situation of a cart, i. 207; entertainments on, i. 214; needs regulation, i. 397; ii. 56–59; iv. 66–69; 280–3; no persons admitted behind the scenes, ii. 435; proposal for more action upon, ii. 503–5; capering and tumbling on, iii. 237; an epitome of the world, iii. 393; Mr. SPECTATOR's interest in, iii. 393–4; regulation of the Athenian, iv. 66; proposed treatise on *S. Morality*, iv. 68; ungraceful dancing on, iv. 146; a stage-maxim, iv. 388.

Stage-Coach, The, i. 130.

Stage-coach: a journey to London in a, ii. 22–25 (referred to, ii. 73); a story heard in a, ii. 143; indecent conversation in a, ii. 439–40; iv. 402–4; slovenly companions in a, iv. 156–7.

Stages of life: we wish each of them at an end, i. 394–5; ii. 322; inconstancy in all, ii. 137; the ancients lenient towards excess in all, iv. 258–9; toys and trifles in all, v. 124–5; force of novelty in all, v. 138–9.

Staincoat Hole, in Cambridge, a memorable place of rendezvous, iii. 484–5.

Staines, dress of a fashionable woman at, ii. 13.

Stair-head, politicians taught the important point of the, iii. 99.

Stammerers, invited together in jest, iii. 397–8.

Stamp Act, imposed on newspapers, iv. 62–64; effects of, iv. 128–30.

Stampiglia, Sylvio (librettist), i. 79.

Stamping of the foot in acting, iv. 436.

Standers-by discovers blots which escape those in the game (prov.), i. 5.

Stanhope, George, translation of Epictetus, i. 224.

Stanhope, Lieut.-Gen. James, a subscriber, i. lxxxix.

Stanier, Sir Samuel (Lord Mayor of London), v. 118.

Stanley, Thomas, *History of Philosophy*, i. 368.

STANZA, TIMOTHY, letter from (enclosing a poem), iv. 176.

Stanzani, Tomaso (librettist), i. 79.

Star(s): shooting of, unlucky, i. 33; go out one after another at rising of sun, i. 274; tail of a blazing s. a prognostication, ii. 6; *stars dropping from the zenith* a term of art in Milton, iii. 64;

and names of pagan gods, iii. 460; each is a sun with its own vortex, iv. 170; reading men's fortunes in, iv. 292; position of, in the celestial globe, iv. 481; beauty of, iv. 529–30; 'tenebrificous', iv. 592; not made merely to please man, v. 125.

Star-Chamber, fined the Stationers' Company for error in printing of the Bible, iv. 580.

Starch, 'that beautiful political s.' in manners of politicians, iii. 99.

Starers: letter from S. C. on, i. 86; letter from a reformed starer, i. 227–8.

Staring: being stared at, the usual triumph of a town lady, ii. 69; an optical contrivance to avoid the impertinence of, ii. 472–3; the art of managing mankind: to make them stare a little, iv. 60; DULCEORELLA's art of, iv. 246. See also Ogling.

Starlings, a school for, i. 151.

'Starting' manner of writing, iii. 491–2.

Starve in the midst of plenty, ii. 248.

Stasicrates, iii. 555.

State-legerdemain, students instructed in feats of, iii. 97.

State-pedant, wrapt up in news, and lost in politics, i. 438.

Statesmen: 'out of business', i. 45; a college of, in France, iii. 95–99; England produces men of integrity rather than, iii. 100.

Station of life: actions suitable to that particular s. in which Providence has placed him, ii. 333; high or low, ii. 371; great actions possible in each, ii. 462–5; each has its duties and employments, iv. 592–3.

Stationer, petition of ANTHONY TITLE-PAGE, iii. 93–94.

Stationers' Company, fined for an error in the Bible, iv. 580.

Statira: in a projected opera, i. 129; in The Rival Queens, i. 167.

STATIRA: 'the agreeable', graceful without affectation, i. 176; letter from, to OROONDATES, ii. 280–2 (referred to, ii. 299).

Statius, Publius Papinius: the Thebaid not on a subject which did honour to his country, i. 300; swelling sentiments in Claudian and, ii. 588; and Claudian guilty of the false sublime, iii. 11; mentioned, v. 109.

Statuary: the art of, compared to education, ii. 338; sight and the work of the, iv. 171.

Statuary: less permanent than literature, ii. 154; the most natural kind of re-

presentation, iii. 559; frequent deviations from the rules in, v. 28.

Statue(s): of Henri IV on the Pont-Neuf, i. 59; of Pasquin in Rome, i. 99; iv. 3; Thessalian, in honour of dancers, i. 284; of kings at the Royal Exchange, i. 296; of Socrates and Silenus, i. 368; and medals of Commodus, ii. 11; erected to Louis XIV, ii. 48; maimed s. at Rome, ii. 390; a ghost or a s. in tragedy, ii. 397; Pygmalion and the, ii. 427; of a Momus dug up at Rome, iii. 351; of Alexander by Lysippus, iii. 555; of Charles II in Stocks-Market, iv. 133.

Statute: regarding the long bow, ii. 133; regarding stabbing, iii. 341.

Stavo ben, ma per star meglio, sto qui, i. 107.

Steel, course of, iv. 460–1.

Steele, Richard: early career, i. xv–xvi; launching of Spectator, i. xvii–xviii; papers in Spectator, i. xliii–xlvi, lvii–lxvi; Victorians' opinion of, i. civ; character of, in Mr. SPECTATOR and Capt. SENTRY, i. 1, 11; a member of Kit-Cat Club, i. 42; his 'short face', i. 75; referred to, in JACK TRUEPENNY (?), i. 352; reminiscence of army career (?), ii. 98; relations with wife alluded to (?), ii. 261, 328, 345; iv. 311–14, 372; his extravagance referred to (?), ii. 349; accused of Protestant demonstrations, ii. 518; v. 106; maiden speech in House of Commons, ii. 552; wore a full-bottomed periwig, iii. 162; son Eugene christened, iii. 265; writer for the Medley, iii. 380; experiments in alchemy, iii. 479; iv. 562; friendship with Whiston, iii. 485; 'the wren on the eagle's wings', iii. 486; praise of Nicolini, iii. 514; letter on the 'multiplication table', iii. 547–8; indirect criticism of Addison (?), iii. 583; friendship with Richard Parker, iv. 181; tribute to Addison, iv. 396; 'a course of Steele' as a cure for spleen, iv. 460; on Addison's share in Spectator, iv. 492–3; and the Academy of Painting, iv. 495. — Apology, i. xvi, lxxiv; — Chit-Chat, iv. 513; — The Christian Hero, i. xvi; in LEONORA's library, i. 156; mentioned, ii. 166; iii. 346; quoted, iii. 327–9; iv. 335–8; — The Conscious Lovers, i. 376; ii. 122, 189, 246; iv. 446; — Dunkirk, pamphlets on, ii. 273; — The Englishman, i. lxxiv; iv. 481, 499; — The Funeral: i. xvi; Penkethman as Trim in, i. 130; immodesty in, i. 216; an incident in, iv. 296; the part of a mute in, v. 47; cited, iii. 476; 480; iii. 320; — The Guardian, i. 346,

ii. *78, 273, 380*; — *The Ladies Library*, i. *159, 195, 391, 405, 463*; ii. *55*; iii. *271*; — *Letters*: quoted, ii. *208*; to Congreve, i. *105*; to Pope, i. *387*; iii. *419, 497*; to 'Prue', ii. *60–64*; iv. *396*; — *The Lover*, ii. *451*; iv. *308, 309, 333, 414*; 'some passages' in, iv. *588*; — *The Lying Lover*: i. *155, 376, 408*; ii. *40, 493*; iv. *311*; — *Poetical Miscellanies*: iii. *514, 585*; — Prologue to *The Distressed Mother*, iii. *31, 239, 250–1*; — *The Tea Table*, i. *21*; — *The Tender Husband*: i. xiv; Penkethman as Humphry Gubbin in, i. *130*; Biddy Tipkin in, i. *154–5*; dispute over marriage-settlements in, iii. *51*; Estcourt as Pounce in, iv. *157*; Bullock as Sir Harry Gubbin in, iv. *388*; Addison's assistance in, iv. *493*; — *The Theatre*, i. *100, 346*; iii. *434*.

Steenkerke, Captain SENTRY's sword used at battle of, iii. 240.

Steenkirk, the, arrived at Newcastle, ii. 15.

Steeple: head-dress and fontange shaped like a, i. 414; a high rock like a parish, ii. 385.

Stephens, Rev. William, referred to(?), iii. *459*.

STERNHOLD, FRANCIS, letter from (a parish clerk), iii. 8–9.

Sternhold, Thomas. *See* Hopkins, John.

Stertinius, Caesar's behaviour to, iii. 408.

Steuart, Mr., of Dalguise, i. lxxxv.

Stevens, Capt. John, *History of Bavaria*, iv. *269*.

Stevens, Robert. *See* Estienne.

STEWARD, JOHN, petition of, ii. 294.

Steward: Mr. SPECTATOR's, i. 351; if the gentleman scorns to be s., the s. becomes the gentleman, ii. 188; the steward's table, ii. 530; 'at the club as', iii. 155; steward's accounts, iv. 210; WILL HONEYCOMB's, iv. 390; often appoints the chaplain, v. 82.

Stewart, Gen. William, a subscriber, i. lxxxix.

Stile: SUSANNAH CROSSSTITCH clambering over a, iii. 418.

Still-life, pictures of, in *PL*, iii. 170.

STINT, JACK, story of, and WILL TRAP, iv. 76–77.

'Stir a matter, To' (legal jargon), iv. 477.

Stobaeus, Johannes: *Florilegium*, iv. *166*; *Anthologium*, v. *33*.

Stockings, men's: i. 351; with golden clocks, i. 197; of different colours, i. 207; silver-clocked, iii. 163; 'about our heels', iii. 168; a blind beggar mending his, iv. 12; 'If you did but see how he rowls his', iv. 184.

Stockings, women's: colours of, iv. 246; freedoms taken with, iv. 588.

Stock-jobber(s): assembly of, at Jonathan's, i. 4; at a great man's levée, ii. 259.

Stock-jobbing, has its seed in the dread of want, i. 469.

Stocks: 'rolling in the public', i. 210; 'asked me how s. went', iii. 154; rise and fall of, iv. 4, 18.

Stoicism, the pedantry of virtue, ii. 444.

Stoics: deny that adversity is an evil, ii. 422; on the excellence of virtue, ii. 444; the chimerical wise man of the, ii. 444; v. 167; the pedantic S. think all crimes alike, ii. 568; their view that pain is not an evil, iii. 130; indifferent to sorrows of others, iii. 486; their indifference to passion an inconsistent belief, iii. 526; the most virtuous sect of philosophers, v. 167.

'Stole away', a hunting cry, i. 477.

Stomach: a young woman who complained that her *stomach ached*, ii. 347; 'how afterwards he came to his', ii. 386; squeamishness of, not the mark of a good constitution, iii. 15; 'had lost his roast-beef s.', iv. 340.

Stomacher(s), iii. 206; v. 73.

Stone, the, i. 105; iv. 564; or gravel, iii. 213; gout and, iv. 169; in the bladder, iv. 510.

Stone-horse, i. 476.

Stones, heaps of, as monuments, iii. 324–5.

Stonesfield, Oxfordshire, Roman pavement discovered at, iii. 339.

Stool-ball, BETTY a romp at, i. 306.

Stop-hounds, i. 476.

Stopping short, an odd humour of, ii. 512.

Stories: surprise the life of, iv. 420; improbable, iv. 420–4.

Storm, laying siege by sap or, iv. 535.

Storm, the Great, foretold in an almanac, ii. 357.

Storm(s): women who are sometimes all s. and tempest, ii. 319; descriptions of, in poets, iv. 234–5; lightnings and s. in the play-house, v. 26.

'Storming', the, a subdivision of the angry, iv. 41.

Story-tellers: who are unduly exact about trifles, ii. 44; who re-tell a story with more veracity, ii. 409–10; among men as well as women, ii. 459–60; the dull generation of, how cured, iii. 399.

Stoughton, R. (apothecary): advertisement for cure of small-pox, iii. *101*; his 'great Cordial Elixir' advertised, iv. *553*.

Stow, John, *Survey of London*, ed. by Strype, i. *14, 61, 95*.

Strada, Famianus: his account of a chimerical correspondence between two lovers, ii. 438; 'the Cleveland of his age', v. 108; translation of a passage in his *Prolusiones Academicae*, v. 109–12.

Strafford, Anne (Johnson) Wentworth, Countess of, ii. *489*.

Strafford, Thomas Wentworth, 3rd Earl of, iii. *439*.

Strahan, George (bookseller), i. *156*.

'Stranger in the candle', i. 31.

Stranger(s): proper behaviour upon meeting, ii. 24; men are s. and sojourners upon earth, ii. 353; iii. 30; our Saviour's injunction to take in the, ii. 405; to be reserved among s. a point of good breeding, iii. 347.

Strap, discipline of the, for a wife, iv. 271.

Strappado, to deserve the, iv. 307.

Stratagem(s): a libidinous man's head full of, ii. 297; Socrates conquers you by, ii. 429; wiles and s. of Satan in *PL*, ii. 564.

Stratford, Francis (Hamburg merchant), referred to (?), iii. 317–18.

Stratford upon Avon, a bonfire at, v. 151.

Stratocles, brought false news of victory to the Athenians, ii. *410*.

Stratonice and Antiochus, ii. 393.

Straw: superstitions regarding a, iv. 292.

'Stream, the purling', in LEONORA's garden, i. 158.

Streams: purling, ii. 11; as a figure of solitude and public life, iii. 517–18.

Street-clubs, i. 41.

Street-room, ii. 7.

Street-vendors, ii. 474–8; iii. 413; v. 41–42.

Streets: gleaning paper in the, iii. 379; well-disposed s. in London, iv. 101.

Streights, 'kept by a sea captain in the', iv. 225.

Strength: folly of desiring s. of youth, ii. 100; gathered through adversity, ii. 422; allegorical figures of S. and Necessity in Aeschylus, iii. 338; bodily s. of Leonardo da Vinci, iv. 489.

STREPHON: in love with a 'demurrer', i. 377; and FLORIO, ii. 86–88; 'there is no resisting', ii. 217; and PHILLIS, ii. 464; and EUDAMIA, iii. 25, 73; 'slain

by a lady's glance', iii. 418; his courtship of GLORIANA, iii. 586–9.

Stretch, a yawn and a, iii. 168.

'Strike a bold stroke' (to lead up a fashion), iii. 163, 225; 'strike home and spare not', iii. 65; strike out new tracks of science, iv. 488.

Strings to one's bow, To have two (prov.), ii. 503.

Strip a servant, i. 443.

'Stripped of his possession' (legal jargon), iv. *477*.

Stripping almost naked, at Bartholomew Fair, i. 218.

'Stroke, Strike a bold', iii. 163, 225; 'stroke of business, as the phrase is', iv. 217.

Strollers, a company of, at Epping, i. 207.

Strops for razors, the author of, iv. 5, 309.

Strumpet, the name of, iii. 16.

Strut, Francis (perfumer), i. *131*.

Strut: an old man creeping with the air of a, ii. 512; 'the King of France had not a better', iii. 241.

Strutt, Joseph, *Sports and Pastimes*, ii. *132, 133*; iii. *372*; iv. *147*.

Strutting, iv. 377; petticoat, ii. 6; by a woman's man, ii. 113.

Strype, John, edition of Stowe's *Survey of London*, i. *14, 61, 95*.

Stubbs, the Rev. Philip, his reading of the Common Prayer praised, ii. 78–79.

Study: the 'Lowngers' enemies to, i. 230; lengthens and enriches life, i. 398; Pascal's too great application to, i. 478–9; affects course of ambition, ii. 370; effect of habit upon, iv. 70.

Stuff, dressing in cloth or in, ii. 526.

Stunsfield. *See* Stonesfield.

Stupid: stupid-note taught, iii. 353; 'from pert to s. sinks supinely down', iv. 398.

Stupidity, allegorical representation of, in vision of painters, i. 354.

STURDY, Mr., iv. 101.

STURDY, JOHN, married the President of the Widow-Club, iv. 558.

Style: writing in a s. suitable to women, i. 21; a low grovelling, i. 245; cultivation of, in the young, ii. 396; mercantile honest s. of a letter, ii. 464; methods of avoiding the idiomatic, iii. 12–15; Milton's, iii. 14, 62–64; Seneca's objection to s. of Calvus, iii. 62; proper for a foreign minister, iii. 98; perspicuity of s. balanced against depth of sense, iv. 137; of epitaphs, iv. 343; of the *Faerie Queene*, iv. 429.

Styleman, John (a Director of E. India Co.), a subscriber, i. *xc*.

Sublime: thoughts, ii. 75; passages in the Old Testament, ii. 127; ideas induced by devotion, ii. 287; instances of virtue, ii. 462; and celebrated reputation, ii. 494; sentiments in the epic must be natural and, ii. 587–8; genius of Milton, iii. 89–91, 141; ideas formed by Homer, iii. 565; pretty and s. sentiments in the same bosom, iv. 396; subjects may be introduced into epistolary verse, v. 113–14; pens, v. 179.

Sublime, the: discussion of nature of true, i. *372*; not relished by little wits, ii. 128; Longinus has given us the same kind of s. which he discusses, ii. 484; the poet should not swell into the false, iii. 11; Aristotle's methods of forming, iii. 11–15; may exist without the pathetic, iii. 254–5; opposed to bombast, iii. 303; greatness as a source of, iv. 233–4; Bunyan not a master of, iv. 365; called the *gusto grande* (in architecture and statuary) by the Italians, v. 28; examples of false and true, v. 117; in oratory, v. 164–7. See also Longinus.

Sublimities, disturbing others with her, iv. 286.

Sublimity: Milton's distinguishing excellence, ii. 587; and perspicuity necessary to language of epic, iii. 10–15; in Milton, iii. 62–63, 85–86.

Submission(s): as a part of fashionable life, i. 486; and deference to superiors, ii. 354.

Substance, materiality of a thinking s. one of the great points of atheism, ii. 230.

Substantial forms: Aristotelians talk unintelligibly of, i. 237; Aristotle's doctrine of, ii. 338.

Sucking malice from his nurse's milk (prov.), ii. 455.

SUDDEN, THOMAS, memorial of, iv. 8–9.

Suet, iii. 153.

Suetonius Tranquillus, Caius: i. *72, 98*; ii. *247, 373, 456, 537*; iii. *41, 152*; on Caesar's baldness, ii. *401*; his *History* an argument against despotic power, iii. 20; on Roman education, iii. 132.

SUFFENUS, an elderly fortune-hunter, iii. 127.

Suffering: spectacle of a brave man superior to, i. 163–4; ii. 422; iii. 409; attitudes towards, iii. 128–30.

Suffolk, Edward Howard, 8th Earl of, iv. *414*.

Sugar: the pith of an Indian cane, i. 295;

in tea and coffee, ii. 82; a plate of brown, ii. 92.

Suicide: a would-be, i. 371; of Negroes in American plantations, ii. 339; from disappointment in love (the Lovers' Leap), ii. 366, 383–5, 406–9; of women in Greece, how prevented, ii. 399–400; less noble than bearing misfortunes, iii. 336; a French novelist on English melancholy leading to, iii. 454; thoughts of, iv. 277.

Suidas, i. *249*; ii. *408*; a story translated from, iv. 385.

SUKEY (a woman of the town), her encounter with Sir ROGER, iii. 532.

Sulla, Lucius Cornelius: the son of, ii. 114; gave himself the title of 'Felix', iii. 43; saw many Mariuses in Caesar, iii. 99; Atticus a friend to S. as well as to Marius, iii. 447.

Sullen, the, a subdivision of the angry, iv. 41.

Sullenness: in a husband, ii. 174; patience exerting itself as s. and despair in savage nations, ii. 339; religion in some little better than s. and reserve, iii. 80.

Sultan: adventures while he held his head in a tub of water, i. 400–1; exercise of, ii. 263; S. Mahmoud and his vizier, iv. 319; S.'s head, v. 118.

Summer: of 1711 moderate, ii. 5; English s. pleasanter than that of any other country in Europe, iii. 474; allegorical depiction of, iii. 595.

Summer-days, a wife who hates your tedious, ii. 11.

Summer-Island suit, an American in a, i. 343.

Summum bonum, equipage the lady's, i. 197.

Sun: the expression 'under the sun', i. 28; v. 117; rising of the, i. 274; ii. 533; Persian Emperor calls himself the Sun of Glory, ii. 128; Persian sacrifices to the, ii. 234; colour only the infraction of rays of, ii. 442; 'the first eye of consequence', ii. 470; makes other lights dim, ii. 533; a map of spots in the, iii. 83; in eclipse in *PL*, iii. 91, 359; the great soul of the universe, cheers the mind of man, iii. 452; rising and setting of, pleasing to the imagination, iii. 544.

Sunday: observance of, i. 459–60; Adam would have kept holy, iv. 586; remonstrance of T. C. against profanation of, v. 116.

Sunderland, Anne Churchill, Countess of, compliment to (?), ii. 479.

Sunderland, Charles Spencer, 3rd Earl of: and Addison, i. xvi; dismissed by the Queen, i. xvii; member of Kit-Cat Club, i. *42*; volume of *Spectator* dedicated to, v. 181–2.

Sun-dial, contemplating over a, i. 230.

Sunshine: influence on many constitutions, ii. 137; in landscapes of Titian, iii. 39; cheerfulness is like a sudden, iii. 430.

Superfluities: of the wealthy supply the necessities of the poor, i. 277; exported from one country to supply the wants of another, i. 294–5; care of, an extravagant vice, i. 469; thrown off by exercise, and prevented by temperance, ii. 264; a humorist who gives away a vast refuse of his, ii. 527.

Superintendent(s): of game, i. 447; of our language needed, ii. 149.

Superior and inferior beings, in the chain of being, i. 459; ii. 136–7.

Superiority: feeling of s. as a cause of laughter, i. 200, 223; ii. 466; absurd ideas of, ii. 185; must be founded on merit and virtue, ii. 292, 351–4; competitions for, ii. 371; as a factor in marriage, iii. 92; and modesty of behaviour, iii. 262.

Superiors: respect to, founded upon instinct, i. 30; proper behaviour of, ii. 354; envy of s. and equals, ii. 494; a silly scholar apt to despise his, ii. 554; intemperate behaviour before, ii. 575; talent of pleasing one's, ii. 592, 599.

Superstition: allegorical figure of, ii. 124; and enthusiasm, ii. 288–90; darkness and s. of Middle Ages, iii. 572; balanced against devotion, iv. 136; the road of s. in the vision of heavenly and worldly wisdom, iv. 369; feigned tales told by, v. 162.

Superstitions: and omens, i. 31–35, 53–54; regarding witches, i. 481–2; referred to, ii. 303; Saint-Evremond's defence of Roman Catholic, ii. 332; destructive to religion, ii. 333; among the vulgar, iv. 292–3; Mahometan, v. 158.

Superstitious: views of the hoop-petticoat, ii. 6; the fool and the s. actuated by unaccountable motives, ii. 250; the s. man is like an insipid courtier, ii. 289; mythology of shepherds used in Philips's *Pastorals*, iv. 363; inquiries into the future, v. 64–65.

Supper, Sir ROGER's, ii. 530.

Supplement, The: read by Sir ROGER, ii. 551; 'read the *S.* and *Daily Courant*', iii. 153.

Surfeits: Estcourt's wine excludes s., fevers, and physic, ii. 530; a quack who offers to cure, iv. 59.

Surgeon(s): work of s. and physician, i. 71; M. Festeau, one of the most considerable s. of Paris, iii. 383; advertisement of a s. in Drury Lane, iv. 59; anecdote of a criminal who tricked a, iv. 290. *See also* Chirurgeon.

Surprise: the life of stories, iv. 420; heightens pleasure, v. 139.

Surprise and delight: essential to wit, i. 264; in detecting appearances of Satan in *PL*, ii. 564.

Surtout, ii. 90; iii. 163.

SUSANNA, wife of HEZEKIAH BROADBRIM, ii. 577.

Susanna, A Paraphrase on the History of, recommended, i. 391.

Susanna, or Innocence Betrayed (puppet-opera), i. 65.

Suspicion(s): of the jealous husband, ii. 168–72; how to ease, ii. 173–6; cunning and s. the companions of little minds, ii. 419; allegorical depiction of, iii. 596.

SWALLOW, Lady CATHERINE, a member of the Widow-Club, iv. 516.

Swan, Mr., the famous punster, i. 261.

Swan, the, at Coleshill-Heath, Warwickshire, ii. 182.

Swan(s): Black S. as a sign, i. 116; Orpheus transformed into a, ii. 326; Sappho transformed into a, ii. 408; in romance-writers, iii. 18.

Swearing: common swearers, i. 36; forbidden in the Two-penny Club, i. 43; in presence of women, ii. 105; indiscriminate charity a worse reproach than, ii. 405; a hush-note to be used against, ii. 389; curing friends of, iii. 398–9; at servants, iv. 46; a kind of habitual perjury, iv. 75; at drivers of coaches, iv. 377. *See also* Profanity.

Sweat: a horse which had but one, ii. 117; asses sweated every morning upon the heath, ii. 182; professed 'she was all over in a', ii. 347.

Sweating: a practice of the Mohocks, iii. 224, 294–5; JACK LIGHTFOOT's adventure with the 'sweaters', iii. 224–5.

Swede, at the Royal Exchange, i. 294.

Sweden, King of. *See* Charles XII.

Swedish general, unhorsing of, at Pultowa, ii. 37.

SWEEPSTAKES, ELIZ., letter from (on JOHN TROTT's dancing), iii. 112–13.

Sweetmeats, i. 46, 241; iv. 232.

Sweetness: and good-humour of EMILIA, iii. 80; of temper necessary in married couples, v. 76.

Swelling sentiments, in Statius and Claudian, ii. 588.

Swepstone, Leicestershire: letter addressed from, iii. 210.

Swift, Jonathan, i. 296; iv. 501; v. 66; suspected of writing Tatlers, i. xv; contributions to Spectator, i. lvi, 215; iv. 567; Thomas Wallace on S.'s style, i. cii; referred to (?), i. 97; ii. 139; iii. 317; iv. 18; addicted to punning, i. 259; on the English language, ii. 32–33; supplied hints to Mrs. Manley, ii. 518; on No. 384, iii. 441; on Stella's admiration of Addison, iii. 583; his 'Hospital' and No. 472, iv. 170. — Battle of the Books, iv. 331; — Baucis and Philemon, ii. 486; — Complete Collection of Conversation, i. 40; — Conduct of the Allies, iv. 33; — Examiner, i. xvii, 16, 17–18, 66, 145, 296, 346; ii. 39, 285, 403; iii. 100, 463; iv. 414; — Journal to Stella, i. xiv, xvii, xcii, 4, 42, 89, 175, 202, 211, 215, 314, 359, 413, 441; ii. 5, 67, 227, 249; iii. 4, 100, 186, 264, 295, 439, 459, 548, 551; iv. 63, 168, 460; — Letters, i. 4, 12, 203, 329, 441; Some Advice to the October Club, i. 42; Tale of a Tub, ii. 288, 519; Tatler, iii. 343; iv. 101; Thoughts on Various Subjects quoted, i. 422; iv. 120; Tritical Essay, i. 5, 19; ii. 449.

Swift, the race not always to the, iii. 44.

Swine, women who resemble, ii. 319.

Swingers, the, a set of familiar romps, iv. 246, 260–1.

Swiny, Owen: one of the managers of the Haymarket Theatre, i. 23; iv. 283; librettist for Camilla, i. 79.

Swiss Cantons: English interest in quarrel of the, iv. 91; the Pope foments division between the, iv. 206.

Swiss musical compositions, i. 132.

Swiss officer, Scaramouche's quarrel with a, iii. 3.

Switzerland: an extraordinary musical genius in, i. 132; advices from Zug, iv. 93.

Swooning, i. 344; ii. 194, 342.

Sword(s): ii. 43, 236; shooting out into long, i. 71; basket-hilt s., i. 450; wearing of, ii. 544; wearing of, by footmen, iii. 69; flash of light upon drawing of, in PL, iii. 89; of Edward III in the Abbey, iii. 215; of Michael, in PL, iii. 231; of Aeneas broke that of Turnus, iii. 231; Maccabeus dreams of receiving s. from Jeremiah, iii. 232; used by Capt. SENTRY at battle of Steenkerke, iii. 240; fighting with, iv.

31; with fine knots, iv. 195–6; Methuen's skill in use of, v. 183.

Sword-combat, account of a, iv. 30–34.

Sword-cutler, the French King's head as sign before door of a, i. 117.

Sword-knot, TOM TAWDRY's rich, iv. 298.

Sword-play, ii. 131.

Sycophant, figure made by the, iii. 152.

Sydenham, Dr. Thomas: his treatise of fevers, i. 105; praises riding as an exercise, i. 473.

Sylla. See Sulla.

Syllables: resemblance of, in echoes and doggerel rhymes, i. 265; iii. 560; insertion or omission of, in PL, iii. 13.

Syllogisms: the schoolman a great friend to, ii. 272; invented by Aristotle, ii. 429.

Sylvan deities, ii. 487.

SYLVANA and HORTENSIUS, iii. 270.

Sylvans: satyrs, fauns, and s. accompanying Bacchus, iii. 596.

Sylvester, Joshua, translation of Du Bartas, i. 247.

SYLVIA: has demurred till she is past child-bearing, i. 377; her perplexity in choosing a husband, ii. 85–88; letter from (on solicitations from her husband's friend), iii. 503–4.

SYLVIUS, 'shot through the sticks of a fan', iii. 417.

Symmetry: of objects, immediately pleasing to the imagination, iii. 538; and proportion of parts pleasing, iii. 544; love of s. and order, natural to mind of man, v. 159.

Sympathy: applications which cure by, i. 225; secret s. of hearts, ii. 132; a generous s. for afflictions of others, iii. 80.

Symposium, rules of a s. in an ancient Greek author, i. 43.

Synaeresis, in a line of verse, iv. 163.

Syncopists, the modern race of, iv. 538.

SYNCROPIUS, a man who does not control his anger, iv. 39–40.

Syntax, a little slip in s. to be overlooked in great poetry, iii. 10.

Syracuse, ladies of, and Vulcan's dogs, iv. 581. See also Sicily.

Syrups, receipts for making, ii. 487.

T, speculations on Spectators signed, ii. 360; iii. 220, 531.

T., A., letter from, to her son, ii. 524.

T., B., his letter proposing marriage, iv. 360.

T., E., letter from (in praise of the Spectator), iv. 486.

T., F., letter from, to his mother, ii. 524–5.

T., J., letter from (in praise of the *Spectator*), iv. 486.

T., M., letter from (is postponing marriage), i. 338–9.

T., M., persuaded not to take the law of the farmer's son, v. 128.

T., P., letter from, to his brother, ii. 463.

T., R., letter from (on Milton), iii. 191–2.

T., S.: letter from (on a show of midgets), ii. 557–8; letter from (on the Chit-Chat Club), iv. 513.

T., T., letter from (on 'Idols' in coffee-houses), i. 371–2.

Tabac de mille fleurs, Scaramouche's invention of, iii. 3.

Tabby: a black t. mantua, iii. 532.

Tabby cat, of a witch, i. 482.

TABITHA, daughter of HEZEKIAH BROADBRIM, ii. 577.

Table: the upper end of the, i. 206; keeping a public, i. 352; dining at a public, i. 466; the high t. at Squire's, ii. 551.

Table-book, i. 357.

Tables, for making Latin verses, ii. 356.

Tables, a game at, iii. 518.

Tablets, one of Charles Mather's fine, iv. 286.

Tabourets, iii. 206.

Tabula Smaragdina, iii. 600.

Tacitus, Publius Cornelius: 'perhaps, with my friend T., fell into observations upon it which were too great for the occasion', ii. 291; describes Germanicus listening in disguise to a soldier, ii. 425–6; displays those outward motives which give birth to the transactions he relates, iii. 528; quoted, i. 424; ii. 495; mentioned, ii. 72; iii. 98.

Tacker, a, fond of the number 134, ii. 249.

Tackle of the coach-window, iv. 100.

Tail, treading upon a lady's, iii. 417.

Tailor(s): playing the role of the lion, i. 57–58; should not use the sign of a lion, i. 117; identifiable by his gait, ii. 271; 'of six foot high', iii. 109; a t.'s bill torn by a husband, v. 80; mentioned, ii. 528; iii. 163; v. 38.

Tailor (a fish), iii. 276.

Take or leave, ii. 355; take the world as we find it, ii. 205.

Tale-bearer(s), i. 83; iii. 123–4, 465.

Talent(s): to be valued only as well used, ii. 178–81, 462; a man with great t., without discretion, like Polyphemus, ii. 376; are set off by modesty, ii. 399; great t. seldom in demand, iii. 235; CLEANTHES an example of t. mis-

applied, iii. 511; proper use of, iv. 487–91.

Talismans: used by absent lovers, ii. 452–3; and other superstitions in Asia, v. 65.

Talk, loose: endangers the credit of the trader, ii. 350–1; referred to, ii. 464.

Talkative, the: a drum the type of the empty and, ii. 23; and the pert, ii. 81–85; temper of the common people, ii. 349; and the inquisitive, ii. 386–9.

Talkers: who bore the company with their narrations, iii. 450–1; THOMAS SUDDEN one of the loud, iv. 8.

Talking: with a friend is thinking aloud, ii. 375; women's love of, ii. 458–62; loud t. the mark of the fortune-hunter, iii. 126.

Talman, M., iii. 154.

Talmud, the, ii. 423.

Tankards, the milk-maid under a pyramid of silver, iii. 372.

Tansy, i. 466.

Tantalism: a kind of T. or Platonic Hell, i. 382.

Tantalus, description of, i. 382.

Tapers, two t. supported by a servant, iii. 296.

TAPERTY, Mrs., an eternal flirt and disturber of families, ii. 293.

Tapestry and wall hangings, i. 361; figures in, ii. 60; iii. 196, 221; embroidery of, recommended to women, v. 72.

Tap (to spend freely), a country gentleman began to, iv. 469.

Tarantula, bite of, cured by music, iv. 590.

Tare and Tret, ii. 40.

Tarentum, HESPERUS of, ii. 408.

Tarpeia, buried under costly ornaments, iii. 372.

Tarsus, Paul of, v. 165.

Tartar(s): example of the wild, ii. 2; T. general's sale of Chinese women, iv. 315; mentioned, ii. 317.

Tartary: incident of the dervish in, iii. 30; ashes of Liszynski shot towards, iii. 462.

Tasso, Torquato: Rinaldo and Armida in, i. 25; 'the *clincant* or tinsel of', i. 26; mixed embellishments of, ii. 588; Milton's imitations of, not worth recording, iii. 392.

Taste: wretched t. in audiences, i. 59; ii. 314; false t. in plays and operas, i. 94; art to conform to, i. 123; the *Spectator's* aim, to establish a t. of polite writing, i. 245; of English poets and readers extremely Gothic, i. 269; a wrong

artificial t. formed on little fanciful authors, i. *297*; a true and unprejudiced t. of nature, i. *362–3*; gross t. in courtship of the present age, i. *386*; of the present age, corrupt, ii. *52*; immoral t. of Shadwell's age, ii. *58–59*; men of t. and gallantry in reign of Charles II, ii. *118*; letter from a gentleman of delicate, ii. *346–7*; proposal for cultivating t. of the young, ii. *395*; trivial t. in show and pomp, ii. *526*; vicious t. prevailing in modern writers, ii. *588*; unanimity of t. and judgement at court of Augustus, ii. *592*; and morals, iii. *15–17*; *The Distressed Mother* 'not busy enough' for the present t. (?), iii. *32*; of ignorant readers, formed on modern poetry, iii. *90*; the nature of: how acquired, iii. *527–31*; of present age, for epigram and conceits, iii. *530*; reasons for differences in, iii. *561*; 'what you call the fine t.', iv. *352*.

Taste(s) (sensitive): those for ever exercising their feeling or tasting, ii. *364*; and colours, why made agreeable to man, iii. *453*; person who could distinguish t. of tea, iii. *527–8*; best pleased with things which at first are disgusting, iv. *70–71*; a remedy for restoring, iv. *462*.

TASTEWELL, DICK, 'slain by a blush', iii. *418*.

Tate, Nahum: adaptation of *King Lear*, i. *170*; and Brady's new version of the Psalms, ii. *305*; hymn by, iv. *12*; his epigram 'On the Spectator', iv. *232–3*.

Tate, Robert (druggist), advertises snuff, iii. *278*.

Tatler: cessation of, i. xiii–xv; iv. *232*; publication of, in volume form, i. xvii, xxiii; Lillie's connexion with, i. xxii, *74*; Addison's assistance in, iv. *492*; quoted [a selection]: on Italian opera, i. *22–23*; on Powell's puppets, i. *61*; on a moving picture, i. *129*; on stage properties, i. *177*, *179*; on punning, i. *259*; on snuff-taking, i. *314*; on conduct of the fan, i. *426–7*; on 'sex in souls', ii. *8*; on man's inconsistency, ii. *136*; on the lottery, ii. *249–50*; on modesty, ii. *399*; on lanterloo, ii. *451*; on the 'pretty fellow', ii. *514*; on pin-money, iii. *51*; on a virtuoso's will, iii. *149*; advertisement for coffee and tea, iii. *207*; on adulteration of wines, iii. *353*; on Powell at the Bath, iii. *401*; advertisement for moving picture, iii. *550–1*; on the naked-shouldered, iv. *38*; on the metaphorically defunct, iv. *178*; on biters, iv. *289*; epitaph from

Stepney, iv. *342*; advertisements for J. More, iv. *458*; on egotism, iv. *520*; on cost of a wig, v. *156*.

TATTLE, LETITIA, wife of THOMAS PRATER, i. *151*.

TATTLE, Mrs., ii. *561*.

TATTLE, TIM, killed by the tap of a fan, iii. *417*.

TATTLE, TOM, an impertinent fellow, i. *393*.

Tauriscus, 'an absent actor', iv. *436*.

Tautologies, in big books, i. *506*.

Tavern(s): each has some old humourist who is master of the house, i. *102*; servants eating at, i. *374*; 'we rambled from t. to t.', i. *407*; to crack a bottle at the next, ii. *411*; open t., ii. *527*; about the Exchange, iii. *401*; tyrants in, iv. *302–4*.

Taverns, inns, and ale-houses:
Bell Ale-house, Wood Street, i. *117*.
Bell Tavern, King Street, Westminster, i. lxxxiii.
Bell Savage Inn, i. *118*.
Bristol, City of (tavern?), i. *40*.
Bull Inn, Bishopsgate Street, iv. *310*.
Bumper Tavern: Richard Estcourt at, ii. *529*; 'the man of the Bumper knows me', ii. *534*; reopened by Thomas Brooke, iii. *353*.
Cannon-Ball (a tavern?), iv. *59*.
Devil Tavern, Fleet Street: manifesto of the Emperor of the Mohocks issued from, iii. *295*.
Feathers (tavern?), i. *40*, *153*.
Fountain Tavern, i. lxxiii, *102*.
George (tavern?), Finch Lane, i. *157*.
George, At the sign of the (tavern?), i. *41*.
George's, at Oxford, i. *182*.
Half-Moon Tavern, Drury Lane, iv. *182*.
Harp, Barbican (tavern?), iv. *62*.
King's Arms Tavern, Wild Street, i. *40*.
King's-Head-Inn, Southwark, iii. *278–9*.
Queen's Arms, Covent Garden, iv. *546*.
Queen's Arms Tavern, Ludgate Hill, i. *102*.
Red Lyon and Ball, the Old Bailey, i. *40*.
Rose Tavern, i. *10*, *149*.
Rummer Tavern, Whitechapel, i. *40*.
Ship Tavern, Greenwich, i. *128*.
Ship and Castle Tavern, Cornhill, i. *40*.
Thatcht House, Ave-Mary-Lane, i. *40*.
Three Tun Tavern, ii. *381*.

INDEX

Taverns (*cont.*)

Trumpet, Sheer Lane (tavern?), ii. *238*.

White-Hart, Long Acre, ii. 473.

Tavern-bill, torn by a wife, v. 80.

Taw (game of marbles), iii. 368.

Taw Waw Eben Zan Kaladar, Emperor of the Mohocks: manifesto of, iii. 293–5; married a rich widow in London, v. 58.

TAWDERY, JACK, should buy him a cane, ii. 512.

TAWDRY, TOM, and FLAVILLA, an unhappy married couple, iv. 298.

Tawny skin, among young women's 'burdens', iv. 507.

Tax, Land: four shillings in the pound, i. 468; iv. 455; party-spirit tends to prejudice of, i. 509; paid for by consumption of products, ii. 284–6.

Tax upon soap, the late, iv. 230.

Taxes, ii. 252; in London, ii. 283–4; for poor relief, ii. 404.

Taylor, James (contractor to the Army), a subscriber, i. *xci*.

Taylor, Jeremy, i. *159*; iv. *71*. — *Holy Living* and *Holy Dying* in LEONORA's library, i. 157.

Taylor, John, iv. *537*.

Taylor, Thomas: translation of Malebranche, i. *155*; translation of Basnage de Beauval, iv. *256–7*.

Tea: 'all well-regulated families, that set apart an hour in every morning for tea and bread and butter', i. 44–45; a dish of tea spilt by CAMILLA on her petticoat, i. 242; the infusion of a China plant, i. 295; sugar in, i. 295, 371; ii. 82; in coffee-houses, i. 371; ii. 92; iv. 408; a dish of, ii. 92, 552; iii. 353; and other India goods sold by Motteux, iii. 25; iv. 479; 'drank a dish of Bohea', iii. 182; 'from nine to twelve, drank my tea, and dressed', iii. 184; 'from dinner to six, drank tea', iii. 184; Green, Imperial, Peco, and Bohea, iii. 207; green tea, iii. 245, 481; cheapening tea, in a China shop, iii. 245; chatting over, iii. 321; those who sip, iii. 485; a person who could distinguish ten kinds of, by tasting, iii. 527; 'drank tea', iv. 378; poem on, by Motteux, iv. 478; sipping their tea for a whole afternoon, v. 71.

Tea-dishes, i. 153, 371; iii. 245.

Tea-equipage, i. 389.

Tea-table(s): i. 228; ii. 119; compliments in use at, i. 152; Mrs. MODISH's, ii. 488; writing to the, ii. 574; 'from ten to eleven, tea-table', iii. 183; appurtenances of, iii. 207; a youth who officiates at the, iii. 367; a particular air at, iii. 415; a *Spectator* to be read at all, iii. 482; of friends, iv. 412; knotting may be done at the, iv. 413; scandal the usual attendant of, v. 72.

Tea-table account, bread and butter in the, iv. 231.

Tea-table reading of the *Spectator*, i. 389; ii. 55, 119, 330, 342, 454; iii. 182, 482; iv. 231; 'your paper part of the equipage of the tea-table', ii. 454.

Tea-table talk: to be furnished by the *Spectator*, i. 21, 44–45; between the sexes, iii. 73.

Teague, in *The Lancashire Witches*, ii. 58.

Tears: an expression of joy, i. 294; true grief beyond relief of, i. 402–4; of OMNAMANTE make you think yourself a brute for your rage, ii. 70; a schoolboy's silent, ii. 116; my heart swells t. into my eyes, ii. 202; the audience at the theatre afraid of letting fall a tear, ii. 315; melting into, ii. 433; the eloquence of, and fainting fits, ii. 480–1; real t. shed by actors in *The Distressed Mother*, iii. 32, 34; heart confesses its humanity and flows out into, iii. 80; Satan's bursting out into (in *PL*), a beautiful circumstance, iii. 86; MOLL COMMON slays with her, iii. 418; allegorical figure of the River of, iv. 276; bring relief to sorrow, iv. 350.

Teasers of the Muses, iii. 26.

Teasing and tormenting a wife, ii. 417.

Teeth: drawing of, i. 96; complaining of 'something that *stuck in her teeth*', ii. 347; fore, ii. 407; 'showed his teeth, some of them very white', ii. 434; sounds which set t. 'an edge', ii. 475; red noses, large lips, and rusty, iv. 507–8; Mr. FONDLE's 'the whitest t. you ever saw', v. 135; whiteness of WILL HONEYCOMB's, v. 185.

Tekel, engraven on a weight, iv. 137.

Telemachus, learnt to keep secrets, iii. 249–50.

Telephus: Peleus and, i. *166*; nursed by a hind, iii. 455.

Telescopes, used in studying stars, iv. 530.

Temper (temperament): variety of, in men and women, ii. 8–9; evenness of, in URANIUS, ii. 66; mutability or unevenness of, ii. 137; easiness of, reduced into an art is good breeding, ii. 165; kinds of, in husbands susceptible of jealousy, ii. 171, 174; dangers of a foolish sanguine, ii. 252; the right t. in disputation, ii. 274; compliances

469

derived from an easy, ii. 281; women of variable and uneven, ii. 319; serenity, or mildness of, the title given to princes, ii. 352; rude, untractable, reserved, and melancholy t. may become agreeable, ii. 425; evenness of, in a wife, ii. 515; women's t. to be neither too untractable nor too complying, ii. 568; men of dull and phlegmatic t. often grow rich, iii. 2; of a person best discovered by his letters, iii. 7; evenness and sweetness of, necessary to married happiness, v. 75–76.

Temper (moderation), women have less than men, i. 243.

Temper, ill: THOMAS SMOAKY's complaint of his master, ii. 293; shown in losing at cards, iv. 10; control of, iv. 39–42.

Temperance: superior to exercise or medicine in promoting health, ii. 264–7; an art which leads to tranquillity, ii. 268–9; without decotion, insipid, ii. 287; as a virtue, ii. 445; representation of, in Spenser, iv. 428–9; importance of t. and sobriety, iv. 448; necessary to a quiet night's sleep, v. 5.

Temperature (middle course), a just t. between indolence and violence, iv. 154.

TEMPEST, MARTHA, letter from (jesting of her husband), ii. 327–8.

Tempest, P. (engraver), ii. 474.

Tempest, The (opera), i. 27.

TEMPLAR, THE: character of, i. 9–10; at a performance of The Pilgrim, i. 94; thinks the Spectator should not criticize members of Inns of Court, i. 142–3; ridicules WILL HONEYCOMB for his poor spelling, i. 437; suspected of writing Spectators signed 'L', ii. 360; his farewell essay, on acting, iv. 432–7; has withdrawn into his own profession, iv. 440, 485; mentioned, i. 144, 425; iv. 389.

Templar: incident of a young T. and his father in the coffee-house, ii. 92–93; conversation of Capt. SENTRY with a, ii. 272–3; who was very arch upon parsons, iv. 18; boasting his third cure, iv. 398; talk with a young, iv. 500; a suitor of the Widow WILDFIRE, iv. 517.

Templars, i. 45; who frequent the playhouse more than Westminster-Hall, i. 90; tempted by Jezebels, ii. 191.

Temple, Sir Richard, a subscriber, i. lxxxix.

Temple, Sir William: his style praised by Melmoth, i. xcviii; wonders why the Northern Hive does not overrun the world now with Goths and Vandals, i. 90; his essays in LEONORA's library, i. 155; his rules for drinking, ii. 266 (an emendation to these, proposed, ii. 306); on mental faculties, i. 19–20; on Chinese writing, i. 255; on genius, ii. 126; on Homer and Virgil, ii. 127, 587; on wealth, ii. 283; on the passions, ii. 373; on differences between animals and human beings, ii. 417; on the French Academy, iii. 96; on variety of English humour, iii. 396; on rules for writing poetry, iii. 451; on English melancholy, iii. 454; on pleasures of sense and imagination, iii. 536, 538; on gardening, iii. 552; iv. 595; on the wall of China, iii. 555.

Temple: monkey discovered in an Egyptian, ii. 7; to Apollo at Leucate, ii. 366, 406; in allegory of love and old age, iii. 76; to Jupiter Belus in Babylon, iii. 554; Solomon's, iv. 583–4; v. 15.

Temptations: called 'opportunities' by the world, ii. 276; of worldly want, ii. 527; dangerous only to madmen or fools, iv. 366.

Ten, the complete number, ii. 361.

Tenant(s): to Sir STEPHEN RACKRENT, i. 406; entertained at Twelfth-Night, ii. 208; to a man of quality, ii. 245; 't., taxes, and law-suits', ii. 252; entertained at Sir ROGER's at Christmas, ii. 550; loss by bad, ii. 598.

Tender: 'that kind of writing which the French critics call the', iii. 333.

Tender-constituted ladies, ii. 6.

Tenderness: of parents for children, ii. 213; and pity incited by dependence, ii. 214; induced more by conferring than by receiving favours, ii. 243; poems of Sappho filled with bewitching, ii. 366; most ills proceed from too much, ii. 387; Raphael's t. for man in PL, ii. 564; of a husband and father in Macbeth, iii. 393–4.

'Tenebrificous' stars, iv. 591.

Tenison, Thomas (Archbishop of Canterbury), a subscriber, i. lxxxviii; mentioned, i. 260.

Tennis, a game of, iii. 578.

TERAMINTA, letter from (on the French doll), ii. 578–9.

Terence (Publius Terentius Afer): proposal that children be taught to act a scene of, ii. 396; no comedy in so polite an author as T. raised upon the violations of the marriage-bed, iv. 68; 'Vos valete & plaudite', iv. 495. — Andria,

quoted, iv. 521; — *Eunuchus*, quoted, ii. 128–9, 169; iv. 486, 521; — *Hecyra*, Prologue to, quoted, iii. 237; — *The Self-Tormentor*, analysis of, iv. 280–2, 356.

Teresias, blind, iv. 512.

TERMAGANT, KITTY, letter from (on a club of she-romps), ii. 345–6.

Terms of art: in painting, ii. 447; use of, in poetry, iii. 63–64; in medicine, iii. 384; in exposition, iv. 6.

Terrae filius, speech of a, ii. 91.

Terrewest, John (prize-fighter), iv. *31, 33.*

Terror: allegorical figures of, iii. 337; aroused by serious poetry, iii. 567; pleasure in, enhanced by sense of our own safety, iii. 568–9.

Terror and pity in tragedy: devices for inducing, i. 177–8, 185–91; Aristotle on the kind of character proper for causing, ii. 565–6.

TERSETT, HARRY, and his lady, an indolent couple, i. 421.

Tertullian, on divining in dreams, iv. 229.

Tester (sixpence), v. 106.

Testimonials: and recommendations, iv. 247–51; to particular *Spectators*, iv. 457–61. *See also* Advertisements.

Testiness of old age, corrected by philosophy, iii. 321–2.

'Testy, Old', v. 39.

Tetrachtys (the number four), ii. 361.

TETTYX, his leap into the Ionian sea, ii. 408.

Texts, beautifying interior of a church, i. 460.

Thales, a saying of, on falsehood, v. 33.

Thammuz, account of, in *PL*, 'finely romantic', iii. 87.

Thank you for nothing (prov.), i. 197; iii. 468.

THANKLEY, DULCIBELLA, letter from (on Duncan Campbell), iv. 181–2.

'That': has supplanted 'who' and 'which', i. 336–7; remonstrance of, i. 344–5; 'that is', a redundant phrase in conversation, iii. 398.

Thatched house, iii. 189, 210.

Theatre(s): the two, in London, i. 4; scenery in, i. 22–27, 63–65, 149–51; pronunciation of the word, ii. 33; to lead out ladies from the, ii. 236; 'the world a t.', ii. 353; persons not allowed behind scenes, ii. 435; only one dramatic theatre licensed in London, ii. 503; trap-doors in, ii. 504; seating arrangements in, ii. *511*; audience composed of two sorts of people, iv.

282; devices for thunder, lightning, &c., v. 25–26.

Theatre, behaviour in the: of an affected woman, i. 194; of women, ii. 314–15; of the Trunk-maker, ii. 413–16; of a beau, ii. 434–5; nose-pulling, ii. 544–5; salutations in, ii. 552–3; of a cluster of coxcombs in, iv. 282.

Theatre of ease, proposed, ii. 503.

Theatre, Roman: defeat of Britons pictured in curtain of, ii. 150; regulation of, iv. 66–68; Cato's visit to, iv. 67.

Theban: general (Epaminondas), ii. 26; Amphion's lute and T. wall, v. 161.

Thebes: wars of, described by Statius, i. 300; anecdote of war between T. and Sparta, iv. 528.

Theft(s): women who engage in, ii. 320; Spartans looked upon it as honourable if it succeeded, iii. 99.

Thémiseul de St-Hyacinthe, Hyacinthe Cordonnier, iv. *161.*

THEMISTA, confidant of ORESTILLA, i. 484.

Themistocles: was helped by others, ii. 44; preferred a man without an estate, to an estate without a man, iii. 126.

Theobald, Lewis, on 'Hero and Leander', i. *265.*

Theocritus: so fine a writer not guilty of false wit, i. 247; quoted, ii. 382–3.

Theodosius, testimony concerning Jesus, iv. 385.

Theodosius and Constantia, story of, ii. 142–8.

Theodosius, or The Force of Love. See Lee.

Theognis, a saying of, iv. 138.

Theophrastus: on beauty, ii. *68*; called Tauriscus an 'absent' actor, iv. 436.

Thermometer, ii. 426, *519*, 595.

Theron, Pindar's praise of, iv. 152.

Thersites: a celebrated ill face, i. 77; a mimic and buffoon, ii. 326, 562, 589; his soul transformed into that of a monkey, ii. 326.

Theseus, ii. 562; in *A Midsummer Night's Dream*, i. 476.

THESPIS, husband of PRAXINOE, ii. 407.

Thespis, the cat-call not older than, iii. 351.

Thessalian statues, in honour of dancers, i. 284.

THESTYLIS and OLPHIS, ii. 407.

Thévenot, Jean de, *Travels into the Levant*, i. *3, 224, 360*; ii. *248.*

Thick and thin, Through (prov.), iii. 414.

Thief: a pleasant t. with the ladies, ii. 112; *worth a halter* (prov.), iii. 189, 210.

THIMBLETON, RALPH, letter from (on his wife), iv. 20.
Thin men, Club of, i. 39–40.
Things, distinguishing between words and, a critic's duty, iii. 36.
Think, thinking: distracted t. of the absent-minded, i. 330–1; materiality of a t. substance, one of the great points of atheism, ii. 230; ill effects of want of, ii. 364; absent lovers t. of each other at a specified time, ii. 437; Cartesian doctrine that the soul always thinks, ii. 460; persons who pretend never to, iii. 6.
Third day (author's benefit), v. 26.
Third Heaven, the particular residence of God, iv. 583.
THIRSIS, in love with a demurrer, i. 377.
Thirteen in company, unlucky (?), i. 33.
'This here' and 'that there', frequently used, i. 345.
Thomas, St., painted by Raphael, ii. 380.
Thomas, in 'The Wanton Wife of Bath', ii. 461.
THOMAS, servant of JACK TOPER, iv. 249.
Thomas, Enos, ii. 117.
'Thomas such a one, Esquire', ii. 226.
THOMPSON, HARRY (a soldier), ii. 98.
THOMSON, JACK, ii. 45.
Thomyris, Queen of Scythia (opera), i. 23.
Thor, subjects of, i. 90.
Thornhill, Sir James: portrait of Steele, i. 75; member of the Academy of Painting, iv. 495.
Thornhill, Richard, duel with Dering, i. 359.
Thought: every t. attended with consciousness, i. 160; no t. can be beautiful which is not just, i. 268; greatness of, in Chevy Chase, i. 303; hunting, a method of drowning t., i. 478; a creature vacant of, ii. 386; purity of, ii. 500, 591; 'when the t. is great and natural', iii. 10.
Thoughts: in the ballad, i. 321, 362–3; immoral t. avoided in Spectator, ii. 205–6, 517; shining t. in writers, ii. 396, 414; lights in pictures represent bright and lively, ii. 447–8; women know how to conceal their, ii. 460; or sentiments in the epic, ii. 585; iii. 84; art of ranging one's t. necessary to the critic, iii. 36; value of putting t. into words, iii. 423; men of warm imaginations and towering, iii. 410.
Thrale, Mrs. Hester (Piozzi), ii. 347.
THRASH, WILL, and his wife, a dull couple, iv. 358.

Thrasybulus, anecdote of, iv. 379.
THREADNEEDLE, ALICE, letter from (how she saved her apprentice maid from seduction), i. 216–18 (this letter praised, iv. 461).
Thread-paper, iii. 189.
Three Nuns and a Hare (sign), i. 117.
THRIFT, HEZEKIAH, letter from (on trade), iv. 306–10.
Thrift: or good husbandry in moral life, ii. 332; the first and best method of gaining riches, iii. 2.
THRIFTY, ABRAHAM, letter from (on his virtuoso nieces), ii. 442–3.
THRIFTY, DEBORAH, letter from (a country maid), iii. 226.
Throstle, and the nightingale, v. 63.
Throwing, a part of the Roman Pentathlum, ii. 133.
Thrush(es): singing of, iii. 593; and jays in a garden, iv. 190; a man who imitates the singing of, iv. 546.
Thucydides, Pericles' funeral oration quoted, i. 349; iii. 105.
Thumb-ring, v. 99.
Thumbs: a treatise of, ii. 469; born with two on one hand, iv. 293.
Thunder: in the opera, i. 24, 64, 150; in The Rehearsal, i. 150; in English tragedy, i. 178, 185–6; the new t. in the playhouse, v. 25–26.
Thunderer to the Playhouse, i. 197; ii. 414; letter from, i. 150–1.
Thunder-bolts, a young girl eating, iv. 16.
Thurmond, John (actor), in All for Love, i. 392.
Thurmonds, Mr., in King's Court, Russell Street, i. 36.
Thwaites, Richard, i. lxxiii.
Thyestes, in The Cruelty of Atreus, i. 65.
THYRSIS: 'shot from a casement in Piccadilly', iii. 417; and SYLVIA, iii. 480.
Tiberius (emperor): letter from Horace to, iv. 250–1; his actions based on jealousy, iv. 524.
Tiberius Nero. See Nero.
Tick-tack. See Trick-track.
Tickell, Thomas: letter quoted, i. liii–liv; contributions to Spectator, i. liv-lv, lxxv, lxxviii–lxxix; iv. 396–9, 494; v. 117–23; 'Kensington Garden', i. 61; iv. 190; edition of Addison's Works, i. 105; notes on Addison, ii. 205–6; part of No. 410 ascribed to, iii. 531; 'The Prospect of Peace', iv. 361; v. 118; translation of Homer, v. 74.
Tickell collection, i. xl.
Tickets, red wax of ball-tickets, black wax of burying-tickets, iv. 15.

Tigellius, the most humorous character in Horace, ii. 137–8, 363.

Tiger(s): in King William's time, i. 56; Bacchus in a chariot drawn by, iii. 596.

Tigress, spots rise in her skin when she is angry, i. 348.

Tilers and masons, ii. 57.

Tillotson, John: ii. *400*; iv. *71*; his sermons preached by Sir ROGER's chaplain, i. 441; the preacher who drew upon T. and Beveridge, ii. 45; passages from sermon on sincerity quoted, i. 430–2; iii. 314–16; iv. 503; on the existence of God, iii. 44; on heaven and hell, iv. 73; subject of evil-speaking nobly handled in a sermon by, iv. 427; on the happiness of the blessed, v. 50; on the idle ('fools at large'), v. 132; used by Steele in *The Ladies Library*, i. *159*; representative of the 'new style', i. *260*; on non-existence, iii. *431*.

'Tilt, Run upon the', iii. 39.

Timber: cutting, ii. 116; destruction of, for the fleets, iv. 594.

Timbrel, sound of the, v. 2.

Time: 't. out of mind', i. 87; waste of, i. 230–2; ii. 54; figure of, with hourglass and scythe, i. 272; allegorical figure of, in vision of painters, i. 356; iii. 76; proper use of, i. 394–7; our notions of duration of, i. 398–402; v. 17–22, 144–5; Locke on our perception of, i. 399; the 'heaviest of loads', i. 421; ii. 112; that portion of eternity called, ii. 123; how to fill up spaces of, with satisfaction, ii. 269; *discovers all things* (prov.), ii. 361; an immense ocean, from which few ancient authors have escaped, ii. 365; 'time will discover the event', a common sentence in newspapers, ii. 388; right use of, differentiates us from slaves, ii. 526; calculation of t. taken up by action of an epic, ii. 543–4; iii. 391; breach of unities of t. and place, ii. 554; 'consistent with my t. of day', iii. 56; refusal to acknowledge ravages of, iii. 75–76; letter on use of, iii. 148–51; two 'journals' illustrating waste of, iii. 153–6, 181–5; proper use of, should be taught children, iii. 250; proper use of, important to young men and women, iii. 346–7; v. 71; 'that t. and chance which is said to happen to every man', iii. 349; rules to be observed in using, iii. 406–8; present, past, and future, iv. 165; judgement the offspring of, iv. 328; present t. an isthmus in an ocean, v. 18.

Time-servers of fashion, iv. 196.

Time-serving, the *Spectator* accused of, iv. 64.

Timotheus (poet and musician), anecdote of, iv. 95.

Timotheus (Athenian general), affected to despise Fortune, iii. 45.

TIMOTHY, Sir, iii. 155.

Tin, English, traded for gold, i. 296.

Tincture(s): to restore sense of smelling, advertised, iv. *462*; of quacks, iv. 553.

Tindal, Matthew, iii. *459*.

Tinker(s): 'give the t. and coblers their presents again', ii. 238; waked by a passing, v. 41.

Tin-mines, income from, iii. 121.

Tippets, i. 248, 295.

Tipping: the wink, ii. 472; iv. 267; the lion, a practice of the Mohocks, iii. 187, 294.

Tipplers, the world filled with, ii. 364.

Tire-woman (-women): English, inferior to French, ii. 578; the most celebrated in Paris, ii. 580; FONTANGE, the, iii. 183; draw their subsistence from fashion, iv. 193.

Tiresias, the Theban soothsayer, iv. 512.

Tirzah, Mount, in southern China, iv. 596, 598; v. 1–2.

Tithe, EUGENIUS reserves a tenth part to charitable uses, ii. 198.

Tithe-stealers, a squire who makes his tenants, i. 462.

Titian (Tiziano Vecellio, or Vecelli): in vision of painters, i. 355; 'that inimitable sunshine diffused over his landscapes', iii. 39.

TITLE-PAGE, ANTHONY, petition to be given unused letters, iii. 93.

'TITLE-PAGE, CROUCHBACK', iii. 93.

Titles: how determined: their emptiness seen at death, ii. 351–2, 352–4; inappropriate in prayers, iii. 130–1; balanced against vanity, iv. 136; folly of desiring, iv. 202; v. 124; and garters, iv. 315; a defence of t. and honours, v. 94–95.

Tividale, in *Chevy-Chase*, i. 317.

Toad: BAREFACE, an impudent, ii. 112; Satan's appearance to Eve in form of a, iii. 172.

Toast(s): Mrs. VIZARD a top t. in the Ugly Club, i. 77; drinking a t. to every letter in a lady's name, i. 126; CAMILLA might be the t. of both parties, i. 242; a celebrated, ii. 304; PATETIA the reigning t. at Oxford, i. 547; most eminent t. in Paris, ii. 578; a first-rate t. at a play, iii. 427; t. and belles, iv. 315; the face and person of a, iv. 316;

'the frolic viscount toasting his miss', iv. 398; English drinking of, iv. 505.

Tobacco, i. 310; a paper of, i. 361; ii. 551; Virginia, ii. 30; iii. 153, 213; smokers of, and takers of snuff, ii. 364; a pipe of John Sly's best, ii. 530. See also Smoking.

Tobacco-box, iii. 153; iv. 540.

Tobacco-pipes: a young girl eating, iv. 15; music played upon, iv. 545.

Tobacco-stopper(s), iv. 539; made by WILL WIMBLE, ii. 550; iii. 215.

Tobacco trade, EPHRAIM WEED bred to the, iv. 82.

Tobacconist. See Sly, John.

Tofts, Mrs. Catherine: in Arsinoe and Camilla, i. 79; the wild boar killed by, in Camilla, i. 93; letter from ('Camilla'), iv. 55–56.

Toilet: women's great scene of business, i. 46; SEMPRONIA at her, i. 193; women who pass their time at their, ii. 320; an incident at a lady's, ii. 548; CLARINDA's, iii. 182–4.

Toilets: quilts, t., &c., made by French Protestants, iii. 206.

Toland, John, ii. 195; iii. 459; referred to (?), ii. 155–6, 412.

TOM: 'the Tyrant' at White's, i. 211; a suitor of BIDDY LOVELESS, ii. 270; Mrs. FREEMAN's footman, ii. 343; eldest son of T. B., iii. 195; 'the bounteous', iii. 289; a bankrupt, iv. 110.

Tomorrow: Never defer that till t. which you can do to-day (prov.), iii. 2; iv. 160.

Tom-tit(s): in the opera, i. 27; transmigration into a, iii. 276; a man who imitates the singing of, iv. 546.

Tone of speech: differs from country to country, i. 120; in acting, iv. 432–7.

Tongs: and gridiron (fable), i. 197; music of t. and key, iv. 546.

Tongue(s): Government of the T., recommended, i. 391; BAREFACE has a spiteful, ii. 112; excess of modesty obstructs the, ii. 398; bold t. and feeble arm of Drances, ii. 399; dissection of a woman's, proposed, ii. 460; Irishman's comment on a woman's, ii. 460 (referred to, ii. 481); good-breeding has made the t. falsify the heart, ii. 479; volubility of women's, ii. 480; noise and strife of, ii. 492; of a coquette has little communication with her heart, ii. 596; 'the sallies of that little, pert, forward, busy person', iii. 123; the porter shows disrespect by stealing out his, iii. 322; cure of a distemper in the, iv. 459.

Tonson, Jacob: secretary of Kit-Cat Club, i. 42; edition of PL, ii. 538; Poetical Miscellanies, v. 103.

Tonson, Jacob, jun.: publisher of the Tatler, i. xxiii; one of the printers of the Spectator, i. xxiii, xxviii–xxix, lviii, lxxii–lxxiii; recommends Bayle's Dictionary for the ladies, i. 390; printer of The Historian (?), iii. 111; mentioned, iv. 272.

Tooth: drawing a t. in a frolic, iii. 341; t. and nail (prov.), iv. 16.

Toothless old lady, ii. 95.

Top, simile of the, in the Aeneid, ii. 542.

Topcliff, Yorkshire, iii. 210.

TOPER, JACK, letter recommending his servant quoted, iv. 249–50.

Top-knots, i. 70.

Torcy, Jean-Baptiste Colbert, Marquis de, protector of new 'Academy for Politics', iii. 96.

Tories: at the Cocoa-Tree Chocolate House, i. 4; and Whigs, i. 5; their aversion to foreigners, i. 213; antipathy to Whigs, i. 213; balanced against Whigs, iv. 137; the Spectator not desirous of increasing the number of Whigs and, iv. 501. See also Whigs.

Tormenting: and teasing a wife, ii. 417; vanity of women in t. their admirers, ii. 553.

Torre, Devonshire, custom of riding the black ram at, v. 101.

Torture: puts human nature, rather than the criminal, to disgrace, i. 410; inflicted by a gay and indifferent wife, ii. 260–1; arguing by, ii. 430; engines of, ii. 431.

Tory: atmosphere at Child's, i. 3; fox-hunters, ii. 3; churchmen of T. sympathies, ii. 195. See also Sir ROGER DE COVERLEY.

Totus mundus agit histrionem, iii. 393.

Touch, sense of, contrasted with that of sight, ii. 536.

'Touched, a little', iv. 574.

Touching for the King's Evil, ii. 456–7.

TOUCHWOOD, Mrs.: an ode to her from the Ugly Club, i. 77; an irreproachable widow, v. 131–2.

Touchwood, Lady (in The Double Dealer), i. 77.

TOUCHY, TOM: 'famous for taking the law of every body', i. 498; dispute with WILL WIMBLE, i. 499; ii. 550.

Toujours gai, the, in French painting, i. 354.

Tour of France and Italy, iii. 367.

Tourille (or Flourilles), Chevalier de, death of, ii. 98.

Tourbillion, each star a sun with its own, iv. 170.

Tout puissant, the (Louis XIV), ii. 211.

Tower: head-dress in shape of a, i. 414; of Lebanon, ii. 127; of Babel, iii. 553–5; the Black T. in vision of heavenly and worldly wisdom, iv. 367–9.

Town, the: 'the vice of', i. 352–3; good breeding in country and, i. 486–9; a country lady hankering after diversions of, ii. 11; the great field of game for the *Spectator*, ii. 19; the present emptiness of, ii. 56; WILL H. thinks it has grown very dull, ii. 93; when the company is in, ii. 112; 'to go upon', ii. 217; 'coming upon', ii. 246; notifying others when one is in, ii. 316; now filling every day, ii. 316; conversation of, ii. 387; Sir ANDREW divides himself between country and, ii. 401; 'newly come upon', ii. 535; wickedness of, iii. 17.

Town-gentleman, ii. 433, 524.

Town-lady, ii. 69.

Town leer, a, iii. 112.

TOWNLEY, TOM, has red hair, iii. 183.

TOWNLY, FRANK, letter from (on the *Spectator*), iv. 514–15.

TOWNLY, TOM, is to marry MELISSA, iv. 183.

Town-rake, transmigration into a, iii. 276.

Toying posture, putting herself in some, iii. 55.

Toymen, iii. 166. *See also* Mather, Charles.

Toys: boys with t. and balls in the streets, iv. 307; folly of prizing t. and trifles, v. 124–5.

Toy-shop(s): excursion to a, i. 46; near Garraway's, ii. 46; buying a cat-call at a, iii. 350; ribbons, brocades, and embroidery in, iv. 271; near Temple Bar, iv. 546.

Trace: 'you may trace him', said of a husbandman, iv. 595.

Trade: Sir ANDREW's notions of, i. 10; education for, rather than learned professions, recommended, i. 91, 448–9; effects of mourning on, i. 276–7; advantages of, to England, i. 296; a beneficial occupation for younger sons, i. 448–9; manufactures, agriculture, and t. employ nineteen men out of twenty, i. 472; indirect *v.* fair methods in, ii. 167; as a means of making a fortune, iii. 4–5; iv. 306–10; right and wrong notions of, iv. 56–57; honesty in, iv. 454.

Trader: credit of, endangered by loose talk, ii. 350–1 (referred to, ii. 464); letter from a merchant to a t. in difficulties, ii. 463–4; known credit is ready cash to a, ii. 591; JACK ANVIL a bold t. both by sea and land, iii. 68; benignity necessary to the, iii. 288–90; adventures all for wealth to his country, iv. 6.

Traders: the family of the CORNELII eminent, ii. 254–5; every day literally add to value of their country, ii. 350; value of, iv. 4–7; letter from R. C. on, iv. 56–57; honesty among, iv. 453–5.

Trades: origin of, in love of pleasure or fear of want, i. 232; cant of particular, iii. 578. *See also* Handicraft(s).

Tradesman: adds to his sign that of the master whom he served, i. 117; letter from a t. about 'Change, i. 285; the insolence to owe no t. a farthing, ii. 505; a true t. looks only into books of accompts, iii. 26; anecdote of a, iii. 66; life story of a, iv. 81–86; an honest t. in Cheapside, iv. 208.

Tradesmen: contemplative, i. 45; in their last year of apprenticeship, ii. 238; breaking, ii. 252; suffer from want of punctuality in others, ii. 334–5; cries of itinerant t. in London, ii. 475; methods of enticing customers, iii. 94–95; who report on likely young gentlemen for marriage, iii. 165; signposts of, iii. 348; recommendation of, iv. 478–83.

Trading interest: importance of, iv. 4–7, 56–57; and the landed interest, ii. 185–9, 401–5.

Tragedy: 'the noblest production of human nature', i. 163; effect of, i. 163–4; modern t. compared to ancient, i. 164–5; the principal design of, i. 169; *Spectators* on t. well received, i. 245; allegorical figure of, i. 274; the moral in modern t., i. 299; the dagger or cup of poison in, ii. 397; superior art of, in *The Distressed Mother*, iii. 32–33; implex fable in, iii. 58–59; last act of a well-written t. draws together all who had a part in it, iii. 329–30; safer than comedy for women, iii. 374; 'dying for love' in modern, iii. 416; writers of, take precedence over writers of comedy, iv. 388; dispute for precedence between writers of t. and epic poetry, iv. 388. *See also* Pity and terror.

Tragedy, ancient: moral effect of, i. 164; iambic verse used in, i. 164; diversity of numbers, i. 165; nobility of sentiments, i. 165; did not make use of 'poetic justice', i. 169; iii. 58–59;

avoided bloodshed upon the stage, i. 189–90; origin of, iii. 516.

Tragedy, English: need of good acting in, i. 59; English have a genius for tragedy, i. 81; language and style of, i. 164–5; vulgarity of sentiments, i. 165; pomposity of expression, i. 166; 'poetic justice' in, i. 168–70; iii. 58–59; iv. 463–5; double plots in, i. 170–1; rants and bombast, i. 171; spectacle in, i. 177–80, 207–8; devices for inducing pity and terror in, i. 177–80, 185–91, 207–8 (thunder and lightning, bells, ghosts, &c.); bloodshed and action on the stage in, i. 187–8; improper reaction of people of quality towards, i. 409; persons of intrigue in 'tragedies of the last age', iii. 513.

Tragedy, French: actors in, seem to speak in one tone, i. 120; absence of drums, trumpets, and huzzas in, i. 179; avoidance of bloodshed on the stage, i. 188–9; is followed by a *petite pièce*, iii. 267.

Tragi-comedy: a monstrous invention, i. 170–1; breaks the tide of the passions, iii. 267; writers of, ranked between writers of tragedy and comedy, iv. 388; mentioned, iii. 352.

Train(s): shooting out into sweeping, i. 71; broad sweeping t. of robes in English tragedy, i. 178; a numerous t. of clients and dependencies, ii. 370; the world intent on t. and equipage, ii. 515.

Trained-Bands: patrolled all night long, i. 183; Colonel JUMPER of, iii. 415.

Trajan (emperor): Pliny's speech in praise of, iv. 150; his chief aim, to conquer, v. 168.

Tranquillity: in conduct of life, i. 470; in the mind, how achieved, ii. 66, 268–9; iii. 431; leaving public life for t. and retirement, ii. 373; public peace and, iii. 19.

TRANSFER, HUMPHREY, letter from (on parish clerks), iii. 401–2.

Transfiguration, the, Raphael's painting of, ii. 381.

Translation: a test of a piece of wit, i. 263; methods of, ii. 319, 427; iv. 127; of Sappho, ii. 367, 390–2; of a Greek MS., ii. 406; by Motteux, iii. 26; of Cato's soliloquy, v. 145.

Transmigration: of human souls into those of animals, ii. 325–6; iii. 524–5; Pugg's account of his, iii. 274–6.

Transport(s): not to be expected on every occasion, ii. 67, 364; of a virtuous love, the least part of its happiness, ii. 281; raised by love, ii. 478.

Transported: Erasmus t. with a passage of Socrates, ii. 334; Sappho t. with the violence of her passion, ii. 366; the Trunk-maker t. at the theatre, ii. 414; the ambitious man t. with praise, ii. 498; with admiration, iii. 81.

TRAP, WILL (RALPH), and JACK STINT, iv. 76–77.

TRAPLAND, the Widow, effect of her ogle, iii. 417.

Trapsticks, legs like, iv. 511.

TRASH, T., letter from (comment on a *Spectator*), iii. 220.

Trash: or treasure met with in reading, iv. 180; vendors of, at the Royal Exchange, iv. 307.

'Trash-eaters', iv. 17.

Travel, travelling: and acquired habits of coquetry, i. 195; like learning, makes a silly man more insufferable, i. 438; misbehaviour in, ii. 22–25, 439; letter from an imaginary traveller, ii. 38; 'accounts of savage nations', ii. 339; travelling ladies in the town, iii. 7; uses of (letter from PHILIP HOMEBRED), iii. 366–70; books of, and the pleasures of the imagination, iii. 574; advertisement of a quack lately come from, iv. 59–60; tendency to admire travellers, iv. 60; books of, more instructive than newspapers, iv. 91; affectation of contempt for, iv. 174; tedious narrators of, iv. 179; to improve one's dress, iv. 195.

TRAY (dog), v. 63.

Treacle, bought at the apothecary's shop, iii. 189, 209.

Treading upon every other board, a whimsical fancy, v. 159.

Treasurer, the Lord, iv. 504.

Treat(s), i. 288; iv. 84; at a house-warming, iv. 342.

Treatises, of thumbs, ears, and noses, ii. 469–70.

Treaty of the Grand Alliance, iii. 51.

Treaty [Latin, politicians instructed in, iii. 98.

Trebonius, example of, in Horace, iii. 248.

Trebutius, Caesar's behaviour to, iii. 408.

Tree(s): and shells in china ware, i. 153; head-dresses like t. new lopped and pruned, i. 413; Jotham's fable of the, ii. 219; WILL MAPLE's genealogical, ii. 296; cut off at the top will shoot out at the bottom, ii. 373; metaphor of laughing, applied to t. in bloom, ii.

468; in cones, globes, and pyramids, iii. 552; kinds of, symbolic of nations, iv. 104-5; preservation of, iv. 398; kinds described by Spenser, iv. 431; destruction of, iv. 594; usefulness of, v. 14-15; legends about, v. 15-17.

Treganey, Mrs., *Spectator* sold by, i. xxiv.

Treillages, contrivers of, like romance-writers, iv. 190.

Trekschuyt, or hackney boat, in Holland, ii. 17.

Trelawny, Jonathan (Bishop of Winchester), iv. 257; v. 175; a subscriber, i. *lxxxviii*.

Trenchard, John, *Natural History of Superstition*, i. 33.

Trent, river, iv. 516.

Trespass, in breaking of hedges, i. 498.

Trespassers, an equity against, ii. 73.

Tresses, golden t. in romance-writers, iii. 18.

Trial of skill, at the Bear-Garden, iv. 30-35.

Tribunes, Roman, represented the people, iii. 20.

TRICE, SARAH, letter from (on MATILDA MOHAIR), iv. 261.

Trick-track, the man of business who played t. in a coffee-house, iii. 478.

Tricks: a husband misled by t. and artifices, ii. 171; and fooleries of a Jezebel, ii. 190; practised by patrons upon their clients, ii. 337; of a fox-hunter, iii. 240.

Trifler(s): T. D.'s fondness for, i. 114; Mr. SPECTATOR deserves to be called a, iv. 76.

Trifles: pursuit after glittering, i. 69; by learned authors, i. 249; WILL WIMBLE wholly employed in, i. 448; undue exactness about t. in speech, ii. 44-46; time spent on, ii. 67; great geniuses sometimes thrown away upon, ii. 130; talking on, ii. 460; in a coquette's heart, ii. 596; incompatible with great designs, iii. 5; in woman's thoughts, iii. 53; importance of, in friendship, iii. 83; men who distinguish themselves by, iv. 570; folly of prizing toys and, v. 124-5; extemporary speculations upon, v. 138.

Trimming, the *Spectator* accused of, iv. 64.

Trimnell's Bagnio, in Castle-Yard, iii. 225.

Trinity, the, represented in *PL*, ii. 564.

Trinity College, Cambridge, letter from, iii. 17-18 (referred to, iii. 483).

Trip(s): Nicolini's variety of Italian, i. 58; to be taught the genteel, ii. 581.

TRIPLETT, JACK, anecdote of, in Lady AIRY's drawing room, iii. 296-7.

Tripodes, on golden wheels, in the *Iliad*, iii. 201.

TRIPPIT, TOM, letter from (on a Greek quotation), ii. 556 (referred to, iii. 161).

TRIPPIT, WILL, 'begins to be smoaked', i. 393.

Triptolemus, ii. 76.

TRISTISSA, letter from (is married to a tyrant), ii. 419.

Triumph(s): gilded, i. 353; satires and invectives a part of a Roman, i. 423; and applause dear to the mind of man, ii. 181; the din attending victories and public, ii. 239; and pomps balanced against vanity, iv. 136.

Triumvirate, Roman, sacrificed friends to furnish out an execution, i. 144.

Troilus, poem inscribed with epitaph of, i. 246.

TROILUS, letter from (on the *Spectator's* Greek mottoes), ii. 453-4.

Trojan fleet, changed into water-nymphs: in the *Aeneid*, iii. 145, 306; v. 15-16; in Ovid, iii. 306.

Trojan horse, building of the, i. 246.

Trojan war: depicted by Homer, iii. 305; in epitaph on Homer, iv. 476.

Trojans: their sacrifices not acceptable to the gods, ii. 312; ruined by over-confidence, iii. 481.

'Trojans' and 'Greeks' in the universities, ii. 429-30, 453-4.

TROPHONIUS, TITUS, letter from (on dreams), iv. 293-4.

Trophonius, cave of, iv. 294; would contribute to the reformation of manners, v. 44; experiences in, v. 46-48.

Tropics: both the, i. 92; jealousy rages most between the, ii. 172.

TROT, NELL, officiates at the table of the Ugly Club, i. 77-78.

TROTT, JOHN: letter from (on his out-of-the-way capers), iii. 57; is setting up 'for a minuit-dancer', iii. 112-13; a second letter from, iii. 137; his unnatural desire for dancing, iii. 149; recommended as teacher of dancing, iii. 415.

Troy, ii. 76, 318, 539, 541; iii. 249; iv. 464, 476; sacking of, an episode in the *Aeneid*, ii. 540; iii. 203; destruction of, in a puppet-show, iii. 401.

True Royal Snuff, advertised, iii. 278.

TRUEBY, Widow: 'Widow Trueby's Water the best thing in the world against the stone or gravel', iii. 212.

TRUELOVE, Mr. and Mrs., i. 244.

TRUELOVE, TOM, has written a sonnet on his mistress, v. 116.

TRUEPENNY, JACK, his good nature leads him into debt, i. 352–3.

Trull, the beggar has his, i. 28.

Trumpery, a beau's head filled with, ii. 571.

Trumpet, a French word imported (?), ii. 151–3.

Trunk-breeches, ii. 7.

Trunk-maker in the Upper Gallery, ii. 413–16 (referred to, ii. 434, 505).

Truss of salad, iii. 532.

Trust: in God, ii. 233; iv. 49–51; qualifications for positions of, iv. 159–61.

TRUSTY, GEORGE, letter from (praising the *Spectator*), ii. 29–30.

TRUSTY, THOMAS: letter from (life story of a servant), i. 405–9; 'slain' by a widow's ogle, iii. 417.

TRUSTY, TOM, undisturbed by noise of his children, iv. 198.

Truth: founder of the family of Humour, i. 146; the basis of wit, i. 268; iv. 362; allegorical figure of, i. 273; reason, t., and nature, the measures of praise and dispraise, i. 278; Persian boys instructed to speak, i. 418; and good sense in Cicero, ii. 75; in painting, ii. 179, 447; the object of argument, ii. 275; our minds chequered with t. and falsehood, ii. 421; the tongue to be tuned by, ii. 462; dashed with fiction in Homer and Virgil, ii. 543; and virtue the standard of delicacy, iii. 15; French t. a conspicuous figure in *nothing*, iii. 100; advantages of, over dissimulation, iii. 314–16; following the dictates of t. and right reason, iii. 479; contrasted with error, iv. 122; captivates with unborrowed charms, iv. 140; is God's body, and light His shadow, iv. 298; and falsehood, iv. 298–301; in Spenser, iv. 431; nothing so delightful as hearing or speaking of, iv. 502; is never the less so, for not being attended to, iv. 570.

Truths, necessity of holding to certain ascertained, iv. 142–3.

Tryphiodorus, a great lipogrammatist, i. 249, 272.

Tub to a whale (prov.), ii. 519.

Tube(s): the body a system of t. and glands, i. 471–2; pipes and t. in the brain, ii. 573; like a weather-glass, ii. 595.

Tuberoses and honeysuckles, iii. 595.

Tucca, Plotius: Virgil praised by, ii. 482.

Tucker: adjusting her, i. 160, 466; iii.

417; a man who could write eloquently upon a, v. 138.

Tudman, Benjamin (contractor to the Army), a subscriber, i. *xc*, *xci*.

TUESDAY, MARY, her letter to an impertinent acquaintance, i. 103–4.

TULIP, TOM, suitor to FLAVIA, i. 385–6.

Tulip(s): *Tulip-mania*, i. 447; women in coloured hoods, like a bed of, ii. 532 (referred to, ii. 577); women at the play, like beds of, ii. 552; a jonquil or, iii. 512; spending time in cultivation of a single, iv. 105; and carnations, v. 14.

Tumbler(s): from Holland, i. 119; on the stage, ii. 56, 504; Mohocks who set women upon their heads, iii. 187, 223, 295.

Tumbling: on the stage, iii. 237; over wares in China shops, iii. 245; 'some *tumble* into fame', iv. 544.

Tumult(s): the magistrate keeps peace in a, ii. 120; ambition raises a secret t. in the soul, ii. 497; Jews always involved in rebellions and, iv. 257.

Tunbridge, i. *102*, 231; ii. 104; letters from, iv. 244–7, 261.

Tunbridge Miscellany, iv. *233, 247, 261.*

Tuningius, G., iv. *542.*

Turban, a 'humourist' who wore a t. instead of a periwig, iv. 571.

Turin: Prince Eugene forced the trenches at, iii. 263.

Turk, the Great, iii. 154; v. 42.

Turk(s): at the masquerade, i. 63; wore pieces of Scanderbeg's bones, iii. 149.

Turkey, Turkish Empire: fleet of, i. 131; Greeks the only musicians in, i. 131; position of women in, i. *224*; trade with, ii. 188; a slave in, ii. 195; massacre of Jews in, iv. 256.

Turkish bassas, in the masquerade, i. 96.

Turkish crescent, arms of the Emperor of the Mohocks, iii. 187.

Turkish divines, v. 7.

Turkish Majesty, His (in *Ibrahim*), i. 218.

Turkish slavery, Greeks under, iii. 22.

Turkish Spy, Letters writ by a, i. *312, 366*; ii. *250, 430*; iii. *424*: iv. *421*; v. 7.

Turkish Tales: story of Mahomet's journey, i. *400*; story of the Sultan of Egypt, i. *400*; story of the Sultan's vizier and the two owls, iv. 318–19.

Turn(s) (quality, disposition), ii. 204, 236, 246, 425; affected by a man's business, ii. 271; of eyes, ii. 470, 471; of features, ii. 596.

Turn(s) or point(s) in style: as a kind of wit, i. 270; in a passage of Ecclesiasti-

cus, i. 290; epigrammatical, i. 316; in Cowley and Ovid, ii. 52–53; in the *bel esprit*, ii. 127; repartee, ii. 191; a finer t. to the thought, ii. 359; in modern lyrics, ii. 366; in Sappho, ii. 367; of expression in Greek, ii. 391; wit consists in giving things that are known an agreeable, ii. 483; epigrammatic t. of Lucan, ii. 588; methods of giving language a poetical, iii. 12; an agreeable t. of poetry in *PL*, iii. 87; little t. of wit in vogue among poets, iii. 90; wit and t. out of place in love poetry, iii. 375–6; taste in England for, iii. 530; in Anacreon, iv. 473–4; of wit and humour, v. 45.

Turns and windings in the hunt, ii. 171.

Turner, —— (singer), in *Camilla*, i. 79, 95.

Turner, Francis (Bishop of Ely), v. 175.

Turner, Sir William, his maxim, iv. 308.

Turnips, cries of sellers of, ii. 476.

TURNOVER, TOM, reply to letter from, iv. 588.

Turnus (in the *Aeneid*), i. 318; his death, i. 302–3; iii. 61; and the phantom of Aeneas, ii. 304; nothing new or particular in his character, ii. 563; dressed himself in spoils of Pallas, iii. 61; combat with Aeneas, iii. 174, 231; iv. 134; as a subject for schoolboys' essays, iii. 248; possessed courage but not piety, iii. 304.

Turnus (in *Camilla*), i. 80.

Turtle(s) [turtle-dove]: cages of, i. 158; in Horace, i. 363; singing of, iv. 452.

Tuscany, Leonardo da Vinci descended from a noble family in, iv. 488.

Tutchin, John, *Observator*, i. 7, 8, 35; iv. 520; v. 101.

Tutor, travelling, 'for thirty pounds a year and a little victuals', iii. 368.

Twanking of a brass kettle or a frying-pan, ii. 475.

Twang on the shoulders, iv. 288.

Tweed, the river (in *Chevy-Chase*), i. 317.

TWEER, TOM, letter from (on physiognomy), iv. 344–5.

Twelfth Night, a yawning-match at, ii. 208.

Twelve Tables, of Roman law, iv. 88.

TWIFORD, SAL, and her children, in WILL MAPLE'S genealogy, ii. 296.

Twilight visits, by ministers of state, iv. 112.

Twine, over a barber's window, forecasting weather, iv. 60.

Twist, a dish of, iii. 154.

Two and two make four, Believe (prov.), ii. 1; we seem to have two souls, iv. 526.

Two Children in the Wood, The: critique of, i. 362–4; the tune of, ii. 207.

Two Golden Balls, boarding-school at, near Stepney, iii. 140, 226, 254.

Two-penny Club, rules of, i. 43.

Tyers, Thomas, i. xxvi.

TYLER, TOM, in the Coronation celebrations, v. 106, 108.

'Tympany, this fashionable' (the hoop-petticoat), ii. 7.

Typographical shapes, poems in, i. 246–7; iii. 560; iv. 288.

Tyranny: allegorical figure of, i. 16; of the old, iii. 243–5; not encouraged by Christianity, iii. 442; William III the check and bridle of, iv. 337.

Tyrant(s): husbands who grow t. that they may seem masters, ii. 418; Mrs. JANE a t. to her lovers, ii. 559; dangerous to a nation, iii. 20–21; a superannuated coquette who plays the, iii. 75–76; in taverns and clubs, iv. 302–4.

Tyrrhene seas, ii. 540; iv. 235.

Tyson, Dr., his Apoplectic Snuff advertised, iii. 279; iv. 61.

Ubiquity, or omnipresence, of God, iv. 582.

Uffenbach, Zacharias Conrad von, description of London quoted, i. 56; ii. 163, 473; iii. 214, 215, 436; iv. 30.

Ugliness and deformity, i. 74–78, 369–70; and aesthetic pleasure, iii. 540.

Ugly Club: its rules, i. 76–78; Mr. SPECTATOR admitted to, i. 133, 205; HECATISSA's application to, i. 205–6, 221–3; originated at Cambridge, i. 335; ROSALINDA's application to, i. 370; referred to, iv. 486.

Ulcers, accompanying the pox, iv. 59.

Ulysses: received bags of wind from Aeolus, i. 17; a poem on, by Tryphiodorus, i. 250; mentioned, ii. 76; iv. 476; his part in the *Odyssey* admired by Aristotle, ii. 564; compared to Satan in *PL*, ii. 564; story of, an example of implex fable, iii. 58; his ship turned into a rock, iii. 145; tradition of, in time of Homer, iii. 305; faithful to Penelope, v. 73–74; a perfect pattern of a prudent man, v. 75.

Unbelief, source of vicious men's, ii. 323.

Unbeliever, a virtuous, under pressure of misfortunes, iii. 43.

Uncharitableness of judging misfortunes of others, iv. 211–14.

Uncle, impertinent behaviour towards an, iii. 506.

Under-citizen of the Bath, ii. 207.

Underhand, ii. 242; detractors of the

Spectator, ii. 519; practices, iv. 469; so much money yearly allowed her, v. 127.

Underhill, [Cave?], as Sampson in *The Fatal Marriage*, iv. 205.

Underpart(s): the husband 'acted but an', i. 32; of his behaviour, i. 324.

Under-petticoat(s): of the PERVERSE WIDOW, iii. 54; quilting an, v. 71.

Under-plot, i. 171; ii. 171.

Understanding: abuse of, i. 28; books which enlighten the, to be preferred, i. 158; conversation with a friend clears and improves the, i. 397; kept clear by physical exercise, i. 471; weak, in witches, i. 480; a man of good u. never a favourite with the ladies, ii. 111; inconstancy of human, ii. 136; goodness of, destroyed by vain dress or discourse, ii. 179; debate over superiority of u. in husband and wife, ii. 195; gold a wonderful clearer of the, ii. 431; the passions awaken the, ii. 490; men resent offences against their virtue less than those against their, ii. 554; good humour which proceeds from the, iii. 80; pleasures of the, iii. 537–9; a good u. necessary to happiness in marriage, iv. 358; and the will: two faculties in the soul, v. 50.

Undertaker, Mr. SPECTATOR sometimes taken for an, iii. 27.

Uneasiness: the 'pretty u.' of the PERVERSE WIDOW, i. 464; a great part of ceremony in women turns upon their, ii. 67; the result of jealousy, ii. 168–9, 175, 340; of a husband, ii. 261; and disquiet arising from ambition, ii. 351; in the married state, ii. 417; at hearing others praised, ii. 426; the luxurious man gains only u. from his enjoyments, ii. 599; an enemy to benevolence, v. 57.

Unfortunate, the, Cardinal Richelieu's view of, iii. 42.

Unguents, phials of, i. 176.

Unities: of time and place, ii. 554; iii. 341; iv. 268; violation of each of the, iii. 352–3; of time, place, and action, iii. 530.

Universal genius, Leonardo da Vinci an example of an, iv. 488.

Universal Spectator, ii. 238.

Universe: the: a kind of theatre filled with pleasant objects, iii. 453; pleasure in contemplating the infinite, iii. 575; variety and harmony of, iv. 442; v. 170–2; infinity of, iv. 529–33.

Universities: syllogisms used in, ii. 429; 'Greeks and Trojans' in, ii. 429–30; might fill rhetoric chairs with she-professors, ii. 458; eloquent speakers of both, ii. 480; should teach men not to be over-modest, iv. 218; public disputes in, iv. 500; Mr. SPECTATOR's respect for both, iv. 587.

Unlearned, *Account of the Works of the*, proposed, iv. 114.

Unlucky, i. 148; ii. 170; stumble in an u. gutter, ii. 191; this u. wag, ii. 207.

Unsight, unseen (prov.), iv. 315.

'Upholsterer, the': the Four Indian Kings lodge with, i. 212; has written to the *Spectator*, v. 116.

Upper end: of the table, i. 206; of the world, iii. 33.

Upper gallery: audience in a playhouse, i. 269; the Trunk-maker in the, ii. 413–16.

URANIUS, his equanimity of temper, ii. 66.

Urfé, Honoré d', *L'Astrée* in LEONORA's library, i. 154.

Uriel in *PL*: always in character, ii. 565; his gliding to earth on a sunbeam a prettiness unworthy of Milton, iii. 174.

Urwin, Will, owner of Will's coffeehouse, i. 3.

Useful: being u. to mankind, the chief end of being, ii. 432.

Usurer: looks to next quarter-day, i. 395; DIAGORAS, the, ii. 408; craft of an, represented on the stage, iii. 394; wife of a rich, iv. 271; Horace's picture of one, iv. 466.

Usury, has its seed in dread of want, i. 469.

Utensils, domestic, in brass and iron, v. 2.

Utrecht: Treaty of, ii. 273; controversy between footmen at, iv. 206; mentioned, iii. 440.

UXANDER and VIRAMIRA, an overfond married couple, iv. 238.

Vacant: methods of filling v. hours of life, i. 394–9; a creature v. of thought, ii. 386.

Vacation, the late long, ii. 389.

VAGELLIUS, a physician without clients who might have been a successful merchant, i. 91.

Vaillant, Paul (bookseller), iv. 41.

Vain: dress or discourse of a man, ii. 179; vainest persons most addicted to laughter, ii. 466; person insufferable, iv. 7.

Vainglorious soldier, in ancient comedy, iv. 68.

VAINLOVE, THO., slain by a woman's glance, iii. 417.

VAINLOVES, the, family of, iv. 100.
Vale of Misery, in the Vision of Mirzah, ii. 123.
Valens, Emperor, law of, concerning libels, iv. 89.
Valentia, Viscount. See Anglesey.
Valentine family, experiments of the, iii. 597–600.
Valentinian, Emperor, law of, concerning libels, iv. 89.
Valentinus, Basilius, i. 398.
VALERIO, affects character of a poet, iii. 511.
Valerius Flaccus, Gaius, wrote of Jason and the Golden Fleece rather than of heroes of his own country, i. 300.
Valerius Maximus, iv. 506.
VALET, RALPH, letter from (complaining of his master), ii. 41–42.
Valet de chambre: of Pluto, i. 123; kept by ladies, i. 192; Sir ROGER's, i. 439.
Valetudinarian(s): i. 15, 105–8 (this letter praised, iv. 438); in society, i. 420; ii. 64–66; in chastity, iii. 481; JOHN RHUBARB, iv. 9–10; Lord FRIDAY, iv. 559; waked by a carman, v. 42.
Valetudinary friendship, subject to heats and colds, iii. 74.
Valiant, the: and wise in all ages have been henpecked, ii. 196; will bear being reproached as rash, iii. 583.
Vallade, J. F., i. 494.
Vallée, Jacques. See Des Barreaux.
Valour: and dancing compared, i. 284; and wisdom essential to manhood, ii. 70; without additional graces would degenerate into brutality, iii. 40.
Value(s): setting a right v. upon men, ii. 178–81; differ among great and low persons, iv. 205.
VAN BRISKET, Madame, a plump Dutch beauty, i. 135.
Vanbrugh, Sir John, a subscriber, i. lxxxix; and the Haymarket Theatre, i. 4; member of Kit-Cat Club, i. 42; architect of Blenheim Palace, i. 251; referred to (?), iv. 66. — Aesop, i. 77, 346; — The Pilgrim, i. 94; — The Recruiting Officer, iv. 155.
Van Effen, Justus, Le Misantrope, iii. 157.
VAN NATH, reply to, who has sent in a letter, iv. 587.
Vandal bishop, introduces an antic dress into Roman Catholic service, ii. 290.
Vandals: and Goths, from the Northern Hive, i. 90; the Spectator not to engage with Goths and, iii. 382.

Vanini, Lucilio, incident at his trial for atheism, iii. 462.
Vanity: the source of extravagancies in dress, i. 70; in women produces 'Idols', i. 312; allegorical representation of, in vision of painters, i. 354; arises from shame of poverty, i. 469; in loud speakers, ii. 83; of an author, ii. 156; the guide of infidels, ii. 232–3; of the courtier, ii. 257; stirred up by the flatterer, ii. 424–5; the natural weakness of the ambitious man, ii. 493; of women in tormenting their admirers, ii. 553; of a beau, ii. 571; to excel, as a motive for pleasing others, ii. 591; Limbo of, in PL, iii. 60, 144; a motive to fortune-hunting, iii. 126; of SYLVANA, iii. 270; of men's wishes, iii. 470; of the creature, a favourite topic, iii. 474; allegorical figure of, iv. 122, 327; titles, honours, pomps and triumphs balanced against, iv. 136; conversation now swelled with, iv. 503; and egotism, iv. 519–22; 'the speck' in WILL WORTHY's heart, v. 8; of this life an argument for immortality, v. 142.
Vapours: 'troubled with', i. 15, 34; iv. 25; advertisement for cure of, i. 226; caused by neglect of exercise, i. 471–2; 'this fashionable reigning distemper', ii. 342; nursing a child, a cure for, ii. 457; 'are terrible things', iii. 245–6; afflict 'women's men', iv. 413; caused by jealousy, iv. 458.
Variable temper, persons of, i. 291–2, 326; ii. 135–9, 319.
Variant readings, in classical authors, iv. 161–5.
Variety: pleasure of greatest v. and simplicity in PL, ii. 540–1; multitude and v. of characters in Homer, ii. 562; of characters in PL, ii. 563; iii. 329; of numbers in PL, iii. 15; of accidents in an implex fable, iii. 58; in epic poetry obtained by similes, iii. 91, 234; of scenes in nature, pleasing to the imagination, iii. 453; refreshing to the mind, iii. 541; v. 52; justness and v. of Spenser's epithets, iv. 431. See also Novelty.
VARILAS, a good-natured man, i. 421.
Various, as a rainbow, i. 276; as the weather, ii. 262.
Varius Rufus, Lucius: Virgil praised by, ii. 482.
Varro, Marcus Terentius, satires of, iii. 468.
Vasari, Giorgio, iv. 488.
Vatican manuscript: a variant reading in

a, iv. 164; of the New Testament, with a fragment of Longinus, v. 165.

Vaulted roofs, effect of, in architecture, iii. 557.

Vaulters on the stage, ii. 504.

Veal, dined on a knuckle of, and bacon, iii. 154.

Venerable: worship, or v. behaviour, the title given to magistrates, ii. 352.

Venereal pleasure, ii. 320.

Venereal maladies, medicine for, advertised, iv. 59.

Venetian, Lewis Cornaro, the, ii. 266.

Venetian ambassador, the late, ii. 267.

Venetian scaramouche, in the Vision of Painters, i. 354.

Venice: the carnival at, i. 96; 'I have commanded the brothels at', ii. 38; fine printing at, iii. 381; letter from, iv. 55–56.

Venienti occurrite morbo, i. 96.

Venison, a haunch of: the best sauce for, iv. 210; dispute over method of cooking, iv. 303.

Venison pasty, iii. 196.

Venison season, i. 335.

Venus: and Adonis painted on a coach, i. 66; a Grecian Venus, i. 140; and Cupids on a fan, i. 227; and Adonis in modern prints, ii. 60; paintings of, ii. 378–9; the dart of, ii. 427; Sappho's hymn to, ii. 367–9, 390; singing a hymn to, ii. 384; represented as delighting in laughter, ii. 468; and Mars in Homer, an example of burlesque, ii. 589; always kind to Mars, iii. 65; girdle given by, to Juno, iii. 311; dressed by the Graces, iii. 337; portrayal of in the first *Aeneid*, iii. 564; and Mars attending the Spring, iii. 594; as Vanity, iv. 122; recognized by her walk, iv. 145–6; Venuses, Graces, Cupids, iv. 196; and Adonis, a painting, iv. 298; in modern poems, iv. 362; 'Beauty's queen', iv. 399; aided in healing of Aeneas, iv. 555; and Vulcan's dogs, iv. 581.

Veny (CLARINDA's dog): combed and washed, iii. 182; borrowed Lady FADDLE's Cupid for, iii. 183; turned off a footman for being rude to, iii. 184.

Verba valent ut nummi, i. 431.

Verbum ardens, can be turned into ridicule, iii. 37.

Verdon, David, i. lxxiii.

Verge: within the v. of the court, i. 425, 437; the v. of nature, ii. 542.

Verjuice, ii. 184.

Vermilion, Nature has touched the face with, i. 415.

Vernacular idiom, our, ii. 150–1.

'Vernal delight', described by Milton, iii. 474 (referred to, iv. 192).

Versailles: 'I have drank champagne at', ii. 159; the French Court at Marly or, iii. 98; iv. 92.

Verses: diversion of making, iv. 287; capping, iv. 287; making golden, iv. 287.

Vertot d'Auboeuf, René-Aubert de, *History of the Revolutions in Portugal*, iii. 301–2.

Vertumnus, a companion of Spring, iii. 594.

Vertuous Wife, The (puppet-show), i. 61.

Vesper and Aurora, attendants of Summer, iii. 595.

Vesta, an attendant of Winter, iii. 596.

Vestal, a: 'in her face but a Messalina in her heart', ii. 70; the severity of, v. 46.

Vestments: ridiculous use of, in Roman Catholic Church, ii. 290.

Vestry, parish, an advertisement from the, ii. 561.

Vetch, Cicero's use of, as rebus, i. 250.

Vetulam suam praetulit immortalitati, v. 75.

Veyssière de Lacroze, Mathurin, iii. 462.

Viande, 'that superstitious *viande*' (a Christmas pie), i. 361.

Vicar: conversation with v. and v.'s wife, ii. 486–8; a boy who puzzled the v. before an assembly of ladies, iii. 367.

Vice: not the individual, but the vice, to be attacked, i. 72 (one exception to this, i. 148); ought to be attacked, wherever met with, i. 143; to be scorned and also pitied, i. 341; 'the v. of the town', i. 352–3; uneasiness follows commission of, i. 457; troubled seasons and angry skies the portion of, ii. 76; plain and simple v. too little for the man of wit and pleasure, ii. 93; and virtue, only disease and health (?), ii. 118; good nature takes off from deformity of, ii. 165; the parent of Misery, ii. 222; means of recovering our souls out of, ii. 341; triumphant in this world, ii. 352; modesty a check to, ii. 400; should be abhorred, though in a friend, ii. 446; that v. which is said to comprehend all others, ii. 449; ridicule to be used to laugh men out of, ii. 467; sexual v. to be pitied rather than condemned, ii. 534; 'pampered v. in the habitations of the wealthy', ii. 537; iii. 16; protests against discussion of, in *Spectator*, ii. 574–5, 577; confounding virtue and, iii. 16; labyrinths of v. and folly, iii.

82; covered by wealth, iv. 138; has learned to mimic virtue, iv. 326; and worldly wisdom, iv. 365–9; attended with greater labour and pains than virtue, v. 134.

Vices: types which are the proper field of the *Spectator*, i. 144; associated with ages of man's life, ii. 271; instructive to compare our v. with those of our forefathers, ii. 317–18; subservience to those of the great, ii. 337; connivance at those of rakes, iii. 64; the incurable v. are those men glory in, iv. 541.

Vicious: writers remain in Purgatory as long as the influence of their writings continues (?), ii. 155; no person so v. who has not some good in him, ii. 223, 517; the v. character to be set up as a scarecrow, ii. 302; parts of each sex satirized, ii. 319, 324–5; desire of fame breeds several v. habits in the mind, ii. 499; persons often prosperous in this life, but will be requited in another, iv. 213; Horace says all men are, iv. 462–3; the v. divided into the covetous, the ambitious, and the sensual, v. 132.

Vicissitude(s): of labour and rest in the lower part of mankind, ii. 269; of day and night, pleasing to the imagination, iii. 453; 'the sweet v. of night and day', iii. 594.

Vickers, William (quack), advertises cures for the 'King's Evil', ii. *457*; iv. *61.*

VICTOR, the genteelest man in the company, ii. 91.

Victor Amadeus of Savoy, v. 183.

Victory (-ies): of Pyrrhus over the Romans, ii. 211; the din attending v. and public triumphs, ii. 239; the man who brought false news of, to the Athenians, ii. 410; as an allegorical figure in Homer and Milton, iii. 337, 338.

Victualling-house, i. 374.

Victualler, the trade of the, ii. 402.

Vienna, i. 277; handicraft-work of Emperor Leopold to be seen at, iii. 319.

'View, In', a hunting cry, i. 477.

Villacerfe, Madame de, account of the death of, iii. 383–5.

Villain, knave, &c.' in modern pamphlets, iv. 537.

Villars, Abbé de Montfaucon de, *Comte de Gabalis*, iii. *425.*

Villars, Louis-Hector, Duc de (Marshal of France): on the battle of Ramillies, iii. *102*; defeated Eugene at Denain, iv.

187; in modern poems, iv. 363; recaptured Bouchain, iv. *407.*

Villeroi, François de Neufville, Duc de, defeated by Eugene, iii. *263.*

Villiers, George. *See* Buckingham.

Vincent, Thomas, advertises soap, iv. *230.*

Vinegar, oil and, i. 374; ii. 264.

Viner, Sir Robert, iv. *99*; anecdote of, and Charles II, iv. 132–3.

Vintner(s): the apothecary employed in countermining the cook and, ii. 264; and funeral-men, iii. 166; who mix adulterated wines, iii. 354–5.

Viol, the bass, i. 450.

Violets, ii. 506; iii. 569, 594; iv. 189; v. 63, 126.

Violin: a certain jigging noise on the, ii. 576; accompanying an Italian recitativo, iii. 352.

Virago: CAMILLA the v. of one party, i. 242.

VIRAMIRA and UXANDER, an over-fond married couple, iv. 238.

Virgil (Publius Vergilius Maro): one verse in, worth all the *clincant* or tinsel of Tasso, i. 26; Ogilby's translation in LEONORA's library, i. 154; has no mixed wit, i. 265; Segrais contrasts Martial and V., i. 269; Homer, V., or Milton will please the plain reader, who would not understand Martial or Cowley, i. 297; comments on the ballad supported by the practice and authority of, i. 321–2; the incidents in *The Children in the Wood* 'are such as V. himself would have touched upon, had the like story been told by that divine poet', i. *362*; Homer has innumerable flights that V. was not able to reach, ii. 127; a 'learned genius', ii. 129; proposal to teach children so that 'the most dangerous page in V. or Homer may be read by them', ii. 395; friendship of V. and Horace, ii. 482; celebrated by Gallus and others, while Bavius and Maevius were his declared foes and calumniators, ii. 482; innumerable verses in, which illustrate suiting of sound to sense, ii. 485; has excelled all others in propriety of his sentiments, but falls short of Homer in the sublime, ii. 589; mean phrases in, no longer shocking, iii. 11; many Hellenisms in, iii. 11–12; no ostentatious display of learning in, iii. 62; his genius inclined him to poetry, iii. 512; 'that divine author', iii. 529; strikes the imagination with what is beautiful, iii. 564; always leaves the

mind composed and softened into an agreeable melancholy, iv. 324–5; an admirer of Musaeus, iv. 329; would never have been heard of, had not his domestic misfortunes driven him out of his obscurity and brought him to Rome, v. 85; mentioned, ii. 79, 115, 154 (*bis*); iii. *538*; iv. 71, 171, 306, 329, 352, 399, 468, 520; v. *109.* — *Eclogues*: Pope's *Messiah*, 'written in imitation of Virgil's Pollio' (Eclogue IV), iii. 419; quoted, ii. 243, 384; iii. 374; — *Georgics*: delightful landskips in, iii. 565; 'those beautiful raptures in', iv. 325; has written a whole book on the art of planting (Book II), iv. 595; Book II quoted, ii. 296; iii. 549; Book III quoted, i. 317; ii. 150; Book IV quoted, i. 255; — *Aeneid*: Camilla an example of female passion for dress and show, i. 69; like Virgil's army: many had not room to use their weapons, i. 89; as Salmoneus, i. 151; v. 26; tragi-comedy as silly as weaving adventures of Aeneas and Hudibras together, i. 170; Camilla and Penthesilea, i. 242; the axe of Epeus, i. 246; half the *Aeneid* turned into Latin rhymes by a monkish writer, i. 254; Dryden's comparison of V. and Ovid in their depiction of Dido, i. 268–9; founded on an important precept of morality, i. 299; his hero the founder of Rome, i. 300; deaths of Camilla and Turnus, i. 302–3; Aeneas's behaviour towards Lausus, i. 303; describes punishment of a voluptuary after death, i. 382; the Sibyl, ii. 129; the Phantom in the [Tenth] Book ran away from Turnus, ii. 304; 'with Dido, in Dryden's Virgil', ii. 384; character of Drances, ii. 399; the Trunk-maker like V.'s ruler of the winds, ii. 415; in passion the eye flashes as with fire, as V. finely describes it, ii. 472; in a rainbow hood, like the Iris in Dryden's Virgil, ii. 532; plunges *in medias res*, ii. 540; some think it lacks unity, ii. 540; describes Carthage and the settlement of Italy, ii. 541; the games, and the simile of the top, ii. 542; an extensive action, diversified by episodes, ii. 542–3; modern critics have estimated the space of time taken by the action, ii. 543–4; iii. 391; his characters inferior to Homer's, in variety and novelty, ii. 562–5; Aristotle's rules would have been more perfect could he have perused the *Aeneid*, ii. 566; Dryden sometimes misrepresents

his way of thinking, ii. 588; criticism of a passage in Book [VII], ii. *588*; but one laugh in the whole poem, ii. 589; why his hero is always directed by a deity, iii. 43; comparison with *PL*, iii. 59–61; the longest digression is in Book X, iii. 61; the catalogue of warriors, iii. 87; use of similes, iii. 90; makes the heroes of the Roman Commonwealth appear in their state of pre-existence, iii. 118; Milton's survey of the creation superior to Virgil's, iii. 142; machinery in (the fleet turned into a shoal of water nymphs, and the myrtle dropping blood), iii. 145; description of Fame, iii. 173, 573; Jupiter weighing the fates of Turnus and Aeneas, iii. 174; iv. 134; beginning of the action, iii. 203; copies Homer's description of piling Pelion upon Ossa, iii. 230; sword of Aeneas broke into pieces that of Turnus, iii. 231; actions of Turnus or Aeneas to be considered by schoolboys, iii. 248; a thousand shining passages which have been lighted up by Homer, iii. 255; Aeneas and the Sibyl before the adamantine gates, iii. 282; Turnus and Aeneas contrasted (from Le Bossu), iii. 304; use of historical fact in, iii. 305; incident of 'eating the tables', iii. 306; changing of the Trojan fleet into water-nymphs, iii. 306; when Dido yielded to temptation, the earth trembled, iii. 311; has been praised for conducting the reader through all the parts of the earth, iii. 332; use of allegorical figures, iii. 337; Aeneas is given a view of his descendants: Milton probably took a hint from this, iii. 361–2, 387; Achates a colourless character, iii. 446; a mathematician who read V. only for the pleasure of tracing Aeneas's voyage by the map, iii. 529; the *Aeneid* like a well-ordered garden, iii. 564; charming picture of Venus, iii. 564–5; makes his hero beautiful, iii. 565; filled with pleasing scenes, iii. 565; use of personification, iii. 573; Aeneas recognizes Venus when she moves, iv. 145; one deity raises a storm and another lays it, iv. 234; compliments his hero by interweaving actions of deities with his achievements, iv. 363; 'with more than mortal charms Aeneas glow'd', iv. 399; poetical justice little observed in, iv. 464; character of Iapis, iv. 551; the machine (turning the fleet into water-nymphs) so much blamed by critics,

v. 15; the great elm tree, a fine metaphorical image of sleep, v. 31; Aeneas's view of his descendants, v. 91; several epic poets, including Milton, have religiously followed V. in the number of his books, v. 159; Book I quoted, ii. 365, 415, 563; iii. 565; Book II quoted, i. 320, 508; iv. 338; Book IV quoted, iii. 579; iv. 228; Book VI quoted, i. 109, 382; iii. 387; Book VII quoted, i. 318; ii. 588; iii. 306; Book VIII quoted, iii. 568; Book IX quoted, i. 318; v. 16 (in Dryden's translation); Book X quoted, i. 303; iii. 61 (in a prose translation); Book XI quoted, i. 69, 302 (in Dryden's translation), 318; ii. 399; Book XII quoted, i. 303, 319, 321; ii. 472; iv. 555–6 (in Dryden's translation).

Virgin: SIMON HONEYCOMB rallied upon being a, ii. 103; tucked up her vestments like a Spartan, ii. 408; letter from a, iii. 64; description of a virginfop, iii. 166.

Virginia (tobacco), ii. 30; iii. 153, 213.

Virtue: decay of public and private, i. 29; the sense of, the mark of a gentleman, i. 324; acts of piety are compliments made to, i. 341; merits double praise when lodged in a seemingly vicious body, i. 367; exercise of, recommended, i. 395; and decency nearly related, i. 433; iii. 40; 'skill of the purse' the cardinal v. of this life, i. 444; satisfaction in practice of, i. 457; and wisdom more important than politics, i. 507; of a nation sunk by party spirit, i. 510; ii. 4; glory the shadow of, ii. 49; extinguished in boys by flogging, ii. 115; Seneca on a natural propensity to, ii. 116; and vice only health and disease (?), ii. 118; good nature shows v. in the fairest light, ii. 165; good nature as a moral, ii. 197–201; the parent of happiness, ii. 222; necessary to acceptable prayers, ii. 311–12; and service the foundation of a high name, ii. 349; the source of honour, ii. 352; iii. 15–16; oppressed in this world, ii. 352; without discretion looks like weakness, ii. 376; modesty a guard to, ii. 399; shamefaced persons who avoid all outward show of, ii. 400–1; heroic v. in common life, ii. 433; beauty and loveliness of, ii. 443–6; Stoic conception of, ii. 444; self-denial the foundation of civil, ii. 462; and good sense make an agreeable friend, ii. 515; women urged to excel in v. and good sense, ii. 533;

required for happiness in marriage, ii. 545; v. 75; men resent offences against v. less than those against their understanding, ii. 554; a man of perfect v. possible in epic, but not in tragedy, ii. 565–6; truth and v. the standard of delicacy, iii. 15; confounding v. and vice, iii. 16; additional graces required in practice of every, iii. 38; Brutus's apostrophe to, iii. 43–44; and beauty, iii. 79; methods of cultivating, in schools, iii. 246–50; in distress, iii. 252, 412; iv. 420; the foundation of modest assurance, iii. 405–6; live according to dictates of v. and right reason, iii. 432; may be dissolved by wine, iii. 479; no charm in women can supply the place of, iii. 482; guarded by true, betrayed by false modesty, iv. 115; covered by poverty, iv. 138; to regulate, not extirpate, the affections of the mind, iv. 254; the reasonableness of, iv. 365; grows by communication, v. 57; attended with fewer labours and pains than is vice, v. 133–4.

Virtues: man not to glory in his own, but in the absence of another's imperfections, i. 311; the social v. recommended, i. 395; ii. 445; instructive to compare our v. with those of our forefathers, ii. 317–18; heathen v. so many shining sins, ii. 331; latent v. brought out by education, ii. 338–9; many incapable of outward representation, ii. 500; domestic v. concern all the world, iii. 32; represented by artists under female shapes, iii. 482; attending Hymen, iv. 326; books written to show the falsity of all human, iv. 416; Spenser's representation of six, iv. 428.

Virtues of Camphire, recommended, i. 391.

Virtuoso(s), i. 329; ii. 356–7, 446, 570; iii. 350–1; activities of, i. 91; young (lawyers), i. 209; two female, ii. 442; treatise found in a poetical v.'s closet, ii. 469; among my foreign correspondents, iii. 96.

Virtuous, the: rigour of, towards prostitutes, ii. 245, 534; the wise man loves only, ii. 444; without a competent knowledge of the world, ii. 450; all parts of life equally pleasant to, ii. 512; 'the outragiously v.', ii. 534; a plea for the strictly v., iii. 65; 'the rigidly v.', iii. 122, 466.

Virtuous: man struggling with misfortunes (Seneca), i. 163–4; ii. 422; iii. 409; the rewards of a v. life, in old age,

ii. 101-3; no person so v. who has not some evil in him, ii. 223; 'a v. mind in a fair body', ii. 445; a private education best for forming a v. man, iii. 133; a conventional epithet applied to women, iii. 466; difficulties in following a v. life will become easier, iv. 70-72; v. persons often unfortunate in this life, but will be rewarded in another, iv. 213; allegorical figure of v. love, iv. 326.

Viscount, 'his miss the frolick v. dreads to toast', iv. 398.

Visé, Jean Donneau de (founder of the *Mercure Galant*), i. xxxvii.

Vision(s): a species of wit giving delight and surprise, i. 265; of 'Erus the Armenian' in Plato, ii. 326; of Adam at the end of *PL*, iii. 59, 361-5; of Aeneas, iii. 361-2, 387; v. 91; mixture of v. and narration in *PL* regrettable, iii. 385-6; many dreams and v. sent in to the *Spectator*, iv. 364-5; of Alnaschar, iv. 411; method of communication called intellectual vision, v. 173. *See also* Allegories, Dream-visions.

Visitant(s): the ladies' complaint of a dumb, ii. 84; regular v. the pleasantest parts of a woman's equipage, ii. 112; of quality at Lady MARY ENVILLE's, iii. 69; Mr. SPECTATOR to be a v. of boarding-schools for young women, iii. 140.

Visiting days: 'the day I keep', i. 104; compliments in use at, i. 152; presents at, iv. 232.

Visits, visitings: i. 342; ii. 316; impertinent and tiresome, i. 103-4; receiving v. in bed, i. 192; making v. and frequenting assemblies, ii. 236; the pleasure of, ii. 299; paid in the country, ii. 448; politicians' manners at levées and, iii. 99; 'twilight visits' by ministers of state, iv. 112.

Vista, in a garden, iii. 569.

Vitellius, Aulus (Roman emperor), ii. 212.

VITRUVIUS, letter from (a 'castle-builder'), ii. 158-60.

Vitruvius Pollio, his works lost, ii. 160.

'Vivacities', iv. 75, 250, 308.

Vivacity: the characteristic of women, ii. 8; of a wife tempered by gravity of a husband, ii. 9; often mistaken for wit, ii. 377; the distinguishing character of the French, iv. 29; balanced against wit, iv. 136.

VIZARD, Mrs., a toast of the Ugly Club, i. 77.

Vizards and masks worn by wits, i. 136.

Vizier: the Grand V. strangled, iii. 154; story of Sultan Mahmoud and his, iv. 319; Alnaschar's reverie of the Grand V.'s daughter, iv. 410-12.

VOCIFER, passes for a 'fine gentleman', i. 324.

Vociferation, a beau distinguishing himself by, ii. 434.

Voice: pipe of Licinius for regulating the, ii. 388-9; iv. 437; of angels compared to thunderings, iii. 331; different sounds of, in acting, iv. 432-7.

'Voice, the common', malignity and wantonness of, ii. 350.

Volscians, Latinus, King of the, i. 228.

Voltager, Prince, and his 'painted vest', i. 185.

Voltaire (François-Marie Arouet): reading of the *Spectator*, i. lxxxvii; *English Notebook*, iii. 424; *Lettres Philosophiques*, iii. 454; *Zadig*, ii. 423.

Volubility: of women's tongues, ii. 480; of WILL HONEYCOMB, v. 184.

Voluntary: sung by a gentleman in the coffee-house, ii. 82; played by the organ, iv. 285; 'laugh a v. to put you in humour', iv. 288; before the First Lesson, v. 153.

Voluntaries, inappropriate v. in church, iii. 253.

Voluntary counsellors, ii. 293.

Volunteers in malice, ii. 559.

Voluptuousness, i. 380-4; punished after death, i. 381-2; story of Pontignan, an example of, i. 382-4.

Vortex: each fixed star a sun with its own, iv. 170.

Vos valete & plaudite, iii. 152; iv. 495.

Vouchers for others, ii. 482; iv. 423.

Vowels: omission of, in termination of preterperfect tense, ii. 33-34; want of, in English, ii. 34; gaping of v. in poetry, illustrated by Pope, ii. 484.

Vows, a beau's head filled with, ii. 571.

Vox & praeterea nihil, i. 263.

Voyages of Ulysses and Satan compared, ii. 564.

Voyce, William (linen-draper), ii. 464.

Vulcan: Cacus, son of, ii. 366; a buffoon among the gods, ii. 562; a burlesque character in Homer, ii. 589; making the twenty *tripodes*, iii. 201; his shop on Lemnos, iii. 230; poured down fire on the river Xanthus, iii. 233; temple to, on Mt. Etna, iv. 580; dogs of, and women of Syracuse, iv. 581-2.

Vulgar: 'Mr. Cowley's *great v.*', i. 470; 'as the v. say', ii. 73; 'the crowd or v. of the rich', ii. 87; the minds of the v. affected by religious superstitions, ii.

333; prostituting learning to the embraces of the, iii. 423; v. errors ridiculed by the virtuosos, ii. 442; the mean and v. to be avoided in the epic, ii. 588; the mouths of the, iii. 10; what v. minds look upon as trifles, iii. 99; 'the great v. and the small', iv. 170.

Vulgarity of a young woman, ii. 346–7.

Vultures: symbols of cares and passions, ii. 124; troubles represented by, iv. 278.

W—, Bully, i. *8*.

W., M., letter from (on education of girls), iii. 139–40.

W., T.: slain by a lady's glance, iii. 418; his remarks on the *Spectator*, iv. 230; his letter proposing marriage, iv. 359–60.

W—, Dr. T—, his system of divinity and spiritual mechanics, iii. 484.

W., Sir T., cuckolded, v. 150.

W., W., 'killed by an unknown hand', iii. 417.

W—n, Mr., 'the learned news-monger', iii. 485.

Wadd, William, *Nugae chirurgicae*, iv. *61, 173*.

WADDLE, Lady, a member of the Widow Club, iv. 516.

WADDLE, Sir SIMON, Kt., iv. 516.

Wade, Lieut.-Gen. George, a subscriber, i. *lxxxix*.

Wafer, politicians instructed how to split a, iii. 97.

Wag(s): names of merry w. in different countries, i. 201–2; a waggish story, i. 241; 'this unlucky w.', ii. 207; wag-wits in London streets, iii. 322.

Wagers: *used for arguments* (prov.), ii. 71, 430; offered in coffee-houses, ii. 71–72; party-liars secured from penalty of, iv. 354.

Wages, relation of, to prices, ii. 403–4.

Wagstaffe, William: *Comment upon Tom Thumb*, i. *322, 364*; iii. *459*; in the *Plain Dealer*, i. *500*; iii. *440–1, 509–10*.

Waistcoat: silk, i. 51; brocade, i. 67; of blue camlet, trimmed with silver, i. 434; silk, unbuttoned to show the shirt, ii. 14; open, ii. 43; without sleeves, iii. 163.

Waiter(s), i. 357; about a sick friend, i. 403; persons of quality followed by, iii. 33.

WAITFORT, The Hon. EDWARD, a suitor of the President of the Widow-Club, iv. 557–61.

Wake, Col. William, anecdote of, iii. 135.

Wake, a country, ii. 130–5.

Walduck, Captain, i. *342*.

Wales: letter addressed from, ii. 384–5; Penmainmaure, the glory of, ii. 384; a letter received from, iii. 263.

Walk: GLYCERA's dancing walk, iv. 245.

Walker, Capt. Charles, ii. *247*.

Walker, Obadiah, *Of Education*, iii. *107*.

Walker, Dr. Thomas, referred to (?), iv. 230.

Walker, William: *Paroemiologia Anglo-Latina*, iv. *527*; *The Royal Grammar*, iv. *425*.

Walking: the art of, to be learned by girls, i. 281–2; a kind of recitative dancing, i. 282; with God, ii. 333; 'I affect a tottering untaught way of', iv. 426; upon hands, iv. 544.

Wall, William, *History of Infant Baptism*, i. 390.

Wall, taking the, iv. 387.

Wall, Great, of China, still to be seen, iii. 555.

Wall-hangings. See Paper, Tapestry.

'Wall-peelers', iv. 17.

Wallace, Thomas, on Addison's style, i. ci–cii.

Waller, Edmund: has a great deal of mixed wit, i. 265; a poet usually has some real or supposed Sacharissa to improve his vein, iv. 371; easiness of WILL HONEYCOMB's favourite W. has made many insipid poets, v. 185; quoted, i. 38; ii. 85, 120, 206, 371, 424, 468; iii. 167.

Wallis, William (contractor to the Army), a subscriber, i. *xci*.

Walls: printed papers on, i. 361; of Babylon, iii. 553–4.

Walmsley, Gilbert, v. *61*.

Walnut(s): the best pickle for a, iv. 210; a pennyworth of, iv. 267.

Walnut-trade, at the Royal Exchange, iv. 307.

Walpole, Horace, v. *146*.

Walpole, Robert: a subscriber, i. lxxxix; member of Kit-Cat Club, i. *42*; mentioned, v. *146*.

Walsh, William: as an original of Sir ROGER, i. *7, 463*; member of Kit-Cat Club, i. *42*.

Walter, Sir John, suppressed country-wakes, ii. 135.

Wanley, Nathaniel, *Wonders of the Little World*, ii. *594*.

Want(s): fear of w. and love of pleasure, the origin of trades and professions, i. 232; fear of w. degenerates into avarice, i. 232; excesses resulting from dread of w. and shame of it, i. 469; relieving the w. of others, ii. 394; one should

speak modestly of his own, ii. 592–3; poverty and w. accompany slavery, iii. 22.

Wanton: carriage in a woman, ii. 179; playing the, ii. 536.

Wanton Wife of Bath, The, quoted, ii. 461.

War(s): a stupid and barbarous way to extend dominion, i. 10; making of, restricted to male sex, i. 312; guilts that attend unjust, ii. 48; unprofitable to princes, ii. 282–3; cripples from the, ii. 335; as a means of arguing, ii. 430; of Pyrrhus regulated by justice and humanity, ii. 444; Adam's vision of, in *PL,* iii. 363; weekly historians: men who delight in, iv. 63; Jews' exemption from, iv. 257.

War of the Spanish Succession, ii. 435, 453; monuments to the dead in, i. 110; the Hebdomadal Meeting on, i. 181–2; has reduced importation of French fashions, i. 192; ii. 577–8; Mr. BEAVER's opinion of, i. 209; taking of the French lines in August, 1711, ii. 50; has adulterated our tongue with French words, ii. 149; raised England to a higher pitch of glory, ii. 150; the confederates in, ii. 159; victories of Her Majesty's armies, ii. 209; iii. 381, 444; news of, cried in London streets, ii. 476; 'if the War continues', iii. 4; poor showing of French generals in, iii. 97; has stimulated interest in news, iv. 91; Marlborough's achievements in, v. 179.

War, the last (with France), iii. 4, 97; v. 8.

Ward, Edward: *Don Quixote,* i. 125; *The London Spy,* i. 36, 61, 90, 131, 146, 350; ii. 206, 257, 295; iii. 292, 294, 350, 507; iv. 265, 307; *Secret History of the Clubs,* i. 39.

Ward, James, a contributor, i. lvi, lxxxi–lxxxii; iii. 533; v. 161.

Ward, John (a Director of the Bank and the East India Co.), a subscriber, i. xc.

Ward, Deputy of the, iv. 284.

Warders of the Tower, v. 137.

Warehouse: an India, ii. 480; of Peter Motteux, iii. 26.

WARLY, WILL, letter from (on the military profession), iv. 533–5.

Warm fellow, warm man, ii. 442; iv. 82, 207.

Warner, John: a subscriber, i. lxxxix, xc; referred to (?), iv. 377; goldsmith near Temple Bar, iv. 483.

Warton, Joseph: on Sir ROGER DE COVERLEY, i. xxxvi; on Addison's method of composition, i. lxv; on

Addison's style, i. xcviii; on the motto of No. 223, ii. 365; on Addison and Pope, ii. 483; on Addison's assistance to Budgell, iii. 251.

Warwick, Charlotte, Dowager Countess of, iv. 499.

Warwick, Edward Henry Rich, 7th Earl of, a subscriber, i. lxxxviii.

Warwickshire; Coleshill-Heath in, ii. 182; Lady BLUEMANTLE lives in a town in, 'famous for much animosity and dissension', iv. 2.

Wash(es), i. 175; Lady BLITHE's, iii. 183.

Washballs, vendor of powder and, ii. 477.

Washing(s): in the Jewish and Mahometan religions, ii. 332; v. 158; the head with cold water, ii. 387; anecdote of a dervish whose mishaps occurred because he failed to wash his hands, v. 158.

Wasp(s): behaving like a, ii. 326; a mean between being wasps and doves, iii. 72.

Wasse's Elixir, i. xxv.

Watch(es): a lady's, with a coronet on the back, i. 38; ladies', i. 428; division of labour in manufacture of, ii. 404.

Watch: beating and putting the w. to rout, ii. 372; iii. 187; alarming the, iv. 249.

WATCHFULL, RACHEL, letter from (on dancing), iii. 414–15.

Watchfulness, in allegory of Avarice and Luxury, i. 235.

Watch-maker, assisted in contriving a puppet, iii. 581.

Watchman: knocking down a, ii. 219; the w.'s thump at midnight, ii. 475; a day-w. followed by a goose, iii. 413–14; bidding good-morrow to another, v. 42; the w.'s cry, v. 105.

Watch-poles, several wounds in the head by, iii. 341.

WATCHWELL, TIM, letter from (on fortune-stealers), iii. 124–6.

Water(s): an entertainment upon the, ii. 191; 'the pure element' the drink of beggars, ii. 402; indecent language upon the, ii. 439; drinking the, iii. 7; the Widow TRUEBY's, iii. 212; a wide expanse of, and falls of, pleasing to the imagination, iii. 540, 542, 544; interpreting dreams by seeing a person's, iv. 294.

Water-gruel, dieted with, iv. 48.

Watering-places (Astrop, Bath, Bury, Epsom, Scarborough, Tunbridge), ii. 104.

Watermen: language of, ii. 439; many

lawyers might have made elegant, iii. 109; on the Thames, iii. 437; amateur w. bred to the law, iv. 268.

Water-nymphs: in sky-coloured garments, ii. 533; Trojan fleet changed into (in the *Aeneid*), iii. 145, 306; v. 15–16; not necessary to the pastoral, iv. 362.

'Watt, Powder', vendor of powder and washballs, ii. 477.

Watts, Isaac, a contributor, i. lvi; iv. *127*.

Watts, Richard (linen-draper), ii. *464*.

Waverland, Philip de, applicant for the flitch of bacon, v. 79.

Wax: an illumination with wax-candles, iii. 69; and wafers necessary for politicians, iii. 97; red wax of ball-tickets, and black wax of burying-tickets, iv. 15; 'wax-nibblers', iv. 17.

Wax-work(s), of Mrs. Salmon, i. 117, 129; v. 82.

Weakness: in a husband as a cause of jealousy, ii. 170; virtue without discretion looks like, ii. 376; advertisement of medicine for, iv. *553*.

Weaknesses: of youth, old age, and manhood, ii. 271; of our temper and inclination, ii. 424; every one has flaws and, ii. 466; pleasure in discovering w. of others, ii. 495–6.

Wealth: only a secondary ingredient in happiness, ii. 158; population the source of, ii. 209, 283, 402–3; expectations of, ii. 597–9; methods of acquiring, iii. 1–5, 477; proper use of, iii. 47–49, 288–91; as a factor in marriage, iii. 92–93; the way to, 'the great article of life', iv. 4; vice is covered by, iv. 138; and poverty, iv. 139; the father of Love, iv. 295; not a title to greatness, v. 84–87.

WEALTHY, SHARLOT, letter from (disadvantages of her upbringing), iv. 405–6.

Wealthy, the: superfluities of, relieve the poor, i. 277; 'pampered vice in the habitations of', ii. 537; iii. 16; foul play to be feared more from the indigent than, iii. 1; attend the poor during Lent in Roman Catholic countries, iii. 400; insolence of, to those below them, iv. 156.

'Wear well': men who (to use our English phrase) *wear well*, iii. 451.

Weather: as a subject of conversation, i. 46; fable of the countryman who desired to control the, i. 108; bad w. induces gloominess, i. 353; influences human constitutions, ii. 137; the

coquette uneasy in all kinds of, ii. 459; prediction of, from pain in the shoulder, iv. 47; a barber's device to denote, iv. 60.

Weather-glass: shows variations of atmosphere, ii. 595; a man serving as a, iv. 47; letter signed, received, iv. 497.

Weaver, John (dancing-master): a contributor, i. lvi; iii. *236*; his treatise on dancing ready to be published, iv. 148.

Weaver, i. 277; anecdote of a, and his wife's lottery-ticket, ii. 440–1; epitaph on a Spittle-fields, iv. 343; burnt for his religion in reign of Queen Mary, v. 92.

Wedding(s): ROBIN BRIDEGROOM wakened by playing of drums after the w.-night, iii. 370; private, iv. 113; w.-customs among the heathens, v. 76.

Wedding-ring, i. 378; ii. 184.

Wedlock, Latitudinarians in, iii. 65.

WEED, EPHRAIM, letter from (how he acquired riches), iv. 81–86.

Weeds, collectors of, i. 91.

Weeds, a widow's, ii. 407; iv. 516, 561; v. 131.

Weekly Comedy, i. *8*.

Weekly historians, men who delight in war, iv. 63.

Weekly Preparations, i. *341*.

Weeping: as an expression of joy, i. 294; not the mark of true grief, i. 403; faculty of, peculiar only to some constitutions, i. 403; and laughter unmanly, ii. 67; over a husband's absence, ii. 436; something moving in the image of w. beauty, iv. 481; of actors in *The Distressed Mother*, iii. 32, 34.

Weibertreue, legend of the, iv. *269*.

WELCH, BETTY, a country girl pitching the bar, ii. 133.

Welford, in *The Scornful Lady*, ii. 554.

WELFORD, Lord, and MARINET, iii. 499.

WELLADAY, RACHAEL, letter from (on the evils of bachelordom), iv. 382–5.

WELLFORD, Mr. ('CYNTHIO'), iii. 493.

Well-wishers: we should have many, but few friends, i. 290.

Welsh: tone of, differs from English and Scotch, i. 120; cruelty of the, ii. 161; letter from a W. correspondent, ii. 384–5; heiress found in a pedigree, v. 93.

Welsted, Leonard: translation of Longinus, ii. *393*; on 'golden verses', iv. *287*.

Wench(es): OMNAMANTE a rapacious, ii. 70; for crowns apiece, ii. 93; 'passed a night with a', ii. 105; a

country, ii. 134, 184; discourse on, ii. 534–7; the shop-maid a pert, ii. 581; at the Royal Exchange, iv. 307.

Wencher(s): a defunct, ii. 95; impotent old, ii. 567.

Wenching, i. 352; ii. 244–8, 279–82, 295–8; the occupation of men of wit and pleasure, ii. 93–96; the enormity of, ii. 216–19; protests against discussion of, ii. 574–7.

Wenham, Jane, trial of, for witchcraft, i. 480.

Wentworth Papers, ii. 489; iv. 537.

West Enborne, Berks., custom at, v. 100, 129.

West Indian, a gay, i. 343.

West Indies: scene of INKLE and YARICO story, i. 49; sugar, i. 295; BRUNETTA and PHILLIS there, i. 343–4; reports of witchcraft in, i. 480; the French masters of, iv. 207; anecdote of the governor in, iv. 248–9; many Jews established in, iv. 256.

West Saxon, WILL FUNNELL the, iv. 542.

Western circuit: a friend upon the, i. 488–9; his observations on country dress, ii. 13–15.

Westminster Assembly, the 'Assembly of divines', v. 150.

Weston, Richard. See Portland.

Weston, Thomas, i. 40.

'Wetting his title', i. 374.

Whale, tubs and barrels thrown out to a, ii. 519.

Whalebone: in petticoats, ii. 6, 74, 579; iii. 417; a prude armed in w. and buckram, ii. 346.

Wharton, Thomas, Earl (and Marquis) of: and Addison, i. xvi; a subscriber, i. lxxxviii; a volume of the Spectator dedicated to, v. 180–1; mentioned, iii. 441.

What-d'ye-call(-him), Mr., i. 19; ii. 560; iv. 206.

What's what, understands (prov.), ii. 23.

WHEADLE, JENNY, iv. 558.

Wheat: the critic who separated chaff from, iii. 38; wheat-ear, iii. 196.

Wheel-barrows: of rotten food sold in streets, iii. 354; and pick-axes, iv. 263; waked by rumbling of, v. 41.

Wheels, living w. in the vision of Ezekiel, iii. 201.

Whet(s): 'to take a', i. 309; sips, drams, and, iv. 542.

Whetters, the world filled with, ii. 364.

Which, petition of Who and, i. 336–7, 344–5.

Whichenovre, manor of, v. 76; Whichenovre-Hall, v. 78–79.

Whifflers, insignificant fellows used like, iv. 414.

Whig(s): frequenting St. James's Coffee-house, i. 4; hostilities with Tories, i. 5, 243, 262; their aversion to kings, i. 213; iii. 216; viewed by the Four Indian Kings, i. 213; dullness among both W. and Tories, i. 262; women partisans of W. and Tories, i. 346–9; iii. 532; v. 72; we should not regard men as W. or Tories, i. 512; jockeys and Tory fox-hunters, ii. 3; Mr. SPECTATOR suspected of being a discarded W., sullen because he is out of place, ii. 20; justice of peace, ii. 183; NATHANIEL HENROOST forced to rail at the times because his wife is a violent, ii. 195; men who see everything in terms of W. or Tory, iv. 64; balanced against Tories, iv. 137; no ambition to increase number of W. and Tories, iv. 501; reconciling the minister of the parish and a W. justice, v. 128; anecdote of a W. criminal, v. 149.

Whiling: time, iv. 75; moments and intervals of life, iv. 358.

Whims and humourists, England noted for, iii. 396.

Whining at a conventicle, v. 155.

Whip(s): and racks used in torture, ii. 431; 'brothers of the' [coachmen], iv. 267; boots, bridles, and, iv. 310.

Whip (to drink quickly), v. 106.

Whip-lash, twisted by WILL WIMBLE, i. 446.

Whipping: of JACK TRUEPENNY for faults of others, i. 352; at school, ii. 115–17, 160–2; children till they cry, and then w. them for crying, ii. 336.

Whisk. See Whist.

Whiskers, i. 500; as a device in comedy, i. 191; beards and, iii. 220–3.

Whisper(s): the desire to be in the w. with great men, ii. 257; credit undone in, ii. 350; gossips who run about with new, ii. 559; domestics causing defamatory, iii. 49; a news-letter of w. proposed, iv. 111–13.

Whisperer(s), i. 484; described, ii. 83–84; in public assemblies, ii. 162–3; employed by the Inquisition on Marriage, iii. 167; about men in power, iii. 479.

Whist(-k): games at whisk, i. 310; whisk not an innocent pastime, ii. 451; throwing away his cards at, iv. 10.

Whistling: a young gentleman who whistles and sings in a coffee-house,

ii. 73; account of a w. match at Bath, ii. 206–8 (referred to, ii. 224); benefits of, ii. 207; a rider whistles to his horse when he would make his waters pass, ii. 207; an amateur whistler, iv. 545–6.

Whiston, William, iii. *484*; iv. 5, *589*; referred to(?), iii. 485.

White, Mr., benefit for, i. *120*.

White, Francis (owner of White's Chocolate House), i. *375*.

White, Francis, *A Treatise of the Sabbath-Day*, iv. *586*.

WHITE, MOLL: a reputed witch, i. 480–2; reports of, ii. 19–20, 57; her death, ii. 550.

White, Thomas (Bishop of Peterborough), v. *175*.

White: hood, ii. 532, 533; sarsenet, ii. 533.

White witch, Mr. SPECTATOR suspected of being a, ii. 20, 57.

Whiteness of hands and teeth, in WILL HONEYCOMB, v. 185.

Whitepot, receipt for a, i. 451.

Whitewash (cosmetic), iii. 418.

Whittington, Richard, and his cat: a projected opera on, i. 27; a puppet-show on, i. 63.

Who and *Which*: petition of, i. 336–7; 'the just remonstrance of affronted *That*', i. 344–5.

Whole Duty of Man, The. See Allestree.

Whoredom, the economy of, described by Fletcher, ii. 535.

Whoremaster(s): 'all the honest w. in the neighbourhood', ii. 219; a cat and a w. will find a way through doors, ii. 296–7; a 'W.'s Journal' received by the *Spectator*, iii. 181; in modern comedies, iv. 68.

Whores, procured from the country, ii. 534–7.

Whorish unresisting good nature, i. 352.

Wicked, the, punishment of, in eternity, ii. 421.

'Wicked Bible, The', iv. *580*.

Widdrington (in *Hudibras*), i. 320.

Widow(s): Mr. SPECTATOR lodges with a widow-woman, i. 52, 425; mourning now worn by w. and heirs, i. 275; a stage-coach companion, ii. 22–25; letters from, ii. 85–86; iv. 425–6; extravagant singing of a widow lady, ii. 305–6; w.'s weeds, ii. 407; iv. 516, 561; v. 131; a young w. and her demands for pin-money, iii. 53; the great game of fortune-hunters, iii. 127; a w. and her froward son, iii. 366–7; Sir ROGER seeing justice done to a widow-woman, iv. 340; devices of a

rich w. to escape suitors, iv. 425–6; account of nine, forming the Widow-Club, iv. 515–18; a half-pay officer laying siege to a, iv. 535; an absolute denial from a maid and from a, v. 23; remarriage of, in ancient Greece, v. 73; the Love-Casuist's report on courtship of, v. 98–101; custom of riding upon the black ram by, v. 100–1, 129–32. *See also* Ephesian Widow. *For* the Perverse Widow *see* Sir ROGER DE COVERLEY.

Widow-Club, The, iv. 515–18, 556–61.

Widow-hunters, secrets of use to, iv. 515.

Widowhood, male, iv. 350.

Wife: account of an over-religious, i. 198–9; *will always have the last word* (prov.), i. 220; and husband complement each other, ii. 9; an affected country, ii. 11; behaviour of, to a jealous husband, ii. 168–78; of a hen-pecked husband, ii. 194–6, 328–30, 342–4; a jealous, ii. 201–4; iv. 380–1; an indifferent, ii. 260–2; story of an unfaithful, ii. 277–9; choice of a, ii. 279–82; iii. 121–3; obedience and tenderness of a faithful, ii. 281; gaiety permissible to the husband, but not to the, ii. 300; reflections of a w. on death, ii. 301–2; nothing better than a good, or worse than a bad, ii. 320; an extravagant, ii. 327; iii. 204–8; *Wanton W. of Bath*, ii. 461; who uses tears and fainting fits, ii. 480–1; qualifications of a good, ii. 514–16, 545–6; a shop-keeper's learned, ii. 582–3; pin-money given to a, iii. 50–54; account of a fashionable, iii. 68–71, 111; EMILIA a pattern, iii. 79–83; a w.'s whims during pregnancy, iii. 195–7; conduct of, in absence of husband, iii. 269–72; a w. solicited by her husband's friend, iii. 503–4; who wears the breeches, iv. 210; the word *wife* most agreeable and delightful, iv. 237; account of death of a, iv. 350–3; passion of love to a mistress contrasted with that to a, iv. 371–2; Pliny's description of his, iv. 372–3; one man, when invited, discards his, iv. 507; saying of an old philosopher about his, iv. 564; a citizen's gay w. in Cave of Trophonius, v. 46; a married couple happy because the w. was dumb, v. 80. *See also* Wives, Husband.

Wig(s): 'a monstrous bush of hair', i. 214; full-bottomed, i. 65; ii. 92; iii. 161; the thick kind in vogue some years ago, i. 248; foretop of, i. 248; a bob wig with black silken bag, ii. 14; a

night-cap wig, ii. 14; iii. 161; letting a wig lie in buckle, ii. 14; a fashionable, ii. 91; a short, ii. 92; iii. 401; a darker, ii. 388; a good w. of advantage to the poor dependant, ii. 593; a fair, iii. 125; a black, iii. 154, 184; a thin natural, iii. 161; black riding, iii. 162; country squires in bob-wigs, iii. 321; burning a long wig in a frolic, iii. 341; long wig of a lawyer, iii. 522; adding white horse-hair to, iv. 221; an immense black, iv. 222; 'she seized his', iv. 224. *See also* Periwig.

Wight, Isle of, ii. 72.

Wildair, Sir Harry (in *The Constant Couple*), iii. 394.

Wilderness: natural genius, like a w. of noble plants, ii. 129; of sweets in *PL*, iii. 202.

WILDFIRE, JOHN, a fox-hunter, iv. 516–17.

WILDFIRE, the Widow, iv. 516–17.

Wild-fowl: a dish of, i. 448; over-roasting of a dish of, iv. 210.

Wilkes, John (contractor to the Army), a subscriber, i. *xci*.

Wilks, Robert (actor and theatre-manager), i. 25; ii. 504; iv. 283; a graceful exit by, ii. 544–5; different roles of, iii. 393–4; other roles, i. 75, 207, 216, 278; ii. 545; iii. 418.

WILL: footman to a Captain of the Guard, i. 375–6; a suitor of BIDDY LOVELESS, ii. 270.

Will: nothing ought to be laudable in a man in which his will is not concerned, i. 133; inconstancy of the human, ii. 136–7; passions enforce the, ii. 490; and understanding: two faculties in the soul, v. 500.

WILLIAM, Sir ROGER's master of the game, i. 484–5.

'WILLIAM, Sir', iii. 210.

William the Conqueror, i. 1; iv. 523; how the Kentish men evaded, iii. 9; 'punished' for pulling down churches, iv. 212.

William III, i. 56; ii. 13–14; revival of Roman noses under, i. 135; 'that glorious monarch', i. 248; defeated at Steenkerke, iii. 240; siege of Namur, iii. 399; Bishop of St. Asaph's tribute to, iii. 440, 443; contrasted with Louis XIV, iv. 335–8.

Williams, John (a Director of South Sea Co.), a subscriber, i. *xc*.

Willis, —— (actor), ii. 57.

Willis, Browne (antiquary), iii. 189.

Willis, Dr. Thomas: *Anatomy of the Brain*, ii. 465; *De anima brutorum*, iv. 69.

WILLOW, KATE, a witty mischievous wench, i. 485.

Willow(s), i. 498; iii. 552; iv. 189.

Wilmot, John. *See* Rochester.

Wilson, George, his Antirheumatick Tincture advertised, iv. 61.

Wilson, Walter, iv. 252.

Wiltshire, gentlemen of, i. 40.

WIMBLE, WILL: character of, i. 446–9; his regard for ceremonial, i. 487–8; dispute with TOM TOUCHY, i. 498–9; ii. 550; suspects Mr. SPECTATOR of being a fanatic and of having killed a man, ii. 4, 19; makes tobacco-stoppers, ii. 550; iii. 215; his thousand roguish tricks at Christmas, ii. 550; mentioned, ii. 21.

Winchester, King Edgar at, v. 70.

Winchilsea, Anne Finch, Countess of, referred to ?), v. 72.

Wind: Spanish jennets impregnate by, ii. 5; *fickle as the* (prov.), ii. 317; bladders filled with, in a beau's head, ii. 571.

Windmill, on Sir ROGER's estate, iii. 54.

Window(s): watchings under, ii. 105; tricks of a Jezebel at her, ii. 190; w.-curtains, ii. 190; iii. 206; poems cut on, ii. 356; use of the w. by a beautiful lady, iii. 55–56; bars to the, iii. 207; a dial cut in a, iii. 318. — BREAKING OF: by rakes, i. 146; ii. 372; by WILL HONEYCOMB, i. 436; 'a breaker of windows in his youth', ii. 576; as the mark of a fashionable man, iv. 569; admired by women, v. 58–59.

Winds: Virgil's ruler of the, ii. 415; drums, w., and enchantments in Lapland, iii. 376; the Almighty making the weight for the, iv. 134; course of, depicted in the terrestrial globe, iv. 482.

Windsor, ii. 62; (the hymn-tune), iii. 8.

Wine, i. 340; ii. 54, 534; *good w. needs no bush* (prov.), ii. 359; Estcourt in the service of wit and, ii. 529; and small-beer, iii. 111; adulteration of, iii. 353–5; as a dissolver of virtue, iii. 479; Montaigne tells us what kind of w. he loves best, iv. 520; and drunkenness, iv. 541–4; if your wife not handsome, 'put less water in your wine', iv. 543; sold at the Queen's Arms, iv. 546.

Wine-press, iii. 596.

Wines: Act for importing French, i. 181; imported into England, i. 295; and spices in a modern meal, ii. 264; green, ii. 530; making w. of fruits of our own growth, iii. 205; counterfeit,

iii. 207; Brooke and Hellier's, iii. 353–5; Port O Port, iii. 355.

Wing, of the peruke, iv. 345.

Wingate, Edmund, *Arithmetique made easie*, i. 391.

Wings, poems in shape of, i. 246, 271; iii. 560.

Wink: to w. at a thing, i. 452; tipping the, ii. 472; took the, iv. 100.

Winstanley, Henry: 'the water-works', ii. *163*; Mrs. Winstanley, his widow, ii. *163*.

Winstanley, William, *New Help to Discourse*, i. *185, 254*; ii. *200*.

Winter: the most dead, uncomfortable time of year, ii. 550; relieved by Christmas, ii. 550; best in Spain, iii. 474; allegorical figure of, iii. 596.

Winter-garden, proposed, iv. 191.

Winter-quarters, shameful for a general to be surprised in, iii. 482.

Winterton, Ralph, *Poetae minores graeci*, i. *55, 246–7, 265*; ii. *296, 318*; iii. *30, 229*; iv. *166, 463*.

Wire(s): lace, and ribbons in head-dresses, i. 414; used in men's coats, ii. 74; sale of patches, pins, and, iv. 102.

Wisdom: and virtue more important than politics, i. 507; and valour essential to manhood, ii. 70; must be justly employed, ii. 180; study of, necessary to right devotion, ii. 311; exerting itself as cunning in savage nations, ii. 339; gravity often mistaken for, ii. 377; divine w. in government of the world, ii. 420; and virtue required for happiness in marriage, ii. 545; and beauty afford a pleasing prospect of human nature, iii. 79; balanced against riches and gravity, iv. 136; allegorical vision of heavenly and worldly, iv. 365–9; the best husbands have been most famous for, v. 75.

Wise, Henry: to be appointed gardener of the play-house, i. 27; and London, our heroic poets, iv. 190.

Wise: whisperers pretend to be, ii. 83; and valiant in all ages have been henpecked, ii. 196; tragical events happen to tbe good and the, ii. 421; 'like w. speeches, they sunk deep into my heart', ii. 446; a w. contrasted with a witty picture, ii. 447; we should not grow too w. for the pleasure of laughter, ii. 466.

Wise man, the: reflections of, contrasted with those of the fool, i. 311; *changes his mind, a fool never will* (prov.), i. 337;

his use of time contrasted with that of the fool, i. 401–2; culls his thoughts for conversation, ii. 375; hates no body, but only loves the virtuous, ii. 444; contrasted with the man of wit, ii. 446–7; of the Stoics, v. 167–8.

Wise men: retrench evils of life by reasonings of philosophy, i. 34; often affected by undue love of praise, i. 161.

WISEACRE, WILLIAM, letter from (wants lessons in the fan for his children), ii. 30–31.

Wiseacre, a: in the pulpit, ii. 46; in a coffee-house, iv. 206.

WISEAKER, WILLIAM, 'drowned in a flood of tears', iii. 418.

Wiseman, Horace, *Several Chirurgicall Treatises*, iii. *214*.

WISHWELL, Cousin, iv. 559.

Wit (great mental capacity; genius): lack of, causes bawdry in plays, i. 216; tempered with candour in Lord Dorset, i. 363; fables the earliest pieces of, ii. 219; a mother who praises the wit of her little boy before he is able to speak, ii. 459; employed by some writers in propagating vice, ii. 517; Estcourt in the service of w. and wine, ii. 529; every kind has a particular science corresponding to it, iii. 107; Pope not ashamed to employ his, in praise of his Maker, iii. 419.

Wit (talent for talking in a brilliant, amusing, or satirical way): affectation of being witty rather than good-natured, the source of most ill habits of life, i. 28; pernicious when not tempered with humanity, i. 99; turned into absurdity by affectation, i. 159–60; among lawyers and clergymen, i. 162; a 'woman's man' has a wonderful deal of, ii. 112; learned at our great schools, ii. 116; less agreeable than good nature, ii. 165; ill nature among ordinary observers passes for, ii. 167; its charms not to be esteemed above virtue, ii. 179; touches of nature more pleasing than touches of wit, ii. 212; without discretion is impertinence, ii. 376; vivacity often mistaken for, ii. 377; vain ostentation of, a motive for attacking others, ii. 494–5; to be tried by the rule of virtue, ii. 554; and ill-nature in ridiculing a new poem, iii. 36; in an improper place is impertinent and absurd, iii. 37; people who pretend to, and write lampoons, iii. 56; degenerates into impudence if innocence is absent, iii. 482; and

raillery, iii. 582–6; impudence and scurrility now pass for, iv. 57–58; balanced against vivacity, iv. 136; substitutes for, in conversation, iv. 287–90; most effective when concealed in gravity, v. 105. *See also* Humour, Lampoons.

Wit (resemblance of ideas, giving delight and surprise): defined by Cowley, i. 146; descended from Good Sense, i. 146; much admired and little understood, i. 244; and judgement contrasted by Locke, i. 263–4; must give delight and surprise, i. 264; consists in resemblance and congruity of ideas, i. 265; iii. 560; various species of, i. 265; Dryden's definition, i. 267–8; truth the basis of, i. 268; opposition of ideas produces a kind of, i. 270; allegory of true, false, and mixed, i. 270–4; superficial strokes of, in Boileau's 8th Satire, ii. 321; letters of Aristaenetus are heightened with a luxuriance of, ii. 427; consists in giving things that are known an agreeable turn, ii. 483; over-use of metaphors savours too much of, iii. 12; out of place in love poetry, iii.375–6; balanced against judgement, iv. 137; allegorical figure of (offspring of Fancy and Judgement), iv. 328. — *Spectators* on wit (Nos. 58–63) made up in sets, i. 507–8; praised, ii. 52.

Wit, false: poems in typographical shapes, i. 246–8; poems excluding certain letters, i. 249–50; the rebus, i. 250–1; echo poems, i. 252–3; the *Aeneid* turned into rhyme, i. 254; a hymn to Mary ringing the changes on eight words, i. 254; anagrams, i. 255; acrostics, i. 255–6; chronograms, i. 256; *bouts-rimés*, i. 256–8; double rhymes, i. 258; puns, i. 259–63; iii. 484 ('mongrel miscreated kind of wit'); distinguished from true wit and mixed wit, i. 263–70; dream-allegory of true and false wit, i. 270–4; epigrammatical turns and points of wit, i. 316; in imitators of Cowley and Ovid, ii. 52–53; various artifices and modes of, ii. 355–7; points, conceits, and turns of wit in modern poems, ii. 366; iii. 90; taste in England for turns of wit, iii. 530; different kinds of, iii. 560; absent from *The Faerie Queene*, iv. 429.

Wit, mixed: consists partly in resemblance of ideas and partly in resemblance of words, i. 265; abounds in Cowley, i. 265; a composition of pun and true wit, i. 267; epigram its only

province, i. 267; allegorical figure of, i. 273.

Wit, man of: example of, i. 28; a handsome fellow not a wit (prov.?), i. 136; near allied to madness, i. 330; MERAB attempts to be both a beauty and a, ii. 69; becoming a wit by commencing a sloven, ii. 90; standards of, in reign of Charles II, ii. 118; genius and invention required to be a wit without immorality, ii. 206; Horace the greatest wit in the Augustan age, ii. 220; contrasted with the wise man, ii. 446–7; capable of exposing a beauty and aggravating a fault, iii. 37.

Wit's Common-wealth. See Bodenham.

Witch(es): in *Macbeth*, i. 194; ii. 58; MOLL WHITE, i. 480–2; spirits and, ii. 21; 'that rabble of broomsticks' in *The Lancashire Witches*, ii. 58; writings about fairies, magicians, and, iii. 570; an old woman that confessed herself a, v. 128.

Witch, a white, ii. 20, 57.

Witches' Prayer, a little epigram called, i. 262.

Witchcraft, i. 480–2; ii. 57–58; oblique vision the mark of bewitchery, ii. 472; stories of, common in England, iv. 572.

WITHER, JOSIAH, slain by a lady's glance, iii. 418.

Witherington, at Chevy Chase, i. 320–1.

Witlings: in the coffee-houses, iv. 129; their ridicule of marriage, iv. 273; about town, iv. 289.

Witnesses: two required by Roman law, iv. 502.

Wits, men of wit: privileged to wear masks and vizards, i. 136; of King Charles's time jested upon the City, i. 142; occupations of German, i. 256; ii. 356; our modern, i. 289; among servants, i. 375, 406; character of, ii. 93–96; preferred by women, ii. 103–6; greatest are eminent for their humanity, ii. 167; many appear dull in print, ii. 167; few in Great Britain are content without being thought, ii. 357; lived together in good understanding in reign of Augustus, ii. 482; corporeal [tumblers on the stage], ii. 504; country wits, iii. 57; types of, iv. 53.

'Wits, little', i. 321, 364; their envy of an anonymous poem, i. 84; to be singled out for attack, i. 148; can laugh at an indecency but not relish the sublime, ii. 128; who ridicule others, ii. 467.

Witt, Johan de, always did one thing at once, iii. 2.

Witticisms: comparing love to fire and flame, i. 266-7; unnatural w. the delight of ordinary readers, ii. 369; constrained, obscene, and painful, ii. 591.

Witty: man does not guide conversation, ii. 376; men often the worst companions, ii. 449; man often sinks into a humorist, ii. 511; the *Spectator* at present forbears any attempt towards being, ii. 544; WILL HONEYCOMB unmercifully w. upon the women, iv. 389; *more w. than wise* (prov.), iv. 539.

Witty Club, at Oxford, i. 76.

Wives: who govern henpecked husbands, ii. 193-6; innocent diversions for, ii. 451-2; impertinent licence in speech of, iii. 72; three errors which may mislead, iii. 208; three country maidens ambitious to become, iii. 226; modern w. of Hensburg, iv. 269-72; 'the English let out their w. to all encounters', iv. 379. *See also* Wife, Husband.

Wizard(s): Mr. SPECTATOR suspected of being a, ii. 20; frequent in England, iv. 292.

Woden, subjects of Thor and, i. 90.

Wolf, Simon, a 'sleeper', ii. 225.

Wolf: one man a w. to another, i. 508; Romulus and Remus nursed by a, ii. 455.

Wolseley, Robert, Preface to *Valentinian*, i. 202.

Wolsey, Thomas, Cardinal: puppet show on, i. 78; his soliloquy (in *Henry VIII*) quoted, iv. 434; egotism of, iv. 520; 'Had I served God . . .', v. 133.

Woman (lady's maid), ii. 39; letter from, ii. 42-43.

Woman (women) of the town, i. 407; ii. 244-8, 536; iv. 225.

Woman-hater: Orpheus was musical, melancholy, and a, ii. 326; sooner or later repents, iv. 389.

Woman-slaughter, the sin of, ii. 113.

Woman's man: Mr. SPECTATOR called, by a gipsy, ii. 16; character of, ii. 110-13, 119-21; letter from one, ii. 120-1; in public assemblies, ii. 163; JACK TRIPLETT, iii. 297; Mr. FANFLY, iv. 332; employment proposed for, iv. 412-13.

Women:
GENERAL COMMENTS: thoughtless creatures who make up the lump of that sex, i. 21; the more powerful part of our people, i. 21; perjuries and levity of, i. 48; resent aspersions on their sex, i. 49; employment of *valets de chambre*, i. 192; fashion of receiving visits in bed, i. 192; ii. 276; sprightliness of, should not degenerate into levity, i. 193; the Four Indian Kings' comments on, i. 214-15; are reasonable creatures, with souls, i. 224; Mahometans' treatment of, i. 224; party-spirit in, i. 242-4, 346-9; Aristaenetus's description of a fine, i. 263; love of praise stronger in ('Idols'), i. 312; snuff-taking by, i. 314; their minds less cultivated with moral precepts, i. 338; seldom write their minds but in their postscripts, i. 339; Roman and Sabine w. prevented war, i. 348; 'the next tender things to children', who laugh and weep readily, i. 403; not generally so ignorant as illtaught, i. 404; their use of the fan, i. 426-9; the old saying, that w. are not to be trusted, i. 456; more gay and joyous than men, ii. 8; their treatment of their maids, ii. 42-43; their concern over ill-health, ii. 66-67; desirable traits in, ii. 68-71; 'the dearer part of mankind', ii. 84; seduction of, ii. 216-19; iii. 15-17; libertines and panders among, ii. 303-5, 567-70; self-esteem in, ii. 308; their behaviour at the theatre, ii. 315, 552-3; notifying others when they are in town, ii. 316; types of (after Semonides), ii. 318-20, 324, 326-8, 448-9; iii. 320; 'the beautiful sex', ii. 445; meaning of the phrase 'a kind woman', iii. 17; EMILIA a pattern, iii. 78-83; an over-worked expression about, iii. 140; most w. actuated by spirit of pride and contradiction, iii. 588; 'I have always hated general satires against', iv. 18; the naked-shouldered, iv. 38; the fine woman in modern comedy a combination of sprightliness and falsehood, iv. 68; FIDELIA, one who deserves the imitation of her sex, iv. 78-80; the modern women of Hensburg, iv. 269-72; insolent behaviour towards, iv. 304-5; 'those dear confounded creatures', iv. 314; sale of unmarried w. at Persian fair, iv. 314-15; Tartar general's sale of Chinese w. in sacks, iv. 315-16; treatment of young w. of beauty and fortune, iv. 405-6.

AFFECTATION IN: an enemy to beauty, i. 139, 159, 206; ii. 69; arises from

Women (*cont.*)
love of praise, i. 160–1; of mispronouncing words, i. 195; account of, in a wife, ii. 11; of general negligence, iii. 6–7; 'our greatest charms are owing to', iv. 332.

BEAUTY IN: 'the most beautiful pieces in human nature', i. 47; undue concern for, i. 137–41; is enhanced by virtue, i. 140, 225, 315, 338–41; ii. 178–9, 533; iii. 482; use of cosmetics, i. 173–7 ('Picts'), 205; ii. 303; the fairest part of the visible creation, i. 224; the most beautiful part of the creation, i. 242; the beautiful part of our species, i. 312; English women excel in, i. 349; iv. 30; too brief for 'demurring', i. 378; the 'fair sex', i. 415, &c.; created, as it were, for ornament, i. 433; dangers of, ii. 68–71; 'the beautiful sex', ii. 445; silent flattery of, ii. 480; whether fair or brown are more beautiful, iii. 17–18; ruined by small-pox, iii. 100–4; v. 96; less important than good nature, iii. 103–4; 'wrinkles' and 'tawny skin' in list of women's burdens, iv. 507.

DRESS. *See* Dress, women's.

EMPLOYMENTS AND DIVERSIONS OF: amusements and occupations, i. 46; fashionable *v.* reasonable diversions, i. 158; women preachers, i. 198–9; gaming, ii. 54; idle ladies of fashion, in China shops, ii. 107–10; iii. 245–6; operas, iii. 55, 374; CLARINDA's journal, iii. 181–5; women poets allowed to use heathen mythology, iv. 364; better employed in tapestry than in writing poetry, v. 72. *See also* Education.

LEARNING IN: effect on LEONORA, i. 158; writers of bawdry, ii. 218–19; pleased with my Greek mottoes, ii. 360; account of two female virtuosos, ii. 442–3; some w. do not understand Greek, ii. 556; iii. 54–55; urged to cultivate their minds as well as adorn their bodies, ii. 583; w. who write Pindarics, iii. 376.

LOQUACITY OF: 'female orators', ii. 458–62; *w.'s tongues made of aspen leaves* (prov.), ii. 461; 'the female loquacious faculty', iii. 55; female conversation, iv. 499.

LOVE OF OUTWARD SHOW: w.'s love of the showy and superficial, i. 66–69, 225; equipage their *summum bonum*, i. 197; 'an animal that delights in finery', ii. 530; manners and not dress the proper ornaments of women, ii. 533, 556. *See also* Dress.

MODESTY AND CHASTITY: modesty the chief ornament of, i. 30; chastity the great point of honour in, i. 416; honour protected by the hoop-petticoat, ii. 6; fear of shame, in w. of ancient Greece, ii. 399–400; modesty the characteristic of, ii. 568; w. should avoid appearance of evil, iii. 463–6.

PROVINCE OF: family and domestic matters their proper sphere, i. 241, 312, 349, 404–5, 433; ii. 442–3; iii. 32, 73, 271–2.

READING FOR: LEONORA's library, i. 153–7; choice of books proposed, i. 159; a catalogue promised, still wanting, i. 340; books of devotion important, i. 341; books recommended by booksellers, by husbands, and by women, i. 389–93; kind of reading important, i. 404–5; the PERVERSE WIDOW 'a reading lady' and 'a desperate scholar', i. 465, 486; further request for advice on reading, ii. 54–55; a lady that reads Locke, ii. 443; catalogue of books not yet given, iv. 382.

RELATIONS WITH THE MALE SEX: are unable to retaliate upon men, i. 49; conversation with men, i. 225; formed to temper mankind, i. 242; iv. 21; their opinion of a 'fine gentleman', i. 323; of dilatory tempers ('Demurrers'), i. 376–80; admire men most for courage, i. 416–17; prefer men of light and volatile humour, ii. 9–10; their love for man is self-love, ii. 10; displeased with grave, silent men, ii. 84; prefer men of gallantry, ii. 103–6; the reigning favourites ('women's men'), ii. 110–13, 119–21; 'Salamanders', ii. 275–6; the eloquence of tears and fainting fits, ii. 480–1; can only advance their fortune in youth, ii. 599; deceived by male jilts, iii. 23–25, 73; their encouragement of rakes, iii. 64–67; 'simonia-cal' ladies, iii. 67; kind of women who most please men, iii. 103–4; dangers in month of May, iii. 371–5, 480–2; iv. 221; 'killing' with their eyes, iii. 416–18; cautioned against designs of men, iii. 496–500; their charms the result of trying to please men, iv. 21; running into freedoms with men, iv. 244–7; their

Women (*cont.*)
power over men, iv. 311–12; methods of winning their favour, v. 58–61; actions which indicate that a woman loves a man, v. 70.

THE SPECTATOR'S ADDRESS TO, i. xix, xcii–xciii; 'the greatest glory of my work, if among reasonable women this paper may furnish *tea-table talk*', i. 21–22; none to whom this paper will be more useful, i. 46–47; some female reactions to, i. 142, 282, 389; ii. 55, 303, 328, 348; iii. 65, 161, 182; iv. 78; hopes to make woman-kind entirely amiable, i. 242; good effects on women's manners, i. 393; ii. 5, 316; the *Spectator* 'a public benefit', i. 404; 'she-disciples who peruse these my daily lectures', iv. 29; women's fondness for, iv. 272; concerned for their happiness and quiet, iv. 377.

WONDER, RALPH, letter from (on 'the Phantom'), iv. 284–7.

Wonders, Inspector of, an order given to, iv. 182.

Wood, Adam (prize-fighter), iv. *31*.

Wood, Anthony à, iv. *252*.

Wood, Charlotte (milliner), ii. *579*.

Wood, Lieut.-Gen. Cornelius, referred to (?), ii. 99.

Wood: counterfeit books carved in, i. 153; 'all the classic authors in', i. 156; price of w. rose during Smithfield executions, ii. 431; Emperor Leopold's handicraft work in, iii. 319.

Woodbines, i. 158; iii. 569; v. 143.

Woodcocks, hunting, i. 472.

Wood-nymphs, not necessary to the pastoral, iv. 362.

Wooden leg, a waterman with a, iii. 436.

Woods: shady w. and purling streams, ii. 11; music of fields and, ii. 474.

Woodstock: mosaic discovered at Stonesfield near, iii. 339; letter from a correspondent at, received, iv. 588.

Woodward, Josiah, *Account of Societies for Reformation of Manners*, i. *35*.

Wooing, a red coat for, ii. 14.

Wool: English w. exchanged by merchants for rubies, i. 296; customers for, ii. 402; linen and woollens, iii. 189, 210.

Woolston, Thomas, referred to (?), iii. 484.

Worcester, Battle of, i. 452.

Worcestershire, seat of Sir ROGER DE COVERLEY in, i. 7; iv. 341, 445.

Word: witty authors try to make one w. look two ways, ii. 53; of a merchant the gold of Ophir, ii. 351; *a w. to the*

wise (prov.), ii. 359, 575; iii. 220; a w. in the ear, iv. 113.

Words: affectation of mispronouncing, i. 195; pedants' concern with obsolete, i. 250; resemblance of, in puns and quibbles, i. 265; iii. 560; *are like money* (prov.), i. 431; contraction of, ii. 34–35; iii. 13; introduction of new w. into English, ii. 34–35; uncouth and antique w. in Milton, ii. 52; iii. 13, 62; importation of French, ii. 149–53; hard w. and dark expressions, ii. 151; a transcript of ideas in the mind, ii. 153; discourses which turn chiefly on w. are irksome, ii. 537; transposition, insertion, and omission of w. in *PL*, iii. 13; coining of w. in *PL*, iii. 13–14; art of distinguishing between w. and things, iii. 36; cant of w. in English critics, iii. 36; jingle of w. in Milton, iii. 63; use of technical terms in *PL*, iii. 63–64; certain w. which give the effect of immense reading, iii. 347; Locke on the abuse of, iii. 403–4; value of putting thoughts into, iii. 423; effect of well-chosen w. in descriptions, iii. 560–1; different ideas affixed to, by different readers, iii. 561; are like leaves, iv. 75, 104, 187; 'a barren superfluity of', iv. 187; choice of, in *The Faerie Queene*, iv. 429.

Wordy orator, like a tree without fruit, iv. 75.

'Work if I had it', the cry of the corn-cutter in the streets, ii. 477.

Work-houses and Bridewells, v. 44.

Working-aprons, ii. 345.

Works of the Unlearned, An Account of the, iv. 114.

World, the (human existence): a theatre, i. 45; ii. 353; love of, i. 112; 'live in and out of, at the same time', i. 115; only a nursery for the next, i. 458; an inn, ii. 353; separating oneself from, ii. 525, 599; freedom in keeping aloof from, ii. 553; Vision of Heavenly and Worldly Wisdom, iv. 364–9; love of, suspends the operations of benevolence, v. 56–57.

World, the (the earth, the universe): in chaos, void of light, distinction, and order, i. 196; 'a citizen of the', i. 294; a wager that the w. is round, ii. 72; a copy or transcript of ideas in the mind of the first Being, ii. 153; casual or eternal formation of w., one of the great points of atheism, ii. 230; divine wisdom in government of, ii. 420; made for man's use and pleasure, iii. 452; contemplation of, iv. 345–9.

World, the (human society): 'one of the housewives of' [above all others], i. 407; the eye(s) of, ii. 135, 352; take the w. as we find it, ii. 205; visiting brothels to see, ii. 248; men of the, their notion of virtue, ii. 443; is more apt to find fault than to commend, ii. 492, 498; not so corrupt as we are apt to imagine, ii. 517; 'the w. says . . .', ii. 560; things at the upper end of, iii. 33; 'a w. of charms': an extended metaphor on this phrase, v. 36.

'Worriers' among tradesmen, iii. 95.

Worship: forms of, paid to an 'Idol', i. 313–14; of the gods, the first rule of Pythagoras, ii. 233–4; propensity of the mind to, ii. 287–8; or venerable behaviour, the title given to magistrates, ii. 352; great men of all ages complied with public forms of, iii. 460. See also Devotion.

Worst, when the w. comes to the (prov.), ii. 19.

Worth, the man of ('as they call him'), v. 68.

Worthier part of mankind, i. 210.

WORTHY, WILL, examination of his heart, v. 8.

Worthy actions: depend on generous and worthy thoughts of ourselves, ii. 321; worthy thoughts the consequence of, ii. 323; consciousness of, an ample reward, ii. 370; possible to all, ii. 462–3.

Wortley, Edward. See Montagu.

Wrangler of the law, Capt. SENTRY's conversation with a young, ii. 272–3.

Wranglers, atheists a generation of, ii. 230.

Wrangling, people who have a certain cheerfulness in, iii. 590.

Wrapping-gowns, the bane of conjugal love, iii. 82.

Wrath, Ajax all w. and fierceness, ii. 326.

Wren, Sir Christopher, i. 4, 212; iv. 215, 479.

Wren, Christopher (the younger), i. 212.

'Wren on the eagle's wings', iii. 486.

Wrestler(s): JAMES, a rough, i. 306; a ring of, on the green, ii. 132; Julius Caesar might have made an excellent, ii. 371.

Wrestling: at country wakes, ii. 132–3; a part of the Roman Pentathlum, ii. 133; and pitching the bar, iv. 24; breaking a leg in, iv. 283.

Wrinkle(s): husbands stung with jealousy at sight of a, ii. 171; HONORIA's fear of w. and old age, iii. 81; in list of women's burdens, iv. 507.

Wrist-bands, 'lays out three pence in a little ribbon for his', ii. 110.

Writer(s): 'like an easy w. or a sonneteer', i. 451; a noble w. should have a vigorous imagination, iii. 563; the mark of a good w.: he makes his reader better pleased with himself, iii. 583; some scatter light, others darkness, iv. 592. See also Authors.

Writing: a dull scheme of party notions is called fine w., i. 511; or printing is the transcript of words, ii. 153; wit and fine w. consists in giving things that are known an agreeable turn, ii. 483; the art of w. unintelligibly, iii. 424; probably a later invention than painting, iii. 559; method in, iv. 186; with one's feet, iv. 544; the itch of, iv. 590.

Writing-master, who transcribed the Old Testament in a periwig, i. 248.

'Wrong side': of forty-three, ii. 39; of thirty, ii. 599.

Wyatt, Rev. Mr. (master of Felsted School), iii. 102.

Wycherley, William: addressed a poem to Swan, i. 261; referred to(?), iv. 66; — The Gentleman Dancing Master, iii. 451; — The Plain Dealer: 'a person of rougher deportment, like Manly in the play', ii. 425; 'the inimitable Dedication to', a masterpiece of raillery on lust, ii. 537; 'red breeches a certain sign of valour', iii. 322.

Wyndham, Sir William, a subscriber, i. lxxxix.

X: a signature which has puzzled the whole town, ii. 360; 'those excellent discourses marked with', iv. 295; Budgell the author of papers marked, iv. 493.

Xanthus, River, Vulcan poured down a storm of fire upon, iii. 233.

Xantippe: Socrates' philosophic resignation to, ii. 196; iv. 199–200, 223; skilled in rhetoric of stirring up the passions, ii. 459; further particulars of, requested, iv. 209; Socrates a good husband, though yoked with, v. 75–76.

XANTIPPE, a letter from, received, iv. 209.

Xenophanes, a saying of, iv. 116.

Xenophon: among the finest prose writers of antiquity writing allegories, ii. 221; mentioned, ii. 360; iv. 329. — Cyropaedia: is always celebrating the philanthropy or good-nature of his hero, ii. 166; on the religious observances of Cyrus, ii. 234; his schools of equity are

sufficiently famous, iii. 248; Cyrus on immortality, quoted, iv. 418–19; anecdote of young Araspas and Panthea, iv. 526–7; Cyrus planted all the Lesser Asia, iv. 593; — *Hellenica*, i. *334*; — *Memorabilia*: the story of Hercules meeting with pleasure and pain, ii. 221; referred to(?), ii. *410*; — *Oeconomicus*, iv. *593*; — *On the Policy of Lacedaemon*: description of Spartan youths' modesty, iii. 321; — *Symposium*: Socrates learned to dance when he was an old man, i. 284; anecdotes of Socrates and Xantippe, iv. 200; Socrates' discourse to bachelors, iv. 272–3.

Xerxes, ii. 360.

Ximena, or the Heroic Daughter. See Cibber, Colley.

Xylander, Wilhelm, translation of Plutarch, v. *75*.

Y: as a signature letter in *Spectator*, ii. 360; cut off by Milton when it precedes a vowel, iii. 15.

YARATILDA, story of MARRATON and, i. 237–40.

Yard of land, iii. 189, 210.

YARICO, story of INKLE and, i. 49, 196.

Yawn, our salutation is a y. and a stretch, iii. 168.

Yawning-match, account of a, ii. 208, 224.

YELLOW, CHARLES, letter from (experiences with jilts), ii. 234–7.

Yellow: hoods, ii. 532; robe of Autumn, iii. *595*.

Yeoman: of an hundred pounds a year, i. 498; found in a genealogy, v. 93.

Yeomen of the Guard: costume of, i. 450; the Beef-Eaters, v. 137.

Yew(s): rebus of, i. 251; a walk bordered with tall, iii. 593; a grove of, in a churchyard, iv. 277; and cypresses, iv. 325.

Yoke-fellow (a wife), i. 32; ii. 134.

Yoke-fellows, pleasure and pain constant, ii. 223.

Yorick, Hamlet's apostrophe to, quoted, iv. 156.

York: letters addressed from, iii. 15–17, 56–57, 112–13, 137; mentioned, iii. 211.

Yorke, Philip (afterwards Earl of Hardwicke), letter on travelling attributed to, i. lvii; iii. *366*.

Yorkshire: Sedbury in, ii. 117; our ladies in, ii. 547; a Y. tone, iii. 112; Topcliff in, iii. 210; letter received from, iii. 373; mentioned, iv. 290.

Young, Edward: on the *Spectator*, i. xcv; on Addison's style, i. xcviii; *Love of Fame*, ii. *207*.

Young, the: idleness of younger sons, i. 448–9; a good-for-nothing young man, i. 501; reformation of a young man, ii. 432–3; envy of an old man for the follies of, ii. 511–12; Fortune, like other females, favours, iii. 44; death of, like destruction of the Spring, iii. 105; have adopted the vices of the aged, iii. 313; Virgil's advice to young people, iii. 374; the youngest child often spoilt by being the parents' darling, iv. 274; love generally accompanied with goodwill in, v. 24.

Youth: who admired his own figure in brass, ii. 71; pleasure makes y. inglorious, age shameful, ii. 94; folly of desiring, ii. 100–3; our schemes of thought in, lost in those of manhood, ii. 137; neither can nor ought to remain at rest, ii. 373; busy inquisitive humour so natural to, ii. 396; of Great Britain laugh at marriage, ii. 417; throwing away vigour of, in arms of harlots, ii. 524; who learned to beat the Grenadiers' March on his chin, iii. 3–4; and beauty powerful in conveying rebukes, iii. 41; allegory of Y. and Love, iii. 76–78; problems of, iii. 217–18; may be frightened by examples of vice, iii. 248; calamities of y. and old age compared, iv. 14; the old rail at the extravagance of, iv. 195; gaiety of, overlooked by the ancients, iv. 259.

Youthier turn, affecting a, iii. 56.

Z: Paul Scarron shaped like the letter, i. 75; as a signature in the *Spectator*, i. xliv–l; ii. 360.

Z., Y.: offers to take Sir ANDREW's place in the Club, iv. 469.

Z—n, Monsieur, iv. 538.

Zeal: for a public cause apt to breed passions, i. 510; for the public good induces uncharitable notions, i. 512; evils of religious, ii. 227–30; iii. 463; of atheists, ii. 230; of the Trunkmaker, ii. 416; z., bigotry, and persecution to be avoided, iii. 495; balanced against charity, iv. 137; 'the godlike z. of doing good', v. 14.

Zealand: part of, in subjection to Burgundy, iv. 241.

ZELINDA: has been courted unsuccessfully for three years, iii. 373; 'wounded by Z.'s scarlet stocking', iii. 417; a love-letter to, v. 143–4.

Zemroude, Queen, consort of Fadlallah, iv. 576.

Zenobius, ii. 243.

Zephon, his rebuke to Satan, in PL, iii. 41, 172.

Zephyrs: and gentle breezes produced by fans, i. 428; and Cupids in paintings, iii. 373; attendants on Summer, iii. 595.

Zeuxis: 'boasts with Z., In eternitatem pingo', i. 221.

ZILPAH, HILPA one of the daughters of, iv. 596, 598; v. 3.

Zimri (in Absalom and Achitophel), character of, ii. 138–9, 363–4.

Zoilus: in Martial, i. 366; his ridicule of Homer, ii. 589; had a long beard and was bald, iii. 221.

ZOILUS, fond of CORINNA, ii. 119.

Zopyrus (physiognomist) and Socrates, i. 368.

Zouch, Francis, advertises snuff, iii. 278.

Zug (in Switzerland), advices from, iv. 93.

&c.: as a signature in the Spectator, ii. 360.

ἀγάπαι (love-feasts), established in England by Gregory the Great, ii. 134.

εἰνοσίφυλλον, applied to Pelion by Homer, iii. 230.

ζῶον φιλόκοσμον, woman defined as, ii. 530.

κακοῦ κόρακος κακὸν ᾠόν (prov.), ii. 243.

πλέον ἥμισυ παντός (prov.), ii. 286.

σκιομαχία (shadow-fighting), i. 474.

στοργή (natural affection to those depending on us), ii. 214.

φιλομμειδής (laughter-loving), applied to Venus, ii. 468; iii. 269.